Teacher's Edition

HARCOURT BRACE SPELLING

LEVEL 3

Thorsten Carlson
Professor Emeritus
Sonoma State University
Rohnert Park, California

Richard Madden
Professor Emeritus
San Diego State University
San Diego, California

Language Arts Advisors

Dorothy S. Strickland
Professor of Education
Teachers College,
   Columbia University
New York, New York

Roger C. Farr
Professor of Education
Indiana University
Bloomington, Indiana

HARCOURT BRACE & COMPANY

Orlando   Atlanta   Austin   Boston   San Francisco   Chicago   Dallas   New York   Toronto   London

http://www.hbschool.com

ISBN 0-15-313660-X
1 2 3 4 5 - 030 - 01 00 99

ACKNOWLEDGMENTS

PHOTO CREDITS

Key: T, Top; B, Bottom; L, Left; C, Center; R, Right.

Pages 56, Ken Lax/The Stock Shop; 72, ZEFA/H.
Armstrong Roberts; 87, Phoebe Dunn/DPI; 92,
Eric Carle/Shostal Associates; 96, Shostal
Associates; 99, Stan Wayman/Photo Researchers;
109(L) G. Trouillet/The Image Bank; 109(C),
Rhoda Galyn; 109(R), Runk/Schoenberger/Grant
Heilman; 117, HB Studio; 118, William Felger/
Grand Heilman; 136, H. Armstrong Roberts; 144,
Ruth Dixon; 163, J. A. Robinson/Photo Research-
ers; 164, Hans Reinhard/Bruce Coleman; 167,
Pat Meyers; 169, Antonio Mendoza/Stock, Boston;
170, Sylvia Johnson/Woodfin Camp & Associates;
171, Stephen Kraseman/Photo Researchers; 172,
Halley Ganges; 173, Leonard Rue III/Photo
Researchers; 174, M. J. Germana/DPI; 175,
George Roos/DPI; 177, Kim Massie/Rainbow;
179, Tana Hoban/DPI; 181, G. Schaller/Bruce
Coleman; 182, Walter Chandoha; 184, Joe
McDonald/Bruce Coleman; 186, A. B. Joyce/Photo
Researchers; 188, Phil Dotson/DPI; 190(L), H.
Armstrong Roberts; 190(R), Sepp Seitz/Woodfin
Camp & Associates; 191, Frost Publishing Group,
Ltd.; 193, Hans Pfletschinger/Peter Arnold; 194,
HB Photo; 196, Florida Dept. of Commerce;
197(L), G. Bordis/De Wys; 197(R), Halley Ganges;
198(L), George Holton/Photo Researchers;
198(R), Ted Horowitz/The Stock Market; 199(L),
Blaine Harrington III/The Stock Market; 199(R),
Joe McDonald/Bruce Coleman; 200(L), Hill/Frost
Publishing Group, Ltd.; 200(R), Mira Atkeson/DPI;
202, Irene Vandermolen/Bruce Coleman.

"Letter Forms and Letter Talk" from *HBJ
HANDWRITING.* Copyright © 1987 by Harcourt
Brace & Company. Reprinted by permission of
Harcourt Brace & Company.

CONTENTS

INTRODUCTION

Development of *Harcourt Brace Spelling*

Research and classroom experience since the beginning of public education have revealed the need for systematic, developmental instruction in spelling. In order for a spelling program to be effective, two essential elements must be considered:

1. **the words to be taught, and**
2. **the strategies of instruction.**

These basic elements must draw on all relevant research and experience. In the creation of *Harcourt Brace Spelling,* the lists of words to be taught and the strategies of instruction evolved together through an examination of published research and the independent research of the authors. The resultant materials were then tested in classrooms throughout the country and reviewed by teachers, researchers, and administrators to determine their usefulness and suitability.

The Importance of Spelling Instruction

Public demand for accountability in the classroom has led to an increase in emphasis on standardized tests. A large majority of school districts in the United States now require students to pass some form of standardized writing assessment at regular intervals throughout their elementary school years. One of the most visible factors in evaluating anyone's writing, student or adult, is this: Are the words spelled correctly? *Harcourt Brace Spelling* will improve students' writing in direct and visible ways through its instructional lessons. It will also help to build competent and able writers through its strong writing strand, which has students applying their spelling knowledge to a challenging variety of writing assignments throughout the year.

Word Lists

The lists of words to be taught in *Harcourt Brace Spelling* were compiled after careful study of words students use in their writing and reading. The authors and consultants have developed and refined the lists over many years of work and research in spelling. They have maintained a database of words, in which they have entered data from the many studies that have been done over the years to determine frequency of use, familiarity, and degree of difficulty. The authors began with data from Rinsland (*A Basic Vocabulary of Elementary School Children*), which is based on children's writing vocabulary; Thorndike-Lorge (*A Teacher's Wordbook of 30,000 Words*); Kucera (*Computational Analysis of Present-Day American English*); *The American Heritage Word Frequency Book*; and several other core vocabulary and word-frequency studies to determine the core of high-frequency words that must be included and to make judgments about the utility of additional words. Harris-Jacobson (*Basic Elementary Reading Vocabularies*) was also consulted in making decisions about which words to include.

The words were grouped to reflect the common and consistent spelling patterns based on sound-letter relationships (phonics), word structures (affixes, inflections, syllable patterns, common roots, compound words), and content area (mathematics, science, social studies, and so on).

For each unit, a principal list was developed, as well as two shorter lists—one for review and the other for extension. The three lists in any one unit illustrate the same spelling generalization.

Strategies of Instruction

The ability to spell correctly is developed through four primary strategies of instruction which should be the focus of an effective program: visual memory, phonics, word structure, and analogy.

- **Visual memory** is undeniably an important factor in spelling ability. We rely on visual memory to test possible spellings, to recognize correct spellings, and to correct misspellings. Visual cues, for example, are probably the most helpful aid in remembering that *through*, *although*, and *enough* are all spelled with the letters *ough*. Visual memory is also important in distinguishing between words that have the some pronunciation but different spellings and meanings.

- **Phonics,** the science of sound-letter relationships, is emphasized throughout **Harcourt Brace Spelling**, particularly in the primary levels. At this stage, children are reading high-utility, high-frequency words with regular and predictable spellings. Systematic, explicit teaching concentrates on the patterns that occur most frequently. For example, while it is true that the long e sound is spelled *eo* in *people*, that spelling is rare. Therefore, more time and attention are given initially to the common spellings of /e/—final *e*, medial *ee*, and *ea*—gradually introducing such other regular spellings as *y* in happy and the *ei* in *receive*.

- **Word structure** has a strong influence on spelling and, like phonics, it must be taught systematically. **Harcourt Brace Spelling** introduces such structural patterns as contractions, compound words, and the addition of inflectional endings or affixes to base or root words. Spelling lists are also organized around meaning-related words. Recognizing the link between spelling and meaning serves as a useful spelling clue. For example, the words *sign* and *signature* are taught together so that the pronounced *g* in *signature* will serve as a reminder of the silent *g* in *sign*.

- **Analogy** is another major strategy that helps us predict the spelling of English words. Common characteristics in *familiar* words can form the basis for an analogy to the spelling of an *unfamiliar* word. Effective use of this strategy is characteristic of proficient spellers, people who have developed an understanding of the underlying regularity of the writing system. In its most elementary form, analogy can be as simple as guessing that words that rhyme might be spelled similarly.

A proficient speller can have a writing vocabulary of about 70,000 words. Spelling knowledge of every one of these 70,000 words is not acquired in formal instruction. However, the ability to use a combination of strategies to predict the spelling of unfamiliar words can be acquired in a comprehensive, developmental spelling program.

Spelling: A Developmental Process

Harcourt Brace Spelling was designed with an understanding and appreciation of the following stages of development.

EMERGENT SPELLERS

- Young children's writing is made up of random strings of letters and sometimes numbers to represent words or a complete message.
- Children use both lowercase and uppercase letters in their writing.
- At this stage, they do not demonstrate a knowledge of letter-sound correspondences.

SEMI-PHONETIC SPELLERS

- Children begin to develop the concept that letters have sounds and that letters are used to represent the sounds in words.
- Several letters may represent a whole word (*GS* for *Gross*, *KT* for *Cot*, *BRZ* for *Birds*). Vowels, medial consonants, and syllables are not represented.
- Children may also use letter names to represent sounds in words (*R* for *Are*, *U* for *You*).
- Spellings may be strung together without spaces before and after words.

PHONETIC SPELLERS

- Children spell words according to the entire sound structure of the word (*KANT* for *Can't*).
- When phonetic spellers are unsure of the correct letter to represent a sound, they often select a letter that represents another sound made in the same part of the mouth. (*CHRAN* for *Train*.)

TRANSITIONAL SPELLERS

- Children's writing reflects features of conventional spelling and phonetic spelling.
- Children use frequently occurring spelling patterns and include vowels in every syllable (*HAMSTUR* for *Hamster*). Although the vowel may be incorrect, it is in the correct position.
- Children rely less on sound structure. They begin to rely on visual memory and word structure.

SYNTACTIC-SEMANTIC SPELLERS

- Children have an understanding of the English spelling system and its basic rules.
- They show an expanded knowledge of word structure and can correctly spell affixes, contractions, and compound words.
- Mature spellers are less dependent on the sound features of words to predict spelling. They make greater use of higher-level strategies.

SPELLING PATTERNS

Sound-Letter Relationships
CONSONANTS

Consonant Sounds and Spellings

The 21 consonant letters—*b, c, d, f, g, h, j, k, l, m, n, p, q, r, s, t, v, w, x, y,* and *z*—spell 23 consonant sounds. The letters *c, q,* and *x* do not represent unique sounds. They stand for consonant sounds that can be represented by other letters. The letter *c* can stand for /k/, as in *can,* or /s/, as in *city.* The letter *q* followed by *u* represents the sounds /kw/, as in *liquid.* The letter *x* represents /ks/, as in *fox* or /gz/, as in *exit.*

Variant Spellings of Consonant Sounds

The consonant sounds /f/, /j/, /k/, /s/, /z/, /ch/, /ng/, and /sh/ are spelled in more than one way.

1. The sound /f/
   initial or final *f* (*fire, leaf*)
   final *ff* (*cuff*)
   initial or final *ph* (*phone, graph*) final *gh* (*laugh*)
2. The sound /j/
   initial *g* before *e* or *i* (*gentle, ginger*)
   final *dge* or *ge* (*edge, image*)
   initial *j* before *a, o,* or *u* (*jar, job, jump*)
3. The sound /k/
   initial *c* before *a, o,* or *u* (*cat, come, cup*)
   initial *k* before /e/, /ē/, /i/, or /ī/ (*kept, keep, kit, kite*)
   final *ck* after short vowel sounds (*back, kick, lock*)
   final *k* after other vowel sounds and consonants (*look, silk, task*)
4. The sound /s/
   initial or final *s* (*see, bus*)
   final *ss* (*miss*)
   initial *c* before *i, e, a, r, y* (*circus, cell, cycle*)
   initial *sc* (*science*)
5. The sound /z/
   initial *z* (*zero, zoo*)
   final *s* (*was, boys*)
6. The sound /ch/
   initial or final *ch* (*child, reach*)
   final *tch* after a short vowel sound (*match, stitch*)
7. The sound /ng/
   final *ng* (*sing, wrong*)
   n before *k* or *g* (*bank, finger*)
8. The sound /sh/
   initial or final *sh* (*ship, wash*)
   in the /sh, n/ syllable, *ti* (*motion, notion*); less frequently *si* (*mission*)
   In a few words /sh/ is spelled in different ways: *sure, machine, patient, social.*

Consonant Clusters

1. The *l* clusters
   Initial: *bl, cl, fl, gl, pl, sl* (*blue, glad,* etc.)
   Final: *ld, lf, lk, lp, lt* (*sold, help,* etc.)
2. The *r* clusters
   Initial: *br, cr, dr, fr, gr, pr, tr* (*bright, cry,* etc.)
   Final: *rd, rk, rm, rn, rt* (*hard, worm,* etc.)
3. Other clusters
   Initial: *sk, sm, sn, sp, st, sw* (*skiff, snow,* etc.)
   Final: *mp, nd, nt, pt, sk, sp, st* (*stamp, risk,* etc.)

Double Consonant Letters

1. Double consonant letters follow short vowel sounds *ss* (*pass*), *dd* (*sudden*), *ll* (*will*), etc.
2. Double consonant letters occur in words in which the final sound of a prefix has been assimilated with the initial sound of the root word (*ad + prove = approve, com + relate = correlate*)

"Silent" Letters

Certain spellings in specific syllable and word locations have lost their phonological function as pronunciations have changed, for example, *k* before *n* (*know*), *w* before *r* (*write*), *b* after *m* (*comb*), *b* before *t* (*debt*).

VOWELS

Vowel Sounds and Spellings

The vowel letters are *a, e, i, o, u*; sometimes *y* as in *story* and *try*; and *w* as in *show* and *cow.*

Short Vowel Sounds

1. The /a/, /e/, /i/, /o/, and /u/ sounds are usually spelled by the letter that is generally associated with the sound (*hat, end, sit, not, up*).
2. In a few words, the short vowel sound is spelled in variant ways, such as /e/ in *head,* or /u/ in *love.*

Grade 3 SHORT VOWEL SOUND LESSON

ng Vowel Sounds

1. The sound /ā/
   usually spelled vowel-consonant-e (VCe) pattern (*save, make*)
   often spelled *ai* when followed by /l/, /d/, /n/, /m/, or /t/ (*mail, paid, rain, claim, wait*)
   often spelled *a* when it is the final sound in a syllable (*pa'per, na'vy*)
   in final position, often spelled *ay* (*stay, away*)
2. The sound /ē/
   most often spelled *ea* and *ee* (*each, pea, meat; tree, sweet*)
   in syllabic final position, often spelled *e* (*detail*)
   at the end of a word, usually spelled *y* (*baby, story*)
   In a few words, /ē/ is spelled in other ways (*eve, field, people, receive, monkey*).
3. The sound /ī/
   most often spelled VCe (*life*) or *i* (*find*)
   at the end of a word, usually spelled *y* (*try, comply*)
4. The sound /ō/
   in most cases spelled *o* (*open, go, piano*)
   often spelled VCe (*rose, hope*)
   in medial position, spelled *oa* (*coat, road*)
   at the end of a word, usually spelled *ow* (*low, know*)

ther Vowel Sounds

1. The sound /yoo/
   most commonly spelled *u* (*union*)
   often spelled VCe (*mule*)
2. The sound /oo/
   most often spelled *oo* (*moon*)
   often spelled *ue* (*blue*), *ew* (*flew*), *u-e* (*rule*)
3. The sound /oo/
   usually spelled *oo* (*book*); also *u* (*put*), *ou* (*could*)
4. The sound /ô/
   usually spelled *o* (*off*) or *a* (*all*)
   before *r*, most often spelled *o* (*or, for*)
   in medial position, *au* (*laundry*)
   in final position, *aw* (*straw*)
5. Vowel and *r*
   The sounds /âr/ can be spelled as in *care, air,* and *bear.*
   The sounds /är/ are often spelled as in *car.*
   The sounds /ûr/ can be spelled as in *turn, term,* and *bird.*
6. The sound /oi/
   The diphthong /oi/ is spelled *oi* in medial position (*spoil*).
   In final position it is most often spelled *oy* (*boy*).
7. The sound /ou/
   The diphthong /ou/ is most often spelled *ou* (*house*).

In final position it is often spelled *ow* (*how*).
8. The sound /ä/
   usually spelled *a* (*calm*)
9. The sound /ə/
   The schwa sound occurs only in multisyllabic words. It is always in an unaccented syllable and can be spelled with any vowel letter (*away, level, pencil, lemon, circus*).

Word Structure

Rules for Adding Suffixes

To most words, simply add the ending without changing the base word (*helping, helps, helpful, helpfully*). Spelling changes are necessary in the following situations.

1. Final *e*
   For most words ending in *e*, drop the *e* before adding endings that begin with vowels (*sense—sensing, sensible, sensory*).
   If the ending begins with a consonant, keep the *e* (*sense—senseless*).
2. Final *y*
   For words ending in a consonant and *y*, change the *y* to *i* when adding endings (*happy—happiest, happily, happiness*).
   But if the suffix begins with *i*, keep the *y* (*carrying*).
3. Doubling
   When a word ends in a single consonant after a single vowel, double the final consonant when adding a suffix that begins with a vowel (*snap—snapping, snapper, snappy*).
   For words of more than one syllable, double the final consonant if the accent is on the last syllable (*forget'—forgetting*, but *mar'ket—marketing*).

Forming Plurals

1. To most nouns, simply add -*s* to form the plural (*dog—dogs*).
2. Add -*es* to words that end in sibilant sounds /s/, /sh/, /ch/, /ks/, /z/ (*buses, glasses, wishes, watches, foxes*).
3. Change the spelling of some words (*mouse—mice, tooth—teeth*).

Spelling Possessives

1. To form the singular possessive, add an apostrophe and *s* (*boy—boy's*).
2. To form the plural possessive, add the apostrophe after the *s* (*girls—girls'*).
3. When the plural is formed by a change in spelling, add an apostrophe and *s* (*men—men's*).

Each unit of **Harcourt Brace Spelling** follows a step-by-step plan to teach a spelling principle. There are two types of units in the program: instructional units and review units.

An Instructional Unit

INTRODUCING THE UNIT

ESTABLISH READINESS FOR LEARNING

This section in the **Teacher's Edition** begins each instructional unit by focusing students' attention on the content of the lesson. Students are presented with what is to be learned and told how this learning will be applied to their written work.

> **Establish Readiness for Learning**
>
> Tell the children that this week they will continue to learn about vowel sounds. In Unit 22 they will study several spellings for the vowel sound /ûr/. Tell the children that they will apply the spelling generalizations to This Week's Words and use those words to write a poem.

APPLY PRIOR LEARNING

This section in the **Teacher's Edition** takes an inductive approach and leads students to formulate the spelling generalizations for the unit. Given specific information, students build on prior knowledge to draw relationships. Students later apply the spelling generalizations to their own writing.

> **Apply Prior Learning**
>
> Have the children apply what they already know about vowel sounds by participating in the following activity.
>
> Write the words *girl, burn, learn,* and *worm* on the chalkboard. Read these words aloud with the children. Ask the children to tell how these words are alike, and help them to recognize that each word has the /ûr/ sound. Ask volunteers to come to the chalkboard and draw a line around the letters that represent /ûr/ in each word. Tell the children that in Unit 22 they will study words that have these spellings for /ûr/. Explain that they can use these words in a variety of writing tasks: they can use the words in a note to a friend, in a letter, or in a book report.

DEVELOPING THE UNIT

THE UNIT WORDS

The numbered Unit word list (called "This Week's Words" in Levels 1–3) is presented in the **Pupil Book** on the first page of each instructional unit in manuscript or cursive. The students read the Unit word list orally and identify the sound-letter or word-structure patterns that are represented. The unit generalization on the page explains the sound-letter or word-structure pattern. Boxed numbers on the word list

indicate that the word has an unusual spelling. A simila box within the unit generalization points out that a discussion of that word follows. A feature titled *Remembe This* often appears on the first page of a unit and provides clues for remembering the spellings of especially troublesome words.

SPELLING PRACTICE

The second page of each instructional unit in the **Pup Book** is a full page of independent spelling practice. Th *Spelling Practice* page presents a series of carefully-organized exercises that lead the students to an understanding of the relationships between the Unit words. Exercises guide the students to observe the spelling pat terns within the words and to recognize regularities. The also give students opportunities to write the words in meaningful contexts. Students write each word at least one time on this page; most words are written more than once.

LANGUAGE STUDY

The third page of each instructional unit in the Pupil Book is devoted to spelling-related language arts skills. Levels 3–6, the page is divided into three parts.

- The first part of this page is *Spelling and Language* This section reinforces the spellings of the Unit word through a review of language principles and gram mar. Most lessons concentrate on areas of spelling difficulty—adding noun and verb inflections, adding prefixes and suffixes, and using context to distinguish homophones.
  - The second part of this page is *Writing on Your Own.* Students apply spelling principles and use spelling words in purposeful writing assignments. Through writing, students test and modify their hypotheses of how words are spelled, thereby extending their knowledge of the English writing system. The lesson emphasizes the importance of correct spelling in communicating effectively and focuses on the fou interrelated stages

Grade 3

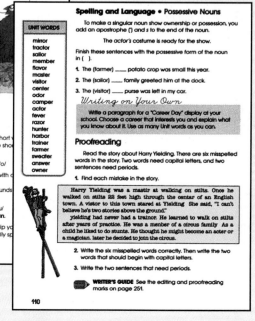

Grade 5

of the writing process: prewriting, composing, revising, and publishing.

- The third part of this page can be either *Using the Dictionary to Spell and Write* or *Proofreading*. (In Level 3, *Using the Dictionary to Spell and Write* and *Proofreading* alternate with *Handwriting*.) The dictionary exercises are more numerous in the first half of the book; the frequency of proofreading exercises increases in the second half. Dictionary exercises are sequentially structured throughout the book and from level to level. The exercises establish the connection between the dictionary and spelling and writing. The proofreading activities cover a wide range of curriculum areas and types of writing, including materials students are likely to produce themselves—for example, social studies and science reports, letters, and news stories. Students focus on finding and correcting a specified number of misspelled words as well as errors in capitalization and punctuation. These activities reinforce what students do when they revise their own writing.

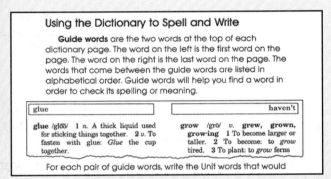

Using the Dictionary to Spell and Write

Guide words are the two words at the top of each dictionary page. The word on the left is the first word on the page. The word on the right is the last word on the page. The words that come between the guide words are listed in alphabetical order. Guide words will help you find a word in order to check its spelling or meaning.

| glue | haven't |

glue /gl⁻oo/ 1 *n.* A thick liquid used for sticking things together. 2 *v.* To fasten with glue: *Glue* the cup together.

grow /grō/ *v.* **grew, grown, growing** 1 To become larger or taller. 2 To become: to *grow* tired. 3 To plant: to *grow* ferns

For each pair of guide words, write the Unit words that would

SPELLING ON YOUR OWN

On the fourth page of each unit in the **Pupil Book** there are exercises for reviewing the Unit words. There is, as well, a list of Mastery words—words that have appeared one or two grades earlier in the program and that demonstrate the spelling principle of the unit. Exercises that accompany the Mastery words are suitable for below-average spellers or as a review for on-level spellers. An additional list of Bonus words completes this page. The Bonus word lists contain words one or two years above grade level. These are geared for use with above-average spellers or as a challenge for on-level

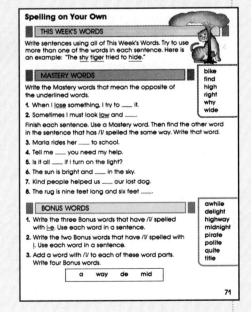

Spelling on Your Own

THIS WEEK'S WORDS

Write sentences using all of This Week's Words. Try to use more than one of the words in each sentence. Here is an example: "The shy tiger tried to hide."

MASTERY WORDS

Write the Mastery words that mean the opposite of the underlined words.

1. When I lose something, I try to ___ it.
2. Sometimes I must look low and ___.

Finish each sentence. Use a Mastery word. Then find the other word in the sentence that has /ī/ spelled the same way. Write that word.

3. Maria rides her ___ to school.
4. Tell me ___ you need my help.
5. Is it all ___ if I turn on the light?
6. The sun is bright and ___ in the sky.
7. Kind people helped us ___ our lost dog.
8. The rug is nine feet long and six feet ___.

bike
find
high
right
why
wide

BONUS WORDS

1. Write the three Bonus words that have /ī/ spelled with i-e. Use each word in a sentence.
2. Write the two Bonus words that have /ī/ spelled with i. Use each word in a sentence.
3. Add a word with /ī/ to each of these word parts. Write four Bonus words.

| a | way | de | mid |

awhile
delight
highway
midnight
pirate
polite
quite
title

71

students. Bonus words also illustrate the spelling principle of the unit.

SUMMARIZE LEARNING

Students are asked to reflect on what they have learned, by summarizing and giving examples. This section in the **Teacher's Edition** appears at two points in the unit:

- after the students have studied the Unit words and completed the *Spelling Practice* page.
- after the students have completed the *Spelling and Language* page and *Spelling on Your Own*.

OF SPECIAL INTEREST

This feature in the **Teacher's Edition** presents interesting facts about how words came into English and how their meanings and spellings evolved over time. The information extends students' word knowledge and gives them a rationale for the spelling and function of words.

CLOSING THE UNIT

APPLY NEW LEARNING

In this section in the **Teacher's Edition**, students are encouraged to apply the spelling principle of the instructional unit when they write independently. Students are provided with several strategies for correcting misspelled words and for spelling unfamiliar words.

TRANSFER NEW LEARNING

This section emphasizes the relationship between spelling, reading, and writing. As students expand their reading vocabulary, they apply what they know about spelling patterns. Reading vocabulary helps to explain spelling, and spelling helps to reinforce reading vocabulary. Once new words are familiar, students should use them in their writing.

ENRICHMENT ACTIVITIES

The **Teacher's Edition** suggests activities that students can do in the classroom or in the home. These activities have students apply prior learning and transfer new learning through written communication. The activities promote higher-level thinking and are appropriate for students of all ability levels.

Activities for the classroom may be individualized by having students use the word list they are studying. One activity in each unit has students use the writing process to complete a paragraph, story, letter, or report. Students may complete each activity individually or in a group.

Students may complete activities for the home independently or with the help of a relative or friend. These activities are designed to build word knowledge and extend the unit spelling generalization to writing.

STUDENT-GENERATED WORD LISTS

In addition to studying the standard lists of spelling words in *Harcourt Brace Spelling*, students may generate their own lists of words based on need and interest. Student-generated spelling words may be those words that students misspell in their writing. They may be words students need to use in the curriculum areas of science/health, social studies, and mathematics, or new vocabulary drawn from their own reading. Students may record their own word lists on the *Study Steps to Learn a Word* copying master provided in the **Teacher's Resource Book** or in a spelling notebook.

To make learning more meaningful and to promote long-term retention of spelling skills, students should be encouraged to organize their own spelling word lists around themes or categories. For example, students may develop a list of words that express emotions, or define the senses, or describe the colonial period in American history.

A Review Unit

Every sixth unit in *Harcourt Brace Spelling*, Levels 2–6, is a review unit. Fifty percent of the Unit words from each of the five preceding units are reviewed. The words selected for review are those with which students are known to have special problems and those which occur frequently in their writing.

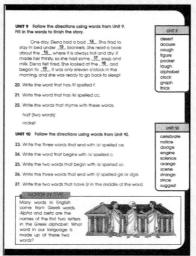

INTRODUCING THE UNIT

Each review unit has the same introductory features as an instructional unit. In *Establish Readiness for Learning*, the teacher sets the purpose of instruction. In *Apply Prior Learning*, the teacher has students formulate the spelling generalizations to be reviewed in the unit.

DEVELOPING THE UNIT

SPELLING REVIEW

The first three pages of each review unit provide additional practice in writing review words. The exercises reinforce sound-letter correspondences and word structure. Thematic passages and completion sentences are frequently used so that students can write words in meaningful contexts.

Study Steps to Learn a Word always precedes the *Spelling Review* exercises. The study steps help students to become independent spellers by giving them a strategy to use when they misspell words and when they encounter unfamiliar words. *Study Steps to*

Learn a Word also appears on the first page of each **Pupil Book** in Levels 1–6.

WORDS IN TIME

This feature appears on one of the three *Spelling Review* pages in each review unit in the **Pupil Book**. It explores the history of a review word, often explaining how the word came into English or how the meaning o spelling changed over time. *Words In Time* creates a logical association for students between the origin of a word and its spelling.

SPELLING AND READING

The fourth page of each review unit in the **Pupil Book** presents a piece of expository, narrative, descriptive, or persuasive writing that students will use later as a model for their own writing. The model contains words from the preceding five units and words that follow the generalizations taught in the preceding five units. After a purpose for reading has been established, students read the model and then answer comprehension questions that involve higher-order thinking of the interpretive, critical, and applicative levels. The comprehension questions have been written to elicit answers that include review words. Students proofread their answers for spelling.

SPELLING AND WRITING

On the fifth page of each review unit, students think about and discuss the writing model presented in *Spelling and Reading* in preparation for their own writing. The students analyze the structure, content, style, and tone of the model. At the conclusion of this section students summarize what they have learned.

On the sixth page students apply what they have learned and complete a writing assignment. The assignment follows the stages of the writing process. Students are encouraged to refer to the *Writer's Guides* at the back of the **Pupil Book** for definitions and models and to the *Spelling Dictionary* and *Spelling Thesaurus*.

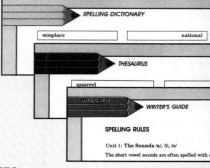

CLOSING THE UNIT

ENRICHMENT ACTIVITIES

The **Teacher's Edition** provides suggested activities that students can do in the home independently or with the assistance of a relative or friend. These activities have students apply prior learning and transfer new learning in written communication in various curriculum areas. They are designed to expand word knowledge and extend the unit spelling generalizations to writing sentences, paragraphs, and stories. The activities promote higher-level thinking and are appropriate for students of all ability levels.

SPELLING AND BEYOND

The Writing Process

Harcourt Brace Spelling emphasizes writing as a process in which a writer actively uses knowledge, experience, and language to express ideas. The writing process depends on the interrelated stages of prewriting, composing, and revising. In this process students imagine the audience, set goals or purposes, develop ideas, produce notes and drafts, and revise to meet the audience's expectations. As the process unfolds, students may return to any one of these activities at any one time to make changes.

- In *Prewriting*, students explore possible topics, identify their purpose and audience, and record and structure ideas and vocabulary. The goal is to expose students to a variety of prewriting activities that will help stimulate ideas for ease of writing their rough, or first, draft.
- In *Composing*, students use their prewriting experiences to structure their own writing. They generate ideas as they match words to thoughts and clarify thoughts according to their purpose and audience.
- In *Revising*, students reread and evaluate their own writing following a set of guidelines. They edit the content of their writing for style, tone, unity, clarity, and coherence. They rethink their original ideas and polish the content of their writing to suit their purpose and the audience for whom they are writing. Then students proofread their work to check for errors in spelling, capitalization, punctuation, and other mechanics.

Note: At this stage of the writing process, it is important to caution students about relying on a software program to do their proofreading for them. While many such programs are helpful tools, they are limited in their abilities. For example, a spellcheck program can determine that the word *sail* is spelled correctly, but it cannot discover that the student actually meant to use the word *sale*.

- *Publishing* students' written compositions means making them public—but not necessarily printed and bound for sale in bookstores. Publishing includes reading a composition aloud to an audience of peers, putting it in a class notebook or other periodical, posting it on a bulletin board for others to read, or including it in an anthology of class compositions to be placed in the school library. This parallels the process of publishing by professional authors and helps students come to a fuller understanding, appreciation, and enjoyment of the process of writing.

Spelling and Handwriting

Effective written communication depends on the writer's ability to transmit information in a manner that is understandable to others. Spelling, therefore, is one important aspect of written communication. Handwriting is the other member of the team. These two skills go hand in hand as basic tools in writing.

Harcourt Brace Spelling includes *Handwriting Models* and *Letter Talk* in English and Spanish at the back of the **Teacher's Edition** in Levels 1–3. *Handwriting Models* are also provided at the back of the **Pupil Book** in Levels 1–6. As students practice writing the Unit words, they should be encouraged to compare their words with the models on the Unit word list.

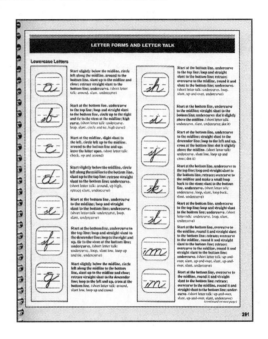

Other Curriculum Areas

On a daily basis students are engaged in some kind of writing that involves other curriculum areas. They may answer chapter questions, write up experiments, take notes and make outlines for a research report, write a summary, or create a time line. When students write in other curriculum areas they should be encouraged to apply their knowledge of spelling and the structure of written language.

Application of spelling principles when writing in other curriculum areas may involve the addition of affixes and inflections. It may also involve the understanding that words related in meaning are often related in spelling despite changes in pronunciation. In the intermediate grades content-area vocabulary often has a high degree of regularity in spelling when examined on the basis of meaning. For example: *compose/composition, define/definition, nation/national.*

MEETING INDIVIDUAL NEEDS

English as a Second Language/ Limited English Proficiency

Harcourt Brace Spelling addresses the needs of students who are learning English as a second language through

- the **Teacher's Edition**
- the **Teacher's Resource Book**
- the **Suggestions and Activities for Limited English Proficient Students**

Special strategies for teaching spelling are necessary to accommodate the needs of limited English proficient (LEP) students. As LEP students are developing a working vocabulary in English, they need to be able to use this vocabulary in their personal writing and in the writing they do in the various content areas. Learning to spell new words as well as familiar words poses difficulties for these students: the sound structure and the correspondence of letters to sounds in English may differ considerably from the sound structure and spelling of their native language.

A variety of strategies that rely on additional materials and alternative teaching methods will ensure continued growth in spelling English words. In *Harcourt Brace Spelling*, additional support materials for reinforcement and reteaching are provided for each unit in the **Teacher's Resource Book** at each level. Since some students may require more direct teaching, you may need to model sample exercises, provide additional examples, read aloud directions, and then have students explain what they are to do.

Learning Difficulties

Students who experience learning difficulties do so for a variety of reasons including language disorders, dyslexia, cognitive deficits, and sensory impairments. Learning to spell places demands on just those areas that are weak or deficient in students with learning difficulties: the basic processes of attention and memory a well as the higher cognitive abilities of language, reasoning, and organization.

Students with learning difficulties need special strategies to strengthen weaknesses or learn compensatory behaviors or skills. In *Harcourt Brace Spelling*, strategies for teaching spelling to these students are provided in each instructional unit in the **Teacher's Edition**. They emphasize a multisensory approach, combining visual, auditory, tactile, and kinesthetic senses to teach and reinforce spelling skills and to strengthen memory and attention. In addition, motivational strategies such as setting goals, earning tangible rewards, and charting progress are suggested to promote learning.

TESTING AND MANAGEMENT

To help you evaluate your students' progress and determine their level of achievement, *Harcourt Brace Spelling* provides a complete testing program. The core testing is found in the **Pupil Book** and **Teacher's Edition**. Additional testing for diagnosis and evaluation is found in the **Teacher's Resource Book** as reproducible copying masters. You should select those testing materials appropriate to the specific needs of your students.

Two methods of evaluation underlie the testing program of *Harcourt Brace Spelling*—Test-Study-Test and Spelling Error Analysis.

Test-Study-Test

Harcourt Brace Spelling uses a Test-Study-Test method with the weekly list of spelling words. Using this method, you dictate a list of words for the students to write. You say each word, use it in a sentence, and then repeat the word. After the test, the students correct their own work by listening to you read the spelling of the words, or by referring to the list of words in the **Pupil Book**.

Each Unit Words Test, Mastery Words Test, and Bonus Words Test in *Harcourt Brace Spelling*, Levels 1–6, is also available on the **Audiocassettes**. On each **Audiocassette** test, students receive pre-test instructions, hear the words clearly spoken, hear the words used in a sentence, and then hear the words spoken again.

Spelling Error Analysis

Spelling errors are faulty predictions based on students' knowledge of written language; they are seldom random. Error analysis examines misspellings in a systematic way by grouping them into error types. You may apply error analysis to students' spelling tests and students' writing in order to identify common error pattern You may then correct students' faulty spelling strategie by introducing and reinforcing the patterns that characterize standard spelling. Two reproducible charts for spelling error analysis—one for Levels 2–3, another for Levels 4–6—are provided in the *Teacher's Resource Book.* You and the students may record error types on the chart to identify common error patterns.

The following chart organizes types of errors according to causal factors.

CAUSE	EXAMPLE OF ERROR	
1. Phonetic substitution		
• Consonant sounds	*sity* for *city*; *kat* for *cat*	
• Vowel sounds	*gloo* for *glue*; *wont* for *want*	
2. Omission and insertion of silent letters	*nit* for *night*; *no* for *know*; *cak* for *cake*	
3. Inaccurate pronunciation	*libery* for *library*; *buder* for *butter*; *ninedy* for *ninety*	
4. Transposition of letters	*littel* for *little*	
5. Double consonants		
• Doubling when not appropriate	*citty* for *city*	
• Leaving out double letters	*litle* for *little*	
• When adding endings	*runing* for *running*	
6. Double vowel confusion	*streem* for *stream*	
7. Homophones		
• Incorrect meaning	*reed* for *read*	
8. Words similar in sound		
• One spelling substituted for another	*advice/advise*; *except/accept*	
9. Common spelling patterns applied to irregular words (overgeneralization)	*wuz* for *was*; *munny* for *money*	
10. Inflectional endings and suffixes Incorrectly added	*skateing* for *skating*; *cherryies* for *cherries*; *judgement* for *judgment*	

Core Testing

SKILLS CHECK INVENTORY

At Levels 2–6 of *Harcourt Brace Spelling* a *Skills Check Inventory* precedes the first unit in the **Pupil Book**. This Inventory evaluates students' mastery of spelling skills taught in the previous level. The results will assist you in determining the level of instruction needed and in deciding which students would benefit from working with the Unit, Mastery, and Bonus word lists.

A *Dictation Test*, given in each **Teacher's Edition**, is part of the *Skills Check Inventory*. It evaluates a student's ability to spell a representative sample of words taught in the previous level. It measures long-term retention of spelling patterns and exceptions as well as auditory discrimination.

TRIAL TEST: WEEKLY UNIT PRETEST

The *Trial Test* is administered before the students study the unit. It is recommended that all students take this pretest on both the Unit and Mastery words. (The Bonus words pretest is given on the second day.) Sentences for the pretest are provided in the opener of each teaching unit in the **Teacher's Edition**. Students correct their own pretests and, with your help, analyze their spelling errors to determine patterns. Based on the results of the Trial Test, you can assign the appropriate word list for study. You may want to use the following guidelines to assign Unit, Mastery, and Bonus word lists.

- Students with one or no errors on the Mastery words, but more than two errors on the Unit words, will study the Unit words. The Bonus words may be an optional challenge.
- Students who make two or more errors on the Mastery words will study the Mastery words and then the Unit words.
- Students who make only one or two errors on the Unit words will study the Bonus words in addition to the regular program.

MIDWEEK TEST

An optional *Midweek Test* may be administered on the third day of each unit's work. You may dictate the words to the students or have them test one another.

UNIT TEST: WEEKLY END-OF-UNIT EVALUATION

The *Unit Test* is administered after the students complete the unit. The Unit words and Mastery words will be dictated to all students. The Bonus words will be dictated only to those students who studied the Bonus words. The sentences for the *Unit Test* are provided in the closing section of each teaching unit in the **Teacher's Edition**.

Students should check and correct their own work and, with your help, analyze their spelling errors to determine patterns. The results of the test may be recorded on the *Pupil Progress Report*, which appears in reproducible form in the **Teacher's Resource Book**. Students should also apply *Study Steps to Learn a Word* to all misspelled words.

DICTATION SENTENCES

The optional *Dictation Sentences* are provided to test students' abilities to spell the words when written in context. The *Dictation Sentences* contain only words previously taught in *Harcourt Brace Spelling*. Words taught in a given unit are in italics. The students should be able to write the entire sentence correctly. You may use the *Dictation Sentences* in place of or in addition to the *Unit Test*.

FORM A: SIX-WEEK EVALUATION (OPTIONAL)

Six *Form A Tests* in formats representative of standardized tests are given in each **Teacher's Edition** for Levels 2–6. The tests are on reproducible copying masters and follow the review units. Each is a multiple-choice test, drawing its words from the six previous units. Directions for administering the test, and the *Answer Key*, are on the back. You may use the *Form A Tests* if your grading period is six weeks.

FORM B: NINE-WEEK EVALUATION (OPTIONAL)

As an alternative to the *Form A Tests*, four *Form B Tests* in formats representative of standardized tests are given in each **Teacher's Edition** for levels 2–6. You may use the *Form B Tests* if your grading period is nine weeks.

MIDYEAR AND END-OF-YEAR TESTS

Midyear and *End-of-Year Tests* are provided in each **Teacher's Edition** for Levels 2–6. The *Midyear Test* follows Unit 18; the *End-of-Year Test* follows Unit 36. For each test, you dictate a list of words for the students to write. A test sentence is provided for each Unit, Mastery, and Bonus word.

Additional Testing

DIAGNOSTIC PRETESTS

At Levels 2–6 of *Harcourt Brace Spelling*, two optional *Diagnostic Pretests* are provided in the *Teacher's Resource Books*.

Diagnostic Pretest A has a standardized-test format and consists of twenty items. The tested words are drawn from the list of spelling words presented at the grade level. Directions for administering the test, and an *Answer Key*, are provided.

Diagnostic Pretest B approximates what students do when they proofread their own writing. The test has the students read a short passage that includes twenty-five spelling words presented at the grade level. Following the passage are twenty-five multiple-choice items. There is an item for each of the underlined spelling words in the passage. The students are asked to identify the correctly-spelled word from four choices. Directions for administering the test and an *Answer Key* are provided.

MASTERY WORDS AND BONUS WORDS TESTS

Six optional *Mastery Words Tests* and *Bonus Words Tests* in standardized-test formats are provided in the **Teacher's Resource Books** for Levels 2–6. The tests may be administered following the review units. Each is a multiple-choice test, drawing its words from the six preceding units.

WRITING SAMPLE TEST

At Levels 2–6, an optional *Writing Sample Test* may be administered following each review unit. The test has the student complete a writing assignment by analyzing a prompt and a picture stimulus, and by reading motivational questions. The student's writing is then analyzed for spelling errors. Using samples of a student's own writing examines spelling in a purposeful context. The student's writing provides a forum for predicting the spelling patterns the student has formulated.

RECORD KEEPING

Progress Reports

In *Harcourt Brace Spelling*, Levels 2–6, there are two types of progress reports for recording students' test results. The *Pupil Progress Report* is a student's personal record of the results of the *Trial* and *Unit Tests*, *Six-week* or *Nine-week Evaluation Tests*, *Midyear Test*, and *End-of-Year Test*. The *Class Progress Report* is the teacher's record of students' test results. Both progress reports appear in reproducible form in the **Teacher's Resource Book** at each level.

Spelling Notebook

Each student may keep a spelling notebook for organizing and retaining written work from these sections of the program.

- *Trial* and *Unit Tests*
- *Spelling on Your Own* activities for Unit words and Bonus words
- *Writing on Your Own*
- *Spelling and Writing*
- *Extending the Lesson*
- Enrichment Activities

ENRICHMENT ACTIVITIES

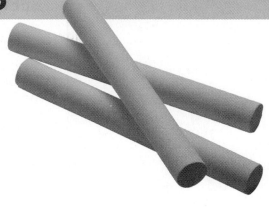

For additional enrichment activities, visit the Harcourt Brace School Publishers Web site at *http://www.hbschool.com.* Click on the Spelling button to find activities for every unit.

The following enrichment activities provide students with opportunities to develop higher-order spelling strategies that will enable them to predict the spelling of English words. The activities do more than have students write spelling words; they also have students apply spelling knowledge to write other words—words they need to use in their writing across the curriculum.

Some activities require whole-class participation, while others are intended for use with small groups or by individual students. The activities may be adapted to reinforce a variety of spelling generalizations. You may select those activities that best suit the needs and interests of your students.

See and Spell

In "See and Spell," the person who is "It" mentally selects an object in plain sight in the classroom. He or she writes the name of the object on a slip of paper and gives it to you or another student. The remaining students have to guess the name by spelling it within a given number of turns. They start by guessing the first letter, then the second, then the third, and so on. The student who is "It" writes the correct letters on the chalkboard as they are guessed. The student who completes the word becomes "It."

SPELLING PASSWORD

"Spelling Password" is played with four people, two on each team. A fifth student is the quiz master. The quiz master has fifteen or twenty cards; a spelling word is written on each card. The quiz master gives a card to one of the players on Team A. That player defines the word for his or her teammate, without using the word itself. If the teammate guesses the word and spells it cor-rectly, Team A gets a point. If the wrong word is guessed, a player from Team B gives his or her teammate a different clue for the same word. If the teammate guesses the word and spells it correctly, Team B gets the point. If not, Team A gets another turn, and so on. Teams take turns at starting each new word.

BEETLES

To play "Beetles," divide the class into two teams. The object of the game is to be the first team to draw a complete *beetle*. Give the first player of one team a word. If the player spells it correctly, he or she draws one part of the beetle's body on the chalkboard. If the word is misspelled, another team member can provide the correct spelling, but the team does not draw the beetle's body. Continue playing by alternating between the two teams until one team has completed a beetle. A completed figure should look like this:

This game may also be played by pairs of students. Have the words written on folded pieces of paper and placed in a paper bag or small box. One player draws a piece of paper and reads the word. The other player spells the word. The first player to create a complete beetle wins.

SPELLING BASEBALL

To play "Spelling Baseball," draw a baseball diamond on the chalkboard. Use four oaktag figures to represent base runners. Divide the class into two teams. Assign each team member a number to indicate the "batting order." Then "pitch" a word to the first batter on Team A. If the player spells the word correctly, he or she moves a runner to first base. If the second batter spells the next word correctly, he or she moves to first base and the first runner advances to second base. If a batter misspells a word, that player gets an out. As play continues, keep track of the runs scored and the number of outs for each inning. Three outs retire a side, and the other team comes to bat.

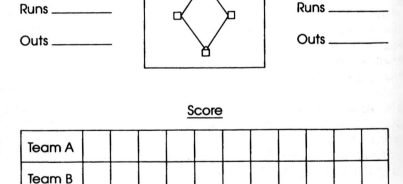

Team A

Runs _____

Outs _____

Team B

Runs _____

Outs _____

Score

Team A											
Team B											

WORD CONSTRUCTIONS

Write beginning, middle, and ending letters on the chalkboard. For example,

f	**ir**	**ly**
w	**ur**	**m**
l	**or**	**th**
t	**ear**	**n**

Have the students see how many words they can spell by combining the letters. When they are finished, make a master list of words on the chalkboard to see how many words were formed. Possibilities include *fear, fir, firm, fur, for, forth, earn, early, earth, worn, wear, worm, worth, learn, tear, torn,* and *turn.*

Other beginning, middle, and ending letters may be used to make "Word Constructions."

COMPOUND CONNECTION

To make "Compound Connections," first have several students write fifteen compound words, drawing a line between the two parts of each compound. Then have them cut thirty cards from oaktag. On each card, students should write one of the smaller words that make up each compound.

To play, the students form groups of two. Students should shuffle the cards well, divide them into two decks, and then place them face down. Students take turns turning up two cards at a time, one from each deck. If the two cards form a compoud word, the student spells the word, keeps the pair, and continues. The other player may challenge if he or she thinks the word is not a real compound. Have the students use a dictionary to determine who is correct. If the two words do not form a compound, the cards are turned face down and put back in the decks. The player with the most cards wins the game.

Other versions may be made for abbreviations, contractions, possessives, base words and inflectional endings, homophones, synonyms, and antonyms.

SYLLABLE WHEELS

Have the students construct six-word, eight-word, or ten-word "Syllable Wheels." Words should contain the VC/CV pattern such as *happen*. Have each student write words that follow the pattern on a sheet of paper. The words should be checked for correct spelling and syllabication. Next the student is ready to make the word wheel by measuring and cutting two circles, one approximately 5" in diameter, and the other about 3" in diameter. The student should place the smaller circle on top of the larger one and fasten them together at their centers. Then the student should divide the circles into six, eight, or ten equal parts. The first syllable of a word should be written in a section of the small wheel and the second syllable in a non-adjoining section of the large wheel.

Have each student work with a partner and exchange wheels. The student turns the wheel. If a word is formed, he or she writes it down. When all possible words have been made, the partner checks the list.

Students can create "Syllable Wheels" for other patterns such as V/CV as in *ro/bot*; VC/V as in *pet/al*.

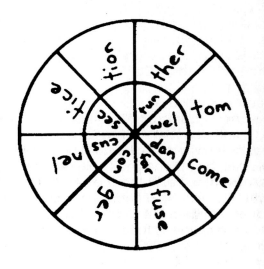

VOWEL TARGET

Have the students complete the "Vowel Target." The target contains six vowel combinations. Students must think of words for each combination. The first letter of each word goes in the outer rim; each word must start with a different letter. However, since all the words meet in the bull's eye, all the words must end with the same letter.

Possible answers include: *meat, boat, pout, feet, wait, root; seal, goal, foul, heel, pail, cool; bead, road, loud, deed, paid, food; dean, loan, noun, seen, vain, moon.*

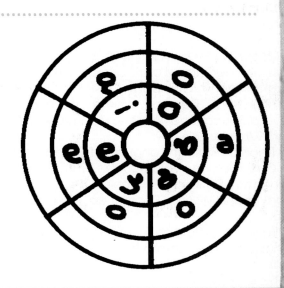

BIBLIOGRAPHY OF SPELLING RESOURCES

Allred, Ruel A., "Integrating Proven Spelling Content and Methods with Emerging Literacy Programs," *Reading Psychology: An International Quarterly*, Volume 14, 1993, pp. 15–31.

Anderson, Kristine F., "The Development of Spelling Ability and Linguistic Strategies," *The Reading Teacher*, November 1985, pp. 140–147.

Axelrod, Penny, and Kathy Shelton Clem, *An Investigation of Spelling Production and Processing in Handicapped Children*. Grant proposal for the U. S. Department of Health, Education, and Welfare, Office of Education, 1977.

Bear, Donald R., "'Learning to Fasten the Seat of My Union Suit Without Looking Around': The Synchrony of Literacy Development," *Theory Into Practice*, Volume 30, Number 3, Summer 1991, pp. 149–157.

Bear, Donald R., and Diane Barone, "The Relationship Between Rapid Automatized Naming and Othographic Knowledge," in J. Zutell and S. McCormick (eds.). *Learner Factors/Teacher Factors: Issues in Literacy Research and Instruction*, pp. 179–184. Chicago, IL: National Reading Conference, 1991.

Beers, Carol Strickland, and James Wheelock Beers, "Three Assumptions About Learning to Spell," *Language Arts*, Volume 58, May 1981, pp. 573–580.

Bissex, G., *Gnys at Wrk: A Child Learns to Write and Read*, Cambridge, MA: Harvard University Press, 1980.

Bolton, Faye, and Diane Snowball, *Teaching Spelling: A Practical Resource*. Portsmouth, NH: Heinemann, 1993.

Boutin, Frances J., "The Effect of a Spelling Approach Used as a Supplement to the Basal Spelling Program with Second Grade Students," Ph.D. dissertation, University of Houston, 1980.

Bradley, Lynette, "The Organization of Visual, Phonological, and Motor Strategies in Learning to Read and to Spell," in Ursula Kirk, ed., *Neuropsychology of Language, Reading, and Spelling*, Academic Press, 1983.

Brown, Ann, and Annmarie Sullivan Palincsar, "Inducing Strategic Learning by Means of Informed Self-Control Training," *Topics in Learning Disabilities*, Volume 2, Number 1, 1982, pp. 1–17.

Carroll, John B., Peter Davis, and Barry Richman, *The American Heritage Word Frequency Book*, Boston: Houghton Mifflin Company, 1971.

Chomsky, Carol, "Reading, Writing, and Phonology," *Harvard Educational Review*, Volume 40, Number 2, May 1970, pp. 287–309.

Cicci, Regina, "Written Language Disorders," *Bulletin of the Orton Society*, Volume XXX, 1980, pp. 240–251.

Cunningham, Patricia M., *Phonics They Use: Words for Reading and Writing*, Second ed. NY: HarperCollins, 1995.

Dale, Edgar, and Joseph O'Rourke, *The Living Word Vocabulary*, Field Enterprises Educational Corporation, 1976.

de Hirsch, Katrina, and Jeanette Jansky, "Patterning and Organizational Deficits in Children with Language and Learning Disabilities," *Bulletin of the Orton Society*, Volume XXX, 1980, pp. 227–239.

Dolch, Edward W., *Better Spelling*, Champaign, IL: Garrard Press, 1942.

Farr, Roger, Cheryl Kelleher, Katherine Lee, and Caroline Beverstock, "An Analysis of the Spelling Patterns of Children in Grades Two Through Eight: A Study of a National Sample of Children's Writing." Center for Reading and Language Studies, Indiana University, 1989.

Fitzsimmons, Robert J., and Bradley M. Loomer, *Spelling: The Research Basis*. University of Iowa, Project Spelling 1980.

Foorman, Barbara R., D. J. Francis, D. M. Novy, and D. Liberman, "How Letter-Sound Instruction Mediates Progress in First-Grade Reading and Spelling," *Journal of Educational Psychology*, Volume 83, 1991, pp. 456–458.

Frith, Uto, ed., *Cognitive Processes in Spelling*. New York: Academic Press, 1980.

Gates, Arthur I., *A List of Spelling Difficulties in 3,876 Words*. New York: Bureau of Publications, Teachers College, Columbia University, 1937.

Gentry, J. Richard, *SPEL . . . Is a Four-Letter Word*. Portsmouth, NH: Heinemann, 1989.

Gill, J. Thomas, Jr., "Development of Word Knowledge As It Relates to Reading, Spelling, and Instruction," *Language Arts*, Volume 69, Number 6, October 1992, pp. 444–453.

Greene, Harry A., *The New Iowa Spelling Scale*. Iowa City: State University of Iowa, 1954.

Hanna, Paul R., Jean S. Hanna, Richard E. Hodges, and Edwin H. Rudorf, Jr., *Phoneme-Grapheme Correspondences as Cues to Spelling Improvement*. U.S. Department of Health, Education, and Welfare, Office of Education, Government Printing Office, Washington: 1976.

Harris, Albert J., and Milton D. Jacobson, *Basic Elementary Reading Vocabularies*. New York: The Macmillan Company, 1972.

Henderson, E., *Teaching Spelling*. Boston: Houghton Mifflin Company, 1995.

Hillerich, Robert L., *A Writing Vocabulary of Elementary Children*. Springfield, IL: Charles C Thomas, 1978.

Hodges, Richard E., "The Conventions of Writing," in *Handbook of Research on Teaching the English Language Arts*, Macmillan, 1991, pp. 775–786.

Horn, Ernest, *A Basic Writing Vocabulary: 10,000 Words Most Commonly Used in Writing*. Iowa City: University of Iowa, 1925.

Jongsma, Kathleen Stumpf, "Reading-Spelling Links: Questions & Answers," *The Reading Teacher*, Volume 43, Number 8, April 1990, pp. 608–610.

učera, Henry, and W. Nelson Francis, *Computational Analysis of Present-Day American English*. Providence, RI: Brown University Press, 1967.

orris, Darrell, "Editorial Comment: Developmental Spelling Theory Revisited," *Reading Psychology: An International Quarterly*, Volume 10, Number 2, 1989, pp. iii–x.

orris, Darrell, "Meeting the Needs of Poor Spellers in the Elementary School: A Developmental Perspective," *National College of Education Occasional Paper No. 14*, November 1986, pp. 3–30.

orris, Darrell, "'Word Sort': A Categorization Strategy for Improving Word Recognition Ability," *Reading Psychology: An International Quarterly*, Volume 3, Number 3, July–September 1982, pp. 247–255.

orton, Donna E., "Spelling," in *The Effective Teaching of Language Arts*. Columbus, OH: Charles E. Merrill Publishing Co., 1985.

artridge, Eric, *A Short Etymological Dictionary of Modern English*, New York: Macmillan Publishing Co., 1979.

ei, Mario, *The Story of English*. Greenwich, CT: Fawcett Publications, 1952.

insland, Henry D., *A Basic Vocabulary of Elementary School Children*. New York: The Macmillan Company, 1945.

Schlagal, Robert C., and Joy Harris Schlagal, "The Integral Character of Spelling," *Language Arts*, Volume 69, Number 6, October 1992, pp. 418–424.

Torgeson, Joseph K., "The Learning Disabled Child as an Inactive Learner: Educational Implications," *Topics in Learning Disabilities*, Volume 2, Number 1, April 1982, pp. 45–52.

Treiman, R., "The Role of Intrasyllabic Units in Learning to Read and Spell," in P. Gough, L. Ehri, and R. Treiman (eds.), *Reading Acquisition*, Hillsdale, NJ: Erlbaum, 1992, pp. 65–106.

Vallecorso, Ada L., Naomi Zigmond, and Lola M. Henderson, "Spelling Instruction in Special Education Classrooms: A Survey of Practices," *Exceptional Children*, Volume 52, Number 1, 1985, pp. 19–24.

Venesky, R. F., "English Orthography: Its Graphical Structure and Its Relation to Sound," *Reading Research Quarterly*, Volume 2, Spring 1967, pp. 75–106.

Walker, Charles Monroe, "High Frequency Word List for Grades 3 Through 9," *The Reading Teacher*, Volume 32, Number 7, April 1979, pp. 803–812.

Zutell, Jerry, and Timothy Rasinski, "Reading and Spelling Connections in Third and Fifth Grade Students," *Reading Psychology: An International Quarterly*, Volume 10, Number 2, 1989, pp. 137–155.

SCOPE AND SEQUENCE

ELEMENTS OF SPELLING	LEVEL 1	LEVEL 2
SOUND-LETTER RELATIONSHIPS		
Spellings for Consonants		
/b/	10–11, 54–55, 110, *10–11, 54–55, 110*	4–8, 29, 31, 115, *4–8, 29, 31, 115*
/d/	22–23, 52–53, 69, 141, *22–23, 52–53, 69, 141*	9–13, 115, *9–13, 115*
/f/	28–29, *28–29*	9–13, 55–59, 115, *9–13, 55–59, 115*
/g/	24–25, 48–49, *24–25, 48–49*	14–18, 30, 55–59, 115, *14–18, 30, 55–59, 115*
/h/	8–9, 69, 110, *8–9, 69, 110*	14–18, 30–31, *14–18, 30–31*
/j/	30–31, *30–31*	14–18, 30, 46, *14–18, 30, 46*
/k/	20–21, 38–39, 141, *20–21, 38–39, 141*	19–23, 31, 101, 115, *19–23, 31, 101, 115*
/kw/		
/l/	4–5, *4–5*	14–18, 30, 35, 55–59, *14–18, 30, 35, 55–59*
/m/	16–17, 50–51, 110, *16–17, 50–51, 110*	4–8, 29, 31, 115, *4–8, 29, 31, 115*
/n/	14–15, 46–47, 69, *14–15, 46–47, 69*	4–8, 29, 115, *4–8, 29, 115*
/p/	18–19, 44–45, *18–19, 44–45*	4–8, 29, *4–8, 29*
/r/	12–13, *12–13*	4–8, 29, 115, *4–8, 29, 115*
/s/	26–27, 110, *26–27, 110*	14–18, 30, 35, 55–59, 115, *14–18, 30, 35, 55–59, 115*
/t/	6–7, 42–43, 69, 110, *6–7, 42–43, 69, 110*	9–13, 115, *9–13, 115*
/th/		76–80, 92, *76–80, 92*
/th̷/	164–167, 172–173, *164–167, 172–173*	81–85, 93, 102, *81–85, 93, 102*
/v/	32–33, *32–33*	9–13, 30, *9–13, 30*
/w/	34–35, 110, 159, *34–35, 110, 159*	9–13, 30, 87, 115, *9–13, 30, 87, 115*
/y/	40–41, *40–41*	9–13, 30, *9–13, 30*
/z/	36–37, *36–37*	55–59, *55–59*
/ks/	56–57, *56–57*	
/gz/		
/zh/		
Consonant Digraphs		
<u>ch</u>	168–171, 174–175, *167–171, 174–175*	81–82, 84–85, 93, *81–82, 84–85, 93*
<u>ng</u>		138–141, *138–141*
<u>sh</u>	164–167, 172–173, *164–167, 172–173*	76–80, 92, *76–80, 92*
<u>th</u>	164–167, 172–173, *164–167, 172–173*	76–80, 81–85, 92, *76–80, 81–85, 92*
<u>wh</u>	168–171, 174–175, *168–171, 174–175*	87, *87*
Consonant Clusters		
Initial clusters with <u>l</u>		66–70, 91, *66–70, 91*
Initial clusters with <u>r</u>		71–75, 92, *71–75, 92*
Initial clusters with <u>s</u>		66–70, 71–75, 91–92, *66–70, 71–75, 91–92*
Initial clusters with digraphs		
Final clusters with <u>d</u>		91, *91*
Final clusters with <u>l</u>		
Final clusters with <u>t</u>		66–70, 91, *66–70*
Spellings for Short Vowel Sounds		
/a/	58–59, 68–71, 76–77, *58–59, 68–71, 76–77*	24–28, 31, 59, *24–28, 31, 59*
/e/	60–61, 84–87, 90–91, *60–61, 84–87, 90–91*	35–39, 59, 60, *35–39, 59, 60*
/i/	62–63, 72–75, 78–79, *62–63, 72–75, 78–79*	40–44, 61, 80, *40–44, 61, 80*
/o/	64–65, 92–95, 100–101, *64–65, 92–95, 100–101*	50–54, 62, *50–54, 62*

***ITALICIZED* NUMBERS REFER TO THE TEACHER'S EDITION**

Section 1

LEVEL 3	LEVEL 4	LEVEL 5	LEVEL 6
153, *153* 8, 25, 153, 155, *8, 25, 153, 155* 8, 25, 69, 128, 143, 145, 155, *8, 25, 69, 128, 143, 145, 155* 128, 153, *128, 153* 128, *128* 38–39, 41, 51, *38–39, 41, 51* 42–43, 45, 52, 61, 128, 153, *42–43, 45, 52, 61, 128, 153* 42, *42* 8, 25, 61, 153, *8, 25, 61, 153* 113, 128, 153, *113, 128, 153* 30–31, 33, 128, 155, *30–31, 33, 128, 155* 153, *153* 113, 115, 128, 153, *113, 115, 128, 153* 8, 25, 46–47, 49, 52, 69, *8, 25, 46–47, 49, 52, 69* 69, 128, 153, *69, 128, 153* 30–31, 33, 50, 128, *30–31, 33, 50, 128* 30–31, 33, 50, 120, *30–31, 33, 50, 120* 61, *61* 115, *115*	120, *120* 46, 49, *46, 49* 38–39, 41, 51, *38–39, 41, 51* 90–91, 95, 97, *90–91, 95, 97* 42–43, 45, 51, 116–117, 119, *42–43, 45, 51, 116–117, 119* 38–39, 41, 51, 116–117, 129, *38–39, 41, 51, 116–117, 129* 143, *143* 49, *49* 125, *125* 46–47, *46–47* 46–47, *46–47* 42–43, 45, 47, 51, 116–117, 119, *42–43, 45, 47, 51, 116–117, 119* 47, *47* 60–61, 63, 76, *60–61, 63, 76* 64–65, 67, 76, *64–65, 67, 76* 38–39, 41, 51, *38–39, 41, 51* 116–117, 119, 129, *116–117, 119, 129*	72–75, 78, *72–75, 78* 72–75, *72–75* 72–75, 78, 151, 156, *72–75, 78, 151, 156* 72–75, 82, *72–75, 82* 42–45, 124, *42–45, 124* 21, 30–33, 39, 50, *21, 30–33, 39, 50* 30–33, 50, *30–33, 50* 72–75, 78, *72–75, 78* 72–75, 78, *72–75, 78* 6, 71, 72–75, *6, 71, 72–75* 72–75, 78, *72–75, 78* 69–71, 72–75, 78, *69–71, 72–75, 78* 6, 20–23, 26, 72–75, *6, 20–23, 26, 72–75* 72–75, 78, *72–75, 78* 38–41, *38–41* 20–23, 26, 72–75, *20–23, 26, 72–75* 153, *153*	25, 94, *25, 94* 149, *149* 31, *31* 85, *85* 30–31, 33, 50, *30–31, 33, 50* 16–17, 68–69, 76, 83, 85, 154, 156, *16–17, 68–69, 76, 83, 85, 154, 156* 20–21, 23, 26, 119, *20–21, 23, 26, 119* 83, 94, *83, 94* 83, 85, *83, 85* 94, *94* 25, 85, *25, 85* 12, 42, 135, 154, *12, 42, 135, 154* 20, *20* 42, 44, 139, *42, 44, 139* 20–21, 23, 26, *20–21, 23, 26* 20–21, 23, 26, *20–21, 23, 26* 34–35, 37, 51, *34–35, 37, 51*

Section 2

LEVEL 3	LEVEL 4	LEVEL 5	LEVEL 6
30–31, 33, 50, *30–31, 33, 50* 30–31, 33, 50, 153, *30–31, 33, 50, 153* 30–31, 33, 50, *30–31, 33, 50* 30–31, 33, 50, 128, *30–31, 33, 50, 128* 124–125, *124–125*	12–13, 15, 25, 64–65, 67, 77, *12–13, 15, 25, 64–65, 67, 77* 60–61, 63, 76, *60–61, 63, 76* 12–13, 15, 25, 60–61, 63, 76, *12–13, 15, 25, 60–61, 63, 76* 11, 60–61, 63, 76, *11, 60–61, 63, 76* 64, 65, 67, *64, 65, 67*	38–41, 42–45, *38–41, 42–45* 38–41, 46–49, 51–52, 151, 156, *38–41, 46–49, 51–52, 151, 156* 38–41, *38–41*	20, 65, *20, 65* 20, 65, 135, *20, 65, 135* 20, *20*

Section 3

LEVEL 3	LEVEL 4	LEVEL 5	LEVEL 6
16–17, 19, 26, 128, *16–17, 19, 26, 128* 16–17, 19, 26, 69, 115, *16–17, 19, 26, 69, 115* 16–17, 19, 26, *16–17, 19, 26* 20–21, 23, 26, 73, *20–21, 23, 26, 73* 20–21, 23, 26, 73, *20–21, 23, 26, 73* 20–21, 23, 26, 128, *20–21, 23, 26, 128*	34–36, 47, *34–36, 47* 6–7, 8–9, 11, 117, *6–7, 8–9, 11, 117* 6–7, 8–9, 11, 34–36, 117, *6–7, 8–9, 11, 34–36, 117* 4–5, *4–5* 4–5, *4–5*	6, 38–41, 51, *6, 38–41, 51* 6, 38–41, 51, 154, *6, 38–41, 51, 154* 6, 38–41, 51, *6, 38–41, 51* 38–41, 51, *38–41, 51* 17, 38–41, *17, 38–41* 6, 17, 38–41, 51, *6, 17, 38–41, 51*	65, 135, *65, 135* 21, 135, *21, 135* 20–21, 135, *20–21, 135*

Section 4

LEVEL 3	LEVEL 4	LEVEL 5	LEVEL 6
4–5, 7, 24, 26, 128, *4–5, 7, 24, 26, 128* 4–5, 7, 9, 24, 26, 41, 155, *4–5, 7, 9, 24, 26, 41, 155* 4–5, 7, 9, 20, 24, 26, 41, 45, 121, 128, 153, *4–5, 7, 9, 20, 24, 26, 41, 45, 121, 128, 153* 4–5, 7, 41, 113, 121, 128, *4–5, 7, 41, 113, 121, 128*	4–5, 7, 24, *4–5, 7, 24* 8–9, 11, 24, 119, *8–9, 11, 24, 119* 4–5, 7, 24, 119, *4–5, 7, 24, 119* 4–5, 7, 24, *4–5, 7, 24*	4–7, 17, 24, 137, 145, *4–7, 17, 24, 137, 145* 4–7, 24, 137, 143, *4–7, 24, 137, 143* 4–7, 24, 71, 73, 143, 145, *4–7, 24, 71, 73, 143, 145* 4–7, 17, 24, 71, *4–7, 17, 24, 71*	4–5, 7, 24, 75, *4–5, 7, 24, 75* 4–5, 7, 12–13, 24, 31, 75, 135, *4–5, 7, 12–13, 24, 31, 75, 135* 4–5, 7, 24, 125, 147, 149, *4–5, 7, 24, 125, 147, 149* 4–5, 7, 24, 31, 125, *4–5, 7, 24, 31, 125*

ELEMENTS OF SPELLING	LEVEL 1	LEVEL 2
/u/	66–67, 80–83, 88–89, *66–67, 80–83, 88–89*	45–49, 59, 61, *45–49, 59, 61*
Spellings for Long Vowel Sounds		
/ā/	120–123, 126–127, 144–147, 150–151, 152–155, 160–161, *120–123, 126–127, 144–147, 150–151, 152–155, 160–161*	97–101, 102–106, 122–123, *97–101, 102–106, 122–123*
/ē/	108–111, 114–115, 140–143, 144–147, 148–149, 150–151, *108–111, 114–115, 140–143, 144–147, 148–149, 150–151*	107–111, 123, *107–111, 123*
/ī/	116–119, 124–125, 132–135, 138–139, *116–119, 124–125, 132–135, 138–139*	112–116, 117–121, 123–124, *112–116, 117–121, 123–124*
/ō/	116–118, 124–125, 132–135, 138–139, 144–147, 150–151, *116–118, 124–125, 132–135, 138–139, 144–147, 150–151*	128–132, 133–137, *128–132, 133–137*
Spellings for Other Vowel Sounds		
/ô/		159–163, 184, *159–163, 184*
/oi/	152–155, 160–161, *152–155, 160–161*	
/ou/		164–168, 184, *164–168, 184*
/o͝o/	140–143, 148–149, *140–143, 148–149*	148–152, *148–152*
/o͞o/		143–147, *143–147*
/yo͝o/		
/yo͞o/		
Spellings for r-controlled Vowel Sounds		
/är/		169–173, 185, *169–173, 185*
/âr/		
/ôr/		169–173, 185, *169–173, 185*
/ûr/		174–178, 185, *174–178, 185*
Spellings for Schwa		
/ər/		179–183, 186, *179–183, 186*
/əl/		
/ən/		
/ə/		
Memory Spellings		
"Silent" Letters	96–99, 102–103, 104–107, 112–113, 128–131, 136–137, 156–159, 162–163, *96–99, 102–103, 104–107, 112–113, 128–131, 136–137, 156–159, 162–163*	112, 128, 148, *112, 128, 148*
Double Letters		55–59, *55–59*
Other-Language Sound-Letter Relationships		
Other Words		86–90, 93, *86–90, 93*
WORD STRUCTURE		
Plural Nouns		
No Base Change	134–135, 154, *134–135, 154*	21, 52, 76, 78, *21, 52, 76, 78*

ITALICIZED NUMBERS REFER TO THE TEACHER'S EDITION

LEVEL 3	LEVEL 4	LEVEL 5	LEVEL 6
4–5, 7, 24, 121, 128, 130, 143, 145, 153, *4–5, 7, 24, 121, 128, 130, 143, 145, 153*	8–9, 11, 24, *8–9, 11, 24*	4–7, 19, 24, 97, *4–7, 19, 24, 73, 97*	4–5, 7, 24, 31, 125, *4–5, 7, 24, 31, 125*
60–61, 63, 75, 77, 121, 130, 153, 156, *60–61, 63, 75, 77, 121, 130, 153, 156*	16–17, 19, 20–21, 23, 25–26, 119, *16–17, 19, 20–21, 23, 25–26, 119*	8–11, 19, 24, 93, 111, 145, *8–11, 19, 24, 93, 111, 145*	8–9, 11, 12–13, 15, 24–25, 75, 125, 151, *8–9, 11, 12–13, 15, 24–25, 75, 125, 151*
31, 64–65, 67, 75, 77, 111, 119, 120, 129–130, 155, *31, 64–65, 67, 75, 77, 111, 119, 120, 129–130, 155*	20–21, 23, 26, *20–21, 23, 26*	12–15, 21, 25, 97, 137, 145, *12–15, 21, 25, 97, 137, 145*	8–9, 11, 12–13, 15, 24–25, 121, 124–125, 147, 151, *8–9, 11, 12–13, 15, 24–25, 121, 124–125, 147, 151*
59, 68–71, 78, 119, 120, 128, 153, 156, *59, 68–71, 78, 119, 120, 128, 153, 156*	16–17, 19, 25, 30–31, 33, 50, 119, *16–17, 19, 25, 30–31, 33, 50, 119*	8–11, 21, 24, 111, 143, 145, *8–11, 21, 24, 111, 143, 145*	8–9, 12–13, 15, 24–25, 125, 139, *8–9, 12–13, 15, 24–25, 125, 139*
9, 72–75, 78, 128, 130, 143, 145, 149, 153, 155–156, *9, 72–75, 78, 128, 130, 143, 145, 149, 153, 155–156*	16–17, 19, 25, 119, *16–17, 19, 25, 119*	12–15, 25, 93, 111, 143, *12–15, 25, 93, 111, 143*	8–9, 11, 24, 125, 135, *8–9, 11, 24, 125, 135*
90–91, 93, 103, 142–143, 145, 153, *90–91, 93, 103, 142–143, 145, 153* 138–139, 141, 155, *138–139, 141, 155* 138–139, 141, 143, 145, 154, 156, *138–139, 141, 143, 145, 154, 156* 134–137, 154, *134–137, 154* 130, 134–137, 154, *130, 134–137, 154*	82–83, 85, 102, *82–83, 85, 102* 82–83, 85, 102, 119, *82–83, 85, 102, 119* 86–87, 89, 102, *86–87, 89, 102* 86–87, 89, 102, *86–87, 89, 102*	60–63, 76, *60–63, 76* 60–63, 76, 137, *60–63, 76, 137* 64–67, 77, *64–67, 77* 64–67, 77, 101, 137, *64–67, 77, 101, 137*	60–62, 63, 77, *60–62, 63, 77* 38–41, 51, *38–41, 51* 38–41, 51, *38–41, 51* 47, 125, *47, 125* 42–45, 52, *42–45, 52* 42–45, *42–45*
98–99, 101, 104, *98–99, 101, 104* 98–99, 101, 104, *98–99, 101, 104* 90–91, 93, 103, *90–91, 93, 103* 94–97, 103, *94–97, 103*	94–95, 97, 103, *94–95, 97, 103* 94–95, 97, 103, *94–95, 97, 103* 94–95, 97, 103, *94–95, 97, 103* 98–99, 101, 104, *98–99, 101, 104*	82–85, 102, *82–85, 102* 137, *137* 82–85, 102, *82–85, 102* 86–89, 93, 102, *86–89, 93, 102*	42–45, 52, *42–45, 52* 47, 68–71, 78, *47, 68–71, 78* 47, 64–66, 67, 77, *47, 64–66, 67, 77*
120–123, 129, 153, *120–123, 129, 153* 120–123, 129, 153, *120–123, 129, 153* 153, *153*	108–109, 111, 128, *108–109, 111, 128* 112–113, 115, 128, *112–113, 115, 128* 112–113, 115, 128, *112–113, 115, 128*	90–93, 103, *90–93, 103* 94–97, 103, 143, *94–97, 103, 143* 94–97, 103, 143, *94–97, 103, 143*	64, 90–92, 93, 103, 116–117, 129, 147, *64, 90–92, 93, 103, 116–117, 129, 147* 42, 116–117, 147, *42, 116–117, 147* 34–35, 42, *34–35, 42* 38, 39, 120–123, 125, 129, 151, *38, 39, 120–123, 125, 129, 151*
46–47, 52, 91, 93, 112–113, 115, 128, *46–47, 52, 91, 93, 112–113, 115, 128* 8–9, 11, 25, 111, 135, 146–147, 149, 155, *8–9, 11, 25, 111, 135, 146–147, 149, 155* 112–115, 128, 142–145, 155, *112–115, 128, 142–145, 155*	16, *16* 20–21, 23, 26, 34–35, 37, 46–47, 49, 50, 52, 86–87, 89, 124–125, 127, 150–151, *20–21, 23, 26, 34–35, 37, 46–47, 49, 50, 52, 86–87, 89, 124–125, 127, 150–151*	68–71, 77, 86, 137, *68–71, 77, 86, 137* 46–47, 59, 72–75, 78, 90, 95, 97, 113, 119, 141, *46–47, 59, 72–75, 78, 90, 95, 97, 113, 119, 141* 68–71, 72–75, *68–71, 72–75*	60, 61, 63, 82–85, 102, *60, 61, 63, 82–85, 102* 56–59, 76, 86–89, 102–103, 125, 127, 130, *56–59, 76, 86–89, 102–103, 125, 127, 130* 68, *68* 12–13, 15, 20–23, 82–85, *12–13, 15, 20–23, 82–85*
6, 34–37, 48, 51, 108–111, 122, 128, 140, *6, 34–37, 48, 51, 108–111, 122, 128, 140*	12–13, 15, 25, 66, *12–13, 15, 25, 66*	34–37, 44, 50, 89, 148, *34–37, 44, 50, 89, 148*	6, 16–19, 25, 33, *6, 16–19, 25, 33*

ITALICIZED **NUMBERS REFER TO THE TEACHER'S EDITION**

SCOPE AND SEQUENCE TE25

ELEMENTS OF SPELLING	LEVEL 1	LEVEL 2
Change y to i		
Change f to v		
Possessive Nouns		
Verbs with Inflections No Base Change		42, 57, 67, 77, 104, 130, 140, *42, 57, 67, 77, 104, 130, 140*
Double Final Consonant		
Drop Final e		130, *130*
Change y to i		
Adjectives with Inflections No Base Change		
Drop Final e Change y to i		
Prefixes		
Suffixes		
Root Words		
Abbreviations		
Contractions		
WORD ANALYSIS **Syllable Patterns**		
Letter Patterns	108, 114, 120, 126, 132, 138, 140, 144, 148, 150, 152, 164, 168, 172, 174, *108, 114, 120, 126, 132, 138, 140, 144, 148, 150, 152, 164, 168, 172, 174*	45, 97, 102, 128, *45, 97, 102, 128*
Pronunciation Changes	71, 73–74, 87, 95, *71, 73–74, 87, 95*	5, 8, 17, 18, 31, 44, 70, 75, 77, 79, 99, 101, 141, 168, *5, 8, 17, 18, 31, 44, 70, 75, 77, 79, 99, 101, 141, 168*
Phonograms		
Rhyming Words *(continued)*	85, 95, 122, 153, 170, 175, *85, 95, 122, 153, 170, 175*	9, 15, 20, 23, 25, 28, 31, 36, 41, 45, 46, 47, 51, 54, 80, 81, 85, 87, 89, 90, 91, 93, 98, 103, 106, 113, 116, 118, 137, 152, 156, 173, 178, *9, 15, 20,*

ITALICIZED NUMBERS REFER TO THE TEACHER'S EDITION

LEVEL 3	LEVEL 4	LEVEL 5	LEVEL 6
108–111, 116–119, 128–129, *108–111, 116–119, 128–129*	12–13, 15, 25, *12–13, 15, 25*	34–37, 50, 89, 148, *34–37, 50, 89, 148* 34–37, 50, *34–37, 50*	
	72–73, 75, 90–93, 103, 110, *72–73, 75, 90–93, 103, 110*	92–93, *92–93*	92, *92*
22, 44, 141, *22, 44, 141* 12–15, *12–15* 56–59, 76, 141, *56–59, 76, 141* 116–119, 129, *116–119, 129*	34–35, 37, 50, 114, *34–35, 37, 50, 114* 34–35, 37, 50, *34–35, 37, 50* 114, *114*	14, 16–17, 19, 25, 56–59, 63, 88, *14, 16–17, 19, 25, 56–59, 63, 88* 16–17, 19, 25, 41, *16–17, 19, 25, 41* 14, 41, 56–59, 63, 76, 88, 140, *14, 41, 56–59, 63, 76, 88, 140* 56–59, 76, *56–59, 76*	10, 15, 56–59, 76, 126, *10, 15, 56–59, 76, 126* 56–59, 76, *56–59, 76* 32, 136, 145, *32, 136, 145* 145, *145*
	68–69, 71, 77, *68–69, 71, 77* 68–69, 71, 77, *68–69, 71, 77* 68–69, 71, 77, 144, *68–69, 71, 77, 144*	40, *40* 39, *39*	23, 86–89, 102–103, *23, 86–89, 102–103* 86–89, 102–103, *86–89, 102–103* 86–89, 98, 102–103, *86–89, 98, 102–103*
94, 151, *94, 151*	138–141, 154, *138–141, 154*	66, 116–119, 129, 134, 152–153, *66, 116–119, 129, 134, 152–153*	26, 67, 73, 94–97, 100, 103, 109, 112–115, 139, 140, *26, 67, 73, 94–97, 100, 103, 109, 112–115, 139, 140*
134, *134*	116–117, 129, 142–143, 145, 146–147, 149, 155–156, *116–117, 129, 142–143, 145, 146–147, 149, 155–156*	47, 66, 110, 113, 115, 120–123, 124–127, 129–130, 134, *47, 66, 110, 113, 115, 120–123, 124–127, 129–130, 134*	14, 26, 45, 73, 75, 96, 98–101, 104, 108–111, 112–115, 117, 128, 138–139, 144, 145, 148, 149, 151–153, *14, 26, 45, 73, 75, 96, 98–101, 104, 108–111, 112–115, 117, 128, 138–139, 144, 145, 148, 149, 151–153*
151, 94, *134, 151*	116–117, 120–121, *116–117, 120–121*	111, *111*	112–115, 138–141, 155, *112–115, 138–141, 155*
	56–57, 59, 76, *56–57, 59, 76*	101, *101*	
86–89, 102, 126, *86–89, 102, 126*	90–91, 93, 103, *90–91, 93, 103*		9, *9*
146–147, 149, 150–151, 153, 155–156, *146–147, 149, 150–151, 153, 155–156*	16–17, 19, 30, 124–125, 127, 130, 134–135, 137, 150–151, 153, 154, 156, *16–17, 19, 30, 124–125, 127, 130, 134–135, 137, 150–151, 153, 154, 156*	138–139, 141, 142–143, 145, 146–149, 154–155, *138–139, 141, 142–143, 145, 146–149, 154–155*	92, 124–125, 127, 130, 134–135, 137, 146–149, 150–151, 153, 154, 156, *92, 124–125, 127, 130, 134–135, 137, 146–149, 150–151, 153, 154, 156*
4–5, 8, 12–15, 16–17, 19, 20–21, 23, 24–26, 30–31, 33, 34, 37, 38, 42–43, 45, 46–47, 49, 50–52, 56–59, 60–61, 63, 64–65, 67, 68–69, 71, 72–73, 76–78, 90–91, 93, 94–97, 98–99, 102–104, 112–113, 116–119, 120–123, 134–135, 137, 142–145, 154–156, *4–5, 8, 12–15, 16–17, 19, 20–21, 23, 24–26, 30–31, 33, 34, 37, 38, 42–43, 45, 46–47, 49, 50–52, 56–59, 60–61, 63, 64–65, 67, 68–69, 71, 72–73, 76–78, 90–91, 93, 94–97, 98–99, 102–104, 112–113, 116–119, 120–123, 134–135, 137, 142–145, 154–156*	16, 115, 124, 151, *16, 115, 124, 151*	8, 12, 24–25, 64–65, 77, *8, 12, 24–25, 64–65, 77*	30–31, 34–35, 82–85, 116–119, *30–31, 34–35, 82–85, 116–119*
7, 19, 23, 45, *7, 19, 23, 45*		98, 142, *98, 142*	44, 56, 84, 137, *44, 56, 84, 137*
	20–21, 23, 30–31, 82–83, 85, *20–21, 23, 30–31, 82–83, 85*	9, 33, 41, 63, 83, *9, 33, 41, 63, 83*	
9, 11, 15, 21, 23, 33, 45, 67, 73, 99, 103–104, 113, 115, 135, 141, 143–144, 147, 155, *9, 11, 15, 21, 23, 33, 45, 67, 73, 99, 103–104, 113, 115*	7, 14, 19, 25, 47, 49, 59, 62, 63, *7, 14, 19, 25, 47, 49, 59, 62, 63*	5, 11, 15, 21, 45, 47, 67, 69, 71, 73, 85, 87, 89, 95, 139, 154, *5, 11, 15, 21, 45, 47, 67, 69, 71, 73, 85, 87, 89, 95, 139, 154*	9, 13, 25, 31, 39, 41, 71, 77, 102, 150, 151, *9, 13, 25, 31, 39, 41, 71, 77, 102, 150, 151*

ITALICIZED NUMBERS REFER TO THE TEACHER'S EDITION

SCOPE AND SEQUENCE

ELEMENTS OF SPELLING	LEVEL 1	LEVEL 2
		23, 25, 28, 31, 36, 41, 45, 46, 47, 51, 54, 80, 81, 85, 87, 89, 90, 91, 93, 98, 103, 106, 113, 116, 118, 137, 152, 156, 173, 178
Compound Words	145, *145*	70, 116, 121, *70, 116, 121*
Related Words		
Word Origins		62, 91, 124, 153, 186, *62, 91, 124, 153, 186*
Mnemonic Devices		71, 81, 86, 117, 128, 138, *71, 81, 86, 117, 128, 138*

SPELLING AND LANGUAGE ARTS	LEVEL 1	LEVEL 2
READING		
Vocabulary **Synonyms**		18, 23, 106, *18, 23, 106*
Antonyms	86, 157, *86, 157*	51, 59, 108, 119, 142, 149, 171, 180, *51, 59, 108, 119, 142, 149, 171, 180*
Homophones	111, *111*	49, 143, 178, *49, 143, 178*
Homographs		14, *14*
Content Area Words		8, 107–110, 116, 164–167, *8, 107–110, 116, 164–167*
Easily Confused Words		81, 83, 84, 86, *81, 83, 84, 86*
Multiple Meanings		68, 83, *68, 83*
Analogies		
Comprehension (Spelling and Reading) Using Context Clues	77, 79, 89, 91, 101, 103, 113, 125, 127, 137, 149, 151, 161, 163, 173, *77, 79, 89, 91, 101, 103, 113, 125, 127, 137, 149, 151, 161, 163, 173*	30, 60, 62, 92, 93, 94, 123, 125, 153, 154, 156, 185, 186, *30, 60, 62, 92, 93, 94, 123, 125, 153, 154, 156, 185, 186*
Identifying the Main Idea		156, 187, *156, 187*
Identifying Details		32, 63, 94, 125, 156, 187, *32, 63, 94, 125, 156, 187*
Sequencing		27, 105, 187, *27, 105, 187*

ITALICIZED NUMBERS REFER TO THE TEACHER'S EDITION

LEVEL 3	LEVEL 4	LEVEL 5	LEVEL 6
135, 141, 143–144, 147, 155			
82–85, 95, 100, 102–104, 111, *82–85, 95, 100, 102–104, 111*	72–73, 75, 78, 120–121, 123, 129, *72–73, 75, 78, 120–121, 123, 129*	11, 67, 98–101, 104, *11, 67, 98–101, 104*	46–49, 52, 73, 78, 153, *46–49, 52, 73, 78, 153*
134, 148, *134, 148*	7, 150, 152, 155, *7, 152, 155*	49, 66, 83, 85, 113, 115, 119, 126–127, 134–137, 145, 147, 152–153, 154–155, *49, 66, 83, 85, 113, 115, 119, 126–127, 134–137, 145, 147, 152–153, 154–155*	15, 36, 37, 41, 59, 71, 73, 78, 85, 95–97, 108–111, 112–115, 117, 122, 128, 138–139, 141, 154–155, 156, *15, 36, 37, 41, 59, 71, 73, 78, 85, 95–97, 108–111, 112–115, 117, 122, 128, 138–139, 141, 154–155, 156*
25, 50, 77, 104, 130, 156, *25, 50, 77, 104, 130, 156*	51, 67, 77, 102, 130, 149, 154, *51, 67, 77, 102, 130, 149, 154*	26, 51, 71, 77, 96–97, 103, 112, 130, 152–153, 155, *26, 51, 71, 77, 96–97, 103, 112, 130, 152–153, 155*	25, 26, 51, 68, 76, 77, 104, 108, 130, 138–141, 144, 155, *25, 26, 51, 68, 76, 77, 104, 108, 130, 138–141, 144, 155*
4, 8, 16, 38, 42, 46, 60, 64, 68, 72, 86, 98, 116, 120, 134, 142, *4, 8, 16, 38, 42, 46, 60, 64, 68, 72, 86, 98, 116, 120, 134, 142*	4, 8, 12, 20, 30, 38, 42, 60, 64, 68, 82, 108, 112, 120, 150, *4, 8, 12, 20, 30, 38, 42, 60, 64, 68, 82, 108, 112, 120, 150*	8, 20, 42, 46, 64, 72, 124, 142, *8, 20, 42, 46, 64, 72, 124, 142*	12, 16, 20, 64, 68, 116, 134, 138, 146, *12, 16, 20, 64, 68, 116, 134, 138, 146*

LEVEL 3	LEVEL 4	LEVEL 5	LEVEL 6
41, 139, *41, 139*	19, 33, 44, 49, 52, 84, 115, 117, 145, *19, 33, 44, 49, 52, 84, 115, 117, 145*	5, 10, 11, 47, 62, 65, 71, 74–75, 83, 89, 91, 95, 97, 108–111, 113, 123, 127, 128–129, 141, 156, *5, 10, 11, 47, 62, 65, 71, 74–75, 83, 89, 91, 95, 97, 108–111, 113, 123, 127, 128–129, 141, 156*	22, 41, 45, 47, 77, 84, 89, 97, 111, 125, 142–145, *22, 41, 45, 47, 77, 84, 89, 97, 111, 125, 142–145*
19, 39, 67, 71, 83, 93, 101, 137, 151, *19, 39, 67, 71, 83, 93, 101, 137, 151*	23, 41, 49, 52, 61, 76, 117, 126, 137, 139, 141, 145, *23, 41, 49, 52, 61, 76, 117, 126, 137, 139, 141, 145*	7, 11, 43, 45, 63, 108–111, 117, 119, 123, 125, 128–129, 147, *7, 11, 43, 45, 63, 108–111, 117, 119, 123, 125, 128–129, 147*	40, 52, 67, 142–145, *40, 52, 67, 142–145*
66, 68, 89, 124–127, 130, *66, 68, 89, 124–127, 130*	16–17, 22–23, 31, 43, 61, 65, 92–93, 97, 103, *16–17, 22–23, 31, 43, 61, 65, 92–93, 97, 103*	9, 22–23, 49, 59, 70–71, 87, 96–97, 112–113, *9, 22–23, 49, 59, 70–71, 87, 96–97, 112–113*	37, 68, 70–71, 78, 85, *37, 68, 70–71, 78, 85*
21, 72, *21, 72*	100, *100*	140, *140*	136, *136*
17, 36, 51, 108–111, 120–123, *17, 36, 51, 108–111, 120–123*	27, 61, 72–75, 116–119, *27, 61, 72–75, 116–119*	112–115, 128, 150–153, 156, *112–115, 128, 150–153, 156*	72–75, 116–119, *72–75, 116–119*
84, *84*	92, 122, *92, 122*	96, *96*	23, 48, *23, 48*
18, 92, 114, 148, *18, 92, 114, 148*	22, 62, 84, 100, *22, 62, 84, 100*	32, 44, 140, *32, 44, 140*	32, 44, 62, 66, 114, 115, 118, 126, *32, 44, 62, 66, 114, 115, 118, 126*
145, *145*			74, 113, 125, 130, 141, *74, 113, 125, 130, 141*
17, 24–25, 26, 51, 52, 78, 103, 129, 155–156, *17, 24–25, 26, 51, 52, 78, 103, 129, 155–156*	27, 53, 79, 105, 131, 157, *27, 53, 79, 105, 131, 157*	84–85, 111, 135, *84–85, 111, 135*	26, 50, 51, 76, 78, 102–104, 128–130, 154, 155, *26, 50, 51, 76, 78, 102–104, 128–130, 154, 155*
80, 131, 157–158, *80, 131, 157–158*	27, 53, 79, 105, 131, 157, *27, 53, 79, 105, 131, 157*	27–28, 53–54, 79–80, 105–106, 131–132, 157–158, *27–28, 53–54, 79–80, 105–106, 131–132, 157–158*	27, 79, 105, 131, 157, *27, 79, 105, 131, 157*
27, 53–54, 79–80, 105–106, 131–132, 157–158, *27, 53–54, 79–80, 105–106, 131–132, 157–158*	27, 53, 79, 105, 131, 157, *27, 53, 79, 105, 131, 157*	131–132, *131–132*	28–29, 106–107, *28–29, 106–107*
10, 11, 13, 15, 19, 32, 40, 41, 54, 57, 71, 75, 104, 132–133, *10, 11, 13, 15, 19, 32, 40, 41, 54, 57, 71, 75, 104, 132–133*	53, *53*	27–28, 53–54, 79–80, 105–106, 131–132, 157–158, *27–28, 53–54, 79–80, 105–106, 131–132, 157–158*	27–29, 106–107, *27–29, 106–107*

SCOPE AND SEQUENCE

SPELLING AND LANGUAGE ARTS	LEVEL 1	LEVEL 2
Drawing Conclusions	77, 83, 89, 103, 113, 115, 125, 127, 139, 149, 163, *77, 83, 89, 103, 113, 115, 125, 127, 139, 149, 163*	63, 94, 125, 156, 187, *63, 94, 125, 156, 187*
Predicting Outcomes	79, 91, 151, 161, *79, 91, 151, 161*	32, 94, *32, 94*
Making Judgments	101, 137, 173, *101, 137, 173*	32, 63, 94, 125, 156, 187, *32, 63, 94, 125, 156, 187*
Distinguishing Between Fact and Opinion		
Identifying Cause-and-Effect Relationships		94, *94*
Response to Literature (Spelling and Reading/Spelling and Writing)		32–34, 63–65, 94–96, 125–127, 156–158, 187–189, *32–34, 63–65, 94–96, 125–127, 156–158, 187–189*
WRITING		
The Writing Process (Prewriting, Composing, Revising, Publishing)		34, 42, 47, 57, 65, 68, 78, 96, 104, 109, 127, 130, 135, 140, 145, 157, 166, 171, 176, 181, 189, *34, 42, 47, 57, 65, 68, 78, 96, 104, 109, 127, 130, 135, 140, 145, 157, 166, 171, 176, 181, 189*
Types of Writing		
Writing Sentences	74, 77, 79, 82, 86, 89, 91, 97, 98, 101, 103, 113, 115, 118, 125, 127, 130, 137, 139, 149, 151, 158, 161, 163, 167, 173, 175, *74, 77, 79, 82, 86, 89, 91, 97, 98, 101, 103, 113, 115, 118, 125, 127, 130, 137, 139, 149, 151, 158, 161, 163, 167, 173, 175*	16, 18, 21, 26, 28, 32, 33–34, 37, 44, 49, 57, 64–65, 69, 70, 73, 83, 85–88, 101, 130, 132, 135, 137, 142, 145, 161, 163, 173, 183, *16, 18, 21, 26, 28, 32, 33–34, 37, 44, 49, 57, 64–65, 69, 70, 73, 83, 85, 88, 101, 130, 132, 135, 137, 142, 145, 161, 163, 173, 183*
Writing Paragraphs		39, 68, 85, 104, 109, 161, 171, 189, *39, 68, 85, 104, 109, 161, 171, 189*
Writing Letters and Social Notes		11, 83, 95–96, *11, 83, 95–96*
Forms of Discourse		
Expository Writing		
Explanations and Directions		42, 52, 68, 75B, 83, 104, 106B, 114, 171, 188–189, *42, 52, 68, 83, 104, 114, 171, 188–189*
Comparisons and Contrasts		
Journals		
Book Reports		
News Stories and Magazine Articles		
Interviews		
Reports		85, *85*
Narrative Writing		
Stories	77, 79, 89, 91, 94, 99, 113, 115, 125, 127, 137, 139, 149, 151, 161, 163, 173, 175, *77, 79, 89, 91, 94, 99, 113, 115, 125, 127, 137, 139, 149, 151, 161, 163, 173, 175*	39, 59, 78, 80, 85, 121, 126–127, 140, 145, 152, 168, 181, *39, 59, 78, 80, 85, 121, 126–127, 140, 145, 152, 168, 181*
Paragraphs		
Biographies and Autobiographies		

ITALICIZED NUMBERS REFER TO THE TEACHER'S EDITION

| --- | --- | --- | --- |
27, 53, 105, 131, 157, *27, 53, 105, 131, 157*	27, 79, 157, *27, 79, 157*	54, 157–158, *54, 157–158*	28, 106–107, *28, 106–107*
27, *27,*	53, *53*	54, 79, 105, *54, 79, 105,*	79, *79*
27, 53, 79, 105, 131, 157, *27, 53, 79, 105, 131, 157*	27, 79, 131, *27, 79, 131*	27, 79, 106, 157–158, *27, 79, 106, 157–158*	
		139, *139*	53, *53*
27, 131, *27, 131*	53, *53,*	80, *80*	10, 28, *10, 28*
27–29, 53–55, 79–81, 105–107, 131–133, 157–159, *27–29, 53–55, 79–81, 105–107, 131–133, 157–159*	27–29, 53–55, 79–81, 105–107, 131–133, 157–159, *27–29, 53–55, 79–81, 105–107, 131–133, 157–159*	27–29, 53–55, 79–81, 105–107, 131–133, 157–159, *27–29, 53–55, 79–81, 105–107, 131–133, 157–159*	27–29, 53–55, 79–81, 105–107, 131–133, 157–159, *27–29, 53–55, 79–81, 105–107, 131–133, 157–159*
6, 10, 14, 18, 22, 28–29, 32, 36, 40, 44, 48, 54–55, 58, 62, 66, 70, 74, 80–81, 84, 88, 92, 96, 100, 106–107, 110, 114, 118, 122, 126, 132–133, 136, 140, 144, 148, 152, 158–159, *6, 10, 14, 18, 22, 28–29, 32, 36, 40, 44, 48, 54–55, 58, 62, 66, 70, 74, 80–81, 84, 88, 92, 96, 100, 106–107, 110, 114, 118, 122, 126, 132–133, 136, 140, 144, 148, 152, 158–159*	6, 10, 14, 18, 22, 28–29, 32, 36, 40, 44, 48, 54–55, 58, 62, 66, 70, 74, 80–81, 84, 88, 92, 96, 100, 106–107, 110, 114, 118, 122, 126, 132–133, 136, 140, 144, 148, 152, 158–159, *6, 10, 14, 18, 22, 28–29, 32, 36, 40, 44, 48, 54–55, 58, 62, 66, 70, 74, 80–81, 84, 88, 92, 96, 100, 106–107, 110, 114, 118, 122, 126, 132–133, 136, 140, 144, 148, 152, 158–159*	6, 10, 14, 18, 22, 28–29, 32, 36, 40, 44, 48, 54–55, 58, 62, 66, 70, 74, 80–81, 84, 88, 92, 96, 100, 106–107, 110, 114, 118, 122, 126, 132–133, 136, 140, 144, 148, 152, 158–159, *6, 10, 14, 18, 22, 28–29, 32, 36, 40, 44, 48, 54–55, 58, 62, 66, 70, 74, 80–81, 84, 88, 92, 96, 100, 106–107, 110, 114, 118, 122, 126, 132–133, 136, 140, 144, 148, 152, 158–159*	6, 10, 14, 18, 22, 28–29, 32, 36, 40, 44, 48, 54–55, 58, 62, 66, 70, 71, 74, 84, 88, 92, 96, 100, 106–107, 110, 114, 118, 122, 126, 132–133, 140, 144, 148, 149, 152, 158–159, *6, 10, 14, 18, 22, 28–29, 32, 36, 40, 44, 48, 54–55, 58, 62, 66, 70, 71, 74, 84, 88, 92, 96, 100, 106–107, 110, 114, 118, 122, 126, 132–133, 140, 144, 148, 149, 152, 158–159*
6, 10, 15, 19, 33, 37, 39, 45, 59, 63, 71, 89, 111, 119, 127, 141, 149, *6, 10, 15, 19, 33, 37, 39, 45, 59, 63, 71, 89, 111, 119, 127, 141, 149*	7, 14–15, 33, 37, 49, 71, 89, 93, 97, 101, 111, 137, 141, 145, *7, 14–15, 33, 37, 49, 71, 89, 93, 97, 101, 111, 137, 141, 145*	7, 14, 18–19, 23, 33, 40, 44–45, 49, 59, 63, 67, 70, 84, 89, 93, 97, 107, 111, 115, 119, 127, 137, 149, 153, *7, 14, 18–19, 23, 33, 40, 44–45, 49, 59, 63, 67, 70, 84, 89, 93, 97, 107, 111, 115, 119, 127, 137, 149, 153*	15, 33, 37, 41, 49, 59, 63, 71, 75, 93, 97, 110, 111, 123, 137, 144, 145, *15, 33, 37, 41, 49, 59, 63, 71, 75, 93, 97, 110, 111, 123, 137, 144, 145*
44, 80–81, 122, *44, 80–81, 122*	28, 33, 48, 63, 66, 110, 118–119, 148, 158–159, *28, 33, 48, 63, 66, 110, 118–119, 148, 158–159*	6, 10, 28–29, 32–33, 36–37, 40, 48, 58, 62, 74, 92, 96, 110, 114, 122, 132–133, 136, 140, 144, 148, 152, 158–159, *6, 10, 28–29, 32–33, 36–37, 40, 48, 58, 62, 74, 92, 96, 110, 114, 122, 132–133, 136, 140, 144, 148, 152, 158–159*	6, 19, 22, 44, 45, 74, 85, 110, 111, 118, 127, 140, 148, 153, *6, 19, 22, 44, 45, 74, 85, 110, 111, 118, 127, 140, 148, 153*
36, 58, 59, 88, 106–107, 148, *36, 58, 59, 88, 106–107, 148*	40, 58–59, 74, 106–107, 114, 136, *40, 58–59, 74, 106–107, 114, 136*	22, 80–81, 118, 126, *22, 80–81, 118, 126*	32, 40, 48, 88, 92, 158–159, *32, 40, 48, 63A, 88, 92, 101A, 158–159*
14, 44, 62, 74, 110, 152, *14, 44, 62, 74, 110, 152*	6, 54–55, 84, 110, 118, 122, *6, 54–55, 84, 110, 118, 122*	18, 96, 158–159, *18, 96, 158–159*	14, 118, *7B, 14, 81A, 115B, 118*
		110, 148, *110, 148*	44, 48, 74, 88, *44, 48, 74, 88*
66, *66*	10, 32, 140, *10, 32, 140*	32, *32*	66, 136, *66, 136*
22, *22*	92, 132–133, *92, 132–133*	136, *136*	126, *126*
84, *84*	22, 66, 144, 148, *22, 66, 144, 148*	48, 74, 132–133, *48, 74, 132–133*	18, 36, 106–107, 111, *11A, 18, 36, 106–107, 111*
		132–133, *132–133*, 145B	96, *96*
92, 158–159, *92, 158–159*	126, *126*	114, *114*	28–29, 70, 100, *23A, 28–29, 70, 100*
18, 40, 54–55, 97, 114, 115, 118, 119, 127, 144, 153, *18, 40, 54–55, 97, 114, 115, 118, 119, 127, 144, 153*	11, 19, 36, 44, 115, 141, *11, 19, 36, 44, 115, 141*	19, 37, 54–55, 59, 62, 75, 89, 101, 140–141, *19, 37, 54–55, 59, 62, 75, 89, 101, 140–141*	7, 10, 33, 62, 114, 132–133, *7, 10, 33, 62, 114, 132–133*
		33, 122, *33, 122*	
		58, *58*	80–81, *80–81*

SPELLING AND LANGUAGE ARTS	LEVEL 1	LEVEL 2
Descriptive Writing		
Paragraphs		73, 109, 161, *73, 109, 161*
Stories		34, 57, 90, 111, *34, 57, 90, 111*
Poetry		47, 75, 119, 157–158, 166, *47, 75, 119, 157–158, 166*
Persuasive Writing		
Paragraphs		
Compositions		
Editorials and Advertisements		
Speeches		
RESOURCES FOR WRITING		
Dictionary		
Locating Words	70, 110, 119, 146, 153, *70, 110, 119, 146, 153*	10, 26, 88, 114, 122, 132, 150, 184, *10, 26, 88, 114, 122, 132, 150, 184*
Alphabetical Order		
Guide Words		
Using Entries	73, 93, 109, 133, 145, 153, 165, *73, 93, 109, 133, 145, 153, 165*	37, 88, 130, *37, 88, 130*
Word Book/Spelling Thesaurus	191–196, *191–196*	52, 65, 73, 145, *52, 65, 73, 145*
Writer's Guide		11, 16, 21, 26, 34, 42, 68, 83, 96, 119, 127, 135, 140, 158, 166, 176, *11, 16, 21, 26, 34, 42, 68, 83, 96, 119, 127, 135, 140, 158, 166, 176*
HANDWRITING		
Legibility of Letter Forms	2, 6, 8, 10, 12, 14, 16, 18, 20, 22, 24, 26, 28, 30, 32, 34, 36, 38, 40, 42, 44, 46, 48, 50, 52, 54, 56, 58, 60, 62, 64, 66, *2, 6, 8, 10, 12, 14, 16, 18, 20, 22, 24, 26, 28, 30, 32, 34, 36, 38, 40, 42, 44, 46, 48, 50, 52, 54, 56, 58, 60, 62, 64, 66*	34, 65, 96, 127, 158, *34, 65, 96, 127, 158*
Common Errors in Letter Formation	200–203, *200–203*	261, 266, *261, 266*
LANGUAGE		
Parts of Speech	69, 122, 134, 143, 154, *69, 122, 134, 143, 154*	42, 68, 78, 104, 109, 130, 140, *42, 68, 78, 104, 109, 130, 140*
LISTENING		
For Sounds of Letters	4, 6, 8, 10, 12, 14, 16, 18, 20, 22, 24, 26, 28, 30, 32, 34, 36, 38, 40, 42, 44,	9, 14, 19, 29, 60, 66, 71, 76, 81, 91, 122, 138, 148, 153, 164, 169, 174,

(continued)

ITALICIZED NUMBERS REFER TO THE TEACHER'S EDITION

LEVEL 3	LEVEL 4	LEVEL 5	LEVEL 6
32, 80–81, 100, *32, 80–81, 100* 40, 54–55, 114, 115, 118, 119, 144, *40, 54–55, 114, 115, 118, 119, 144* 70, 96, 136, *70, 96, 136*	28, 29, 33, 48, 63, 84, 148, 158, 159, *28, 29, 33, 48, 63, 84, 148, 158, 159* 11, 19, 36, 44, 115, 141, *11, 19, 36, 44, 115, 141* 14, 62, 96, *14, 62, 96* 119, *119* 18, 88, 152, *18, 88, 152*	6, 28–29, 40, 144, *6, 28–29, 40, 144* 88, 100, *88, 100* 10, 92, 152, *10, 92, 152* 36, 66, *36, 66* 110, *110*	6, 54–55, 58, 115, *6, 54–55, 58, 115* 122, 152, *122, 152* 18, *18* 55A, 115A, 123B
10, 84, 100, *10, 84, 100* 32, 114, *32, 114* 18, 58, 66, 92, 128, *18, 58, 66, 92, 128*	6–7, 19, 21, 41, 66–67, 75, 111, 127, *6–7, 19, 21, 41, 66–67, 75, 111, 127* 10, 66, *10, 66* 6, 10, 14–15, 22, 32, 36, 40, 44, 48, 62, 70, 84, 92, 100, 114, 122, 136, 144, 152, *6, 10, 14–15, 22, 32, 36, 40, 44, 48, 62, 70, 84, 92, 100, 114, 122, 136, 144, 152*	6, 10, 15, 33, 48, 59, 93, 95, 153, *6, 10, 15, 33, 48, 59, 93, 95, 153* 10, 48, *10, 48* 6, 10, 14, 22, 32, 36, 40, 44–45, 48–49, 62–63, 66, 70, 74, 84, 88, 96–97, 110, 115, 118, 126, 140, 148, *6, 10, 14, 22, 32, 36, 40, 44–45, 48–49, 62–63, 66, 70, 74, 84, 88, 96–97, 110, 115, 118, 126, 140, 148*	11, 71, *11, 71* 10, 33, *10, 33* 6, 10, 14, 18, 32, 36, 40, 44, 48–49, 66, 70, 84, 92, 100, 114, 122, 123, 136, 144, 152, *6, 10, 14, 18, 32, 36, 40, 44, 48–49, 66, 70, 84, 92, 100, 114, 122, 123, 136, 144, 152*
29, 32, 81, 107, 133, *29, 32, 81, 107, 133*	29, 44, 48, 55, 81, 107, 118, 152, 159, *29, 44, 48, 55, 81, 107, 118, 152, 159*	29, 55, 74, 107, 133, *29, 55, 74, 107, 133*	6, 22, 29, 55, 63, 81, 84, 107, 133, 159, *6, 22, 29, 55, 63, 81, 84, 107, 133, 159*
6, 14, 22, 29, 36, 40, 44, 48, 55, 58, 62, 66, 70, 74, 81, 84, 88, 92, 96, 110, 118, 122, 126, 133, 136, 144, 152, 159, *6, 14, 22, 29, 36, 40, 44, 48, 55, 58, 62, 66, 70, 74, 81, 84, 88, 92, 96, 110, 118, 122, 126, 133, 136, 144, 152, 159*	6, 10, 14, 18, 22, 29, 32, 36, 40, 55, 58, 62, 74, 81, 84, 88, 92, 96, 100, 107, 110, 114, 122, 126, 133, 136, 140, 144, 148, *6, 10, 14, 18, 22, 29, 32, 36, 40, 55, 58, 62, 74, 81, 84, 88, 92, 96, 100, 107, 110, 114, 122, 126, 133, 136, 140, 144, 148*	18, 22, 29, 32, 36, 44, 58, 62, 66, 84, 88, 92, 96, 107, 110, 118, 126, 133, 144, 148, 152, 159, *18, 22, 29, 32, 36, 44, 58, 62, 66, 84, 88, 92, 96, 107, 110, 118, 126, 133, 144, 148, 152, 159*	10, 14, 18, 22, 29, 32, 36, 40, 44, 48, 55, 58, 66, 70, 74, 81, 88, 96, 100, 107, 110, 114, 118, 126, 133, 136, 140, 148, 159, *10, 14, 18, 22, 29, 32, 36, 40, 44, 48, 55, 58, 66, 70, 74, 81, 88, 96, 100, 107, 110, 114, 118, 126, 133, 136, 140, 148, 159*
6, 14, 29, 36, 40, 48, 55, 62, 70, 81, 126, 152, *6, 14, 29, 36, 40, 48, 55, 62, 70, 81, 126, 152*	29, 55, 81, 107, 133, 159, *29, 55, 81, 107, 133, 159*	55, 81, *55, 81*	29, 55, 81, 107, 133, *29, 55, 81, 107, 133*
40, 48, 62, 70, 262–269, *40, 48, 62, 70, 262–269*			
12–15, 18, 22, 27–28, 44, 47, 52, 56–59, 74, 75, 79–80, 92, 108–110, 114, 116–119, 122, 136, 148, *12–15, 18, 22, 27–28, 44, 47, 52, 56–59, 74, 75, 79–80, 92, 108–110, 114, 116–119, 122, 136, 148*	10, 12–13, 18, 32, 34, 40, 48, 66, 88, 96, 100–101, 110, 114, 122, 136, 144, 148, 152, *10, 12–13, 18, 32, 34, 40, 48, 66, 88, 96, 100–101, 110, 114, 122, 136, 144, 148, 152*	14, 16–17, 19, 25, 32, 34–37, 40, 47, 49, 50, 56–59, 63, 67, 76, 88–89, 100, 110–111, 114, 118–119, 121, 123, 127, 130, 136, 140, 144, 148–149, 150–151, 156, *14, 16–17, 19, 25, 32, 34–37, 40, 47, 49, 50, 56–59, 63, 67, 76, 88–89, 100, 110–111, 114, 118–119, 121, 123, 127, 130, 136, 140, 144, 148–149, 150–151, 156*	8, 10, 14, 18, 32, 35, 37, 44, 45, 56–59, 62, 66, 67, 86–89, 92, 96, 99, 100, 102, 104, 108–111, 114, 115, 126, 128, 136, 144, 148, 152–153, *8, 10, 14, 18, 32, 35, 37, 44, 45, 56–59, 62, 66, 67, 86–89, 92, 96, 99, 100, 102, 104, 108–111, 114, 115, 126, 128, 136, 144, 148, 152–153*
4, 8, 16, 20, 24, 30, 50, 64, 76, 102, 112, 120, 128, 138, 142, 154, *4, 8, 16,*	4, 8, 12, 16, 24, 50, 60, 64, 72, 82, 86, 94, 102, 108, 112, 128, 134, 150,	21, 24, 50, 76, 90, 102, 128, 146, 151, *21, 24, 50, 76, 90, 102, 128, 146,*	1, 15, 24, 34, 42, 50, 76, 90, 94, 102, 120, 124, 128, 154, *1, 15, 24, 34, 42,*

SCOPE AND SEQUENCE

SPELLING AND LANGUAGE ARTS	LEVEL 1	LEVEL 2
	46, 48, 50, 52, 54, 56, 58, 60, 62, 64, 66, 68, 72, 76, 78, 80, 84, 88, 90, 92, 96, 100, 102, 104, 108, 112, 114, 116, 120, 124, 126, 128, 132, 136, 138, 140, 144, 148, 150, 152, 156, 160, 162, 164, 168, 172, 174, *4, 6, 8, 10, 12, 14, 16, 18, 20, 22, 24, 26, 28, 30, 32, 34, 36, 38, 40, 42, 44, 46, 48, 50, 52, 54, 56, 58, 60, 62, 64, 66, 68, 72, 76, 78, 80, 84, 88, 90, 92, 96, 100, 102, 104, 108, 112, 114, 116, 120, 124, 126, 128, 132, 136, 138, 140, 144, 148, 150, 152, 156, 160, 162, 164, 168, 172, 174*	184, *9, 14, 19, 29, 60, 66, 71, 76, 81, 91, 122, 138, 148, 153, 164, 169, 174, 184*
For Rhyme, Rhythm, and Alliteration	85, 95, 122, 153, 170, 175, *85, 95, 122, 153, 170, 175*	
For Appreciation		127, *127*
SPEAKING		
Correct Enunciation of Words	4, 6, 8, 10, 12, 14, 16, 18, 20, 22, 24, 26, 28, 30, 32, 34, 36, 38, 40, 42, 44, 46, 48, 50, 52, 54, 56, 58, 60, 62, 64, 66, 68, 72, 76, 78, 80, 84, 88, 90, 92, 96, 100, 102, 104, 108, 112, 114, 116, 120, 124, 126, 128, 132, 136, 138, 140, 144, 148, 150, 152, 156, 160, 162, 164, 168, 172, 174, *4, 6, 8, 10, 12, 14, 16, 18, 20, 22, 24, 26, 28, 30, 32, 34, 36, 38, 40, 42, 44, 46, 48, 50, 52, 54, 56, 58, 60, 62, 64, 66, 68, 72, 76, 78, 80, 84, 88, 90, 92, 96, 100, 102, 104, 108, 112, 114, 116, 120, 124, 126, 128, 132, 136, 138, 140, 144, 148, 150, 152, 156, 160, 162, 164, 168, 172, 174*	9, 14, 19, 29, 60, 66, 71, 76, 81, 91, 122, 138, 148, 153, 164, 169, 174, 184, *9, 14, 19, 29, 60, 66, 71, 76, 81, 91, 122, 138, 148, 153, 164, 169, 174, 184*
Discussions		33, 64, *33, 64*

SPELLING AND OTHER CURRICULUM	LEVEL 1	LEVEL 2
SCIENCE/HEALTH	91, 101, 125, 129, 131, 149, 155, 173, *9A, 9B, 17A, 25A, 25B, 33B, 41A, 41B, 49A, 49B, 57A, 57B, 61B, 67A, 67B, 75B, 83A, 87A, 91, 95B, 99A, 101, 107A, 107B, 111A, 111B, 115A, 119A, 119B, 123B, 125, 129, 131, 131A, 131B, 143A, 143B, 147A, 149, 151A, 155, 155B, 167A, 167B, 171B, 173, 175A*	8, *8, 8A, 8B, 13B, 18A, 18B, 28A, 34A, 39A, 39B, 44A, 44B, 49A, 49B, 59B, 65A, 70A, 80A, 80B, 85A, 85B, 101A, 101B, 111B, 121A-121B, 127A, 132A, 132B, 137A, 142A, 147A, 152A, 152B, 158A, 163B, 168B, 173B, 178B, 189A*
SOCIAL STUDIES	127, 139, 159, 161, 166, *9B, 17B, 25B, 41B, 49B, 57B, 61B, 67B, 71A, 71B, 75B, 83B, 87B, 99B, 103A, 107B, 111B, 115A, 123A, 123B, 127, 135A, 135B, 139, 139A, 143A, 147B, 155A–155B, 159, 159A, 159B, 161, 163A, 166, 175A*	164–167, *18B, 23A, 34A, 44A, 44B, 49B, 54A, 54B, 70B, 75B, 85B, 90A, 90B, 96A, 106A, 111A, 111B, 116A, 127A, 132B, 147B, 164–167, 168B, 173A, 178A, 178B, 183B, 189A*
MATHEMATICS	154, 158, 163, *33A, 83B, 95A, 103A, 131B, 135B, 139A, 147B, 154, 158, 163, 163A, 171A*	107–110, 116A, *23B, 54B, 59B, 107–110, 116, 116A-116B, 142B, 152B*
FINE ARTS	135, *61A, 79A, 91A, 119B, 135, 167A*	102–105, *8B, 23B, 28B, 44B, 80B, 85B, 90B, 96A, 101B, 102–105, 116A, 121B, 137B, 142B, 163A, 173B, 183B*

ITALICIZED NUMBERS REFER TO THE TEACHER'S EDITION

LEVEL 3	LEVEL 4	LEVEL 5	LEVEL 6
20, 24, 30, 50, 64, 76, 102, 112, 120, 128, 138, 142, 154	154, 4, 8, 12, 16, 24, 50, 60, 64, 72, 82, 86, 94, 102, 108, 112, 128, 134, 150, 154	151	50, 76, 90, 94, 102, 120, 124, 128, 154
		55, 55	81, 96, 133, 81, 96, 133
4, 8, 16, 20, 24, 30, 50, 64, 76, 102, 112, 118, 120, 126, 128, 148, 151, 154, 4, 8, 16, 20, 24, 30, 50, 64, 76, 102, 112, 118, 120, 126, 128, 148, 151, 154	4, 8, 12, 16, 24, 50, 60, 64, 72, 82, 94, 102, 108, 112, 128, 134, 154, 4, 8, 12, 16, 24, 50, 60, 64, 72, 82, 94, 102, 108, 112, 128, 134, 154	21, 24, 50, 76, 90, 102, 142, 146, 21, 24, 50, 76, 90, 102, 142, 146	1, 15, 16, 24, 50, 76, 82, 90, 102, 120, 124, 128, 146, 154, 1, 15, 16, 24, 50, 76, 82, 90, 102, 120, 124, 128, 146, 154
29, 81, 133, 29, 81, 133		28, 54–55, 80–81, 106–107, 132–133, 158–159, 28, 54–55, 80–81, 106–107, 132–133, 158–159	29, 55, 29, 55

LEVEL 3	LEVEL 4	LEVEL 5	LEVEL 6
17, 65, 96, 110, 111, 122, 11B, 15B, 17, 19B, 23B, 33B, 37B, 41B, 45B, 49B, 55A, 59B, 63B, 65, 67B, 75B, 81A, 85B, 89B, 93B, 96, 101B, 110–111, 111B, 115B, 122, 123B, 127B, 133A, 137B, 141B, 149B, 153B	53, 116–119, 7B, 11B, 15B, 19B, 23B, 29A, 33A, 37B, 41B, 45B, 53, 55A, 63B, 75B, 85B, 89B, 97B, 101B, 111B, 115B, 116–119, 119B, 123B, 127B, 137B, 141B, 145B, 159A	32, 144, 148, 7B, 11B, 15B, 23A, 23B, 32, 41A, 41B, 45B, 49B, 55A, 63A, 63B, 67B, 75B, 85A, 85B, 89B, 93B, 97B, 101B, 111A, 119B, 123B, 137B, 144, 145A, 148, 149A, 149B	27–28, 72, 75, 127, 7A, 7B, 11A, 11B, 15A, 15B, 19A, 19B, 23B, 27–28, 29A, 33A, 37A, 41A, 41B, 67B, 71A, 72, 75, 75A, 75B, 81A, 85B, 89A, 93B, 97A, 101B, 107A, 111A, 127, 127B, 133A, 137A, 141B, 145B, 149A, 149B, 153A
131, 157, 7B, 11B, 23A, 29A, 37A, 37B, 49B, 63B, 67B, 71B, 81A, 85B, 89B, 97B, 119B, 123B, 127B, 131, 133A, 145B, 149B, 153B, 157, 159A	72–75, 7B, 11B, 19A, 19B, 23B, 33B, 37B, 41B, 49B, 55A, 59A, 59B, 71B, 72–75, 75A, 75B, 81A, 85B, 97B, 101B, 107A, 141B, 149B, 153B, 159A	112–115, 128, 7A, 11A, 19A, 19B, 29A, 33B, 45A, 45B, 49A, 55A, 59B, 71B, 75B, 81A, 93A, 93B, 97B, 101B, 107A, 111B, 112–115, 115A, 115B, 119B, 127A, 128, 133A, 137A, 145B, 153B, 159A	27–28, 11B, 15B, 23A, 23B, 27–28, 33B, 37B, 49A, 49B, 55B, 59B, 63A, 63B, 67A, 67B, 71B, 85A, 85B, 89B, 93B, 97B, 111A, 115B, 123B, 137B, 141A, 141B, 145A, 149A, 149B, 153A, 153B, 159A
71B, 97B, 111B, 119B, 145B	41A, 49B, 63B, 115B, 137B	37A, 37B, 59B, 63B, 67A, 127B, 137B, 145A, 153B, 159A	116–119, 37A, 37B, 116–119, 119A, 119B
51, 79, 19B, 51, 75B, 79, 93B, 107A, 141B, 159A	27, 23A, 27, 29A, 37A, 67B, 93B, 107A, 111B, 123B, 153B	10, 153, 7B, 10, 15B, 19B, 29A, 37B, 41B, 49B, 67B, 71B, 81A, 85B, 89B, 97A, 111B, 119A, 123A, 127B, 133A, 141A, 149B, 153	45, 19A, 29A, 33B, 45, 45B, 49B, 63B, 81A, 127B, 133A, 137B, 145B

NOTES

HARCOURT BRACE SPELLING

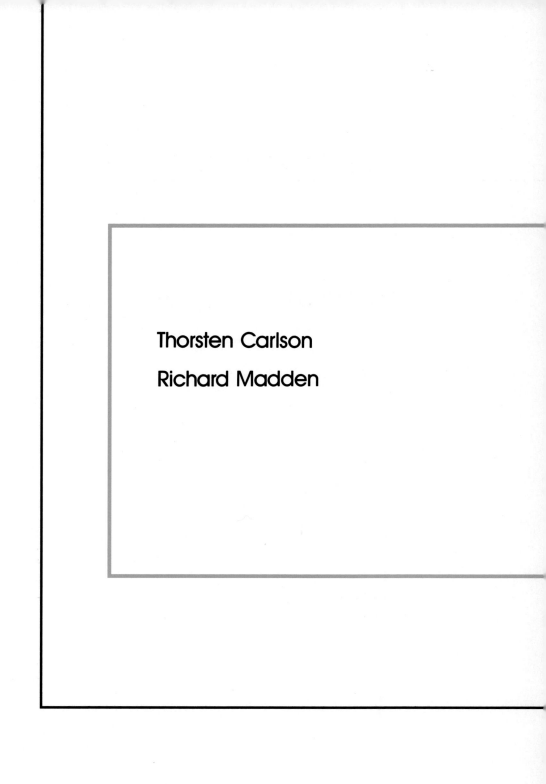

Thorsten Carlson

Richard Madden

HARCOURT BRACE SPELLING

HARCOURT BRACE & COMPANY

Orlando Atlanta Austin Boston San Francisco Chicago Dallas New York Toronto London

http://www.hbschool.com

Acknowledgments

Letter forms from *HBJ Handwriting.* Copyright © 1987 by Harcourt Brace & Company. Definitions and the pronunciation key in the "Spelling Dictionary" are from the *HBJ School Dictionary.* Copyright © 1985, 1977 by Harcourt Brace & Company. Reprinted by permission of Harcourt Brace & Company.

PHOTO CREDITS

Key: T, Top; B, Bottom; L, Left; C, Center; R, Right.

Page 56, Ken Lax/The Stock Shop; 72, ZEFA/H, Armstrong Roberts; 87, Phoebe Dunn/DPI; 92, Eric Carle/Shostal Associates; 96, Shostal Associates; 99, Stan Wayman/Photo Researchers; 109(L), G. Trouillet/The Image Bank; 109(C), Rhoda Galyn; 109(R), Runk/Schoenberger/Grant Heilman; 117, HB Studio; 136, H.Armstrong Roberts; 144, Ruth Dixon; 163, J. A. Robinson/Photo Researchers; 164, Hans Reinhard/Bruce Coleman; 167, Pat Meyers; 169, Antonio Mendoza/Stock, Boston; 170, Sylvia Johnson/Woodfin Camp & Associates; 171, Stephen Kraseman/ Photo Researchers; 172, Halley Ganges; 173, Leonard Rue III/Photo Researchers; 174, M.J. Germana/DPI; 175, George Roos/DPI; 177, Kim Massie/Rainbow; 179, Tana Hoban/DPI; 181, G. Schaller/Bruce Coleman; 182, Walter Chandoha; 184, Joe McDonald/Bruce Coleman; 186, A. B. Joyce/Photo Researchers; 188, Phil Dotson/DPI; 190(L), H. Armstrong Roberts; 190(R), Sepp Seitz/Woodfin Camp & Associates;191, Frost Publishing Group. Ltd.; 193, Hans Pfletschinger/Peter Arnold; 194, HB Photo; 196, Florida Dept. of Commerce; 197(L), G. Bordis/De Wys; 197(R), Halley Ganges; 198(L), George Holton/Photo Researchers; 198(R), Ted Horowitz/The Stock Market; 199(L), Blaine Harrington III/The Stock Market; 199(R), Joe McDonald/Bruce Coleman; 200(L), Hill/Frost Publishing Group. Ltd.; 200(R), Mira Atkeson/DPI; 202, Irene Vandermolen/Bruce Coleman.

Printed in the United States of America
ISBN 0-15-313652-9

Spelling

Grade 4
  Mikayla
  Emily H. Unit 1
  ✗ Jessica - fixes U1-3
  ? Sydney - all units

Grade
Jacob I Unit 4
Alyssa Unit 3 I.
✗

Grade 5 -
  Jared - U3 I

Teaching is
❤ **a work**
of heart!

Introduction to the Book

Contents

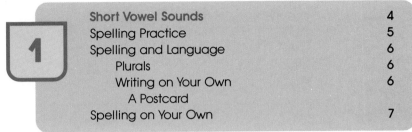

Review with the children the Contents pages for *Harcourt Brace Spelling* to acquaint them with the book's features. Explain to them the purpose of a table of contents.

Guide the children through the major features of the Contents and have them identify the pages on which each feature appears.

- The book opens with *Study Steps to Learn a Word.* Have the children turn to the Study Steps on page 1. Read the Study Steps to the children or have a volunteer read it. Ask them to explain how the Study Steps might be helpful.

- Following Study Steps is the **Skills Check.** Explain to the children that they will take the **Skills Check** to identify those spelling skills they have mastered from the previous level.

- The next part in the Contents identifies the **36 Spelling Lessons** the children will study. Point out that every sixth lesson is a review unit. Have the children identify the sections of the first instructional unit and the first review unit. Ask them to turn to the first page of each section and briefly describe the contents.

- Direct the children's attention to the resources that follow Unit 36. Discuss with them how they can make use of these resources.

 SPELLING DICTIONARY

Explain that all the spelling words in their book are listed in the dictionary. Have the children turn to page 162. Point out the **Pronunciation Key** and explain that the key lists the sound symbols and the spellings that stand for the sounds. The key will help them to pronounce unfamiliar words and to identify the possible spellings for a sound.

 SPELLING THESAURUS

Have the children turn to the **Spelling Thesaurus** and ask them to describe its purpose and organization. Explain that they can use the thesaurus to help them write.

WRITER'S GUIDE

Explain to the children that the **Writer's Guide** is a valuable resource that they can use when they write. Have the children turn to the first page of each section and briefly describe the contents. Then discuss how each section might be helpful.

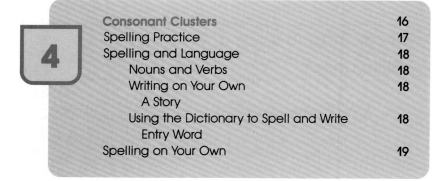
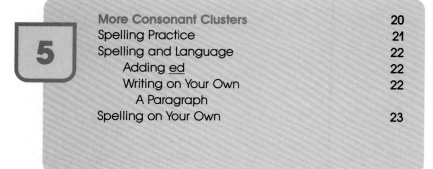
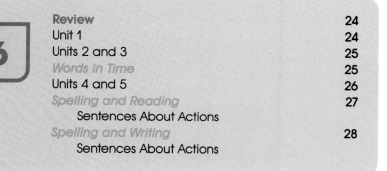

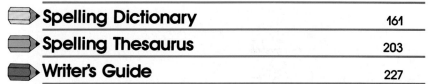

Study Steps to Learn a Word

SAY the word. Listen to each sound. Think about what the word means.

LOOK at the word. See how the letters are made. Try to see the word in your mind.

SPELL the word to yourself. Think about the way each sound is spelled.

WRITE the word. Copy it from your book. Check the way you made your letters. Write the word again.

CHECK your learning. Cover the word and write it. Did you spell it correctly? If not, do these steps until you know how to spell the word.

1

OVERVIEW

Study Steps to Learn a Word is a lifelong strategy that will help children become successful, independent spellers.

The *first step* has the child relate the word to its meaning. It taps the child's prior experience with the word.

The *second step* has the child look at the word critically and then form a visual image of the word.

The *third step* has the child use sound-letter cues to help reinforce the spelling of a word.

The *fourth step* develops the child's visual memory for the word through writing—a kinesthetic mode of learning. It reminds the child to write legibly to avoid spelling inaccuracies.

The *fifth step* has the child strengthen the visual memory of the word through writing.

Children may apply *Study Steps to Learn a Word* in the following situations:

- when they misspell words on the Trial Test.
- when they misspell words on the Unit Test.
- when they encounter unfamiliar words or words they are unsure of how to spell.
- when they misspell words in their writing.
- when they misspell words in other content-area assignments.

PROCEDURE

Before the children begin their work in the **Pupil Book,** you may want to introduce them to *Study Steps to Learn a Word.* Use the Study Steps **Teaching Aids Transparency.** Guide the children through the steps using the word *listen.* To aid them in practicing the steps, you may want to reproduce and distribute *Study Steps to Learn a Word* copying master.

Encourage the children to use the Study Steps throughout the year as they learn to spell new words. Children may refer to *Study Steps to Learn a Word* on page 1 of the **Pupil Book** or on the first page of each Review Unit; they may also refer to the Study Steps poster on display in the classroom.

Skills Check

OVERVIEW

At Levels 2 through 6 of **Harcourt Brace Spelling,** an optional diagnostic inventory is provided. This Skills Check inventory is in two parts. The first part, on pages 2 and 3 of the **Pupil Book,** includes multiple choice and fill-in questions to evaluate the children's mastery and retention of the spelling skills taught at the previous level. The second part of the inventory, on page 3A of the **Teacher's Edition,** is a list of words taught at the previous level to be used for dictation.

This diagnostic inventory will help you to determine the general level of instruction at which both individuals and groups can function effectively and to pinpoint areas of particular spelling difficulty.

PROCEDURE

Have the children complete the Skills Check on pages 2 and 3 first. Briefly discuss the directions for each part; then have the children complete the inventory independently. You may check the answers yourself or have the children correct their own. A quick review of their responses to the inventory will help you assess the children's individual abilities and recognize any special problems they may have.

See page 3A for the list of words from Level 2 to be used for dictation.

Name _____ **Date** _____

A. Write a word you know that has each vowel sound.

SAMPLE ANSWERS

1. short a	hat	**6.** long a	game
2. short e	pet	**7.** long e	feel
3. short i	sit	**8.** long i	five
4. short o	hop	**9.** long o	rope
5. short u	fun		

number right

A. ___ (9)

B. Add beginning letters. Use different letters to write two different words each time.

SAMPLE ANSWERS

10. ___op	top	hop
11. ___an	can	ran
12. ___ame	same	name
13. ___ee	tree	see
14. ___ide	ride	wide
15. ___ut	cut	but

number right

B. ___ (12)

C. Two words in each row rhyme. One does not. Write the word that does not rhyme.

16. gave	have	save	have
17. near	hear	bear	bear
18. hair	there	were	were
19. what	that	cat	what

number right

C. ___ (4)

2

D. Write each list of words in ABC order.

20. please _____ **made**
    paint
    neck _____ **neck**
    made
    _____ **paint**
    _____ **please**

21. why _____ **why**
    your
    winter _____ **winter**
    wrong
    _____ **wrong**
    _____ **your**

number right
D. ___ (6)

Score three (3) points for each group of words that is in the correct order. Score zero (0) if there are any errors.

E. Write the words that mean the opposite.

22. up _____ **down**
23. left _____ **right**
24. on _____ **off**
25. before _____ **after**
26. in _____ **out**
27. stop _____ **go**

number right
E. ___ (6)

F. Write an action word to finish each sentence.
SAMPLE ANSWERS

28. Robin will _____ **tell or read** _____ us a story.
29. Dennis will _____ **eat** _____ dinner with us.
30. Tammy will _____ **ride** _____ her bike to school.
31. Brian will _____ **play** _____ the game with us.
32. Wendy will _____ **swim** _____ in the pool.

number right
F. ___ (5)

G. Say each word to yourself. Write a word that sounds the same but is not spelled the same.

33. wood _____ **would**
34. there _____ **their**
35. hear _____ **here**
36. rode _____ **road**
37. right _____ **write**
38. no _____ **know**
39. blew _____ **blue**
40. deer _____ **dear**

number right
G. ___ (8)

total
right ___ (50)

3

Skills Check

ANALYSIS OF RESULTS

Determine the total number of correct items on each child's Skills Check. Then review his or her performance on each lettered section of the inventory. Note that each separate section assesses a particular spelling skill, short vowel sounds for example. On the back of each child's **Progress Report,** keep a record of the spelling skills evaluated in the inventory, noting especially those areas in which the child is weak. Use the charts to individualize instruction or to group children with common spelling problems.

The following references will tell you where, at this level and at the previous level, you can find practice exercises for each skill in the inventory. Boldface numbers indicate that a skill is the major focus of a unit; light numbers indicate that the skill is the focus of **Spelling and Language** in the unit.

A. Short Vowel Sounds
Level 2: Units **5, 7, 8, 9, 10**
Level 3: Unit **1**

B. Initial Consonants and Phonograms
Level 2: Units **1, 2, 3,** 7, 19
Level 3: Units 2, 14

C. Unusual Sound-Letter Correspondences
Level 2: Units **17,** 2, 19, 22
Level 3: Units **33,** 23, 31

D. Alphabetical Order
Level 2: Units 5, 17, 19, 22, 29
Level 3: Units 2, 10, 19, 23

E. Spelling Familiar Words
Level 2: Units **11, 23, 26, 32, 35**
Level 3: Units **2, 16, 17, 28, 32**

F. Writing Familiar Words in Context
Level 2: Units **11, 13, 14, 20, 21, 22,** 2, 8, 25, 27
Level 3: Units **2, 4, 14, 15, 16,** 17, 21, 26, 34

G. Homophones
Level 2: Units 16, 28
Level 3: Units **29,** 15

DICTATED WORD LIST

The list of dictated words will help you assess the children's spelling ability with a representative sample of words taught in Level 2. It measures retention of regular spelling patterns and exceptions, as well as auditory discrimination.

PROCEDURE

To administer the test, say each word and use it in the sentence provided. Then repeat the word. Have the children write the words on a separate piece of paper or in their spelling notebooks.

Collect the children's papers after they have corrected their own tests, or check their responses yourself. Note the kinds of errors each child makes. As children work with Level 3, regularly check their work for skill mastery.

1. *fast*   Emily can run very *fast.*   **fast**
2. *help*   Mom will *help* us wash the dog.   **help**
3. *fill*   Please *fill* the cat's water bowl.   **fill**
4. *shop*   We *shop* at the new supermarket.   **shop**
5. *truck*   A big *truck* passed us on the highway.   **truck**
6. *face*   Reggie has a big grin on his *face.*   **face**
7. *paint*   We are going to *paint* the living room white.   **paint**
8. *stay*   Please *stay* here until we get back.   **stay**
9. *leave*   Ben and Beth *leave* for school at eight o'clock.   **leave**
10. *street*   Always cross the *street* at the corner.   **street**
11. *write*   Alice can *write* very neatly.   **write**
12. *night*   Last *night* Mike went to bed early.   **night**
13. *stone*   Susan made the *stone* skip across the water.   **stone**
14. *road*   The *road* through the woods is very narrow.   **road**
15. *know*   We all *know* the right answer.   **know**
16. *room*   Charlie's *room* is upstairs.   **room**
17. *took*   Angela *took* the dog for a walk.   **took**
18. *start*   The movie will *start* in ten minutes.   **start**
19. *before*   Think carefully *before* you answer the question.   **before**
20. *other*   This pencil is longer than the *other* one.   **other**

ANALYSIS OF RESULTS

A high percentage of misspelled words may indicate that a child should concentrate on the Mastery words and work with This Week's Words secondarily.

Children who miss few or no words on the dictated test should benefit from working with the Bonus words.

Short Vowel Sounds

PREVIEWING THE UNIT

Unit Materials

Instruction and Practice

Pupil Book   pages 4–7
Teacher's Edition
  Teaching Plans   4–7
  Enrichment Activities
    For the Classroom   page 7A
    For the Home   page 7B
  Reteaching Strategies   page 7C

Testing

Teacher's Edition
  Trial Tests   pages 3C–3D
  Unit Test   page 7B
  Dictation Test   page 7B

Additional Resources

PRACTICE AND REINFORCEMENT
Extra Practice Master 1: This Week's Words
Extra Practice Master 1: Mastery Words
Extra Practice Master 1: Bonus Words
LEP Practice Master 1
Spelling and Language Master 1
Study Steps to Learn a Word Master

RETEACHING FOLLOW-UP

Reteaching Follow-up Master 1A:
  Discovering Spelling Ideas
Reteaching Follow-up Master 1B: Word
  Shapes
LEP Reteaching Follow-up Master 1

TEACHING AIDS
Spelling Generalizations Transparency 1
Home Letter 1

Click on the SPELLING banner to find activities for this unit.

Learner Objectives

Spelling

- To spell words that demonstrate these sound-letter relationships: /a/a, /e/e, /i/i, /o/o, /u/u.
- To form the plurals of nouns.
- To build words using phonograms and initial consonant substitutions.

Reading

- To follow written directions.
- To use context clues to complete sentences given spelling words.

Writing

- To write a postcard.
- To use the writing process.
- To proofread for spelling, capitalization, and punctuation.
- To write legible manuscript and cursive letters.

Listening

- To listen for consonant and short vowel sounds in words.
- To follow oral directions.

Speaking

- To contribute ideas and information in group discussions.
- To respond to questions.
- To present rhymes to the class.

THIS WEEK'S WORDS

- flag
- fed
- hid
- dot
- hunt
- apple
- bring
- club
- else
- happy
- pen
- river
- rock
- shall
- sunny

MASTERY WORDS

- and
- last
- leg
- sit
- top
- until

BONUS WORDS

- struck
- smash
- dwell
- melt
- flock
- crop
- strap
- swift

Assignment Guide

This guide shows how you teach a typical spelling unit in either a five-day or a three-day sequence, while providing for individual differences. **Boldface type** indicates essential classwork. Steps shown in light type may be done in class or assigned as homework.

Five Days	○ = average spellers ☆ = better spellers ✓ = slower spellers	Three Days
Day **1** ▶ a	○ ☆ **Take This Week's Words Trial Test and correct** ○ ✓ **Take Mastery word Trial Test and correct** ○ ☆ **Read This Week's Words and discuss generalization page 4**	Day **1**
Day **2** ◀ b	○ Complete Spelling Practice page 5 ○ ✓ Complete Extra Practice Master 1: This Week's Words (optional) ✓ Complete Spelling on Your Own: Mastery Words page 7 ☆ **Take Bonus word Trial Test and correct**	
Day **3** ▶ c	○ ☆ ✓ **Complete Spelling and Language page 6** ○ ☆ ✓ Complete Writing on Your Own page 6 ○ ✓ Take Midweek Test (optional) ☆ Complete Spelling on Your Own: Bonus words page 7 ○ ✓ Complete Spelling and Language Master 1 (optional)	Day **2**
Day **4** ◀ d	○ Complete Spelling on Your Own: This Week's Words page 7 ✓ Complete Extra Practice Master 1: Mastery words (optional) ☆ Complete Extra Practice Master 1: Bonus words (optional)	
Day **5** ▶ e	○ **Take Unit Test on This Week's Words** ○ Complete Reteaching Follow-up Masters 1A and 1B (optional) ○ ✓ **Take Unit Test on Mastery words** ☆ **Take Unit Test on Bonus words**	Day **3**

Enrichment Activities for the **classroom** and for the **home** included at the end of this unit may be assigned selectively on any day of the week.

INTRODUCING THE UNIT

Establish Readiness for Learning

Tell the children that this week they will study words with short vowel sounds. In Unit 1 they will review the five short vowel sounds /a/, /e/, /i/, /o/, and /u/. Tell the children that they will apply what they are learning about short vowel sounds to This Week's Words and use those words to write a postcard.

Assess Children's Spelling Ability

Administer the Trial Test before the children study This Week's Words. Use the test sentences provided. Say each word and use it in a sentence. Then repeat the word. Have the children write the words on a separate sheet of paper or in their spelling notebooks. Test sentences are also provided for Mastery and Bonus words.

Have the students check their own work by listening to you read the spelling of the words or by referring to This Week's Words in the left column of the **Pupil Book.** For each misspelled word, have the students follow the **Study Steps to Learn a Word** on page 1 in the **Pupil Book** or use the copying master to study and write the words. Students should record the number correct on their **Progress Report.**

Trial Test Sentences

This Week's Words
1. **flag** Our *flag* is red, white, and blue. **flag**
2. **fed** Victor *fed* the dog. **fed**
3. **hid** Mary *hid* behind a tree. **hid**
4. **dot** Put a *dot* over the letter. **dot**
5. **hunt** A treasure *hunt* is fun. **hunt**
6. **apple** This *apple* is juicy. **apple**
7. **bring** Everyone may *bring* a friend to the party. **bring**
8. **club** Rachel belongs to a book *club*. **club**

FOCUS

- Establishes objectives
- Relates to prior learning
- Sets purpose of instruction

9. **else** See what *else* you can find. **else**
10. **happy** We were *happy* to see Grandma. **happy**
11. **pen** This *pen* is out of ink. **pen**
12. **river** We fished in the *river*. **river**
13. **rock** A big *rock* rolled off the mountain. **rock**
14. **shall** What *shall* we do next? **shall**
15. **sunny** If it is *sunny*, we will go to the beach. **sunny**

Mastery Words

1. **and** Anne *and* Glenda are here. **and**
2. **last** Brendan was *last* in line. **last**
3. **leg** The bird stood on one *leg*. **leg**
4. **sit** You may *sit* here if you like. **sit**
5. **top** Nell cannot reach the *top* shelf. **top**
6. **until** I will wait *until* he is ready. **until**

Bonus Words

1. **struck** Lightning *struck* that tree. **struck**
2. **smash** You will *smash* the box if you sit on it. **smash**

3. **dwell** Tigers *dwell* in jungles. **dwell**
4. **melt** The sun will *melt* the snow. **melt**
5. **flock** A *flock* of birds flew over. **flock**
6. **crop** The farmer grew a fine *crop* of corn. **crop**
7. **strap** The *strap* on this shoe is broken. **strap**
8. **swift** A deer is a *swift* animal. **swift**

Apply Prior Learning

Have the children apply what they already know about short vowel sounds by using the following activity.

Write the following words on the chalkboard: *mop, slept, funny, mask, stick*. Ask children how the vowels are alike in each of the words. Elicit from the children that all these words have short vowel sounds. Have children name a word for each of the short vowel sounds. Explain that they can use words which have short vowel sounds in a variety of writing tasks: they can use the words in a note to a friend, in a letter, in a science report, or in a social studies assignment.

FOR CHILDREN WITH SPECIAL NEEDS

Learning Difficulties

Since some children with learning problems have difficulty remembering the correct association for a sound and a letter, it is best to review just one vowel sound each day. On the first day, use the following activities to review the short vowel sound for the letter *a*. Then use the same activities on subsequent days to review the short vowel sound for the letters *e, i, o, u*.

Write the words *glad, chat,* and *last* on the chalkboard. Have the children read these words aloud with you. Point out that each word contains the vowel sound that is heard at the beginning of the word *apple*, which is the short vowel sound for the letter *a*. Have the children name some words which contain the short vowel sound for the letter *a*. List their responses on the chalkboard. Read the words listed on the chalkboard aloud with the children.

Read pairs of words in which one word contains the short vowel sound for the letter *a* and one word does not. Have the children identify the word which contains

the short vowel sound for the letter *a*. Words such as the following may be used in this activity: *tin, tan; band, bend; fun, fan; sick, sack.*

Write the letter *a* in the center of a large piece of butcher paper. Have the children cut out from old magazines pictures of objects whose names contain the short vowel sound for the letter *a*. Ask volunteers to name the object in each of their pictures and then paste the picture on the butcher paper to create a collage.

Limited English Proficiency

To help limited English proficient children work with the spelling generalizations for Unit 1, you may wish to refer to the booklet "Suggestions and Activities for Limited English Proficient Students."

TEACHING PLAN

Objective To spell words that demonstrate these sound-letter relationships: /a/a, /e/e, /i/i, /o/o, /u/u.

1. Have the children think of names that have short vowel sounds. *Pat, Ted, Kim, Bob,* and *Gus* are possibilities. Write the names as column heads on the chalkboard together with the symbols for the short vowel sounds: /a/, /e/, /i/, /o/, /u/. Leave the names on the chalkboard for use later.

2. Read the generalization on page 4 aloud. Stress that if the children remember the sentence "Fat hens will not run," they will always be able to identify the short vowel sounds and their most common spellings.

You may wish to introduce the lesson by using **Spelling Generalizations Transparency 1.**

3. Have volunteers read This Week's Words aloud. As each word is read, the children should indicate under which name the word should be listed on the chalkboard.

You may wish to assign **LEP Practice Master 1** for reinforcement in writing spelling words.

1 Short Vowel Sounds

THIS WEEK'S WORDS

1.	flag
2.	fed
3.	hid
4.	dot
5.	hunt
6.	apple
7.	bring
8.	club
9.	else
10.	happy
11.	pen
12.	river
13.	rock
14.	shall
15.	sunny

This Week's Words

All of This Week's Words have short vowel sounds. These are the signs for the short vowel sounds.

/a/   /e/   /i/   /o/   /u/

These sounds are usually spelled with one vowel letter.

You hear all the short vowel sounds in this sentence:

/a/ /e/ /i/ /o/ /u/
Fat hens will not run.

Remember this sentence. It will help you to remember which sounds are usually spelled with only one vowel letter.

4

Extra Practice: This Week's Words

Name
Extra Practice   This Week's Words   UNIT **1**

Finish the sentences with This Week's Words. A short vowel sound is given before each blank. This is the short vowel sound heard in the missing word.

1. Peggy /e/ ___**fed**___ an
   /a/ ___**apple**___ to the pony.
2. Jack and Hector /i/ ___**hid**___ behind the big /o/ ___**rock**___.
3. We forgot to /i/ ___**bring**___ the beach ball!
4. Some friends and I are starting a chess /u/ ___**club**___
5. Jamie is /a/ ___**happy**___ with her new kite.
6. Hold on to that fishing pole, or /e/ ___**else**___!
7. It was warm and /u/ ___**sunny**___ today.
8. Watch the birds /u/ ___**hunt**___ for worms.
9. Pedro put his /e/ ___**pen**___ in his pocket.
10. The ink made a black /o/ ___**dot**___ on his shirt.
11. The /a/ ___**flag**___ outside the post office waved in the breeze.
12. "We ___**shall**___ find a great treasure!" cried the pirate.
13. The ship sailed up the /i/ ___**river**___

apple	fed	pen
bring	flag	river
club	happy	rock
dot	hid	shall
else	hunt	sunny

Extra Practice • 1

Extra Practice: Mastery Words

Name
Extra Practice   Mastery Words   UNIT **1**

A. Find the Mastery words in the puzzle. The words go across and down. Circle the words you find.

```
z m f t r a h l p l
n l k o g f x b n a
a n d p s y w u f s
x i r q s n l e g t
o o t d i f e v n g
a a c w t z r w t y
b n r w e x l j u i
l u n t i h p n d
```

B. Finish the sentences with Mastery words. Write each word in the boxes next to the right number.

1. Write your name at the ___ of the page.
2. Do not begin the test ___ I say so.
3. Please ___ in that chair, David.
4. Cathy hit two home runs ___ week.
5. Mike ___ Eric are best friends.
6. Diana hurt her ___ when she jumped over the fence.

1	t	o	p
2	u	n	t	i	l
3	s	i	t
4	l	a	s	t
5	a	n	d
6	l	e	g

C. Find in the boxes above the three words with short vowel sounds. The words go down, not across. Circle those words.

| and | last | leg |
| sit | top | until |

2 • Extra Practice

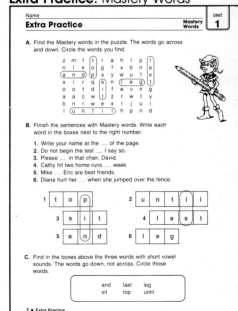

Spelling Practice

A. Finish the sentences. Use This Week's Words.

1. The vowel sound /a/ is spelled with __a__ in <u>fat</u>,

   _____flag_____, _____apple_____

   _____happy_____, and _____shall_____.

2. The vowel sound /e/ is spelled with __e__ in <u>hens</u>,

   _____fed_____, _____else_____

   and _____pen_____.

3. The vowel sound /i/ is spelled with __i__ in <u>will</u>,

   _____hid_____ _____bring_____,

   and _____river_____.

4. The vowel sound /o/ is spelled with __o__ in <u>not</u>,

   _____dot_____, and _____rock_____.

5. The vowel sound /u/ is spelled with __u__ in <u>run</u>,

   _____hunt_____, _____club_____,

   and _____sunny_____.

B. Write the words that start with the same sounds as the picture names.

6. _____bring_____

7. _____club_____

C. Write the words that end with the same sounds as the picture names.

8. _____hunt_____

9. _____rock_____

5

flag
fed
hid
dot
hunt
apple
bring
club
else
happy
pen
river
rock
shall
sunny

Extra Practice: Bonus Words

Summarize Learning

Have the children summarize what they have learned on pages 4 and 5. *Ask:*

• What letter sounds have you learned about in the lesson? (/a/a, /e/e, /i/i, /o/o, /u/u)

• What are examples of words that have short vowel sounds? (flag, fed, hid, dot, hunt; accept other examples)

TEACHING PLAN

Objectives To write words given vowel sound clues; to write words given initial and final consonant sounds.

1. Briefly discuss the directions on page 5.
2. You may wish to work through the page orally with the children before they complete the activities independently. Remind them to use legible handwriting. You may wish to demonstrate the correct form of the letters *a, e, i, o,* and *u* and then have the children practice writing the letters. For **Handwriting Models,** refer the children to page 258 in the **Pupil Book.**
3. The activities in Exercises **B** and **C** provide readiness for subsequent units on consonant clusters (Unit 4) and the *ck* spelling for final /k/ (Unit 10). When the children have completed the page, ask them to say the picture names and the words they wrote for Exercise **B.** (bread, bring; cloud, club) Have them listen for the two consonant sounds that begin each word. Similarly, in Exercise **C,** have them listen for the two consonant sounds at the end of *tent* and *hunt.* Point out that the final /k/ in *duck* and *rock* is spelled *ck.*
4. To correct the children's work, ask volunteers to write the answers on the chalkboard. Let the children check their own work.

For reinforcement in writing spelling words, you may wish to assign *Extra Practice Master 1: This Week's Words.*

⟳ EXTENDING THE LESSON

Challenge the children to write sentences in which all the words have the same short vowel sound. Offer these examples to get them started.

/a/ Happy Hal shall have an apple.
/e/ Beth fed ten hens.
/i/ Six fish hid in this river.
/o/ Bob spots dots on rocks.
/u/ Gus hunts bugs.

TEACHING PLAN

SPELLING AND LANGUAGE

> **Objective** To form the plurals of nouns by adding *s*.

1. Have a volunteer read the introduction to Plurals on page 6 aloud. Ask the children to look at the pictures and the words *hen* and *hens* beneath them. Compare the number of hens and the spelling of each word. Point out that the *s* in *hens* indicates more than one hen.
2. Have the children complete the exercise independently.
3. To correct the children's work, have a volunteer write the plural nouns on the chalkboard. Let the children check their own work.

For extended practice in writing plural nouns, you may wish to assign *Spelling and Language Master 1*.

WRITING ON YOUR OWN

> **Objectives** To write a postcard using the plural forms of given spelling words; to proofread for spelling.

1. Review the directions with the children.
2. As a *prewriting* activity, have the children discuss some things that might happen on a boat trip. Have them *compose* a postcard about an imaginary boat trip, using the plural forms of the given spelling words. When the children are ready to *revise* their postcards, remind them to check spelling. For additional help, you may wish to refer them to the *Revising Checklist* on page 247 of the **Writer's Guide**. To *publish* the children's work, have the children draw pictures to go with their postcards, and display their postcards and pictures on a bulletin board entitled "Our Boat Trip."

THIS WEEK'S WORDS

flag
fed
hid
dot
hunt
apple
bring
club
else
happy
pen
river
rock
shall
sunny

Spelling and Language • Plurals

A **plural** names more than one. Add <u>s</u> to make most words plural.

Finish the sentences. Use the plurals of some of This Week's Words.

hen   **hens**

1. Do you have enough _____apples_____ to make a pie?
2. Craig has lots of pencils and _____pens_____.
3. Pete and I belong to different book _____clubs_____.
4. Tina and Jim carried _____flags_____ in the parade.

Writing on Your Own

Write a postcard to your friends to tell them about a boat trip. Use the plural forms of these words: <u>rock</u>, <u>river</u>.

 WRITER'S GUIDE How did you end each sentence? For help with periods and question marks, turn to page 249.

HANDWRITING

i I   t T   l L   e E

The lowercase letters **i**, **t**, **l**, and **e** begin with this undercurve stroke. ____⌐

1. Practice writing **i I, t T, l L, e E** in cursive.

2. Write this sentence: *I let Eli tell it.*

6

HANDWRITING

> **Objective** To practice writing cursive letter forms: *il, tT, lL, eE*.

1. Read the introductory sentence on page 6 aloud.
2. Have the children examine the models for the cursive letters. Point out that *i* and *t* do not have loops; *e* is formed with a small loop; and *l* is formed with a tall loop.
3. Have the children practice the letter forms and write the sentence.
4. Ask the children to compare their letter forms with the models.

Extra Practice: Spelling and Language

Name _____
Spelling and Language   UNIT 1

A. In each sentence, circle the word that should be plural. Then write the sentence using the plural of the word you circled.

happy
fed
apple
bring
hid
else
river
flag
rock
club
shall
pen
hunt
sunny
dot

1. Two (club) had a big picnic.
   Two clubs had a big picnic.
2. The picnic was near (river) and lakes.
   The picnic was near rivers and lakes.
3. There were many (rock) on the picnic grounds.
   There were many rocks on the picnic grounds.
4. It is fun to draw (flag).
   It is fun to draw flags.
5. You can put (dot) and lines on the flags.
   You can put dots and lines on the flags.
6. You need many different (pen) to draw the colors.
   You need many different pens to draw the colors.

B. Use the plurals of two of This Week's Words to answer the questions.

7. What are red things that grow on trees?   apples
8. What are thin things that make marks?   pens

4 • Extra Practice

Spelling on Your Own

THIS WEEK'S WORDS

Words can make you think of other words. For example, <u>leap</u> might make you think of frog. And quiet as a might make you think of <u>mouse</u>. Write This Week's Words to go with these words.

1. treasure ___
2. ___ and ink
3. join the ___
4. ___ the i
5. bright and ___
6. anything ___
7. ___ it here
8. ___ ending
9. cross the ___
10. ___ or will
11. ___ the dog
12. ___ pie
13. hard as a ___
14. wave a ___
15. ran and ___

See answers below.

MASTERY WORDS

Follow the directions. Use the Mastery words.

and
last
leg
sit
top
until

1. Write the two words that begin with a vowel letter.

   and   until

2. Write the two words that have short a.

   and   last

Write the Mastery word that rhymes with each word.

3. beg   leg
4. hit   sit
5. hop   top
6. fast   last

BONUS WORDS

struck
smash
dwell
melt
flock
crop
strap
swift

Add the missing letters to write Bonus words.

1. ___ ift
2. ___ock
3. ___elt
4. ___ash
5. ___rap
6. ___op
7. ___ruck
8. ___ell

Now add different beginning consonant letters to the word parts above. For example, you can add l to <u>ift</u> to make <u>lift</u> or <u>dr</u> to make <u>drift</u>. See how many different words you can make.

See answers below.

7

Spelling on Your Own Answers

THIS WEEK'S WORDS

1. hunt 2. pen 3. club 4. dot 5. sunny
6. else 7. bring 8. happy 9. river 10. shall
11. fed 12. apple 13. rock 14. flag 15. hid

BONUS WORDS

1. swift 2. flock 3. melt 4. smash 5. strap
6. crop 7. struck 8. dwell

Some words that may be formed are:

ift	drift	rap	trap	ruck	truck
	gift		wrap	ell	bell
ock	clock	op	chop		sell
	knock		drop		smell
elt	belt		hop		spell
	felt		shop		tell
ash	cash				well
	crash				

Summarize Learning

Have the children summarize what they have learned in this unit. Ask:

- What have you learned about forming plurals? (The plurals of some nouns can be formed by adding s.) Give examples. (apples, pens, clubs; accept other examples)
- What spelling generalizations have you learned? How did you use these generalizations?

TEACHING PLAN

Objective To apply the unit spelling generalization to spell This Week's Words, Mastery words, and Bonus words independently.

THIS WEEK'S WORDS

1. Read the directions on page 7 aloud.
2. Have the children complete the activity independently on a separate piece of paper or in their spelling notebooks.

MASTERY WORDS

1. Read the Mastery words aloud. As each word is read, have the children identify the short vowel sound.
2. Read the directions on page 7 and work through the activities orally.

BONUS WORDS

1. Review the unit generalization on page 4.
2. Ask a volunteer to read the Bonus words aloud. Have the children look up the meanings of any unfamiliar words in the **Spelling Dictionary.**
3. Read the directions on page 7 aloud.
4. Have the children complete the exercise independently.

For reinforcement in writing spelling words, you may wish to assign **Extra Practice Master 1: Mastery Words** or **Bonus Words.**

CLOSING THE UNIT

Apply New Learning

Tell the children that if they misspell words with short vowel sounds in their writing, they should use one or more of the following strategies:

- think about the possible spellings for a short vowel sound and try to picture the word in their minds.
- think of words that rhyme and compare in their minds how the words are spelled.
- think of a known word that is related in meaning and spelling.

Transfer New Learning

Tell the children that when they encounter new words in their personal reading and in other content areas, they should learn the meaning of those words and then apply the generalizations they have studied to the spelling of those words. Tell them that once the words are familiar in both meaning and spelling, they should use the new words in their writing.

ENRICHMENT ACTIVITIES

Classroom activities and **home activities** may be assigned to children of all ability levels. The activities provide opportunities for children to use their spelling words in new contexts.

For the Classroom

To individualize classroom activities, you may have the children use the word list they are studying in this unit.

- *Basic:* Use **Mastery** words to complete the activity.
- *Average:* Use **This Week's Words** to complete the activity.
- *Challenging:* Use **Bonus** words to complete the activity.

1. Language Arts/Writing Rhyming Words Have the children write six pairs of rhyming words using spelling words and other words. Then have them use each word pair in a sentence. If the rhyming words are *river* and *shiver,* the sentence might be *I shiver by the river.* Next have the children create an exercise for a classmate by scrambling the rhyming words and copying the sentences, omitting the rhyming words. The other child must complete the sentences by choosing from the list of rhyming words.

   ■ COOPERATIVE LEARNING: Have each group create a rhyming word exercise. Each child within a group should write word pairs using three of the spelling words. Have the group check each word pair to be sure the words rhyme. One group member should record while the others take turns incorporating each word pair into a sentence. Have the group then work cooperatively to scramble the word pairs and copy each of the sentences, omitting the word pairs. Have the groups exchange exercises and complete the other group's exercise.

2. Language Arts/Writing Sentences Have each child choose five spelling words, each containing a different short vowel sound. For example: *flag, fed, hid, dot, hunt.* The children should then write a sentence for each of the spelling words. Every word in each sentence should have the same vowel sound. Give the children this model sentence for words with short *u: Ducks hunt funny bugs.*

   ■ COOPERATIVE LEARNING: Have each group write sentences. Each sentence should contain a spelling word that has a short vowel sound; all the other words in the sentence should have the same short vowel sound as the spelling word. Each child in the group should work with a different vowel sound. For example, a child working with /a/ might write this sentence using the spelling word *happy: Cats act happy.* Tell group members to check each other's sentences to see if all the words have the same short vowel sound. One member from each group should read the group's sentences aloud and have the other children identify the short vowel sound featured in each sentence.

3. Language Arts/Writing Rhyming Poetry Have each child write rhyming two-line poems using some of the spelling words. As a **prewriting** activity, direct the children to look over the spelling lists in search of words for which they can think of rhyming words. For example, a child might rhyme *sunny* with *bunny.* Have the children write the spelling words and the rhyming words on their papers. To **compose** the poem, have the children choose one pair of rhyming words and write a two-line poem. The children may refer to page 254 of the **Writer's Guide** for a model of a rhyme. Then have the children **revise** their poems by checking to see that the lines rhyme and the words are correctly spelled. **Publish** the rhymes by having the children read their rhymes aloud.

   ■ COOPERATIVE LEARNING: Have each group write three two-line rhymes using some of the spelling words. As a **prewriting** activity, have each child review the three spelling lists for words for which he or she can think of rhyming words. Have the children record the rhyming pairs. Have the children share their rhyming words and choose one of each group member's rhyming pairs to include in each rhyme. When the children are ready to **compose** the rhymes, have the group select a recorder. Have them choose one child to suggest a line of the poem that ends with the first word of a pair. Another child should complete that two-line rhyme. The group should follow the same procedure to compose the other two-line rhymes. Children may refer to the **Writer's Guide** on page 254 for a model of a rhyme. The group should revise the poems, checking to see that the lines rhyme and the spelling is correct. Each group can **publish** its poems by displaying them for the class to read.

For the Home

Children may complete home activities independently or with the assistance of a relative or friend in the home.

1. Language Arts/Writing Clues for a Treasure Hunt Tell the children to write a set of directions for a treasure hunt. Directions should lead to at least three places where clues direct the treasure hunter to the next clue. The final clue should reveal the treasure. Tell children to include as many of their spelling words as possible in their directions.

2. Language Arts/Making New Words from Spelling Words Tell the children to make other words by replacing the short vowel in five of their spelling words with another short vowel. Have the children use a dictionary to make sure they have written real words. Then tell them to write five sentences, each of which includes both the spelling word and the new word. Have the children check their sentences for spelling and then share them with a family member.

3. Social Studies/Writing a Paragraph on the Flag Tell the children to write a paragraph about the symbols on a flag. Point out that the stars on the United States flag stand for the fifty states. Have the children use some of the spelling words to write a paragraph describing the symbols on another flag. The flag might represent a country, a class, or a club, or the children might make up a flag. Remind the children to refer to the **Writer's Guide** on page 250 for a model of a descriptive paragraph and to use the **Revising Checklist** on page 247 to revise their work.

EVALUATING SPELLING ABILITY

Unit Test

This Week's Words

1. *flag*   There is a *flag* in front of the post office.   *flag*
2. *fed*   My baby sister *fed* herself this morning.   *fed*
3. *hid*   Jesse *hid* the marbles from the baby.   *hid*
4. *dot*   The clown had a red *dot* on his nose.   *dot*
5. *hunt*   Greg likes to *hunt* for pretty red stones.   *hunt*
6. *apple*   This *apple* is not ripe yet.   *apple*
7. *bring*   Grandpa will *bring* us back home after dinner.   *bring*
8. *club*   We need more members in our *club*.   *club*
9. *else*   Hurry or *else* we will be late.   *else*
10. *happy*   Larry sings when he is *happy*.   *happy*
11. *pen*   My brother gave me a new *pen* for my birthday.   *pen*

12. *river*   This *river* is too deep to wade across.   *river*
13. *rock*   We dug up a big *rock* in the garden.   *rock*
14. *shall*   What *shall* we have for dinner?   *shall*
15. *sunny*   A *sunny* day is nicer than a rainy day.   *sunny*

Mastery Words

1. *and*   Herb *and* I went roller skating.   *and*
2. *last*   Marty ate the *last* peanut.   *last*
3. *leg*   Jenny has a scratch on her *leg*.   *leg*
4. *sit*   Carlos likes to *sit* in the rocking chair.   *sit*
5. *top*   The *top* button on my jacket is missing.   *top*
6. *until*   The baby sitter will stay *until* Dad gets home.   *until*

Bonus Words

1. *struck*   The wheel of her bike *struck* the curb.   *struck*
2. *smash*   The waves *smash* against the rocks.   *smash*
3. *dwell*   Two families *dwell* in this house.   *dwell*
4. *melt*   Butter will *melt* on a hot potato.   *melt*
5. *flock*   The man was feeding a *flock* of chickens.   *flock*
6. *crop*   They planted a *crop* of wheat.   *crop*
7. *strap*   Kate fastened the *strap* on her book bag.   *strap*
8. *swift*   The runner is as *swift* as a deer.   *swift*

Dictation Sentences

This Week's Words

1. We can *hunt* for a big *rock* by the *river*.
2. I *shall bring* the *apple* with me.
3. I *hid* the *pen* so no one *else* can find it.
4. We made a *flag* for our new *club*.
5. My cat was *happy* after I *fed* it.
6. The pretty kite was a *dot* in the *sunny* sky.

Mastery Words

1. Her left *leg and* foot hurt after she fell.
2. We can *sit* on *top* of this box.
3. We will wait here *until* the *last* bus comes.

Bonus Words

1. The rock *struck* the glass but did not *smash* it.
2. The *flock* of birds was *swift* to fly away.
3. It will *melt* in the sun.
4. Each year we grow a *crop* of nuts.
5. Some people *dwell* in boats on the water.
6. The *strap* keeps the baby in his chair.

RETEACHING STRATEGIES FOR SPELLING

Children who have made errors on the Unit Test may require reteaching. Use the following **Reteaching Strategies** and **Follow-up Masters 1A** and **1B** for additional instruction and practice of This Week's Words. (You may wish to assign **LEP Reteaching Follow-up Master 1** for reteaching of spelling words.)

A. Discovering Spelling Ideas

1. Say the following words as you write them on the chalkboard.

   sad   leg   pig   clock   fun

2. Ask the children to identify the short vowel sound in each word. (/a/, /e/, /i/, /o/, and /u/)
3. Ask the children what letters are used to spell the short vowel sounds. (a, e, i, o, u)
4. Ask the children what they have learned about the spellings of short vowel sounds. (They are usually spelled with one vowel letter.)

B. Word Shapes

1. Explain to the children that each word has a shape and that remembering the shape of a word can help them to spell the word correctly.
2. On the chalkboard, write the words *tap* and *pick*. Have the children identify "short," "tall," and "tail" letters.
3. Draw the configuration of each word on the chalkboard, and ask the children which word fits in each shape.

Use **Reteaching Follow-up Master 1A** to reinforce spelling generalizations taught in Unit 1.

Use **Reteaching Follow-up Master 1B** to reinforce spellings of This Week's Words for Unit 1.

Name _____
Reteaching Follow-up A   Discovering Spelling Ideas   UNIT 1

THIS WEEK'S WORDS

flag	fed	dot	apple	club
happy	river	rock	hunt	hid
pen	bring	else	shall	sunny

1. Study This Week's Words. Say each word to yourself.
2. Write the words that have the sound /a/.

   flag   apple

   happy   shall

3. Write the words that have the sound /e/.

   fed   else   pen

4. Write the words that have the sound /i/.

   hid   bring   river

5. Write the words that have the sound /o/.

   dot   rock

6. Write the words that have the sound /u/.

   hunt   club   sunny

7. Write how each short vowel sound is spelled.

   /a/ ___a___   /e/ ___e___   /i/ ___i___

   /o/ ___o___   /u/ ___u___

8. What do the words have in common?

   All the words have short vowel sounds spelled with one vowel letter.

Reteaching • 1

Name _____
Reteaching Follow-up B   Word Shapes   UNIT 1

THIS WEEK'S WORDS

flag	fed	dot	apple	club
happy	river	rock	hunt	hid
pen	bring	else	shall	sunny

Write each of This Week's Words in its correct shape. The first one has been done for you. Children may interchange answers that fit the same configuration.

1. p e n   2. s h a l l

3. h i d   4. f l a g

5. h u n t   6. s u n n y

7. b r i n g   8. d o t

9. e l s e   10. r i v e r

11. r o c k   12. f e d

13. c l u b   14. a p p l e

15. h a p p y

2 • Reteaching

PREVIEWING THE UNIT

Unit Materials

Instruction and Practice

Pupil Book	pages 8–11
Teacher's Edition	
Teaching Plans	pages 8–11
Enrichment Activities	
For the Classroom	pages 11A–11B
For the Home	page 11B
Reteaching Strategies	page 11C

Testing

Teacher's Edition	
Trial Test	pages 7E–7F
Unit Test	page 11B
Dictation Test	page 11B

Additional Resources

PRACTICE AND REINFORCEMENT
Extra Practice Master 2: This Week's Words
Extra Practice Master 2: Mastery Words
Extra Practice Master 2: Bonus Words
LEP Practice Master 2
Spelling and Language Master 2
Study Steps to Learn a Word Master

RETEACHING FOLLOW-UP
Reteaching Follow-up Master 2A:
   Discovering Spelling Ideas
Reteaching Follow-up Master 2B: Word
   Shapes
LEP Reteaching Follow-up Master 2

TEACHING AIDS
Spelling Generalizations Transparency 2

Visit our Web site
http://www.hbschool.com

Click on the SPELLING banner to find activities for this unit.

Learner Objectives

Spelling

- To spell words that demonstrate these final sound-letter relationships: /l/ll, /f/ff, /s/ss, /d/dd.
- To form new words by changing letters in given words.
- To use the dictionary to check alphabetical order.

Reading

- To follow written directions.
- To read a classmate's story.
- To use context clues to complete a story.

Writing

- To write a story.
- To use the writing process.
- To proofread for spelling, capitalization, and punctuation.
- To write legible manuscript and cursive letters.

Listening

- To listen for letter-sound clues when writing words.
- To follow oral directions.
- To listen for rhyming words.

Speaking

- To contribute ideas and information in group discussions.
- To respond to questions.
- To present a story to the class.
- To express feelings and ideas about a piece of writing.

THIS WEEK'S WORDS

spill
drill
ill
shell
spell
smell
stuff
cliff
kiss
less
mess
unless
add
odd
roll

MASTERY WORDS

egg
fell
grass
off
pull
still

BONUS WORDS

foggy
fossils
pillow
pudding
recess
sudden
valley
village

Assignment Guide

This guide shows how you teach a typical spelling unit in either a five-day or a three-day sequence, while providing for individual differences. **Boldface type** indicates essential classwork. Steps shown in light type may be done in class or assigned as homework.

Five Days		⊂ = average spellers ⋆ = better spellers ✓ = slower spellers	Three Days
Day 1	a	• ⋆ **Take This Week's Words Trial Test and correct** • ✓ **Take Mastery word Trial Test and correct** • ⋆ **Read This Week's Words and discuss generalization on page 8**	Day 1
Day 2	b	• Complete Spelling Practice page 9 • ✓ Complete Extra Practice Master 2: This Week's Words (optional) ✓ Complete Spelling on Your Own: Mastery Words page 11 ⋆ **Take Bonus word Trial Test and correct**	
Day 3	c	• ⋆ ✓ **Complete Spelling and Language page 10** • ⋆ ✓ Complete Writing on Your Own page 10 • ⋆ ✓ **Complete Using the Dictionary to Spell and Write page 10** • ✓ Take Midweek Test (optional) ⋆ Complete Spelling on Your Own: Bonus words page 11 • ✓ Complete Spelling and Language Master 2 (optional)	Day 2
Day 4	d	• Complete Spelling on Your Own: This Week's Words page 11 ✓ Complete Extra Practice Master 2: Mastery words (optional) ⋆ Complete Extra Practice Master 2: Bonus words (optional)	
Day 5	e	• Take Unit Test on This Week's Words • Complete Reteaching Follow-up Masters 2A and 2B (optional) • ✓ **Take Unit Test on Mastery words** ⋆ **Take Unit Test on Bonus words**	Day 3

Enrichment Activities for the **classroom** and for the **home** included at the end of this unit may be assigned selectively on any day of the week.

INTRODUCING THE UNIT

Establish Readiness for Learning

Tell the children that this week they will continue to study words with short vowel sounds. In Unit 2 they will study words that end with the double consonants *ll, ff, ss,* and *dd.* Tell the children that they will apply the spelling generalizations to This Week's Words and use those words to write a story.

Assess Children's Spelling Ability

Administer the Trial Test before the children study This Week's Words. Use the test sentences provided. Say each word and use it in a sentence. Then repeat the word. Have the children write the words on a separate sheet of paper or in their spelling notebooks. Test sentences are also provided for Mastery and Bonus words.

Have the children check their own work by listening to you read the spelling of the words or by referring to This Week's Words in the left column of the **Pupil Book.** For each misspelled word, have the children follow the **Study Steps to Learn a Word** on page 1 in the **Pupil Book** or use the copying master to study and write the words. Children should record the number correct on their **Progress Report.**

Trial Test Sentences

This Week's Words
1. *spill*   Try not to *spill* your milk.   *spill*
2. *drill*   Mom will *drill* a hole in the wall.   *drill*
3. *ill*   Ben was *ill* and had to go home.   *ill*
4. *shell*   A turtle has a hard *shell*.   *shell*
5. *spell*   Alice can *spell* some hard words.   *spell*
6. *smell*   David likes the *smell* of paint.   *smell*

FOCUS
• Establishes objectives
• Relates to prior learning
• Sets purpose of instruction

7. *stuff*   Joan keeps all kinds of *stuff* in her old toy box.   **stuff**
8. *cliff*   The eagle's nest is on a high *cliff*.   **cliff**
9. *kiss*   Eric gave his mom a good-by *kiss*.   **kiss**
10. *less*   Six is four *less* than ten.   **less**
11. *mess*   Francie's room is a *mess*.   **mess**
12. *unless*   Benjy won't go *unless* you go too.   **unless**
13. *add*   Kevin can *add* numbers in his head.   **add**
14. *odd*   That purple and pink house is *odd*.   **odd**
15. *roll*   Linda taught her dog to *roll* over.   **roll**

Mastery Words

1. *egg*   Ruth had an *egg* for breakfast.   **egg**
2. *fell*   Henry *fell* down.   **fell**
3. *grass*   The *grass* looks very green after it rains.   **grass**
4. *off*   Carrie fell *off* her bike.   **off**
5. *pull*   Don't *pull* the cat's tail.   **pull**
6. *still*   Alex is eight, but Doug is *still* only seven.   **still**

Bonus Words

1. *foggy*   It was a wet and *foggy* day.   **foggy**
2. *fossils*   We saw dinosaur *fossils* at the museum.   **fossils**
3. *pillow*   There are feathers in this *pillow*.   **pillow**

4. *pudding*   This *pudding* is too sweet.   **pudding**
5. *recess*   Most children enjoy *recess*.   **recess**
6. *sudden*   The car made a *sudden* stop.   **sudden**
7. *valley*   The river flows down the mountain and into the *valley*.   **valley**
8. *village*   Only 63 people live in that *village*.   **village**

Apply Prior Learning

Tell the children that they can discover spelling generalizations by applying what they already know about words with double consonants. Use the following activity.

Have the children name some words that end with the sounds /l/, /f/, /s/, and /d/. Write their responses on the chalkboard. Continue writing their responses until words containing final /l/ll, /f/ff, /s/ss, and /d/dd are among the words listed. Have children note that some words end with single consonants and some end with double consonants. Ask volunteers to come to the chalkboard and circle the words that end with double consonants. Tell the children that they will study words that end with double consonants. Explain that they can use these words in a variety of writing tasks: they can use the words in a note to a friend, in a letter, in a science report, or in a creative writing assignment.

FOCUS

- Relates to prior learning
- Draws relationships
- Applies spelling generalizations to new contexts

FOR CHILDREN WITH SPECIAL NEEDS

Learning Difficulties

Children with auditory memory deficits often find it easier to remember a spelling generalization they have learned through inductive reasoning. Ask the children to be detectives and try to solve the mystery of the generalization themselves.

Example: spill
          stuff
          unless
          odd

Ask a volunteer to come to the chalkboard and draw a line under the vowel and final double consonant in each word as you and the other children read the word aloud. Ask the children to formulate a generalization based on

the words on the chalkboard. Elicit from the children that the final consonant sound in these words is represented by double consonant letters, and that each of these words has a short vowel sound.

Limited English Proficiency

To help limited English proficient children work with the spelling generalizations for Unit 2, you may wish to refer to the booklet "Suggestions and Activities for Limited English Proficient Students."

TEACHING PLAN

Objective To spell words that demonstrate these sound-letter relationships: final /l/ll, final /f/ff, final /s/ss, final /d/dd.

1. Write these groups of words on the chalkboard, omitting the circles:

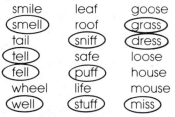

smile   leaf   goose
(smell)   roof   (grass)
tail   (sniff)   (dress)
(tell)   safe   loose
(fell)   (puff)   house
wheel   life   mouse
(well)   (stuff)   (miss)

Ask the children what the words in each group have in common. Help them to recognize that all the words in each group have the same final consonant sound. Then ask volunteers to read the words aloud, and have the children indicate if each word has a short vowel sound. Circle the words that have short vowel sounds, and help the children draw the conclusion that all the words that have short vowel sounds end with double consonant letters.

2. Have volunteers read This Week's Words aloud. A box ☐ around the number that precedes a word in the list indicates that the relationship between sounds and letters in the word is in some way unusual. Such words are commented on either in the generalization following a similar box or in **Remember This.**

You may wish to introduce the lesson by using **Spelling Generalizations Transparency 2**.

3. Read the generalization on page 8 aloud, and have a volunteer identify the vowel sound heard in *roll*. (/ō/)

4. Read the verses in **Remember This** aloud. *Add* and *odd* are the only words in the English language in which final /d/ is spelled *dd*.

You may wish to assign **LEP Practice Master 2** for reinforcement in writing spelling words.

---

2 Double Letters

THIS WEEK'S WORDS

1. spill
2. drill
3. ill
4. shell
5. spell
6. smell
7. stuff
8. cliff
9. kiss
10. less
11. mess
12. unless
13. add
14. odd
15. roll

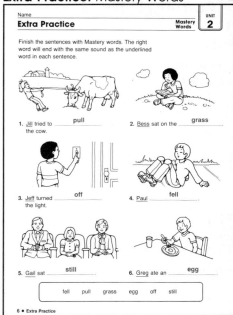

This Week's Words

Most of This Week's Words have a short vowel sound. Most of them end with the consonant sound /l/, /f/, or /s/. These consonant sounds are spelled with two consonant letters.

- /l/ is spelled **ll** in spill
- /f/ is spelled **ff** in stuff
- /s/ is spelled **ss** in kiss

Double consonant letters also spell /d/ in add and odd.
☐ The word roll does not have a short vowel sound. What vowel sound do you hear in roll?

REMEMBER THIS

One d is enough for bad and sad
And lad and had and even mad.
But when it comes to spelling add,
Another d you'll have to add.

One d will do for cod and nod,
And one's enough for rod and pod.
But odd is odd, as you see—
It needs a second letter d.

8

Extra Practice: This Week's Words

Name ___
Extra Practice   This Week's Words   UNIT **2**

Finish each group of sentences with This Week's Words. Use words that end with the same sound as the picture words.

A. 1. We will **stuff** the turkey now.
   2. Keep away from the edge of the **cliff** !

B. 3. Reggie feels **ill** today.
   4. A clam lives in its **shell**
   5. The worker will **drill** through the wall.
   6. Did you **roll** out the dough?
   7. Can you **spell** this word?
   8. Don't **spill** the water!
   9. I **smell** something cooking!

C. 10. This orange is **less** sweet than that one.
   11. Lucy gave Grandpa a hug and a **kiss**
   12. Joan will not call us **unless** she cannot go to the ball game.
   13. Please help me clean up this **mess**

D. 14. Five is an **odd** number.
   15. Did you **add** rice to the soup?

| spill | ill | drill | shell | smell | spell | stuff | cliff |
| kiss | less | mess | unless | add | odd | roll | |

Extra Practice • 5

Extra Practice: Mastery Words

Name ___
Extra Practice   Mastery Words   UNIT **2**

Finish the sentences with Mastery words. The right word will end with the same sound as the underlined word in each sentence.

1. Jill tried to **pull** the cow.
2. Bess sat on the **grass**
3. Jeff turned **off** the light.
4. Paul **fell**
5. Gail sat **still**
6. Greg ate an **egg**

| fell | pull | grass | egg | off | still |

6 • Extra Practice

Spelling Practice

A. Follow the directions. Use This Week's Words.

1. Write the six words that have the vowel sound /e/.

shell	spell	smell
less	mess	unless

2. Write the five words that have the vowel sound /i/.

spill	drill	ill
cliff	kiss	

3. Write the word that has a long o. ___roll___

4. Write the word that rhymes with <u>nod</u>. ___odd___

5. Write the word that rhymes with <u>sad</u>. ___add___

B. Finish the story with This Week's Words. The consonant sound that ends each word is given to help you. One is done for you.

My room is a __6__ /s/. Dad says I can't go to Ben's party __7__ /s/ I clean my room today. But cleaning my room makes me feel __8__ /l/. There is so much __9__ /f/ to put away. Here is the __10__ /d/ little __11__ /l/ I found on the beach. I could __12__ /l/ a hole in it and wear it on a chain. But it has a funny __13__ /l/. I guess I should throw it away.

6. mess	7. unless	8. ill
9. stuff	10. odd	11. shell
12. drill	13. smell	

Handwriting column:
spill
drill
ill
shell
spell
smell
stuff
cliff
kiss
less
mess
unless
add
odd
roll

9

Summarize Learning

Have the children summarize what they have learned on pages 8 and 9. *Ask:*

- What consonant sounds have you learned about in the lesson? (/l/, /f/, /s/, and /d/)
- What did you learn about these final consonant sounds? (They are sometimes spelled with double consonants when preceded by a short vowel.)
- What are some words in which the final consonant sounds are spelled with double consonants? (spill, stuff, less, odd; accept other examples)

TEACHING PLAN

> **Objectives** To write words given vowel sound clues; to write rhyming words; to write words that complete a story.

1. Briefly discuss the directions on page 9. You might prepare the children for completing Exercise **B** by reading the paragraph aloud and having the children supply the missing words. Make certain that the children understand that the letters between the lines / / represent sounds. When correcting the children's responses in Exercise **B**, you should be primarily concerned with correct spelling.

2. Have the children complete the page independently. Remind the children to use legible handwriting. You may wish to demonstrate the correct form of the letters *l, f, s,* and *d* and then have the children practice writing the letters. For **Handwriting Models,** refer the children to page 258 in the **Pupil Book.**

3. To correct the children's work, have volunteers read their answers aloud. The children should check their own work.

For reinforcement in writing spelling words, you may wish to assign *Extra Practice Master 2: This Week's Words.*

TEACHING PLAN

SPELLING AND LANGUAGE

Objective To write a different word by changing one letter in a given word.

1. Write *odd* on the chalkboard. Ask the children what word you would spell if you changed o to a.
2. Read the directions on page 10 aloud. Then have a volunteer say the picture words and identify the first letter in each word. Be sure the children understand that they must write the new letter over the ▲.

   If you are using the hardcover book, have the children write the first word in each word ladder and refer to their books to find out where to write the new letter. Tell them to write each new word carefully under the previous word.
3. Have two volunteers reproduce their completed word ladders on the chalkboard. Children may check their own work.

For extended practice in forming new words, you may wish to assign **Spelling and Language Master 2.**

WRITING ON YOUR OWN

Objectives To write a story using spelling words; to proofread for spelling.

1. Review the directions with the children.
2. As a **prewriting** activity, have the children discuss what is happening in the picture on page 8 and what might happen next. Have them **compose** a story about the cat. When the children **revise** their stories, remind them to check spelling. For additional help, you may wish to refer them to the **Revising Checklist** on page 247 of the **Writer's Guide.** To **publish** the children's work, have them read their stories aloud.

Spelling and Language • Word Ladders

THIS WEEK'S WORDS
spill
drill
ill
shell
spell
smell
stuff
cliff
kiss
less
mess
unless
add
odd
roll

Changing one letter can make a different word. Take add. If you write o in place of a, you spell odd. Change the words below. Put a new letter where the ▲ is. The new letter is the first letter in the picture word. Then make another new word the same way.

1.
k	i	s	s
m	i	s	s
m	e	s	s
l	e	s	s

2.
s	t	i	l	l
s	p	i	l	l
s	p	e	l	l
s	m	e	l	l

Writing on Your Own

Look at the picture on page 8. Write sentences for your classmates about the cat. First tell what is happening in the picture. Then tell what happens next. Use some of This Week's Words.

Using the Dictionary to Spell and Write

A good writer uses the dictionary to check if a word was used correctly. The words in a dictionary are in alphabetical order. **Alphabetical order** is the order of letters from a to z. Write these groups of words in alphabetical order.

1. cliff
   ill
   add
   roll

   add
   cliff
   ill
   roll

2. spell
   stuff
   shell
   smell

   shell
   smell
   spell
   stuff

 SPELLING DICTIONARY Remember to use your **Spelling Dictionary** when you write.

10

USING THE DICTIONARY

Objective To write words in alphabetical order by first or second letter.

1. Read the introductory paragraph on page 10 aloud. Review the procedure for alphabetizing words by writing the words below on the chalkboard and having the children tell you how to arrange them in order:

   bread blue bed boat

2. Have the children complete the activity independently.
3. To check the children's work, ask volunteers to read their lists. Have the children check their own work.

Extra Practice: Spelling and Language

Name	UNIT
Spelling and Language	**2**

A. Change one letter of the word in dark print. Use the new word to finish the sentence. The new word will be one of This Week's Words.

spill
drill
ill
shell
spell
smell
stuff
cliff
kiss
less
mess
unless
add
odd
roll

1. **swell** Our class is learning how to ___**spell**___ many different words.
2. **old** We know all about even numbers and ___**odd**___ numbers.
3. **and** We can ___**add**___ numbers together.
4. **stiff** Some children have lots of ___**stuff**___ in their desks.
5. **miss** If you don't clean your desk, it becomes a ___**mess**___
6. **all** When children feel ___**ill**___ , they don't come to school.
7. **skill** At lunch, we try not to ___**spill**___ our milk.

B. Use one of This Week's Words to complete each item.

8. Change one letter of **shall** to make a word that rhymes with spell. ___**shell**___
9. Change one letter of **loss** to make a word that rhymes with mess. ___**less**___
10. Change one letter of **droll** to make a word that rhymes with spill. ___**drill**___

8 • Extra Practice

Spelling on Your Own

THIS WEEK'S WORDS

`add add add` / `d d drill`

Make a "word chain" with This Week's Words. Write one word. Use a letter in that word to write another word. Then keep going, writing words across and down. Try to link all the words in one chain. You may also make more than one chain.

MASTERY WORDS

| egg |
| fell |
| grass |
| off |
| pull |
| still |

Follow the directions. Use the Mastery words.

1. Write the two words that begin with two consonant letters.

grass   still

2. Write the two words that begin with a vowel letter.

egg   off

Write the Mastery word that rhymes with each word below.

3. well _____fell_____   **4.** hill _____still_____

5. pass _____grass_____   **6.** full _____pull_____

Write the Mastery words that go with these words.

7. on and _____off_____   **8.** chicken and _____egg_____

BONUS WORDS

| foggy |
| fossils |
| pillow |
| pudding |
| recess |
| sudden |
| valley |
| village |

Write the Bonus word that goes with each meaning.

1. play period   **2.** place to rest your head

3. creamy dessert   **4.** without warning

5. small town   **6.** place between mountains

7. full of mist   **8.** marks of very old plants and animals

Write a short story. Try to use all the Bonus words.   **See answers below.**

11

Summarize Learning

Have the children summarize what they have learned in this unit. *Ask:*

- What have you learned about word ladders? (A new word can sometimes be formed by changing one letter in a word.) Give examples (add, odd; m*i*ss, mess; accept other examples)
- What did you learn about how words are arranged in a dictionary? (They are arranged in alphabetical order.)
- What spelling generalizations have you learned? How did you use these generalizations?

Spelling on Your Own

TEACHING PLAN

Objective   To apply the unit spelling generalization to spell This Week's Words, Mastery words, and Bonus words independently.

THIS WEEK'S WORDS

1. Read the directions on page 11 aloud. Copy the third step of the sample word chain given in the **Pupil Book** on the chalkboard. Then ask the children to find a word on the list that can be linked up with *drill*.
2. Have the children complete the activity independently.

MASTERY WORDS

1. Ask a volunteer to read the Mastery words aloud.
2. Read the directions on page 11. Work through the activities orally.

BONUS WORDS

1. Point out that double consonant letters can also occur in the middle of a word. Remind the children that double consonant letters usually follow short vowel sounds.
2. Ask a volunteer to read the Bonus words aloud.
3. Briefly discuss the directions on page 11. Then have the children complete the activities independently on a separate piece of paper. If the children are having problems getting started, suggest that they write about someone who lives in a village in a valley and finds fossils on the playground.

For reinforcement in writing spelling words, you may wish to assign **Extra Practice Master 2: Mastery Words** or **Bonus Words**

CLOSING THE UNIT

Apply New Learning

Tell the children that if they misspell words with double consonants in their writing, they should use one or more of the following strategies:

- think of words that rhyme, and compare in their minds how they are spelled.
- think about whether the spelling of the word could be unusual.

Transfer New Learning

Tell the children that when they encounter new words in their personal reading and in other context areas, they should learn the meaning of those words and then apply the generalizations they have studied to the spelling of those words. Tell the children that once the words are familiar in both meaning and spelling, they should use the new words in their writing.

ENRICHMENT ACTIVITIES

Classroom activities and **home activities** may be assigned to children of all ability levels. The activities provide opportunities for children to use their spelling words in new contexts.

For the Classroom

To individualize classroom activities, you may have the children use the word list they are studying in this unit.

- *Basic:* Use **Mastery** words to complete the activity.
- *Average:* Use **This Week's Words** to complete the activity.
- *Challenging:* Use **Bonus** words to complete the activity.

1. **Language Arts/Writing Riddles** Have the children write riddles about spelling words. Tell the children that you are going to ask a riddle. They are to answer it by using one of their new spelling words. Ask the following riddle: *I am thinking of a word that has a short vowel sound, and means "to name or write in order the letters of a word." What word am I thinking of?* (spell) Tell the children to write similar riddles for five other spelling words, giving one clue about sound or spelling, and one clue about meaning. Have the children share their riddles.

■ COOPERATIVE LEARNING: Have each group create a riddle book using spelling words. Each child within a group should write clues for one riddle to contribute to the book. Riddles should have at least two clues, one related to sound or spelling, and one related to meaning. Group members should try out their riddles on each other to see if the clues are effective. They may consult a dictionary to check definitions. When each group is

satisfied with its riddles, the riddles should be combined into book form.

2. **Language Arts/Creating Sentences** Have the children use their spelling words to build sentences based on specific phrases. To clarify the task, first write the phrase *the soup* on the chalkboard, and brainstorm ways that spelling words can be used to say things about *the soup*. For example, *Add pepper to the soup.* Tell the children to use spelling words from all three lists to create ten sentences which contain the following phrases: *at the beach, the dog will, over the rocks, in the room, Fred runs to.* Have them share their sentences.

■ COOPERATIVE LEARNING: Have each group create sentences based on given themes, using one of the above phrases as the basis for as many sentences as they can create. Tell each child in a group to use the phrase in written sentences that include one or more spelling words. Have group members check each other's sentences to see if they include both the phrase and spelling words. One member from each group should read his or her group's sentences aloud.

3. **Language Arts/Writing a Descriptive Paragraph** Have the children write a descriptive paragraph. As a ***prewriting*** activity, first direct the children's attention to page 249 of the **Writer's Guide** to read about descriptive paragraphs. Then have them look over the spelling list in search of words that they might use to describe a particular scene. Tell each child to select a scene he or she wants to describe and to make a cluster drawing. Draw this model of a cluster on the chalkboard.

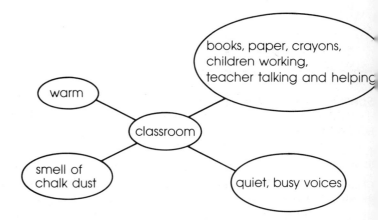

When the children have finished the ***prewriting*** activity, tell them to use the cluster drawing to **compose** the paragraph. Remind the children to use as many spelling words as possible. Then have the children **revise** the paragraph, making sure it gives a clear picture of what a place is like. Remind the children to proofread for spelling, capitalization, and punctuation errors. **Publish** the children's work in a class booklet.

■ COOPERATIVE LEARNING: Have each group write a

descriptive paragraph. As a **prewriting** activity, first have each group brainstorm scenes they might describe, using the three spelling lists for ideas. After each group chooses one scene, have group members make a cluster drawing, writing the word that names the place in a central circle. Members should list details around the place.

When the children are ready to **compose** the descriptive paragraph, tell each group to select one child to begin the paragraph by providing a first sentence. Other children should build on that sentence, each contributing one or more sentences that tell more about the place. Each group should select one child to record as other group members **revise** the paragraph, checking to see if it names a place and gives details that describe it. Have each child within a group check the paragraph for spelling, capitalization, and punctuation errors. Children may use the **Revising Checklist** on page 247 for help. Have one child in the group rewrite the paragraph. Each group should **publish** its paragraph by having a group member read it aloud or by displaying it for the class to read.

For the Home

Children may complete home activities independently or with the assistance of a relative or friend in the home.

1. **Social Studies/Creating a Dictionary of Geographical Terms** Tell the children to begin a book of geographical features, using as many spelling words as possible. The children should look through old magazines to find pictures of such things as cliffs, rocks, rivers, mountains, oceans, and beaches. Next, the pictures should be cut out and pasted on a separate piece of paper. The children may use a dictionary to help them as they label each picture. Have the children use their spelling words to write a sentence relating to the picture. After several pages have been completed, the children can arrange the entries alphabetically and gather them into a booklet. The booklet may be shared with a friend or a relative.

2. **Science/Writing Sentences About Plants** Tell the children to choose spelling words from the three lists and write sentences about growing plants from seeds. Encourage them to use as many spelling words in each sentence as possible. *The seed will not grow into a plant* <u>unless</u> *you* <u>add</u> *plenty of water.* Have the children underline each spelling word they have used. The children may ask a friend or relative to read their sentences.

3. **Language Arts/Writing a Humorous Paragraph** Have the children write a humorous paragraph called "The Odd Mess." Tell the children to begin their paragraphs with the sentence *You won't believe what I saw just now!* Ask them to use as many spelling words as possible. Remind them to check for spelling, capitalization, and punctuation. The children might enjoy reading their paragraphs to a friend or relative.

4. **Science/Making a List of Living Things** Have the children compile a list of living things that have shells, such as turtles, snails, lobsters, clams, oysters, crabs, or armadillos; or living things that come from shells, such as robins, roosters, sparrows, or swallows. Then have the children choose five words from the list and write each in a sentence.

EVALUATING SPELLING ABILITY

Unit Test

This Week's Words
1. *spill*   Pedro wiped up the *spill* with a sponge.   **spill**
2. *drill*   The dentist has a new *drill*.   **drill**
3. *ill*   Lacey is *ill* with the flu.   **ill**
4. *shell*   Pat found a pretty *shell* on the beach.   **shell**
5. *spell*   You need three *a*'s to *spell* <u>banana</u>.   **spell**
6. *smell*   My dog likes to *smell* flowers.   **smell**
7. *stuff*   Tim tried to *stuff* everything in one suitcase.   **stuff**
8. *cliff*   We watched the mountain climbers go up the *cliff*.   **cliff**
9. *kiss*   They *kiss* their mother every day.   **kiss**
10. *less*   Pam likes winter *less* than summer.   **less**
11. *mess*   The cat made a *mess* of the yarn.   **mess**
12. *unless*   We can walk *unless* it is raining.   **unless**
13. *add*   Jed knows how to *add* and subtract.   **add**
14. *odd*   An anteater is an *odd* animal.   **odd**
15. *roll*   Please help me *roll* up this sleeping bag.   **roll**

Mastery Words
1. *egg*   A robin's *egg* has a blue shell.   **egg**
2. *fell*   The book *fell* on the floor.   **fell**
3. *grass*   The *grass* is dry and brown.   **grass**
4. *off*   Terry turned *off* the lights.   **off**
5. *pull*   Ralph will *pull* us on his sled.   **pull**
6. *still*   Emma never sits *still* for long.   **still**

Bonus Words
1. *foggy*   It is hard to drive when it is *foggy*.   **foggy**
2. *fossils*   Andy and Carol are digging for *fossils*.   **fossils**
3. *pillow*   Carol cannot sleep without a *pillow*.   **pillow**
4. *pudding*   We had rice *pudding* for dessert.   **pudding**
5. *recess*   We do a lot of work before *recess*.   **recess**
6. *sudden*   All of a *sudden* Mary remembered the right answer.   **sudden**
7. *valley*   The farmers in the *valley* raise sheep.   **valley**
8. *village*   There is a library in the *village*.   **village**

Dictation Sentences

This Week's Words
1. We saw the *shell roll* off the *cliff*.
2. You will make a *mess* if you *spill* this *odd stuff*.
3. Children *add* and *spell* in school.
4. She is *ill* and will miss school *unless* she gets well soon.
5. They use a saw *less* than they use a *drill*.
6. All of us like to *kiss* the baby.
7. That is a nice *smell*.

Mastery Words
1. The *grass fell off* the truck.
2. We sit *still* so he can *pull* us along.
3. That *egg* will be good to eat.

Bonus Words
1. She found these *fossils* in the *valley* on a *foggy* day.
2. All of a *sudden*, *recess* was over at the *village* school.
3. He sat on a *pillow* to eat the *pudding*.

RETEACHING STRATEGIES FOR SPELLING

Children who have made errors on the Unit Test may require reteaching. Use the following *Reteaching Strategies* and *Follow-up Masters 2A* and *2B* for additional instruction and practice of This Week's Words. (You may wish to assign *LEP Reteaching Follow-up Master 2* for reteaching of spelling words.)

A. Discovering Spelling Ideas

1. Say the following words as you write them on the chalkboard.

   grill   pass   puff

2. Ask the children to identify the final consonant sound in each word. (/l/, /s/, /f/)
3. Ask the children to identify the letters used to spell the final consonant sounds. (*ll, ss, ff*)
4. Ask the children what they have learned about spelling of /l/, /f/, and /s/ at the end of a word. (They are often spelled with double letters.)

B. Word Shapes

1. Explain to the children that each word has a shape and that remembering the shape of the word can help them to spell the word correctly.
2. On the chalkboard, write the words *swell* and *pass.* Have the children identify "short," "tall," and "tail" letters.
3. Draw the configuration of each word on the chalkboard, and ask the children which word fits in each shape.

Use *Reteaching Follow-up Master 2A* to reinforce spelling generalizations taught in Unit 2.

Use *Reteaching Follow-up Master 2B* to reinforce spellings of This Week's Words for Unit 2.

Name _____ **UNIT 2**
Reteaching Follow-up A   Discovering Spelling Ideas

THIS WEEK'S WORDS

spill	ill	shell	smell	kiss
mess	unless	odd	drill	add
spell	stuff	less	roll	cliff

1. Study This Week's Words. Say each word to yourself.

2. Write the words that end with the sound /l/.

   spill   ill   shell

   smell   drill   spell

   roll

3. Write the words that end with the sound /f/.

   stuff   cliff

4. Write the words that end with the sound /s/.

   kiss   mess

   less   unless

5. Write the words that end with the sound /d/.

   odd   add

6. Draw a line under the letters that make the final sound in each word you wrote for 2–5.

7. What do This Week's Words have in common?

   They all end with double consonant letters.

Reteaching • 3

Name _____ **UNIT 2**
Reteaching Follow-up B   Word Shapes

THIS WEEK'S WORDS

spill	ill	shell	smell	kiss
mess	unless	odd	drill	add
spell	stuff	less	roll	cliff

Write each of This Week's Words in its correct shape. The first one has been done for you.   Children may interchange answers that fit the same configuration.

1. s m e l l
2. i l l
3. s h e l l
4. o d d
5. u n l e s s
6. m e s s
7. c l i f f
8. s p i l l
9. l e s s
10. a d d
11. d r i l l
12. s t u f f
13. r o l l
14. s p e l l
15. k i s s

4 • Reteaching

11C   UNIT 2 *Double Letters*

PREVIEWING THE UNIT

Unit Materials

Instruction and Practice

Pupil Book	pages 12–15
Teacher's Edition	
Teaching Plans	pages 12–15
Enrichment Activities	
For the Classroom	page 15A
For the Home	page 15B
Reteaching Strategies	page 15C

Testing

Teacher's Edition	
Trial Test	pages 11E–11F
Unit Test	page 15B
Dictation Test	page 15B

Additional Resources

PRACTICE AND REINFORCEMENT
Extra Practice Master 3: This Week's Words
Extra Practice Master 3: Mastery Words
Extra Practice Master 3: Bonus Words
LEP Practice Master 3
Spelling and Language Master 3
Study Steps to Learn a Word Master

RETEACHING FOLLOW-UP
Reteaching Follow-up Master 3A:
   Discovering Spelling Ideas
Reteaching Follow-up Master 3B: Word
   Shapes
LEP Reteaching Follow-up Master 3

TEACHING AIDS
Spelling Generalizations Transparency 3

Visit our Web site
http://www.hbschool.com

Click on the SPELLING banner to find activities for this unit.

Learner Objectives

Spelling

- To spell words in which the final consonant letter is doubled before *ed* or *ing* is added.
- To spell base forms and inflected forms of verbs.

Reading

- To follow written directions.
- To use context clues to complete sentences given spelling words.
- To read a paragraph written by a classmate.
- To recognize that some words can function as nouns or verbs.
- To use a dictionary for word meaning.

Writing

- To write a paragraph.
- To use the writing process.
- To proofread for spelling, capitalization, and punctuation.
- To write legible manuscript and cursive letters.

Listening

- To listen to identify words in which the final consonant letter is doubled before *ed* or *ing* is added.
- To follow oral directions.

Speaking

- To respond to a question.
- To speak clearly to a group.
- To express feelings and ideas about a piece of writing.
- To present a "how-to" paragraph.
- To contribute ideas and information in group discussions.

THIS WEEK'S WORDS

bat
chop
clap
drop
nap
pin
step
skinned
stopped
trapped
tripped
tagging
planning
wagging
tapping

MASTERY WORDS

hop
pat
rub
pet
spot
pop

BONUS WORDS

scrub
swap
prop
plot
grabbed
shopped
wrapping
stirring

Assignment Guide

This guide shows how you teach a typical spelling unit in either a five-day or a three-day sequence, while providing for individual differences. **Boldface type** indicates essential classwork. Steps shown in light type may be done in class or assigned as homework.

Five Days	○ = average spellers ★ = better spellers ✓ = slower spellers			Three Days
Day 1 ▶a	○ ★	**Take This Week's Words Trial Test and correct**		
	○ ✓	**Take Mastery word Trial Test and correct**		
	○ ★	**Read This Week's Words and discuss generalization on page 12**		**Day 1**
Day 2	○	Complete Spelling Practice page 13	◀b	
	○ ✓	Complete Extra Practice Master 3: This Week's Words (optional)		
	✓	Complete Spelling on Your Own: Mastery words page 15		
	★	**Take Bonus word Trial Test and correct**		
Day 3 ▶c	○ ★ ✓	**Complete Spelling and Language page 14**		
	○ ★ ✓	Complete Writing on Your Own page 14		
	○ ✓	Take Midweek Test (optional)		**Day 2**
	★	Complete Spelling on Your Own: Bonus words page 15		
	○ ✓	Complete Spelling and Language Master 3 (optional)		
Day 4	○	Complete Spelling on Your Own: This Week's Words page 15	◀d	
	✓	Complete Extra Practice Master 3: Mastery words (optional)		
	★	Complete Extra Practice Master 3: Bonus words (optional)		
Day 5 ▶e	○	Take Unit Test on This Week's Words		
	○	Complete Reteaching Follow-up Masters 3A and 3B (optional)		**Day 3**
	○ ✓	**Take Unit Test on Mastery words**		
	★	**Take Unit Test on Bonus words**		

Enrichment Activities for the **classroom** and for the **home** included at the end of this unit may be assigned selectively on any day of the week.

INTRODUCING THE UNIT

Establish Readiness for Learning

Tell the children that this week they will continue to study words with short vowel sounds. In Unit 3 they will study action words or verbs in which the final consonant letter is doubled before adding *ed* or *ing.* Tell the children that they will apply the spelling generalization to This Week's Words and use those words to write a paragraph.

Assess Children's Spelling Ability

Administer the Trial Test before the children study This Week's Words. Use the test sentences provided. Say each word and use it in a sentence. Then repeat the word. Have the children write the words on a separate sheet of paper or in their spelling notebooks. Test sentences are also provided for Mastery and Bonus words.

Have the children check their own work by listening to you read the spelling of the words or by referring to This Week's Words in the left column of the **Pupil Book.** For each misspelled word, have the children follow the **Study Steps to Learn a Word** on page 1 in the **Pupil Book** or use the copying master to study and write the words. Children should record the number correct on their **Progress Report.**

Trial Test Sentences

This Week's Words
1. *bat*   It is Allan's turn to *bat.*   *bat*
2. *chop*   We need to *chop* up some onions.   *chop*
3. *clap*   People *clap* after a good show. *clap*
4. *drop*   Do not *drop* the groceries. *drop*
5. *nap*   Some children *nap* in the afternoon.   *nap*
6. *pin*   Try to *pin* the tail on the donkey. *pin*

- Establishes objectives
- Relates to prior learning
- Sets purpose of instruction

7. **step**   Don't *step* in the mud puddle.
   step
8. **skinned**   Sharon *skinned* her knee.
   skinned
9. **stopped**   Mrs. Alvarez *stopped* to pick
   us up.   **stopped**
10. **trapped**   Jack *trapped* a bug in a jar.
    trapped
11. **tripped**   Nancy *tripped* on the stairs.
    tripped
12. **tagging**   My brother is always *tagging*
    after me.   **tagging**
13. **planning**   We are *planning* a picnic.
    planning
14. **wagging**   Fido is *wagging* her tail.
    wagging
15. **tapping**   Who is *tapping* on the
    window?   **tapping**

Mastery Words

1. **hop**   Rabbits know how to *hop*.   **hop**
2. **pat**   You must *pat* a baby's back
   gently.   **pat**
3. **rub**   Bears *rub* their backs on trees.   **rub**
4. **pet**   Do not *pet* strange dogs.   **pet**
5. **spot**   Can you *spot* Freddy in this crowd?
   spot
6. **pop**   Balloons *pop* when they break.
   pop

Bonus Words

1. **scrub**   Dad will *scrub* the bathroom
   floor.   **scrub**
2. **swap**   Joe and Tina *swap* baseball
   cards.   **swap**

3. **prop**   We need a stick to *prop* up the
   plant.   **prop**
4. **plot**   Let's *plot* a way to surprise Philip.
   plot
5. **grabbed**   The hungry lion *grabbed* the
   meat.   **grabbed**
6. **shopped**   Mr. Medford *shopped* around
   for a tractor.   **shopped**
7. **wrapping**   The clerk is *wrapping* our
   package.   **wrapping**
8. **stirring**   Abby is *stirring* the pudding.
   stirring

Apply Prior Learing

Have the children apply what they already know about doubling consonants before adding *ed* or *ing* by using the following activity.

Write the words *running, sitting, stopped,* and *chatted* on the chalkboard. Ask the children to find some characteristics that all these words have in common. (They all have short vowel sounds; they have double consonants in the middle; they have been formed by adding endings to base words; they are all action words, or verbs.) Have volunteers circle the base word in each word. Tell the children that they will study words that have some of the same characteristics that they discovered about the words on the chalkboard. Explain that the children can use these words in a variety of writing tasks: they can use the words in a note to a friend, in a letter, in a science report, or to complete a social studies assignment.

FOCUS

- Relates to prior learning
- Draws relationships
- Applies spelling generalizations to new contexts

FOR CHILDREN WITH SPECIAL NEEDS

Learning Difficulties

Children with language and memory deficits may have problems learning and remembering the generalization about when to double and when not to double the consonant ending of the verb before adding *er* or *ing*.

To reinforce the generalizations in this unit, use activities that involve the motor skills and visual feedback. At the top of a sheet of paper in the spelling notebook, have the children write the generalization: "When an action word (verb) ends with one vowel and one consonant, double the last letter when adding *ed* or *ing*." You may wish to prepare this on a duplicating master for those children who are not able to copy accurately.

Have the children write a base word and immediately under it write that word with a double final consonant and the letters *ed.* Under that have them write the base

word again, this time adding the letters *ing.* Ask them to use all forms of the word in sentences to ensure that the children understand its meaning. Finally, have the children trace each word in the set (base word, base word + *ed,* base word + *ing*) saying the letters aloud as they do so. The tracing activity may be done as many as three times per word for emphasis.

Limited English Proficiency

To help limited English proficient children work with the spelling generalizations for Unit 3, you may wish to refer to the booklet "Suggestions and Activities for Limited English Proficient Students."

TEACHING PLAN

Objective   To spell words in which the final consonant letter is doubled before *ed* or *ing* is added.

1. Write this sentence on the chalkboard:

   I pet the dog.

   Ask a child to read it aloud. Then ask the children to change the sentence to make it tell what already happened. (I petted the dog.) Write the new sentence below the first one. Then write these incomplete sentences beside those already on the chalkboard:

   I am __ the dog.
   I was __ the dog.

   Ask the children to supply the missing word. (petting) Explain that these are different ways to talk about "now" and "before." Then point out that *pet* has only one *t,* whereas *petted* and *petting* both have two *t*'s.
2. Read the generalization on page 12 aloud.

You may wish to introduce the lesson by using **Spelling Generalizations Transparency 3.**

3. Have volunteers read this week's words aloud. Ask the children to identify the letter that was doubled in words 8–15.

You may wish to assign **LEP Practice Master 3** for reinforcement in writing spelling words.

3 Verbs

THIS WEEK'S WORDS

1. bat
2. chop
3. clap
4. drop
5. nap
6. pin
7. step
8. skinned
9. stopped
10. trapped
11. tripped
12. tagging
13. planning
14. wagging
15. tapping

The dogs <u>wag</u> their tails.

This Week's Words

The word <u>wag</u> is a **verb,** or action word. It ends with one vowel letter and one consonant letter. You can add <u>ed</u> to <u>wag</u> to make a word that tells about the past. When you add <u>ed</u>, you must double the last letter.

The dogs <u>wagged</u> their tails.

You can also add <u>ing</u> to <u>wag</u>. When you add <u>ing</u>, you must also double the last letter.

The dogs were <u>wagging</u> their tails.

All of This Week's Words are verbs. They all follow this pattern:

wag   wagged   wagging

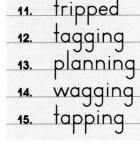

12

Extra Practice: This Week's Words

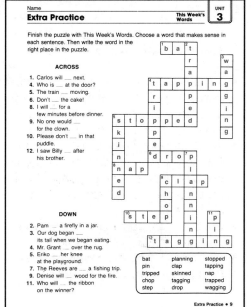

Name
Extra Practice   This Week's Words   UNIT 3

Finish the puzzle with This Week's Words. Choose a word that makes sense in each sentence. Then write the word in the right place in the puzzle.

ACROSS

1. Carlos will __ next.
4. Who is __ at the door?
5. The train __ moving.
6. Don't __ the cake!
8. I will __ for a few minutes before dinner.
9. No one would __ for the clown.
10. Please don't __ in that puddle.
12. I saw Billy __ after his brother.

DOWN

2. Pam __ a firefly in a jar.
3. Our dog began __ its tail when we began eating.
4. Mr. Grant __ over the rug.
5. Eriko __ her knee at the playground.
7. The Reeves are __ a fishing trip.
9. Denise will __ wood for the fire.
11. Who will __ the ribbon on the winner?

bat	planning	stopped
pin	clap	tapping
tripped	skinned	nap
chop	tagging	trapped
step	drop	wagging

Extra Practice • 9

Extra Practice: Mastery Words

Name
Extra Practice   Mastery Words   UNIT 3

A. Be a detective. Which Mastery word goes with each sentence clue? Write the word in the blank.

1. Stick a pin in a balloon and you will hear this. __pop__
2. Drop some juice on a rug and you will make this. __spot__
3. Touch someone lightly on the arm and you do this. __pat__
4. Go near a rabbit and it might do this. __hop__
5. To make a table shine you do this. __rub__
6. A dog or cat might be this. __pet__

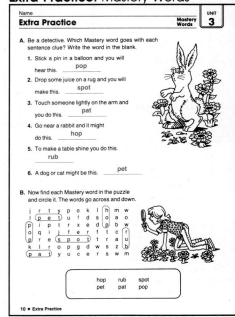

B. Now find each Mastery word in the puzzle and circle it. The words go across and down.

```
j r t y p o k l h m w
l p e t u f d s o a o
p i p t r x e d b w r
o q i f e r f t c u
p r e s p o t r a b
k l r o p g d w s z b
p a t y u c e r s w m
```

| hop | rub | spot |
| pet | pat | pop |

10 • Extra Practice

Spelling Practice

A. Write the verbs that go with the pictures. Use This Week's Words.

1. _____nap_____   2. _____bat_____   3. _____pin_____

B. Add <u>ed</u> to each of these words.

4. trip _____tripped_____   5. skin _____skinned_____

6. stop _____stopped_____   7. trap _____trapped_____

C. Add <u>ing</u> to each of these words.

8. wag _____wagging_____   9. plan _____planning_____

10. tap _____tapping_____   11. tag _____tagging_____

D. Finish the sentences. Use This Week's Words.

12. A _____clap_____ of thunder surprised Chee.

13. She was helping her dad _____chop_____ wood.

14. The first _____drop_____ of rain hit her hand.

15. They decided to watch the rain from the

_____step_____.

E. Try this "word math."

16. stopped – ed = _____stop_____ + ing = _____stopping_____

17. planning – ing = _____plan_____ + ed = _____planned_____

18. tripped – ed = _____trip_____ + ing = _____tripping_____

13

This Week's Words list (right margin, cursive):
bat
chop
clap
drop
nap
pin
step
skinned
stopped
trapped
tripped
tagging
planning
wagging
tapping

Extra Practice: Bonus Words

Extra Practice

Name _____   Bonus Words   UNIT 3

A. Read each sentence. Draw a line under the word that makes no sense.

1. The thieves grobbed a holdup.
2. Grandma protted for new shoes.
3. We swagged the presents.
4. Dad spluted the bathtub.
5. Ken platted the ball and ran.
6. David and Lena plapped baseball cards.
7. We crotted up the plant with a stick.
8. Annie is dribbing the soup.

scrub
swap
prop
plot
grabbed
shopped
wrapping
stirring

B. Use the puzzle to find the right word. First find the number of each sentence. Then follow the arrows to find the letters that spell the right word. Write the word after the sentence.

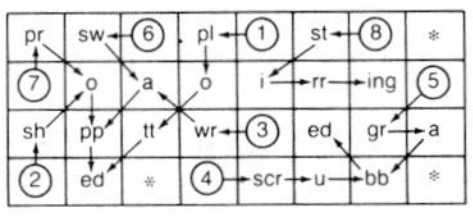

C. Now write the sentences correctly. Use the word you found in the puzzle in place of the silly word.

1. The thieves plotted a holdup.
2. Grandma shopped for new shoes.
3. We wrapped the presents.
4. Dad scrubbed the bathtub.
5. Ken grabbed the ball and ran.
6. David and Lena swapped baseball cards.
7. We propped up the plant with a stick.
8. Annie is stirring the soup.

Extra Practice • 11

Summarize Learning

Have the children summarize what they have learned on pages 12 and 13. *Ask:*

- What have you learned about final consonants in this lesson? (The final consonant letter is doubled in some words before adding *ed* or *ing*.)
- What are examples of words in which the final consonant must be doubled before adding *ed* or *ing*? (stopped, tagging; accept other examples)
- What sort of words are This Week's Words? (action words, or verbs)
- What are some examples of verbs? (clap, stopped; accept other examples)

TEACHING PLAN

Objectives To write base forms and inflected forms of verbs; to write words in sentence context.

1. Briefly discuss the directions on page 13. Ask volunteers to identify the pictures in Exercise **A** and suggest a verb that tells about each picture. Do the first item in Exercise **E** on the chalkboard as an example.
2. Have the children complete the page independently. Remind the children to use legible handwriting. Point out the unit verbs used as nouns in items 12, 14, and 15. You may wish to demonstrate the correct form of the letters *ed* and *ing* and then have the children practice writing the letters. For **Handwriting Models,** refer the children to page 258 in the **Pupil Book.**
3. To correct the children's work, have volunteers write the answers on the chalkboard. Let the children check their own work.

For reinforcement in writing spelling words, you may wish to assign *Extra Practice Master 3: This Week's Words.*

★ *of special interest*

The verb *tag* has two distinct meanings. One is derived from the Middle English noun *tag,* "small decorative bit of metal fixed to an article of clothing." This *tag* has come to refer to any small appendage, such as a price tag or the ticket that a police officer leaves under the windshield wiper when *tagging* an illegally parked car. The other meaning of *tag* comes from the name of a game originally known as *tig*—a variant of the word *tick,* "tap or touch."

TEACHING PLAN

SPELLING AND LANGUAGE

Objective To write inflected forms of given verbs in sentence context.

1. Read the introductory paragraph on page 14 aloud. Remind the children to double the final consonant before adding *ed* or *ing* to This Week's Words.
2. Have the children complete the activity independently.
3. To correct the children's work, ask for volunteers to copy their completed sentences on the chalkboard. Let the children check their own work.

For extended practice in writing inflected verb forms, you may wish to assign **Spelling and Language Master 3.**

WRITING ON YOUR OWN

Objectives To write a paragraph using spelling words; to proofread for spelling.

1. Review the directions with the children.
2. As a **prewriting** activity, have the children name some of their favorite games as you list them on the chalkboard. Have them **compose** a paragraph in which they describe how to play their favorite game. When the children are ready to **revise** their paragraphs, remind them to check spelling. For additional help, you may wish to refer them to the **Revising Checklist** on page 247 of the **Writer's Guide.** To **publish** the children's work, have them exchange their paragraphs and allow them to try to follow one another's directions.

HANDWRITING

Objective To practice writing cursive letter forms: *r R, s S, p P.*

1. Read the first sentence on page 14. Have the children examine the beginning stroke in the models.
2. Have the children examine the models for cursive letters. Help them to notice where the letters touch or intersect the lines.
3. Have the children practice the letter forms and write the sentence.
4. When they have finished, ask the children to compare their letter forms with the models.

Spelling and Language • Adding ed and ing

THIS WEEK'S WORDS
bat
chop
clap
drop
nap
pin
step
skinned
stopped
trapped
tripped
tagging
planning
wagging
tapping

You add *ed* to a word to tell what has already happened. You add *ing* to a word to tell what is or was happening.

Finish the sentences. Add *ed* to the words in dark print.

1. **pin** Mom ____pinned____ Tom's blue ribbon to his shirt.

2. **clap** We ____clapped____ until our hands were red.

Finish the sentences. Add *ing* to the words in dark print.

3. **chop** Jeff is ____chopping____ mushrooms for the pizza.

4. **tag** Sam's dog was ____tagging____ along after us.

Writing on Your Own

Write a paragraph for a friend telling how to play your favorite game. Be sure to give all the steps in the game. Use some of This Week's Words. Use the *ed* and *ing* endings.

WRITER'S GUIDE For a sample how-to paragraph, turn to page 250.

HANDWRITING

rR   sS   pP

Notice where the beginning undercurve stroke stops in each lowercase letter.

r   s   p

1. Practice writing **r R, s S, p P** in cursive.

2. Write this sentence: *Peter sells pies.*

14

Extra Practice: Spelling and Language

Name _____
Spelling and Language   UNIT **3**

A. The first sentence in each group has an underlined word. Finish the other sentences in the group by adding ed or ing to the underlined word.

bat
nap
pin
chop
drop
planning
clap
step
tapping
skinned
stopped
tripped
trapped
tagging
wagging

1. a. The cat wants to trap the mouse.
   b. The cat is good at ____trapping____ mice.
   c. The mouse has never been ____trapped____ by a cat.

2. a. We chop wood for our fireplace.
   b. Last year, we ____chopped____ wood all winter long.
   c. We were ____chopping____ wood every day from morning to night.

3. a. Rita likes to plan long trips.
   b. She ____planned____ a trip around the world.
   c. Some of Rita's friends are ____planning____ to go with her.

B. Each sentence has a word with ed or ing. Write the word without ed or ing.

4. The dog is wagging its tail. ____wag____
5. The cats napped all day long. ____nap____
6. The horse stepped over the log. ____step____
7. Some young birds are tapping on trees. ____tap____

12 • Extra Practice

Spelling on Your Own

THIS WEEK'S WORDS

All of This Week's Words are **verbs.** But they can also be used as **nouns,** or naming words. <u>Bat</u> is a verb when you say "<u>Bat</u> the ball." But it is a noun when you say "Use my <u>bat</u>."

Write sentences using This Week's Words as nouns. You will have to take <u>ed</u> and <u>ing</u> off such words as <u>skinned</u> and <u>planning</u>.

MASTERY WORDS

Follow the directions. Use the Mastery words.

| hop |
| pat |
| rub |
| pet |
| spot |
| pop |

1. Write the three words that begin like <u>paw</u>.

    pat   pet   pop

2. Write the three words that end like <u>cat</u>.

    pat   pet   spot

Finish each sentence pair. Use a Mastery word.

3. Rabbits are hopping.

Rabbits   hop   .

4. I am petting the dog.

I   pet   the dog.

5. Balloons are popping.

Balloons   pop   .

6. I am rubbing my eyes.

I   rub   my eyes.

BONUS WORDS

Write the Bonus word that rhymes with each word.

| scrub |
| swap |
| prop |
| plot |
| grabbed |
| shopped |
| wrapping |
| stirring |

1. clapping   **2.** club   **3.** purring   **4.** hot

Follow the directions. Use the Bonus words.

5. Write the word that rhymes with <u>pop</u> but isn't spelled with <u>o</u>.

6. Make all the words end in ed. You will have to take <u>ing</u> off two words before you add <u>ed</u>. Then use each word in a sentence.   **See answers below.**

15

Spelling on Your Own **Answers**

BONUS WORDS

1. wrapping 2. scrub 3. stirring 4. plot
5. swap 6. scrubbed, swapped, propped, plotted, grabbed, shopped, wrapped, stirred
EXAMPLE: We <u>scrubbed</u> the floor yesterday.

TEACHING PLAN

> **Objectives** To apply the unit spelling generalization to spell This Week's Words, Mastery words, and Bonus words independently.

THIS WEEK'S WORDS

1. Read the directions on page 15 aloud. Prepare the children for the activity by discussing some of the more difficult noun meanings. Use these examples.

   I had a pork *chop* for dinner. There was a loud *clap* of thunder. Shep knocked over the lamp with a *wag* of his tail.

2. Have the children complete the activity independently on a separate piece of paper.

MASTERY WORDS

1. Ask a volunteer to read the Mastery Words aloud.
2. Read the directions on page 15. Work through the activities orally with the children.

BONUS WORDS

1. Review the unit generalization on page 12.
2. Ask a volunteer to read the Bonus Words aloud. Have the children look up the meanings of any unfamiliar words in the **Spelling Dictionary**. Tell them that to find the meanings of words with *ed* or *ing* added, they must look up the word without the ending.
3. Briefly discuss the directions on page 15. Then have the children complete the activities independently on a separate piece of paper.

For reinforcement in writing spelling words, you may wish to assign *Extra Practice Master 3*: *Mastery Words* or *Bonus Words.*

Summarize Learning

Have the children summarize what they have learned in this unit. *Ask*:

- What have you learned about adding endings to verbs? (The ending *ed* is added to a word to tell what has already happened. The ending *ing* can be added to make a word that can be used with words such as *am, is, are, was,* and *were.* You add *ing* to a word to tell what *is* or *was* happening.)
- What spelling generalizations have you learned? How did you use these generalizations?

CLOSING THE UNIT

Apply New Learning

Tell the children that if they misspell verbs with double letters, they should use one or more of the following strategies:

- think about the possible spelling for a sound within the word and use the dictionary to find the correct spelling.
- think of words that rhyme and compare in their minds how they are spelled.
- say the word to themselves and check to see if letters have been left out.

Transfer New Learning

Tell the children that when they encounter new words in their personal reading and in other content areas, they should learn the meaning of those words and then apply the generalizations they have studied to the spelling of those words. Tell the children that once the words are familiar in both meaning and spelling, they should use the new words in their writing.

ENRICHMENT ACTIVITIES

Classroom activities and **home activities** may be assigned to children of all ability levels. The activities provide opportunities for children to use their spelling words in new contexts.

For the Classroom

To individualize classroom activities, you may have the children use the word list they are studying in this unit to complete the activities.

- *Basic:* Use **Mastery** words to complete the activity.
- *Average:* Use **This Week's Words** to complete the activity.
- *Challenging:* Use **Bonus** words to complete the activity.

1. Language Arts/Writing Synonyms Have each child write synonyms for at least five spelling words. Remind the

children that synonyms are words that mean the same, or almost the same, thing. Have the children use all ten words to make a matching exercise for another child to complete. The children who need help may use a dictionary or the **Spelling Thesaurus** on page 203.

■ COOPERATIVE LEARNING: Have each group create a matching exercise with synonyms. Each child within a group should write synonyms for two of the spelling words. Have the group check each pair of synonyms to be sure they are accurate. Together the group should create a matching exercise using the spelling words and their synonyms. If the children choose different synonyms for a spelling word, have the group choose the pair they judge the best. When they are ready, have the groups exchange their work and complete the exercises. Refer children to the **Spelling Thesaurus** on page 203 if they need help.

2. Language Arts/Writing Stories Using Present or Past Tense Verbs Have the children use words from their spelling lists to write a story about an imaginary pet dog. The children may use any of the base words and the endings *ing* or *ed*. As a **prewriting** activity, have the children list things that the dog might do or that they might like to do with the dog. Have them think of a name for the imaginary dog and picture what it looks like. Have them use these ideas to **compose** their stories. As they **revise** the stories, remind them that all verbs must be in the same tense. A sample story might be as follows: *My dog Rocky starts wagging his tail as soon as he sees me. Rocky is always tagging along with me. This summer I am planning to take Rocky on a trip. We will be stopping in many places.* Have the children **proofread** their stories for spelling, capitalization, and punctuation. **Publish** the stories by having the children read them to a classmate.

■ COOPERATIVE LEARNING: Have each group write a story about a pet dog. As a **prewriting** activity, the group should decide on a name for the dog and use their spelling words to make a list of things the dog might do. Each group should select one child to be the group secretary. To **compose** the story, each group member should dictate a sentence while the secretary writes the sentences. The children should then read the story and **revise** it by recommending changes and proofreading for spelling, capitalization, and punctuation. Remind the children to use the **Revising Checklist** on page 247 for help. Encourage them to illustrate their stories. **Publish** the stories by having one group member read the story aloud while another member displays the illustrations.

For the Home

Children may complete home activities independently or with the assistance of a relative or friend in the home.

1. **Language Arts/Adding Word Endings** Tell the children to choose four of the first seven spelling words and write new forms of the words by adding the endings *ing* and *ed*. Have them check a dictionary to be sure that they have spelled the new forms of the base words correctly. Then have the children write a paragraph using either *ing* or *ed* forms of at least six of their spelling words. The children may read their paragraph to a friend or family member.

2. **Language Arts/Writing a How-to Paragraph** Tell the children to write directions for playing an outdoor game. The game may be a real one, such as "Hide and Seek," or one that the children invent. They should list at least five steps and include several of the spelling words in their directions. Remind the children to write each of the steps either in the present or in the past tense. Remind the children to use the **Writer's Guide** on page 250 for a model of a "how-to" paragraph. Have the children proofread their directions for spelling, capitalization, and punctuation and use the **Revising Checklist** on page 247 for help. The children may share their work with a friend or relative.

3. **Science/Listing Uses for an Object** Tell the children to think of an object and list as many uses for the object as possible. For example, *a pencil might be used for writing, as a stick for a puppet, to support a vine, or to serve as a ruler.* Have the children include as many spelling words in their lists as possible. Remind the children to check the spelling of their words. Suggest to the children that they bring their lists in to share with the class.

4. **Language Arts/Writing a Descriptive Paragraph** Have the children write a paragraph which describes a picture. Tell the children to first review their spelling words to see what verbs are included. Tell them to then look through some magazines or books to find an exciting action picture which they can describe using some of the words from their spelling list. Remind the children to proofread their paragraph for spelling, capitalization, and punctuation, using the **Revising Checklist** on page 247 for help. The children may share their paragraphs with a family member or friend.

EVALUATING SPELLING ABILITY

Unit Test

This Week's Words

1. **bat**   The baby likes to *bat* her teddy bear.   **bat**
2. **chop**   Let's *chop* some wood for the fire.   **chop**
3. **clap**   You may *clap* when the music stops.   **clap**
4. **drop**   Karen will *drop* the letter in the mailbox.   **drop**
5. **nap**   If you are sleepy, you should *nap*.   **nap**
6. **pin**   Help me *pin* this flower on my coat.   **pin**
7. **step**   Please *step* this way.   **step**
8. **skinned**   Tina *skinned* her elbow.   **skinned**
9. **stopped**   Kenny's watch *stopped* because he forgot to wind it.   **stopped**
10. **trapped**   The raccoon was *trapped* in the garage.   **trapped**
11. **tripped**   Wendell *tripped* on his shoelace.   **tripped**
12. **tagging**   Mother is *tagging* things for the garage sale.   **tagging**
13. **planning**   We are *planning* a trip.   **planning**
14. **wagging**   The angry cat is *wagging* its tail.   **wagging**
15. **tapping**   Sandy is *tapping* her toes.   **tapping**

Mastery Words

1. **hop**   Kangaroos can *hop* very fast.   **hop**
2. **pat**   Mom will *pat* the dough into a ball.   **pat**
3. **rub**   You should not *rub* your eyes.   **rub**
4. **pet**   Our dog is happiest when you *pet* it.   **pet**
5. **spot**   We tried to *spot* a deer in the woods.   **spot**
6. **pop**   The toast will *pop* up when it's ready.   **pop**

Bonus Words

1. **scrub**   We must *scrub* the bathtub.   **scrub**
2. **swap**   Ben wants to *swap* an apple for an orange.   **swap**
3. **prop**   Use the pillow to *prop* up your head.   **prop**
4. **plot**   The spies will *plot* a way to steal the secret plans.   **plot**
5. **grabbed**   The baby *grabbed* for the toy.   **grabbed**
6. **shopped**   Neil *shopped* for some boots.   **shopped**
7. **wrapping**   George is *wrapping* some presents.   **wrapping**
8. **stirring**   Tanya is *stirring* raisins into the oatmeal.   **stirring**

Dictation Sentences

This Week's Words

1. He *tripped* and *skinned* his leg.
2. I am *planning* to *chop* some wood and then I will *nap*.
3. My dog's tail stops *wagging* when my cat is *tagging* along.
4. We *stopped* to *pin* a note on her door.
5. Our hands *clap* when our feet are *tapping*.
6. *Step* up and *bat* the ball but do not *drop* it.
7. We were *trapped* in the house by the rain.

Mastery Words

1. When I *pet* my cat, it will *rub* my leg.
2. I ate so much that dad says I will *pop*.
3. If the frog will *hop* to me, I will *pat* it.
4. Can you *spot* a good place to sit?

Bonus Words

1. Jim *grabbed* the dish when I was *stirring* the mix.
2. She *shopped* for flower seeds to plant.
3. I want to *swap* jobs with you and *scrub* the car.
4. Help me *prop* up this box so I can start *wrapping* it.
5. We can *plot* the best way to do it.

RETEACHING STRATEGIES FOR SPELLING

Children who have made errors on the Unit Test may require reteaching. Use the following *Reteaching Strategies* and *Follow-up Masters 3A* and *3B* for additional instruction and practice of This Week's Words. (You may wish to assign *LEP Reteaching Follow-up Master 3* for reteaching of spelling words.)

A. Discovering Spelling Ideas

1. Say the following words as you write them on the chalkboard.

   drip   dripped   dripping

2. Ask the children to identify the two types of letters that end the word *drip*. (a vowel and a consonant)
3. Ask the children to tell what happens to the final consonant when you add *ed* and *ing*. (You double the final consonant.)

B. Word Shapes

1. Explain to the children that each word has a shape and that remembering the shape of a word can help them to spell the word correctly.
2. On the chalkboard, write the words *mopping* and *batted*. Have the children identify "short," "tall," and "tail" letters.
3. Draw the configuration of each word on the chalkboard, and ask the children which word fits in each shape.

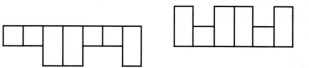

Use *Reteaching Follow-up Master 3A* to reinforce spelling generalizations taught in Unit 3.

Use *Reteaching Follow-up Master 3B* to reinforce spellings of This Week's Words for Unit 3.

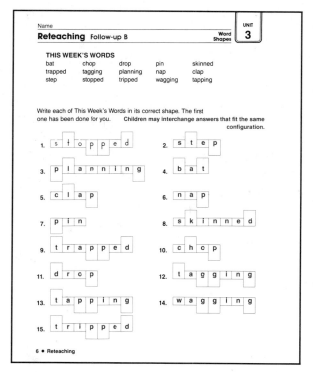

PREVIEWING THE UNIT

Unit Materials

Instruction and Practice

Pupil Book	pages 16–19
Teacher's Edition	
Teaching Plans	pages 16–19
Enrichment Activities	
For the Classroom	pages 19A–19B
For the Home	page 19B
Reteaching Strategies	page 19C

Testing

Teacher's Edition	
Trial Test	pages 15E–15F
Unit Test	page 19B
Dictation Test	page 19B

Additional Resources

PRACTICE AND REINFORCEMENT
Extra Practice Master 4: This Week's Words
Extra Practice Master 4: Mastery Words
Extra Practice Master 4: Bonus Words
LEP Practice Master 4
Spelling and Language Master 4
Study Steps to Learn a Word Master

RETEACHING FOLLOW-UP
Reteaching Follow-up Master 4A:
    Discovering Spelling Ideas
Reteaching Follow-up Master 4B: Word
    Shapes
LEP Reteaching Follow-up Master 4

TEACHING AIDS
Spelling Generalizations Transparency 4

Visit our Web site
http://www.hbschool.com

Click on the SPELLING banner to find activities for this unit.

Learner Objectives

Spelling

- To spell words that demonstrate these sound-letter relationships: /kl/cl; /fl/fl; /dr/dr; /pr/pr; /tr/tr; /str/str; /spr/spr.
- To combine initial consonant clusters and phonograms to spell words.

Reading

- To follow written directions.
- To use context clues to complete sentences given spelling words.
- To use a dictionary to locate information.
- To use a dictionary for word meaning.

Writing

- To write a mystery story.
- To use the writing process.
- To proofread for spelling, capitalization, and punctuation.
- To write legible manuscript and cursive letters.

Listening

- To follow oral directions.
- To listen for letter-sound clues when writing.

Speaking

- To respond to a question.
- To contribute ideas and information in group discussions.
- To speak clearly to a group.
- To present a story to the class.
- To express feelings and ideas about a piece of writing.

THIS WEEK'S WORDS

clear
close
drawer
drive
flat
floor
print
snow
star
state
stick
trick
string
spray
spring

MASTERY WORDS

from
glad
small
start
stay
swim

BONUS WORDS

blast
flash
frame
planet
scratch
space
split
spread

Assignment Guide

This guide shows how you teach a typical spelling unit in either a five-day or a three-day sequence, while providing for individual differences. **Boldface type** indicates essential classwork. Steps shown in light type may be done in class or assigned as homework.

Five Days	○ = average spellers ★ = better spellers ✓ = slower spellers	Three Days
Day **1**	**a** ● ★ **Take This Week's Words Trial Test and correct** ● ✓ **Take Mastery word Trial Test and correct** ● ★ **Read This Week's Words and discuss generalization on page 16**	Day **1**
Day **2**	● Complete Spelling Practice page 17 ● ✓ Complete Extra Practice Master 4: This Week's Words (optional) ✓ Complete Spelling on Your Own: Mastery Words page 19 ★ **Take Bonus word Trial Test and correct**	**b**
Day **3**	**c** ● ★ ✓ **Complete Spelling and Language page 18** ● ★ ✓ Complete Writing on Your Own page 18 ● ★ ✓ **Complete Using the Dictionary to Spell and Write page 18** ● ✓ Take Midweek Test (optional) ★ Complete Spelling on Your Own: Bonus words page 19 ● ✓ Complete Spelling and Language Master 4 (optional)	Day **2**
Day **4**	● Complete Spelling on Your Own: This Week's Words page 19 ✓ Complete Extra Practice Master 4: Mastery Words (optional) ★ Complete Extra Practice Master 4: Bonus Words (optional)	**d**
Day **5**	**e** ● Take Unit Test on This Week's Words ● Complete Reteaching Follow-up Masters 4A and 4B (optional) ● ✓ **Take Unit Test on Mastery words** ★ **Take Unit Test on Bonus words**	Day **3**

Enrichment Activities for the **classroom** and for the **home** included at the end of this unit may be assigned selectively on any day of the week.

INTRODUCING THE UNIT

Establish Readiness for Learning

Tell the children that this week they will study words with the initial consonant clusters *cl, dr, fl, pr, tr, str,* and *spr.* Explain that they will apply what they have learned to This Week's Words and will use those words to write a mystery story.

Assess Children's Spelling Ability

Administer the Trial Test before the children study This Week's Words. Use the test sentences provided. Say each word and use it in a sentence. Then repeat the word. Have the children write the words on a separate sheet of paper or in their spelling notebooks. Test sentences are also provided for Mastery and Bonus words.

Have the children check their own work by listening to you read the spelling of the words or by referring to This Week's Words in the left column of the **Pupil Book.** For each misspelled word, have the children follow the **Study Steps to Learn a Word** on page 1 in the **Pupil Book** or use the copying master to study and write the words. Children should record the number correct on their **Progress Report.**

Trial Test Sentences

This Week's Words
1. *clear* You can see stars on a *clear* night. **clear**
2. *close* Fern lives *close* to Sylvia. **close**
3. *drawer* Betsy's sweater is in the *drawer.* **drawer**
4. *drive* It is a long *drive* to Dallas. **drive**
5. *flat* The car had a *flat* tire. **flat**
6. *floor* Raymond spilled water on the *floor.* **floor**

FOCUS
- Establishes objectives
- Relates to prior learning
- Sets purpose of instruction

7. *print* Please *print* your name neatly.
print

8. *snow* Manuelo has never seen *snow*.
snow

9. *star* Rhoda watched a shooting *star*.
star

10. *state* Rhode Island is the smallest *state*.
state

11. *stick* The dog carried the *stick* in its mouth. **stick**

12. *trick* The zookeeper taught the dolphin a *trick*. **trick**

13. *string* We can tie up the box with this *string*. **string**

14. *spray* We should *spray* some water on the plants. **spray**

15. *spring* Flowers bloom in the *spring*.
spring

Mastery Words

1. *from* Martina comes *from* Peru. **from**

2. *glad* I'm *glad* she lives here now.
glad

3. *small* We need a *small* paper bag.
small

4. *start* Issac will *start* the game. **start**

5. *stay* Jessica will *stay* at Sally's house.
stay

6. *swim* Paul likes to *swim* in the ocean.
swim

Bonus Words

1. *blast* The rocket will *blast* off tomorrow. **blast**

2. *flash* A *flash* of lightning came before the thunder. **flash**

3. *frame* Let's buy this picture *frame*.
frame

4. *planet* Mars is called the red *planet*.
planet

5. *scratch* I'm afraid the cat will *scratch* you. **scratch**

6. *space* Leave some *space* between the chairs. **space**

7. *split* Dad *split* the log with an ax. **split**

8. *spread* Marcia *spread* peanut butter on her toast. **spread**

Apply Prior Learning

Have the children name some words that contain initial consonant clusters with which they are familiar. List these words on the chalkboard. Encourage children to name some words that contain clusters with two consonants and clusters with three consonants. If the children need help with this activity, use these words: *clean, drip, flower, pretty, trip, strap,* and *spread*. Write these words on the chalkboard and have volunteers underline the letters that stand for the initial consonant clusters. Have the children add other words to the list, using these or other initial consonant clusters. Have the children note which words have clusters with two consonants and which have clusters with three consonants.

FOCUS

- Relates to prior learning
- Draws relationships
- Applies spelling generalizations to new contexts

FOR CHILDREN WITH SPECIAL NEEDS

Learning Difficulties

Children with language disorders have persistent deficits in analyzing the component sounds of words and in blending the sounds within a word. Practice in segmenting and blending words is recommended to help them with these skills. Motivate the children by involving them in making and working with manipulative materials.

Have the children write each of the consonant clusters *cl, dr, fl, pr, tr, sn, st, str,* and *spr* on a separate card. Then have them write each of the word endings *ear, ose, awer, ive, at, oor, int, ow, ar, ate, ick, ing,* and *ay* on a separate card. Have the children work together to match the consonant clusters with the word endings to form words. Remind the children that some combinations will not form real words. When the children have completed this activity, have them name all the real words

that they have formed as you list their responses on the chalkboard. Have the children compare the list on the chalkboard to This Week's Words. Have them note that they were able to create more words than there are in This Week's Words by combining each of the consonant clusters with each of the different word endings.

Limited English Proficiency

To help limited English proficient children work with the spelling generalizations for Unit 4, you may wish to refer to the booklet "Suggestions and Activities for Limited English Proficient Students."

TEACHING PLAN

Objective To spell words with initial consonant clusters.

1. Write *rip* on the chalkboard. Have the children say the word and tell you how many consonant sounds they hear at the beginning of the word. Then add a *t* to the beginning of the word. Ask the children to say the new word and indicate the number of sounds heard at the beginning of *trip*. Then add an *s* to the beginning of the word and have the children say the new word. Help them to recognize that the three sounds /s/, /t/, and /r/ are all heard together at the beginning of *strip*.
2. Read the generalization on page 16 aloud.

You may wish to introduce the lesson by using **Spelling Generalizations Transparency 4.**

3. Have volunteers read This Week's Words aloud. As each word is read, ask the children to identify the number of consonant sounds heard at the beginning of the word.
4. Direct the children's attention to **Remember This** at the bottom of the page. Ask a child to read the paragraph aloud. Then write these incomplete sentences on the chalkboard:

___ the door.
Put your chair ___ to mine.

Have the children say the missing word in each sentence and spell it orally.

You may wish to assign **LEP Practice Master 4** for reinforcement in writing spelling words.

---

4 Consonant Clusters

THIS WEEK'S WORDS

1. clear
2. close
3. drawer
4. drive
5. flat
6. floor
7. print
8. snow
9. star
10. state
11. stick
12. trick
13. string
14. spray
15. spring

This Week's Words

Say the word <u>clear</u> to yourself. You hear two consonant sounds at the beginning of <u>clear</u>—/k/ and /l/. These sounds are spelled with **c** and **l**.

The letters **cl** in <u>clear</u> are called a **consonant cluster.** The letters are written together. You hear both consonant sounds.

Sometimes three consonant letters make up a consonant cluster. The letters **spr** in <u>spray</u> are a consonant cluster. You hear all three consonant sounds at the beginning of <u>spray</u>.

REMEMBER THIS

The word <u>close</u> can be said two ways. You say it one way when you say "<u>Close</u> your eyes." You say it another way when you say "Stand <u>close</u> to the table." But either way you say it, it is spelled the same: <u>close</u>.

16

Extra Practice: This Week's Words

Name
Extra Practice   This Week's Words   UNIT **4**

Help Princess find her way to the stick. Draw a line to connect the words that begin with consonant clusters.

Now write all the words you found that begin with consonant clusters.

1. drive
2. trick
3. star
4. clear
5. drawer
6. state
7. spray
8. flat
9. string
10. close
11. snow
12. floor
13. spring
14. print
15. stick

clear	close	drawer	drive	flat
floor	print	snow	star	state
stick	trick	spray	spring	string

Extra Practice • 13

Extra Practice: Mastery Words

Name
Extra Practice   Mastery Words   UNIT **4**

Finish the puzzle with Mastery words. First write the word that fits each sentence. The consonant cluster that begins the word is given to help you. Then write the word in the right place in the puzzle.

ACROSS

2. When does the race
   (st) **start** ?

3. Frank likes to
   (sw) **swim**
   in the ocean.

4. Will you go or will you
   (st) **stay** ?

5. Luis was (gl) **glad**
   when he won the race.

DOWN

1. I threw the ball
   (fr) **from**
   here to there.

3. If a thing is not very big,
   it is (sm) **small**

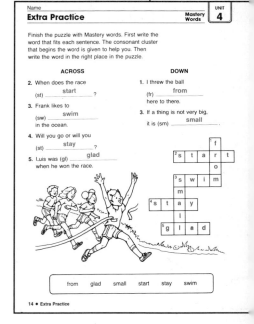

| from | glad | small | start | stay | swim |

14 • Extra Practice

Spelling Practice

A. Follow the directions. Use This Week's Words.

1. Write the four words that have **l** in the consonant cluster.

clear   close

flat   floor

2. Write the seven words that have **r** in the consonant cluster.

drawer   drive   print

trick   spray   string

spring

3. Write the three words that begin with the same cluster as <u>stop</u>.

star   state   stick

4. Write the three words that have a three-letter cluster.

spray   string   spring

5. Write the word that ends with <u>er</u>.   drawer

B. Finish the story with This Week's Words. The consonant clusters in ( ) will help you.

Jake was cold. He got up to (cl) **6** the window. The (fl) **7** felt icy under his feet. He looked out. There was fresh (sn) **8** on the ground. The sky was (cl) **9** . He saw a falling (st) **10** . It made a (str) **11** of light in the sky.

6. close   **7.** floor   **8.** snow

9. clear   **10.** star   **11.** string

(right margin word list, cursive)
clear
close
drawer
drive
flat
floor
print
snow
star
state
stick
trick
string
spray
spring

17

TEACHING PLAN

Objectives To write words that have *l* or *r* in the initial consonant cluster; to write words given spelling clues; to write words that complete a story.

1. Briefly discuss the directions on page 17. You might prepare the children for completing Exercise **B** by reading the paragraph aloud and having the children supply the missing words. Point out that the beginning cluster in each missing word is given in parentheses.
2. Have the children complete the page independently. Remind them to use legible handwriting. You may wish to demonstrate the correct form of the letters *l* and *r* and have the children practice writing the letters. For **Handwriting Models,** refer the children to page 258 in the **Pupil Book.**
3. To correct the children's work, have volunteers write their answers on the chalkboard. Let the children check their own work.

For reinforcement in writing spelling words, you may wish to assign *Extra Practice Master 4: This Week's Words.*

⭐ *of special interest*

The letter *s* is followed by several different consonants in initial consonant clusters. Other consonants, however, are followed only by a liquid (*l* or *r*) or a glide (*w* in *dwell*).

	b	bl, br
sc	**c**	cl, cr
	d	dr, dw
	f	fl, fr
	g	gl, gr
sk	**k**	
sl	**l**	
sm	**m**	
sn	**n**	
sp	**p**	pl, pr
sq	**q**	
st	**t**	tr, tw
sw	**w**	

Summarize Learning

Have the children summarize what they have learned on pages 16 and 17. *Ask:*

- What have you learned about initial consonant clusters in this lesson? (Consonant clusters can contain two or three consonants; each consonant sound in a cluster can be heard.)
- What are examples of words that have consonant clusters? (clear, print, string; accept other examples)

TEACHING PLAN

SPELLING AND LANGUAGE

Objective To write words in sentence context and recognize which are verbs and nouns.

1. To introduce this activity, write these sentences on the chalkboard:

   Joan will <u>star</u> in the show.
   Joan is a <u>star</u>.

   Ask volunteers to read the sentences aloud. Point out that in the first sentence, *star* is a verb. It tells what Joan will do. In the second sentence, *star* is a noun. It tells what Joan is.
2. Read the introductory paragraph on page 18 aloud.
3. Have the children complete the activity independently.
4. To correct the children's work, ask volunteers to read their completed sentences aloud. Let the children check their own work.

For extended practice in writing words in sentence context, you may wish to assign *Spelling and Language Master 4.*

WRITING ON YOUR OWN

Objectives To write a mystery story using spelling words; to proofread for spelling.

1. Review the directions with the children.
2. As a **prewriting** activity, make a chart on the chalkboard using the headings *Who, What, When, Where,* and *Why.* Have the children suggest entries for each heading and list their responses. Then have them **compose** their mystery stories. When they are ready to **revise,** remind them to check spelling. For additional help, you may wish to refer them to the **Revising Checklist** on page 247 of the **Writer's Guide.** To **publish** the children's work, have volunteers read their stories to the class.

18 UNIT 4 *Consonant Clusters*

USING THE DICTIONARY

Objective To recognize entry words; to locate given entry words in the **Spelling Dictionary.**

1. Read the introductory paragraph on page 18 aloud. Have the children identify the three entry words—*busy, butter,* and *butterfly*—in the dictionary sample. Ask volunteers to read the meanings for each entry word.
2. Have the children complete the exercise independently.

THIS WEEK'S WORDS
clear
close
drawer
drive
flat
floor
print
snow
star
state
stick
trick
string
spray
spring

Spelling and Language • Nouns and Verbs

A **noun** names a person, a place, or a thing. A **verb** shows action or being. Finish each pair of sentences with one of This Week's Words. The word will be a verb in the first sentence and a noun in the second sentence.

1. Tomorrow we will _____ **drive** _____ to the mountains.
2. It is a beautiful _____ **drive** _____ in the fall.
3. Let's _____ **trick** _____ Mimi into thinking we're not going.
4. Mimi will laugh about our _____ **trick** _____.

Writing on Your Own

Write a mystery story for your teacher. Tell about two people who are cleaning a house. Suddenly they find a note. Tell what the note says and what the two people do. Use some of This Week's Words.

Using the Dictionary to Spell and Write

On a dictionary page, an **entry word** is a word in dark print that is followed by its meaning. Entry words appear in alphabetical order. This helps you find a word quickly to check its spelling or meaning.

> **bus·y** /biz'ē/ *adj.* **1** Doing things: I'm *busy* making lunch. **2** Full of things to do: I had a *busy* day.
> **but·ter** /but'ər/ *n.* A yellow spread made from cream, used on bread. —*v.* To spread butter on.
> **but·ter·fly** /but'ər·flī'/ *n., pl.* **butterflies** An insect with four brightly colored wings.

Look up each word below in the **Spelling Dictionary.** Then write the entry word that follows it.

1. start _____ **state** _____
2. princess _____ **print** _____
3. draw _____ **drawer** _____
4. spread _____ **spring** _____

SPELLING DICTIONARY Remember to use your **Spelling Dictionary** when you write.

18

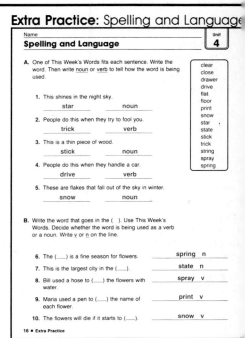

Extra Practice: Spelling and Language

Name
Spelling and Language Unit 4

A. One of This Week's Words fits each sentence. Write the word. Then write <u>noun</u> or <u>verb</u> to tell how the word is being used.

clear
close
drawer
drive
flat
floor
print
snow
star
state
stick
trick
string
spray
spring

1. This shines in the night sky.
   star — noun
2. People do this when they try to fool you.
   trick — verb
3. This is a thin piece of wood.
   stick — noun
4. People do this when they handle a car.
   drive — verb
5. These are flakes that fall out of the sky in winter.
   snow — noun

B. Write the word that goes in the ( ). Use This Week's Words. Decide whether the word is being used as a verb or a noun. Write *v* or *n* on the line.

6. The (___) is a fine season for flowers. spring n
7. This is the largest city in the (___). state n
8. Bill used a hose to (___) the flowers with water. spray v
9. Maria used a pen to (___) the name of each flower. print v
10. The flowers will die if it starts to (___). snow v

16 • Extra Practice

Spelling on Your Own

THIS WEEK'S WORDS

```
I S T A T E S
O T V E M U N
K A F R U E O
D R A W E R W
```

Use all of This Week's Words to make a word search puzzle. You can write the words across or down. Fill in the empty spaces with other letters. Let someone else solve the puzzle.

MASTERY WORDS

Write the Mastery word that begins with the same two letters as each word.

1. smile	small	**2.** free	from
3. sweet	swim	**4.** glass	glad

from
glad
small
start
stay
swim

Write Mastery words that mean the opposite.

5. stop	start	**6.** go	stay
7. large	small	**8.** sad	glad

Put the words in order to make two sentences.

9. from   beginning.   Start   the

Start from the beginning.

10. stay   some   Let's   and   swim   more.

Let's stay and swim some more.

BONUS WORDS

1. Combine the beginning consonant clusters at the left with the word endings at the right. Spell as many words as you can.

spr	scr	sp	pl
fr	bl	fl	spl

ead	atch	ace	ame
ast		ash	it

blast
flash
frame
planet
scratch
space
split
spread

2. Write the Bonus word you could not make in **1.**
3. Write sentences about outer space with Bonus words.   **See answers below.**

19

Spelling on Your Own Answers

BONUS WORDS

1. *Bonus words*   *Others*

spread	spit
scratch	*plead
space	place
frame	blame
blast	flame
flash	flit
split	splash

*Point out that the vowel sound in *plead* /plēd/ is different from the vowel sound in *spread* /spred/.

NOTE: **The words listed under *Others* are possible answers. Children should not be expected to list them all.**

2. planet
3. Children will write as directed. Be sure to check spelling.

Summarize Learning

Have the children summarize what they have learned in this unit. *Ask:*

- What have you learned about nouns and verbs? (Some words can be used both as nouns and as verbs.) Give examples. (drive, trick; accept other examples)
- What did you learn about dictionary entry words? (They are the words in dark print; the entry word is followed by its meaning; they are listed in alphabetical order.)
- What spelling generalizations have you learned? How did you use these generalizations?

Spelling on Your Own UNIT 4d

TEACHING PLAN

Objective To apply the unit spelling generalization to spell This Week's Words, Mastery words, and Bonus words independently.

THIS WEEK'S WORDS

1. Read the directions on page 19 aloud. Explain that this puzzle contains words written across or down the page with extra letters in the empty spaces to "hide" the words.
2. Have the children make up their puzzles independently on graph paper.
3. Let the children exchange their work with classmates and solve one another's puzzles.

MASTERY WORDS

1. Review the unit generalization on page 16.
2. Read the Mastery words aloud. Have the children identify each consonant cluster.
3. Read the directions on page 19 aloud and review the concept of opposites. Then have the children put the words in **9** and **10** in sentence order and read the sentences aloud.
4. Have the children complete the activities independently.

BONUS WORDS

1. Review the unit generalization on page 16.
2. Ask a volunteer to read the Bonus words aloud.
3. Have the children complete the exercises independently.

For reinforcement in writing spelling words, you may wish to assign **Extra Practice Master 4: Mastery Words** or **Bonus Words.**

CLOSING THE UNIT

Apply New Learning

Tell the children that if they misspell words with consonant clusters in their writing, they should use one or more of the following strategies:

- think of a known word that is related in meaning and spelling.
- write the word using different spellings and compare it with the spelling they picture in their minds.
- pronounce the word very carefully to see that the correct letter or letters have been used to spell the sounds in the word.

Transfer New Learning

Tell the children that when they encounter new words in their personal reading and in other content areas, they should learn the meaning of those words and then apply the generalizations they have studied to the spelling of those words. Tell the children that once the words are familiar in both meaning and spelling, they should use the new words in their writing.

ENRICHMENT ACTIVITIES

Classroom activities and *home activities* may be assigned to children of all ability levels. The activities provide opportunities for children to use their spelling words in new contexts.

For the Classroom

To individualize classroom activities, you may have the children use the word list they are studying in this unit.

- *Basic:* Use **Mastery** words to complete the activity.
- *Average:* Use **This Week's Words** to complete the activity.
- *Challenging:* Use **Bonus** words to complete the activity.

1. **Language Arts/Writing Words with Initial Consonant Clusters** Have the children write each of the different initial consonant clusters from their spelling words. (*cl, dr, fl, pr, tr, str, spr*) Then ask them to write new words that begin with each initial cluster. Tell the children to check the dictionary to make sure that their new words have been spelled correctly. Then have the children list the initial consonant clusters in a column on the left and the word endings in mixed-up order on the right. Have them include endings of some of the spelling words. The children should exchange papers and combine word parts from both columns to form words.

   ■ COOPERATIVE LEARNING: Have each group create a matching exercise using initial consonant clusters and word endings. Each group should work together to review

the spelling list for initial consonant clusters. Group members should divide the clusters among themselves. Then each child should write at least three new words beginning with his or her initial consonant clusters. Have group members check each other's words to be sure they are real words. Together, the group members should create a matching exercise. Tell the group to choose a recorder to list the clusters on the left and word endings from each child's list on the right. Endings from some spelling words should be included. When the children have finished, have the groups exchange and complete the exercises.

2. **Language Arts/Writing Coded Messages** Have each group make up a secret code. To make a code, the children should replace letters of the alphabet with other symbols that stand for those letters. Children may use such symbols as other letters, numerals in sequence, shapes, or pictures. For example: If *6 = f, 12 = l, 1 = a, and 20 = t,* then *6–12–1–20 = flat.* The children should write messages in their code containing as many spelling words as possible. After the children have written their coded messages, have them send their messages to friends for deciphering.

   ■ COOPERATIVE LEARNING: Have each group make up a code, replacing the alphabet with other letters, numerals, or any other symbols they want to use. Then have each child write a message to someone in the group using the code. The children should use as many spelling words as possible in their messages. Have group members decode each other's messages. Each group can give one of their messages to the class to decode.

3. **Language Arts/Writing a Friendly Letter** As a *prewriting* activity, have the children turn to page 251 in the **Writer's Guide** to read about friendly letters. Remind them that a friendly letter has five parts: *heading, greeting, body, closing,* and *signature.* Suggest that they write about some interesting things that they have done recently. Tell them to look over all three spelling lists in search of topics to develop in the body of the letter. Have them write down a few key words from the lists and focus on one or two topics to write about. After each child has selected topics, have him or her jot down a few notes about how to develop each one. Finally, have the child decide to which friend the letter will be written. When the child has finished the *prewriting* activities, tell him or her to use the notes to *compose* the letter. Remind the child to use as many spelling words as possible in the letter. Then have the child *revise* the letter, making sure it has the correct parts. Remind the child to refer to the **Revising Checklist** on page 247 and to proofread for spelling, capitalization, and punctuation errors. *Publish* the children's work by having them fold their letters and drop them into a class "mailbox" for other children to read.

   ■ COOPERATIVE LEARNING: Have each group collaborate to write a friendly letter. As a *prewriting* activity, first direc the group's attention to page 251 of the **Writer's Guide** to read about friendly letters. Have each group member review the three spelling lists for interesting topics, write down some key words, and jot down ideas for developing some of the topics. Tell group members to share ideas and select one or two to include in the body of the letter. When the children are ready to **compose** the letter, tell them to choose one child to begin the letter orally by naming its recipient. Other children should each contribute one or more sentences until the letter is fully developed through the closing. Tell the children to use as many spelling words as possible. One child should record the letter as others **revise** it, checking to see if the letter has all five parts, and if spelling, capitalization, and punctuation are correct. Remind the children to refer to the **Revising Checklist** on page 247 for help. Ask one child to rewrite the letter and have all the children sign it. Each group can **publish** its letter by exchanging with other groups. One child in each group should read another group's letter aloud. Letters can also be displayed for the class to read.

For the Home

Children may complete these activities independently or with the assistance of a relative or friend in the home.

1. Language Arts/Writing **Word Comparisons** Have the children make up word comparisons using some of their spelling words. A word comparison is a definition that compares one word with another word. For example: *A stick is like a board, but smaller and thinner. Both are made out of wood. Both come from trees.* Have the children proofread their word comparisons for spelling, capitalization, and punctuation.

2. Language Arts/Writing **Alliterative Sentences** Have the children write four sentences using their spelling words. They should identify the initial consonant cluster in the spelling word, and then write a sentence using as many other words beginning with the same initial cluster as they can. For example: *Don't drop the dripping dress into the drawer.* Have the children check their sentences for spelling errors.

3. Health/Writing **Safety Rules for Car Passengers** Tell the children to make a list of safety rules for automobile passengers, using as many of their spelling words as possible. Suggest that they visualize themselves riding in a car and try to think of ways they can make the trip safer. For example: *Don't stick things out the window.* The children may ask a friend or relative to add to the automobile safety rules.

4. Fine Arts/Writing **Sentence Captions** Tell the children to use some of the spelling words to think of ideas for artwork. Have the children create the artwork and then write sentences describing their work. One example would be: *Cotton could be glued down to make snow.* The children should check the spelling, capitalization, and punctuation of their sentences.

EVALUATING SPELLING ABILITY

Unit Test

This Week's Words

1. *clear*   The water in the pool is very *clear*.   clear
2. *close*   Susan will *close* the door.   close
3. *drawer*   Put the spoons in the *drawer*.   drawer
4. *drive*   Let's *drive* to the park.   drive
5. *flat*   Lie *flat* on your back.   flat
6. *floor*   The living room *floor* has a carpet on it.   floor
7. *print*   There is a paw *print* in the mud.   print
8. *snow*   Larry helped shovel *snow*.   snow
9. *star*   Brenda will *star* in the school play.   star
10. *state*   My room is in a sorry *state*.   state
11. *stick*   This stamp won't *stick* on the letter.   stick
12. *trick*   Rubin played a *trick* on his brother.   trick
13. *string*   Marjorie likes to *string* beads.   string
14. *spray*   We used bug *spray* to stop the ants.   spray
15. *spring*   This water came from a *spring*.   spring

Mastery Words

1. *from*   Jack rode his bike home *from* school.   from
2. *glad*   He was *glad* it was not raining.   glad
3. *small*   Mr. Peabody has a *small* car.   small
4. *start*   Yesterday the car would not *start*.   start
5. *stay*   Please *stay* here until I get back.   stay
6. *swim*   We can *swim* at the city pool.   swim

Bonus Words

1. *blast*   There was a *blast* of cold air when Tricia opened the door.   blast
2. *flash*   Those signs *flash* on and off.   flash
3. *frame*   We need a *frame* for this picture.   frame
4. *planet*   The spaceship will travel to another *planet*. planet
5. *scratch*   Josh had a *scratch* on his hand.   scratch
6. *space*   We could not find a parking *space*.   space
7. *split*   Dan and Cindy *split* a box of raisins.   split
8. *spread*   We *spread* newspapers on the floor before we painted.   spread

Dictation Sentences

This Week's Words

1. I use a *stick* and a *string* for my *trick*.
2. Fold your shirts *flat* so the *drawer* will *close*.
3. He found a *clear* paw *print* in the *snow*.
4. Rachel was the *star* of the play about her *state*.
5. Dad will *drive* us to the *spring* to get water.
6. We put bug *spray* on the *floor* to keep the bugs away.

Mastery Words

1. We will *start from* my house and race to the *small* pond.
2. I am *glad* you can *stay* and *swim*.

Bonus Words

1. With a *blast* and a *flash* we left the *planet* and went out into *space*.
2. The cat made a long *scratch* on the door *frame*.
3. We *split* up the bird seed and *spread* it out for the birds to eat.

RETEACHING STRATEGIES FOR SPELLING

Children who have made errors on the Unit Test may require reteaching. Use the following **Reteaching Strategies** and **Follow-up Masters 4A** and **4B** for additional instruction and practice of This Week's Words. (You may wish to assign **LEP Reteaching Follow-up Master 4** for reteaching of spelling words.)

A. Discovering Spelling Ideas

1. Say the following words as you write them on the chalkboard.

     class   dress   stick   stripe

2. Ask the children to identify the consonant sounds at the beginning of each word. (/k/ and /l/; /d/ and /r/; /s/ and /t/; /s/, /t/, and /r/)
3. Ask the children to identify the letters for these sounds and how they are written. (cl, dr, st, str; the letters are written together at the beginning of each word)
4. Ask the children what they have learned about these groups of letters that are called consonant clusters. (Consonant clusters are groups of two or three letters that are written together. Each consonant sound is heard. They all appear at the beginning of these words.)

B. Word Shapes

1. Explain to the children that each word has a shape and that remembering the shape of a word can help them to spell the word correctly.
2. On the chalkboard, write the words *clap* and *stray*. Have the children identify "short," "tall," and "tail" letters.
3. Draw the configuration of each word on the chalkboard, and ask the children which word fits in each shape.

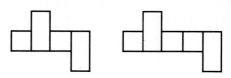

Use **Reteaching Follow-up Master 4A** to reinforce spelling generalizations taught in Unit 4.

Use **Reteaching Follow-up Master 4B** to reinforce spellings of This Week's Words for Unit 4.

Name

Reteaching Follow-up A

Discovering Spelling Ideas

UNIT 4

THIS WEEK'S WORDS

clear	drive	flat	print	stick
drawer	spray	spring	close	floor
snow	state	trick	string	star

1. Study This Week's Words. Say each word to yourself.

2. Write the words that begin with these sounds.

/k/ + /l/	/f/ + /l/	/s/ + /p/ + /r/
(cl)ear	(fl)oor	(spr)ing
(cl)ose	(fl)at	(spr)ay

/s/ + /t/	/d/ + /r/	/t/ + /r/
(st)ate	(dr)awer	(tr)ick
(st)ick	(dr)ive	
(st)ar		

/s/ + /n/	/p/ + /r/	/s/ + /t/ + /r/
(sn)ow	(pr)int	(str)ing

3. Circle the letters in your answers that spell those sounds.

4. What is it called when you hear two or three consonant sounds together?

   a consonant cluster

5. What have you learned about consonant clusters?

   A consonant cluster occurs when two or three consonant

   letters are written together and you hear each consonant

   sound. It can appear at the beginning of a word.

Reteaching • 7

Name

Reteaching Follow-up B

Word Shapes

UNIT 4

THIS WEEK'S WORDS

clear	drive	flat	print	stick
drawer	spray	spring	close	floor
snow	state	trick	string	star

Write each of This Week's Words in its correct shape. The first one has been done for you.   Children may interchange answers that fit the same configuration.

1. s t a t e   2. p r i n t

3. d r i v e   4. s p r a y

5. s n o w   6. s t a r

7. s t r i n g   8. f l a t

9. c l o s e   10. f l o o r

11. t r i c k   12. s t i c k

13. s p r i n g   14. d r a w e r

15. c l e a r

8 • Reteaching

19C   UNIT 4 *Consonant Clusters*

More Consonant Clusters

Unit Materials

Instruction and Practice

Pupil Book	pages 20–23
Teacher's Edition	
Teaching Plans	pages 20–23
Enrichment Activities	
For the Classroom	pages 23A–23B
For the Home	page 23B
Reteaching Strategies	page 23C

Testing

Teacher's Edition	
Trial Test	pages 19E–19F
Unit Test	page 23B
Dictation Test	page 23B

Additional Resources

PRACTICE AND REINFORCEMENT
Extra Practice Master 5: This Week's Words
Extra Practice Master 5: Mastery Words
Extra Practice Master 5: Bonus Words
LEP Practice Master 5
Spelling and Language Master 5
Study Steps to Learn a Word Master

RETEACHING FOLLOW-UP
Reteaching Follow-up Master 5A:
  Discovering Spelling Ideas
Reteaching Follow-up Master 5B: Word
  Shapes
LEP Reteaching Follow-up Master 5

TEACHING AIDS
Spelling Generalizations Transparency 5

Visit our Web site
http://www.hbschool.com

Click on the SPELLING banner to find activities for this unit.

Learner Objectives

Spelling

- To spell words that demonstrate these sound-letter relationships: /kt/ct; /nd/nd; /lk/lk; /ft/ft; /ld/ld; /mp/mp.
- To spell words by adding initial consonants and consonant clusters.
- To add *ed* to verbs to tell what already happened.
- To spell new words by changing one letter in a given word.

Reading

- To follow written directions.
- To develop facility in oral reading for an audience.
- To use context clues to complete sentences given spelling words.

Writing

- To write a paragraph.
- To use the writing process.
- To proofread for spelling, capitalization, and punctuation.
- To write legible manuscript and cursive letters.

Listening

- To listen to words for consonant sounds.
- To listen to identify rhyming words.
- To follow oral directions.

Speaking

- To speak clearly to a group.
- To contribute ideas and information in group discussions.
- To express feelings and ideas about a piece of writing.
- To present a paragraph to the group.

THIS WEEK'S WORDS

act
dust
east
test
west
lift
bend
grand
ground
wind
build
child
wild
milk
bump

MASTERY WORDS

felt
hand
help
hold
left
want

BONUS WORDS

adult
blend
burst
insect
prompt
pumpkin
stamp
tramp

Assignment Guide

This guide shows how you teach a typical spelling unit in either a five-day or a three-day sequence, while providing for individual differences. **Boldface type** indicates essential classwork. Steps shown in light type may be done in class or assigned as homework.

Five Days	• = average spellers ★ = better spellers ✓ = slower spellers	Three Days
Day **1** a	• ★ **Take This Week's Words Trial Test and correct** • ✓ **Take Mastery word Trial Test and correct** • ★ **Read This Week's Words and discuss generalization on page 20**	Day **1**
Day **2**	• Complete Spelling Practice page 21 • ✓ Complete Extra Practice Master 5: This Week's Words (optional) ✓ Complete Spelling on Your Own: Mastery Words page 23 ★ **Take Bonus word Trial Test and correct**	b
Day **3** c	• ★ ✓ **Complete Spelling and Language page 22** • ★ ✓ Complete Writing on Your Own page 22 • ✓ Take Midweek Test (optional) ★ Complete Spelling on Your Own: Bonus words page 23 • ✓ Complete Spelling and Language Master 5 (optional)	Day **2**
Day **4**	• Complete Spelling on Your Own: This Week's Words page 23 ✓ Complete Extra Practice Master 5: Mastery words (optional) ★ Complete Extra Practice Master 5: Bonus words (optional)	d
Day **5** e	• Take Unit Test on This Week's Words • Complete Reteaching Follow-up Masters 5A and 5B (optional) • ✓ **Take Unit Test on Mastery Words** ★ **Take Unit Test on Bonus Words**	Day **3**

Enrichment Activities for the **classroom** and for the **home** included at the end of this unit may be assigned selectively on any day of the week.

INTRODUCING THE UNIT

Establish Readiness for Learning

Tell the children that this week they will continue to study words with consonant clusters, but that in this lesson the clusters are at the end of the word. Tell the children that they will apply what they learn to This Week's Words and use those words to write a paragraph.

Assess Children's Spelling Ability

Administer the Trial Test before the children study This Week's Words. Use the test sentences provided. Say each word and use it in a sentence. Then repeat the word. Have the children write the words on a separate sheet of paper or in their spelling notebooks. Test sentences are also provided for Mastery and Bonus words.

Have the children check their own work by listening to you read the spelling of the words

or by referring to This Week's Words in the left column of the **Pupil Book.** For each misspelled word, have the children follow the **Study Steps to Learn a Word** on page 1 in the **Pupil Book** or use the copying master to study and write the words. Children should record the number correct on their **Progress Report.**

Trial Test Sentences

This Week's Words
1. *act* Please don't *act* silly. *act*
2. *dust* Help me *dust* the living room. *dust*
3. *east* North Carolina is *east* of Tennessee. *east*
4. *test* The math *test* was not hard. *test*
5. *west* The pioneers traveled *west* in covered wagons. *west*
6. *lift* Kent could not *lift* the heavy box. *lift*
7. *bend* A twig breaks when you *bend* it. *bend*

FOCUS
- Establishes objectives
- Relates to prior learning
- Sets purpose of instruction

8. *grand*   We had a *grand* time at the zoo.   **grand**

9. *ground*   Bob dug a hole in the *ground*.   **ground**

10. *wind*   The *wind* is blowing very hard.   **wind**

11. *build*   Let's *build* a snowman.   **build**

12. *child*   Every *child* got a prize.   **child**

13. *wild*   There are *wild* animals in the woods.   **wild**

14. *milk*   Fred drank two glasses of *milk*.   **milk**

15. *bump*   Do not *bump* your head.   **bump**

Mastery Words

1. *felt*   I *felt* cold.   **felt**

2. *hand*   Meg held the baby chick in her *hand*.   **hand**

3. *help*   Vera will *help* us clean up.   **help**

4. *hold*   Please *hold* my jacket.   **hold**

5. *left*   Sarah *left* her mittens on the bus.   **left**

6. *want*   Hank and Mary *want* hamburgers.   **want**

Bonus Words

1. *adult*   A grown-up person is an *adult*.   **adult**

2. *blend*   The recipe says to *blend* the butter and the honey.   **blend**

3. *burst*   Arnie *burst* the soap bubble with his finger.   **burst**

4. *insect*   A spider is an *insect*.   **insect**

5. *prompt*   People who are *prompt* are never late.   **prompt**

6. *pumpkin*   Let's make a *pumpkin* pie.   **pumpkin**

7. *stamp*   Jacob put a *stamp* on the letter.   **stamp**

8. *tramp*   The scouts will *tramp* through the woods.   **tramp**

Apply Prior Learning

Tell the children that they can learn about final consonant clusters by using what they already know about initial consonant clusters. Have children generate words with initial and final consonant clusters by using the following activity.

Write the following on the chalkboard:

1. spoke	2. hand
sport	kind
spill	bend

Read the words in each list with the children. Have the children decide on a common element for each word list (initial consonant clusters *sp*; final consonant clusters *nd*.)

Now write the following chart on the chalkboard. Ask the children to supply words to complete the chart, and write correct responses on the chalkboard.

Initial	Final	Initial and Final
sp____	____ft	____st
dr____	____nd	st____
fl____	____ld	

Lead the children to the generalization that consonant clusters may appear either at the beginning or end of a word. Explain to the children that in this unit, they will study words that have these consonant clusters at the end of words.

FOCUS

- Relates to prior learning
- Draws relationships
- Applies spelling generalizations to new contexts

FOR CHILDREN WITH SPECIAL NEEDS

Learning Difficulties

Children with auditory processing disorders have difficulty segmenting and blending the component sounds of words. This activity provides practice in attention to detail and fine motor coordination.

Using tachistoscopes will help children blend letters with final consonant clusters to make words. For this activity, make eight tachistoscopes. Cut a 1 × 2 inch window in a piece of heavy paper. On the right side of the window, write one of the seven consonant clusters: *ct, st, ft, nd, lk, ld, mp*. Staple the window paper on top of another paper of the same size. Then cut a 14 × 2 inch strip of paper. On that paper at 2-inch intervals, have the children write the beginning letters of the words that can be combined with the ending cluster to form a word. For example, the children could write the letters *du, ea, te,* and *we* to go with the final cluster *st*. Place the strip in the ta-

chistoscope and move it until the beginning letters are lined up with the final consonant cluster. Have the children blend the two parts of the work together.

The children may work independently with these materials, making words in the window and then copying them into their spelling notebooks.

Limited English Proficiency

To help limited English proficient children work with the spelling generalizations for Unit 5, you may wish to refer to the booklet "Suggestions and Activities for Limited English Proficient Students."

TEACHING PLAN

Objective To spell words with final consonant clusters.

1. Write these pairs of words on the chalkboard:

bell – belt   fell – felt   win – wind
mill – milk

Ask the children to say the words carefully, and help them to conclude that the first word in each pair ends with one consonant sound and the second word ends with two consonant sounds. Point out that the two consonant sounds are spelled with two consonant letters.

2. Read the generalization on page 20 aloud.

You may wish to introduce the lesson by using **Spelling Generalizations Transparency 5.**

3. Have volunteers read This Week's Words aloud. Encourage them to pronounce the end of each word. As each word is read, ask the children to identify the last letter in the word.

4. Direct the children's attention to **Remember This** at the bottom of the page, and ask a child to read the paragraph aloud. Suggest to the children that they can remember the correct order of *u* and *i* in *build* by recalling that *you* should always come before *I* in the sentence: "*You* and *I* can *build* a model plane."

You may wish to assign **LEP Practice Master 5** for reinforcement in writing spelling words.

UNIT 5   *More Consonant Clusters*

---

5 More Consonant Clusters

THIS WEEK'S WORDS

1. act
2. dust
3. east
4. test
5. west
6. lift
7. bend
8. grand
9. ground
10. wind
11. build
12. child
13. wild
14. milk
15. bump

act   lift
wind build
milk bump

This Week's Words

The letters **cl** in <u>clear</u> are called a consonant cluster. Consonant clusters do not always come at the beginning of words. Often they come at the end of words.

Say the word <u>act</u> to yourself. Listen carefully for the consonant sounds /k/ and /t/ at the end of <u>act</u>. The letters **ct** in <u>act</u> are a consonant cluster.

I spell it with **i.**
You spell it with **u.**

Then **you** and **I** will spell it with **ui**!

REMEMBER THIS

The vowel sound /i/ in <u>build</u> is spelled <u>ui</u>. Here is the reason why. Hundreds of years ago, the word was sometimes spelled with <u>u</u>, <u>buld</u>, and sometimes spelled with <u>i</u>, <u>bild</u>. No one could decide which was right — <u>u</u> or <u>i</u>. So they decided to use them both!

20

Extra Practice: This Week's Words

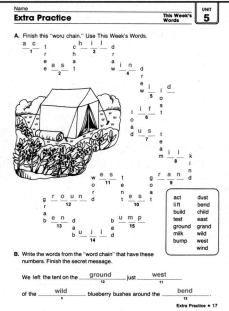

Name
Extra Practice   This Week's Words   UNIT 5

A. Finish this "word chain." Use This Week's Words.

act	dust
lift	bend
build	child
test	east
ground	grand
milk	wild
bump	west
	wind

B. Write the words from the "word chain" that have these numbers. Finish the secret message.

We left the tent on the __ground__ just __west__
                          12   11

of the __wild__ blueberry bushes around the __bend__.
          5   13

Extra Practice • 17

Extra Practice: Mastery Words

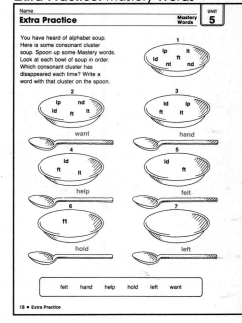

Name
Extra Practice   Mastery Words   UNIT 5

You have heard of alphabet soup. Here is some consonant cluster soup. Spoon up some Mastery words. Look at each bowl of soup in order. Which consonant cluster has disappeared each time? Write a word with that cluster on the spoon.

| felt | hand | help | hold | left | want |

18 • Extra Practice

Spelling Practice

A. Follow the directions. Use This Week's Words.

1. Write the two words that begin with the same consonant cluster and end with the same cluster.

grand   ground

2. Write the three words that end with <u>ld</u>.

build   child   wild

B. Write the word that rhymes with each word.

3. jump   bump   **4.** drift   lift

5. fact   act   **6.** silk   milk

C. Finish the sentences. Use one of This Week's Words.

7. I forgot to (wind) my watch.

8. The wind blew the leaves around.

Circle the word you wrote that rhymes with <u>kind</u>.

D. Write the words that end with the same cluster as each picture word does.

band   **last**

9. bend   **10.** dust

grand   east

ground   test

wind   west

This Week's Words list (handwritten):

act
dust
east
test
west
lift
bend
grand
ground
wind
build
child
wild
milk
bump

Extra Practice: Bonus Words

Summarize Learning

Have the children summarize what they have learned on pages 20 and 21. *Ask:*

- What words in this lesson end with the same consonant clusters? (dust, east, test, west; bend, grand, ground, wind; build, child, wild)
- How do you know which pronunciation of the word *wind* to use? (by the context of the sentence)

TEACHING PLAN

Objectives To write words given spelling clues; to write rhyming words; to recognize the two pronunciations and meanings of *wind*.

1. Briefly discuss the directions on page 21. You might prepare the children for completing Exercise **C** by reading the two sentences and having the children supply the missing words. Point out that both words have the same spelling but they are pronounced differently. Be sure that the children understand that in Exercise **D** they should write words that end with the same consonant cluster as *band* and *last.*

2. Have children complete the page independently. Remind children to use legible handwriting. You may wish to demonstrate the correct form of the letters *lt, nd,* and *lk* and then have the children practice writing the letters. For **Handwriting Models,** refer the children to page 258 in the **Pupil Book.**

3. To correct the children's work, have volunteers write their answers on the chalkboard. Let the children check their own work.

For reinforcement in writing spelling words, you may wish to assign **Extra Practice Master 5: This Week's Words.**

★ of special interest

Final consonant clusters may present some problems for children since the second sound in many final clusters is frequently not pronounced. Spelling This Week's Words correctly may be particularly difficult for children for whom final consonant cluster reduction is a characteristic of their dialect. It is important to help these children *hear* the final sounds and remember the letters that spell these sounds in the words.

TEACHING PLAN

SPELLING AND LANGUAGE

Objective To add *ed* to verbs and rewrite sentences in the past tense.

1. Write these sentences on the board:

   Today I dust the house.
   Yesterday I dusted the house.

   Ask what letters were added to *dust* to make the word tell about something that happened yesterday.
2. Read the directions on page 22 aloud. Tell the children to write only the missing word.
3. Have the children complete the activity independently.
4. Ask volunteers to read the sentences aloud. Let the children check their work.

For extended practice in writing inflected verb forms, you may wish to assign **Spelling and Language Master 5**.

WRITING ON YOUR OWN

Objective To write a paragraph about a book; to proofread for spelling.

1. Review the directions.
2. As a **prewriting** activity have the children write the title of the book they would like to write about. Then have them brainstorm ideas around the title: facts about the story, how they liked the story, whether other children would like the story and why. Then have the children **compose** their paragraphs. They should **revise** their paragraphs by checking for correct spelling. To **publish** the children's work, have them read their paragraphs aloud.

HANDWRITING

Objective To practice writing cursive letter forms: *h H, k K, b B, f F.*

THIS WEEK'S WORDS

act
dust
east
test
west
lift
bend
grand
ground
wind
build
child
wild
milk
bump

Spelling and Language • Adding ed

You just add *ed* to most verbs to tell what already happened. Add *ed* to the words in parentheses ( ). Make the sentences tell about the past.

1. Carlos and Hilda (milk) __**milked**__ cows every day.

2. Then they (lift) __**lifted**__ the pails onto a shelf.

3. They (bump) __**bumped**__ into the cows.

4. Laughing, they (dust) __**dusted**__ themselves off.

Writing on Your Own

Write a paragraph for your classmates about a book you have read. Tell a little about the story. Tell if you think your classmates would like the book. Use some of This Week's Words.

 WRITER'S GUIDE For help editing and proofreading, use the marks on page 248.

HANDWRITING

h H   k K   b B   f F

The lowercase letters **h, k, b,** and **f** all begin with the same undercurve stroke.

1. Practice writing **h H, k K, b B, f F** in cursive.

2. Write this sentence: *Help Beth lift her bike.*

22

1. Read the introductory sentence on page 22 aloud. Have the children examine the model of the beginning stroke.
2. Have the children examine the models for the cursive letters. Help them to note where the letters touch or intersect the lines. Point out that all the letters have tall open loops, and note the difference between lowercase *h* and *k*.
3. Have the children practice the letter forms and write the sentence.
4. Ask the children to compare their letter forms with the models.

Extra Practice: Spelling and Language

Name _____ UNIT **5**
Spelling and Language

Use This Week's Words to finish the story. Add *ed* to each verb.

One morning, long ago, a farmer __1__ her
cows and put the milk in pails. Then she __2__ the
milk. The milk was good, so she __3__ the pails
onto her wagon. Her wagon __4__ along the rocky
road. One bump was so bad that a pail fell out of
the wagon. The pail landed on the __5__. The
farmer got down to get the pail.

All of a sudden, the cold north __6__ started
blowing very hard. It was strong and __7__. The
farmer was cold, but she __8__ very brave. "I am
no longer a __9__," she said. "People in town need
the __10__ that I bring in pails." So she put the pail
back in the wagon and rode into town.

1. __milked__
2. __tested__
3. __lifted__
4. __bumped__
5. __ground__
6. __wind__
7. __wild__
8. __acted__
9. __child__
10. __milk__

dust	east	build	west	lift
bend	grand	act	bump	ground
wind	test	child	wild	milk

20 • Extra Practice

Spelling on Your Own

THIS WEEK'S WORDS

Change the underlined letter in each word. Write one of This Week's Words.

1. b<u>a</u>nd	**2.** buil<u>t</u>	**3.** l<u>i</u>st	**4.** du<u>s</u>k	**5.** a<u>n</u>t
6. te<u>n</u>t	**7.** gran<u>t</u>	**8.** win<u>k</u>	**9.** we<u>n</u>t	**10.** <u>m</u>ild
11. <u>h</u>ump	**12.** <u>a</u>round	**13.** eas<u>y</u>	**14.** mil<u>l</u>

Use the word you haven't written yet in a sentence.

See answers below.

MASTERY WORDS

1. Write the three Mastery words that have **t** in the consonant cluster.

    felt   left   want

2. Write the two words that have **d** in the consonant cluster.

    hand   hold

3. Write the three words that have short **e**.

    felt   help   left

4. Add **ed** to **help**. Use the word in a sentence.

    EXAMPLE: Bruce helped with dinner.

felt
hand
help
hold
left
want

BONUS WORDS

1. Write the four Bonus words that begin and end with consonant clusters.
2. Write the three words that have two vowel sounds.
3. Write the word that rhymes with <u>first</u> and <u>worst</u>.
4. The words <u>stamp</u> and <u>tramp</u> both end with <u>amp</u>. Add different beginning consonants to <u>amp</u>. Spell as many words as you can. Then do the same thing with <u>end</u> in <u>blend</u>.

See answers below.

adult
blend
burst
insect
prompt
pumpkin
stamp
tramp

23

Summarize Learning

Have the children summarize what they have learned in this unit. *Ask:*

- What have you learned about consonant clusters? (They can come at the beginning or the end of words.)
- What are examples of words that have consonant clusters at the beginning and end? (grind, chalk; accept other examples)

Spelling on Your Own — UNIT 5d

TEACHING PLAN

Objective To apply the unit spelling generalization to spell This Week's Words, Mastery words, and Bonus words independently.

THIS WEEK'S WORDS

1. Read the directions on page 23 aloud. Do **1** and **2** orally with the children. Point out that children must use the remaining word in a sentence.
2. Have the children complete the activity independently.

MASTERY WORDS

1. Review the unit generalization on page 20.
2. Read the Mastery words aloud. As each word is read, have the children identify the last letter in each word.
3. Read the directions on page 23 aloud. Remind the children to begin their sentence with a capital letter and end it with a period.
4. Have the children complete the activities independently.

BONUS WORDS

1. Review the unit generalization on page 20.
2. Ask a volunteer to read the Bonus words aloud. Have the children look up the meanings of any unfamiliar words in the **Spelling Dictionary**.
3. Briefly discuss the directions on page 23. Then let the children complete the activity independently on a separate piece of paper or in their spelling notebooks.

For reinforcement in writing spelling words, you may wish to assign *Extra Practice Master 5: Mastery Words* or *Bonus Words.*

More Consonant Clusters

CLOSING THE UNIT

Apply New Learning

Tell the children that if they misspell words with consonant clusters in their writing, they should use one or more of the following strategies:

- think of a known word that is related in meaning and spelling.
- think of words that rhyme, and compare in their minds how they are spelled.
- pronounce the word carefully to see that the correct letter or letters have been used to spell the sounds in the word.

Transfer New Learning

Tell the children that when they encounter new words in their personal reading and in other content areas, they should learn the meaning of those words and then apply the generalizations they have studied to the spelling of those words. Tell them that once the words are familiar in both meaning and spelling, they should use them in their writing.

ENRICHMENT ACTIVITIES

Classroom activites and **home activites** may be assigned to children of all ability levels. The activities provide opportunities for children to use their spelling words in new context.

For the Classroom

To individualize classroom activities you may have the children use the word list they are studying in this unit.

- *Basic:* Use **Mastery** words to complete the activity.
- *Average:* Use **This Week's Words** to complete the activity.
- *Challenging:* Use **Bonus** words to complete the activity.

1. Language Arts/Writing Rhyming Words Have the children write three pairs of rhyming words. First have them find any rhyming pairs on their spelling list, *(test, west).* Then have them think of words that rhyme with other words on their list, checking the spelling of the new words. Have them use all six words to make a word search puzzle.

 ■ COOPERATIVE LEARNING: Have each group create a word search puzzle. Each child should write rhyming word pairs, each containing one spelling word and one other word. Children should check each other's word pairs to be sure they rhyme and are spelled correctly. Together, the children should create one puzzle using all the rhyming word pairs. The finished puzzle should be distributed to the other children to solve.

2. Language Arts/Writing Context Clues for Words Have the children use their spelling words in five sentences that provide contextual meaning for those words. Explain to them that the meaning of each spelling word should

be clear from the meaning of other words in the sentence. After they finish writing, the children should copy their sentences on another paper, leaving a blank in place of the spelling word. Have each child ask another child to supply the word that belongs to each sentence.

■ COOPERATIVE LEARNING: Have each group use spelling words in sentences that provide contextual meaning for those words. Each child should write two sentences, using one spelling word in each. The children should check each other's sentences to see if they can figure out the spelling words from the meaning of the other words in the sentences. The group should then choose two recorders to share the task of copying the sentences, leaving a blank in place of each spelling word. Groups should exchange sentences and group members should work together to complete another group's sentences.

3. Social Studies/Writing a Fictionalized Report Have the children write a fictionalized report on the topic *An Early Plane Flight.* For a model of a report, refer to page 254 in the **Writer's Guide.** As a *prewriting* activity, have the children refer to an encyclopedia or other reference book for information about the history of flying and early pilots. Tell the children they should describe part of the flight, such as the take-off or landing, from the pilot's point of view. Suggest that individual children brainstorm as they develop a cluster drawing, writing the pilot's name in the center and adding words or phrases that are associated with the pilot or the flight. When children have finished the prewriting activities, tell them to use both the information gathered during research and the cluster drawing to **compose** the report. Remind the children to include spelling words as they write. Then have the children *revise* their report, making sure the report tells a clear story of an event. Tell the children to proofread for spelling, capitalization, and punctuation errors. **Publish** the reports by giving the children an opportunity to read them to the class.

■ COOPERATIVE LEARNING: Have each group write a fictionalized story of an early pilot's flight. As a *prewriting* activity, have each group look in an encyclopedia or in other reference sources for information on the history of airplanes and early pilots, and take notes to share with group members. Then have each group work together to develop a cluster drawing, writing the name of the pilot in the center and adding words or phrases that are associated with the pilot. Have the children be sure to include spelling words as they work. When the children are ready to **compose** the report, tell them to select one child who should refer to the cluster drawing as he or she contributes the first sentence. Other children should build on that sentence, each offering sentences until the group is satisfied that the pilot's report is complete. The group should then select one member to record the report. Other group members should *revise* the report, checking to see if it clearly describes an event. Each child within the group should check the report for spelling, capitalization, and punctuation errors, using the **Revising Checklist** on page 247. Then have the group select one child to rewrite the report. Each group should ***publish*** its report by having a group member read it aloud.

For the Home

Children may complete these activities independently or with the assistance of a relative or friend in the home.

1. Science/Comparing and Contrasting Flying Things Have each child develop a chart comparing and contrasting things that fly. Tell the children to find at least two pictures of things that fly (examples: birds, insects, planes, kites and blimps). Have the children draw or cut out pictures and paste them along the left side of a piece of paper. Across the top of the paper, the children should write the headings *Alike* and *Different.* Tell the children to keep their spelling words in mind as they think about ways the things are alike and ways they are different. Have the children use at least three spelling words as they record information on the chart. For example, a kite and a bird are alike because they both can lift off the ground; they are different because a bird is alive and you must build a kite.

2. Language Arts/Writing Similes Have the children use spelling words to write as many comparisons as they can. Tell the children to use the words *as* or *like.* For example: *Milk is as white as snow; The runner was as fast as the wind.* Encourage the children to use the same spelling words in different comparisons.

3. Science/Writing a Paragraph About the Weather Have the children use their spelling words to write a paragraph about the weather. Tell the children to use the following as the main idea sentence for their paragraphs: *The weather this week has been _____.* Remind the children to check page 250 in the **Writer's Guide** for a model of a descriptive paragraph before they begin to write. After they have finished their paragraphs, the children should check to see that they have written clear paragraphs, using the **Revising Checklist** on page 247.

4. Health/Charting Physical Growth Have the children develop a list of some things they can do now that they could not do when they were younger. The list should include ways they take care of themselves, things they do to help others, and ways they have fun. Tell the children to use words from the three spelling lists. When they have finished, the children should use words from the three lists to write about three things they expect to be able to do when they are older.

EVALUATING SPELLING ABILITY

Unit Test

This Week's Words

1. **act** Benjy will *act* in the school play. **act**

2. **dust** There is *dust* on the piano. **dust**
3. **east** The wind is coming from the *east.* **east**
4. **test** Evan passed the *test.* **test**
5. **west** The sun sets in the *west.* **west**
6. **lift** No one can *lift* a car. **lift**
7. **bend** Do not *bend* your sore elbow. **bend**
8. **grand** It is a *grand* day for a picnic. **grand**
9. **ground** David planted the seeds in the *ground.* **ground**
10. **wind** Jerry forgot to *wind* his watch. **wind**
11. **build** Mom is going to *build* a bookcase. **build**
12. **child** When Dad was a *child,* he lived on a farm. **child**
13. **wild** Dell and Tim had a *wild* race. **wild**
14. **milk** Amy learned how to *milk* a cow. **milk**
15. **bump** Carol has a *bump* on her head. **bump**

Mastery Words

1. **felt** The children *felt* the rabbit's soft fur. **felt**
2. **hand** Simon scratched his *hand.* **hand**
3. **help** Carly needs our *help.* **help**
4. **hold** Betty let me *hold* her kitten. **hold**
5. **left** Dennis *left* the party early. **left**
6. **want** Kim and Jane *want* to bake bread. **want**

Bonus Words

1. **adult** An *adult* should help you use the oven. **adult**
2. **blend** Ellen will *blend* the colors. **blend**
3. **burst** Ted *burst* through the door. **burst**
4. **insect** Will wrote a report about an *insect.* **insect**
5. **prompt** Our teacher likes us to be *prompt* for school. **prompt**
6. **pumpkin** Lonnie loves *pumpkin* bread. **pumpkin**
7. **stamp** Please don't *stamp* your foot. **stamp**
8. **tramp** Hikers like to *tramp* along forest trails. **tramp**

Dictation Sentences

This Week's Words

1. The *wind* from the *east* blew the *dust* to the *west.*
2. Why did you *lift* the box off the *ground*?
3. You must *bend* down and clean up the *milk* that the *child* spilled.
4. They *want* to *build* a *grand* house by the water.
5. I hope my dog does not *act wild* at the pet show.
6. Please do not *bump* me while I am taking the *test.*

Mastery Words

1. His *left hand felt* cold.
2. I *want* to *help* her *hold* the kite.

Bonus Words

1. The *pumpkin burst* when it fell on the ground.
2. That *adult* can help us find the name of that pretty *insect.*
3. The colors in the *stamp blend* well.
4. You can not *tramp* in the rain if you want to be *prompt.*

Children who have made errors on the Unit Test may require reteaching. Use the following **Reteaching Strategies** and **Follow-up Masters 5A** and **5B** for additional instruction and practice of This Week's Words. (You may wish to assign **LEP Reteaching Follow-up Master 5** for reteaching of spelling words.)

A. Discovering Spelling Ideas

1. Say the following words as you write them on the chalkboard.

    chest   sand   gold   stump

2. Ask the children to identify the consonant sounds at the end of each word. (/s/ and /t/, /n/ and /d/, /l/ and /d/, /m/ and /p/)
3. Ask the children to identify the letters for these sounds and how they are written. (st, nd, ld, mp. The letters are written together at the end of each word.)
4. Ask the children what they have learned about these letters that are called consonant clusters. (Consonant clusters are groups of two letters that are written together. Each consonant sound is heard. They all appear at the end of these words.)

B. Word Shapes

1. Explain to the children that each word has a shape and that remembering the shape of the word can help them to spell the word correctly.
2. On the chalkboard, write the words best and lump. Have the children identify "short," "tall," and "tail" letters.
3. Draw the configuration of each word on the chalkboard, and ask the children which word fits in each shape.

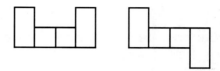

Use **Reteaching Follow-up Master 5A** to reinforce spelling generalizations taught in Unit 5.

Use **Reteaching Follow-up Master 5B** to reinforce spellings of This Week's Words for Unit 5.

Name _____

Reteaching Follow-up A   Discovering Spelling Ideas   UNIT **5**

THIS WEEK'S WORDS

dust	test	lift	grand	wind
milk	ground	act	east	west
bend	build	wild	bump	child

1. Study This Week's Words. Say each word to yourself.

2. Write the words that end with these sounds.

/s/ + /t/	/l/ + /d/	/n/ + /d/
dus(t)	bui(l)(d)	grou(n)(d)
tes(t)	wi(l)(d)	be(n)(d)
eas(t)	chi(l)(d)	gra(n)(d)
wes(t)		wi(n)(d)

/l/ + /k/	/f/ + /t/
mi(l)(k)	li(f)(t)

/m/ + /p/	/k/ + /t/
bu(m)(p)	a(c)(t)

3. Circle the letters in your answers that spell those sounds.

4. What is it called when you hear two consonant sounds together?

    a consonant cluster

5. What have you learned about consonant clusters?

    A consonant cluster occurs when two or three consonant letters are

    written together and you hear each consonant sound. They can

    appear at the beginning or end of a word.

Reteaching • 9

Name _____

Reteaching Follow-up B   Word Shapes   UNIT **5**

THIS WEEK'S WORDS

dust	test	lift	grand	wind
milk	ground	act	east	west
bend	build	wild	bump	child

Write each of This Week's Words in its correct shape. The first one has been done for you. Children may interchange answers that fit the same configuration.

1. w i l d
2. w i n d
3. g r a n d
4. b e n d
5. e a s t
6. d u s t
7. b u m p
8. b u i l d
9. l i f t
10. c h i l d
11. w e s t
12. t e s t
13. m i l k
14. g r o u n d
15. a c t

10 • Reteaching

PREVIEWING THE UNIT

Unit Materials

Instruction and Practice

Pupil Book	pages 24–29
Teacher's Edition	
Teaching Plans	pages 24–29
Enrichment Activities	
For the Home	page 29A

Testing

Teacher's Edition	
Trial Test	pages 23E–23F
Unit Test	page 29A
Form *A** Test 1	Page T1

If your grading period is six weeks, you may want to use the **Form A Test at the end of this unit.*

Additional Resources

PRACTICE AND REINFORCEMENT
Review Master 6A: Units 1 and 2
Review Master 6B: Units 3 and 4
Review Master 6C: Unit 5 and Test Exercise
Dictionary and Proofreading Master 1
Study Steps to Learn a Word Master
Mastery Words Review: Units 1–5
Bonus Words Review: Units 1–5

TESTING (optional)
Mastery Words Test: Units 1–5
Bonus Words Test: Units 1–5
Writing Test 1

TEACHING AIDS
Spelling and Writing Transparency 1
Home Letter 2

Visit our Web site
http://www.hbschool.com

Click on the SPELLING banner to find activities for this unit.

Learner Objectives

Spelling

- To review words that demonstrate these sound-letter relationships: /a/a, /e/e, /i/i, /o/o, /u/u.
- To review words that demonstrate these sound-letter relationships: final /l/ll, final /f/ff, final /s/ss, final /d/dd.
- To review words in which final consonant letter is doubled before *ed* or *ing* is added.
- To review words with initial consonant clusters.
- To review words with final consonant clusters.

Reading

- To recognize action verbs in a story.
- To analyze and respond to a story.
- To follow written directions.
- To use the dictionary for word meaning.

Writing

- To write sentences incorporating action verbs.
- To use the writing process.
- To edit for content, style, and tone.
- To revise using editing and proofreading marks.
- To proofread for spelling, capitalization, and punctuation.
- To write legible manuscript and cursive letters.

Listening

- To listen to action sentences.

Speaking

- To express feelings and ideas about a piece of writing.
- To present definitions and action sentences.
- To contribute ideas and information in group discussions.

REVIEW WORDS

UNIT 1
apple ✓
bring ✓
else
flag
shall ✓
hunt
river ✓
happy

UNIT 2
add
ill ✓
spell
stuff ✓
unless ✓
mess ✓
roll
less

UNIT 3
chop
nap ✓
step
tripped ✓
wagging
drop ✓
planning ✓
stopped

UNIT 4
close
drawer
floor ✓
print
spring ✓
drive ✓
state ✓
spray

UNIT 5
act
build ✓
ground ✓
milk ✓
test
east ✓
west
lift

Assignment Guide

This guide shows how you teach a typical spelling unit in either a five-day or a three-day sequence, while providing for individual differences. **Boldface type** indicates essential classwork. Steps shown in light type may be done in class or assigned as homework.

Five Days	◡ = average spellers ★ = better spellers ✓ = slower spellers	Three Days
Day 1	**a** ● ★ ✓ **Take Review Words Trial Test and correct**	
Day 2	● ★ ✓ Complete Spelling Review pages 24, 25, 26 ● ★ ✓ Complete Review Master 6 A, 6 B, 6 C (optional) ✓ Complete Mastery Words Review Master: Units 1–5 (optional) ★ Complete Bonus Words Review Master: Units 1–5 (optional) **b**	Day 1
Day 3	**c** ● ★ ✓ **Complete Spelling and Reading page 27**	
Day 4	● ★ ✓ Complete Spelling and Writing pages 28–29 ● ★ ✓ Complete Dictionary and Proofreading Master 1 (optional) **d**	Day 2
Day 5	**e** ● ★ ✓ **Take Review Words Unit Test** ✓ Take Mastery Words Test: Unit 1–5 (optional) ★ Take Bonus Words Test: Units 1–5 (optional)	Day 3

Enrichment Activities for the **home** included at the end of this unit may be assigned selectively on any day of the week.

INTRODUCING THE UNIT

Establish Readiness for Learning

Tell the children they will review words from the previous five units. In Unit 6 they will review:

- words with short vowel sounds.
- words with final double letters.
- using verb inflections.
- words with consonant clusters.

Tell the children they will use some of the review words to write sentences with action verbs.

Assess Children's Spelling Ability

Administer the Trial Test before the children study the review words. Use the test sentences provided. Say each word and use it in a sentence. Then repeat the word. Have the children write the words on a separate sheet of paper or in their spelling notebooks.

Have the children check their own work by listening to you read the spelling of the words or by referring to the review words lists in the side boxes of the **Pupil Book.** For each misspelled word, have the children follow the **Study Steps to Learn a Word** on page 24 in

the **Pupil Book,** or use the copying master to study and write the words. Children should record the number correct on their **Progress Report.**

Trial Test Sentences

1. **apple** Ron bit into the shiny red *apple*. **apple**
2. **bring** Everyone may *bring* a friend to the party. **bring**
3. **else** Mary needs something *else*. **else**
4. **flag** Anna carried a *flag* in the parade. **flag**
5. **shall** We *shall* play at recess. **shall**
6. **hunt** Tom will help you *hunt* for the lost kitten. **hunt**
7. **river** The fishing boats went out early on the *river*. **river**
8. **happy** I'm so *happy* that my kitten has been found. **happy**
9. **add** Mitch can *add* those numbers in his head. **add**
10. **ill** Emma stayed home because she was *ill*. **ill**
11. **spell** Todd can *spell* some very long words. **spell**
12. **stuff** Put all that *stuff* in this bag. **stuff**

FOCUS

- Establishes objectives
- Relates to prior learning
- Sets purpose of instruction

13. **unless** Marianne won't play *unless* we all play. **unless**
14. **mess** What a *mess* we made when we spilled the paint! **mess**
15. **roll** Pigs like to *roll* in the mud to keep cool. **roll**
16. **less** In *less* than ten days vacation begins. **less**
17. **chop** We must *chop* down that dead tree. **chop**
18. **nap** Our cats seem to *nap* all the time. **nap**
19. **step** Please do not *step* on the flowers. **step**
20. **tripped** Jane accidentally *tripped* on the stairs. **tripped**
21. **wagging** The dog was *wagging* its tail. **wagging**
22. **drop** Tracy will *drop* the package if it's heavy. **drop**
23. **planning** Our family is *planning* a trip this summer. **planning**
24. **stopped** Kim *stopped* running after she hurt her foot. **stopped**
25. **close** Juan wants to *close* the door. **close**
26. **drawer** The ruler is in the top *drawer* of the desk. **drawer**
27. **floor** The children sat on the *floor*. **floor**
28. **print** Janet can *print* very neatly. **print**
29. **spring** The cat will *spring* at the mouse. **spring**
30. **drive** Leon is learning to *drive* a car. **drive**
31. **state** My mother was born in the *state* of Iowa. **state**
32. **spray** *Spray* some water on these flowers. **spray**
33. **act** Laura likes to *act* in plays. **act**
34. **build** They will *build* a cabin in the woods. **build**

35. **ground** The *ground* is covered with leaves. **ground**
36. **milk** Brenda likes cold *milk*. **milk**
37. **test** We had a math *test* at school yesterday. **test**
38. **east** The sun always rises in the *east*. **east**
39. **west** The sun always sets in the *west*. **west**
40. **lift** John will help you *lift* this heavy box. **lift**

Apply Prior Learning

Have the children apply what they know about the generalizations found in Units 1-5. Use the following activities.

Write these words on the chalkboard: *drag* and *slap*. Ask the children what these words have in common. (They both have the /a/ sound.) Have the children underline the spelling for the short vowel sounds. (dr<u>a</u>g, sl<u>a</u>p) Now write these words on the chalkboard: *spill, dress*. Ask the children what *spill* and *dress* have in common. (Both *spill* and *dress* end with double consonants.) Have the children underline the double consonant in each word. (spi<u>ll</u>, dre<u>ss</u>) Ask them to give examples of other words that end in double consonants.

Now write these words on the chalkboard: *spill, mop*. Have the children add *ed* and *ing* to these words and underline the spellings for the endings. (spill<u>ed</u>, spill<u>ing</u>, mopp<u>ed</u>, mopp<u>ing</u>). Ask them to explain how the spelling changes when *ed* and *ing* are added. (For most words, such as *spill*, the spelling does not change when *ed* and *ing* are added; however, in a one-syllable word with a short vowel sound and a single final consonant like *mop*, the consonant is doubled as in *mop, mopped, mopping*.) Tell the children that they will review words that follow these generalizations and then use the words to write sentences.

FOCUS

- Relates to prior learning
- Draws relationships
- Applies spelling generalizations to new contexts

TEACHING PLAN

Objectives To review words that demonstrate these sound-letter relationships: /a/a, /e/e, /i/i, /u/u.

1. Review the directions to the exercises on page 24. Remind the children that the answers to the exercises are to be found only among the eight review words on page 24.
2. Have the children complete the exercises independently. You may refer them to the **Writer's Guide** at the back of the **Pupil Book** for a review of the spelling generalization for Unit 1.

Review

Do these steps if you are not sure how to spell a word.
● **Say** the word. Listen to each sound. Think about what the word means.
● **Look** at the word. See how the letters are made. Try to see the word in your mind.
● **Spell** the word to yourself. Think about the way each sound is spelled.
● **Write** the word. Copy it from your book. Check the way you made your letters. Write the word again.
● **Check** your learning. Cover the word and write it. Did you spell it correctly? If not, do these steps until you know how to spell the word.

UNIT 1 Follow the directions. Use words from Unit 1.

UNIT 1
apple
bring
else
flag
shall
hunt
river
happy

1. Write the two words that begin with a short vowel sound.
Word order may vary.
apple   else

2. Write the four words that have /a/.
Word order may vary.
apple   flag
shall   happy

3. Write the two words that have /i/.
Word order may vary.
bring   river

4. Write the word that has /u/.
hunt

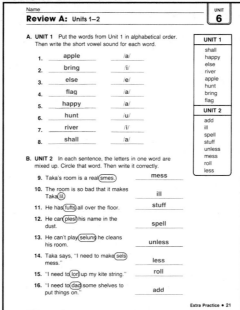

Finish these sentences.

5. We decided to ____hunt____ for treasure today.
6. We started our search on the banks of the ____river____ that flows past my house.
7. Under an ____apple____ tree we saw a watch.

24

Review: Units 1 and 2

Name
Review A: Units 1–2   UNIT **6**

A. UNIT 1 Put the words from Unit 1 in alphabetical order. Then write the short vowel sound for each word.

1.	apple	/a/
2.	bring	/i/
3.	else	/e/
4.	flag	/a/
5.	happy	/a/
6.	hunt	/u/
7.	river	/i/
8.	shall	/a/

UNIT 1
shall
happy
else
river
apple
hunt
bring
flag

UNIT 2
add
ill
spell
stuff
unless
mess
roll
less

B. UNIT 2 In each sentence, the letters in one word are mixed up. Circle that word. Then write it correctly.

9. Taka's room is a real (smes.) — mess
10. The room is so bad that it makes Taka (lil) — ill
11. He has (tufts) all over the floor. — stuff
12. He can (ples) his name in the dust. — spell
13. He can't play (seluns) he cleans his room. — unless
14. Taka says, "I need to make (sels) mess." — less
15. "I need to (lorl) up my kite string." — roll
16. "I need to (dad) some shelves to put things on." — add

Extra Practice • 21

Review: Units 3 and 4

Name
Review B: Units 3–4   UNIT **6**

A. UNIT 3 Use a word from Unit 3 to complete each sentence.

1. You use a knife to ____ food. — chop
2. You go to bed to ____, or sleep. — nap
3. To cross a puddle, ____ over it. — step
4. The man ____ over the brick. — tripped
5. The dog is ____ its tail. — wagging
6. If you ____ a glass, you might break it. — drop
7. The teacher is ____ a test. — planning
8. The car ____ at the red light. — stopped

UNIT 3
stopped
step
drop
chop
planning
nap
wagging
tripped

UNIT 4
spray
drawer
spring
close
state
floor
drive
print

B. UNIT 4 Write a word from Unit 4 that fits the meaning of each sentence.

9. You do this with a door. — close
10. It's part of a desk. — drawer
11. It's under your feet. — floor
12. You do this with a pencil. — print
13. This is a season of the year. — spring
14. People in cars do this. — drive
15. You live in one. — state
16. You do this with a hose. — spray

22 • Extra Practice

8. I was _____happy_____ we had found at least one treasure.

9. I asked my friend to _____bring_____ it to me.

10. We wondered what _____else_____ we would find that day.

UNIT 2 Follow the directions. Use words from Unit 2. Write the words that end with these sounds. **Word order may vary.**

11. /f/ _____stuff_____   12. /d/ _____add_____

13. /l/ (three words) _____ill_____   _____spell_____   _____roll_____

Word order may vary.

14. /s/ (three words) _____unless_____   _____mess_____   _____less_____

Finish these sentences.

15. Another word for <u>sick</u> is _____ill_____ .

16. You _____add_____ <u>un</u> to <u>less</u> to spell _____unless_____ .

UNIT 2
add
ill
spell
stuff
unless
mess
roll
less

UNIT 3 Finish this story with words from Unit 3.

Meg's dad was __17__ to build a fire. He began to __18__ the wood. Meg helped by carrying logs. She was careful not to __19__ any on the ground. Then Meg's puppy Pokey ran up. It __20__ right in Meg's path, barking and __21__ its tail. Meg did not want to __22__ on Pokey. She could not see where she was going. She __23__ over a rock and almost fell. Meg said, "Pokey, I wish you would go into the house and take a __24__ when I work."

UNIT 3
chop
nap
step
tripped
wagging
drop
planning
stopped

17. _____planning_____   18. _____chop_____   19. _____drop_____

20. _____stopped_____   21. _____wagging_____   22. _____step_____

23. _____tripped_____   24. _____nap_____

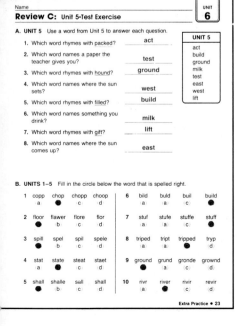

WORDS IN TIME

The word <u>spell</u> came from the old word <u>spellen</u>. <u>Spellen</u> meant "to read out." Why do you think <u>spellen</u> became <u>spell</u>?

25

Spelling Review   UNIT 6b

TEACHING PLAN

Objectives To review words that demonstrate these sound-letter relationships: final /l/ll, final /f/ff, final /s/ss, final /d/dd; to review words in which the final consonant letter is doubled before *ed* or *ing* is added.

1. Review the directions to the exercises on page 25. Remind the children that the answers to the exercises are to be found only among the sixteen review words on page 25.
2. Have the children complete the exercises independently. You may refer them to the **Writer's Guide** at the back of the **Pupil Book** for a review of the spelling generalizations for Units 2 and 3.

⊃ EXTENDING THE LESSON

Have the children make up five complete sentences using review words from Units 2 and 3. Suggest that they write about imaginary encounters with strange creatures, perhaps visitors from another planet. Have them use at least two review words per sentence.

Remind the children to proofread the sentences for spelling.

---

eview: Unit 5

Name	UNIT
Review C: Unit 5·Test Exercise	**6**

A. UNIT 5 Use a word from Unit 5 to answer each question.

1. Which word rhymes with packed? _____act_____
2. Which word names a paper the teacher gives you? _____test_____
3. Which word rhymes with <u>hound</u>? _____ground_____
4. Which word names where the sun sets? _____west_____
5. Which word rhymes with <u>filled</u>? _____build_____
6. Which word names something you drink? _____milk_____
7. Which word rhymes with <u>gift</u>? _____lift_____
8. Which word names where the sun comes up? _____east_____

UNIT 5
act
build
ground
milk
test
east
west
lift

B. UNITS 1–5 Fill in the circle below the word that is spelled right.

1	copp	chop ●	choppp	choop	6	bild	buld	buil	build ●
	a	b	c	d		a	b	c	d
2	floor ●	flawer	flore	flor	7	stuf	stufe	stuffe	stuff ●
	a	b	c	d		a	b	c	d
3	spill ●	spel	spil	spele	8	triped	tript	tripped ●	tryp
	a	b	c	d		a	b	c	d
4	stat	state ●	steat	staet	9	ground ●	grund	gronde	growd
	a	b	c	d		a	b	c	d
5	shall ●	shalle	sall	shall	10	rivr	river ●	rivir	revir
	a	b	c	d		a	b	c	d

Extra Practice • 23

UNIT B   *Review*   **25**

TEACHING PLAN

Objectives To review words with initial consonant clusters; to review words with final consonant clusters.

1. Review the directions to the exercises on page 26. Remind the children that the answers to the exercises are to be found only among the sixteen review words on page 26.
2. Have the children complete the exercises independently. You may refer them to the **Writer's Guide** at the back of the **Pupil Book** for a review of the spelling generalizations for Units 4 and 5.
3. Review the children's answers on pages 24–26 orally, or have volunteers write them on the chalkboard.

For reinforcement in writing review words for Units 1–5, you may wish to assign *Review Masters 6A, 6B,* and *6C.*

--- WORDS IN TIME ---

Have a volunteer read **Words in Time** aloud. Tell the children that many words have their origins in Old English as well as other languages.

As a COOPERATIVE LEARNING activity, have the children examine these four unit words that have more than one meaning: *roll, spring, spell,* and *state.* On the chalkboard, give the following example:

(1) spell (n), a state of magic power;
(2) spell (v), to form words with letters.

Point out that the different meanings have to do with the way the words are used. Have a group take one or two words. Have each child or pair of children choose one meaning of the word and (1) research its origin; (2) find its definition; (3) write a statement of the findings; (4) draw a picture to illustrate the meaning of the word. Have children in the group read the statements, share the pictures, and discuss why they think the same word came to have different meanings.

UNIT 4
close
drawer
floor
print
spring
drive
state
spray

UNIT 5
act
build
ground
milk
test
east
west
lift

UNIT 4 Add consonant clusters to these word parts to make words from Unit 4.

25. ___oor — floor
26. ___ose — close
27. ___awer — drawer
28. ___ing — spring
29. ___ive — drive
30. ___ate — state
31. ___ay — spray
32. ___int — print

UNIT 5 Follow the directions. Use words from Unit 5.

33. Write the word that has /a/.
act

34. Write the three words that have /i/.
build   milk   lift

35. Write the two words that have /e/.
test   west

36. Write the word that begins with a consonant cluster.
ground

Finish these sentences. Use words from Unit 5.

37. There are lots of sticks lying on the ____ ground
38. Let's use them to ____ build ____ some toy boats.
39. Then we'll go to the pond and ____ test ____ them.
40. A good wind is blowing from ____ east ____ to west.
41. The wind will ____ lift ____ the sails and move the boats.
42. We can ____ act ____ like sailors sailing off to sea.

26

Spelling and Reading
Sentences About Actions

Read the following story. Look for all the action verbs.

After a long <u>drive</u>, the Romero family came to the <u>river</u>. They were <u>planning</u> to camp on the <u>west</u> bank. They put up a tent and unloaded food. Then they <u>stopped</u> and decided to take a <u>nap</u>.

Some strange sounds woke them up. They rushed out of the tent. Their <u>stuff</u> was scattered everywhere. Apples and <u>milk</u> had spilled onto the <u>ground</u>. Everything was a <u>mess</u>!

"Watch your <u>step</u>," warned Mr. Romero. "Act calmly and stay <u>close</u> together. Can someone <u>bring</u> me a light?"

"I have a flashlight," said Mrs. Romero. "Let's take a look around."

"Paw <u>prints</u>," whispered Maria. Then everyone shouted, "<u>Raccoons</u>!"

"We should have left our food in the car," Yolanda sighed.

"I guess we flunked the raccoon test!" laughed Maria.

Write the answers to the questions.   *See answers below.*

1. What did the Romeros decide after they unloaded food? *Literal*
2. What did Mr. Romero tell everyone to do after they found the mess? *Literal*
3. How did the Romeros know raccoons took the food? *Interpretive*
4. Do you think the Romeros will still have a good time camping? Why or why not? *Critical*

Underline the review words in your answers. Check to see that you spelled the words correctly.

27

Spelling and Reading **Answers**

1. They decided to take a <u>nap</u>. 2. He told them to <u>act</u> calmly and stay <u>close</u> together. 3. They saw the paw <u>prints</u>. 4. Accept all reasonable answers. Possible answer: The Romeros will probably still have a good time because they seem cheerful at the end.

On this page the children will read:
• This Week's Words from the preceding five units;
• words reviewed in this unit;
• words that follow the generalizations taught in the preceding five units.

TEACHING PLAN

Objectives   To analyze and respond to sentences about actions; to proofread written answers for spelling.

1. Tell the children that they will read a story that includes a number of spelling words from Units 1–5. Explain that most stories have action sentences that tell the reader what is happening. A good writer chooses the words and phrases in the action sentences very carefully. For example, he or she chooses clear and interesting verbs to help the reader picture the action. Interesting action sentences make the reader want to read to find out what will happen next. Tell the children that the story will serve as a model for their own writing.

2. Have the children read about the Romero family and how one action leads to another. Tell the children to look for words that express the actions.

3. Have the children answer the questions independently. Tell them to underline the review words in their answers and to proofread their answers for spelling.

4. Spot-check the children's answers as they work. Review answers orally.

TEACHING PLAN

Objectives To identify verbs used in action sentences; to evaluate illustrations of story scenes.

1. Have the children read the first paragraph of **Think and Discuss** on page 28. Ask them to recall stories they have read that were full of action and give examples of action verbs. Ask them to look over the story on page 27 again and decide if it contains clear and interesting action verbs.

2. Have the children study the illustrations and accompanying sentences on page 28. Ask them if the verb in each sentence fits the action shown in each picture. Ask them if they would have illustrated either picture differently.

3. Have the children read the rest of **Think and Discuss** independently and answer the questions. Ask them to give examples of other clear and interesting action verbs the writer could have used to describe what happens in the story.

4. Have the children read **Apply** at the bottom of page 28. Tell them that they will use some of their spelling words to write sentences that tell about the actions of something that moves. Discuss with them the importance of keeping their audience in mind as they write. Explain that whoever reads their sentences may not be familiar with the object they are describing. Tell the children to be careful to use clear and interesting verbs in their descriptions.

Summarize Learning

Have the children identify the characteristics of a good description of action. (use of clear and interesting verbs that tell exactly what is happening and make the story exciting for the reader)

Spelling and Writing
Sentences About Actions

Think and Discuss

Words that show actions are called action verbs. Look at the pictures.

Words to Help You Write
bring
roll
spring
tripped
drop
hunt

They put up the tent.   **They unloaded the food.**

The pictures show some of the actions described in the story on page 27. Read the sentence that goes with each picture. What verb describes the action in the first picture?[A] What verb describes the action in the second picture?[B]

The story is filled with action. The characters in the story do many different things. The writer uses action verbs to tell what they do. Read the second paragraph on page 27. What verb describes what the Romeros did when strange sounds woke them up?[C] Look at the third paragraph. What verbs does Mr. Romero use when he tells his family what to do?[D]

Sometimes several verbs can describe one action. A good writer will choose the verb that best describes what is happening. For example, there are many verbs that describe how a person can speak. Look at the fifth paragraph of the story. What action verb does the writer use to describe how Maria spoke?[E]

Apply

Write **sentences that tell about actions** for your classmates. Use the guidelines on the next page.

28

Think and Discuss Answers

A. put up B. unloaded C. rushed D. watch, act, stay, bring E. whispered

Prewriting

● Think of something that moves. The pictures may help you.
● Make a list of your subject's actions. Start each idea with a clear and different verb.

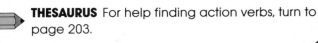

THESAURUS For help finding action verbs, turn to page 203.

Composing

Use your list to write the first draft of your action sentences.
● Make each idea on your list a complete sentence.
● Write at least six sentences telling how your subject moves.

Revising

Read your action sentences and show them to a classmate. Follow these guidelines to improve your work. Use the editing and proofreading marks to show changes.

Editing

● Make sure your sentences use clear and interesting verbs.
● Change the verbs that do not describe actions clearly.

Proofreading

● Look over your spelling and correct any mistakes.
● Check your capitalization and punctuation.

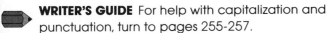

WRITER'S GUIDE For help with capitalization and punctuation, turn to pages 255-257.

Copy your action sentences onto a clean paper. Write carefully and neatly.

Publishing

Read your sentences aloud to the class. Ask your classmates what verbs helped them <u>see</u> the action best.

29

Editing and Proofreading Marks

☰	capitalize
⊙	make a period
∧	add something
⋀	add a comma
⌿	take something away
◯	spell correctly
⁋	indent the paragraph
/	make a lowercase letter

For additional practice in using the dictionary to spell and write and in proofreading, you may wish to assign *Dictionary and Proofreading Master 1.*

Spelling and Writing — UNIT 6d

TEACHING PLAN

Objectives To write sentences describing actions; to edit for content, style, and tone; to proofread for spelling, capitalization, and punctuation.

1. **Prewriting** Have the children choose a moving subject to describe. Tell them that they may write about a person, an animal, or an object. Point out that the subject should move in a variety of ways. Have the children imagine the subject in action. Tell them to visualize the movements involved, and list action verbs describing each movement. Suggest that they use the **Spelling Thesaurus** on page 203 to help them select action verbs.

2. **Composing** Before the children begin composing, remind them that they must use complete sentences. Explain that each sentence should contain an action verb that gives a clear picture of what the subject is doing. Have the children write first drafts of the six sentences.

3. **Revising (Editing and Proofreading)** Have the children ask classmates to read their sentences to see if they can picture what was described. Children should consider their classmates' comments as they revise the sentences. Have the children follow the guidelines on page 29 to revise their sentences. Remind them to use the **Spelling Dictionary** to check their spelling. To help the children prepare a legible copy of the sentences, have them consult the **Handwriting Models** in the **Writer's Guide** on page 258.

For reinforcement in editing and proofreading, you may wish to use *Spelling and Writing Transparency 1.*

4. **Publishing** Have the children read their action sentences to their classmates.

ENRICHMENT ACTIVITIES

Home Activities may be assigned to children of all ability levels. The activities provide opportunities for children to use their spelling words in new contexts.

For the Home

The children may complete home activities independently or with the assistance of a relative or friend in the home.

1. Language Arts/Categorizing Spelling Words Have the children review the spelling words and group them into categories. Tell the children to write a heading for each category they find. For example, *Food: apple, milk; Directions: east, west.* Have the children add other words to the categories. Tell them to check for spelling. The children can share the word categories with a friend or relative.

2. Language Arts/Writing a Rhyming Poem Tell the children to write a rhyming poem using some of the spelling words. Refer them to page 254 in the **Writer's Guide** for a model of a rhyming poem. Tell the children that the poem can tell a funny little story or it can create a word picture. Tell the children to share their poems with a friend or relative.

3. Social Studies/Writing a Paragraph About the Environment Have the children use some of the spelling words to write a paragraph about the importance of keeping the outdoors attractive and clean. Remind the children to look on page 250 of the **Writer's Guide** for a model of a paragraph. Suggest that the children use the **Thesaurus** to enrich their writing. Have them proofread the paragraphs for spelling, capitalization, and punctuation. The children may read the paragraphs to a friend or family member.

4. Social Studies/Writing Facts About States Tell the children to use some of the spelling words to write five sentences containing facts about the state they live in. For example, *We have a big river that runs through this state.* Tell the children that when they have completed the sentences, they should do the following: circle words with short vowel sounds; underline all double consonants; and draw a double line below the consonant clusters *st* and *nd.*

EVALUATION

Unit Test

1. *apple*   A shiny, red *apple* is a delicious snack.   **apple**
2. *bring*   Flora will *bring* her turtle to school.   **bring**
3. *else*   Hiroshi chose someone *else* as his partner.   **else**
4. *flag*   The American *flag* has a star for each state.   **flag**

5. *shall*   We *shall* bake some wheat bread today.   **shall**
6. *hunt*   I decided to *hunt* for my lost mitten.   **hunt**
7. *river*   The *river* flowed past towns and fields.   **river**
8. *happy*   I am *happy* to be home after my long trip.   **happy**
9. *add*   First beat the eggs, and then *add* the sugar.   **add**
10. *ill*   Pedro stayed home because he was *ill.*   **ill**
11. *spell*   Some words are very hard to *spell.*   **spell**
12. *stuff*   Our attic is full of really old *stuff.*   **stuff**
13. *unless*   I will not play well *unless* I practice.   **unless**
14. *mess*   When the baby eats, she makes a big *mess.* **mess**
15. *roll*   Our dog loves to *roll* in the grass.   **roll**
16. *less*   My little brother weighs *less* than I do.   **less**
17. *chop*   We need to *chop* some wood for our wood stove.   **chop**
18. *nap*   The baby takes a *nap* in the afternoon.   **nap**
19. *step*   Ramon took one *step* into the cold waves.   **step**
20. *tripped*   Peg *tripped* over a rock on the path.   **tripped**
21. *wagging*   The pup jumped up, *wagging* his tail.   **wagging**
22. *drop*   Maria did not *drop* any dishes.   **drop**
23. *planning*   My family is *planning* a long trip.   **planning**
24. *stopped*   The cars *stopped* at the red light.   **stopped**
25. *close*   The dog kept his nose *close* to the ground.   **close**
26. *drawer*   Gloria put her papers in the *drawer.* **drawer**
27. *floor*   Miguel spread the newspapers on the *floor.* **floor**
28. *print*   The boys saw a strange *print* in the thick dust.   **print**
29. *spring*   In the *spring,* the world seems new.   **spring**
30. *drive*   My sister learned to *drive* our car.   **drive**
31. *state*   Miyoshi moved here from another *state.* **state**
32. *spray*   We felt the cool *spray* from the fountain.   **spray**
33. *act*   Juan will *act* as captain in this game.   **act**
34. *build*   We watched the ants *build* their nest.   **build**
35. *ground*   Rivers flow under the *ground.*   **ground**
36. *milk*   Andrea bought *milk* to drink with her lunch.   **milk**
37. *test*   I passed my swimming *test* last week.   **test**
38. *east*   We will travel *east* to New York City.   **east**
39. *west*   The early settlers kept moving *west.*   **west**
40. *lift*   My father can *lift* that heavy box.   **lift**

Mastery and Bonus Words Review and Assessment

For additional practice you may wish to assign **Mastery Words Review Master: Units 1–5** or **Bonus Words Review Master: Units 1–5.** To assess children's spelling ability with these words, use **Mastery Words Test: Units 1–5** or **Bonus Words Test: Units 1–5.**

Mastery Words Review

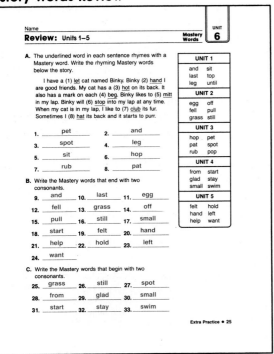

Name
Review: Units 1–5   UNIT 6 Mastery Words

A. The underlined word in each sentence rhymes with a Mastery word. Write the rhyming Mastery words below the story.

I have a (1) let cat named Binky. Binky (2) hand I are good friends. My cat has a (3) hot on its back. It also has a mark on each (4) beg. Binky likes to (5) mitt in my lap. Binky will (6) stop into my lap at any time. When my cat is in my lap, I like to (7) club its fur. Sometimes I (8) hat its back and it starts to purr.

1. pet   2. and
3. spot   4. leg
5. sit   6. hop
7. rub   8. pat

B. Write the Mastery words that end with two consonants.
9. and   10. last   11. egg
12. fell   13. grass   14. off
15. pull   16. still   17. small
18. start   19. felt   20. hand
21. help   22. hold   23. left
24. want

C. Write the Mastery words that begin with two consonants.
25. grass   26. still   27. spot
28. from   29. glad   30. small
31. start   32. stay   33. swim

UNIT 1
and · sit
last · top
leg · until

UNIT 2
egg · off
fell · pull
grass · still

UNIT 3
hop · pet
pat · spot
rub · pop

UNIT 4
from · start
glad · stay
small · swim

UNIT 5
felt · hold
hand · left
help · want

Extra Practice ● 25

Bonus Words Review

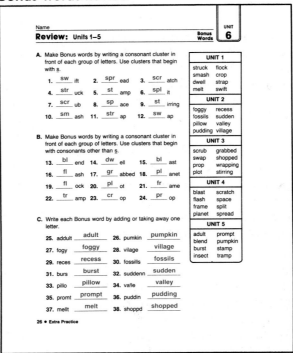

Name
Review: Units 1–5   UNIT 6 Bonus Words

A. Make Bonus words by writing a consonant cluster in front of each group of letters. Use clusters that begin with s.
1. sw ift   2. spr ead   3. scr atch
4. str uck   5. st amp   6. spl it
7. scr ub   8. sp ace   9. st irring
10. sm ash   11. str ap   12. sw ap

B. Make Bonus words by writing a consonant cluster in front of each group of letters. Use clusters that begin with consonants other than s.
13. bl end   14. dw ell   15. bl ast
16. fl ash   17. gr abbed   18. pl anet
19. fl ock   20. pl ot   21. fr ame
22. tr amp   23. cr op   24. pr op

C. Write each Bonus word by adding or taking away one letter.
25. addult   adult   26. pumkin   pumpkin
27. fogy   foggy   28. vilage   village
29. reces   recess   30. fossills   fossils
31. burs   burst   32. suddenn   sudden
33. pillo   pillow   34. valle   valley
35. promt   prompt   36. puddin   pudding
37. mellt   melt   38. shoppd   shopped

UNIT 1
struck · flock
smash · crop
dwell · strap
melt · swift

UNIT 2
foggy · recess
fossils · sudden
pillow · valley
pudding · village

UNIT 3
scrub · grabbed
swap · shopped
prop · wrapping
plot · stirring

UNIT 4
blast · scratch
flash · space
frame · split
planet · spread

UNIT 5
adult · prompt
blend · pumpkin
burst · stamp
insect · tramp

26 ● Extra Practice

Mastery Words Test

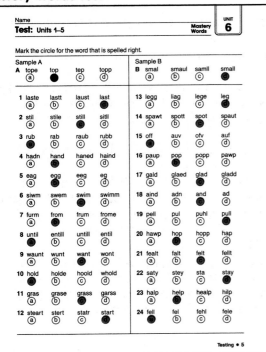

Name
Test: Units 1–5   UNIT 6 Mastery Words

Mark the circle for the word that is spelled right.

Sample A
A tope **top** tep topp
   ⓐ ● ⓒ ⓓ

Sample B
B smal smaul samll **small**
   ⓐ ⓑ ⓒ ●

1 laste lastt laust **last**
   ⓐ ⓑ ⓒ ●

2 stil stile **still** sitll
   ⓐ ⓑ ● ⓓ

3 **rub** rab raub rubb
   ● ⓑ ⓒ ⓓ

4 hadn **hand** haned haind
   ⓐ ● ⓒ ⓓ

5 eag **egg** eeg eg
   ⓐ ● ⓒ ⓓ

6 siwm swem **swim** swimm
   ⓐ ⓑ ● ⓓ

7 furm **from** frum frome
   ⓐ ● ⓒ ⓓ

8 **until** entill untill entil
   ● ⓑ ⓒ ⓓ

9 waunt wunt **want** wont
   ⓐ ⓑ ● ⓓ

10 **hold** holde hoold whold
   ● ⓑ ⓒ ⓓ

11 gras grase **grass** garss
   ⓐ ⓑ ● ⓓ

12 steart stert statr **start**
   ⓐ ⓑ ⓒ ●

13 legg liag lege **leg**
   ⓐ ⓑ ⓒ ●

14 spawt spott **spot** spaut
   ⓐ ⓑ ● ⓓ

15 **off** auv ofv auf
   ● ⓑ ⓒ ⓓ

16 paup **pop** popp pawp
   ⓐ ● ⓒ ⓓ

17 gald glaed **glad** gladd
   ⓐ ⓑ ● ⓓ

18 aind adn **and** ad
   ⓐ ⓑ ● ⓓ

19 pell pul puhl **pull**
   ⓐ ⓑ ⓒ ●

20 hawp **hop** hopp hap
   ⓐ ● ⓒ ⓓ

21 fealt falt **felt** fellt
   ⓐ ⓑ ● ⓓ

22 saty stey sta **stay**
   ⓐ ⓑ ⓒ ●

23 halp **help** healp hilp
   ⓐ ● ⓒ ⓓ

24 **fell** fel fehl fele
   ● ⓑ ⓒ ⓓ

Testing ● 5

Bonus Words Test

Name
Test: Units 1–5   UNIT 6 Bonus Words

Mark the circle for the word that is spelled right.

Sample A
A struk strauk **struck** struc
   ⓐ ⓑ ● ⓓ

Sample B
B shopt **shopped** shoped shouped
   ⓐ ● ⓒ ⓓ

1 vally vallie **valley** vallee
   ⓐ ⓑ ● ⓓ

2 spred **spread** spredd spraed
   ⓐ ● ⓒ ⓓ

3 skrub scub skerub **scrub**
   ⓐ ⓑ ⓒ ●

4 dewell dwel drell **dwell**
   ⓐ ⓑ ⓒ ●

5 pumkin **pumpkin** paumkin pumpken
   ⓐ ● ⓒ ⓓ

6 villaje vilage villaje **village**
   ⓐ ⓑ ⓒ ●

7 floke flokc **flock** flauk
   ⓐ ⓑ ● ⓓ

8 **wrapping** repping wraping reping
   ● ⓑ ⓒ ⓓ

9 planit plainet **planet** plannet
   ⓐ ⓑ ● ⓓ

10 skrach scratch skratch scaratch
   ⓐ ● ⓒ ⓓ

11 puding pooding **pudding** poudding
   ⓐ ⓑ ● ⓓ

12 **recess** rescess reesess reccess
   ● ⓑ ⓒ ⓓ

13 incect **insect** inseck inseckt
   ⓐ ● ⓒ ⓓ

14 swift swiftt **swiftt** swieft
   ● ⓑ ⓒ ⓓ

15 berst birst burrst **burst**
   ⓐ ⓑ ⓒ ●

16 stirring **sturring** stiring sturing
   ⓐ ● ⓒ ⓓ

17 foscils fosills **fossills** fossils
   ⓐ ⓑ ⓒ ●

18 blasst balast **blast** blastt
   ⓐ ⓑ ● ⓓ

19 adalt edult **adult** adlult
   ⓐ ⓑ ● ⓓ

20 **pillow** pilloe pilow pellow
   ● ⓑ ⓒ ⓓ

21 smach **smash** samsh smasch
   ⓐ ● ⓒ ⓓ

22 grabed **grabbed** garabed garabbed
   ⓐ ● ⓒ ⓓ

23 **stamp** stemp staump stummp
   ● ⓑ ⓒ ⓓ

24 spilt splet spelit **split**
   ⓐ ⓑ ⓒ ●

6 ● Testing

NOTES

Six-Week Evaluation

Mark the circle for the word that is spelled right.

Sample A

A anothr   unother   another   unothr
ⓐ   ⓑ   ●ⓒ   ⓓ

Sample B

B shine   shyne   shien   shin
ⓐ   ⓑ   ⓒ   ⓓ

---

1 apple   appel   aple   epple
ⓐ   ⓑ   ⓒ   ⓓ

11 waggeng   wagin   wagging   waggin
ⓐ   ⓑ   ⓒ   ⓓ

2 brng   birng   bring   buring
ⓐ   ⓑ   ⓒ   ⓓ

12 planing   plannin   planin   planning
ⓐ   ⓑ   ⓒ   ⓓ

3 elss   else   esle   elce
ⓐ   ⓑ   ⓒ   ⓓ

13 kloz   close   kloze   cloze
ⓐ   ⓑ   ⓒ   ⓓ

4 hut   hunt   hnt   hunnt
ⓐ   ⓑ   ⓒ   ⓓ

14 drawer   drawur   drauer   draur
ⓐ   ⓑ   ⓒ   ⓓ

5 add   adde   ad   aid
ⓐ   ⓑ   ⓒ   ⓓ

15 prit   printe   printt   print
ⓐ   ⓑ   ⓒ   ⓓ

6 spele   spell   spall   spel
ⓐ   ⓑ   ⓒ   ⓓ

16 spary   spuray   spraiy   spray
ⓐ   ⓑ   ⓒ   ⓓ

7 stuf   stuff   stugh   stoff
ⓐ   ⓑ   ⓒ   ⓓ

17 actt   akt   act   axt
ⓐ   ⓑ   ⓒ   ⓓ

8 unlese   unles   unless   unleass
ⓐ   ⓑ   ⓒ   ⓓ

18 build   bild   biuld   biled
ⓐ   ⓑ   ⓒ   ⓓ

9 stepp   steppe   step   stepe
ⓐ   ⓑ   ⓒ   ⓓ

19 ground   grownd   gruond   groun
ⓐ   ⓑ   ⓒ   ⓓ

10 triped   tripped   tript   trippt
ⓐ   ⓑ   ⓒ   ⓓ

20 testt   tesst   text   test
ⓐ   ⓑ   ⓒ   ⓓ

FORM A TEST 1

Administering the Test

1. Tell the children that today they will take a spelling test on some of the words they have studied in Units 1-5. Pass out the test papers. Tell the children to leave them turned upside down until you are ready to begin.

2. Have the children turn their tests over. Direct their attention to Sample A. Read this sentence: *another* Would you like *another* glass of milk? *another* Point out that the test shows four ways to spell *another,* and that only one way is correct. Have them note that circle c under the correct spelling is filled in.

3. Now direct the children's attention to Sample B. Read this sentence: *shine* The sun may *shine* today. *shine* Point out that this test shows four ways to spell *shine.* Ask a child to tell you which spelling is right by spelling the word—*s-h-i-n-e.* Repeat the right spelling, *s-h-i-n-e,* and have the children fill in circle a in pencil.

4. After you have checked to see that all children have completed Sample B correctly, proceed with the test. Use these sentences.

   1. **apple** Erin fed an *apple* to the horse. **apple**
   2. **bring** You must *bring* the book back today. **bring**
   3. **else** Do you want green beans or something *else*? **else**
   4. **hunt** Andy wants to *hunt* for lost treasure. **hunt**
   5. **add** We can *add* four-digit numbers. **add**
   6. **spell** We are learning to *spell* new words. **spell**
   7. **stuff** Todd tried to *stuff* the books into his bag. **stuff**
   8. **unless** You will never do it *unless* you try. **unless**
   9. **step** The dancers must *step* in time with the music. **step**
   10. **tripped** Tess *tripped* over her own shoelaces. **tripped**
   11. **wagging** The puppy's tail is always *wagging*. **wagging**
   12. **planning** We are *planning* to have a party next week. **planning**
   13. **close** Please *close* the window. **close**
   14. **drawer** Marty put the socks in his *drawer*. **drawer**
   15. **print** That big book has very small *print*. **print**
   16. **spray** Use this hose to *spray* water on the plants. **spray**
   17. **act** Sometimes people like to *act* silly. **act**
   18. **build** It took years to *build* that long bridge. **build**
   19. **ground** The *ground* was still damp from the rain. **ground**
   20. **test** Althea studied hard for the *test*. **test**

Evaluating the Results

Use the following **Answer Key** to correct the children's tests and to determine whether they need more practice with particular units. The chart shows the units in which each answer word is taught.

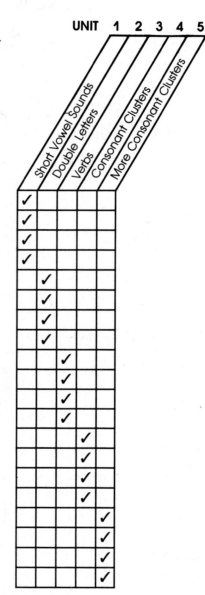

ANSWER KEY

1. a ⓑ ⓒ ⓓ — (a)
2. a ⓑ ⓒ ⓓ — (c)
3. a ⓑ ⓒ ⓓ — (b)
4. a ⓑ ⓒ ⓓ — (b)
5. a ⓑ ⓒ ⓓ — (a)
6. a ⓑ ⓒ ⓓ — (b)
7. a ⓑ ⓒ ⓓ — (b)
8. a ⓑ ⓒ ⓓ — (c)
9. a ⓑ ⓒ ⓓ — (c)
10. a ⓑ ⓒ ⓓ — (b)
11. a ⓑ ⓒ ⓓ — (c)
12. a ⓑ ⓒ ⓓ — (d)
13. a ⓑ ⓒ ⓓ — (b)
14. a ⓑ ⓒ ⓓ — (a)
15. a ⓑ ⓒ ⓓ — (d)
16. a ⓑ ⓒ ⓓ — (d)
17. a ⓑ ⓒ ⓓ — (c)
18. a ⓑ ⓒ ⓓ — (a)
19. a ⓑ ⓒ ⓓ — (a)
20. a ⓑ ⓒ ⓓ — (d)

More Letters Than Sounds

PREVIEWING THE UNIT

Unit Materials

Instruction and Practice

Pupil Book	pages 30–33
Teacher's Edition	
Teaching Plans	pages 30–33
Enrichment Activities	
For the Classroom	page 33A
For the Home	page 33B
Reteaching Strategies	page 33C

Testing

Teacher's Edition	
Trial Test	pages 29E–29F
Unit Test	page 33B
Dictation Test	page 33B

Additional Resources

PRACTICE AND REINFORCEMENT
Extra Practice Master 7: This Week's Words
Extra Practice Master 7: Mastery Words
Extra Practice Master 7: Bonus Words
LEP Practice Master 7
Spelling and Language Master 7
Study Steps to Learn a Word Master

RETEACHING FOLLOW-UP
Reteaching Follow-up Master 7A:
   Discovering Spelling Ideas
Reteaching Follow-up Master 7B:
   Word Shapes
LEP Reteaching Follow-up Master 7

TEACHING AIDS
Spelling Generalizations Transparency 6

Click on the SPELLING banner to find activities for this unit.

Learner Objectives

Spelling

- To spell words that demonstrate these sound-letter relationships: /th/ *th*; /ch/ *ch, tch*; /sh/ *sh*; /ng/ *ng, n*.
- To spell words by supplying the letters for consonant sounds.
- To alphabetize.

Reading

- To recognize the function of guide words in the dictionary.
- To use context clues to complete sentences given spelling words.
- To follow written directions.

Writing

- To write a paragraph.
- To use the writing process.
- To proofread for spelling, capitalization, and punctuation.
- To write legible manuscript and cursive letters.

Listening

- To listen to identify sounds spelled with consonant digraphs.
- To listen to identify the sound /ē/.
- To follow oral directions.

Speaking

- To respond to a question.
- To speak clearly to a group.
- To express feelings and ideas about a piece of writing.
- To present a story.
- To contribute ideas and information in group discussions.

THIS WEEK'S WORDS
another
together
weather
chin
reach
which
teacher
catch
kitchen
shine
shout
crash
strong
angry
hungry

MASTERY WORDS
father
each
lunch
shut
push
sing

BONUS WORDS
clothing
fresh
gather
pitcher
porch
rather
shack
whether

Assignment Guide

This guide shows how you teach a typical spelling unit in either a five-day or a three-day sequence, while providing for individual differences. **Boldface type** indicates essential classwork. Steps shown in light type may be done in class or assigned as homework.

Five Days	● = average spellers ★ = better spellers ✓ = slower spellers	Three Days
Day **1** ▶a	● ★ **Take This Week's Words Trial Test and correct** ● ✓ **Take Mastery Word Trial Test and correct** ● ★ **Read This Week's Words and discuss generalization page 30**	Day **1**
Day **2** ◀b	● Complete Spelling Practice page 31 ● ✓ Complete Extra Practice Master 7: This Week's Words (optional) ✓ Complete Spelling on Your Own: Mastery Words page 33 ★ **Take Bonus Word Trial Test and correct**	
Day **3** ▶c	● ★ ✓ **Complete Spelling and Language page 32** ● ★ ✓ Complete Writing on Your Own page 32 ● ★ ✓ **Complete Using the Dictionary to Spell and Write page 32** ● ✓ Take Midweek Test (optional) ★ Complete Spelling on Your Own: Bonus Words page 33 ● ✓ Complete Spelling and Language Master 7 (optional)	Day **2**
Day **4** ◀d	● Complete Spelling on Your Own: This Week's Words page 33 ✓ Complete Extra Practice Master 7: Mastery Words (optional) ★ Complete Extra Practice Master 7: Bonus Words (optional)	
Day **5** ▶e	● **Take Unit Test on This Week's Words** ● Complete Reteaching Follow-up Masters 7A and 7B (optional) ● ✓ **Take Unit Test on Mastery Words** ★ **Take Unit Test on Bonus Words**	Day **3**

Enrichment Activities for the **classroom** and for the **home** included at the end of this unit may be assigned selectively on any day of the week.

INTRODUCING THE UNIT

Establish Readiness for Learning

Tell children that this week they will continue to study consonant sounds. In Unit 7, they will be learning about consonant digraphs. Explain that consonant digraphs are two consonants that, together, have a single sound that is different from the sound of either consonant. Tell the children that they will apply what they learn about the digraphs *th, ch, sh,* and *ng* to This Week's Words and will use those words to write a paragraph.

Assess Children's Spelling Ability

Administer the Trial Test before the children study This Week's Words. Use the test sentences provided. Say each word and use it in a sentence. Then repeat the word. Have the children write the words on a separate sheet of paper or in their spelling notebooks. Test

sentences are also provided for Mastery and Bonus words.

Have the children check their own work by listening to you read the spelling of the words or by referring to This Week's Words in the left column of the **Pupil Book.** For each misspelled word, have the children follow the **Study Steps to Learn a Word** on page 1 in the **Pupil Book** or use the copying master to study and write the words. Children should record the number correct on their **Progress Report.**

Trial Test Sentences

This Week's Words
1. *another* Emily would like *another* sandwich. *another*
2. *together* Todd and Missy walk to school *together*. *together*
3. *weather* The *weather* is getting colder. *weather*
4. *chin* Molly bumped her *chin.* *chin*

FOCUS
- Establishes objectives
- Relates to prior learning
- Sets purpose of instruction

5. **reach** Henry cannot *reach* the top shelf. **reach**
6. **which** Rosa cannot decide *which* book to read. **which**
7. **teacher** The *teacher* marked the papers. **teacher**
8. **catch** Irene can *catch* a fish. **catch**
9. **kitchen** Dad is cooking in the *kitchen.* **kitchen**
10. **shine** George will *shine* his shoes. **shine**
11. **shout** Do not *shout* in the halls. **shout**
12. **crash** The dish fell with a *crash.* **crash**
13. **strong** An elephant is a *strong* animal. **strong**
14. **angry** Margo is *angry* with her friend. **angry**
15. **hungry** You will be *hungry* if you skip breakfast. **hungry**

Mastery Words

1. **father** My *father* took us fishing. **father**
2. **each** The clown gave a balloon to *each* child. **each**
3. **lunch** Paula had soup for *lunch.* **lunch**
4. **shut** Please *shut* the front door. **shut**
5. **push** When you are in line, don't *push.* **push**
6. **sing** Our class will *sing* at the P.T.A. meeting. **sing**

Bonus Words

1. **clothing** It is cold out, so wear warm *clothing.* **clothing**
2. **fresh** These tomatoes are *fresh.* **fresh**
3. **gather** We will *gather* up all the toys. **gather**
4. **pitcher** Kathy made a *pitcher* of iced tea. **pitcher**

5. **porch** Grandma is sitting on the *porch.* **porch**
6. **rather** I would *rather* play. **rather**
7. **shack** We keep tools in a *shack* in the backyard. **shack**
8. **whether** Vera is deciding *whether* or not to come with us. **whether**

Apply Prior Learning

Tell children that they can discover spelling generalizations by applying what they already know about consonant sounds. Use the following activity. Write the words *shore, crush,* and *washer* on the chalkboard. Read each word to the children and ask them to identify what is the same about each of the words. (Each word contains the sound /sh/.) Then ask the children to add other words to the list. Have them draw conclusions about how the sound /sh/ is spelled and where it may occur in a word. (The sound /sh/ is spelled *sh* and may occur at the beginning, in the middle, or at the end of a word.)

Repeat the procedure for the sounds /th/*th*, /ch/*ch*, *tch*, and /ng/*ng*, *n* using the following words:

/th/*th* – the, feather
/ch/*ch, tch* – check, watch, reach
/ng/*ng* – long, finger

Tell the children that they will study words that have these sounds spelled with more than one letter. Explain that they can use these words in a variety of writing tasks; they can use the words in a letter, in a science report, or to complete a social studies assignment.

FOR CHILDREN WITH SPECIAL NEEDS

Learning Difficulties

Visual-motor manipulatives are effective teaching tools for children with visual-memory deficits. Having children make these manipulatives helps them become aware of the components of words as they construct the materials.

Guide the child as he or she makes square "tiles" on which this week's digraphs will be written. Draw lines on a sheet of construction paper to divide it into twenty-six 2-inch squares. Make the number of tiles with each digraph equal to the number of This Week's Words that have that digraph.

Write This Week's Words on pieces of paper, omitting the digraph and leaving enough space for the "tiles" to be inserted. An example follows.

Tile	Word	Tile	Word
sh	ine	tch	ki en

Ask the child to select the "tile" that will complete each word and place it in the space on the word card. After you have checked for accuracy, have the child copy each word, placing all words with the same digraph in one list.

Save the "tiles" and cards in an envelope labeled "Consonant Digraphs" so the child can use the activity independently at another time.

Limited English Proficiency

To help limited English proficient children work with the spelling generalizations for Unit 7, you may wish to refer to the booklet "Suggestions and Activities for Limited English Proficient Students."

TEACHING PLAN

Objective To spell words that demonstrate these sound-letter relationships: /ŧħ/*th*, /ch/*ch, tch*, /sh/*sh*, /ng/*ng, n*.

1. Write these sets of words on the chalkboard:

ten	care	seat	ran
hen	hair	heat	rag
then	chair	sheet	rang

Have a volunteer say the first set of words. Point out that the three words are the same except for the beginning consonant sound. Then help the children recognize that /ŧħ/ is a distinct sound and quite different from the sounds /t/ and /h/. Follow a similar procedure for the other sets of words, making certain that the children recognize that the sounds of the words are the same except for the first or last sound. Help them to recognize each time that the sound represented by the consonant digraph is different from the sounds of the two separate letters.

2. Read the generalization on page 30 aloud. Encourage the children to remember the sentence "That child should sing" to help them identify the consonant sounds that are spelled with more than one letter.

You may wish to introduce the lesson by using **Spelling Generalizations Transparency 6.**

3. Have volunteers read This Week's Words aloud. As each word is read, ask the children to identify the letters that spell /ŧħ/, /ch/, /sh/, or /ng/ in the word. Point out that in *angry* and *hungry* you can hear the sound /g/. Explain that in these words, the sound /ng/ is represented by *n* alone.

You may wish to assign **LEP Practice Master 7** for reinforcement in writing spelling words.

---

7 More Letters Than Sounds

THIS WEEK'S WORDS

1. another
2. together
3. weather
4. chin
5. reach
6. which
7. teacher
8. catch
9. kitchen
10. shine
11. shout
12. crash
13. strong
14. angry
15. hungry

That child should sing.

This Week's Words

The words this week have consonant sounds that are spelled with more than one letter. You hear those sounds in this sentence.

/ŧħ/   /ch/   /sh/   /ng/
That child should sing.

● The first sound in <u>that</u> is spelled **th**.

another

● The first sound in <u>child</u> is spelled **ch** or **tch**.

chin   reach   catch

● The first sound in <u>should</u> is spelled **sh**.

shine   crash

● The last sound in <u>sing</u> is spelled **ng** or **n**.

strong   angry

30

Extra Practice: This Week's Words

Name
Extra Practice   This Week's Words   UNIT 7

Each of the words below has two or three letters that are underlined. Under each word, write This Week's Words that are spelled with the same letters.

this	**ring**
another	angry
weather	strong
together	hungry

fish	**pitch**
crash	kitchen
shout	catch
shine	

chair	
which	
reach	
chin	
teacher	

another	crash	kitchen
which	weather	angry
shout	catch	reach
together	strong	shine
teacher	chin	hungry

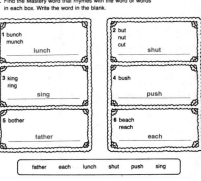

Extra Practice ● 27

Extra Practice: Mastery Words

Name
Extra Practice   Mastery Words   UNIT 7

A. Choose the Mastery words that have the letter pairs *ch, sh, th,* or *ng*. Write each Mastery word under the right letter pair.

ch	**sh**
each	shut
lunch	push

th	**ng**
father	sing

B. Find the Mastery word that rhymes with the word or words in each box. Write the word in the blank.

1 bunch munch	2 but nut cut
lunch	shut

3 king ring	4 bush
sing	push

5 bother	6 beach reach
father	each

| father | each | lunch | shut | push | sing |

28 ● Extra Practice

Spelling Practice

A. Finish the sentences. Use This Week's Words that have /ch/.

1. Nicole ran to the _____kitchen_____ to get a snack.

2. She had to _____catch_____ her bus in five minutes.

3. She didn't know _____which_____ fruit to take.

4. She remembered her _____teacher_____ said apples were a good snack.

5. She stood on her tiptoes to _____reach_____ the fruit.

6. An apple fell, hitting her nose and _____chin_____

B. Follow the directions. Use This Week's Words.

7. Write the two words that begin with consonant clusters.

_____crash_____   _____strong_____

8. Write the four words that end with <u>er</u>. Then draw a line under the two consonant letters that stand for one sound in each word.

_____ano<u>th</u>er_____   _____toge<u>th</u>er_____

_____wea<u>th</u>er_____   _____tea<u>ch</u>er_____

9. Write the two words that end with the long <u>e</u> sound.

_____angry_____   _____hungry_____

10. Write the word that sounds like <u>witch</u>.

_____which_____

C. Write This Week's Words that go with these words. Use words that start with /sh/.

11. Don't _____shout_____! **12.** Rise and _____shine_____!

This Week's Words (handwritten):
another
together
weather
chin
reach
which
teacher
catch
kitchen
shine
shout
crash
strong
angry
hungry

31

Summarize Learning

Have the children summarize what they have learned on pages 30 and 31. *Ask:*

- What consonant sounds did you learn in this lesson? (/th/, /sh/, /ch/, /ng/)

- What did you learn about these sounds? (They may occur at the beginning, middle, or end of a word; they are spelled as follows: th, sh, ch, tch, ng, and n.)

- What are examples of words containing the sounds /sh/, /th/, /ch/, and /ng/ in different places? (shine, crash, another, chin, reach, kitchen, strong, angry; accept other examples)

TEACHING PLAN

Objectives To write words with given consonant sounds; to recognize initial consonant clusters; to write words with given vowel sounds; to write a homophone; to write words given context clues.

1. Briefly discuss the directions on page 31. Remind the children that a consonant cluster is two or three letters written together that stand for two or three sounds that are said together. Be certain that the children can identify the sound /ē/; if necessary, define /ē/ as the vowel sound heard at the end of *tree* and *happy*.

2. Have the children complete the exercises independently. Remind them to use legible handwriting. You may wish to demonstrate the correct form of the letters *th, ch, tch, sh,* and *ng* and then have the children practice writing the letters. For **Handwriting Models,** refer the children to page 258 in the **Pupil Book.**

3. To correct the children's work, have volunteers write their answers on the chalkboard. Let the children check their own work.

For reinforcement in writing spelling words, you may wish to assign *Extra Practice Master 7: This Week's Words.*

⭐ *of special interest*

The consonant digraphs *ch, sh,* and *th* are relatively late additions to the English orthography. Before the Norman Conquest, the sound /ch/ was written c, as in *cild,* "child"; the sound /sh/ was written *sc,* as in *scal,* "shall"; and the sounds /th/ and /th/ were written with þ (*thorn*) and ð (*edh*). *Thorn* and *edh* were both used somewhat indiscriminately to represent unvoiced and voiced *th*.

TEACHING PLAN

SPELLING AND LANGUAGE

Objective To write words in sentence order.

1. Read the directions on page 32 aloud. Remind the children to look for the capitalized word and the word with a period to find out how the sentence begins and ends.
2. Ask a child to read the first group of words in the correct order.
3. Have the children complete the activity independently.
4. Have volunteers write the sentences on the chalkboard. Let the children check their own work.

For extended practice in writing words in sentence order, you may wish to assign *Spelling and Language Master 7.*

WRITING ON YOUR OWN

Objectives To write a paragraph; to proofread for spelling.

1. Review the directions.
2. As a **prewriting** activity, have the children generate a list of details that appear in the picture. Help the children formulate a main idea sentence. Then have them **compose** their paragraphs. When they are ready to **revise**, remind the children to check for spelling. To **publish** the children's work, have them compile their paragraphs into a booklet.

USING THE DICTIONARY

Objectives To recognize the function of guide words; to write words that come between two given words in alphabetical order.

1. Read and discuss the introductory paragraph on page 32.
2. Ask the children to look up *shine* in the **Spelling Dictionary** and to tell you the guide words that appear

on the page. (secret—should) Then ask them to tell you if *shout* is on this page. (no)
3. Read the directions on page 32. Remind the children to look for words that come after the first word and before the second word in alphabetical order.
4. Have the children complete the activity independently.
5. To correct the children's work, have volunteers read the words aloud. Let the children check their own work.

THIS WEEK'S WORDS

another
together
weather
chin
reach
which
teacher
catch
kitchen
shine
shout
crash
strong
angry
hungry

32

Spelling and Language • Writing Sentences

Write the words in order so they make a sentence. Remember that a sentence begins with a capital letter and ends with a period.

1. kitchen - went for I the sandwich. to a

   I went to the kitchen for a sandwich.

2. peanut could the butter reach jar. I not

   I could not reach the peanut butter jar.

Writing on Your Own

Write a paragraph for your teacher telling about the picture on page 30. Use as many of This Week's Words as you can.

THESAURUS For help finding descriptive words, turn to page 203.

Using the Dictionary to Spell and Write

Guide words help you find a word quickly if you need to check its spelling or meaning. There are two **guide words** at the top of each dictionary page. The word on the left is the first word on the page. The word on the right is the last word. All the other words on the page are in alphabetical order between those words.

ear	everyday
ear[1] /ir/ *n.* What people and animals use for hearing. **ear**[2] /ir/ *n.* Where grain grows on	—*v.* **emptied, emptying** To make empty: Ben *emptied* his pockets. **en·e·my** /en'ə-mē/ *n., pl.* **enemies** A

Here are two pairs of guide words. Write two of This Week's Words that would be on each page.

1. all   apple   ___angry___   ___another___

2. cent   day   ___chin___   ___crash___

Extra Practice: Spelling and Language

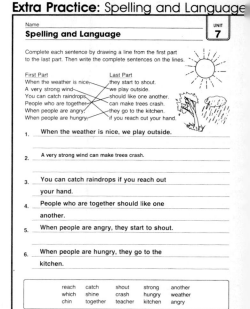

Name _____
Spelling and Language   UNIT **7**

Complete each sentence by drawing a line from the first part to the last part. Then write the complete sentences on the lines.

First Part | Last Part
When the weather is nice, | they start to shout.
A very strong wind | we play outside.
You can catch raindrops | should like one another.
People who are together | can make trees crash.
When people are angry, | they go to the kitchen.
When people are hungry, | if you reach out your hand.

1. When the weather is nice, we play outside.
2. A very strong wind can make trees crash.
3. You can catch raindrops if you reach out your hand.
4. People who are together should like one another.
5. When people are angry, they start to shout.
6. When people are hungry, they go to the kitchen.

reach	catch	shout	strong	another
which	shine	crash	hungry	weather
chin	together	teacher	kitchen	angry

30 • Extra Practice

Spelling on Your Own

THIS WEEK'S WORDS

Letters that spell a consonant sound are missing from each of This Week's Words. Add the missing letters. Write the whole word.

1. stro___
2. whi___
3. toge___er
4. cra___
5. ___ine
6. rea___
7. hu___gry
8. ki___en
9. ___out
10. a___gry
11. ___in
12. wea___er
13. ano___er
14. tea___er
15. ca___   See answers below.

MASTERY WORDS

Follow the directions. Use the Mastery words.

father
each
lunch
shut
push
sing

1. Write the two words that end with /ch/.

    each   lunch

2. Write two words. One ends the way the other begins.

    push   shut

Write Mastery words to go with these words.

3. __lunch__ and dinner 4. mother and __father__

5. __sing__ and dance 6. __each__ and every

BONUS WORDS

clothing
fresh
gather
pitcher
porch
rather
shack
whether

1. Write the Bonus word that sounds like <u>weather</u>.
2. Write the two words that rhyme.
3. Write the two words that begin with a consonant cluster.
4. Write the word that can name someone who throws a ball or something that holds milk. Write a sentence that uses both meanings.
5. Write sentences about a farm. Try to use all the Bonus words.

See answers below.

33

Spelling on Your Own Answers

THIS WEEK'S WORDS

1. ng strong 2. ch which 3. th together 4. sh crash 5. sh shine 6. ch reach 7. n hungry 8. tch kitchen 9. sh shout 10. n angry 11. ch chin 12. th weather 13. th another 14. ch teacher 15. tch catch

BONUS WORDS

1. whether 2. gather, rather 3. clothing, fresh 4. pitcher EXAMPLE: The baseball <u>pitcher</u> drank a <u>pitcher</u> of milk. 5. Children will write as directed. Be sure to check spelling.

Summarize Learning

Have the children summarize what they have learned in this unit. *Ask:*

- What have you learned about writing words in sentence order? (The words must express a complete thought. A capital letter belongs at the beginning. A period belongs at the end.)
- What have you learned about guide words in the dictionary? (There are two guide words at the top of each dictionary page. The word on the left is the first word on the page and the word on the right is the last word on the page.)
- What spelling generalizations have you learned? How did you use them?

TEACHING PLAN

Objective To apply the unit spelling generalization to spell This Week's Words, Mastery words, and Bonus words independently.

THIS WEEK'S WORDS

1. Read the directions on page 33 aloud. Help the children get started by completing the first two words with them orally.
2. Have the children complete the activity independently.
3. To correct the children's work, have volunteers write the words on the chalkboard. Ask the children to exchange papers to check the work.

MASTERY WORDS

1. Review the sounds /th/, /ch/, /sh/, and /ng/, using the sentence "That child should sing." Then read each Mastery word, having the children repeat the word and identify the two letters that spell one sound.
2. Read the directions on page 33 aloud.
3. Have the children complete the activities independently.

BONUS WORDS

1. Briefly review the unit generalization on page 30.
2. Have volunteers read the Bonus words aloud. Have the children look up the meanings of any unfamiliar words in the **Spelling Dictionary.**
3. Ask volunteers to make up oral sentences.
4. Have the children complete the exercises independently on a separate piece of paper.

For reinforcement in writing spelling words, you may wish to assign *Extra Practice Master 7: Mastery Words* or *Bonus Words.*

CLOSING THE UNIT

Apply New Learning

Tell the children that if they misspell words with consonant digraphs in their writing, they should use one or more of the following strategies:

- think of words that rhyme, and compare in their minds how they are spelled.
- pronounce the word very carefully to see that the correct letters have been used to spell the sounds in the word.

Transfer New Learning

Tell children that when they encounter new words in their personal reading and in other content areas, they should learn the meaning of those words and then apply the generalizations they have studied to the spelling of those words. Tell them that once the words are familiar in both meaning and spelling, they should use the new words in their writing.

ENRICHMENT ACTIVITIES

Classroom activities and **home activities** may be assigned to children of all ability levels. The activities provide opportunities for children to use their spelling words in new contexts.

For the Classroom

To individualize classroom activities, you may have the children use the word list they are studying in this unit.

- *Basic:* Use **Mastery** words to complete the activity.
- *Average:* Use **This Week's Words** to complete the activity.
- *Challenging:* Use **Bonus** words to complete this activity.

1. **Language Arts/Writing a Commercial** Have each child write a short commercial. Each child should think of an imaginary product that some of the words on the spelling list could help describe. Have each child make up a name for the product and then write two or three sentences to "sell" it to classrooms. Have them use at least three spelling words. For example: "SMILE-O—It makes people like one *another* when they are *angry*. Don't *shout*—use SMILE-O!" Have the children read five commercials aloud. Introduce each child by saying, "And now, a word from our sponsor."

■ COOPERATIVE LEARNING: Have each group create a commercial. First the group should collaborate to make up and name an imaginary product that could be described using spelling words. Then each child should write two or three sentences praising the product, using at least one spelling word in each sentence. The group should then agree on which sentences to use in the final commercial. One child should write down the final version. The group should check to be sure the handwriting is legible and the words are correctly spelled. Another

child should be chosen as "announcer" to read the commercial aloud to the class.

2. **Language Arts/Writing Fact and Opinion Sentences** Have the children use four of the spelling words to write four pairs of fact and opinion sentences. Explain that a fact is a statement that can be proven; an opinion is a statement about what one person thinks. Have them exchange papers with a classmate, label each sentence *Fact or Opinion,* and see if the classmate agrees.

■ COOPERATIVE LEARNING: Have each group write three pairs of facts and opinion sentences. Each child should use one spelling word twice, once in a statement of fact, once to state an opinion. Group members should read each other's statements to check whether each pair actually gives one fact and one opinion. The group should discuss their judgments. Then each group member should copy his or her statements onto clean paper without identifying them as fact or opinion, and the papers should be distributed for other children to identify.

3. **Language Arts/Writing a Story** Have each child use the spelling words to write a story. As a **prewriting** activity, have the children first read about the structure of a story on page 252 of the **Writer's Guide.** Then have the children review the spelling lists in search of nouns, verbs, and other words that might contribute to an interesting story. Tell the children to write down some story ideas, and choose the one that they like best. Have the children make a chart with the following headings: *Character(s), Setting,* and *Plot.* Tell the children to list a few details under the appropriate heading. Under *Plot,* have the children list the problem and the steps the character will take to solve it. Then have them use the chart to **compose** the story. Remind the children to use as many spelling words as possible. Then have the children **revise** the story, making sure it has a clear beginning, middle, and ending. Remind the children to proofread for spelling, capitalization, and punctuation errors and to use the **Revising Checklist** on page 247 for help. Then have them give the story a title. **Publish** the children's work in a class booklet or bulletin-board display.

■ COOPERATIVE LEARNING: Have each group write a story using as many spelling words as possible. As a **prewriting** activity, have the group make a chart with the headings *Character(s), Setting,* and *Plot.* Tell each member to list details about each story element. When the children are ready to **compose,** tell them to select one child to begin the story orally by introducing the main character. Another child should describe the setting, and a third, the problem. Have children continue contributing sentences until the story has reached a natural conclusion. The group should select one member to record the story draft and another, the final version. Group members should **revise** the story by checking for a clear beginning, middle, and ending. Each group should **publish** their story by having a group member read it to the class.

For the Home

Children may complete these activities independently or with the assistance of a relative or friend in the home.

1. **Language Arts/Writing Words with Digraph Spellings** Have the children build words with *ng, tch, th, sh,* and *ch.* Tell the children to identify the digraphs in *another, chin, crash, catch,* and *strong* and then write two new words containing each digraph. Then have them write a paragraph containing five of the new words. The children may ask a friend or family member to contribute words to the lists.

2. **Language Arts/Writing a News Report** Tell the children to use some of the spelling words to write a news report about something exciting that happened. Before writing, the children may wish to go over some news items in a newspaper with a relative. When the children are finished writing the news report, they should check their work for correct spelling, punctuation, and capitalization, using the **Revising Checklist** on page 247. The children may add a catchy headline that sums up the report in only a few words. Ask the children to look for and underline any words in the report containing the digraphs *sh, ch, tch, th,* and *ng.* The children may read the news stories to a friend or relative.

3. **Science/Writing a Weather Report** Tell the children to make a word map to enrich the concept of *weather.* Remind them that they must write the concept word in the center and circle it. Then they must write related words around that central word, and draw lines from the central word to the words to which it is related. A word map developing the concept of weather will use words that tell all about possible kinds of weather. The children should use some of the words from the word map to write a weather report. Have the children proofread their work for spelling, then show it to a family member or friend.

4. **Health/Writing Sentences** Tell the children to use several of the spelling words to write tips for keeping healthy. Suggest that health tips can pertain to such topics as healthy snacks, clothing suitable for different weather conditions, and accident prevention. Tell the children to check for spelling, capitalization, and punctuation. Children may ask a friend or relative to add to their list of health tips.

EVALUATING SPELLING ABILITY

Unit Test

This Week's Words

1. **another** My aunt lives in *another* town. **another**
2. **together** They may work *together.* **together**
3. **weather** If the *weather* is rainy, we will stay inside. **weather**
4. **chin** Uncle Mark has a beard on his *chin.* **chin**
5. **reach** George will *reach* the finish line first. **reach**

6. **which** I don't know *which* bus goes downtown. **which**
7. **teacher** The *teacher* read the class a story. **teacher**
8. **catch** Laura ran to *catch* the ball. **catch**
9. **kitchen** The bread was in the *kitchen.* **kitchen.**
10. **shine** The sun does not *shine* at night. **shine**
11. **shout** Everyone started to *shout* when our team won. **shout**
12. **crash** No one was hurt in the car *crash.* **crash**
13. **strong** Onions have a *strong* smell. **strong**
14. **angry** Frank counts to ten when he is *angry.* **angry**
15. **hungry** Playing all day makes you *hungry.* **hungry**

Mastery Words

1. **father** Grandpa Kelly is Mom's *father.* **father**
2. **each** We need to feed *each* kitten. **each**
3. **lunch** We eat *lunch* at school. **lunch**
4. **shut** Please *shut* off the TV. **shut**
5. **push** You must *push* hard to open the door. **push**
6. **sing** Kevin can *sing* many songs. **sing**

Bonus Words

1. **clothing** Bibi found a suitcase of old *clothing.* **clothing**
2. **fresh** We had *fresh* strawberries. **fresh**
3. **gather** Children always *gather* around the clown. **gather**
4. **pitcher** The *pitcher* threw the ball. **pitcher**
5. **porch** Everyone helped paint the front *porch.* **porch**
6. **rather** Ron would *rather* not help. **rather**
7. **shack** There is a small *shack* near the pond. **shack**
8. **whether** Julie cannot decide *whether* she likes camp or not. **whether**

Dictation Sentences

This Week's Words

1. The *teacher* did not *reach* to *catch another* ball.
2. The *hungry* cats are all in the *kitchen together.*
3. I did not know *which* doctor to call when I hurt my *chin.*
4. The *strong* spring sun will *shine* after the winter *weather.*
5. I saw the car *crash* and the *angry* man *shout.*

Mastery Words

1. My *father* likes to *sing* when he fixes *lunch.*
2. I will *push each* door *shut.*

Bonus Words

1. We will *gather fresh* apples and store them in the *shack.*
2. Would you *rather* drink milk from the *pitcher* on the *porch?*
3. I do not know *whether* I like this new *clothing.*

RETEACHING STRATEGIES FOR SPELLING

Children who have made errors on the Unit Test may require reteaching. Use the following **Reteaching Strategies** and **Follow-up Masters 7A** and **7B** for additional instruction and practice of This Week's Words. (You may wish to assign **LEP Reteaching Follow-up Master 7** for reteaching of spelling words.)

A. Discovering Spelling Ideas

1. Say the following words as you write them on the chalkboard.

   there   chill   match   sharp   long

2. Ask the children to identify the consonant sounds they hear that are spelled with more than one letter. (/th/, /ch/, /sh/, and /ng/)
3. Ask the children to identify how the consonant sounds /th/, /ch/, /sh/ and /ng/ are spelled in the words. *(th, ch, tch, sh, ng)* Point out that /ng/ can also be spelled *n* as in *anger.*
4. Ask the children what they have learned about the spellings of those words. (All the consonant sounds are spelled with more than one letter. The sound /th/ is spelled *th,* the sound /ch/ is spelled *ch* or *tch,* the sound /sh/ is spelled *sh,* and the sound /ng/ is spelled *ng.* It can also be spelled *n.*)

B. Word Shapes

1. Explain to the children that each word has a shape and that remembering the shape of a word can help them to spell the word correctly.
2. On the chalkboard, write the words *brother* and *ship.* Have the children identify "short," "tall," and "tail" letters.
3. Draw the configuration of each word on the chalkboard, and ask the children which word fits in each shape.

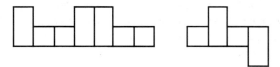

Use **Reteaching Follow-up Master 7A** to reinforce spelling generalizations taught in Unit 7.

Use **Reteaching Follow-up Master 7B** to reinforce spellings of This Week's Words for Unit 7.

Name				UNIT 7
Reteaching Follow-up A			Discovering Spelling Ideas	

THIS WEEK'S WORDS

another   reach   teacher   catch   shout
strong   together   chin   weather   which
kitchen   shine   crash   hungry   angry

1. Study This Week's Words. Say each word to yourself.

2. Write the words that use the same letters as *there* to spell the sound /th/.

   another   together   weather

3. Write the words that use the same letters as *chair* or *match* to spell the sound /ch/.

   chin   reach   which
   teacher   catch   kitchen

4. Write the words that use the same letters as *ship* to spell the sound /sh/.

   shine   shout   crash

5. Write the words that use the same letters as *long* or *anger* to spell the sound /ng/.

   strong   angry   hungry

6. What do the words have in common?

   They all have consonant sounds that are spelled with more than one letter.

   Reteaching • 11

Name				UNIT 7
Reteaching Follow-up B			Word Shapes	

THIS WEEK'S WORDS

another   reach   teacher   catch   shout
strong   together   chin   weather   which
kitchen   shine   crash   hungry   angry

Write each of This Week's Words in its correct shape. The first one has been done for you.   Children may interchange answers that fit the same configuration.

1. s t r o n g   2. s h i n e
3. w h i c h   4. s h o u t
5. c r a s h   6. k i t c h e n
7. t e a c h e r   8. r e a c h
9. a n o t h e r   10. c a t c h
11. h u n g r y   12. a n g r y
13. t o g e t h e r   14. w e a t h e r
15. c h i n

12 • Reteaching

PREVIEWING THE UNIT

Unit Materials

Instruction and Practice

Pupil Book   pages 34–37
Teacher's Edition
   Teaching Plans   pages 34–37
   Enrichment Activities
      For the Classroom   pages 37A–37B
      For the Home   page 37B
   Reteaching Strategies   page 37C

Testing

Teacher's Edition
   Trial Test   pages 33E–33F
   Unit Test   page 37B
   Dictation Test   page 37B

Additional Resources

PRACTICE AND REINFORCEMENT
Extra Practice Master 8: This Week's Words
Extra Practice Master 8: Mastery Words
Extra Practice Master 8: Bonus Words
LEP Practice Master 8
Spelling and Language Master 8
Study Steps to Learn a Word Master

RETEACHING FOLLOW-UP
Reteaching Follow-up Master 8A:
   Discovering Spelling Ideas
Reteaching Follow-up Master 8B: Word
   Shapes
LEP Reteaching Follow-up Master 8

TEACHING AIDS
Spelling Generalizations Transparency 7

Visit our Web site
http://www.hbschool.com

Click on the SPELLING banner to find activities for this unit.

Learner Objectives

Spelling

- To spell plural nouns formed by adding *s* and *es.*

Reading

- To follow written directions.
- To read a friendly letter.
- To use context clues to complete sentences, given spelling words.

Writing

- To write a friendly letter.
- To use the writing process.
- To proofread for spelling, capitalization, and punctuation.
- To write legible manuscript and cursive letters.

Listening

- To listen for vowel sounds in words.
- To follow oral directions.

Speaking

- To contribute ideas and information in group discussions.
- To respond to questions.
- To express feelings and ideas about a piece of writing.
- To present a report to the class.

THIS WEEK'S WORDS

paths
desks
lists
fingers
robins
pictures
uncles
circuses
guesses
classes
bushes
churches
inches
ranches
beaches

MASTERY WORDS

dishes
ducks
glasses
lights
paws
wishes

BONUS WORDS

bandages
branches
headaches
parents
patches
peaches
pickles
sandwiches

Assignment Guide

This guide shows how you teach a typical spelling unit in either a five-day or a three-day sequence, while providing for individual differences. **Boldface type** indicates essential classwork. Steps shown in light type may be done in class or assigned as homework.

Five Days	● = average spellers ★ = better spellers ✓ = slower spellers	Three Days
Day **1**	● ★ **Take This Week's Words Trial Test and correct** ● ✓ **Take Mastery Word Trial Test and correct** ● ★ **Read This Week's Words and discuss generalization on page 34**	Day **1**
Day **2**	● Complete Spelling Practice page 35 ● ✓ Complete Extra Practice Master 8: This Week's Words (optional) ✓ Complete Spelling on Your Own: Mastery words page 37 ★ **Take Bonus Word Trial Test and correct**	Day **1**
Day **3**	● ★ ✓ **Complete Spelling and Language page 36** ● ★ ✓ Complete Writing on Your Own page 36 ● ✓ Take Midweek Test (optional) ★ Complete Spelling on Your Own: Bonus Words page 37 ● ✓ Complete Spelling and Language Master 8 (optional)	Day **2**
Day **4**	● Complete Spelling on Your Own: This Week's Words page 37 ✓ Complete Extra Practice Master 8: Mastery Words (optional) ★ Complete Extra Practice Master 8: Bonus Words (optional)	Day **2**
Day **5**	● Take Unit Test on This Week's Words ● Complete Reteaching Follow-up Masters 8A and 8B (optional) ● ✓ **Take Unit Test on Mastery Words** ★ **Take Unit Test on Bonus Words**	Day **3**

Enrichment Activities for the **classroom** and for the **home** included at the end of this unit may be assigned selectively on any day of the week.

INTRODUCING THE UNIT

Establish Readiness for Learning

Tell the children that this week they will learn a spelling generalization that will help them to know when to add *s* or *es* to words to make them plural. Tell them that they will apply this spelling generalization to This Week's Words and use those words to write a friendly letter.

Assess Children's Spelling Ability

Administer the Trial Test before the children study This Week's Words. Use the test sentences provided. Say each word and use it in a sentence. Then repeat the word. Have the children write the words on a separate sheet of paper or in their spelling notebooks. Test sentences are also provided for Mastery and Bonus words.

Have the children check their own work by listening to you read the spelling of the words or by referring to This Week's Words in the left column of the **Pupil Book.** For each misspelled word, have the children follow the **Study Steps to Learn a Word** on page 1 in the **Pupil Book** or use the copying master to study and write the words. Children should record the number correct on their **Progress Report.**

Trial Test Sentences

This Week's Words

1. *paths* The two *paths* lead in different directions. *paths*
2. *desks* Mrs. Thompson asked the children to put their *desks* in a circle. *desks*
3. *lists* People take shopping *lists* to the supermarket. *lists*
4. *fingers* The little child counted on his *fingers.* *fingers*
5. *robins* There were many *robins* in our yard this morning. *robins*
6. *pictures* Holly showed us *pictures* of her cat. *pictures*

7. *uncles*   Melissa has two aunts and two uncles.   **uncles**

8. *circuses*   Randy loves carnivals and circuses.   **circuses**

9. *guesses*   I will give you three *guesses*.   **guesses**

10. *classes*   Three *classes* went to the museum today.   **classes**

11. *bushes*   The dog was hiding in the bushes.   **bushes**

12. *churches*   My mother likes to visit old churches.   **churches**

13. *inches*   The book is eight *inches* wide.   **inches**

14. *ranches*   There are cattle *ranches* in Texas.   **ranches**

15. *beaches*   There are three *beaches* near our town.   **beaches**

Mastery Words

1. *dishes*   Mark and Deb will wash the dishes.   **dishes**

2. *ducks*   Ten *ducks* were swimming in the pond.   **ducks**

3. *glasses*   The *glasses* are in the cabinet.   **glasses**

4. *lights*   Martha turned off the *lights*.   **lights**

5. *paws*   A dog has four *paws*.   **paws**

6. *wishes*   The princess had three *wishes*.   **wishes**

Bonus Words

1. *bandages*   Carmen has *bandages* on both of her knees.   **bandages**

2. *branches*   There was snow on the *branches* of the tree.   **branches**

3. *headaches*   Joe had a lot of *headaches* before he got his glasses.   **headaches**

4. *parents*   Peggy's *parents* bought a new car.   **parents**

5. *patches*   Karen has colorful *patches* on her jacket.   **patches**

6. *peaches*   We ate sliced *peaches* for dessert.   **peaches**

7. *pickles*   Tom bought a jar of *pickles*.   **pickles**

8. *sandwiches*   Eva brought peanut butter sandwiches.   **sandwiches**

Apply Prior Learning

Have children apply what they already know about forming plurals by using the following activity.

Write the words *dogs, lunches, tacks, glasses, tents, dishes,* and *circuses* on the chalkboard. Ask children to try to discover what all these words have in common. Elicit from the children that all these words are plurals and end with the letter *s*. Tell the children to examine these words again to find out what additional similarities are shared by four of the words on the chalkboard. Elicit that the words *lunches, glasses, dishes,* and *circuses* end with the letters *es*. Tell the children that in Unit 8 they will study words whose plurals are formed by adding the letters *s* or *es*. Explain that they can use these words in a variety of writing tasks: they can use the words in a note to a friend, in a letter, in a science report, or in a creative writing assignment.

UNIT 8a

FOCUS

- Relates to prior learning
- Draws relationships
- Applies spelling generalizations to new contexts

FOR CHILDREN WITH SPECIAL NEEDS

Learning Difficulties

Children with auditory memory and language disorders may have difficulty recalling spelling generalizations. Help the children learn these generalizations so that they become automatic. One strategy that has been helpful in aiding memory in language-disordered individuals is to set language to music.

Think of a song that is familiar to both you and the children. Substitute the words of the song with the words of the spelling generalization in this lesson. (To make a plural, add *es* to words that end with *s, ss, sh,* or *ch.*) Teach the song to the children and have them sing it with you. Write the words *circus, cat, class, bush, band,* and *ranch* on the chalkboard. Have the children sing the generalization softly to themselves. Ask them to name the words to which the generalization cannot be applied. (*cat* and *band*) Have the children name the words to which the generalization can be applied. (*circus, class, bush,* and *ranch*) Then have volunteers come to the chalkboard and write the plurals for these words.

Limited English Proficiency

To help limited English proficient children work with the spelling generalizations for Unit 8, you may wish to refer to the booklet "Suggestions and Activities for Limited English Proficient Students."

TEACHING PLAN

Objective To spell plural nouns formed by adding *s* and *es*.

1. Read the following phrases to the children and ask them to supply the missing words. Record their responses on the chalkboard.

   one *path;* two___ (paths)
   one *robin;* two___ (robins)
   one *desk;* two___ (desks)
   one *beach;* two___ (beaches)
   one *guess;* two___ (guesses)
   one *circus;* two___ (circuses)

   Point out that each word on the chalkboard is a plural noun and names more than one. Help the children to recognize that some of the plurals end with *s* and others end with *es*.

You may wish to introduce the lesson by using *Spelling Generalizations Transparency 7.*

2. Read the generalization on page 34 aloud. Then have a volunteer read **Remember This** at the bottom of the page aloud. Let the children test the usefulness of this hint. Say these words one at a time:

   sandwich toothbrush address
   stitch wristwatch hippopotamus

   Have the children say the plural of each word and indicate if they hear the extra vowel sound. Then write the singular and plural nouns on the chalkboard, pointing out that *es* is added to form the plural each time.

3. Read This Week's Words aloud, and have the children identify the letter or letters that were added to form the plural.

You may wish to assign *LEP Practice Master 8* for reinforcement in writing spelling words.

 Plurals

THIS WEEK'S WORDS

1. paths
2. desks
3. lists
4. fingers
5. robins
6. pictures
7. uncles
8. circuses
9. guesses
10. classes
11. bushes
12. churches
13. inches
14. ranches
15. beaches

paths
path

This Week's Words

A word that names just one thing is **singular**. A word that names more than one thing is **plural**. Here are two ways to make a word plural.

1. Add <u>s</u> to most words.

   path paths

2. Add <u>es</u> to words that end with s, ss, sh, or ch.

   circus circuses
   class classes
   bush bushes
   beach beaches

REMEMBER THIS

Say <u>beach</u>. Now say <u>beaches</u>. Listen to the extra vowel sound before the s in <u>beaches</u>. That extra vowel sound tells you to add <u>es</u>. But this doesn't work with a word like <u>faces</u>. The e is already there in <u>face</u>.

34

Extra Practice: This Week's Words

Name
Extra Practice   This Week's Words   UNIT **8**

Finish the puzzles with This Week's Words. Read each sentence and choose the word that fits. Then write the word in the boxes.

1. A hand has five of these.
2. Children sit at these in school.
3. People go to the store with these.
4. You walk through the forest on these.
5. The husbands of your aunts are these.
6. Some birds are these.
7. Artists paint these.

1. f i n g e r s
2. d e s k s
3. l i s t s
4. p a t h s
5. u n c l e s
6. r o b i n s
7. p i c t u r e s

8. Clowns are found in these.
9. You might get the answer with these.
10. People relax and swim at these.
11. People gather on Sunday at these.
12. Horses are kept at these.
13. Some front yards have these.
14. One foot is twelve of these.
15. A school is made up of these.

8. c i r c u s e s
9. g u e s s e s
10. b e a c h e s
11. c h u r c h e s
12. r a n c h e s
13. b u s h e s
14. i n c h e s
15. c l a s s e s

paths   beaches   bushes   churches   circuses
classes desks   fingers   guesses   inches
lists   pictures   ranches   robins   uncles

Extra Practice • 31

Extra Practice: Mastery Words

Name
Extra Practice   Mastery Words   UNIT **8**

A. Write the plural of each word.

1. dish ___dishes___   2. duck ___ducks___
3. glass ___glasses___ 4. light ___lights___
5. paw ___paws___   6. wish ___wishes___

B. Look at each picture. Then write the Mastery word that fits the sentence.

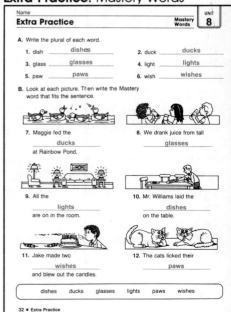

7. Maggie fed the ___ducks___ at Rainbow Pond.
8. We drank juice from tall ___glasses___.
9. All the ___lights___ are on in the room.
10. Mr. Williams laid the ___dishes___ on the table.
11. Jake made two ___wishes___ and blew out the candles.
12. The cats licked their ___paws___.

dishes   ducks   glasses   lights   paws   wishes

32 • Extra Practice

Spelling Practice

A. Write the plural of each word.

1. church ___churches___
2. beach ___beaches___
3. inch ___inches___
4. ranch ___ranches___
5. guess ___guesses___
6. class ___classes___

B. Finish the sentences. Write the plural of each word in dark print.

7. **desk** We sat at our ___desks___ and waited.

8. **finger** We couldn't keep our ___fingers___ still.

9. **robin** Even the ___robins___ outside seemed excited.

10. **uncle** Today, my ___uncles___ invited the class for a field trip to their horse ranch.

11. **path** The students would get to ride horses on ___paths___ all through the ranch.

12. **list** The teacher checked her ___lists___ for the names of the students signed up to go.

C. Write the word that goes with each picture. Then write the plural.

13. ___circus___
   ___circuses___

14. ___bush___
   ___bushes___

15. ___picture___
   ___pictures___

paths
desks
lists
fingers
robins
pictures
uncles
circuses
guesses
classes
bushes
churches
inches
ranches
beaches

35

Extra Practice: Bonus Words

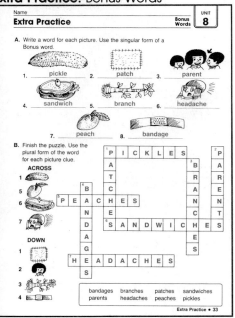

TEACHING PLAN

Objectives To write the plurals of given singular nouns; to write singular and plural nouns, given picture clues.

1. Briefly discuss the directions on page 35. Have a volunteer identify the three pictures in Exercise **C**.
2. Have the children complete the page independently. Remind them to use legible handwriting. You may wish to demonstrate the correct form of the letters e and s and then have the children practice writing the letters. For **Handwriting Models,** refer the children to page 258 in the **Pupil Book.**
3. Review the children's responses for Exercise **A** orally, writing the plural nouns on the chalkboard and directing the children's attention to final ch or ss and the ending es. Have volunteers write the answers for Exercises **B** and **C** on the chalkboard. Let the children check their own work.

For reinforcement in writing spelling words, you may wish to assign *Extra Practice Master 8: This Week's Words.*

⭐ of special interest

The original meaning of the Latin word *circus* was "circle." In Roman times, *circus* took on the specialized meaning of "circular arena for spectator sports." This meaning is the basis of the modern use of *circus* to describe the circular arena in which acrobats, clowns, and trained animals perform, and by extension to describe the acts performed in such an arena and the troupe who performs these acts. The use of *circus* to mean "circle" survives, however, in British English—the evidence being Piccadilly Circus, a traffic circle in London.

Summarize Learning

Have the children summarize what they have learned on pages 34 and 35. *Ask:*

- What have you learned about forming plurals in this lesson? (The plurals of most words are formed by adding s. The plurals of words that end with s, ss, sh, or ch are formed by adding es.)
- What are examples of words to which this generalization can be applied? (paths, robins, guesses, classes; accept other examples)

TEACHING PLAN

SPELLING AND LANGUAGE

Objective To write singular or plural nouns in sentence context.

1. To introduce this activity, write these sentence frames on the chalkboard:

> I see these ___.
> I see that___.
> Some___are there.
> One___is here.

Have volunteers use the singular and plural forms of several of This Week's Words in the sentence frames. Help the children to recognize that the words *these* and *that, some* and *one,* and the verbs *are* and *is* signal whether a singular or plural noun fits in the blank.

2. Read the directions on page 36 aloud, and have volunteers complete the first sentence orally. Then have the children complete the activity.

3. Ask volunteers to read each completed sentence aloud. Have the children identify the words that helped them decide whether the singular or plural was correct. Let the children check their own work.

For extended practice in writing singular or plural nouns in sentence contexts, you may wish to assign *Spelling and Language Master 8.*

WRITING ON YOUR OWN

Objectives To write a friendly letter; to proofread for spelling.

1. Read the directions.
2. As a **prewriting** activity, have the children tell how they would describe their school. Write their responses on the chalkboard. Then have each child **compose** a friendly letter to describe the school to a friend. When the children are ready to **revise** their letters, remind them to check spelling. For additional help, you may wish to refer them to the **Revising Checklist** on

page 247 of the **Writer's Guide**. To *publish* the children's work, have them exchange letters with their classmates.

HANDWRITING

Objective To practice writing cursive letter forms: c C, o O, a A.

1. Read the first two sentences, and have the children examine and compare the models of os and as.
2. Have the children study the models of the letter forms. Ask them to note the ending stroke in each letter.
3. Have the children practice the letter forms and write the sentence.

THIS WEEK'S WORDS
paths
desks
lists
fingers
robins
pictures
uncles
circuses
guesses
classes
bushes
churches
inches
ranches
beaches

Spelling and Language • One or More

Write one of This Week's Words to finish each sentence. Decide if the singular or the plural fits. For example, you would use the plural of path to finish the sentence: "These ___ lead to the woods." You would use the singular to finish the sentence "This ___ leads to the woods."

1. Adam built a sand castle at the ___beach___ .

2. He took a ___picture___ of it with his camera.

3. Can you tell how many ___inches___ tall it was?

Writing on Your Own

Pretend you have a pen pal. Write a letter to your friend describing your school. Use some of This Week's Words.

 WRITER'S GUIDE For help with the parts of a friendly letter, turn to page 251.

HANDWRITING

c C o O a A

Join **o** to other letters at the midline.   *os*

Join **a** to other letters at the bottom line.   *as*

1. Practice writing c C, o O, a A in cursive.

2. Practice writing **os, as, co, ca** in cursive.

3. Write this sentence: *Carlos spoke to the class.*

36

Extra Practice: Spelling and Language

Name _____ UNIT **8**
Spelling and Language

A. Circle the word in each sentence that should be plural. Then write the sentence using the plural of the word you circled.

1. I have many (uncle) but only one Uncle Mel.
   I have many uncles, but only one Uncle Mel.

2. Mel owns one of the biggest (ranch) in the state.
   Mel owns one of the biggest ranches in the state.

3. The ranch has lakes, rivers, and (beach).
   The ranch has lakes, rivers, and beaches.

4. (Robin) and other birds live in these bushes.
   Robins and other birds live in these bushes.

5. One of those birds is just two (inch) tall.
   One of those birds is just two inches tall.

B. Make the plural words singular. Make the singular words plural.

6. desks   desk   7. church   churches
8. class   classes   9. guess   guesses
10. circuses circus

paths	robins	pictures	fingers	bushes
ranches	churches	guesses	lists	beaches
desks	uncles	circuses	classes	inches

34 • Extra Practice

Spelling on Your Own

THIS WEEK'S WORDS

Write sentences using all of This Week's Words. Try to use as many of the words as you can in each sentence. You may use the singular or the plural. Here is an example: "I have lots of <u>pictures</u> of <u>circuses</u> in my <u>desk</u>."

MASTERY WORDS

Write the plural of each word. Draw a line under the letters you added to spell the plural.

1. glass _____glass<u>es</u>_____
2. wish _____wish<u>es</u>_____
3. dish _____dish<u>es</u>_____
4. duck _____duck<u>s</u>_____

Finish the sentences. Use the Mastery words.

5. Please turn off the _____lights_____.
6. That dog has muddy _____paws_____.
7. Do _____wishes_____ ever come true?
8. Jesse drank three _____glasses_____ of milk.
9. Sara fed bread to the _____ducks_____ at the pond.
10. Joan and Chet will wash the _____dishes_____.

dishes
ducks
glasses
lights
paws
wishes

BONUS WORDS

1. Write the singular of each Bonus word. Circle each singular word that ends with <u>e</u>.
2. Write the names of three things you might take on a picnic.
3. Write the word that means mother and father.
4. Write sentences about a picnic. Try to use the singular or plural of each Bonus word.

See answers below.

bandages
branches
headaches
parents
patches
peaches
pickles
sandwiches

37

Spelling on Your Own Answers

BONUS WORDS
1. (bandage)
   branch
   (headache)
   parent
   patch
   peach
   (pickle)
   sandwich
2. peaches, pickles, sandwiches
3. parents
4. Children will write as directed. Be sure to check spelling.

Summarize Learning

Have the students summarize what they have learned in this unit. *Ask:*
- What have you learned about using singular or plural words to complete sentences? (Reading the sentence will help you to know whether to use the singular or plural form of a word to complete the sentence.)
- What spelling generalizations have you learned? How did you use these generalizations?

TEACHING PLAN

Objective To apply the unit spelling generalization to spell This Week's Words, Mastery words, and Bonus words independently.

THIS WEEK'S WORDS

1. Read the directions on page 37 aloud. To help the children begin, ask volunteers to give oral sentences that use at least two of This Week's Words.
2. Have the children complete the activity independently on a separate piece of paper.
3. This activity may be extended by asking volunteers to read their sentences aloud. Ask other children to write the forms of This Week's Words used in the sentences on the chalkboard.

MASTERY WORDS

1. Review the unit generalization on page 34. Read the Mastery words aloud, and have volunteers identify the letter or letters that make each word a plural.
2. Briefly discuss the directions on page 37 to be sure that the children understand what they are to do. Then have the children complete the activities independently.

BONUS WORDS

1. Briefly review the unit generalization and **Remember This** on page 34.
2. Have volunteers read the Bonus words aloud.
3. Have the children complete the exercise independently on a separate piece of paper.
4. Check the children's work orally, giving volunteers the opportunity to read their stories aloud.

For reinforcement in writing spelling words, you may wish to assign *Extra Practice Master 8: Mastery Words* or *Bonus Words.*

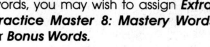

CLOSING THE UNIT

Apply New Learning

Tell the children that if they misspell plural nouns in their writing, they should use one or more of the following strategies:

- write the word using different spellings and compare it with the spelling they picture in their minds.
- try to find patterns and causes of their errors.
- use the origin of a word to help remember the correct spelling.
- pronounce the word very carefully to see that the correct letter or letters have been used to spell the sounds.

Transfer New Learning

Tell the children that when they encounter new words in their personal reading and in other context areas, they should learn the meaning of those words and then apply the generalizations they have studied to the spelling of those words. Tell them that once the words are familiar in both meaning and spelling, they should use the new words in their writing.

ENRICHMENT ACTIVITIES

Classroom activities and **home activities** may be assigned to children of all ability levels. The activities provide opportunities for children to use their spelling words in new contexts.

For the Classroom

To individualize classroom activities, you may have the children use the word list they are studying in this unit.

- *Basic:* Use **Mastery** words to complete the activity.
- *Average:* Use **This Week's Words** to complete the activity.
- *Challenging:* Use **Bonus** words to complete the activity.

1. **Language Arts/Making Words Plural** Tell the children to write the following headings on a sheet of paper: *circus, class, bush,* and *beach.* Have them underline the letter(s) of the final sound in each word and write at least four of the final sound in each word and write other nouns that have the same ending under each appropriate heading. Then tell them to write five sentences using the plural form of some of the words they listed. Have children rewrite the sentences, leaving a blank in place of a spelling word. Have children ask other children to supply the missing spelling word in each sentence.

   ■ COOPERATIVE LEARNING: Tell each group to write the following headings: *circus, class, bush,* and *beach.* Have different group members underline the letter(s) of the final sound in each word. Then have each child choose

one heading, write nouns that end the same way, and use the plural form of the nouns in three sentences. Group members should check each other's words for correct spelling. Each group can then choose five sentences, leaving a blank for the plural word, and exchange their sentences with another group.

2. **Language Arts/Writing Questions** Tell each child to choose spelling words and write two questions about each word. For example, *What do you call your father's brothers? To whom are aunts married?* (uncles) Then have the children make a matching exercise by copying the questions in a left-hand column on their papers and the scrambled spelling words in a right-hand column. Children can exchange papers and have a classmate complete the exercise by matching the questions to the spelling word that answers them.

   ■ COOPERATIVE LEARNING: Have each group write questions about spelling words. The group members should divide up the spelling words, and each member should write two questions about each of his or her words. The group should then read over all the questions and create a matching exercise. Then have the groups exchange and solve each other's matching exercises.

3. **Social Studies/Writing a Report** Have the children use spelling words to write a brief report about a social studies community. As a **prewriting** activity, have the children search the spelling list for an idea of the type of community to choose as a topic. Then have the children each choose a topic and make a cluster drawing of it.

   Tell the children to convert the subtopics on their cluster drawings to headings. Then have the children use the encyclopedia and other books to learn about their topics, and write notes under some of their headings. To **compose** their reports, the children should reread their notes to see which subheading has enough information to form a good paragraph. Tell children to include spelling words and other plural words, and to remember to give their reports a title. Have the children **revise** their reports by checking to see that the paragraph has a topic sentence and supporting details, and that spelling and punctuation are correct. Children may refer to the **Writer's Guide** on page 249 for information about paragraph structure and to the **Revising Checklist** on page 247 for help with revising their work. **Publish** the reports by having each one read to the class, and then display the reports on a bulletin board.

   ■ COOPERATIVE LEARNING: Have each group write a brief report about a social studies community. As a **prewriting** activity, tell each group to decide on one topic. Each group should select a recorder to make a cluster drawing of the topic while other group members create it. Have each group member choose two subtopics, read about them in an encyclopedia or other books, and take notes on their subtopics. When children are ready to **compose** the report, tell them to select the subtopics on which they obtained the most information, and have each member of the group write a paragraph about it. Have the group members **revise** by reading each other's paragraphs to check for correct paragraph structure, spelling, and punctuation. Then group members should combine their paragraphs into a unified report, give it a title, and **publish** it by having one member read it aloud to the class. After the reports have been read aloud, they can be displayed on a bulletin board.

For the Home

Children may complete these activities independently or with the assistance of a relative or friend in the home.

1. **Language Arts/Writing a Journal** Children should make up a journal entry, using words in plural form. Have children pretend to write a journal entry about a place they just visited where everything they saw was double. For example, *While I was walking past two stores, I saw two robins sitting in two bushes.* Children should try to use as many words as possible from the three spelling lists and should underline the spelling words in the journal entry. Have children share the journal entry with a family member or a friend.

2. **Social Studies/Creating a Dictionary of Geographical Terms** Tell the children to add to their book of geographical features, using spelling words from the current unit. Have the children look through magazines to find pictures of geographical features and then cut out and paste each picture on a separate sheet of paper. Encourage the children to use a dictionary to help them as they label each picture. Have the children use their spelling words to write a sentence related to each picture. Children should alphabetize their pages.

3. **Science/Making a Dictionary of Science Words** Have the children skim through the lists of spelling words and locate those words that would be found in a science dictionary. Examples of a few words are *robins, bushes,* and *beaches.* Then have the children use a dictionary and write each word, its pronunciation, its meaning, and a sentence using the word on a separate sheet of paper. Finally, the words should be alphabetized and placed in booklet form. At a later time, the children may want to add words from other spelling units to the dictionary.

4. **Language Arts/Writing Rhyming Words** Have the children write rhyming word pairs using both spelling words and new words. Have them check the dictionary to see if each new word is a real word and is correctly spelled. Then have the children use the word pairs to write five humorous sentences. For example, *I make shopping lists on my wrists.* Children may read their sentences to a family member or friend.

EVALUATING SPELLING ABILITY

Unit Test

This Week's Words
1. *paths* Three *paths* lead through the woods. **paths**
2. *desks* The *desks* are made of wood. **desks**
3. *lists* Fran forgot both shopping *lists*. **lists**
4. *fingers* Peter's *fingers* are cold. **fingers**
5. *robins* The *robins* have a nest in that tree. **robins**
6. *pictures* We all drew *pictures* of our pets. **pictures**
7. *uncles* My *uncles* own a grocery store. **uncles**
8. *circuses* Two *circuses* are in town. **circuses**
9. *guesses* I made three *guesses*. **guesses**
10. *classes* Many *classes* are in the play. **classes**
11. *bushes* These *bushes* are green. **bushes**
12. *churches* Some *churches* are white. **churches**
13. *inches* The table is sixty *inches* long. **inches**
14. *ranches* Cattle are raised on *ranches*. **ranches**
15. *beaches* Sandy *beaches* are wide. **beaches**

Mastery Words
1. *dishes* Please don't drop the *dishes*. **dishes**
2. *ducks* We could hear the *ducks* quacking. **ducks**
3. *glasses* Grandma wears *glasses* to read. **glasses**
4. *lights* The porch *lights* were turned on. **lights**
5. *paws* My dog's *paws* are wet. **paws**
6. *wishes* I hope my *wishes* come true. **wishes**

Bonus Words
1. *bandages* He has *bandages* on his wrist. **bandages**
2. *branches* The storm broke some *branches* off the tree. **branches**
3. *headaches* Bright sun gives some people *headaches*. **headaches**
4. *parents* Everyone's *parents* are here. **parents**
5. *patches* We put *patches* on our pants. **patches**
6. *peaches* Ann likes sliced *peaches*. **peaches**
7. *pickles* Max brought *pickles* for the picnic. **pickles**
8. *sandwiches* We ate tuna *sandwiches*. **sandwiches**

Dictation Sentences

This Week's Words
1. We took *pictures* of the *robins* in the *bushes*.
2. My brothers keep *lists* of their *classes* in their *desks*.
3. Those *paths* go to the *ranches* and on to the *beaches*.
4. My *uncles* helped build two *churches* in our town.
5. You have two *guesses* to tell how many *circuses* I saw.
6. I know how many *inches* long all my *fingers* are.

Mastery Words
1. Dad *wishes* you would put away the *dishes* and *glasses* and turn out the *lights*.
2. Dogs have *paws* and *ducks* have feet.

Bonus Words
1. My *parents* ate *sandwiches, pickles,* and *peaches*.
2. We put *patches* on the dresses where the tree *branches* had torn them.
3. You can not use *bandages* to fix *headaches*.

RETEACHING STRATEGIES FOR SPELLING

Children who have made errors on the Unit Test may require reteaching. Use the following **Reteaching Strategies** and **Follow-up Masters 8A** and **8B** for additional instruction and practice of This Week's Words. (You may wish to assign **LEP Reteaching Follow-up Master 8** for reteaching of spelling words.)

A. Discovering Spelling Ideas

1. Say the following words as you write them on the chalkboard.

   cups   glasses   bunches   wishes   choruses

2. Ask the children what letters were added to these words to make them name more than one thing. (s, es)
3. Ask the children to identify the consonant letter or letters that appear before the es. (ss, ch, sh, s)
4. Ask the children what two ways they have learned to make words plural. (Add s to most words; add es to words that end with s, ss, sh, or ch.)

1. Explain to the children that each word has a shape and that remembering the shape of a word can help them to spell the word correctly.
2. On the chalkboard, write the words books and porches. Have the children identify "short," "tall," and "tail" letters.
3. Draw the configuration of each word on the chalkboard, and ask the children which word fits in each shape.

Use **Reteaching Follow-up Master 8A** to reinforce spelling generalizations taught in Unit 8.

Use **Reteaching Follow-up Master 8B** to reinforce spellings of This Week's Words for Unit 8.

Name _____

Reteaching Follow-up A   Discovering Spelling Ideas   UNIT **8**

THIS WEEK'S WORDS

paths	fingers	robins	pictures	classes
bushes	churches	lists	desks	guesses
uncles	circuses	ranches	inches	beaches

1. What do all of This Week's Words have in common?

   They are plural words; they name more than one thing.

2. Write the words that have the same ending as the first word in each column.

laps	porches
paths	circuses
desks	guesses
lists	classes
fingers	bushes
robins	churches
pictures	inches
uncles	ranches
	beaches

3. What have you learned about making words plural?

   To make a word plural, add s to most words, add es to words ending with s, ss, sh, or ch.

Reteaching • 13

Name _____

Reteaching Follow-up B   Word Shapes   UNIT **8**

THIS WEEK'S WORDS

paths	fingers	robins	pictures	classes
bushes	churches	lists	desks	guesses
uncles	circuses	ranches	inches	beaches

Write each of This Week's Words in its correct shape. The first one has been done for you. Children may interchange answers that fit the same configuration.

1. b u s h e s
2. p i c t u r e s
3. d e s k s
4. b e a c h e s
5. f i n g e r s
6. c i r c u s e s
7. i n c h e s
8. l i s t s
9. r a n c h e s
10. p a t h s
11. c l a s s e s
12. r o b i n s
13. u n c l e s
14. c h u r c h e s
15. g u e s s e s

14 • Reteaching

PREVIEWING THE UNIT

Unit Materials

Instruction and Practice

Pupil Book   pages 38–41
Teacher's Edition
  Teaching Plans   pages 38–41
  Enrichment Activities
    For the Classroom   pages 41A–41B
    For the Home   page 41B
  Reteaching Strategies   page 41C

Testing

Teacher's Edition
  Trial Test   pages 37E–37F
  Unit Test   page 41B
  Dictation Test   page 41B
  Form *B** Test 1   pages T3–T4

*If your grading period is nine weeks, you may want to use
the **Form B Test** at the end of this unit.

Additional Resources

Teacher's Resource Package

PRACTICE AND REINFORCEMENT
  Extra Practice Master 9: This Week's Words
  Extra Practice Master 9: Mastery Words
  Extra Practice Master 9: Bonus Words
  LEP Practice Master 9
  Spelling and Language Master 9
  Study Steps to Learn a Word Master

RETEACHING FOLLOW-UP
  Reteaching Follow-up Master 9A:
    Discovering Spelling Ideas
  Reteaching Follow-up Master 9B: Word
    Shapes
  LEP Reteaching Follow-up Master 9

TEACHING AIDS
  Spelling Generalizations Transparency 8

Visit our Web site
http://www.hbschool.com

Click on the SPELLING banner to find activities for this unit.

Learner Objectives

Spelling

- To spell words that demonstrate these sound-letter relationships: initial /j/*j, g;* medial /j/*g;* final/j/*ge, dge.*
- To make a word chain using spelling words.

Reading

- To follow written directions.
- To arrange given words in sentence order.
- To read a classmate's story.

Writing

- To write a story.
- To use the writing process.
- To proofread for spelling, capitalization, and punctuation.
- To write legible manuscript and cursive letters.

Listening

- To listen for consonant and vowel sounds in words.
- To follow oral directions.

Speaking

- To contribute ideas and information in group discussions.
- To respond to questions.
- To present a story.
- To express feelings and ideas about a piece of writing.

THIS WEEK'S WORDS

giraffe
danger
jam
jug
juice
gentle
giant
magic
age
cage
large
page
bridge
edge
judge

MASTERY WORDS

jar
jet
job
jump
just
give

BONUS WORDS

join
jungle
gingerbread
gym
package
strange
fudge
ledge

Assignment Guide

This guide shows how you teach a typical spelling unit in either a five-day or a three-day sequence, while providing for individual differences. **Boldface type** indicates essential classwork. Steps shown in light type may be done in class or assigned as homework.

Five Days	○ = average spellers ★ = better spellers ✓ = slower spellers		Three Days
Day 1	**a**	● ★ **Take This Week's Words Trial Test and correct** ● ✓ **Take Mastery Word Trial Test and correct** ● ★ **Read This Week's Words and discuss generalization on page 38**	**Day 1**
Day 2	**b**	● Complete Spelling Practice page 39 ● ✓ Complete Extra Practice Master 9: This Week's Words (optional) ✓ Complete Spelling on Your Own: Mastery Words page 41 ★ **Take Bonus Word Trial Test and correct**	
Day 3	**c**	● ★ ✓ **Complete Spelling and Language page 40** ● ★ ✓ Complete Writing on Your Own page 40 ● ✓ Take Midweek Test (optional) ★ Complete Spelling on Your Own: Bonus Words page 41 ● ✓ Complete Spelling and Language Master 9 (optional)	**Day 2**
Day 4	**d**	● Complete Spelling on Your Own: This Week's Words page 41 ✓ Complete Extra Practice Master 9: Mastery Words (optional) ★ Complete Extra Practice Master 9: Bonus Words (optional)	
Day 5	**e**	● **Take Unit Test on This Week's Words** ● Complete Reteaching Follow-up Masters 9A and 9B (optional) ● ✓ **Take Unit Test on Mastery Words** ★ **Take Unit Test on Bonus Words**	**Day 3**

Enrichment Activities for the **classroom** and for the **home** included at the end of this unit may be assigned selectively on any day of the week.

INTRODUCING THE UNIT

Establish Readiness for Learning

Tell the children that this week they will continue to study consonant sounds. In Unit 9 they will study several spellings for /j/. Tell the children that they will apply the spelling generalizations to This Week's Words and use those words to write a story.

Assess Children's Spelling Ability

Administer the Trial Test before the children study This Week's Words. Use the test sentences provided. Say each word and use it in a sentence. Then repeat the word. Have the children write the words on a separate sheet of paper or in their spelling notebooks. Test sentences are also provided for Mastery and Bonus words.

Have the children check their own work by listening to you read the spelling of the words

or by referring to This Week's Words in the left column of the **Pupil Book.** For each misspelled word, have the children follow the **Study Steps to Learn a Word** on page 1 in the **Pupil Book** or use the copying master to study and write the words. Children should record the number correct on their **Progress Report.**

Trial Test Sentences

This Week's Words
1. *giraffe*   We saw a *giraffe* at the zoo.   *giraffe*
2. *danger*   The sign warned people of the *danger.*   *danger*
3. *jam*   Leo likes to eat *jam* and bread.   *jam*
4. *jug*   We brought a *jug* of lemonade to the picnic.   *jug*
5. *juice*   Mandy drinks orange *juice* at breakfast.   *juice*
6. *gentle*   Mom woke Terry with a *gentle* nudge.   *gentle*

7. *giant* We read a story about a *giant*. *giant*

8. *magic* Wanda knows several *magic* tricks. *magic*

9. *age* Angie and Brad are the same age. *age*

10. *cage* Our parakeet lives in a *cage*. *cage*

11. *large* A butterfly has *large* colorful wings. *large*

12. *page* Read to the end of the *page*. *page*

13. *bridge* The cars and buses went across the *bridge*. *bridge*

14. *edge* Do not stand near the *edge* of the cliff. *edge*

15. *judge* A *judge* works in a courtroom. *judge*

Mastery Words

1. *jar* Pickles come in a *jar*. *jar*
2. *jet* A *jet* moves very fast. *jet*
3. *job* My mom got a new *job*. *job*
4. *jump* The horse will *jump* over that fence. *jump*
5. *just* We got there *just* in time. *just*
6. *give* Please *give* me some help. *give*

Bonus Words

1. *join* Keith wants to *join* the club. *join*
2. *jungle* Many wild animals live in the *jungle*. *jungle*

3. *gingerbread* Bob likes *gingerbread* cookies. *gingerbread*

4. *gym* We can run and play in the *gym*. *gym*

5. *package* Alex could not wait to open the *package*. *package*

6. *strange* Brandy and Doreen made a *strange* animal with clay. *strange*

7. *fudge* You need lots of sugar to make *fudge*. *fudge*

8. *ledge* Put the plant on the window *ledge*. *ledge*

Apply Prior Learning

Have the children apply what they already know about /j/ by involving them in the following activity.

Have the children name some words that contain /j/ as you write them on the chalkboard. Continue writing the children's responses until words that contain initial /j/j, g, medial /j/g, and final /j/ge, dge are among the words listed on the chalkboard. Have volunteers come to the chalkboard and draw a line around the four different spellings of /j/. Tell the children that in Unit 9 they will study words that have this /j/. Explain that they can use these words in a variety of writing tasks: they can use the words in a note to a friend, in a letter, or in a story.

FOCUS

- Relates to prior learning
- Draws relationships
- Applies spelling generalizations to new contexts

FOR CHILDREN WITH SPECIAL NEEDS

Learning Difficulties

Learning-disabled children are often passive learners. Encourage their active participation in the visual identification of words with /j/ by involving them in the following activity.

Have the children fold a piece of lined, letter-size paper to form three columns. Have them write the title, "Words with the sound /j/," at the top of their papers. Under the title have them write the letter *j* in the first column, *g* in the second column, and *dge* in the third column. Tell the children to write each of their spelling words under the appropriate column. Tell them that they are to act as word detectives as they continue searching for more words to add to their lists. Suggest that they look for words in books, magazines, and newspapers. You may

wish to have the children continue this activity as a homework assignment. When the children have completed their lists, have them read their words aloud and spell them. Have them underline the letter or letters that spell the /j/ in each word.

Limited English Proficiency

To help limited English proficient children work with the spelling generalizations for Unit 9, you may wish to refer to the booklet "Suggestions and Activities for Limited English Proficient Students."

UNIT 9a
This Week's Words

TEACHING PLAN

Objective To spell words that demonstrate these sound-letter relationships: initial /j/*j, g*; medial /j/*g*; final /j/*ge, dge*.

1. Write this sentence on the chalkboard:

> The gentle giant carried a jug of juice and a jar of jam across the large bridge.

Read the sentence aloud. Read it a second time, asking the children to stop you every time they hear /j/. As the children respond, underline the letter or letters that spell /j/. Help the children to recognize that there are four ways to spell /j/: *g* and *j* at the beginning of words; *ge* and *dge* at the end of words.

You may wish to introduce the lesson by using **Spelling Generalizations Transparency 8.**

2. Read the generalization on page 38 aloud.
3. Have volunteers read This Week's Words aloud. As each word is read, ask the children to identify the letter or letters that spell the sound /j/ in the word. In words that have /j/ spelled *g*, have the children name the vowel letter that follows *g*. In words with final /j/, ask them to indicate if the preceding vowel sound is a short vowel sound.
4. Direct the children's attention to **Remember This** at the bottom of the page. Have a child read the sentence aloud and comment on the picture of the giraffe.

You may wish to assign **LEP Practice Master 9** for reinforcement in writing spelling words.

---

9 The Sound /j/

THIS WEEK'S WORDS

1. *giraffe*
2. *danger*
3. *jam*
4. *jug*
5. *juice*
6. *gentle*
7. *giant*
8. *magic*
9. *age*
10. *cage*
11. *large*
12. *page*
13. *bridge*
14. *edge*
15. *judge*

This Week's Words

All the words this week have the sound /j/. Here are four ways to spell /j/.

- with **j**

  jam

- with **g** before **e** or **i**

  gentle   ma**g**ic

- with **ge** at the end of a word

  a**ge**

- with **dge** after a short vowel sound

  e**dge**

REMEMBER THIS

There is an e at the tail end of giraffe.

38

Extra Practice: This Week's Words

Name
Extra Practice   This Week's Words   UNIT 9

Use This Week's Words to do both puzzles. Finish the first puzzle with words that have /j/ at the beginning or middle. Finish the second puzzle with words that end with /j/.

ACROSS
1. Pour the milk from the ___.
4. The ___ ate ten bowls of stew for supper.
6. Beware of ___!
7. Stan drinks grape ___.

DOWN
1. The lawyer spoke to the ___.
2. The ___ is a tall animal.
3. Be ___ with the puppy.
5. Rosie knows ___ tricks.
7. I like strawberry ___.

(Puzzle 1 grid)
j u g
u   i
d   r
g i a n t
e   f
m
d a n g e r
j u i c e
a
m

ACROSS
4. There is a ___ over the river.
6. The bird lives in a ___.
7. We walked to the ___ of the water.

DOWN
1. Something big is ___.
2. Mrs. Stone is a ___ in court.
3. My friend and I are the same ___.
5. Start on this ___.

(Puzzle 2 grid)
j   a
a   u
b r i d g e
p   g
c a g e
g
e d g e

jug   jam   judge   juice   gentle   giant   giraffe   danger
cage   large   page   bridge   edge   magic   age

Extra Practice • 35

Extra Practice: Mastery Words

Name
Extra Practice   Mastery Words   UNIT 9

Put the words in order. Write six sentences to answer the questions. First choose a Mastery word that makes sense in each sentence. Write it in the box. The missing word in the first sentence is given to help you. Remember that a sentence begins with a capital letter and ends with a period.

job
jump
jet
just
jar
give

1. Where is the jam?

in   is   the | jar. | The   jam

The jam is in the jar.

2. What does the frog like to do?

likes | jump. | It   to

It likes to jump.

3. What do you see in the sky?

see   I | jet. | a

I see a jet.

4. Why is Carla happy?

has   new   a | job. | She

She has a new job.

5. What should I do with this key?

Please   it   me.   to | give |

Please give it to me.

6. When did the movie start?

five   started   It | just | ago.   minutes

It just started five minutes ago.

36 • Extra Practice

Spelling Practice

A. Follow the directions. Use This Week's Words.

1. Write the three words that start with /j/ spelled <u>g</u>.

<u>gentle</u>   <u>giant</u>   <u>giraffe</u>

2. Write the three words that end with /j/ and have long <u>a</u>.

<u>age</u>   <u>cage</u>   <u>page</u>

3. Write the word that ends with /j/ and means the opposite of <u>small</u>.

<u>large</u>

4. Write the three words that end with /j/ and have short vowel sounds.

<u>bridge</u>   <u>edge</u>   <u>judge</u>

B. Add the letter that spells /j/ in each word. Write the words.

5. dan__er   <u>danger</u>   **6.** ma__ic   <u>magic</u>

C. Tell what the giant uses when he makes breakfast. Write sentences. Use the three words that start with /j/ spelled j and end with another consonant sound. Then circle all the words you used that have the sound /j/.

The three words children should use

are <u>jam</u>, <u>juice</u>, **and** <u>jug</u>. **Other words with**

the sound /j/ that children might use and

should then circle are <u>giant</u>, <u>jar</u>, <u>jelly</u>, **and**

<u>orange</u>.

39

giraffe
danger
jam
jug
juice
gentle
giant
magic
age
cage
large
page
bridge
edge
judge

Spelling Practice   UNIT 9b

TEACHING PLAN

Objectives To write words given spelling and vowel sound clues; to write sentences that describe a picture.

1. Briefly discuss the directions for Exercises **A** and **B** on page 39.
2. Have the children complete Exercises **A** and **B** independently. Remind them to use legible handwriting. You may wish to demonstrate the correct form of the letters g and j and then have the children practice writing the letters. For **Handwriting Models,** refer the children to page 258 in the **Pupil Book.**
3. Then read the directions for Exercise **C** aloud and make sure that the children understand what they are to do. Encourage them to look at the picture and tell about what they see on the table. Remind them to begin sentences with capital letters and end them with periods.
4. Have the children complete Exercise **C** independently.
5. To correct the children's work, have volunteers write their answers for Exercises **A** and **B** on the chalkboard. Then ask one or two children to read what they have written for Exercise **C**. Let the children check their own work.

For reinforcement in writing spelling words, you may wish to assign *Extra Practice Master 9: This Week's Words.*

Extra Practice: Bonus Words

Name		UNIT
Extra Practice	Bonus Words	**9**

A. Write the Bonus word that names a place where you might find each of these things. Then write another Bonus word that has /j/ spelled with the same letter or letters.

1. gym — gingerbread
2. jungle — join
3. ledge — fudge
4. package — strange

gym	gingerbread	fudge	join
jungle	ledge	strange	package

B. Each sentence describes a Bonus word. It also describes one of the words in the box at the right. Write the Bonus word and the other word for each sentence.

connect	forest
windowsill	carton
playground	unusual

5. This word describes something odd.
   strange — unusual
6. Wild animals live here.
   jungle — forest
7. This is something like a narrow shelf.
   ledge — windowsill
8. Games are played here.
   gym — playground
9. This thing holds other things.
   package — carton
10. This verb means "to put together."
   join — connect

Extra Practice • 37

Summarize Learning

Have the children summarize what they have learned on pages 38 and 39. *Ask:*
- What have you learned about /j/ in this lesson? (Initial /j/ is spelled j, g; final /j/ is spelled ge, dge.)
- What are examples of words to which these generalizations can be applied? (giraffe, jam, cage, bridge; accept other examples)

UNIT 9c Language Study

TEACHING PLAN

SPELLING AND LANGUAGE

> **Objective** To write given sets of words in sentence order.

1. Write these words on the chalkboard:

   giraffe in The zoo. the is

   Ask a volunteer to arrange the words in correct sentence order and write the complete sentence on the chalkboard. (The giraffe is in the zoo.)
2. Read the directions on page 40 aloud.
3. Have the children complete the exercises independently.
4. To correct the children's work, have volunteers read the sentence aloud. Let the children check their work.

For extended practice in writing words in sentence order, you may wish to assign *Spelling and Language Master 9.*

WRITING ON YOUR OWN

> **Objectives** To write a story using some spelling words; to proofread for spelling.

1. Read the directions aloud.
2. As a **prewriting** activity, have the children make a list of some things they might see in a magic land where gentle giants live. Then have each child **compose** a story that tells about this magic land. Remind them to use as many of This Week's Words as they can in their stories. Refer to a model of a story on page 253 of the **Writer's Guide.** When the children are ready to **revise** their paragraphs, remind them to check spelling. To **publish** the children's work, have them exchange papers and read each other's stories orally.

HANDWRITING

> **Objective** To practice writing cursive letter forms: *j J, u U, w W.*

THIS WEEK'S WORDS

giraffe
danger
jam
jug
juice
gentle
giant
magic
age
cage
large
page
bridge
edge
judge

Spelling and Language • Writing Sentences

Put the words in order to write two sentences. Remember that a sentence starts with a capital letter and ends with a period.

1. judge   The   went   zoo.   to   gentle   the

   The gentle judge went to the zoo.

2. giant   saw   there.   He   a   giraffe

   He saw a giant giraffe there.

Writing on Your Own

Write a story for a young friend. Tell about a magic land where gentle giants live. Use as many of This Week's Words as you can.

WRITER'S GUIDE Can your friend read your story? If you need help writing any letters, turn to page 261.

HANDWRITING

j J   u U   w W

Notice how the letters **u** and **w** are alike.   u   w

1. Practice writing j J, u U, w W in cursive.

2. Write this sentence: *We sip fruit juice.*

40

---

1. Read the introductory sentence on page 40 aloud. Have the children examine the models for lowercase *u* and *w*. Ask a child to explain the similarity between the two letters.
2. Have the children examine the models for the cursive letters. Help them to note where the letters touch or intersect the lines.
3. Have the children practice the letter forms and write the sentence.
4. When they have finished, ask the children to compare their letter forms with the models. Review each child's work to note specific handwriting problems.

Extra Practice: Spelling and Language

Name _____   UNIT 9
Spelling and Language

Complete each sentence by drawing a line from the first part to the last part. Then write the complete sentences on the lines.

First Part	Last Part
A tall giraffe has to duck	straight out of a jug.
When the tiger is in a cage,	we are out of danger.
A whale may be a giant animal,	"Son, act your age."
A busy boy spilled paint	but it is very gentle.
The man drank juice	to walk under a bridge.
A kind judge said,	all over a page.

1. A tall giraffe has to duck to walk under a bridge.
2. When the tiger is in a cage, we are out of danger.
3. A whale may be a giant animal, but it is very gentle.
4. A busy boy spilled paint all over a page.
5. The man drank juice straight out of a jug.
6. A kind judge said, "Son, act your age."

jam	juice	danger	magic	cage
age	bridge	judge	edge	giraffe
jug	giant	gentle	large	page

38 • Extra Practice

Spelling on Your Own

THIS WEEK'S WORDS

```
a g e    a g e      a g e
            d          d
            g          g
            e  j u i c e
```

Make a "word chain" with This Week's Words. Write one word. Use a letter in that word to write another word. Keep going, writing words across and down. Try to link all the words in one chain. You may also make more than one chain.

MASTERY WORDS

jar
jet
job
jump
just
give

Follow the directions. Use the Mastery words.

1. Write the word that does not begin with /j/. _____give_____

2. Write the two words that end with consonant clusters.

   _____jump_____   _____just_____

Write the Mastery words with these vowel sounds.

3. /e/ _____jet_____   4. /o/ _____job_____

5. /i/ _____give_____

Write the Mastery word that goes with each word.

6. _____jump_____ rope   7. _____jet_____ plane

8. _____just_____ right   9. pickle _____jar_____

BONUS WORDS

join
jungle
gingerbread
gym
package
strange
fudge
ledge

1. Write the Bonus word that sounds the same as Jim.
2. Write the Bonus words that start with /j/ spelled j.
3. Rewrite these questions. Use Bonus words in place of the underlined words.

   What is in the odd box on the shelf? Is it spicy cake? Is it chocolate candy?

4. Write the names of other things that might be in the box. Use words that have /j/.   **See answers below.**

41

Spelling on Your Own Answers

BONUS WORDS

1. gym 2. join, jungle 3. What is in the strange package on the ledge? Is it gingerbread? Is it fudge? 4. Possible answers: *vegetables, jellybeans, gingersnaps.* Words do not necessarily have to be food names.

Summarize Learning

Have the children summarize what they have learned in this unit. *Ask:*

• What have you learned about writing words in sentence order? (The words must be placed in order so that they express a complete thought. The word that begins with a capital letter belongs at the beginning of the sentence. The word that is followed by a period belongs at the end of the sentence.)

• What spelling generalizations have you learned? How did you use these generalizations?

TEACHING PLAN

Objective To apply the unit spelling generalization to spell This Week's Words, Mastery words, and Bonus words independently.

THIS WEEK'S WORDS

1. Read the directions on page 41 aloud. Copy on the chalkboard the third step of the sample word chain given in the **Pupil Book.** Then ask the children to find a word on the list that can be linked up with *juice.* Add the word to the chain.
2. Have the children complete the activity independently.

MASTERY WORDS

1. Read the Mastery words aloud. Have the children repeat each word after you and identify the letter that spells /j/. Be sure the children recognize that g does not stand for /j/ in *give.*
2. Discuss the directions on page 41.
3. Have the children complete the activities independently.

BONUS WORDS

1. Have volunteers read the Bonus words aloud.
2. Briefly discuss the directions for **3** and **4.** Be sure the children understand that in **3** they should rewrite each question using Bonus words that have the same meaning as the underlined words. Also point out that in **4** the contents need not be food.
3. Have the children complete the activities on a separate piece of paper.

For reinforcement in writing spelling words, you may wish to assign *Extra Practice Master 9: Mastery Words* or *Bonus Words.*

CLOSING THE UNIT

Apply New Learning

Tell the children that if they misspell words with the sound /j/ in their writing, they should use one of the following strategies:

- think about the possible spellings for the /j/ sound and try to picture the word in their minds.
- write the word using different spellings and compare it with the spelling they picture in their minds.
- think of words that rhyme, and compare in their minds how they are spelled.

Transfer New Learning

Tell the children that when they encounter new words in their personal reading and in other content areas, they should learn the meaning of those words and then apply the generalizations they have studied to the spelling of those words. Tell the children that once the words are familiar in both meaning and spelling, they should use the new words in their writing.

ENRICHMENT ACTIVITIES

Classroom activities and **home activities** may be assigned to children of all ability levels. The activities provide opportunities for children to use their spelling words in new contexts.

For the Classroom

To individualize classroom activities, you may have the children use the word list they are studying in this unit:

- *Basic:* Use **Mastery** words to complete the activity.
- *Average:* Use **This Week's Words** to complete the activity.
- *Challenging:* Use **Bonus** words to complete the activity.

1. Language Arts/Writing Categories for Words Tell the children to classify spelling words into larger categories. Have the children write five spelling words across their papers. Above each word, have the children decide under what larger group, or category, each word belongs, and write the name of the category above that word. The children should add two or three new words to each of their categories.

■ COOPERATIVE LEARNING Have each group classify spelling words into larger categories. Tell each group to select as many words from the spelling list as there are group members and then work collaboratively to assign each word to a larger category. Each child within a group should then take one of the categories and add as many words to it as he or she can. Have group members check each other's words to see if they have been assigned to the proper categories. Then one member from each group should read the group's categories and words aloud, pausing to allow other children to give more words for the same category.

2. Language Arts/Writing Sentences About Fantasy and Reality Have the children use their spelling words to write four pairs of sentences, one of each pair based on reality, the other on fantasy. Tell the children to change the first sentence of each pair into fantasy by making as few changes as possible. Have the children copy one of each pair of sentences onto another piece of paper, leaving a blank in place of the spelling word. Then have them ask other children to supply the missing spelling words, and to label each sentence *Reality* or *Fantasy.*

■ COOPERATIVE LEARNING Each child within the group should use four spelling words to write realistic sentences. Group members should read their sentences aloud and exchange them. Then have group members change the sentences they received into fantasy, changing as few words as possible. One child in each group should collect and write the group's sentence pairs. Another child can read the pairs aloud and the other children can label them *Reality* or *Fantasy.*

3. Language Arts/Writing a Story Have the children write a brief story using the spelling words for this unit. As a **prewriting** activity, have the children look at the spelling words and try to group words into categories that might lead to a story idea. For example, the words *giraffe, danger, gentle, cage,* and *large* might be used in a story about zoo animals. After several story ideas have been discussed, have the children choose one idea and **compose** their stories. Remind the children to use as many spelling words as possible in their stories. When the children have completed their stories, have them **revise** their work. Remind them to check to see that there is a problem and a solution in their stories. You may wish to **publish** these stories in a class book or use them for a bulletin board display. You may make the stories available for the other children to read.

■ COOPERATIVE LEARNING Have each group write a story using the spelling words for this unit. Direct the children to page 252 in the **Writer's Guide** to read about stories. As a **prewriting** activity, have each child categorize some of the spelling words into a group that gives an idea for a story. Then have the children read these words to the rest of the group. As a group, have the children choose which category to write their story about. Remind the children to include the elements of character, plot, and setting in their story. Also remind them their story must have a problem and a solution. The children should work as a group to **compose** the story. One child should write the story. When the story is complete, another child should read it aloud. Then other children should make suggestions for **revising** the story. Remind the children to refer to the **Revising Checklist** on page 247 for help with revising their work. When the children are completely satisfied, have them **publish** their work by writing and illustrating the story for the other members of the class to read.

For the Home

Children may complete these activities independently or with the assistance of a relative or friend in the home.

1. **Language Arts/Writing a Descriptive Paragraph** Tell the children to write a paragraph describing an experience that could have taken place at the zoo. Refer the children to page 250 of the **Writer's Guide** for a model of a descriptive paragraph. Suggest that the paragraph might involve the child, an animal, and danger. Tell the children to review their spelling list for ideas, and use at least three spelling words in their paragraphs. Children should proofread their work for spelling, capitalization, and punctuation. Remind the children to use the **Revising Checklist** on page 247 for help. Then have the children share their work with a friend or relative.

2. **Science/Building Vocabulary on Animals** Tell the children to make a word map illustrating a zoo-related concept, using spelling words from this and previous units. Remind the children to write the concept word in the center of the page and circle it. They should then write words related to the concept word around that word, draw boxes around those words, and draw lines from the concept word to the other words to see how they are related. The children may ask a friend or relative to add to their maps. Provide the following model:

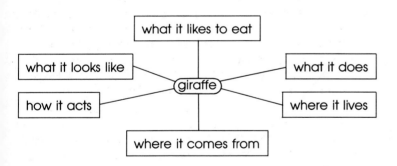

3. **Health/Writing Safety Rules for a Trip to the Zoo** Tell the children to write a list of rules to follow at the zoo. Remind them to consider the dangers, such as *being hurt by or hurting an animal,* and *getting lost.* Have the children use as many spelling words from this and previous lists as they can. The children may wish to add to their lists after discussing them with a family member. Have the children underline all spelling words and proofread their work for spelling, capitalization, and punctuation.

4. **Language Arts/Writing Sentences Using Words with /j/** Tell the children to write five sentences using their spelling words. They should identify the letters that stand for the /j/ sound in each spelling word, and then write a sentence using each spelling word and one or more words in which the same consonants stand for the /j/ sound. For example: *Janet enjoys juice.* Have the children check their sentences for spelling, and then share them with a family member.

EVALUATING SPELLING ABILITY

Unit Test

This Week's Words
1. *giraffe* A *giraffe* is a tall animal. **giraffe**
2. *danger* Stay here out of *danger.* **danger**
3. *jam* Micky makes strawberry *jam.* **jam**
4. *jug* Please pass the *jug* of milk. **jug**
5. *juice* Nan likes grape *juice.* **juice**
6. *gentle* Be *gentle* with the baby kitten. **gentle**
7. *giant* There is a *giant* tree in Tom's backyard. **giant**
8. *magic* The *magic* show was fun to watch. **magic**
9. *age* Pedro is tall for his *age.* **age**
10. *cage* We keep the hamsters in a *cage.* **cage**
11. *large* A hippopotamus is a *large* animal. **large**
12. *page* Fran finished reading the *page* first. **page**
13. *bridge* There is a new *bridge* over the river. **bridge**
14. *edge* Stand at the *edge* of the pond. **edge**
15. *judge* Arlene will *judge* the picture contest. **judge**

Mastery Words
1. *jar* That *jar* is full of jelly beans. **jar**
2. *jet* We flew on a *jet* to Florida. **jet**
3. *job* Deborah's *job* is to feed the animals. **job**
4. *jump* Ellen loves to *jump* rope. **jump**
5. *just* This will *just* take a few minutes. **just**
6. *give* Carl will *give* his sister a present. **give**

Bonus Words
1. *join* Sarah will *join* us for dinner. **join**
2. *jungle* Tigers live in the *jungle.* **jungle**
3. *gingerbread* Bill ate some *gingerbread.* **gingerbread**
4. *gym* The band will practice in the *gym.* **gym**
5. *package* Dorrie bought a *package* of flower seeds. **package**
6. *strange* Our cat hissed at the *strange* cat. **strange**
7. *fudge* Stephanie thinks *fudge* is too sweet. **fudge**
8. *ledge* Put the keys on the *ledge* by the door. **ledge**

Dictation Sentences

This Week's Words
1. The *giant giraffe* has a *magic cage.*
2. The *judge* turned the *large page* with his *gentle* hands.
3. There may be *danger* near the *edge* of the *bridge.*
4. A child his *age* can drink a small *jug* of *juice* with his *jam* sandwich.

Mastery Words
1. Please *give* me the *jar* before the bugs *jump* away.
2. His new *job* is not *just* to fly a *jet.*

Bonus Words
1. We left the *strange package* on the *ledge* near the *jungle gym.*
2. You can *join* us to make *fudge* and *gingerbread.*

Children who have made errors on the Unit Test may require reteaching. Use the following *Reteaching Strategies* and *Follow-up Masters 9A* and *9B* for additional instruction and practice of This Week's Words. (You may wish to assign *LEP Reteaching Follow-up Master 9* for reteaching of spelling words.)

A. Discovering Spelling Ideas

1. Say the following words as you write them on the chalkboard.

   job   general   gigantic   urge   ledge

2. Ask the children to identify the letters that spell the sound /j/ in these words. (*j, g, ge, dge*)
3. Ask the children to identify the vowels following the /j/ in *general* and *gigantic*. (*e* and *i*)
4. Ask the children where the /j/ appears in the word *urge*. (at the end of the word)
5. Ask the children what type of vowel comes before the /j/ in *ledge*. (short)
6. Ask the children what they have learned about spelling /j/. (It can be spelled with *j, g* before *e* or *i, ge* at the end of a word, or *dge* after a short vowel sound.)

B. Word Shapes

1. Explain to the children that each word has a shape and that remembering the shape of a word can help them to spell the word correctly.
2. On the chalkboard, write the words *jump* and *barge*. Have the children identify "short," "tall," and "tail" letters.
3. Draw the configuration of each word on the chalkboard, and ask the children which word fits in each shape.

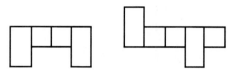

Use *Reteaching Follow-up Master 9A* to reinforce spelling generalizations taught in Unit 9.

Use *Reteaching Follow-up Master 9B* to reinforce spellings of This Week's Words for Unit 9.

Name _____
Reteaching Follow-up A   Discovering Spelling Ideas   UNIT **9**

THIS WEEK'S WORDS

danger	jam	juice	magic	cage
edge	bridge	giraffe	gentle	jug
giant	large	page	age	judge

1. Study This Week's Words. Say each word to yourself.

2. Write the words that have /j/ spelled like the /j/ in *jar*.
   jam   jug
   juice   judge

3. Write the words that have /j/ spelled like the /j/ in *ledge*.
   bridge   edge   judge

4. Write the words that have /j/ at the end spelled like the /j/ in *rage*.
   age   cage
   page   large

5. Write the words that have /j/ spelled like the /j/ in *gem* or *aging*.
   giraffe   danger   magic
   gentle   giant

6. Circle the letters in each word you wrote in **2–5** that spell the sound /j/.

7. What do This Week's Words show you about ways to spell /j/?

   /j/ can be spelled with a j, with g before e or i, with ge
   at the end of a word, or with dge after a short vowel sound.

   Reteaching • 15

Name _____
Reteaching Follow-up B   Word Shapes   UNIT **9**

THIS WEEK'S WORDS

danger	jam	juice	magic	cage
edge	bridge	giraffe	gentle	jug
giant	large	page	age	judge

Write each of This Week's Words in its correct shape. The first one has been done for you.   Children may interchange answers that fit the same configuration.

1. p a g e   2. l a r g e

3. j u i c e   4. a g e

5. d a n g e r   6. b r i d g e

7. e d g e   8. j u g

9. g e n t l e   10. m a g i c

11. c a g e   12. g i a n t

13. j u d g e   14. g i r a f f e

15. j a m

16 • Reteaching

Nine-Week Evaluation

Mark the circle for the word that is spelled right.

Sample A				
A	peice ⓐ	piec ⓑ	piece Ⓒ	peece ⓓ

Sample B				
B	byk ⓐ	bik ⓑ	byke Ⓒ	bike ⓓ

1	flag ⓐ	flagg ⓑ	fleg Ⓒ	flog ⓓ
2	aple ⓐ	appel ⓑ	apple Ⓒ	epple ⓓ
3	chall ⓐ	shal ⓑ	shall Ⓒ	shell ⓓ
4	unles ⓐ	unlese ⓑ	unleass Ⓒ	unless ⓓ
5	stuf ⓐ	stugh ⓑ	stuff Ⓒ	stoff ⓓ
6	triped ⓐ	tripped ⓑ	tript Ⓒ	trippt ⓓ
7	waging ⓐ	waggin ⓑ	wagin Ⓒ	wagging ⓓ
8	close ⓐ	kloz ⓑ	cloze Ⓒ	kloze ⓓ
9	draur ⓐ	drauer ⓑ	drawer Ⓒ	drawur ⓓ
10	floor ⓐ	flore ⓑ	flor Ⓒ	flour ⓓ

11	bild ⓐ	build ⓑ	biuld Ⓒ	billed ⓓ
12	grownd ⓐ	gruond ⓑ	groun Ⓒ	ground ⓓ
13	teecher ⓐ	teacher ⓑ	techer Ⓒ	teechur ⓓ
14	showt ⓐ	shout ⓑ	chout Ⓒ	chowt ⓓ
15	picture ⓐ	pictures ⓑ	pitcher Ⓒ	picteres ⓓ
16	uncles ⓐ	uncels ⓑ	unkles Ⓒ	uncle ⓓ
17	gueses ⓐ	gesses ⓑ	guesses Ⓒ	geusses ⓓ
18	danjur ⓐ	danger ⓑ	dangor Ⓒ	dainger ⓓ
19	larg ⓐ	larj ⓑ	larje Ⓒ	large ⓓ
20	juse ⓐ	juice ⓑ	juze Ⓒ	juise ⓓ

FORM B TEST 1

Administering the Test

1. Tell the children that today they will take a spelling test on some of the words they have studied in Units 1–9. Pass out the test papers. Tell the children to leave them turned upside down until you are ready to begin.

2. Have the children turn their tests over. Direct their attention to Sample A. Read this sentence: *piece* He ate a *piece* of pie. *piece* Point out that the test shows four ways to spell *piece*. Only one way is correct. Have the children note that circle *c* under the correct spelling is filled in.

3. Now direct the children's attention to Sample B. Read this sentence: *bike* The boy rode on his *bike*. *bike* Point out that this test shows four ways to spell *bike*. Ask a child to tell you which spelling is right by spelling the word—*b-i-k-e*. Repeat the right spelling, *b-i-k-e*, and have the children fill in circle *d* in pencil.

4. After you have checked to see that all children have completed Sample B correctly, have the children proceed with the test. Use these sentences.

1. **flag**   He raised the *flag*.   **flag**
2. **apple**   The *apple* is sweet.   **apple**
3. **shall**   I *shall* go too.   **shall**
4. **unless**   We will go *unless* it rains.   **unless**
5. **stuff**   He put the *stuff* away.   **stuff**
6. **tripped**   He *tripped* on the rock.   **tripped**
7. **wagging**   The dog is *wagging* his tail.   **wagging**
8. **close**   Please *close* the door.   **close**
9. **drawer**   Put the clothes in the *drawer*.   **drawer**
10. **floor**   She played on the *floor*.   **floor**
11. **build**   They will *build* the house.   **build**
12. **ground**   The *ground* is dry.   **ground**
13. **teacher**   The *teacher* will help me.   **teacher**
14. **shout**   We heard her *shout*.   **shout**
15. **pictures**   He painted several *pictures*.   **pictures**
16. **uncles**   They have four *uncles*.   **uncles**
17. **guesses**   She will have three *guesses*.   **guesses**
18. **danger**   The *danger* from the storm has passed.   **danger**
19. **large**   My dog is very *large*.   **large**
20. **juice**   My favorite drink is orange *juice*.   **juice**

Evaluating the Results

Use the following **Answer Key** to correct the children's tests and to determine whether they need more practice with particular units. The chart shows the units in which each answer word is taught.

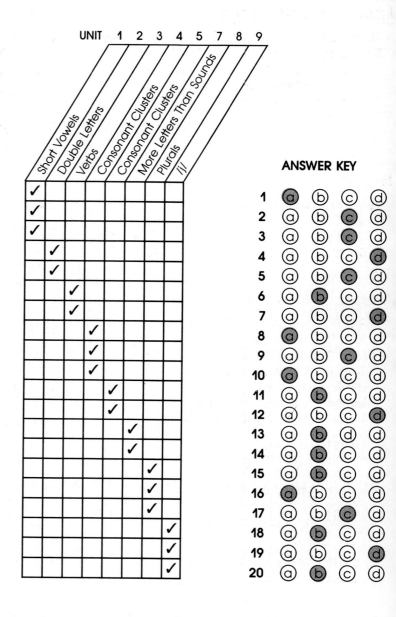

	UNIT 1 Short Vowels	2 Double Letters	3 Verbs	4 Consonant Clusters	5 Consonant Clusters	7 More Letters Than Sounds	8 Plurals	9 /j/
1	✓							
2	✓							
3	✓							
4		✓						
5		✓						
6			✓					
7			✓					
8			✓					
9				✓				
10				✓				
11					✓			
12					✓			
13						✓		
14						✓		
15							✓	
16							✓	
17							✓	
18								✓
19								✓
20								✓

ANSWER KEY

1. ⓐ ⓑ ⓒ ⓓ
2. ⓐ ⓑ ⓒ ⓓ
3. ⓐ ⓑ ⓒ ⓓ
4. ⓐ ⓑ ⓒ ⓓ
5. ⓐ ⓑ ⓒ ⓓ
6. ⓐ ⓑ ⓒ ⓓ
7. ⓐ ⓑ ⓒ ⓓ
8. ⓐ ⓑ ⓒ ⓓ
9. ⓐ ⓑ ⓒ ⓓ
10. ⓐ ⓑ ⓒ ⓓ
11. ⓐ ⓑ ⓒ ⓓ
12. ⓐ ⓑ ⓒ ⓓ
13. ⓐ ⓑ ⓒ ⓓ
14. ⓐ ⓑ ⓒ ⓓ
15. ⓐ ⓑ ⓒ ⓓ
16. ⓐ ⓑ ⓒ ⓓ
17. ⓐ ⓑ ⓒ ⓓ
18. ⓐ ⓑ ⓒ ⓓ
19. ⓐ ⓑ ⓒ ⓓ
20. ⓐ ⓑ ⓒ ⓓ

PREVIEWING THE UNIT

Unit Materials

Instruction and Practice

Pupil Book	pages 42–45
Teacher's Edition	
Teaching Plans	pages 42–45
Enrichment Activities	
For the Classroom	pages 45A–45B
For the Home	page 45B
Reteaching Strategies	page 45C

Testing

Teacher's Edition	
Trial Test	pages 41E–41F
Unit Test	page 45B
Dictation Test	page 45B

Additional Resources

PRACTICE AND REINFORCEMENT
Extra Practice Master 10: Unit Words
Extra Practice Master 10: Mastery Words
Extra Practice Master 10: Bonus Words
LEP Practice Master 10
Spelling and Language Master 10
Study Steps to Learn a Word Master

RETEACHING FOLLOW-UP
Reteaching Follow-up Master 10A:
 Discovering Spelling Ideas
Reteaching Follow-up Master 10B: Word
 Shapes
LEP Reteaching Follow-up Master 10

TEACHING AIDS
Spelling Generalizations Transparency 9

Click on the SPELLING banner to find activities for this unit.

Learner Objectives

Spelling

- To spell words that demonstrate these sound-letter relationships: /k/c, k at the beginning of words; /k/k, ck at the end of words.
- To recognize /k/c before a and o, /k/k before e and i.
- To recognize /kw/qu.
- To review alphabetical order.

Reading

- To follow directions.
- To use context clues to complete sentences given spelling words.
- To read a how-to paragraph.

Writing

- To write a how-to paragraph.
- To use the writing process.
- To proofread for spelling, capitalization, and punctuation.
- To write legible manuscript and cursive letters.

Listening

- To listen for consonant and vowel sounds in words.
- To listen for rhyming words.
- To follow oral directions.

Speaking

- To contribute ideas and information in group discussions.
- To respond to questions.
- To present a pantomime.
- To express feelings and ideas about a piece of writing.

THIS WEEK'S WORDS
kick
camp
candy
cane
cost
kept
key
kindness
kitten
speak
back
lucky
neck
pack
quick

MASTERY WORDS
sick
cold
cup
keep
cat
pick

BONUS WORDS
cabin
camera
creek
jacket
kettle
pocket
smoke
tickle

Assignment Guide

This guide shows how you teach a typical spelling unit in either a five-day or a three-day sequence, while providing for individual differences. **Boldface type** indicates essential classwork. Steps shown in light type may be done in class or assigned as homework.

Five Days	○ = average spellers ☆ = better spellers ✓ = slower spellers	Three Days
Day 1	• ☆ **Take This Week's Words Trial Test and correct** • ✓ **Take Mastery Word Trial Test and correct** • ☆ **Read This Week's Words and discuss generalization page 42**	Day 1
Day 2	• Complete Spelling Practice page 43 • ✓ Complete Extra Practice Master 10: This Week's Words (optional) ✓ Complete Spelling on Your Own: Mastery Words page 45 ☆ **Take Bonus Word Trial Test and correct**	
Day 3	• ☆ ✓ **Complete Spelling and Language page 44** • ☆ ✓ Complete Writing on Your Own page 44 • ☆ ✓ **Complete Using the Dictionary to Spell and Write page 44** • ✓ Take Midweek Test (optional) ☆ Complete Spelling on Your Own: Bonus Words page 45 • ✓ Complete Spelling and Language Master 10 (optional)	Day 2
Day 4	• Complete Spelling on Your Own: This Week's Words page 45 ✓ Complete Extra Practice Master 10: Mastery Words (optional) ☆ Complete Extra Practice Master 10: Bonus Words (optional)	
Day 5	• Take Unit Test on This Week's Words • Complete Reteaching Follow-up Masters 10A and 10B (optional) • ✓ **Take Unit Test on Mastery Words** ☆ **Take Unit Test on Bonus Words**	Day 3

Enrichment Activities for the **classroom** and for the **home** included at the end of this unit may be assigned selectively on any day of the week.

INTRODUCING THE UNIT

Establish Readiness for Learning

Tell the children that this week they will continue to study consonant sounds. In Unit 10 they will study several spellings for /k/ and learn when these spellings should be used. Tell the children that they will apply the spelling generalizations to This Week's Words and use those words to write a how-to paragraph.

Assess Children's Spelling Ability

Administer the Trial Test before the children study This Week's Words. Use the test sentences provided. Say each word and use it in a sentence. Then repeat the word. Have the children write the words on a separate sheet of paper or in their spelling notebooks. Test sentences are also provided for Mastery and Bonus words.

Have the children check their own work by listening to you read the spelling of the words or by referring to This Week's Words in the left column of the **Pupil Book.** For each misspelled word, have the children follow the **Study Steps to Learn a Word** on page 1 in the **Pupil Book** or use the copying master to study and write the words. Children should record the number correct on their **Progress Report.**

Trial Test Sentences

This Week's Words
1. *kick*   Robbie will *kick* the ball.   *kick*
2. *camp*   Erica went to *camp* last summer.   *camp*
3. *candy*   Too much *candy* is bad for your teeth.   *candy*
4. *cane*   Mr. Smythe walks with a *cane.* *cane*
5. *cost*   How much does this book *cost*? *cost*

FOCUS

- Establishes objectives
- Relates to prior learning
- Sets purpose of instruction

6. *kept* Grandma *kept* the picture I drew. **kept**

7. *key* This *key* will open that lock. **key**

8. *kindness* Always treat other people with *kindness.* **kindness**

9. *kitten* The *kitten* is asleep in the sun. **kitten**

10. *speak* Please *speak* clearly. **speak**

11. *back* A camel has a hump on its *back.* **back**

12. *lucky* Mindy feels *lucky* today. **lucky**

13. *neck* A giraffe has a long *neck.* **neck**

14. *pack* Mom helped Barry *pack* his suitcase. **pack**

15. *quick* Amos was *quick* to answer. **quick**

Mastery Words

1. *sick* Gail feels *sick.* **sick**
2. *cold* She has a bad *cold.* **cold**
3. *cup* I'd like a *cup* of hot soup. **cup**
4. *keep* I *keep* my marbles in a box. **keep**
5. *cat* We have a *cat* named Boots. **cat**
6. *pick* Let's *pick* some flowers. **pick**

Bonus Words

1. *cabin* Who lives in that log *cabin?* **cabin**
2. *camera* Rita took these pictures with her *camera.* **camera**

3. *creek* We went swimming in the *creek.* **creek**

4. *jacket* Alan's new *jacket* is bright red. **jacket**

5. *kettle* We heated water in a tea *kettle.* **kettle**

6. *pocket* Put your mittens in your *pocket.* **pocket**

7. *smoke* We smelled the *smoke* from the campfire. **smoke**

8. *tickle* Please don't *tickle* me. **tickle**

Apply Prior Learning

Have children apply what they already know about /k/ by using the following activity.

Write the words *tack, came, beak, kit* on the chalkboard. Ask children to try to discover what all these words have in common. Elicit from the children that all these words have /k/. Ask volunteers to come to the chalkboard and draw a line around the letter or letters that represent /k/ in each word. Have children note that /k/ is spelled *c* or *k* at the beginning of some words and /k/ is spelled *k* or *ck* at the end of some words. Tell the children that in Unit 10 they will study words that have these spellings for /k/. Explain that they can use these words in a variety of writing tasks: they can use the words in a note to a friend, in a letter, or in a story.

FOR CHILDREN WITH SPECIAL NEEDS

Learning Difficulties

Children with visual memory deficits will spell phonetically. For example, they may spell the word *lucky* as *luky* or the word *cap* as *kap.* These children rely on phonetically transcribing letter sounds instead of developing a visual image of the way a word is supposed to look. The following activity will help children to develop a visual image of their spelling words.

Write This Week's Words on the chalkboard. Point out the letters that represent /k/ in each word. Have the children write each word while saying each letter aloud. Then have them use a crayon to underline the letter that represents /k/ in each word. Repeat this activity at least three times for each word to reinforce the visual image of the words. Next erase the letters that represent /k/ in

each of This Week's Words on the chalkboard. Ask volunteers to come to the chalkboard and write the letter that represents /k/ in each spelling word.

Limited English Proficiency

To help limited English proficient children work with the spelling generalizations for Unit 10, you may wish to refer to the booklet "Suggestions and Activities for Limited English Proficient Students."

TEACHING PLAN

Objective To spell words that demonstrate these sound-letter relationships: initial /k/c, k; final /k/k, ck.

1. Have the children think of words that have the sound /k/. Write the words suggested on the chalkboard, grouping together words with initial /k/ and words with final /k/. When a number of words have been written on the chalkboard, help the children to recognize that /k/ is usually spelled c before a, o, and u and k before e and i. Help them also to see that /k/ is spelled ck after short vowel sounds and k after long vowel sounds.
2. Read the generalization on page 42 aloud.

You may wish to introduce the lesson by using **Spelling Generalizations Transparency 10.**

3. Have volunteers read This Week's Words aloud. As each word is read, ask the children to identify the letter or letters that spell /k/ in the word. If /k/ is in the initial position, have the child also name the vowel letter that follows the letter for /k/. If /k/ is in the final position (in a word or syllable), ask the child to indicate if the vowel sound that precedes /k/ is short or long.
4. Direct the children's attention to **Remember This** at the bottom of the page. Read the introductory sentence and the poem aloud. Have the children find the six words in the poem that begin like *quick*. Point out that *qu* represents the sound combination /kw/.

You may wish to assign **LEP Practice Master 10** for reinforcement in writing spelling words.

---

10 The Sound /k/

THIS WEEK'S WORDS

1. kick
2. camp
3. candy
4. cane
5. cost
6. kept
7. key
8. kindness
9. kitten
10. speak
11. back
12. lucky
13. neck
14. pack
15. quick

This Week's Words

All the words this week have the sound /k/. Here are the ways /k/ is spelled.

- with **c** or **k** at the beginning of a word

  <u>c</u>amp   <u>k</u>ey

- with **k** after a long vowel sound

  spea<u>k</u>

- with **ck** after a short vowel sound

  ba<u>ck</u>

REMEMBER THIS

The consonant sounds that begin <u>quick</u> are spelled **qu**.

**That queer old letter q
Would be quite quiet without a <u>u</u>.
It cannot question or quarrel or quack
Unless a <u>u</u> is right at its back.**

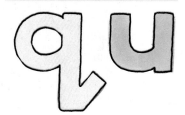

42

Extra Practice: This Week's Words

Name
Extra Practice   This Week's Words   UNIT 10

Finish the sentences with This Week's Words. Use each word only once.

1. Mark __kept__ the __key__ to his house in his pocket.
2. Aunt Ann gave Lenny a birthday gift. Lenny wrote Aunt Ann a note. It said, "Thank you for your __kindness__."
3. Jackie's __kitten__ wears a bell around its __neck__.
4. Peggy hung a __candy__ __cane__ on the Christmas tree.
5. "How much does this coat __cost__?"
6. Karen leaves for summer __camp__ in July.
7. "May I __speak__ to Mrs. Clark?" asked Donna.
8. The runner had a number on the __back__ of her shirt.
9. The football player tried to __kick__ the ball far.
10. Leroy's __lucky__ number is five.
11. The Nelsons began to __pack__ clothing for their weekend at the beach.
12. The mouse was too __quick__ for the cat. The mouse got away.

kick	camp	candy	cane	cost
kept	key	kindness	kitten	speak
back	lucky	neck	pack	quick

Extra Practice • 39

Extra Practice: Mastery Words

Name
Extra Practice   Mastery Words   UNIT 10

A. Write the Mastery word or words that rhyme with each word below. Then underline the letters that spell /k/.

told __cold__   deep __keep__

fat __cat__   pup __cup__

tick (two words) __sick__   __pick__

B. Finish each sentence with a Mastery word. There is a word with the sound /k/ in each sentence. The missing word has /k/ spelled with the same letter or letters.

1. Be sure to __keep__ your keys in a safe place.
2. Could I have some __cold__ orange juice, please?
3. Don't __pick__ up that black bug!
4. Melody's __cat__ has a soft coat.
5. I'm afraid my pet duck is __sick__.
6. Add a __cup__ of corn to the soup.

| sick | cold | cup | keep | cat | pick |

40 • Extra Practice

Spelling Practice

A. Follow the directions. Use This Week's Words.

1. Write the four words that begin with /k/ spelled <u>c</u>.

camp	candy
cane	cost

2. What vowel letters come after <u>c</u> in these words? <u>a</u>   <u>o</u>

3. Write the five words that begin with /k/ spelled <u>k</u>.

kept	key	kindness
kitten	kick	

4. What vowel letters come after <u>k</u> in these words? <u>e</u>   <u>i</u>

5. Write the six words that end with /k/. Circle the word that has a long vowel sound.

(speak)	back	kick
neck	pack	quick

6. What letter spells /k/ in the word you circled? <u>k</u>

B. Finish the sentences. Use This Week's Words. The underlined name shows how /k/ is spelled in the missing word.

7. <u>Kevin</u> dropped the <u>key</u> to his house.

8. <u>Carol</u> saw him drop it near the fire in the <u>camp</u>.

9. <u>Vicky</u> was <u>quick</u> to pick it up and give it back.

10. <u>Chuck</u> said it was <u>lucky</u> Kevin didn't lose it.

This Week's Words: kick, camp, candy, cane, cost, kept, key, kindness, kitten, speak, back, lucky, neck, pack, quick

43

TEACHING PLAN

Objectives To write words given the letters that spell /k/; to recognize that /k/ is spelled c before a and o; to recognize that /k/ is spelled k before e and i; to recognize that /k/ is spelled k after long vowel sounds; to write words in sentence context.

1. Briefly discuss the directions on page 43. Be sure the children understand that in Exercise **B** the proper noun gives a clue about the spelling for /k/ in the missing word.
2. Have the children complete the page independently. Remind them to use legible handwriting. You may wish to demonstrate the correct form of the letters c and k and then have the children practice writing the letters. For **Handwriting Models,** refer the children to page 258 in the **Pupil Book.**
3. To correct the children's work, have volunteers write the answers on the chalkboard, or check the answers orally. Let the children check their own responses.

For reinforcement in writing spelling words, you may wish to assign *Extra Practice Master 10: This Week's Words.*

★ *of special interest*

The letter q followed by u is regularly used in Latin to represent the double sound /kw/. However, this orthography did not occur in English until after the Norman Conquest and was not used with any regularity until the end of the 13th century. In Old English and early Middle English, the sounds /kw/ were represented by cw or cu.

Extra Practice: Bonus Words

Extra Practice   Bonus Words   UNIT 10

A. Read the story. Some of the words don't make sense. They are in the wrong place. Find the words that don't make sense and draw a line under each one. Then write each wrong word below the story.

Ernie and his uncle had walked all day. At last they came to the <u>pocket.</u> They would sleep there that night. Uncle John built a fire in the fireplace. Ernie watched the <u>tickle</u> go up the chimney. They hung a tin <u>camera</u> over the fire to heat some stew.

Uncle John said, "I'm going to the <u>smoke</u> to get some water. Put your <u>cabin</u> on, Ernie, and come along."

When Ernie was getting the water, Ernie pulled a <u>creek</u> out of his left <u>kettle.</u> "Smile, Uncle John!" he shouted. Ernie backed up to get all of Uncle John in the picture. He felt something <u>jacket</u> his face. He thought it was a bug or something awful, but it was just some pine needles. Ernie had backed up into a pine tree!

Correct words appear in right margin above: cabin, smoke, kettle, creek, jacket, camera, pocket, tickle

1. pocket	2. tickle	3. camera
4. smoke	5. cabin	6. creek
7. kettle	8. jacket	

B. Now write the story over on another piece of paper. Put each word you wrote in the right place.   Correct words appear in right margin above.

cabin camera creek jacket kettle pocket smoke tickle

Extra Practice • 41

Summarize Learning

Have the children summarize what they have learned on pages 42 and 43. *Ask:*
- What have you learned about /k/ in this lesson? (Initial /k/ is spelled c, k; final /k/ is spelled k, ck; /k/ is spelled c before a and o; /k/ is spelled k before e and i; /k/ is spelled ck after a short vowel sound.)
- What are examples of words to which these generalizations can be applied? (kick, kept, camp, cost; accept other examples)

TEACHING PLAN

SPELLING AND LANGUAGE

Objective   To write the past tense of given verbs.

1. To introduce this activity, write this question on the chalkboard:

    Did you *pick* a book to read?

    Elicit an answer that uses the word *picked*. Write *picked* on the board, and point out how *ed* is added to *pick* to spell the word *picked*.
2. Have the children complete the exercises independently.
3. Review the work orally, having the children check their own answers.

For extended practice in writing inflected verb forms, you may wish to assign **Spelling and Language Master 10.**

WRITING ON YOUR OWN

Objectives   To write a how-to paragraph; to proofread for spelling.

1. Review the directions.
2. As a **prewriting** activity, have the children name some steps one would take to prepare a dinner, and list their responses on the chalkboard. Then have each child **compose** a how-to paragraph which tells how to cook dinner. When the children are ready to **revise** their paragraphs, remind them to check spelling. For additional help, you may wish to refer them to the **Revising Checklist** on page 247 of the **Writer's Guide.** To **publish** the children's work, have them exchange their how-to paragraphs with their classmates. Invite volunteers to pantomime how to cook dinner as described in their classmates' paragraphs.

THIS WEEK'S WORDS

kick
camp
candy
cane
cost
kept
key
kindness
kitten
speak
back
lucky
neck
pack
quick

44

USING THE DICTIONARY

Objective   To write words in alphabetical order by first or second letter.

1. Read the introductory paragraph on page 44 aloud. Briefly review alphabetical order by writing the words below on the chalkboard and having the children put them in alphabetical order:
    sick sack sock
2. Have the children complete this activity independently.
3. Have volunteers write their alphabetical lists on the chalkboard. Let the children check their work.

Spelling and Language • Adding *ed*

You add *ed* to most verbs to tell what already happened. Add *ed* to the words in dark print. Finish the sentences.

1. camp   We _____ **camped** _____ near the river last night.

2. back   Mom _____ **backed** _____ the car up to our tent.

3. pack   Dad and I unloaded the _____ **packed** car.

4. kick   Then Angela and I _____ **kicked** _____ rocks into the water.

Writing on Your Own

Write a paragraph telling your classmates how you cooked dinner. Remember to add *ed* to most verbs to tell what already happened.

WRITER'S GUIDE For help with the past tense, turn to page 240.

Using the Dictionary to Spell and Write

A dictionary gives you information that will help you when you write. The words in a dictionary are in alphabetical order. If the first letters of words are the same, look at the next letter. <u>C</u>at, <u>c</u>ome, <u>c</u>ut are in order by the second letter—<u>a</u>, <u>o</u>, <u>u</u>.

Write each group of words in alphabetical order.

1. candy   **back**
kick   **candy**
back
cost   **cost**
key
            key

            kick

2. lucky   **kept**
kindness   **kindness**
quick
kept   **lucky**
speak
            quick

            speak

Spelling on Your Own

camp · stamp

THIS WEEK'S WORDS

Write each of This Week's Words. Think of a word that rhymes with that word. Then write the rhyming word.

See answers below.

MASTERY WORDS

sick
cold
cup
keep
cat
pick

Follow the directions. Use the Mastery words.

1. Write the two words that have the sound /i/.

_____sick_____   _____pick_____

2. Write the two words that end with the sound /k/.

_____sick_____   _____pick_____

3. Write the four words that begin with the sound /k/.

_____cold_____   _____cup_____

_____keep_____   _____cat_____

Change the first letter of each word. Write a Mastery word.

4. hold _____cold_____   **5.** hat _____cat_____

6. deep _____keep_____   **7.** pup _____cup_____

BONUS WORDS

cabin
camera
creek
jacket
kettle
pocket
smoke
tickle

1. Write the six Bonus words that have two or more vowel sounds.

2. Write the two words that begin with consonant clusters.

3. Write the two words that end the way <u>pickle</u> does.

4. Write the two words that end the way <u>ticket</u> does.

5. Write the word that begins and ends with /k/.

6. Write sentences using all the Bonus words. Try to make them tell a story. Your story could be about camping.

See answers below.

45

Spelling on Your Own Answers

THIS WEEK'S WORDS

Possible rhyming words are:

kick	**sick**	kitten	**mitten**
camp	**stamp**	speak	**weak**
candy	**handy**	back	**sack**
cane	**pane**	luck	**duck**
cost	**lost**	or	
kept	**slept**	lucky	**plucky**
key	**see**	neck	**check**
kind	**find**	pack	**crack**
or		quick	**stick**
kindness	**blindness**		

BONUS WORDS

1. cabin, camera, jacket, kettle, pocket, tickle **2.** creek, smoke **3.** kettle, tickle **4.** jacket, pocket **5.** creek **6.** Children will write as directed. Be sure to check spelling.

Summarize Learning

Have the children summarize what they have learned in this unit. *Ask:*

- What have you learned about verbs with the *ed* ending? (You add *ed* to most verbs to tell what already happened.)
- What did you learn about how words are arranged in a dictionary? (They are arranged in alphabetical order. If the first letters of words are the same, then the words are placed in order by the next letter.)
- What spelling generalizations have you learned? How did you use these generalizations?

Spelling on Your Own   UNIT 10d

TEACHING PLAN

Objective To apply the unit spelling generalization to spell This Week's Words, Mastery words, and Bonus words independently.

THIS WEEK'S WORDS

1. Read the directions on page 45 aloud. Help children get started by asking them to suggest words that rhyme with *kick*. For *lucky* and *kindness*, tell them that they may write words that rhyme with the base words, *luck* and *kind*.
2. Have the children complete the activity independently on a separate piece of paper.

MASTERY WORDS

1. Review the unit generalization on page 42. Then read the Mastery words aloud, and have children repeat each word after you. Have volunteers identify the letter or letters that stand for /k/.
2. Briefly discuss the directions on page 45 to be sure that the children understand them.
3. Have the children complete the activities independently.

BONUS WORDS

1. Briefly review the unit generalization on page 42.
2. Have volunteers read the Bonus words aloud. Encourage the children to look up the meaning of any unfamiliar words in the **Spelling Dictionary.**
3. Have the children complete the exercises independently on a separate piece of paper.

For reinforcement in writing spelling words, you may wish to assign ***Extra Practice Master 10: Mastery Words*** or ***Bonus Words.***

CLOSING THE UNIT

Apply New Learning

Tell the children that if they misspell words with the sound /k/ in their writing, they should use one or more of the following strategies:

- think about the possible spellings for /k/ and try to picture the word in their minds.
- think of words that rhyme and compare in their minds how they are spelled.
- look at the changes in spelling that occur in related words.
- say the word to themselves and check to see if letters have been left out.

Transfer New Learning

Tell the children that when they encounter new words in their personal reading and in other content areas, they should learn the meaning of those words and then apply the generalizations they have studied to the spelling of those words. Tell them that once the words are familiar in both meaning and spelling, they should use them in their writing.

ENRICHMENT ACTIVITIES

Classroom activities and **home activities** may be assigned to children of all ability levels. The activities provide opportunities for children to use their spelling words in new contexts.

For the Classroom

To individualize classroom activities, you may have the children use the word list they are studying in this unit.

- *Basic:* Use **Mastery** words to complete the activity.
- *Average:* Use **This Week's Words** to complete the activity.
- *Challenging:* Use **Bonus** words to complete the activity.

1. Language Arts/Writing Analogies Tell the children to use some of the spelling words to write analogies. Explain that an analogy is a special kind of comparison. To illustrate analogies, have children complete these examples: *boy is to man as girl is to _____; happy is to sad as large is to _____; foot is to shoe as hand is to _____.* Tell children that when they write an analogy, they must think about how the first two words are related. For example, a *man* is an adult *boy; happy* is the opposite of *sad;* a *foot* goes into a *shoe.* Then they must think of two more words that are related in the same way as the first two words. For example, a *woman* is an adult *girl; small* is the opposite of *large;* a *hand* goes into a *glove.* Ask the children to use their spelling words to write three analogies. Then have the children copy their analogies,

leaving the last words blank. Tell the children to exchange papers and complete each other's analogies.

■ COOPERATIVE LEARNING: Tell each group to use spelling words to write analogies. Explain that an analogy is a special kind of comparison. Make sure that each group has worked through and understands the three examples given above. Then have each group member use spelling words to write three analogies. Tell group members to respond to their group's analogies, discussing how the pairs of words are related, and whether the analogies are successful. When each group has six satisfactory analogies, have a group recorder copy them, leaving the last words blank for other members of the class to complete. You may wish to keep each group's analogies in a class book, or keep them available for other members of the class to read.

2. Language Arts/Writing a Friendly Letter Have each child write a letter to a friend. As a *prewriting* activity, have the children review page 251 in the **Writer's Guide,** which tells about friendly letters. Suggest that the children go over the spelling lists in search of interesting topics to develop their letters. After they have written down a few key ideas, have the children select one or two and then jot down notes about what they will write. After the prewriting acitivties are completed, have the children use the notes to *compose* their letters. Remind the children to use as many spelling words as possible. Then have the children *revise,* making sure their letters have the five correct parts. Remind the children to refer to the **Revising Checklist** on page 247 and to proofread for spelling, capitalization, and punctuation errors. The children may make an envelope out of a large sheet of paper and address it to a friend. *Publish* the children's work by having each child fold the letter, enclose it in its envelope, and send it to the person for whom it is intended.

■ COOPERATIVE LEARNING: Have each group collaborate to write a friendly letter. As a *prewriting* activity, first direct the group's attention to page 251 of the **Writer's Guide** to read about friendly letters. Have each group member go over the spelling lists for topic ideas for the body of the letter. Tell group members to share ideas and select one or two topics to include in the letter. When the children are ready to *compose* the letter, have them choose one child to record while the other children each contribute a sentence or two. The children should use as many spelling words as possible. Then each group member should help to *revise* the letter, checking to see if it has all five parts, and whether spelling, capitalization, and punctuation are correct. Have one child rewrite the letter and have all the children sign it. One child can fold a large sheet of paper into an envelope shape and address it.

Each group can then **publish** their letters by putting them in their envelopes and exchanging the letters with other groups.

For the Home

Children may complete these activities independently or with the assistance of a relative or friend in the home.

1. Language Arts/Writing an Advertisement Have the children write an advertisement trying to convince someone to buy a kitten. The children should first generate a list of reasons why buying a kitten is a good idea. Advertisements might mention what the kitten looks like, how it acts, its care, and its cost. Tell the children to use several words with the /k/ sound, and underline each one after they have finished writing their ads.

2. Science/Writing Guidelines for Pet Care Tell the children to use several of the spelling words to write a two-column list of do's and do not's for taking care of a pet kitten. Suggest that they consider ways to identify the animal in case it gets lost, to make the animal feel good, to be healthy, and to trust its owner. Tell the children to include other words with the /k/ sound along with spelling words. The children should check their work for spelling errors, then read their lists to a relative or friend.

3. Language Arts/Building New Words from Spelling Words Have the children replace the /k/ sound in at least five spelling words and add one or more letters to make new words. The children should check a dictionary to see if the new words are spelled correctly, then use each one in a sentence. The children may wish to read their sentences to someone.

EVALUATING SPELLING ABILITY

Unit Test

This Week's Words
1. **kick**   Beth gave the ball a hard *kick*.   **kick**
2. **camp**   Let's *camp* here by the stream.   **camp**
3. **candy**   Don't eat *candy* between meals.   **candy**
4. **cane**   The man tapped his *cane* on the floor.   **cane**
5. **cost**   New cars *cost* a lot of money.   **cost**
6. **kept**   They *kept* the surprise party a secret.   **kept**
7. **key**   This is the *key* to the front door.   **key**
8. **kindness**   We thanked them for their *kindness*.   **kindness**

9. **kitten**   A *kitten* is cute and playful.   **kitten**
10. **speak**   Our teacher will *speak* at the meeting.   **speak**
11. **back**   We sat in the *back* row.   **back**
12. **lucky**   Are four-leaf clovers really *lucky*?   **lucky**
13. **neck**   I wrapped a scarf around my *neck*.   **neck**
14. **pack**   The hiker carried a *pack* on her back.   **pack**
15. **quick**   Diane made a *quick* trip to the store.   **quick**

Mastery Words
1. **sick**   No one likes being *sick*.   **sick**
2. **cold**   We wear warm clothes in *cold* weather.   **cold**
3. **cup**   I dropped the *cup* of juice on the floor.   **cup**
4. **keep**   You may *keep* that pencil.   **keep**
5. **cat**   My *cat* has long whiskers.   **cat**
6. **pick**   Mom will *pick* us up after school.   **pick**

Bonus Words
1. **cabin**   The Logans have a *cabin* in the woods.   **cabin**
2. **camera**   Greg put film in the *camera*.   **camera**
3. **creek**   This path leads down to the *creek*.   **creek**
4. **jacket**   Please hang up your *jacket*.   **jacket**
5. **kettle**   We cooked the spaghetti in a big *kettle*.   **kettle**
6. **pocket**   Sally put the money in her *pocket*.   **pocket**
7. **smoke**   The *smoke* made our eyes burn.   **smoke**
8. **tickle**   A *tickle* in my throat made me cough.   **tickle**

Dictation Sentences

This Week's Words
1. He was *lucky* to get his *kitten* back.
2. He *kept* a *candy* cane in his *pack* at *camp*.
3. The bike *cost* us very little because of their *kindness*.
4. He *kept* the *key* on a string hanging on his *neck*.
5. I will *speak* to her about that *quick kick*.

Mastery Words
1. You should *keep* drinking juice when you are *sick* with a *cold*.
2. Please *pick* up the *cup* of milk so the *cat* will not drink it.

Bonus Words
1. I left the *kettle* in the *cabin* by the *creek*.
2. The *smoke* from the fire started to *tickle* my nose.
3. He put his *camera* in the *pocket* of his *jacket*.

Children who have made errors on the Unit Test may require reteaching. Use the following **Reteaching Strategies** and **Follow-up Masters 10A** and **10B** for additional instruction and practice of This Week's Words. (You may wish to assign **LEP Reteaching Follow-up Master 10** for reteaching of spelling words.)

A. Discovering Spelling Ideas

1. Say the following words as you write them on the chalkboard.

   cold   kangaroo   leak   sack

2. Ask the children to identify the consonant sound that all the words have. (/k/)
3. Ask the children to identify the letters used to spell /k/ in *cold* and *kangaroo* and their position in the words. (*c* and *k* at the beginning of the words)
4. Ask the children to identify the type of vowel sounds before /k/ in *leak* and *sack*. (long, short)
5. Ask the children what they have learned about spelling /k/. (It can be spelled with *c* or *k* at the beginning of a word, *k* after a long vowel sound, and *ck* after a short vowel sound.)

B. Word Shapes

1. Explain to the children that each word has a shape and that remembering the shape of a word can help them to spell the word correctly.
2. On the chalkboard, write the words *cast* and *snack*. Have the children identify "short," "tall," and "tail" letters.
3. Draw the configuration of each word on the chalkboard, and ask the children which word fits in each shape.

Use **Reteaching Follow-up Master 10A** to reinforce spelling generalizations taught in Unit 10.

Use **Reteaching Follow-up Master 10B** to reinforce spellings of This Week's Words for Unit 10.

PREVIEWING THE UNIT

Unit Materials

Instruction and Practice

Pupil Book	pages 46–49
Teacher's Edition	
Teaching Plans	pages 46–49
Enrichment Activities	
For the Classroom	page 49A
For the Home	page 49B
Reteaching Strategies	page 49C

Testing

Teacher's Edition	
Trial Test	pages 45E–45F
Unit Test	page 49B
Dictation Test	page 49B

Additional Resources

Teacher's Resource Package

PRACTICE AND REINFORCEMENT
Extra Practice Master 11: This Week's Words
Extra Practice Master 11: Mastery Words
Extra Practice Master 11: Bonus Words
LEP Practice Master 11
Spelling and Language Master 11
Study Steps to Learn a Word Master

RETEACHING FOLLOW-UP
Reteaching Follow-up Master 11A:
  Discovering Spelling Ideas
Reteaching Follow-up Master 11B: Word
  Shapes
LEP Reteaching Follow-up Master 11

TEACHING AIDS
Spelling Generalizations Transparency 10

Visit our Web site
http://www.hbschool.com

Click on the SPELLING banner to find activities for this unit.

Learner Objectives

Spelling

- To spell words that demonstrate these sound-letter relationships: initial /s/s, c; final /s/ce, ss.
- To form the plurals of nouns by adding s or es.

Reading

- To follow written directions.
- To use context clues to write words.
- To use the dictionary.

Writing

- To write a paragraph.
- To use the writing process.
- To proofread for spelling, capitalization, and punctuation.
- To write legible manuscript and cursive letters.

Listening

- To listen for consonant and vowel sounds in words.
- To follow oral directions.

Speaking

- To contribute ideas and information in group discussions.
- To respond to questions.
- To present poems to the class.
- To express feelings and ideas about a piece of writing.

THIS WEEK'S WORDS

six
city
police
suit
ask
listen
decide
ice
pencil
price
princess
fence
once
piece
sentence

MASTERY WORDS

face
seed
nice
sent
place
soft

BONUS WORDS

bicycle
certain
notice
peace
recite
secret
silver
since

Assignment Guide

This guide shows how you teach a typical spelling unit in either a five-day or a three-day sequence, while providing for individual differences. **Boldface type** indicates essential classwork. Steps shown in light type may be done in class or assigned as homework.

Five Days	○ = average spellers ★ = better spellers ✓ = slower spellers	Three Days
Day **1**	**a** ○ ★ **Take This Week's Words Trial Test and correct** ○ ✓ **Take Mastery Word Trial Test and correct** ○ ★ **Read This Week's Words and discuss generalization on page 46**	Day **1**
Day **2**	○ Complete Spelling Practice page 47 ○ ✓ Complete Extra Practice Master 11: This Week's Words (optional) ✓ Complete Spelling on Your Own: Mastery Words page 49 ★ **Take Bonus Word Trial Test and correct** **b**	
Day **3**	**c** ○ ★ ✓ **Complete Spelling and Language page 48** ○ ★ ✓ Complete Writing on Your Own page 48 ○ ✓ Take Midweek Test (optional) ★ Complete Spelling on Your Own: Bonus Words page 49 ○ ✓ Complete Spelling and Language Master 11 (optional)	Day **2**
Day **4**	○ Complete Spelling on Your Own: This Week's Words page 49 ✓ Complete Extra Practice Master 11: Mastery words (optional) ★ Complete Extra Practice Master 11: Bonus words (optional) **d**	
Day **5**	**e** ○ Take Unit Test on This Week's Words ○ Complete Reteaching Follow-up Masters 11A and 11B (optional) ○ ✓ **Take Unit Test on Mastery Words** ★ **Take Unit Test on Bonus Words**	Day **3**

Enrichment Activities for the **classroom** and for the **home** included at the end of this unit may be assigned selectively on any day of the week.

INTRODUCING THE UNIT

Establish Readiness for Learning

Tell the children that this week they will continue to learn about the different spellings of initial and final consonant sounds. In Unit 11 they will study several spellings for the /s/ sound. Tell the children that they will apply the spelling generalizations to This Week's Words and use those words to write a pararaph.

Assess Children's Spelling Ability

Administer the Trial Test before the children study This Week's Words. Use the test sentences provided. Say each word and use it in a sentence. Then repeat the word. Have the children write the words on a separate sheet of paper or in their spelling notebooks. Test sentences are also provided for Mastery and Bonus words.

Have the children check their own work by listening to you read the spelling of the words or by referring to This Week's Words in the left column of the **Pupil Book.** For each misspelled word, have the children follow the **Study Steps to Learn a Word** on page 1 in the **Pupil Book** or use the copying master to study and write the words. Children should record the number correct on their **Progress Report.**

Trial Test Sentences

This Week's Words
1. *six*   The cat has *six* kittens.   **six**
2. *city*   Dallas is a big *city.*   **city**
3. *police*   They called the *police* to get help.   **police**
4. *suit*   Dave has a new *suit.*   **suit**
5. *ask*   Joanne called to *ask* me a question.   **ask**
6. *listen*   Let's *listen* to this record next.   **listen**
7. *decide*   Maria must *decide* what to do.   **decide**

FOCUS

- Establishes objectives
- Relates to prior learning
- Sets purpose of instruction

Spelling on Your Own

THIS WEEK'S WORDS

Write some funny story titles. Use This Week's Words. Try to use more than one of the words in each title. Here is an example: "The Princess and the Pencil."

MASTERY WORDS

| face |
| seed |
| nice |
| sent |
| place |
| soft |

Follow the directions. Use the Mastery words.

1. Write the three words that begin with /s/.

seed   sent   soft

2. Write the three words that end with /s/.

face   nice   place

3. Write the three words that have consonant clusters.

sent   place   soft

Finish the sentences. Use the Mastery words.

4. Mr. Witter is a _____nice_____ person.

5. He always has a smile on his _____face_____ .

BONUS WORDS

| bicycle |
| certain |
| notice |
| peace |
| recite |
| secret |
| silver |
| since |

Follow the directions. Use the Bonus words.

1. Write the word that sounds just like <u>piece</u>. Then use the two words in sentences.

2. Write the word that begins and ends with /s/.

3. Rewrite this sentence: "Are you <u>sure</u> you didn't <u>see</u> anything odd?" Use Bonus words in place of the underlined words.

Write the Bonus words that go with these words.

4. ___ a poem **5.** ride a ___ **6.** keep a ___ **7.** ___ spoon

See answers below.

49

Spelling on Your Own Answers

BONUS WORDS

1. peace EXAMPLES: May I have a <u>piece</u> of cake? After the war there was <u>peace</u>. 2. since 3. Are you <u>certain</u> you didn't <u>notice</u> anything odd? 4. recite 5. bicycle 6. secret 7. silver

Summarize Learning

Have the children summarize what they have learned in this unit. *Ask:*

● What have you learned about forming the plurals of nouns? (The plurals of some nouns can be formed by adding *s*. The plurals of words that end with *s, ss, sh, ch,* or *x* must be formed by adding *es*.) Give examples. (suits, sixes; accept other

● What spelling generalizations have you learned? How did you use these generalizations?

Spelling on Your Own

UNIT 11d

TEACHING PLAN

> **Objective** To apply the unit spelling generalization to spell This Week's Words, Mastery words, and Bonus words independently.

THIS WEEK'S WORDS

1. Read the directions on page 49 aloud. To help the children get started, have volunteers suggest some titles using This Week's Words.
2. Have the children complete the activity on a piece of paper. Tell them to use each word at least once.
3. Allow time for volunteers to share some of their story titles.
4. This activity may be extended by having the children choose one of their titles and write a story.

MASTERY WORDS

1. Review these spellings for initial and final /s/: s and ce. Then read the Mastery words aloud, having the children repeat each one after you.
2. Read the directions on page 49 aloud. Remind the children that the symbol /s/ stands for a sound. Briefly review consonant clusters.
3. Have the children complete the activities independently.

BONUS WORDS

1. Briefly review the unit generalization on page 46.
2. Have volunteers read the Bonus words aloud. Discuss the meanings of the words, and have the children look up unfamiliar words in the **Spelling Dictionary.**
3. Have the children complete the exercises independently on a separate piece of paper.

For reinforcement in writing spelling words, you may wish to assign **Extra Practice Master 11: Mastery Words** or **Bonus Words.**

CLOSING THE UNIT

Apply New Learning

Tell the children that when they misspell a word with the /s/ sound in their writing they should use one or more of the following strategies:

- think about the possible spellings for the /s/ sound and try to picture the word in their minds.
- write the word using different spellings and compare it with the spellings they picture in their minds.
- say the word to themselves and check to see if letters have been left out.

Transfer New Learning

Tell the children that when they encounter new words in their personal reading and in other content areas, they should learn the meaning of those words and then apply the generalizations they have studied to the spelling of those words. Tell them that once the words are familiar in both meaning and spelling, they should use the new words in their writing.

ENRICHMENT ACTIVITIES

Classroom activities and **home activities** may be assigned to children of all ability levels. The activities provide opportunities for children to use their spelling words in new contexts.

For the Classroom

To individualize classroom activities, you may have the children use the word list they are studying in this unit.

- *Basic:* Use **Mastery** words to complete the activity.
- *Average:* Use **This Week's Words** to complete the activity.
- *Challenging:* Use **Bonus** words to complete the activity.

1. **Language Arts/Writing Guide Words** Tell each child to choose five spelling words and then decide on two new words that might serve as the guide words at the top of a dictionary page listing each of the spelling words. When the children have finished this activity, have them copy only the five sets of guide words onto a sheet of paper. Children can exchange guide words and write the spelling word that belongs under each set.

   ■ COOPERATIVE LEARNING: Have each group write guide words that might be at the top of the dictionary page on which each of four spelling words might be found. Assign different words to each group. After group members have written four sets of guide words, have all the children within the group share and discuss whether the guide words are acceptable. Then have the children

add at least five other words that would appear on each dictionary page. Have the children make the four pages into a small dictionary. Ask the children to illustrate some of the words. Display the dictionaries from each group on a bulletin board for the rest of the class to read.

2. **Language Arts/Writing Rhyming Poetry** Have the children use some of the spelling words to write rhyming poetry. Ask the children to write rhyming pairs, thinking of a rhyming word for as many spelling words as they can. Then have them write some short poems using the words, and share the poems orally.

   ■ COOPERATIVE LEARNING: Have each group write a rhyming poem. Have each group member write rhyming words for as many spelling words as possible. The group should then compare lists and choose the rhyming pair they like best for each spelling word. Then the group should begin to write a rhyming poem, using the rhyming pairs they have chosen. One child should write down the lines as the children suggest them. When the group has used all the word pairs, the group should read the poem and revise it as necessary. They should then choose one member to rewrite the poem and read it aloud to the entire class.

3. **Language Arts/Writing a Story** Have each child use the spelling words to write a mystery story. Explain that a mystery story has the three basic elements: characters, setting, and plot. Point out that writers of mystery stories give clues so the reader can try to guess the answer to the mystery. As a **prewriting** activity, have each child brainstorm possible mysteries or crimes, using the spelling lists for ideas. Then tell the children to make a chart with the headings *Character(s)*, *Setting*, and *Plot*. Under *Plot*, have them list the mystery, and how it will be solved. When the children have finished, have them use their list and chart to **compose** the story. Then have the children **revise** their stories, making sure they have invented a mystery, a character who solves it, and clues for the reader to pick up before the story ends. Remind the children to give their stories a title. Have each child design an intriguing cover for his or her story. **Publish** the stories by displaying them on a mystery table.

   ■ COOPERATIVE LEARNING: Have each group write a mystery story using as many spelling words as possible. As a **prewriting** activity, tell each group to brainstorm kinds of mysteries. Have each group choose a person to write down the details on a chart headed *Character(s)*, *Setting*, and *Plot*. Each child should **compose** sections of the actual story. One child should write it down. Group members should **revise** the story by checking to see if a mystery has been introduced, puzzled over, and solved. The children should all check for correct spelling, capitalization, and punctuation. Every group can **publish** its work by illustrating a cover for the story and making it available to classmates on a mystery table.

For the Home

Children may complete these activities independently or with the assistance of a relative or friend in the home.

1. **Language Arts/Writing Word Comparisons** Have the children make up word comparisons using some of their spelling words. Remind them that a word comparison is a definition that compares one word to another word. For example: a *city* is a community where people live and work; a *city* is like a village, but much, much bigger; a *city* has many neighborhoods, while a village may have only one. Have the children proofread their word comparisons for spelling, punctuation, and capitalization. Children may share their word comparisons with a friend or a member of their family.

2. **Language Arts/Writing an Opinion** Have the children write a paragraph in which they give their opinion on a particular topic. Remind children that an opinion is made up of statements with which people may disagree. Children should refer to the **Writer's Guide** on page 249 to read about paragraph structure. Then they should begin their paragraph by stating their opinion. The other sentences in the paragraph should support that opinion. For example, a first sentence might be: Every country should have a *princess*. Other sentences should go on to tell why this is so. Tell the children to use several spelling words and words with the sound /s/ in their opinion paragraphs. Remind the children to proofread their paragraphs for spelling, capitalization, and punctuation, and to use the **Revising Checklist** on page 247 for help.

3. **Social Studies/Writing a Factual Paragraph on Police Services** Tell the children to write a paragraph telling what services the police perform in their city or community. To stimulate their ideas, ask the children to first imagine a community with no police. The paragraphs should begin with a statement of the main idea and continue with sentences that relate to that main idea. Remind the children to use spelling words and other words with the /s/ sound in their paragraphs. The children may ask a family member for ideas before they write. They should proofread their work for spelling, capitalization, and punctuation and use the **Revising Checklist** on page 247 for help. The children may bring their work in to school to share with classmates.

4. **Science/Writing Observations of an Ice Cube** Tell the children to write a report based upon their observations of an ice cube. For one week, the children should watch a piece of ice under as many conditions as possible. For example, in cold juice, in soapy water, on the stove, in a glass on the window sill. Then have the children write about the various things they did with the ice and what happened to the ice in each case. The report may be in prose or chart form. Tell the children to use spelling words from this and earlier units, as well as other words with the /s/ sound. Have children proofread their work for spelling errors. Children may share their findings with a family member, a friend, or the class.

EVALUATING SPELLING ABILITY

Unit Test

This Week's Words
1. *six*   Trisha ate *six* pancakes.   *six*
2. *city*   Miguel plays in the *city* park.   *city*
3. *police*   The *police* found the child.   *police*
4. *suit*   The clown wore a baggy *suit*.   *suit*
5. *ask*   Aunt Jane will come if we *ask* her.   *ask*
6. *listen*   Please *listen* to the story carefully.   *listen*
7. *decide*   Artie cannot *decide* which book to buy.   *decide*
8. *ice*   The *ice* on the sidewalk is slippery.   *ice*
9. *pencil*   The red *pencil* is Harry's.   *pencil*
10. *price*   The *price* of food has gone up.   *price*
11. *princess*   Cinderella became a *princess*.   *princess*
12. *fence*   There is a *fence* around our yard.   *fence*
13. *once*   We had a brown dog *once*.   *once*
14. *piece*   I'll use this *piece* of paper for my letter.   *piece*
15. *sentence*   A *sentence* starts with a capital letter.   *sentence*

Mastery Words
1. *face*   Troy had a grin on his *face*.   *face*
2. *seed*   Karen found a *seed* in her orange juice.   *seed*
3. *nice*   George did a *nice* job.   *nice*
4. *sent*   Mom *sent* Larry to the store.   *sent*
5. *place*   We need a *place* to hide the gift.   *place*
6. *soft*   A baby's skin is very *soft*.   *soft*

Bonus Words
1. *bicycle*   Mom has a ten-speed *bicycle*.   *bicycle*
2. *certain*   Lisa wants a *certain* kind of boots.   *certain*
3. *notice*   Nick did not *notice* Ed's new glasses.   *notice*
4. *peace*   We want *peace* in the world.   *peace*
5. *recite*   The children will *recite* their poems.   *recite*
6. *secret*   Rachel has a *secret* pocket in her coat.   *secret*
7. *silver*   The dentist put a *silver* filling in the tooth.   *silver*
8. *since*   Kristin has been waiting *since* two o'clock.   *since*

Dictation Sentences

This Week's Words
1. I had to *ask* the *police* for help *once*.
2. Will you *listen* and *decide* if the *sentence* is right?
3. I made *six* pictures with my *pencil*.
4. The *princess* fell on a *piece* of *ice* near the *fence*.
5. The *city* store has the *suit* at a good *price*.

Mastery Words
1. The cat sat in a *nice soft place*.
2. I *sent* the *seed* for him to plant.
3. He had a smile on his *face*.

Bonus Words
1. They are *certain* to *notice* my new *silver bicycle*.
2. He will *recite* a story about a *secret* door.
3. They have been happy *since peace* came to their town.

RETEACHING STRATEGIES FOR SPELLING

Children who have made errors on the Unit Test may require reteaching. Use the following *Reteaching Strategies* and *Follow-up Masters 11A* and *11B* for additional instruction and practice of This Week's Words. (You may wish to assign *LEP Reteaching Follow-up Master 11* for reteaching of spelling words.)

A. Discovering Spelling Ideas

1. Say the following words as you write them on the chalkboard.

    sad   decent   nice

2. Ask the children to identify the consonant sound that each word has. (/s/)
3. Ask the children to identify what letters are used to spell /s/ in *sad* and *decent*. (s, c)
4. Ask the children to identify the letters used to spell /s/ in *nice* and where they appear in the word. (ce; at the end of the word)
5. Ask the children what they have learned about spelling /s/. (It can be spelled with s, c, or ce at the end of a word.)

B. Word Shapes

1. Explain to the children that each word has a shape and that remembering the shape of a word can help them to spell the word correctly.
2. On the chalkboard, write the words *seem* and *brace*. Have the children identify "short," "tall," and "tail" letters.
3. Draw the configuration of each word on the chalkboard, and ask the children which word fits in each shape.

Use *Reteaching Follow-up Master 11A* to reinforce spelling generalizations taught in Unit 11.

Use *Reteaching Follow-up Master 11B* to reinforce spellings of This Week's Words for Unit 11.

PREVIEWING THE UNIT

Unit Materials

Instruction and Practice

Pupil Book	pages 50–55
Teacher's Edition	
Teaching Plans	pages 50–55
Enrichment Activities	
For the Home	page 55A

Testing

Teacher's Edition	
Trial Test	pages 49E–49F
Unit Test	page 55A
Form *A** Test	pages T5–T6

*If your grading period is six weeks, you may want to use the **Form A Test** at the end of this unit.

Additional Resources

PRACTICE AND REINFORCEMENT
Review Master 12A: Units 7 and 8
Review Master 12B: Units 9 and 10
Review Master 12C: Unit 11 and Test
    Exercise
Dictionary and Proofreading Master 2
Study Steps to Learn a Word Master
Mastery Words Review: Units 7–11
Bonus Words Review: Units 7–11

TESTING (OPTIONAL)
Mastery Words Test: Units 7–11
Bonus Words Test: Units 7–11
Writing Test 2

TEACHING AIDS
Spelling and Writing Transparency 2
Home Letter 3

Visit our Web site
http://www.hbschool.com

Click on the SPELLING banner to find activities for this unit.

Learner Objectives

Spelling

- To review words with these consonant digraphs: /sh/, /ch/, /ng/, /th/.
- To review plural nouns formed by adding *s* and *es.*
- To review words that demonstrate these sound-letter relationships: initial /j/*j,g;* medial /j/*g,* final /j/*ge,dge.*
- To review words that demonstrate these sound-letter relationships: initial /k/*c,k;* final /k/*k,ck.*
- To review nouns that end with /s/ spelled *ce;* to review verbs that have /s/ spelled *c.*

Reading

- To look for the beginning, middle, and end of a story.
- To use spelling words and context clues to answer questions.
- To follow written directions.
- To use the dictionary for word meaning.

Writing

- To write a story.
- To use the writing process.
- To edit for content, style, and tone.
- To revise using editing and proofreading marks.
- To proofread for spelling, capitalization, and punctuation.
- To write legible manuscript and cursive letters.

Listening

- To listen to stories.

Speaking

- To contribute ideas and information in group discussions.
- To express feelings and ideas about a piece of writing.
- To present stories.

REVIEW WORDS

UNIT 7
✓hungry
kitchen
✓shine
shout
✓teacher
together
✓weather
✓strong

UNIT 8
✓classes
inches
✓pictures
guesses
✓uncles
desks
✓fingers
✓beaches

UNIT 9
✓juice
giant
✓danger
large
✓bridge
gentle
✓age
✓edge

UNIT 10
✓kept
key
✓speak
quick
✓lucky
back
✓kindness
✓cost

UNIT 11
✓listen
city
✓pencil
piece
✓ask
decide
✓sentence
✓police

Assignment Guide

This guide shows how you teach a typical spelling unit in either a five-day or a three-day sequence, while providing for individual differences. **Boldface type** indicates essential classwork. Steps shown in light type may be done in class or assigned as homework.

Five Days	° = average spellers ★ = better spellers ✓ = slower spellers	Three Days
Day **1**	**a** ° ★ ✓ **Take Review Words Trial Test and correct**	
Day **2**	° ★ ✓ Complete Spelling Review pages 50, 51, 52 ° ★ ✓ Complete Review Master 12A, 12B, 12C (optional) ✓ Complete Mastery Words Review Master: Units 7–11 (optional) ★ Complete Bonus Words Review Master: Units 7–11 (optional) **b**	Day **1**
Day **3**	**c** ° ★ ✓ **Complete Spelling and Reading page 53**	Day **2**
Day **4**	° ★ ✓ Complete Spelling and Writing pages 54–55 ° ★ ✓ Complete Dictionary and Proofreading Master 2 (optional) **d**	
Day **5**	**e** ° ★ ✓ **Take Review Words Unit Test** ✓ Take Mastery Words Test: Units 7–11 (optional) ★ Take Bonus Words Test: Units 7–11 (optional)	Day **3**

Enrichment Activities for the **home** included at the end of this unit may be assigned selectively on any day of the week.

INTRODUCING THE UNIT

Establish Readiness for Learning

Tell the children that they will review words from the previous five units. In Unit 12 they will review:

- plural nouns
- words with the following consonant digraphs: /th/, /ch/, /sh/, /ng/
- words with /s/, /j/, /k/

Tell the children that they will use some of the review words to write a story.

Assess Children's Spelling Ability

Administer the Trial Test before the children study the review words. Use the test sentences provided. Say each word and use it in a sentence. Then repeat the word. Have the children write the words on a separate sheet of paper or in their spelling notebooks.

Have the children check their own work by listening to you read the spelling of the words or by referring to the review words lists in the side boxes of the **Pupil Book.** For each misspelled word, have the children follow the **Study Steps to Learn a Word** on page 50 in

the **Pupil Book,** or use the copying master to study and write the words. Children should record the number correct on their **Progress Report.**

Trial Test Sentences

1. *hungry* Dave is *hungry* for a good breakfast. *hungry*
2. *kitchen* You will find the milk in the kitchen. *kitchen*
3. *shine* These shoes will *shine* when I polish them. *shine*
4. *shout* The team gave a *shout* when they won the game. *shout*
5. *teacher* The music *teacher* taught the class to sing. *teacher*
6. *together* The boys will ride to the show *together.* *together*
7. *weather* Our family watches the *weather* report on TV. *weather*
8. *strong* The elephant is very *strong.* *strong*
9. *classes* I have math and reading *classes* every day. *classes*
10. *inches* There are 12 *inches* in one foot. *inches*
11. *pictures* Dad likes to take *pictures* with his camera. *pictures*
12. *guesses* Cindy picked the number of beans after two *guesses.* *guesses*

13. *uncles*   Billy has four *uncles* and two aunts.   **uncles**
14. *desks*   The students sat at their *desks* in the classroom.   **desks**
15. *fingers*   Your *fingers* help you hold things.   **fingers**
16. *beaches*   Sandy *beaches* are good places to walk.   **beaches**
17. *juice*   Michael has cereal and *juice* every morning.   **juice**
18. *giant*   The *giant* tree stood out in the forest.   **giant**
19. *danger*   Watch out for places where there is *danger*.   **danger**
20. *large*   Small is the opposite of *large*.   **large**
21. *bridge*   We stood on the *bridge* to fish in the stream.   **bridge**
22. *gentle*   Be *gentle* when you pick up the puppy.   **gentle**
23. *age*   I can tell you your *age*.   **age**
24. *edge*   This path leads to the *edge* of the river.   **edge**
25. *kept*   Brooks *kept* his schoolwork in his desk.   **kept**
26. *key*   The gold *key* opened a secret door.   **key**
27. *speak*   Mary Lou is learning to *speak* French.   **speak**
28. *quick*   Be *quick* or we will miss our bus.   **quick**
29. *lucky*   We were *lucky* to get good seats for the show.   **lucky**
30. *back*   Front is the opposite of *back*.   **back**
31. *kindness*   Mr. Sanchez treated us with *kindness*.   **kindness**
32. *cost*   How much does a new bike *cost*?   **cost**
33. *listen*   Terry will *listen* for the signal.   **listen**
34. *city*   A *city* has many tall buildings.   **city**
35. *pencil*   The lead in my *pencil* is broken.   **pencil**
36. *piece*   I am missing a *piece* of my puzzle.   **piece**
37. *ask*   I will *ask* him to come.   **ask**
38. *decide*   Cliff will *decide* which flowers to plant.   **decide**
39. *sentence*   The *sentence* was easy to read.   **sentence**
40. *police*   The *police* helped solve the crime.   **police**

Apply Prior Learning

Have the children apply what they know about the generalizations for Units 7–11. Use the following activity.

Write the following words on the chalkboard: *pens* and *glasses*. Ask the children to explain how the two plural endings are different. (The plural of *pen* is made by adding *s* and the plural of *glass* is made by adding *es*.) Ask them if the plural of either word forms an extra vowel sound. (yes) Which word has the extra vowel sound? *(glasses)* Now write these words on the chalkboard in two columns:

robin	*beach*
snake	*dress*

Ask the children how they would form the plural of the nouns in the first column. (add *s*) Then ask if adding an *s* to make the nouns plural makes an extra vowel sound. (no) Ask how they would form the plural of the nouns in the second column. (add *es*) Then ask if adding an *es* to make the nouns plural makes an extra vowel sound. (yes) Tell the children to keep these ideas in mind when forming noun plurals. Have volunteers give examples of other words that add *s* or *es* to form the plurals.

Write the following sentence on the chalkboard: *The general is sick on a barge with a cold.* Read the sentence with the class and ask them to identify the words that contain the following sounds: /s/, /j/, and /k/. (/s/ sick; /j/: general, barge; /k/: sick, cold) Then ask the children to state what they know about how to spell /s/ /j/, and /k/. (/s/ may be spelled *s* or *c*; /j/ may be spelled *g*, *ge*, or *j*; /k/ may be spelled *k* or *c*)

Tell the children that they will review words that follow these generalizations and then use the words to write a story.

FOCUS

- Relates to prior learning
- Draws relationships
- Applies spelling generalizations to new contexts

TEACHING PLAN

Objective To review words with /sh/, /ch/, /th/, and /ng/.

1. Review the directions to the exercises on page 50. Remind the children that the answers to the exercises are to be found only among the eight review words on page 50.
2. Have the children complete the exercises independently. You may refer them to the **Writer's Guide** at the back of the book for a review of the spelling generalization for Unit 7.

— **WORDS IN TIME** —————

Have a volunteer read **Words in Time** aloud. Have the children give a reason why *coquere* came to mean "kitchen." (because a kitchen is used for cooking) Tell the children that they will be finding more words that come from other languages.

As a COOPERATIVE LEARNING activity, have the group compose a word origin list of three of their review words from Units 7–11. Explain that the children are to find word origins in the following languages: Latin, French, German, Old English, or Greek. Briefly discuss with the children how they may locate the word origin in a dictionary. Provide some examples on the chalkboard. Then have the children refer to the dictionary, the encyclopedia, or books on the origins of words. Have one of the children write a list of review words the group has selected. Have one or two other volunteers write the Latin, French, German, or Greek word origin next to the corresponding review word. Encourage children to think about things such as spelling derivations and meanings.

---

12 Review

Do these steps if you are not sure how to spell a word.
● **Say** the word. Listen to each sound. Think about what the word means.
● **Look** at the word. See how the letters are made. Try to see the word in your mind.
● **Spell** the word to yourself. Think about the way each sound is spelled.
● **Write** the word. Copy it from your book. Check the way you made your letters. Write the word again.
● **Check** your learning. Cover the word and write it. Did you spell it correctly? If not, do these steps until you know how to spell the word.

UNIT 7
hungry
kitchen
shine
shout
teacher
together
weather
strong

UNIT 7 **Follow the directions. Use words from Unit 7.**

1. Write the two words that begin with /sh/.
Word order may vary.
(sh)ine   (sh)out

2. Write the two words that have /ch/. Word order may vary.
ki(tch)en   tea(ch)er

3. Write the two words that have /th/. Word order may vary.
toge(th)er   wea(th)er

4. Write the two words that have /ng/. Word order may vary.
hu(ng)ry   stro(ng)

Circle the letters that spell /sh/, /ch/, /th/, and /ng/ in the words you wrote for 1 through 4 above.
Word order may vary.

WORDS IN TIME

Many of our words come from other languages. The word kitchen came from the old word coquere. Coquere meant "to cook." People began to use coquere to mean kitchen. Why do you think this happened?

50

Review: Units 7 and 8

Name _____
Review A: Units 7–8

UNIT
12

A. UNIT 7 Circle the word from Unit 7 in each sentence that is missing some consonants. Then write the whole word.

1. Today the (weaer) is very bad. ___weather___
2. A (stro) wind is blowing. ___strong___
3. The sun will not (ine) at all today. ___shine___
4. Our (teaer) tells us to stay inside. ___teacher___
5. The children usually play (togeer) outside. ___together___
6. They like to jump (out) and run. ___shout___
7. Sometimes they get (hury) and tired. ___hungry___
8. Then the teacher brings them a snack from the school (kien). ___kitchen___

UNIT 7
hungry
kitchen
shine
shout
teacher
together
weather
strong
UNIT 8
classes
inches
pictures
guesses
uncles
desks
fingers
beaches

B. UNIT 8 Use the plural or singular form of a word from Unit 8 to finish each sentence.

9. Hector has one aunt and one ___uncle___
10. He has ten ___fingers___ on his hands.
11. His mother hangs many ___pictures___ on his wall.
12. Hector's pencil is three ___inches___ long.
13. He knows kids in all the ___classes___
14. Hector likes to sit at his ___desk___
15. He never makes wild ___guesses___
16. Hector likes to swim at a sandy ___beach___

Extra Practice • 47

Review: Units 9 and 10

Name _____
Review B: Units 9–10

UNIT
12

A. UNIT 9 Some of these words are spelled correctly; others are spelled wrong. Write each word correctly. Then circle the letter or letters that make the /j/ sound.

1. aje ___a(g)e___
2. juice ___(j)uice___
3. larj ___lar(g)e___
4. jentle ___(g)entle___
5. ej ___ed(g)e___
6. bridge ___bri(dg)e___
7. jiant ___(g)iant___
8. dandger ___dan(g)er___

UNIT 9
juice
giant
danger
large
bridge
gentle
age
edge
UNIT 10
kept
key
speak
quick
lucky
back
kindness
cost

B. UNIT 10 Write the words from Unit 10 that have the same meaning as the words below. Then circle the letter or letters in each answer that make the /k/ sound.

9. goodness ___(k)indness___
10. saved ___(k)ept___
11. fast ___qui(ck)___
12. price ___(c)ost___
13. rear ___ba(ck)___
14. clue ___(k)ey___
15. talk ___spea(k)___
16. in luck ___lu(ck)y___

48 • Extra Practice

UNIT 8 Follow the directions. Use words from Unit 8. Finish the sentences in the paragraph.

We painted __5__ in my art class today. We wanted to hang them in all our __6__ for other students to see. Then we could look at them as we sat at our __7__. One picture was ten __8__ high. It was a drawing of Danielle's favorite aunts and __9__. Another showed sand castles built at nearby __10__. Some students had even used their __11__ to paint with. It took several __12__ to figure out what they had drawn.

UNIT 8

classes
inches
pictures
guesses
uncles
desks
fingers
beaches

5. ___pictures___ 6. ___classes___ 7. ___desks___

8. ___inches___ 9. ___uncles___ 10. ___beaches___

11. ___fingers___ 12. ___guesses___

Circle the letters in your answers that make the words plural.

UNIT 9 Follow the directions. Use words from Unit 9.

13. Write the three words that start with /j/.
Word order may vary.
___juice___ ___giant___ ___gentle___

14. Write the four words that end with /j/. Then underline the letters in each word that spell /j/. Word order may vary.

___large___ ___bridge___

___age___ ___edge___

UNIT 9

juice
giant
danger
large
bridge
gentle
age
edge

Finish the sentences that tell about the picture.

15. The ___gentle, giant, or large___ giraffe came to drink at the river.

16. The giraffe saw a lion at the ___edge___ of the grass.

17. So the giraffe ran from ___danger___

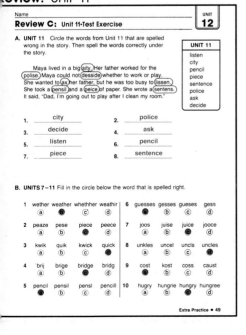

51

TEACHING PLAN

Objectives To review plural nouns; to review words with initial /j/j, g; medial /j/g; final /j/ge, dge.

1. Review the directions to the exercises on page 51. Remind the children that the answers to the exercises are to be found only among the sixteen review words on page 51.
2. Have the children complete the exercises independently. You may refer them to the **Writer's Guide** at the back of the book for a review of the spelling generalizations for Units 8 and 9.

EXTENDING THE LESSON

Have the children write letters to a favorite relative, using some of the review words. Explain that the main object in writing is to communicate thoughts. Ask the children to think of something special they would like to communicate to their relative.

Remind the children to proofread their letters for spelling, punctuation, and capitalization.

Review: Unit 11

Name _____
Review C: Unit 11·Test Exercise **UNIT 12**

A. UNIT 11 Circle the words from Unit 11 that are spelled wrong in the story. Then spell the words correctly under the story.

Maya lived in a big (sity.) Her father worked for the (polise.) Maya could not (desside) whether to work or play. She wanted to (ax) her father, but he was too busy to (lissen.) She took a (pensil) and a (peice) of paper. She wrote a (sentens.) It said, "Dad, I'm going out to play after I clean my room."

UNIT 11

listen
city
pencil
piece
sentence
police
ask
decide

1. ___city___ 2. ___police___
3. ___decide___ 4. ___ask___
5. ___listen___ 6. ___pencil___
7. ___piece___ 8. ___sentence___

B. UNITS 7–11 Fill in the circle below the word that is spelled right.

1	wether	weather	whetther	weathir	6	guesses	gesses	gueses	gess
	ⓐ	●	ⓒ	ⓓ		●	ⓑ	ⓒ	ⓓ
2	peaze	pese	piece	peece	7	joos	juise	juice	jooce
	ⓐ	ⓑ	●	ⓓ		ⓐ	ⓑ	●	ⓓ
3	kwik	quik	kwick	quick	8	unkles	uncel	uncls	uncles
	ⓐ	ⓑ	ⓒ	●		ⓐ	ⓑ	ⓒ	●
4	'brij	brige	bridge	bridg	9	cost	kost	coss	caust
	ⓐ	ⓑ	●	ⓓ		●	ⓑ	ⓒ	ⓓ
5	pencil	pensil	pensl	pencill	10	hugry	hungrie	hungry	hungree
	●	ⓑ	ⓒ	ⓓ		ⓐ	ⓑ	●	ⓓ

Extra Practice • 49

Spelling Review

TEACHING PLAN

Objective To spell words that demonstrate these sound-letter relationships: initial /k/ c, k; final /k/ k, ck; initial /s/ s, c.

1. Review the directions to the exercises on page 52. Remind the children that the answers to the exercises are to be found only among the sixteen review words on page 52.
2. Have the children complete the exercises independently. You may refer them to the **Writer's Guide** at the back of the book for a review of the spelling generalizations for Units 10 and 11.
3. Review the children's answers on pages 50–52 orally, or have volunteers write them on the chalkboard.

For reinforcement in writing review words for Units 7–11, you may wish to assign **Review Masters 12A, 12B,** and **12C.**

UNIT 10

kept
key
speak
quick
lucky
back
kindness
cost

UNIT 10 Finish the sentences with words from Unit 10. Then draw a line under all the letters in each sentence that spell /k/

18. I don't feel too ___ lu<u>ck</u>y ___ today.

19. I lost the ___ key ___ that unlo<u>ck</u>s my bi<u>k</u>e.

20. I should have ___ kept ___ it in a safer place.

21. I hope the ___ <u>c</u>ost ___ of a new one won't be much

22. I will ___ speak ___ to Mom about a small loan.

23. I <u>c</u>an repay her ___ kindness ___ by <u>c</u>leaning the house.

Write the word from Unit 10 that rhymes with each word below.

24. tack ___ back ___ **25.** slept ___ kept ___

26. sneak ___ speak ___ **27.** trick ___ quick ___

UNIT 11

listen
city
pencil
piece
ask
decide
sentence
police

UNIT 11 Follow the directions. Use words from Unit 11. Remember that nouns are words that name a person, place, or thing. Verbs are words that show action.

28. Write the three nouns that end with /s/ spelled ce. Circle the word that has short vowel sounds. **Word order may vary.**

piece (sentence) police

29. Write the two verbs that have /s/ spelled s. Circle the silent letter in one word.

ask lis(t)en

30. Write the verb that has /s/ spelled c. ___ decide

Write the two nouns that go with these words.

31. sharpen a ___ pencil **32.** live in a ___ city

Spelling and Reading
A Story

Read the following story. Look for the beginning, middle, and ending.

Long ago, a <u>gentle</u> <u>giant</u> lived in a <u>large</u> house by a river. He had built a <u>strong</u> <u>bridge</u> over the river so that travelers could cross without <u>danger</u>.

One day the <u>giant</u> looked <u>out</u> and frowned at the <u>weather</u>. Thick, heavy storm clouds filled the black sky. Soon, a wild wind tore the <u>giant's</u> <u>bridge</u> apart.

When the storm was over, the <u>giant</u> heard a girl shouting to him from across the river.

"Can you help me?" the girl <u>asked</u>. "I'm in <u>danger</u>. I must reach the other side!"

The <u>giant</u> jumped over the river in one long leap.

"We must be <u>quick</u>," the giant said. "Hold on!" They leaped <u>back</u> just as a <u>hungry</u> bear came out of the bushes.

The girl wanted to thank the <u>giant</u> for his <u>kindness</u>. She gave him a <u>shining</u> gold <u>key</u>. She had found it long ago, but never knew its owner.

The <u>giant</u> needed no <u>guesses</u> to name the <u>key's</u> owner. The <u>key</u> to his long-locked chest had finally come <u>back</u> to him. Now he could share the chest's wealth of treasures and jewels.

Write the answers to the questions.   **See answers below.**

1. In this story, why did the giant build the bridge over the river? *Literal*
2. What did a wild wind do? *Literal*
3. Why was the girl in danger? *Interpretive*
4. What kind of person is the giant? How do you know? *Critical*

Underline the review words in your answers. Check to see that you spelled the words correctly.

53

TEACHING PLAN

Objectives To analyze and respond to a story; to identify elements of plot and characterization; to proofread written answers for spelling.

1. Tell the children that they will read a story that includes a number of spelling words from Units 7–11. Explain that a writer plans a story before actually writing it. He or she decides who the main character or characters will be, where and when the story will take place, and what the story will be about. Tell the children that the story will be a model for their own writing.
2. Tell the children that in every story there is a problem that the main character or characters must try to solve. Have the children identify the problem and the solution in the story.
3. Have the children answer the questions independently. Tell them to underline the review words in the answers and to proofread the answers for spelling.
4. Spot-check the children's answers as they work. Review answers orally.

Spelling and Reading Answers

1. He wanted travelers to cross without <u>danger</u>. 2. It tore the <u>giant's</u> <u>bridge</u> apart. 3. There was a <u>hungry</u> bear near her. 4. Accept all reasonable answers. Possible answers: He is kind and helpful; he built a <u>bridge</u> to help travelers; he rescued the girl from the <u>hungry</u> bear; he wanted to share his treasures with his friends and travelers.

On this page, students will read:
• This Week's Words from the preceding five units;
• words reviewed in this unit;
• words that follow the generalizations taught in the preceding five units.

Spelling and Writing

TEACHING PLAN

Objective To identify story elements.

1. Have the children read the first paragraph of **Think and Discuss** on page 54. Ask them to read the beginning of the story on page 53, to name the main character, to tell when the story takes place, and to tell where the main character lives. Have the children recall other stories in which the main character was a giant. Ask whether the giant in those stories solved problems or caused them for others.

2. Have the children read the rest of **Think and Discuss** independently and answer the questions. Ask the children to suggest other ways the story might have ended.

3. Have the children study the illustration on page 53. Ask them whether the picture illustrates the beginning, the middle, or the ending of the story.

4. Have the children read **Apply** at the bottom of page 54. Tell them that they will write a story using some of the spelling words. Explain that their classmates will be the audience for the story. Discuss the importance of planning the story before they begin to write.

Summarize Learning

Have the children identify the three most important elements of a story. (character(s), setting, and a plot which involves a problem that the main character encounters and tries to solve)

Spelling and Writing
A Story

Words to Help You Write

shout
together
strong
giant
danger
large
gentle
quick
lucky
kindness
city

Think and Discuss

A story beginning tells about the main character or characters in the story. It also tells when and where the story takes place. Look at the beginning of the story on page 53. Who is the main character? When does the story take place? Where does the main character live?

The middle of the story is the main part of the story. It tells about a problem. It also tells how the character or characters try to solve the problem. What other character is introduced in the middle of the story on page 53? What problem does this character have? What does she ask the giant to do?

The ending tells how the characters solve their problem. It finishes the story. What does the giant do to rescue the girl? What else happens at the end of the story?

Apply

Write a **story** for your classmates to read. Follow the writing guidelines on the next page.

54

Think and Discuss Answers

A. giant B. long ago C. in a large house by a river D. a girl E. She has to get across the river before a hungry bear gets to her. F. She asks him to help her reach the other side of the river. G. He jumps over the river and brings her back. H. The girl gives the giant a key he had lost. It opens a treasure chest.

Prewriting

Plan your story. Make a chart with four headings: **Main character, Where, When,** and **Problem.**
- Fill in the chart.
- Make a list of the ways the character could solve the problem. Choose the one you like best.

Composing

Use your chart to help you write the first draft of your story.
- Write the beginning of your story. Tell whom your story is about. Write where and when the story takes place.
- Write the middle of your story. Describe the problem the character has. Tell how he or she solves the problem.
- Write the ending. Tell how everything works out.

Revising

Read your story and show it to a classmate. Follow these guidelines to improve your work. Use the editing and proofreading marks to show changes.

WRITER'S GUIDE For help revising your story, use the checklist on page 247.

Editing

- Be sure your story has a beginning, middle, and ending.

Proofreading

- Check your spelling and correct any mistakes.
- Check your capitalization and punctuation.

Copy your story onto a clean paper. Write carefully and neatly.

Publishing

Put your story in a class notebook with those of your classmates. Then you can read each other's stories.

55

Editing and Proofreading Marks	
≡	capitalize
⊙	make a period
∧	add something
⋏	add a comma
꜀	take something away
◯	spell correctly
¶	indent the paragraph
/	make a lowercase letter

Extra Practice: Dictionary/Proofreading

Dictionary and Proofreading 2 | UNIT 12

Using the Dictionary to Spell and Write

A. Here are three pairs of guide words. Write words from the box that would come between each pair of guide words.

| kitchen, ask, danger, giant, speak, large, key, fingers, piece, city, shout, hungry, uncles, back, shine, beaches, gentle, quick, kindness, police |

1. age   classes
   - ask
   - beaches
   - back
   - city

2. sentence   strong
   - shine
   - speak
   - shout

3. kept   listen
   - key
   - kitchen
   - kindness
   - large

Proofreading

B. Circle the nine misspelled words in the story. Then write the words correctly.

Slim was a tall, thin giant. His fingers were as tall as trees. He was quik on his feet and gentel in his ways. When he was hunry, he ate a pece of a mountain. The poliece liked Slim. "He is no danjer to us," they said. "It's his four uncle who are really tall."

4. giant   5. fingers
6. quick   7. gentle
8. hungry   9. piece
10. police 11. danger
12. uncles

50 • Extra Practice

For additional practice in using the dictionary to spell and write and in proofreading, you may wish to assign **Dictionary and Proofreading Master 2.**

ENRICHMENT ACTIVITIES

Home activities may be assigned to children of all ability levels. The activities provide opportunities for the children to use their spelling words in new contexts.

For the Home

The children may complete home activities independently or with the assistance of a relative or friend in the home.

1. **Health/Writing Signs** Have the children design and write signs. Tell them to review the spelling lists in this unit for ideas for signs. Suggest that the children make warning signs, road signs, and zoo signs. Remind them to use as many spelling words as possible in writing the text for the signs. Children should design each sign differently and then show the signs to a relative or a friend.

2. **Science/Categorizing by Animal, Vegetable, Mineral** Have the children build a word chart, using the following headings: *Animals, Vegetables, Minerals, Other.* Have the children review the spelling words in this unit and, under each heading, list the words that can be categorized with the heading. Point out that the animal category includes all living beings. The vegetable category includes anything related to plants, as well as plant products such as paper or wood. Minerals include air, earth, water, and chemicals. Sometimes a word may be used in more than one category or may not seem to fit any category but "other." Have the children share the word charts with a relative or a friend.

3. **Language Arts/Writing Directions** Tell the children to write directions for doing or making something at home. Children should incorporate some of their spelling words. For example, children may write a set of directions for using the telephone. Have children work with a relative or friend to test the directions and then write them in sequential order. Have children proofread the directions for spelling.

4. **Language Arts/Writing Alliterative Sentences** Have the children use the spelling words to write sentences with alliterations. Explain that an alliteration is a phrase in which the first letter of almost every word is the same. For example, if the spelling word is *robins,* a sentence with an alliteration would be *Red robins return.* Children should use spelling words from Units 7 through 11 and try to incorporate more than one spelling word into each sentence.

EVALUATION

Unit Test

1. *hungry* After the game, we were *hungry.* **hungry**
2. *kitchen* Ari raided the *kitchen* for a snack. **kitchen**
3. *shine* Ken used black polish to *shine* his shoes. **shine**
4. *shout* We heard a *shout* from the boat. **shout**
5. *teacher* The new *teacher* asked us our names. **teacher**
6. *together* We went to the movies *together.* **together**
7. *weather* In good *weather* we play in the park. **weather**
8. *strong* A *strong* person could lift these boxes. **strong**
9. *classes* All the *classes* will go on the trip. **classes**
10. *inches* There are twelve *inches* in one foot. **inches**
11. *pictures* My parents took *pictures* of the play. **pictures**
12. *guesses* We took three *guesses* at how many beans were in the jar. **guesses**
13. *uncles* My *uncles* taught me how to whistle. **uncles**
14. *desks* We shall empty our *desks* when school is over. **desks**
15. *fingers* My *fingers* were sticky from the glue. **fingers**
16. *beaches* Some *beaches* are rocky and others have beautiful white sand. **beaches**
17. *juice* We squeezed fresh orange *juice.* **juice**
18. *giant* Jack met a *giant* taller than a house. **giant**
19. *danger* The sign on the thin ice warned us of the *danger.* **danger**
20. *large* A steam shovel dug a *large* hole. **large**
21. *bridge* Traffic was stuck on the *bridge* over the river. **bridge**
22. *gentle* She gave the horse a *gentle* pat. **gentle**
23. *age* Some people don't like to tell their *age.* **age**
24. *edge* We stood on the *edge* of the cliff. **edge**
25. *kept* We *kept* our books in our desks. **kept**
26. *key* Mitsumi forgot the *key* to the front door. **key**
27. *speak* I can *speak* Spanish and English. **speak**
28. *quick* I gave my mother a *quick* hug and rushed off to school. **quick**
29. *lucky* Elena is *lucky* to have her own room. **lucky**
30. *back* Jerry sits at the *back* of the room. **back**
31. *kindness* Thank you for the *kindness* you showed me when I hurt my knee. **kindness**
32. *cost* We have to find out how much the food will cost. **cost**
33. *listen* We *listen* carefully to the directions. **listen**
34. *city* The *city* bustles with cars and people hurrying in all directions. **city**
35. *pencil* Tom wrote the answers with a *pencil.* **pencil**
36. *piece* Lily found the missing *piece* of the puzzle. **piece**
37. *ask* We will *ask* her where the nearest post office is. **ask**
38. *decide* I must *decide* what to give my sister for her birthday. **decide**
39. *sentence* I will finish writing this *sentence* and stop. **sentence**
40. *police* The *police* are trained to help people in trouble. **police**

Mastery and Bonus Words Review and Assessment

For additional practice you may wish to assign **Mastery Words Review Master: Units 7–11** or **Bonus Words Review Master: Units 7–11**. To assess children's spelling ability with these words, use **Mastery Words Test: Units 7–11** or **Bonus Words Test: Units 7–11**.

Mastery Words Review

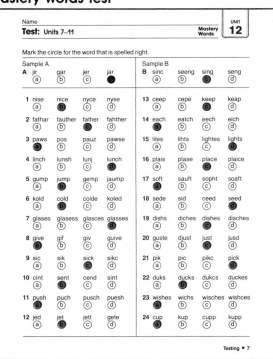

Bonus Words Review

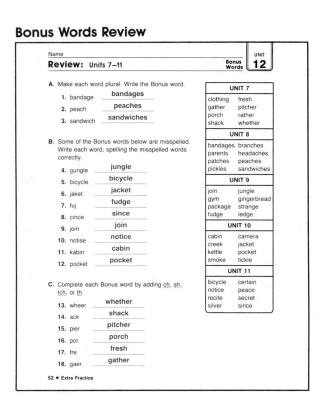

Mastery Words Test

Bonus Words Test

NOTES

Mark the circle for the word that is spelled right.

Sample A					Sample B			
A noat	note	not	nowt		**B** ryd	rid	ride	ryde
ⓐ	⬤b	ⓒ	ⓓ		ⓐ	ⓑ	ⓒ	ⓓ

1 lisen	lissen	listen	liten		**11** polis	polic	polise	police
ⓐ	ⓑ	ⓒ	ⓓ		ⓐ	ⓑ	ⓒ	ⓓ
2 wether	wethir	weather	weathr		**12** classes	classis	classs	classus
ⓐ	ⓑ	ⓒ	ⓓ		ⓐ	ⓑ	ⓒ	ⓓ
3 bridge	brige	brij	brigde		**13** bac	bak	back	backe
ⓐ	ⓑ	ⓒ	ⓓ		ⓐ	ⓑ	ⓒ	ⓓ
4 kost	cost	quost	ckost		**14** aks	asc	asq	ask
ⓐ	ⓑ	ⓒ	ⓓ		ⓐ	ⓑ	ⓒ	ⓓ
5 pencil	pensil	penssil	penkil		**15** speak	speake	speack	speac
ⓐ	ⓑ	ⓒ	ⓓ		ⓐ	ⓑ	ⓒ	ⓓ
6 hsout	chout	schout	shout		**16** deskes	deskess	desks	deskz
ⓐ	ⓑ	ⓒ	ⓓ		ⓐ	ⓑ	ⓒ	ⓓ
7 jiant	giant	jyant	geant		**17** juce	guce	juice	guice
ⓐ	ⓑ	ⓒ	ⓓ		ⓐ	ⓑ	ⓒ	ⓓ
8 hunkry	hungre	hungry	hungrie		**18** picturez	pictures	picturs	picturz
ⓐ	ⓑ	ⓒ	ⓓ		ⓐ	ⓑ	ⓒ	ⓓ
9 larg	larj	large	larje		**19** kitchan	kitchen	ketchin	citchin
ⓐ	ⓑ	ⓒ	ⓓ		ⓐ	ⓑ	ⓒ	ⓓ
10 inches	inchess	inchez	inchs		**20** cept	cetp	kept	kupt
ⓐ	ⓑ	ⓒ	ⓓ		ⓐ	ⓑ	ⓒ	ⓓ

FORM A TEST 2

Administering the Test

1. Tell the children that today they will take a spelling test on some of the words they have studied in Units 7–11. Pass out the test papers. Tell the children to leave them turned upside down until you are ready to begin.

2. Have the children turn their tests over. Direct their attention to Sample A. Read this sentence: *note* Sally wrote a *note* to her grandmother. *note* Point out that the test shows four ways to spell *note*. Only one way is correct. Have the children note that circle *b* under the correct spelling is filled in.

3. Now direct the children's attention to Sample B. Read this sentence: *ride* George can *ride* his bike to the park. *ride* Point out that this test shows four ways to spell *ride*. Ask a child to tell you which spelling is right by spelling the word—*r-i-d-e*. Repeat the right spelling, *r-i-d-e,* and have the children fill in circle *c* in pencil.

4. After you have checked to see that all children have completed Sample B correctly, have the children proceed with the test. Use these sentences.

1. *listen*   Sally likes to *listen* to records.   *listen*
2. *weather*   John wears boots in rainy *weather*.   *weather*
3. *bridge*   Four ducks swam under the *bridge*.   *bridge*
4. *cost*   These shoes *cost* fifteen dollars.   *cost*
5. *pencil*   Sally made a sketch with a *pencil*.   *pencil*
6. *shout*   Please don't *shout* in the hallway.   *shout*
7. *giant*   My favorite tale is about a *giant*.   *giant*
8. *hungry*   Playing baseball makes Jack *hungry*.   *hungry*
9. *large*   That shirt has a *large* hole.   *large*
10. *inches*   The worm was two *inches* long.   *inches*
11. *police*   The *police* solved the case.   *police*
12. *classes*   Becky enjoys her art *classes*.   *classes*
13. *back*   Amy scratched her *back*.   *back*
14. *ask*   I will *ask* the police officer for directions.   *ask*
15. *speak*   The mayor will *speak* to the class.   *speak*
16. *desks*   Leave your papers on your *desks*.   *desks*
17. *juice*   Paul drinks *juice* with his breakfast.   *juice*
18. *pictures*   Ann drew two *pictures* of flowers.   *pictures*
19. *kitchen*   The stove is in the *kitchen*.   *kitchen*
20. *kept*   Hats are not usually *kept* on in a building.   *kept*

Evaluating the Results

Use the following **Answer Key** to correct the children's tests and to determine whether they need more practice with particular units. The chart shows the units in which each answer word is taught.

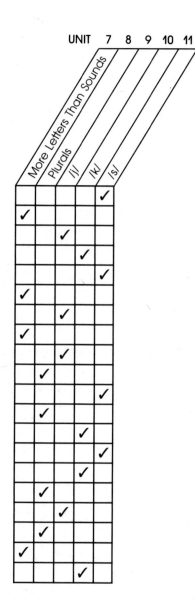

ANSWER KEY

1	ⓐ	ⓑ	**ⓒ**	ⓓ
2	ⓐ	ⓑ	**ⓒ**	ⓓ
3	**ⓐ**	ⓑ	ⓒ	ⓓ
4	ⓐ	**ⓑ**	ⓒ	ⓓ
5	**ⓐ**	ⓑ	ⓒ	ⓓ
6	ⓐ	ⓑ	ⓒ	**ⓓ**
7	ⓐ	**ⓑ**	ⓒ	ⓓ
8	ⓐ	ⓑ	**ⓒ**	ⓓ
9	ⓐ	ⓑ	**ⓒ**	ⓓ
10	**ⓐ**	ⓑ	ⓒ	ⓓ
11	ⓐ	ⓑ	ⓒ	**ⓓ**
12	**ⓐ**	ⓑ	ⓒ	ⓓ
13	ⓐ	ⓑ	**ⓒ**	ⓓ
14	ⓐ	ⓑ	ⓒ	**ⓓ**
15	**ⓐ**	ⓑ	ⓒ	ⓓ
16	ⓐ	ⓑ	**ⓒ**	ⓓ
17	ⓐ	ⓑ	**ⓒ**	ⓓ
18	ⓐ	**ⓑ**	ⓒ	ⓓ
19	ⓐ	**ⓑ**	ⓒ	ⓓ
20	ⓐ	ⓑ	**ⓒ**	ⓓ

Verbs That End with e

Unit Materials

Instruction and Practice

Pupil Book pages 56–59
Teacher's Edition
Teaching Plans pages 56–59
Enrichment Activities
For the Classroom page 59A
For the Home page 59B
Reteaching Strategies page 59C

Testing

Teacher's Edition
Trial Test pages 55E–55F
Unit Test page 59B
Dictation Test page 59B

Additional Resources

PRACTICE AND REINFORCEMENT
Extra Practice Master 13: This Week's Words
Extra Practice Master 13: Mastery Words
Extra Practice Master 13: Bonus Words
LEP Practice Master 13
Spelling and Language Master 13
Study Steps to Learn a Word Master

RETEACHING FOLLOW-UP
Reteaching Follow-up Master 13A:
   Discovering Spelling Ideas
Reteaching Follow-up Master 13B: Word
   Shapes
LEP Reteaching Follow-up Master 13

TEACHING AIDS
Spelling Generalizations Transparency 11

Click on the SPELLING banner to find activities for this unit.

Learner Objectives

Spelling

• To spell base forms and inflected forms of verbs that end with e.

Reading

• To follow written directions.
• To use context clues to complete sentences given spelling words.
• To use the dictionary to locate information.
• To use the dictionary for word meaning.

Writing

• To write an invitation.
• To use the writing process.
• To proofread for spelling, capitalization, and punctuation.
• To write legible manuscript and cursive letters.

Listening

• To follow oral directions.
• To listen to identify nouns and their meaning in a sentence.
• To listen to identify verbs with inflected forms.

Speaking

• To speak clearly to a group.
• To use visual aids in making oral presentations.
• To respond to a question.
• To read aloud a written invitation.
• To express feelings and ideas about a piece of writing.
• To contribute ideas and information in group discussions.

THIS WEEK'S WORDS

invite
paste
skate
stare
tape
taste
wipe
cared
hiked
loved
moved
dancing
hoping
living
smiling

MASTERY WORDS

bake
name
race
save
use
wave

BONUS WORDS

manage
prepare
suppose
surprise
divided
promised
behaving
chasing

Assignment Guide

This guide shows how you teach a typical spelling unit in either a five-day or a three-day sequence, while providing for individual differences. **Boldface type** indicates essential classwork. Steps shown in light type may be done in class or assigned as homework.

Five Days	● = average spellers　★ = better spellers　✓ = slower spellers	Three Days
Day **1**	**a** ● ★ **Take This Week's Words Trial Test and correct** ● ✓ **Take Mastery Word Trial Test and correct** ● ★ **Read This Week's Words and discuss generalization page 56**	Day **1**
Day **2**	● Complete Spelling Practice page 57 ● ✓ Complete Extra Practice Master 13: This Week's Words (optional) ✓ Complete Spelling on Your Own: Mastery Words page 59 ★ **Take Bonus Word Trial Test and correct**	
Day **3**	**c** ● ★ ✓ **Complete Spelling and Language page 58** ● ★ ✓ Complete Writing on Your Own page 58 ● ★ ✓ **Complete Using the Dictionary to Spell and Write page 58** ● ✓ Take Midweek Test (optional) ★ Complete Spelling on Your Own: Bonus Words page 59 ● ✓ Complete Spelling and Language Master 13 (optional)	Day **2**
Day **4**	● Complete Spelling on Your Own: This Week's Words page 59 ✓ Complete Extra Practice Master 13: Mastery Words (optional) ★ Complete Extra Practice Master 13: Bonus Words (optional)	
Day **5**	**e** ● **Take Unit Test on This Week's Words** ● Complete Reteaching Follow-up Masters 13A and 13B (optional) ● ✓ **Take Unit Test on Mastery Words** ★ **Take Unit Test on Bonus Words**	Day **3**

Enrichment Activities for the **classroom** and for the **home** included at the end of this unit may be assigned selectively on any day of the week.

INTRODUCING THE UNIT

Establish Readiness for Learning

Tell the children that they will learn to spell verbs that end in e. They will also learn how to add endings to those verbs. They will apply what they learn to This Week's Words and use some of those words to write an invitation.

Assess Children's Spelling Ability

Administer the Trial Test before the children study This Week's Words. Use the test sentences provided. Say each word and use it in a sentence. Then repeat the word. Have the children write the words on a separate sheet of paper or in their spelling notebooks. Test sentences are also provided for Mastery and Bonus words.

Have the children check their own work by listening to you read the spelling of the words

or by referring to This Week's Words in the left column of the **Pupil Book.** For each misspelled word, have the children follow the **Study Steps to Learn a Word** on page 1 in the **Pupil Book** or use the copying master to study and write the words. Children should record the number correct on their **Progress Report.**

Trial Test Sentences

This Week's Words
1. *invite*　I will *invite* you to my party.　*invite*
2. *paste*　Let's *paste* these stars on your costume.　*paste*
3. *skate*　We can *skate* at the new rink tomorrow.　*skate*
4. *stare*　Cats often *stare* at things.　*stare*
5. *tape*　Please *tape* this note to the door.　*tape*

6. *taste*   These apples *taste* very good.   **taste**

7. *wipe*   Please *wipe* your hands on this towel.   **wipe**

8. *cared*   We played for fun, and no one *cared* who won.   **cared**

9. *hiked*   The scouts *hiked* up the mountain.   **hiked**

10. *loved*   We *loved* our trip to the zoo.   **loved**

11. *moved*   She *moved* to Chicago last week.   **moved**

12. *dancing*   Everyone was *dancing* to the music.   **dancing**

13. *hoping*   I am *hoping* to win first prize.   **hoping**

14. *living*   My big sister is *living* in Denver.   **living**

15. *smiling*   The baby was laughing and *smiling*.   **smiling**

Mastery Words

1. *bake*   Let's *bake* bread for dinner.   **bake**

2. *name*   Candy can *name* all 50 states.   **name**

3. *race*   I'll *race* you to the corner.   **race**

4. *save*   A seat belt can *save* your life.   **save**

5. *use*   We can *use* this stick for a bat.   **use**

6. *wave*   We will *wave* good-bye when you leave.   **wave**

Bonus Words

1. *manage*   It will be hard to *manage* without you.   **manage**

2. *prepare*   I will *prepare* lunch right away.   **prepare**

3. *suppose*   I *suppose* you know what happened.   **suppose**

4. *surprise*   Let's *surprise* Grandpa by raking the yard.   **surprise**

5. *divided*   Kara and Louise *divided* the apple between them.   **divided**

6. *promised*   They *promised* to get home on time.   **promised**

7. *behaving*   The children were *behaving* like grown-ups.   **behaving**

8. *chasing*   The dog was *chasing* the cat.   **chasing**

Apply Prior Learning

Have the children be spelling detectives. Tell them that they can discover spelling generalizations by applying what they already know. Write the words *save* and *name* on the chalkboard. Then write *saved* and *saving*, *named* and *naming*. Ask the children to look at the words and draw conclusions. (Each word ends with the letter e. When the ending *ed* or *ing* is added, the e is dropped before adding the ending.) Tell the children that they will study words than end in e and will learn to add endings *ed* and *ing*. Explain that they can use these words in a variety of spelling tasks: writing stories, writing letters, or writing notes to friends.

FOCUS

• Relates to prior learning
• Draws relationships
• Applies spelling generalizations to new contexts

FOR CHILDREN WITH SPECIAL NEEDS

Learning Difficulties

Children with learning disabilities are often inconsistent and disorganized in their approach to problem solving. They can be more consistent in their spelling if they learn to follow generalizations and execute a step-by-step approach to applying those generalizations. The strategy in teaching this unit's spelling generalization is to provide the children with an example so that they can follow the step-by-step approach used in the example as they apply the spelling generalization to words.

Have the children write the spelling generalization at the top of a sheet of lined paper. (For most words ending in e, drop the e before adding *ed* or *ing*.) Then have the children write two examples at the top of their paper. (sav¢ + ed = saved; sav¢ + ing = saving) Have the children use these examples as they write This Week's Words and add *ed* and *ing* to each word. Ask the children to look in books and magazines available in the classroom to find more words to which this generalization can be applied. Have them add these words to their list.

Limited English Proficiency

To help limited English proficient children work with the spelling generalizations for Unit 13, you may wish to refer to the booklet "Suggestions and Activities for Limited English Proficient Students."

TEACHING PLAN

Objective   To spell the base forms and the inflected forms of verbs that end with *e*.

1. Direct the children's attention to the photograph on page 56, and have a child read the sentence under the photograph.
2. Read the generalization on page 56 aloud. Write these words horizontally on the chalkboard.

    smile   smiled   smiling

   Then write *invite* under *smile*. Ask a volunteer to come to the board and use the pattern of *smile – smiled – smiling* to write *invite* with *ed* and *ing*. Then write *cared* under *invited*. Have another child come to the board and write the other two forms of *cared*. Finally write *dancing* under *caring,* and ask a third child to supply the missing forms of that verb.

You may wish to introduce the lesson by using ***Spelling Generalizations Transparency 11.***

3. Have volunteers read This Week's Words aloud. As words **8–15** are read, ask the children to identify and spell each word without *ed* or *ing*.

You may wish to assign **LEP Practice Master 13** for reinforcement in writing spelling words.

---

13 Verbs That End with e

THIS WEEK'S WORDS

1. *invite*
2. *paste*
3. *skate*
4. *stare*
5. *tape*
6. *taste*
7. *wipe*
8. *cared*
9. *hiked*
10. *loved*
11. *moved*
12. *dancing*
13. *hoping*
14. *living*
15. *smiling*

Smile

56

These happy people smile.

This Week's Words

The word smile is a verb in the sentence above. It ends with the letter e. You can add ed to smile to make a word that tells about the past. When you add ed, you must drop the final e.

These happy people smiled.

You can also add ing to smile. When you add ing, you must also drop the final e.

These happy people are smiling.

All of This Week's Words are verbs. They all follow this pattern.

smile   smiled   smiling

Extra Practice: This Week's Words

Name
Extra Practice   This Week's Words   UNIT **13**

Find all fifteen of This Week's Words in the puzzle. The words go across and down. Circle each word. Then write it in one of the blanks under the puzzle.

invite	wipe	tape
paste	loved	skate
hoping	living	moved
stare	hiked	smiling
taste	dancing	cared

Order may vary.

invite	paste	skate	stare	tape
taste	wipe	cared	hiked	loved
moved	dancing	hoping	living	smiling

Extra Practice • 53

Extra Practice: Mastery Words

Name
Extra Practice   Mastery Words   UNIT **13**

Finish the sentences below with Mastery words. First look at the capital letters under each blank. Then use the code. Match the capital letters with small letters. The small letters will spell the Mastery word that fits the sentence.

| E N U Q X I Z K B T M V S A F W C L J G P H D Y R O |
| a b c d e f g h i j k l m n o p q r s t u v w x y z |

1. Matthew needs flour and eggs. He is going to ___**bake**___ some bread.
   NEMX

2. Joyce just won the spelling bee. Her mother and father ___**wave**___ to her and smile.
   DEHX

3. Simon wants to speak to his grandmother. He will ___**use**___ the telephone.
   PJX

4. Natasha brought an apple to school. She will ___**save**___ it until lunch.
   JEHX

5. Tina sees a new girl next door. "I'm Tina," she says. "What is ycur ___**name**___?"
   AESX

6. Nick wakes up early Saturday. He is going to run in the ___**race**___ at nine o'clock.
   LEUX

| name   save   bake   use   race   wave |

54 • Extra Practice

Spelling Practice

A. Write the verbs that go with the pictures. Use This Week's Words.

1. __paste__   2. __skate__   3. __taste__

B. Add <u>ed</u> to each of these words.

4. love __loved__   5. care __cared__

6. wipe __wiped__   7. move __moved__

C. Add <u>ing</u> to each of these words.

8. smile __smiling__   9. hope __hoping__

10. dance __dancing__   11. live __living__

D. Finish the sentences. Use This Week's Words.

12. Did José __invite__ Beth to his party?

13. It is not polite to __stare__ at people.

14. Do you want to __taste__ this soup?

15. I watched Mom __tape__ a bandage on Eva's knee.

E. Try this "word math."

16. dancing − ing = __dance__ + ed = __danced__

17. hiked − ed = __hike__ + ing = __hiking__

18. hoping − ing = __hope__ + ed = __hoped__

This Week's Words:
invite
paste
skate
stare
tape
taste
wipe
cared
hiked
loved
moved
dancing
hoping
living
smiling

57

Summarize Learning

Have the children summarize what they have learned on pages 56 and 57. *Ask:*

- What have you learned in this lesson about adding endings to verbs? (When the base form of a verb ends with the letter e, the e must be dropped before adding *ed* or *ing*.)
- What are some examples of verbs to which this generalization applies? (paste, wipe; accept other examples).

TEACHING PLAN

Objectives To write words given picture clues; to write the base forms and inflected forms of verbs; to write verbs in sentence context.

1. Briefly discuss the directions on page 57. Ask the children to identify the pictures. Briefly review what happens with final e when endings are added.
2. Have the children complete the page independently. Remind them to use legible handwriting. You may wish to demonstrate the correct form of the letters *ed* and *ing* and then have the children practice writing the letters. For **Handwriting Models,** refer the children to page 258 in the **Pupil Book.**
3. To correct the children's work, have volunteers write their answers for Exercises **B, C,** and **E** on the chalkboard. For Exercise **E,** ask them to copy the entire line. Have the children read their answers for Exercises **A** and **D** aloud. Let the children check their own work.

For reinforcement in writing spelling words, you may wish to assign *Extra Practice Master 13: This Week's Words.*

⭐ *of special interest*

It is possible to mix flour and water and create paste. This fact gives insight into the etymology of the word *paste.* In Greek the word *pastē* meant "barley porridge." This Greek word was borrowed by Latin as *pasta* to name a sticky dough. Latin *pasta* is the origin of the Italian word *pasta,* the French word *paté,* and the English word *paste* – which in Middle English named a flour and water mixture that could be baked to make bread, dried to make noodles, or used to glue things together.

TEACHING PLAN

SPELLING AND LANGUAGE

Objective To write inflected forms of verbs in sentence context.

1. Read the introductory paragraph on page 58 aloud. Have volunteers give sample sentences using a verb with *ed* and *ing*.
2. Have the children complete the exercises independently.
3. To correct the children's work, ask volunteers to write the verbs with *ed* and *ing*. Ask the children to exchange work to check answers.

For extended practice in writing inflected verb forms, you may wish to assign **Spelling and Language Master 13.**

WRITING ON YOUR OWN

Objectives To write an invitation; to proofread for spelling.

1. Review the directions with the children.
2. As a **prewriting** activity, refer to page 251 in the **Writer's Guide** for a model of the parts of a letter. Discuss with the children what information about the skating party should be included in an invitation (date, time, place), and list their responses on the chalkboard. Then have the children **compose** their invitations using some of This Week's Words. When the children are ready to **revise,** remind them to check spelling and to make sure they have included all important information. For additional help, you may wish to refer them to the **Revising Checklist** on page 247 of the **Writer's Guide.** To **publish,** have the children read their invitations to the class.

USING THE DICTIONARY

Objectives To recognize that only base forms of verbs appear as entry words; to write the base forms of verbs given inflected forms; to use the dictionary to locate words.

1. Ask a volunteer to read the introductory paragraph on page 58 aloud. Then have the children locate the inflected forms of the verb in the dictionary entry for *stare.*
2. Have the children complete the activity independently.
3. Let the children check their own work by locating the words they wrote in the **Spelling Dictionary.**

THIS WEEK'S WORDS
invite
paste
skate
stare
tape
taste
wipe
cared
hiked
loved
moved
dancing
hoping
living
smiling

Spelling and Language • Adding *ed* and *ing*

You add *ed* to a word to tell what already happened. You add *ing* to a word to tell what is or was happening.

Finish the sentences. Add *ed* or *ing* to each word in dark print. Remember to drop the *e* before adding *ed* or *ing*.

1. **paste** Danielle was _____ **pasting** _____ stars on blue paper.
2. **skate** Then she _____ **skated** _____ to the corner store.
3. **tape** She was _____ **taping** _____ her notes up all over.
4. **invite** Danielle _____ **invited** _____ everyone to her party.

Writing on Your Own

Pretend you are going to have a birthday party at a skating rink. Write an invitation to send to your grandmother, grandfather, or other relative. Use as many of This Week's Words as you can. Try to use *ed* or *ing* with some of the words.

 WRITER'S GUIDE For help with the parts of a letter, turn to page 251.

Using the Dictionary to Spell and Write

Look at this dictionary sample. The entry word is *stare.* The word with *ed* and *ing* comes after *stare.* To find *stared* or *staring* in the dictionary, you must look up *stare.*

> **stare** /stâr/ *v.* **stared, staring** To look hard, often without blinking: The dog *stared* at the cat.
> —*n.* A long, hard look.

Suppose you want to check the spelling of these words in the dictionary. Write each word you would look up.

1. dancing _____ **dance** _____ 2. moved _____ **move**
3. hoping _____ **hope** _____ 4. cared _____ **care**

58

Spelling on Your Own

Spelling on Your Own   UNIT 13d

THIS WEEK'S WORDS

This Week's Words are all verbs, but some of them can also be nouns. Choose words that can be nouns. Use them to finish these sentences.

1. David broke the shoestring on his ___skate___.

2. He tried to use ___tape___ to hold it together.

Now write a sentence for each of the rest of This Week's Words.

MASTERY WORDS

bake
name
race
save
use
wave

Write these words without _ed_ to make Mastery words.

1. waved ___wave___   2. raced ___race___

3. named ___name___   4. used ___use___

Write these words without _ing_ to make Mastery words.

5. baking ___bake___   6. using ___use___

7. saving ___save___   8. racing ___race___

When Leo doesn't listen, he must ask questions. Finish his questions with Mastery words.

9. Al: I baked a cake.   Leo: What did you ___bake___?
10. Al: I saved some for you.   Leo: What did you

___save___?

BONUS WORDS

manage
prepare
suppose
surprise
divided
promised
behaving
chasing

1. Add _ed_ and _ing_ to the first four Bonus words.
2. Write the last four words without _ed_ or _ing_.
3. Write the two words that have long _i_.
4. Write a letter to a friend about a birthday party. Try to use all the Bonus words in your letter.   See answers below.

59

Spelling on Your Own Answers

BONUS WORDS

1. managed, managing, prepared, preparing, supposed, supposing, surprised, surprising 2. divide, promise, behave, chase 3. surprise, divided 4. Children will write as directed. Be sure to check spelling.

TEACHING PLAN

> **Objective**   To apply the unit spelling generalization to spell This Week's Words, Mastery words, and Bonus words independently.

THIS WEEK'S WORDS

1. Have a volunteer read the directions on page 59 aloud.
2. Have the children complete the activity independently on a separate piece of paper.

MASTERY WORDS

1. Have volunteers read the Mastery words aloud. As each word is read, have the children say the word with _ed_ and _ing_ added. Write these forms on the chalkboard.
2. Read the directions on page 59 aloud and have the children complete the activity independently.

BONUS WORDS

1. Briefly review the unit generalization on page 56.
2. Have a volunteer read the Bonus words aloud. Discuss the meanings of the words and have the children look up any unfamiliar words in the **Spelling Dictionary.**
3. Have the children complete the activity on a separate piece of paper.

For reinforcement in writing spelling words, you may wish to assign **Extra Practice Master 13: Mastery Words** or **Bonus Words.**

Summarize Learning

Have the children summarize what they have learned in this unit. _Ask:_

• What have you learned about writing verbs in sentence context? (You add _ed_ to a word to tell what already happened. You add _ing_ to make a word that can be used with words such as _am, is, are, was,_ and _were._ You add _ing_ to a word to tell what _is_ or _was_ happening.)

• What have you learned about entry words in the dictionary? (Only the base forms of verbs are used as entry words.)

• What spelling generalizations have you learned? How did you use these generalizations?

CLOSING THE UNIT

Apply New Learning

Tell the children that if they misspell words ending in e in their writing, they should use one or more of the following strategies:

- write the word using different spellings and compare it with the spelling they picture in their minds.
- try to find patterns and causes of their errors.
- look at the changes in spelling that occur in related words.

Transfer New Learning

Tell the children that when they encounter new words in their personal reading and in other content areas, they should learn the meaning of those words and then apply the generalizations they have studied to the spelling of those words. Tell them that once the words are familiar in both meaning and spelling, they should use the new words in their writing.

ENRICHMENT ACTIVITIES

Classroom activities and **home activities** may be assigned to children of all ability levels. The activities provide opportunities for children to use their spelling words in new contexts.

For the Classroom

To individualize classroom activities, you may have the children use the word list they are studying in this unit.

- *Basic:* Use **Mastery** words to complete the activity.
- *Average:* Use **This Week's Words** to complete the activity.
- *Challenging:* Use **Bonus** words to complete the activity.

1. **Language Arts/Writing Riddles** Have the children write riddles about spelling words. Tell them to follow this format as they write a riddle: *I am eating, sleeping, breathing, and thinking. What word am I?* (living) Have the children write similar riddles for five other spelling words. When the children have completed their riddles, invite them to share their riddles with one another.

■ COOPERATIVE LEARNING: Have each group create riddles for as many spelling words as there are group members. Each child within a group should write clues for one riddle. Riddles should take the following form: *I am eating, sleeping, breathing, and thinking. What word am I?* (living) Group members should try out their riddles on each other to see if their clues are effective. They may check definitions in a dictionary. Each group should exchange and guess riddles.

2. **Language Arts/Writing Sentences Using Words as Nouns and Verbs** Tell each child to use two spelling words in pairs of sentences. The first sentence of each pair should be a question in which a spelling word is used as a verb. The second sentence should answer the question and use the same spelling word as a noun. For example, May I *skate* this afternoon? (verb) No, your *skate* is broken. (noun) Tell children they may use any of the base words on their spelling list. After they have finished writing their sentences, children can ask each other their questions and answer them by using their classmate's spelling word as a noun.

■ COOPERATIVE LEARNING: Have each group write pairs of sentences using spelling words as nouns and verbs. Each child should use two spelling words in two sentence pairs. The first sentence of each pair should use the word as a verb and ask a question; the second sentence should use the word as a noun and answer the question. For example, May I *skate* this afternoon? (verb) No, your *skate* is broken. (noun) Group members should check each other's sentences to see if the spelling words have been used correctly. The group should then choose several questions and copy them for other children to answer, using the same spelling word as a noun.

3. **Language Arts/Writing Rhyming Poetry** Have each child write rhyming two-line poems using some of their spelling words. As a ***prewriting*** activity, direct the children to look over the spelling lists in search of words for which they can think of rhyming words. Children's rhymes should express actions. For example, a child might rhyme the spelling word *taste* with *chased: I asked for a taste, But away I was chased.* Have the children write the spelling words and rhyming words on paper. To **compose** the poem, have the children choose four pairs of rhyming words and write four two-line poems. Have the children ***revise*** their poems by checking to see that the lines rhyme and the words are correctly spelled. ***Publish*** the rhymes by having the children read them aloud.

■ COOPERATIVE LEARNING: Have each group write four two-line rhymes using some of their spelling words. As a ***prewriting*** activity, have each child record the rhyming pairs. Tell each group to share their rhyming words and choose one of each group member's rhyming pairs to include in each rhyme. When the children are ready to **compose** the rhymes, have the group select a recorder. Tell the group to choose one child to suggest a line of the poem that ends with the first word of a pair; another child can complete that two-line rhyme. The group should follow the same procedure to compose the other rhymes. The group can then ***revise*** their poems, checking to see that the lines rhyme and the spelling is correct. Each group can ***publish*** their poems by displaying them for the class to read.

For the Home

Children may complete these activities independently or with the assistance of a relative or friend in the home.

1. **Language Arts/Writing Directions** Tell the children to write directions for doing or making something. Children should incorporate some of their spelling words. For example, children might write a set of directions about how to roller skate or ice skate. Suggest that children work with someone else to test the directions, and then write them in sequential order. Have children proofread their directions for spelling.

2. **Health/Making a Chart of Health Tips** Tell the children to use verbs on the spelling list and other verbs to develop a chart that gives health tips. Children may refer to *HBJ Health,* grade 3, for ideas. In a column on the left, children should list five verbs. Across from each verb, they should write the corresponding health tip, and the reason for suggesting it. For example, *Wipe: Wipe your face dry after washing it. Then it won't become chapped.*

3. **Language Arts/Writing Sentence Captions** Tell the children to find pictures of active people. Have children review their spelling lists and use as many verbs as possible to guide them in their picture search. Tell children to paste each picture on a separate page, and beneath each one write the describing verb. Children should then use the verb in a sentence telling about the picture.

4. **Language Arts/Writing Synonyms** Have each child write synonyms for at least four spelling words. Encourage the children to use the **Spelling Thesaurus** on page 203 to find synonyms. Tell them to use each synonym in a sentence. Children may ask a relative or friend to replace each synonym with another word that means the same, or almost the same, thing. If the replacement chosen is the word from the spelling list, the children will know they have used a good synonym.

EVALUATING SPELLING ABILITY

Unit Test

This Week's Words

1. *invite* We will *invite* our neighbors to the picnic. *invite*
2. *paste* You can *paste* the pictures in this book. *paste*
3. *skate* Let's *skate* in the park. *skate*
4. *stare* The dogs *stare* at the birds. *stare*
5. *tape* Please *tape* the box shut. *tape*
6. *taste* I like to *taste* new foods. *taste*
7. *wipe* Use the sponge to *wipe* off the table. *wipe*
8. *cared* Charles *cared* about doing well on the test. *cared*
9. *hiked* Joyce *hiked* five miles today. *hiked*
10. *loved* Daddy *loved* the present we gave him. *loved*
11. *moved* The neighbors *moved* their piano. *moved*
12. *dancing* Andrea was *dancing* around the room. *dancing*
13. *hoping* I keep *hoping* to find a four-leaf clover. *hoping*
14. *living* Joe is *living* in your old house now. *living*
15. *smiling* Marta was *smiling* at David. *smiling*

Mastery Words

1. *bake* We will *bake* some potatoes for dinner. *bake*
2. *name* They did *name* the baby Charles. *name*
3. *race* Let's *race* on our bikes. *race*
4. *save* My parents are trying to *save* money. *save*
5. *use* We did not *use* all the paper. *use*
6. *wave* Look at the camera and *wave*. *wave*

Bonus Words

1. *manage* I think I can *manage* by myself. *manage*
2. *prepare* We will *prepare* everything for the picnic. *prepare*
3. *suppose* I *suppose* I should make my bed. *suppose*
4. *surprise* Nothing would *surprise* Mom. *surprise*
5. *divided* The girl *divided* the paper in half. *divided*
6. *promised* Jeb *promised* to mow the lawn. *promised*
7. *behaving* The gerbil is *behaving* strangely. *behaving*
8. *chasing* Hector was *chasing* Billy. *chasing*

Dictation Sentences

This Week's Words

1. Please *wipe* off the desk after you *paste* and *tape*.
2. I am *hoping* they will *invite* me to *skate* or go *dancing*.
3. She was *smiling* as she *moved* on and *hiked* up the hill.
4. No one *cared* that he wanted to *taste* the apple juice.
5. The cat *loved* to *stare* at the place where the fish were *living*.

Mastery Words

1. I will *wave* as you *race* by.
2. Please *save* me some milk to *use* when I *bake*.
3. What will we *name* the baby bird?

Bonus Words

1. Do you *suppose* we can *manage* to *prepare* lunch as we *promised*?
2. The dog was not *behaving* when it was *chasing* cats.
3. He *divided* the orange in two.
4. We will jump out and *surprise* Tim.

RETEACHING STRATEGIES FOR SPELLING

Children who have made errors on the Unit Test may require reteaching. Use the following **Reteaching Strategies** and **Follow-up Masters 13A** and **13B** for additional instruction and practice of This Week's Words. (You may wish to assign **LEP Reteaching Follow-up Master 13** for reteaching of spelling words.)

A. Discovering Spelling Ideas

1. Say the following words as you write them on the chalkboard.

dare   dared   daring

2. Ask the children to identify the last letter of the verb *dare*.
3. Ask the children to identify the word parts that were added to the verb. (*ed* and *ing*)
4. Ask the children what happened to the final *e* when *ed* or *ing* were added. (It was dropped.)
5. Ask the children what they have learned about adding *ed* and *ing* to verbs that end with *e*. (Drop the final *e* before adding *ed* or *ing*.)

B. Word Shapes

1. Explain to the children that each word has a shape and that remembering the shape of a word can help them to spell the word correctly.
2. On the chalkboard, write the words *like* and *taping*. Have the children identify "short," "tall," and "tail" letters.
3. Draw the configuration of each word on the chalkboard, and ask the children which word fits in each shape.

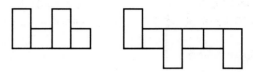

Use **Reteaching Follow-up Master 13A** to reinforce spelling generalizations taught in Unit 13.

Name				UNIT 13
Reteaching Follow-up A			Discovering Spelling Ideas	

THIS WEEK'S WORDS

invite	paste	stare	tape	cared
loved	dancing	living	hoping	skate
taste	wipe	hiked	moved	smiling

1. Study This Week's Words. Complete the chart below.

Verbs	Verbs with ed	Verbs with ing
live	lived	**living**
hike	**hiked**	hiking
love	**loved**	loving
smile	smiled	**smiling**
care	**cared**	caring
hope	hoped	**hoping**
move	**moved**	moving
dance	danced	**dancing**

2. What letter did you drop when you added *ed* or *ing*?

     e

Reteaching • 21

Use **Reteaching Follow-up Master 13B** to reinforce spellings of This Week's Words for Unit 13.

Name				UNIT 13
Reteaching Follow-up B			Word Shapes	

THIS WEEK'S WORDS

invite	paste	stare	tape	cared
loved	dancing	living	hoping	skate
taste	wipe	hiked	moved	smiling

Write each of This Week's Words in its correct shape. The first one has been done for you. Children may interchange answers that fit the same configuration.

1. t a s t e
2. l i v i n g
3. s m i l i n g
4. s t a r e
5. p a s t e
6. m o v e d
7. l o v e d
8. t a p e
9. h i k e d
10. h o p i n g
11. d a n c i n g
12. c a r e d
13. s k a t e
14. w i p e
15. i n v i t e

22 • Reteaching

PREVIEWING THE UNIT

Unit Materials

Instruction and Practice

Pupil Book   pages 60–63
Teacher's Edition
Teaching Plans   pages 60–63
Enrichment Activities
    For the Classroom   page 63A
    For the Home   page 63B
Reteaching Strategies   page 63C

Testing

Teacher's Edition
Trial Test   pages 59E–59F
Unit Test   page 63B
Dictation Test   page 63B

Additional Resources

PRACTICE AND REINFORCEMENT
Extra Practice Master 14: This Week's Words
Extra Practice Master 14: Mastery Words
Extra Practice Master 14: Bonus Words
LEP Practice Master 14
Spelling and Language Master 14
Study Steps to Learn a Word Master

RETEACHING FOLLOW-UP
Reteaching Follow-up Master 14A:
    Discovering Spelling Ideas
Reteaching Follow-up Master 14B: Word
    Shapes
LEP Reteaching Follow-up Master 14

TEACHING AIDS
Spelling Generalizations Transparency 12

Click on the SPELLING banner to find activities for this unit.

Learner Objectives

Spelling

- To spell words that demonstrate the sound-letter relationships: /ā/a-consonant-e, *ai, ay, ey, eigh.*
- To form new words by changing letters in given words.

Reading

- To follow written directions.
- To use context clues to complete sentences given spelling words.

Writing

- To write a how-to paragraph.
- To use the writing process.
- To proofread for spelling, capitalization, and punctuation.
- To write legible manuscript and cursive letters.

Listening

- To listen to identify words with the sound /ā/.
- To listen to respond to a speaker by asking questions and contributing information.
- To follow oral directions.

Speaking

- To speak clearly to a group.
- To contribute ideas and information in group discussions.
- To present a story to the class.
- To express feelings and ideas about a piece of writing.

THIS WEEK'S WORDS

awake
brave
clay
gate
hay
lake
lay
mail
paid
safe
snake
today
trail
obey
eight

MASTERY WORDS

late
may
nail
paint
same
they

BONUS WORDS

crayon
delay
faint
grape
mistake
railroad
raisin
snail

Assignment Guide

This guide shows how you teach a typical spelling unit in either a five-day or a three-day sequence, while providing for individual differences. **Boldface type** indicates essential classwork. Steps shown in light type may be done in class or assigned as homework.

Five Days	● = average spellers ★ = better spellers ✓ = slower spellers	Three Days
Day **1**	a ● ★ **Take This Week's Words Trial Test and correct** ● ✓ **Take Mastery Word Trial Test and correct** ● ★ **Read This Week's Words and discuss generalization page 60**	Day **1**
Day **2**	● Complete Spelling Practice page 61 ● ✓ Complete Extra Practice Master 14: This Week's Words (optional) ✓ Complete Spelling on Your Own: Mastery Words page 63 ★ **Take Bonus Word Trial Test and correct** b	
Day **3**	c ● ★ ✓ **Complete Spelling and Language page 62** ● ★ ✓ Complete Writing on Your Own page 62 ● ✓ Take Midweek Test (optional) ★ Complete Spelling on Your Own: Bonus Words page 63 ● ✓ Complete Spelling and Language Master 14 (optional)	Day **2**
Day **4**	● Complete Spelling on Your Own: This Week's Words page 63 ✓ Complete Extra Practice Master 14: Mastery Words (optional) ★ Complete Extra Practice Master 14: Bonus Words (optional) d	
Day **5**	e ● Take Unit Test on This Week's Words ● Complete Reteaching Follow-up Masters 14A and 14B (optional) ● ✓ **Take Unit Test on Mastery Words** ★ **Take Unit Test on Bonus Words**	Day **3**

Enrichment Activities for the **classroom** and for the **home** included at the end of this unit may be assigned selectively on any day of the week.

INTRODUCING THE UNIT

Establish Readiness for Learning

Tell the children that this week they will continue to study words with long vowel sounds. In Unit 14 they will study four spellings for the long vowel sound /ā/. Tell the children that they will apply the spelling generalizations to This Week's Words and use those words to write a how-to paragraph.

Assess Children's Spelling Ability

Administer the Trial Test before the children study This Week's Words. Use the test sentences provided. Say each word and use it in a sentence. Then repeat the word. Have the children write the words on a separate sheet of paper or in their spelling notebooks. Test sentences are also provided for Mastery and Bonus words.

Have the children check their own work by

listening to you read the spelling of the words or by referring to This Week's Words in the left column of the **Pupil Book.** For each misspelled word, have the children follow the **Study Steps to Learn a Word** on page 1 in the **Pupil Book** or use the copying master to study and write the words. Children should record the number correct on their **Progress Report.**

Trial Test Sentences

This Week's Words

1. *awake*   It is late at night, but I am wide *awake.*   **awake**
2. *brave*   Even *brave* people are sometimes scared.   **brave**
3. *clay*   Clarissa made an elephant out of *clay.*   **clay**
4. *gate*   Please close the *gate.*   **gate**
5. *hay*   The horses are eating *hay.*   **hay**
6. *lake*   We went swimming in the *lake.*   **lake**
7. *lay*   The hen will *lay* eggs.   **lay**

FOCUS

- Establishes objectives
- Relates to prior learning
- Sets purpose of instruction

8. **mail**   Anna got a letter in the *mail*.
   mail
9. **paid**   Jeremy *paid* for the toy
   himself.   *paid*
10. **safe**   The key will be *safe* here.   *safe*
11. **snake**   That woman has a pet *snake*.
    snake
12. **today**   We can go *today* or
    tomorrow.   *today*
13. **trail**   We followed the *trail* up the hill.
    trail
14. **obey**   We must all *obey* the law.   *obey*
15. **eight**   There are *eight* robins in the
    yard.   *eight*

Mastery Words

1. **late**   If we miss the bus, we'll be *late*.
   late
2. **may**   We *may* have to walk.   *may*
3. **nail**   Joan hung the picture on a *nail*.
   nail
4. **paint**   The house needs some *paint*.
   paint
5. **same**   Let's paint it the *same*
   color.   *same*
6. **they**   I think *they* will like it.   *they*

Bonus Words

1. **crayon**   Doug wrote the sign with a
   crayon.   *crayon*
2. **delay**   Please do this without *delay*.
   delay

3. **faint**   Sherry was so hungry she felt *faint*.
   faint
4. **grape**   Brad ate a *grape*.   *grape*
5. **mistake**   Isabelle made a *mistake* in the
   math problem.   *mistake*
6. **railroad**   The *railroad* station is up the
   street.   *railroad*
7. **raisin**   A *raisin* is a dried grape.   *raisin*
8. **snail**   The *snail* moved slowly along the
   branch.   *snail*

Apply Prior Learning

Have the children apply what they already know about the long vowel sound of the letter *a* by participating in the following activity.

Write the words *make, rail, bay, survey,* and *sleigh* on the chalkboard. Read these words aloud with the children. Ask the children to tell how these words are alike, and help them to recognize that each word has the long vowel sound for the letter *a*. Ask volunteers to come to the chalkboard and draw a line around the letters that represent the /ā/ sound in each word. Tell the children that in Unit 14 they will study words that have these long vowel spellings. Explain that they can use these words in a variety of writing tasks; they can use the words in a note to a friend, in a letter, or in a book report.

FOR CHILDREN WITH SPECIAL NEEDS

Learning Difficulties

Information-processing disabilities result in inconsistent learning. A multi-sensory approach is effective in teaching children with this disability.

Unlined paper and pencil are the only materials needed for this activity. Divide This Week's Words into the words that demonstrate three different spellings of the long vowel sound of the letter *a*. (*a*-consonant-*e*—*awake, brave, lake, safe, snake;* ai—*mail, paid, trail;* ay—*clay, hay, lay, today*). Teach only one of these spellings each day.

Write This Week's Words on the chalkboard. Ask the children to say one of the words aloud and copy it onto their papers. Point out the spelling of that word. Have the children close their eyes and recall the letters in the

word. Then have them write the word on their papers without looking at a model. Direct their attention to the sensation of making each of the letters. Have the children look at their word and compare it with the word at the top of their papers, one letter at a time. If the word is written correctly, ask the children to say the word. If the word is misspelled, have them repeat the sequence.

Limited English Proficiency

To help limited English proficient children work with the spelling generalizations for Unit 14, you may wish to refer to the booklet "Suggestions and Activities for Limited English Proficient Students."

TEACHING PLAN

Objective To spell words that demonstrate these sound-letter relationships: /ā/ a-consonant-e, ai, ay, ey, eigh.

1. Write the letter *a* on the chalkboard and have the children say the letter name. Remind them that this is the sound that is called a long *a*. Then ask the children to say words that have the sound /ā/. As words are suggested, write them on the chalkboard. Help the children to identify the letters that spell /ā/ in each word, and to recognize that medial /ā/ can be spelled *a*-consonant-e or *ai* and the final /ā/ is usually spelled *ay*.

You may wish to introduce the lesson by using **Spelling Generalizations Transparency 12.**

2. Read the generalization on page 60 aloud. Help the children to identify *ey* as the spelling for /ā/ in *obey* and *eigh* as the spelling for /ā/ in *eight*.
3. Direct the children's attention to **Remember This** at the bottom of the page. Have a volunteer read the verse aloud.
4. Have volunteers read This Week's Words aloud. As each word is read, ask the children to identify the letters that spell /ā/ in the word.

You may wish to assign **LEP Practice Master 14** for reinforcement in writing spelling words.

---

14 The Vowel Sound /ā/

THIS WEEK'S WORDS

1. *awake*
2. *brave*
3. *clay*
4. *gate*
5. *hay*
6. *lake*
7. *lay*
8. *mail*
9. *paid*
10. *safe*
11. *snake*
12. *today*
13. *trail*
14. *obey*
15. *eight*

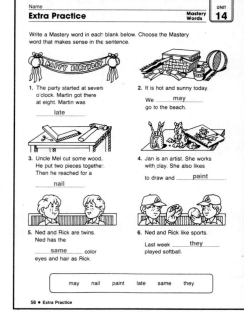

This Week's Words

All the words this week have the vowel sound /ā/. Here are three ways to spell /ā/.

- with **a**-consonant-e, as in <u>lake</u>
- with **ai**, as in <u>trail</u>
- with **ay** at the end of a word, as in <u>today</u>

☐ The words obey and eight also have the vowel sound /ā/. How is /ā/ spelled in each of these words?

REMEMBER THIS

In <u>clay</u> and <u>hay</u> and <u>lay</u> and <u>day</u>,
The letters <u>a-y</u> spell long <u>a</u>.
But <u>obey</u> is spelled another way.
It ends with <u>e-y</u>, just like <u>they</u>.
Then there's <u>gate</u> and <u>late</u>, you see,
Both spelled the same with <u>a-t-e</u>.
So who would expect <u>8</u> to be
Spelled with <u>e-i-g-h-t</u>?

60

Extra Practice: This Week's Words

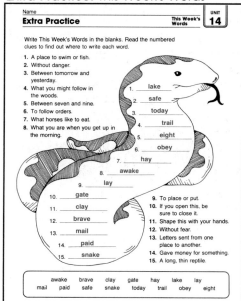

Name
Extra Practice   This Week's Words   UNIT 14

Write This Week's Words in the blanks. Read the numbered clues to find out where to write each word.

1. A place to swim or fish.
2. Without danger.
3. Between tomorrow and yesterday.
4. What you might follow in the woods.
5. Between seven and nine.
6. To follow orders.
7. What horses like to eat.
8. What you are when you get up in the morning.

1. lake
2. safe
3. today
4. trail
5. eight
6. obey
7. hay
8. awake
9. lay
10. gate
11. clay
12. brave
13. mail
14. paid
15. snake

9. To place or put.
10. If you open this, be sure to close it.
11. Shape this with your hands.
12. Without fear.
13. Letters sent from one place to another.
14. Gave money for something.
15. A long, thin reptile.

| awake | brave | clay | gate | hay | lake | lay |
| mail | paid | safe | snake | today | trail | obey | eight |

Extra Practice • 57

Extra Practice: Mastery Words

Name
Extra Practice   Mastery Words   UNIT 14

Write a Mastery word in each blank below. Choose the Mastery word that makes sense in the sentence.

1. The party started at seven o'clock. Martin got there at eight. Martin was _____ late

2. It is hot and sunny today. We _____ may go to the beach.

3. Uncle Mel cut some wood. He put two pieces together. Then he reached for a _____ nail

4. Jan is an artist. She works with clay. She also likes to draw and _____ paint

5. Ned and Rick are twins. Ned has the _____ same color eyes and hair as Rick.

6. Ned and Rick like sports. Last week _____ they played softball.

| may | nail | paint | late | same | they |

58 • Extra Practice

Spelling Practice

A. Follow the directions. Use This Week's Words.

1. Write the six words that have /ā/ spelled as it is in <u>same</u>.

awake	brave	gate
lake	safe	snake

2. Write the five words that end with /ā/.

clay	hay	lay
today	(obey)	

3. Circle the word you wrote for **2** that does not end with <u>ay</u>.

4. Write the word that sounds just like <u>ate</u>. _____eight_____

B. Write the words that begin and end with these letters.

5. m___l ___mail___   6. p___d ___paid___

7. tr___l ___trail___

C. Finish the story. Use This Week's Words. The last sound in each word is given to help you. Write one word twice.

Eric and Ed hiked to the ___8___ /k/. Next to the ___9___ /l/ they saw a ___10___ /k/. Ed was afraid, but Eric was ___11___ /v/.

"We will be perfectly ___12___ /f/. But you must ___13___ /ā/ me. Do not make a sound. That ___14___ /k/ is not ___15___ /k/!"

8.	lake	9.	trail	10.	snake
11.	brave	12.	safe	13.	obey
14.	snake	15.	awake		

Word list (right margin):
awake
brave
clay
gate
hay
lake
lay
mail
paid
safe
snake
today
trail
obey
eight

61

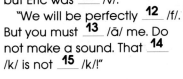

TEACHING PLAN

> **Objectives** To write words given spelling clues; to write words given the position of /ā/; to write words given initial and final consonants; to write words that complete a story.

1. Read the directions on page 61 aloud. Briefly discuss the directions for Exercise **C**. Be sure the children understand that they are to write words that end with the sounds given.

2. Have the children complete the page independently. Remind them to use legible handwriting. You may wish to demonstrate the correct form of the letters *a* and *e* and then have the children practice writing the letters. For **Handwriting Models,** refer the children to page 258 in the **Pupil Book.**

3. To correct the children's work, have volunteers write their answers for Exercises **A** and **B** on the chalkboard. Let the children check their own answers. Then ask a volunteer to read the completed story in Exercise **C** to the class.

For reinforcement in writing spelling words, you may wish to assign *Extra Practice Master 14: This Week's Words.*

⭐ **of special interest**

The word *mail* is an example of the semantic change called *transference*. Originally the word *mail* named a pouch, or traveling bag and later specifically the pouch in which letters and parcels were transported. Eventually the word was applied to the contents of the bag.

Summarize Learning

Have the children summarize what they have learned on pages 60 and 61. *Ask:*
- What have you learned about how to spell the /ā/ sound? (The /ā/ sound may be spelled *a*-consonant-*e*, *ai*, *ay*, *ey*, and *eigh*.)
- What are examples of words using the different spellings for /ā/? (*awake, mail, clay, obey, eight;* accept other examples)

TEACHING PLAN

SPELLING AND LANGUAGE

Objective To write different words by changing beginning letters, given picture clues.

1. Write *made* on the chalkboard. Ask the children what word you would spell if you changed *d* to *k*. Work in a similar way through the next two steps in this word ladder: made—make—fake—tale.
2. Read the directions on page 62 aloud. Then have a volunteer say the picture words and identify the first letter in each word.

   If you are using the hardcover book, have the children write the first word in each word ladder and refer to their books to find out where to write the new letter. Tell them to write each new word carefully under the previous word.
3. To correct the children's work, have two volunteers write their word ladders on the board. Let the children check their own work.

For extended practice in writing new words by substituting letters, you may wish to assign *Spelling and Language Master 14.*

WRITING ON YOUR OWN

Objectives To write a how-to paragraph; to proofread for spelling.

1. Read the directions aloud.
2. As a **prewriting** activity, make a chart of different types of playground equipment and ways to use each safely. Then have the children **compose** their paragraphs. When they are ready to **revise,** remind them to check for spelling. To **publish,** display the children's work on hall bulletin boards for other children to read.

HANDWRITING

Objective To practice writing cursive letter forms: *vV, xX, yY, zZ*; to write a sentence using cursive writing.

Spelling and Language • Word Ladders

THIS WEEK'S WORDS
awake
brave
clay
gate
hay
lake
lay
mail
paid
safe
snake
today
trail
obey
eight

Many of This Week's Words have the same endings. If you change a letter or letters at the beginning of a word, you make a new word. Take <u>g</u>ate. If you write l in place of g, you spell late. Start with the words below. Change the underlined letters to make new words. Use the pictures to help you.

1. <u>aw</u> a k e
   <u>l</u> a k e
   <u>s n</u> a k e
   <u>r</u> a k e

2. <u>t r</u> a i l
   <u>m</u> a i l
   <u>p</u> a i l
   <u>s</u> a i l

Writing on Your Own

Write a paragraph for a young friend. Tell how to play safely on the playground. Use some of This Week's Words.

WRITER'S GUIDE Did you write neatly? If you need help writing any letters, turn to page 261.

HANDWRITING

v V   x X   z Z

The lowercase letters **v, x,** and **z** begin with this overcurve stroke. ⟋

1. Practice writing **v V, x X, z Z** in cursive.

2. Write this sentence: *Val saw six zebras.*

62

1. Read the first sentence on page 62 aloud. Have the children examine the model of the beginning stroke.
2. Have the children examine the models for the cursive letters. Help them to note where the letters touch or intersect the lines.
3. Have the children practice the letter forms and write the sentence independently.
4. When they have finished, ask the children to compare their letter forms with the models.

Extra Practice: Spelling and Language

Name _____   UNIT 14

Spelling and Language

A. Underline the word in each sentence that does not make sense. Then change one letter of the word so that it makes sense. Write the new word on the line.

1. A <u>brake</u> woman carried letters in her pack. — brave
2. She walked on a long and dusty <u>grail</u>. — trail
3. The path she took was not <u>sale</u>. — safe
4. It seemed to wind and slither through the trees like a <u>slake</u>. — snake
5. The path was made of wet red <u>clam</u>. — clay
6. In one spot, it went past a cold and dark <u>make</u>. — lake
7. The woman was <u>maid</u> to do her job. — paid
8. Her job was to deliver <u>sail</u> to each home on the path. — mail

B. Add letters to the vowels in dark print. Write some of This Week's Words.

9. __ay	10. __ai__	11. __a__e
clay	paid	gate
hay	trail	lake
lay	mail	safe
today		brave
		snake
		awake

| awake | clay | hay | lake | paid | snake | trail | obey |
| brave | gate | lay | mail | safe | today | eight | |

60 • Extra Practice

Spelling on Your Own

THIS WEEK'S WORDS

Add <u>a-e</u>, <u>ai</u>, or <u>ay</u> to each group of letters. Write This Week's Words.

1. tr l   **2.** aw k   **3.** cl   **4.** m l   **5.** h
6. sn k   **7.** g t   **8.** p d   **9.** l k   **10.** l
11. br v   **12.** s f   **13.** tod

Now write the words that aren't spelled with <u>a-e</u>, <u>ai</u>, or <u>ay</u>. **See answers below.**

MASTERY WORDS

Follow the directions. Use the Mastery words.

late
may
nail
paint
same
they

1. Write the two words that rhyme with <u>day</u>.

_____may_____   _(they)_

2. Circle the word that is not spelled with <u>ay</u>.

3. Name two things you could use to make a doghouse.

_____nail_____   _____paint_____

Read each word. Then write two Mastery words that have /ā/ spelled the same way.

4. make _____late_____   _____same_____

5. train _____nail_____   _____paint_____

BONUS WORDS

Follow the directions. Use the Bonus words.

crayon
delay
faint
grape
mistake
railroad
raisin
snail

1. Write the three Bonus words that begin with consonant clusters.
2. Write the words that start with <u>de</u> and <u>mis</u>.
3. Write the four words that have /ā/ spelled as it is in <u>train</u>.
4. Write two words that name things that can be purple.
5. Write four sentences. Use two Bonus words in each sentence. **See answers below.**

63

Summarize Learning

Have the children summarize what they have learned in this unit. *Ask:*

● What did you learn about adding different letters in front of some word endings? (You can often make new words.)
● What spelling generalizations have you learned? How did you use these generalizations?

Spelling on Your Own | UNIT 14d

TEACHING PLAN

Objective To apply the unit spelling generalization to spell This Week's Words, Mastery words, and Bonus words independently.

THIS WEEK'S WORDS

1. Read the directions on page 63 aloud. Help the children get started by having a volunteer indicate the letters that must be added in **1** to spell one of This Week's Words.
2. Have the children complete the activity independently on a separate piece of paper. Encourage them to try to complete the activity without referring to the word list.

MASTERY WORDS

1. Briefly review the unit generalization.
2. Have volunteers read the Mastery words aloud. As each word is read, have the children identify the letters that spell /ā/ in the word.
3. Read the directions on page 63 aloud. Ask the children to identify the letters that spell /ā/ in the words given for **4** and **5**.
4. Have the children complete the activity independently.

BONUS WORDS

1. Briefly review the unit generalization.
2. Have volunteers read the Bonus words aloud. As each word is read, have the children identify the letters that spell /ā/ in the word.
3. Have the children complete the work independently on a separate piece of paper.

For reinforcement in writing spelling words, you may wish to assign *Extra Practice Master 14: Mastery Words* or *Bonus Words.*

CLOSING THE UNIT

Apply New Learning

Tell the children that if they misspell words with the /ā/ sound in their writing, they should use one or more of the following strategies:

- think about the possible spellings for the /ā/ sound and try to picture the word in their minds.
- write the word using different spellings and compare it with the spelling they picture in their minds.
- think of words that rhyme and compare in their minds how the words are spelled.

Transfer New Learning

Tell the children that when they encounter new words in their personal reading and in other content areas, they should learn the meaning of those words and then apply the generalizations they have studied to the spelling of those words. Tell the children that once the words are familiar in both meaning and spelling, they should use the new words in their writing.

ENRICHMENT ACTIVITIES

Classroom activities and **home activities** may be assigned to children of all ability levels. The activities provide opportunities for children to use their spelling words in new contexts.

For the Classroom

To individualize classroom activities, you may have the children use the word list they are studying in this unit.

- *Basic:* Use **Mastery** words to complete the activity.
- *Average:* Use **This Week's Words** to complete the activity.
- *Challenging:* Use **Bonus** words to complete the activity.

1. **Language Arts/Writing Rhyming Words** Have the children write rhyming word pairs using at least four spelling words. Then have them use all eight words to make a word search puzzle.

   ■ COOPERATIVE LEARNING: Have each group create a word search puzzle. The group should divide up the words on the list and each child should write a rhyming word for as many of his or her assigned words as possible. The children should check each other's word pairs to be sure that they rhyme. Together, the group should create one word search puzzle using all the rhyming word pairs. Once the puzzle is completed, have the group exchange puzzles with another group for solving.

2. **Language Arts/Writing Context Sentences** Have the children use their spelling words in five sentences that provide contextual meaning for those words. Explain that

the meaning of each spelling word should be clear from the meaning of the other words in the sentence. After they write their sentences, the children should copy them onto another sheet of paper, leaving a blank in place of the spelling word. Then have the children ask each other to supply the missing spelling word.

■ COOPERATIVE LEARNING: Have each group use spelling words in contextual sentences. Each child should write two sentences using one of the spelling words in each sentence. The children should check each other's sentences to see if they are able to figure out the spelling words from the meaning of the other words in the sentences. The group should then choose two recorders to share the task of copying the sentences, leaving a blank in place of each spelling word.

3. **Language Arts/Writing a Realistic Adventure Story** Have each child use the spelling words to write a realistic adventure story. As a *prewriting* activity, have the children review the spelling list to find words to use in their stories. Suggest that a snake can be an important part of their stories. Have children develop cluster drawings based on the concept word *snake.* Such a cluster drawing might begin like this:

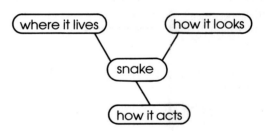

Children should use their clusters, along with ideas taken from words on the spelling list, to decide on the details of the story. When the children are ready, have them **compose** their adventure stories. Then have them **revise** their stories, checking to see that each story is realistic and exciting, and has a beginning, middle, and ending. Then have them **publish** the stories by displaying them in the classroom.

■ COOPERATIVE LEARNING: Have each group write a realistic adventure story using as many spelling words as possible. As a *prewriting* activity, have each group create a cluster drawing. Tell the groups to use both the cluster drawing and the spelling list as they decide on a story plot. When the children are ready to **compose,** group members should take turns contributing to the parts of the story, while one child records each part. Each group should **revise** the story by reading it aloud to see if it has a beginning, middle and ending, and whether it presents an exciting, but realistic, adventure. Then have groups **publish** the stories by choosing one member to read each story aloud to the class.

For the Home

Children may complete these activities independently or with the assistance of a relative or friend in the home.

1. **Language Arts/Writing Two-line Rhymes** Tell the children to match the spelling words *brave, clay, mail, obey,* and *eight* with rhyming words in which the same letters produce the /ā/ sound. Then have the children write two-line rhymes for three of the rhyming pairs. The children may share their rhymes with a relative or friend.

2. **Science/Drawing and Labeling Nature Trails** Have the children use as many spelling words as possible to draw and label a map of a nature trail. Tell them to first refer to their spelling words for ideas about things for which there might be signs on a nature trail. The children should also think of new words containing the /ā/ sound. For example: *blue jays, lane, tame, grapes.*

3. **Social Studies/Writing a Paragraph About a Courageous Person** Have the children write a paragraph about a person who is brave. The children may write about a famous historical person or a living person (for example, a fire fighter or a relative). Tell the children to use some of their spelling words to describe the person's brave actions. After the children have finished their paragraphs, have them proofread their work for spelling, capitalization, and punctuation.

4. **Language Arts/Writing Antonyms** Have the children write antonyms for five of their spelling words. They may refer to earlier units if necessary. The children should use all ten words to make a word search puzzle. They may give the puzzle to a friend or relative to solve.

EVALUATING SPELLING ABILITY

Unit Test

This Week's Words

1. **awake** It is late, but Ed is still wide *awake*. **awake**
2. **brave** The *brave* girl rescued the cat. **brave.**
3. **clay** Lizzie's mother makes bowls out of *clay*. **clay**
4. **gate** I must have heard the *gate* squeak. **gate**
5. **hay** Fred brought *hay* to the horses. **hay**
6. **lake** Let's row across the *lake*. **lake**
7. **lay** You can just *lay* your coats on the bed. **lay**
8. **mail** I must *mail* this letter. **mail**
9. **paid** We *paid* three dollars to see the movie. **paid**
10. **safe** It is not *safe* to play in the street. **safe**
11. **snake** A *snake* was asleep in the sun. **snake**
12. **today** It is not my birthday *today*. **today**
13. **trail** The *trail* went through the woods. **trail**
14. **obey** Barbie did not *obey* the rule. **obey**
15. **eight** Brian has *eight* cousins. **eight**

Mastery Words

1. **late** It is getting *late*. **late**
2. **may** The game *may* be over by now. **may**
3. **nail** Please *nail* this sign to the post. **nail**
4. **paint** The *paint* is not dry yet. **paint**
5. **same** Our birthdays are on the *same* day. **same**
6. **they** Amy and Kim hope *they* can come. **they**

Bonus Words

1. **crayon** My red *crayon* is almost used up. **crayon**
2. **delay** Heavy traffic will *delay* us. **delay**
3. **faint** We heard a *faint* scratching sound. **faint**
4. **grape** Mark likes *grape* juice best. **grape**
5. **mistake** Nina made a small *mistake*. **mistake**
6. **railroad** Uncle Jim works for the *railroad*. **railroad**
7. **raisin** Marcia likes toasted *raisin* bread. **raisin**
8. **snail** A *snail* lives in a shell. **snail**

Dictation Sentences

This Week's Words

1. The *trail* to the *lake* starts at the *gate*.
2. He got *eight* pieces of *mail today*.
3. The *snake lay* in the *clay* by the river.
4. The man was *safe* because the *brave* girl helped him.
5. The horse was *awake* and ate some *hay*.
6. They *paid* the fine when the judge asked them to *obey*.

Mastery Words

1. I hope *they* stay *late* and *paint* the room.
2. We *may* use the *same nail* again.

Bonus Words

1. There was a *delay* on the *railroad* because of a *mistake*.
2. Did you know that a *raisin* is a dried *grape*?
3. My *crayon* picture of the *snail* is too *faint*.

RETEACHING STRATEGIES FOR SPELLING

Children who have made errors on the Unit Test may require reteaching. Use the following **Reteaching Strategies** and **Follow-up Masters 14 A** and **14B** for additional instruction and practice of This Week's Words. (You may wish to assign **LEP Reteaching Follow-up Master 14** for reteaching of spelling words.)

A. Discovering Spelling Ideas

1. Say the following words as you write them on the chalkboard.

   make   pain   say

2. Ask the children to identify the vowel sound that each word has. (/ā/)
3. Ask the children to identify the letters that spell /ā/. (a-consonant-e, ai, ay)
4. Ask the children what they have learned about spelling /ā/. (It can be spelled a-consonant-e, ai, or ay at the end of a word.)

B. Word Shapes

1. Explain to the children that each word has a shape and that remembering the shape of a word can help them t spell the word correctly.
2. On the chalkboard, write the words *mate* and *pay*. Have the children identify "short," "tall," and "tail" letters.
3. Draw the configuration of each word on the chalkboard and ask the children which word fits in each shape.

Use **Reteaching Follow-up Master 14A** to reinforce spelling generalizations taught in Unit 14.

Use **Reteaching Follow-up Master 14B** to reinforce spellings of This Week's Words for Unit 14.

24 • Reteaching

The Vowel Sound /ē/

PREVIEWING THE UNIT

Unit Materials

Instruction and Practice

Pupil Book — pages 64–67
Teacher's Edition
  Teaching Plans — pages 64–67
  Enrichment Activities
    For the Classroom — page 67A
    For the Home — page 67B
  Reteaching Strategies — page 67C

Testing

Teacher's Edition
  Trial Test — pages 63E–63F
  Unit Test — page 67B
  Dictation Test — page 67B

Additional Resources

PRACTICE AND REINFORCEMENT
Extra Practice Master 15: This Week's Words
Extra Practice Master 15: Mastery Words
Extra Practice Master 15: Bonus Words
LEP Practice Master 15
Spelling and Language Master 15
Study Steps to Learn a Word Master

RETEACHING FOLLOW-UP
Reteaching Follow-up Master 15A:
  Discovering Spelling Ideas
Reteaching Follow-up Master 15B: Word
  Shapes
LEP Reteaching Follow-up Master 15

TEACHING AIDS
Spelling Generalizations Transparency 13

Visit our Web site
http://www.hbschool.com

Click on the SPELLING banner to find activities for this unit.

Learner Objectives

Spelling

- To spell words that demonstrate the sound-letter relationships /ē/ea, ee, e, y.
- To recognize homophones.
- To spell words given dictionary pronunciations.

Reading

- To follow written directions.
- To use context clues to complete sentences.
- To use the dictionary as a key to pronunciation.
- To use the dictionary as a key to word meaning.

Writing

- To write in a journal.
- To use the writing process.
- To proofread for spelling, capitalization, and punctuation.
- To write legible manuscript and cursive letters.

Listening

- To listen to identify words with the sound /ē/.
- To follow oral directions.

Speaking

- To respond to a question.
- To speak clearly to a group.
- To present a story to the class.
- To express feelings and ideas about a piece of writing.
- To contribute ideas and information in group discussions.

THIS WEEK'S WORDS

dream
asleep
any
between
busy
cheek
even
every
meal
meat
only
really
seen
team
weak

MASTERY WORDS

deep
easy
feel
free
mean
neat

BONUS WORDS

cozy
daisy
evening
feast
freedom
geese
measles
sneeze

Assignment Guide

This guide shows how you teach a typical spelling unit in either a five-day or a three-day sequence, while providing for individual differences. **Boldface type** indicates essential classwork. Steps shown in light type may be done in class or assigned as homework.

Five Days	○ = average spellers ☆ = better spellers ✓ = slower spellers	Three Days
Day **1**	**a** ○ ☆ **Take This Week's Words Trial Test and correct** ○ ✓ **Take Mastery Word Trial Test and correct** ○ ☆ **Read This Week's Words and discuss generalization page 64**	Day **1**
Day **2**	○ Complete Spelling Practice page 65 ○ ✓ Complete Extra Practice Master 15: This Week's Words (optional) ✓ Complete Spelling on Your Own: Mastery Words page 67 ☆ **Take Bonus Word Trial Test and correct** **b**	
Day **3**	**c** ○ ☆ ✓ **Complete Spelling and Language page 66** ○ ☆ ✓ Complete Writing on Your Own page 66 ○ ☆ ✓ **Complete Using the Dictionary to Spell and Write page 66** ○ ✓ Take Midweek Test (optional) ☆ Complete Spelling on Your Own: Bonus Words page 67 ○ ✓ Complete Spelling and Language Master 15 (optional)	Day **2**
Day **4**	○ Complete Spelling on Your Own: This Week's Words page 67 ✓ Complete Extra Practice Master 15: Mastery Words (optional) ☆ Complete Extra Practice Master 15: Bonus Words (optional) **d**	
Day **5**	**e** ○ Take Unit Test on This Week's Words ○ Complete Reteaching Follow-up Masters 15A and 15B (optional) ○ ✓ **Take Unit Test on Mastery Words** ☆ **Take Unit Test on Bonus Words**	Day **3**

Enrichment Activities for the **classroom** and for the **home** included at the end of this unit may be assigned selectively on any day of the week.

INTRODUCING THE UNIT

Establish Readiness for Learning

Tell the children that this week they will continue to study words with long vowel sounds. In Unit 15 they will study four spellings for the long vowel sound /ē/. Tell the children that they will apply the spelling generalizations to This Week's Words and use those words in writing in a journal.

Assess Children's Spelling Ability

Administer the Trial Test before the children study This Week's Words. Use the test sentences provided. Say each word and use it in a sentence. Then repeat the word. Have the children write the words on a separate sheet of paper or in their spelling notebooks. Test sentences are also provided for Mastery and Bonus words.

FOCUS

- Establishes objectives
- Relates to prior learning
- Sets purpose of instruction

Have the children check their own work by listening to you read the spelling of the words or by referring to This Week's Words in the left column of the **Pupil Book.** For each misspelled word, have the children follow the **Study Steps to Learn a Word** on page 1 in the **Pupil Book** or use the copying master to study and write the words. Children should record the number correct on their **Progress Report.**

Trial Test Sentences

This Week's Words
1. *dream*   Jeff had a strange *dream* last nig⟩ *dream*
2. *asleep*   He was fast *asleep*.   *asleep*
3. *any*   There isn't *any* milk left.   *any*
4. *between*   He sits *between* Ray and Janet.   *between*
5. *busy*   We are too *busy* to go shopping.   ⟩
6. *cheek*   Ryan has a scratch on his *cheek*.   *cheek*

7. **even** These two pieces are not *even*.
   even
8. **every** We walk by your house *every*
   day. **every**
9. **meal** Lunch is my favorite *meal*. **meal**
10. **meat** There were vegetables and
    meat in the soup. **meat**
11. **only** There is *only* one muffin
    left. **only**
12. **really** Miranda is a *really* nice
    girl. **really**
13. **seen** Paco has *seen* the new
    movie. **seen**
14. **team** Let's ask Roberta to be on our
    team. **team**
15. **weak** The sick puppy was too *weak* to
    bark. **weak**

Mastery Words

1. **deep** The lake is *deep* in the
   middle. **deep**
2. **easy** It is *easy* to do a
   somersault. **easy**
3. **feel** Darin's hands *feel* cold. **feel**
4. **free** We all got *free* balloons. **free**
5. **mean** I didn't *mean* to break it. **mean**
6. **neat** Ruth raked the leaves into a *neat*
   pile. **neat**

Bonus Words

1. **cozy** It is *cozy* by the fireplace. **cozy**
2. **daisy** Rona put the *daisy* in her
   hair. **daisy**

3. **evening** Come over to my house this
   evening. **evening**
4. **feast** The birds had a *feast* on the
   sunflower seeds. **feast**
5. **freedom** Wild animals need their
   freedom. **freedom**
6. **geese** A flock of *geese* flew over the
   field. **geese**
7. **measles** Tony's brother has the *measles*.
   measles
8. **sneeze** Pepper can make you *sneeze*.
   sneeze

Apply Prior Learning

Have the children apply what they already
know about the /ē/ sound by having them
participate in the following activity.

Have the children name words that contain
the long vowel sound for the letter e. Write their
responses on the chalkboard. Continue listing
the children's responses until words that contain
ea, ee, e, and *y* are among the words listed. Have
volunteers come to the chalkboard and draw
a line around the four different spellings for /ē/.
Tell the children that in Unit 15 they will study
words that have the long vowel sound for the
letter e. Explain that they can use these words
in a variety of writing tasks: they can use the
words in a note to a friend, in a letter, or in a
creative writing assignment.

FOCUS

- Relates to prior
  learning
- Draws relationships
- Applies spelling
  generalizations to
  new contexts

FOR CHILDREN WITH SPECIAL NEEDS

Learning Difficulties

Using additional sensory input helps the child with
Attention Deficit Disorder (ADD) focus on the spelling task
by involving multiple sensory systems.

For this activity you will need glue in a squeezable
container and tagboard. Ask the child to use the glue to
write one of This Week's Words that contains the /ē/
sound. Have the child use cursive writing, as the steady
flow seems to be easier for many children with visual-
motor difficulties. After the glue has dried, have the child
trace the letters of the word with the index finger of the
preferred writing hand. Have the child name each letter
aloud while tracing, for additional auditory reinforcement.

Have the children do this activity three times for each
of This Week's Words to reinforce the four spellings of /ē/.

Limited English Proficiency

To help limited English proficient children work with the
spelling generalizations for Unit 15, you may wish to refer
to the booklet "Suggestions and Activities for Limited English Proficient Students."

TEACHING PLAN

Objective To spell words that demonstrate these sound-letter relationships: /ē/ ea, ee, e, y.

1. Write this sentence on the chalkboard:

    She feels very clean.

    Ask the children how the words in the sentence are alike, and help them to recognize that each word has the sound /ē/. Then help the children identify the letter or letters that spell /ē/ in each word. (e, ee, y, ea.)

You may wish to introduce the lesson by using **Spelling Generalizations Transparency 13.**

2. Read the generalization on page 64 aloud.
3. Have volunteers read This Week's Words aloud. As each word is read, have the children identify the letter or letters that spell /ē/ in the word.
4. Direct the children's attention to **Remember This**, and read the paragraph aloud. Help the children to recognize that *every* is usually pronounced /ev'rē/ but that thinking of *every* as *ever+y* will help them spell the word correctly.

You may wish to assign **LEP Practice Master 15** for reinforcement in writing spelling words.

---

15 The Vowel Sound /ē/

THIS WEEK'S WORDS

1. dream
2. asleep
3. any
4. between
5. busy
6. cheek
7. even
8. every
9. meal
10. meat
11. only
12. really
13. seen
14. team
15. weak

64

This Week's Words

All the words this week have the vowel sound /ē/. Here are four ways to spell /ē/.

● with **ea,** as in dream
● with **ee,** as in asleep
● with **e,** as in even
● with **y** at the end of a word, as in any

REMEMBER THIS

You don't always hear the sound of the second e in every. Here's something that can help you remember to put it in.

ever + y = every

Extra Practice: This Week's Words

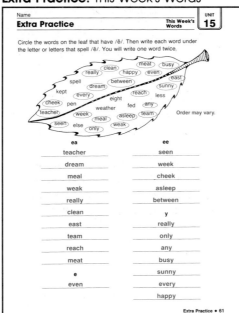

Extra Practice: Mastery Words

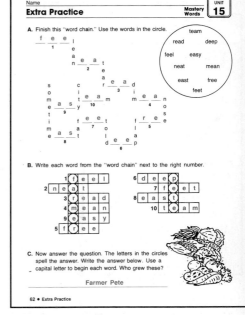

Spelling Practice

A. First write the words that go with the pictures. Then follow the directions. Use This Week's Words.

dream
asleep
any
between
busy
cheek
even
every
meal
meat
only
really
seen
team
weak

1. _____team_____   2. _____cheek_____

3. How is /ē/ spelled in the word you wrote for **1**? __ea__

4. Write the other five words that have /ē/ spelled this way.

dream	meal	meat
really	weak	

5. How is /ē/ spelled in the word you wrote for **2**? __ee__

6. Write the other three words that have /ē/ spelled this way.

| asleep | between | seen |

7. Write the word that begins with /ē/. __even__

8. Write the five words that end with /ē/. Circle the word that has /ē/ twice.

any	busy	every
only	(really)	

B. Finish the sentences. Use This Week's Words.

9. Jean's six cats keep her very _____busy_____.

10. She must feed them each and _____every_____ day.

11. Just _____between_____ you and me, Jean has too many cats.

65

TEACHING PLAN

Objectives To write words given picture clues; to write words given spelling clues; to write words with final /ē/; to write words in sentence context.

1. Read the directions for Exercise **A** on page 65 aloud, and complete **1** and **2** with the children. Be sure that everyone has written the correct answers for **1** and **2** before continuing with the activities.
2. Have the children complete the page independently. Remind them to use legible handwriting. You may wish to demonstrate the correct form of the letters *a* and *y* and then have the children practice writing the letters. For **Handwriting Models,** refer the children to page 258 in the **Pupil Book.**
3. To correct the children's work, have volunteers write the answers for **3–8** on the chalkboard. Let the children check their own work. Then have volunteers read the completed sentences for **9–11** aloud.
4. Extend the lesson by having the children identify the other words in the sentences for **9–11** that have the sound /ē/. (Jean's, keep, very, She, feed, each, me, Jean, many)

For reinforcement in writing spelling words, you may wish to assign *Extra Practice Master 15: This Week's Words.*

Extra Practice: Bonus Words

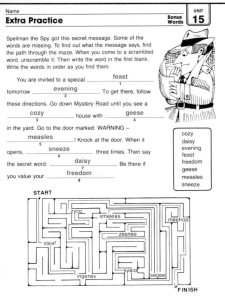

Summarize Learning

Have the children summarize what they have learned on pages 64 and 65. *Ask:*

• What have you learned about the way the /ē/ sound can be spelled? (/ē/ can be spelled with *ea, ee, e,* or *y.*)
• What are examples of words to which this generalization can be applied? (dream, asleep, even, only; accept other examples)

Language Study

TEACHING PLAN

SPELLING AND LANGUAGE

Objectives To recognize homophones; to write homophones in sentence context.

1. To introduce this activity, write this sentence on the chalkboard:

   Henry ate eight peanuts.

   Ask a child to read the sentence aloud. Help the children to recognize that *ate* and *eight* sound alike but have different spellings and meanings.
2. Read the introductory paragraph and the directions on page 66.
3. Have the children complete the exercise independently.
4. To correct the children's work, have volunteers read the answers for **1** and **2** aloud and copy their completed sentence for **3** on the chalkboard. Let the children check their own answers.

For extended practice in writing homophones in sentence context, you may wish to assign **Spelling and Language Master 15.**

WRITING ON YOUR OWN

Objectives To write in a journal; to proofread for spelling.

1. Read the directions aloud.
2. As a **prewriting** activity, have the children make lists of events for their journals. Then have them **compose** one or two journal entries. When the children are ready to **revise** their entries, have them check spelling, capitalization, and punctuation. To **publish** the children's work, bind the entries into a Class Journal.

USING THE DICTIONARY

Objectives To recognize and use dictionary pronunciations; to spell words given dictionary pronunciations.

THIS WEEK'S WORDS

dream
asleep
any
between
busy
cheek
even
every
meal
meat
only
really
seen
team
weak

Spelling and Language • Homophones

<u>Sea</u> and <u>see</u> are **homophones.** They sound alike, but they are not spelled alike. They also have different meanings.

Write the homophones for these words.

1. meet _____ meat _____   **2.** week _____ weak _____

Finish the sentence. Use one pair of homophones.

3. I will _____ meet _____ you at the _____ meat _____ market.

Writing on Your Own

Start keeping a daily journal to help you remember things you do each day. Write the day and date each time you write in your journal. Begin by writing about what you did yesterday. Use some of This Week's Words.

 WRITER'S GUIDE For a sample of a journal entry, turn to page 252.

Using the Dictionary to Spell and Write

A **pronunciation** is given after each entry word in a dictionary. A pronunciation is a special way of writing a word. It shows you how to say the word. Knowing how to pronounce a word can help you remember how to spell it.

> **an•y** /en'ē/ *adj.* No special one: *Any* coat will do.

A **pronunciation key** helps you read the pronunciation. It gives all the special signs and the sounds they stand for.

act, āte, câre, ärt;	egg, ēven;	if, īce;	on, ōver, ôr;	bŏŏk, fŏŏd;	up, tûrn;
ə = a in *ago*, e in *listen*, i in *giraffe*, o in *pilot*, u in *circus*;		yŏō = u in *music*;		oil;	out;
	chair; sing; shop; thank; that; zh in *treasure*.				

Write the word that goes with each pronunciation.

1. /rē'lē/ _____ really _____   **2.** /ōn'lē/ _____ only _____

3. /ev'rē/ _____ every _____   **4.** /mēl/ _____ meal _____

66

---

1. Read the introductory paragraph on page 66 aloud. Have the children locate the pronunciation of the word *any* in the sample dictionary entry. Then direct the children's attention to the pronunciation key and help them to pronounce *any*.
2. Before you have the children complete the activity, ask them to pronounce the words, using the pronunciations.
3. To correct the children's work, have volunteers write the words on the chalkboard. Let the children check their own spellings.

Extra Practice: Spelling and Language

Name _____   UNIT 15
Spelling and Language

A. Circle the homophone in each sentence. If the homophone does not fit in the sentence, write the correct homophone.

1. Tim eats ham once a (week.)   week
2. Tim likes ham because it's tasty (meat)
3. If you don't eat (meat) you'll soon get thin.   meat
4. You'll get so thin that you can't be (scene.)   seen
5. Jan wants to (meet) a man who can act.
6. She wants him to act in a (seen) from a play.   scene
7. She has been looking for over a (weak.)   week
8. "I haven't (scene) anybody I like," she says.   seen

B. Answer each question with a homophone.

9. What is seven days long? a _____ week _____
10. What is another way of saying "not strong"?
    _____ weak _____
11. What does a butcher cut? _____ meat _____
12. What do you do when you get to know somebody for the first time? You _____ meet _____ him or her.
13. What is one part of a play? a _____ scene _____

---

dream asleep busy meal only team every between
cheek really even meat seen weak any

64 • Extra Practice

Spelling on Your Own

THIS WEEK'S WORDS

Divide This Week's Words into groups by the way /ē/ is spelled. You will have four groups: ea, ee, e, and y. Then write as many other words as you can that fit into each group. Remember that one of the words fits into two groups.

See answers below.

MASTERY WORDS

Add ea or ee. Write the Mastery words.

1. fr___ _____ free

2. ___sy _____ easy

3. m___n _____ mean

4. d___p _____ deep

5. n___t _____ neat

6. f___l _____ feel

Write Mastery words that mean the opposite of the underlined words.

7. My room is messy, but Jo's is _____ neat

8. Cleaning is hard for me but _____ easy for her.

Write the Mastery words that rhyme with these words.

9. tree _____ free

10. keep _____ deep

11. heel _____ feel

| deep |
| easy |
| feel |
| free |
| mean |
| neat |

BONUS WORDS

Follow the directions. Use the Bonus words.

1. Write the word that begins with /ē/.

2. Write the two words that end with /ē/.

3. Write the three words that have consonant clusters.

4. Write the two words that are plurals.

Find the Bonus word that rhymes with each word. Then write a sentence using each rhyming pair.

5. beast   **6.** breeze   **7.** crazy   **8.** peace

See answers below.

| cozy |
| daisy |
| evening |
| feast |
| freedom |
| geese |
| measles |
| sneeze |

67

Spelling on Your Own Answers

Spelling on Your Own Answers

THIS WEEK'S WORDS

ea	dream	e	even	ee	asleep
	meal				between
	meat	y	any		cheek
	really		busy		seen
	team		every		
	weak		only		
			really		

Children will write other words as directed. Be sure to check spelling.

BONUS WORDS

1. evening 2. cozy, daisy 3. feast, freedom, sneeze 4. measles, geese 5. feast EXAMPLE: The beast had a feast. 6. sneeze EXAMPLE: A cold breeze makes me sneeze. 7. daisy EXAMPLE: He goes crazy when he sees a yellow daisy. 8. geese EXAMPLE: The geese give us no peace and quiet.

Summarize Learning

Have the children summarize what they have learned in this unit. Ask:

• What have you learned about homophones? (They are two words that sound alike but are not spelled alike and do not have the same meaning. (sea/see, meet/meat)

• What have you learned about a dictionary pronunciation key? (It shows you how to say a word.)

• What spelling generalizations have you learned? How did you use these generalizations?

Spelling on Your Own   UNIT 15d

TEACHING PLAN

Objective To apply the unit spelling generalization to spell This Week's Words, Mastery words, and Bonus words independently.

THIS WEEK'S WORDS

1. Read the directions on page 67 aloud. Ask the children to divide their papers into four columns and to write a spelling for /ē/ at the top of each column: ea, ee, e, y. Have them write each of This Week's Words in the correct column and then write other words with /ē/ spelled with the same letters.
2. Have the children complete the activity independently.
3. Have volunteers write their lists on the chalkboard. Provide correct spellings for new words, if necessary.

MASTERY WORDS

1. Briefly review the unit generalization on page 64.
2. Have volunteers read the Mastery words aloud. As each word is read, have the children identify the letters that spell /ē/ in the word.
3. Read the directions on page 67 and review the concept of opposites. Then have the children complete the exercises independently.

BONUS WORDS

1. Briefly review the unit generalization on page 64.
2. Have volunteers read the Bonus words aloud. Encourage the children to look up the meaning of any unfamiliar word in the **Spelling Dictionary.**
3. Have the children complete the activities independently on a separate piece of paper.

For reinforcement in writing spelling words, you may wish to assign *Extra Practice Master 15: Mastery Words* or *Bonus Words.*

UNIT 15 *The Vowel Sound /ē/*   **67**

CLOSING THE UNIT

Apply New Learning

Tell the children that when they misspell words with the vowel sound /ē/ in their writing, they should use one or more of the following strategies:

- think about the possible spellings for /ē/ and try to picture the word in their minds.
- think of words that rhyme and compare in their minds how they are spelled.
- pronounce the word carefully to see that the correct letter or letters have been used to spell the sounds in the word.

Transfer New Learning

Tell the children that when they encounter new words in their personal reading and in other content areas, they should learn the meaning of those words and then apply the generalizations they have studied to the spelling of those words. Tell the children that once the words are familiar in both meaning and spelling, they should use the new words in their writing.

ENRICHMENT ACTIVITIES

Classroom activities and **home activities** may be assigned to children of all ability levels. The activities provide opportunities for children to use their spelling words in new contexts.

For the Classroom

To individualize classroom activities, you may have the children use the word list they are studying in this unit.

- *Basic:* Use **Mastery** words to complete the activity.
- *Average:* Use **This Week's Words** to complete the activity.
- *Challenging:* Use **Bonus** words to complete the activity.

1. **Language Arts/Writing Sentences** Have each child choose spelling words in which different letters represent the /ē/ sound. For example: *dream, asleep, any, even.* Tell the children to write one sentence using each of these spelling words. Other words in each sentence should have words that use the same letter or letters to represent the /ē/ sound. Give the children this model: *Even Peter has a secret.* After the children have written their sentences, they should copy them with blanks for the letters that represent the /ē/ sound and give them to a classmate to complete.

   ◼ COOPERATIVE LEARNING: Have each group write sentences using words with the same spelling for the sound /ē/. Assign each group a key word from their spelling list. For example: *dream* or *asleep.* Each child should write a sentence containing several words with /ē/ spelled as it is in the key word. They may use spelling words and other words. Have group members check each other's sentences to be sure the appropriate spelling for /ē/ is used. One child should copy the group's sentences, using blanks instead of the letters that have the /ē/ sound. Other children should be asked to fill in the blanks.

2. **Language Arts/Writing a Fantasy Story** Have each child use the spelling words to write a fantasy story. Explain that in a fantasy story people or animals can do things that real people and animals cannot do. Direct the children to the **Writer's Guide** on page 253 for a model of a story. As a *prewriting* activity, have the children make a Fantasy Chart. The chart should list actions that would be possible only in a fantasy. Provide the following as a starter model:

	Fantasy	
People	fly	travel back in time
	walk through walls	
Animals	talk	
	wear clothes	

Tell the children to use the chart to plan their story. When they have decided on characters, setting, and plot, have them *compose* their story. Remind the children to use as many spelling words as they can. Have the children *revise* their story by checking for a beginning, middle, and ending. Remind the children to check spelling, capitalization, and punctuation and to refer to the **Revising Checklist** on page 247 for help. *Publish* the children's stories by having each child read his or her story to the class. Then display the stories on a bulletin board.

◼ COOPERATIVE LEARNING: Have each group write a fantasy story using as many spelling words as possible. As a *prewriting* activity, have each group work collaboratively to make a Fantasy Chart that lists things people and animals might do in a fantasy. Tell the members of each group to work individually to plan the story elements, using the chart for ideas. Then have group members share their plans with each other and choose what they like best about each to fashion a final plan. Each group should divide the task of writing the story among its members by having each child write several sentences. When the groups are ready, have them *compose* their fantasy stories. Then have the group members respond to each other's work and combine it into one story. Remind the children to give the story a title. Have groups *revise* their stories by making sure the story is unified and has a satisfactory beginning, middle, and ending. The children should **proofread** for spelling, capitalization, and punctuation errors. *Publish* the fantasy stories by having each group read its story to the class and then display the stories on a bulletin board.

For the Home

Children may complete these activities independently or with the assistance of a relative or friend in the home.

1. **Language Arts/Writing Sentences with Homophones** Tell the children to write homophones for spelling words. Have them choose eight spelling words, from both the current and earlier units, and list another word that sounds the same but has a different meaning from each of the spelling words. For example: *weak/week*. The children should then use four of their homophone pairs in two sets of sentences.

2. **Social Studies/Making a Good-Deeds Chart** Have the children make a chart listing helpful tasks that various children could perform both at home and in the community. Tell the children to make up a Good Deeds Team by listing five names down the left side of the chart, each of which contains the /ē/ sound. For example, *Jean.* Then have children list jobs to be done by each person named, using as many words with the /ē/ sound as possible. For example, *clean, leaves, sweep, weeds, feed,* and *seeds.* The children should check the spelling of new words.

3. **Health/Writing a List of Healthful Snacks** Tell the children to use spelling words and other words with the /ē/ sound to write a list of healthful snacks. Explain that healthful snacks are foods that provide energy but do not contain too much sugar. Good snack foods include fruits, vegetables, dairy products, and peanut butter. Suggest that the children be imaginative in combining foods to make up their snack lists.

4. **Language Arts/Writing Up an Interview** Tell the children to use spelling words to write a paragraph based on a fictional interview with one member of any kind of school team for example: sports or spelling. The person interviewed should tell about how he or she trained, how team members work together, and what it is like to do one's best. The children should use new words containing the /ē/ sound. For example: *eat, sleep, meet.* After they have finished writing their paragraphs, the children should proofread their work for spelling, capitalization, and punctuation errors, using the **Revising Checklist** on page 247. Have the children share their interviews with someone in their families.

EVALUATING SPELLING ABILITY

Unit Test

This Week's Words
1. **dream**   I *dream* every night.   **dream**
2. **asleep**   Helen fell *asleep* early.   **asleep**
3. **any**   We can play *any* game you want to play.   **any**
4. **between**   Bob has a lot to do *between* now and Tuesday.   **between**
5. **busy**   Rachel is very *busy* doing homework.   **busy**
6. **cheek**   Gordie kissed Grandma on the *cheek.*   **cheek**
7. **even**   Charlie ran fast, but Pia ran *even* faster.   **even**
8. **every**   The twins wash the dishes *every* night.   **every**
9. **meal**   We eat every *meal* in the kitchen.   **meal**
10. **meat**   Kay likes gravy on her *meat.*   **meat**
11. **only**   This is the *only* suitcase Joe has.   **only**
12. **really**   Is that *really* what happened?   **really**
13. **seen**   I haven't *seen* Anna for a year.   **seen**
14. **team**   Our *team* is playing the Jets tonight.   **team**
15. **weak**   Jenny's knees felt *weak* after skating.   **weak**

Mastery Words
1. **deep**   The dog dug a *deep* hole.   **deep**
2. **easy**   Paul thought the test was *easy.*   **easy**
3. **feel**   The mittens *feel* nice and warm.   **feel**
4. **free**   They are giving away *free* puppies.   **free**
5. **mean**   Julie played a *mean* trick on her sister.   **mean**
6. **neat**   Sam's room is *neat* and clean.   **neat**

Bonus Words
1. **cozy**   The blanket keeps me warm and *cozy.*   **cozy**
2. **daisy**   Marcie picked a *daisy* in the field.   **daisy**
3. **evening**   It gets colder in the *evening.*   **evening**
4. **feast**   We always *feast* on holidays.   **feast**
5. **freedom**   Everyone wants to live in *freedom.*   **freedom**
6. **geese**   Two fat *geese* waddled across the barnyard.   **geese**
7. **measles**   This shot will keep you from getting the *measles.*   **measles**
8. **sneeze**   A *sneeze* may be the sign of a cold.   **sneeze**

Dictation Sentences

This Week's Words
1. You may *even dream every* time you are *asleep.*
2. We have *meat* for *only* one *meal* a day.
3. Our *team* was *really busy* planning for the game.
4. Have you *seen any* flowers *between* the bushes?
5. Her *cheek* was hot and she felt *weak.*

Mastery Words
1. It is *easy* to be *neat.*
2. He likes to *feel* the *deep* grass with his feet.
3. Do you *mean* that the lunch is *free*?

Bonus Words
1. The *geese* will *feast* in a *cozy* place this *evening.*
2. The *daisy* is the one flower that makes him *sneeze.*
3. You must give up your *freedom* when you have the *measles.*

RETEACHING STRATEGIES FOR SPELLING

Children who have made errors on the Unit Test may require reteaching. Use the following *Reteaching Strategies* and *Follow-up Masters 15A* and *15B* for additional instruction and practice of This Week's Words. (You may wish to assign *LEP Reteaching Follow-up Master 15* for reteaching of spelling words.)

A. Discovering Spelling Ideas

1. Say the following words as you write them on the chalkboard.

   scream deep equal many

2. Ask the children to identify the long vowel sound in each word. (/ē/)

3. Ask the children to identify the letters that spell /ē/. (ea, ee, e, y)

4. Ask the children what they have learned about spelling /ē/. (It can be spelled with ea, ee, e, or y.)

B. Word Shapes

1. Explain to the children that each word has a shape and that remembering the shape of a word can help them spell the word correctly.

2. On the chalkboard, write the words *beam* and *seem*. Have the children identify "short," "tall," and "tail" letters.

3. Draw the configuration of each word on the chalkboard and ask the children which word fits in each shape.

Use *Reteaching Follow-up Master 15A* to reinforce spelling generalizations taught in Unit 15.

Use *Reteaching Follow-up Master 15B* to reinforce spellings of This Week's Words for Unit 15.

Name _____
Reteaching Follow-up A   Discovering Spelling Ideas   UNIT **15**

THIS WEEK'S WORDS

dream	asleep	busy	meal	only
team	between	any	cheek	really
even	meat	seen	weak	every

1. Study This Week's Words. Say each word to yourself. What sound do This Week's Words have in common?

   They all have the sound /ē/.

2. Look at the word at the top of each column. Write each of This Week's Words in the column that spells /ē/ the same way as the word in dark print. One word will be used twice.

lean	peep	pretty
dream	cheek	really
really	asleep	busy
meal	seen	every
meat	between	any
team		only
weak		

3. Which of This Week's Words spells /ē/ with e?

   even

4. What are the four ways that the sound /ē/ is spelled in This Week's Words?

   /ē/ can be spelled with ea, ee, e, and y at the end of the word.

5. Using four different spellings for /ē/, write four other words.

   POSSIBLE ANSWERS: sunny, steam, feed, event

Reteaching • 25

Name _____
Reteaching Follow-up B   Word Shapes   UNIT **15**

THIS WEEK'S WORDS

dream	asleep	busy	meal	only
team	between	any	cheek	really
even	meat	seen	weak	every

Write each of This Week's Words in its correct shape. The first one has been done for you. Children may interchange answers that fit the same configuration.

1. e v e n
2. a s l e e p
3. w e a k
4. t e a m
5. o n l y
6. a n y
7. b u s y
8. m e a l
9. e v e r y
10. b e t w e e n
11. d r e a m
12. c h e e k
13. s e e n
14. m e a t
15. r e a l l y

26 • Reteaching

PREVIEWING THE UNIT

Unit Materials

Instruction and Practice

Pupil Book   pages 68–71
Teacher's Edition
Teaching Plans   pages 68–71
Enrichment Activities
For the Classroom   page 71A
For the Home   page 71B
Reteaching Strategies   page 71C

Testing

Teacher's Edition
Trial Test   pages 67E–67F
Unit Test   page 71B
Dictation Test   page 71B

Additional Resources

PRACTICE AND REINFORCEMENT
Extra Practice Master 16: This Week's Words
Extra Practice Master 16: Mastery Words
Extra Practice Master 16: Bonus Words
LEP Practice Master 16
Spelling and Language Master 16
Study Steps to Learn a Word Master

RETEACHING FOLLOW-UP
Reteaching Follow-up Master 16A:
   Discovering Spelling Ideas
Reteaching Follow-up Master 16B: Word
   Shapes
LEP Reteaching Follow-up Master 16

TEACHING AIDS
Spelling Generalizations Transparency 14

Visit our Web site
http://www.hbschool.com

Click on the SPELLING banner to find activities for this unit.

Learner Objectives

Spelling

● To spell words that demonstrate the sound-letter relationships /ī/i-consonant-e, *igh, i, y, uy.*

Reading

● To follow written directions.
● To use context clues for word identification.
● To use a dictionary to locate information.
● To use the dictionary for word meaning.

Writing

● To write rhyming sentences.
● To use the writing process.
● To proofread for spelling, capitalization, and punctuation.
● To write legible manuscript and cursive letters.

Listening

● To listen to identify words with the vowel sound /ī/.
● To follow oral directions.
● To appreciate sound devices of rhythm and rhyming.

Speaking

● To speak clearly to a group.
● To read stories and poems.
● To respond to a question.
● To express feelings and ideas about a piece of writing.
● To present rhyming sentences and poems.
● To contribute ideas and information in group discussions.

THIS WEEK'S WORDS

nine
lion
bite
bright
fight
hide
life
line
myself
prize
shy
sight
tiger
wise
buy

MASTERY WORDS

bike
find
high
right
why
wide

BONUS WORDS

awhile
delight
highway
midnight
pirate
polite
quite
title

Assignment Guide

This guide shows how you teach a typical spelling unit in either a five-day or a three-day sequence, while providing for individual differences. **Boldface type** indicates essential classwork. Steps shown in light type may be done in class or assigned as homework.

Five Days	○ = average spellers ★ = better spellers ✓ = slower spellers	Three Days
Day 1 **a**	○ ★ **Take This Week's Words Trial Test and correct** ○ ✓ **Take Mastery Word Trial Test and correct** ○ ★ **Read This Week's Words and discuss generalization page 68**	**Day 1**
Day 2 **b**	○ Complete Spelling Practice page 69 ○ ✓ Complete Extra Practice Master 16: This Week's Words (optional) ✓ Complete Spelling on Your Own: Mastery Words page 71 ★ **Take Bonus Word Trial Test and correct**	
Day 3 **c**	○ ★ ✓ **Complete Spelling and Language page 70** ○ ★ ✓ Complete Writing on Your Own page 70 ○ ✓ Take Midweek Test (optional) ★ Complete Spelling on Your Own: Bonus Words page 71 ○ ✓ Complete Spelling and Language Master 16 (optional)	**Day 2**
Day 4 **d**	○ Complete Spelling on Your Own: This Week's Words page 71 ✓ Complete Extra Practice Master 16: Mastery Words (optional) ★ Complete Extra Practice Master 16: Bonus Words (optional)	
Day 5 **e**	○ **Take Unit Test on This Week's Words** ○ Complete Reteaching Follow-up Masters 16A and 16B (optional) ○ ✓ **Take Unit Test on Mastery Words** ★ **Take Unit Test on Bonus Words**	**Day 3**

Enrichment Activities for the **classroom** and for the **home** included at the end of this unit may be assigned selectively on any day of the week.

INTRODUCING THE UNIT

Establish Readiness for Learning

Tell the children that this week they will continue to study words with long vowel sounds and that they will be studying the /ī/ sound. They will apply what they learn to This Week's Words and use some of those words to write rhyming sentences.

Assess Children's Spelling Ability

Administer the Trial Test before the children study This Week's Words. Use the test sentences provided. Say each word and use it in a sentence. Then repeat the word. Have the children write the words on a separate sheet of paper or in their spelling notebooks. Test sentences are also provided for Mastery and Bonus words.

Have the children check their own work by listening to you read the spelling of the words

or by referring to This Week's Words in the left column of the **Pupil Book.** For each misspelled word, have the children follow the **Study Steps to Learn a Word** on page 1 in the **Pupil Book** or use the copying master to study and write the words. Children should record the number correct on their **Progress Report.**

Trial Test Sentences

This Week's Words
1. *nine*   Barry is *nine* years old.   *nine*
2. *lion*   The *lion* roared.   *lion*
3. *bite*   That dog doesn't *bite*.   *bite*
4. *bright*   The light is very *bright*.   *bright*
5. *fight*   Diane and her sister seldom *fight*. *fight*
6. *hide*   Rodney found a good place to *hide*.   *hide*
7. *life*   Shelley has had a dog all her *life*. *life*
8. *line*   The runners were at the starting *line*. *line*

FOCUS
- Establishes objectives
- Relates to prior learning
- Sets purpose of instruction

9. *myself*   I can do it *myself*.   **myself**
10. *prize*   Carrie won first *prize*.   **prize**
11. *shy*   Ted doesn't talk much because he is *shy*.   **shy**
12. *sight*   The sailboats on the lake are a beautiful *sight*.   **sight**
13. *tiger*   The striped cat looks like a *tiger*.   **tiger**
14. *wise*   An owl looks very *wise*.   **wise**
15. *buy*   Please *buy* some milk at the store.   **buy**

Mastery Words
1. *bike*   Jeff rode his *bike* to school.   **bike**
2. *find*   Lou couldn't *find* her other shoe.   **find**
3. *high*   The plane flew *high* in the sky.   **high**
4. *right*   You gave the *right* answer.   **right**
5. *why*   I don't know *why* I did that.   **why**
6. *wide*   Main Street is very *wide*.   **wide**

Bonus Words
1. *awhile*   I hope you can stay *awhile*.   **awhile**
2. *delight*   Sunny days *delight* everybody.   **delight**
3. *highway*   The express bus takes the *highway*.   **highway**

4. *midnight*   Penny was asleep at *midnight*.   **midnight**
5. *pirate*   Captain Hook is the *pirate* in *Peter Pan*.   **pirate**
6. *polite*   Alistair is *polite* to older people.   **polite**
7. *quite*   We need *quite* a big piece of paper.   **quite**
8. *title*   Make up a funny *title* for your story.   **title**

Apply Prior Learning

Tell the children that they can discover spelling generalizations by applying what they already know about long vowel sounds. Say the words *bike* and *night* and write them on the chalkboard. Ask the children to name other words that have the same /ī/ sound. As the children suggest words, write them in columns according to the spelling of the sound. Ask the children what they can conclude about the /ī/ sound and the way it is spelled. (All the words have the same vowel sound, but it is spelled differently.) Tell the children that they will learn words that have these and other spellings for the long *i* sound. They can use the words in a variety of writing tasks: stories, a note to a friend, or a science assignment.

FOCUS

- Relates to prior learning
- Draws relationships
- Applies spelling generalizations to new contexts

FOR CHILDREN WITH SPECIAL NEEDS

Learning Difficulties

To assist children with language disabilities in learning the spellings for the /ī/ sound, concentrate on teaching only one spelling at a time.

Use the strategy of drawing attention to the characteristic spelling *i*-consonant-e by writing the words *nine, bite, kite, life, line, prize,* and *wise* on the chalkboard. Have the children copy the words and then trace over each word using both a pencil and colored, fine point markers. Have the children begin writing over the pre-written letters with a pencil. When each child comes to the /ī/ sound spelled *i*-consonant-e, he or she is to use the colored marker and trace over the letters *i* and *e*. Then instruct the children to switch back to the pencil for

the remainder of the word. Follow this procedure for all of the spellings *igh, i,* and *y* at the end of a word.

You may wish to have each child do this work in his or her spelling notebook. For additional reinforcement, continue the activity as work to be done at home using the Mastery words.

Limited English Proficiency

To help limited English proficient children work with the spelling generalizations for Unit 16, you may wish to refer to the booklet "Suggestions and Activities for Limited English Proficient Students."

TEACHING PLAN

Objective To spell words that demonstrate these sound-letter relationships: /ī/ i-consonant-e, igh, i, y, uy.

1. Write these words in a column on the chalkboard:

   neat beat leaf seat

   Ask a volunteer to read the words. Remind the children that each of these words has the sound /ē/. Then ask the children to say a word that begins and ends with the same consonant sounds as each word but has long *i* instead of long *e*. As the children say the words, write *night, bite, life, sight* next to the other words. Then help the children to recognize the two spellings for /ī/ in these words: *igh,* in *night* and *sight; i-consonant-e,* in *bite* and *life.*

You may wish to introduce the lesson by using **Spelling Generalizations Transparency 14.**

2. Read the generalization on page 68 aloud. Help the children to recognize that /ī/ is spelled with *uy* in *buy.*
3. Direct the children's attention to **Remember This** at the bottom of the page, and read the paragragh aloud. Then write *by* on the chalkboard, and ask a volunteer to use the word in a sentence. Write *buy* on the chalkboard, and ask a volunteer to use this word in a sentence.
4. Have volunteers read This Week's Words. As each word is read, ask the children to identify the letter or letters that spell /ī/ in the word.

You may wish to assign **LEP Practice Master 16** for reinforcement in writing spelling words.

---

16 The Vowel Sound /ī/

THIS WEEK'S WORDS

1. nine
2. lion
3. bite
4. bright
5. fight
6. hide
7. life
8. line
9. myself
10. prize
11. shy
12. sight
13. tiger
14. wise
15. buy

This Week's Words

All the words this week have the vowel sound /ī/. Here are four ways to spell /ī/.

- with **i-consonant-e**, as in <u>nine</u>
- with **igh**, as in <u>bright</u>
- with **i**, as in <u>lion</u>
- with **y** at the end of a word or word part, as in <u>myself</u>

☐ The word <u>buy</u> also has the vowel sound /ī/. What letter are you surprised to find in <u>buy</u>?

REMEMBER THIS

By is a very useful word. It helps you tell where and how. You can sit <u>by</u> the fire. You can win <u>by</u> one point. But if you want to talk about what you'll get at the store, remember: you need buy and buy needs u.

68

Extra Practice: This Week's Words

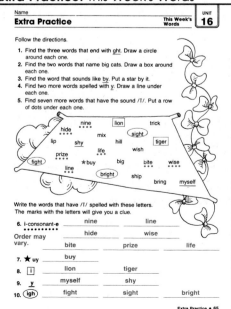

Extra Practice: Mastery Words

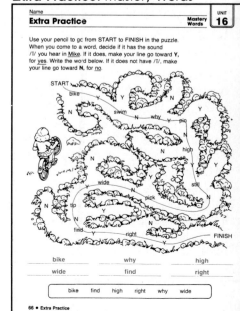

Spelling Practice

A. Follow the directions. Use This Week's Words.

1. Write the word for the number 9. ___nine___

2. Write the six other words that have /ī/ spelled this way.

bite	hide	life
line	prize	wise

3. Write the two words that name animals.

lion	tiger

4. There are three words you can use to talk about yourself. Write the missing one.

   me, ___myself___ , and I

5. Write the two words that rhyme with <u>try</u>. Then circle the word that sounds just like <u>by</u>.

   ___shy___   (buy)

6. Finish the answer to the riddle. Use a word that sounds almost like the word lying. What do you call a big cat that tells fibs?

   A lying ___lion___

B. Write This Week's Words that end with /t/ and begin with these letters.

7. f ___fight___   8. br ___bright___

9. s ___sight___

C. Write the words that go with these words. Use This Week's Words.

10. ___hide___ and seek   11. pillow ___fight___

12. all by ___myself___   13. ___buy___ and sell

Word list (right column):
nine
lion
bite
bright
fight
hide
life
line
myself
prize
shy
sight
tiger
wise
buy

69

TEACHING PLAN

Objectives To write words given spelling clues; to write words given meaning clues; to write rhyming words; to write words given sound and spelling clues; to write words given context clues.

1. Briefly discuss the directions on page 69.
2. Have the children complete the page independently. Remind them to use legible handwriting. You may wish to demonstrate the correct form of the letter *i* and then have the children practice writing the letter. For **Handwriting Models,** refer the children to page 258 in the **Pupil Book.**
3. To correct the children's work, have volunteers write the answers for **1–5** and **7–9** on the chalkboard. Review the answer to the riddle in **6** and the responses for **10–13** orally. Let the children check their own work.

For reinforcement in writing spelling words, you may wish to assign *Extra Practice Master 16: This Week's Words.*

Extra Practice: Bonus Words

Name
Extra Practice   Bonus Words UNIT 16

Finish the puzzle. Some of the answers are not Bonus words. These words have * before their clues. Decide which word fits each clue. Then write the word in the right place in the puzzle.

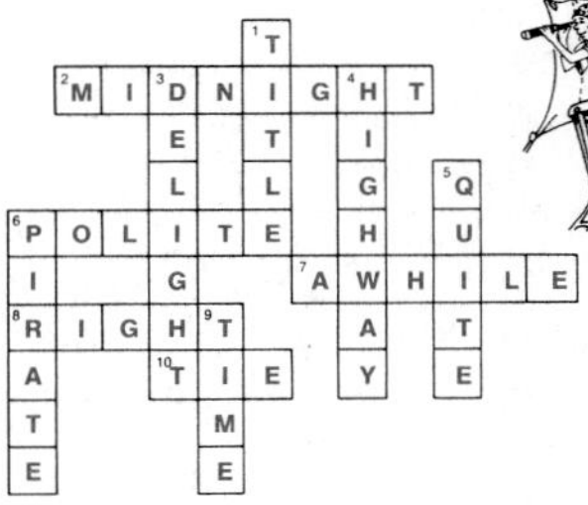

ACROSS
2. 12 o'clock at night.
6. It is the opposite of <u>rude</u>.
7. This word means "for a short time."
* 8. It is the opposite of <u>left</u>.
*10. Do this with your shoelaces so you won't trip.

DOWN
1. This word means "the name of something."
3. This word means "great joy."
4. Cars travel on this.
5. This word means "completely."
6. Captain Hook was one.
* 9. A clock tells you this.

polite	awhile	delight	midnight
highway	pirate	title	quite

Extra Practice • 67

Summarize Learning

Have the children summarize what they have learned on pages 68 and 69. *Ask:*

• What have you learned about the way the /ī/ sound can be spelled? (/ī/ can be spelled with *i*-consonant-*e*, *igh*, *i*, *y*, or *uy*.)

• What are examples of words to which these generalizations can be applied? (nine, bright, lion, shy, buy; accept other examples)

TEACHING PLAN

SPELLING AND LANGUAGE

Objective To write rhyming words to complete a poem.

1. Read the directions on page 70 aloud. Have the children locate and read the words in boldface type for which they must find rhyming words. Tell them that the the words they write should rhyme with these words and also have the same spelling for /ī/.
2. Have the children complete the activity independently.
3. When the children have finished, ask a volunteer to read the poem and supply the missing words. Let the children check their own work.

For extended practice in writing rhyming words, you may wish to assign *Spelling and Language Master 16.*

WRITING ON YOUR OWN

Objectives To write rhyming sentences; to proofread for spelling.

1. Review directions with the children.
2. As a **prewriting** activity, have the children think of rhyming words for some of This Week's Words, and list them on the chalkboard. Then have the children **compose** their rhyming sentences. When they are ready to **revise**, remind the children to check for spelling. For additional help, you may also wish to refer them to the **Revising Checklist** on page 247 of the **Writer's Guide**. To **publish,** have the children read their sentences to the class.

HANDWRITING

Objectives To practice writing cursive letter forms: n N, m M; to write a sentence using cursive writing.

1. Read the introductory sentences on page 70. Have the children

examine the models for lowercase *n* and *m*.
2. Have the children examine the models for capital *N* and *M*. Help them to note where the letters touch or intersect the lines.
3. Have the children practice the letter forms and write the sentence independently.
4. When they have finished, ask the children to compare their letter forms with the models. Review each child's work to note any problems he or she may be having with forming the letters.

Spelling and Language • Rhyming Words

Finish the poem with words that rhyme with the words in dark print. Use This Week's Words. Write your answers below the poem.

THIS WEEK'S WORDS
nine
lion
bite
bright
fight
hide
life
line
myself
prize
shy
sight
tiger
wise
buy

On a night so warm and **fine,**
As the clock was striking ___ 1 ,
I met a frog, quite by **surprise,**
That looked so very old and ___ 2 .
As it chewed upon a **fly,**
It asked me why I was so ___ 3 .

1. ____ nine ____   2. ____ wise ____   3. ____ shy ____

Writing on Your Own

Write two rhyming sentences that end with <u>bright</u> and <u>sight</u>. Then write some more rhyming sentences using This Week's Words.

 WRITER'S GUIDE For an example of a rhyming poem, turn to page 254.

HANDWRITING

n N   m M

The lowercase letter **n** touches the midline two times.   *n*

The lowercase letter **m** touches the midline three times.   *m*

1. Practice writing n N, m M in cursive.

_____

_____

2. Write this sentence: *I went to Maine.*

_____

_____

70

Extra Practice: Spelling and Language

Name ___
Spelling and Language

UNIT 16

A. Use This Week's Words to answer the questions. Each answer rhymes with the word in dark print.

1. **tight**	What is something you do with your teeth?	bite
2. **eyes**	What do you get if you win a race?	prize
3. **lies**	What do we call someone who knows a lot?	wise
4. **pine**	How many planets are there?	nine
5. **wife**	What does an animal lose when it dies?	life
6. **light**	What can't you have without eyes?	sight
7. **mine**	What do people stand in when they want to buy tickets?	line
8. **might**	What is the opposite of <u>dark</u>?	bright
9. **fly**	What is the opposite of <u>sell</u>?	buy
10. **sly**	What is the opposite of <u>bold</u>?	shy
11. **tide**	What do you do if you don't want to be found?	hide

B. The first word in each line is mixed up. Unscramble the word so that it rhymes with the word in dark print.

12. trihgb	bright	kite
13. eswi	wise	eyes
14. etbi	bite	night
15. dieh	hide	lied

nine	bite	bright	fight	life	shy	prize	wise
lion	hide	myself	sight	line	buy	tiger	

68 • Extra Practice

Spelling on Your Own

THIS WEEK'S WORDS

Write sentences using all of This Week's Words. Try to use more than one of the words in each sentence. Here is an example: "The shy tiger tried to hide."

MASTERY WORDS

Write the Mastery words that mean the opposite of the underlined words.

| bike |
| find |
| high |
| right |
| why |
| wide |

1. When I lose something, I try to ___find___ it.

2. Sometimes I must look low and ___high___.

Finish each sentence. Use a Mastery word. Then find the other word in the sentence that has /ī/ spelled the same way. Circle that word.

3. Maria (rides) her ___bike___ to school.

4. Tell me ___why___ you need (my) help.

5. Is it all ___right___ if I turn on the (light?)

6. The sun is (bright) and ___high___ in the sky.

7. (Kind) people helped us ___find___ our lost dog.

8. The rug is (nine) feet long and six feet ___wide___.

BONUS WORDS

1. Write the three Bonus words that have /ī/ spelled with i-e. Use each word in a sentence.

2. Write the two Bonus words that have /ī/ spelled with i. Use each word in a sentence.

3. Add a word with /ī/ to each of these word parts. Write four Bonus words.

| awhile |
| delight |
| highway |
| midnight |
| pirate |
| polite |
| quite |
| title |

a	way	de	mid

See answers below.

71

Summarize Learning

Have the children summarize what they have learned in this unit. *Ask:*

- What have you learned about words that rhyme? (Rhyming words have the same ending sounds, but might be spelled differently.)
- What spelling generalizations have you learned? How did you use these generalizations?

TEACHING PLAN

Objective To apply the unit spelling generalization to spell This Week's Words, Mastery words, and Bonus words independently.

THIS WEEK'S WORDS

1. Read the directions on page 71 aloud. Ask volunteers to make up oral sentences that include two or more of This Week's Words.

2. Have the children complete the activity on a separate piece of paper.

MASTERY WORDS

1. Briefly review the unit generalization on page 68.

2. Have volunteers read each Mastery Word and identify the letter or letters that spell /ī/ in the word.

3. Read the directions on page 71 aloud. Be sure the children understand that in **3–18** they should write the word that completes the sentence and then find another word in the sentence that has the same spelling for /ī/.

   If you are using the hardcover book, have the children write the missing word in **3–18** and also the word with the same spelling for /ī/.

4. Have the children complete the activities independently.

BONUS WORDS

1. Briefly review the unit generalization.

2. Have volunteers read the Bonus words aloud. Encourage the children to look up the meaning of any unfamiliar word in the **Spelling Dictionary**.

3. Have the children complete the activity on a separate piece of paper.

For reinforcement in writing spelling words, you may wish to assign *Extra Practice Master 16: Mastery Words* or *Bonus Words.*

The Vowel Sound /ī/

CLOSING THE UNIT

Apply New Learning

Tell the children that if they misspell words with the long vowel sound /ī/ in their writing, they should use one of the following strategies:

- think about the possible spellings for the long vowel sound /ī/ and try to picture the word in their minds.
- think of words that rhyme and compare in their minds how the words are spelled.
- look at changes in spelling that occur in related words.

Transfer New Learning

Tell the children that when they encounter new words in their personal reading and in other content areas, they should learn the meaning of those words and then apply the generalizations they have studied to the spelling of those words. Tell them that once the words are familiar in both meaning and spelling, they should use the new words in their writing.

ENRICHMENT ACTIVITIES

Classroom activities and **home activities** may be assigned to children of all ability levels. These activities provide opportunities for children to use their spelling words in new contexts.

For the Classroom

To individualize classroom activities, you may have the children use the word list they are studying in this unit.

- *Basic:* Use **Mastery** words to complete the activity.
- *Average:* Use **This Week's Words** to complete the activity.
- *Challenging:* Use **Bonus** words to complete the activity.

1. **Language Arts/Building Vocabulary** Have each child build sets of words for the following phonograms: *ide* as in *tide; ight* as in *tight; ine* as in *pine.* Tell the children to begin with spelling words that have the target phonogram and then to list as many other words with the same phonogram as they can. After children have completed their lists, compile class lists on strips of butcher paper. Ask children to use the words that they suggest in sentences that show the meanings of the words.

   ■ COOPERATIVE LEARNING: Have each group build sets of words for the phonograms listed above. After the lists are compiled, group members should check the spelling of each word and be sure every group member can use each word in a sentence. Each group should present one list to the class. Allow the class to ask a group member to use one word from the group's list in a sentence that shows its meaning and to challenge the group on any misspelled words.

2. **Language Arts/Writing Sentences** Have each child write sentences that use all three words in each of the following rows in a sentence. Tell them that their sentences may be humorous.

prize	clay	between
hike	today	busy
window	joke	follow

   ■ COOPERATIVE LEARNING: Have the children work as a group to create three different sentences that use each set of words listed above. Each group member will be responsible for leading the discussion and recording the group's sentences for one set of words. Then have the group share the sentences with the class.

3. **Language Arts/Writing an Acrostic** Tell the children that they are going to write acrostics using some of their spelling words. Explain that an acrostic is based on the letters of a word that is written vertically. Each letter is used as the first letter of the first word in that line. The content of the acrostic should tell a story about the word. Begin the ***prewriting*** activity by directing the children to choose a word from their spelling lists to use for their acrostics and write it in the middle of their papers. Have them think of words and phrases associated with their words and create word clusters. When the children finish the prewriting activity, tell them to use their word clusters to help them ***compose*** their acrostics. Remind them to use as many spelling words as possible. Then have the children ***revise*** their acrostics, making sure the content describes or tells a story about the vertical word. ***Publish*** the children's work in a bulletin board display or in a class booklet.

   ■ COOPERATIVE LEARNING: Have the children create an acrostic as a group. As a ***prewriting*** activity, have the group choose a word from their spelling list to use as the base of the acrostic and make a word cluster. When the children are ready to ***compose*** the acrostic, tell them to select one child to record as each child suggests lines. After all group members have contributed their suggestions, tell the group to come to a consensus on the best lines to use. Have groups ***revise*** their acrostics, making sure the content describes or tells a story about the vertical word. Each child within the group should check the acrostic for spelling and punctuation. Have the group select one child to copy the acrostic onto construction paper. ***Publish*** the children's work in a bulletin board display or in a class booklet.

For the Home

Children may complete these activities independently or with the assistance of a relative or friend in the home.

1. **Language Arts/Writing an Imaginary Dream** Tell the children to write an imaginary dream. Have them look at their spelling list and let it suggest to them the events of their dream. Encourage them to write a strange or funny adventure, using as many spelling words as they can. At the end of their dream paragraph, have them write, "And then I woke up."

2. **Social Studies/Writing Questions About People or Places** Tell the children to write three questions about people or places in the world. Explain that each question must contain at least one spelling word. Encourage the children to use their social studies book or consult a family member for help. Have the children bring their questions to class for others to answer, or have them ask someone in their home to answer the questions.

3. **Language Arts/Writing a Sequence of Events** Have the children write five sentences telling five things they did today. Tell them to be sure to include words with /ī/. When the children have written five sentences, have them rearrange the sentences sequentially and draw a line around the word that has the /ī/ sound. Children can read their sentences to someone.

4. **Mathematics/Writing Word Problems** Tell the children to write four word problems requiring addition or subtraction. Have the children include as many words as they can containing long i. For example, Ivy has *five* dimes and she finds *nine* more. How many dimes does Ivy have? Children may bring their word problems to school for other children to solve.

EVALUATING SPELLING ABILITY

Unit Test

This Week's Words

1. **nine** Cats don't really have *nine* lives. **nine**
2. **lion** There is a new *lion* at the zoo. **lion**
3. **bite** Gladys took a *bite* out of the apple. **bite**
4. **bright** We need a *bright* light in the hall. **bright**
5. **fight** Dad broke up the pillow *fight*. **fight**
6. **hide** The children will play *hide* and seek. **hide**
7. **life** Monique has wanted a pet all her *life*. **life**
8. **line** Ethan was the first in *line*. **line**
9. **myself** I bought this book for *myself*. **myself**
10. **prize** The *prize* was a ticket to the circus. **prize**
11. **shy** The child was too *shy* to ask a question. **shy**
12. **sight** Thelma came around the corner and into *sight*. **sight**
13. **tiger** A *tiger* is part of the cat family. **tiger**
14. **wise** Wasting time is not a *wise* thing to do. **wise**
15. **buy** Elisa wants to *buy* a puzzle. **buy**

Mastery Words

1. **bike** My *bike* is bright red. **bike**
2. **find** I hope Jerry will *find* his dog. **find**
3. **high** The new building is 40 stories *high*. **high**
4. **right** Try to do it the *right* way. **right**
5. **why** Tell me *why* you were late. **why**
6. **wide** Chee left the window *wide* open. **wide**

Bonus Words

1. **awhile** Myra slept *awhile*. **awhile**
2. **delight** A visit would *delight* Grandpa. **delight**
3. **highway** The *highway* was built last year. **highway**
4. **midnight** We stayed up until *midnight*. **midnight**
5. **pirate** Carmine wrote about a *pirate*. **pirate**
6. **polite** Try to be *polite* at the party. **polite**
7. **quite** Paula's hat is not *quite* big enough. **quite**
8. **title** Gabe knows the *title* of the book. **title**

Dictation Sentences

This Week's Words

1. The *tiger* was *shy* when the *lion* came in *sight*.
2. It is *wise* to *buy* the *prize* now and *hide* it.
3. She got in *line* to see the *nine bright* stars.
4. The angry dogs started to *fight* and *bite*.
5. I have wanted a pet for *myself* all my *life*.

Mastery Words

1. You will *find* the *bike* on the *right* side.
2. He will tell you *why* the road is *high* and *wide*.

Bonus Words

1. It was *quite* a *delight* to ride on this *highway awhile*.
2. The *pirate* took the boat at *midnight*.
3. He was *polite* when he asked the *title* of the book.

who have made errors on the Unit Test may require reteaching. Use the following
aching Strategies and **Follow-up Masters 16A** and **16B** for additional instruction and
practice of This Week's Words. (You may wish to assign **LEP Reteaching Follow-up Master 16**
for reteaching of spelling words.)

A. Discovering Spelling Ideas

1. Say the following words as you write them on the chalkboard:

    nine   sight   item   fly

2. Ask the children to identify the vowel sound in each word. (/ī/)
3. Ask the children to identify the letters that spell /ī/ in the words. (i-consonant-e, igh, i, y)
4. Ask the children what they have learned about spelling /ī/. (It can be spelled with i-consonant-e, igh, i, or y.)

B. Word Shapes

1. Explain to the children that each word has a shape an that remembering the shape of a word can help them spell the word correctly.
2. On the chalkboard, write the words *fine* and *light*. Have the children identify "short," "tall," and "tail" letters.
3. Draw the configuration of each word on the chalkboa and ask the children which word fits in each shape.

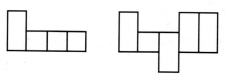

Use **Reteaching Follow-up Master 16A** to reinforce spelling generalizations taught in Unit 16.

Use **Reteaching Follow-up Master 16B** to reinforce spellings of This Week's Words for Unit 16.

The Vowel Sound /ō/

PREVIEWING THE UNIT

Unit Materials

Instruction and Practice

Pupil Book	pages 72–75
Teacher's Edition	
Teaching Plans	pages 72–75
Enrichment Activities	
For the Classroom	pages 75A–75B
For the Home	page 75B
Reteaching Strategies	page 75C

Testing

Teacher's Edition	
Trial Test	pages 71E–71F
Unit Test	page 75B
Dictation Test	page 75B

Additional Resources

PRACTICE AND REINFORCEMENT
Extra Practice Master 17: This Week's Words
Extra Practice Master 17: Mastery Words
Extra Practice Master 17: Bonus Words
LEP Practice Master 17
Spelling and Language Master 17
Study Steps to Learn a Word Master

RETEACHING FOLLOW-UP
Reteaching Follow-up Master 17A:
  Discovering Spelling Ideas
Reteaching Follow-up Master 17B: Word
  Shapes
LEP Reteaching Follow-up Master 17

TEACHING AIDS
Spelling Generalizations Transparency 15

Visit our Web site
http://www.hbschool.com

Click on the SPELLING banner to find activities for this unit.

Learner Objectives

Spelling

- To spell words that demonstrate the sound-letter relationships /ō/o-consonant-e, oa, o, ow.
- To recognize the relationship between the present and past form of irregular verbs.

Reading

- To follow written directions.
- To use context clues for word identification.
- To use the dictionary as a key to word meaning.

Writing

- To write a how-to paragraph.
- To use the writing process.
- To proofread for spelling, capitalization, and punctuation.
- To write legible manuscript and cursive letters.

Listening

- To listen to identify words with the long vowel sound /ō/.
- To follow oral directions.

Speaking

- To respond to a question.
- To speak clearly to a group.
- To present a how-to paragraph to the class.
- To express feelings and ideas about a piece of writing.
- To contribute ideas and information in group discussions.

THIS WEEK'S WORDS

both
float
blow
fold
follow
hello
joke
load
old
rose
sold
spoke
stove
window
bow

MASTERY WORDS

also
grow
low
oak
own
those

BONUS WORDS

slope
vote
boast
throat
narrow
shadow
scold
stroll

Assignment Guide

This guide shows how you teach a typical spelling unit in either a five-day or a three-day sequence, while providing for individual differences. **Boldface type** indicates essential classwork. Steps shown in light type may be done in class or assigned as homework.

Five Days	● = average spellers　　★ = better spellers　　✓ = slower spellers	Three Days
Day **1**	**a** ● ★　**Take This Week's Words Trial Test and correct** ● ✓　**Take Mastery Word Trial Test and correct** ● ★　**Read This Week's Words and discuss generalization page 72**	
Day **2**	●　Complete Spelling Practice page 73 ● ✓　Complete Extra Practice Master 17: This Week's Words (optional) ✓　Complete Spelling on Your Own: Mastery words page 75 ★　**Take Bonus word Trial Test and correct**　**b**	Day **1**
Day **3**	**c** ● ★ ✓　**Complete Spelling and Language page 74** ● ★ ✓　Complete Writing on Your Own page 74 ● ★ ✓　**Complete Proofreading page 74** ● ✓　Take Midweek Test (optional) ★　Complete Spelling on Your Own: Bonus words page 75 ● ✓　Complete Spelling and Language Master 17 (optional)	
Day **4**	●　Complete Spelling on Your Own: This Week's Words page 75 ✓　Complete Extra Practice Master 17: Mastery words (optional) ★　Complete Extra Practice Master 17: Bonus words (optional)　**d**	Day **2**
Day **5**	**e** ●　Take Unit Test on This Week's Words ●　Complete Reteaching Follow-up Masters 17A and 17B (optional) ● ✓　**Take Unit Test on Mastery words** ★　**Take Unit Test on Bonus words**	Day **3**

Enrichment Activities for the **classroom** and for the **home** included at the end of this unit may be assigned selectively on any day of the week.

INTRODUCING THE UNIT

Establish Readiness for Learning

Tell the children that this week they will continue to study words with long vowel sounds. In Unit 17 they will study four spellings for the long vowel sound /ō/. Tell the children that they will apply the spelling generalization to This Week's Words and use those words in writing a how-to paragraph.

Assess Children's Spelling Ability

Administer the Trial Test before the children study This Week's Words. Use the test sentences provided. Say each word and use it in a sentence. Then repeat the word. Have the children write the words on a separate sheet of paper or in their spelling notebooks. Test sentences are also provided for Mastery and Bonus words.

Have the children check their own work by listening to you read the spelling of the words or by referring to This Week's Words in the left column of the **Pupil Book.** For each misspelled word, have the children follow the **Study Steps to Learn a Word** on page 1 in the **Pupil Book** or use the copying master to study and write the words. Children should record the number correct on their **Progress Report.**

Trial Test Sentences

This Week's Words
1. *both*　Becky and Ted *both* do well in math.　*both*
2. *float*　Wood and cork are things that *float*.　*float*
3. *blow*　The wind will *blow* the leaves around.　*blow*
4. *fold*　Maggie will help you *fold* the laundry.　*fold*
5. *follow*　Raul's dogs always *follow* him to school.　*follow*

FOCUS

- Establishes objectives
- Relates to prior learning
- Sets purpose of instruction

6. **hello**   Akiko said *hello* to her friend.
   hello
7. **joke**   Basil told a *joke* about an
   elephant.   *joke*
8. **load**   Rosalie helped *load* the stuff into
   the car.   *load.*
9. **old**   I like my *old* shoes better than my
   new ones.   *old*
10. **rose**   Everyone *rose* when the principal
    walked into the room.   *rose*
11. **sold**   Mel's family *sold* their car.   *sold*
12. **spoke**   She *spoke* quietly to the
    children.   *spoke*
13. **stove**   Do not turn on the *stove.*   *stove*
14. **window**   Olivia washed the *window.*
    window
15. **bow**   Hank tied the ribbon in a *bow.*
    bow

Mastery Words

1. **also**   Dorothy wants to draw *also.*   *also*
2. **grow**   Many flowers *grow* in our
   garden.   *grow*
3. **low**   That chair is too *low* for you.   *low*
4. **oak**   An *oak* tree grows in our
   yard.   *oak*
5. **own**   Carol has her *own* bike.   *own*
6. **those**   Jorge drew all *those* pictures.
   those

Bonus Words

1. **slope**   We skied down the *slope.*   *slope*

2. **vote**   Many people will *vote* for the next
   President.   *vote*
3. **boast**   Some children *boast* about what
   they can do.   *boast*
4. **throat**   Tina has a sore *throat.*   *throat*
5. **narrow**   We walked down a *narrow*
   trail.   *narrow*
6. **shadow**   The cat stared at its own
   shadow.   *shadow*
7. **scold**   The birds seem to *scold* each
   other.   *scold*
8. **stroll**   John and Mike will *stroll* through
   the park.   *stroll*

Apply Prior Learning

Have the children apply what they already know about the /ō/ sound by having them participate in the activity that follows.

Have the children name words that contain the long vowel sound for the letter o. Write their responses on the chalkboard. Continue listing the children's responses until words which contain /ō/o-consonant-e, oa, o, and ow are among those words listed. Have volunteers come to the chalkboard and draw a line around the four different spellings for /ō/. Tell the children that in Unit 17 they will study words that have the long vowel sound for the letter o. Explain that they can use these words in a variety of writing tasks: they can use the words in a note to a friend, in a letter, or in a creative writing assignment.

FOCUS

- Relates to prior learning
- Draws relationships
- Applies spelling generalizations to new contexts

FOR CHILDREN WITH SPECIAL NEEDS

Learning Difficulties

Children with learning disabilities seem to have better retention of the correct spellings of words when given a model or pattern to follow.

Divide This Week's Words into four groups for each of the spellings of the /ō/ sound as follows: o-consonant-e — *joke, rose, spoke, stove;* oa — *float, load;* o — *both, fold, hello, old, sold;* ow — *blow, follow, window,* and *bow.* First ask the children to spell This Week's Words. Then provide them with the correct spelling, either on the chalkboard or in a list that they have at their desks. Have them check their work for accuracy and underline any misspelled words with a colored marker or crayon. For each misspelled word, have the children copy the word correctly onto a new piece of paper, and then cover it and write the word from memory. Have the children

compare the word they wrote with the word on their spelling list. If it is not correctly spelled, have them repeat the procedure.

During the week of study for This Week's Words, ask the children to spell the words that they misspelled. Follow the strategy described above if any other misspellings occur.

Limited English Proficiency

To help limited English proficient children work with the spelling generalizations for Unit 17, you may wish to refer to the booklet "Suggestions and Activities for Limited English Proficient Students."

TEACHING PLAN

Objective To spell words that demonstrate these sound-letter relationships: /ō/ o-consonant-e, *oa*, *o*, *ow*.

1. Direct the children's attention to the photograph on page 72 and ask them to think of a sentence that tells about the picture. Work with the children until you have developed this sentence:

   Both those polar bears know how to float.

   Write the sentence on the chalk-board, and help the children to identify the words with /ō/ and the letters that spell /ō/ in the words. (both, o; those, o-e; polar, o; know, ow; float, oa)
2. Read the generalization on page 72 aloud.

You may wish to introduce the lesson by using **Spelling Generalizations Transparency 15.**

3. Have volunteers read This Week's Words aloud. As each word is read, have the children identify the letter or letters that spell /ō/ in the word.
4. Direct the children's attention to **Remember This** at the bottom of the page and read the paragraph aloud. Ask volunteers to use *bow* /bō/ and *bow* /bou/ in oral sentences.

You may wish to assign **LEP Practice Master 17** for reinforcement in writing spelling words.

---

17 The Vowel Sound /ō/

THIS WEEK'S WORDS

1. both
2. float
3. blow
4. fold
5. follow
6. hello
7. joke
8. load
9. old
10. rose
11. sold
12. spoke
13. stove
14. window
15. bow

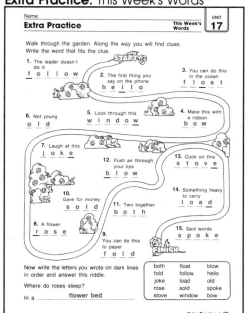

72

This Week's Words

All the words this week have the vowel sound /ō/. Here are four ways to spell /ō/.

- with **o-consonant-e**, as in <u>joke</u>
- with **oa**, as in <u>float</u>
- with **o**, as in <u>both</u> and <u>fold</u>
- with **ow**, as in <u>blow</u>

> **REMEMBER THIS**
>
> The word <u>bow</u> can be said two ways. <u>Bow</u> has /ō/ when you say "Tie the ribbon in a <u>bow</u>." <u>Bow</u> has the vowel sound heard in <u>cow</u> when you say "Take a <u>bow</u>." But either way, it is spelled the same: <u>bow</u>.

Extra Practice: This Week's Words

Name
Extra Practice This Week's Words UNIT **17**

Walk through the garden. Along the way you will find clues. Write the word that fits the clue.

1. The leader doesn't do it
   f o l l o w START

3. You can do this in the ocean
   f l o a t

2. The first thing you say on the phone
   h e l l o

6. Not young
   o l d

5. Look through this
   w i n d o w

4. Make this with a ribbon
   b o w

7. Laugh at this
   j o k e

12. Push air through your lips
   b l o w

13. Cook on this
   s t o v e

10. Gave for money
   s o l d

11. Two together
   b o t h

14. Something heavy to carry
   l o a d

8. A flower
   r o s e

9. You can do this to paper
   f o l d FINISH

15. Said words
   s p o k e

Now write the letters you wrote on dark lines in order and answer this riddle.

Where do roses sleep?

In a ___flower bed___

both	float	blow
fold	follow	hello
joke	load	old
rose	sold	spoke
stove	window	bow

Extra Practice • 69

Extra Practice: Mastery Words

Name
Extra Practice Mastery Words UNIT **17**

This is a strange tree. It has six different kinds of leaves. Each leaf has a letter on it. Write the letter or letters you find on each kind of leaf. Then add the letters that spell /ō/ and write a Mastery word.

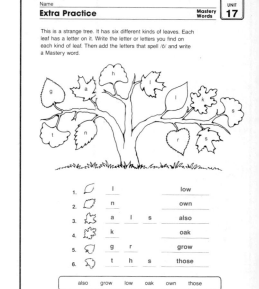

1. l ___ low
2. n ___ own
3. a l s ___ also
4. k ___ oak
5. g r ___ grow
6. t h s ___ those

| also | grow | low | oak | own | those |

70 • Extra Practice

Spelling Practice

A. Follow the directions. Use This Week's Words.

1. Write the four words that have /ō/ spelled as it is in <u>nose</u>.

joke	rose
spoke	stove

2. Write the five words that end with /ō/.

blow	follow	(hello)
window	bow	

3. Circle the word you wrote for **2** that does not end with <u>ow</u>.

4. Write the three words that end with the cluster <u>ld</u>.

fold	old	sold

5. Write the word that means "two." ___ **both**

B. Write This Week's Words that rhyme with these words.

6. boat ___ **float**   **7.** toad ___ **load**

C. Finish the sentences. Use This Week's Words. You will use one word twice.

8. Pablo called me on the phone to say ___ **hello** .

9. He told me a funny ___ **joke** .

10. He said, "What's big and gray and has a trunk and a rear ___ **window** ?"

11. I said, "An ___ **old** gray car."

12. He said, "No, an elephant. I made up the part about the ___ **window** ."

13. We ___ **both** laughed a lot.

both
float
blow
fold
follow
hello
joke
load
old
rose
sold
spoke
stove
window
bow

73

Extra Practice: Bonus Words

Summarize Learning

Have the children summarize what they have learned on pages 72 and 73. *Ask:*

- What have you learned about /ō/ in this lesson? (The /ō/ sound is heard when a word is spelled with o-consonant-e, oa, o, or ow.)
- What are some examples of words to which this generalization can be applied? (*both, float, joke, load, bow;* accept other examples)

TEACHING PLAN

Objectives To write words given spelling clues; to write words that end with /ō/; to write words that rhyme with given words; to write words in sentence context.

1. Briefly discuss the directions on page 73. If necessary, read the sentences in Exercise **C** aloud and have the children supply the missing words.
2. Have the children complete the exercises independently. Remind them to use legible handwriting. You may wish to demonstrate the correct form of the letters *o* and *w* and then have the children practice writing the letters. For **Handwriting Models,** refer the children to page 258 in the **Pupil Book.**
3. To correct the children's work, have volunteers write their answers for Exercises **A** and **B** on the chalkboard. Ask a volunteer to read the completed sentences in Exercise **C** aloud. Let the children check their own work.

For reinforcement in writing spelling words, you may wish to assign *Extra Practice Master 17: This Week's Words.*

⭐ *of special interest*

The words used to describe a window in Old English and Middle English reveal something about daily life during these periods. In Old English, a window was called *eāgthyrel* ("eye-hole") or *eāgduru* ("eye-door") —in other words, peephole. The name suggests that the function of windows was to allow people to peer out and observe approaching danger. In the Middle Ages, the Norse word *vindauga* ("wind-eye," whence *window*) began to replace the older terms. The new choice of name may suggest a new understanding of windows as a means of providing ventilation.

TEACHING PLAN

SPELLING AND LANGUAGE

Objectives To recognize the relationship between the present and past forms of irregular verbs; to write irregular verb forms in sentence context.

1. To introduce this activity, write this question on the chalkboard:

   What did Alan say?

   Ask the children to answer the question, using *said*. Help the children to recognize the relationship between *say* and *said*.
2. Read the directions on page 74.
3. Have the children complete the activity independently.
4. To correct the children's work, have volunteers read the questions and answers aloud. Let the children check their own work.

For extended practice in writing the past tense form of verbs, you may wish to assign *Spelling and Language Master 17.*

WRITING ON YOUR OWN

Objectives To write a how-to paragraph; to proofread for spelling, capitalization, and punctuation.

1. Review the directions.
2. As a **prewriting** activity, discuss with children the jobs they might do around the house. List one job on the chalkboard and ask children to identify each step necessary to complete it. Remind children to list steps in the correct order. Then have each child choose a job and **compose** a how-to paragraph explaining each step. When the children are ready to **revise** their paragraphs, remind them to check spelling, capitalization, and punctuation. To **publish** the children's work, have each paragraph read to the class.

Spelling and Language • Using Verbs

THIS WEEK'S WORDS
both
float
blow
fold
follow
hello
joke
load
old
rose
sold
spoke
stove
window
bow

Finish the answers to these questions. Use This Week's Words. You will write verbs that tell what already happened.

1. When did Lucy rise today?

She ___rose___ at 7:00 this morning.

2. Did she go out to sell juice?

Yes, she ___sold___ twenty glasses of juice.

3. Did you speak to Lucy when she got home?

Yes, I ___spoke___ with her when she returned.

Writing on Your Own

Do you help your parents around the house? Write a paragraph which tells how you do one home job. Give all the steps and helpful tips. Use some of This Week's Words.

Proofreading

Doug wrote this secret message. He misspelled six words.

Stand under the front windo. Take six steps toward the roze garden. Point boath feet east. Follo your nose to the old tree. Look for a yellow boe. This is no joak.

1. Circle each of Doug's mistakes.
2. Write the six misspelled words correctly.

window	rose	both
follow	bow	joke

WRITER'S GUIDE See the editing and proofreading marks on page 248.

74

PROOFREADING

Objectives To proofread a message for spelling errors; to write misspelled words correctly.

1. Read the introductory sentences and the directions on page 74.
2. Ask the children to follow as you read and look for spelling errors.
3. Have the children read the message again and mark the errors according to the directions.

   If you are using the hardcover book, the children should simply locate the misspelled words and write them correctly in their spelling notebooks.

Extra Practice: Spelling and Language

Name _____ UNIT **17**
Spelling and Language

A. Each sentence has one verb. Add *ed* to each verb and write the new word.

1. Many boats float on the sea. ___floated___
2. Big boats follow little boats near land. ___followed___
3. On sailboats, sailors fold sails. ___folded___
4. Sailors load boats with boxes and bags. ___loaded___
5. The sailors joke with each other. ___joked___

B. Finish each sentence. Use This Week's Words.

6. At our garage sale, Mom ___spoke___ to everyone who passed the door or the ___window___
7. Once, when she ___rose___ to say ___hello___, she knocked over our dirty ___old___ stove.
8. We had two bikes, but Mom ___sold___ them ___both___
9. She even got rid of a whole ___load___ of coal!

C. Answer each question with a verb. Use This Week's Words.

10. What did the sun do this morning? It ___rose___
11. What do actors do at the end of a play? They ___bow___
12. What do strong winds do? They ___blow___
13. What do you do when someone leads? You ___follow___

| both | float | fold | follow | load | old | spoke | sold |
| blow | hello | joke | window | rose | bow | stove | |

72 • Extra Practice

Spelling on Your Own

THIS WEEK'S WORDS

1. Write NOUN, VERB, and OTHER at the top of your paper.
2. Write each of This Week's Words under the right word. A word like <u>load</u> can be a noun or a verb, but write it in just one place. Three of This Week's Words are not nouns or verbs. Write them under OTHER.
3. Think of a describing word that goes with each noun. Write the two words. Here's an example: <u>funny joke</u>.
4. Then think of a noun that goes with each verb. Write the words. Here is an example: <u>corks float</u>. **See answers below.**

HEAVY **LOAD**

LOAD THE CAR

also
grow
low
oak
own
those

MASTERY WORDS

1. Write the three Mastery words that end with /ō/.

   also   grow   low

2. Write the two Mastery words that begin with /ō/.

   oak   own

3. Write the Mastery word that rhymes with <u>nose</u>.   those

4. Use the word you just wrote in a sentence.

   EXAMPLE: **Acorns grow on those oak trees.**

BONUS WORDS

Follow the directions. Use the Bonus words.
1. Write all the words in alphabetical order.
2. After each word, write how /ō/ is spelled in that word.

Try this "word math."
3. <u>three</u> − /ē/ + /ō/ + <u>t</u> = ____
4. <u>say</u> − /ā/ + <u>tea</u> − /ē/ + <u>roll</u> = ____
5. <u>show</u> − /ō/ + <u>ad</u> + /ō/ = ____

Now make up your own "word math" problems. Use the Bonus words.
See answers below.

75

slope
vote
boast
throat
narrow
shadow
scold
stroll

Spelling on Your Own Answers

THIS WEEK'S WORDS

1.–2. NOUN   **VERB**   **OTHER**

joke*	float*	both
load*	blow*	hello
rose*	fold*	old
stove	follow	
window	sold	
bow*	spoke*	

*These words can function as nouns or verbs and could be listed in either column.

3. Answers will vary.
4. Answers will vary.

BONUS WORDS

1. boast   oa
   narrow   ow
   scold   o
   shadow   ow
   slope   o-e
   stroll   o
   throat   oa
   vote   o-e
2. See above.
3. throat
4. stroll
5. shadow

Children will write as directed. Be sure to check spelling.

Summarize Learning

Have the children summarize what they have learned in this unit. *Ask:*
- What have you learned about making the past tense for the words *rise, sell,* and *speak*? (They are **not** made by adding *ed;* the past tense is a new word.)
- What have you learned about proofreading in this lesson? (To reread sentences to look for and correct words that are misspelled.)
- What spelling generalizations have you learned? How did you use these generalizations?

Spelling on Your Own UNIT 17d

TEACHING PLAN

> **Objective** To apply the unit spelling generalization to spell This Week's Words, Mastery words, and Bonus words independently.

THIS WEEK'S WORDS

1. Read the directions for **1** on page 75, and have the children write NOUN, VERB, and OTHER on a separate piece of paper.
2. Read the directions for **2**. Have volunteers read This Week's Words, and help the children to decide in which column each word should be written.
3. Read the directions for **3** and **4**. Make sure that the children understand what they are to do.

MASTERY WORDS

1. Review the unit generalization on page 72.
2. Have volunteers read each Mastery word aloud and identify the letter or letters that spell /ō/.
3. Briefly discuss the directions on page 75.

BONUS WORDS

1. Have volunteers read the Bonus words aloud. Encourage the children to look up the meaning of any unfamiliar word in the **Spelling Dictionary.**
2. Make sure the children understand how to do the "word math." Remind them that the pronunciations in the **Spelling Dictionary** can help them write their "word math" problems.
3. Have the children complete the exercise on a separate piece of paper.

For reinforcement in writing spelling words, you may wish to assign *Extra Practice Master 17: Mastery Words* or *Bonus Words.*

CLOSING THE UNIT

Apply New Learning

Tell the children that if they misspell words with the long vowel sound /ō/ in their writing, they should use one of the following strategies:

- think about the possible spellings for a long vowel sound /ō/ and try to picture the word in their minds.
- think of words that rhyme and compare in their minds how they are spelled.
- think of a known word that is related in meaning and spelling.

Transfer New Learning

Tell the children that when they encounter new words in their personal reading and in other content areas, they should learn the meaning of those words and then apply the generalizations they have studied to the spelling of those words. Tell the children that once the words are familiar in both meaning and spelling, they should use the new words in their writing.

ENRICHMENT ACTIVITIES

Classroom activities and **home activities** may be assigned to children of all ability levels. The activities provide opportunities for children to use their spelling words in new contexts.

For the Classroom

To individualize **classroom activities**, you may have the children use the word list they are studying in this unit.

- *Basic:* Use **Mastery** words to complete the activity.
- *Average:* Use **This Week's Words** to complete the activity.
- *Challenging:* Use **Bonus** words to complete the activity.

1. **Language Arts/Writing a Friendly Letter** Have each child write a friendly letter to another student in the class. You may wish to assign partners to the children so that each child receives a letter. The children should use as many spelling words as possible in the bodies of their letters. Before they write, direct the children to page 251 in the **Writer's Guide** for a model of the form of a friendly letter. Remind the children to use the **Revising Checklist** on page 247 to revise their letters, checking for spelling and punctuation. Encourage the children to "send" the letters to their classmates.

   ■ COOPERATIVE LEARNING: Have each group write a friendly letter to another group. All the group members should brainstorm for details that they would like to include in the letter. As they do so, one member should make a list of possible details. The group should decide

on a sequence, and divide the details among the children. Have each child write a brief paragraph for the body of the letter. The group should then revise the letter, checking it for spelling, capitalization, and punctuation. One member should be chosen to read the letter aloud to the other group.

2. **Language Arts/Writing Sentences to Show Multiple Meanings** Have the children use the dictionary to find two meanings for one of the following spelling words: *blow, rose, spoke.* Tell the children to jot down the meanings of the words. Then have them write example sentences that might be used in a dictionary to explain each of the word's meanings.

   ■ COOPERATIVE LEARNING: Have each child in the group use the dictionary to find two meanings of one of these spelling words: *blow, rose, spoke.* Then have each child write example sentences to show the word's meaning. Group members should then discuss the effectiveness of each member's sentences and suggest revisions as needed. Each group should compile a list of the words and sentences to share with the class.

3. **Language Arts/Writing a Journal Entry** Have each child write a journal entry for an imaginary person. The entry should use as many spelling words as possible. Tell the children that each will pretend to be an imaginary person and write about something that person did one day. Direct the children to page 252 in the **Writer's Guide** to read about journals. As a *prewriting* activity, have each child create an imaginary person and write the person's name at the top of a piece of paper. Then direct the children to look over the spelling word list to get ideas for an event about which they can write. Give the following examples: *The First Person to Cross the New Bridge; Why This Circus Was Better Than Other Circuses I Have Seen.* Have each child write topics under the name of the character and then list events that might have happened to that person. When the children finish the *prewriting* activities, tell them to use their lists to *compose* their journal entries. Tell the children that they should use "I" as they write. Remind them to use as many spelling words as possible. Then have the children *revise* their entries by checking that events are logically sequenced and that they have used the first person. Remind the children to proofread for spelling, capitalization, and punctuation errors, using the **Revising Checklist** on page 247 for help. Then tell the children to write the day and date at the top of their journal entries. *Publish* the children's work on a bulletin-board display.

   ■ COOPERATIVE LEARNING: Have each group write a journal entry for an imaginary person. As a *prewriting* activity, have each group create an imaginary person. Then have the group look over the spelling word list in search of appropriate topics and list them. Tell each group member to choose a different topic to use for a diary entry and list the things that happened. Group members should **compose** their entries individually. Have the group work together to **revise** each member's entry. Group members should suggest ways to make each member's entry clearer, and check for spelling, capitalization, and punctuation errors. Have the group **publish** their entries by compiling them in a diary and making a cover page with a title and the name of their imaginary person.

For the Home

Children may complete these activities independently or with the assistance of a relative or friend in the home.

1. Science/Categorizing Objects Tell the children to think about things that float when they are placed in water. Have the children make a chart on a sheet of paper. In the left column, have them write a list of things that float. In the right column, have them write a list of things that do not float. Have the children use some of the spelling words and other words that have the long /ō/ sound on this chart.

2. Language Arts/Writing a Telephone Conversation Tell the children to imagine a brief telephone conversation between two friends. Ask the children to think of a topic that the friends might be discussing, then write at least six lines of conversation. Remind the children that when we read or write exactly what someone says, the person's words begin and end with quotation marks. Have the children use several spelling words in their conversations.

3. Language Arts/Writing Persuasive Sentences Have the children write five sentences trying to convince someone to go to a birthday party. Each sentence should include a spelling word. For example, You will get a *load* of great presents. Children may ask a friend to suggest more reasons for attending a birthday party, then add those to their lists. When the sentences are complete, the children can read them to someone else.

4. Fine Arts/Writing and Illustrating Sentences Have the children choose two spelling words and write sentences about each word. Then have the children select a sentence and illustrate either the word or what is happening in the sentence.

EVALUATING SPELLING ABILITY

Unit Test

This Week's Words
1. **both**   Soon *both* children will be good swimmers.   **both**
2. **float**   If you don't tie the boat, it will *float* away.   **float**
3. **blow**   Make a wish before you *blow* out the candles.   **blow**
4. **fold**   Miguel will *fold* his paper in half.   **fold**
5. **follow**   Mr. Jackson will *follow* us in his car.   **follow**
6. **hello**   Margo called to say *hello*.   **hello**
7. **joke**   Elaine told a good *joke*.   **joke**
8. **load**   We will *load* the clothes into the washing machine.   **load**
9. **old**   Jim wore his *old* clothes for painting.   **old**
10. **rose**   Katie picked a yellow *rose*.   **rose**
11. **sold**   Sally *sold* lemonade at the baseball game.   **sold**
12. **spoke**   The vet *spoke* to the class about animals.   **spoke**
13. **stove**   The cabin has a wood-burning *stove*.   **stove**
14. **window**   Charlie broke the *window*.   **window**
15. **bow**   Tie your shoelaces in a *bow*.   **bow**

Mastery Words
1. **also**   Randy *also* knows how to sing.   **also**
2. **grow**   Our kitten will *grow* a lot in a year.   **grow**
3. **low**   Dad cut off the *low* branch.   **low**
4. **oak**   Let's sit here under this *oak* tree.   **oak**
5. **own**   Sean would like to *own* a horse.   **own**
6. **those**   These mittens are mine, and *those* are yours.   **those**

Bonus Words
1. **slope**   The roof has a steep *slope*.   **slope**
2. **vote**   Eighteen-year-olds are old enough to *vote*.   **vote**
3. **boast**   Evan wanted to *boast* about his prize.   **boast**
4. **throat**   Pat said she had a frog in her *throat*.   **throat**
5. **narrow**   Lucia tied a *narrow* ribbon in her hair.   **narrow**
6. **shadow**   Dee saw her *shadow* on the wall.   **shadow**
7. **scold**   Brenda's father did not *scold* her.   **scold**
8. **stroll**   Alan took a *stroll* along the beach.   **stroll**

Dictation Sentences

This Week's Words
1. He *sold* his *old* *stove*.
2. They *both* *spoke* to us from the *window*.
3. The bird can say *hello* and tell a *joke*.
4. The boat will not *float* if it has a big *load*.
5. He wanted to *follow* the smell of the *rose*.
6. The boy with the *bow* tie will *blow* the whistle.
7. Do not *fold* that note.

Mastery Words
1. I know *those* *low* *oak* trees will *grow* tall.
2. He *also* wants to *own* a dog and cat.

Bonus Words
1. Did she *scold* Pat for taking a *stroll*?
2. He had to *boast* until his *throat* hurt to get every *vote*.
3. The *shadow* of the tree fell on the *narrow* slope.

RETEACHING STRATEGIES FOR SPELLING

Children who have made errors on the Unit Test may require reteaching. Use the following **Reteaching Strategies** and **Follow-up Masters 17A** and **17B** for additional instruction and practice of This Week's Words. (You may wish to assign **LEP Reteaching Follow-up Master 17** for reteaching of spelling words.)

A. Discovering Spelling Ideas

1. Say the following words as you write them on the chalkboard.

> pole   boat   post   crow

2. Ask the children to identify the vowel sound that each word has in common. (/ō/)
3. Ask the children to identify the letters that spell /ō/ in the words. *(o-consonant-e, oa, o, ow)*
4. Ask the children what they have learned about spelling /ō/. (It can be spelled with o-consonant-e, oa, o, or ow at the end of a word.)

B. Word Shapes

1. Explain to the children that each word has a shape and that remembering the shape of a word can help them t spell the word correctly.
2. On the chalkboard, write the words *row* and *coat*. Have the children identify "short" and "tall" letters.
3. Draw the configuration of each word on the chalkboard and ask the children which word fits in each shape.

Use **Reteaching Follow-up Master 17A** to reinforce spelling generalizations taught in Unit 17.

Use **Reteaching Follow-up Master 17B** to reinforce spellings of This Week's Words for Unit 17.

Name _____

Reteaching Follow-up A   Discovering Spelling Ideas   UNIT 17

THIS WEEK'S WORDS

both	float	fold	follow	load
old	spoke	sold	blow	hello
joke	window	rose	bow	stove

1. Study This Week's Words. Say each word to yourself. What do This Week's Words have in common?

They all have the sound /ō/.

2. Look at the spelling for /ō/ above each column. Write each of This Week's Words in the column that has the same spelling as the word.

o-consonant-e	o	ow
joke	fold	blow
rose	old	follow
spoke	sold	window
stove	both	bow
	hello	

oa
float
load

3. What are the four ways to spell /ō/ in This Week's Words?

/ō/ is spelled o-consonant-e, oa, o, or ow.

Reteaching • 29

Name _____

Reteaching Follow-up B   Word Shapes   UNIT 17

THIS WEEK'S WORDS

both	float	fold	follow	load
old	spoke	sold	blow	hello
joke	window	rose	bow	stove

Write each of This Week's Words in its correct shape. The first one has been done for you. Children may interchange answers that fit the same configuration.

1. w i n d o w   2. h e l l o
3. s p o k e   4. o l d
5. s o l d   6. f l o a t
7. b o t h   8. r o s e
9. s t o v e   10. l o a d
11. b l o w   12. f o l d
13. b o w   14. f o l l o w
15. j o k e

30 • Reteaching

75C   UNIT 17 *The Vowel Sound /ō/*

PREVIEWING THE UNIT

Unit Materials

Instruction and Practice

Pupil Book	pages 76–81
Teacher's Edition	
Teaching Plans	pages 76–81
Enrichment Activities	
For the Home	page 81A

Testing

Teacher's Edition	
Trial Test	pages 75E–75F
Unit Test	page 81A
Form *A** Test 3	page T7
Form *B** Test 2	page T9
Midyear Test*	page T11

*At midyear there are three testing options. If your grading period is six weeks, you may want to use **Form A**; if your grading period is nine weeks, you may want to use **Form B.** In addition, you may want to use the **Midyear Test** to assess spelling ability for Units 1–18.

Additional Resources

PRACTICE AND REINFORCEMENT
Review Master 18A: Units 13 and 14
Review Master 18B: Units 15 and 16
Review Master 18C: Unit 17 and Test
   Exercise
Dictionary and Proofreading Master 3
Study Steps to Learn a Word Master
Mastery Words Review: Units 13–17
Bonus Words Review: Units 13–17

TESTING (optional)
Mastery Words Test: Units 13–17
Bonus Words Test: Units 13–17
Writing Test 3

TEACHING AIDS
Spelling and Writing Transparency 3
Home Letter 4

Visit our Web site
http://www.hbschool.com

Click on the SPELLING banner to find activities for this unit.

Learner Objectives

Spelling

- To review base forms and inflected forms of verbs that end with -e.
- To review words that demonstrate these sound-letter relationships: /ā/a-consonant-e, *ai, ay, ey, eigh.*
- To review words that demonstrate these sound-letter relationships: /ē/ea, ee, e, y.
- To review words that demonstrate these sound-letter relationships: /ī/i-consonant-e, *igh, i, y, uy.*
- To review words that demonstrate these sound-letter relationships: /ō/o-consonant-e, *oa, o, ow.*

Reading

- To read a description.
- To follow written directions.
- To look for colorful words in a description.

Writing

- To write a descriptive paragraph.
- To use the writing process.
- To edit for content, style, and tone.
- To revise using editing and proofreading marks.
- To proofread for spelling, capitalization, and punctuation.
- To write legible manuscript and cursive letters.

Listening

- To listen to recognize and write words with short and long vowel sounds.
- To follow a series of oral directions.

Speaking

- To contribute ideas and information in group discussions.
- To express feelings and ideas about a piece of writing.
- To present descriptive paragraphs.

REVIEW WORDS

UNIT 13
invite
skate
taste
cared
smiling
loved
living
paste

UNIT 14
brave
mail
today
eight
obey
lake
gate
paid

UNIT 15
team
weak
between
busy
every
even
only
really

UNIT 16
life
hide
bright
myself
buy
prize
nine
sight

UNIT 17
both
hello
joke
float
follow
sold
window
fold

Assignment Guide

This guide shows how you teach a typical spelling unit in either a five-day or a three-day sequence, while providing for individual differences. **Boldface type** indicates essential classwork. Steps shown in light type may be done in class or assigned as homework.

Five Days	⚬ = average spellers ★ = better spellers ✓ = slower spellers	Three Days
Day **1** ▶a	⚬ ★ ✓ **Take Review Word Trial Test and correct**	
Day **2**	⚬ ★ ✓ Complete Spelling Review pages 76, 77, 78 ⚬ ★ ✓ Complete Review Master 8A, 8B, 8C (optional) ✓ Complete Mastery Words Review Master: Units 13 – 17 (optional) ★ Complete Bonus Words Review Master: Units 13 – 17 (optional) ◀b	Day **1**
Day **3** ▶c	⚬ ★ ✓ **Complete Spelling and Reading page 79**	
Day **4**	⚬ ★ ✓ Complete Spelling and Writing pages 80 – 81 ⚬ ★ ✓ Complete Dictionary and Proofreading Master 3 (optional) ◀d	Day **2**
Day **5** ▶e	⚬ ★ ✓ **Take Review Words Unit Test** ✓ Take Mastery Words Test: Units 13 – 17 (optional) ★ Take Bonus Words Test: Units 13 – 17 (optional)	Day **3**

Enrichment Activities for the **home** included at the end of this unit may be assigned selectively on any day of the week.

INTRODUCING THE UNIT

Establish Readiness for Learning

Tell the children they will review words from the previous five units. In Unit 18 they will review:

- verbs with different endings.
- words with the long vowel sound /ā/.
- words with the long vowel sound /ē/.
- words with the long vowel sound /ī/.
- words with the long vowel sound /ō/.

Tell the children they will use some of the review words to write a descriptive paragraph.

Assess Children's Spelling Ability

Administer the Trial Test before the children study the review words. Use the test sentences provided. Say each word and use it in a sentence. Then repeat the word. Have the children write the words on a separate sheet of paper or in their spelling notebooks.

Have the children check their own work by listening to you read the spelling of the words or by referring to the review words lists in the side boxes of the **Pupil Book.** For each miss-

pelled word, have the children follow the **Study Steps to Learn a Word** on page 76 in the **Pupil Book,** or use the copying master to study and write the words. Children should record the number correct on their **Progress Report.**

Trial Test Sentences

1. *invite*   I hope they *invite* us to their party.   *invite*
2. *skate*   A wheel came off Barry's *skate.* *skate*
3. *taste*   Lemons *taste* sour.   *taste*
4. *cared*   The zoo keeper *cared* for the animals.   *cared*
5. *smiling*   Mrs. Easton is always *smiling.* *smiling*
6. *loved*   Suzie *loved* her old teddy bear.   *loved*
7. *living*   My friend is *living* in that old brown house.   *living*
8. *paste*   Please *paste* these pictures in the scrapbook.   *paste*
9. *brave*   Lion tamers must be very *brave.* *brave*

FOCUS

- Establishes objectives
- Relates to prior learning
- Sets purpose of instruction

10. *mail*   Mark got a letter in the *mail*.
    mail

11. *today*   If yesterday was Sunday, then
    today is Monday.   **today**

12. *eight*   The number *eight* comes after the
    number seven.   **eight**

13. *obey*   He should always *obey* the
    rules.   **obey**

14. *lake*   The ducks like to dive in the *lake*.
    lake

15. *gate*   Open this *gate* and go into the
    garden.   **gate**

16. *paid*   Mr. Brown *paid* Brad to mow his
    lawn.   **paid**

17. *team*   Jenny will play on our *team*.
    team

18. *weak*   A cold makes you feel *weak*.
    weak

19. *between*   Maggie sits *between* Ben and
    Sally.   **between**

20. *busy*   Tommy is *busy* washing his bike.
    busy

21. *every*   We have dinner at six o'clock
    every night.   **every**

22. *even*   Andy likes soccer *even* more than
    softball.   **even**

23. *only*   His car will hold *only* four people.
    only

24. *really*   Joe *really* hit a home run.   **really**

25. *life*   Gina has lived in Cleveland all her
    life.   **life**

26. *hide*   You *hide*, and I will try to find
    you.   **hide**

27. *bright*   The *bright* light hurt my eyes.
    bright

28. *myself*   I fixed *myself* a sandwich.
    myself

29. *buy*   Let's *buy* Mom a present.   **buy**

30. *prize*   I hope he wins first *prize*.   **prize**

31. *nine*   The number *nine* comes before
    the number ten.   **nine**

32. *sight*   We will watch that car and keep it
    in *sight*.   **sight**

33. *both*   Alex and Leah *both* love pizza.
    both

34. *hello*   Say *hello* to Aunt Sarah for me.
    hello

35. *joke*   Jim told a *joke* about a canary.
    joke

36. *float*   A rock will not *float* on the
    water.   **float**

37. *follow*   You go first, and I will *follow*
    you.   **follow**

38. *sold*   The man *sold* the kittens for five
    dollars each.   **sold**

39. *window*   Tracy will open the *window*
    and let in some air.   **window**

40. *fold*   After you *fold* your letter, put it in
    an envelope.   **fold**

Apply Prior Learning

Write these words on the chalkboard: *snake, beak, bite,* and *rose.* Ask the children to explain the difference among the four words. (Each has a different vowel sound.) Then ask if there are any similarities among the words. (Yes, they are all one-syllable words and all have a long vowel sound.) Have a volunteer underline the long vowel sound in each word. (sn<u>a</u>ke, b<u>ea</u>k, b<u>i</u>te, r<u>o</u>se) Ask the children to name other words with long vowel sounds and list them with the appropriate word on the chalkboard. Have the children make a statement of what they know about spelling each long vowel sound. Write their responses on the chalkboard. Additional spellings may be added as children go through the Review Unit. Tell the children that they will review words that follow these generalizations and then use the words to write a description.

Write these words on the chalkboard:

paste	(pasted)	(pasting)
dare	(dared)	(daring)
rake	(raked)	(raking)
date	(dated)	(dating)

Ask the children what two things these words have in common. (They all have /ā/ and end in e.) Have the children add *ed* and *ing* to each word. Ask the children what general statement can be made about adding *ing* and *ed* to these verbs. (When a verb ends in e, drop the e and add *ed* or *ing*.)

FOCUS

- Relates to prior learning
- Draws relationships
- Applies spelling generalizations to new contexts

TEACHING PLAN

Objective To review base forms and inflected forms of verbs that end with e.

1. Review the directions to the exercises on page 76. Remind the children that the answers to the exercises are to be found only among the eight review words on page 76.

2. Have the students complete the exercises independently. You may refer them to the **Writer's Guide** at the back of the book for a review of the spelling generalization for Unit 13.

18

Review

Do these steps if you are not sure how to spell a word.
- **Say** the word. Listen to each sound. Think about what the word means.
- **Look** at the word. See how the letters are made. Try to see the word in your mind.
- **Spell** the word to yourself. Think about the way each sound is spelled.
- **Write** the word. Copy it from your book. Check the way you made your letters. Write the word again.
- **Check** your learning. Cover the word and write it. Did you spell it correctly? If not, do these steps until you know how to spell the word.

UNIT 13

invite
skate
taste
cared
smiling
loved
living
paste

UNIT 13 Follow the directions. Use words from Unit 13. Add **ed** or **ing** to these words.

1. care + ed _____ cared
2. love + ed _____ loved
3. live + ing _____ living
4. smile + ing _____ smiling

Write the words that rhyme with these words.

5. kite _____ invite
6. plate _____ skate
7. waste _____ taste *or* paste
8. piling _____ smiling

Finish each sentence. Use a word that begins with the same sound as the person's name used in the sentence.

9. Ingrid and her friends will _____ invite _____ us to a party.

10. Peter will make invitations with paper and _____ paste _____ .

11. Tony will cook a new dish for us to _____ taste _____ .

76

Review: Units 13 and 14

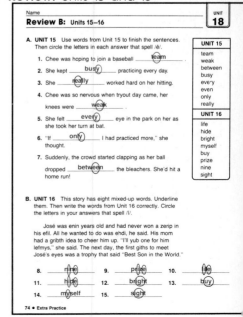

Name _____
Review A: Units 13–14

UNIT
18

A. UNIT 13 Finish each sentence by adding ed or ing to the word in dark print. Write words from Unit 13.

UNIT 13
invite
skate
taste
cared
smiling
loved
living
paste

1. **care** My grandfather _____ cared _____ for my sister and me while my parents were on a trip.

2. **live** While he was _____ living _____ with us, he was always making us laugh.

3. **smile** He seemed to be telling us jokes and _____ smiling _____ all the time.

4. **love** We _____ loved _____ to hear him tell stories.

UNIT 14
brave
mail
today
eight
obey
lake
paid
gate

B. Try this "word math." Write words from Unit 13.

5. inviting – ing = _____ invite
6. skated – ed = _____ skate
7. tasted – ed = _____ taste

C. UNIT 14 This story has eight misspelled words from Unit 14. Circle the misspelled words and write them correctly.

Ramón and his dog live near a laike. The dog is ate years old todai, but it isn't very breighve. Every time anyone comes with the meyle, the dog runs away and hides on the muddy banks. Ramón is tired of washing his dog every day, so he has peyed a friend to help him build a gait. Now the dog will have to obay Ramón and stay away from the water.

8. _____ lake
9. _____ eight
10. _____ today
11. _____ brave
12. _____ mail
13. _____ paid
14. _____ gate
15. _____ obey

Extra Practice • 73

Review: Units 15 and 16

Name _____
Review B: Units 15–16

UNIT
18

A. UNIT 15 Use words from Unit 15 to finish the sentences. Then circle the letters in each answer that spell /ē/.

UNIT 15
team
weak
between
busy
every
even
only
really

1. Chee was hoping to join a baseball _____ team _____ .

2. She kept _____ busy _____ practicing every day.

3. She _____ really _____ worked hard on her hitting.

4. Chee was so nervous when tryout day came, her knees were _____ weak _____ .

5. She felt _____ every _____ eye in the park on her as she took her turn at bat.

6. "If _____ only _____ I had practiced more," she thought.

7. Suddenly, the crowd started clapping as her ball dropped _____ between _____ the bleachers. She'd hit a home run!

UNIT 16
life
hide
bright
myself
buy
prize
nine
sight

B. UNIT 16 This story has eight mixed-up words. Underline them. Then write the words from Unit 16 correctly. Circle the letters in your answers that spell /ī/.

José was enin years old and had never won a zerip in his efil. All he wanted to do was ehdi, he said. His mom had a gribth idea to cheer him up. "I'll yub one for him lefmys," she said. The next day, the first giths to meet José's eyes was a trophy that said "Best Son in the World."

8. _____ nine
9. _____ prize
10. _____ life
11. _____ hide
12. _____ bright
13. _____ buy
14. _____ myself
15. _____ sight

74 • Extra Practice

UNIT 14 Follow the directions. Use words from Unit 14.

12. Write the three words that spell /ā/ with a-consonant-e.
Word order may vary.

brave   lake   gate

13. Write the two words that end with /ā/.
Word order may vary.

obey   today

Add letters that spell /ā/ to finish these words.

14. _ _ _ _ t   eight   **15.** g _ t _   gate

16. m _ _ l   mail   **17.** p _ _ d   paid

UNIT 15 Follow the directions. Use words from Unit 15.

18. Write the four words that end with /ē/.
Word order may vary.

busy   every

only   really

Add letters that spell /ē/ to finish these words.

19. t _ _ m   team   **20.** betw _ _ n   between

21. _ ven   even   **22.** ever _   every

Finish these sentences.

23. My room is ____ really ____ a mess!

24. I can't even walk ____ between ____ the bed and the desk.

UNIT 14
brave
mail
today
eight
obey
lake
gate
paid

UNIT 15
team
weak
between
busy
every
even
only
really

WORDS IN TIME

The word <u>mail</u> started out as the old word <u>male</u>. <u>Male</u> meant "bag" or "pouch." Why do you think the word <u>male</u> became <u>mail</u>?

77

TEACHING PLAN

Objectives To review words that demonstrate these sound-letter relationships: /ā/ a-consonant-e, *ai*, *ay*, *ey*, *eigh*. To review words that demonstrate these sound-letter relationships: /ē/ *ea*, *ee*, *e*, *y*.

1. Review the directions to the exercises on page 77. Remind the children that the answers to the exercises are to be found only among the sixteen review words on page 77.
2. Have the children complete the exercises independently. You may refer them to the **Writer's Guide** at the back of the book for a review of the spelling generalizations for Units 14 and 15.

WORDS IN TIME

Have a volunteer read **Words in Time** aloud. Ask the children why they think the word *male* became *mail*. (because the mail was carried in a bag or pouch) Tell the children that many common words in the English language come from French words.

As a COOPERATIVE LEARNING activity, have each group trace the history of one of the following words; *obey, eight, team,* and *paid.* One or two children within each group should find the word's origin and the others should find the word's current definition. The children may use the dictionary and books on word origins. Then have one child use the information to enter each word on a group chart showing its root word, its original meaning, and its current meaning. Other children should proofread for spelling, capitalization, and punctuation errors. Have the group display the chart on a bulletin board.

Review: Unit 17

Name ____

Review C: Unit 17•Test Exercise   UNIT 18

A. UNIT 17 Answer the questions with words from Unit 17.

UNIT 17
both
hello
joke
float
follow
sold
window
fold

1. What do you do if you don't sink? ____ float
2. What are you looking through if you can see outside? a ____ window
3. What do you say when you answer the phone? ____ hello
4. What do you do if you don't lead? ____ follow
5. What do you tell that makes people laugh? a ____ joke
6. What can make a piece of paper half as big? a ____ fold
7. If two people tie for first place, who gets a prize? ____ both
8. What means the opposite of <u>bought</u>? ____ sold

B. UNITS 13 – 17 Look at the word with a line under it. Fill in the circle marked **r** if the word is spelled right. Fill in the circle marked **w** if the word is spelled wrong.

1 Does it <u>taste</u> good?   ⓡ ⓦ   8 I am <u>rilly</u> happy.   ⓡ ⓦ
2 The best <u>teme</u> won.   ⓡ ⓦ   9 He can <u>scate</u> fast.   ⓡ ⓦ
3 That is a funny <u>joak</u>.   ⓡ ⓦ   10 She <u>soald</u> cars.   ⓡ ⓦ
4 She is <u>smiling</u>.   ⓡ ⓦ   11 She's an <u>only</u> child.   ⓡ ⓦ
5 They have <u>nine</u> cats.   ⓡ ⓦ   12 We will <u>hide</u> here.   ⓡ ⓦ
6 Did he <u>mail</u> the card?   ⓡ ⓦ   13 It's raining <u>todeigh</u>.   ⓡ ⓦ
7 She <u>pade</u> in cash.   ⓡ ⓦ   14 I will wash <u>myself</u>.   ⓡ ⓦ

Extra Practice • 75

EXTENDING THE LESSON

Show the children some simple acrostics using some of the spelling words, such as the following:

city
lake
asleep
skate
stare

Then have the children compose their own acrostics using some of the review words.

TEACHING PLAN

Objectives   To review words that demonstrate these sound-letter relationships: /ī/ *i-consonant-e, igh, i, y, uy;* to review words that demonstrate these sound-letter relationships: /ō/ *o-consonant-e, oa, o, ow.*

1. Review the directions to the exercises on page 78. Remind the children that the answers to the exercises are to be found only among the sixteen review words on page 78.
2. Have the children complete the exercises independently. You may refer them to the **Writer's Guide** at the back of the book for a review of the spelling generalizations for Units 16 and 17.
3. Review the children's answers on pages 76–78 orally, or have volunteers write them on the chalkboard.

UNIT 16

life
hide
bright
myself
buy
prize
nine
sight

UNIT 16   **Change the underlined letter or letters in each word to make a word from Unit 16.**

25. li<u>n</u>e _____ life
26. <u>it</u>self _____ myself
27. <u>w</u>ide _____ hide
28. l<u>igh</u>t _____ sight
29. <u>f</u>ine _____ nine
30. b<u>o</u>y _____ buy

Finish these sentences with words from Unit 16. Then circle the letters that spell /ī/ in the words.

31. I won a _____ pri(ze)

32. I was so proud of _____ m(y)self

33. I had a _____ br(igh)t _____ smile on my face.

UNIT 17

both
hello
joke
float
follow
sold
window
fold

UNIT 17   **Follow the directions. Use words from Unit 17. Write the words that are the opposite of these words.**

34. lead _____ follow
35. good-bye _____ hello
36. sink _____ float
37. bought _____ sold

Finish these sentences.

Just __38__ these directions. Hold this stick with __39__ hands. Stamp your foot and cough. What's the matter? Can't you get your motorcycle started?
Isn't that a funny __40__?

38. _____ follow
39. _____ both
40. _____ joke

Write the words that finish these sentences.

41. Please _____ follow _____ the leader.

42. Simon says open the _____ window

43. Simon says _____ fold _____ the paper in half.

Spelling and Reading
A Description

Read the following description. Look for the colorful words.

The painter sat in a small blue boat in the middle of the lake. A cool breeze was blowing, but she was warm in her bright red sweater and cap. The painter ate a fresh, juicy orange. Then she placed a clean, white canvas between her paint and her brushes.

The painter felt the weak rays of the sun turn warm. She watched a family of ducks swim into sight. The painter loved little ducks. She wanted to paint them.

Soon the painter saw two tall boats. They seemed to skate across the lake. Their white sails were floating on the wind, like clouds in the sky. The boats seemed to invite her to paint them. The painter grabbed a brush and started to paint.

Write the answers to the questions. *See answers below.*
Literal
1. In this description, where does the writer say the boat is?
2. What verb does the writer use to describe how the two tall boats moved across the lake? *Literal*
3. What does the writer mean by saying that the boats seemed to invite the painter to paint them? *Interpretive*
4. How does the painter feel about being on the lake? Why do you think as you do? *Critical*

Underline the review words in your answers. Check to see that you spelled the words correctly.

79

TEACHING PLAN

Objectives To analyze and respond to a description; to identify sensory details in a description; to proofread written answers for spelling.

1. Tell the children that they will read a description that includes a number of spelling words from Units 13 – 17. Explain that a good writer paints a picture with words. If the writer chooses his or her words with care, a word picture can seem as real as life. Ask the children to think of stories they have read in which descriptions were vivid enough to be real. Explain that the story on page 79 will serve as a model for their own writing.
2. Have the children read the description and try to visualize the scene the writer describes. Tell them to try to imagine what they might see, hear, smell, and feel if they were actually in the scene.
3. Have the children answer the questions independently. Tell them to underline the review words in the answers and to proofread the answers for spelling.
4. Spot-check the children's answers. Review answers orally.

Spelling and Reading Answers

1. The boat is in the middle of a lake. 2. skate 3. The writer means that the boats looked so pretty that they seemed as if they should be a painting. 4. Accept any reasonable answer. (Possible answers: happy, calm, relaxed; because she was painting things she enjoyed)

On this page, students will read:
• This Week's Words from the preceding five units;
• words reviewed in this unit;
• words that follow the generalizations taught in the preceding five units.

TEACHING PLAN

> **Objectives**   To identify sensory details used in a description; to evaluate illustrations for a description.

1. Have the children read the first paragraph of **Think and Discuss** on page 80. Ask them to study the illustrations on page 80. Have the children tell whether the illustrations match the scene they pictured as the read the description. Tell the children to recall past experiences that helped them "see" the writer's description in their minds. Then ask the children if they would have illustrated the description differently.

2. Have the children identify the describing words in the first paragraph of the story that tell what the writer saw and tasted.

3. Have the children read the rest of **Think and Discuss** independently, and answer the questions. Ask them to give examples of other vivid and colorful words the writer could have used to describe the scene.

4. Have the children read **Apply** at the bottom of page 80. Tell them that they will write a descriptive paragraph about their favorite food using some of the spelling words. Suggest that they write as if they were describing their favorite food to someone who may not be familiar with that food. Explain that their description should make the food sound so tasty that the person reading the description would want to taste the food immediately. Tell the children to be sure to use vivid and colorful words and phrases.

Spelling and Writing
A Description

Think and Discuss

Words to Help You Write
taste
paste
eight
weak
even
really
bright
sight
float
fold

In a description, a writer uses describing words. These words tell the reader what the writer has seen, heard, smelled, felt, or tasted.

Look at the pictures on this page. Do they show what you saw in your mind as you read the story on page 79? Read the first paragraph of the story. What describing words does the writer use to tell about the boat? What words does the writer use to describe the canvas? These words help the reader see what the writer saw. What sentence in the first paragraph tells the reader about taste?

Read the second paragraph on page 79. How does the writer describe the sun's rays? This description helps the reader feel the weather.

In a description, a writer can use verbs to help the reader see actions. What verbs in the last sentence of the story describe what the painter did?

Apply

Write a description of your favorite food to share with your classmates. Follow the writing guidelines on the next page.

80

Summarize Learning

Have the children identify the characteristics of a good description. (use of vivid and colorful words that appeal to the senses, details that make the word picture seem as real as life)

Think and Discuss **Answers**

A. small, blue
B. clean, white
C. The painter ate a fresh, juicy orange.
D. The weak rays turn warm.
E. grabbed (a brush), started to paint

Prewriting

- Think of your favorite food. The pictures on this page might help you.
- Make a chart with these five columns: <u>See</u>, <u>Hear</u>, <u>Touch</u>, <u>Smell</u>, <u>Taste</u>.
- List colorful words in each column that describe the food.

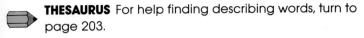 **THESAURUS** For help finding describing words, turn to page 203.

Composing

Use your chart to write the first draft of your description.

- Write a topic sentence that tells what your favorite food is.
- Write detail sentences about the food. Use colorful words from your chart that describe the food.

Revising

Read your paragraph and show it to a classmate. Follow these guidelines to improve your work. Use the editing and proofreading marks to show changes.

Editing

- Make sure your descriptions are clear.
- Make sure you used colorful words.

Proofreading

- Check your spelling and correct any mistakes.
- Check your capitalization and punctuation.

WRITER'S GUIDE If you need help with capitalization and punctuation, turn to pages 255-257.

Copy your story onto a clean paper. Write carefully and neatly.

Publishing

Share your description. Ask your classmates to tell which words make them want to taste your favorite food.

81

Editing and Proofreading Marks

≡	capitalize
⊙	make a period
∧	add something
⩘	add a comma
ℒ	take something away
◯	spell correctly
⁋	indent the paragraph
/	make a lowercase letter

Spelling and Writing — UNIT 18d

TEACHING PLAN

Objectives To write a descriptive paragraph using sensory details; to edit for content, style, and tone; to proofread for spelling, capitalization, and punctuation.

1. **Prewriting** Have the children select a food and then close their eyes to recall how it looks, smells, and tastes. Tell the children to complete the charts with vivid, colorful words that appeal to the senses. Suggest that they use the **Writer's Word Bank** to help them select descriptive words.

2. **Composing** Before the children begin composing, remind them that a paragraph must contain a topic that tells the main idea. Explain that the detail sentences in a paragraph tell about the topic. Remind the children to use colorful and vivid words that appeal to the senses. Have the children write the first drafts. They may use some spelling words listed on pages 76–78 or other spelling words in the paragraphs. Children may refer to the **Writer's Guide** for a definition and a model of a descriptive paragraph.

3. **Revising (Editing and Proofreading)** Have the children ask classmates to read the paragraphs to see whether they evoke a strong sense of what it is like to see, smell, and eat the food described. Children should consider their classmates' comments as they revise the paragraphs. Have the children follow the guidelines on page 81 to revise the paragraphs. Remind them to use the **Spelling Dictionary** to check the spelling.

For reinforcement in editing and proofreading, you may wish to use *Spelling and Writing Transparency 3.*

4. **Publishing** have the children share the paragraphs with the class.

Extra Practice: Dictionary/Proofreading

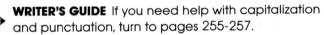

Name _____

Dictionary and Proofreading 3 — UNIT 18

Using the Dictionary to Spell and Write

A. The pronunciations below show words that you know. Use these words to answer the questions.

/păst/	/āt/	/ē'vən/	/wēk/
/brīt/	/bī/	/hĕ-lō'/	/wĭn'dō/

paste, eight, weak, even, bright, buy, window, hello, loved, every, busy, sight, both, follow, cared, obey

1. What is the opposite of <u>dark</u>? __bright__
2. What do you use to glue things? __paste__
3. What's another way of saying "hi"? __hello__
4. What's a piece of glass in a wall? __window__
5. What's six plus two? __eight__
6. What's the opposite of <u>strong</u>? __weak__
7. What's the opposite of <u>sell</u>? __buy__
8. What's the opposite of <u>odd</u>? __even__

Proofreading

B. Circle the eight misspelled words in this story. Then spell the words correctly.

Theo (luvd) his dog Mitch. Mitch (caird) for Theo in many ways and knew how to (obeigh) orders (Eviry) day they went for a walk near a (bizee) street. Mitch would lead and Theo would (follo) Theo had no (site) so Mitch took care of them (boath)

9. __loved__   10. __cared__   11. __obey__
12. __Every__   13. __busy__   14. __follow__
15. __sight__   16. __both__

76 • Extra Practice

For additional practice in using the dictionary to spell and write and in proofreading, you may wish to assign *Dictionary and Proofreading Master 3.*

UNIT 18 *Review* **81**

ENRICHMENT ACTIVITIES

Home activities may be assigned to children of all ability levels. The activities provide opportunities for children to use their spelling words in new contexts.

For the Home

The children may complete home activities independently or with the assistance of a relative or friend in the home.

1. **Language Arts/Writing a Limerick** Tell the children to write a limerick using some of the spelling words. Tell them a limerick is a humorous verse consisting of five lines and having a rhyme scheme of *aabba*. Explain that this means that lines 1, 2, and 5 rhyme, and lines 3 and 4 rhyme. Tell the children that a limerick also has a certain rhythm. Provide this example:

   There once was a sad-looking clown
   Who went everywhere with a frown.
   When told he should smile
   He said, "Not my style.
   But instead I'll go 'round upside-down."

   Tell the children to use as many spelling words as possible in the limericks. Suggest that they share their limericks with a friend or relative.

2. **Language Arts/Writing a Why-Tale** Tell the children that many stories have been told to explain why natural things happen, such as why we have snow or why giraffes don't bark or roar. Point out that long ago, people often made up stories to explain such things. In one such story, whenever it snowed, it meant a woman who lived in the sky was shaking her quilt filled with feathers. Tell the children to write explanations for why the tiger has stripes, why lions roar, or why ice melts. They should include other spelling words and use their imaginations to make the stories interesting. Suggest that children read their stories to a friend.

3. **Social Studies/Writing Consumer Guidelines** Tell the children to discuss guidelines for being a smart shopper with a family member. Otherwise, children should generate their own list of guidelines, using as many spelling words as possible. Each guideline should tell ways to get a good value for one's money. For example, *Don't buy everything in sight.* Children might bring their lists in to share with the class.

4. **Health/Writing About Fitness** Have the children write a paragraph telling how they plan to keep fit for life. Ask them to scan the list of review words for ideas about sports and activities they may want to write about. They should state their age *today* (most will be *eight* or *nine* years old), and tell how they believe their plan will affect their future. Have them give their composition a title that includes the word *life*.

EVALUATION

Unit Test

1. *invite*   We will *invite* them to the party.   *invite*
2. *skate*   Raoul will *skate* to my house later.   *skate*
3. *taste*   The boys *taste* the soup.   *taste*
4. *cared*   My grandmother *cared* for me.   *cared*
5. *smiling*   Max is *smiling* at something funny.   *smiling*
6. *loved*   I *loved* the book you sent me.   *loved*
7. *living*   Joanne is *living* in Mexico.   *living*
8. *paste*   We could *paste* the pictures on a piece of cardboard.   *paste*
9. *brave*   When I had my shots, I was very *brave*. *brave*
10. *mail*   I wait for the *mail* to come every day.   *mail*
11. *today*   Perhaps my letter will come *today*.   *today*
12. *eight*   An octopus has *eight* arms.   *eight*
13. *obey*   When we drive, we must *obey* the laws.   *obey*
14. *lake*   Billy likes to swim in the *lake*.   *lake*
15. *gate*   The *gate* was open.   *gate*
16. *paid*   My dad *paid* for our carnival rides.   *paid*
17. *team*   The *team* has won every game.   *team*
18. *weak*   He was too *weak* to stand.   *weak*
19. *between*   I walked *between* Sue and Peg.   *between*
20. *busy*   We ate at the *busy* restaurant.   *busy*
21. *every*   I think *every* seat is taken.   *every*
22. *even*   I was so full, I couldn't *even* eat dessert.   *even*
23. *only*   We have *only* two puppies left.   *only*
24. *really*   The poem you wrote is *really* beautiful.   *really*
25. *life*   The Pilgrims did not have an easy *life* in the new land.   *life*
26. *hide*   Everyone will *hide* at the surprise party.   *hide*
27. *bright*   The baby blinked at the *bright* lights.   *bright*
28. *myself*   I taught *myself* to ride a skateboard.   *myself*
29. *buy*   We need to *buy* some food.   *buy*
30. *prize*   Ray's story won first *prize* in the contest.   *prize*
31. *nine*   I put my light out at *nine* o'clock.   *nine*
32. *sight*   The city lights are a beautiful *sight*.   *sight*
33. *both*   I took *both* books home from the library.   *both*
34. *hello*   My friend Ina came by to say *hello*.   *hello*
35. *joke*   I have heard that old *joke* before.   *joke*
36. *float*   You can *float* in the water.   *float*
37. *follow*   We will *follow* the path.   *follow*
38. *sold*   We *sold* bread to raise money.   *sold*
39. *window*   Please open the *window*.   *window*
40. *fold*   I helped *fold* the clothes.   *fold*

Mastery and Bonus Words Review and Assessment

For additional practice you may wish to assign *Mastery Words Review Master: Units 13–17* or *Bonus Words Review Master: Units 13–17*. To assess children's spelling ability with these words, use *Mastery Words Test: Units 13–17* or *Bonus Words Test: Units 13–17*.

Mastery Words Review

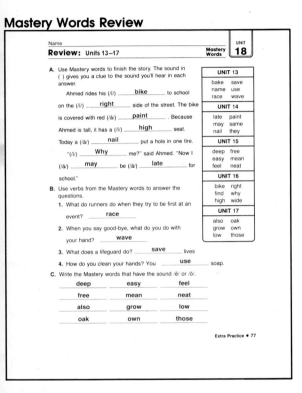

Name _____
Review: Units 13–17   Mastery Words / UNIT 18

A. Use Mastery words to finish the story. The sound in ( ) gives you a clue to the sound you'll hear in each answer.

Ahmed rides his (/ī/) __bike__ to school on the (/ī/) __right__ side of the street. The bike is covered with red (/ā/) __paint__ . Because Ahmed is tall, it has a (/ī/) __high__ seat. Today a (/ā/) __nail__ put a hole in one tire. "(/ī/) __Why__ me?" said Ahmed. "Now I (/ā/) __may__ be (/ā/) __late__ for school."

UNIT 13
bake · save
name · use
race · wave

UNIT 14
late · paint
may · same
nail · they

UNIT 15
deep · free
easy · mean
feel · neat

UNIT 16
bike · right
find · why
high · wide

UNIT 17
also · oak
grow · own
low · those

B. Use verbs from the Mastery words to answer the questions.
1. What do runners do when they try to be first at an event? __race__
2. When you say good-bye, what do you do with your hand? __wave__
3. What does a lifeguard do? __save__ lives
4. How do you clean your hands? You __use__ soap.

C. Write the Mastery words that have the sound /ē/ or /ō/.

deep	easy	feel
free	mean	neat
also	grow	low
oak	own	those

Extra Practice • 77

Bonus Words Review

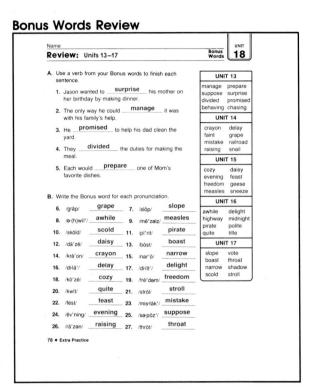

Name _____
Review: Units 13–17   Bonus Words / UNIT 18

A. Use a verb from your Bonus words to finish each sentence.
1. Jason wanted to __surprise__ his mother on her birthday by making dinner.
2. The only way he could __manage__ it was with his family's help.
3. He __promised__ to help his dad clean the yard.
4. They __divided__ the duties for making the meal.
5. Each would __prepare__ one of Mom's favorite dishes.

UNIT 13
manage · prepare
suppose · surprise
divided · promised
behaving · chasing

UNIT 14
crayon · delay
faint · grape
mistake · railroad
raising · snail

UNIT 15
cozy · daisy
evening · feast
freedom · geese
measles · sneeze

UNIT 16
awhile · delight
highway · midnight
pirate · polite
quite · title

UNIT 17
slope · vote
boast · throat
narrow · shadow
scold · stroll

B. Write the Bonus word for each pronunciation.
6. /grāp/ __grape__ 7. /slōp/ __slope__
8. /ə·(h)wīl'/ __awhile__ 9. /mē'zəlz/ __measles__
10. /skōld/ __scold__ 11. /pī'rit/ __pirate__
12. /dā'zē/ __daisy__ 13. /bōst/ __boast__
14. /krā'on/ __crayon__ 15. /nar'ō/ __narrow__
16. /di·lā'/ __delay__ 17. /di·līt'/ __delight__
18. /kō'zē/ __cozy__ 19. /frē'dəm/ __freedom__
20. /kwīt/ __quite__ 21. /strōl/ __stroll__
22. /fēst/ __feast__ 23. /mis·tāk'/ __mistake__
24. /ēv'ning/ __evening__ 25. /sə·pōz'/ __suppose__
26. /rā'zən/ __raising__ 27. /thrōt/ __throat__

78 • Extra Practice

Mastery Words Test

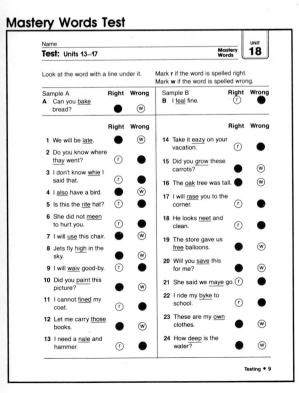

Name _____
Test: Units 13–17   Mastery Words / UNIT 18

Look at the word with a line under it. Mark **r** if the word is spelled right. Mark **w** if the word is spelled wrong.

Sample A — **A** Can you <u>bake</u> bread? ● (w)
Sample B — **B** I <u>feal</u> fine. (r) ●

	Right	Wrong
1 We will be <u>late</u>.	●	(w)
2 Do you know where <u>thay</u> went?	(r)	●
3 I don't know <u>whie</u> I said that.	(r)	●
4 I <u>also</u> have a bird.	●	(w)
5 Is this the <u>rite</u> hat?	(r)	●
6 She did not <u>meen</u> to hurt you.	(r)	●
7 I will <u>use</u> this chair.	●	(w)
8 Jets fly <u>high</u> in the sky.	●	(w)
9 I will <u>waiv</u> good-by.	(r)	●
10 Did you <u>paint</u> this picture?	●	(w)
11 I cannot <u>fined</u> my coat.	(r)	●
12 Let me carry <u>those</u> books.	●	(w)
13 I need a <u>nale</u> and hammer.	(r)	●

	Right	Wrong
14 Take it <u>eazy</u> on your vacation.	(r)	●
15 Did you <u>grow</u> these carrots?	●	(w)
16 The <u>oak</u> tree was tall.	●	(w)
17 I will <u>rase</u> you to the corner.	(r)	●
18 He looks <u>neet</u> and clean.	(r)	●
19 The store gave us <u>free</u> balloons.	●	(w)
20 Will you <u>save</u> this for me?	●	(w)
21 She said we <u>maye</u> go.	(r)	●
22 I ride my <u>byke</u> to school.	(r)	●
23 These are my <u>own</u> clothes.	●	(w)
24 How <u>deep</u> is the water?	●	(w)

Testing • 9

Bonus Words Test

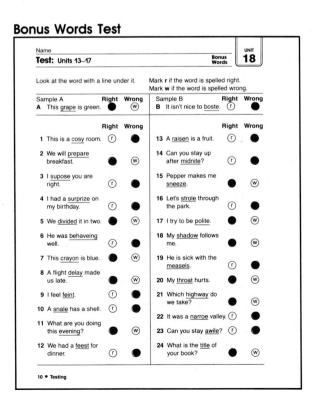

Name _____
Test: Units 13–17   Bonus Words / UNIT 18

Look at the word with a line under it. Mark **r** if the word is spelled right. Mark **w** if the word is spelled wrong.

Sample A — **A** This <u>grape</u> is green. ● (w)
Sample B — **B** It isn't nice to <u>boste</u>. (r) ●

	Right	Wrong
1 This is a <u>cosy</u> room.	(r)	●
2 We will <u>prepare</u> breakfast.	●	(w)
3 I <u>supose</u> you are right.	(r)	●
4 I had a <u>surprize</u> on my birthday.	(r)	●
5 We <u>divided</u> it in two.	●	(w)
6 He was <u>behaveing</u> well.	(r)	●
7 This <u>crayon</u> is blue.	●	(w)
8 A flight <u>delay</u> made us late.	●	(w)
9 I feel <u>feint</u>.	(r)	●
10 A <u>snale</u> has a shell.	(r)	●
11 What are you doing this <u>evening</u>?	●	(w)
12 We had a <u>feest</u> for dinner.	(r)	●

	Right	Wrong
13 A <u>raisen</u> is a fruit.	(r)	●
14 Can you stay up after <u>midnite</u>?	(r)	●
15 Pepper makes me <u>sneeze</u>.	●	(w)
16 Let's <u>strole</u> through the park.	(r)	●
17 I try to be <u>polite</u>.	●	(w)
18 My <u>shadow</u> follows me.	●	(w)
19 He is sick with the <u>measels</u>.	(r)	●
20 My <u>throat</u> hurts.	●	(w)
21 Which <u>highway</u> do we take?	●	(w)
22 It was a <u>narroe</u> valley.	(r)	●
23 Can you stay <u>awile</u>?	(r)	●
24 What is the <u>title</u> of your book?	●	(w)

10 • Testing

NOTES

Six-Week Evaluation

Look at the word with a line under it.
Mark **r** if the word is spelled right.
Mark **w** if the word is spelled wrong.

Sample A	Right	Wrong		Sample B	Right	Wrong
A She wrote that <u>sentance</u>.	(r)	(w) filled	**B** You may use my <u>pencil</u>.	(r)	(w)
1 She will <u>invit</u> us to go.	(r)	(w)	**11** She was <u>buzy</u> working.	(r)	(w)
2 They <u>cared</u> for our cat.	(r)	(w)	**12** Make each pile <u>even</u>.	(r)	(w)
3 We like <u>liveing</u> here.	(r)	(w)	**13** The sun is too <u>birght</u>.	(r)	(w)
4 <u>Paste</u> it on the paper.	(r)	(w)	**14** I will go all by <u>myself</u>.	(r)	(w)
5 Is there any <u>mail</u> for me?	(r)	(w)	**15** She wants to <u>beye</u> a bike.	(r)	(w)
6 She will play ball <u>tooday</u>.	(r)	(w)	**16** I got first <u>priz</u>.	(r)	(w)
7 I saw <u>aite</u> eggs in the box.	(r)	(w)	**17** That was a funny <u>joke</u>.	(r)	(w)
8 I will open the <u>gayt</u>.	(r)	(w)	**18** The boat will not <u>float</u>.	(r)	(w)
9 Our <u>team</u> lost the game.	(r)	(w)	**19** Try to <u>folow</u> the tracks.	(r)	(w)
10 Put it <u>between</u> the two chairs.	(r)	(w)	**20** The store <u>sold</u> kites.	(r)	(w)

FORM A TEST 3

Administering the Test

1. Tell the children that today they will take a spelling test on some of the words they have studied in Units 13–17. Pass out the test papers. Tell the children to leave them turned upside down until you are ready to begin.

2. Have the children turn their tests over. Direct their attention to Sample A. Read this sentence: She wrote that *sentence.* Point out that *sentence* is spelled wrong, so the circle under *Wrong* is filled in. The *w* stands for *Wrong.* If the word were spelled correctly, the circle under *Right* would be filled in. The *r* stands for *Right.*

3. Now direct the children's attention to Sample B. Read this sentence: You may use my *pencil.* Ask a child to tell you if *pencil* is spelled right by spelling the word—*p-e-n-c-i-l.* Repeat the right spelling, *p-e-n-c-i-l,* and have the children fill in circle *r* in pencil.

4. After you have checked to see that all children have completed Sample B correctly, have the children proceed with the test.

Evaluating the Results

Use the following **Answer Key** to correct the children's tests and to determine whether they need more practice with particular units. The chart shows the units in which each answer word is taught.

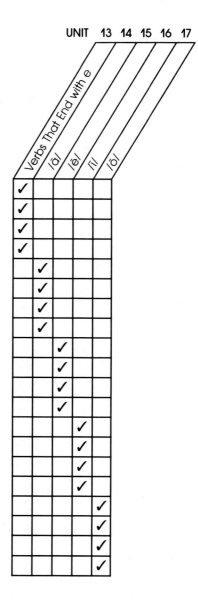

ANSWER KEY

1	r	**w**
2	**r**	w
3	r	**w**
4	**r**	w
5	**r**	w
6	r	**w**
7	r	**w**
8	r	**w**
9	**r**	w
10	**r**	w
11	r	**w**
12	**r**	w
13	r	**w**
14	**r**	w
15	r	**w**
16	r	**w**
17	**r**	w
18	**r**	w
19	r	**w**
20	**r**	w

Look at the word with a line under it.
Mark **r** if the word is spelled right.
Mark **w** if the word is spelled wrong.

		Right	Wrong
Sample A			
A	They will <u>bild</u> a new house.	(r)	(w) ●

		Right	Wrong
Sample B			
B	There is <u>dust</u> in the air.	(r)	(w)

1 The <u>key</u> opened the door. (r) (w)

2 Ask her to <u>speek</u> to our group. (r) (w)

3 We were <u>lucky</u> to win. (r) (w)

4 We live in a large <u>city</u>. (r) (w)

5 He has a pen and a <u>pencle</u>. (r) (w)

6 She wrote a long <u>sentance</u>. (r) (w)

7 She likes to roller <u>skait</u>. (r) (w)

8 Did you <u>invit</u> him to the party? (r) (w)

9 They <u>cared</u> for the garden. (r) (w)

10 Everyone is here <u>tedey</u>. (r) (w)

11 There was a letter in the <u>male</u>. (r) (w)

12 She has <u>ate</u> marbles. (r) (w)

13 Our <u>team</u> will win. (r) (w)

14 I feel <u>week</u> and hungry. (r) (w)

15 Stand <u>between</u> us. (r) (w)

16 The dog will <u>hide</u> from us. (r) (w)

17 It is a <u>brite</u> day. (r) (w)

18 I will go <u>myself</u>. (r) (w)

19 He said <u>hello</u> to me. (r) (w)

20 The <u>joak</u> was on us. (r) (w)

FORM B TEST 2

Administering the Test

1. Tell the children that today they will take a spelling test on some of the words they have studied in Units 10–17. Pass out the test papers. Tell the children to leave them turned upside down until you are ready to begin.

2. Have the children turn their tests over. Direct the children's attention to Sample A. Read this sentence: They will *build* a new house. Point out that *build* is spelled wrong, so the circle under *Wrong* is filled in. The *w* stands for *Wrong*. If the word were spelled correctly, the circle under *Right* would be filled in. The *r* stands for *Right*.

3. Now direct the children's attention to Sample B. Read this sentence: There is *dust* in the air. Ask a child to tell you if *dust* is spelled right by spelling the word—*d-u-s-t*. Repeat the right spelling, *d-u-s-t*, and have the children fill in circle *r* in pencil.

4. After you have checked to see that all children have completed Sample B correctly, have the children proceed with the test.

Evaluating the Results

Use the following **Answer Key** to correct the children's tests and to determine whether they need more practice with particular units. The chart shows the units in which the answer word is taught.

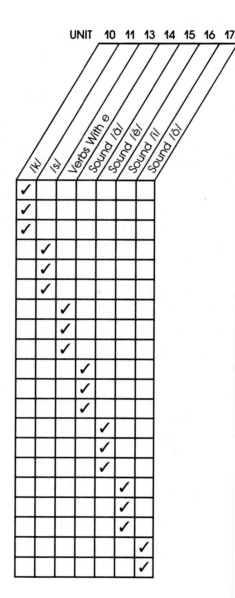

		ANSWER KEY	
1	● r	●	ⓦ w
2	ⓡ r		● w
3	● r		ⓦ w
4	● r		ⓦ w
5	ⓡ r		● w
6	ⓡ r		● w
7	ⓡ r		● w
8	ⓡ r		● w
9	● r		ⓦ w
10	ⓡ r		● w
11	ⓡ r		● w
12	ⓡ r		● w
13	● r		ⓦ w
14	ⓡ r		● w
15	● r		ⓦ w
16	● r		ⓦ w
17	ⓡ r		● w
18	● r		ⓦ w
19	● r		ⓦ w
20	ⓡ r		● w

MIDYEAR TEST

This Week's Words

1. *bring*   Please *bring* me some water.   *bring*
2. *happy*   Aunt Laura was *happy* to see us.   *happy*
3. *spell*   Gordie knows how to *spell* that word.   *spell*
4. *add*   You must *add* up these numbers.   *add*
5. *skinned*   Nate *skinned* his elbow.   *skinned*
6. *planning*   Our class is *planning* a trip to the museum.   *planning*
7. *floor*   The book fell on the *floor*.   *floor*
8. *string*   Penny tied *string* around the box.   *string*
9. *lift*   Help me *lift* this box.   *lift*
10. *build*   Let's *build* a snowman.   *build*
11. *catch*   I hope I don't *catch* a cold.   *catch*
12. *together*   Nancy and Mimi play *together*.   *together*
13. *pictures*   Brenda draws *pictures* of horses.   *pictures*
14. *guesses*   I will give you three *guesses*.   *guesses*
15. *desks*   Let's push our *desks* together.   *desks*
16. *bridge*   The *bridge* crosses the river.   *bridge*
17. *giant*   Dinosaurs were *giant* animals.   *giant*
18. *quick*   Linda was *quick* to give the answer.   *quick*
19. *listen*   Let's *listen* to some music.   *listen*
20. *piece*   We fed the dog a *piece* of meat.   *piece*
21. *smiling*   Everyone was *smiling* at the baby.   *smiling*
22. *awake*   Paul stayed *awake* until 9:00.   *awake*
23. *every*   We work hard *every* day.   *every*
24. *myself*   Sometimes I sing to *myself*.   *myself*
25. *follow*   Don't let the dog *follow* us.   *follow*

Mastery Words

1. *last*   Mindy studied her spelling words *last* night.   *last*
2. *fell*   Andrew *fell* off his bike.   *fell*
3. *still*   His leg *still* hurts.   *still*
4. *from*   Sandy got a letter *from* her cousin.   *from*
5. *start*   Don't *start* until everyone is here.   *start*
6. *help*   Ms. Biggs will *help* us clean up.   *help*
7. *want*   David and Miguel *want* to play checkers.   *want*
8. *push*   You must *push* hard to open the heavy door.   *push*

9. *lights*   Please turn off the *lights*.   *lights*
10. *glasses*   Martha drank two *glasses* of milk.   *glasses*
11. *give*   I want to *give* you this present.   *give*.
12. *just*   Ted got there *just* in time.   *just*
13. *jump*   Missy likes to *jump* rope.   *jump*
14. *sick*   Pat was *sick* last week.   *sick*
15. *face*   Chuck has a sad look on his *face*.   *face*
16. *name*   That girl's *name* is Lisa.   *name*
17. *they*   I hope *they* get here soon.   *they*
18. *easy*   This game is *easy* to learn.   *easy*
19. *those*   These oranges are bigger than *those* are.   *those*
20. *grow*   We *grow* vegetables in our garden.   *grow*

Bonus Words

1. *recess*   The children played tag at *recess*.   *recess*
2. *wrapping*   My brother is *wrapping* Mom's present.   *wrapping*
3. *scratch*   That cat will not *scratch* you.   *scratch*
4. *spread*   Pia *spread* peanut butter on her toast.   *spread*
5. *adult*   An *adult* must go with you on the plane.   *adult*
6. *whether*   He doesn't know *whether* he will go or not.   *whether*
7. *sandwiches*   Beth made *sandwiches* for lunch.   *sandwiches*
8. *parents*   Jan's *parents* are always so friendly.   *parents*
9. *gym*   We can play volleyball in the *gym*.   *gym*
10. *package*   Todd bought a *package* of sunflower seeds.   *package*
11. *secret*   Brad would not tell his *secret* to anybody.   *secret*
12. *promised*   Karen *promised* never to tease the dog again.   *promised*
13. *surprise*   Let's fix breakfast and *surprise* Mom.   *surprise*
14. *crayon*   Adam used a red *crayon* to make the sign.   *crayon*
15. *throat*   Eubie has a sore *throat* and a fever.   *throat*

NOTES

Compound Words

Unit Materials

Instruction and Practice

Pupil Book	pages 82–85
Teacher's Edition	
Teaching Plans	pages 82–85
Trial Test	pages 81E–81F
Unit Test	page 85B
Dictation Test	page 85B

Testing

Teacher's Edition	
Trial Test	pages 81E–81F
Unit Test	page 85B
Dictation Test	page 85B

Additional Resources

PRACTICE AND REINFORCEMENT
Extra Practice Master 19: This Week's Words
Extra Practice Master 19: Mastery Words
Extra Practice Master 19: Bonus Words
LEP Practice Master 19
Spelling and Language Master 19
Study Steps to Learn a Word Master

RETEACHING FOLLOW-UP
Reteaching Follow-up Master 19A:
    Discovering Spelling Ideas
Reteaching Follow-up Master 19B: Word
    Shapes
LEP Reteaching Follow-up Master 19

TEACHING AIDS
Spelling Generalizations Transparency 16

Visit our Web site
http://www.hbschool.com

**Click on the
SPELLING
banner to
find activities
for this unit.**

Learner Objectives

Spelling

- To spell compound words.
- To alphabetize.

Reading

- To follow written directions.
- To use context clues for word identification.
- To use a dictionary to locate information.
- To recognize consonant clusters.
- To use a dictionary for word meaning.

Writing

- To write a news story.
- To use the writing process.
- To proofread for spelling, capitalization, and punctuation.
- To write legible manuscript and cursive letters.

Listening

- To listen to identify rhyming words.
- To listen to identify words as compounds or as two words in sentence context.
- To follow oral directions.

Speaking

- To speak clearly to a group.
- To respond to a question.
- To contribute ideas and information in group discussions.
- To express feelings and ideas about a piece of writing.
- To present a news story.

THIS WEEK'S WORDS

anyone
anyway
bedroom
cannot
everybody
football
grandfather
grandmother
herself
himself
maybe
outside
playground
sometimes
yourself

MASTERY WORDS

into
within
anything
onto
without
inside

BONUS WORDS

everyday
forever
meanwhile
downstairs
everywhere
cupboard
whoever
ourselves

Assignment Guide

This guide shows how you teach a typical spelling unit in either a five-day or a three-day sequence, while providing for individual differences. **Boldface type** indicates essential classwork. Steps shown in light type may be done in class or assigned as homework.

Five Days	○ = average spellers ☆ = better spellers ✓ = slower spellers	Three Days
Day **1** (a)	○ ☆ **Take This Week's Words Trial Test and correct** ○ ✓ **Take Mastery Word Trial Test and correct** ○ ☆ **Read This Week's Words and discuss generalization page 82**	Day **1**
Day **2** (b)	○ **Complete Spelling Practice page 83** ○ ✓ Complete Extra Practice Master 19: This Week's Words (optional) ✓ Complete Spelling on Your Own: Mastery Words page 85 ☆ **Take Bonus Word Trial Test and correct**	Day **1**
Day **3** (c)	○ ☆ ✓ **Complete Spelling and Language page 84** ○ ☆ ✓ Complete Writing on Your Own page 84 ○ ☆ ✓ **Complete Using the Dictionary to Spell and Write page 84** ○ ✓ Take Midweek Test (optional) ☆ Complete Spelling on Your Own: Bonus Words page 85 ○ ✓ Complete Spelling and Language Master 19 (optional)	Day **2**
Day **4** (d)	○ Complete Spelling on Your Own: This Week's Words page 85 ✓ Complete Extra Practice Master 19: Mastery Words (optional) ☆ Complete Extra Practice Master 19: Bonus Words (optional)	Day **2**
Day **5** (e)	○ **Take Unit Test on This Week's Words** ○ Complete Reteaching Follow-up Masters 19A and 19B (optional) ○ ✓ **Take Unit Test on Mastery Words** ☆ **Take Unit Test on Bonus Words**	Day **3**

Enrichment Activities for the **classroom** and for the **home** included at the end of this unit may be assigned selectively on any day of the week.

INTRODUCING THE UNIT

Establish Readiness for Learning

Tell the children that they will learn to spell words that are made up of two smaller words. They will apply what they learn to This Week's Words and use some of those words to write a news story.

Assess Children's Spelling Ability

Administer the Trial Test before the children study This Week's Words. Use the test sentences provided. Say each word and use it in a sentence. Then repeat the word. Have the children write the words on a separate sheet of paper or in their spelling notebooks. Test sentences are also provided for Mastery and Bonus words.

Have the children check their own work by listening to you read the spelling of the words

or by referring to This Week's Words in the left column of the **Pupil Book.** For each misspelled word, have the children follow the **Study Steps to Learn a Word** on page 1 in the **Pupil Book** or use the copying master to study and write the words. Children should record the number correct on their **Progress Report.**

Trial Test Sentences

This Week's Words

1. *anyone*   Did *anyone* remember to feed the fish?   *anyone*
2. *anyway*   Carly doesn't want to go *anyway.*   *anyway*
3. *bedroom*   Tammy cleaned her *bedroom.*   *bedroom*
4. *cannot*   We *cannot* find the parrot. *cannot*
5. *everybody*   Georgia wants *everybody* to come to her birthday party.   *everybody*

6. **football** Gina's family watches *football* games on TV. **football**

7. **grandfather** Daryl's *grandfather* came to visit. **grandfather**

8. **grandmother** Francie's *grandmother* lives in Philadelphia. **grandmother**

9. **herself** Yolanda is always singing to *herself*. **herself**

10. **himself** Mike wants to go by *himself*. **himself**

11. **maybe** If we ask Pablo, *maybe* he will help us. **maybe**

12. **outside** Chad and Howie played *outside* all day. **outside**

13. **playground** Everyone was at the *playground*. **playground**

14. **sometimes** Glenn only makes mistakes *sometimes*. **sometimes**

15. **yourself** Please don't burn *yourself*. **yourself**

Mastery Words

1. **into** If you are cold, go back *into* the house. **into**

2. **within** All children must be kept *within* the playground area during recess. **within**

3. **anything** Sam doesn't have *anything* to do. **anything**

4. **onto** The baby climbed *onto* his mother's lap. **onto**

5. **without** Don't go out *without* your jacket. **without**

6. **inside** We had to stay *inside* because it was raining. **inside**

Bonus Words

1. **everyday** Megan wore her *everyday* shoes to play outside. **everyday**

2. **forever** Carla would like to stay at camp *forever*. **forever**

3. **meanwhile** I'll do the dishes, and *meanwhile*, you sweep the floor. **meanwhile**

4. **downstairs** The furnace is *downstairs* in the basement. **downstairs**

5. **everywhere** We looked *everywhere* for her pen. **everywhere**

6. **cupboard** Put the dishes in the *cupboard*. **cupboard**

7. **whoever** Mrs. Graham wants *whoever* spilled the milk to mop it up. **whoever**

8. **ourselves** We'll do it *ourselves*. **ourselves.**

Apply Prior Learning

Have the children be spelling detectives. Tell them that they can discover spelling generalizations about compound words by applying what they already know. Write the words *into, without,* and *anything* on the chalkboard. Ask the children to look at the words and draw conclusions. (Each word is made up of two smaller words.) Ask the children if they know what these words are called. (compound words) Tell the children that they will learn to write words that are made up of two other words. Explain that they can use these words in a variety of spelling tasks: writing stories, writing letters, or writing a social studies report.

FOCUS

- Relates to prior learning
- Draws relationships
- Applies spelling generalizations to new contexts

FOR CHILDREN WITH SPECIAL NEEDS

Learning Difficulties

Children with visual-spatial and visual analysis deficits may have trouble recognizing the beginnings and endings of words. The following strategy emphasizes the spacing of words in sentences.

Draw the child's attention to the meaning of a compound word. Tell the child that although a compound word is made up of two words, each of which has a separate meaning, when the words are combined to form a compound word, the compound word has a meaning of its own. A word that is written with no space between its component words is a compound word.

Use this opportunity to focus on the spelling of the component words if the child continues to make errors in his or her spelling.

Have the child complete sentences using This Week's Words. Provide additional visual cues for spacing and

spelling by making a space for each letter of the word and, if necessary, each word in the sentence as follows:

After school I go to the └┴┴┴┘ground.
My grand└┴┴┴┴┴┘ lives
by └┴┴┘self.

Children can check their own or each other's work if you write the words on the chalkboard or on individual cards.

Limited English Proficiency

To help limited English proficient children work with the spelling generalizations for Unit 19, you may wish to refer to the booklet "Suggestions and Activities for Limited English Proficient Students."

TEACHING PLAN

Objective   To spell compound words.

1. Have the children look at the picture on page 82. Ask the children to notice the words on the children's T-shirts. Have volunteers look at each pair of children, read the two words on their T-shirts, and then read the compound word formed by the two words.
2. Read the generalization on page 82 aloud.

You may wish to introduce the lesson by using **Spelling Generalizations Transparency 19.**

3. Have volunteers read This Week's Words aloud. Remind the children that when they read compounds, just as when they spell compounds, they should look for the smaller words that make up the compound word. As each word is read, have the children identify the two words that make up the compound.

You may wish to assign **LEP Practice Master 19** for reinforcement in writing spelling words.

---

19 **Compound Words**

THIS WEEK'S WORDS

1. anyone
2. anyway
3. bedroom
4. cannot
5. everybody
6. football
7. grandfather
8. grandmother
9. herself
10. himself
11. maybe
12. outside
13. playground
14. sometimes
15. yourself

82

This Week's Words

Sometimes two words are put together to make a new word. The new word is called a **compound word.**

All the words this week are compound words. Remember how the smaller words that make up each word are spelled. That will make writing the long word easier.

Extra Practice: This Week's Words

Name
Extra Practice   This Week's Words   UNIT **19**

Draw a line from each word on the left to a word on the right to make This Week's Words. Write each compound word in the blank.

1. any	self	1. _____
2. foot	side	2. football
3. grand	one	3. grandfather
4. your	father	4. yourself
5. out	ball	5. outside

1. anyone
2. football
3. grandfather
4. yourself
5. outside

6. bed	mother	6. bedroom
7. play	self	7. playground
8. grand	room	8. grandmother
9. every	ground	9. everybody
10. him	body	10. himself

6. bedroom
7. playground
8. grandmother
9. everybody
10. himself

11. any	times	11. anyway
12. her	not	12. herself
13. some	be	13. sometimes
14. can	way	14. cannot
15. may	self	15. maybe

11. anyway
12. herself
13. sometimes
14. cannot
15. maybe

anyone	anyway	bedroom	cannot	everybody
football	grandfather	grandmother	herself	himself
maybe	outside	playground	sometimes	yourself

Extra Practice • 79

Extra Practice: Mastery Words

Name
Extra Practice   Mastery Words   UNIT **19**

A. There are five words in each box. Use them to write three compound words that are Mastery words.

in	any	
to	thing	side

1. into
2. anything
3. inside

to	on	with
in	out	

4. onto
5. without
6. within

B. Now use the words you wrote to finish these sentences.

7. The cat jumped ___onto___ the chair.

8. There is a puppy ___inside___ that basket.

9. Mrs. Wayne left work ___without___ her umbrella.

10. Is there ___anything___ wrong?

11. I live ___within___ two miles of him.

12. Jean threw the paper ___into___ the basket.

into
anything
within
onto
without
inside

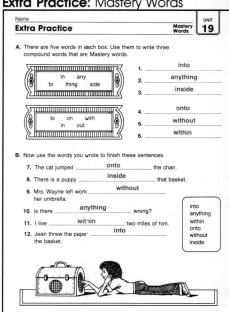

80 • Extra Practice

Spelling Practice

A. Follow the directions. Use This Week's Words.

1. Add a word from the red box to a word in the green box. Write six compound words.

bed	may	play
can	foot	some

ball	not	times
room	be	ground

bedroom	maybe	playground
cannot	football	sometimes

2. Write two different words made from <u>any</u> and another word.

anyone	anyway

3. Write three words made from <u>self</u> and another word.

herself	himself	yourself

4. Write the two words that name your parent's parents.

grandfather	grandmother

5. The first part rhymes with <u>day</u>. The second part rhymes with <u>sound</u>. Write the compound word. Then write the three consonant clusters in the word.

playground	pl	gr	nd

B. Change one of the smaller words in each compound word. Make a word that means the opposite.

6. inside ___outside___   **7.** nobody ___everybody___

C. Finish the sentences. Use This Week's Words.

Hector can ride by __8__ . The baby girl can walk by __9__ . What can you do by __10__ ?

8. ___himself___   **9.** ___herself___   **10.** ___yourself___

anyone
anyway
bedroom
cannot
everybody
football
grandfather
grandmother
herself
himself
maybe
outside
playground
sometimes
yourself

83

Extra Practice: Bonus Words

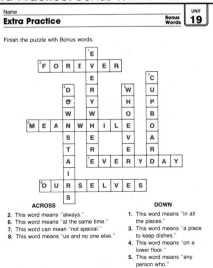

Summarize Learning

Have the children summarize what they have learned on pages 82 and 83. *Ask:*

- What have you learned about compound words? (Sometimes two words put together make a compound word.)
- What are examples of words to which these generalizations can be applied? (playground, grandfather, football; accept other examples)

TEACHING PLAN

SPELLING AND LANGUAGE

Objective To write words as compounds or as two words in sentence context.

1. Read the introductory paragraph on page 84 aloud.
2. Write these sentences on the chalkboard:

> Maybe we'll jog today.
> He may be here by seven.

Have volunteers read the sentences aloud. Help the children to recognize the difference between *maybe* and *may be* by showing them that *maybe* can be dropped and a complete sentence remains. This is not true for *may be.*
3. Have the children complete the exercises independently.
4. Have volunteers read the completed sentences aloud and indicate whether they wrote one word or two words.

For extended practice in writing compound words, you may wish to assign *Spelling and Language Master 19.*

WRITING ON YOUR OWN

Objectives To write a news story; to proofread for spelling.

1. Review the directions.
2. As a *prewriting* activity, discuss the pretend fair with the children. Write the word *fair* in a circle on the chalkboard and have the children generate ideas about what information should be included in a news story about the fair. Write their responses in cluster circles around the core word *fair.* Then have each child **compose** a news story. When they are ready to **revise,** remind them to check for spelling. To **publish,** compile the children's work into a newspaper for display in the classroom.

Spelling and Language • One Word or Two

THIS WEEK'S WORDS
anyone
anyway
bedroom
cannot
everybody
football
grandfather
grandmother
herself
himself
maybe
outside
playground
sometimes
yourself

In the sentence "Maybe I'll see you tomorrow," you write maybe as one word. But in the sentence "I may be here tomorrow," you write may be as two words. The same thing happens with anyway and any way. It is one word in the sentence "I didn't want it anyway." But it is two words if you write "You may color the picture any way you like."

Finish the sentences with maybe or may be.

1. _____Maybe_____ this path leads to the zoo.

2. This ____may be____ a shorter way to the zoo.

Finish the sentences with anyway or any way.

3. Is there ____any way____ we can help you?

4. We will try to help you ____anyway____

Writing on Your Own

Pretend your school had a spring fair on the playground. Write a news story for the school newspaper. Tell who came and what they did. Use as many of This Week's Words as you can.

 WRITER'S GUIDE For a sample of a news story, turn to page 253.

Using the Dictionary to Spell and Write

A good writer uses the dictionary all the time. The words in a dictionary are listed in alphabetical order. Use This Week's Words. Write the word that would come right after each of these words in a dictionary.

1. grand ____grandfather____   2. plant ____playground____

3. become ____bedroom____   4. follow ____football____

 SPELLING DICTIONARY Look in the **Spelling Dictionary** to check your answers.

84

USING THE DICTIONARY

Objective To write words that come immediately after given words in alphabetical order.

1. Read the directions on page 84.
2. Remind the children that if the first letters in words are the same, they must keep looking until they find letters that are different.
3. Have the children complete the activity independently.
4. Remind children to check their answers by looking up the words in the **Spelling Dictionary.**

Extra Practice: Spelling and Language

Name _____
Spelling and Language   UNIT 19

A. Some sentences have two words that should be a compound word. Other sentences have a compound word that should be two words. In each sentence, circle the word or words that need to be changed. Then write the sentence correctly.

1. Everybody knows the (foot ball) coach named Thelma.
   Everybody knows the football coach named Thelma.

2. Thelma is a grandmother who likes to be (out side.)
   Thelma is a grandmother who likes to be outside.

3. Her team (maybe) the best that anyone has ever seen.
   Her team may be the best that anyone has ever seen.

4. Our team (some times) plays against Thelma's team.
   Another team sometimes plays against Thelma's team.

5. Is there (anyway) that anyone can beat Thelma's team?
   Is there any way that anyone can beat Thelma's team?

B. Look at the sentences you have written correctly. Now write all the different compound words you see in those sentences. Write a word only once.

Everybody	football	grandmother
outside	anyone	sometimes
cannot		

| anyone |
| anyway |
| bedroom |
| cannot |
| everybody |
| football |
| grandfather |
| grandmother |
| herself |
| himself |
| maybe |
| outside |
| playground |
| sometimes |
| yourself |

82 • Extra Practice

Spelling on Your Own

THIS WEEK'S WORDS

Add the missing words. Write the compound words that are This Week's Words.

1. can + ___
2. your + ___
3. ___ + way
4. ___ + side
5. foot + ___
6. ___ + room
7. her + ___
8. ___ + times
9. play + ___
10. him + ___
11. ___ + be
12. ___ + one
13. ___ + father
14. every + ___
15. ___ + mother

See answers below.

into
within
anything
onto
without
inside

MASTERY WORDS

1. Write two Mastery words made from <u>with</u> and another word.

within   without

2. Write two Mastery words made from <u>to</u> and another word.

into   onto

3. Match the words. Write three Mastery words.

with	thing	without
any	side	anything
in	out	inside

BONUS WORDS

1. Write the Bonus word that does not sound like the two words it is made from.
2. Write the four Bonus words made with <u>ever</u> or <u>every</u>.
3. Replace the underlined words with Bonus words. Then finish the story.

    Jason looked <u>in all places</u> for the lost whistle. <u>At the same time</u> I searched <u>on the floor below</u>. We told <u>our own minds</u> it was lost <u>for the rest of time</u>. But then…

See answers below.

everyday
forever
meanwhile
downstairs
everywhere
cupboard
whoever
ourselves

85

Spelling on Your Own Answers

THIS WEEK'S WORDS

1. cannot 2. yourself 3. anyway 4. outside
5. football 6. bedroom 7. herself
8. sometimes 9. playground 10. himself
11. maybe 12. anyone 13. grandfather
14. everybody 15. grandmother

BONUS WORDS

1. cupboard 2. whoever, forever, everyday, everywhere 3. Jason looked <u>everywhere</u> for the lost whistle. <u>Meanwhile</u> I searched <u>downstairs</u>. We told <u>ourselves</u> that it was lost <u>forever</u>. But then …

Children will write as directed. Be sure to check spelling.

Summarize Learning

    Have the children summarize what they have learned in this unit. *Ask:*
- What have you learned about the words *maybe* and *anyway*? (Sometimes they are written as compound words; sometimes they are written as two separate words— *may be* and *any way*.)
- What have you learned about dictionaries in this lesson? (Words are listed in alphabetical order in a dictionary.)
- What spelling generalizations have you learned? How did you use these generalizations?

Spelling on Your Own UNIT 19d

TEACHING PLAN

Objectives To apply the unit spelling generalization to spell This Week's Words, Mastery words, and Bonus words independently.

THIS WEEK'S WORDS

1. Read the directions on page 85. Help the children begin by going through the first three items.
2. Have the children complete the activity independently on a separate piece of paper.

MASTERY WORDS

1. Have volunteers read the Mastery words aloud. As each word is read, have the children identify the two words that make up each compound word.
2. Briefly discuss the directions on page 85.
3. Have the children complete the exercises independently.

BONUS WORDS

1. Have volunteers read the Bonus words aloud. As each word is read, have the children identify the two words that make up the compound word. Compare the pronunciation of *cupboard* /kub'erd/ and its components *cup*/kup/ and *board*/bôrd/. Encourage the children to look up the meaning of any unfamiliar words in the **Spelling Dictionary.**
2. Briefly discuss the directions on page 85. Be sure that the children understand what they are to do in **3.**
3. Have the children complete the exercises independently on a separate piece of paper.

For reinforcement in writing spelling words, you may wish to assign *Extra Practice Master 19: Mastery Words* or *Bonus Words.*

CLOSING THE UNIT

Apply New Learning

Tell the children that if they misspell compound words in their writing, they should use one or more of the following strategies:

- write the word using different spellings and compare it with the spelling they picture in their minds.
- think of words that rhyme, and compare in their minds how they are spelled.
- use the two original words to help remember the correct spelling.

Transfer New Learning

Tell the children that when they encounter new words in their personal reading and in other content areas, they should learn the meaning of those words and then apply the generalizations they studied to the spelling of those words. Tell them that once the words are familiar in both meaning and spelling, they should use the new words in their writing.

ENRICHMENT ACTIVITIES

Classroom activities and **home activities** may be assigned to children of all ability levels. The activities provide opportunities for children to use their spelling words in new contexts.

For the Classroom

To individualize classroom activities, you may have the children use the word list they are studying in this unit.

- *Basic:* Use **Mastery** words to complete the activity.
- *Average:* Use **This Week's Words** to complete the activity.
- *Challenging:* Use **Bonus** words to complete the activity.

1. **Language Arts/Writing Compound Words** Have the children choose and write six compound words from the spelling list. Ask them to draw a line between the two words of each compound word. Tell the children to think of as many new compound words as possible, using the two words that form each word. After the children have completed the activity, have them share their new compound words with the class.

   ■ COOPERATIVE LEARNING: Have each group create a list of new compound words. Each group member should write as many new compound words as possible, using both words of any one compound word from all three of the lists. Group members should illustrate the new compound words and write them in sentences. Have them share the results with the class.

2. **Language Arts/Writing Sentences** Have the children use their spelling words to create sentences using sentence parts provided by you. As an example, write *at the playground* on the chalkboard and brainstorm ways that spelling words can be used to make the phrase into a complete sentence. Tell the children to use one or more of the spelling words as well as other words to make complete sentences using phrases such as the following: *my brother, jumped over, maybe tomorrow.* When they have completed the activity, have the children share their sentences with the class.

   ■ COOPERATIVE LEARNING: Have each group write complete sentences using one of the above phrases. Each child should write a sentence using the phrase and one or more spelling words. Tell group members to check each other's sentences for spelling, capitalization, and punctuation and to make sure that the phrase and at least one spelling word were included. When the sentences have been written, have one member from the group identify the phrase for the class and then share the group's sentences with them.

3. **Language Arts/Writing a News Story** Have each child write a short news story. As a ***prewriting*** activity, have the children look over the spelling word list in search of possible ideas for a news story. Tell the children to list their ideas and then choose one. Then have the children make a chart with the following headings: *who, what, where, when, why.* Tell the children to list details about the news event under each heading. When they have completed the prewriting activities, have them use their charts to ***compose*** the news story, beginning with a sentence such as *Yesterday morning the P.T.A. of Lincoln School opened the new school playground.* Then have the children ***revise*** their news stories, making sure they have included all the details from the chart that they considered important. Tell them to also proofread for spelling, capitalization, and punctuation. ***Publish*** the children's stories in a class newspaper or bulletin board display.

   ■ COOPERATIVE LEARNING: Have each group write a news story. As a ***prewriting*** activity, have the group members select an idea and make the chart. When the children are ready to ***compose*** the news story, have them select one child to begin the story orally by giving an opening sentence telling who or what the story is about. Have the other children in the group build on the opening sentence until the news story is fully developed. Another child can then record the story. Other group members should ***revise*** the story, making sure that all the details have been included. Each child within a group should proofread for spelling, capitalization, and punctuation. Have each group then select a child to rewrite the story. Each group should ***publish*** the story by displaying it for the class to read.

For the Home

Children may complete these activities independently or with the assistance of a relative or friend in the home.

1. **Language Arts/Writing a Riddle** Tell the children to write a riddle for some of their spelling words. Clues for each word can be about meaning and spelling or sound. Provide the children with this example: *I am a word made from two words. I am a place to sleep in a house. What am I? (bedroom)*

2. **Health/Writing a Description on Exercise** Discuss with the children the importance of getting enough exercise. Tell them to make a list of the different kinds of exercise they get each day. Then have them write a paragraph describing their favorite way to exercise. Have the children refer to the **Writer's Guide** on page 249 to read about paragraphs. Encourage them to use compound words in their writing. Remind the children to proofread their paragraphs for spelling, capitalization, and punctuation, using the **Revising Checklist** on page 247.

3. **Social Studies/Writing Travel Directions** Tell the children to make a map to show their route from home to another point in town, such as school, the library, a friend's house, or the playground, and then write a how-to paragraph giving a set of directions. Remind the children to use as many of their spelling words as possible. Tell the children to check the directions with someone in the home. Children should then proofread their directions for spelling, capitalization, and punctuation.

4. **Language Arts/Writing a Paragraph About Someone You Like** Tell the children to write a paragraph about a neighbor or relative they particularly like. Have them list some reasons why they like the person. Tell the children to write a paragraph stating the reasons, making sure to use some of their spelling words. After revising and proofreading, have the children share the paragraphs with someone at home.

EVALUATING SPELLING ABILITY

Unit Test

This Week's Words

1. *anyone* Vera asked if *anyone* had seen her dog. **anyone**
2. *anyway* Benjy didn't want dessert *anyway.* **anyway**
3. *bedroom* Please put your things in the *bedroom.* **bedroom**
4. *cannot* Katherine *cannot* come with us. **cannot**
5. *everybody* We wanted *everybody* to have a good time. **everybody**
6. *football* One of Alonzo's favorite sports is *football.* **football**
7. *grandfather* Yoshiro's *grandfather* is sixty years old. **grandfather**
8. *grandmother* I want to meet Christine's *grandmother.* **grandmother**
9. *herself* Angie made the scrambled eggs *herself.* **herself**
10. *himself* Vinnie ate too much and gave *himself* a stomach ache. **himself**
11. *maybe* If we are careful, *maybe* we can fix it. **maybe**
12. *outside* Nadine is playing *outside.* **outside**
13. *playground* The swings at the *playground* are being repaired. **playground**
14. *sometimes* Mrs. O'Brien *sometimes* reads to us. **sometimes**
15. *yourself* You can tie your shoelaces *yourself.* **yourself**

Mastery Words

1. *into* A squirrel got *into* our attic. **into**
2. *within* He held his feelings *within* himself. **within**
3. *anything* Louisa wondered if there was *anything* to eat. **anything**
4. *onto* They loaded the wood *onto* the truck. **onto**
5. *without* Chris left *without* his little brother. **without**
6. *inside* The dog cannot come *inside.* **inside**

Bonus Words

1. *everyday* Wear your *everyday* jacket on the hike. **everyday**
2. *forever* The dog cannot bark *forever,* I hope. **forever**
3. *meanwhile* Cathy went for help, and *meanwhile,* we waited. **meanwhile**
4. *downstairs* Please come *downstairs* and have breakfast. **downstairs**
5. *everywhere* There were flowers *everywhere.* **everywhere**
6. *cupboard* The cereal is in the *cupboard.* **cupboard**
7. *whoever* I want *whoever* is going to the library to line up. **whoever**
8. *ourselves* We cleaned the room *ourselves.* **ourselves**

Dictation Sentences

This Week's Words

1. The *bedroom* is a place for my *grandmother* to be by *herself.*
2. We hope *everybody* will go *outside* to the *playground.*
3. My *grandfather* is always willing to play *football* with *anyone.*
4. Do you think *maybe* it is good to be by *yourself* *sometimes*?
5. Tim *cannot* come by *himself* *anyway.*

Mastery Words

1. The cat got *onto* the chair and *into* the milk.
2. I won't go *within* a mile of that house *without* my dog.
3. Is there *anything* you haven't put *inside* that box?

Bonus Words

1. In the *meanwhile,* we looked for the dog *everywhere* *downstairs.*
2. I set the *everyday* dishes in the *cupboard.*
3. I want *whoever* wants some juice to get it now.
4. We told *ourselves* we would not wait *forever.*

RETEACHING STRATEGIES FOR SPELLING

Children who have made errors on the Unit Test may require reteaching. Use the following **Reteaching Strategies** and **Follow-up Masters 19A** and **19B** for additional instruction and practice of This Week's Words. (You may wish to assign **LEP Reteaching Follow-up Master 19** for reteaching of spelling words.)

A. Discovering Spelling Ideas

1. Say the following words as you write them on the chalkboard.
   myself   somewhere   campground
2. Ask the children to identify how the words are alike. (They're all made up of two smaller words.)
3. Ask the children to identify the two small words that make up each compound word. (my, self; some, where; camp, ground)
4. Ask the children what they have learned about compound words. (They're made up of two smaller words.)

B. Word Shapes

1. Explain to the children that each word has a shape and that remembering the shape of a word can help them spell the word correctly.
2. On the chalkboard, write the words *nobody* and *someone*. Have the children identify "short," "tall," and "tail" letters.
3. Draw the configuration of each word on the chalkboard and ask the children which word fits in each shape.

Use **Reteaching Follow-up Master 19A** to reinforce spelling generalizations taught in Unit 19.

Use **Reteaching Follow-up Master 19B** to reinforce spellings of This Week's Words for Unit 19.

Name _____
Reteaching Follow-up A   Discovering Spelling Ideas   UNIT **19**

THIS WEEK'S WORDS

anyone	bedroom	everybody	football	grandfather
himself	playground	anyway	herself	sometimes
yourself	grandmother	outside	cannot	maybe

1. Study This Week's Words. Say each word to yourself. Then finish the "word math." You will write This Week's Words.

any	+	one	=	anyone		her	+	self	=	herself
any	+	way	=	anyway		him	+	self	=	himself
bed	+	room	=	bedroom		may	+	be	=	maybe
can	+	not	=	cannot		out	+	side	=	outside
every	+	body	=	everybody		play	+	ground	=	playground
foot	+	ball	=	football		some	+	times	=	sometimes
grand	+	father	=	grandfather		your	+	self	=	yourself
grand	+	mother	=	grandmother						

2. What have you learned about compound words?

   __Two smaller words make up a compound word.__

   _____

3. Write five other compound words.
      POSSIBLE ANSWERS: anything, butterfly, cartwheel,

      downpour, downstairs

Reteaching • 31

Name _____
Reteaching Follow-up B   Word Shapes   UNIT **19**

THIS WEEK'S WORDS

anyone	bedroom	everybody	football	grandfather
himself	playground	anyway	herself	sometimes
yourself	grandmother	outside	cannot	maybe

Write each of This Week's Words in its correct shape. The first one has been done for you. Children may interchange answers that fit the same configuration.

1. h i m s e l f   2. y o u r s e l f
3. b e d r o o m   4. s o m e t i m e s
5. m a y b e   6. e v e r y b o d y
7. a n y o n e   8. a n y w a y
9. o u t s i d e   10. h e r s e l f
11. c a n n o t   12. f o o t b a l l
13. g r a n d f a t h e r
14. g r a n d m o t h e r
15. p l a y g r o u n d

32 • Reteaching

85C   UNIT 19   *Compound Words*

PREVIEWING THE UNIT

Unit Materials

Instruction and Practice

Pupil Book	pages 86–89
Teacher's Edition	
Teaching Plans	pages 86–89
Enrichment Activities	
For the Classroom	page 89A
For the Home	page 89B
Reteaching Strategies	page 89C

Testing

Teacher's Edition	
Trial Test	pages 85E–85F
Unit Test	page 89B
Dictation Test	page 89B

Additional Resources

PRACTICE AND REINFORCEMENT
Extra Practice Master 20: This Week's Words
Extra Practice Master 20: Mastery Words
Extra Practice Master 20: Bonus Words
LEP Practice Master 20
Spelling and Language Master 20
Study Steps to Learn a Word Master

RETEACHING FOLLOW-UP
Reteaching Follow-up Master 20A:
   Discovering Spelling Ideas
Reteaching Follow-up Master 20B: Word
   Shapes
LEP Reteaching Follow-up Master 20

TEACHING AIDS
Spelling Generalizations Transparency 17

Click on the SPELLING banner to find activities for this unit.

Learner Objectives

Spelling

- To spell contractions.
- To recognize the function of the apostrophe in contractions.
- To spell words that are parts of known contractions.

Reading

- To follow written directions.
- To use context clues for word identification.

Writing

- To write a letter.
- To use the writing process.
- To proofread for spelling, capitalization, and punctuation.
- To write legible manuscript and cursive letters.

Listening

- To listen to identify contractions.
- To listen to determine if a contraction fits in a given sentence.
- To follow oral directions.

Speaking

- To speak clearly to a group.
- To respond to a question.
- To express feelings and ideas about a piece of writing.
- To present a letter.
- To contribute ideas and information in group discussions.

THIS WEEK'S WORDS

can't
didn't
don't
he's
I'll
I'm
isn't
it's
let's
she's
that's
there's
we'll
we're
won't

MASTERY WORDS

do
is
not
their
there
will

BONUS WORDS

aren't
doesn't
haven't
they're
wasn't
weren't
what's
you're

Assignment Guide

This guide shows how you teach a typical spelling unit in either a five-day or a three-day sequence, while providing for individual differences. **Boldface type** indicates essential classwork. Steps shown in light type may be done in class or assigned as homework.

Five Days	● = average spellers ★ = better spellers ✓ = slower spellers		Three Days
Day 1 **a**	● ★ **Take This Week's Words Trial Test and correct** ● ✓ **Take Mastery Word Trial Test and correct** ● ★ **Read This Week's Words and discuss generalization page 86**		**Day 1**
Day 2 **b**	● Complete Spelling Practice page 87 ● ✓ Complete Extra Practice Master 20: This Week's Words (optional) ✓ Complete Spelling on Your Own: Mastery Words page 89 ★ **Take Bonus Word Trial Test and correct**		**Day 1**
Day 3 **c**	● ★ ✓ **Complete Spelling and Language page 88** ● ★ ✓ Complete Writing on Your Own page 88 ● ★ ✓ Take Midweek Test (optional) ● ★ ✓ **Complete Proofreading page 88** ★ Complete Spelling on Your Own: Bonus Words page 89 ● ✓ Complete Spelling and Language Master 20 (optional)		**Day 2**
Day 4 **d**	● Complete Spelling on Your Own: This Week's Words page 89 ✓ Complete Extra Practice Master 20: Mastery Words (optional) ★ Complete Extra Practice Master 20: Bonus Words (optional)		**Day 2**
Day 5 **e**	● Take Unit Test on This Week's Words ● Complete Reteaching Follow-up Masters 20A and 20B (optional) ● ✓ **Take Unit Test on Mastery Words** ★ **Take Unit Test on Bonus Words**		**Day 3**

Enrichment Activities for the **classroom** and for the **home** included at the end of this unit may be assigned selectively on any day of the week.

INTRODUCING THE UNIT

Establish Readiness for Learning

Remind the children that they have learned to combine two words into one to make a compound word. Tell them that this week they will learn to combine two words into contractions. They will apply what they learn to This Week's Words and use some of those words to write a letter.

Assess Children's Spelling Ability

Administer the Trial Test before the children study This Week's Words. Use the test sentences provided. Say each word and use it in a sentence. Then repeat the word. Have the children write the words on a separate sheet of paper or in their spelling notebooks. Test sentences are also provided for Mastery and Bonus words.

Have the children check their own work by listening to you read the spelling of the words or by referring to This Week's Words in the left column of the **Pupil Book.** For each misspelled word, have the children follow the **Study Steps to Learn a Word** on page 1 in the **Pupil Book** or use the copying master to study and write the words. Children should record the number correct on their **Progress Report.**

Trial Test Sentences

This Week's Words
1. *can't*   Doreen *can't* find her sweater. *can't*
2. *didn't*   Warren *didn't* come to school today. *didn't*
3. *don't*   Please *don't* shout. *don't*
4. *he's*   Hal says *he's* not sure. *he's*
5. *I'll*   If you go, *I'll* go with you. *I'll*
6. *I'm*   On Saturday *I'm* going to play baseball. *I'm*
7. *isn't*   That animal *isn't* a raccoon. *isn't*
8. *it's*   I think *it's* a woodchuck. *it's*

FOCUS

- Establishes objectives
- Relates to prior learning
- Sets purpose of instruction

9. *let's* When we are finished, *let's* play a game. **let's**
10. *she's* Alicia thinks *she's* lost. **she's**
11. *that's* I hope *that's* Clio at the door. **that's**
12. *there's* I think *there's* some milk left. **there's**
13. *we'll* Dominic says *we'll* be there at eight. **we'll**
14. *we're* Howard knows *we're* waiting for him. **we're**
15. *won't* Hilary and Angela *won't* disobey their parents. **won't**

Mastery Words

1. *do* Juan and Nora *do* not want to go to the party. **do**
2. *is* It *is* a sunny day. **is**
3. *not* Joe is *not* sad. **not**
4. *their* Floyd and Justin put on *their* boots. **their**
5. *there* I hope *there* is more cake. **there**
6. *will* Jonathan *will* not clean his room. **will**

Bonus Words

1. *aren't* We *aren't* ready to give the dog a bath. **aren't**
2. *doesn't* Travis *doesn't* want a cookie. **doesn't**

3. *haven't* Eloise and Danny *haven't* finished their work. **haven't**
4. *they're* The teacher hopes *they're* having a good time. **they're**
5. *wasn't* That *wasn't* a scary movie. **wasn't**
6. *weren't* Josie knows they *weren't* laughing at her. **weren't**
7. *what's* I wonder *what's* for lunch. **what's**
8. *you're* I am glad *you're* here. **you're**

Apply Prior Learning

Have the students be spelling detectives. Tell them that they can discover spelling generalizations about contractions by applying what they already know. Write the words *do* and *not* on the chalkboard. Then write *don't*. Ask the children to suggest other pairs of words that combine into one word. Write them on the chalkboard. Ask the children to look at the words and draw conclusions. (Each pair of two words is combined into one word, with a letter or letters omitted and replaced with an apostrophe.) Tell the children that they will study words that are contractions. Explain that they can use these words in a variety of spelling tasks: writing stories, writing letters, or writing notes to friends.

FOCUS

• Relates to prior learning
• Draws relationships
• Applies spelling generalizations to new contexts

FOR CHILDREN WITH SPECIAL NEEDS

Learning Difficulties

Organizing, planning, and executing a task in a systematic and accurate manner typically presents problems for children with learning disabilities. These deficiencies may be seen in the spelling words in which an apostrophe must be placed in a particular location and selected letters deleted. This activity is designed to give the child a systematic problem-solving strategy.

Have the children write the first word + the second word that form the contraction, then the base word and the contracted ending, and finally, the contracted word. An example might be *did + not = did + n't = didn't*.

To teach letters that are to be omitted to make a contracted word, have the children write the two words. Have them write the two words a second time, drawing lines through the letters to be omitted and adding the

apostrophe. Finally, have them write the contracted word. An example might be *I will = I wi̶l̶l = I'll*. Organization will be emphasized if the work is divided into columns so that the patterns are clearly seen.

Limited English Proficiency

To help limited English proficient children work with the spelling generalizations for Unit 20, you may wish to refer to the booklet "Suggestions and Activities for Limited English Proficient Students."

TEACHING PLAN

Objectives To spell contractions; to recognize which letters are dropped to form contractions; to recognize the function of the apostrophe in contractions.

1. Write *can + not* on the chalkboard and ask the children to identify the compound they learned in Unit 19 that is made up of these two words. Write *cannot* on the chalkboard, and remind the children that all of the letters in *can* and *not* are also in *cannot.* Then tell the children that there is a way to put *can* and *not* together to make a shorter word. Write the word *can't* on the chalkboard, and ask a child to read it. Tell the children that *can't* is a contraction.

2. Direct the children's attention to the frogs on page 86. Have the children look at the pictures of the frogs as you read the generalization aloud.

You may wish to introduce the lesson by using *Spelling Generalizations Transparency 17.*

3. Read This Week's Words. As each word is read, have a volunteer identify the two words that make up the contraction. Then ask the children to identify the letters that have been left out of each contraction. Help the children to recognize *will not* as the source of *won't* by using *won't* in a sentence.

4. Direct the children's attention to **Remember This** at the bottom of the page. Read the verse aloud. Discuss the verse and the accompanying drawing with the children.

You may wish to assign *LEP Practice Master 20* for reinforcement in writing spelling words.

20 Contractions

THIS WEEK'S WORDS

1. can't
2. didn't
3. don't
4. he's
5. I'll
6. I'm
7. isn't
8. it's
9. let's
10. she's
11. that's
12. there's
13. we'll
14. we're
15. won't

86

This Week's Words

A **contraction** is a short way of writing two words together. Some of the letters are left out. An **apostrophe** takes their place.

<u>Can't</u> is the contraction of <u>can</u> and <u>not</u>. The apostrophe takes the place of <u>n</u> and <u>o</u>.

All the words this week are contractions. What words make up the contractions? What letters are left out?

REMEMBER THIS

How <u>do</u> <u>not</u> becomes <u>don't</u> is easy to tell.
But <u>will</u> <u>not</u> to <u>won't</u>—what happens then?
Why, the <u>i</u> runs away with the double <u>l</u>,
And the <u>o</u> jumps over the <u>n</u>.

Extra Practice: This Week's Words

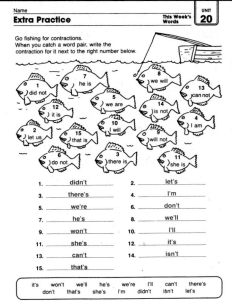

Name
Extra Practice   This Week's Words   UNIT 20

Go fishing for contractions.
When you catch a word pair, write the contraction for it next to the right number below.

7 he is
1 did not
13 can not
8 we will
12 it is
5 we are
14 is not
2 let us
10 I will
4 I am
15 that is
3 there is
9 will not
6 do not
11 she is

1. didn't   2. let's
3. there's   4. I'm
5. we're   6. don't
7. he's   8. we'll
9. won't   10. I'll
11. she's   12. it's
13. can't   14. isn't
15. that's

| it's | won't | we'll | he's | we're | I'll | can't | there's |
| don't | that's | she's | I'm | didn't | isn't | let's |

Extra Practice • 83

Extra Practice: Mastery Words

Name
Extra Practice   Mastery Words   UNIT 20

A. In each pair of boxes, write the two Mastery words that make up each contraction.

1. don't = do + not
2. isn't = is + not
3. won't = will + not
4. there's = there + is

B. Finish each sentence using the word <u>there</u> or the word <u>their</u>.

5. The Morans drove _____their_____ car to Plum Beach.
6. They brought _____their_____ dog, Fluffy.
7. The Morans went _____there_____ for the day.
8. They met _____their_____ friends Norman and Sally Fox _____there_____
9. Fluffy had a good time _____there_____

| do |
| is |
| not |
| their |
| there |
| will |

C. Finish each sentence with the two words that make up the contraction. Write the words in the blanks.

10. Smoky and Felix (don't) _____do_____ _____not_____ like the new cat food.
11. They (won't) _____will_____ _____not_____ touch it.
12. There (isn't) _____is_____ _____not_____ a thing I can do to make them try it.

84 • Extra Practice

Spelling Practice

A. Write the contractions of these words.

1. I will _____ I'll

2. we will _____ we'll

3. let us _____ let's

4. we are _____ we're

5. I am _____ I'm

B. Follow the directions. Use This Week's Words.

6. Write the five words that are contractions of <u>not</u> and another word.

can't   didn't   don't

isn't   won't

7. Write the six words that are contractions of <u>is</u> and another word.

he's   isn't   it's

she's   that's   there's

8. Rewrite this sentence twice. **It is not raining now.** Use <u>it's</u> the first time. Use <u>isn't</u> the second time.

It's not raining now.

It isn't raining now.

C. Rewrite each sentence. Use two contractions each time.

9. Linda will not tell us about the party she is planning.

Linda won't tell us about the party she's planning.

10. She says we will have more fun if we do not know.

She says we'll have more fun if we don't know.

11. I cannot think what it is going to be like.

I can't think what it's going to be like.

can't
didn't
don't
he's
I'll
I'm
isn't
it's
let's
she's
that's
there's
we'll
we're
won't

87

TEACHING PLAN

Objectives To write contractions given the words that make up the contractions; to rewrite sentences using contractions.

1. Read the directions on page 87 aloud. Be sure the children understand that in **8** they are to write two different sentences. Also emphasize that in Exercise **C** they should use two contractions in each sentence they write.

2. Have the children complete the page independently. Remind them to use legible handwriting. You may wish to demonstrate the correct form of the letters *n* and *t* and then have the children practice writing the letters. For **Handwriting Models,** refer the children to page 258 in the **Pupil Book.**

3. To correct the children's work, have volunteers write the answers on the chalkboard. Ask the children who are writing the sentences for **8–11** on the chalkboard to draw a line under each contraction. Let the children check their own responses.

For reinforcement in writing spelling words, you may wish to assign *Extra Practice Master 20: This Week's Words.*

⟲ EXTENDING THE LESSON

To provide more practice with contractions, have the children rewrite these three sentences, using two contractions in each:

I am sure it will not rain today.
(*I'm* sure it *won't* rain today.)
They do not know that we are here.
(They *don't* know that *we're* here.)
That is why he did not come.
(*That's* why he *didn't* come.)

Extra Practice: Bonus Words

Name _____

Extra Practice   Bonus Words   UNIT 20

Whenever you see a number on the graph, put the word at the side and the word at the top together to form a contraction. Write your answers below.

	am	are	is	will	have	do	does	did	were	can	was
I	1			2	3						
you		4		5	6						
he			7	8							
she			9	10							
it			11	12							
we	13		14	15							
they	16		17	18							
not	19	20	21	22	23	24	25	26	27	28	
what			29								
there			30								

1. I'm   2. I'll   3. I've
4. you're   5. you'll   6. you've
7. he's   8. he'll   9. she's
10. she'll   11. it's   12. it'll
13. we're   14. we'll   15. we've
16. they're   17. they'll   18. they've
19. aren't   20. isn't   21. won't
22. haven't   23. don't   24. doesn't
25. didn't   26. weren't   27. can't
28. wasn't   29. what's   30. there's

Extra Practice • 85

Summarize Learning

Have the children summarize what they have learned on pages 86 and 87. *Ask:*

• What have you learned about a contraction? (It is a short way of writing two words together.)

• Why is it called a contraction? (It is called a contraction because some letters are left out and an apostrophe is used to take their place.)

• What are some examples of words that are contractions? (can't, won't, I'm, she's, didn't; accept other examples)

TEACHING PLAN

SPELLING AND LANGUAGE

Objectives To use negative contractions; to write sentences that mean the opposite of given sentences.

1. Read the introductory paragraph on page 88 aloud.
2. Write these sentences on the chalkboard:

   We want to go home.
   Yesterday we wanted to stay.

   Help the children to think of negative sentences for the sentences above using *don't* and *didn't*. Help the children to recognize that *don't* tells about the present and *didn't* tells about the past.
3. Read the directions on page 88 aloud, and have the children complete the activity independently.
4. When the children have finished, ask volunteers to write their sentences on the chalkboard and draw a line under the contraction.

For extended practice in writing negative contractions, you may wish to assign *Spelling and Language Master 20.*

WRITING ON YOUR OWN

Objectives To write a letter; to proofread for spelling.

1. Read the directions aloud.
2. As a **prewriting** activity, discuss with the children the information that should be included in their letters. List their responses on the chalkboard. You may also wish to refer to a model of a letter on page 251 of the **Writer's Guide.** Then have the children **compose** their letters. When they are ready to **revise,** remind them to check for spelling. For additional help, you may also wish to refer them to the **Revising Checklist** on page 247 of the **Writer's Guide.** To **publish** children's work, have them read their letters to the class.

Spelling and Language • Negative Sentences

THIS WEEK'S WORDS
can't
didn't
don't
he's
I'll
I'm
isn't
it's
let's
she's
that's
there's
we'll
we're
won't

I can't sing means the opposite of I can sing. They didn't sing means the opposite of They sang. I can't sing and They didn't sing are negative sentences.

Write the sentences as negative sentences. Use This Week's Words.

1. Mike and Charles will play in the park.

   Mike and Charles won't play in the park.

2. They want to ride on the swings.

   They don't want to ride on the swings.

Writing on Your Own

Write a letter to your grandmother, grandfather, or other relative. Ask if you can visit. Ask when you can come to visit and what you should bring. Use some of This Week's Words.

 WRITER'S GUIDE How did you end your sentences? For help with periods and questions marks, turn to page 238.

Proofreading

1. Read the letter Darin wrote to his grandmother. Find the three spelling mistakes he made. Circle each one.

> *Dear Grandma,*
> *Wer coming to visit you next month. Thats what Mom said today. I donnt know when will get there. Dad says he's going to call you.*
> *I'm going to bed now. Il write again soon.*
> *Love,*
> *Darin*

2. Write the three misspelled words correctly.

   We're _____   don't _____   I'll _____

 WRITER'S GUIDE Use the editing and proofreading marks on page 248.

88

PROOFREADING

Objectives To proofread a letter for spelling errors; to write misspelled words correctly.

1. Read the directions aloud.
2. Have the children read through the letter independently, looking for errors. Then ask them to go back and circle each misspelled word.

   If you are using the hardcover book, the children should simply locate the misspelled words and write them correctly in their notebooks.

Extra Practice: Spelling and Language

Name
Spelling and Language   UNIT 20

A. Finish the answer for each question. Use a contraction in the second answer to each question.

	can't
	didn't
	don't
	he's
	I'll
	I'm
	isn't
	it's
	let's
	she's
	that's
	there's
	we'll
	we're
	won't

1. Is the sun shining today?
   Yes, _____ the sun is shining today.
   No, _____ the sun isn't shining today.

2. Did you eat lunch today?
   Yes, _____ I did eat lunch today.
   No, _____ I didn't eat lunch today.

3. Do you like watching football?
   Yes, _____ I do like watching football.
   No, _____ I don't like watching football.

4. Will you come to the beach?
   Yes, _____ I will come to the beach.
   No, _____ I won't come to the beach.

B. You can make each sentence negative by making a negative contraction with one of the verbs in the sentence. Circle the verb you would use in your contraction. Then write the contraction on the line.

5. The kids do like to play cards.   don't
6. They can play many card games.   can't
7. They did play with red cards.   didn't
8. John is a very good card player.   isn't
9. He will play again tomorrow.   won't

86 • Extra Practice

Spelling on Your Own

THIS WEEK'S WORDS

Use all of This Week's Words in sentences. Draw a line under the contraction in each sentence. After the sentence, write the two words that make up the contraction. Here is an example.

I <u>can't</u> find my mittens.   can not

MASTERY WORDS

Write the two Mastery words that make up each contraction.

do
is
not
their
there
will

1. isn't _____ is _____ not

2. don't _____ do _____ not

3. there's _____ there _____ is

4. won't _____ will _____ not

<u>There</u> tells where. <u>Their</u> tells whose. Finish the sentences. Use <u>there</u> or <u>their</u>.

5. Peg and Brian invited me to _____ their _____ house.

6. I was _____ there _____ all afternoon.

7. I had fun playing with _____ their _____ dog.

BONUS WORDS

Follow the directions. Use the Bonus words.

aren't
doesn't
haven't
they're
wasn't
weren't
what's
you're

1. Use their, there, and they're in sentences.

2. Use your and you're in sentences.

3. Write the word that is a contraction of <u>is</u> and another word.

Answer these questions. Use a Bonus word contraction made from <u>not</u> and another word in each answer.

4. Have you eaten?   **5.** Were you there?   **6.** Are we next?

7. Does Paul like nuts?   **8.** Were they sad?   **See answers below.**

89

Spelling on Your Own Answers

BONUS WORDS

1. EXAMPLES: Jill and Leon lost <u>their</u> mittens. The mittens were <u>there</u> on the shelf before. But <u>they're</u> gone now. 2. EXAMPLES: May I use <u>your</u> pencil? <u>You're</u> not using it, are you? 3. <u>what's</u> 4. No, I <u>haven't</u> eaten. 5. No, I <u>wasn't</u> there. 6. <u>No, we aren't</u> next. 7. No, he <u>doesn't</u> like them. 8. No, they <u>weren't</u> sad.

Summarize Learning

Have the children summarize what they have learned in this unit. *Ask:*

- What have you learned about writing contractions? (You leave out some letters and use an apostrophe in their place.)
- What have you learned about using negative contractions? (Negative contractions are the opposite of positive words.)
- What spelling generalizations have you learned? How did you use these generalizations?

Spelling on Your Own

Spelling on Your Own UNIT 20d

TEACHING PLAN

Objectives To apply the unit spelling generalization to spell This Week's Words, Mastery words, and Bonus words independently.

THIS WEEK'S WORDS

1. Read the directions on page 89 aloud. Help the children get started by asking volunteers to use *didn't, he's,* and *let's* in oral sentences. As each sentence is suggested, write the contraction on the chalkboard and have the children identify the words that make up the contraction.
2. Have the children complete the activity independently on a separate piece of paper.

MASTERY WORDS

1. Have volunteers read the Mastery words aloud. Have volunteers name contractions of which *do, is, not, there,* and *will* are a part. Help the children to distinguish between *their* and *there* by using each word in a sentence.
2. Briefly discuss the directions on page 89. Then have the children complete the exercises.

BONUS WORDS

1. Briefly review the unit generalization.
2. Have volunteers read the Bonus words. As each word is read, ask the children to identify the words that make up the contraction.
3. Review the correct usage of *their, there, they're* and *your, you're*. Have the children tell which two words are possessive pronouns and which two words are contractions.
4. Have them complete the exercises on a separate piece of paper.

For reinforcement in writing spelling words, you may wish to assign **Extra Practice Master 20: Mastery Words** or **Bonus Words.**

CLOSING THE UNIT

Apply New Learning

Tell the children that if they misspell words with contractions in their writing, they should use one or more of the following strategies:

- think about possible spellings for the contraction and try to picture the word in their minds.
- write the word using different spellings and compare it with the spelling they picture in their minds.
- use the two original words to help remember the correct spelling.

Transfer New Learning

Tell the children that when they encounter new words in their personal reading and in other content areas, they should learn the meaning of those words and then apply the generalizations they have studied to the spelling of those words. Tell them that once the words are familiar in both meaning and spelling, they should use the new words in their writing.

ENRICHMENT ACTIVITIES

Classroom activities and **home activities** may be assigned to children of all ability levels. The activities provide opportunities for children to use their spelling words in new contexts.

For the Classroom

To individualize classroom activities, you may have the children use the word list they are studying in this unit.

- *Basic:* Use **Mastery** words to complete the activity
- *Average:* Use **This Week's Words** to complete the activity.
- *Challenging:* Use **Bonus** words to complete the activity.

1. **Language Arts/Writing Contrasting Sentences** Have the children make up contrasting sentences using contractions from their spelling lists. To illustrate the activity, write the following examples on the chalkboard:

   Billy did, but I didn't.
   Ann can, but Mary _____. (can't)
   Ben will, but Lee _____. (won't)

   After completing the model sentences, the children should write their own sentences. Then have them rewrite the sentences, leaving a blank in place of the contraction. Children should then exchange papers with one another and complete the sentences. Those children studying the Mastery words should use verbs from the Mastery words list and add the word *not* to the second part of the sentence, for example:

   Cats do, but dogs _____. (do not)

■ COOPERATIVE LEARNING: Have each group create a set of contrasting sentences using contractions from the spelling lists. Each member of the group should write a sentence using a spelling word. When the group is satisfied with all the sentences, have each member rewrite his or her sentence, leaving a blank in place of each contraction. Then have the groups complete each other's sentences. Those children studying the Mastery words should work with these sentences:

What _____ you say?
It is _____.
We are _____ friends.

2. **Language Arts/Writing Sentences** Have the children complete the sentences that follow with as many different spelling words as make sense.

   Mom said _____ leaving at noon.
   My sister _____ go.
   _____ my brother.

Then have the children create their own sentences. Tell them to write the sentences so that more than one spelling word can be used to complete each sentence. Have them exchange their sentences with one another.

■ COOPERATIVE LEARNING: Have each group complete the sentences. Have each member be responsible for writing specific sentences. When each group is certain that they have found all the possible responses, have them share their sentences with the class. Then have each group create a set of their own sentences. Have each member write a sentence. Tell the group to check the sentences to make sure they make sense. Then have one member rewrite the sentences, leaving a blank space for the spelling word. Have other groups complete their sentences.

3. **Language Arts/Writing a Story** Have each student write the middle and ending of a story. Provide the following story starter:

   The doorbell rang. When I opened the door, I found a huge box on the front steps. The tab had my name on it. A very strange sound was coming from inside the box. I _____

As a **prewriting** activity, have the children make a chart with the following headings: *What did I do? What is in the box? What does it look like?* Tell the children to write possibilities in each of the columns. Then have them use the ideas listed on the chart to **compose** the story. Remind them to use as many spelling words as they can. Have the children **revise** the story, making sure they told what they did, what was in the box, and what it looked like. **Publish** the stories in a class book, on a bulletin board display.

■ COOPERATIVE LEARNING: Have each group complete the story. As a *prewriting* activity, have the members of the group work together to complete the chart. As the group discusses the possibilities, have one member record the responses. After deciding which possibilities they like best, the members should work together to *compose* the story. Each member should write a paragraph to answer one question. Group members should then *revise* the story, checking to see that all the important details from the chart have been included. Each group should *publish* the story by including it in a class book, or by displaying it on the bulletin board.

For the Home

Children may complete these activities independently or with the help of a relative or friend in the home.

1. **Language Arts/Writing Sentences with Contractions** Have the children look for contractions with *n't* in magazines, books, or newspapers. After finding a contraction, have them copy the sentence and underline the contraction. Then tell the children to write the two words that make up the contraction as well as its opposite. As an example, present the following: The big, bad wolf *couldn't* blow the house down. (could not, could) Then have the children look for other types of contractions.

2. **Science/Writing True and False Statements About Animals** Have the children write true and false statements about animals. Each sentence should include a spelling word from any of the lists: for example, *A frog can't fly* and *Birds don't fly*. Encourage children to use a dictionary, an encyclopedia, or a science book for help. The children can set the page up as a quiz for friends or classmates to do.

3. **Language Arts/Writing a Rhyming Poem** Tell the children to write a four-line poem using as many spelling words as possible. The second and fourth lines should rhyme. Refer them to page 254 of the **Writer's Guide** to read about rhyming poems. Then provide this example.

   "Didn't you hear me?"
   Asked Bobby B. Blatt.
   "I can't, so I won't!
   Now really, that's that!"

   Tell the children to share their rhymes with a friend or family member.

4. **Social Studies/Writing About a News Event** Tell the children to listen to the news on the radio or television. Then have them write several sentences using some of their spelling words to tell about what they heard. Have them share their sentences with a family member or friend.

EVALUATING SPELLING ABILITY

Unit Test

This Week's Words

1. **can't**   Amelia *can't* find her mittens.   **can't**

2. **didn't**   I *didn't* see Dick yesterday.   **didn't**
3. **don't**   Cindy and Anita *don't* know what happened.   **don't**
4. **he's**   Bill is sure *he's* hiding somewhere.   **he's**
5. **I'll**   If it is cold, *I'll* wear my new coat.   **I'll**
6. **I'm**   I go to bed when *I'm* sleepy.   **I'm**
7. **isn't**   It *isn't* a nice day.   **isn't**
8. **it's**   We cannot skate if *it's* raining.   **it's**
9. **let's**   After we read, *let's* do some math.   **let's**
10. **she's**   I think *she's* in the living room.   **she's**
11. **that's**   Consuelo knows *that's* the right answer.   **that's**
12. **there's**   I think *there's* someone at the door.   **there's**
13. **we'll**   Luke hopes *we'll* have art today.   **we'll**
14. **we're**   Connie knows *we're* watching her.   **we're**
15. **won't**   This science test *won't* be difficult.   **won't**

Mastery Words

1. **do**   Those dogs *do* not bark.   **do**
2. **is**   Owen thinks it *is* going to rain.   **is**
3. **not**   They did *not* put anything away.   **not**
4. **their**   The children hung up *their* jackets.   **their**
5. **there**   Anthony thought *there* were more raisins in the box.   **there**
6. **will**   The show *will* not start for another hour.   **will**

Bonus Words

1. **aren't**   The animals *aren't* hungry.   **aren't**
2. **doesn't**   Sandy *doesn't* have the book.   **doesn't**
3. **haven't**   We *haven't* been here long.   **haven't**
4. **they're**   I don't know if *they're* in the kitchen.   **they're**
5. **wasn't**   That *wasn't* a very funny joke.   **wasn't**
6. **weren't**   They *weren't* paying attention.   **weren't**
7. **what's**   Guess *what's* in the package.   **what's**
8. **you're**   We will get on the bus if *you're* sure it is the right one.   **you're**

Dictation Sentences

This Week's Words

1. I hope *that's* where *we're* going to live.
2. They *won't* go if *it's* raining.
3. He *didn't* tell them *I'm* here.
4. If *there's* a bus coming, *let's* catch it.
5. If *we'll* be there late, *I'll* call.
6. I *don't* know if *she's* coming with us.
7. You *can't* use the bike if *he's* riding it.
8. *I'm* sure he *isn't* at the store today.

Mastery Words

1. They *do* not have *their* hats.
2. He *is* happy that *there will* be a game today.

Bonus Words

1. I know *they're* waiting to see what *you're* going to do.
2. I hope you *haven't* seen *what's* in the bag.
3. They *aren't* going if he *doesn't* take them.
4. We *weren't* walking on a street that *wasn't* safe.

RETEACHING STRATEGIES FOR SPELLING

Children who have made errors on the Unit Test may require reteaching. Use the following **Reteaching Strategies** and **Follow-up Masters 20A** and **20B** for additional instruction and practice of This Week's Words. (You may wish to assign **LEP Reteaching Follow-up Master 20** for reteaching of spelling words.)

A. Discovering Spelling Ideas

1. Say the following words as you write them on the chalkboard.

    have + not = haven't

2. Ask the children if *haven't* means the same thing as *have not*. (yes)
3. Ask the children to tell what happened when the two words were added together to make a shorter word. (One of the letters was left out, and an apostrophe was added.)
4. Point out that this shorter way of writing two words is called a contraction.
5. Ask the children what they have learned about contractions. (They're made up of two words; an apostrophe shows where a letter or letters are missing.)

B. Word Shapes

1. Explain to the children that each word has a shape and that remembering the shape of a word can help them to spell the word correctly.
2. On the chalkboard, write the words *hasn't* and *you'll*. Have students identify "short," "tall," and "tail" letters, as well as apostrophes.
3. Draw the configuration of each word on the chalkboard, and ask students which word fits in each shape.

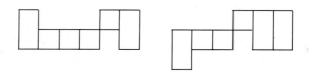

Use **Reteaching Follow-up Master 20A** to reinforce spelling generalizations taught in Unit 20.

Use **Reteaching Follow-up Master 20B** to reinforce spellings of This Week's Words for Unit 20.

Name
Reteaching Follow-up A — Discovering Spelling Ideas — UNIT 20

THIS WEEK'S WORDS

can't	didn't	he's	isn't	she's
we'll	it's	there's	don't	that's
I'll	let's	won't	we're	I'm

1. Write each pair of words as a contraction. You will write This Week's Words.

can not	**can't**	let us	**let's**
did not	**didn't**	she is	**she's**
do not	**don't**	that is	**that's**
he is	**he's**	there is	**there's**
I will	**I'll**	we will	**we'll**
I am	**I'm**	we are	**we're**
is not	**isn't**	will not	**won't**
it is	**it's**		

2. What takes the place of the missing letters in the words you wrote?

    An apostrophe takes the place of the missing letter or letters.

3. What have you learned about contractions?

    A contraction is a short way of writing two words together.
    an apostrophe takes the place of the missing letter or letters.

4. Write two other contractions and show the two words that make up each contraction.

    POSSIBLE ANSWERS: she'll—she will
    they're—they are

Reteaching • 33

Name
Reteaching Follow-up B — Word Shapes — UNIT 20

THIS WEEK'S WORDS

can't	didn't	he's	isn't	she's
we'll	it's	there's	don't	that's
I'll	let's	won't	we're	I'm

Write each of This Week's Words in its correct shape. The first one has been done for you. **Children may interchange answers that fit the same configuration.**

1. w e 'l l
2. i s n ' t
3. d i d n ' t
4. w o n ' t
5. s h e ' s
6. w e ' r e
7. d o n ' t
8. I ' l l
9. t h e r e ' s
10. l e t ' s
11. I ' m
12. i t ' s
13. h e ' s
14. t h a t ' s
15. c a n ' t

34 • Reteaching

PREVIEWING THE UNIT

Unit Materials

Instruction and Practice

Pupil Book	pages 90–93
Teacher's Edition	
Teaching Plans	pages 90–93
Enrichment Activities	
For the Classroom	pages 93A–93B
For the Home	page 93B
Reteaching Strategies	page 93C

Testing

Teacher's Edition	
Trial Test	pages 89E–89F
Unit Test	page 93B
Dictation Test	page 93B

Additional Resources

PRACTICE AND REINFORCEMENT
Extra Practice Master 21: This Week's Words
Extra Practice Master 21: Mastery Words
Extra Practice Master 21: Bonus Words
LEP Practice Master 21
Spelling and Language Master 21
Study Steps to Learn a Word Master

RETEACHING FOLLOW-UP
Reteaching Follow-up Master 21A:
  Discovering Spelling Ideas
Reteaching Follow-up Master 21B: Word
  Shapes
LEP Reteaching Follow-up Master 21

TEACHING AIDS
Spelling Generalizations Transparency 18

Click on the SPELLING banner to find activities for this unit.

Learner Objectives

Spelling

- To spell words that demonstrate these sound-letter relationships: /ô/a, aw, au; /ôr/or, our.

Reading

- To follow written directions.
- To use the dictionary to recognize multiple meanings.
- To identify the meaning of a word used in sentence context.

Writing

- To write a report.
- To use the writing process.
- To proofread for spelling, capitalization, and punctuation.
- To write legible manuscript and cursive letters.

Listening

- To listen to identify the word or words using /ô/, /ôr/.
- To listen to identify rhyming words and homophones.
- To listen to determine if a word functions as a noun or a verb in a sentence context.
- To follow oral directions.

Speaking

- To speak clearly to a group.
- To respond to a question.
- To present reports.
- To express feelings and ideas about a piece of writing.
- To contribute ideas and information in group discussions.

THIS WEEK'S WORDS

straw
horse
born
cause
corn
course
four
horn
jaw
north
short
talk
taught
walk
wash

MASTERY WORDS

before
crawl
draw
fall
more
tall

BONUS WORDS

acorn
corral
court
daughter
downpour
fawn
pause
stalk

Assignment Guide

This guide shows how you teach a typical spelling unit in either a five-day or a three-day sequence, while providing for individual differences. **Boldface type** indicates essential classwork. Steps shown in light type may be done in class or assigned as homework.

Five Days	○ = average spellers ★ = better spellers ✓ = slower spellers	Three Days
Day **1**	**a** ○ ★ **Take This Week's Words Trial Test and correct** ○ ✓ **Take Mastery Word Trial Test and correct** ○ ★ **Read This Week's Words and discuss generalization page 90**	Day **1**
Day **2**	○ Complete Spelling Practice page 91 ○ ✓ Complete Extra Practice Master 21: This Week's Words (optional) ✓ Complete Spelling on Your Own: Mastery Words page 93 ★ **Take Bonus Word Trial Test and correct** **b**	
Day **3**	**c** ○ ★ ✓ **Complete Spelling and Language page 92** ○ ★ ✓ Complete Writing on Your Own page 92 ○ ★ ✓ **Complete Using the Dictionary to Spell and Write page 92** ○ ✓ Take Midweek Test (optional) ★ Complete Spelling on Your Own: Bonus Words page 93 ○ ✓ Complete Spelling and Language Master 21 (optional)	Day **2**
Day **4**	○ Complete Spelling on Your Own: This Week's Words page 93 ✓ Complete Extra Practice Master 21: Mastery Words (optional) ★ Complete Extra Practice Master 21: Bonus Words (optional) **d**	
Day **5**	**e** ○ Take Unit Test on This Week's Words ○ Complete Reteaching Follow-up Masters 21A and 21B (optional) ○ ✓ **Take Unit Test on Mastery Words** ★ **Take Unit Test on Bonus Words**	Day **3**

Enrichment Activities for the **classroom** and for the **home** included at the end of this unit may be assigned selectively on any day of the week.

INTRODUCING THE UNIT

Establish Readiness for Learning

Tell the children that this week they will learn to spell more words with vowel sounds. They have learned many words with short and long vowels. Now they will learn some variant vowel sounds, the ones they hear in words such as *horn* and *cause.* They will learn several spellings for these sounds and will apply these spelling patterns to This Week's Words. Then they will use these words to write a paragraph.

Assess Children's Spelling Ability

Administer the Trial Test before the children study This Week's Words. Use the test sentences provided. Say each word and use it in a sentence. Then repeat the word. Have the children write the words on a separate sheet of paper or in their spelling notebooks. Test

sentences are also provided for Mastery and Bonus words.

Have the children check their own work by listening to you read the spelling of the words or by referring to This Week's Words in the left column of the **Pupil Book.** For each misspelled word, have the children follow the **Study Steps to Learn a Word** on page 1 in the **Pupil Book** or use the copying master to study and write the words. Children should record the number correct on their **Progress Report.**

Trial Test Sentences

This Week's Words
1. *straw*   The farmer put the *straw* in the barn. *straw*
2. *horse*   She rode a *horse* to the fair. *horse*
3. *born*   That kitten was *born* last month. *born*

4. *cause* They are trying to learn the *cause* of the fire. **cause**

5. *corn* Chickens often eat *corn*. **corn**

6. *course* Of *course* we can go to the circus. **course**

7. *four* Kent will be home at *four* o'clock. **four**

8. *horn* A rhinoceros has a *horn* on its snout. **horn**

9. *jaw* The ball hit Ellen in the *jaw*. **jaw**

10. *north* Toronto is *north* of New Orleans. **north**

11. *short* Those jeans are too *short* for me. **short**

12. *talk* Please don't *talk* during the test. **talk**

13. *taught* Ms. Ferguson *taught* the children a new game. **taught**

14. *walk* Let's *walk* to the library. **walk**

15. *wash* Derek will *wash* his hands before dinner. **wash**

Mastery Words

1. *before* Rhea got to school *before* 8:30. **before**

2. *crawl* Babies *crawl* before they learn to walk. **crawl**

3. *draw* Alexis can *draw* well. **draw**

4. *fall* Sometimes I *fall* when I skate. **fall**

5. *more* Stacy wants some *more* grapes. **more**

6. *tall* The giraffe is a *tall* animal. **tall**

Bonus Words

1. *acorn* The squirrel is eating an *acorn*. **acorn**

2. *corral* The horses are in a *corral*. **corral**

3. *court* The lawyer will go to *court* today. **court**

4. *daughter* Mrs. Green's *daughter* is named Robin. **daughter**

5. *downpour.* We got soaking wet in the *downpour*. **downpour**

6. *fawn* A *fawn* is a baby deer. **fawn**

7. *pause* Rory will *pause* before answering the question. **pause**

8. *stalk* The flowers grew on a tall *stalk*. **stalk**

Apply Prior Learning

Write the words *draw, talk, fall,* and *daughter* on the chalkboard and read them aloud. Ask the children what is alike about these words. (They have the same vowel sound.) Ask the children to notice how the vowel is spelled in each word. (Children should notice that there is an *a* in each word. They may also notice that the *a* is followed by an *l* in two words, and by a *u* or *w* in the other two words.) Some children may pronounce words such as *dog* and *frog* with the /ô/ sound. If so, you may want to remind them that this is yet another way to spell the sound. Tell the children that they will learn several ways to spell words with this vowel.

Write the words *for* and *board* on the chalkboard. Ask the children to listen for the sounds /ôr/ as you read them aloud. Tell the children that they will learn ways to spell these sounds.

FOCUS

- Relates to prior learning
- Draws relationships
- Applies spelling generalizations to new contexts

FOR CHILDREN WITH SPECIAL NEEDS

Learning Difficulties

Children with Attention Deficit Disorder (ADD) may require special teaching techniques to help them learn multiple spellings for the same sound. Using a multisensory approach captures their attention and reinforces the material to be learned.

In cursive script, have the child write on a sheet of paper each of This Week's Words that is spelled with the /ô/ sound spelled *a, aw,* and *au.* Then have the child take the following actions: 1) say each word; 2) using the forefinger of the preferred writing hand, trace over the letters of the word, saying the letter names aloud; 3) using a pencil, trace over the letters of the word, saying the letter names aloud; 4) write the word beneath the one that has just been traced; 5) cover up the two previously written words and write the word from memory.

Follow this procedure for the /ô/ sounds that are spelled *or* and *our.*

Limited English Proficiency

To help limited English proficient children work with the spelling generalizations for Unit 21, you may wish to refer to the booklet "Suggestions and Activities for Limited English Proficient Students."

TEACHING PLAN

Objective To spell words that demonstrate these sound-letter relationships: /ô/a, aw, au; /ôr/or, our.

1. Direct the children's attention to the pictures on page 90, and ask them to identify the things shown. When they have identified *straw* and *horse*, write the two words on the chalkboard. Help the children to hear the sound /ô/ at the end of *straw* and the sounds /ôr/ in *horse*.
2. Read the generalization on page 90 aloud.

You may wish to introduce the lesson by using **Spelling Generalizations Transparency 18.**

3. Have volunteers read This Week's Words aloud. As each word is read, ask the children to indicate if the word is a "straw word" or a "horse word"—that is, if /ô/ or /ôr/ is heard in the word. Then have them identify the letter or letters that spell the given sound. In some dialects, there is no distinction between the sounds /ô/ and /ôr/. *Horse, course,* and *moss* may be pronounced as rhyming words. If the children have difficulty hearing /r/, pay special attention to the *r* that follows o and ou in This Week's Words.
4. The word *wash* has several pronunciations: /wôsh/, /wosh/, /woish/, /wô(e)rsh/, /wärsh/. If *wash* is not pronounced /wôsh/ in your area, relate the letter *a* to the vowel sound heard in *wash*. If the sound /r/ is heard in the children's pronunciation, stress that the letter *r* does not appear in the word *wash*.

You may wish to assign **LEP Practice Master 21** for reinforcement in writing spelling words.

21 The Sounds /ô/ and /ôr/

THIS WEEK'S WORDS

1. straw
2. horse
3. born
4. cause
5. corn
6. course
7. four
8. horn
9. jaw
10. north
11. short
12. talk
13. taught
14. walk
15. wash

/ô/ /ôr/

90

This Week's Words

The sound /ô/ is heard in <u>straw</u>. It can be spelled with these letters.

● **a,** as in <u>talk</u>

● **aw,** as in <u>straw</u>

● **au,** as in <u>cause</u>

The sounds /ôr/ are heard in <u>horse</u>. The sound /ô/ with <u>r</u> in this word is spelled <u>or</u>.

☐ The words <u>course</u> and <u>four</u> spell the sounds /ôr/ with **our.**

Extra Practice: This Week's Words

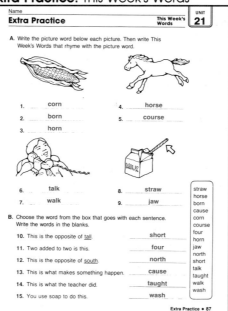

Name
Extra Practice   This Week's Words   UNIT 21

A. Write the picture word below each picture. Then write This Week's Words that rhyme with the picture word.

1. corn
2. born
3. horn

4. horse
5. course

6. talk
7. walk

8. straw
9. jaw

| straw |
| horse |
| born |
| cause |
| corn |
| course |
| four |
| horn |
| jaw |
| north |
| short |
| talk |
| taught |
| walk |
| wash |

B. Choose the word from the box that goes with each sentence. Write the words in the blanks.

10. This is the opposite of <u>tall</u>.   short
11. Two added to two is this.   four
12. This is the opposite of <u>south</u>.   north
13. This is what makes something happen.   cause
14. This is what the teacher did.   taught
15. You use soap to do this.   wash

Extra Practice • 87

Extra Practice: Mastery Words

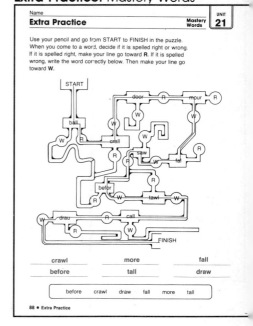

Name
Extra Practice   Mastery Words   UNIT 21

Use your pencil and go from START to FINISH in the puzzle. When you come to a word, decide if it is spelled right or wrong. If it is spelled right, make your line go toward **R**. If it is spelled wrong, write the word correctly below. Then make your line go toward **W**.

| crawl | more | fall |
| before | tall | draw |

| before | crawl | draw | fall | more | tall |

88 • Extra Practice

Spelling Practice

A. Follow the directions. Use This Week's Words.

1. Write the two words that have /ô/ spelled as it is in <u>paw</u>.

   <u>straw</u>   <u>jaw</u>

2. Write the word that sounds just like <u>for</u>. <u>four</u>

3. Write the six words that have /ôr/ spelled as it is in <u>for</u>.

   <u>horse</u>   <u>born</u>   <u>corn</u>

   <u>horn</u>   <u>north</u>   <u>short</u>

4. Write the other word that has /ôr/ spelled as it is in <u>four</u>.

   <u>course</u>

5. Write the word that rhymes with <u>caught</u>. <u>taught</u>

6. Write the three words that have the sound /ô/ spelled
   with <u>a</u>. Circle the words that have a "silent" letter <u>l</u>.

   (talk)   (walk)   <u>wash</u>

B. Add the letters that spell /ô/ and /ôr/. Write the words
that finish the story.

A unicorn looks like a
(**7**) h___se. But it has a long,
straight (**8**) h___n on its
forehead. Unicorns like to
(**9**) w___sh their horns in water.
This makes the water magic for
a (**10**) sh___t time. It can
(**11**) c___se people to have
good luck. Of (**12**) c___se, there
is really no such thing as a
unicorn.

7. <u>horse</u>   8. <u>horn</u>   9. <u>wash</u>

10. <u>short</u>   11. <u>cause</u>   12. <u>course</u>

This Week's Words list (right column):
straw
horse
born
cause
corn
course
four
horn
jaw
north
short
talk
taught
walk
wash

91

TEACHING PLAN

Objectives To write words given
sound-letter clues; to write words
given homophones; to write rhyming
words; to write words that complete
a story.

1. Read the directions for Exercise **A**
   on page 91, and work through the
   activities orally with the children.
   Then read the directions for Exercise
   B to be sure that the children understand what they are to do.
2. Have the children complete the
   activities independently. Remind
   them to use legible handwriting. You
   may wish to demonstrate the
   correct form of the letters *a, o, r, u,*
   and *w,* and then have the children
   practice writing the letters. For
   Handwriting Models, refer the
   children to page 258 in the **Pupil
   Book.**
3. To correct the children's work, have
   volunteers write their answers for Exercise **A** on the chalkboard. Have a
   volunteer read the completed story
   for Exercise **B** aloud. Let the children
   check their own work.

For reinforcement in writing spelling
words, you may wish to assign **Extra
Practice Master 21: This Week's
Words.**

★ *of special interest*

The word *corn* was originally applied
to all edible grains. When English
colonists came to America and were
introduced to American Indian maize,
they called it "Indian corn." In time, the
grain the American Indians called
maize came to be known simply as
corn, and in American usage, the word
corn lost its general meaning "grain."

Extra Practice: Bonus Words

Name _____
Extra Practice   **UNIT 21** Bonus Words

A. Say the name for this:

The name is said /ôr/. Write the three Bonus words with the
sounds /ôr/ in alphabetical order on the oars.

1. acorn
2. court
3. downpour

B. Now try this "word math." Write a Bonus word.

4. fin − /i/ + /ô/ = _____ fawn
5. steak − /ā/ + /ô/ = _____ stalk
6. day − /ā/ + /ô/ + /tər/ = _____ daughter
7. cart − /är/ + /ôr/ = _____ court
8. down + pair − /âr/ + /ôr/ = _____ downpour

C. <u>Paws</u> and <u>pause</u> sound just alike: /pôz/. Decide which word
fits each sentence. Then write the right spelling.

9. There was a /pôz/ before everyone started clapping. _____ pause
10. That cat's back /pôz/ each have six toes. _____ paws
11. These tracks were made by a bear's /pôz/. _____ paws
12. Let's /pôz/ for a while and sit on this rock. _____ pause

stalk daughter pause fawn corral downpour court acorn

Extra Practice • 89

Summarize Learning

Have the children summarize what
they have learned on pages 90 and
91. *Ask:*

- What vowel sounds have you
  learned about in this lesson? (/ô/ and
  /ôr/)
- What did you learn about these
  sounds? (three ways to spell the
  vowel sound /ô/a, aw, au: two ways
  to spell the vowel sounds /ôr/or, our)
- What are some examples of words
  using the different spellings of /ô/
  and /ôr/? (talk, straw, cause, horse,
  course; accept other examples)

TEACHING PLAN

SPELLING AND LANGUAGE

Objective To write words in sentence context and recognize whether a word is used as a verb or a noun.

1. Read the introductory sentences and the directions on page 92. Remind the children to choose one of This Week's Words that will complete both sentences in each pair.
2. Have the children complete the activity independently.
3. Have volunteers read each pair of sentences aloud. Let the children check their own work.

For extended practice in recognizing parts of speech, you may wish to assign *Spelling and Language Master 21.*

WRITING ON YOUR OWN

Objectives To write a report; to proofread for spelling.

1. Review the directions.
2. As a **prewriting** activity, discuss with the children some of their favorite animals. Write the name of one animal in a circle on the chalkboard, and have the children generate facts about it. Write these facts in a cluster around the core word. Then have the children **compose** their reports. When they are ready to **revise,** remind them to check for spelling. To **publish,** have children read their reports to the class.

USING THE DICTIONARY

Objectives To recognize multiple meanings; to identify the meaning of a word used in sentence context.

1. Read the introductory paragraph on page 92 aloud. Remind the children that a noun names a

person, place, or thing, and that a verb shows action or being.
2. Ask a child to read the noun definition of *cause* and the illustrative sentence given in the sample entry. Ask a second child to read the verb definition of *cause* and the illustrative sentence.
3. Read the directions on page 92. Remind the children to refer to the dictionary entry to help them determine if *cause* is a noun or a verb in each sentence.
4. Have the children complete the activity independently.
5. Review the activity orally with the children and let them check their own work.

THIS WEEK'S WORDS
straw
horse
born
cause
corn
course
four
horn
jaw
north
short
talk
taught
walk
wash

Spelling and Language • Nouns and Verbs

A **noun** names a person, a place, or a thing. A **verb** shows action or being. Finish each pair of sentences with one of This Week's Words. The word will be a verb in the first sentence and a noun in the second.

1. The boys _____ wash _____ their clothes.
2. When the _____ wash _____ is done, they have lunch.
3. Aunt Ann always listens when I _____ talk _____ to her.
4. I feel good after a long _____ talk _____ with her.

Writing on Your Own

Write a report about your favorite animal for your teacher. Use some of This Week's Words as both nouns and verbs.

 WRITER'S GUIDE For a sample report, turn to page 254.

Using the Dictionary to Spell and Write

A **definition** tells what a word means. Some words have more than one definition. You need to know the different definitions of a word to make sure you used the word correctly in your writing. Read the definitions for the word cause. One is a noun (n.). The other is a verb (v.).

> **cause** /kôz/ *n.* A person or thing that makes something happen; reason: He was the *cause* of the trouble.
> —*v.* **caused, causing** To make something happen: A traffic jam *caused* us to be late.

Write n. or v. to show how cause is used in each sentence.

1. __v.__ What could have caused Taro to stay at home?
2. __n.__ No one knows the cause of the fire.
3. __n.__ You have no cause to be angry.

92

Extra Practice: Spelling and Language

Name	UNIT
Spelling and Language	**21**

A. Write noun or verb to tell if the underlined word in each sentence is a noun or a verb.

1. Cesar and Peter really like to talk.   **verb**
2. Today they went for a walk in the woods.   **noun**
3. They had to wash their clothes when they got home.   **verb**
4. They were dirty, and dusty paths were the cause.   **noun**
5. Their mother gave them a talk about keeping clean.   **noun**
6. They will hang their wash on a line.   **noun**
7. The sun will cause the clothes to dry.   **verb**
8. Then Cesar and Peter can walk in the woods again.   **verb**

straw	
horse	
born	
cause	
corn	
course	
four	
horn	
jaw	
north	
short	
talk	
taught	
walk	
wash	

B. Write the noun in each sentence.

9. A straw horse cannot run.   **horse**
10. Old straw smells good.   **straw**
11. Corn grows slowly.   **corn**
12. Drive around the course!   **course**
13. Honk your horn!   **horn**

90 • Extra Practice

Spelling on Your Own

THIS WEEK'S WORDS

Make a "word chain" with This Week's Words. Write one word. Use a letter in that word to write another word. Keep going, writing words across and down. Try to link all the words in one chain. You may also make more than one chain.

```
                    f         f
                    o         o
h o r n   h o r n   h o r n
                    u         u
          f         r   s t r a w
          o
          u
          r
```

MASTERY WORDS

Follow the directions. Use the Mastery words.

1. Write the two words that have /ô/ spelled <u>a</u>.

　　fall　　　　　　　tall

2. Write the two words that have /ô/ spelled <u>aw</u>.

　　crawl　　　　　　draw

3. Write the two words that have the sounds /ôr/.

　before　　　　　　more

Write the Mastery words that are the opposite of these words.

4. less 　　more　　　**5.** after 　before

6. short 　　tall

> before
> crawl
> draw
> fall
> more
> tall

BONUS WORDS

Write a Bonus word to go with each definition.

1. girl child　　**2.** place for horses　　**3.** rainstorm
4. baby deer　　**5.** place for a judge　　**6.** seed of oak trees

Follow the directions. Use the Bonus words.

7. Write the word that sounds just like <u>paws</u>.
8. Write the word with a "silent" letter <u>l</u>.
9. Use the Bonus words in sentences. Try to make your sentences tell a story. Read your story to a friend.

See answers below.

> acorn
> corral
> court
> daughter
> downpour
> fawn
> pause
> stalk

93

Spelling on Your Own Answers

BONUS WORDS

1. daughter 2. corral 3. downpour 4. fawn
5. court 6. acorn 7. pause 8. stalk
9. Children will write as directed. Be sure to check spelling.

Summarize Learning

Have the children summarize what they have learned in this unit. *Ask:*

• What have you learned about verbs and nouns in this lesson? (A noun names a person, a place, or a thing. A verb shows action or being. Some words can be used as both verbs and nouns.)
• What have you learned about dictionary definitions? (A definition tells what a word means. Some words have more than one definition.)
• What spelling generalizations have you learned? How did you use these generalizations?

TEACHING PLAN

> **Objective**　To apply the unit spelling generalization to spell This Week's Words, Mastery words, and Bonus words independently.

THIS WEEK'S WORDS

1. Read the directions on page 93. Copy onto the chalkboard the third step of the sample word chain given in the **Pupil Book.** Ask the children to find a word on the list that can be linked up with *straw.*
2. Have the children complete the activity independently.

MASTERY WORDS

1. Review the sounds /ô/ and /ôr/. Remind the children that /ô/ is heard in *straw* and /ôr/ is heard in *horse.*
2. Have volunteers read the Mastery words aloud. As each word is read, indicate whether the word has the sound /ô/ or the sounds /ôr/, and identify the letter or letters that spell the given sound in the word.
3. Have the children complete the exercises independently.

BONUS WORDS

1. Briefly review the unit generalization on page 90.
2. Have volunteers read the Bonus words aloud. As each word is read, help the children to identify the letters that spell /ô/ or /ôr/ in the word. Point out to the children that neither the sound /ô/ nor the sounds /ôr/ is heard in *corral.*
3. Have the children complete the exercises independently on a separate piece of paper.

For reinforcement in writing spelling words, you may wish to assign *Extra Practice Master 21: Mastery Words* or *Bonus Words.*

CLOSING THE UNIT

Apply New Learning

Tell the children that if they misspell words with the sound /ô/ in their writing, they should use one or more of the following strategies:

- think about the possible spellings for the sound /ô/ and try to picture the word in their minds.
- think about the possible spellings for the sound within the word and use the dictionary to find the correct spelling.
- think of words that rhyme and compare in their minds how they are spelled.

Transfer New Learning

Tell the children that when they encounter new words in their personal reading and in other content areas, they should learn the meaning of those words and then apply the generalizations they have studied to the spelling of those words. Tell them that once the words are familiar in both meaning and spelling, they should use the new words in their writing.

ENRICHMENT ACTIVITIES

Classroom activities and **home activities** may be assigned to children of all ability levels. The activities provide opportunities for children to use their spelling words in new contexts.

For the Classroom

To individualize classroom activities, you may have the children use the word list they are studying in this unit.

- *Basic:* Use **Mastery** words to complete the activity.
- *Average:* Use **This Week's Words** to complete the activity.
- *Challenging:* Use **Bonus** words to complete the activity.

1. Language Arts/Writing Definitions Have the children choose five spelling words for which they will write definitions. Tell the children that you will give them a definition for one of This Week's Words. They will have to choose the right word. Present this definition: *a number that comes after three and before five.* After the children name *four,* have them write their own definitions for each of the five words they have chosen. When they have completed their definitions, have the children exchange papers with one another and guess the word that matches each definition.

   ■ COOPERATIVE LEARNING: Have each group create a set of definitions for as many spelling words as there are group members. Each child within the group should write a definition. Then have the group members read their definitions to one another to see if their meanings are

clear and effective. When each group is satisfied that their definitions are good ones, have classmates read them and guess the word that matches each definition.

2. Language Arts/Using Alliteration Have the children write sentences with alliteration, using the words from all three spelling lists. Explain that alliteration is the repetition of the same initial sound in the words of a sentence. Provide the children with this example: *Teddy T. Thompson taught toothless Tony Taylor to talk.* After writing the sentences, have the children exchange papers and read them aloud. Each child may want to make a booklet of favorite sentences.

   ■ COOPERATIVE LEARNING: Have each group make up a set of sentences with alliteration using words from the three spelling lists. Have the group members decide which spelling words they will each use according to the initial sound of each word. Then have each member write his or her own sentences. When everyone in the group has completed the sentences, have them share the sentences, combine and extend where necessary, and proofread for correct spelling, capitalization, and punctuation. When the group is satisfied with the corrections and changes, have the members select one child to rewrite the sentences into a booklet. Then have the group share their work with other classmates.

3. Language Arts/Writing a Friendly Letter Have the children write a letter to Farmer Smith to thank him for allowing them to visit his farm. First, direct the children's attention to page 251 of the **Writer's Guide** to read about friendly letters. As a *prewriting* activity have the children look over the words from their spelling lists and note which ones might be used in the letter. Then tell them to list anything they may have seen or done, and what they liked best and why. Have the children **compose** their letters, using their list and as many spelling words as they can. Next, tell them to *revise* their letters, making sure they have followed the format for writing a letter and that they have included everything they wanted to say. Remind the children to proofread for spelling, capitalization, and punctuation, using the **Revising Checklist** on page 247 for help. Have them draw a picture of something they saw or did at the farm and *publish* their letters on a bulletin board.

   ■ COOPERATIVE LEARNING: Have each group write a letter to Farmer Smith thanking him for allowing them to visit. Direct the children's attention to page 251 of the **Writer's Guide** to read about friendly letters. As a *prewriting* activity, have the members of the group discuss the things they saw, did, or enjoyed most of all. Then have one member of the group make a list. When the children are ready to **compose** the letter, have them choose one child to begin orally by providing the first sentence of the letter and another child to record the letter. Each child should build on the first sentence, each adding one or more sentences. Group members should then **revise** the letter, making sure that it includes everything they wanted to say about the visit. Each child within the group should also proofread for spelling, capitalization, and punctuation. Then have the group select one person to rewrite the letter. Each group should **publish** their letter by reading it aloud.

For the Home

Children may complete these activities independently or with the assistance of a relative or friend in the home.

1. **Language Arts/Categorizing Nouns and Verbs** Have the children make two columns at the top of a sheet of paper. Tell them to label the first column *Nouns* and the second column *Verbs*. Remind the children that *nouns* name people, places, and things, and that *verbs* are action words. Tell the children to decide which spelling words are nouns and which words are verbs. Have them list the words accordingly. For example, *Nouns: straw, horse, corn; Verbs: talk, walk, wash.* Then have the children add other words to these categories. They may wish to illustrate the words and keep them in a notebook for future reference. Have them share their lists with a friend or relative.

2. **Science/Writing a Factual Paragraph on Babies** Discuss with the children that when many animal babies are born, they are able to walk or move about almost immediately. Point out that human babies, on the other hand, are not able to walk at birth. Have the children write a paragraph explaining the steps human babies go through before they are able to walk. Tell the children to use time-order words such as *first, next, then,* and *finally,* as well as spelling words from all three lists. The children can also illustrate their paragraphs. Tell them to share their paragraphs with a friend or family member.

3. **Language Arts/Writing a Description** Tell the children to look at the words on all three spelling lists. Then have them use as many of these words as possible to describe something without actually naming it. Refer the children to page 250 of the **Writer's Guide** for a model of a descriptive paragraph. After checking for correct spelling, capitalization, and punctuation, using the **Revising Checklist** on page 247 for help, have the children share their descriptions with someone at home to see if that person can guess what is being described.

4. **Fine Arts/Writing and Illustrating Sentences** Have the children write five sentences using the spelling words that have to do with life on a farm, such as *straw, horse,* and *corn.* Then have the children draw pictures to illustrate these sentences. The children may also use other words that have the /ôr/ or /ô/ sounds in their sentences.

EVALUATING SPELLING ABILITY

Unit Test

This Week's Words
1. **straw** The scarecrow was stuffed with *straw.* **straw.**
2. **horse** Kelly is learning how to ride a *horse.* **horse**
3. **born** Taro was *born* in 1976. **born**
4. **cause** Lightning can *cause* a forest fire. **cause**
5. **corn** We grow *corn* in our garden. **corn**
6. **course** Mr. Lopez is taking a *course* at State College. **course**
7. **four** I need *four* children to help me. **four**
8. **horn** Arnie can play the *horn.* **horn**
9. **jaw** Jessie had a bruise on her *jaw.* **jaw**
10. **north** Our family will travel *north* this summer. **north**
11. **short** Our dog's tail is very *short.* **short**
12. **talk** Mr. Bearheels and I had a long *talk.* **talk**
13. **taught** Dad *taught* me how to fix my bicycle. **taught**
14. **walk** Let's take a *walk* on the beach. **walk**
15. **wash** Maureen and Neal did the *wash.* **wash**

Mastery Words
1. **before** We must leave *before* seven. **before**
2. **crawl** That baby is learning how to *crawl.* **crawl**
3. **draw** Gretchen will *draw* a mural for our room. **draw**
4. **fall** The school year begins in the *fall.* **fall**
5. **more** I wish we had *more* time to play. **more**
6. **tall** Vicki is a very *tall* girl. **tall**

Bonus Words
1. **acorn** Let's plant this *acorn* and see if it will grow. **acorn**
2. **corral** The *corral* is near the barn. **corral**
3. **court** Russell is going to the tennis *court.* **court**
4. **daughter** Mrs. Benson's *daughter* is a schoolteacher. **daughter**
5. **downpour** The *downpour* soaked everyone on the field. **downpour**
6. **fawn** We saw a *fawn* in the woods. **fawn**
7. **pause** There was a short *pause* before the music started again. **pause**
8. **stalk** A *stalk* of corn can grow several feet high. **stalk**

Dictation Sentences

This Week's Words
1. Our teacher *taught four* boys to ride the *horse.*
2. Of *course* I will take a *short walk* with you.
3. His *jaw* hurts too much to *talk* or play the *horn.*
4. The *north* wind will blow down the *corn.*
5. The baby pigs were *born* on the *straw* in the pen.
6. A hard rain can *cause* some plants to *wash* away.

Mastery Words
1. The *tall* bird ate the bug *before* it could *crawl* away.
2. She will *draw more* pictures of the *fall* leaves.

Bonus Words
1. The *fawn* seemed to *pause* in the woods when the *downpour* started.
2. The corn *stalk* near the horse *corral* is taller than my *daughter.*
3. An *acorn* rolled onto the tennis *court.*

RETEACHING STRATEGIES FOR SPELLING

Children who have made errors on the Unit Test may require reteaching. Use the following **Reteaching Strategies** and **Follow-up Masters 21A** and **21B** for additional instruction and practice of This Week's Words. (You may wish to assign **LEP Reteaching Follow-up Master 21** for reteaching of spelling words.)

A. Discovering Spelling Ideas

1. Say the following words as you write them on the chalkboard.

   balk   for
   law   source
   pause

2. Ask the children to identify the common sound in each column of words. (/ô/ and /ôr/)
3. Ask the children to identify the letters that spell /ô/. (a, aw, au)
4. Ask the children to identify the letters that spell /ôr/. (or, our)
5. Ask the children what they have learned about spelling /ô/ and /ôr/. (/ô/ can be spelled with a, aw, or au, /ôr/ can be spelled with or or our)

B. Word Shapes

1. Explain to the children that each word has a shape and that remembering the shape of a word can help them to spell the word correctly.
2. On the chalkboard, write the words torn and paw. Have the children identify "short," "tall," and "tail" letters.
3. Draw the configuration of each word on the chalkboard, and ask the children which word fits in each shape.

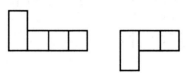

Use **Reteaching Follow-up Master 21A** to reinforce spelling generalizations taught in Unit 21.

Use **Reteaching Follow-up Master 21B** to reinforce spellings of This Week's Words for Unit 21.

Name _____
Reteaching Follow-up A   Discovering Spelling Ideas   UNIT 21

THIS WEEK'S WORDS

straw	born	cause	course	four
talk	short	jaw	horse	corn
north	taught	horn	walk	wash

1. Study This Week's Words. Say each word to yourself.

2. In each column, write the words that have the same vowel sound as the first word in the column. Circle the letters that make the sound.

paw	porch
straw	born
cause	course
talk	-four
jaw	short
taught	horse
walk	corn
wash	north
	horn

3. What vowel sound do the words in the first column have? ___ /ô/

4. What sounds do the words in the second column have? ___ /ôr/

5. What have you learned about the spellings of the sound /ô/?
   /ô/ can be spelled a, aw, and au.

6. What have you learned about the spellings of the sounds /ôr/?
   /ôr/ can be spelled or and our

Reteaching • 35

Name _____
Reteaching Follow-up B   Word Shapes   UNIT 21

THIS WEEK'S WORDS

straw	born	cause	course	four
talk	short	jaw	horse	corn
north	taught	horn	walk	wash

Write each of This Week's Words in its correct shape. The first one has been done for you. Children may interchange answers that fit the same configuration.

1. taught
2. cause
3. straw
4. short
5. course
6. horn
7. wash
8. corn
9. horse
10. walk
11. born
12. four
13. jaw
14. north
15. talk

36 • Reteaching

93C   UNIT 21 *The Sounds /ô/ and /ôr/*

PREVIEWING THE UNIT

Unit Materials

Instruction and Practice

Pupil Book   pages 94–97
Teacher's Edition
  Teaching Plans   pages 94–97
  Enrichment Activities
    For the Classroom   pages 97A–97B
    For the Home   page 97B
  Reteaching Strategies   page 97C

Testing

Teacher's Edition
  Trial Test   pages 93E–93F
  Unit Test   page 97B
  Dictation Test   page 97B

Additional Resources

PRACTICE AND REINFORCEMENT
Extra Practice Master 22: This Week's Words
Extra Practice Master 22: Mastery Words
Extra Practice Master 22: Bonus Words
LEP Practice Master 22
Spelling and Language Master 22
Study Steps to Learn a Word Master

RETEACHING FOLLOW-UP
Reteaching Follow-up Master 22A:
  Discovering Spelling Ideas
Reteaching Follow-up Master 22B: Word
  Shapes
LEP Reteaching Follow-up Master 22

TEACHING AIDS
Spelling Generalizations Transparency 19

Click on the SPELLING banner to find activities for this unit.

Learner Objectives

Spelling

● To spell words that demonstrate these sound-letter relationships: /ûr/*ir, ur, ear, or.*

Reading

● To follow written directions.

Writing

● To write a poem.
● To use the writing process.
● To proofread for spelling, capitalization, and punctuation.
● To write legible manuscript and cursive letters.

Listening

● To listen to identify compound words.
● To listen to identify words with /ûr/*ir, ur, ear, or.*
● To follow oral directions.

Speaking

● To speak clearly to a group.
● To respond to a question.
● To present poems to the class.
● To express feelings and ideas about a piece of writing.
● To contribute ideas and information in group discussions.

THIS WEEK'S WORDS

sir
fur
learn
world
birthday
bluebird
burn
circle
early
earn
earth
heard
return
skirt
worry

MASTERY WORDS

bird
hurt
work
turn
girl
word

BONUS WORDS

pearl
purpose
search
thirsty
turtle
whirl
worst
worth

Assignment Guide

This guide shows how you teach a typical spelling unit in either a five-day or a three-day sequence, while providing for individual differences. **Boldface type** indicates essential classwork. Steps shown in light type may be done in class or assigned as homework.

Five Days	○ = average spellers ★ = better spellers ✓ = slower spellers	Three Days
Day **1**	**a** ● ★ **Take This Week's Words Trial Test and correct** ● ✓ **Take Mastery Word Trial Test and correct** ● ★ **Read This Week's Words and discuss generalization page 94**	Day **1**
Day **2**	● Complete Spelling Practice page 95 ● ✓ Complete Extra Practice Master 22: This Week's Words (optional) ✓ Complete Spelling on Your Own: Mastery Words page 97 ★ **Take Bonus Word Trial Test and correct** **b**	Day **1**
Day **3**	**c** ● ★ ✓ **Complete Spelling and Language page 96** ● ★ ✓ Complete Writing on Your Own page 96 ● ★ ✓ **Complete Proofreading page 96** ● ✓ Take Midweek Test (optional) ★ Complete Spelling on Your Own: Bonus Words page 97 ● ✓ Complete Spelling and Language Master 22 (optional)	Day **2**
Day **4**	● Complete Spelling on Your Own: This Week's Words page 97 ✓ Complete Extra Practice Master 22: Mastery Words (optional) ★ Complete Extra Practice Master 22: Bonus Words (optional) **d**	Day **2**
Day **5**	**e** ● Take Unit Test on This Week's Words ● Complete Reteaching Follow-up Masters 22A and 22B (optional) ● ✓ **Take Unit Test on Mastery Words** ★ **Take Unit Test on Bonus Words**	Day **3**

Enrichment Activities for the **classroom** and for the **home** included at the end of this unit may be assigned selectively on any day of the week.

INTRODUCING THE UNIT

Establish Readiness for Learning

Tell the children that this week they will continue to learn about vowel sounds. In Unit 22 they will study several spellings for the vowel sound /ûr/. Tell the children that they will apply the spelling generalizations to This Week's Words and use those words to write a poem.

Assess Children's Spelling Ability

Administer the Trial Test before the children study This Week's Words. Use the test sentences provided. Say each word and use it in a sentence. Then repeat the word. Have the children write the words on a separate sheet of paper or in their spelling notebooks. Test sentences are also provided for Mastery and Bonus words.

Have the children check their own work by

listening to you read the spelling of the words or by referring to This Week's Words in the left column of the **Pupil Book.** For each misspelled word, have the children follow the **Study Steps to Learn a Word** on page 1 in the **Pupil Book** or use the copying master to study and write the words. Children should record the number correct on their **Progress Report.**

Trial Test Sentences

This Week's Words

1. *sir* "Good morning, *sir*," said the cab driver. *sir*
2. *fur* A bear has a heavy *fur* coat. *fur*
3. *learn* Martin wants to *learn* to do a cartwheel. *learn*
4. *world* Some people have traveled all over the *world*. *world*
5. *birthday* Lucy's *birthday* is next week. *birthday*

FOCUS

- Establishes objectives
- Relates to prior learning
- Sets purpose of instruction

6. *bluebird*   Robbie spotted a *bluebird* in the tree.   **bluebird**

7. *burn*   We can *burn* this wood in the fireplace.   **burn**

8. *circle*   The children sat in a *circle* and told stories.   **circle**

9. *early*   We woke up *early* this morning.   **early**

10. *earn*   My sister and brother *earn* money by baby-sitting.   **earn**

11. *earth*   Dudley dug a hole in the *earth*.   **earth**

12. *heard*   Sal *heard* his mother calling.   **heard**

13. *return*   The plane will *return* to San Francisco tonight.   **return**

14. *skirt*   Nell is wearing a *skirt* today.   **skirt**

15. *worry*   You don't have to *worry* about getting lost.   **worry**

Mastery Words

1. *bird*   Becky knows the name of almost every *bird*.   **bird**

2. *hurt*   The dog will not *hurt* you.   **hurt**

3. *work*   All children have finished their *work*.   **work**

4. *turn*   We must *turn* left at the next corner.   **turn**

5. *girl*   That *girl* is my friend Belinda.   **girl**

6. *word*   Pancho can spell that *word*.   **word**

Bonus Words

1. *pearl*   Maybe there is a *pearl* ring in that box.   **pearl**

2. *purpose*   I didn't hit you with the ball on purpose.   **purpose**

3. *search*   We will *search* everywhere for the lost key.   **search**

4. *thirsty*   Max is *thirsty* after playing football.   **thirsty**

5. *turtle*   Cindy saw a *turtle* in the road.   **turtle**

6. *whirl*   Do ice skaters get dizzy when they *whirl* around?   **whirl**

7. *worst*   The *worst* storm of the winter was in February.   **worst**

8. *worth*   That gold watch is *worth* a lot of money.   **worth**

Apply Prior Learning

Have the children apply what they already know about vowel sounds by participating in the following activity.

Write the words *girl, burn, learn,* and *worm* on the chalkboard. Read these words aloud with the children. Ask the children to tell how these words are alike, and help them to recognize that each word has the /ûr/ sound. Ask volunteers to come to the chalkboard and draw a line around the letters that represent /ûr/ in each word. Tell the children that in Unit 22 they will study words that have these spellings for /ûr/. Explain that they can use these words in a variety of writing tasks: they can use the words in a note to a friend, in a letter, or in a book report.

FOCUS

- Relates to prior learning
- Draws relationships
- Applies spelling generalizations to new contexts

FOR CHILDREN WITH SPECIAL NEEDS

Learning Difficulties

Children with information-processing deficiencies may need additional help in learning which of the four spellings of /ûr/ apply to This Week's Words. Use an approach such as the following which emphasizes visual imaging.

Write This Week's Words on the chalkboard. On a sheet of lined paper, have each child copy a spelling word from the chalkboard. Spell the word aloud with the children. Have them cover the word with a piece of paper and close their eyes. Ask them to visualize the word as you spell it aloud for them. With eyes still closed, they should spell the word aloud. With eyes open, they should then try to visualize the word on their papers. Direct the children to trace the image of the word onto the paper.

Then have them say the letters of the word aloud while writing each one. Finally, have the children check their spelling to see that it matches the word that was first written. If it is misspelled, have them cross it out and write it correctly so that the correct spelling is reinforced.

Limited English Proficiency

To help limited English proficient children work with the spelling generalizations for Unit 22, you may wish to refer to the booklet "Suggestions and Activities for Limited English Proficient Students."

TEACHING PLAN

Objective To spell words that demonstrate these sound-letter relationships: /ûr/ *ir, ur, ear, or.*

1. Have the children look at the picture on page 94 and ask a child to read the sentence below the picture. Tell the children that the same vowel sound with *r* is heard in four of the words in the sentence. Help them to recognize that *early, bird, purple,* and *worm* have the sounds /ûr/, and to identify the letters that spell /ûr/ in each word.
2. Read the generalization on page 94 aloud.

You may wish to introduce the lesson by using **Spelling Generalizations Transparency 19.**

3. Have volunteers read This Week's Words. As each word is read, have the children identify the letters that spell /ûr/ in the word. Then ask the children to identify the two words that are compound words. (birthday, bluebird) Point out the letters *re* at the beginning of *return.* Ask children what it means to *redo* a paper or to *retell* a story. (*do it again, tell it again*). Explain that the letters *re* at the beginning of a word often mean *again.*

You may wish to assign **LEP Practice Master 22** for reinforcement in writing spelling words.

---

22 The Sounds /ûr/

THIS WEEK'S WORDS

1. sir
2. fur
3. learn
4. world
5. birthday
6. bluebird
7. burn
8. circle
9. early
10. earn
11. earth
12. heard
13. return
14. skirt
15. worry

The early bird catches the purple worm.

This Week's Words

The sound /û/ with <u>r</u> is heard in all the words this week. Here are four ways to spell /ûr/.

- with **ir**, as in <u>bird</u> and <u>sir</u>
- with **ur**, as in <u>purple</u> and <u>fur</u>
- with **ear**, as in <u>early</u> and <u>learn</u>
- with **or**, as in <u>worm</u> and <u>world</u>

94

Extra Practice: This Week's Words

Name
Extra Practice
This Week's Words | UNIT 22

Finish the puzzle with This Week's Words. Each clue tells something about one of the words. Choose the word and write it where it belongs in the puzzle.

ACROSS
3. A fire does this.
4. The planet we live on.
5. Used ears to listen.
7. To be afraid something is wrong.
9. A word used instead of a man's name.
10. It is blue and can fly.
12. Make money by working.
13. The opposite of <u>late</u>.

DOWN
1. The shape of a ring or ball.
2. It keeps an animal warm.
3. You have one once a year.
6. The United States is on one side of this. China is on the other.
8. To give back.
9. Something a girl might wear.
11. What you do in school.

sir	fur	learn	world	birthday
bluebird	burn	circle	early	earn
earth	heard	return	skirt	worry

Extra Practice • 91

Extra Practice: Mastery Words

Name
Extra Practice
Mastery Words | UNIT 22

Circle the Mastery word in each box that is spelled correctly.

burd berd (bird)	tern tirn (turn)
werk wurk (work)	(hurt) hirt hert
wurd (word) wird	gerl gurl (girl)

Write each word you circled under the letters that spell /ûr/ in that word.

ir	**or**
bird	work
girl	word

| **ur** |
| turn |
| hurt |

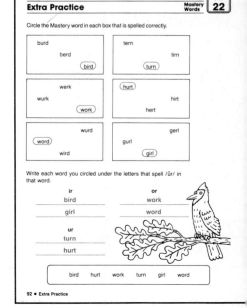

| bird | hurt | work | turn | girl | word |

92 • Extra Practice

Spelling Practice

A. Follow the directions. Use This Week's Words.

1. Write the words that have /ûr/ spelled the same as it is in these words.

   purple *worm*

fur	world	return
burn	worry	

2. Write the compound word made from <u>bird</u> and another word.

   bluebird

3. Write the four other words that have /ûr/ spelled <u>ir</u>.

sir	(birthday)
circle	skirt

4. Circle the compound word you wrote for **3**.

5. Write the three words that begin with /ûr/.

early	earn	earth

6. Put a letter in front of <u>earn</u>. Write another word.

   learn

7. Answer this question. Use one of This Week's Words.

   Did you hear the phone ring?

   Yes, __I heard the phone ring.__

B. Write the words that have these meanings. Use This Week's Words.

8. find out ___learn___

9. come back ___return___

10. too soon ___early___

11. round shape ___circle___

95

Word list (right column):
sir
fur
learn
world
birthday
bluebird
burn
circle
early
earn
earth
heard
return
skirt
worry

Summarize Learning

Have the children summarize what they have learned on pages 94 and 95. *Ask:*

- What have you learned about the way /ûr/ can be spelled? (/ûr/ can be spelled *ir, ur, ear,* or *or*)
- What are examples of words to which these generalizations can be applied? (*sir, fur, learn, world;* accept other examples)

TEACHING PLAN

Objectives   To write words given spelling clues; to recognize compound words; to write words that begin with (ûr/; to write the past tense of *hear;* to write words given definitions.

1. Briefly discuss the directions on page 95. Be sure the children understand that they should write a complete sentence for **7**.
2. Have the children complete the page independently. Remind them to use legible handwriting. You may wish to demonstrate the correct form of the letters *u, r, i, e, a,* and *o* and then have the children practice writing the letters. For **Handwriting Models,** refer the children to page 258 in the **Pupil Book.**
3. To correct the children's work, have volunteers read their answers aloud. Let the children check their own work.

For reinforcement in writing spelling words, you may wish to assign **Extra Practice Master 22: This Week's Words.**

⭐ *of special interest*

The words *skirt* and *shirt,* as well as *scissors* and *shears,* all come from an Indo-European root word that means "cut." The immediate source for *skirt* is the Old Norse word *skyrta;* the immediate source for *shirt* is the Old English word *scyrte.* Both *skyrta* and *scyrte* named tunic-like garments worn by men and women alike. In time, the *skyrta* evolved into something resembling a modern skirt and was worn almost exclusively by women. The *scyrte* eventually became a garment for the upper part of the body worn, until recently, primarily by men.

TEACHING PLAN

SPELLING AND LANGUAGE

Objective To write rhyming words to complete a poem.

1. Read the directions on page 96 aloud. Have the children locate and read the words in boldface type for which they must find rhyming words. Remind them that words do not have to be spelled the same way to rhyme, and briefly review the four spellings for /ûr/.
2. Have the children complete the activity independently.
3. Ask a volunteer to read the poem and supply the missing words. Let the children check their own work.

For extended practice in writing rhyming words, you may wish to assign *Spelling and Language Master 22.*

WRITING ON YOUR OWN

Objectives To write a poem; to proofread for spelling.

1. Review the directions.
2. As a *prewriting* activity, have the children make a list of rhyming words to use as they *compose* their poems. You may wish to refer them to the model of a poem on page 254 of the **Writer's Guide**. When they are ready to *revise*, remind the children to check for spelling. For additional help, you may also wish to refer them to the **Revising Checklist** on page 247 of the **Writer's Guide**. To *publish*, have the children read their poems to the class.

PROOFREADING

Objectives To proofread a report for spelling errors; to write misspelled words correctly.

Spelling and Language • Rhyming Words

THIS WEEK'S WORDS

sir
fur
learn
world
birthday
bluebird
burn
circle
early
earn
earth
heard
return
skirt
worry

Finish the poem with words that rhyme with the words in dark print. Use This Week's Words. Remember that /ûr/ can be spelled in different ways.

Late one night, something **stirred.**
What could have made the noise I __1__?
1. ___heard___

Something was hiding behind a **fern.**
What could it be? I had to __2__.
2. ___learn___

Then I heard a friendly **purr,**
And touched my cat's soft, silky __3__.
3. ___fur___

Writing on Your Own

Write a poem for your friends. Begin your poem with the first two lines of the poem above. Use as many of This Week's Words as you can.

Proofreading

Keisha wrote this report. She misspelled five words.

1. Circle each mistake.

Raccoons have thick (fir) They have black (curcles) around their tails. They hunt at night and (retearn) to their dens (erly) in the morning. Baby raccoons stay with their mother. They (lurn) from her how to hunt and climb trees.

2. Write the five misspelled words correctly.

___fur___   ___circles___   ___return___

___early___   ___learn___

 WRITER'S GUIDE See the editing and proofreading marks on page 248.

---

1. Read the introductory sentences and the directions on page 96 aloud to be sure that the children understand what they are to do.
2. Have the children read through the report independently, looking for errors. Then ask them to go back and circle each misspelled word. Remind the children that they should write the misspelled words correctly on the lines provided.

If you are using the hardcover book, the children should simply locate the misspelled words and write them correctly in their notebooks.

Extra Practice: Spelling and Language

Name _____
Spelling and Language   UNIT **22**

A. The silly words in the story rhyme with the correct words. Circle the silly words. Then write the correct words on the lines. Use This Week's Words.

Jessica wants to (lurd) all she can about the (curled) She wants to know why the (birth) is round and why wood (learns) She wants to know why cats have (sir) and why a knight is called (Her). (third) that she wants to (burn) enough money to go around the world. I never (furry) about Jessica. She knows just what she wants.

1. ___learn___   2. ___world___
3. ___earth___   4. ___burns___
5. ___fur___   6. ___Sir___
7. ___heard___   8. ___earn___
9. ___worry___

B. Write This Week's Words that rhyme with the words in dark print.

turn	**her**	**third**
burn	fur	bluebird
learn	sir	heard
earn		
return		

sir	fur	learn	world	birthday
bluebird	burn	earn	circle	return
early	earth	heard	skirt	worry

94 • Extra Practice

Spelling on Your Own

THIS WEEK'S WORDS

In place of <u>ûr</u>, write the letters that spell /ûr/. Write each word.

1. sûr
2. retûrn
3. skûrt
4. bûrn
5. bûrthday
6. fûr
7. cûrcle
8. ûrth
9. lûrn
10. bluebûrd
11. ûrn
12. wûrry
13. ûrly
14. hûrd
15. wûrld

See answers below.

MASTERY WORDS

bird
hurt
work
turn
girl
word

1. Write the Mastery word that begins with <u>t</u>. Write the word that ends with <u>t</u>. Then write two other letters that are alike in these two words.

turn   hurt   ur

2. Write the two Mastery words that have the letters <u>or</u>.

work   word

3. My friend Holly has a parrot named Polly. Write the Mastery words that tell what Holly is and what Polly is.

girl   bird

BONUS WORDS

pearl
purpose
search
thirsty
turtle
whirl
worst
worth

1. Write the Bonus word that goes with <u>hungry</u>.
2. What animal carries its house on its <u>back</u>? Write the name.
3. Write the Bonus word that means "seek, or look for."
4. Write the Bonus word that is the opposite of <u>best</u>.
5. Next to each word you wrote for **1–4**, write another Bonus word that has /ûr/ spelled the same.
6. Write a story you could read to a three- or four-year-old. Your story could be about a baby turtle.

See answers below.

97

Spelling on Your Own Answers

THIS WEEK'S WORDS

1. sir 2. return 3. skirt 4. burn 5. birthday
6. fur 7. circle 8. earth 9. learn
10. bluebird 11. earn 12. worry 13. early
14. heard 15. world

BONUS WORDS

1. thirsty   whirl
2. turtle   purpose
3. search   pearl
4. worst   worth
5. See above.
6. Children will write as directed. Be sure to check spelling.

Summarize Learning

Have the children summarize what they have learned in this unit. *Ask:*

• What have you learned about rhyming words in this lesson? (Two words that end in the same sound are called rhyming words; poems often contain rhyming words.)

• What spelling generalizations have you learned? How did you use these generalizations?

TEACHING PLAN

Objective To apply the unit spelling generalization to spell This Week's Words, Mastery words, and Bonus words independently.

THIS WEEK'S WORDS

1. Read the directions on page 97 aloud. Point out that *ûr* in the words stands for the sounds /ûr/. Help the children get started by doing the first two words orally.
2. Have the children complete the activity independently on a separate piece of paper.

MASTERY WORDS

1. Review the unit generalization on page 94.
2. Have volunteers read the Mastery words aloud. As each word is read, have the children identify the letters that spell /ûr/ in the word.
3. Briefly discuss the directions on page 97. Then have the children complete the activities independently.

BONUS WORDS

1. Briefly review the unit generalization on page 94.
2. Have volunteers read the Bonus words aloud. As each word is read, have the children identify the letters that spell /ûr/ in the word.
3. Have the children complete the exercises independently on a separate piece of paper.

For reinforcement in writing spelling words, you may wish to assign **Extra Practice Master 22: Mastery Words** or **Bonus Words.**

CLOSING THE UNIT

Apply New Learning

Tell the children that if they misspell words with the sounds /ûr/ in their writing, they should use one or more of the following strategies:

- think about the possible spellings for the sounds /ûr/ and try to picture the word in their minds.
- write the word using different spellings and compare it with the spelling they picture in their minds.
- think about whether the spelling of the word could be unusual.

Transfer New Learning

Tell the children that when they encounter new words in their personal reading and in other content areas, they should learn the meaning of those words and then apply the generalizations they have studied to the spelling of those words. Tell them that once the words are familiar in both meaning and spelling, they should use new words in their writing.

ENRICHMENT ACTIVITIES

Classroom activities and **home activities** may be assigned to children of all ability levels. The activities provide opportunities for children to use their spelling words in new contexts.

For the Classroom

To individualize classroom activities, you may have the children use the word list they are studying in this unit:

- *Basic:* Use **Mastery** words to complete the activity.
- *Average:* Use **This Week's Words** to complete the activity.
- *Challenging:* Use **Bonus** words to complete the activity.

1. **Language Arts/Writing Riddles** Have the children write riddles about spelling words. Have the children choose four spelling words that they can define. Explain to the children that they will be writing riddles. As an example, present this riddle. *I am not a person or a place. I can be short or long. I am usually seen on girls and women. I end like* shirt. After the children name *skirt,* have them write their own riddles, using at least two clues. One clue should be related to sound or spelling, and the other clue should be related to word meaning. After they finish their riddles, have the children exchange them.

■ COOPERATIVE LEARNING: Have each group create a riddle book using spelling words. Have each group member write clues for one riddle. Riddles should give at least two clues. Have each group member try out his or her riddle on other group members to see if it is effective.

Members should help one another revise the clues when necessary. After each group is satisfied with the results, have the group make a booklet of riddles.

2. **Language Arts/Writing Clues** Have the children write coded messages using spelling words. Tell the children to make up a code and then use the code to write a message. The messages should include some of the spelling words. Numbers, shapes, or symbols can be used to represent letters of the alphabet. When the children have completed the messages, have them send the messages to other children in the classroom.

■ COOPERATIVE LEARNING: Have each group write a coded message using spelling words. Tell each group to decide on the numbers, shapes, or symbols to represent letters of the alphabet. Then have each group member contribute a word that is part of the message. Have groups exchange messages and decode them. The groups may wish to compile the messages into a booklet.

3. **Language Arts/Writing in a Journal** Have each child write a journal entry. First direct the children's attention to the **Writer's Guide** to read about journals. Then as a *prewriting* activity, have the children look over the lists of words that might be used to tell about something special that happened or about something special they saw or did. Tell the children to decide what they want to write about and then make a cluster drawing with the word or phrase that names the idea in the center. Around the idea, have the children write details about the event and about how they felt. Then have the children refer to the cluster drawing to **compose** the paragraph. Encourage them to use as many spelling words as possible. Have the children **revise** the entry, making sure they have included all the details from the cluster drawing. Remind them also to proofread for spelling, capitalization, and punctuation. **Publish** the children's entries in a class journal. Some children may also want to illustrate the journal entries.

■ COOPERATIVE LEARNING: Have each group write a journal entry. As a *prewriting* activity have the group members select what they want to write about in the journal. Then have them make a cluster drawing with the word or phrase that names the topic in the center circle. Have members take turns listing details about what happened, how they felt, or what they saw. When the group is ready to **compose** the journal entry, have them choose one group member to begin the entry with a sentence such as, *Early yesterday morning, we saw the most amazing thing.* Have each of the other members build on that sentence, adding details from the cluster. Group members should use as many spelling words as possible from all three lists. One group member can record the journal entry. Group members should **revise,** checking to see if all the details are included. Each child should also proofread for spelling, capitalization, and punctuation. Have the group choose one child to rewrite the entry. Each group can then **publish** their entry in a class journal.

For the Home

Children may complete these activities independently or with the assistance of a relative or friend in the home.

1. Social Studies/Writing Interview Questions for People in the News Have the children imagine that they will be interviewing a personality in the news, such as a famous astronaut. Have them write six questions that they would ask using as many spelling words as possible. Have them share the questions with someone at home and then try to find out the answers.

2. Language Arts/Writing Word Associations Have the children choose six spelling words. Tell them to write a word that makes them think of each spelling word. Encourage children to use the **Thesaurus** on page 203 to locate words that might be written. The word might be a synonym, an antonym, or a word commonly associated with the spelling word. For example, *hop* and *jump* are synonyms, *up* and *down* are antonyms, and *salt* and *pepper* are commonly associated with each other. Have the children give the word to someone at home to see if he or she can guess the spelling word.

3. Language Arts/Writing a Spelling Test Have the children prepare a spelling test to give to a family member or friend. Tell the children to choose ten of the spelling words and present the words in a multiple-choice format. Tell them that one answer choice should be spelled correctly and the other three choices should be misspelled. Tell the children to have the person fill in the circle next to the correctly spelled word. Present the following example:

1. ⓐ lurn   ⓑ learn   ⓒ laern   ⓓ leurn

4. Mathematics/Writing Word Problems Have the children write two or three word problems using as many spelling words as possible. Children may use models from a math book. Then have children proofread for spelling, punctuation, capitalization, and also for the correct answers.

EVALUATING SPELLING ABILITY

Unit Test

This Week's Words
1. *sir*   The clerk said, "May I help you, *sir*?"   *sir*
2. *fur*   A raccoon's *fur* is brown and black.   *fur*
3. *learn*   Mary will *learn* to play the violin.   *learn*
4. *world*   Erin found Scotland on a map of the *world*.   *world*

5. *birthday*   Earl's *birthday* is in March.   *birthday*
6. *bluebird*   A *bluebird* was in the birdbath.   *bluebird*
7. *burn*   Don't *burn* your fingers on the iron.   *burn*
8. *circle*   Draw a *circle* on your math paper.   *circle*
9. *early*   Everyone should arrive *early*.   *early*
10. *earn*   Eli wants to *earn* some money.   *earn*
11. *earth*   There are many kinds of animals on the *earth*.   *earth*
12. *heard*   Stephen *heard* that radio program.   *heard*
13. *return*   I must *return* this book to the library.   *return*
14. *skirt*   A green sweater will go with that *skirt*.   *skirt*
15. *worry*   If we don't go home now, Mom will *worry*.   *worry*

Mastery Words
1. *bird*   A canary is a *bird*.   *bird*
2. *hurt*   Jared *hurt* his arm.   *hurt*
3. *work*   Doctors and nurses *work* in hospitals.   *work*
4. *turn*   When you have finished, *turn* the page.   *turn*
5. *girl*   That *girl* just moved into our neighborhood.   *girl*
6. *word*   Jacqueline didn't say a *word*.   *word*

Bonus Words
1. *pearl*   Gwen lost a *pearl* earring.   *pearl*
2. *purpose*   I don't know the *purpose* of that tool.   *purpose*
3. *search*   We will *search* for the lost cat.   *search*
4. *thirsty*   That dog must be *thirsty*.   *thirsty*
5. *turtle*   We found this *turtle* at the lake.   *turtle*
6. *whirl*   The pinwheels *whirl* in the wind.   *whirl*
7. *worst*   That was the *worst* cold I ever had.   *worst*
8. *worth*   That movie is not *worth* seeing.   *worth*

Dictation Sentences

This Week's Words
1. I *heard* a *bluebird* *early* in the morning.
2. My new *skirt* hides the *burn* on my leg.
3. He said he would *return* on my *birthday*.
4. She drew a *circle* around the word.
5. He will *learn*, *sir*.
6. I *worry* about how on *earth* he will *earn* a living.
7. He grows the best apple trees in the *world*.
8. The *fur* on the kitten was so soft.

Mastery Words
1. The *girl* saw a little *bird* that was *hurt*.
2. It was his *turn* to wash the dishes.
3. He went to *work* without a *word*.

Bonus Words
1. Her *purpose* was to *search* for a *turtle* in the woods.
2. The lost *pearl* was *worth* finding.
3. We were *thirsty* at the *worst* time of all.
4. The fall leaves *whirl* in the wind.

RETEACHING STRATEGIES FOR SPELLING

Children who have made errors on the Unit Test may require reteaching. Use the following **Reteaching Strategies** and **Follow-up Masters 22A** and **22B** for additional instruction and practice of This Week's Words. (You may wish to assign **LEP Reteaching Follow-up Master 22** for reteaching of spelling words.)

A. Discovering Spelling Ideas

1. Say the following words as you write them on the chalkboard.

   stir   turn   earnest   worm

2. Ask the children to identify the sounds that all the words have in common. (/ûr/)
3. Ask the children to identify the letters that spell /ûr/. *(ir, ur, ear, or)*
4. Ask the children what they have learned about spelling /ûr/. *(It can be spelled ir, ur, ear, or or.)*

B. Word Shapes

1. Explain to the children that each word has a shape and that remembering the shape of a word can help them to spell the word correctly.
2. On the chalkboard, write the words *pearl* and *churn*. Have the children identify "short," "tall," and "tail" letters.
3. Draw the configuration of each word on the chalkboard, and ask the children which word fits in each shape.

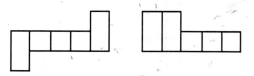

Use **Reteaching Follow-up Master 22A** to reinforce spelling generalizations taught in Unit 22.

Use **Reteaching Follow-up Master 22B** to reinforce spellings of This Week's Words for Unit 22.

Name _____

Reteaching Follow-up A   Discovering Spelling Ideas   UNIT **22**

THIS WEEK'S WORDS

sir	learn	birthday	burn	circle
early	heard	worry	fur	world
bluebird	earn	return	earth	skirt

1. Study This Week's Words. Say each word to yourself. What do This Week's Words have in common?

   They all have the sounds /ûr/.

2. Write the words that spell /ûr/ with the letters at the top of each list.

ir	ear
sir	learn
birthday	early
bluebird	earn
circle	earth
skirt	heard

ur	or
fur	world
burn	worry
return	

3. What have you learned about the ways to spell /ûr/?

   /ûr/ can be spelled with ir, ur, ear, and or.

Reteaching • 37

Name _____

Reteaching Follow-up B   Word Shapes   UNIT **22**

THIS WEEK'S WORDS

sir	learn	birthday	burn	circle
early	heard	worry	fur	world
bluebird	earn	return	earth	skirt

Write each of This Week's Words in its correct shape. The first one has been done for you. Children may interchange answers that fit the same configuration.

1. w o r r y
2. e a r l y
3. l e a r n
4. h e a r d
5. e a r n
6. f u r
7. r e t u r n
8. b l u e b i r d
9. w o r l d
10. e a r t h
11. s i r
12. c i r c l e
13. b u r n
14. s k i r t
15. b i r t h d a y

38 • Reteaching

PREVIEWING THE UNIT

Unit Materials

Instruction and Practice

Pupil Book	pages 98–101
Teacher's Edition	
Teaching Plans	pages 98–101
Enrichment Activities	
For the Classroom	pages 101A–101B
For the Home	page 101B
Reteaching Strategies	page 101C

Testing

Teacher's Edition	
Trial Test	pages 97E–97F
Unit Test	page 101B
Dictation Test	page 101B

Additional Resources

PRACTICE AND REINFORCEMENT
Extra Practice Master 23: This Week's Words
Extra Practice Master 23: Mastery Words
Extra Practice Master 23: Bonus Words
LEP Practice Master 23
Spelling and Language Master 23
Study Steps to Learn a Word Master

RETEACHING FOLLOW-UP
Reteaching Follow-up Master 23A:
   Discovering Spelling Ideas
Reteaching Follow-up Master 23B: Word
   Shapes
LEP Reteaching Follow-up Master 23

TEACHING AIDS
Spelling Generalizations Transparency 20

Visit our Web site
http://www.hbschool.com

**Click on the
SPELLING
banner to
find activities
for this unit.**

Learner Objectives

Spelling

- To spell words that demonstrate these sound-letter relationships: /är/ *ar, ear;* /âr/ *air, ear.*
- To alphabetize by third letter.

Reading

- To follow written directions.
- To use a dictionary to locate information.

Writing

- To write a paragraph.
- To use the writing process.
- To proofread for spelling, capitalization, and punctuation.
- To write legible manuscript and cursive letters.

Listening

- To listen to identify the sounds /är/ and /âr/ in words.
- To listen to respond to a question.
- To follow oral directions.

Speaking

- To speak clearly to a group.
- To express feelings and ideas about a piece of writing.
- To contribute ideas and information in group discussions.
- To present sentences and descriptive paragraphs.

THIS WEEK'S WORDS

park
stairs
art
bark
barn
card
farm
yard
air
fair
hair
pair
bear
pear
heart

MASTERY WORDS

arm
chair
start
far
hard
part

BONUS WORDS

argue
barber
garden
repair
alarm
haircut
artist
market

Assignment Guide

This guide shows how you teach a typical spelling unit in either a five-day or a three-day sequence, while providing for individual differences. **Boldface type** indicates essential classwork. Steps shown in light type may be done in class or assigned as homework.

Five Days	● = average spellers ★ = better spellers ✓ = slower spellers	Three Days
Day **1** ▶ **a**	● ★ **Take This Week's Words Trial Test and correct** ● ✓ **Take Mastery Word Trial Test and correct** ● ★ **Read This Week's Words and discuss generalization page 98**	Day **1**
Day **2**	● Complete Spelling Practice page 99 ● ✓ Complete Extra Practice Master 23: This Week's Words (optional) ✓ Complete Spelling on Your Own: Mastery Words page 101 ★ **Take Bonus Word Trial Test and correct** ◀ **b**	
Day **3** ▶ **c**	● ★ ✓ **Complete Spelling and Language page 100** ● ★ ✓ Complete Writing on Your Own page 100 ● ★ ✓ **Complete Using the Dictionary to Spell and Write page 100** ● ✓ Take Midweek Test (optional) ★ Complete Spelling on Your Own: Bonus Words page 101 ● ✓ Complete Spelling and Language Master 23 (optional)	Day **2**
Day **4**	● Complete Spelling on Your Own: This Week's Words page 101 ✓ Complete Extra Practice Master 23: Mastery Words (optional) ★ Complete Extra Practice Master 23: Bonus Words (optional) ◀ **d**	
Day **5** ▶ **e**	● Take Unit Test on This Week's Words ● Complete Reteaching Follow-up Masters 23A and 23B (optional) ● ✓ **Take Unit Test on Mastery Words** ★ **Take Unit Test on Bonus Words**	Day **3**

Enrichment Activities for the **classroom** and for the **home** included at the end of this unit may be assigned selectively on any day of the week.

INTRODUCING THE UNIT

Establish Readiness for Learning

Tell the children that this week they will learn more about vowels that come before the letter r. Also, they will learn to form compound words using words they know. Tell them they will apply the spelling generalizations to This Week's Words and use those words in a description they will write.

Assess Children's Spelling Ability

Administer the Trial Test before the children study This Week's Words. Use the test sentences provided. Say each word and use it in a sentence. Then repeat the word. Have the children write the words on a separate sheet of paper or in their spelling notebooks. Test sentences are also provided for Mastery and Bonus words.

Have the children check their own work by listening to you read the spelling of the words or by referring to This Week's Words in the left column of the **Pupil Book.** For each misspelled word, have the children follow the **Study Steps to Learn a Word** on page 1 in the **Pupil Book** or use the copying master to study and write the words. Children should record the number correct on their **Progress Report.**

Trial Test Sentences

This Week's Words
1. *park*   Children like to play in the *park*. *park*
2. *stairs*   Don't leave your skates on the *stairs*. **stairs**
3. *art*   We will have an *art* lesson today. *art*
4. *bark*   The dogs *bark* when someone comes to the door. **bark**
5. *barn*   The cows are in the *barn*.   **barn**

6. **card**   Fern sent Richie a birthday *card*.
   card
7. **farm**   There are sheep on the *farm*.
   farm
8. **yard**   The swings are in the *yard*.   **yard**
9. **air**   The kite is up in the *air*.   **air**
10. **fair**   Dorrie won a prize at the school
    fair.   **fair**
11. **hair**   Chip has very curly *hair*.   **hair**
12. **pair**   Lillie has a new *pair* of glasses.
    pair
13. **bear**   Ling's favorite animal is a panda
    bear.   **bear**
14. **pear**   This yellow *pear* is very
    juicy.   **pear**
15. **heart**   Your *heart* pumps blood through
    your body.   **heart**

Mastery Words

1. **arm**   I could reach it if my *arm* were a
   little longer.   **arm**
2. **chair**   That new *chair* is bright red.   **chair**
3. **start**   The car couldn't *start* this morning.
   start
4. **far**   My cousins live *far* away.   **far**
5. **hard**   Mitchell always works very *hard*.
   hard
6. **part**   The drumstick is Ernest's favorite *part*
   of the chicken.   **part**

Bonus Words

1. **argue**   Do not *argue* with your
   sister.   **argue**
2. **barber**   The *barber* will cut your
   hair.   **barber**
3. **garden**   Mother is planting flowers in the
   garden.   **garden**

4. **repair**   The mechanic will *repair* the
   car.   **repair**
5. **alarm**   Everyone knew what to do when
   the fire *alarm* went off.   **alarm**
6. **haircut**   Diana does not like her new
   haircut.   **haircut**
7. **artist**   We watched an *artist* painting in
   the park.   **artist**
8. **market**   Gilbert bought vegetables at the
   market.   **market**

Apply Prior Learning

Have the children be spelling detectives. Tell them that they can discover spelling generalizations by applying what they already know. Write the words *part* and *chair* on the chalkboard. Ask the children to say words that rhyme with these words. (start, art, heart/fair, bear) If children suggest such words as *care* or *there*, acknowledge that they have the correct sound, but their spellings are not part of this week's lesson. Write these words under the word with which they rhyme. Ask the children what is alike and what is different about the words you have written. (The words under *part* have the same vowel sound. In some words it is spelled *ar*. In some words it is spelled *ear*. The words under *chair* have the same vowel sound. In some it is spelled *air*. In others it is spelled *ear*.) Tell the children that they will study words that have the vowel sound they hear in *part* and *chair*. Explain that they can use these words in a variety of spelling tasks: writing stories, writing poems, or writing a social studies report.

FOCUS

- Relates to prior learning
- Draws relationships
- Applies spelling generalizations to new contexts

FOR CHILDREN WITH SPECIAL NEEDS

Learning Difficulties

Children with auditory discrimination and auditory analysis deficits will have difficulty detecting the subtle differences between /är/ and /âr/ sounds.

Engage the children in an auditory discrimination activity. To ensure their active participation, have them prepare the needed materials. Use a 3 x 5 index card or cut out a rectangle of that approximate size. In one color crayon, have children write /är/; in another color, write /âr/. After the materials are made, prepare the children for a listening activity. Say one of This Week's Words. In response, have the children hold up the card on which the sound is printed. Check to make certain that all children choose the correct representation.

Because of the two spellings for each of the sounds in

this unit, you may wish to use a tactile-kinesthetic method for reinforcement. Have the children write This Week's Words with the /âr/ sound and make two separate lists for the **air** and **ear** spellings. Trace over the words, asking the children to say the letter names as they spell the words.

Limited English Proficiency

To help limited English proficient children work with the spelling generalizations for Unit 23, you may wish to refer to the booklet "Suggestions and Activities for Limited English Proficient Students."

TEACHING PLAN

Objective To spell words that demonstrate these sound-letter relationships: /är/ ar, ear; /âr/ air, ear.

1. Write these pairs of words on the chalkboard:

    far—fair star—stair bar—bear

   Ask volunteers to read each pair aloud. Help the children to distinguish between the sounds /är/ in the first word in each pair and the sounds /âr/ in the second word. Point out that the first words are all spelled with *ar,* and the second words are spelled with *air* or *ear.*

You may wish to introduce the lesson by using *Spelling Generalizations Transparency 20.*

2. Read the generalization on page 98 aloud.
3. Have volunteers read This Week's Words. As each word is read, have the children identify the letters that spell /är/ or /âr/ in the word.
4. Remind the children that a box around the number preceding a word in the list shows that the word has an unusual spelling.
5. Direct the children's attention to **Remember This** at the bottom of the page and ask a child to read the paragraph aloud. Point out that the letters *hear* in *heart* are not pronounced the same as the verb *hear,* but that remembering that the letters that spell *hear* are also in *heart* can help them spell *heart* correctly.

You may wish to assign *LEP Practice Master 23* for reinforcement in writing spelling words.

23 The Sounds /är/ and /âr/

THIS WEEK'S WORDS

1. park
2. stairs
3. art
4. bark
5. barn
6. card
7. farm
8. yard
9. air
10. fair
11. hair
12. pair
13. bear
14. pear
15. heart

This Week's Words

The sounds /är/ can be spelled **ar,** as in park.
☐ The sounds /är/ are spelled **ear** in heart.
The sounds /âr/ can be spelled **air,** as in stairs.
The sounds /âr/ can also be spelled **ear,** as in bear.

REMEMBER THIS

Here's a way to remember the e in heart. "You can hear your heart." The first four letters in heart are the letters that spell hear.

98

Extra Practice: This Week's Words

Name
Extra Practice   This Week's Words   UNIT 23

Work your way down the alphabet stairs. Write This Week's Words where they fit in alphabetical order. Start by writing air in the first blank. Remember, if the first two or three letters are the same, keep looking. Put the words in order by the first different letter.

air
art
bark
barn
bear
card
chair
fair
farm
hair
heart
mark
pair
park
pear
stairs
yard

park
card
hair
stairs
farm
pair
art
yard
bear
bark
air
pear
barn
fair
heart

Extra Practice • 95

Extra Practice: Mastery Words

UNIT 23

A. The letters a and r appear in all the Mastery words. Use the clues to help you fill in the missing letters.

a r __m__ connects the hand to the body
__h__ a r __d__ as marble
__s__ t a r __t__ at the beginning
__p__ a r __t__ your hair
__f__ a r to go

You've done so well, just lean back and relax in your
__c__ __h__ a i r .

B. Finish the story. Use Mastery words.
    José liked the ____start____ of the magic
show. In this early ____part____ of the act, it was
dark and a little ____hard____ to see. The magician
put a tall hat on the ____chair____. She put her
____arm____ into the hat as ____far____
as it would go. Then the lights got brighter. The
magician pulled a white rabbit from the hat!

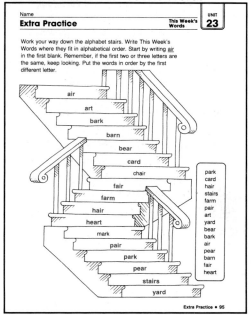

| arm | chair | start | far | hard | part |

96 • Extra Practice

Spelling Practice

A. Follow the directions. Use This Week's Words.

1. Write the word for something you cannot see that is all around you.

   <u>air</u>

2. Add one letter at a time to the word you wrote for **1.** Write three words.

   <u>fair</u>   <u>hair</u>   <u>pair</u>

3. Write the two words that sound alike.

   <u>pair</u>   <u>pear</u>

4. Finish this sentence with two of This Week's Words.

   I walked down the <u>stairs</u> to get a juicy

   <u>pear</u> from the fruit bowl.

5. Answer this riddle. Use two words that rhyme. What do you call a panda's fur?

   <u>bear</u>   <u>hair</u>

B. Write two words that rhyme with each of these words.

6. dark   <u>park</u>   <u>bark</u>

7. hard   <u>card</u>   <u>yard</u>

8. part   <u>art</u>   <u>heart</u>

C. Add one letter to the end of each word. Write some of This Week's Words.

9. car   <u>card</u>   10. far   <u>farm</u>

11. bar (two words)   <u>bark</u>   <u>barn</u>

99

This Week's Words

park
stairs
art
bark
barn
card
farm
yard
air
fair
hair
pair
bear
pear
heart

TEACHING PLAN

Objectives To write words given meaning clues; to write words given spelling clues; to write homophones; to write words in sentence context; to write rhyming words; to write words by adding letters to known words.

1. Briefly discuss the directions on page 99. Point out that in Exercise **B** the children must write two words that rhyme with each word given. Also be sure the children understand that in Exercise **C** they must add a consonant letter to the end of each given word to spell one of This Week's Words.

2. Have the children complete the page independently. Remind them to use legible handwriting. You may wish to demonstrate the correct form of the letters *a, i, e* and *r* and then have the children practice writing the letters. For **Handwriting Models,** refer the children to page 258 in the **Pupil Book.**

3. To check the children's work, have volunteers write the answers on the chalkboard. Let the children check their own responses.

For reinforcement in writing spelling words, you may wish to assign **Extra Practice Master 23: This Week's Words.**

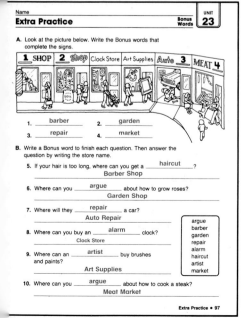

Summarize Learning

Have the children summarize what they have learned on pages 98 and 99. *Ask:*

- What vowel sounds did you learn in this lesson? (/är/ and /âr/)
- What did you learn about these sounds? (two ways to spell /är/*ar, ear;* two ways to spell /âr/*air, ear*)
- What are some examples of words using the different spellings of /är/ and /âr/? (*park, stairs, bear, heart;* accept other examples)

★ of special interest

Speakers of dialects characterized by the loss of /r/ after vowel sounds will pronounce *ar* in *park* and *art* like the first vowel sound in *father.* This should not cause serious spelling problems since the pronunciation /ä/ for *ar* is consistent. For example, a speaker of such a dialect might say: /päk the kä in hä'väd yäd/. To help children who speak an *r*-less dialect, relate the sound /ä/ to the letters *ar.*

TEACHING PLAN

SPELLING AND LANGUAGE

Objective To write compound words by combining given words.

1. Read the introductory sentences on page 100 aloud. Briefly review compound words, and ask the children to name compound words they have learned. If necessary, refer them to Unit 19, page 82.
2. Read the directions on page 100. Have the children name the two words that form the compound for the first definition.
3. Have the children complete the exercise independently.
4. To correct the children's work, have volunteers read the compound words aloud. Let the children check their own work.

For extended practice in writing compound words, you may wish to assign *Spelling and Language Master 23.*

WRITING ON YOUR OWN

Objectives To write a paragraph; to proofread for spelling.

1. Review the directions with the children.
2. As a *prewriting* activity, discuss what the children know about their town. Have them make a list of things that they would like to tell someone about it. Then have the children **compose** a description of their town. Encourage them to include an illustration with their description. When the children are ready to **revise** their work, remind them to proofread for spelling. For additional help, you may wish to refer them to the **Revising Checklist** on page 247 of the **Writer's Guide.** **Publish** the children's stories, placing them together in a class book called *Our Town.*

THIS WEEK'S WORDS

park
stairs
art
bark
barn
card
farm
yard
air
fair
hair
pair
bear
pear
heart

road
robin
rock
rode

100

USING THE DICTIONARY

Objective To write words in alphabetical order by third letter.

1. Read the introductory paragraph. Then write these sets of words vertically on the chalkboard: sat, sad, sale; better, bed, bell, best. Then have the children put the words in alphabetical order on the chalkboard. (sad, sale, sat; bed, bell, best, better)
2. Have the children complete this activity independently.
3. To correct the children's work, have volunteers read their alphabetized lists aloud. Let the children check their own work.

Spelling and Language • Compound Words

Two words can be put together to make a new word. The new word is called a **compound word.**

board	plane	up

Put three of This Week's Words together with three words from the box. Make compound words to go with these definitions.

1. It flies in the sky. **airplane**

2. It is what boxes are made from. **cardboard**

3. You climb the steps to get there. **upstairs**

Writing on Your Own

Tell what your town is like for a friend who does not live there. You may wish to make compound words of some of This Week's Words to use in your description.

Using the Dictionary to Spell and Write

A good place to look for the correct spelling of a word is the dictionary. The words in a dictionary are in alphabetical order. If the first letters of words are the same, look at the second letter. If the second letters are the same, look at the third letter. Back, bad, bag are in order by third letter—c, d, g.

Write each group of words in alphabetical order.

1. stairs **pair**
   park **park**
   straw **stairs**
   pair
   straw

2. heart **fair**
   farm **farm**
   herself **heart**
   fair
   herself

SPELLING DICTIONARY Remember to use your **Spelling Dictionary** when you write.

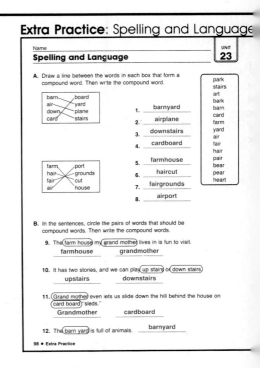

Extra Practice: Spelling and Language

Spelling on Your Own

THIS WEEK'S WORDS

```
M B E A R
F A I R E
T R H D I
N K S T H
```

Use all the words to make a word search puzzle. You can write the words across or down. Fill in the empty spaces with other letters. Then let someone else solve the puzzle.

MASTERY WORDS

> arm
> chair
> start
> far
> hard
> part

Change one letter in each word. Write Mastery words.

1. park __part__   2. card __hard__

3. car __far__   4. art __arm__

Add two letters to each word. Write Mastery words.

5. art __start__   6. air __chair__

Follow the directions. Write the Mastery words.

7. Take away the first letter in <u>farm</u>. __arm__

8. Take away the last letter in <u>farm</u>. __far__

Write the Mastery words that mean the opposite of each word.

9. soft __hard__   10. finish __start__

BONUS WORDS

> argue
> barber
> garden
> repair
> alarm
> haircut
> artist
> market

Write the Bonus words that go with these words.

1. ___ clock   2. ___ shop   3. flea ___   4. rose ___

Follow the directions. Use the Bonus words.

5. Write the two words that have the sounds /âr/.
6. Write all the words in alphabetical order.
7. Write a story about an artist and a barber. Try to use all the Bonus words in your story.   **See answers below.**

101

Spelling on Your Own Answers

BONUS WORDS

1. alarm 2. barber (repair, garden) 3. market
4. garden 5. haircut, repair 6. alarm argue
artist barber garden haircut market repair
7. Children will write as directed. Be sure to check spelling.

Summarize Learning

Have the children summarize what they have learned in this unit. *Ask:*
- What have you learned about writing compound words? (Two words can be put together to make a new word.)
- What have you learned about the order of words in a dictionary? (The words are listed in alphabetical order.)
- What spelling generalizations have you learned? How did you use these generalizations?

TEACHING PLAN

> **Objective** To apply the unit spelling generalization to spell This Week's Words, Mastery words, and Bonus words independently.

THIS WEEK'S WORDS

1. Read the directions on page 101 aloud. Remind the children that a word-search puzzle contains words written across or down the paper with extra letters in the empty spaces to "hide" the words. Point out the example at the top of the page in the **Pupil Book.**
2. Have the children make their puzzles on graph paper.
3. Let the children exchange their work and solve each other's puzzles.

MASTERY WORDS

1. Briefly review these sounds and spellings: /är/ar, /âr/air.
2. Have volunteers read the Mastery words aloud. Indicate whether /är/ or /âr/ is heard in each word, and have the children identify the letters that spell the given sounds in the word.
3. Read the directions for each activity on page 101 to make sure that the children understand what they are to do.
4. Have the children complete the activities independently.

BONUS WORDS

1. Briefly review these sounds and spellings: /är/ ar; /âr/ air.
2. Have volunteers read the Bonus words aloud. As each word is read, have the children identify the letters that spell /är/ or /âr/ in the word.
3. Have the the children complete the exercises independently on a separate piece of paper.

For reinforcement in writing spelling words, you may wish to assign *Extra Practice Master 23: Mastery Words* or *Bonus Words.*

UNIT 23 *The Sounds /är/ and /â*

CLOSING THE UNIT

Apply New Learning

Tell the children that if they misspell words with the sounds /är/ and /âr/ in their writing, they should use one or more of the following strategies:

- think of words that rhyme and compare in their minds how they are spelled.
- think about whether the spelling of the word could be unusual.
- think about whether the word might sound like another but be spelled differently (homophone). Use sentence context to help them know which spelling is appropriate.

Transfer New Learning

Tell the children that when they encounter new words in their personal reading and in other content areas, they should learn the meaning of those words and then apply the generalizations they have studied to the spelling of those words. Tell them that once the words are familiar in both meaning and spelling, they should use the new words in their writing.

ENRICHMENT ACTIVITIES

Classroom activities and **home activities** may be assigned to children of all ability levels. The activities provide opportunities for children to use their spelling words in new contexts.

For the Classroom

To individualize classroom activities, you may have the children use the word list they are studying in this unit.

- *Basic:* Use **Mastery** words to complete the activity.
- *Average:* Use **This Week's Words** to complete the activity.
- *Challenging:* Use **Bonus** words to complete the activity.

1. Language Arts/Writing Sentences Tell the children to choose any five spelling words. Then have them write a sentence with good context clues for each of the words. Next, have them rewrite the sentence, leaving a blank in place of the spelling word. Present this example: *Our dogs **bark** when the doorbell rings. Our dogs _____ when the doorbell rings.* After they have completed their sentences, have the children exchange papers with one another and write the missing words.

   ■ COOPERATIVE LEARNING: Have each group create a set of fill-in-the-blank sentences. Each child in the group should choose a spelling word and write a sentence with good context clues. Next, have them rewrite the sentence leaving a blank space in place of the spelling word. Present this example: *Our dogs **bark** when the doorbell*

rings. *Our dogs _____ when the doorbell rings.* Group members should then try out one another's sentences to see if the context clues help to determine the correct spelling word. After the group is satisfied with all the sentences, have one member write the sentences with blanks for the missing spelling word. These can then be shared with the class.

2. Language Arts/Writing Headlines Have the children use their spelling words to create imaginative newspaper headlines. Point out that when something unusual or important happens, a newspaper will print a headline in bold letters to attract the attention of its readers. Explain that headlines are always written in the present tense and that *a, an,* and *the* are often not used. As an example, present the following headline, explaining that it is about Goldilocks and the Three Bears: *Girl with Fair Hair Breaks Chair of Baby Bear!* When the children are finished, have them share their headlines with the class. At a later time, children may want to write stories for their headlines.

   ■ COOPERATIVE LEARNING: Have each group write a newspaper headline. Explain that a headline appears on the front page of a newspaper in bold print to announce something unusual or important that has taken place. Present this headline, explaining that it is about Goldilocks and the Three Bears: *Girl with Fair Hair Breaks Chair of Baby Bear!* Have the members of the group look over their spelling words, discuss possible news events, and then choose one they would like to write about. Have one child in the group begin orally as another child records the idea. Then have the other members of the group work together to revise the headline. When the group is satisfied with the headline, have one person rewrite it and then read it aloud to the class. The group may also want to add drawings that illustrate the headline.

3. Language Arts/Writing a Lost and Found Ad Have the children write a paragraph for a Lost and Found column in a newspaper. As a **prewriting** activity, have the children look over their spelling words for possible ideas and list them. Next, tell them to decide what they will write about. Then have the children make a chart with the following headings: where it was lost (found), when it was lost (found), what it looks like. Tell the children to list possible details in each category. When they have completed these prewriting activities, have them refer to the chart to **compose** the paragraph. Remind them that in order for the reader to get a clear picture, the writer must be very specific when describing the object that was lost or found. Have the children **revise** their paragraphs, making sure that they have included all the necessary details listed on their charts. Tell them also to proofread for spelling, capitalization, and punctuation. **Publish** the paragraphs in a class newspaper.

■ COOPERATIVE LEARNING: Have each group write a paragraph. As a **prewriting** activity, have the children make a chart with the following headings: *where it was lost (found), when it was lost (found), what it looks like.* Tell the members to list the details in the appropriate column. When the group is ready to **compose** the paragraph, tell them to choose one child to begin the paragraph orally by providing the first sentence. Each of the other children in the group should build on that sentence. The group should select one child to record the paragraph. The group members should next **revise** the paragraph, keeping in mind that anyone who reads the paragraph must be able to get a clear picture of what was lost or found. Have one child in the group write the final copy. Each group can **publish** their paragraph by putting it in a class newspaper.

For the Home

Children may complete these activities independently or with the assistance of a relative or friend in the home.

1. Language Arts/Categorizing Spelling Words Tell the children to make up word categories using some of their spelling words. Explain that to form a category, they must look for specific features that certain words share. Present these examples: *String beans, broccoli, and carrots are vegetables. Lions, tigers, and leopards are wild cats.* Have the children add other words to their categories.

2. Social Studies/Writing About Jobs Tell the children to think about the people they know and the types of jobs they do. Then have them write a short paragraph using some of their spelling words to describe a specific job.

3. Language Arts/Writing Mnemonic Devices Tell the children to write a spelling clue to help them remember how to spell words they have misspelled on a test. As an example, refer them to **Remember This** on page 98.

4. Science/Writing Facts About Human Beings Have the children use some of their spelling words to write five facts about human beings. Explain that a fact is something that is known to be true. Tell them to use a dictionary, an encyclopedia, or a health or science book to check their facts.

EVALUATING SPELLING ABILITY

Unit Test

This Week's Words

1. **park**   Dad will *park* the car.   **park**
2. **stairs**   Mei ran up the *stairs*.   **stairs**
3. **art**   The *art* museum opens at ten o'clock.   **art**

4. **bark**   That little dog has a very loud *bark*.   **bark**
5. **barn**   The colt was born in our *barn*.   **barn**
6. **card**   Richard wrote the words on a *card*.   **card**
7. **farm**   The class visited a dairy *farm*.   **farm**
8. **yard**   The *yard* is muddy today.   **yard**
9. **air**   There is a lot of dust in the *air*.   **air**
10. **fair**   We saw many animals at the *fair*.   **fair**
11. **hair**   Molly has a ribbon in her *hair*.   **hair**
12. **pair**   Lance bought a *pair* of shoes.   **pair**
13. **bear**   The *bear* growled and snarled.   **bear**
14. **pear**   She put a *pear* in the fruit basket.   **pear**
15. **heart**   Randy was so frightened that his *heart* was beating very fast.   **heart**

Mastery Words

1. **arm**   Bonnie's *arm* was in a sling.   **arm**
2. **chair**   The soft *chair* was very comfortable.   **chair**
3. **start**   I hope the car will *start* this morning.   **start**
4. **far**   Japan is *far* away.   **far**
5. **hard**   That is a *hard* mattress.   **hard**
6. **part**   Only *part* of your work is finished.   **part**

Bonus Words

1. **argue**   We will not *argue* about the camera.   **argue**
2. **barber**   That *barber* is a funny person.   **barber**
3. **garden**   Everyone worked in the *garden*.   **garden**
4. **repair**   The *repair* shop was closed.   **repair**
5. **alarm**   When the fire *alarm* rings, walk out of the building.   **alarm**
6. **haircut**   This afternoon Jacob will get a *haircut*.   **haircut**
7. **artist**   Danielle wants to be an *artist*.   **artist**
8. **market**   There is a new food *market* in our neighborhood.   **market**

Dictation Sentences

This Week's Words

1. We can *park* in the *yard* by the *barn*.
2. I painted a *heart* and a *bear* in *art* class.
3. The *farm* dog will *bark* if there is danger.
4. I ate a *pear* at the *fair*.
5. She will dry her wet *hair* in the *air*.
6. The *card* has a picture of a *pair* of cats on the *stairs*.

Mastery Words

1. The *arm* of the *chair* was *hard*.
2. That *part* of the race is *far* from the *start*.

Bonus words

1. Dad did not *argue* with the *barber* about his *haircut*.
2. The *artist* painted in our *garden* and at the *market*.
3. Can you *repair* our fire *alarm*?

RETEACHING STRATEGIES FOR SPELLING

Children who have made errors on the Unit Test may require reteaching. Use the following **Reteaching Strategies** and **Follow-up Masters 23A** and **23B** for additional instruction and practice of This Week's Words. (You may wish to assign **LEP Reteaching Follow-up Master 23** for reteaching of spelling words.)

A. Discovering Spelling Ideas

1. Say the following words as you write them on the chalkboard.

far	fairy
hearth	tear

2. Ask the children to identify the common sound in each column of words. (/är/ and /âr/)
3. Ask the children to identify the letters that spell /är/ and /âr/. (ar, ear, air, ear)
4. Ask the children what they have learned about spelling /är/ and /âr/. (/är/ is spelled with ar or ear, /âr/ is spelled with air or ear.)

B. Word Shapes

1. Explain to the children that each word has a shape and that remembering the shape of a word can help them to spell the word correctly.
2. On the chalkboard, write the words *garden* and *airport*. Have the children identify "short," "tall," and "tail" letters.
3. Draw the configuration of each word on the chalkboard, and ask the children which word fits in each shape.

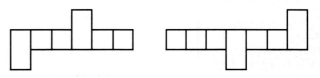

Use **Reteaching Follow-up Master 23A** to reinforce spelling generalizations taught in Unit 23.

Use **Reteaching Follow-up Master 23B** to reinforce spellings of This Week's Words for Unit 23.

Name _____

Reteaching Follow-up A

Discovering Spelling Ideas

UNIT **23**

THIS WEEK'S WORDS

park	art	barn	farm	fair
pair	heart	stairs	bark	air
card	yard	hair	bear	pear

1. Study This Week's Words. Say each word to yourself.

2. In each column, write the words that have the same sounds as the word at the top of the list.

far	fairy
park	fair
art	pair
barn	stairs
farm	air
heart	hair
bark	bear
card	pear
yard	

3. What sounds do the words in the first column have in common?

They all have the sounds /är/.

4. What sounds do the words in the second column have in common?

They all have the sounds /âr/.

5. What have you learned about the spellings for /är/ and /âr/?

/är/ can be spelled ar or ear, /âr/ can be spelled air or ear.

Reteaching • 39

Name _____

Reteaching Follow-up B

Word Shapes

UNIT **23**

THIS WEEK'S WORDS

park	art	barn	farm	fair
pair	heart	stairs	bark	air
card	yard	hair	bear	pear

Write each of This Week's Words in its correct shape. The first one has been done for you. Children may interchange answers that fit the same configuration.

1. h a i r
2. p a i r
3. b a r k
4. p a r k
5. h e a r t
6. a r t
7. c a r d
8. f a i r
9. p e a r
10. y a r d
11. f a r m
12. s t a i r s
13. a i r
14. b e a r
15. b a r n

40 • Reteaching

01C   UNIT 23 *The Sounds /är/ and /âr/*

PREVIEWING THE UNIT

Unit Materials

Instruction and Practice

Pupil Book	pages 102–107
Teacher's Edition	
Teaching Plans	pages 102–107
Enrichment Activities	
For the Home	page 107A

Testing

Teacher's Edition	
Trial Test	pages 101E–101F
Unit Test	page 107A
Form *A** Test 4	page T12

*If your grading period is six weeks, you may want to use the **Form A Test** at the end of this unit.

Additional Resources

PRACTICE AND REINFORCEMENT
Review Master 24A: Units 19 and 20
Review Master 24B: Units 21 and 22
Review Master 24C: Unit 23 and Test
    Exercise
Dictionary and Proofreading Master 4
Study Steps to Learn a Word Master
Mastery Words Review Master: Units 19–23
Bonus Words Review Master: Units 19–23

TESTING (optional)
Mastery Words Test: Units 19–23
Bonus Words Test: Units 19–23
Writing Test 4

TEACHING AIDS
Spelling and Writing Transparency 4
Home Letter 5

Visit our Web site
http://www.hbschool.com

Click on the SPELLING banner to find activities for this unit.

Learner Objectives

Spelling

- To review compound words.
- To review contractions.
- To review words that demonstrate these sound-letter relationships: /ô/a, aw, au; /ôr/or, our.
- To review words that demonstrate these sound-letter relationships: /ūr/ ir, ur, ear, or.
- To review words that demonstrate these sound-letter relationships: /är/ar,ear; /â/air,ear.

Reading

- To recognize the five parts of a friendly letter.
- To use spelling review words to answer questions.
- To follow written directions.
- To use the dictionary for word meaning.

Writing

- To write a friendly letter.
- To use the writing process.
- To edit for structure and content.
- To revise using editing and proofreading marks.
- To proofread for spelling, capitalization, and punctuation.
- To write legible manuscript and cursive letters.

Listening

- To listen to write words given sound-letter clues.
- To follow a series of oral directions.

Speaking

- To express feelings and ideas about a piece of writing.
- To present a friendly letter.
- To contribute ideas and information in group discussions.

Assignment Guide

This guide shows how you teach a typical spelling unit in either a five-day or a three-day sequence, while providing for individual differences. **Boldface type** indicates essential classwork. Steps shown in light type may be done in class or assigned as homework.

Five Days	• = average spellers ★ = better spellers ✓ = slower spellers	Three Days
Day **1**	**a** • ★ ✓ **Take Review Word Trial Test and correct**	Day **1**
Day **2**	• ★ ✓ Complete Spelling Review pages 102, 103, 104 • ★ ✓ Complete Review Master 24A, 24B, 24C (optional) ✓ Complete Mastery Words Review Master: Units 19-23 (optional) ★ Complete Bonus Words Review Master: Units 19-23 (optional) **b**	
Day **3**	**c** • ★ ✓ **Complete Spelling and Reading page 105**	Day **2**
Day **4**	• ★ ✓ Complete Spelling and Writing pages 106-107 • ★ ✓ Complete Dictionary and Proofreading Master 4 (optional) **d**	
Day **5**	**e** • ★ ✓ **Take Review Words Unit Test** ✓ Take Mastery Words Test: Units 19-23 (optional) ★ Take Bonus Words Test: Units 19-23 (optional)	Day **3**

Enrichment Activities for the **home** included at the end of this unit may be assigned selectively on any day of the week.

INTRODUCING THE UNIT

Establish Readiness for Learning

Tell the children that they will review words from the previous five units. In Unit 24 they will review:

- compound words
- contractions
- the following sound-letter relationships: /ô/ a, aw, au; /ôr/ or, our; /ûr/ ir, ur, ear, or; /är/ ar, ear; /âr/ air, ear

Tell the children that they will use some of the review words to write a friendly letter.

Assess Children's Spelling Ability

Administer the Trial Test before the children study the review words. Use the test sentences provided. Say each word and use it in a sentence. Then repeat the word. Have the children write the words on a separate sheet of paper or in their spelling notebooks.

Have the children check their own work by listening to you read the spelling of the words or by referring to the review words lists in the side boxes of the **Pupil Book.** For each misspelled word, have the children follow the **Study Steps to Learn a Word** on page 102 in the **Pupil Book,** or use the copying master to

study and write the words. Children should record the number correct on their **Progress Report.**

Trial Test Sentences

1. *anyway*   It was raining, but we walked home *anyway.*   *anyway*
2. *bedroom*   Marcia's *bedroom* is upstairs.   *bedroom*
3. *everybody*   We want *everybody* to come to the party.   *everybody*
4. *maybe*   He said *maybe* we can go to the movies.   *maybe*
5. *sometimes*   We go out for dinner *sometimes.*   *sometimes*
6. *outside*   We went *outside* to play ball.   *outside*
7. *grandfather*   I see my *grandfather* every summer.   *grandfather*
8. *grandmother*   Gina looks like her *grandmother.*   *grandmother*
9. *didn't*   Matt *didn't* finish his work.   *didn't*
10. *I'll*   If you go, *I'll* go with you.   *I'll*
11. *let's*   We don't have school today, so *let's* go on a picnic.   *let's*
12. *there's*   I know *there's* time to fix it.   *there's*
13. *won't*   I *won't* start until you get here.   *won't*

14. **can't** We *can't* find the key. **can't**
15. **that's** We think *that's* a good place to start. **that's**
16. **we're** I hope *we're* all going together. **we're**
17. **talk** Kevin's baby sister is learning to *talk*. **talk**
18. **taught** Leanne *taught* her dog to do tricks. **taught**
19. **straw** Dennis drank his milk with a *straw*. **straw**
20. **short** We can stay for only a *short* while. **short**
21. **four** The table has *four* legs. **four**
22. **born** Roberto was *born* in New York. **born**
23. **walk** Anne and Mary *walk* to school together. **walk**
24. **north** Can you find *north* on this map? **north**
25. **birthday** Maria has a party on her *birthday*. **birthday**
26. **heard** We *heard* a noise in the hall. **heard**
27. **learn** Brent wants to *learn* to play tennis. **learn**
28. **return** You must *return* this book to the library. **return**
29. **world** We can find the country on a *world* map. **world**
30. **circle** I drew a *circle* to show the sun. **circle**
31. **early** We got up *early* to go fishing. **early**
32. **worry** My mom will *worry* if I get home late. **worry**
33. **park** Terry will *park* the car. **park**
34. **yard** Rose bushes grow in our *yard*. **yard**
35. **heart** The valentine was shaped like a *heart*. **heart**

36. **stairs** These *stairs* lead to the attic. **stairs**
37. **bear** We saw a black *bear* in the forest. **bear**
38. **card** I got a funny *card* from my cousin. **card**
39. **hair** My dad says my *hair* is too long. **hair**
40. **air** The *air* feels cold today. **air**

Apply Prior Learning

words.)

Then write *it's* and *they're* on the chalkboard. Ask the children what *it's* and *they're* have in common. (They are contractions.) Have them explain the spelling generalization for contractions. (The second word is shortened and an apostrophe takes the place of one or more letters that are left out.) Tell the children that they will review words that follow these generalizations and then use the words to write a friendly letter.

TEACHING PLAN

Objectives To spell compounds; to spell contractions.

1. Review the directions to the exercises on page 102. Remind the children that the answers are to be found only among the sixteen review words on page 102.
2. Have the children complete the exercises independently. You may refer them to the **Writer's Guide** at the back of the book for a review of the spelling generalizations for Units 19 and 20.

24 Review

Do these steps if you are not sure how to spell a word.

● **Say** the word. Listen to each sound. Think about what the word means.
● **Look** at the word. See how the letters are made. Try to see the word in your mind.
● **Spell** the word to yourself. Think about the way each sound is spelled.
● **Write** the word. Copy it from your book. Check the way you made your letters. Write the word again.
● **Check** your learning. Cover the word and write it. Did you spell it correctly? If not, do these steps until you know how to spell the word.

UNIT 19

anyway
bedroom
everybody
maybe
sometimes
outside
grandfather
grandmother

UNIT 20

didn't
I'll
let's
there's
won't
can't
that's
we're

UNIT 19 **Add one of the words from the box to each word below. Write words from Unit 19.**

times	side	way	be	father	room	mother	body

1. may ___maybe___
2. every ___everybody___
3. bed ___bedroom___
4. some ___sometimes___
5. out ___outside___
6. any ___anyway___

Word order may vary.

7. grand (two words) ___grandmother___ ___grandfather___

UNIT 20 **Follow the directions. Use words from Unit 20. Write the contractions for these words.**

8. that is ___that's___
9. let us ___let's___
10. did not ___didn't___
11. there is ___there's___
12. we are ___we're___
13. can not ___can't___
14. I will ___I'll___
15. will not ___won't___

102

Review: Units 19 and 20

Name _____
Review A: Units 19–20   UNIT 24

A. UNIT 19 Write the compound word in each sentence.

1. My grandfather lives on a ranch. ___grandfather___
2. My grandmother lives there, too. ___grandmother___
3. I stay at the ranch sometimes. ___sometimes___
4. My bedroom is near the kitchen. ___bedroom___
5. I can hear the cows moving outside my window at night. ___outside___
6. Everybody at the ranch is very nice to me. ___Everybody___
7. Maybe I will live on a ranch when I grow up. ___maybe___
8. It would be a lot of work, but it would be fun anyway. ___anyway___

UNIT 19
anyway
bedroom
everybody
maybe
sometimes
outside
grandfather
grandmother

UNIT 20
didn't
I'll
let's
there's
won't
can't
that's
we're

B. UNIT 20 Circle the words that can be made into contractions in the sentences. Then write the contractions.

9. Since it will not quit raining, we can not play outside today. ___won't___ ___can't___
10. I know there is a game that is fun to play inside. ___there's___ ___that's___
11. Let us play checkers. ___Let's___
12. I will even let you make the first move. ___I'll___
13. We are having so much fun! ___We're___
14. I did not know you could play so well. ___didn't___

Extra Practice • 99

Review: Units 21 and 22

Name _____
Review B: Units 21–22   UNIT 24

A. UNIT 21 Fill in each blank with a word from Unit 21. The sound before each blank gives you a clue.

1. Clarissa was /ôr/ ___born___ on a ranch.
2. Today Clarissa is /ôr/ ___four___ years old.
3. Clarissa is /ôr/ ___short___ for her age.
4. She likes to /ô/ ___walk___ all over the ranch.
5. She likes to /ô/ ___talk___ to all the pigs and cows.
6. Clarissa's father has /ô/ ___taught___ her many things.
7. Clarissa knows that cold winds come from the /ôr/ ___north___
8. She also knows that /ô/ ___straw___ comes from grain.

UNIT 21
talk
taught
straw
short
four
born
walk
north

UNIT 22
birthday
heard
learn
return
world
circle
early
worry

B. UNIT 22 Each word is missing two or three letters. Write the missing letters. Then write the word from Unit 22.

9. bthday ___ir___ ___birthday___
10. ly ___ear___ ___early___
11. wld ___or___ ___world___
12. retn ___ur___ ___return___
13. wry ___or___ ___worry___
14. hd ___ear___ ___heard___
15. ln ___ear___ ___learn___
16. ccle ___ir___ ___circle___

100 • Extra Practice

UNIT 21

Follow the directions. Use words from Unit 21. Finish the story. The clues /ô/ and /ôr/ are given. You will use some words twice.

My aunt /ô/ __16__ us a funny game. You draw straws. There are /ôr/ __17__ long ones and one that is /ôr/ __18__ . Whoever gets the short /ô/ __19__ must /ô/ __20__ only in rhymes. I got the /ôr/ __21__ /ô/ __22__ . So wherever I /ô/ __23__ , in rhymes I must /ô/ __24__ .

UNIT 21
talk
taught
straw
short
four
born
walk
north

16. ___taught___ 17. ___four___ 18. ___short___

19. ___straw___ 20. ___talk___ 21. ___short___

22. ___straw___ 23. ___walk___ 24. ___talk___

Write the word that rhymes with each word.

25. horn ___born___ 26. forth ___north___

27. caught ___taught___ 28. pour ___four___

UNIT 22

Follow the directions. Use words from Unit 22.

29. Write the three words that have /ûr/ spelled e_a_r.
Word order may vary.
___heard___ ___learn___ ___early___

30. Write the two words that have /ûr/ spelled _or_.
Word order may vary.
___world___ ___worry___

UNIT 22
birthday
heard
learn
return
world
circle
early
worry

31. Write the two words that have /ûr/ spelled _ir_.
Word order may vary.
___birthday___ ___circle___

32. Write the word that has /ûr/ spelled _ur_.
___return___

103

TEACHING PLAN

Objectives To review words that demonstrate these sound-letter relationships: /ô/a, aw, au; /ôr/or, our; to review words that demonstrate these sound-letter relationships: /ûr/ir, ur, ear, or.

1. Review the directions to the exercises on page 103. Remind the children that the answers to the exercises are to be found only among the sixteen review words on page 103.
2. Have the children complete the exercises independently. You may refer them to the **Writer's Guide** at the back of the book for a review of the spelling generalizations for Units 21 and 22.

EXTENDING THE LESSON

Have the children write four or five eye-catching story titles using review words. Explain that eye-catching titles that catch the reader's interest are usually short and to the point. Some examples are:

Last Straw
An Early Birthday

Remind the children to proofread the titles for spelling.

Review: Unit 23

Name	UNIT 24
Review C: Unit 23 · Test Exercise	

A. UNIT 23 Answer each question with a word from Unit 23. Then circle the sound the answer makes: /är/, as in _art_, or /âr/, as in _care_.

UNIT 23
park
yard
heart
stairs
bear
card
hair
air

1. What growls and has four legs?
   a ___bear___ /är/(/âr/)

2. What is always three feet long?
   a ___yard___ (/är/)/âr/

3. What do cars do in a garage?
   ___park___ (/är/)/âr/

4. What grows on top of your head? ___hair___ /är/(/âr/)

5. What stiff piece of paper is sent on birthdays? a ___card___ (/är/)/âr/

6. What do you climb to the second floor? ___stairs___ /är/(/âr/)

7. What beats in your chest? a ___heart___ (/är/)/âr/

8. What do you use to fill a balloon? ___air___ /är/(/âr/)

B. UNITS 19—23 Fill in the circle below the word that is spelled wrong.

1	maybee ●	anyway ⓑ	everybody ⓒ	4	won't ⓐ	can't ⓑ	din't ●
2	taught ⓐ	tawk ●	straw ⓒ	5	four ⓐ	bourn ●	short ⓒ
3	lurn ●	heard ⓑ	return ⓒ	6	air ⓐ	bair ●	hair ⓒ

Extra Practice • 101

TEACHING PLAN

Objective   To spell words that demonstrate these sound-letter relationships: /är/ar, ear; /âr/air, ear.

1. Review the directions to the exercises on page 104. Remind the children that the answers to the exercises are to be found only among the eight review words on page 104.
2. Have the children complete the exercises independently. You may refer them to the **Writer's Guide** at the back of the book for a review of the spelling generalization for Unit 23.
3. Review the children's answers on pages 102 – 104 orally, or have volunteers write them on the chalkboard.

For reinforcement in writing review words for Units 19 – 23, you may wish to assign **Review Masters 24A, 24B,** and **24C.**

WORDS IN TIME

Have a volunteer read **Words in Time** aloud. Tell the children that other names of animals also have interesting word histories.

As a COOPERATIVE LEARNING activity, have the group compose a word history for an animal. Ask the group to choose one animal. (Examples are a giraffe, gerbil, deer, lion, cow.) Refer the children in the group to resource materials, such as the dictionary, encyclopedia, and books on the origins of words. Have each child record the information on a group chart. Have one child use the information to write a word history. Have other children illustrate the word history by drawing pictures of the animal or cutting pictures out of magazines. Ask another child to revise the word history, checking spelling, punctuation, and capitalization. The group should display the word history on the bulletin board.

UNIT 23

park •
yard
heart •
stairs •
bear
card
hair •
air

UNIT 23   Follow the directions. Use words from Unit 23.

33. Write the four words that have /är/. Draw a line under the letters that spell /är/ in each word.   **Word order may vary.**

p<u>ar</u>k   y<u>ar</u>d

h<u>ear</u>t   c<u>ar</u>d

34. Write the four words that have /âr/. Draw a line under the letters that spell /âr/ in each word.   **Word order mary vary.**

st<u>air</u>s   b<u>ear</u>

h<u>air</u>   <u>air</u>

35. Write the word from **34** that is a plural word.

stairs

Add a word to each word below to make a compound word. Then write the compound word.

36. back + ___yard___ = ___backyard___

37. up   + ___stairs___ = ___upstairs___

38. Write the two words that rhyme with <u>air</u>.
   Word order may vary.

___hair___   ___bear___

39. Finish this sentence.

Amanda drew a red ___heart___ on the birthday

___card___ she gave to her mother.

WORDS IN TIME

The word <u>bear</u> comes from the old word <u>bera</u>. <u>Bera</u> meant "the brown one." Can you guess why people gave this name to a bear?

104

Spelling and Reading

A Friendly Letter

Read the following friendly letter. Look at the five parts.

> 387 First Street
> Boulder, Colorado 80302
> July 15, 19—
>
> Dear Gail,
>
> I can't wait for you to come next month. We're going to have a lot of fun.
>
> It's going to be my birthday while you're here. Mom is planning a party for me. It will be outside in our yard.
>
> I'll talk to my dad about taking us fishing. He just taught me how to fish. I only wish your visit were going to be longer. Four days is such a short time!
>
> What is new with you? Write soon and tell me.
>
> Your friend,
> Mary

Heading

Greeting

Body

Closing
Signature

Write the answers to the questions.
See answers below.
1. In the letter, where does Mary say her birthday party will take place? *Literal*
2. How long will Gail's visit be? *Literal*
3. How does Mary feel about the length of Gail's visit? *Interpretive*
4. Why do you think Mary asked Gail what's new with her? *Critical*

Underline the review words in your answers. Check to see that you spelled the words correctly.

105

TEACHING PLAN

Objectives To analyze and respond to a friendly letter; to identify details about a friendly letter; to proofread written answers for spelling.

1. Tell the children that they will read a friendly letter that includes a number of spelling words from Units 19–23. Point out that a friendly letter has five parts: the heading, the greeting, the body, the closing, and the signature, and that it is usually written to a friend or relative to tell about what you have been doing. Explain that the friendly letter will serve as a model for their own writing.
2. Have the children read the friendly letter to learn what Mary has written to her friend Gail. Tell them to notice the details about what is being planned.
3. Have the children answer the questions independently. Tell them to underline the review words in the answers and to proofread the answers for spelling.
4. Spot-check the children's answers as they work. Review answers orally.

Spelling and Reading **Answers**

1. It will take place outside in the <u>yard</u>.
2. <u>four</u> days
3. She is sad that it will be so <u>short</u>. 4. Accept all reasonable answers. Possible answer: Mary is curious about what Gail has been doing.

On this page students will read:
- This Week's Words from the preceding five units;
- words reviewed in this unit;
- words that follow the generalizations taught in the preceding five units.

TEACHING PLAN

> **Objectives** To recognize the
> purpose of a friendly letter; to
> identify the details of a friendly
> letter; to evaluate the form and
> mechanics of a friendly letter.

1. Have the children read the first
   paragraph of **Think and Discuss** on
   page 106. Ask the children to recall
   a friendly letter that they might
   have received and then give
   examples of the type of information
   it contained. Ask the children if the
   letter on page 105 fits the definition
   of a friendly letter.

2. Have the children read the rest of
   Think and Discuss independently
   and answer the questions. Ask the
   children to give examples of what
   the writer told her friend and what
   she wanted to know. Have them
   discuss what other types of
   information might have been
   included.

3. Have the children read **Apply** at the
   bottom of page 106. Tell them that
   they will write a friendly letter using
   some of the spelling words. Discuss
   with them the parts of a friendly
   letter and the types of information
   that are included.

Spelling and Writing
A Friendly Letter

Words to Help You Write
grandmother
grandfather
didn't
I'll
let's
there's
we're
talk
learn
early
park
yard

Think and Discuss

A friendly letter is a letter you write to a friend or a
relative. You can tell about things you did, or other news. You
can also ask what your friend or relative is doing.

Look at Mary's letter on page 105. To whom did she write?
What did she tell Gail about? What question did Mary ask
Gail?

Look at the five parts of Mary's letter. Where did she use
capital letters? Where did she use commas?

Apply

Now you will write a **friendly letter.** Follow the writing
guidelines on the next page.

Summarize Learning

Have the children identify the
purpose of a friendly letter (a letter
written to a friend or relative to tell
about things the writer has done), the
parts of a friendly letter (heading,
greeting, body, closing, signature), and
the mechanics of a friendly letter
(capitalization and punctuation).

Think and Discuss Answers

A. Gail B. She told Gail about the things
they'll do when Gail visits. C. What is new
with you? D. She used capital letters in
the heading, greeting, at the beginning of
all sentences in the body, at the
beginning of the closing, and in her
signature. E. She used commas in the
second and third lines of the heading,
and at the end of the greeting and
closing.

Prewriting

Get ready to write a friendly letter to a friend or relative who lives in another town.
- Choose someone to receive your letter.
- Make a list of some things you did that might interest the person to whom you are writing.
- Make a list of some things you would like to know about the person.

 THESAURUS If you need more words to tell about things you did, turn to page 203.

Composing

Use your lists to write your letter.
- Write about what you have been doing.
- Ask about news your friend or relative might have.

Revising

Read your letter. Follow these guidelines to improve your work. Use the editing and proofreading marks to show changes.

Editing

- Make sure your letter has all five parts.
- Check that you told something about yourself.
- Be sure you asked about the other person.

Proofreading

- Check your spelling and correct any mistakes.
- Check your capitalization and punctuation.

Copy your letter onto a clean paper. Write carefully and neatly.

Publishing

Send your letter to your friend or relative. Or share your letter with your classmates by posting it on a class bulletin board. See what information other children included in their letters.

107

Editing and Proofreading Marks	
≡	capitalize
⊙	make a period
∧	add something
⋏	add a comma
⌿	take something away
◯	spell correctly
⊓	indent the paragraph
/	make a lowercase letter
∿ tr	transpose

TEACHING PLAN

Objectives To write a friendly letter; to edit for structure and content; to proofread for spelling, capitalization, and punctuation.

1. **Prewriting** Have the children list some possible things that they might like to include in a friendly letter. Children might like to tell about what they are learning in school, a visit from their grandparents, a special gift they have received. Explain that listing details can help them to organize their ideas before they write their letters.

To help the children use more precise language in their writing, you may wish to have them use **Writer's Word Bank**.

2. **Composing** Have the children write the first draft of a friendly letter. Tell them to use some of the spelling words on page 106 or other review words in the paragraphs. The children may refer to the **Writer's Guide** on page 251 for a definition and a model of a friendly letter.

3. **Revising (Editing and Proofreading)** Have the children ask classmates to read the friendly letters. Have the reader check to see if the five parts of the letter are included and if the body of the letter is clearly written and makes sense. Have the children consider their classmates' comments as they revise their letters. Remind them to use the **Spelling Dictionary** to check the spelling. To help the children prepare a legible copy of the letters, have them consult the **Handwriting Models** in the **Writer's Guide** on page 258.

For reinforcement in editing and proofreading, you may wish to use **Spelling and Writing Transparency 4.**

4. **Publishing** Have the children share the letters by sending them to a friend or relative.

---

xtra Practice: Dictionary/Proofreading

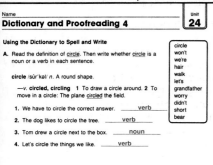

For additional practice in using a dictionary to spell and write and in proofreading, you may wish to assign **Dictionary and Proofreading Practice Master 4.**

ENRICHMENT ACTIVITIES

For the Home

Home activities may be assigned to children of all ability levels. The activities provide opportunities for children to use their spelling words in new contexts. The children may complete these activities independently or with the assistance of a relative or friend in the home.

1. **Language Arts/Making a Word Search Puzzle Using Rhyming Words** Have each child write rhyming words for five of the spelling words. Then have the children use all ten words to make a word search puzzle. Tell the children to share the puzzles with a friend or family member.

2. **Language Arts/Writing Sentences** Explain to the children that homophones are words with the same sound but different meanings. The words *two, to,* and *too* are examples. Tell the children that the following pairs of words are homophones: *four, for; heard, herd; bear, bare; hair, hare.* Have the children use a dictionary to check for word meanings and then write a sentence to illustrate each word. Tell the children to share the sentences with a friend or a relative at home. Children may wish to put these words in a notebook and add to the list as they find other examples of homophones.

3. **Health/Writing Directions for a Game** Tell the children to think about a game that they like to play in physical education. Have them write a paragraph giving directions for playing the game to someone who has never played it before. When they have finished, have them share the paragraph with a friend or someone at home.

4. **Fine Arts/Listening to Music and Writing a Description** Tell the children to listen to a piece of music that they do not normally listen to, perhaps with a friend or another member of the family. Have them close their eyes as they listen. Then have them write several sentences describing how they feel when they hear it. Tell them to use as many review words in the sentences as possible. Tell them to compare the sentences and share them with other friends or family members.

EVALUATION

Unit Test

1. *anyway* I didn't think I'd get a part in the play, but I tried out *anyway.* **anyway**
2. *bedroom* It took me all day to clean my *bedroom.* **bedroom**
3. *everybody* At my house, *everybody* helps do the chores. **everybody**
4. *maybe* I think that *maybe* I'll take guitar lessons. **maybe**

5. *sometimes* My grandfather *sometimes* tells us stories. **sometimes**
6. *outside* In the summer we play *outside.* **outside**
7. *grandfather* My *grandfather* came to this country when he was seven years old. **grandfather**
8. *grandmother* My *grandmother* knitted this hat and sweater for me. **grandmother**
9. *didn't* I *didn't* see the TV program about whales. **didn't**
10. *I'll* First *I'll* ask if I can go with you. **I'll**
11. *let's* We can go to the supermarket, but first *let's* make a list of what we need. **let's**
12. *there's* I heard *there's* a new tiger cub at the zoo. **there's**
13. *won't* This door *won't* open. **won't**
14. *can't* Laura *can't* come with us on Saturday. **can't**
15. *that's* I think *that's* Mario's jacket. **that's**
16. *we're* Miss Sanchez said *we're* going to sing a song. **we're**
17. *talk* I wonder what my cat would say if she could *talk.* **talk**
18. *taught* My mother *taught* me how to ride a bicycle. **taught**
19. *straw* David drank his milk with a *straw.* **straw**
20. *short* These pants are much too *short.* **short**
21. *four* There are *four* trails that lead to the top of the mountain. **four**
22. *born* My sister was *born* on New Year's Day. **born**
23. *walk* I usually *walk* to school with Inez. **walk**
24. *north* We turn *north* on Oak Street. **north**
25. *birthday* Joe's *birthday* is today. **birthday**
26. *heard* In the park we *heard* the ducks. **heard**
27. *learn* Raul and Elizabeth will *learn* how to throw a soccer ball. **learn**
28. *return* Norman wants to *return* for a visit. **return**
29. *world* People from all over the *world* visit New York City. **world**
30. *circle* We formed a *circle* and began to dance. **circle**
31. *early* I wake up so *early* that the birds are still asleep. **early**
32. *worry* Diane does not have to *worry* about passing the test. **worry**
33. *park* Our neighborhood wants to make a *park* out of that empty lot. **park**
34. *yard* My puppy likes to play in our *yard.* **yard**
35. *heart* I was so scared, I thought my *heart* would jump right out. **heart**
36. *stairs* The *stairs* to the second floor are at the end of the hall. **stairs**
37. *bear* The big black *bear* scratched himself on a rock. **bear**
38. *card* When my friend was in the hospital, I sent her a *card* and some flowers. **card**
39. *hair* Roberto is getting his *hair* cut today. **hair**
40. *air* The airplane sailed through the *air.* **air**

Mastery and Bonus Words Review and Assessment

For additional practice you may wish to assign *Mastery Words Review Master: Units 9–23* or *Bonus Words Review Master: Units 9–23*. To assess students' spelling ability with these words, use *Mastery Words Test: Units 19–23* or *Bonus Words Test: Units 19–23*.

Mastery Words Review

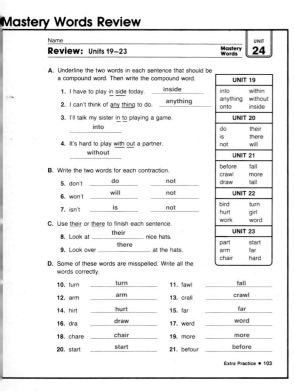

Name
Review: Units 19–23 — Mastery Words — UNIT 24

A. Underline the two words in each sentence that should be a compound word. Then write the compound word.

1. I have to play in side today. __inside__
2. I can't think of any thing to do. __anything__
3. I'll talk my sister in to playing a game. __into__
4. It's hard to play with out a partner. __without__

B. Write the two words for each contraction.

5. don't — do / not
6. won't — will / not
7. isn't — is / not

C. Use their or there to finish each sentence.

8. Look at __their__ nice hats.
9. Look over __there__ at the hats.

D. Some of these words are misspelled. Write all the words correctly.

10. turn — turn
11. fawl — fall
12. arm — arm
13. crall — crawl
14. hirt — hurt
15. far — far
16. dra — draw
17. werd — word
18. chare — chair
19. more — more
20. start — start
21. befour — before

UNIT 19
into / within
anything / without
onto / inside

UNIT 20
do / their
is / there
not / will

UNIT 21
before / fall
crawl / more
draw / tall

UNIT 22
bird / turn
hurt / girl
work / word

UNIT 23
part / start
arm / far
chair / hard

Extra Practice • 103

Bonus Words Review

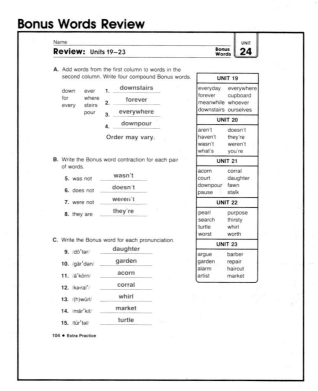

Name
Review: Units 19–23 — Bonus Words — UNIT 24

A. Add words from the first column to words in the second column. Write four compound Bonus words.

down / ever
for / where
every / stairs
 / pour

1. downstairs
2. forever
3. everywhere
4. downpour

Order may vary.

B. Write the Bonus word contraction for each pair of words.

5. was not — wasn't
6. does not — doesn't
7. were not — weren't
8. they are — they're

C. Write the Bonus word for each pronunciation.

9. /dô´tər/ — daughter
10. /gär´dən/ — garden
11. /ā´kôrn/ — acorn
12. /kə-ral´/ — corral
13. /(h)wûrl/ — whirl
14. /mär´kit/ — market
15. /tûr´təl/ — turtle

UNIT 19
everyday / everywhere
forever / cupboard
meanwhile / whoever
downstairs / ourselves

UNIT 20
aren't / doesn't
haven't / they're
wasn't / weren't
what's / you're

UNIT 21
acorn / corral
court / daughter
downpour / fawn
pause / stalk

UNIT 22
pearl / purpose
search / thirsty
turtle / whirl
worst / worth

UNIT 23
argue / barber
garden / repair
alarm / haircut
artist / market

104 • Extra Practice

Mastery Words Test

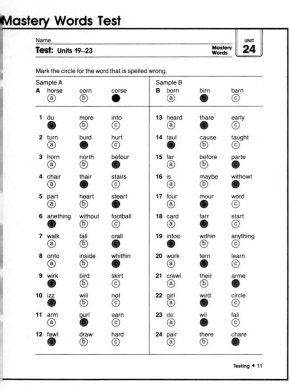

Name
Test: Units 19–23 — Mastery Words — UNIT 24

Mark the circle for the word that is spelled wrong.

Sample A			Sample B		
A horse ⓐ	corn ⓑ	corse ●	B born ●	birn ⓐ	barn ⓒ
1 du ●	more ⓑ	into ⓒ	13 heard ⓐ	thare ●	early ⓒ
2 turn ⓐ	burd ●	hurt ⓒ	14 taul ●	cause ⓑ	taught ⓒ
3 horn ⓐ	north ⓑ	befour ●	15 far ⓐ	before ⓑ	parte ●
4 chair ⓐ	thair ●	stairs ⓒ	16 is ⓐ	maybe ⓑ	withowt ●
5 part ⓐ	heart ⓑ	steart ●	17 four ⓐ	mour ●	word ⓒ
6 anething ●	without ⓑ	football ⓒ	18 card ⓐ	farr ●	start ⓒ
7 walk ⓐ	tall ⓑ	crall ●	19 intoo ●	within ⓑ	anything ⓒ
8 onto ⓐ	inside ⓑ	whithin ●	20 work ⓐ	tern ●	learn ⓒ
9 wirk ●	bird ⓑ	skirt ⓒ	21 crawl ⓐ	their ⓑ	arme ●
10 izz ●	will ⓑ	not ⓒ	22 girl ⓐ	wird ●	circle ⓒ
11 arm ⓐ	gurl ●	earn ⓒ	23 do ⓐ	wil ●	fall ⓒ
12 fawl ●	draw ⓑ	hard ⓒ	24 pair ⓐ	there ⓑ	chare ●

Testing • 11

Bonus Words Test

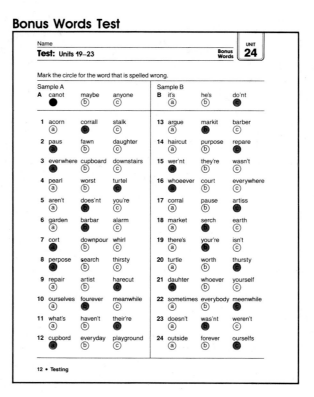

Name
Test: Units 19–23 — Bonus Words — UNIT 24

Mark the circle for the word that is spelled wrong.

Sample A			Sample B		
A canot ●	maybe ⓑ	anyone ⓒ	B it's ⓐ	he's ⓑ	do'nt ●
1 acorn ⓐ	corrall ●	stalk ⓒ	13 argue ⓐ	markit ●	barber ⓒ
2 paus ●	fawn ⓑ	daughter ⓒ	14 haircut ⓐ	purpose ⓑ	repare ●
3 everwhere ●	cupboard ⓑ	downstairs ⓒ	15 wer'nt ●	they're ⓑ	wasn't ⓒ
4 pearl ⓐ	worst ⓑ	turtel ●	16 whoever ⓐ	court ⓑ	everywhere ⓒ
5 aren't ⓐ	does'nt ●	you're ⓒ	17 corral ⓐ	pause ⓑ	artiss ●
6 garden ⓐ	barbar ●	alarm ⓒ	18 market ⓐ	serch ●	earth ⓒ
7 cort ●	downpour ⓑ	whirl ⓒ	19 there's ⓐ	your're ●	isn't ⓒ
8 perpose ●	search ⓑ	thirsty ⓒ	20 turtle ⓐ	worth ⓑ	thursty ●
9 repair ⓐ	artist ⓑ	harecut ●	21 dauhter ●	whoever ⓑ	yourself ⓒ
10 ourselves ⓐ	fourever ●	meanwhile ⓒ	22 sometimes ⓐ	everybody ⓑ	meenwhile ●
11 what's ⓐ	haven't ⓑ	their're ●	23 doesn't ⓐ	was'nt ●	weren't ⓒ
12 cupbord ●	everyday ⓑ	playground ⓒ	24 outside ⓐ	forever ⓑ	ourselfs ●

12 • Testing

NOTES

Six-Week Evaluation

Mark the circle for the word that is spelled wrong.

Sample A			Sample B		
A bright ⓐ	every ⓑ	prise ⊙	**B** team ⓐ	todey ⓑ	only ⓒ

1 owtside ⓐ	anyone ⓑ	grandmother ⓒ	**11** walk ⓐ	stairs ⓑ	fouer ⓒ
2 can't ⓐ	everbody ⓑ	grandfather ⓒ	**12** she's ⓐ	nohrth ⓑ	taught ⓒ
3 bedrum ⓐ	heard ⓑ	outside ⓒ	**13** berthday ⓐ	circle ⓑ	sir ⓒ
4 outside ⓐ	walk ⓑ	grandfater ⓒ	**14** lern ⓐ	fur ⓑ	bluebird ⓒ
5 we'er ⓐ	early ⓑ	didn't ⓒ	**15** early ⓐ	retern ⓑ	hair ⓒ
6 didn't ⓐ	ther's ⓑ	playground ⓒ	**16** burn ⓐ	jaw ⓑ	wurld ⓒ
7 let's ⓐ	I'm ⓑ	wont ⓒ	**17** haert ⓐ	yard ⓑ	four ⓒ
8 that's ⓐ	I'ell ⓑ	yourself ⓒ	**18** aire ⓐ	worry ⓑ	learn ⓒ
9 return ⓐ	tolk ⓑ	straw ⓒ	**19** heard ⓐ	skirt ⓑ	kard ⓒ
10 born ⓐ	didn't ⓑ	strahw ⓒ	**20** bear ⓐ	yaird ⓑ	it's ⓒ

FORM A TEST 4

Administering the Test

1. Tell the children that today they will take a spelling test on some of the words they have studied in Units 19 – 23. Pass out the test papers. Tell the children to leave them turned upside down until you are ready to begin.

2. Have the children turn their tests over. Direct the children's attention to Sample A. Have the children look for the incorrect spelling. Ask a child to tell you the word that is spelled incorrectly. Point out that circle c under the misspelling *p-r-i-s-e* is filled in.

3. Now direct the children's attention to Sample B. Have the children look for the incorrect spelling. Ask a child to tell you the word that is spelled incorrectly by spelling it correctly. (*t-o-d-a-y*) Then have the children fill in circle *b* in pencil.

4. After you have checked to see that all children have completed Sample B correctly, have the children proceed with the test.

Evaluating the Results

Use the following **Answer Key** to correct the children's tests and to determine whether they need more practice with particular units. The chart shows the units in which each answer word is taught.

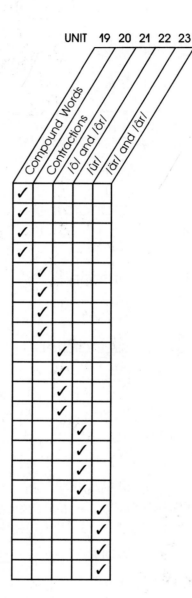

ANSWER KEY

	a	b	c
1	●		
2		●	
3	●		
4			●
5	●		
6		●	
7			●
8		●	
9		●	
10			●
11			●
12		●	
13	●		
14	●		
15		●	
16			●
17	●		
18	●		
19			●
20		●	

PREVIEWING THE UNIT

Unit Materials

Instruction and Practice

Pupil Book	pages 108–111
Teacher's Edition	
Teaching Plans	pages 108–111
Enrichment Activities	
For the Classroom	page 111A
For the Home	page 111B
Reteaching Strategies	page 111C

Testing

Teacher's Edition	
Trial Test	pages 107E–107F
Unit Test	page 111B
Dictation Test	page 111B

Additional Resources

PRACTICE AND REINFORCEMENT
Extra Practice Master 25: This Week's Words
Extra Practice Master 25: Mastery Words
Extra Practice Master 25: Bonus Words
LEP Practice Master 25
Spelling and Language Master 25
Study Steps to Learn a Word Master

RETEACHING FOLLOW-UP
Reteaching Follow-up Master 25A:
    Discovering Spelling Ideas
Reteaching Follow-up Master 25B: Word
    Shapes
LEP Reteaching Follow-up Master 25

TEACHING AIDS
Spelling Generalizations Transparency 21

Click on the SPELLING banner to find activities for this unit.

Learner Objectives

Spelling

- To spell plurals formed by adding *s* or by changing *y* to *i* and adding *es*.

Reading

- To follow written directions.
- To use context clues for word identification.

Writing

- To write a paragraph.
- To use the writing process.
- To proofread for spelling, capitalization, and punctuation.
- To write legible manuscript and cursive letters.

Listening

- To listen to identify the difference between singular and plural nouns in sentence context.
- To listen to respond to a speaker.
- To follow oral directions.

Speaking

- To speak clearly to a group.
- To contribute ideas and information in group discussions.
- To express feelings and ideas about a piece of writing.
- To present a how-to paragraph.

THIS WEEK'S WORDS
pancakes
ears
eyes
grades
lands
marbles
newspapers
shapes
wheels
buddies
butterflies
fairies
guppies
puppies
spies

MASTERY WORDS
trains
tires
streets
stones
plants
ants

BONUS WORDS
blueberries
stories
cartwheels
chances
cherries
details
hobbies
puddles

Assignment Guide

This guide shows how you teach a typical spelling unit in either a five-day or a three-day sequence, while providing for individual differences. **Boldface type** indicates essential classwork. Steps shown in light type may be done in class or assigned as homework.

Five Days	○ = average spellers ★ = better spellers ✓ = slower spellers	Three Days
Day **1**	**a** ● ★ **Take This Week's Words Trial Test and correct** ● ✓ **Take Mastery Word Trial Test and correct** ● ★ **Read This Week's Words and discuss generalization page 108**	Day **1**
Day **2**	● Complete Spelling Practice page 109 ● ✓ Complete Extra Practice Master 25: This Week's Words (optional) **b** ✓ Complete Spelling on Your Own: Mastery Words page 111 ★ **Take Bonus Word Trial Test and correct**	
Day **3**	**c** ● ★ ✓ **Complete Spelling and Language page 110** ● ★ ✓ Complete Writing on Your Own page 110 ● ✓ Take Midweek Test (optional) ● ★ ✓ **Complete Proofreading page 110** ● ✓ Take Midweek Test (optional) ● ✓ Complete Spelling and Language Master 25 (optional)	Day **2**
Day **4**	● Complete Spelling on Your Own: This Week's Words page 109 ✓ Complete Extra Practice Master 25: Mastery Words (optional) **d** ★ Complete Extra Practice Master 25: Bonus Words (optional)	
Day **5**	**e** ● **Take Unit Test on This Week's Words** ● Complete Reteaching Follow-up Masters 25A and 25B (optional) ● ✓ **Take Unit Test on Mastery Words** ★ **Take Unit Test on Bonus Words**	Day **3**

Enrichment Activities for the **classroom** and for the **home** included at the end of this unit may be assigned selectively on any day of the week.

INTRODUCING THE UNIT

Establish Readiness for Learning

Tell the children that this week they will learn more about spelling the plural forms of words. Tell them that learning more about the plural forms will help them spell This Week's Words and many new words. They will use the words they learn to write a paragraph.

Assess Children's Spelling Ability

Administer the Trial Test before the children study This Week's Words. Use the test sentences provided. Say each word and use it in a sentence. Then repeat the word. Have the children write the words on a separate sheet of paper or in their spelling notebooks. Test sentences are also provided for Mastery and Bonus words.

Have the children check their own work by listening to you read the spelling of the words

or by referring to This Week's Words in the left column of the **Pupil Book.** For each misspelled word, have the children follow the **Study Steps to Learn a Word** on page 1 in the **Pupil Book** or use the copying master to study and write the words. Children should record the number correct on their **Progress Report.**

Trial Test Sentences

This Week's Words
1. *pancakes* Tomás put maple syrup on his *pancakes.* ***pancakes***
2. *ears* People hear with their *ears.* ***ears***
3. *eyes* People see with their *eyes.* ***eyes***
4. *grades* Jackson likes to get good *grades* on his report card. ***grades***
5. *lands* In many *lands* people ride bicycles to work. ***lands***
6. *marbles* Put your *marbles* in a bag. ***marbles***
7. *newspapers* Mr. Henderson sells *newspapers* and magazines. ***newspapers***

FOCUS

- Establishes objectives
- Relates to prior learning
- Sets purpose of instruction

8. *shapes* Circles and squares are *shapes*.
 shapes
9. *wheels* The *wheels* of the train went clickety-clack. **wheels**
10. *buddies* Neil and José are *buddies*.
 buddies
11. *butterflies* We saw ten *butterflies* in the field. **butterflies**
12. *fairies* That story is about elves and *fairies*. **fairies**
13. *guppies* We have *guppies* in a fishbowl in our classroom. **guppies**
14. *puppies* My dog had five *puppies*.
 puppies
15. *spies* The good guys caught all the *spies*. **spies**

Mastery Words
1. *trains* Two *trains* leave for Benningburg every day. **trains**
2. *tires* The *tires* on Wayne's bike need air. **tires**
3. *streets* The *streets* in our city are cleaned twice a week. **streets**
4. *stones* We put pretty *stones* around the rosebushes. **stones**
5. *plants* All the *plants* need to be watered. **plants**
6. *ants* Lauren loves to watch the *ants* in the ant colony. **ants**

Bonus Words
1. *blueberries* We picked *blueberries* for lunch. **blueberries**
2. *stories* Clem likes adventure *stories*.
 stories

3. *cartwheels* Conchita can turn *cartwheels*. **cartwheels**
4. *chances* You have two *chances* to guess the answer. **chances**
5. *cherries* Put the *cherries* in the bowl. **cherries**
6. *details* David told us all the *details*.
 details
7. *hobbies* Manuel's *hobbies* are stamp collecting and skiing. **hobbies**
8. *puddles* The child splashed in all the *puddles*. **puddles**

Apply Prior Learning

 Have the children be spelling detectives. Tell them that they can discover spelling generalizations by applying what they already know. Write the words *train* and *stone* on the chalkboard. Ask the children to read these words and then say the word that tells you more than one. (trains, stones) Write these words on the chalkboard. What do we call words that mean more than one? (plural) Ask the children to give you other words in both singular and plural forms. Write them on the chalkboard. Some of the words may end with *consonant-y*. If so, ask the children what they notice about the way plurals are formed. (Sometimes you just add *s*. Sometimes you change the *y* to *i* and add *es*.) If no words ending in *consonant-y* have been suggested, tell the children they will learn about another way to spell plurals for certain words. Explain that they can use these words in a variety of spelling tasks: writing stories, writing poems, or writing a social studies report.

FOR CHILDREN WITH SPECIAL NEEDS

Learning Difficulties

 Recalling a spelling generalization presents difficulties for some children with language disorders and auditory memory deficits. Help the children learn these generalizations so that they become automatic.

 At the top of a piece of lined paper, write the generalization: *Words that end with a consonant and* y, *change* y *to* i *and add* es. Have the children write This Week's Words that end in *y* on the left side of the paper. Prior to writing the plural form of This Week's Words, have the children say the spelling generalization aloud. Then, with a colored marker, have them underline the *y*, cross it out, add the letters *i* and *es*, and write the plural form of each word.

 As independent work or a homework assignment, have the children find other words in classroom reading materials or in the library to which this generalization applies. Carry out the activity as described.

Limited English Proficiency

To help limited English proficient children work with the spelling generalizations for Unit 25, you may wish to refer to the booklet "Suggestions and Activities for Limited English Proficient Students."

TEACHING PLAN

Objective To spell plurals formed by adding *s* or by changing *y* to *i* and adding *es*.

1. Write *dog* on the chalkboard. Ask the children to say the word for more than one dog. Write *dogs* on the chalkboard, and have a child tell you how the words are different. Then ask the children to tell you what a young dog is called. Write *puppy* on the chalkboard, and ask the children to say the word for more than one *puppy*. Write *puppies* on the chalkboard, and help the children to recognize how the words are different.

2. Read the generalization on page 108 aloud.

You may wish to introduce the lesson by using **Spelling Generalizations Transparency 21.**

3. Have volunteers read This Week's Words. As each word is read, ask the children to identify the letter or letters that form the plural.

You may wish to assign **LEP Practice Master 25** for reinforcement in writing spelling words.

---

25 More Plurals

THIS WEEK'S WORDS

1. *pancakes*
2. *ears*
3. *eyes*
4. *grades*
5. *lands*
6. *marbles*
7. *newspapers*
8. *shapes*
9. *wheels*
10. *buddies*
11. *butterflies*
12. *fairies*
13. *guppies*
14. *puppies*
15. *spies*

This Week's Words

A **plural noun** names more than one thing. You add <u>s</u> to most nouns to make the plural.

pancake　pancakes
ear　　　ears

Just <u>s</u> is not enough for words like <u>buddy</u> and <u>spy</u>. These words end with a consonant and <u>y</u>. To make them plural, change <u>y</u> to <u>i</u> and add <u>es</u>.

buddy　　buddies
spy　　　spies

108

Extra Practice: This Week's Words

Name
Extra Practice · This Week's Words · UNIT 25

Finish the puzzle with This Week's Words. Each sentence tells something about one of the words. Choose the word and write it where it belongs in the puzzle.

ears　　guppies
butterflies　lands
eyes　　wheels
pancakes　puppies
fairies　marbles
grades　buddies
shapes　spies
newspapers

ACROSS

1. Many people read these every day.
5. These have bright-colored wings.
7. These might be circles or squares.
11. You need these to hear.
12. You need these to see.
13. Pupils get these on tests.
14. A bicycle has two of these.

DOWN

2. These grow up to be dogs.
3. These must live in water.
4. Their work is to find out secrets.
5. This is another word for <u>friends</u>.
6. These do magic in make-believe stories.
8. These are good for breakfast.
9. These are small, round, and hard and are used in games.
10. Countries may be called this.

Extra Practice • 105

Extra Practice: Mastery Words

Name
Extra Practice · Mastery Words · UNIT 25

A. Write the Mastery word that goes with each sentence.

1. These are hard and are found on the ground.
   stones

2. These are found on bicycles and cars. They are round.
   tires

3. These are tiny. They are hard workers.
   ants

B. Add letters to these words to spell Mastery words. The boxes show how many letters and where they go. Then write the whole words.

4. P | l | ant | s
   plants

5. s | tree | t | s
   streets

6. t | rain | s
   trains

tires　streets　stones　ants　trains　plants

106 • Extra Practice

Spelling Practice

A. Write the plural of each word.

1. guppy ___guppies___
2. fairy ___fairies___
3. buddy ___buddies___
4. spy ___spies___

B. Write the plural of the words in dark print. Finish the sentences.

5. **newspaper** Mr. Ito reads four ___newspapers___ every day.

6. **land** Some are sent to him from other ___lands___ .

C. Write the singular of these words.

7. grades ___grade___
8. pancakes ___pancake___
9. shapes ___shape___
10. marbles ___marble___

D. Write the singular and plural words for each picture.

11. ___puppy___
    ___puppies___

12. ___wheel___
    ___wheels___

13. ___butterfly___
    ___butterflies___

E. Write the plural of the words in dark print. Finish the sentences.

14. **eye** He has ___eyes___ in the back of his head.

15. **ear** Tell me—I'm all ___ears___ .

109

---

pancakes
ears
eyes
grades
lands
marbles
newspapers
shapes
wheels
buddies
butterflies
fairies
guppies
puppies
spies

TEACHING PLAN

Objectives To write plurals of given singular nouns; to write the singular of given plural nouns; to write words given picture clues.

1. Briefly discuss the directions on page 109.
2. Have the children complete the page independently. Remind them to use legible handwriting. You may wish to demonstrate the correct form of the letters *i, y, e,* and *s* and then have the children practice writing the letters. For **Handwriting Models,** refer the children to page 258 in the **Pupil Book.**
3. To correct the children's work, have volunteers write the answers on the chalkboard. Let the children check their own work.

For reinforcement in writing spelling words, you may wish to assign **Extra Practice Master 25: This Week's Words.**

⟳ EXTENDING THE LESSON

Direct the children's attention to Exercise **E** on page 109. Have a child read each completed sentence aloud, and ask the child to explain what the sentence means. If necessary, help the children to recognize that the actual meaning of the sentences is "He notices everything" and "I'm eager to listen." Then, just for fun, have the children draw pictures to show what the sentences *say.* Ask them to label their pictures with one of the sentences in Exercise **E.**

Extra Practice: Bonus Words

Extra Practice — Name — Bonus Words — UNIT 25

Read each clue. Decide which word fits the clue. Write the singular form of the Bonus word in the blank. Then write the plural form of the word in the right place in the puzzle.

ACROSS
1. You must jump over this if you don't want wet feet. ___puddle___
4. This is a compound word. The first word names what a horse pulls. ___cartwheel___
6. This is a compound word. The first word names a color. ___blueberry___
7. It grows on the kind of tree George Washington chopped down. ___cherry___

DOWN
2. To spell this word, add *de* to the word that names what a dog wags. ___detail___
3. This word names something you do, like collecting stamps or making model planes. ___hobby___
4. You take this if you take a try. ___chance___
5. People enjoy reading this. ___story___

hobbies
cartwheels
blueberries
details
stories
chances
cherries
puddles

Extra Practice • 107

Summarize Learning

Have the children summarize what they have learned on pages 108 and 109. *Ask:*

- What did you learn about plural forms in this lesson? (The letter *s* is added to most nouns to make them plural. Words that end with a consonant and *y* are made plural by changing *y* to *i* and adding *es.*)
- What are some examples of words that follow these generalizations? (ears, guppies; accept other examples)

TEACHING PLAN

SPELLING AND LANGUAGE

Objective To write singular or plural nouns in sentence context.

1. To introduce this activity, write these sentence frames on the chalkboard:

   Those _____ wag their tails.
   This _____ wags its tail.

   Then ask the children whether *puppy* or *puppies* fits in each blank. Help them to recognize that in the first sentence, *those, wag, their,* and *tails* are clues that tell you the missing word is plural. In the second sentence, *this, wags, its,* and *tail* tell you that the missing word is singular.
2. Read the directions on page 110.
3. Have the children complete the activity independently.
4. To correct the children's work, have volunteers read the completed sentences aloud. Then ask them to identify the word or words in the sentence that helped them decide whether to use the singular or plural. (1. A caterpillar; a; 2. get)

For extended practice in writing singular or plural nouns in sentence context you may wish to assign *Spelling and Language Master 25.*

WRITING ON YOUR OWN

Objectives To write a paragraph; to proofread for spelling.

1. Review the directions.
2. As a **prewriting** activity, have the children list what they would have to do to care for pets. Then have the children **compose** a paragraph in which they tell how to take care of a pet. When the children are ready to **revise** their work, remind them to proofread for spelling. **Publish** the children's paragraphs by placing them together in a class booklet.

PROOFREADING

Objectives To proofread for spelling errors and capital letters.

1. Read the introductory sentences and the directions on page 110.
2. Have the children read through the entry independently, looking for errors. Then ask them to circle each spelling mistake and draw three lines under letters that should be capitalized. Have them write the misspelled words correctly.
3. **If you are using the hardcover book,** the children should simply locate the errors and then write the incorrect words correctly.

THIS WEEK'S WORDS
pancakes
ears
eyes
grades
lands
marbles
newspapers
shapes
wheels
buddies
butterflies
fairies
guppies
puppies
spies

Spelling and Language • One or More

One of This Week's Words will finish each sentence. Decide if the singular or plural word fits. For example, *puppies* fits the sentence "Those _____ wag their tails." But *puppy* fits the sentence "That _____ wags its tail." Write the words that fit the sentences.

1. A caterpillar becomes a beautiful ___butterfly___

2. Jay's ___grades___ get better with each report card.

Writing on Your Own

Write a paragraph for a class booklet called "How We Take Care of Our Pets." Tell how to take care of the pet you have or would like to have. Use some of This Week's Words and some other plurals.

WRITER'S GUIDE For a sample of a how-to paragraph, turn to page 250.

Proofreading

Jill wrote this in her journal. She misspelled six words and forgot two capital letters.

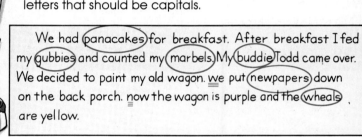

1. Circle each of Jill's mistakes. Draw three lines under the letters that should be capitals.

We had (panacakes) for breakfast. After breakfast I fed my (gubbies) and counted my (marbels). My (buddie) Todd came over. We decided to paint my old wagon. we put (newpapers) down on the back porch. now the wagon is purple and the (wheals) are yellow.

2. Write the six misspelled words correctly.

pancakes	guppies	marbles
buddy	newspapers	wheels

Extra Practice: Spelling and Language

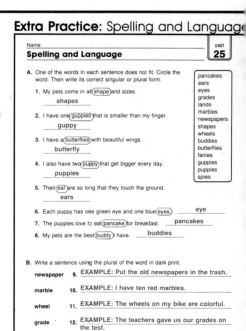

Name ___
Spelling and Language
UNIT 25

A. One of the words in each sentence does not fit. Circle the word. Then write its correct singular or plural form.

1. My pets come in all (shape) and sizes.
   shapes
2. I have one (guppies) that is smaller than my finger.
   guppy
3. I have a (butterflies) with beautiful wings.
   butterfly
4. I also have two (puppy) that get bigger every day.
   puppies
5. Their (ear) are so long that they touch the ground.
   ears
6. Each puppy has one green eye and one blue (eyes).   eye
7. The puppies love to eat (pancake) for breakfast.   pancakes
8. My pets are the best (buddy) I have.   buddies

pancakes
ears
eyes
grades
lands
marbles
newspapers
shapes
wheels
buddies
butterflies
fairies
guppies
puppies
spies

B. Write a sentence using the plural of the word in dark print.
newspaper 9. EXAMPLE: Put the old newspapers in the trash.
marble 10. EXAMPLE: I have ten red marbles.
wheel 11. EXAMPLE: The wheels on my bike are colorful.
grade 12. EXAMPLE: The teachers gave us our grades on the test.

108 • Extra Practice

Spelling on Your Own

THIS WEEK'S WORDS

Write some funny story titles. Use This Week's Words. Try to use more than one of the words in each title. You may use the singular or the plural. Here are some examples: "Why Wheels Are That Shape" and "Life with Puppies and Guppies."

MASTERY WORDS

Follow the directions. Use the Mastery words.

1. Write three words that name things in the picture.

ants	stones	plants

2. Write the word that has the sound /ē/. _____ streets

Finish the sentences. Use the Mastery words.

3. Jenny played with her electric _____ trains _____ .

4. Then she watered the _____ plants _____ in her room.

5. Next, she pumped up the _____ tires _____ on her bike.

Mastery words box:
- trains
- tires
- streets
- stones
- plants
- ants

BONUS WORDS

1. Write the singular of each Bonus word. Tell what happens to make the word plural.
2. Write the two Bonus words that are compound words.
3. Write the five Bonus words that have double letters.
4. Write the six Bonus words with long vowel sounds.
5. Write sentences using the Bonus words. Try to use two of the words in each sentence.   **See answers below.**

Bonus words box:
- blueberries
- stories
- cartwheels
- chances
- cherries
- details
- hobbies
- puddles

111

Spelling on Your Own Answers

BONUS WORDS

1.
blueberry	Change y to i, add es.
story	Change y to i, add es.
cartwheel	Add s.
chance	Add s.
cherry	Change y to i, add es.
detail	Add s.
hobby	Change y to i, add es.
puddle	Add s.

2. blueberries, cartwheels
3. blueberries, cartwheels, cherries, hobbies, puddles
4. blueberries, stories, cartwheels, cherries, details, hobbies
5. EXAMPLE: Tell me all the <u>details</u> about your <u>hobbies</u>.

Summarize Learning

Have the children summarize what they have learned in this unit.
Ask:

- What have you learned about writing singular or plural nouns in sentence context? (The sentence must be read carefully in order to decide whether the singular or plural form of a word belongs in the sentence.)
- What spelling generalizations have you learned? How did you use these generalizations?

TEACHING PLAN

Objective   To apply the unit spelling generalization to spell This Week's Words, Mastery words, and Bonus words independently.

THIS WEEK'S WORDS

1. Read the directions on page 111 aloud. Help the children get started by having volunteers suggest additional examples. Encourage them to use each one of This Week's Words in a title.
2. Have the children complete the activity independently on a separate piece of paper.
3. When the children have finished writing their titles, ask each child to read his or her best title. Write the titles on the chalkboard.

MASTERY WORDS

1. Briefly review the concept of plurals.
2. Have volunteers read the Mastery words aloud. As each word is read, ask the children to identify the singular form of the word.
3. Briefly discuss the directions on page 111. Then have the children complete the activities.
4. Review each child's work, noting any difficulty in following directions.

BONUS WORDS

1. Briefly review plurals formed by changing y to i before adding es.
2. Have volunteers read the Bonus words aloud. As each word is read, ask other children to explain how the plural of the word is formed.
3. Have the children complete the exercises independently on a separate piece of paper.

For reinforcement in writing spelling words, you may wish to assign ***Extra Practice Master 25: Mastery Words*** or ***Bonus Words.***

CLOSING THE UNIT

Apply New Learning

Tell the children that if they misspell plural words in their writing, they should use one or more of the following strategies:

- use the origin of a word to help remember the correct spelling.
- think of words that rhyme and compare in their minds how they are spelled.
- write the word using different spellings and compare it with the spellings they picture in their minds.

Transfer New Learning

Tell the children that when they encounter new words in their personal reading and in other content areas, they should learn the meaning of those words and then apply the generalizations they have studied to the spelling of those words. Tell the children that once the words are familiar in both meaning and spelling, they should use the new words in their writing.

ENRICHMENT ACTIVITIES

Classroom activities and **home activities** may be assigned to children of all ability levels. The activities provide opportunities for children to use their spelling words in new contexts.

For the Classroom

To individualize classroom activities, you may have the children use the word list they are studying in this unit.

- *Basic:* Use **Mastery** words to complete the activity.
- *Average:* Use **This Week's Words** to complete the activity.
- *Challenging:* Use **Bonus** words to complete the activity.

1. **Language Arts/Writing Word Associations** Have the children choose several spelling words from this lesson for which they can name two synonyms or two other words commonly associated with the word. Present this example: *Name a spelling word that belongs with books and magazines.* After the children name *newspapers,* have them write their own word groups, leaving a blank space for the spelling word. After they have completed their groups, have the children switch with one another and guess the answers.

   ▪ COOPERATIVE LEARNING: Have each group create a set of word associations. Each child within the group should choose one word for which he or she can name two synonyms or two other words commonly associated with the word. Children should try out their word associations with one another to see if they are effective. They can revise them together. After each group is satisfied with all the word associations, groups can share with classmates.

2. **Language Arts/Writing Contrasting Sentences** Have the children choose several spelling words to make sentences based on the following pattern provided by you: Mark ate only one *pancake.* I ate six *pancakes.* After writing their sentences, have the children rewrite them leaving a blank space for the spelling word. Have the children exchange their sentences with one another and fill in the missing spelling words.

   ▪ COOPERATIVE LEARNING Have each group create a set of contrasting sentences. Each member of the group should write a pair of sentences for a different spelling word. After they have tried out their sentences and revised where necessary, have the group select one person to rewrite all the sentences, leaving a blank space for each spelling word. Then have the group share its sentences with classmates.

3. **Language Arts/Writing a Report** Have the children write a report. First, direct the children's attention to page 254 of the **Writer's Guide** to read about reports. Then as a *prewriting* activity, have the children look over the spelling lists in search of words that suggest a possible topic, for example, *transportation on land, choosing a pet, how ants live.* Ask each child to select a topic he or she wants to write about, read about their topic, and then list any important details. When the children have completed the prewriting activity, tell them to use their lists to **compose** their reports. Remind them to use as many spelling words as possible. Then have the children *revise* their reports, making sure their detail sentences support the main idea of the report. Have the children proofread for spelling, capitalization, and punctuation, using the **Revising Checklist** on page 247 for help. After they have rewritten their reports, have the children **publish** their work by reading the reports aloud to the class. Some children may also wish to illustrate their reports.

   ▪ COOPERATIVE LEARNING: Have each group write a report. As a *prewriting* activity, have the children look over the spelling lists in search of words that suggest a possible topic. Have the members of the group decide what they will write about, read about their topic, and then make a list of important details. When the group is ready to **compose,** have them select one child to begin the report orally by providing a topic sentence. The other members of the group should then use the list to formulate detail sentences that build on the topic sentence. The group can select one person to record the report. Other members should *revise,* checking to make sure that the details support the main idea of the report. Each child should also proofread the report for spelling, capitalization, and punctuation. Have the group select one person to rewrite the report. Other children may want to provide illustrations. Each group can then **publish** its report by displaying it on the bulletin board.

For the Home

Children may complete these activities independently or with the assistance of a relative or friend in the home.

1. **Language Arts/Writing Humorous Sentences** Tell the children to write two silly sentences using as many spelling words as they can. Present this example: *Butterflies chased puppies through the streets of the town.* Have the children underline the spelling words in each sentence. Children may enjoy illustrating their sentences. Then have them share their work with a friend or family member.

2. **Language Arts/Writing Clues for Spelling Words** Tell the children to write a short description for some of their spelling words without actually naming the word. Present this example: *They are round and flat and taste good at breakfast.* (pancakes) Then have the children share their descriptions with friends or family members to see if that person can guess what is being described.

3. **Mathematics/Describing Shapes** Tell the children to choose a shape and write a description of it. Have them include everyday items as examples of the shape they have chosen to describe. Point out that some of their spelling words may be helpful as examples. Remind the children to proofread for spelling, capitalization, and punctuation, using the **Revising Checklist** on page 247. They may also wish to cut out pictures from old magazines that illustrate the shape. When the children have finished, have them share their descriptions with a friend or family member.

4. **Science/Writing Questions About Plants and Animals** Have children think of a plant or animal they would like to know about. Tell them to write five questions about the plant or animal, using some of their spelling words. Then tell the children to use a dictionary, an encyclopedia, or a science book to find the answers to their questions. When they have completed the activity, have them share their findings with a friend or someone at home.

EVALUATING SPELLING ABILITY

Unit Test

This Week's Words

1. *pancakes* You may have *pancakes* for breakfast. **pancakes**
2. *ears* My *ears* are cold. **ears**
3. *eyes* Alicia covered her *eyes*. **eyes**
4. *grades* The second and third *grades* will go to the circus. **grades**
5. *lands* Children in many *lands* go to school. **lands**
6. *marbles* Those are my best *marbles*. **marbles**
7. *newspapers* My father reads two *newspapers* every day. **newspapers**
8. *shapes* Pasta comes in all different *shapes*. **shapes**
9. *wheels* Leo painted the wagon *wheels*. **wheels**
10. *buddies* My *buddies* and I are going downtown. **buddies**
11. *butterflies* Some *butterflies* have beautiful wings. **butterflies**
12. *fairies* The *fairies* in that story are very clever. **fairies**
13. *guppies* Neville bought some *guppies* at the pet store. **guppies**
14. *puppies* We saw some *puppies* in the pet store. **puppies**
15. *spies* Rodney thinks all *spies* wear dark glasses. **spies**

Mastery Words

1. *trains* Donny has a set of electric *trains*. **trains**
2. *tires* Mom bought new *tires* for the car. **tires**
3. *streets* Five *streets* come together at this corner. **streets**
4. *stones* There are *stones* in the bottom of the aquarium. **stones**
5. *plants* Mrs. Kwan has three *plants* in her room. **plants**
6. *ants* We don't want *ants* in the kitchen. **ants**

Bonus Words

1. *blueberries* Liz likes *blueberries* and cream. **blueberries**
2. *stories* These *stories* are about pioneers. **stories**
3. *cartwheels* Willis learned to do *cartwheels*. **cartwheels**
4. *chances* Everyone will get two *chances* to bat. **chances**
5. *cherries* The dessert has *cherries* in it. **cherries**
6. *details* Donna remembered all the *details* of the trip. **details**
7. *hobbies* Cheryl enjoys her *hobbies*. **hobbies**
8. *puddles* There were many *puddles* after the storm. **puddles**

Dictation Sentences

This Week's Words

1. My *buddies* and I ate *pancakes* before we played *marbles*.
2. The *fairies* in the story can fly like *butterflies*.
3. Pictures of the *spies* were in all the *newspapers*.
4. He can draw the *shapes* of *eyes* and *ears*.
5. Children from all *lands* like *puppies*.
6. A car has four *wheels*.
7. I showed my *guppies* to boys and girls in many *grades*.

Mastery Words

1. Most *trains* do not have *tires*.
2. The *ants* hid in *plants* and near *stones*.
3. Cars drive on the *streets*.

Bonus Words

1. That girl takes *chances* doing *cartwheels* over *puddles*.
2. One of my *hobbies* is picking *blueberries* and *cherries*.
3. Tell me some *details* from the *stories* you heard.

RETEACHING STRATEGIES FOR SPELLING

Children who have made errors on the Unit Test may require reteaching. Use the following **Reteaching Strategies** and **Follow-up Masters 25A** and **25B** for additional instruction and practice of This Week's Words. (You may wish to assign **LEP Reteaching Follow-up Master 25** for reteaching of spelling words.)

A. Discovering Spelling Ideas

1. Say the following words as you write them on the chalkboard.

   bags   flames   ladies   babies

2. Ask the children to identify how all the words are alike. (They all name more than one thing.)
3. Ask the children to identify what letter or letters were added to the nouns to make them name more than one thing, or become plural. (*s* and *es*)
4. Ask the children what the singular forms of *ladies* and *babies* are. (lady, baby) Ask the children what happened to the *y* when *es* was added to make the words plural. (The *y* was changed to *i*.)
5. Ask the children what they have learned about spelling plurals. (Add *s* to most nouns; for nouns that end with *y*, change the *y* to *i* and add *es*.)

B. Word Shapes

1. Explain to the children that each word has a shape and that remembering the shape of a word can help them to spell the word correctly.
2. On the chalkboard, write the words *parties* and *cups*. Have the children identify "short," "tall," and "tail" letters.
3. Draw the configuration of each word on the chalkboard, and ask the children which word fits in each shape.

Use **Reteaching Follow-up Master 25A** to reinforce spelling generalizations taught in Unit 25.

Use **Reteaching Follow-up Master 25B** to reinforce spellings of This Week's Words for Unit 25.

Name _____

Reteaching Follow-up A
Discovering Spelling Ideas
UNIT **25**

THIS WEEK'S WORDS

ears	grades	lands	marbles	guppies
fairies	butterflies	pancakes	eyes	shapes
spies	buddies	puppies	wheels	newspapers

1. Study This Week's Words. Say each word to yourself. What do This Week's Words have in common?

   They are all plural nouns.

2. Write each of This Week's Words next to the singular form of the word. The first one has been done for you.

puppy	**puppies**	pancake	pancakes
fairy	fairies	grade	grades
butterfly	butterflies	wheel	wheels
guppy	guppies	marble	marbles
buddy	buddies	land	lands
spy	spies	shape	shapes
		newspaper	newspapers
		ear	ears
		eye	eyes

3. What happens to the letter *y* when you add *es*?

   The *y* is changed to *i*.

4. What letter did you add to make the words in the second column plural?

   s

Reteaching • 41

Name _____

Reteaching Follow-up B
Word Shapes
UNIT **25**

THIS WEEK'S WORDS

ears	grades	lands	marbles	guppies
fairies	butterflies	pancakes	eyes	shapes
spies	buddies	puppies	wheels	newspapers

Write each of This Week's Words in its correct shape. The first one has been done for you. Children may interchange answers that fit the same configuration.

1. f a i r i e s   2. p a n c a k e s
3. b u d d i e s   4. m a r b l e s
5. g r a d e s   6. e y e s
7. g u p p i e s   8. l a n d s
9. e a r s   10. w h e e l s
11. s p i e s   12. p u p p i e s
13. s h a p e s
14. n e w s p a p e r s
15. b u t t e r f l i e s

42 • Reteaching

PREVIEWING THE UNIT

Unit Materials

Instruction and Practice

Pupil Book	pages 112–115
Teacher's Edition	
Teaching Plans	pages 112–115
Enrichment Activities	
For the Classroom	pages 115A–115B
For the Home	page 115B
Reteaching Strategies	page 115C

Testing

Teacher's Edition	
Trial Test	pages 111E–111F
Unit Test	page 115B
Dictation Test	page 115B

Additional Resources

PRACTICE AND REINFORCEMENT
Extra Practice Master 26: This Week's Words
Extra Practice Master 26: Mastery Words
Extra Practice Master 26: Bonus Words
LEP Practice Master 26
Spelling and Language Master 26
Study Steps to Learn a Word Master

RETEACHING FOLLOW-UP
Reteaching Follow-up Master 26A:
   Discovering Spelling Ideas
Reteaching Follow-up Master 26B: Word
   Shapes
LEP Reteaching Follow-up Master 26

TEACHING AIDS
Spelling Generalizations Transparency 22

Visit our Web site
http://www.hbschool.com

Click on the SPELLING banner to find activities for this unit.

Learner Objectives

Spelling

- To spell words with "silent" letters.

Reading

- To follow written directions.
- To recognize that given words can function as verbs or nouns.
- To recognize verb tenses.
- To recognize the function of guide words in a dictionary.
- To use a dictionary for word meanings.

Writing

- To write a story.
- To use the writing process.
- To proofread for spelling, capitalization, and punctuation.
- To write legible manuscript and cursive letters.

Listening

- To listen to identify a word as noun or verb in sentence context.
- To identify silent letters in words read aloud.
- To follow oral directions.

Speaking

- To speak clearly to a group.
- To present a story.
- To express feelings and ideas about a piece of writing.
- To contribute ideas and information in group discussions.

THIS WEEK'S WORDS

knee
knew
knit
knock
knot
known
calf
half
climb
lamb
thumb
wren
written
wrote
gnat

MASTERY WORDS

know
listen
should
walk
who
write

BONUS WORDS

crumbs
chalk
knead
kneel
knife
limb
wreck
wrist

Assignment Guide

This guide shows how you teach a typical spelling unit in either a five-day or a three-day sequence, while providing for individual differences. **Boldface type** indicates essential classwork. Steps shown in light type may be done in class or assigned as homework.

Five Days	○ = average spellers ☆ = better spellers ✓ = slower spellers	Three Days
Day **1**	**a** ● ☆ **Take This Week's Words Trial Test and correct** ● ✓ **Take Mastery Word Trial Test and correct** ● ☆ **Read This Week's Words and discuss generalization page 112**	Day **1**
Day **2**	● Complete Spelling Practice page 113 ● ✓ Complete Extra Practice Master 26: This Week's Words (optional) ✓ Complete Spelling on Your Own: Mastery Words page 115 ☆ **Take Bonus Word Trial Test and correct** **b**	
Day **3**	**c** ● ☆ ✓ **Complete Spelling and Language page 114** ● ☆ ✓ Complete Writing on Your Own page 114 ● ☆ ✓ **Complete Using the Dictionary to Spell and Write page 114** ● ✓ Take Midweek Test (optional) ☆ Complete Spelling on Your Own: Bonus Words page 115 ● ✓ Complete Spelling and Language Master 26 (optional)	Day **2**
Day **4**	● Complete Spelling on Your Own: This Week's Words page 115 ✓ Complete Extra Practice Master 26: Mastery Words (optional) ☆ Complete Extra Practice Master 26: Bonus Words (optional) **d**	
Day **5**	**e** ● Take Unit Test on This Week's Words ● Complete Reteaching Follow-up Masters 26A and 26B (optional) ● ✓ **Take Unit Test on Mastery Words** ☆ **Take Unit Test on Bonus Words**	Day **3**

Enrichment Activities for the **classroom** and for the **home** included at the end of this unit may be assigned selectively on any day of the week.

INTRODUCING THE UNIT

Establish Readiness for Learning

Tell the children that usually they can tell how to spell a word by listening to it carefully, but this week they will learn to spell words that have silent letters. Explain that they will learn and apply the spelling patterns for words with silent letters to This Week's Words and use those words to write a funny how-to story.

Assess Children's Spelling Ability

Administer the Trial Test before the children study This Week's Words. Use the test sentences provided. Say each word and use it in a sentence. Then repeat the word. Have the children write the words on a separate sheet of paper or in their spelling notebooks. Test sentences are also provided for Mastery and Bonus words.

Have the children check their own work by listening to you read the spelling of the words or by referring to This Week's Words in the left column of the **Pupil Book.** For each misspelled word, have the children follow the **Study Steps to Learn a Word** on page 1 in the **Pupil Book** or use the copying master to study and write the words. Children should record the number correct on their **Progress Report.**

Trial Test Sentences

This Week's Words
1. *knee* Sonia skinned her *knee*. *knee*
2. *knew* Malcolm *knew* the answer. *knew*
3. *knit* Grandma will *knit* us all mittens. *knit*
4. *knock* Go to the door when you hear someone *knock*. *knock*
5. *knot* Harry tied a *knot* in the rope. *knot*

FOCUS

- Establishes objectives
- Relates to prior learning
- Sets purpose of instruction

6. *known* We have *known* each other for a long time. **known**
7. *calf* The *calf* follows its mother everywhere. **calf**
8. *half* Give *half* the apple to Sue. **half**
9. *climb* Clinton likes to *climb* trees. **climb**
10. *lamb* The *lamb* is in the pasture. **lamb**
11. *thumb* Ralph has a bandage on his *thumb*. **thumb**
12. *wren* A *wren* is living in our birdhouse. **wren**
13. *written* That story was *written* by my friend. **written**
14. *wrote* Nell *wrote* a poem. **wrote**
15. *gnat* A *gnat* is buzzing near my ear. **gnat**

Mastery Words

1. *know* Maggie doesn't *know* this game. **know**
2. *listen* All the children *listen* well. **listen**
3. *should* We *should* go home now. **should**
4. *walk* Marnie took a *walk* around the neighborhood. **walk**
5. *who* Craig knows *who* won the school election. **who**
6. *write* Leroy will *write* a letter to his cousin. **write**

Bonus Words

1. *crumbs* There were *crumbs* all over the floor. **crumbs**

2. *chalk* I cannot find the *chalk*. **chalk**
3. *knead* We must *knead* the bread dough. **knead**
4. *kneel* The people in the front should *kneel* down. **kneel**
5. *knife* Cut the bread with a *knife*. **knife**
6. *limb* The storm blew a *limb* off the tree. **limb**
7. *wreck* You will *wreck* the sand castle if you step on it. **wreck**
8. *wrist* Valerie wears a bracelet on her *wrist*. **wrist**

Apply Prior Learning

Have the children apply what they already know about silent letters by having them participate in the following activity.

Write the words *knife, comb, write, ghastly,* and *halfway* on the chalkboard. Read the words aloud with the children. Have them tell what is alike about these words. Help them to recognize that each of these words contains a silent letter. Ask volunteers to come to the chalkboard and draw a line around the silent letters in each word. Ask the children to name some more words that have silent letters as you list them on the chalkboard. Tell the children that they will study words that have these silent letters. Explain that they can use the words in a variety of writing tasks: they can use the words in a note to a friend, in a letter, or in a creative writing assignment.

FOR CHILDREN WITH SPECIAL NEEDS

Learning Difficulties

Children with learning difficulties have trouble with words that must be learned by visual memory. The following strategy uses guided reduction of cues, which will reinforce the correct spelling in a manner that holds the child's attention.

Make a tachistoscope by cutting a 1/2 inch by 2 inch window in a piece of cardboard. On another piece of paper write a series of words as shown:

```
k n o w n
kn_____n
_____own
_ _ _ _ _
_____
```

Display the first spelling in the tachistoscope window and ask the child to spell the word aloud. Show the next word in the sequence; the word with missing letters. Ask the child to spell the word again. Follow this procedure until the child has spelled the entire word from memory without the aid of any cues. Use this strategy for all of the silent letter words in this unit.

Limited English Proficiency

To help limited English proficient children work with the spelling generalizations for Unit 26, you may wish to refer to the booklet "Suggestions and Activities for Limited English Proficient Students."

TEACHING PLAN

Objective To spell words that demonstrate these sound-letter relationships: /n/*kn*, /f/*lf*, /m/*mb*, /r/*wr*, /n/*gn*.

Read this sentence aloud to the class, pronouncing the initial /k/ in all the words:

I knew my knees were knocking.
/ī knōō mī knēz wûr knok'ing/

1. Ask the children to tell you what was wrong with what you said. When they have responded, explain to them that hundreds of years ago people would have said this sentence in almost the same way.
2. Direct the children's attention to the picture at the top of page 112. Ask a child to read the pronunciation /knē/.

You may wish to introduce the lesson by using **Spelling Generalizations Transparency 22.**

3. Read the generalization on page 112 aloud.
4. Have volunteers read This Week's Words and identify the "silent" letter in each word.
5. Then ask a child to read the "knock-knock" riddle at the bottom of the page.

You may wish to assign **LEP Practice Master 26** for reinforcement in writing spelling words.

26 "Silent" Letters

THIS WEEK'S WORDS

1. knee
2. knew
3. knit
4. knock
5. knot
6. known
7. calf
8. half
9. climb
10. lamb
11. thumb
12. wren
13. written
14. wrote
15. gnat

This Week's Words

Say the word <u>knee</u>. Listen to the beginning sound /n/. Hundreds of years ago, people said both /k/ and /n/ at the beginning of <u>knee</u>. Now the sound /k/ is not heard. But the letter <u>k</u> is still written. When the sound of a letter is not heard, we call it a "silent" letter.

Read each of the words to yourself. Decide which letter is a "silent" letter in each word.

Knock, knock — Who's there? — Ellen. — Ellen who? — L in calf is silent.

112

Extra Practice: This Week's Words

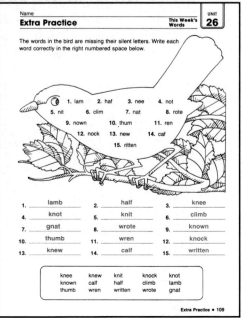

Name
Extra Practice | This Week's Words | UNIT 26

The words in the bird are missing their silent letters. Write each word correctly in the right numbered space below.

1. lam 2. haf 3. nee 4. not
5. nit 6. clim 7. nat 8. rote
9. nown 10. thum 11. ren
12. nock 13. new 14. caf
15. ritten

1. ____lamb____ 2. ____half____ 3. ____knee____
4. ____knot____ 5. ____knit____ 6. ____climb____
7. ____gnat____ 8. ____wrote____ 9. ____known____
10. ____thumb____ 11. ____wren____ 12. ____knock____
13. ____knew____ 14. ____calf____ 15. ____written____

knee	knew	knit	knock	knot
known	calf	half	climb	lamb
thumb	wren	written	wrote	gnat

Extra Practice • 109

Extra Practice: Mastery Words

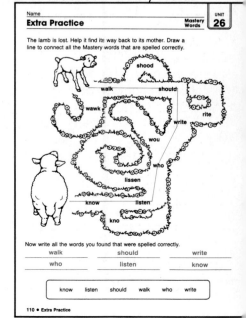

Name
Extra Practice | Mastery Words | UNIT 26

The lamb is lost. Help it find its way back to its mother. Draw a line to connect all the Mastery words that are spelled correctly.

shood
walk   should
wawk   rite
            write
        wou
        who
    lissen
know   listen
    kno

Now write all the words you found that were spelled correctly.

walk ____ should ____ write ____
who ____ listen ____ know ____

| know | listen | should | walk | who | write |

110 • Extra Practice

Spelling Practice

A. Follow the directions. Use This Week's Words.

1. Write the three words that begin with the sound /r/.

<u>wren</u> <u>written</u> <u>wrote</u>

2. Write the three words that end with the sound /m/.

<u>climb</u> <u>lamb</u> <u>thumb</u>

3. Write the two words that have a "silent" letter <u>l</u>.

<u>calf</u> <u>half</u>

4. Write the word that has a "silent" g. <u>gnat</u>

B. Add a "silent" letter and another letter. Write This Week's Words.

5. _ _ it <u>knit</u> **6.** _ _ ock <u>knock</u>

7. _ _ ee <u>knee</u> **8.** _ _ ot <u>knot</u>

C. Write This Week's Words that rhyme with these words.

9. jam <u>lamb</u> **10.** time <u>climb</u>

11. hum <u>thumb</u>

D. Read the first sentence in each group. Find the word that has a "silent" letter. Then finish the next two sentences. Use words that have the same "silent" letter.

12. Luis and Cissy know how to solve the puzzle.

I should have <u>known</u> they'd figure it out.

I wish I <u>knew</u> how they did it so quickly.

13. Debbie writes long letters to Mary Jane.

The one she <u>wrote</u> today was very long.

It may be the longest letter she's ever <u>written</u>!

knee
knew
knit
knock
knot
known
calf
half
climb
lamb
thumb
wren
written
wrote
gnat

113

Spelling Practice UNIT 26b

TEACHING PLAN

> **Objectives** To write words given sound and letter clues; to write words given spelling clues; to write rhyming words; to write the past tense and past participle of words.

1. Briefly discuss the directions on page 113. Emphasize that in Exercise **D**, the children should begin by finding the word with a "silent" letter in the first sentence. They are to finish the other two sentences with words that begin with the same letters.
2. Have the children complete the page independently. Remind them to use legible handwriting. You may wish to demonstrate the correct form of the letters *k, n, l, f, m, b, w, r, g* and *h* and then have the children practice writing the letters. For **Handwriting Models,** refer the children to page 258 in the **Pupil Book.**
3. To correct the children's work, have volunteers write their answers for Exercises **A, B,** and **C** on the chalkboard. When these have been checked, ask two children to read their completed sentences for Exercise **D** aloud. Let the children check their own work.

For reinforcement in writing spelling words, you may wish to assign *Extra Practice Master 26: This Week's Words.*

⭐ *of special interest*

Thumb and *thigh* both come from an old Indo-European root which apparently meant "thickness, or swelling." The derivation seems quite logical if you think of the thumb as a thick or swollen finger and of the thigh as a thick or swollen part of the leg.

---

xtra Practice: Bonus Words

Name _____

Extra Practice Bonus Words UNIT 26

A. Read the story. Some of the words don't make sense. They are in the wrong place. Find the words that don't make sense and draw a line under each one. Then write each wrong word below the story.

Mr. Diaz taught the class to bake bread. He wrote the directions in crumbs on the board. Mark copied them in his notebook.

The next Saturday Mark decided to try to bake bread. He asked his mom to help. "I don't want to kneel it," said Mark.

First they mixed the dough. Then they had to wreck it. That was hard. It made Mark's knife hurt. After they let it rise, they baked it.

When it was done, Mom got the bread limb. When she cut the bread, some chalk fell on the floor. She asked Mark to knead down and sweep them up. Mark said, "Let's feed the leftover bread to the birds. We'll put it in the feeder on the wrist of the tree."

1. <u>crumbs</u> 2. <u>kneel</u> 3. <u>wreck</u>

4. <u>knife</u> 5. <u>limb</u> 6. <u>chalk</u>

7. <u>knead</u> 8. <u>wrist</u>

B. Now write the story over on another piece of paper. Put each word you wrote in the right place. Children will write as directed. Be sure to check for spelling.

| crumbs | chalk | knead | kneel |
| knife | limb | wreck | wrist |

Extra Practice • 111

Summarize Learning

Have the children summarize what they have learned on pages 112 and 113. *Ask:*

- What have you learned about "silent" letters in this lesson? (The sounds /n/, /f/, /m/, and /r/ can be spelled by "silent" letters.)
- What are the "silent" letters that spell these sounds? (/n/kn, gn, /f/lf, /m/mb, /r/wr)
- What are some examples of words that follow these generalizations? (knew, gnat, calf, lamb, wren; accept other examples)

TEACHING PLAN

SPELLING AND LANGUAGE

Objective To write words in sentence context and recognize which are nouns and verbs.

1. Review the idea of words functioning as verbs and nouns:

    Bruno will <u>bark</u> at you.
    Bruno has a fierce <u>bark</u>.

    Help the children to recognize that *bark* is a verb in the first sentence because it tells what Bruno will do. In the second sentence, *bark* is a noun because it names something Bruno has.
2. Read the instructions on page 114.
3. Have the children complete the activity independently.
4. Let the children check their own work as volunteers read each pair of sentences aloud.

For extended practice in writing nouns and verbs in sentence context, you may wish to assign *Spelling and Language Master 26.*

WRITING ON YOUR OWN

Objectives To write a story; to proofread for spelling.

1. Review the directions.
2. As a **prewriting** activity, discuss some funny things that could happen to a lamb that knew how to knit. Then have the children **compose** a funny story. When they are ready to **revise,** remind them to proofread for spelling. **Publish** the children's stories by inviting them to read their stories.

USING THE DICTIONARY

Objectives To recognize the function of guide words; to write words that come between two given words in alphabetical order.

THIS WEEK'S WORDS
knee
knew
knit
knock
knot
known
calf
half
climb
lamb
thumb
wren
written
wrote
gnat

Spelling and Language • Nouns and Verbs

A **noun** names a person, a place, or a thing. A **verb** shows action or being. Finish each pair of sentences with one of This Week's Words. The word will be a verb in the first sentence and a noun in the second.

1. Let's ____climb____ up the mountain on Saturday.
2. It's a rough ____climb____, so wear heavy shoes.
3. Just ____knock____ on the door when you get here.
4. I will come out as soon as I hear your ____knock____.

Writing on Your Own

Write a funny story for your family. Tell about a lamb that knew how to knit.

Using the Dictionary to Spell and Write

Suppose you want to check the spelling of a word in the dictionary. The quickest way to find the word is to use the guide words. Two **guide words** appear at the top of every page. The word on the left is the first word on the page. The word on the right is the last word. All the other words on the page are in alphabetical order between the guide words.

trail	until

trail /trāl/ *n.* **1** A path. **2** The marks left by a person or animal. —*v.* To follow behind: Jacob *trailed* everyone in the race.

Tues. Abbreviation for *Tuesday.*
Tues·day /t(y)ōͻz′dē/ *or* /t(y)ōͻz′dā/ *n.* The third day of the week.

Here are three pairs of guide words. Write two of This Week's Words that would be on each page.

1. cabin color   ____calf____   ____climb____
2. game   help   ____gnat____   ____half____
3. kind   knife   ____knee____   ____knew____

114

---

1. Read the introductory paragraph on page 114 aloud.
2. Have the children look at the sample dictionary guide words. Write these words on the chalkboard:

    turn   use   unless

    Have the children indicate whether or not each word would be found on the sample page. (*Turn* and *unless* would appear on the page.)
3. Read the directions on page 114. Have the children complete the work independently.
4. Have volunteers read their answers. Let the children check their own work.

Extra Practice: Spelling and Language

Name	UNIT
Spelling and Language	26

A. Write the underlined word from each sentence. Then write whether the word is used as a noun or a verb.

		knee
1. Jan <u>knew</u> a farmer who lived in the hills.		knew
knew	**verb**	knit
		knock
2. The farmer had three sheep and a <u>lamb</u>.		knot
lamb	**noun**	known
		calf
3. The sheep liked to <u>climb</u> on rocks.		half
climb	**verb**	climb
		lamb
4. The older animals liked the steep <u>climb</u>.		thumb
climb	**noun**	wren
		written
5. The lamb stayed behind, tied to a tree that had a large <u>knot</u> on its trunk.		wrote
knot	**noun**	gnat
6. Jan had held the lamb so the farmer could <u>knot</u> the rope around the tree.		
knot	**verb**	
7. Later that day they heard a <u>knock</u> at the door.		
knock	**noun**	
8. The lamb had gotten loose and <u>knocked</u> on the door with its hoof.		
knocked	**verb**	

B. Use This Week's Words to complete the items.

9. This noun names a part of your hand.	**thumb**
10. This verb names something you do with wool.	**knit**
11. This noun names a type of bird.	**wren**
12. This verb names something you do to rope.	**knot**

112 • Extra Practice

Spelling on Your Own

Spelling on Your Own   UNIT 26d

THIS WEEK'S WORDS

What two letters are needed to finish each word? Add the letters and write This Week's Words.

1. _ _ at
2. thu _ _
3. _ _ ock
4. _ _ it
5. la _ _
6. _ _ en
7. ca _ _
8. _ _ ot
9. _ _ ote
10. _ _ ee
11. cli _ _
12. _ _ own
13. _ _ ew
14. ha _ _
15. _ _ itten

See answers below.

MASTERY WORDS

Follow the directions. Use the Mastery words.

| know |
| listen |
| should |
| walk |
| who |
| write |

1. Write the three words that start with the letter w.

walk   who   write

2. Write the word that starts with the sound /r/. _____ write

3. Write a question. Start with the word that rhymes with you.

EXAMPLE: Who knows the answer?

Add the "silent" letters. Write Mastery words.

4. lis _ en _____ listen
5. _ now _____ know
6. shou _ d _____ should
7. wa _ k _____ walk

BONUS WORDS

Write the Bonus words that rhyme with these words.

1. seal
2. peck
3. him
4. seed
5. comes
6. fist
7. talk
8. life

| crumbs |
| chalk |
| knead |
| kneel |
| knife |
| limb |
| wreck |
| wrist |

Follow the directions. Use the Bonus words.

9. Write the word that sounds just like need. Use both words in a sentence.

10. Write a story about Silent Kay, the girl who never talked. Use as many words as you can that start with kn.   See answers below.

115

TEACHING PLAN

Objective To apply the unit spelling generalization to spell This Week's Words, Mastery words, and Bonus words independently.

THIS WEEK'S WORDS

1. Read the directions on page 115. Help the children begin by completing the first word with them.
2. Have the children complete the activity independently on a separate piece of paper.
3. Have volunteers write the words on the chalkboard. Ask the children to exchange papers to check the work.

MASTERY WORDS

1. Review the concept of "silent" letters.
2. Have volunteers read the Mastery words aloud. As each word is read, help the children to identify the "silent" letter in the word.
3. Briefly discuss the directions on page 115. Then have the children complete the exercises.
4. Check each child's work individually.

BONUS WORDS

1. Have volunteers read the Bonus words aloud. As each word is read, have the children identify the "silent" letter in the word.
2. Have the children complete the exercises independently on a separate piece of paper.
3. To correct the children's work, have volunteers write the words for **1–9** on the chalkboard. Let the children check their own work. Then have five volunteers read their stories aloud to the class.

For reinforcement in writing spelling words, you may wish to assign *Extra Practice Master 26: Mastery Words* or *Bonus Words.*

Spelling on Your Own Answers

THIS WEEK'S WORDS

1. gnat 2. thumb 3. knock 4. knit
5. lamb 6. wren 7. calf 8. knot 9. wrote
10. knee 11. climb 12. known 13. knew
14. half 15. written

BONUS WORDS

1. kneel 2. wreck 3. limb 4. knead 5. crumbs
6. wrist 7. chalk 8. knife 9. knead
EXAMPLE: How long do I <u>need</u> to <u>knead</u> the bread? 10. Children will write as directed. Be sure to check spelling.

Summarize Learning

Have the children summarize what they have learned in this unit. *Ask:*

- What have you learned about nouns and verbs? (Some words can be used as both nouns and verbs.)
- What have you learned about guide words in the dictionary? (Two guide word appear at the top of every dictionary page. The word on the left is the first word on the page and the word on the right is the last word.)
- What spelling generalizations have you learned? How did you use these generalizations?

CLOSING THE UNIT

Apply New Learning

Tell the children that if they misspell words with silent letters in their writing, they should use one of the following strategies:

- write the word using different spellings and compare it with the spelling they picture in their minds.
- think about whether the spelling of the word could be unusual.
- think about the possible spellings for a sound within the word and use the dictionary to find the correct spelling.

Transfer New Learning

Tell the children that when they encounter new words in their personal reading and in other content areas, they should learn the meaning of those words and then apply the generalizations they have studied to the spelling of those words. Tell them that once the words are familiar in both meaning and spelling, they should use the new words in their writing.

ENRICHMENT ACTIVITIES

Classroom activities and **home activities** may be assigned to children of all ability levels. The activities provide opportunities for children to use their spelling words in new contexts.

For the Classroom

To individualize classroom activities, you may have the children use the word list they are studying in this unit.

- *Basic:* Use **Mastery** words to complete the activity.
- *Average:* Use **This Week's Words** to complete the activity.
- *Challenging:* Use **Bonus** words to complete the activity.

1. **Language Arts/Writing Word Clues** Have the children look over their spelling words and notice which ones have smaller words within them. Tell them they are going to write clues using words within words. To demonstrate the activity, present this example: *I am looking at a word. Here's a clue for you. I can see a smaller word in it. The word is* limb. *What is the word I am looking at?* After the children name *climb,* have them choose additional words and write clues for each one. After they have completed their clues, have the children exchange with one another and guess the answers.

■ COOPERATIVE LEARNING: Have each group make a set of clues for spelling words. Have the group look over their spelling words to notice which ones have smaller words within them. Have each child in the group write clues for one word. Have them try out their clues on each other.

If everyone in the group is satisfied, have them share their clues with their classmates.

2. **Language Arts/Writing Sentences** Have the children use their spelling words to build sentences based on sentence starters which you provide. To illustrate the activity, write the words *Last night I . . .* on the chalkboard and brainstorm ways that spelling words can be used to complete the sentence. Possible responses would be; *Last night I heard a knock at the door; Last night I saw a ghost; Last night I hurt my thumb.* Have the children use one or more of their spelling words, as well as other words, to complete the following sentence starters: *Did you hear about; Have you ever; On the way to school we; Tell me why you.* When they are finished, have the children share their sentences with the class.

■ COOPERATIVE LEARNING: Have each group develop sentences. Have them use one of the above sentence starters. Have each child in the group use the sentence starter in a complete sentence that includes one or more spelling words. Tell group members to check one another's sentences to see if they include both the sentence starter and one or more spelling words. When the sentences are written, one member from each group should first identify the phrase used for the class, then share the group's sentences.

3. **Language Arts/Writing a Book Report** Have the children write a book report. As a **prewriting** activity, have the children look over their spelling word lists in search of words that might suggest books they have read and words that might be used in their book reports. Have them list their ideas. Ask each child to select a book for a report and then make notes that answer each of the following questions:

What is the title?
Who is the author?
When does the story take place?
Where does the story take place?
Who is the main character?
What happens to the main character?

When the children have completed this activity, tell them to use their notes to **compose** the first draft of the report. Remind them to use as many spelling words as they can in their reports. Then have the children **revise** their reports, using their notes to make sure they have included all the important details. Remind the children to proofread for spelling, capitalization, and punctuation. Children may also want to include an illustration of an important event or a main character from the book. Have the children **publish** their reports by reading to the class or by displaying them on the bulletin board.

■ COOPERATIVE LEARNING: Have each group write a book report or a report on a short story. As a **prewriting** activity, have each group select a book (short story) that everyone in the group has read. Then have them brainstorm to answer questions such as the following:

What is the title?
Who is the author?
When does the story take place?
Where does the story take place?
Who is the main character?
What happens to the main character?

Have the group select one person to take notes. When the children are ready to **compose**, have one person begin by providing a topic sentence. The other children should build on the sentence, each adding one or more sentences until the report is complete and all the questions are answered. One person should be selected to write the first draft. The other children should **revise**, making sure that the details support the topic sentence. Each group member should proofread for spelling, capitalization, and punctuation. One child should rewrite the book report. Someone in the group may also want to illustrate an event or character from the book. Have the group **publish** the report by having one person read it aloud or by displaying it for the class to read.

For the Home

Children may complete these activities independently or with the assistance of a relative or friend in the home.

1. **Language Arts/Writing Word Families** Tell the children to choose four spelling words and write as many words as they can think of that are in the same word family. Give the following example: *walk, walks, walking, walked, walker.* Have the children check a dictionary to be sure they have written actual words and that they are spelled correctly. Then tell them to write sentences using all the words from one family.

2. **Language Arts/Categorizing Spelling Words** Have the children make a word chart with the following headings for each column: *body parts, animals, eating utensils, things to write with.* Then tell the children to review the spelling words and list each word under the correct heading. Present this example; *knee* is under *body parts.* When they have reviewed the spelling words, have them add any other words they can think of under each heading.

3. **Health/Writing Safety Rules** Tell the children to think about some of the safety rules they have learned over the years and why they are so important to follow. Ask the children to write the four rules that they consider to be most important, using some of their spelling words. The children may want to illustrate their rules.

4. **Science/Writing Names for Animal Young** Tell the children that the young of some animals have special names. For example, a *cat* has *kittens* and a *dog* has *puppies.* Tell the children to review their spelling words and write any words that are names for the young of animals. If the children do not know the parent for each young animal, have them use a dictionary. Have them add any other names for young animals that they can.

EVALUATING SPELLING ABILITY

Unit Test

This Week's Words
1. *knee* Cary's *knee* is sore. **knee**
2. *knew* Mr. Yung *knew* where Chi was going. **knew**
3. *knit* My mother will *knit* a sweater. **knit**
4. *knock* I heard a *knock* at the door. **knock**
5. *knot* Denny can untie that *knot.* **knot**
6. *known* I wish I had *known* this before. **known**
7. *calf* The *calf* was born last week. **calf**
8. *half* This carton of milk is *half* empty. **half**
9. *climb* They will *climb* over the fence. **climb**
10. *lamb* A baby *lamb* has wobbly legs. **lamb**
11. *thumb* Press this button with your *thumb.* **thumb**
12. *wren* We saw a robin and a *wren.* **wren**
13. *written* Louis has not *written* his report yet. **written**
14. *wrote* Lynn *wrote* her report yesterday. **wrote**
15. *gnat* A *gnat* is a tiny insect. **gnat**

Mastery Words
1. *know* I *know* how you feel. **know**
2. *listen* Let's *listen* to the record player. **listen**
3. *should* Gordie doesn't know if he *should* stay. **should**
4. *walk* Let's take a *walk.* **walk**
5. *who* Miriam knows the people *who* live in that house. **who**
6. *write* Holly can *write* very neatly. **write**

Bonus Words
1. *crumbs* The bird ate the bread *crumbs.* **crumbs**
2. *chalk* The *chalk* is in my drawer. **chalk**
3. *knead* Pizza dough is sticky and hard to *knead.* **knead**
4. *kneel* We had to *kneel* down and pick up the pennies. **pennies**
5. *knife* Be careful when you use a sharp *knife.* **knife**
6. *limb* The swing hangs from a tree *limb.* **limb**
7. *wreck* That car is a *wreck.* **wreck**
8. *wrist* Gloria broke her *wrist* when she fell. **wrist**

Dictation Sentences

This Week's Words
1. I *wrote* what I *knew* about the life of the *gnat.*
2. We saw the *lamb* and the *calf climb* the hill.
3. I hurt my *knee* and my *thumb* in the game.
4. She has *written half* of her story about the *wren.*
5. I wish I had *known* about the *knot* in the string.
6. A man in a *knit* hat started to *knock* at the door.

Mastery Words
1. We *should listen* to the birds as we *walk* in the park.
2. I *know who* will *write* the story.

Bonus Words
1. You will *wreck* the *knife* if you use it to cut into the tree *limb.*
2. You can *kneel* and draw the starting line with this *chalk.*
3. We can give these *crumbs* to the birds.
4. I take the watch off my *wrist* when I *knead* rolls.

RETEACHING STRATEGIES FOR SPELLING

Children who have made errors on the Unit Test may require reteaching. Use the following **Reteaching Strategies** and **Follow-up Masters 26A** and **26B** for additional instruction and practice of This Week's Words. (You may wish to assign **LEP Reteaching Follow-up Master 26** for reteaching of spelling words.)

A. Discovering Spelling Ideas

1. Say the following words as you write them on the chalkboard.

   knob   limb   wring

2. Ask the children to identify how the words are alike. (They all have letters you cannot hear.)
3. Ask the children to identify the "silent" letter in each word. *(k, b, w)*
4. Ask the children why it is important to remember that some words have "silent" letters. (so they can be spelled correctly)

B. Word Shapes

1. Explain to the children that each word has a shape and that remembering the shape of a word can help them to spell the word correctly.
2. On the chalkboard, write the words *knife* and *wrong*. Have the children identify "short," "tall," and "tail" letters.
3. Draw the configuration of each word on the chalkboard, and ask the children which word fits in each shape.

Use **Reteaching Follow-up Master 26A** to reinforce spelling generalizations taught in Unit 26.

Use **Reteaching Follow-up Master 26B** to reinforce spellings of This Week's Words for Unit 26.

Name _____

Reteaching Follow-up A

Discovering Spelling Ideas — UNIT 26

THIS WEEK'S WORDS

knee	knit	knock	calf	climb
lamb	wrote	written	knew	knot
known	half	thumb	wren	gnat

1. Add a "silent" letter to each group of letters. Write This Week's Words.

thum	thum(b)	nit	(k)nit
nat	(g)nat	nee	(k)nee
rote	(w)rote	caf	cal(f)
nock	(k)nock	clim	clim(b)
new	(k)new	ren	(w)ren
lam	lam(b)	not	(k)not
nown	(k)nown	haf	hal(f)
ritten	(w)ritten		

2. What do all of This Week's Words have in common?
   They all have "silent" letters.

Draw a circle around the "silent" letter in each word you wrote for 1.

Write four other words that have "silent" letters. Then circle the "silent" letter in each word.

POSSIBLE ANSWERS: (k)nead, (k)now, (w)rap, (w)rist

Reteaching • 43

Name _____

Reteaching Follow-up B

Word Shapes — UNIT 26

THIS WEEK'S WORDS

knee	knit	knock	calf	climb
lamb	wrote	written	knew	knot
known	half	thumb	wren	gnat

Write each of This Week's Words in its correct shape. The first one has been done for you. **Children may interchange answers that fit the same configuration.**

1. w r i t t e n
2. k n o t
3. h a l f
4. k n e w
5. g n a t
6. k n i t
7. t h u m b
8. k n o w n
9. w r o t e
10. k n o c k
11. k n e e
12. c a l f
13. c l i m b
14. l a m b
15. w r e n

44 • Reteaching

Words That End with y

PREVIEWING THE UNIT

Unit Materials

Instruction and Practice

Pupil Book	pages 116–119
Teacher's Edition	
Teaching Plans	pages 116–119
Enrichment Activities	
For the Classroom	pages 119A–119B
For the Home	page 119B
Reteaching Strategies	page 119C

Testing

Teacher's Edition	
Trial Test	pages 115E–115F
Unit Test	page 119B
Dictation Test	page 119B
Form *B** Test 3	page T14

*If your grading period is nine weeks, you may want to use the **Form *B* Test** at the end of this unit.

Additional Resources

PRACTICE AND REINFORCEMENT
Extra Practice Master 27: This Week's Words
Extra Practice Master 27: Mastery Words
Extra Practice Master 27: Bonus Words
LEP Practice Master 27
Spelling and Language Master 27
Study Steps to Learn a Word Master

RETEACHING FOLLOW-UP
Reteaching Follow-up Master 27A:
   Discovering Spelling Ideas
Reteaching Follow-up Master 27B: Word
   Shapes
LEP Reteaching Follow-up Master 27

TEACHING AIDS
Spelling Generalizations Transparency 23

Click on the SPELLING banner to find activities for this unit.

Learner Objectives

Spelling

- To spell base forms and inflected forms of nouns and verbs that end with a consonant and *y.*

Reading

- To follow written directions.
- To recognize the function of an accent mark in dictionary pronunciation.
- To recognize accented syllables given pronunciations.

Writing

- To write a story.
- To use the writing process.
- To proofread for spelling, capitalization, and punctuation.
- To write legible manuscript and cursive letters.

Listening

- To listen to identify the syllables in words.
- To listen to identify word endings *ed* or *ing.*
- To follow oral directions.

Speaking

- To speak clearly to a group.
- To respond to a question.
- To read stories.
- To express feelings and ideas about a piece of writing.
- To present a story.
- To contribute ideas and information in group discussions.

THIS WEEK'S WORDS

family
hurry
body
company
lady
library
party
penny
pony
carry
copy
cry
empty
marry
study

MASTERY WORDS

city
try
baby
sky
dry
candy

BONUS WORDS

bury
colony
deny
enemy
envy
factory
memory
supply

Assignment Guide

This guide shows how you teach a typical spelling unit in either a five-day or a three-day sequence, while providing for individual differences. **Boldface type** indicates essential classwork. Steps shown in light type may be done in class or assigned as homework.

Five Days	● = average spellers ★ = better spellers ✓ = slower spellers		Three Days
Day **1**	**a**	● ★ **Take This Week's Words Trial Test and correct** ● ✓ **Take Mastery Word Trial Test and correct** ● ★ **Read This Week's Words and discuss generalization page 116**	Day **1**
Day **2**	**b**	● Complete Spelling Practice page 117 ● ✓ Complete Extra Practice Master 27: This Week's Words (optional) ✓ Complete Spelling on Your Own: Mastery Words page 119 ★ **Take Bonus Word Trial Test and correct**	
Day **3**	**c**	● ★ ✓ **Complete Spelling and Language page 118** ● ★ ✓ Complete Writing on Your Own page 118 ● ★ ✓ **Complete Using the Dictionary to Spell and Write page 118** ● ✓ Take Midweek Test (optional) ★ Complete Spelling on Your Own: Bonus Words page 119 ● ✓ Complete Spelling and Language Master 27 (optional)	Day **2**
Day **4**	**d**	● Complete Spelling on Your Own: This Week's Words page 119 ✓ Complete Extra Practice Master 27: Mastery Words (optional) ★ Complete Extra Practice Master 27: Bonus Words (optional)	
Day **5**	**e**	● Take Unit Test on This Week's Words ● Complete Reteaching Follow-up Masters 27A and 27B (optional) ● ✓ **Take Unit Test on Mastery Words** ★ **Take Unit Test on Bonus Words**	Day **3**

Enrichment Activities for the **classroom** and for the **home** included at the end of this unit may be assigned selectively on any day of the week.

INTRODUCING THE UNIT

Establish Readiness for Learning

Have the children recall that in Unit 25 they learned how to form plurals of words ending with a consonant and *y* by changing the *y* to *i* and adding *es*. Tell them that this week they will learn more about spelling words ending in a consonant and *y*. Explain that they will apply these spelling generalizations to This Week's Words and use the words to write a story about a pony.

Assess Children's Spelling Ability

Administer the Trial Test before the children study This Week's Words. Use the test sentences provided. Say each word and use it in a sentence. Then repeat the word. Have the children write the words on a separate sheet of paper or in their spelling notebooks. Test

---
FOCUS

- Establishes objectives
- Relates to prior learning
- Sets purpose of instruction

sentences are also provided for Mastery and Bonus words.

Have the children check their own work by listening to you read the spelling of the words or by referring to This Week's Words in the left column of the **Pupil Book.** For each misspelled word, have the children follow the **Study Steps to Learn a Word** on page 1 in the **Pupil Book** or use the copying master to study and write the words. Children should record the number correct on their **Progress Report.**

Trial Test Sentences

This Week's Words
1. *family*   My *family* lives in Houston.
   family
2. *hurry*   Let's *hurry* or we'll be late.
   hurry
3. *body*   Your arm is part of your *body*.
   body

4. **company**   Mr. Eaton works for that *company*.   **company**

5. **lady**   We handed our tickets to the *lady* at the door.   **lady**

6. **library**   Noah likes to go to the *library*. **library**

7. **party**   The third grade is having a *party*. **party**

8. **penny**   I found a *penny*.   **penny**

9. **pony**   Noel rode a *pony*.   **pony**

10. **carry**   Milo offered to *carry* the suitcase.   **carry**

11. **copy**   Please *copy* this sentence.   **copy**

12. **cry**   We heard the kittens *cry*.   **cry**

13. **empty**   Lance's job is to *empty* the waste baskets.   **empty**

14. **marry**   Aunt Eloise will *marry* Nathan.   **marry**

15. **study**   Rafael and Pam *study* hard.   **study**

Mastery Words

1. **city**   Seattle is a big *city*.   **city**

2. **try**   Sheldon and I *try* to behave.   **try**

3. **baby**   The *baby* is crying.   **baby**

4. **sky**   The *sky* is cloudy today.   **sky**

5. **dry**   Use this towel to *dry* your hands. **dry**

6. **candy**   Wallace gave me some *candy*. **candy**

Bonus Words

1. **bury**   The dog will *bury* the bone in the backyard.   **bury**

2. **colony**   A *colony* of ants lives in that anthill.   **colony**

3. **deny**   Oscar and Mickey *deny* that they broke the window.   **deny**

4. **enemy**   An owl is a mouse's *enemy*. **enemy**

5. **envy**   I try not to *envy* people who can paint better than I can.   **envy**

6. **factory**   Shoes are made in that *factory*. **factory**

7. **memory**   Mary Anne has a good *memory*.   **memory**

8. **supply**   We keep a *supply* of pencils in the cupboard.   **supply**

Apply Prior Learning

Have the children be spelling detectives. Tell them that they can discover spelling generalizations by applying what they already know. Write the word *spoon* on the chalkboard. Ask the children to tell you the plural and how to spell it. (spoons) Write *puppy* on the chalkboard. What kind of word is *puppy*? (noun) What is the plural of *puppy* and how do you spell it? (puppies) Ask the children to recall the generalization about plurals of words ending in a consonant and *y*. Write *try* on the chalkboard. Then ask what kind of word *try* is. (verb) How do we change it to mean you already did it? (tried) Write *tried* on the chalkboard. Ask the children what they notice about adding the *ed* to *try*. (Change the *y* to *i* before adding *ed*.) Ask how you would change *try* to *trying*. (If children suggest changing the *y* to *i*, write it that way to show that it looks silly. Then write it the correct way and have the children conclude that when adding *ing*, the *y* stays.) Add additional examples if necessary. Explain that the children will learn to spell nouns and verbs that end in *y* and that they can use these words in a variety of spelling tasks: writing stories, writing poems, or writing a social studies report.

FOR CHILDREN WITH SPECIAL NEEDS

Learning Difficulties

A child with learning problems is seldom systematic and organized about problem solving. The following strategy is designed to help the child become more systematic and therefore more accurate when spelling words that require deleting letters prior to adding suffixes.

Write the three generalizations with one example for each at the top, middle, and bottom thirds of a duplicating master. The generalizations are as follows: change *y* to *i* and add *es*; change *y* to *i* and add *ed*; *y* stays when you add *ing*. For each generalization, have the child write the unit word and add the ending.

For each word to which an ending is added, have the child write the word followed by + and the ending. If a letter is to be changed, have the child place a line through it and write *i* beside it as a reminder. Then the child should write the entire word. Sample: *carry* i + ed = *carried*.

To several of the unit words, more than one ending may be added. For example: *marry* i + es = *marries*, *marry* i + ed = *married*, *marry* + ing = *marrying*.

Limited English Proficiency

To help limited English proficient children work with the spelling generalizations for Unit 27, you may wish to refer to the booklet "Suggestions and Activities for Limited English Proficient Students."

TEACHING PLAN

Objectives To spell nouns and verbs that end with a consonant and *y*; to spell inflected forms of nouns and verbs that end with a consonant and *y*.

1. Write this sentence on the chalkboard:

   This family will hurry.

   Ask the children to tell how the sentence would read if it told about more than one family. Then write this sentence on the chalkboard:

   These families will hurry.

   Ask the children to make the sentence tell what already happened. Write this sentence on the chalkboard:

   These families hurried.

   Have the children compare *family/families* and *hurry/hurried*.

2. Read the generalization on page 116 aloud, or ask a volunteer to read it.

You may wish to introduce the lesson by using *Spelling Generalizations Transparency 23.*

3. Have volunteers read This Week's Words aloud. As each word is read, have the children decide if *es* can be added to form a word that names more than one or if *ed* and *ing* can be added. Then identify the words as nouns or verbs.

4. Direct the children's attention to **Remember This** at the bottom of the page. Ask a volunteer to read the paragraph aloud.

You may wish to assign *LEP Practice Master 27* for reinforcement in writing spelling words.

---

27 Words That End with y

THIS WEEK'S WORDS

1. *family*
2. *hurry*
3. *body*
4. *company*
5. *lady*
6. *library*
7. *party*
8. *penny*
9. *pony*
10. *carry*
11. *copy*
12. *cry*
13. *empty*
14. *marry*
15. *study*

These families are hurrying.

This Week's Words

All of the words this week end with a consonant and *y*. Some are nouns. Some are verbs.

To make the nouns plural, change *y* to *i* and add *es*.

family   families

To make the verbs tell about the past, change *y* to *i* and add *ed*.

hurry   hurried

The *y* stays when you add *ing*.

hurry   hurrying

REMEMBER THIS

There are two r's in li**b**rary. They come before and after the **c**. Think of this. In the library you **reach** **and** **read**.

116

Extra Practice: This Week's Words

Name _____
Extra Practice   This Week's Words   UNIT 27

Finish the puzzle with This Week's Words. Write the singular of each noun. Remember to change *i* and drop *es*. Write the verbs without *ed*. Remember to change a letter.

ACROSS
4. bodies (NOUN)
6. married (VERB)
7. emptied (VERB)
10. libraries (NOUN)
11. hurried (VERB)
12. parties (NOUN)
13. ponies (NOUN)
14. ladies (NOUN)

DOWN
1. cried (VERB)
2. copied (VERB)
3. companies (NOUN)
5. families (NOUN)
8. studied (VERB)
9. carried (VERB)
12. pennies (NOUN)

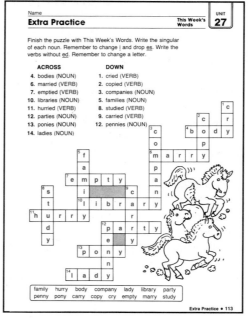

family   hurry   body   company   lady   library   party
penny   pony   carry   copy   cry   empty   marry   study

Extra Practice • 113

Extra Practice: Mastery Words

Name _____
Extra Practice   Mastery Words   UNIT 27

Follow the directions below the picture.

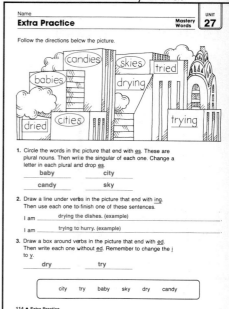

1. Circle the words in the picture that end with *es*. These are plural nouns. Then write the singular of each one. Change a letter in each plural and drop *es*.

   baby _____   city _____

   candy _____   sky _____

2. Draw a line under verbs in the picture that end with *ing*. Then use each one to finish one of these sentences.

   I am _____ drying the dishes. (example)

   I am _____ trying to hurry. (example)

3. Draw a box around verbs in the picture that end with *ed*. Then write each one without *ed*. Remember to change the *i* to *y*.

   dry _____   try _____

   city   try   baby   sky   dry   candy

114 • Extra Practice

Spelling Practice

A. Write the singular of each plural noun.

1. bodies _____body_____   2. ladies _____lady_____

3. ponies _____pony_____   4. pennies _____penny_____

B. Write these words without _ed_. Remember to change a letter.

5. emptied _____empty_____   6. cried _____cry_____

7. studied _____study_____   8. married _____marry_____

C. Add _ing_ to the word in dark print. Finish each sentence.

9. **hurry** Melissa is _____hurrying_____ down the street.

10. **carry** She is _____carrying_____ a bag of groceries.

D. Finish the first sentence with _copy_ + _ed_. Finish the second sentence with _copy_ + _es_.

11. Steve _____copied_____ his paper until it was perfect.

12. He made five _____copies_____ before he was done.

E. Finish the sentences. Use This Week's Words.

13. There are three people in Hamad's

_____family_____

14. Hamad's father works for a

_____company_____ that makes bikes.

15. Hamad's mother works in a

_____library_____ that has many books.

16. I met them both at Hamad's birthday

_____party_____

family
hurry
body
company
lady
library
party
penny
pony
carry
copy
cry
empty
marry
study

117

TEACHING PLAN

Objectives To write the singulars of given plural nouns; to write the base forms and inflected forms of verbs; to write words in sentence context.

1. Briefly discuss the directions on page 117. Remind the children that _y_ is changed to _i_ before _es_ is added to a noun and before _ed_ is added to a verb, but _y_ is not changed before _ing_ is added.

2. Have the children complete the exercises independently. Remind them to use legible handwriting. You may wish to demonstrate the correct form of the letter _y_ and then have the children practice writing the letter. For **Handwriting Models**, refer the children to page 258 in the **Pupil Book**.

3. To correct the children's work, have volunteers write the answers for Exercises **A, B, C,** and **D** on the chalkboard. Have volunteers read the sentences for Exercise **E** aloud. Let the children check their own work.

For reinforcement in writing spelling words, you may wish to assign **Extra Practice Master 27: This Week's Words.**

Extra Practice: Bonus Words

Name		Bonus Words	UNIT 27

Extra Practice

A. Read each sentence. One word in each sentence is in code. Here's how to break the code. Write the letter that comes just before each letter in alphabetical order. For example, if the code word is tqbdf, the real word is _space_.

factory
supply
colony
deny
enemy
bury
memory
envy

Write the word for each code word. Then add _ed_ or _es_ to write a word that fits the sentence.

1. The Terrans built four space dpmpoz.
colony   colonies

2. Each one had several large gbdupsz.
factory   factories

3. They tvqqmz energy for Terra.
supply   supplied

4. Energy receivers were cvsz in the ground.
bury   buried

5. No one efoz their success.
deny   denied

6. Their fofnz tried to steal their plans.
enemy   enemies

7. They fowz the new source of energy.
envy   envied

8. But the plans were stored in the Terrans' nfnpsz.
memory   memories

B. Now complete this "word math."

9. buried – ed = _____bury_____ + ing = _____burying_____

10. denying – ing = _____deny_____ + ed = _____denied_____

11. envied – ed = _____envy_____ + ing = _____envying_____

Extra Practice • 115

Summarize Learning

Have the children summarize what they have learned on pages 116 and 117. _Ask:_

- What did you learn about words that end with a consonant and _y_? (to make the nouns plural, the _y_ is changed to _i_ before adding _es_; to make the verbs tell about the past, the _y_ is changed to _i_ before _ed_ is added; the _y_ remains when _ing_ is added)

- What are some examples of words that follow these generalizations? (families, carried, marrying; accept other examples)

TEACHING PLAN

SPELLING AND LANGUAGE

Objectives To write inflected forms of given verbs in sentence context; to write the plural forms of given nouns in sentence context.

1. Read the introductory paragraph and the first set of directions on page 118 aloud.
2. Read the statement about plural nouns (midway through activity) and briefly review singular and plural nouns. Then read the second set of directions on page 118.
3. Have the children complete both parts of the activity independently.
4. Have volunteers write the inflected forms on the chalkboard. Let the children check their own work.

For extended practice in writing inflected verb forms and plurals, you may wish to assign **Spelling and Language Master 27**.

WRITING ON YOUR OWN

Objectives To write a story; to proofread for spelling.

1. Review the directions.
2. As a **prewriting** activity, have the children write the word *pony* in the center of a piece of paper and cluster words and ideas around the word *pony*. Then have the children **compose** a story about a pony. When the children are ready to **revise** their work, remind them to proofread for spelling. **Publish** the children's stories by having them read one another's stories.

USING THE DICTIONARY

Objectives To recognize the function of an accent mark in dictionary pronunciations; to write words given pronunciations.

1. Read the introductory paragraph on page 118 aloud. Have the

---

THIS WEEK'S WORDS
family
hurry
body
company
lady
library
party
penny
pony
carry
copy
cry
empty
marry
study

Spelling and Language • Verbs and Plurals

You add <u>ed</u> to a verb to tell what already happened. You add <u>ing</u> to make a verb that can be used with <u>am</u>, <u>is</u>, <u>are</u>, <u>was</u>, and <u>were</u>.

Write the verbs. Add <u>ed</u> or <u>ing</u> to the words in dark print.

1. hurry Lena _____hurried_____ to her desk.

2. study She is _____studying_____ about animals that work.

A plural noun names more than one thing. Write the plural of the word in dark print.

3. pony Lena read a book about Shetland _____ponies_____ .

Writing on Your Own

Write a story for your classmates about a pony. Use as many of This Week's Words as you can. Add <u>ed</u> and <u>ing</u> to some of the verbs in your story.

 WRITER'S GUIDE Do you need help revising your story? If so, turn to the checklist on page 247.

Using the Dictionary to Spell and Write

A dictionary gives you information that will help you when you write. There are two vowel sounds in <u>pony</u>. So <u>pony</u> has two **syllables**. The pronunciation for <u>pony</u> has this mark: ′. It is an **accent mark**. It shows which syllable is said with more force.

po·ny /pō′nē/ *n., pl.* **ponies** A very small horse.

act, āte, câre, ärt; egg, ēven; if, īce; on, ōver, ôr; bŏŏk, fōōd; up, tûrn; ə = a in *ago*, e in *listen*, i in *giraffe*, o in *pilot*, u in *circus*; yŏŏ = u in *music*; oil; out; chair; sing; shop; thank; that; zh in *treasure*.

Find the accent mark in each pronunciation. Write **1**, **2**, or **3** to show which syllable the mark follows. Then write the word.

1. /emp′tē/ __1__ _____empty_____ **2.** /fam′ə·lē/ __1__ _____family_____

118

---

children say the word *pony* several times, listening for the two syllables. Have them say the word *pony* again, listening for the syllable that is said with greater force.
2. Read the directions on page 118 aloud, and help the children read the pronunciations. Point out the "upside down" e in the pronunciation for *family*. Explain that /ə/ is the sign for *schwa* /shwä/, a weak vowel sound that is heard only in unaccented syllables.
3. Have the children complete the exercise independently.

Extra Practice: Spelling and Language

Name	UNIT 27

Spelling and Language

A. Add *ed* or *ing* to make the verb fit in each sentence. Write the new verb on the line.

1. Yesterday Hector hurry home from school. _____hurried_____	family hurry body company lady library party penny pony carry copy cry empty marry study
2. He was carry many big books in a bag. _____carrying_____	
3. That night he empty the books on his desk. _____emptied_____	
4. Then he study as hard as he could. _____studied_____	
5. He spent hours copy important sentences. _____copying_____	
6. The next day he almost cry with joy when he saw his good spelling grade _____cried_____	

B. Use the plurals of This Week's Words to answer the questions.

7. What do we call small horses? _____ponies_____
8. What do we call coins worth one cent? _____pennies_____
9. What do we call big buildings with books? _____libraries_____
10. What do we call offices where people work? _____companies_____
11. What's another word for <u>women</u>? _____ladies_____
12. What do we call birthday events? _____parties_____

116 • Extra Practice

Spelling on Your Own

THIS WEEK'S WORDS

1. Write **NOUN** and **VERB** at the top of your paper.
2. Write each of This Week's Words under the right word. The words hurry, copy, cry, and study can be nouns or verbs. Write them in both lists.
3. Use one noun and one verb together in a sentence. You can make the noun plural. You can add ed or ing to the verb. Here is an example: "The ladies hurried to the bus stop."
4. Use the nouns and verbs to write two more sentences.

See answers below.

MASTERY WORDS

city
try
baby
sky
dry
candy

Follow the directions. Use the Mastery words.

1. Write the three words that end with /ī/.

   sky   dry   try

2. Write the three words that end with /ē/.

   baby   candy   city

Write the singular of each plural noun. Remember to change a letter.

3. cities ___city___   4. candies ___candy___

5. skies ___sky___   6. babies ___baby___

Write these Mastery words without ed.

7. tried ___try___   8. dried ___dry___

BONUS WORDS

bury
colony
deny
enemy
envy
factory
memory
supply

1. Write the Bonus word that has two p's. Write two sentences, using it as a noun and as a verb.
2. Write the plurals of the four other nouns.
3. Add ed and ing to the three other verbs.
4. Write a story about hidden treasure. Use the Bonus words.

See answers below.

119

Spelling on Your Own Answers

THIS WEEK'S WORDS

NOUN	VERB
~~f~~amily	hurry
~~h~~urry	carry
~~b~~ody	copy
~~c~~ompany	cry
~~l~~ady	empty
~~l~~ibrary	marry
~~p~~arty	study
~~p~~enny	
~~p~~ony	
~~c~~opy	
~~c~~ry	
~~s~~tudy	

Children will write as directed. Be sure to check spelling.

1. **supply** EXAMPLE: Dell will supply me with a large supply of pencils. 2. colonies, enemies, factories, memories 3. buried, burying, denied, denying, envied, envying 4. Children will write as directed. Be sure to check spelling.

Summarize Learning

Have the children summarize what they have learned in this unit. *Ask:*
- What have you learned about adding endings to words that end with y? (See unit generalizations.)
- What have you learned about accent marks in dictionary pronunciations? (An accent mark shows which syllable of a word is said with more force.)
- What spelling generalizations have you learned? How did you use these generalizations?

TEACHING PLAN

Objective To apply the unit spelling generalization to spell This Week's Words, Mastery words, and Bonus words independently.

THIS WEEK'S WORDS

1. Read the directions on page 119. Remind the children that a noun names a person, place, or thing, and that you can add s or es to a noun to make it name more than one. Remind the children that a verb tells about action, and that you can add ed or ing to a verb.
2. Have the children complete the first two steps of the activity under your direction.
3. Select a noun and a verb, and have volunteers use the words in a sentence.
4. Have the children complete the activity independently.

MASTERY WORDS

1. Briefly review the unit generalization on page 116.
2. Have volunteers read the Mastery words aloud. As each word is read, help the children to decide if es can be added to form a word that names more than one or if ed and ing can be added.
3. Briefly discuss the directions on page 119. Then have the children complete the activities independently.

BONUS WORDS

1. Briefly review the unit generalization on page 116.
2. Have volunteers read the Bonus words aloud.
3. Have the children complete the exercise on a separate piece of paper.

For reinforcement in writing spelling words, you may wish to assign **Extra Practice Master 27: Mastery Words** or **Bonus Words.**

CLOSING THE UNIT

Apply New Learning

Tell the children that if they misspell words that end with *y* in their writing, they should use one or more of the following strategies:

- write the word using different spellings and compare it with the spelling they picture in their minds.
- think of words that rhyme and compare in their minds how they are spelled.
- use the origin of a word to help remember the correct spelling.

Transfer New Learning

Tell the children that when they encounter new words in their personal reading and in other content areas, they should learn the meaning of those words and then apply the generalizations they have studied to the spelling of those words. Tell them that once the words are familiar in both meaning and spelling, they should use the new words in their writing.

ENRICHMENT ACTIVITIES

Classroom activities and **home activities** may be assigned to children of all ability levels. The activities provide opportunities for children to use their spelling words in new contexts.

For the Classroom

To individualize classroom activities, you may have the children use the word list they are studying in this unit.

- *Basic:* Use **Mastery** words to complete the activity.
- *Average:* Use **This Week's Words** to complete the activity.
- *Challenging:* Use **Bonus** words to complete the activity.

1. **Language Arts/Writing Clues** Have the children choose six spelling words and then write clues for each one. Clues can be a brief definition, a synonym, or an antonym. Then have them use all six words in a matching exercise for another child to complete. Children who need help may use the **Spelling Dictionary,** or you may refer them to the **Thesaurus** on page 203.

   ■ COOPERATIVE LEARNING: Have each group create a matching exercise with definitions, synonyms, and antonyms. After the group decides which spelling words to use, have each member be responsible for writing a definition, a synonym, or an antonym for certain words. Have the group check the definitions, synonyms, and antonyms to be sure the clues are accurate. Together the group should develop a matching exercise using the spelling words and their definitions, synonyms,

and antonyms. Once the matching exercise is complete, have the group distribute it to other groups to complete.

2. **Language Arts/Writing Sentences** Have the children choose two nouns and two verbs from their list of spelling words. Tell them they will write pairs of sentences using the singular and plural forms of the nouns and the *ing* and *ed* forms of the verbs. Present these examples for nouns: *The pony trotted away. The ponies trotted away.* Present these examples for verbs: *The boys are hurrying to the game. The boys hurried to the game.* When they have finished their sentences, have the children share with the class.

   ■ COOPERATIVE LEARNING: Have each group create sentences for the nouns and the verbs on the spelling lists. Have each child write two pairs of sentences as described above. Children should use words from all three lists. Tell group members to check each other's sentences to see if they include the correct form of the noun or verb. When the sentences have been written, have one member from the group identify the spelling words for the class, then share the group's sentences with them.

3. **Language Arts/Writing a How-to Paragraph** Have the children write a how-to paragraph. First direct their attention to page 250 of the **Writer's Guide** to read about how-to paragraphs. As a *prewriting* activity, have the children look over the spelling word list in search of possible ideas for a how-to paragraph and then list their ideas. For example, children may wish to write about how to find a book in the library, how to plan a party, or how to ride a pony. After choosing a topic, have them list the steps they would use to explain how to do it. When they have completed the prewriting activities, have them use the list to **compose** the paragraph. Remind them to use as many spelling words as possible and to consider the use of time order words such as *first, next, then, last,* or *finally.* Then have the children **revise** the paragraph, making sure that the steps are clearly written and in order. Remind them to proofread for spelling, capitalization, and punctuation. Children may also want to illustrate their how-to paragraphs. **Publish** their paragraphs by having the children read them aloud or by displaying them on the bulletin board for the class to read.

   ■ COOPERATIVE LEARNING: Have each group write a how-to paragraph. As a *prewriting* activity, have the group search the spelling word list for possible ideas for a how-to paragraph and list them. Have the group share their ideas and then decide what to write about. Suggest that they make a list of the steps. To **compose** the how-to paragraph, one child in the group should write a topic sentence. The other children should add the detail sentences. All the children should **revise,** checking to make sure that the steps are clearly written and in order. Each child should also proofread for spelling, capitalization, and punctuation. Where appropriate, individual members of the group may want to illustrate the steps. The group should select one child to copy the paragraph. Have the group **publish** its how-to paragraph by having one member read it aloud to the class.

For the Home

Children may complete these activities independently or with the assistance of a relative or friend in the home.

1. **Language Arts/Writing Word Families** Tell the children to choose some verbs from their spelling lists and write as many forms of the verbs as they can. For example, *study, studies, studying, studied* are forms of one word. Have the children look in a dictionary to be sure they have written actual words and that they are spelled correctly. Then have the children write a sentence for each word. Children should share their words and sentences with a friend or someone at home.

2. **Language Arts/Writing Sentences with Rhyming Word Pairs** Have the children create sentences in which they use a spelling word and a word that rhymes with it in the same sentence. Present these examples:

    Please *try* not to *cry*.
    Tony has a little *pony*.

    Then have the children rewrite their sentences, leaving a blank for each spelling word. Have them ask a friend or someone at home to guess the missing spelling word.

3. **Mathematics/Writing Word Problems** Have the children use as many spelling words as possible to write several word or story problems. Children should refer to their mathematics books for models if necessary. When they have checked their problems for clarity and correct answers, have the children ask a friend or family member to solve the problems.

4. **Social Studies/Writing a Paragraph About a Community** Tell the children to write a paragraph about their community. Have them review the spelling words on all three lists for words that they might use in their paragraphs. Refer them to page 249 of the **Writer's Guide** to read about paragraphs.

EVALUATING SPELLING ABILITY

Unit Test

This Week's Words
1. *family*   My *family* has gone on vacation.   *family*
2. *hurry*   Everyone should *hurry* to the gym.   *hurry*
3. *body*   Your heart pumps blood through your whole *body*.   *body*
4. *company*   That *company* manufactures chairs.   *company*
5. *lady*   A *lady* is waiting for the bus.   *lady*
6. *library*   We found many interesting books at the *library*.   *library*

7. *party*   Juanita is having a *party*.   *party*
8. *penny*   I gave the clerk two quarters and a *penny*.   *penny*
9. *pony*   Lucy has never ridden a *pony*.   *pony*
10. *carry*   Franklin will help us *carry* the groceries.   *carry*
11. *copy*   Please *copy* your report neatly.   *copy*
12. *cry*   She could hear the kitten *cry*.   *cry*
13. *empty*   Let's throw out these *empty* boxes.   *empty*
14. *marry*   The rabbi will *marry* Louise and Melvin.   *marry*
15. *study*   I hope everyone will *study* the homework.   *study*

Mastery Words
1. *city*   A million people live in that *city*.   *city*
2. *try*   We will *try* to find the dog.   *try*
3. *baby*   The *baby* is in the playpen.   *baby*
4. *sky*   The *sky* is blue today.   *sky*
5. *dry*   Please *dry* your hair.   *dry*
6. *candy*   Paulina bought some *candy*.   *candy*

Bonus Words
1. *bury*   Ostriches *bury* their heads in the sand.   *bury*
2. *colony*   The Pilgrims started a *colony* at Plymouth Rock.   *colony*
3. *deny*   You cannot *deny* that you forgot your homework.   *deny*
4. *enemy*   The dog is not really the cat's *enemy*.   *enemy*
5. *envy*   The boys *envy* Geoffrey's new bike.   *envy*
6. *factory*   The *factory* workers get out of work at five.   *factory*
7. *memory*   Many facts are stored in your *memory*.   *memory*
8. *supply*   Mom will *supply* the potato salad for the picnic.   *supply*

Dictation Sentences

This Week's Words
1. The *lady* helped us *carry* the books to the *library*.
2. We must *hurry*; we are having *company* for our *party*.
3. The child started to *cry* for the *penny*.
4. Grown-ups may wish to *marry* and have a *family*.
5. We can *study* in the *empty* room.
6. You can *copy* this picture of how the heart works in the *body*.
7. Let's give the *pony* an apple.

Mastery Words
1. The *baby* will *try* to get the *candy*.
2. The *sky* is sunny in the *city*.
3. I need to *dry* my wet hair.

Bonus Words
1. The *factory* would not *supply* trucks to the *enemy*.
2. She could not *deny* her *envy* of his good *memory*.
3. The people in the farming *colony* watched the snow *bury* the land.

RETEACHING STRATEGIES FOR SPELLING

Children who have made errors on the Unit Test may require reteaching. Use the following **Reteaching Strategies** and **Follow-up Masters 27A** and **27B** for additional instruction and practice of This Week's Words. (You may wish to assign **LEP Reteaching Follow-up Master 27** for reteaching of spelling words.)

A. Discovering Spelling Ideas

1. Say the following words as you write them on the chalkboard.

country	worry
countries	worried
	worrying

2. Ask the children to identify which type of words are in each column. (The first column has nouns; the second has verbs.)
3. Ask the children to identify the last letter in *country* and *worry.* (y) Ask whether a consonant or vowel comes before that letter. (a consonant)
4. Ask the children to identify the plural of *country* and tell what happened when the noun was made plural. (*countries,* the *y* changed to *i* and *es* was added.)
5. Ask the children to identify what happened to the verb *worry* when *ed* and *ing* were added. (The *y* changed to *i* when *ed* was added. The *y* did not change when *ing* was added.)
6. Ask the children what they have learned about making nouns that end with a consonant and *y* plural. (Change the *y* to *i* and add *es*).
7. Ask the children what they have learned about adding *ed* and *ing* to verbs that end with a consonant and *y.* (Change the *y* to *i* and add *ed*; keep the *y* when you add *ing.*)

B. Word Shapes

1. Explain to the children that each word has a shape and that remembering the shape of a word can help them to spell the word correctly.
2. On the chalkboard, write the words *baby* and *fry.* Have the children identify "short," "tall," and "tail" letters.
3. Draw the configuration of each word on the chalkboard, and ask the children which word fits in each shape.

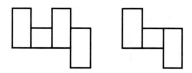

Use **Reteaching Follow-up Master 27A** to reinforce spelling generalizations taught in Unit 27.

Use **Reteaching Follow-up Master 27B** to reinforce spellings of This Week's Words for Unit 27.

Name _____

Reteaching Follow-up A   Discovering Spelling Ideas   UNIT 27

THIS WEEK'S WORDS

hurry	company	lady	empty	family
party	library	pony	marry	study
body	copy	penny	carry	cry

1. Study This Week's Words. Say each word to yourself. How are the words alike?
   <u>They all end with a consonant and y.</u>

2. Write the singular form of each noun below.

families	**family**	bodies	**body**
companies	**company**	ladies	**lady**
libraries	**library**	parties	**party**
pennies	**penny**	ponies	**pony**

3. Look at the singular noun and its plural form. What happened to the noun when it was made plural? <u>The y changed to i and es was added.</u>

4. Write these verbs without ed.

hurried	**hurry**	carried	**carry**
copied	**copy**	married	**marry**

5. Look at the verb you wrote and the verb with ed. What happened to the verb when ed was added? <u>The y changed to i.</u>

6. Write the following verbs without the ing ending.

emptying	**empty**	crying	**cry**
studying	**study**	carrying	**carry**

Reteaching • 45

Name _____

Reteaching Follow-up B   Word Shapes   UNIT 27

THIS WEEK'S WORDS

family	company	party	carry	empty
hurry	lady	penny	copy	marry
body	library	pony	cry	study

Write each of This Week's Words in its correct shape. The first one has been done for you. Children may interchange answers that fit the same configuration.

1. p e n n y
2. f a m i l y
3. s t u d y
4. m a r r y
5. h u r r y
6. c o p y
7. c a r r y
8. e m p t y
9. c o m p a n y
10. b o d y
11. p o n y
12. l a d y
13. p a r t y
14. c r y
15. l i b r a r y

46 • Reteaching

Nine-Week Evaluation

Mark the circle for the word that is spelled wrong.

Sample A			Sample B		
A right	cheek	prise	**B** team	trale	grape
ⓐ	ⓑ	● c	ⓐ	ⓑ	ⓒ

1	grandfather	owtside	anyway	**11**	circle	earley	worry
	ⓐ	ⓑ	ⓒ		ⓐ	ⓑ	ⓒ
2	bedroom	grandmother	somtimes	**12**	haert	yard	park
	ⓐ	ⓑ	ⓒ		ⓐ	ⓑ	ⓒ
3	everbody	maybe	anyone	**13**	card	bark	staers
	ⓐ	ⓑ	ⓒ		ⓐ	ⓑ	ⓒ
4	I'll	diden't	isn't	**14**	ears	marbels	newspapers
	ⓐ	ⓑ	ⓒ		ⓐ	ⓑ	ⓒ
5	wont	there's	let's	**15**	puppys	grades	wheels
	ⓐ	ⓑ	ⓒ		ⓐ	ⓑ	ⓒ
6	can't	that's	we'ere	**16**	butterflies	eyes	buddys
	ⓐ	ⓑ	ⓒ		ⓐ	ⓑ	ⓒ
7	nourth	talk	straw	**17**	hafe	thumb	knock
	ⓐ	ⓑ	ⓒ		ⓐ	ⓑ	ⓒ
8	short	four	tought	**18**	knit	written	kneu
	ⓐ	ⓑ	ⓒ		ⓐ	ⓑ	ⓒ
9	berthday	heard	learn	**19**	empty	libary	hurry
	ⓐ	ⓑ	ⓒ		ⓐ	ⓑ	ⓒ
10	return	earn	wold	**20**	partie	study	carry
	ⓐ	ⓑ	ⓒ		ⓐ	ⓑ	ⓒ

FORM B TEST 3

Administering the Test

1. Tell the children that today they will take a spelling test on some of the words they have studied in Units 19 – 27. Pass out the test papers. Tell the children to leave them turned upside down until you are ready to begin.

2. Have the children turn their tests over. Direct the children's attention to Sample A. Have the children look for the incorrect spelling. Ask a child to tell you the word that is spelled incorrectly. Point out that circle c under the misspelling p-r-i-s-e is filled in.

3. Now direct the children's attention to Sample B. Have the children look for the incorrect spelling. Ask a child to tell you the word that is spelled incorrectly by spelling it correctly. (t-r-a-i-l) The have the children fill in circle b in pencil.

4. After you have checked to see that all children have completed Sample B correctly, have the children proceed with the test.

Evaluating the Results

Use the following **Answer Key** to correct the children's tests and to determine whether they need more practice with particular units. The chart shows the units in which each answer word is taught.

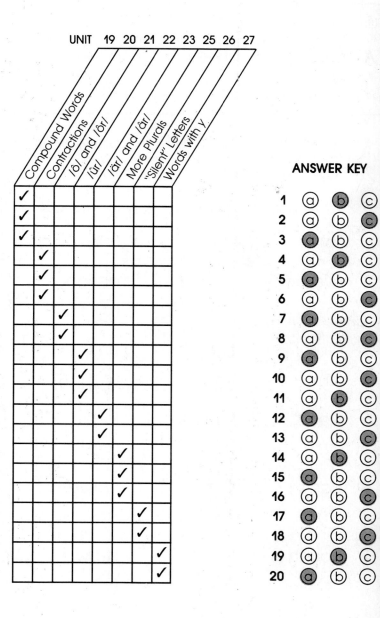

ANSWER KEY

1. ⓐ **b** ⓒ
2. ⓐ ⓑ **c**
3. **a** ⓑ ⓒ
4. ⓐ **b** ⓒ
5. **a** ⓑ ⓒ
6. ⓐ ⓑ **c**
7. **a** ⓑ ⓒ
8. ⓐ **b** ⓒ
9. **a** ⓑ ⓒ
10. ⓐ ⓑ **c**
11. ⓐ **b** ⓒ
12. **a** ⓑ ⓒ
13. ⓐ ⓑ **c**
14. ⓐ **b** ⓒ
15. **a** ⓑ ⓒ
16. ⓐ ⓑ **c**
17. **a** ⓑ ⓒ
18. ⓐ ⓑ **c**
19. ⓐ **b** ⓒ
20. **a** ⓑ ⓒ

PREVIEWING THE UNIT

Unit Materials

Instruction and Practice

Pupil Book   pages 120–123
Teacher's Edition
  Teaching Plans   pages 120–123
  Enrichment Activities
    For the Classroom   pages 123A–123B
    For the Home   page 123B
  Reteaching Strategies   page 123C

Testing

Teacher's Edition
  Trial Test   pages 119E–119F
  Unit Test   page 123B
  Dictation Test   page 123B

Additional Resources

PRACTICE AND REINFORCEMENT
  Extra Practice Master 28: This Week's Words
  Extra Practice Master 28: Mastery Words
  Extra Practice Master 28: Bonus Words
  LEP Practice Master 28
  Spelling and Language Master 28
  Study Steps to Learn a Word Master

RETEACHING FOLLOW-UP
  Reteaching Follow-up Master 28A:
    Discovering Spelling Ideas
  Reteaching Follow-up Master 28B: Word
    Shapes
  LEP Reteaching Follow-up Master 28

TEACHING AIDS
  Spelling Generalizations Transparency 24

Visit our Web site
http://www.hbschool.com

Click on the SPELLING banner to find activities for this unit.

Learner Objectives

Spelling

- To spell words that demonstrate these sound-letter relationships: /əl/*le, el; /ər/er, ar.*
- To form the plural of nouns by adding *s.*

Reading

- To follow written directions.
- To use the dictionary to locate information.
- To use the dictionary for word meaning.

Writing

- To write a paragraph.
- To use the writing process.
- To proofread for spelling, capitalization, and punctuation.
- To write legible manuscript and cursive letters.

Listening

- To listen to identify two syllables in a word.
- To listen to identify the letters that spell /əl/ and /ər/ in a word.
- To follow oral directions.

Speaking

- To speak clearly to a group.
- To respond to a question.
- To express feelings and ideas about a piece of writing.
- To present a descriptive paragraph.
- To contribute ideas and information in group discussions.

THIS WEEK'S WORDS
purple
camel
cover
able
bottle
eagle
people
table
level
nickel
shovel
either
letter
summer
sugar

MASTERY WORDS
after
dollar
ever
other
over
river

BONUS WORDS
answer
clever
collar
paddle
polar
puzzle
travel
tunnel

Assignment Guide

This guide shows how you teach a typical spelling unit in either a five-day or a three-day sequence, while providing for individual differences. **Boldface type** indicates essential classwork. Steps shown in light type may be done in class or assigned as homework.

Five Days	○ = average spellers ★ = better spellers ✓ = slower spellers	Three Days
Day 1 (a)	○ ★ **Take This Week's Words Trial Test and correct** ○ ✓ **Take Mastery Word Trial Test and correct** ○ ★ **Read This Week's Words and discuss generalization page 120**	**Day 1**
Day 2 (b)	○ Complete Spelling Practice page 121 ○ ✓ Complete Extra Practice Master 28: This Week's Words (optional) ✓ Complete Spelling on Your Own: Mastery Words page 123 ★ **Take Bonus Word Trial Test and correct**	
Day 3 (c)	○ ★ ✓ **Complete Spelling and Language page 122** ○ ★ ✓ Complete Writing on Your Own page 122 ○ ★ ✓ **Complete Proofreading page 122** ○ ✓ Take Midweek Test (optional) ★ Complete Spelling on Your Own: Bonus Words page 123 ○ ✓ Complete Spelling and Language Master 28 (optional)	**Day 2**
Day 4 (d)	○ Complete Spelling on Your Own: This Week's Words page 123 ✓ Complete Extra Practice Master 28: Mastery Words (optional) ★ Complete Extra Practice Master 28: Bonus Words (optional)	
Day 5 (e)	○ **Take Unit Test on This Week's Words** ○ Complete Reteaching Follow-up Masters 28A and 28B (optional) ○ ✓ **Take Unit Test on Mastery Words** ★ **Take Unit Test on Bonus Words**	**Day 3**

Enrichment Activities for the **classroom** and for the **home** included at the end of this unit may be assigned selectively on any day of the week.

INTRODUCING THE UNIT

Establish Readiness for Learning

Tell the children that this week they will study words that end with the /əl/ and /ər/ sounds. Tell them that they will discover spelling patterns for those words. Tell the children they will use what they learn to spell This Week's Words and to write a paragraph.

Assess Children's Spelling Ability

Administer the Trial Test before the children study This Week's Words. Use the test sentences provided. Say each word and use it in a sentence. Then repeat the word. Have the children write the words on a separate sheet of paper or in their spelling notebooks. Test sentences are also provided for Mastery and Bonus words.

Have the children check their own work by

listening to you read the spelling of the words or by referring to This Week's Words in the left column of the **Pupil Book.** For each misspelled word, have the children follow the **Study Steps to Learn a Word** on page 1 in the **Pupil Book** or use the copying master to study and write the words. Children should record the number correct on their **Progress Report.**

Trial Test Sentences

This Week's Words
1. *purple*   Maya is wearing a *purple* shirt.   *purple*
2. *camel*   That *camel* has two humps.   *camel*
3. *cover*   Please *cover* the bike before it rains.   *cover*
4. *able*   Rex is *able* to climb the rope.   *able*
5. *bottle*   The ketchup will not come out of the *bottle*.   *bottle*

FOCUS

- Establishes objectives
- Relates to prior learning
- Sets purpose of instruction

6. **eagle** The *eagle* soared high above our heads. **eagle**
7. **people** Some *people* wear glasses. **people**
8. **table** Put the napkins on the *table*. **table**
9. **level** The floor in the old house is not *level*. **level**
10. **nickel** Priscilla needs another *nickel* to buy milk. **nickel**
11. **shovel** Use the *shovel* to dig in the garden. **shovel**
12. **either** I want *either* Peter or Jill to feed the dog. **either**
13. **letter** Mother wrote a *letter*. **letter**
14. **summer** Jimmy is going to camp this *summer*. **summer**
15. **sugar** Eleanor doesn't put *sugar* on her cereal. **sugar**

Mastery Words
1. **after** You may watch TV *after* dinner. **after**
2. **dollar** Timothy has a *dollar* in his bank. **dollar**
3. **ever** Have you *ever* seen a hippopotamus? **ever**
4. **other** I saw Sal the *other* day. **other**
5. **over** The ball flew *over* the fence. **over**
6. **river** We went fishing on the *river*. **river**

Bonus Words
1. **answer** I hope Rob can *answer* the question. **answer**
2. **clever** That joke is very *clever*. **clever**
3. **collar** Joleen's coat has a fur *collar*. **collar**

4. **paddle** Don't drop the canoe *paddle*. **paddle**
5. **polar** A *polar* bear is white. **polar**
6. **puzzle** Kenny bought a jigsaw *puzzle*. **puzzle**
7. **travel** My family likes to *travel* to new places. **travel**
8. **tunnel** We drove through a *tunnel* on the way to the city. **tunnel**

Apply Prior Learning

Have the children be spelling detectives. Tell them that they can discover spelling generalizations by applying what they already know. Write the words *after* and *dollar* on the chalkboard. Ask the children to tell you how many syllables each word has. (two) Ask which syllable is softest, or not accented. (the second) Ask the children what they notice about the second syllables. (They sound the same, but one is spelled er and the other is spelled ar.) Ask the children to suggest other two-syllable words. Write them on the chalkboard. Each time, elicit which is the softer syllable. There should be a variety of examples of the /ər/ sound spelled with different vowels. Encourage children to conclude that the sound can be spelled in many ways in the unaccented syllables. Tell the children that they will learn two-syllable words and how to spell the unaccented syllables. Explain that they can use these words in a variety of spelling tasks: writing stories, writing poems, or writing a social studies report.

FOCUS
- Relates to prior learning
- Draws relationships
- Applies spelling generalizations to new contexts

FOR CHILDREN WITH SPECIAL NEEDS

Learning Difficulties

One of the characteristics of some children with learning disabilities is impulsivity, leading to inconsistency and a scattered approach to problem solving. The following activity is one way in which you can help the children develop strategies for step-by-step problem solving.

Have the children create word lists of This Week's Words. The first step is to have them make two columns on each of two lined pieces of paper or in their spelling notebooks. At the top of the columns on the first piece of paper, have the children write /əl/ = el and /əl/ = le and on the second piece of paper, /ər/ = er and /ər/ = ar. To encourage a systematic approach to a multistep activity, have them next list all the words that end in el to the appropriate column of their paper. Follow this approach for the words ending le, er, and ar. When the

children have finished their lists, tell them to count the total number of words to be sure they have fifteen. If they do not have fifteen, tell them to start at the top of the list of This Week's Words and find each word on their paper. When they realize a word is missing from their paper, the children should add that word to the appropriate list.

Limited English Proficiency

To help limited English proficient children work with the spelling generalizations for Unit 28, you may wish to refer to the booklet "Suggestions and Activities for Limited English Proficient Students."

TEACHING PLAN

Objective To spell words that demonstrate these sound-letter relationships: /əl/le, el; /ər/er, ar.

1. Direct the children's attention to the pictures on page 120 and ask a child to read the caption for the pictures. Just for fun, ask the children to explain how the two pictures are different and to offer captions that would clarify that difference. Then have them say *purple, camel,* and *cover* and indicate whether they say the first part of the word or the second part with more force.
2. Read the generalization on page 120 aloud.

You may wish to introduce the lesson by using *Spelling Generalizations Transparency 24.*

3. Have volunteers read This Week's Words aloud. As each word is read, have the children identify the last two letters in the word.
4. Direct the children's attention to **Remember This** at the bottom of the page, and read the paragraph aloud. You might poll the class to find out how the children pronounce *either.* (Chances are most, if not all, of the children say /ē′thər/.) Use the results of the poll to help the children conclude that the way most of them say *either* gives a hint about which vowel letter comes first.

You may wish to assign *LEP Practice Master 28* for reinforcement in writing spelling words.

---

28 The Sounds /əl/ and /ər/

THIS WEEK'S WORDS

1. purple
2. camel
3. cover
4. able
5. bottle
6. eagle
7. people
8. table
9. level
10. nickel
11. shovel
12. either
13. letter
14. summer
15. sugar

purple camel cover

purple camel cover

This Week's Words

All the words this week have two vowel sounds. We say that they have two **syllables**. The first syllable in each word is said with more force. The second syllable has a weak vowel sound called a **schwa**. We use this sign to show the schwa: /ə/.

/əl/   The schwa with /l/ is spelled **le** in <u>purple</u> and **el** in <u>camel</u>.

/ər/   The schwa with /r/ is often spelled **er**, as in <u>cover</u>. But it can be spelled with other vowel letters. It is spelled **ar** in <u>sugar</u>.

REMEMBER THIS

There are two ways to say <u>either</u>. One way begins with long <u>e</u>: /ē′thər/. The other way begins with long <u>i</u>: /ī′thər/. That's good. It helps us remember to put <u>e</u> and <u>i</u> in <u>either</u>.

120

Extra Practice: This Week's Words

Name
Extra Practice   This Week's Words   UNIT 28

Use This Week's Words to answer the fifteen questions below. Write the answer words in the blanks.

1. What do you write to a friend? — letter
2. What do you keep juice in? — bottle
3. What are children, women, and men? — people
4. What word means this one or that one, but not both? — either
5. What is sweet? — sugar
6. What buys something? — nickel
7. What can you put over something? — cover
8. What color is grape juice? — purple
9. What means "can"? — able
10. What is a time of year? — summer
11. What is a bird? — eagle
12. What is a place to put dinner? — table
13. What is used to dig? — shovel
14. What means "flat and even"? — level
15. What is an animal found in the desert? — camel

purple	eagle	shovel
camel	cover	able
bottle	people	table
level	nickel	sugar
either	letter	summer

Extra Practice • 117

Extra Practice: Mastery Words

Name
Extra Practice   Mastery Words   UNIT 28

A. Here are the Mastery words. The vowel letters are missing. Write the words over. Put the right vowel letters in place of the shapes. The first one has been done for you. Write each word just once.

1. △ v △ r — ever
2. ☐ ft △ r — after
3. ◠ th △ r — other
4. r ◇ v △ r — river
5. ◠ v △ r — over
6. d ◠ ll ☐ r — dollar

B. Look at the words you wrote. Each shape stands for a different vowel letter. Write the letter you wrote for each shape.

☐ = a   △ = e
◇ = i   ◠ = o

C. Now you know what the shapes stand for. Write some more words. Use vowel letters in place of the shapes.

7. w ◠ nd △ r — wonder
8. m ◠ t △ r — motor
9. f ☐ rth △ r — farther
10. c △ nt △ r — center
11. t ◇ g △ r — tiger
12. m ◠ th △ r — mother

| after | dollar | ever | other | over | river |

118 • Extra Practice

Spelling Practice

A. Follow the directions. Use This Week's Words.

1. Write the three words that name things in the picture.

bottle

table

people

2. Write three more words that have /əl/ spelled the same way.

purple   _able_   _eagle_

3. Write the word for this picture.

nickel

4. Write three more words that have /əl/ spelled this way.

camel   _level_   _shovel_

5. Write the three words that begin with vowel sounds.

able   _eagle_   _either_

B. Add the letters that stand for /ər/. Write the words.

6. cov___   _cover_   **7.** lett___   _letter_

8. eith___   _either_   **9.** sug___   _sugar_

10. summ___   _summer_

C. Read the clues. Then write This Week's Words to answer the riddles.

11. I have four legs and a long <u>a</u>.   _table_

12. I have the sound /u/ and I dig.   _shovel_

13. I have a head on one side and a short <u>i</u>.   _nickel_

purple
camel
cover
able
bottle
eagle
people
table
level
nickel
shovel
either
letter
summer
sugar

121

Summarize Learning

Have the children summarize what they have learned on pages 120 and 121. _Ask:_

- What vowel sounds have you learned in this lesson? (/əl/, /ər/)
- What have you learned about these sounds? Give examples. (Two ways to spell the sound /əl/, are le, el; table, camel. Two ways to spell the sound /ər/, are er, ar; cover, sugar.)

TEACHING PLAN

Objectives To write words given picture clues; to write words given spelling clues; to write words given accented syllables; to write words given meaning clues.

1. Briefly discuss the directions on page 121. Ask the children to identify the three things in the picture for **1** (bottle, table, people) and the picture for **3** (nickel). Be sure that the children understand the riddles in **C**. If necessary, read the riddles in Exercise **C**. If necessary, read the riddles aloud and have the children respond orally.

2. Have the children complete the activities independently. Remind them to use legible handwriting. You may wish to demonstrate the correct form of the letters e, l, a, and r and then have the children practice writing the letters. For **Handwriting Models,** refer the children to page 258 in the **Pupil Book.**

3. To correct the children's work, have volunteers write the answers on the chalkboard. Let the children check their own answers.

For reinforcement in writing spelling words, you may wish to assign **Extra Practice Master 28: This Week's Words.**

⟲ EXTENDING THE LESSON

Ask the children to write their own riddles for some of This Week's Words following the pattern of the riddles in Exercise **C.** Point out that their riddles should include a meaning clue and a vowel sound clue. Give the children an opportunity to share their riddles with the class.

TEACHING PLAN

SPELLING AND LANGUAGE

Objectives To form the plural of nouns by adding *s*; to write nouns in sentence context.

1. Read the introductory paragraph and the directions on page 122 aloud.
2. Have the children complete the exercises independently.

For extended practice in writing plural forms, you may wish to assign **Spelling and Language Master 28.**

WRITING ON YOUR OWN

Objectives To write a paragraph; to proofread for spelling.

1. Review the directions with the children.
2. As a **prewriting** activity, discuss what the children know about eagles and camels. Write the word *eagle* on the chalkboard and draw a line around it. Have the children name some things that they know about eagles. Write the children's responses on the chalkboard and cluster them around the word *eagle*. Do the same with the word *camel*. Then have the children **compose** stories about an eagle or a camel. When the children are ready to **revise** their work, remind them to proofread for spelling. For additional help, you may wish to refer them to the **Revising Checklist** on page 247 of the **Writer's Guide**. **Publish** the children's work by having them read their stories to younger children from another class.

THIS WEEK'S WORDS
purple
camel
cover
able
bottle
eagle
people
table
level
nickel
shovel
either
letter
summer
sugar

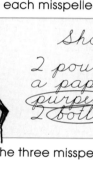

122

Spelling and Language • Plural Nouns

A plural noun names more than one thing. You add <u>s</u> to most nouns to make them plural.

Finish the sentences. Use plurals of This Week's Words.

1. Bald _____**eagles**_____ have white feathers on their heads.

2. Some _____**camels**_____ have one hump and oth have two.

3. There are seven _____**letters**_____ in the word <u>animals</u>.

Writing on Your Own

Write a paragraph for a young child telling about an eagle or a camel. Use plural nouns and some of This Week's Words.

 WRITER'S GUIDE For help revising your paragraph, see the checklist on page 247.

Proofreading

Wendy made up a shopping list. She made three spelling mistakes in her list.

1. Circle each misspelled word.

Shopping List
2 pounds of ⟨suger⟩
a paper tablecloth
⟨purpel⟩ grapes
2 ⟨bottes⟩ of apple juice

2. Write the three misspelled words correctly.

sugar   **purple**   **bottles**

 WRITER'S GUIDE See the editing and proofreading marks on page 248.

PROOFREADING

Objectives To proofread a shopping list for spelling errors; to write misspelled words correctly.

1. Read the directions on page 122 aloud.
2. Have the children read the list and circle each error. Then ask them to write the misspelled words correctly. **If you are using the hardcover book,** the children should simply locate the misspelled words and write them correctly.

Extra Practice: Spelling and Language

Name _____
Spelling and Language

Unit
28

A. Circle the word in each sentence that should be plural. Then write the sentence using the plural of the word you circled.

1. Two ⟨summer⟩ ago, I worked at a zoo.
   Two summers ago, I worked at a zoo.
2. The zoo had many ⟨camel⟩ and goats.
   The zoo had many camels and goats.
3. The zoo also had two ⟨eagle⟩ and three hawks.
   The zoo also had two eagles and three hawks.
4. The baby animals drank milk from ⟨bottle⟩.
   The baby animals drank milk from bottles.
5. People could use one of the picnic ⟨table⟩ on the zoo grounds.
   People could use one of the picnic tables on the zoo grounds.
6. Our job was to use ⟨shovel⟩ to pick up any trash they left.
   Our job was to use shovels to pick up any trash they left.

B. Use plurals of This Week's Words to answer the questions.

7. What birds did the zoo have?
   ____**eagles**____ and hawks.
8. How did some baby animals get milk? from ____**bottles**____
9. Where did people eat? at picnic ____**tables**____
10. What was used to pick up trash? ____**shovels**____

purple	camel	eagle	people	shovel	letter	level	able
bottle	cover	table	nickel	either	summer	sugar	

120 • Extra Practice

Spelling on Your Own

THIS WEEK'S WORDS

Here are the first syllables of all of This Week's Words. Add the missing syllable to each one. Write the whole word.

1. sum	**2.** lev	**3.** bot	**4.** pur	**5.** ea
6. cam	**7.** ta	**8.** cov	**9.** shov	**10.** let
11. ei	**12.** nick	**13.** peo	**14.** a	**15.** sug

See answers below.

MASTERY WORDS

Add the vowel letters. Write the Mastery words.

1. d_ll_r _____ dollar _____   **2.** _th_r _____ other _____

3. r_v_r _____ river _____   **4.** _ft_r _____ after _____

Finish the sentences. Use the Mastery words that mean the opposite of the words in dark print.

5. I went **under** the bridge as she went _____ over _____ it.

6. My sister was born **before** me, but _____ after _____ my brother.

Write Mastery words to finish the sentence.

7. And they lived happily _____ ever _____ _____ after _____ .

> after
> dollar
> ever
> other
> over
> river

BONUS WORDS

Write the Bonus words that go with these words.

1. jigsaw _____   **2.** _____ fox   **3.** underground
4. _____ the phone   **5.** canoe _____   **6.** _____ bear
7. _____ far   **8.** leash and _____

Use these pairs of Bonus words in sentences.

9. The two words that end with <u>le</u>.
10. The two words that end with <u>el</u>.
11. The two words that end with <u>er</u>.   See answers below.

> answer
> clever
> collar
> paddle
> polar
> puzzle
> travel
> tunnel

123

Spelling on Your Own Answers

THIS WEEK'S WORDS

1. summer 2. level 3. bottle 4. purple
5. eagle 6. camel 7. table 8. cover
9. shovel 10. letter 11. either 12. nickel
13. people 14. able 15. sugar

BONUS WORDS

1. puzzle 2. clever 3. tunnel 4. answer
5. paddle 6. polar 7. travel 8. collar

EXAMPLES:

9. Can you solve the <u>puzzle</u> of the missing Ping-Pong <u>paddle</u>?
10. Buses <u>travel</u> slowly through the <u>tunnel</u>.
11. Andrea gave a <u>clever</u> <u>answer</u>.

Summarize Learning

Have the children summarize what they have learned in this unit. *Ask:*

● What did you learn about plural forms in this lesson? (The letter *s* is added to most nouns to make them plural.)
● What spelling generalizations have you learned? How did you use these generalizations?

TEACHING PLAN

> **Objective** To apply the unit spelling generalization to spell This Week's Words, Mastery words, and Bonus words independently.

THIS WEEK'S WORDS

1. Read the directions on page 123 aloud. Help the children begin by having volunteers tell what letters must be added to *sum* to spell one of This Week's Words. Write *summer* on the chalkboard.
2. Have the children complete the activity independently on a separate piece of paper.

MASTERY WORDS

1. Review the spelling for /ər/: er, ar.
2. Have volunteers read the Mastery words aloud. As each word is read, help the children identify the letters that spell /ər/ in the word.
3. Briefly discuss the directions for **7** on page 123. Remind the children that many stories end this way.

BONUS WORDS

1. Review these spellings: /əl/le, el and /ər/er, ar.
2. Have volunteers read the Bonus words aloud. As each word is read, have the children identify the letters that spell /əl/ or /ər/ in the word. Encourage the children to look up the meaning of any unfamiliar words in the **Spelling Dictionary**.
3. Have the children complete the exercise independently on a separate piece of paper.

For reinforcement in writing spelling words, you may wish to assign *Extra Practice Master 28: Mastery Words* or *Bonus Words*.

CLOSING THE UNIT

Apply New Learning

Tell the children that if they misspell words with the schwa sounds /əl/ and /ər/ in their writing, they should use one of the following strategies:

- think about the possible spellings for the schwa sound and try to picture the word in their minds.
- think about the possible spellings for a sound within the word and use the dictionary to find the correct spelling.
- pronounce the word very carefully to see that the correct letter or letters have been used to spell the sounds in the word.

Transfer New Learning

Tell the children that when they encounter new words in their personal reading and in other content areas, they should learn the meaning of those words and then apply the generalizations they have studied to the spelling of those words. Tell them that once the words are familiar in both meaning and spelling, they should use the new words in their writing.

ENRICHMENT ACTIVITIES

Classroom activities and **home activities** may be assigned to children of all ability levels. The activities provide opportunities for children to use their spelling words in new contexts.

For the Classroom

To individualize classroom activities, you may have the children use the word list they are studying in this unit.

- *Basic:* Use **Mastery** words to complete the activity.
- *Average:* Use **This Week's Words** to complete the activity.
- *Challenging:* Use **Bonus** words to complete the activity.

1. **Language Arts/Writing Context Sentences** Have the children choose six spelling words and write a sentence for each. After proofreading for correct spelling, capital-ization, and punctuation, the children should rewrite their sentences, leaving a blank for the spelling word. Have the children then exchange sentences and fill in the missing spelling word.

   ■ COOPERATIVE LEARNING: Have each group make a set of sentences using their spelling words. Have each child in the group choose two words and write a sentence for each. Then have the children rewrite their sentences, leaving a blank for each spelling word. Have the group members test one another's sentences. When the sentences have been revised and proofread, have the group select one person to rewrite all the sentences with blanks. These sentences can then be shared with the class.

2. **Language Arts/Writing Codes** Have the children make a treasure map that includes directions to a hidden treasure. The directions should include as many spelling words as possible. When the children have completed their maps and directions, have them exchange with one another to try and find where the treasure is hidden.

   ■ COOPERATIVE LEARNING: Have each group make a treasure map and directions to a hidden treasure. After making the map, each member of the group should make up one direction to the treasure. After checking each other's directions for accuracy and revising the map, the group should select one person to rewrite the directions and another to draw the map. This can be given to the class to decode.

3. **Language Arts/Writing a Story** Have each child write a story. First, direct the children's attention to page 252 of the **Writer's Guide** to read about stories. As a *prewriting* activity, have the children look over the spelling list for words that suggest possible ideas for a story and for words that might be used to write the story. Tell the children to list their ideas and then decide what to write about. Possible stories might include the tale of a purple camel, the mystery of a secret tunnel, or the way a clever eagle outsmarted a lion. Then have the children make a chart with headings for where and when the story takes place, the main characters, what happens, and how the story ends. Tell them to write the possibilities in the appropriate columns. When the children have completed the prewriting activities, have them use the chart to *compose* the story. Remind them to use as many spelling words as they can. Then have the children *revise* the story, making sure they have included all the details from the chart. Tell them to proofread for spelling, capitalization, and punctuation. Then have the children illustrate their stories. *Publish* the stories in a class book, or have the children read their stories aloud and show their illustrations.

   ■ COOPERATIVE LEARNING: Have each group write a story. As a *prewriting* activity, have the group look over the spelling lists and brainstorm for possible story ideas. After deciding what their story will be about, the group should make a chart with headings where and when the story takes place, the main characters, what happens, and how the story ends. Have the group select one child to write their ideas in the appropriate columns. When they have completed these activities, have them refer to the chart as they *compose* the story. Have one child begin the story. The other children should build on the first sentence. Remind them to refer to the chart and to use as many spelling words as they can. Group members should then **revise** and proofread the story. Have the group select one student to rewrite the story and another to illustrate it. Each group should **publish** the story by having a student read it aloud, by including it in a class book, or by displaying it on the bulletin board.

For the Home

Children may complete these activities independently or with the assistance of a relative or friend in the home.

1. **Language Arts/Writing Word Associations** Tell the children to choose six spelling words for which they can name two other words commonly associated with the word. For example, the spelling word *purple* could be included with *green* and *red* because they are all colors. Have the children write the two words and leave a blank for the spelling word. Tell then to ask a friend or someone at home to guess which spelling word belongs with each pair of words.

2. **Language Arts/Writing Tongue Twisters** Tell the children to write a tongue twister using as many spelling words as possible that begin with the same sound. Tell them they may use words from all three lists. Present this sentence as an example: *The puzzled people paddled past a purple polar bear.* Tell the children to share their sentences with friends or relatives.

3. **Social Studies/Writing a Description of a Place** Ask the children to think about a special place they have visited, such as another city or another state. Tell them to write several sentences that describe the place, using some of their spelling words. When the children have completed their descriptions, they may wish to draw a picture of the place they have visited.

4. **Science/Writing a How-to Paragraph About a Garden** Tell the children to write a how-to paragraph about planting and caring for a garden. Refer them to page 250 of the **Writer's Guide** to read about how-to paragraphs, if necessary. Remind them to use some of their spelling words.

EVALUATING SPELLING ABILITY

Unit Test

This Week's Words
1. *purple* Grape jelly is *purple*. **purple**
2. *camel* We saw a *camel* at the zoo. **camel**
3. *cover* There is a nice picture on the *cover* of that book. **cover**
4. *able* Christy is not *able* to come. **able**
5. *bottle* Willie spilled the *bottle* of orange juice. **bottle**
6. *eagle* It is illegal to hunt a bald *eagle*. **eagle**
7. *people* Many *people* ride buses every day. **people**

8. *table* Dinner is on the *table*. **table**
9. *level* The bulldozer made the ground *level*. **level**
10. *nickel* Becky has a *nickel*. **nickel**
11. *shovel* Please help Dad *shovel* the snow. **shovel**
12. *either* You may have *either* a pear or an apple. **either**
13. *letter* Every name should start with a capital *letter*. **letter**
14. *summer* Last *summer* Lenore learned how to build a campfire. **summer**
15. *sugar* Too much *sugar* is not good for your teeth. **sugar**

Mastery Words
1. *after* It is *after* ten o'clock. **after**
2. *dollar* Four quarters equal one *dollar*. **dollar**
3. *ever* Hilda wondered if she would *ever* go to England. **ever**
4. *other* All the *other* children remembered their lunch. **other**
5. *over* Put the books *over* there. **over**
6. *river* Let's take a walk down by the *river*. **river**

Bonus Words
1. *answer* The *answer* to the problem is six. **answer**
2. *clever* René is *clever* enough to solve any puzzle. **clever**
3. *collar* Buy the dog a new *collar*. **collar**
4. *paddle* Libby broke the canoe *paddle*. **paddle**
5. *polar* We wondered if the *polar* bear was cold. **polar**
6. *puzzle* Franco finished the crossword *puzzle*. **puzzle**
7. *travel* Many people like to *travel* by train. **travel**
8. *tunnel* The *tunnel* was dark and scary. **tunnel**

Dictation Sentences

This Week's Words
1. Two *people* were *able* to lift the *table*.
2. The book with the *purple cover* costs a *nickel*.
3. We can use *either shovel* to make the land *level*.
4. Her *letter* said she saw a *camel* last *summer*.
5. I put the *sugar* in a *bottle* with an *eagle* on it.

Mastery Words
1. There is the bridge *over* the *river*.
2. My *other* friends will come *after* lunch.
3. Did you *ever* find the *dollar* you lost?

Bonus Words
1. The *clever* child knew the *answer* to the *puzzle*.
2. The train will soon *travel* into the *tunnel*.
3. The *polar* bear started to *paddle* across the water.
4. Your cat should have a *collar*.

RETEACHING STRATEGIES FOR SPELLING

Children who have made errors on the Unit Test may require reteaching. Use the following *Reteaching Strategies* and *Follow-up Masters 28A* and *28B* for additional instruction and practice of This Week's Words. (You may wish to assign *LEP Reteaching Follow-up Master 28* for reteaching of spelling words.)

A. Discovering Spelling Ideas

1. Say the following words as you write them on the chalkboard.

   simple   tunnel   butter   cougar

2. Ask the children to identify the last two letters of each word. *(le, el, er, ar)*

3. Point out that each word has two parts, each with a vowel sound. The first part, or **syllable,** is said with more force. The second syllable has a weak vowel sound call a **schwa.** Ask the children to identify the two spellings for /ə/ and the consonant *l*, or /əl/, and the two spellings for /ə/ and the consonant *r*, or /ər/. *(le, el; er, ar)*

4. Ask the children what they have learned about spelling /əl/ and /ər/. (/əl/ can be spelled *le* or *el;* /ər/ can be spelled *er* or *ar*)

B. Word Shapes

1. Explain to the children that each word has a shape and that remembering the shape of a word can help them to spell the word correctly.

2. On the chalkboard, write the words *couple* and *under.* Have the children identify "short," "tall," and "tail" letters.

3. Draw the configuration of each word on the chalkboard, and ask the children which word fits in each shape.

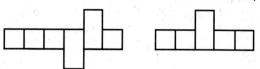

Use *Reteaching Follow-up Master 28A* to reinforce spelling generalizations taught in Unit 28.

Use *Reteaching Follow-up Master 28B* to reinforce spellings of This Week's Words for Unit 28.

Name				UNIT
Reteaching Follow-up A			Discovering Spelling Ideas	28

THIS WEEK'S WORDS

purple	eagle	people	letter	level
bottle	table	nickel	summer	sugar
camel	cover	shovel	either	able

1. Study This Week's Words. Say each word to yourself. How many vowel sounds do you hear in each word? __two__

2. The last vowel sound in each of This Week's Words is a weak vowel sound called a schwa, or /ə/. Write This Week's Words below the schwa and final consonant you hear in the word.

/əl/	/ər/
purple	letter
camel	cover
eagle	either
people	summer
shovel	sugar
level	
bottle	
nickel	
able	
table	

3. Look at the /əl/ column. How is /əl/ spelled in these words? __le, el__

4. Look at the /ər/ column. How is /ər/ spelled in these words? __er, ar__

Reteaching • 47

Name				UNIT
Reteaching Follow-up B			Word Shapes	28

THIS WEEK'S WORDS

purple	able	people	nickel	letter
camel	bottle	table	shovel	summer
cover	eagle	level	either	sugar

Write each of This Week's Words in its correct shape. The first one has been done for you. Children may interchange answers that fit the same configuration.

1. s u g a r   2. b o t t l e

3. p u r p l e   4. c o v e r

5. l e v e l   6. s h o v e l

7. p e o p l e   8. c a m e l

9. n i c k e l   10. t a b l e

11. e i t h e r   12. l e t t e r

13. a b l e   14. s u m m e r

15. e a g l e

48 • Reteaching

PREVIEWING THE UNIT

Unit Materials

Instruction and Practice

Pupil Book	pages 124–127
Teacher's Edition	
Teaching Plans	pages 124–127
Enrichment Activities	
For the Classroom	pages 127A–127B
For the Home	page 127B
Reteaching Strategies	page 127C

Testing

Teacher's Edition	
Trial Test	pages 123E–123F
Unit Test	page 127B
Dictation Test	page 127B

Additional Resources

Teacher's Resource Package

PRACTICE AND REINFORCEMENT
Extra Practice Master 29: This Week's Words
Extra Practice Master 29: Mastery Words
Extra Practice Master 29: Bonus Words
LEP Practice Master 29
Spelling and Language Master 29
Study Steps to Learn a Word Master
Reteaching Follow-up Master 29A:
    Discovering Spelling Ideas
Reteaching Follow-up Master 29B: Word
    Shapes
LEP Reteaching Follow-up Master 29

TEACHING AIDS
Spelling Generalizations Transparency 25

Visit our Web site
http://www.hbschool.com

Click on the SPELLING banner to find activities for this unit.

Learner Objectives

Spelling

- To spell homophones.
- To spell pairs of homophones given pronunciations.

Reading

- To follow written directions.
- To understand the meaning of homophones in sentence context.
- To use a dictionary as a key to pronunciation.
- To use a dictionary for word meaning.

Writing

- To write signs.
- To use the writing process.
- To proofread for spelling, capitalization, and punctuation.
- To write legible manuscript and cursive letters.

Listening

- To listen to recognize a speaker's purpose for a presentation.
- To listen to identify homophones.
- To follow oral directions.

Speaking

- To speak clearly to a group.
- To respond to a question.
- To express feelings and ideas about a piece of writing.
- To present a story.
- To contribute ideas and information in group discussions.

THIS WEEK'S WORDS

sale
sail
beat
beet
break
brake
main
mane
read
reed
meet
rode
son
whose
won

MASTERY WORDS

here
too
would
to
wood
hear

BONUS WORDS

groan
hole
pain
scent
whole
cent
grown
pane

Assignment Guide

This guide shows how you teach a typical spelling unit in either a five-day or a three-day sequence, while providing for individual differences. **Boldface type** indicates essential classwork. Steps shown in light type may be done in class or assigned as homework.

Five Days	• = average spellers ★ = better spellers ✓ = slower spellers	Three Days
Day **1** **a**	• ★ **Take This Week's Words Trial Test and correct** • ✓ **Take Mastery Word Trial Test and correct** • ★ **Read This Week's Words and discuss generalization page 124**	Day **1** **b**
Day **2**	• Complete Spelling Practice page 125 • ✓ Complete Extra Practice Master 29: This Week's Words (optional) ✓ Complete Spelling on Your Own: Mastery Words page 127 ★ **Take Bonus Word Trial Test and correct**	
Day **3** **c**	• ★ ✓ **Complete Spelling and Language page 126** • ★ ✓ Complete Writing on Your Own page 126 • ★ ✓ **Complete Using the Dictionary to Spell and Write page 126** • ✓ Take Midweek Test (optional) ★ Complete Spelling on Your Own: Bonus Words page 127 • ✓ Complete Spelling and Language Master 29 (optional)	Day **2**
Day **4**	• Complete Spelling on Your Own: This Week's Words page 127 ✓ Complete Extra Practice Master 29: Mastery Words (optional) ★ Complete Extra Practice Master 29: Bonus Words (optional)	**d**
Day **5** **e**	• **Take Unit Test on This Week's Words** • Complete Reteaching Follow-up Masters 29A and 29B (optional) • ✓ **Take Unit Test on Mastery Words** ★ **Take Unit Test on Bonus Words**	Day **3**

Enrichment Activities for the **classroom** and for the **home** included at the end of this unit may be assigned selectively on any day of the week.

FOCUS

- Establishes objectives
- Relates to prior learning
- Sets purpose of instruction

INTRODUCING THE UNIT

Establish Readiness for Learning

Tell the children that this week they will learn about homophones. Tell the children that they will apply the spelling generalizations to This Week's Words and use those words to write signs.

Assess Children's Spelling Ability

Administer the Trial Test before the children study This Week's Words. Use the test sentences provided. Say each word and use it in a sentence. Then repeat the word. Have the children write the words on a separate sheet of paper or in their spelling notebooks. Test sentences are also provided for Mastery and Bonus words.

Have the children check their own work by

listening to you read the spelling of the words or by referring to This Week's Words in the left column of the **Pupil Book.** For each misspelled word, have the children follow the **Study Steps to Learn a Word** on page 1 in the **Pupil Book** or use the copying master to study and write the words. Children should record the number correct on their **Progress Report.**

Trial Test Sentences

This Week's Words
1. *sale*   There was a *sale* on sheets at the department store.   *sale*
2. *sail*   We bought a new *sail* for our boat.   *sail*
3. *beat*   Charette *beat* the eggs with a fork.   *beat*
4. *beet*   A *beet* grows underground, like a carrot.   *beet*
5. *break*   Don't *break* your glasses.   *break*

6. *brake*   Mr. Perez stepped on the *brake* to stop the car.   **brake**
7. *main*   Peter read the paragraph to find the *main* idea.   **main**
8. *mane*   A male lion has a *mane*.   **mane**
9. *read*   Franklin can *read* well.   **read**
10. *reed*   Laura picked a *reed* in the marsh.   **reed**
11. *meet*   The children will *meet* after school.   **meet**
12. *rode*   Everyone *rode* the school bus in the morning.   **rode**
13. *son*   Robert is Mrs. Casey's *son*.   **son**
14. *whose*   I don't know *whose* paper this is.   **whose**
15. *won*   Our team *won* the game.   **won**

Mastery Words

1. *here*   Please come *here*.   **here**
2. *too*   Molly should come, *too*.   **too**
3. *would*   Ron *would* like to help.   **would**
4. *to*   Please go *to* the office.   **to**
5. *wood*   We burned *wood* in the fireplace.   **wood**
6. *hear*   I hope that everyone can *hear* me.   **hear**

Bonus Words

1. *groan*   We heard a *groan* in the haunted house.   **groan**

2. *hole*   We dug a *hole* to plant the bulbs.   **hole**
3. *pain*   Martin has a *pain* in his ear.   **pain**
4. *scent*   The *scent* of a skunk is very unpleasant.   **scent**
5. *whole*   The *whole* class will go outdoors for recess.   **whole**
6. *cent*   A *cent* is a penny.   **cent**
7. *grown*   Katy has *grown* two inches this year.   **grown**
8. *pane*   A *pane* of glass in the window was broken.   **pane**

Apply Prior Learning

Have the children apply what they already know about homophones by having them participate in the following activity.

Write the words *ad* and *add* on the chalkboard. Have the children tell what is alike and what is different about these words. Help them to recognize that these words sound alike but are not spelled alike and that these words have different meanings. Ask volunteers to dictate a sentence for each of these words. Ask the children to think of more word pairs that are homophones as you list them on the chalkboard.

FOCUS

- Relates to prior learning
- Draws relationships
- Applies spelling generalizations to new contexts

FOR CHILDREN WITH SPECIAL NEEDS

Learning Difficulties

Children with memory deficiencies have difficulty spelling homophones. They do not realize that they need sentence context for the spelling of the homophone in addition to a learned spelling generalization or a sound-symbol relationship. The following strategy gives the children practice spelling This Week's Words in sentence context as well as providing additional sensory input.

Tell the children that homophones are words that sound alike but are not spelled alike. Say one of the homophones, such as *sale*, and ask a volunteer to dictate a sentence using this word. Write his or her sentence on a duplicating master, leaving a blank space in place of the homophone. Then ask a volunteer to dictate another sentence using the homophone *sail*. Write that sentence on the duplicating master, leaving a blank space in

place of the homophone. Continue in this manner until the children have dictated one sentence for each homophone. Write the homophones from This Week's Words in a box at the top of the duplicating master. Reproduce the duplicating master and have the children complete it independently.

Limited English Proficiency

To help limited English proficient children work with the spelling generalizations for Unit 29, you may wish to refer to the booklet "Suggestions and Activities for Limited English Proficient Students."

TEACHING PLAN

Objective To spell homophones.

1. Direct the children's attention to the cartoon at the top of page 124 and have a child read the cartoon dialogue. Then ask the children to comment on the cartoon character's confusion and explain the meanings of *sale* and *sail*.
2. Read the generalization on page 124 aloud.

You may wish to introduce the lesson by using ***Spelling Generalizations Transparency 25.***

3. Direct the children's attention to the cartoon at the bottom of the page. Have a child read the dialogue and comment on the use and meaning of *beat* and *beet*.
4. Have volunteers read This Week's Words aloud. As the first five pairs of homophones are read, ask the children to define each word. For the last five words, have the children think of another word that sounds the same but has different spelling and meaning. Write these homophone pairs on the chalk-board:

    meet-meat rode-road son-sun
    whose-who's won-one

5. Have volunteers use each homo-phone (including those written on the chalkboard) in an oral sentence.

You may wish to assign ***LEP Practice Master 29*** for reinforcement in writing spelling words.

Homophones

THIS WEEK'S WORDS

1. sale
2. sail
3. beat
4. beet
5. break
6. brake
7. main
8. mane
9. read
10. reed
11. meet
12. rode
13. son
14. whose
15. won

This Week's Words

Sale and sail are **homophones.** They sound alike, but they are not spelled alike. They also have different meanings.

Homophones can be tricky. You must pay attention to what the words mean. Then you can write the words that make sense in your sentences.

124

Extra Practice: This Week's Words

Name
Extra Practice   This Week's Words   UNIT **29**

A. The pronunciations for some of This Week's Words are given. Write the correct spelling of each word.

1. Phil's face was as red as a /bēt/. — beet
2. The boat needs a new /sāl/. — sail
3. Maria used the /brāk/ to stop her bike. — brake
4. A flute is made with a /rēd/. — reed
5. Please /bēt/ the eggs, Kevin. — beat
6. Mrs. Ray bought two books on /sāl/. — sale
7. She began to /rēd/ one book today. — read
8. Apple Street is the /mān/ street in my town. — main
9. The lion shook its thick /mān/. — mane
10. Did you /brāk/ this window? — break

B. Write the correct homophone in each sentence.

11. Let's <u>meat</u> at the zoo. — meet
12. Do you know <u>who's</u> pen this is? — whose
13. Dad bought me a shirt on <u>sail</u>. — sale
14. The toy lion had a soft <u>main</u>. — mane
15. I will <u>reed</u> the baby a story. — read
16. Our team has <u>one</u> again! — won
17. We <u>road</u> in the back seat of the car. — rode
18. The Taylors have a <u>sun</u> in college. — son
19. Did you <u>beet</u> the eggs for the cake? — beat
20. Andy fixed the <u>sale</u> on my boat. — sail

word box: sale / read / sail / reed / beat / meet / beet / rode / break / son / brake / whose / main / won / mane

Extra Practice • 121

Extra Practice: Mastery Words

Name
Extra Practice   Mastery Words   UNIT **29**

Kim sent a letter to Carmen. One word in each underlined sentence is wrong. Write the right Mastery word next to the sentence number below.

Dear Carmen,

How are you?

It is very cold <u>hear</u>. Robert is chopping <u>would</u> in the yard. Mom and Dad say it's going <u>too</u> be a hard winter. <u>Wood</u> you visit me soon? Let me know when.

You should <u>here</u> me play the drums! Carrie, Danny, and I are in a band. Mom and Dad think drums are to noisy. They wish I played the flute like Todd!

That's all for <u>row</u>. Please write soon.

Your friend,

Kim

1. ___ here   2. ___ wood
3. ___ to   4. ___ Would
5. ___ hear   6. ___ too

word box: here   too   would   to   wood   hear

122 • Extra Practice

Spelling Practice

A. Write the homophones for these words. Use This Week's Words.

1. who's ___whose___
2. sun ___son___
3. road ___rode___
4. one ___won___
5. meat ___meet___

B. A word in each sentence doesn't make sense. Draw a line under that word. Then write the right word.

6. The horse has a long, white <u>main</u>. ___mane___
7. You step on the <u>break</u> to stop a car. ___brake___
8. The store is having a <u>sail</u> on jeans. ___sale___
9. Pablo's face is as red as a <u>beat</u>. ___beet___
10. Gail made a flute out of a <u>read</u>. ___reed___

C. Finish each sentence. Use the word that has the right meaning.

11. Miko and Chris ___read___ a book every week.
12. I hope our team can ___beat___ the other team.
13. Children ___sail___ their toy boats on this pond.
14. Dad can ___break___ open an egg with one hand.
15. What is the ___main___ street in your town called?

D. Rewrite this sentence. Use <u>road</u> and its homophone.

16. We took a ride down the road.

    We rode down the road.

sale
sail
beat
beet
break
brake
main
mane
read
reed
meet
rode
son
whose
won

125

TEACHING PLAN

Objectives To write words given homophones; to write the correct homophone in sentence context; to write a sentence using a homophone pair.

1. Briefly discuss the directions on page 125.
2. Have the children complete the page independently. Remind them to use legible handwriting. For **Handwriting Models,** refer the children to page 258 in the **Pupil Book.**
3. To correct the children's work, have volunteers write their answers on the chalkboard. Let the children check their own work.

For reinforcement in writing spelling words, you may wish to assign **Extra Practice Master 29: This Week's Words.**

⭐ *of special interest*

The distinctions between *homophone, homograph,* and *homonym* are often not clear. All three words derive from Greek. *Homophone* ("same sound") refers to words that are pronounced the same but have different meanings and spellings. *Meat* and *meet* are homophones. *Homograph* ("same writing") refers to words that are spelled the same but have different meanings and sometimes also have different pronunciations. *Yard* ("enclosure") and *yard* ("unit of measure") are homographs, as are *wind* /wind/ and *wind* /wīnd/. *Homonym* ("same name") is often used to refer generally to both homophones and homographs.

Extra Practice: Bonus Words

Extra Practice — Bonus Words — UNIT 29

A. Read each sentence. One word is given as a pronunciation. Write the correct spelling for that word.

1. Howard fell against a /pān/ of glass. — pane
2. The glass didn't break, but Howard has a /pān/ in his arm. — pain
3. These flowers have a nice /sent/. — scent
4. We must dig a large /hōl/ to plant this tree. — hole
5. It may take us the /hōl/ day. — whole
6. Mom let out a /grōn/ when Linda tried on her summer clothes. — groan
7. Linda had /grōn/ so much that everything was too small. — grown

B. Finish the two puzzles. First find the two Bonus words for each pronunciation. Then write the homophone that comes first in alphabetical order in Puzzle 1. Write the other homophone in Puzzle 2. Use the numbers with the pronunciations to write the words in the right places.

8. /grōn/
9. /sent/
10. /hōl/
11. /pān/

Puzzle 1 / Puzzle 2

cent grown whole pane hole pain groan scent

Extra Practice • 123

Summarize Learning

Have the children summarize what they have learned on pages 124 and 125. *Ask:*

• What have you learned about homophones in this lesson? (They are words that sound alike but are not spelled alike and have different meanings.)
• What are some examples of homophones? (*tale, tail; main, mane;* accept other examples)

TEACHING PLAN

SPELLING AND LANGUAGE

Objective To write *whose* and *who's* correctly in sentence context.

1. Read the introductory paragraph on page 126 aloud. Then read each of these sentences aloud:

   a. Who's finished the work?
   b. Whose book is that?
   c. Who's older, you or Janet?
   d. Who's been to a circus?

   Ask the children to indicate how /hōōz/ should be spelled in each sentence. Suggest that if they can put *who is* or *who has* in place of /hōōz/, the word is *who's*; if they cannot, the word is *whose*.

2. Read the directions on page 126 aloud. Remind the children that sentences or questions always begin with capital letters.

3. Have the children complete the exercises independently.

4. To correct the children's work, read the sentences aloud and have a volunteer write *whose* or *who's* on the chalkboard each time. Let the children check their own work.

For extended practice in writing *whose* and *who's* in sentence context, you may wish to assign *Spelling and Language Master 29.*

WRITING ON YOUR OWN

Objectives To write signs using homophone pairs; to proofread for spelling.

1. Read the directions aloud.

2. As a **prewriting** activity, have each child make a list of homophones, including some from This Week's Words. Then have the children choose three pairs to use as they **compose** their signs. When they are ready to **revise,** remind the children to check for spelling. To **publish,** display the children's work on a bulletin board.

THIS WEEK'S WORDS
sale
sail
beat
beet
break
brake
main
mane
read
reed
meet
rode
son
whose
won

126

USING THE DICTIONARY

Objective To spell pairs of homophones given pronunciations.

1. Read the introductory paragraph. Help the children to read the pronunciation /hōōz/.

2. Read the directions on page 126 aloud. Have volunteers say each pronunciation in the exercise.

3. Have the children complete the exercises independently.

4. Have volunteers write each pair of homophones on the chalkboard. Let the children check their own work.

Spelling and Language • <u>Whose</u> and <u>Who's</u>

You use <u>whose</u> to ask questions about who owns something: "<u>Whose</u> pencil is this?" The word <u>who's</u> is a contraction for <u>who is</u> or <u>who has</u>. You use <u>who's</u> to ask this kind of question: "<u>Who's</u> using my pencil?"

Start each of these questions with <u>Whose</u> or <u>Who's</u>.

1. _____Who's_____ going camping with you?

2. _____Whose_____ tent will you use?

3. _____Who's_____ doing the cooking?

Writing on Your Own

Write three signs using homophone pairs from This Week's Words. Here is an example: "Sail for Sale." Share your signs with your class.

WRITER'S GUIDE Can your classmates read your signs? For help writing any letters, turn to page 258.

Using the Dictionary to Spell and Write

Knowing how to pronounce a word can help you remember how to spell it. A **pronunciation** is a special way of writing a word. It shows you how to say the word. As you can see, the pronunciations for <u>who's</u> and <u>whose</u> are the same.

> **who's** /hōōz/ 1 Who is: *Who's* ready for recess?
> 2 Who has: *Who's* got my notebook?
> **whose** /hōōz/ *pron.* Belonging to which person: *Whose* book is this?

act, āte, câre, ärt; egg, ēven; if, īce; on, ōver, ôr; bŏŏk, fōōd; up, tûrn;
ə = a in *ago*, e in *listen*, i in *giraffe*, o in *pilot*, u in *circus*; yōō = u in *music*; oil; out;
chair; sing; shop; thank; that; zh in *treasure*.

Write the two words for each pronunciation.

1. /brāk/ _____break_____ _____brake_____

2. /sāl/ _____sale_____ _____sail_____

Spelling on Your Own

THIS WEEK'S WORDS

Write sentences using homophone pairs. Use This Week's Words. Use the homophones you know for <u>meet</u>, <u>rode</u>, <u>son</u>, <u>whose</u>, and <u>won</u>, too. Here is an example: "Let's <u>meet</u> at the <u>meat</u> store."

MASTERY WORDS

Follow the directions. Use the Mastery words.

| here |
| too |
| would |
| to |
| wood |
| hear |

1. Write the word that means almost the same as "listen." Then write the word that sounds the same.

<u>   hear   </u>   <u>   here   </u>

2. Write the word that names what comes from trees. Then write the word that sounds the same.

<u>   wood   </u>   <u>   would   </u>

Finish the sentences. Use two Mastery words.

3. Juan walks his little brother <u> to </u> school.

4. His brother is <u> too </u> little to go alone.

BONUS WORDS

Some homophones are mixed up in this story. Write the story correctly. Then finish the story.

| groan |
| hole |
| pain |
| scent |
| whole |
| cent |
| grown |
| pane |

    The night had groan cold. Nan could smell the cent of pine needles. The wind whistled through a whole in the window pain. It sounded like the grown of someone in pane. Nan thought, "For two scents I'd leave this cabin and go home." Still, she knew the hole situation would seem better in the morning.
    Suddenly Nan heard a loud cracking sound.

Spelling on Your Own Answers

BONUS WORDS

The night had <u>grown</u> cold. Nan could smell the <u>scent</u> of pine needles. The wind whistled through a <u>hole</u> in the window <u>pane</u>. It sounded like the <u>groan</u> of someone in <u>pain</u>. Nan thought, "For two <u>cents</u> I'd leave this cabin and go home." Still, she knew the <u>whole</u> situation would seem better in the morning.
    Suddenly Nan heard a loud cracking sound.
    Children will write as directed. Be sure to check spelling.

Summarize Learning

Have the children summarize what they have learned in this unit. *Ask:*
- What have you learned about writing *whose* and *who's* in sentence context? (The word *whose* is used to ask questions about who owns something. The word *who's* is a contraction for *who is* or *who has*.)
- What have you learned about dictionary pronunciations? (A pronunciation shows how a word should be said.)
- What spelling generalizations have you learned? How did you use these generalizations?

TEACHING PLAN

> **Objectives** To apply the unit spelling generalization to spell This Week's Words, Mastery words, and Bonus words independently.

THIS WEEK'S WORDS

1. Read the directions on page 127 aloud. Help the children get started by having volunteers give sentences using *sale* and *sail*. Write their responses on the chalkboard.
2. Have the children complete the activity independently on a separate piece of paper.
3. To review the children's work, have volunteers read their sentences aloud.

MASTERY WORDS

1. Review the definition of *homophones* on page 124.
2. Have volunteers read the Mastery words aloud. When all the words have been read, ask the children to identify the homophone pairs and tell what each homophone means.
3. Briefly discuss the directions on page 127 to be sure that the children understand what they are to do.
4. Have the children complete the activity independently.

BONUS WORDS

1. Briefly review the definition of *homophones* on page 124.
2. Have volunteers read the Bonus words aloud. Have other children match the homophone pairs and tell what each homophone means.
3. Have the children complete the exercise independently.
4. Collect the children's papers to review their work.

For reinforcement in writing spelling words, you may wish to assign **Extra Practice Master 29: Mastery Words** or **Bonus Words**.

CLOSING THE UNIT

Apply New Learning

Tell the children that if they misspell homophones in their writing, they should use one or more of the following strategies:

- write the word using different spellings and compare it with the spelling they picture in their minds.
- think about whether the word might sound like another word but be spelled differently. Use sentence context to help know which spelling is appropriate.
- use the dictionary to find the correct spelling.

Transfer New Learning

Tell the children that when they encounter new words in their personal reading and in other content areas, they should learn the meaning of those words and then apply the generalizations they have studied to the spelling of those words. Tell them that once the words are familiar in both meaning and spelling, they should use the new words in their writing.

ENRICHMENT ACTIVITIES

Classroom activities and **home activities** may be assigned to children of all ability levels. The activities provide opportunities for children to use their spelling words in new contexts.

For the Classroom

To individualize classroom activities, you may have the children use the word list they are studying in this unit.

Basic: Use **Mastery** words to complete the activity.
Average: Use **This Week's Words** to complete the activity.
Challenging: Use **Bonus** words to complete the activity.

1. **Language Arts/Writing Definitions** Have the children choose several spelling words for which they will write definitions. Tell the children you will give them a definition for one of This Week's Words. They will have to choose and spell the correct word. Present this definition: *a type of tall grass with a hollow stalk that grows in wet places.* After the children name and spell *reed,* have them write their own definitions for each of the words they have chosen. When they have completed their definitions, have the children exchange papers with one another and select the word that matches the definition.

■ COOPERATIVE LEARNING: Have each group create a set of definitions for as many spelling words as there are group members. Each child within the group should write a definition. Then have the group members try out their definitions on each other to see if their meanings are clear and effective. When each group is satisfied that the definitions are good ones, have classmates read the definitions and name and spell the word that matches the definition.

2. **Language Arts/Writing Sentences** Have the children choose two pairs of homophones and write a sentence for each pair. Present this example. *The horse with the white mane ran down the main street of town.* Then have the children rewrite their sentences leaving blanks for the homophones. Have them exchange papers and write the correct homophone in each blank.

■ COOPERATIVE LEARNING: Have each group make a set of sentences using a pair of homophones in each sentence. Provide the children with this example: *The horse with the white mane ran down the main street of town.* Have each group member choose a pair of homophones and then write his or her own sentence using both words. Tell the children to test out their sentences on one another. When the group is satisfied with the corrections and changes, have the members select one child to rewrite the sentences leaving blanks for each pair of homophones. Then have the group share their sentences with other classmates.

3. **Language Arts/Writing a News Story** Have each child write a news story about a sporting event. First direct the children's attention to page 253 of the **Writer's Guide** to read about news stories. As a *prewriting* activity, have the children look over the spelling word list in search of possible ideas for a news story about a sporting event, such as a horse race, a sailboat race, or a car race. Tell the children to list their ideas and then choose one. Then have the children make a chart with the following headings: *who, what, where, when, why.* Tell the children to list details about each category. When they have completed the prewriting activities, have them use their charts to **compose** the news story. Remind the children to use as many spelling words as possible. Then have the children **revise** their news stories, making sure they have included all the details from the chart that they considered important. Tell them to also proofread for spelling, capitalization, and punctuation using the **Revising Checklist** on page 247 for help. **Publish** the children's stories in a class newspaper.

■ COOPERATIVE LEARNING: Have each group write a news story about a sporting event. As a *prewriting* activity, have the group members select an idea by looking over the spelling words. Then have them make a chart with the following headings: *who, what, where, when, why.* Tell the group to list details about each category. When the children are ready to **compose** the news story, have them select one group member to begin the story orally by giving an opening sentence telling who or what the story is about. Have the other members in the group build on the opening sentence.

Each child should add a sentence or two until the news story is fully developed. One child can then record the story. Other group members should **revise** the story, making sure that all the details have been included. Each child within the group should proofread for spelling, capitalization, and punctuation. Have each group then select a child to rewrite the story. Each group should **publish** the story by having a member read it aloud.

or the Home

Children may complete these activities independently or ith the assistance of a relative or friend in the home.

Language Arts/Writing Word Families Tell the children to choose some verbs from their spelling lists and write as many words as they can think of that are in the same word family. For example, *break, breaks, broke, breaking, broken* are in the same word family. Have the children check a dictionary to be sure thay have written actual words and that they are spelled correctly. Then have the children write a sentence for each word in one word family. Children should share their words and sentences with a friend or someone at home.

Science/Writing True and False Statements About Animals and Plants Have the children write true and false statements using their spelling words. For example, *Beets grow on trees* and *Monkeys can't read.* Encourage the children to use a dictionary, the encyclopedia, or their textbooks for help. Then tell the children to share their statements by asking a friend or family member to guess which ones are true and which ones are false.

Social Studies/Writing a Biographical Sketch Tell the children to write a brief biographical sketch about a famous person in American History, such as George Washington or Paul Revere. Have them list some facts about the person, using an encyclopedia or history book if needed. Tell the children to write a paragraph using the facts and some of their spelling words. After revising and proofreading, have the children share their sketches with someone at home.

Language Arts/Writing a Why-Tale Tell the children that there is a scientific explanation for such things as thunder, lightning, volcanic eruptions, and earthquakes. Tell them that long ago, people often made up stories to explain these occurrences. Tell the children to write their own imaginative explanation of thunder and lightning, a volcano, or an earthquake, using some of their spelling words. Have them read their stories to a friend or relative.

VALUATING SPELLING ABILITY

Unit Test

This Week's Words

1. *sale*   Dishes were on *sale* this week.   *sale*
2. *sail*   Many people like to *sail* boats.   *sail*
3. *beat*   Rock music has a strong *beat*.   *beat*

4. *beet*   When Clyde is embarrassed, his face gets as red as a *beet*.   *beet*
5. *break*   We tried not to *break* the thin ice.   *break*
6. *brake*   Dad will fix the *brake* on my bike.   *brake*
7. *main*   Broad Street is the *main* street of the village.   *main*
8. *mane*   Jody brushed the horse's *mane*.   *mane*
9. *read*   Irene likes to *read* mystery stories.   *read*
10. *reed*   The *reed* snapped when I stepped on it.   *reed*
11. *meet*   Libby will *meet* Ralph at the corner.   *meet*
12. *rode*   Maria *rode* the white horse.   *rode*
13. *son*   Mrs. Jackson's oldest *son* is a professor.   *son*
14. *whose*   I wonder *whose* shoes these are.   *whose*
15. *won*   I hope Bill *won* the prize.   *won*

Mastery Words

1. *here*   Put the glasses *here* on the shelf.   *here*
2. *too*   Cal will have a sandwich, *too*.   *too*
3. *would*   I had hoped you *would* not be late.   *would*
4. *to*   Let's go *to* the bookstore.   *to*
5. *wood*   This table is made of *wood*.   *wood*
6. *hear*   I cannot *hear* what he is saying.   *hear*

Bonus Words

1. *groan*   We heard the sick animal *groan*.   *groan*
2. *hole*   The dog is digging a *hole* in the garden.   *hole*
3. *pain*   Carlos has a *pain* in his leg.   *pain*
4. *scent*   The *scent* of the flowers is lovely.   *scent*
5. *whole*   I hope you finished the *whole* job.   *whole*
6. *cent*   That gum costs one *cent*.   *cent*
7. *grown*   The plants have *grown* an inch this week.   *grown*
8. *pane*   We replaced the broken *pane* in the door.   *pane*

Dictation Sentences

This Week's Words

1. She *rode* down the *main* street to *meet* her *son*.
2. I know *whose* story I will *read* next.
3. The horse with the white *mane* *beat* the other horses in the race.
4. Both a *reed* and a *beet* are plants.
5. She needs a new *brake* for her bike.
6. We *won* a trip to *sail* on a big boat.
7. Do not *break* any of the dishes on the *sale* table.

Mastery Words

1. We can stand *here* and *hear* the bird sing.
2. Tell me if you *would* like *to* chop some *wood*, *too*.

Bonus Words

1. He will *groan* when he sees how big the *hole* in his shoe has *grown*.
2. She felt a *pain* in her back when she washed the *whole* window *pane*.
3. He won't pay a *cent* for a dog that can't follow a *scent*.

RETEACHING STRATEGIES FOR SPELLING

Children who have made errors on the Unit Test may require reteaching. Use the following **Reteaching Strategies** and **Follow-up Masters 29A** and **29B** for additional instruction and practice of This Week's Words. (You may wish to assign **LEP Reteaching Follow-up Master 29** for reteaching of spelling words.)

A. Discovering Spelling Ideas

1. Say the following words as you write them on the chalkboard.

   pear   pair   we've   weave

2. Ask the children to tell how the words in each pair are alike. (The words sound alike.)
3. Ask the children to define each pair of words. (*Pear* is a fruit and *pair* means "two of something;" *we've* is a contraction of *we have* and *weave* means "to make something by winding in and out.")
4. Ask the children what else besides their meanings makes the words in each pair of words different. (They are spelled differently.)
5. Tell the children that words that sound alike but are not spelled alike and do not have the same meaning are called **homophones.** Ask the children why it is important to know the meanings of homophone pairs. (So that they can write the word that makes sense in a sentence.)

B. Word Shapes

1. Explain to the children that each word has a shape and that remembering the shape of a word can help them spell the word correctly.
2. On the chalkboard, write the words *pail* and *pale*. Have the children identify "short," "tall," and "tail" letters.
3. Draw the configuration of each word on the chalkboard and ask the children which word fits in each shape.

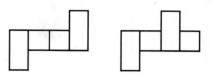

Use **Reteaching Follow-up Master 29A** to reinforce spelling generalizations taught in Unit 29.

	UNIT 29
Name	
Reteaching Follow-up A	Discovering Spelling Ideas

THIS WEEK'S WORDS

sale	beet	main	reed	son
sail	break	mane	meet	whose
beat	brake	read	rode	won

1. Study This Week's Words. Say each word to yourself.

2. For each word below, write the word that sounds the same. You will write This Week's Words. The first one has been done for you.

sale	**sail**	who's	**whose**
main	**mane**	meat	**meet**
beat	**beet**	reed	**read**
brake	**break**	road	**rode**
read	**reed**	sail	**sale**
one	**won**	beet	**beat**
break	**brake**	sun	**son**
mane	**main**		

3. Read each pair of sound-alike words. Are the words in the pair spelled the same way? _____**no**_____

Words that sound alike but are spelled differently and have different meanings are called **homophones.** How many of This Week's Words are homophones? _____**all of them**_____

5. Write four other pairs of homophones.

   POSSIBLE ANSWERS: bear, bare; heal, heel; not, knot; pain, pane

Reteaching • 49

Use **Reteaching Follow-up Master 29B** to reinforce spellings of This Week's Words for Unit 29.

	UNIT 29
Name	
Reteaching Follow-up B	Word Shapes

THIS WEEK'S WORDS

son	reed	beet	sale	main
whose	meet	break	sail	mane
won	rode	brake	beat	read

Write each of This Week's Words in its correct shape. The first one has been done for you. **Children may interchange answers that fit the same configuration.**

1. w o n
2. b e a t
3. m a n e
4. s a l e
5. w h o s e
6. m a i n
7. m e e t
8. r o d e
9. s a i l
10. r e e d
11. b r e a k
12. s o n
13. r e a d
14. b e e t
15. b r a k e

50 • Reteaching

REVIEWING THE UNIT

nit Materials

struction and Practice

Pupil Book   pages 128–133
Teacher's Edition
  Teaching Plans   pages 128–133
  Enrichment Activities
    For the Home   page 133A

esting

Teacher's Edition
  Trial Test   pages 127E–127F
  Unit Test   page 133A
  Form A* Test 5   page T16

your grading period is six weeks, you may want to use
e **Form A Test** at the end of this unit.

dditional Resources

PRACTICE AND REINFORCEMENT
Review Master 30A: Units 25 and 26
Review Master 30B: Units 27 and 28
Review Master 30C: Unit 29 and Test
  Exercise
Dictionary and Proofreading Master 5
Study Steps to Learn a Word Master
Mastery Words Review Master: Units 25–29
Bonus Words Review Master: Units 25–29

TESTING (optional)
Mastery Words Test: Units 25–29
Bonus Words Test: Units 25–29
Writing Test 5

TEACHING AIDS
Spelling and Writing Transparency 5
Home Letter 6

Visit our Web site
http://www.hbschool.com

Click on the SPELLING banner to find activities for this unit.

Learner Objectives

Spelling

- To review plurals formed by adding *s* or by changing *y* to *i* and adding *es*.
- To review words with "silent" letters.
- To review base forms and inflected forms of nouns and verbs that end with a consonant and *y*.
- To review words that demonstrate these sound-letter relationships: /əl/*le, el;* /ər/*er, ar.*
- To review and write homophones.

Reading

- To use context clues to answer questions.
- To recognize number words and time-clue words in given sequence.
- To follow written directions.
- To use the dictionary to locate information.

Writing

- To write a how-to article.
- To use the writing process.
- To edit for content.
- To revise using editing and proofreading marks.
- To proofread for spelling, capitalization, and punctuation.
- To write legible manuscript and cursive letters.

Listening

- To listen to recognize and write words given long and short vowel sounds.
- To follow a series of oral directions.

Speaking

- To contribute ideas and information in group discussions.
- To express feelings and ideas about a piece of writing.
- To present how-to paragraphs.

REVIEW WORDS

UNIT 25
ears
eyes
marbles
butterflies
puppies
grades
wheels
buddies

UNIT 26
climb
gnat
half
knock
wrote
knew
thumb
written

UNIT 27
family
empty
hurry
library
study
party
cry
copy

UNIT 28
either
nickel
letter
people
sugar
summer
table
purple

UNIT 29
break
read
rode
sale
whose
won
meet
son

Assignment Guide

This guide shows how you teach a typical spelling unit in either a five-day or a three-day sequence, while providing for individual differences. **Boldface type** indicates essential classwork. Steps shown in light type may be done in class or assigned as homework.

Five Days	○ = average spellers ☆ = better spellers ✓ = slower spellers	Three Days
Day **1**	**a** ○ ☆ ✓ **Take Review Word Trial Test and correct**	
Day **2**	○ ☆ ✓ Complete Spelling Review pages 128, 129, 130 ○ ☆ ✓ Complete Review Master 30A, 30B, 30C (optional) ✓ Complete Mastery Words Review Master: Units 25–29 (optional) ☆ Complete Bonus Words Review Master: Units 25–29 (optional) **b**	Day **1**
Day **3**	**c** ○ ☆ ✓ **Complete Spelling and Reading page 131**	
Day **4**	○ ☆ ✓ Complete Spelling and Writing pages 132–133 ○ ☆ ✓ Complete Dictionary and Proofreading Master 5 (optional) **d**	Day **2**
Day **5**	**e** ○ ☆ ✓ **Take Review Word Unit Test** ✓ Take Mastery Words Test: Units 25–29 (optional) ☆ Take Bonus Words Test: Units 25–29 (optional)	Day **3**

Enrichment Activities for the **home** included at the end of this unit may be assigned selectively on any day of the week.

INTRODUCING THE UNIT

Establish Readiness for Learning

Tell the children they will review words from the previous five units. In Unit 30 they will review:

- plural nouns
- words with silent letters
- words that end in *y*
- the sounds /əl/ and /ər/
- homophones

Tell the children that they will use some of the review words to write a how-to article.

Assess Children's Spelling Ability

Administer the Trial Test before the children study the review words. Use the test sentences provided. Say each word and use it in a sentence. Then repeat the word. Have the children write the words on a separate sheet of paper or in their spelling notebooks.

Have the children check their own work by listening to you read the spelling of the words or by referring to the review words lists in the side boxes of the **Pupil Book.** For each mis-spelled word, have the children follow the **Study Steps to Learn a Word** on page 128 in the **Pupil Book,** or use the copying master to study and write the words. Children should

record the number correct on their **Progress Report.**

Trial Test Sentences

1. *ears*   My dog has long, floppy *ears.* **ears**
2. *eyes*   My mother's *eyes* are blue. **eye**
3. *marbles*   Mr. Chan collects *marbles.* **marbles**
4. *butterflies*   The *butterflies* are fluttering above the meadow. **butterflies**
5. *puppies*   Our dog had three *puppies.* **puppies**
6. *grades*   I got better *grades* in school this year. **grades**
7. *wheels*   Betty needs new *wheels* for her bike. **wheels**
8. *buddies*   Peter likes to play with his *buddies.* **buddies**
9. *climb*   It is dangerous to *climb* trees. **climb**
10. *gnat*   The *gnat* is a type of fly. **gnat**
11. *half*   I'll share *half* of my apple with you. **half**
12. *knock*   Bill will *knock* at the door before he enters. **knock**
13. *wrote*   Tim *wrote* a letter to his cousin. **wrote**

FOCUS

- Establishes objectives
- Relates to prior learning
- Sets purpose of instruction

14. *knew*   Twana *knew* she would do well on the test.   **knew**
15. *thumb*   The *thumb* is a useful finger.   **thumb**
16. *written*   The words are *written* in large letters.   **written**
17. *family*   There are five people in my family.   **family**
18. *empty*   Our classroom is *empty* at four o'clock.   **empty**
19. *hurry*   If we *hurry*, we will arrive on time.   **hurry**
20. *library*   The school *library* is down the hall.   **library**
21. *study*   Sam must *study* for the test.   **study**
22. *party*   My birthday *party* is on Saturday.   **party**
23. *cry*   The baby started to *cry*.   **cry**
24. *copy*   When you have finished, *copy* your story on a clean piece of paper.   **copy**
25. *either*   We can have *either* fish or chicken for dinner.   **either**
26. *nickel*   Bradley found a *nickel* on the sidewalk.   **nickel**
27. *letter*   Sally received a *letter* from her friend.   **letter**
28. *people*   I know the *people* who live in that house.   **people**
29. *sugar*   Lily measured the *sugar*.   **sugar**
30. *summer*   The weather is warm in the summer.   **summer**
31. *table*   Six people can sit at this *table*.   **table**
32. *purple*   I like to wear my *purple* sweater.   **purple**
33. *break*   The dish will *break* if you drop it.   **break**
34. *read*   I decided to *read* a book about the planets.   **read**
35. *rode*   We *rode* down the street.   **rode**
36. *sale*   Oranges are on *sale* at the supermarket.   **sale**

37. *whose*   I know *whose* coat this is.   **whose**
38. *won*   Our team *won* the soccer game.   **won**
39. *meet*   We will *meet* our new teacher today.   **meet**
40. *son*   The Riveras are proud of their *son*.   **son**

Apply Prior Learning

Have the children apply what they know about the generalizations for Units 25–29. Use the following activity.

Write words on the chalkboard in two columns. In the column on the left, write the following words: *fiddle, knot, penny, pony, lamb, dollar, party, daisy.* In the column on the right, write the plural forms opposite *fiddle* (fiddles) and *knot* (knots). Have the children identify a common element for the words on the right. (They are the plural forms and end with *s.*) Have them tell you how the plural forms were made. (by adding *s* to each word on the left) Ask the children to give the plural forms of the rest of the words on the left.

Ask them to tell in which words the plural was formed in a different way from the first two words. (pony, daisy, penny, party) Then ask what these words have in common. (They all end with *y.*) Have them explain how the spelling changes when these words are made plural. (Change the *y* to *i* and add *es.*) Have the children divide the remaining words into two groups according to a common element. (words with the /ə/ sound in the second syllable: *fiddle, dollar;* words with "silent" letters: *lamb, knot*) Ask the children to explain the spelling generalizations for each group and to give more words like those listed.

Write these sentences on the chalkboard: The lion had a huge _____ (main, mane). Did you _____ (break, brake) the balloon? I forgot to _____ (reed, read) today's lesson. We set _____ (sail, sale) in a little boat. Ask the children what the words in parentheses have in common. (They sound the same but are spelled differently.) Have them fill in the blanks with the right word. Tell the children that they will review words that follow these generalizations and then use the words to write a how-to article.

FOCUS
- Relates to prior learning
- Draws relationships
- Applies spelling generalizations to new contexts

TEACHING PLAN

Objectives To write the plurals of words; to write words with "silent" letters.

1. Review the directions to the exercises on page 128. Remind the children that the answers are to be found only among the sixteen review words on page 128.

2. Have the children complete the exercises independently. You may refer them to the **Writer's Guide** at the back of the **Pupil Book** for a review of the spelling generalizations for Units 25 and 26.

Review

Do these steps if you are not sure how to spell a word.
- **Say** the word. Listen to each sound. Think about what the word means.
- **Look** at the word. See how the letters are made. Try to see the word in your mind.
- **Spell** the word to yourself. Think about the way each sound is spelled.
- **Write** the word. Copy it from your book. Check the way you made your letters. Write the word again.
- **Check** your learning. Cover the word and write it. Did you spell it correctly? If not, do these steps until you know how to spell the word.

UNIT 25

ears
eyes
marbles
butterflies
puppies
grades
wheels
buddies

UNIT 26

climb
gnat
half
knock
wrote
knew
thumb
written

UNIT 25 Follow the directions. Use words from Unit 25. Write the plurals of these words.

1. puppy ___puppies___   2. marble ___marbles___

3. eye ___eyes___   4. butterfly ___butterflies___

5. buddy ___buddies___   6. wheel ___wheels___

7. ear ___ears___   8. grade ___grades___

UNIT 26 Follow the directions. Use words from Unit 26. Write the words for these pronunciations.

9. /rōt/ ___wrote___   10. /nok/ ___knock___

11. /klīm/ ___climb___   12. /haf/ ___half___

13. /nat/ ___gnat___   14. /thum/ ___thumb___

15. /n(y)oo/ ___knew___   16. /rit'(ə)n/ ___written___

 SPELLING DICTIONARY If you need help, use the pronunciation key on page 162.

128

Review: Units 25 and 26

Name
Review A: Units 25–26

UNIT
30

A. **UNIT 25** Circle the word in each sentence that should be plural. Write the word from Unit 25 on the line.

1. I played all day with two of my best (buddy.)
   buddies

2. First we played with red glass (marble)
   marbles

3. Next, we fixed both (wheel) on my bike.
   wheels

4. Then we watched (butterfly) in the flower garden.
   butterflies

5. Finally, we visited the (four puppy) born yesterday.
   puppies

6. Their (eye) were still closed. ___eyes___

7. Their (ear) are so big and soft. ___ears___

8. I wish my teacher gave (grade) for playing all day.
   grades

B. **UNIT 26** Unscramble each group of letters to make a word from Unit 26. Then circle the silent letter in the word.

9. eortw (wrote)   10. cknok (knock)
11. tentirw (written)   12. tang (gnat)
13. mhtub thum(b)   14. afhl ha(l)f
15. licmb clim(b)   16. wnek (k)new

UNIT 25

ears
eyes
marbles
butterflies
puppies
grades
wheels
buddies

UNIT 26

climb
gnat
half
knock
wrote
knew
thumb
written

Extra Practice • 125

Review: Units 27 and 28

Name
Review B: Units 27–28

UNIT
30

A. **UNIT 27** Solve the word math problems. Use words from Unit 27.

1. families – es = ___family___
2. hurried – ed = ___hurry___
3. libraries – es = ___library___
4. parties – es = ___party___
5. studied – ed = ___study___
6. copied – ed = ___copy___
7. cries – es = ___cry___
8. emptied – ed = ___empty___

B. **UNIT 28** In the paragraph, circle the words that end with /əl/. Underline the words that end with /ər/. Write the words in the correct column below the paragraph.

Bree couldn't wait for summer to come. She planned to set up a lemonade stand again this year. She had a pretty (purple) tablecloth for the (table). She had a great recipe that used no sugar. Even the letter she would post beside the stand was written. It would let (people) know that each (nickel) she earned would go for either a new bike or school clothes.

Words that end with /əl/   Words that end with /ər/
___purple___   ___summer___
___table___   ___sugar___
___people___   ___letter___
___nickel___   ___either___

UNIT 27

family
empty
hurry
library
study
party
cry
copy

UNIT 28

either
nickel
letter
people
sugar
summer
table
purple

126 • Extra Practice

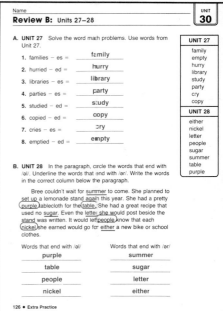
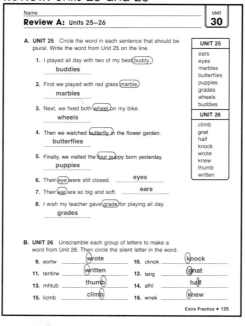

UNIT 27 Follow the directions. Use words from Unit 27. Write the singular of each word.

17. families ___family___   18. parties ___party___

19. libraries ___library___   20. copies ___copy___

Write each word without ___ed___. Remember to change a letter.

21. studied ___study___   22. cried ___cry___

23. emptied ___empty___   24. hurried ___hurry___

Finish each sentence by adding ___ing___ to a Unit 27 word.

25. No one heard the baby ___crying___ this morning.

26. Dad was ___hurrying___ to get breakfast ready.

27. Ryan was ___copying___ his story in his room.

UNIT 27
family
empty
hurry
library
study
party
cry
copy

UNIT 28 Follow the directions. Use words from Unit 28.

28. Write the four words that end with /ər/.
Word order may vary.

___either___   ___letter___

___sugar___   ___summer___

29. Write the four words that end with /əl/.
Word order may vary.

___nickel___   ___people___

___table___   ___purple___

30. Write the two words that have /ē/. Word order may vary.

___either___   ___people___

Write the word that goes with each meaning.

31. a color ___purple___   32. a five-cent coin ___nickel___

33. a season ___summer___   34. one or the other ___either___

UNIT 28
either
nickel
letter
people
sugar
summer
table
purple

129

TEACHING PLAN

Objectives To write words that end with /ər/, /əl/, and /ē/; to spell inflected nouns and verbs that end with a consonant and *y*.

1. Review the directions to the exercises on page 129. Remind the children that the answers to the exercises are to be found only among the sixteen review words on page 129.

2. Have the children complete the exercises independently. You may refer them to the **Writer's Guide** at the back of the **Pupil Book** for a review of the spelling generalizations for Units 27 and 28.

⭔ EXTENDING THE LESSON

Have the children write a descriptive paragraph using review words. Some topics might be:

A Family Picnic
A Day in School

Remind the children to use a topic sentence to present the main idea and detail sentences to tell more about the topic. Tell them to use as many review words as they can. Remind the children to proofread the paragraphs for spelling.

Review: Unit 29

Name _____

Review C: Unit 29 • Test Exercise   **UNIT 30**

A. UNIT 29 Answer the questions with words from Unit 29.

1. When a store lowers its prices, what is it having? A ___sale___

2. What happens when you get to know somebody for the first time? You ___meet___ him or her.

3. What did you do if you didn't lose? You ___won___

4. What do parents call the boy in the family? ___son___

5. What word asks who owns something? ___whose___

6. What have you done if you've sat in something while it moved? ___rode___

7. What happens when you drop a glass? You ___break___ it.

8. What do you do with a book? You ___read___ it.

UNIT 29
break
read
rode
sale
whose
won
meet
son

B. UNITS 25 — 29 Fill in the circle below the word that is spelled wrong.

1	ears (a)	eys ●	whose (c)	6	climb (a)	hal: (b)	nat ●
2	party (a)	hury ●	empty (c)	7	leter ●	people (b)	sugar (c)
3	grades (a)	marbles (b)	wheles ●	8	library (a)	fam:y ●	copy (c)
4	rede ●	buddies (b)	knock (c)	9	purpel ●	table (b)	nickel (c)
5	wrote (a)	knew (b)	writen ●	10	break (a)	roed ●	won (c)

Extra Practice • 127

30b Spelling Review

TEACHING PLAN

Objective To write homophones

1. Review the directions to the exercises on page 130. Remind the children that the answers to the exercises are to be found only among the review words on page 130.
2. Have the children complete the exercises independently. You may refer them to the **Writer's Guide** at the back of the **Pupil Book** for a review of the spelling generalization for Unit 29.
3. Review the children's answers on pages 128-130 orally, or have volunteers write them on the chalkboard.

For reinforcement in writing review words for Units 25-29, you may wish to assign **Review Masters 30A, 30B,** and **30C.**

WORDS IN TIME

Have a volunteer read **Words in Time** aloud. Point out to the students that writing and reading are ways of *communicating*. People have many ways of communicating, or sharing ideas with one another.

As a COOPERATIVE LEARNING activity, have a group of children think of as many words as they can to describe ways to communicate. (speak, listen, write, read) Have the group plan a large picture or mural that will illustrate these different modes. Each child should choose a word and draw pictures of people engaging in that form of communication to add to the mural. Each child should label his or her picture and paste or tape it to the group's mural. Have the children proofread the labels for spelling, and check the pictures for clarity of meaning.

UNIT 29

break
read
rode
sale
whose
won
meet
son

UNIT 29 Follow the directions. Use words from Unit 29. Write the homophone for each of these words.

35. sail _____ sale   **36.** who's _____ whose

37. road _____ rode   **38.** brake _____ break

39. one _____ won   **40.** sun _____ son

Write the words that have these vowel sounds.

41. Write the two words that have /ā/.   Word order may vary

_____ break   _____ sale

42. Write the two words that have /ē/.   Word order may vary

_____ read   _____ meet

43. Write the word that has /ō/.   _____ rode

44. Write the word that has /o͞o/.   _____ whose

45. Write the two words that have /u/.   Word order may vary

_____ won   _____ son

WORDS IN TIME

The word <u>read</u> comes from the old word <u>raeden</u>. <u>Raeden</u> meant "to guess" or "to find the meaning of." Long ago, people did not know why things in nature happened. They thought that when there was a rainbow or a falling star, nature was telling them something. They asked special people to <u>raeden</u>, or guess the meaning of, such events. Since most people did not know how to read then, they would also ask special people to <u>raeden</u>, or find the meaning of, words.

130

Spelling and Reading
A How-to Article

Read the following how-to article. Look for the way the steps are in order.

A good way to make money during the <u>summer</u> is to sell orange juice from a stand. You can do this alone, or you can ask your <u>buddies</u> to help you.

The first step in opening a juice stand is to gather the materials. You will need a <u>table</u>, paper cups, a money box, orange juice, a pitcher, and ice. You will also need heavy paper, crayons, and tacks for your sign.

The second step is to make the sign for your stand. Use brightly colored crayons, such as orange and <u>purple</u>, to catch the <u>eyes</u> of <u>people</u> walking by. Make the <u>letters</u> of your sign large.

Next set up your stand. Place the <u>table</u> on level ground. Put your cups and money box on it. Then tack the sign you have <u>written</u> on or near the stand.

The last step is to get the juice ready. Pour juice into a pitcher and add ice. Now you're ready to sell orange juice from your own stand.

Write the answers to the questions.   **See answers below.**

1. In this how-to article, who does the writer say you can ask to help you set up an orange juice stand? *Literal*
2. What materials do you need to set up an orange juice stand? *Literal*
3. Why should you make the letters of your sign large? *Interpretative*
4. Why is summer a good time to sell orange juice? *Critical*

Underline the review words in your answers. Check to see that you spelled the words correctly.

131

TEACHING PLAN

Objectives   To analyze and respond to a how-to article; to identify details about a how-to article; to proofread written answers for spelling.

1. Tell the children that they will read a how-to article that includes a number of spelling words from Units 25–29. Point out that a how-to article gives directions for making or doing something, tells in order the steps to complete it, and gives the materials needed. A how-to article uses time-clue words to help the reader follow the steps. Explain that the how-to article will serve as a model for their own writing.
2. Have the children read the how-to article to learn a good way to make money during the summer. Tell them to notice the way the steps are in order.
3. Have the children answer the questions independently. Tell them to underline the review words in their answers and to proofread their answers for spelling.
4. Spot-check the children's answers as they work. Review answers orally.

Spelling and Reading **Answers**

1. You can ask your <u>buddies</u>. 2. You need a <u>table</u>, paper cups, a money box, orange juice, a pitcher, ice, heavy paper, crayons, and tacks. 3. <u>People</u> can <u>read</u> large <u>letters</u> easily. 4. <u>People</u> are likely to be hot and thirsty.

On this page students will read:
- This Week's Words from the preceding five units;
- words reviewed in this unit;
- words that follow the generalizations taught in the preceding five units.

TEACHING PLAN

Objectives To recognize the purpose of a how-to article; to identify the details of a how-to article; to evaluate the form of a how-to article.

1. Have the children read the first paragraph of **Think and Discuss** on page 132. Ask the children to recall a how-to article that they might have read and then give examples of the type of information it contained. Ask the children if the how-to article on page 131 is a good example of a how-to article.

2. Have the children read the next paragraph of **Think and Discuss** and answer the questions. Then have them study the illustration at the top of page 132. Ask the children to describe the scene pictured and to explain what the scene represents. (The scene indicates that the children have followed all the steps and are now ready to sell orange juice.)

3. Have the children read the rest of **Think and Discuss** independently and answer the questions. Ask the children to think of any other time-clue words the writer might have used.

4. Have the children read **Apply** at the bottom of page 132. Tell them that they will write a how-to article using some of their spelling words. Discuss with them the importance of writing the steps of a how-to article in the correct order and including all the materials needed.

Spelling and Writing
A How-to Article

Words to Help You Write

eyes
ears
marbles
butterflies
puppies
ghost
half
thumb
empty
buddies
either
people
table
purple
read

Think and Discuss

A how-to article gives directions for making or doing something. What does the article on page 131 tell you how to do?

A how-to article lists the materials and steps needed to do the task. It tells the order in which the steps have to be done. What is the first step in opening an orange juice stand? What materials are needed to do the second step?

A how-to article uses time-clue words, such as <u>first</u>, <u>then</u>, and <u>next</u>. What time-clue words can you find in the how-to article? Why do you think time-clue words are helpful in a how-to article?

Apply

Now it's time for you to write a **how-to article** for a younger friend. Follow the writing guidelines on the next page.

132

Summarize Learning

Have the children identify the purpose of a how-to article (give directions for making or doing something), what the article lists (materials and steps in order), and the types of words used to indicate order (time-clue words: first, then, next, last).

Think and Discuss **Answers**

A. It tells you how to set up an orange juice stand. B. First you gather the materials. C. You'll need heavy paper, crayons, and tacks. D. first, second, next, last E. They help the reader follow the steps in the correct order.

Prewriting

- Think of something you know how to make or do. Choose something that has only a few steps.
- Make a list of the things needed.
- Make a list of steps to follow.

 THESAURUS For help finding more words to tell about the steps, turn to page 203.

Composing

Use your lists to write the first draft of your how-to article.

- Write a sentence that tells what your article will be about.
- Tell what materials are needed.
- Write simple detail sentences to explain each step.
- Use time-clue words to make the order of the steps clear.

Revising

Read your article and show it to a classmate. Follow these guidelines to improve your work. Use the editing and proofreading marks to show changes.

 WRITER'S GUIDE For help revising your article, use the checklist on page 247.

Editing

- Make sure your first sentence tells what your article is about.
- Make sure you listed all the materials needed.
- Make sure the steps are in the correct order.
- Check to be sure you used time-clue words.

Proofreading

- Check your spelling and correct any mistakes.
- Check your capitalization and punctuation.

Copy your article onto clean paper. Write carefully and neatly.

Publishing

Show your article to your younger friend. Ask if he or she would like to make or do the thing you tell about.

133

Editing and Proofreading Marks

≡	capitalize
⊙	make a period
∧	add something
⋏	add a comma
﹏	take something away
◯	spell correctly
¶	indent the paragraph
/	make a lowercase letter
∼tr	transpose

Extra Practice: Dictionary/Proofreading

Name _____

Dictionary and Proofreading   UNIT **30**

Using the Dictionary to Spell and Write

A. Find the accent mark in each pronunciation. Write 1 or 2 to show which syllable the mark follows. Then write the word. You may wish to use your **Spelling Dictionary** to help you.

table
nickel
marbles
written
people
letter
hurry
study
son
empty
rode
grades
won
wheels
buddies
summer
break
knew
half
wrote

1. /mär'bəlz/ __1__ _marbles_
2. /tā'bəl/ __1__ _table_
3. /stud'ē/ __1__ _study_
4. /rit'ən/ __1__ _written_
5. /nik'əl/ __1__ _nickel_
6. /pē'pəl/ __1__ _people_
7. /let'ər/ __1__ _letter_
8. /hûr'ē/ __1__ _hurry_

Proofreading

B. Circle the misspelled words in the story. Draw three lines under letters that should be capitalized. Then spell the words correctly.

Last sumer we roed our bikes in a race down an emty road. Kids knue from all graeds were there. Half of my budies had bikes with red weels and half with blue. we all tried to brake the record, but we were too slow. Alvin one the race. he is the sun of a woman who rote a book about bikes.

9. _summer_   10. _rode_   11. _empty_
12. _knew_   13. _grades_   14. _half_
15. _buddies_   16. _wheels_   17. _break_
18. _won_   19. _son_   20. _wrote_

128 • Extra Practice

TEACHING PLAN

Objectives To write a how-to article; to edit for content; to proofread for spelling, capitalization, and punctuation.

1. **Prewriting** Have the children list some things that they know how to make or do. Tell them to choose something that does not require many steps. Have the children think about all the materials needed to complete the process, as well as all the steps involved. The children should make lists of each. Suggest that the children use their spelling lists or the **Spelling Thesaurus** on page 203 to help select words.

To help the children use more precise language in their writing, you may wish to have them use the **Writer's Word Bank**.

2. **Composing** Remind the children that the first sentence should tell what the article is about. Detail sentences should explain each step, and time-clue words will help to make the order of the steps clear. Have the children write their first drafts.

3. **Revising (Editing and Proofreading)** Have each child ask a classmate to read the how-to article. Have the reader check to see if the article includes all the materials needed as well as all the steps. Have the children consider their classmates' comments as they revise their work. Tell them to follow the guidelines on page 133. Remind them to use their **Spelling Dictionary** to check their spelling. To help the children prepare a legible copy of their articles, have them consult the **Handwriting Models** in the **Writer's Guide** on page 258.

For reinforcement in editing and proofreading, you may wish to use **Spelling and Writing Transparency 5.**

4. **Publishing** Have the children share their articles with a younger friend.

For additional practice in using a dictionary to spell and write and in proofreading, you may wish to assign **Dictionary and Proofreading Practice Master 5.**

ENRICHMENT ACTIVITIES

For the Home

Home activities may be assigned to children of all ability levels. The activities provide opportunities for children to use their spelling words in new contexts. The children may complete these activities independently or with the assistance of a relative or friend in the home.

1. Social Studies/Writing Interview Questions for People in the News Tell the children to think of someone who is currently in the news. Have them write five questions that they would ask the person. Tell them to use as many spelling words as they can in the questions. Then have the children discuss the questions with a friend or relative.

2. Science/Writing Statements on the Five Senses Tell the children to write as many statements as they can about the five senses, using the spelling words. Have them use a science book or an encyclopedia to check their facts if necessary. After revising and proofreading, have them share and discuss their statements with a friend or relative.

3. Language Arts/Writing a Picture Description Have the children look through magazines or books for a picture of a painting, a drawing, or a sculpture. Children should think of words to describe how they feel when they look at the artwork. Have them write several sentences about the artwork, using a spelling word in each sentence. Have them show the artwork to a friend or relative.

4. Language Arts/Writing a Rhyming Poem Have the children write a rhyming poem. Tell them to look over the spelling words for ideas. They may wish to write about a ghost, a puppy, or butterflies. If necessary, refer them to page 254 of the **Writer's Guide** to read about rhyming poems. When they have finished, have them read their poems to friends or relatives.

EVALUATION

Unit Test

1. *ears* My dog's *ears* are black. **ears**
2. *eyes* At the top of the roller coaster, I closed my eyes. **eyes**
3. *marbles* Sam and Polly play *marbles* in the schoolyard. **marbles**
4. *butterflies* Two orange and black *butterflies* perched like flowers on a bush. **butterflies**
5. *puppies* The three *puppies* wrestled playfully with each other. **puppies**
6. *grades* Children in all four *grades* attended the school assembly. **grades**
7. *wheels* My mother took the training *wheels* off the bike. **wheels**
8. *buddies* Joey and Tim have been close *buddies* since kindergarten. **buddies**
9. *climb* Marie had to *climb* the hill. **climb**
10. *gnat* Mimi did a science report on the *gnat.* **gnat**
11. *half* I gave *half* of my sandwich to Kira. **half**
12. *knock* We thought we heard a *knock.* **knock**
13. *wrote* The class *wrote* a letter to the mayor. **wrote**
14. *knew* Alfredo *knew* all the answers to the quiz. **knew**
15. *thumb* Without a *thumb,* we would have a hard time holding things. **thumb**
16. *written* Judy has *written* an exciting story for the school magazine. **written**
17. *family* The Rodriguez *family* lives there. **family**
18. *empty* The custodian took away all the *empty* boxes. **empty**
19. *hurry* If we *hurry,* we can still get to the movie on time. **hurry**
20. *library* Today's *library* has records and videotapes as well as books for you to borrow. **library**
21. *study* Sometimes I *study* in the kitchen. **study**
22. *party* For my birthday this year we had a bowling *party.* **party**
23. *cry* We heard the *cry* of a sea bird. **cry**
24. *copy* I tried to *copy* this picture, but it didn't turn out well. **copy**
25. *either* We can *either* go out for pizza or eat at home. **either**
26. *nickel* I have two dimes, and I need a *nickel* to make a quarter. **nickel**
27. *letter* The mailman brought Joan a *letter* from her friend in Japan. **letter**
28. *people* Many *people* came to the opening of the new restaurant. **people**
29. *sugar* The recipe for these cookies calls for one cup of *sugar.* **sugar**
30. *summer* None of my *summer* clothes from last year fit. **summer**
31. *table* We set the *table* with pretty paper plates. **table**
32. *purple* At sunset the sky turned pink, orange, and *purple.* **purple**
33. *break* If you *break* something in a store, you have to pay for it. **break**
34. *read* I like to *read* adventure stories. **read**
35. *rode* At the zoo we *rode* on a camel. **rode**
36. *sale* The toy store is having a big *sale* on swing sets. **sale**
37. *whose* We don't know *whose* sneakers these are. **whose**
38. *won* Our basketball team *won* the league championship this year. **won**
39. *meet* We will *meet* you on the corner after school. **meet**
40. *son* Jason said he would like to have a *son* someday. **son**

Mastery and Bonus Words Review and Assessment

For additional practice you may wish to assign **Mastery Words Review Master: Units 25–29** or **Bonus Words Review Master: Units 25–29.** To assess students' spelling ability with these words, use **Mastery Words Test: Units 25–29** or **Bonus Words Test: Units 25–29.**

Mastery Words Review

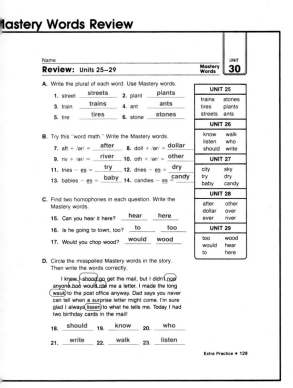

Name _____
Review: Units 25–29 — Mastery Words — UNIT **30**

A. Write the plural of each word. Use Mastery words.

1. street ___streets___ 2. plant ___plants___
3. train ___trains___ 4. ant ___ants___
5. tire ___tires___ 6. stone ___stones___

UNIT 25
trains stones
tires plants
streets ants

B. Try this "word math." Write the Mastery words.

7. aft + /ər/ = ___after___ 8. doll + /ər/ = ___dollar___
9. riv + /ər/ = ___river___ 10. oth + /ər/ = ___other___
11. tries − es = ___try___ 12. dries − es = ___dry___
13. babies − es = ___baby___ 14. candies − es = ___candy___

UNIT 26
know walk
listen who
should write

UNIT 27
city sky
try dry
baby candy

C. Find two homophones in each question. Write the Mastery words.

15. Can you hear it here? ___hear___ ___here___
16. Is he going to town, too? ___to___ ___too___
17. Would you chop wood? ___would___ ___wood___

UNIT 28
after other
dollar over
ever river

UNIT 29
too wood
would hear
to here

D. Circle the misspelled Mastery words in the story. Then write the words correctly.

I knew I shood go get the mail, but I didn't noe anyone hoo would rite me a letter. I made the long wauk to the post office anyway. Dad says you never can tell when a surprise letter might come. I'm sure glad I always lissen to what he tells me. Today I had two birthday cards in the mail!

18. ___should___ 19. ___know___ 20. ___who___
21. ___write___ 22. ___walk___ 23. ___listen___

Extra Practice • 129

Bonus Words Review

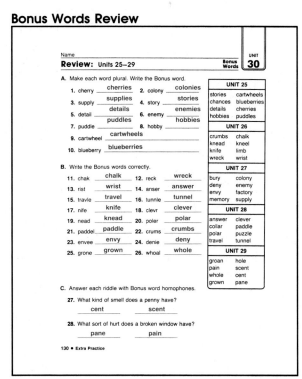

Name _____
Review: Units 25–29 — Bonus Words — UNIT **30**

A. Make each word plural. Write the Bonus word.

1. cherry ___cherries___ 2. colony ___colonies___
3. supply ___supplies___ 4. story ___stories___
5. detail ___details___ 6. enemy ___enemies___
7. puddle ___puddles___ 8. hobby ___hobbies___
9. cartwheel ___cartwheels___
10. blueberry ___blueberries___

UNIT 25
stories cartwheels
chances blueberries
details cherries
hobbies puddles

UNIT 26
crumbs chalk
knead kneel
knife limb
wreck wrist

B. Write the Bonus words correctly.

11. chak ___chalk___ 12. reck ___wreck___
13. rist ___wrist___ 14. anser ___answer___
15. travle ___travel___ 16. tunnle ___tunnel___
17. nife ___knife___ 18. clevr ___clever___
19. nead ___knead___ 20. poler ___polar___
21. paddel ___paddle___ 22. crums ___crumbs___
23. envee ___envy___ 24. denie ___deny___
25. grone ___grown___ 26. whoal ___whole___

UNIT 27
bury colony
deny enemy
envy factory
memory supply

UNIT 28
answer clever
collar paddle
polar puzzle
travel tunnel

UNIT 29
groan hole
pain scent
whole cent
grown pane

C. Answer each riddle with Bonus word homophones.

27. What kind of smell does a penny have?
___cent___ ___scent___

28. What sort of hurt does a broken window have?
___pane___ ___pain___

130 • Extra Practice

Mastery Words Test

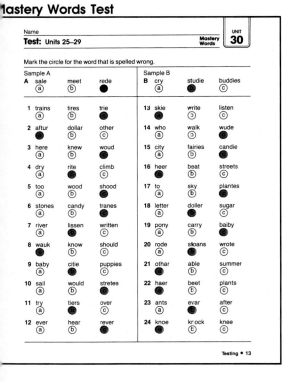

Name _____
Test: Units 25–29 — Mastery Words — UNIT **30**

Mark the circle for the word that is spelled wrong.

Sample A
A sale meet **rede**

Sample B
B cry studie buddies

1 trains tires **trie**
2 **aftur** dollar other
3 here knew **woud**
4 dry **rite** climb
5 too wood **shood**
6 stones candy **tranes**
7 river **lissen** written
8 **wauk** know should
9 baby **citie** puppies
10 sail would **stretes**
11 try **tiers** over
12 ever hear **rever**
13 **skie** write listen
14 who walk **wude**
15 city fairies **candie**
16 **heer** beat streets
17 to sky **plantes**
18 letter **doller** sugar
19 pony carry **baiby**
20 rode **sloans** wrote
21 **othar** able summer
22 **haer** beet plants
23 ants **evar** after
24 **knoe** kr ock knee

Testing • 13

Bonus Words Test

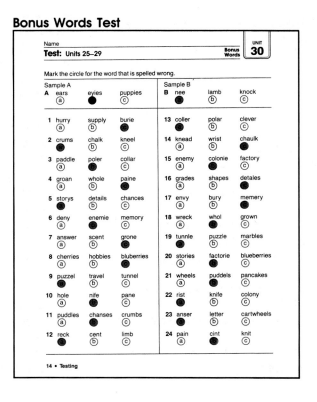

Name _____
Test: Units 25–29 — Bonus Words — UNIT **30**

Mark the circle for the word that is spelled wrong.

Sample A
A ears **eyies** puppies

Sample B
B **nee** lamb knock

1 hurry supply **burie**
2 **crums** chalk kneel
3 **paddle** poler collar
4 groan whole **paine**
5 **storys** details chances
6 deny **enemie** memory
7 answer scent **grone**
8 cherries hobbies **bluberies**
9 **puzzel** travel tunnel
10 hole **nife** pane
11 puddles **chanses** crumbs
12 **reck** cent limb
13 coller polar clever
14 knead wrist **chaulk**
15 enemy **colonie** factory
16 grades shapes **detales**
17 envy bury **memery**
18 wreck **whol** grown
19 **tunnle** puzzle marbles
20 stories **factorie** blueberries
21 wheels **puddels** pancakes
22 **rist** knife colony
23 **anser** letter cartwheels
24 pain **cint** knit

14 • Testing

NOTES

Six-Week Evaluation

Mark the circle for the word that is spelled wrong.

Sample A				Sample B		
A add ⓐ	akt ⓫	nap ⓒ		**B** step ⓐ	chop ⓑ	dropp ⓒ

1 wun ⓐ	whose ⓑ	ghost ⓒ		**11** shovel ⓐ	rode ⓑ	sael ⓒ
2 ears ⓐ	either ⓑ	eyez ⓒ		**12** knewe ⓐ	knock ⓑ	knee ⓒ
3 puppies ⓐ	people ⓑ	perple ⓒ		**13** marbles ⓐ	nickle ⓑ	knit ⓒ
4 suger ⓐ	letter ⓑ	summer ⓒ		**14** whoose ⓐ	party ⓑ	eyes ⓒ
5 haf ⓐ	calf ⓑ	lamb ⓒ		**15** studdy ⓐ	son ⓑ	lady ⓒ
6 climb ⓐ	thum ⓑ	written ⓒ		**16** beet ⓐ	main ⓑ	meit ⓒ
7 butterflys ⓐ	buddies ⓑ	guppies ⓒ		**17** pupies ⓐ	grades ⓑ	study ⓒ
8 table ⓐ	wheels ⓑ	marbuls ⓒ		**18** copy ⓐ	rode ⓑ	gohst ⓒ
9 library ⓐ	embty ⓑ	hurry ⓒ		**19** company ⓐ	famly ⓑ	empty ⓒ
10 letter ⓐ	eether ⓑ	eagle ⓒ		**20** main ⓐ	calf ⓑ	cri ⓒ

FORM A TEST 5

Administering the Test

1. Tell the children that today they will take a spelling test on some of the words they have studied in Units 25–29. Pass out the test papers. Tell the children to leave them turned upside down until you are ready to begin.

2. Have the children turn their tests over. Direct their attention to Sample A. Have the children look for the incorrect spelling. Ask the child to tell you the word that is spelled incorrectly. Point out that circle *b* under the misspelling *a-k-t* is filled in.

3. Now direct the children's attention to Sample B. Have the children look for the incorrect spelling. Ask a child to tell you the word that is spelled incorrectly by spelling it correctly. (*d-r-o-p*) The have the children fill in circle c in pencil.

4. After you have checked to see that all children have completed Sample B correctly, have the children proceed with the test.

Evaluating the Results

Use the following **Answer Key** to correct the children's tests and to determine whether they need more practice with particular units. The chart shows the units in which each answer word is taught.

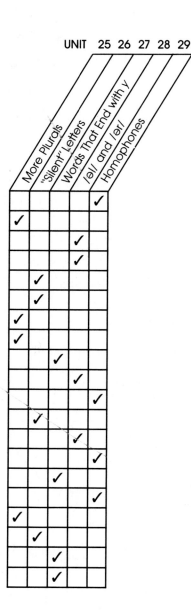

UNIT   25 26 27 28 29

ANSWER KEY

1 (a●) (b) (c)
2 (a) (b) (c●)
3 (a) (b) (c●)
4 (a●) (b) (c)
5 (a●) (b) (c)
6 (a) (b●) (c)
7 (a●) (b) (c)
8 (a) (b) (c●)
9 (a) (b●) (c)
10 (a) (b●) (c)
11 (a) (b) (c●)
12 (a●) (b) (c)
13 (a) (b●) (c)
14 (a●) (b) (c)
15 (a●) (b) (c)
16 (a) (b) (c●)
17 (a●) (b) (c)
18 (a) (b) (c●)
19 (a) (b●) (c)
20 (a) (b) (c●)

The Sounds /o͝o/ and /o͞o/

PREVIEWING THE UNIT

Unit Materials

Instruction and Practice

Pupil Book pages 134–137
Teacher's Edition
  Teaching Plans pages 134–137
  Enrichment Activities
    For the Classroom pages 137A–137B
    For the Home page 137B
  Reteaching Strategies page 137C

Testing

Teacher's Edition
  Trial Test pages 133E–133F
  Unit Test page 137B
  Dictation Test page 137B

Additional Resources

PRACTICE AND REINFORCEMENT
  Extra Practice Master 31: This Week's Words
  Extra Practice Master 31: Mastery Words
  Extra Practice Master 31: Bonus Words
  LEP Practice Master 31
  Spelling and Language Master 31
  Study Steps to Learn a Word Master

RETEACHING FOLLOW-UP
  Reteaching Follow-up Master 31A:
    Discovering Spelling Ideas
  Reteaching Follow-up Master 31B: Word
    Shapes
  LEP Reteaching Follow-up Master 31

TEACHING AIDS
  Spelling Generalizations Transparency 26

Click on the SPELLING banner to find activities for this unit.

Learner Objectives

Spelling

- To spell words that demonstrate these sound-letter relationships: /o͝o/oo; /o͞o/oo, ou, ew, o.
- To spell words by adding initial consonants to *ew* and *ook*.

Reading

- To follow written directions.
- To use the dictionary for word meaning.

Writing

- To write a poem.
- To use the writing process.
- To proofread for spelling, capitalization, and punctuation.
- To write legible manuscript and cursive letters.

Listening

- To listen to identify the letters that spell the vowel sounds /o͝o/ and /o͞o/.
- To listen to identify rhyming words.
- To follow oral directions.

Speaking

- To speak clearly to a group.
- To present poems and descriptive paragraphs.
- To respond to a question.
- To express feelings and ideas about a piece of writing.
- To contribute ideas and information in group discussions.

THIS WEEK'S WORDS
balloon
brook
shook
stood
goodness
choose
noon
raccoon
roof
tooth
group
soup
flew
grew
lose

MASTERY WORDS
took
room
soon
wool
new
school

BONUS WORDS
chew
crooked
lookout
shampoo
smooth
stew
tourist
wooden

Assignment Guide

This guide shows how you teach a typical spelling unit in either a five-day or a three-day sequence, while providing for individual differences. **Boldface type** indicates essential classwork. Steps shown in light type may be done in class or assigned as homework.

Five Days	● = average spellers ★ = better spellers ✓ = slower spellers	Three Days
Day **1** (a)	● ★ **Take This Week's Words Trial Test and correct** ● ✓ **Take Mastery Word Trial Test and correct** ● ★ **Read This Week's Words and discuss generalization on page 134**	Day **1**
Day **2** (b)	● Complete Spelling Practice page 135 ● ✓ Complete Extra Practice Master 31: This Week's Words (optional) ✓ Complete Spelling on Your Own: Mastery Words page 137 ★ **Take Bonus Word Trial Test and correct**	
Day **3** (c)	● ★ ✓ **Complete Spelling and Language page 136** ● ★ ✓ Complete Writing on Your Own page 136 ● ★ ✓ **Complete Proofreading page 136** ● ✓ Take Midweek Test (optional) ★ Complete Spelling on Your Own: Bonus Words page 137 ● ✓ Complete Spelling and Language Master 31 (optional)	Day **2**
Day **4** (d)	● Complete Spelling on Your Own: This Week's Words page 137 ✓ Complete Extra Practice Master 31: Mastery Words (optional) ★ Complete Extra Practice Master 31: Bonus Words (optional)	
Day **5** (e)	● **Take Unit Test on This Week's Words** ● Complete Reteaching Follow-up Masters 31A and 31B (optional) ● ✓ **Take Unit Test on Mastery Words** ★ **Take Unit Test on Bonus Words**	Day **3**

Enrichment Activities for the **classroom** and for the **home** included at the end of this unit may be assigned selectively on any day of the week.

INTRODUCING THE UNIT

Establish Readiness for Learning

Tell the children that this week they will continue to learn about vowel sounds. In Unit 31 they will study several spellings for the vowel sounds /o͞o/ and /o͝o/. Tell the children that they will apply the spelling generalizations to This Week's Words and use those words to write a poem.

Assess Children's Spelling Ability

Administer the Trial Test before the children study This Week's Words. Use the test sentences provided. Say each word and use it in a sentence. Then repeat the word. Have the children write the words on a separate sheet of paper or in their spelling notebooks. Test sentences are also provided for Mastery and Bonus words.

Have the children check their own work by listening to you read the spelling of the words or by referring to This Week's Words in the left column of the **Pupil Book.** For each misspelled word, have the children follow the **Study Steps to Learn a Word** on page 1 in the **Pupil Book** or use the copying master to study and write the words. Children should record the number correct on their **Progress Report.**

Trial Test Sentences

This Week's Words

1. *balloon* Mavis has a red *balloon*. **balloon**
2. *brook* We waded in the little *brook*. **brook**
3. *shook* The wind *shook* the leaves off the tree. **shook**
4. *stood* The lost dog *stood* on the sidewalk looking sad. **stood**
5. *goodness* Everyone helped the homeless people out of the *goodness* of their hearts. **goodness**

6. **choose** Let's *choose* up sides for the game. **choose**

7. **noon** At *noon* we will have lunch. **noon**

8. **raccoon** Walter saw a *raccoon* in the woods. **raccoon**

9. **roof** The *roof* needs to be fixed. **roof**

10. **tooth** Sammy's *tooth* needs to be filled. **tooth**

11. **group** A *group* of children gathered around the clown. **group**

12. **soup** That pea *soup* is delicious! **soup**

13. **flew** The geese *flew* south for the winter. **flew**

14. **grew** Alexander *grew* radishes in his garden. **grew**

15. **lose** Bertram did not *lose* his jacket. **lose**

Mastery Words

1. **took** Natalie *took* the dog for a walk. **took**

2. **room** Please clean your *room*. **room**

3. **soon** It will *soon* be time for recess. **soon**

4. **wool** That sweater is made of *wool*. **wool**

5. **new** Annette is reading her *new* book. **new**

6. **school** Alice and Roberto walk to *school* together. **school**

Bonus Words

1. **chew** You should always *chew* your food well. **chew**

2. **crooked** Reynold drew a *crooked* line on his paper. **crooked**

3. **lookout** The guard stood at the *lookout* post. **lookout**

4. **shampoo** Mom bought *shampoo* at the drugstore. **shampoo**

5. **smooth** A marble is *smooth* and round. **smooth**

6. **stew** Felicia likes beef *stew*. **stew**

7. **tourist** We gave the *tourist* directions to the museum. **tourist**

8. **wooden** Perry mixed the batter with a *wooden* spoon. **wooden**

Apply Prior Learning

Have the children apply what they already know about the vowel sounds /ŏŏ/ and /ōō/ by participating in the following activity.

Write the words *wood, took,* and *book* on the chalkboard and read them aloud with the children. Ask the children to tell what is alike in all these words. Help them to recognize that in each word, /ŏŏ/ is represented by the letters oo. Then write the words *soon, stew, prove,* and *soup* on the chalkboard. Ask the children to tell what is alike in all these words. Help them to recognize that /ōō/ is represented by the letters oo, ou, o, and ew. Tell the children that in Unit 31 they will study words that have these vowel spellings. Explain that they can use these words in a variety of writing tasks; they can use the words in a note to a friend, in a letter, or in a story.

FOCUS

- Relates to prior learning
- Draws relationships
- Applies spelling generalizations to new contexts

FOR CHILDREN WITH SPECIAL NEEDS

Learning Difficulties

For children with learning disabilities, recalling two different spellings for the same sound can be confusing. Making a mental picture of the words helps to reinforce the visual image of the words.

Read This Week's Words aloud with the children. Have them name the words that contain /ōō/ as you list them on the chalkboard. Then have the children name the words that contain /ŏŏ/ as you list those words in a separate column on the chalkboard. Point out the letters that represent the vowel sound in each list of words.

Have the children first practice writing all of the words from one list. Then, on large, unlined sheets of paper, have them write the words, saying each letter name as it is written. Check the accuracy of the spelling, and have the children correct any errors. Before writing the words

a third time, have the children close their eyes, try to recall the picture of the word, say the spelling aloud, and then "copy" it from their mental image onto paper. Once again, check each child's work for accuracy and have the children correct any errors immediately. Repeat the activity with words from the second list.

Limited English Proficiency

To help limited English proficient children work with the spelling generalizations for Unit 31, you may wish to refer to the booklet "Suggestions and Activities for Limited English Proficient Students."

TEACHING PLAN

Objective To spell words that demonstrate these sound-letter relationships: /ŏŏ/ oo; /ōō/ oo, ou, ew, o.

1. Write *school books* on the chalkboard and ask a child to read the two words aloud. Help the children to recognize that both words are spelled with *oo*, but that the vowel sounds in the words are different.
2. Read the generalizations on page 134 aloud.

You may wish to introduce the lesson by using **Spelling Generalizations Transparency 26.**

3. Have volunteers read This Week's Words. It is not necessary to have the children indicate whether the vowel sound is /ŏŏ/ or /ōō/ in those words in which the vowel sound is spelled oo. This is particularly true for *roof*, which may also be pronounced /rōof/ or /rŏof/. As the last five words are read, however, you should ask the children to identify the letters that spell /ōō/.
4. Point out the letters *ness* at the end of This Week's Word *goodness*. Tell children that the letters *ness* at the end of a word often mean that an adjective, such as *kind* or *fair*, has been turned into a noun, such as *kindness* or *fairness*.

You may wish to assign **LEP Practice Master 31** for reinforcement in writing spelling words.

---

31 The Sounds /ŏŏ/ and /ōō/

THIS WEEK'S WORDS

1. *balloon*
2. *brook*
3. *shook*
4. *stood*
5. *goodness*
6. *choose*
7. *noon*
8. *raccoon*
9. *roof*
10. *tooth*
11. *group*
12. *soup*
13. *flew*
14. *grew*
15. *lose*

This Week's Words

There are two sounds that are spelled with **oo**: /ŏŏ/, heard in <u>brook</u>, and /ōō/, heard in <u>noon</u>.

The sound /ōō/ can also be spelled with these letters.

- **ou**, as in <u>group</u>
- **ew**, as in <u>flew</u>
- ☐ **o**, as in <u>lose</u>

REMEMBER THIS

A **word family** is a group of words that are related. Think of <u>balloon</u> as a member of the same word family as <u>ball</u>.

134

Extra Practice: This Week's Words

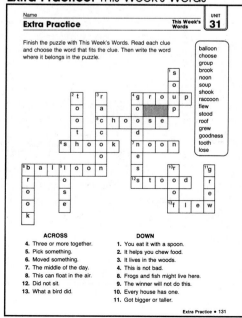

Name
Extra Practice   This Week's Words   UNIT **31**

Finish the puzzle with This Week's Words. Read each clue and choose the word that fits the clue. Then write the word where it belongs in the puzzle.

balloon
choose
group
brook
noon
soup
shook
raccoon
flew
stood
roof
grew
goodness
tooth
lose

ACROSS
4. Three or more together.
5. Pick something.
6. Moved something.
7. The middle of the day.
8. This can float in the air.
12. Did not sit.
13. What a bird did.

DOWN
1. You eat it with a spoon.
2. It helps you chew food.
3. It lives in the woods.
4. This is not bad.
8. Frogs and fish might live here.
9. The winner will not do this.
10. Every house has one.
11. Got bigger or taller.

Extra Practice • 131

Extra Practice: Mastery Words

Name
Extra Practice   Mastery Words   UNIT **31**

A. Add the letters that spell /ŏŏ/ or /ōō/ to these consonants. Write the Mastery words.

1. sch__l   s c h o o l
2. r__m   r o o m
3. w__l   w o o l
4. t__k   t o o k
5. s__n   s o o n
6. n__   n e w

B. Which word rhymes with the word in dark print? Write that word.

7. **June**	soon	bone	7.	soon
8. **cool**	school	stroll	8.	school
9. **broom**	some	room	9.	room
10. **pull**	wool	tool	10.	wool
11. **too**	toe	new	11.	new
12. **look**	took	lock	12.	took

C. Write the words you chose in **B** after the right numbers in the puzzle. If you chose correctly, the words will fit together and spell two more little words going down. Circle those words.

took   room   soon
wool   new   school

132 • Extra Practice

Spelling Practice

A. Follow the directions. Use This Week's Words.

1. Write the four words that have the same vowel sound as look. **Word order may vary.**

brook	shook
stood	goodness

2. Write the three words that have double consonant letters. **Word order may vary.**

balloon	goodness	raccoon

3. Write the two words that rhyme with <u>new</u>.
Word order may vary.

flew	grew

4. Write the two words that rhyme but have /o͞o/ spelled in different ways. **Word order may vary.**

choose	lose

5. Write the word that is the same forward and backward.

noon

B. Finish the story. Use This Week's Words.

One night I dreamed that a dragon __6__ over our house. It landed on the __7__. The whole house __8__ when it landed. A large __9__ of people came to look at the dragon. When it saw all the people, it smiled. It had only one big __10__ in its mouth. The dragon looked hungry. So we fed it some __11__.

6. flew	7. roof	8. shook
9. group	10. tooth	11. soup

Words list (right margin):
balloon
brook
shook
stood
goodness
choose
noon
raccoon
roof
tooth
group
soup
flew
grew
lose

135

Summarize Learning

Have the children summarize what they have learned on pages 134 and 135. *Ask:*

- What vowel sounds did you learn in this lesson? (/o͝o/ and /o͞o/)
- What did you learn about these sounds? (one way to spell /o͝o/oo; four ways to spell /o͞o/oo, ou, ew, o)
- What are some examples of words using the different spellings of /o͝o/ and /o͞o/? (brook, roof, group, flew, lose; accept other examples)

TEACHING PLAN

> **Objectives** To write words given spelling clues; to write words that rhyme; to write words that complete a story.

1. Briefly discuss the directions on page 135. Be sure the children understand that in Exercise **B** they must use the other words in the story to help them decide which word makes sense in each sentence. If necessary, read the passage aloud and have the children supply the missing words.

2. Have the children complete the activities independently. Remind them to use legible handwriting. You may wish to demonstrate the correct form of the letters o, u, e, and w and then have the children practice writing the letters. For **Handwriting Models,** refer the children to page 258 in the **Pupil Book.**

3. To correct the children's work, have volunteers write the correct answers for Exercise **A** on the chalkboard. Let the children check their own answers. If you have not already read through the story in preparation for the activities, have a volunteer read the completed story for Exercise **B** aloud.

For reinforcement in writing spelling words, you may wish to assign *Extra Practice Master 31: This Week's Words.*

★ of special interest

The *raccoon* is an animal native to North America and has an American Indian name. The word *raccoon* is derived from the Algonquian name *aroughcoune* or *arathkone*. The first mention of raccoons in English work appears in the writings of Captain John Smith. In 1608, Captain Smith described the land around Jamestown as "covered with a great covering of Rahaugcums."

TEACHING PLAN

SPELLING AND LANGUAGE

Objectives To recognize the relationship between present and past forms of irregular verbs; to write past forms of irregular verbs given present forms; to write present forms of irregular verbs given past forms.

1. Read the introductory paragraph on page 136 aloud.
2. Read the directions on page 136. Point out that the verb on the left tells about now and the children must write the verb that tells what already happened. The verb on the right tells what already happened and the children must write the verb that tells about now. Be sure the children understand that they should work in numerical order.
3. Ask a child to write each answer, and then have a volunteer use the verb in a sentence. Let the children check their own work.

For extended practice in writing irregular verb forms, you may wish to assign **Spelling and Language Master 31.**

WRITING ON YOUR OWN

Objectives To write a poem; to proofread for spelling.

1. Review the directions with children.
2. As a **prewriting** activity, have the children make a list of rhyming words to use as they **compose** their poems. Remind them to use as many of This Week's Words as they can. When they are ready to **revise,** remind the children to check for spelling. For additional help, you may also wish to refer them to the **Revising Checklist** on page 247 of the **Writer's Guide.** To **publish,** have the children read their poems to the class.

136   UNIT 31 *The Sounds /o͞o/ and /o͝o/*

THIS WEEK'S WORDS

balloon
brook
shook
stood
goodness
choose
noon
raccoon
roof
tooth
group
soup
flew
grew
lose

Spelling and Language • Using Verbs

Often you add <u>ed</u> to a verb to talk about what already happened. "Dogs <u>bark</u>. Dogs <u>barked</u>." Sometimes the whole word changes. "Dogs <u>eat</u> meat. Dogs <u>ate</u> meat."

Finish the chart. Use This Week's Words.

NOW	BEFORE		BEFORE	NOW
eat	**ate**		**saw**	**see**
1. fly	flew		3. lost	lose
2. shake	shook		4. chose	choose

Writing on Your Own

Write a scary poem for a friend. You can finish this one or you can make up your own.

As I stood beside the brook,
I looked, I saw, and then I shook!

 WRITER'S GUIDE For a sample poem, see page 254.

Proofreading

Pam wrote this story. She made six mistakes in spelling.

1. Circle each mistake Pam made.

> Once upon a time a little boy had a red balloon. He was afraid he would loose his balloon. So he tied it to his hand. But the string came loose. The balloon floo away. The boy chased it. The baloon flew over a brook. The boy stod and watched it. It greu smaller and smaller.
>
> Two weeks later the boy saw a racoon. The raccoon was carrying something red. It was the lost red balloon!

2. Write the six misspelled words correctly.

lose	flew	balloon
stood	grew	raccoon

PROOFREADING

Objectives To proofread a story for spelling errors; to write misspelled words correctly.

1. Read the introductory sentences on page 136 aloud.
2. Read the story aloud, and have the children follow along in their books.
3. Have the children reread the story, circle the misspelled words, and write them correctly.

   If you are using the hardcover book, the children should simply locate the misspelled words and write them correctly in their notebooks.

Extra Practice: Spelling and Language

Name
Spelling and Language   UNIT 31

A. In the story, circle the verbs that are not right. Then write the verbs correctly.

A baby bird did not want to (flew.) Every day, the bird (grow) larger. Once, the bird (stand) on the edge of its nest. The bird shook when it looked at the ground far below. "I do not (chose) to fly," it said. "If I fly, I may (lost) my life."
The bird started to grow even larger. All its brothers and sisters (fly) away. The bird's mother made it (stood) on the edge of the nest. Suddenly, the bird (lose) its grip and started to fall. The bird (shake) so much that its wings started to flap. Then the bird (fly) all over the sky.

1.	fly	2.	grew
3.	stocd	4.	choose
5.	lose	6.	flew
7.	stand	8.	lost
9.	shook	10.	flew

B. Tell whether the verbs below show what is happening or what has already happened by writing now or before next to each verb.

11. shook	before	12. flew	before
13. chose	before	14. stood	before
15. fly	now	16. grow	now
17. lost	before	18. shake	now

balloon	brook	stood	noon	soup
grew	choose	goodness	lose	group
raccoon	shook	tooth	roof	flew

134 • Extra Practice

Spelling on Your Own

```
r o o f   r o o f   r o o f
                l         l
                e         e
                w   g r e w
```

THIS WEEK'S WORDS

Make a "word chain" with This Week's Words. Write one word. Use a letter in that word to write another word. Keep going, writing words across and down. Try to link all the words in one chain. You may also make more than one chain.

MASTERY WORDS

Follow the directions. Use the Mastery words.

took
room
soon
wool
new
school

1. Write the two words that have the same vowel sound as <u>book</u>.

    <u>took</u>   <u>wool</u>

2. Write the four words that have the same vowel sound as <u>noon</u>.

    <u>room</u>   <u>soon</u>

    <u>new</u>   <u>school</u>

3. Write the word that tells when.   <u>soon</u>

4. Write the word that is not spelled with <u>oo</u>.   <u>new</u>

Write the Mastery words that mean the opposite.

5. old <u>new</u>   **6.** gave <u>took</u>

BONUS WORDS

chew
crooked
lookout
shampoo
smooth
stew
tourist
wooden

1. Write the three Bonus words that end with /o͞o/.

2. Write the five Bonus words spelled with <u>oo</u>.

3. Write this sentence over. Use three Bonus words that mean the opposite of the underlined words. "The <u>local person</u> drove down a <u>straight</u> but <u>bumpy</u> road."

4. <u>Chew</u> and <u>stew</u> both end with <u>ew</u>. Use other consonants with <u>ew</u>. Spell as many words as you can. Then do the same thing with <u>ook</u>.   **See answers below.**

137

Spelling on Your Own **Answers**

BONUS WORDS

1. chew, shampoo, stew
2. crooked, lookout, shampoo, smooth, wooden
3. The <u>tourist</u> drove down a <u>crooked</u> but <u>smooth</u> road.
4. EXAMPLES:

ew	ook
blew	book
crew	brook
dew	cook
few	hook
flew	look
drew	shook
grew	took
mew	
new	

Summarize Learning

Have the children summarize what they have learned in this unit. *Ask:*

- What did you learn about using irregular verbs? (Often *ed* is added to a verb to talk about what already happened. Sometimes a whole word changes as in the words <u>eat</u> and <u>ate</u>.)
- What spelling generalizations have you learned? How did you use these generalizations?

TEACHING PLAN

> **Objective** To apply the unit spelling generalization to spell This Week's Words, Mastery words, and Bonus words independently.

THIS WEEK'S WORDS

1. Read the directions on page 137 aloud. Copy the third step of the sample word chain on the chalkboard. Then ask the children to find a word on the list that can be linked up with *grew*. Add that word to the chain.
2. Have the children complete the activity independently.

MASTERY WORDS

1. Briefly review these sounds and spellings: /o͝o/ oo; /o͞o/ oo, ew.
2. Have volunteers read the Mastery words. Help them to identify the vowel sounds /o͝o/ and /o͞o/. Ask the children to indicate which letters spell the vowel sounds.
3. Briefly discuss the directions on page 137. Then have the children complete the activities.

BONUS WORDS

1. Briefly review these sounds and spellings: /o͝o/ oo; /o͞o/ oo, ou, ew.
2. Have volunteers read the Bonus words aloud. Encourage the children to look up the meaning of any unfamiliar words in the **Spelling Dictionary**.
3. Have the children complete the exercise on a piece of paper.
4. Have the children read their lists of words spelled with *ew* and *ook*, and ask a volunteer to make a master list of the words on the chalkboard.

For reinforcement in writing spelling words, you may wish to assign *Extra Practice Master 31: Mastery Words* or *Bonus Words.*

CLOSING THE UNIT

Apply New Learning

Tell the children that if they misspell words with the vowel sounds /o͝o/ and /o͞o/ in their writing they should use one or more of the following strategies:

● think about the possible spellings for the vowel sound /o͝o/ (or /o͞o/) and try to picture the word in their minds.
● think of words that rhyme and compare in their minds how they are spelled.
● try to find patterns and causes of their errors.

Transfer New Learning

Tell the children that when they encounter new words in their personal reading and in other content areas, they should learn the meaning of those words and then apply the generalizations they have studied to the spelling of those words. Tell them that once the words are familiar in both meaning and spelling, they should use the new words in their writing.

ENRICHMENT ACTIVITIES

Classroom activities and **home activities** may be assigned to children of all ability levels. The activities provide opportunities for children to use their spelling words in new contexts.

For the Classroom

To individualize classroom activities, you may have the children use the word list they are studying in this unit.

● *Basic:* Use **Mastery** words to complete the activity.
● *Average:* Use **This Week's Words** to complete the activity.
● *Challenging:* Use **Bonus** words to complete the activity.

1. **Language Arts/Building Vocabulary** Have each child build sets of words for the following phonograms: *oon* as in *balloon; ew* as in *flew; ook* as in *brook.* Tell the children to begin with any spelling words that have the target phonogram and then to list as many other words with the same phonogram as they can. Tell the children to be sure that each word is spelled correctly and that they understand the meaning of each word. After the children have completed their lists, make a class list. Ask the children to use their words in sentences to show their meanings. You may wish to have the children add words to the lists as they find them.

   ■ COOPERATIVE LEARNING: Have each group build sets of words for the following phonograms: *oon* as in *balloon; ew* as in *flew; ook* as in *brook.* Each set should begin with any spelling words that have the target phonogram and then the children should list as many other words with the phonogram as they can.

After compiling the lists, group members should check the spelling of each word. Every group member should be able to use each word in a sentence. Each group should make a copy of their list. Have a classmate ask a member of the group to use one word from the list in a sentence that shows the meaning of the word and to challenge the group on any misspelled words.

2. **Language Arts/Writing Sentences** Have the children write sentences that use all three words in each of the following sets: *group, stood, roof; lose, tooth, soup; balloon, grew, flew.* Present the following sentence as an example: *The raccoon came to the brook at noon.* Tell the children that their sentences may be funny.

   ■ COOPERATIVE LEARNING: Have each group create two different sentences that use each set of words listed above. As the children discuss possibilities, have each member record the group's sentences. Then have the group select a sentence to share with the class.

3. **Language Arts/Writing a Descriptive Paragraph** Have the children write a descriptive paragraph. Direct their attention to page 250 of the **Writer's Guide** to read about descriptive paragraphs. As a **prewriting** activity, have the children look over their spelling words in search of words that they might use to describe a scene such as a bathroom after giving a dog a bath, a kitchen after someone has prepared dinner, or a school cafeteria at lunchtime. Ask each child to select a scene they want to describe and make a cluster drawing with the word that names the place written in the center. Have the children write details around the circle. Remind the children that details can tell how something looks, sounds, smells, and feels. Present this model of a cluster drawing:

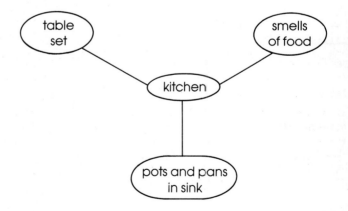

Have the children use their cluster drawings to **compose** their paragraphs. Tell the children to use as many spelling words as they can. Then have the children **revise** the paragraph, making sure it gives a clear picture of the place or thing being described. Children should also proofread for spelling, capitalization, and punctuation. **Publish** the children's paragraphs in a class book or bulletin board display.

■ COOPERATIVE LEARNING: Have each group write a descriptive paragraph. As a **prewriting** activity, have each group select a scene to describe in the paragraph. Then have them make a cluster drawing with the place named in the center circle. Tell the children to write details about how the place looks, sounds, smells, and feels. One child in the group can begin to **compose** by providing the first sentence orally. Each child in the group should then continue by adding one or more sentences that tell about the place. Remind the children to use as many of their spelling words as they can. One group member can record the paragraph. The other children in the group should **revise** the paragraph. Each child should also proofread for spelling, capitalization, and punctuation. One child can then rewrite the paragraph. **Publish** the paragraph by having a group member read it aloud to the class.

For the Home

Children may complete these activities independently or with the assistance of a relative or friend in the home.

1. Language Arts/Writing Word Associations Tell the children to choose several spelling words and write two synonyms or two other words commonly associated with each word. For example: *school, library, post office.* Have them rewrite each of their word groups leaving a blank space for the spelling word. Children can ask a friend or someone at home to guess the missing spelling word to complete each group.

2. Language Arts/Writing Sentence Pairs Using Antonyms Tell the children to choose several spelling words for which they can name antonyms. Tell them to write sentences for each antonym pair. For example: *We stood for an hour waiting for the bus to leave. We sat for an hour waiting for the bus to leave.* After writing their sentences, have the children share them with a friend or someone at home.

3. Health/Writing Statements About Nutrition Tell the children to write three statements about nutrition. Tell them that each sentence should contain one spelling word. For example: *Vegetable soup has many important vitamins.*

4. Science/Naming and Defining Bodies of Water Tell the children that a *brook* is a small stream. Have them list words that name other bodies of water. Children should check the spelling of the words in a dictionary (pond, stream, river, bay, ocean, lake) and then write the meaning for each.

Evaluating Spelling Ability

Unit Test

This Week's Words

1. *balloon*   The Angstrums took a ride in a hot-air *balloon.*   **balloon**
2. *brook*   There is a *brook* running through the meadow.   **brook**
3. *shook*   The dog *shook* the water off its coat.   **shook**
4. *stood*   Luke *stood* in the last row.   **stood**
5. *goodness*   Mary shows her *goodness* by always being helpful.   **goodness**
6. *choose*   I didn't know which book to *choose.*   **choose**
7. *noon*   The factory workers have a break at *noon.*   **noon**
8. *raccoon*   A *raccoon* dips its food in water.   **raccoon**
9. *roof*   We could hear the rain on the *roof.*   **roof**
10. *tooth*   Margaret has a loose *tooth.*   **tooth**
11. *group*   A *group* of parents helped with the paper drive.   **group**
12. *soup*   Mom gave Josh chicken *soup* when he had the flu.   **soup**
13. *flew*   The pigeons *flew* away.   **flew**
14. *grew*   Mr. Rodriguez *grew* a mustache.   **grew**
15. *lose*   She didn't want to *lose* her money.   **lose**

Mastery Words

1. *took*   Mother *took* us to the park.   **took**
2. *room*   This *room* is sunny.   **room**
3. *soon*   I hope dinner will be ready *soon.*   **soon**
4. *wool*   Manuel is wearing a *wool* sweater.   **wool**
5. *new*   These are the *new* library books.   **new**
6. *school*   Our *school* has a big playground.   **school**

Bonus Words

1. *chew*   No one may *chew* gum in school.   **chew**
2. *crooked*   The picture was *crooked,* so Jack straightened it.   **crooked**
3. *lookout*   Be on the *lookout* for Otis and Sue.   **lookout**
4. *shampoo*   Don't get *shampoo* in your eyes.   **shampoo**
5. *smooth*   We roller-skate here because the sidewalk is *smooth.*   **smooth**
6. *stew*   You can reheat the *stew* for dinner.   **stew**
7. *tourist*   The *tourist* visited the state park.   **tourist**
8. *wooden*   Grandpa made a *wooden* rocking horse for Tracy.   **wooden**

Dictation Sentences

This Week's Words

1. My *balloon flew* over the *roof.*
2. The *raccoon stood* by the *brook.*
3. Our *group* may *choose* to have *soup* at *noon.*
4. The baby *grew* another *tooth.*
5. She did not *lose* her job because of the *goodness* of a friend.
6. The leaves *shook* in the wind.

Mastery Words

1. I *took* my *new* pen to *school.*
2. Hang up your *wool* coat as *soon* as you come into the *room.*

Bonus Words

1. The *tourist* was on the *lookout* for a store that sold *shampoo.*
2. The meat in the *stew* was hard to *chew.*
3. My *wooden* stick is *crooked* but *smooth.*

Children who have made errors on the Unit Test may require reteaching. Use the following **Reteaching Strategies** and **Follow-up Masters 31A** and **31B** for additional instruction and practice of This Week's Words. (You may wish to assign **LEP Reteaching Follow-up Master 31** for reteaching of spelling words.)

A. Discovering Spelling Ideas

1. Say the following words as you write them on the chalkboard.

   book   moon   you   stew   move

2. Ask the children to identify the vowel sounds heard in the words. (/o͞o/ and /o͝o/)
3. Ask the children to identify what letters spell the sound /o͝o/ in book. (oo)
4. Ask the children to identify what letters spell the sound /o͞o/ in the other words. (oo, ou, ew, o)
5. Ask the children what they have learned about spelling /o͝o/ and /o͞o/. (/o͝o/ is spelled with oo; /o͞o/ can be spelled with oo, ou, ew, or o.)

B. Word Shapes

1. Explain to the children that each word has a shape and that remembering the shape of a word can help them to spell the word correctly.
2. On the chalkboard, write the words *spoon* and *crook*. Have the children identify "short," "tall," and "tail" letters.
3. Draw the configuration of each word on the chalkboard, and ask the children which word fits in each shape.

Use **Reteaching Follow-up Master 31A** to reinforce spelling generalizations taught in Unit 31.

Use **Reteaching Follow-up Master 31B** to reinforce spellings of This Week's Words for Unit 31.

Name _____ **Reteaching** Follow-up A   Discovering Spelling Ideas   **UNIT 31**

THIS WEEK'S WORDS

balloon	stood	noon	grew	choose
raccoon	tooth	roof	lose	group
brook	shook	soup	flew	goodness

1. In each list, write the words that have the same vowel sound as the first word in the column.

look /o͝o/
- brook
- stood
- goodness
- shook

moon /o͞o/
- balloon
- noon
- soup
- grew
- choose
- raccoon
- tooth
- roof
- flew
- lose
- group

2. What vowel sound do all the words in the first column have in common?
   ___/o͝o/___ Circle the letters that spell that sound.

3. What vowel sound do all the words in the second column have in common?
   ___/o͞o/___ Circle the letters that spell that sound.

Reteaching • 51

Name _____ **Reteaching** Follow-up B   Word Shapes   **UNIT 31**

THIS WEEK'S WORDS

balloon	stood	noon	tooth	flew
brook	goodness	raccoon	group	grew
shook	choose	roof	soup	lose

Write each of This Week's Words in its correct shape. The first one has been done for you. Children may interchange answers that fit the same configuration.

1. l o s e
2. s h o o k
3. g r o u p
4. r a c c o o n
5. g o o d n e s s
6. n o o n
7. s t o o d
8. s o u p
9. t o o t h
10. b a l l o o n
11. g r e w
12. f l e w
13. b r o o k
14. c h o o s e
15. r o o f

52 • Reteaching

The Sounds /ou/ and /oi/

REVIEWING THE UNIT

Unit Materials

Instruction and Practice

Pupil Book — pages 138–141
Teacher's Edition
  Teaching Plans — pages 138–141
  Enrichment Activities
    For the Classroom — page 141A
    For the Home — page 141B
  Reteaching Strategies — page 141C

Testing

Teacher's Edition
  Trial Test — pages 137E–137F
  Unit Test — page 141B
  Dictation Test — page 141B

Additional Resources

PRACTICE AND REINFORCEMENT
  Extra Practice Master 32: This Week's Words
  Extra Practice Master 32: Mastery Words
  Extra Practice Master 32: Bonus Words
  LEP Practice Master 32
  Spelling and Language Master 32
  Study Steps to Learn a Word Master

RETEACHING FOLLOW-UP
  Reteaching Follow-up Master 32A:
    Discovering Spelling Ideas
  Reteaching Follow-up Master 32B: Word
    Shapes
  LEP Reteaching Follow-up Master 32

TEACHING AIDS
  Spelling Generalizations Transparency 27

Visit our Web site
http://www.hbschool.com

Click on the SPELLING banner to find activities for this unit.

Learner Objectives

Spelling

- To spell words that demonstrate these sound-letter relationships: /ou/ *ou, ow;* /oi/ *oi, oy.*
- To review plural nouns formed by adding *s.*

Reading

- To identify the appropriate meaning of a word with multiple meanings using sentence context.
- To follow written directions.
- To use a dictionary for word meaning.

Writing

- To write a how-to paragraph.
- To use the writing process.
- To proofread for spelling, capitalization, and punctuation.
- To write legible manuscript and cursive letters.

Listening

- To listen to identify the vowel sounds /ou/ and /oi/ in words.
- To follow oral directions.

Speaking

- To speak clearly to a group.
- To contribute ideas and information in group discussions.
- To express feelings and ideas about a piece of writing.

THIS WEEK'S WORDS

loud
noise
cloud
mouse
mouth
sound
brown
clown
crown
owl
oil
point
voice
joy
enjoy

MASTERY WORDS

about
found
house
our
shout
town

BONUS WORDS

spoil
coins
loyal
destroy
bounce
proud
frown
towel

Assignment Guide

This guide shows how you teach a typical spelling unit in either a five-day or a three-day sequence, while providing for individual differences. **Boldface type** indicates essential classwork. Steps shown in light type may be done in class or assigned as homework.

Five Days	° = average spellers ★ = better spellers ✓ = slower spellers	Three Days
Day **1**	**a** ° ★ **Take This Week's Words Trial Test and correct** ° ✓ **Take Mastery Word Trial Test and correct** ° ★ **Read This Week's Words and discuss generalization on page 138**	Day **1**
Day **2**	° Complete Spelling Practice page 139 ° ✓ Complete Extra Practice Master 32: This Week's Words (optional) ✓ Complete Spelling on Your Own: Mastery Words page 141 ★ **Take Bonus Word Trial Test and correct** **b**	Day **1**
Day **3**	**c** ° ★ ✓ **Complete Spelling and Language page 140** ° ★ ✓ Complete Writing on Your Own page 140 ° ★ ✓ **Complete Using the Dictionary to Spell and Write page 140** ° ✓ Take Midweek Test (optional) ★ Complete Spelling on Your Own: Bonus Words page 141 ° ✓ Complete Spelling and Language Master 32 (optional)	Day **2**
Day **4**	° Complete Spelling on Your Own: This Week's Words page 141 ✓ Complete Extra Practice Master 32: Mastery Words (optional) ★ Complete Extra Practice Master 32: Bonus Words (optional) **d**	Day **2**
Day **5**	**e** ° **Take Unit Test on This Week's Words** ° Complete Reteaching Follow-up Masters 32A and 32B (optional) ° ✓ **Take Unit Test on Mastery Words** ★ **Take Unit Test on Bonus Words**	Day **3**

Enrichment Activities for the **classroom** and for the **home** included at the end of this unit may be assigned selectively on any day of the week.

INTRODUCING THE UNIT

Establish Readiness for Learning

Remind children that in the last unit they learned words which used two vowels to make one vowel sound. In Unit 32 they will learn the spelling pattern for more words that have two vowels together. Explain that they will apply these spelling patterns to This Week's Words and use those words to write a how-to paragraph.

Assess Children's Spelling Ability

Administer the Trial Test before the children study This Week's Words. Use the test sentences provided. Say each word and use it in a sentence. Then repeat the word. Have the children write the words on a separate sheet of paper or in their spelling notebooks. Test sentences are also provided for Mastery and Bonus words.

Have the children check their own work by listening to you read the spelling of the words or by referring to This Week's Words in the left column of the **Pupil Book.** For each misspelled word, have the children follow the **Study Steps to Learn a Word** on page 1 in the **Pupil Book** or use the copying master to study and write the words. Children should record the number correct on their **Progress Report.**

Trial Test Sentences

This Week's Words
1. *loud*   Please don't talk in a *loud* voice.   *loud*
2. *noise*   The car was making a strange *noise.*   *noise*
3. *cloud*   There was a *cloud* in front of the sun.   *cloud*
4. *mouse*   He was as quiet as a *mouse.*   *mouse*

FOCUS

- Establishes objectives
- Relates to prior learning
- Sets purpose of instruction

5. *mouth*   The dentist looked into her *mouth*.   **mouth**
6. *sound*   Thunder makes a loud booming *sound*.   **sound**
7. *brown*   Skip's new shoes are *brown*.   **brown**
8. *clown*   She acts like a *clown*.   **clown**
9. *crown*   A king wears a *crown*.   **crown**
10. *owl*   The *owl* slept in the tree.   **owl**
11. *oil*   The car needs *oil*.   **oil**
12. *point*   This pencil has a sharp *point*.   **point**
13. *voice*   Tim heard a *voice* outside the door.   **voice**
14. *joy*   A visit brings *joy* to a sick person.   **joy**
15. *enjoy*   I *enjoy* reading.   **enjoy**

Mastery Words

1. *about*   Akiko read a book *about* a puppet.   **about**
2. *found*   Gretchen *found* a nickel.   **found**
3. *house*   Their *house* is painted green.   **house**
4. *our*   We painted *our* house yellow.   **our**
5. *shout*   Don't *shout* in the hall.   **shout**
6. *town*   Laura lives on the other side of *town*.   **town**

Bonus Words

1. *spoil*   The rain will *spoil* our picnic.   **spoil**

2. *coins*   We found some *coins* in the sand.   **coins**
3. *loyal*   A dog is a *loyal* pet.   **loyal**
4. *destroy*   A fire can *destroy* the forest.   **destroy**
5. *bounce*   A ball will *bounce* if you drop it.   **bounce**
6. *proud*   Pedro was *proud* of his good report card.   **proud**
7. *frown*   Making mistakes makes James *frown*.   **frown**
8. *towel*   Use this *towel* to dry your hands.   **towel**

Apply Prior Learning

Write the list of This Week's Words on the chalkboard. Have the children read the words aloud and ask them what the words have in common. (the /ou/ and /oi/ sounds) Have the children group the words according to these sounds and label each group. Have them underline the letters that represent the /ou/ or /oi/ sound in each word. Then have the children give additional examples for each group and underline the letters that represent the /ou/ and /oi/ sounds. Finally, ask the children what they see and can say about the ways the /ou/ and /oi/ sounds are spelled. (The /ou/ sound is spelled *ou* and *ow*. The /oi/ sound can be spelled *oi* and *oy*.)

FOCUS

- Relates to prior learning
- Draws relationships
- Applies spelling generalizations to new contexts

FOR CHILDREN WITH SPECIAL NEEDS

Learning Difficulties

Use tactile sensation to help children with Attention Deficit Disorder (ADD) distinguish the two different spellings of the /oi/ sound: *oi* and *oy*, and of the /ou/ sound: *ou* and *ow*.

Divide This Week's Words into lists that contain the different spellings of the two sounds so that one spelling can be taught at a time. This helps the child learn one spelling very well prior to learning the second spelling.

Have the child write each word three times, first with you slowly dictating the spelling and the child writing. As you come to the letters that stand for the /oi/ or /ou/ sound, raise your voice slightly for emphasis. Next, you and the child simultaneously spell the word as the child writes it. Finally, have the child spell the word aloud as he or she writes it.

If the child seems to need additional experience in spelling these words, follow the tactile strategy introduced in Unit 15. Have the child write the words with liquid glue and, after it has dried, trace the shape of the letters with the finger of the preferred writing hand.

Limited English Proficiency

To help limited English proficient children work with the spelling generalizations for Unit 32, you may wish to refer to the booklet "Suggestions and Activities for Limited English Proficient Students."

TEACHING PLAN

Objective To spell words that demonstrate these sound-letter relationships: /ou/ou, ow; /oi/oi, oy.

1. Direct the children's attention to the picture on page 138. Have a child read the two words that accompany the picture, and help the children to identify the vowel sound in each word—/ou/ in *loud*; /oi/ in *noise*.
2. Read the generalization on page 138 aloud.

You may wish to introduce the lesson by using **Spelling Generalizations Transparency 29.**

3. Have volunteers read This Week's Words aloud. As each word is read, have the children indicate whether the sound /ou/ or /oi/ is heard in the word. Then have the children identify the letters that spell the vowel sound in the word. Help them to recognize that /oi/ is spelled with *oi* at the beginning and middle of words and with *oy* at the end of words or syllables.

You may wish to assign **LEP Practice Master 32** for reinforcement in writing spelling words.

---

32 The Sounds /ou/ and /oi/

THIS WEEK'S WORDS

1. loud
2. noise
3. cloud
4. mouse
5. mouth
6. sound
7. brown
8. clown
9. crown
10. owl
11. oil
12. point
13. voice
14. joy
15. enjoy

This Week's Words

The vowel sound /ou/ is heard in <u>loud</u>. This sound is spelled two ways.

● /ou/ is spelled **ou** in <u>loud</u>
● /ou/ is spelled **ow** in <u>brown</u>

The vowel sound /oi/ is heard in <u>noise</u>. This sound is also spelled two ways.

● /oi/ is spelled **oi** in <u>noise</u>
● /oi/ is spelled **oy** at the end of <u>joy</u>

138

Extra Practice: This Week's Words

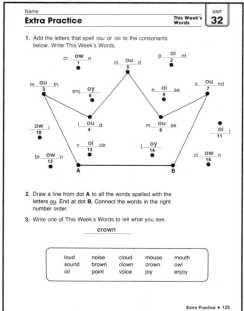

Extra Practice: Mastery Words

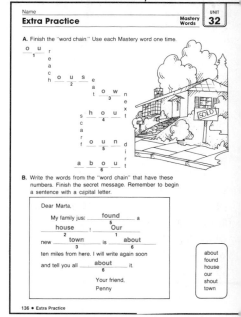

Spelling Practice

A. Follow the directions. Use This Week's Words.

1. Write the three words that name things in the picture.

clown

crown

owl

2. Write the word for the color of the bird. __brown__

3. Write two words that mean about the same thing. Here is a hint. They both name things a horn makes.

noise   sound

4. Write three more words that have /oi/ spelled <u>oi</u>.

oil   point   voice

5. Write four more words that have /ou/ spelled <u>ou</u>.

loud   cloud

mouse   mouth

6. What should you never use in the library? Write a word with /ou/ and a word with /oi/.

loud   voice

7. Write the word that means about the same thing as happiness. Then add two letters. Spell another one of This Week's Words.

joy   enjoy

B. Change the underlined letter in each word. Write one of This Week's Words.

8. c<u>l</u>own ____ crown   **9.** <u>r</u>ound ____ sound

10. <u>h</u>ouse ____ mouse   **11.** <u>s</u>outh ____ mouth

139

Words list:
loud
noise
cloud
mouse
mouth
sound
brown
clown
crown
owl
oil
point
voice
joy
enjoy

TEACHING PLAN

Objectives To write words given picture clues; to write words given meaning clues; to write words given vowel sound clues; to write words by adding or changing letters in given words.

1. Briefly discuss the directions on page 139. If necessary, have a volunteer identify the three things in the picture for **1**.
2. Have the children complete the page independently. Remind them to use legible handwriting. You may wish to demonstrate the correct form of the letters o, w, and y and then have the children practice writing the letters. For **Handwriting Models,** refer the children to page 258 in the **Pupil Book.**
3. To correct the children's work, have volunteers write the answers on the chalkboard. Ask the children to exchange their work and check one another's responses.

For reinforcement in writing spelling words, you may wish to assign **Extra Practice Master 32: This Week's Words.**

★ of special interest

The next time you hear a very loud noise, you will no doubt recall this word history. *Noise* and *nausea* share the Greek root—*nausia* ("seasickness"). The Romans used the word *nausea* to describe any unpleasant or unsettling situation. *Nausea,* with this extended meaning, became the Old French word *noyse,* and hence the English word *noise.*

Extra Practice: Bonus Words

Summarize Learning

Have the children summarize what they have learned on pages 138 and 139. *Ask:*

• What vowel sounds have you learned in this lesson? (/ou/, /oi/)
• What have you learned about these sounds? Give examples. (Two ways to spell the vowel sound /ou/, *ou, ow; sound, brown.* Two ways to spell /oi/, *oi, oy; voice, joy.*)

TEACHING PLAN

SPELLING AND LANGUAGE

> **Objectives** To form the plural of nouns by adding *s*; to write plural nouns in sentence context.

1. Read the introductory paragraph and the directions on page 140 aloud. Be sure the children understand that they should choose the plural form of the word that best fits each sentence.
2. Have the children complete the activity independently.
3. Ask volunteers to read their completed sentences aloud. Let the children check their own work.

For extended practice in writing plural nouns, you may wish to assign **Spelling and Language Master 32.**

WRITING ON YOUR OWN

> **Objectives** To write a how-to paragraph; to proofread for spelling.

1. Review the directions.
2. As a **prewriting** activity, write the words *circus clown* in a circle on the chalkboard. Discuss with the children the things clowns do to make people laugh, and write their responses in a cluster around the core words. Then have the children **compose** their paragraphs. When they are ready to **revise**, remind them to check for spelling. To **publish**, have the children illustrate their paragraphs. Then mount their pictures and paragraphs on a class bulletin board.

USING THE DICTIONARY

> **Objectives** To recognize multiple meanings; to identify the meaning of a word in sentence context.

1. Read the introductory paragraph on page 140 aloud. Have the

children look at the sample dictionary entries for *noise* and *sound*, and read the definitions aloud.
2. Write these sentences on the chalkboard:

   a. The bell will sound at 9:00.
   b. We heard a sound outside.
   c. That sounds like a good idea.

Ask the children if *noise* can take the place of *sound*.
3. Read the directions on page 140 aloud. Then have the children complete the activity.
4. Check the children's work orally.

THIS WEEK'S WORDS
loud
noise
cloud
mouse
mouth
sound
brown
clown
crown
owl
oil
point
voice
joy
enjoy

Spelling and Language • Plural Nouns

A plural noun names more than one thing. You add <u>s</u> to most nouns to make them plural.
Finish the sentences. Write plurals of This Week's Words.

1. There were dark _____clouds_____ in the sky.
2. Ned could hear the _____sounds_____ of thunder and wind.

Writing on Your Own

Imagine you are a clown in a circus. Write a paragraph for people who want to learn to be a clown. Tell what you do during a show. Explain how to make people laugh. Use some plurals and some of This Week's Words.

WRITER'S GUIDE For a sample of a how-to paragraph, turn to page 250.

Using the Dictionary to Spell and Write

Knowing the definition of a word can help you check if you used a word correctly in your writing. A **definition** tells what a word means. Read the definitions for <u>noise</u> and <u>sound</u>. <u>Noise</u> has one definition. <u>Sound</u> has more than one.

> **noise** /noiz/ *n.* Sound, especially loud sound: The crowd made a lot of *noise*.

> **sound** /sound/ *n.* Anything that can be heard: Don't make a *sound*!
> —*v.* **1** To make a sound: *Sound the horn.* **2** To seem: *It sounds right to me.*

Read each sentence. Can <u>noise</u> take the place of <u>sound</u>? If it can, write <u>noise</u> or <u>noises</u> in the blank.

1. The story <u>sounds</u> exciting. _____
2. The cat was making angry <u>sounds</u>. ___noises___
3. Shall I <u>sound</u> the dinner bell? _____
4. Isabel heard a banging <u>sound</u> outside. ___noise___

Extra Practice: Spelling and Language

Name		UNIT
Spelling and Language		**32**

A. Circle the word in each sentence that should be plural. Then write the sentence again. Use the plural of the word you circled.

1. Two (clown) had a funny act.
   Two clowns had a funny act.
2. They wore (crown) on their ears.
   They wore crowns on their ears.
3. They made many different (sound)
   They made many different sounds.
4. They could hoot like (owl)
   They could hoot like owls.
5. They could make their (voice) roar.
   They could make their voices roar.
6. They could make ten (noise) at once.
   They could make ten noises at once.

B. Answer the questions by writing plural nouns. Use plurals of This Week's Words.

7. What does a basketball team score?   points
8. What are fluffy and float in the sky?   clouds
9. What birds say "hoot"?   owls

noise	mouse	sound	clown	owl
point	loud	enjoy	voice	joy
cloud	mouth	brown	crown	oil

138 • Extra Practice

Spelling on Your Own

THIS WEEK'S WORDS

Add the letters that spell /ou/. Write This Week's Words.

1. cl__d   **2.** cr__n   **3.** m__th   **4.** __l   **5.** br__n   **6.** m__se
7. l__d   **8.** s__nd   **9.** cl__n

Add the letters that spell /oi/. Write This Week's Words.

10. n__se   **11.** __l   **12.** enj__   **13.** p__nt   **14.** v__ce   **15.** j__

See answers below.

MASTERY WORDS

about
found
house
our
shout
town

Follow the directions. Use the Mastery words.

1. Write the word that starts with /ou/. _____ our _____

2. Write the two words that have <u>out</u> in them.

_____ about _____   _____ shout _____

Write Mastery words that rhyme with these words.

3. sound _____ found _____   **4.** down _____ town _____

5. mouse _____ house _____   **6.** out _____ shout _____

Write the Mastery words that mean the opposite.

7. whisper _____ shout _____   **8.** lost _____ found _____

BONUS WORDS

spoil
coins
loyal
destroy
bounce
proud
frown
towel

Follow the directions. Use the Bonus words.

1. Write the four words that have the sound /ou/.
2. Write the four words that have the sound /oi/.
3. Write the two verbs that mean "wreck, or ruin."

Add <u>ed</u> to each of these words. Then use the words with <u>ed</u> in sentences.

4. spoil   **5.** destroy   **6.** bounce   **7.** frown

See answers below.

141

Spelling on Your Own Answers

THIS WEEK'S WORDS

1. cloud 2. crown 3. mouth 4. owl 5. brown
6. mouse 7. loud 8. sound 9. clown
10. noise 11. oil 12. enjoy 13. point
14. voice 15. joy

BONUS WORDS

1. bounce, proud, frown, towel 2. spoil,
coins, loyal, destroy 3. spoil, destroy
EXAMPLES:
4. spoiled Ellen told Mike and spoiled the surprise. 5. destroyed The rabbit destroyed the
cabbage patch. 6. bounced Raymond
bounced the ball for ten minutes without stopping. 7. frowned Susan frowned when I said I
couldn't go.

Summarize Learning

Have the children summarize what they have learned in this unit. *Ask:*

- What have you learned about adding *s* to nouns? Give examples. (Plurals can be formed by adding *s* to nouns: cloud, clouds; sound, sounds.)
- What have you learned about the definitions of words? Give examples. (Some words have more than one definition. *Sound* can mean "to make a noise" or "to seem.")
- What spelling generalizations have you learned? How did you use these generalizations?

TEACHING PLAN

Objectives To apply the unit spelling generalization to spell This Week's Words, Mastery words, and Bonus words independently.

THIS WEEK'S WORDS

1. Read the directions on page 141 aloud. Help the children get started by asking them to tell what words result if the sound /ou/ is added to the letters given in **1–9** and the sound /oi/ is added to the letters given in **10–15**.
2. Have the children complete the activity. Encourage them to write the words *without* looking at the list on page 140.
3. When the children have completed the activity, ask them to check their own spelling against the list on page 140.

MASTERY WORDS

1. Briefly review the spellings for /ou/: *ou, ow*.
2. Have volunteers read the Mastery words aloud. As each word is read, have the children identify the letters that spell /ou/ in the word.
3. Briefly discuss the directions on page 141. Then have the children complete the activity.

BONUS WORDS

1. Briefly review the unit generalization on page 138.
2. Have volunteers read each Bonus word aloud and identify the letters that spell /ou/ or /oi/. Point out that /oi/ is spelled with *oy* in *loyal* because /oi/ is heard at the end of a syllable.
3. Have the children complete the exercise independently on a piece of paper.

For reinforcement in writing spelling words, you may wish to assign *Extra Practice Master 32: Mastery Words* or *Bonus Words*.

CLOSING THE UNIT

Apply New Learning

Tell the children that if they misspell words with the vowel sounds /ou/ and /oi/ in their writing, they should use one or more of the following strategies:

- think of words that rhyme and compare in their minds how they are spelled.
- think about whether the spelling of the word could be unusual.
- write the words using different spellings and compare these spellings with the spelling they picture in their minds.

Transfer New Learning

Tell the children that when they encounter new words in their personal reading and in other content areas, they should learn the meaning of those words and then apply the generalizations they have studied to the spelling of those words. Tell them that once the words are familiar in both meaning and spelling, they should use the new words in their writing.

ENRICHMENT ACTIVITIES

Classroom activities and **home activities** may be assigned to children of all ability levels. The activities provide opportunities for children to use their spelling words in new contexts.

For the Classroom

To individualize classroom activities, you may have the children use the word list they are studying in this unit:

- *Basic:* Use **Mastery** words to complete the activity.
- *Average:* Use **This Week's Words** to complete the activity.
- *Challenging:* Use **Bonus** words to complete the activity.

1. **Language Arts/Writing a Poem** Have the children write a poem using spelling words and words that rhyme with them. Have the children choose four of the spelling words and write a rhyming word for each one. Then have the children use each pair of rhyming words to write two-line rhymes for the poem. Then tell the children to try to put together three or more pairs of rhyming lines (six lines) about the same topic to compose a poem. Have the children check the poem for spelling, punctuation, and capitalization errors. Ask the children to share their poems by reading them aloud.

   ■ COOPERATIVE LEARNING: Have each group write a poem using spelling words and words that rhyme with them. Have each group member choose a spelling word and write a word that rhymes with it. Have the group choose a topic for the poem. Then have each group

member write two-line rhymes about the topic, using the rhyming word pair. Ask each member to write his or her two-line rhymes on chart paper. Have one member read the completed poem for spelling, punctuation, and capitalization errors. Then have one member share the poem with the other groups by reading it aloud.

2. **Language Arts/Writing Sentences to Show Multiple Meanings** Have the children use the dictionary to find two meanings for one of the following spelling words: *sound, point, brown.* Tell them to write down the meanings of the word. Then have them write example sentences to explain each of the word's meanings. Have the children share their sentences.

   ■ COOPERATIVE LEARNING Have each child in the group use a dictionary to find two meanings of the following spelling words: *sound, point, brown.* Each child should choose a different word and write example sentences. The group should then discuss the effectiveness of each member's sentences and revise them where necessary. Have the group then share the sentences with the class.

3. **Language Arts/Writing a Friendly Letter** Have the children write a friendly letter using some of their spelling words. First, direct children's attention to page 251 of the **Writer's Guide** to read about friendly letters. As a *prewriting* activity, have the children look over their spelling word lists in search of possible ideas that might be included in a friendly letter and record their ideas. For example, children may wish to write to a friend about something special they heard or saw. Have the children **compose** their letters using their ideas. Next, tell them to *revise* their letters, making sure they have followed the format for writing a letter and that each paragraph has a main idea sentence followed by detail sentences. Remind the children to proofread for spelling, capitalization, and punctuation, using the **Revising Checklist** on page 247 for help. Have them **publish** their letters by reading them aloud to the class.

   ■ COOPERATIVE LEARNING: Have each group write a friendly letter using some of their spelling words. As a *prewriting* activity, have the members of the group look over their spelling word lists for possible ideas for a letter and record these ideas. Have the group share their ideas and decide which they will use in a letter. When the children are ready to **compose** the letter, have them choose one child to begin orally by providing the first sentence of the letter. Each child should build on the first sentence by adding one or more sentences. Group members should then *revise,* making sure that they followed the format for writing a letter and that each paragraph has a main idea sentence followed by detail sentences. Each child should also proofread for spelling, capitalization, and punctuation. Then have the group select one person to rewrite the letter. Each group should **publish** its letter by reading it aloud.

or the Home

Children may complete these activities independently or with the assistance of a relative or friend in the home.

Science/Writing Questions About Sound Tell the children to write three questions about *sound,* using a spelling word in each. For example: *How can a loud noise hurt your ears?* Encourage the children to use their science books as a reference. Tell the children to ask someone at home to answer the questions or bring them to class for classmates to answer.

Language Arts/Writing Two-line Rhymes Have the children write rhyming words using three spelling words with the sound /ou/ and three spelling words with the sound /oi/. Then have the children use one of the rhyming pairs to write a two-line rhyme whose lines end with the rhyming words. For example:

> There once was a *mouse*
> Who lived in our *house.*

Language Arts/Writing a FOR-SALE Ad Tell the children to write a three-line FOR-SALE ad using as many spelling words with the sounds /ou/ and /oi/ as they can. Read aloud several ads from the classified section of a newspaper, explaining that to save space complete sentences are not always used. For example:

> FOR SALE Small brown mouse needs home. Enjoys people. Doesn't eat much or make noise.

Fine Arts/Illustrating Words to Show Meaning Tell the children to illustrate spelling words by arranging the letters to form a picture of the word they represent. Use the examples below:

EVALUATING SPELLING ABILITY

Unit Test

Dictation Sentences

RETEACHING STRATEGIES FOR SPELLING

Children who have made errors on the Unit Test may require reteaching. Use the following **Reteaching Strategies** and **Follow-up Masters 32A** and **32B** for additional instruction and practice of This Week's Words. (You may wish to assign **LEP Reteaching Follow-up Master 32** for reteaching of spelling words.)

A. Discovering Spelling Ideas

1. Say the following words as you write them on the chalkboard.

proud	coil
crowd	boy

2. Ask the children to identify the vowel sound that the words in each pair have in common. (proud, crowd, /ou/; coil, boy, /oi/)
3. Ask the children to identify the letters that spell /ou/ and /oi/. (ou and ow; oi and oy)
4. Ask the children what they have learned about spelling /ou/ and /oi/. (/ou/ can be spelled ou or ow; /oi/ can be spelled oi or oy.)

B. Word Shapes

1. Explain to the children that each word has a shape and that remembering the shape of a word can help them to spell the word correctly.
2. On the chalkboard, write the words *foil* and *plow*. Have the children identify "short," "tall," and "tail" letters.
3. Draw the configuration of each word on the chalkboard, and ask the children which word fits in each shape.

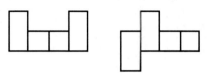

Use **Reteaching Follow-up Master 32A** to reinforce spelling generalizations taught in Unit 32.

Use **Reteaching Follow-up Master 32B** to reinforce spellings of This Week's Words for Unit 32.

Name _____

Reteaching Follow-up A Discovering Spelling Ideas **UNIT 32**

THIS WEEK'S WORDS

noise	brown	crown	voice	loud
cloud	clown	point	enjoy	joy
mouse	sound	owl	oil	mouth

1. Study This Week's Words. Say each word to yourself.

2. In each column, write the words that have the same vowel sound as the first word in the list.

how	boil
mouse	noise
brown	voice
crown	point
owl	oil
loud	enjoy
mouth	joy
cloud	
sound	
clown	

3. What vowel sound do all the words in the first column have in common?

   ___/ou/___ Circle the letters that spell that sound.

4. What vowel sound do all the words in the second column have in common?

   ___/oi/___ Circle the letters that spell that sound.

Reteaching • 53

Name _____

Reteaching Follow-up B Word Shapes **UNIT 32**

THIS WEEK'S WORDS

loud	mouse	brown	owl	voice
noise	mouth	clown	oil	joy
cloud	sound	crown	point	enjoy

Write each of This Week's Words in its correct shape. The first one has been done for you. Children may interchange answers that fit the same configuration.

1. n o i s e
2. o w l
3. p o i n t
4. o i l
5. m o u s e
6. c l o w n
7. c r o w n
8. m o u t h
9. c l o u d
10. s o u n d
11. j o y
12. e n j o y
13. v o i c e
14. l o u d
15. b r o w n

54 • Reteaching

141C   UNIT 32 *The Sounds /ou/ and /oi/*

PREVIEWING THE UNIT

Unit Materials

Instruction and Practice

Pupil Book	pages 138–145
Teacher's Edition	
Teaching Plans	pages 138–145
Enrichment Activities	
For the Classroom	pages 145A–145B
For the Home	page 145B
Reteaching Strategies	page 145C

Testing

Teacher's Edition	
Trial Test	pages 141E–141F
Unit Test	page 145B
Dictation Test	page 145B

Additional Resources

PRACTICE AND REINFORCEMENT
Extra Practice Master 33: This Week's Words
Extra Practice Master 33: Mastery Words
Extra Practice Master 33: Bonus Words
LEP Practice Master 33
Spelling and Language Master 33
Study Steps to Learn a Word Master

RETEACHING FOLLOW-UP
Reteaching Follow-up Master 33A:
    Discovering Spelling Ideas
Reteaching Follow-up Master 33B: Word
    Shapes
LEP Reteaching Follow-up Master 33

TEACHING AIDS
Spelling Generalizations Transparency 28

Click on the SPELLING banner to find activities for this unit.

Learner Objectives

Spelling

- To spell words that demonstrate these sound-letter relationships: /u/ou; /ou/ou; /ô/ough; /ō/ough; /uf/ough.
- To spell words with similar patterns but different vowel sounds.

Reading

- To follow written directions.
- To identify rhyming words.
- To use context clues for word identification.
- To identify sound-letter relationships.
- To use a dictionary to locate information.
- To use a dictionary for word meaning.

Writing

- To write a story.
- To use the writing process.
- To proofread for spelling, capitalization, and punctuation.
- To write legible manuscript and cursive letters.

Listening

- To listen to identify the relationship between sounds and letters.
- To follow oral directions.

Speaking

- To speak clearly to a group.
- To read stories and poems.
- To respond to a question.
- To express feelings and ideas about a piece of writing.
- To present a story.
- To contribute ideas and information in group discussions.

THIS WEEK'S WORDS

double
country
cousin
touch
count
flour
round
bought
brought
thought
although
though
tough
rough
enough

MASTERY WORDS

row
slow
own
bow
how
tower

BONUS WORDS

couple
southern
south
county
trousers
cough
fought
shoulder

This guide shows how you teach a typical spelling unit in either a five-day or a three-day sequence, while providing for individual differences. **Boldface type** indicates essential classwork. Steps shown in light type may be done in class or assigned as homework.

Five Days	● = average spellers ★ = better spellers ✓ = slower spellers	Three Days
Day **1** a	● ★ **Take This Week's Words Trial Test and correct** ● ✓ **Take Mastery word Trial Test and correct** ● ★ **Read This Week's Words and discuss generalization page 142**	Day **1**
Day **2** b	● Complete Spelling Practice page 143 ● ✓ Complete Extra Practice Master 33: This Week's Words (optional) ✓ Complete Spelling on Your Own: Mastery Words page 145 ★ **Take Bonus word Trial Test and correct**	
Day **3** c	● ★ ✓ **Complete Spelling and Language page 144** ● ★ ✓ Complete Writing on Your Own page 144 ● ★ ✓ **Complete Proofreading page 144** ● ✓ Take Midweek Test (optional) ★ Complete Spelling on Your Own: Bonus words page 145 ● ✓ Complete Spelling and Language Master 33 (optional)	Day **2**
Day **4** d	● Complete Spelling on Your Own: This Week's Words page 145 ✓ Complete Extra Practice Master 33: Mastery words (optional) ★ Complete Extra Practice Master 33: Bonus words (optional)	
Day **5** e	● Take Unit Test on This Week's Words ● Complete Reteaching Follow-up Masters 33A and 33B (optional) ● ✓ **Take Unit Test on Mastery words** ★ **Take Unit Test on Bonus words**	Day **3**

Enrichment Activities for the **classroom** and for the **home** included at the end of this unit may be assigned selectively on any day of the week.

INTRODUCING THE UNIT

Establish Readiness for Learning

Tell the children that this week they will learn about words that contain the letters *ou* and *ough*. Explain that these spellings represent different vowel sounds in different words. Tell the children they will apply what they learn to spell This Week's Words and use some of the words to write a funny adventure story.

Assess Children's Spelling Ability

Administer the Trial Test before the children study This Week's Words. Use the test sentences provided. Say each word and use it in a sentence. Then repeat the word. Have the children write the words on a separate sheet of paper or in their spelling notebooks. Test

sentences are also provided for Mastery and Bonus words.

Have the children check their own work by listening to you read the spelling of the words or by referring to This Week's Words in the left column of the **Pupil Book.** For each misspelled word, have the children follow the **Study Steps to Learn a Word** on page 1 in the **Pupil Book** or use the copying master to study and write the words. Children should record the number correct on their **Progress Report.**

Trial Test Sentences

This Week's Words

1. *double*   We saw a *double* feature at the movies.   *double*
2. *country*   My uncle lives on a farm in the *country*.   *country*
3. *cousin*   My *cousin* lives next door. *cousin*

4. *touch*   Do not *touch* the wet paint.
   touch

5. *count*   We must *count* the people in
   the room.   **count**

6. *flour*   We need *flour* to bake bread.
   flour

7. *round*   Oranges and grapefruits are
   round.   **round**

8. *bought*   Chico *bought* a new yo-yo.
   bought

9. *brought*   He *brought* the yo-yo to
   school.   **brought**

10. *thought*   Arlene *thought* before she
    answered the question.   **thought**

11. *although*   I'm glad you're here, *although*
    you're very late.   **although**

12. *though*   We will go even *though* it is
    raining.   **though**

13. *tough*   A rhinoceros has a *tough* skin.
    tough

14. *rough*   A cat's tongue is *rough.*   **rough**

15. *enough*   One hamburger is *enough* for
    me.   **enough**

Mastery Words

1. *row*   Effie put the chairs in a *row.*   **row**
2. *slow*   This bus is very *slow.*   **slow**
3. *own*   Someday I will *own* a horse.   **own**
4. *bow*   Miko put a *bow* on the package.
   bow
5. *how*   This is *how* to do it.   **how**
6. *tower*   The town hall has a clock *tower.*
   tower

Bonus Words

1. *couple*   I have a *couple* of things to
   do.   **couple**
2. *southern*   Joanie lives in the *southern*
   part of the state.   **southern**

3. *south*   California is *south* of Oregon.
   south

4. *county*   Mr. Greene is the sheriff in this
   county.   **county**

5. *trousers*   The tailor mended Thad's
   trousers.   **trousers**

6. *cough*   A tickle in your throat makes you
   cough.   **cough**

7. *fought*   The firefighters *fought* the
   blaze.   **fought**

8. *shoulder*   The parrot sat on the woman's
   shoulder.   **shoulder**

Apply Prior Learning

Write the words *must, cow, show* and *taught*
on the chalkboard. Ask the children to name
other words that have each of these vowel
sounds. If any of the words have the same
vowel sound spelled with *ou*, write them on the
chalkboard. (Possible responses: *touch* or
cousin, house, though, bought) If none are
suggested with *ou* spelling the vowel sound,
proceed with the following orally. Say the word
touch and ask which word on the chalkboard
has the same vowel sound. (must) Ask the
children if they would expect the vowel sound
to be spelled the same way. (Children will
probably say yes.) Do the same with the words
house, though, and *bought.* Tell the children
that they will learn that in some words, each of
these vowel sounds is spelled with different
letters. Tell the children that they will learn
about the different ways to spell these sounds
as they learn This Week's Words. Then they can
use these words in a variety of writing tasks:
writing letters, writing lists, or preparing reports.

FOCUS

- Relates to prior
  learning
- Draws relationships
- Applies spelling
  generalizations to
  new contexts

FOR CHILDREN WITH SPECIAL NEEDS

Learning Difficulties

Using music to facilitate language learning is effective
in teaching spelling to children with language and
learning difficulties.

In preparation you will need two tape recorders and
two tapes: one blank and the other with prerecorded in-
strumental music. Review the spelling of This Week's
Words with the children and have them make a list of
those words that present problems for them. With the
taped music playing on one tape recorder as background music, and the other tape in the record mode,
have each child say the spelling word, spell it slowly, and
repeat the word into the tape recorder, then pause for
about 10–15 seconds before saying the next word.

To study This Week's Words, have the children play their

own personal spelling-accompanied-by-music tape. At
the pause in the tape, have the children write the spelling
word.

Have the children check their own spelling from their
original list. Any misspelled words should be crossed out or
erased and written correctly.

Limited English Proficiency

To help limited English proficient children work with the
spelling generalizations for Unit 33, you may wish to refer
to the booklet "Suggestions and Activities for Limited English Proficient Students."

TEACHING PLAN

Objective To spell words that demonstrate these sound-letter relationships: /u/ou, /ou/ou, /ô/ough, /uf/ough.

1. Write these two columns on the chalkboard:

touch	caught
tough	show
though	much
thought	stuff

   Ask a child to read each word in the first column and then find a word in the second column that rhymes with it. Help the children to recognize that each word in the first column is spelled with *ou* or *ough* but that these letters represent a number of different sounds—sounds that are often spelled with different letters.

2. Read the poem, which is the generalization, on page 142.

You may wish to introduce the lesson by using *Spelling Generalizations Transparency 28.*

3. Have volunteers read This Week's Words aloud. As each word is read, have the children indicate whether *ou* or *ough* represents the vowel sound heard in *much* (double, country, cousin, touch), in *howl* (count, flour, round), in *paw* (bought, brought, thought), at the end of *shadow* (although, though), or in *huff* and *puff* (tough, rough, enough). Also draw the children's attention to the *le* spelling for /əl/ in *double,* the *in* spelling for /ən/ in *cousin,* the *y* spelling for /ē/ in *country,* and the *al* spelling for /ôl/ in *although.*

4. Discuss the meaning and use of any unfamiliar word. Have volunteers look up such words in the **Spelling Dictionary.**

You may wish to assign *LEP Practice Master 33* for reinforcement in writing spelling words.

---

33 Words with ou and ough

THIS WEEK'S WORDS

1. double
2. country
3. cousin
4. touch
5. count
6. flour
7. round
8. bought
9. brought
10. thought
11. although
12. though
13. tough
14. rough
15. enough

This Week's Words

In double, country, cousin, and touch,
The o-u sounds like the u in much.

In count and flour and also in round,
The o-u has a howling sound.

With g-h in bought, brought, and thought,
The o-u sounds like the end of paw.

The o-u-g-h in although and though
Sounds surprised—scared of a shadow.

These same four letters huff and puff
In tough and rough and in enough.

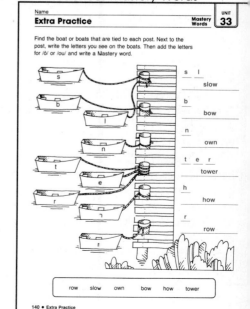

142

Extra Practice: This Week's Words

Name
Extra Practice This Week's Words UNIT 33

1. Circle the three words that rhyme with *stuff.* Then circle the four other words that have a short *u* sound.

2. Draw a box around the word that sounds like *flower.* Then draw a box around the two other words that have the sound /ou/.

3. Draw a line under the two words that rhyme with *go.*

4. Make an X under each word that rhymes with *ough.*

5. Write the seven words you circled.

touch	rough	tough
enough	cousin	country
double		

6. Write the three words you put a box around.

flour	round	count

7. Write the two words you drew a line under.

though	although

8. Write the three words you put an X under.

bought	brought	thought

Extra Practice • 139

Extra Practice: Mastery Words

Name
Extra Practice Mastery Words UNIT 33

Find the boat or boats that are tied to each post. Next to the post, write the letters you see on the boats. Then add the letters for /ô/ or /ou/ and write a Mastery word.

s l	slow
b	bow
n	own
t e r	tower
h	how
r	row

row	slow	own	bow	how	tower

140 • Extra Practice

Spelling Practice

A. Follow the directions. Use This Week's Words.

This Week's Words (word list on right):
double
country
cousin
touch
count
flour
round
bought
brought
thought
although
though
tough
rough
enough

1. Write a word that means "hard to chew." (It rhymes with stuff.)   _tough_

2. Add an <u>h</u> to make a word that means "even if." (It rhymes with go.)   _though_

3. Add a <u>t</u> to make a word that means "did think." (It rhymes with caught.)   _thought_

4. Write the three words that end with the sound /f/.
   rough   _tough_   _enough_

5. Write four more words that have the sound /u/ as in up.
   double   _country_
   cousin   _touch_

6. Write the two words that end with /ō/.
   though   _although_

7. Write the three words that have the sound /ou/.
   count   _flour_   _round_

8. Write the three words that rhyme with <u>caught</u>.
   bought   _brought_   _thought_

B. Use This Week's Words to answer the questions.

9. Did she buy her friend a tie?
   Yes, she _bought_ her friend a tie.

10. Did she bring it to his birthday party?
    Yes, she _brought_ it to his birthday party.

11. Did he think the tie was nice?
    Yes, he _thought_ the tie was nice.

143

---

xtra Practice: Bonus Words

Name

Extra Practice — Bonus Words — UNIT 33

Kevin wrote this letter to his friend Amos. He made eleven spelling mistakes. Some of the words he spelled wrong are Bonus words. Some of them are This Week's Words.

1. Find the spelling mistakes and draw a line under each one.

Dear Amos,
My whole family went on a bicycle trip last week. Mom and Dad took a cuple of days off from work. We wint souht to Green Countie. That's in the sothern part of the state.
Things were pretty ruff at the beginning. My brother fell off his bike. He tore his trowsers and bumped his sholder. Ned is tuff, though, and he was all right.
We were going to camp out Saturday night, but it started to rain. Mom and Dad decided we should go to a motel. Ned faught with them about it. He wanted to stay in the tent. Then he started to coff. Mom said, "That's enuff. We are going to a motel before we all catch colds." So we stayed in a motel that night.
Please write to me soon.
Your friend,
Kevin

2. Write the eleven misspelled words correctly.

couple	south	County
southern	rough	trousers
shoulder	tough	fought
cough	enough	

couple	south	trousers	cough
county	southern	fought	shoulder

Extra Practice • 141

Summarize Learning

Have the children summarize what they have learned on pages 142 and 143. *Ask:*

- What sounds have you learned about in this lesson? (/u/, /ou/, /ô/, /uf/)
- What have you learned about these sounds? Give examples. (/u/ can be spelled *ou*, *touch*; /ou/ can be spelled *ou*, *count*; /ô/ can be spelled *ough*, *bought*; /uf/ can be spelled *ough*, *rough*)

TEACHING PLAN

Objectives To write words given meaning clues; to write words given consonant and vowel sound clues; to write rhyming words; to write words in sentence context.

1. Briefly discuss the directions on page 143. Be sure the children understand that in **1-3** they will start with one word and add letters to spell two other words. Also check to be sure that the children can identify the sounds represented by /ō/ and /ou/ in **6** and **7**.

2. Have the children complete the page independently. Remind them to use legible handwriting. You may wish to demonstrate the correct form of the letters *g* and *u* and then have the children practice writing the letters. For **Hand-writing Models,** refer the children to page 258 in the **Pupil Book.**

3. To correct the children's work, have volunteers write the answers for the activities in Exercise **A** on the chalkboard. Let the children check their own answers. Then have volunteers read the completed sentences in Exercise **B** aloud. Point out that in each sentence, the word they wrote is the past form of an irregular verb. Ask the children to identify the other form of the verb in the question that precedes each sentence. (buy, bring, think)

For reinforcement in writing spelling words, you may wish to assign *Extra Practice Master 33: This Week's Words.*

TEACHING PLAN

SPELLING AND LANGUAGE

> **Objective** To write rhyming words that complete a poem.

1. To prepare children for this activity, discuss the steps involved in making bread. Explain the terms *yeast, knead,* and *rise,* if necessary.
2. Read the directions on page 144 aloud. It may be helpful to read the poem aloud and have the children supply the missing rhyming words.
3. Have the children complete the poem independently.

For extended practice in writing rhyming words, you may wish to assign *Spelling and Language Master 33.*

WRITING ON YOUR OWN

> **Objectives** To write a story; to proofread for spelling.

1. Review the directions with the children.
2. As a **prewriting** activity, discuss with the children the differences between city life and country life, and possible humorous incidents in both places. Make a chart to show parallels between children's responses, such as:

	CITY	COUNTRY
Traffic	heavy	light
Hobbies	museums	picnics

Then have the children **compose** their stories. You may wish to refer children to a model of a story on page 253 of the **Writer's Guide.** When they are ready to **revise,** remind them to check for spelling. For additional help, you may also wish to refer them to the **Revising Checklist** on page 247 of the **Writer's Guide.** To **publish,** have children read their stories to the class.

THIS WEEK'S WORDS

double
country
cousin
touch
count
flour
round
bought
brought
thought
although
though
tough
rough
enough

Spelling and Language • Rhyming Words

Finish the poem with This Week's Words. The words must rhyme with the words in dark print. Write your answers below.

Come to my house in about an **hour,**
And help me make bread from yeast and __1__ .
Then after all the kneading and **trouble,**
We'll leave it to rise until it is __2__ .
After we bake it just as we **ought,**
We'll have fresh bread—quicker than you __3__ .

1. _____flour_____   2. _____double_____   3. _____thought_____

Writing on Your Own

Write a story for your classmates called "The City Cousin." Tell about the funny adventures of a city cousin who comes to visit a country cousin. Use some of This Week's Words.

✏️ **WRITER'S GUIDE** For a sample of a story, turn to page 252.

Proofreading

David wrote down this phone message for his mother. He made six spelling mistakes.
1. Circle each of David's mistakes.

> *Mrs. Logan called at 3:00. She visited her* (cosin) *in the* (contry). *She* (broght) *back* (enuff) *fresh corn for everybody. We can* (cont) *on having some for dinner. Please get in* (tuch) *with her.*

2. Write the six misspelled words correctly.

cousin	country	brought
enough	count	touch

✏️ **WRITER'S GUIDE** See the editing and proofreading marks on page 248.

PROOFREADING

> **Objectives** To proofread a message for spelling errors; to write misspelled words correctly.

1. Read the introductory sentences and the directions on page 144.
2. Have the children read through the message independently, looking for errors. Then ask them to circle the misspelled words and write them correctly.
   If you are using the hardcover book, the children should simply locate the misspelled words and write them correctly in their notebooks.

Extra Practice: Spelling and Language

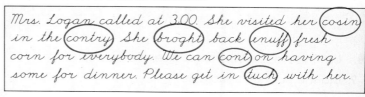

Name
Spelling and Language   UNIT 33

In each sentence, circle the word that doesn't make sense. Then write the sentence again using one of This Week's Words. The word will rhyme with the word that doesn't make sense.

1. Yesterday I (caught) a new blue bike.
   Yesterday I bought a new blue bike.
2. Its wheels were nice and (pound).
   Its wheels were nice and round.
3. Its tires were as (huff) as nails.
   Its tires were as tough as nails.
4. The seat was nice to (much).
   The seat was nice to touch.
5. It felt smooth, not (puff).
   It felt smooth, not rough.
6. I (taught) the bike home to show to my mom.
   I brought the bike home to show to my mom.
7. She said, "I (bought) you wanted a red bike."
   She said, "I thought you wanted a red bike."
8. I answered, "Blue is good (rough) for me."
   I answered, "Blue is good enough for me."

double	touch	flour	country	bought
tough	rough	enough	although	thought
cousin	count	round	brought	though

142 • Extra Practice

Spelling on Your Own

THIS WEEK'S WORDS

Use all the words to make a word search puzzle. You can write the words across or down. Fill in the empty spaces with other letters. Then let someone else solve the puzzle.

```
C A C R O F E
G D O U B L E
C O U S I N M
R E N N I E A
R K T O U G H
```

MASTERY WORDS

Follow the directions. Use the Mastery words.

row	slow
own	bow
how	tower

1. Write the four words with /ō/ as in <u>low</u>.

_____row_____   _____slow_____   **Word order may vary.**

_____own_____   _____bow_____

2. Write the three words with /ou/ as in <u>cow</u>.

_____bow_____   _____how_____   **Word order may vary.**
                                    _____tower_____

3. Write the word you wrote for both **1** and **2.** _____bow_____

Use one Mastery word to finish both sentences.

4. Take the oars and _____row_____ the boat.

5. Tall people must stand in the back _____row_____.

BONUS WORDS

couple
southern
south
county
trousers
cough
fought
shoulder

Write the two words in each group that have the same vowel sound.

1. couple   **2.** cough   **3.** trousers   **4.** shoulder
   cup   tough   trouble   cold
   soup   off   houses   should

Finish these sentences with Bonus words.

5. <u>Think</u> is to <u>thought</u> as <u>fight</u> is to _____.

6. <u>North</u> is to <u>northern</u> as <u>south</u> is to _____.

Write sentences using the Bonus words. **See answers below.**

145

Summarize Learning

Have the children summarize what they have learned in this unit. *Ask:*

- What have you learned about in this unit? Give examples. (/u/ spelled *ou*, *touch*; /ou/ spelled *ou*, *count*; /ô/ spelled *ough*, *bought*; /uf/ spelled *ough*, *rough*)
- What generalizations have you learned? How did you use these generalizations?

Spelling on Your Own   UNIT 33d

TEACHING PLAN

Objective   To apply the unit spelling generalization to spell This Week's Words, Mastery words, and Bonus words independently.

THIS WEEK'S WORDS

1. Read the directions on page 145 aloud. Help the children get started by demonstrating on the chalkboard how the sample puzzle in the **Pupil Book** was developed.
2. Have the children make up their puzzles independently.
3. Let the children exchange their work and solve each other's puzzles.

MASTERY WORDS

1. Put a simple drawing of a bow and of a stick figure bowing on the chalkboard. Have the children identify each drawing and write *bow* under each one. Help the children to recognize that *ow* spells /ō/ in one of the words and /ou/ in the other.
2. Have volunteers read the Mastery words aloud. As each word is read, help the children to recognize the vowel sound spelled with *ow* and to relate it to /bō/ or /bou/.
3. Have the children complete the activities independently.

BONUS WORDS

1. Review the sounds represented by *ou* and *ough* in This Week's Words and introduce *ough* for /ôf/ in *cough* and *ou* for /ō/ in *shoulder*.
2. Have volunteers read the Bonus words aloud.
3. Have the children complete the activities independently.

For reinforcement in writing spelling words, you may wish to assign *Extra Practice Master 33: Mastery Words* or *Bonus Words.*

CLOSING THE UNIT

Apply New Learning

Tell the children that if they misspell words with *ou* and *ough* in their writing, they should use one or more of the following strategies:

- think about the possible spellings for a sound within the word and use the dictionary to find the correct spelling.
- write the word using different spellings and compare it with the spelling they picture in their minds.
- think of words that rhyme and compare in their minds how they are spelled.

Transfer New Learning

Tell the children that when they encounter new words in their personal reading and in other content areas, they should learn the meaning of those words and then apply the generalizations they have studied to the spelling of those words. Tell them that once the words are familiar in both meaning and spelling, they should use the new words in their writing.

ENRICHMENT ACTIVITIES

Classroom activities and **home activities** may be assigned to children of all ability levels. The activities provide opportunities for children to use their spelling words in new contexts.

For the Classroom

To individualize classroom activities, you may have the children use the word list they are studying in this unit.

- *Basic:* Use **Mastery** words to complete the activity.
- *Average:* Use **This Week's Words** to complete the activity.
- *Challenging:* Use **Bonus** words to complete the activity.

1. **Language Arts/Writing Example Sentences** Have the children look up five spelling words in the dictionary and note one of the meanings for each word. Then have them write an example sentence which shows that meaning. Use this example for the word *count* with the meaning "to name numbers in order": *My little sister can count to one hundred by ones.* When the children are satisfied with their sentences, have them write the sentences on another sheet of paper, leaving a blank for the spelling word. Have the children exchange papers and write the missing spelling word to complete each of the sentences. Then have them try to give the meaning of the word based on the example sentence.

 ■ COOPERATIVE LEARNING: Have each group write a set of example sentences for spelling words. After group members decide which words will be used, have each

child look up one word in the dictionary and note one of its meanings. Then each child should write an example sentence which shows that meaning. After the group revises and proofreads the sentences, have one person rewrite all the sentences, leaving a blank space for each spelling word. Have the group ask classmates to complete each sentence and try to give the meaning of the word as used in the sentence.

2. **Language Arts/Writing Sentences** Have students use their spelling words to write sentences, using sentence parts provided by you. As an example, write *I thought* on the chalkboard and brainstorm ways to use as many spelling words as possible to complete the sentence. An example would be: *I thought you brought the flour we bought at the country store.* Tell the children to make complete sentences using phrases such as the following: *Although we, called to say, is not so, Don't.* When they have completed the activity, have the children share the sentences with the class.

 ■ COOPERATIVE LEARNING: Have each group make complete sentences using one of the following phrases: *Although we, called to say, is not so, Don't.* Children should use as many spelling words as they can from all three lists. Tell group members to check one another's sentences to make sure that the phrase and other spelling words have been included. When the sentences have been written, have one member from each group identify the group's phrase for the class and then share the group's sentences with them.

3. **Language Arts/Writing a Journal Entry** Have the children write a journal entry about a story character they have read about. Tell them to use as many spelling words as possible. Direct their attention to page 252 of the **Writer's Guide** to read about journals. Tell the children to write about what the story character did. As a *prewriting* activity, have the children decide upon the character. Have them look over the spelling word lists to get ideas about an event they can write about. Give these examples: *a visit with George Washington, my adventure with Goldilocks and the three bears.* Have the children write their topics and then list the things that might have happened. Tell them to choose three or four things that happened and put them in the proper order. When children complete the prewriting activities, tell them to use their lists to *compose* their journal entries. Remind them to use as many spelling words as possible. Then have the children *revise* their journal entries by checking to make sure the events are in the proper order. Remind them to proofread for spelling, capitalization, and punctuation. *Publish* their journal entries in a bulletin board display.

 ■ COOPERATIVE LEARNING: Have each group write a journal entry that describes a story character they have read about. As a *prewriting* activity, have each group choose the character. Then have the group look over the spelling word lists in search of appropriate topics and list them. When the group is ready to **compose,** have one group member begin by contributing the first sentence or two. The other children in the group should then build on the first sentences, using as many spelling words as possible. Have the group work together to **revise,** suggesting ways to make the entry more clear, interesting, or complete. Each member of the group should also proofread for spelling, capitalization, and punctuation. Have the group **publish** the journal entry by reading it aloud to the class or by displaying it on the bulletin board.

r the Home

Children may complete these activities independently or th the assistance of a relative or friend in the home.

Language Arts/Writing Word Families Tell the children to choose four spelling words and write as many words as they can think of that are in the same word family. As an example, present the following group of words: *touch, touches, touched, touching, touchy.* Tell the children to check a dictionary to be sure their words are spelled correctly. Then have the children write a sentence for each word in one word family.

Language Arts/Writing Alliterative Phrases Tell the children to use spelling words to write original alliterative phrases of three or four words, using at least one spelling word. Give these examples: *country cousins count* catfish, *tough* Tommy *touches* turtles.

Mathematics/Writing an Explanation on Multiplication Tell the children to write as many sentences as necessary to explain how to multiply four times two to someone who does not know how to multiply. Remind them to use some of their spelling words in their explanations and to include a drawing if necessary.

Social Studies/Writing a Comparison of the City and the Country Tell the children to think about differences be- tween a big city and a country town. Tell them to write a short paragraph that compares the two. They may want to draw a picture or cut pictures from old magazines to accompany their paragraphs. Refer children to page 249 of the **Writer's Guide** to read about paragraphs if necessary.

VALUATING SPELLING ABILITY

nit Test

1. **double** When you *double* 12 you get 24. **double**
2. **country** Liechtenstein is a very small *country.* **country**
3. **cousin** My aunt and my *cousin* came to visit us. **cousin**
4. **touch** Roberto can *touch* his toes. **touch**
5. **count** Little Jeffie can *count* to ten. **count**

6. **flour** You can make paste with *flour* and water. **flour**
7. **round** The clock has a *round* face. **round**
8. **bought** We *bought* the food for the picnic. **bought**
9. **brought** We *brought* it home with us. **brought**
10. **thought** Estelle *thought* the story was wonderful. **thought**
11. **although** We watched a movie *although* we were tired. **although**
12. **though** We enjoyed it even *though* it was long. **though**
13. **tough** This meat is too *tough* to chew. **tough**
14. **rough** You shouldn't be *rough* with the baby. **rough**
15. **enough** Michelle has *enough* apples for everyone. **enough**

Mastery Words
1. **row** You may *row* the boat. **row**
2. **slow** Turtles and snails are very *slow.* **slow**
3. **own** Kim has her *own* telephone. **own**
4. **bow** The singer will *bow* to the audience. **bow**
5. **how** I wonder *how* cold it is today. **how**
6. **tower** The ranger watched from the lookout *tower.* **tower**

Bonus Words
1. **couple** The *couple* next door are away. **couple**
2. **southern** Alabama is in the *southern* part of the country. **southern**
3. **south** Mexico is *south* of the United States. **south**
4. **county** That is the biggest *county* in the state. **county**
5. **trousers** Alex spilled soup on his *trousers.* **trousers**
6. **cough** The dust made Lucia *cough.* **cough**
7. **fought** The dogs *fought* over the bone. **fought**
8. **shoulder** I will carry the box on my *shoulder.* **shoulder**

Dictation Sentences

This Week's Words
1. My *cousin bought* this *flour* in a *country* store.
2. I *thought* we *brought enough* for everybody.
3. The rock was *rough* to the *touch.*
4. We ate the meat even *though* it was *tough.*
5. She caught *double* her last *count* of fish, *although* the fish were small.
6. The table is *round.*

Mastery Words
1. Do you know *how* to tie this *bow?*
2. I will put the things that I *own* in a *row.*
3. We are *slow* when we take the stairs to the top of the *tower.*

Bonus Words
1. Give me a *couple* of taps on the *shoulder* if I *cough.*
2. We'll drive *south* to the *southern* part of the *county.*
3. He *fought* to get his *trousers* over his boots.

RETEACHING STRATEGIES FOR SPELLING

Children who have made errors on the Unit Test may require reteaching. Use the following *Reteaching Strategies* and *Follow-up Masters 33A* and *33B* for additional instruction and practice of This Week's Words. (You may wish to assign *LEP Reteaching Follow-up Master 33* for reteaching of spelling words.)

A. Discovering Spelling Ideas

1. Say the following words as you write them on the chalkboard.

   fought   dough   rough   trouble   sour

2. Ask the children to identify the letters that are the same in the first group of words. *(ough)*
3. Ask the children to identify the different sounds *ough* spells. (fought – /ô/ as in *raw*, dough – /ō/ as in *blow*, rough – /uf/ as in *puff*)
4. Ask the children to identify the letters that are the same in the next group of words. *(ou)*
5. Ask the children to identify the different sounds *ou* spells. (trouble – /u/ as in *much*, sour – /ou/ as in *round*)
6. Ask the children what they have learned about *ou* and *ough*. (The letters *ou* can spell two sounds: /u/ as in *much* and /ou/ as in *round*; *ough* can spell three sounds: /ô/ as in *raw*, /ō/ as in *blow*, /uf/ as in *puff*.)

B. Word Shapes

1. Explain to the children that each word has a shape and that remembering the shape of a word can help them to spell the word correctly.
2. On the chalkboard, write the words *couple* and *ought*. Have the children identify "short," "tall," and "tail" letters.
3. Draw the configuration of each word on the chalkboard, and ask the children which word fits in each shape.

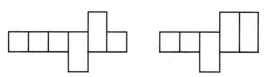

Use *Reteaching Follow-up Master 33A* to reinforce spelling generalizations taught in Unit 33.

Use *Reteaching Follow-up Master 33B* to reinforce spellings of This Week's Words for Unit 33.

Name _____
Reteaching Follow-up A   Discovering Spelling Ideas   UNIT **33**

THIS WEEK'S WORDS

double	touch	flour	t<u>ough</u>	although
cousin	count	round	r<u>ough</u>	thought
country	brought	bought	th<u>ough</u>	enough

1. Underline the words above that contain *ough*.

2. Look at the underlined words and follow the directions. Write the words in which *ough* has the same vowel sound as in *raw*.

   | bought | brought | thought |

   Write the words in which *ough* has the same vowel sound as in *blow*.

   | although | though |

   Write the words in which *ough* rhymes with *puff*.

   | tough | enough | rough |

3. Look at the words above that are not underlined and follow the directions.
   Write the words in which *ou* has the same vowel sound as in *luck*.

   | double | country |
   | cousin | touch |

   Write the words in which *ou* has the same vowel sound as in *pound*.

   | flour | count | round |

4. How many different sounds does *ough* spell in This Week's Words?

   three

5. How many different sounds does *ou* by itself stand for in This Week's Words?

   two

Reteaching • 55

Name _____
Reteaching Follow-up B   Word Shapes   UNIT **33**

THIS WEEK'S WORDS

double	touch	round	thought	tough
country	count	bought	although	rough
cousin	flour	brought	though	enough

Write each of This Week's Words in its correct shape. The first one has been done for you. **Children may interchange answers that fit the same configuration.**

1. a l t h o u g h
2. c o u s i n
3. t h o u g h t
4. t o u c h
5. d o u b l e
6. r o u g h
7. c o u n t r y
8. t h o u g h
9. r o u n d
10. f l o u r
11. c o u n t
12. t o u g h
13. b o u g h t
14. b r o u g h t
15. e n o u g h

56 • Reteaching

REVIEWING THE UNIT

Unit Materials

Instruction and Practice

Pupil Book	pages 146–149
Teacher's Edition	
Teaching Plans	pages 146–149
Enrichment Activities	
For the Classroom	pages 149A–149B
For the Home	page 149B
Reteaching Strategies	page 149C

Testing

Teacher's Edition	
Trial Test	pages 145E–145F
Unit Test	page 149B
Dictation Test	page 149B

Additional Resources

PRACTICE AND REINFORCEMENT
Extra Practice Master 34: This Week's Words
Extra Practice Master 34: Mastery Words
Extra Practice Master 34: Bonus Words
LEP Practice Master 34
Spelling and Language Master 34
Study Steps to Learn a Word Master

RETEACHING FOLLOW-UP
Reteaching Follow-up Master 34A:
   Discovering Spelling Ideas
Reteaching Follow-up Master 34B: Word
   Shapes
LEP Reteaching Follow-up Master 34

TEACHING AIDS
Spelling Generalizations Transparency 29

Visit our Web site
http://www.hbschool.com

Click on the SPELLING banner to find activities for this unit.

Learner Objectives

Spelling

- To spell words that have the VC/CV syllable pattern.

Reading

- To follow written directions.
- To recognize accented syllables given dictionary pronunciations.
- To use context clues for word identification.
- To use a dictionary as a key to pronunciation.
- To use a dictionary for word meanings.
- To recognize accented syllables given dictionary pronunciations.

Writing

- To write a letter.
- To use the writing process.
- To proofread for spelling, capitalization, and punctuation.
- To write legible manuscript and cursive letters.

Listening

- To listen to recognize how words can be divided into syllables.
- To follow oral directions.

Speaking

- To speak clearly to a group.
- To respond to a question.
- To express feelings and ideas about a piece of writing.
- To present a how-to paragraph and a story.
- To contribute ideas and information in group discussions.

THIS WEEK'S WORDS

butter
cattle
dinner
funny
happen
lesson
matter
middle
rabbit
corner
forgot
number
perhaps
problem
wonder

MASTERY WORDS

follow
happy
hello
pretty
sunny
sister

BONUS WORDS

stammer
swallow
hollow
allow
tonsils
seldom
welcome
practice

Assignment Guide

This guide shows how you teach a typical spelling unit in either a five-day or a three-day sequence, while providing for individual differences. **Boldface type** indicates essential classwork. Steps shown in light type may be done in class or assigned as homework.

Five Days	○ = average spellers ★ = better spellers ✓ = slower spellers	Three Days
Day **1**	○ ★ **Take This Week's Words Trial Test and correct** ○ ✓ **Take Mastery Word Trial Test and correct** ○ ★ **Read This Week's Words and discuss generalization page 146**	Day **1**
Day **2**	○ Complete Spelling Practice page 147 ○ ✓ Complete Extra Practice Master 34: This Week's Words (optional) ✓ Complete Spelling on Your Own: Mastery Words page 149 ★ **Take Bonus Word Trial Test and correct**	
Day **3**	○ ★ ✓ **Complete Spelling and Language page 148** ○ ★ ✓ Complete Writing on Your Own page 148 ○ ★ ✓ **Complete Using the Dictionary to Spell and Write page 148** ○ ✓ Take Midweek Test (optional) ★ Complete Spelling on Your Own: Bonus Words page 149 ○ ✓ Complete Spelling and Language Master 34 (optional)	Day **2**
Day **4**	○ Complete Spelling on Your Own: This Week's Words page 149 ✓ Complete Extra Practice Master 34: Mastery Words (optional) ★ Complete Extra Practice Master 34: Bonus Words (optional)	
Day **5**	○ **Take Unit Test on This Week's Words** ○ Complete Reteaching Follow-up Masters 34A and 34B (optional) ○ ✓ **Take Unit Test on Mastery Words** ★ **Take Unit Test on Bonus Words**	Day **3**

Enrichment Activities for the **classroom** and for the **home** included at the end of this unit may be assigned selectively on any day of the week.

INTRODUCING THE UNIT

Establish Readiness for Learning

Tell the children that this week they will learn more about syllables. In Unit 34 they will study the VC/CV syllable pattern. Tell the children that they will apply the spelling generalizations to This Week's Words and use those words to write a letter.

Assess Children's Spelling Ability

Administer the Trial Test before the children study This Week's Words. Use the test sentences provided. Say each word and use it in a sentence. Then repeat the word. Have the children write the words on a separate sheet of paper or in their spelling notebooks. Test sentences are also provided for Mastery and Bonus words.

Have the children check their own work by

listening to you read the spelling of the words or by referring to This Week's Words in the left column of the **Pupil Book**. For each misspelled word, have the children follow the **Study Steps to Learn a Word** on page 1 in the **Pupil Book** or use the copying master to study and write the words. Children should record the number correct on their **Progress Report.**

Trial Test Sentences

This Week's Words
1. *butter* I don't use *butter* on my toast. *butter*
2. *cattle* We get milk and beef from *cattle*. *cattle*
3. *dinner* We had fish for *dinner*. *dinner*
4. *funny* Dad told us a *funny* story about losing his hat. *funny*
5. *happen* It won't *happen* again. *happen*
6. *lesson* This is a spelling *lesson*. *lesson*
7. *matter* Something is the *matter* with my bike. *matter.*

FOCUS

- Establishes objectives
- Relates to prior learning
- Sets purpose of instruction

8. *middle*   Jan woke up in the *middle* of the night.   **middle**

9. *rabbit*   We saw a *rabbit* hop across the trail.   **rabbit**

10. *corner*   Isaac's house is on the *corner*.   **corner**

11. *forgot*   Joanie *forgot* to bring her book.   **forgot**

12. *number*   Please give me your phone number.   **number**

13. *perhaps*   If Lyle goes skating, *perhaps* I will go, too.   **perhaps**

14. *problem*   Amelia could not solve the last problem.   **problem**

15. *wonder*   I *wonder* how this story ends   **wonder**

Mastery Words

1. *follow*   The puppy will *follow* you home.   **follow**

2. *happy*   Dean is *happy* that it is spring.   **happy**

3. *hello*   She said *hello* to him.   **hello**

4. *pretty*   Brad's mother is very *pretty*.   **pretty**

5. *sunny*   We like to swim on a *sunny* day.   **sunny**

6. *sister*   My *sister* is older than I.   **sister**

Bonus Words

1. *stammer*   Some people *stammer* when they are nervous.   **stammer**

2. *swallow*   This soup is too hot to *swallow*.   **swallow**

3. *hollow*   The squirrels live in a *hollow* tree.   **hollow**

4. *allow*   They do not *allow* dogs in here.   **allow**

5. *tonsils*   Arnie had his *tonsils* out.   **tonsils**

6. *seldom*   Ruth *seldom* watches TV because she prefers to read.   **seldom**

7. *welcome*   You are *welcome* to join us.   **welcome**

8. *practice*   Wayne must *practice* catching the ball.   **practice.**

Apply Prior Learning

Have the children apply what they already know about syllable patterns by participating in the following activity.

Write the words *silly, lumber, happy,* and *slumber* on the chalkboard. Ask the children to tell what is alike in all these words. Help them to recognize that each word has two vowel sounds with two consonant letters between those two sounds, and that each word has two syllables. Have volunteers come to the chalkboard and divide each word into syllables. Point out the VC/CV pattern as they divide the words into syllables. Tell the children that in Unit 34 they will study words that have these syllable patterns. Explain that they can use these words in a variety of writing tasks; they can use the words in a note to a friend, in a letter, or in a creative writing assignment.

FOR CHILDREN WITH SPECIAL NEEDS

Learning Difficulties

Children with disabilities in auditory analysis of words may benefit from learning some mnemonic devices that will help them remember the generalizations taught in this unit. Help children learn the unit generalizations by telling them that syllables may be divided between two consonants when the consonants are "sandwiched" in between two vowels. Have the children underline the two vowels and divide the "sandwich filling" in two with a line, e.g., *din/ner.*

If you describe the concept of "sandwich" in a humorous, exaggerated way, this will help the children to remember. For example, the word is *forgot*. The *o* is a special type of bread used to wrap around the two slices of *rg*. To make two open-face sandwiches, we'll separate the *r* and the *g* so that each piece of bread has a slice of filling.

Limited English Proficiency

To help limited English proficient children work with the spelling generalizations for Unit 34, you may wish to refer to the booklet "Suggestions and Activities for Limited English Proficient Students."

TEACHING PLAN

Objectives To spell words that have the VC/CV syllable pattern; to recognize how words can be divided into syllables.

1. Write these syllables on the chalkboard:

> hap   py   pen
> win   ter   ner
> but   ton   ter

Explain to the children that two words can be formed from each set of three word parts. Help them to form *happy, happen; winter, winner; button, butter.* Help them to recognize that each of the word parts they used to form the words has one vowel sound. Then remind them that these word parts are called syllables.

2. Read the generalization on page 146 aloud.

You may wish to introduce the lesson by using **Spelling Generalizations Transparency 29.**

3. Have volunteers read This Week's Words. As each word is read, ask the children to identify the two consonants in the middle of the word. Have them tell where each word would be divided into syllables.

You may wish to assign **LEP Practice Master 34** for reinforcement in writing spelling words.

34 Syllable Patterns

THIS WEEK'S WORDS

1. *butter*
2. *cattle*
3. *dinner*
4. *funny*
5. *happen*
6. *lesson*
7. *matter*
8. *middle*
9. *rabbit*
10. *corner*
11. *forgot*
12. *number*
13. *perhaps*
14. *problem*
15. *wonder*

This Week's Words

All the words this week have two vowel sounds. We say that they have two **syllables.**

Some of the words have double consonant letters in the middle: bu<u>tt</u>er. These words are divided into syllables between the double consonant letters.

Some of the words have two different consonant letters in the middle: co<u>rn</u>er. These words are divided into syllables between those consonant letters.

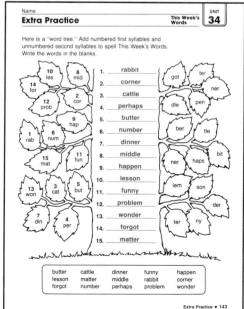

146

Extra Practice: This Week's Words

Name

Extra Practice   This Week's Words   UNIT 34

Here is a "word tree." Add numbered first syllables and unnumbered second syllables to spell This Week's Words. Write the words in the blanks.

1. rabbit
2. corner
3. cattle
4. perhaps
5. butter
6. number
7. dinner
8. middle
9. happen
10. lesson
11. funny
12. problem
13. wonder
14. forgot
15. matter

butter	cattle	dinner	funny	happen
lesson	matter	middle	rabbit	corner
forgot	number	perhaps	problem	wonder

Extra Practice • 143

Extra Practice: Mastery Words

Name

Extra Practice   Mastery Words   UNIT 34

A. Write the Mastery word that goes with each clue.

1. She is part of a family.   `s i s t e r`
2. A rainy day is not this.   `s u n n y`
3. Say this when you meet a friend.   `h e l l o`
4. This word tells about how someone looks.   `p r e t t y`
5. The leader does not do this.   `f o l l o w`
6. Someone who feels good is this.   `h a p p y`

B. Now finish the story. Write the first syllable of each Mastery word. Match the numbers here with the numbers in A.

It was a bright and <u>sun</u> (2) ny morning, but Bruce was not <u>hap</u> (6) py. He and his <u>sis</u> (1) ter Gwen were going to fight a dragon. Gwen was a year older and was very <u>pret</u> (4) ty.

Bruce and Gwen left early to look for the trail of the dragon. They said <u>hel</u> (3) lo to the wise owl. The owl knew all about the forest. "You must <u>fol</u> (5) low that path," it said. They thanked the owl and set off to find the dragon.

| follow | happy | hello |
| pretty | sunny | sister |

144 • Extra Practice

Spelling Practice

A. Write This Week's Words that have these double consonant letters. Then draw a line between the two syllables.

1. bb   rab|bit
2. ss   les|son
3. pp   hap|pen
4. nn (two words)   **Word order may vary.**

    din|ner   fun|ny

5. tt (three words)   **Word order may vary.**

    but|ter   cat|tle   mat|ter

6. Now write the word that tells where you divided the words.   middle

B. Add one of the syllables in the box to one of the numbered syllables. Write some of This Week's Words.

lem	ner	der	got	ber	haps

7. num   number
8. prob   problem
9. per   perhaps
10. cor   corner
11. for   forgot
12. won   wonder

C. Write one of This Week's Words that rhymes with each word. Then draw a line between the two syllables in each pair.

13. winner   din|ner
14. batter   mat|ter
15. sunny   fun|ny
16. riddle   mid|dle
17. mutter   but|ter
18. battle   cat|tle

This Week's Words:
butter
cattle
dinner
funny
happen
lesson
matter
middle
rabbit
corner
forgot
number
perhaps
problem
wonder

147

TEACHING PLAN

Objectives To write words given spelling clues; to divide words into syllables; to write words given syllables; to write rhyming words.

1. Briefly review how This Week's Words can be divided into syllables between two middle consonants.
2. Discuss the directions on page 147. Be sure the children understand that in Exercise **C** they should write the word that rhymes with each word given and then draw a line through *both* words to show how the words are divided into syllables.

   If you are using the hardcover book, the children should copy the words given in the book for Exercise **C**, write the word that rhymes with each one, and draw lines through both words to show syllable division.
3. Have the children complete the activities independently. Remind them to use legible handwriting. For **Handwriting Models,** refer the children to page 258 in the **Pupil Book.**
4. To correct the children's work, have volunteers write the answers on the chalkboard. Ask them to write both words for each item in Exercise **C**. Let the children check their own work.

For reinforcement in writing spelling words, you may wish to assign ***Extra Practice Master 34: This Week's Words.***

Extra Practice: Bonus Words

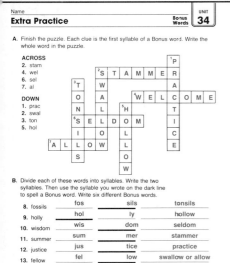

Summarize Learning

Have the children summarize what they have learned on pages 146 and 147. *Ask:*

- What did you learn about the VC/CV syllable pattern in this lesson? (Words that have two syllables with two consonants in the middle are divided between those consonant letters.)
- What are some examples of words that follow this generalization? (rabbit, problem; accept other examples)

TEACHING PLAN

SPELLING AND LANGUAGE

> **Objective**   To write words in sentence context and recognize which are nouns and verbs.

1. To prepare the children for this activity, briefly review the difference between a noun and a verb. Then write the word *row* on the chalkboard. Ask volunteers to use the word as a noun in a sentence and then as a verb.
2. Read the directions on page 148.
3. Have the children complete the activity independently.
4. Have volunteers read the completed sentences aloud. Let the children check their own work.

For extended practice in writing nouns and verbs in sentence context, you may wish to assign *Spelling and Language Master 34.*

WRITING ON YOUR OWN

> **Objectives**   To write a letter to a relative; to proofread for spelling.

1. Review the directions.
2. As a **prewriting** activity, have the children think of something funny that happened to them and list details that relate to the incident. Then have them **compose** their letters. When they are ready to **revise,** remind them to check for spelling. To **publish** have the children send their letters to their relatives.

USING THE DICTIONARY

> **Objectives**   To write words given dictionary pronunciations; to recognize accented syllables given dictionary pronunciations.

Spelling and Language • Nouns and Verbs

THIS WEEK'S WORDS
butter
cattle
dinner
funny
happen
lesson
matter
middle
rabbit
corner
forgot
number
perhaps
problem
wonder

A **noun** names a person, a place, or a thing. A **verb** shows action or being. Finish each pair of sentences with one of This Week's Words. The word will be a noun in the first sentence and a verb in the second.

1. Wally chased the dog around the ___corner___
2. Finally he was able to ___corner___ it.
3. Start with the ___number___ 1.
4. Then ___number___ your paper from 1 to 25.

Writing on Your Own

Write a letter to a relative telling about something funny that happened to you. Use some of This Week's Words. Try to use words as nouns and as verbs, or words from the same word family.

Using the Dictionary to Spell and Write

A good speller sometimes uses the pronunciation of a word to remember how to spell the word. The pronunciation for a two-syllable word has an accent mark. It shows which syllable is said with more force. The first syllable in <u>butter</u> is the accented syllable.

but·ter   /but'ər/

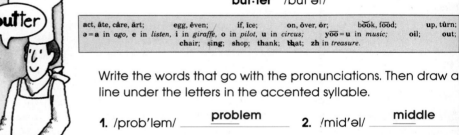

act, āte, câre, ärt;   egg, ēven;   if, īce;   on, ōver, ôr;   bŏŏk, fōōd;   up, tûrn;
ə = a in *ago,* e in *listen,* i in *giraffe,* o in *pilot,* u in *circus;*   yōō = u in *music;*   oil;   out;
chair;   sing;   shop;   thank;   that;   zh in *treasure.*

Write the words that go with the pronunciations. Then draw a line under the letters in the accented syllable.

1. /prob'ləm/ ___problem___
2. /mid'əl/ ___middle___
3. /per·haps'/ ___perhaps___
4. /fər·got'/ ___for<u>got</u>___

✏ **SPELLING DICTIONARY** Remember to use your **Spelling Dictionary** when you write.

148

---

1. Read the introductory paragraph on page 148 aloud. Ask the children to look up *enough, cousin,* and *although* in the **Spelling Dictionary** and use the pronunciation to identify the accented syllable in each word.
2. Read the directions on page 148 aloud and ask volunteers to say the words given as pronunciations.
3. Have the children complete the activity independently.
4. Have volunteers write the words on the chalkboard. Let the children check their own work.

Extra Practice: Spelling and Language

> Name _____   UNIT **34**
> **Spelling and Language**
>
> **A.** Write the underlined word on the first line. On the second line, write **noun** or **verb** to tell how the word is used in the sentence.
>
> | | butter |
> | --- | --- |
> | | lesson |
> | | forgot |
> | | cattle |
> | | matter |
> | | number |
> | | dinner |
> | | middle |
> | | perhaps |
> | | funny |
> | | rabbit |
> | | problem |
> | | happen |
> | | corner |
> | | wonder |
>
> 1. Strange things always <u>happen</u> to Sarah.
>   __happen__   __verb__
> 2. Yesterday she <u>forgot</u> to put on her watch.
>   __forgot__   __verb__
> 3. She said, "I <u>wonder</u> what time it is?"
>   __wonder__   __verb__
> 4. She walked to the <u>corner</u> to find a clock in a store.
>   __corner__   __noun__
> 5. None of the <u>stores</u> had clocks.
>   __stores__   __noun__
> 6. "Oh, well," she went on, "it doesn't <u>matter</u> to me what time it is."
>   __matter__   __verb__
> 7. "I'll find out when I go home for <u>dinner</u>."
>   __dinner__   __noun__
>
> **B.** Write one of This Week's Words to tell what is described in each sentence.
>
> 8. This noun names an animal that hops.   __rabbit__
> 9. This noun names animals that moo.   __cattle__
> 10. This noun names something you spread on bread.   __butter__
> 11. This noun names something you use for counting.   __number__
>
> 146 • Extra Practice

Spelling on Your Own

THIS WEEK'S WORDS

Write some funny story titles. Use This Week's Words. Try to use more than one of the words in each title. Here are some examples: "The Rabbit Who Forgot How to Hop" and "The Mad Hatter's Funny Dinner."

MASTERY WORDS

follow
happy
hello
pretty
sunny
sister

Follow the directions. Use the Mastery words.

1. Write the two words that have double l.

follow   hello

2. Draw a line under the letters that spell /ō/ in the words you just wrote. Then use both words in a sentence.

EXAMPLE: **I said hello to the dog that seemed to follow me.**

Add the letters that spell the second syllable of each Mastery word. Write the whole word.

3. sis   sister   **4.** sun   sunny

5. hap   happy   **6.** pret   pretty

7. hel   hello   **8.** fol   follow

BONUS WORDS

stammer
swallow
hollow
allow
tonsils
seldom
welcome
practice

1. Write all the Bonus words in alphabetical order. Then draw a line between the two syllables in each word.

2. Write the three words that are spelled with double l. Then circle the word that ends with the vowel sound in cow.

3. Use swallow and tonsils in a sentence.

4. Write sentences using welcome, practice, and swallow as nouns. Then write sentences using each word as a verb.

See answers below.

149

Spelling on Your Own Answers

BONUS WORDS

. al|low hol|low prac|tice sel|dom
tam|mer swal|low ton|sils wel|come

. swallow, hollow, (allow)

. EXAMPLE: I couldn't swallow after I had
my tonsils out.

. EXAMPLES: They gave George a warm
welcome. Everyone welcomed him. Band
practice is tonight. We must practice for
the parade. Lonnie took a big swallow of
water. Then she swallowed the pill.

Summarize Learning

Have the children summarize what they have learned in this unit. *Ask:*

* What have you learned about nouns and verbs? (Some words can be both nouns and verbs.) Give examples. (butter, corner, accept other examples)
* What have you learned about accent marks in dictionary pronunciations? (The pronunciation of a two-syllable word has an accent mark. An accent mark shows which syllable is said with more force.)
* What spelling generalizations have you learned? How did you use these generalizations?

TEACHING PLAN

Objectives To apply the unit spelling generalization to spell This Week's Words, Mastery words, and Bonus words independently.

THIS WEEK'S WORDS

1. Read the directions on page 149 aloud. Help the children get started by having volunteers suggest story titles using two or more of This Week's Words.
2. Have the children complete the activity independently on a separate piece of paper.
3. Give the children an opportunity to share their story titles with the class.

MASTERY WORDS

1. Briefly review the unit generalization on page 146.
2. Have volunteers read the Mastery words aloud. As each word is read, have the children indicate how each word can be divided into syllables.
3. Read the directions on page 149 aloud. Be sure that the children recognize the symbol for long o: /ō/.
4. Have the children complete the activities independently.
5. Check each child's work.

BONUS WORDS

1. Briefly review the unit generalization on page 146.
2. Have volunteers read the Bonus words aloud. Discuss word meanings and have volunteers look up unfamiliar words in the **Spelling Dictionary.**
3. Have the children complete the exercise independently on a separate piece of paper.

For reinforcement in writing spelling words, you may wish to assign *Extra Practice Master 34: Mastery Words* or *Bonus Words.*

CLOSING THE UNIT

Apply New Learning

Tell the children that if they misspell words that have the VC/CV syllable patterns in their writing they should use one or more of the following strategies:

- think of words that rhyme and compare in their minds how they are spelled.
- write the word using different spellings and compare it with the spelling they picture in their minds.
- pronounce the word very carefully to see that the correct letter or letters have been used to spell the sounds in the word.

Transfer New Learning

Tell the children that when they encounter new words in their personal reading and in other content areas, they should learn the meaning of those words and then apply the generalizations they have studied to the spelling of those words. Tell them that once the words are familiar both in meaning and spelling, they should use the new words in their writing.

ENRICHMENT ACTIVITIES

Classroom activities and **home activities** may be assigned to children of all ability levels. The activities provide opportunities for children to use their spelling words in new contexts.

For the Classroom

To individualize classroom activities, you may have the children use the word list they are studying in this unit.

- *Basic:* Use **Mastery** words to complete the activity.
- *Average:* Use **This Week's Words** to complete the activity.
- *Challenging:* Use **Bonus** words to complete the activity.

1. **Language Arts/Writing Clues** Have the children choose three spelling words that they are able to define. Tell them to write two or three clues for each of the words, making each clue easier as they go. After completing the clues, have the children read one clue at a time to another child. The listener must try to guess and write the spelling word with the fewest number of clues. Give this example for *butter: The word I am thinking of comes from cream. It is yellow and melts with heat.*

   ■ COOPERATIVE LEARNING: Have each group create word clues for as many spelling words as there are group members. Each child within a group should write two or three clues, each one easier than the last. Children should try out their clues, reading one clue at a time. After each clue the listener gets an opportunity to guess

the word. The object is to guess and write the spelling word with the fewest number of clues.

2. **Language Arts/Writing Questions** Have each child write five questions using the spelling words. Encourage the children to look through their textbooks for ideas. For example, present this science-related question: *What kind of food do rabbits eat?* After finishing, have the children exchange questions and write the answers. Encourage children to check the answers in their textbooks.

   ■ COOPERATIVE LEARNING: Have each group write a set of content-area questions using their spelling words. Have each child in the group write a question related to a different content area, such as science, social studies, mathematics, health, and reading. Have the group members test each other's questions and revise where necessary. When they are satisfied, have the group select one member to rewrite all the questions. These can be shared with their classmates.

3. **Language Arts/Writing a How-to Paragraph** Have the children write a how-to paragraph. First direct their attention to page 250 of the **Writer's Guide** to read about how-to paragraphs. As a *prewriting* activity, have the children look over the spelling word list in search of possible ideas for a how-to paragraph and list them. For example, children may wish to write about how to prepare a meal or how to cross a street safely. After they have chosen a topic, have them list the steps they should use to explain how to do it. When they have completed the prewriting activities, have them **compose** the paragraph. Remind them to use as many spelling words as possible. Suggest that they also use time-clue words such as *first, next, then, last,* or *finally.* Then have the children **revise** the paragraph, making sure that the steps are clearly written and in order. Remind them to proofread for spelling, capitalization, and punctuation. Children may also want to illustrate their how-to paragraphs. **Publish** their paragraphs by having the children read them aloud.

   ■ COOPERATIVE LEARNING: Have each group write a how-to paragraph. As a *prewriting* activity, have the group search the spelling word list for possible ideas for a how-to paragraph and list them. Have the group members share their ideas and then decide what to write about. For example, they may write about how to prepare a meal or how to cross a street safely. Suggest that they list the steps that would have to be followed in order to complete the process. To **compose** the how-to paragraph, one child in the group should begin with a topic sentence. The other children should add detail sentences. Remind them to use as many spelling words as possible. Suggest that they also use time-clue words such as *first, next, third, then, last,* and *finally.* One child in the group may be selected to write the paragraph. All the children should **revise,** checking to make sure that the steps are clearly written and in order. Each child should also proofread for spelling, capitalization, and punctuation. Where appropriate, the group may want to illustrate the steps. The group should select one child to rewrite the paragraph. Have the group **publish** their how-to paragraph by having one member read it aloud to the class.

For the Home

Children may complete these activities independently or with the assistance of a relative or friend in the home.

1. **Language Arts/Categorizing Parts of Speech** Tell the children to make up word categories using the words from all three lists. Children should fill in words under each of the following category headings: words that name people, places, and things; action words; and words that describe. Then have the children write two or three sentences using a word from each category in each sentence.

2. **Language Arts/Writing Answers to Questions** Tell the children to write a sentence that has at least one spelling word to answer each of the following questions:
   a. What do you usually do after school?
      Sample answer: I feed my pet rabbit, do my lessons, and then have dinner.
   b. What might a fox say to a rabbit?
   c. What would you do to help a child who is lost?

3. **Science/Writing Statements About Animal Groups** Tell the children to write four facts about animal groups using some of their spelling words. Remind the children that a fact is something that is known to be true. Encourage the children to use their science books or an encyclopedia for reference.

4. **Social Studies/Writing a News Story** Tell the children to imagine that they are news reporters. Have them write the first paragraph of a news story. It should be about something thay have studied in social studies or have read about recently in a newspaper or magazine. Explain to the children that the first paragraph usually tells *who, what, where, when,* and *why.* Remind the children to use some of their spelling words. When they have completed their paragraphs, have them share their news story with a friend or someone at home.

Evaluating Spelling Ability

Unit Test

This Week's Words
1. **butter**   Bruce likes *butter* on his toast.   *butter*
2. **cattle**   The *cattle* were in the field.   *cattle*
3. **dinner**   I can smell *dinner* cooking.   *dinner*
4. **funny**   This is a *funny* movie.   *funny*
5. **happen**   She does not know what will *happen* next.   *happen*
6. **lesson**   We will finish the science *lesson* soon.   *lesson*

7. **matter**   It doesn't *matter* what time it is.   *matter*
8. **middle**   The ball rolled into the *middle* of the street.   *middle*
9. **rabbit**   The magician pulled a *rabbit* out of a hat.   *rabbit*
10. **corner**   Bill wrote his name in the *corner* of the picture.   *corner*
11. **forgot**   Harvey *forgot* to buy the bread.   *forgot*
12. **number**   We need a *number* of things at the store.   *number*
13. **perhaps**   Victor can't go, but *perhaps* Marquita can.   *perhaps*
14. **problem**   Ants can be a *problem* at a picnic.   *problem*
15. **wonder**   I *wonder* if it will rain.   *wonder*

Mastery Words
1. **follow**   Please *follow* directions.   *follow*
2. **happy**   He will be *happy* to see you.   *happy*
3. **hello**   We can say *hello* to Mary.   *hello*
4. **pretty**   The flowers are very *pretty*.   *pretty*
5. **sunny**   The cat was lying in a *sunny* spot.   *sunny*
6. **sister**   Erin's little *sister* is only two.   *sister*

Bonus Words
1. **stammer**   You may *stammer* when you are excited.   *stammer*
2. **swallow**   It is hard to *swallow* a big pill.   *swallow*
3. **hollow**   Is the door solid, or is it *hollow* inside?   *hollow*
4. **allow**   My parent's won't *allow* me to do that.   *allow*
5. **tonsils**   Ursula must have her *tonsils* out.   *tonsils*
6. **seldom**   You *seldom* see a fox in these woods.   *seldom*
7. **welcome**   Let's *welcome* our friends at the door.   *welcome*
8. **practice**   It takes *practice* to do this well.   *practice*

Dictation Sentences

This Week's Words
1. I *forgot* to get *butter* for *dinner*.
2. I *wonder* how to do this *number problem*.
3. A *funny* toy *rabbit* sat in the *corner* of the store.
4. We can put the *cattle* in the *middle* of the barn.
5. Does it *matter* if I study the *lesson* in the morning?
6. No one knows what will *happen*.
7. I cannot help, but *perhaps* they can.

Mastery Words
1. My *sister* is *happy* on a *sunny* day.
2. Let's *follow* him and say *hello*.
3. That picture is *pretty*.

Bonus Words
1. It is hard to *swallow* if your *tonsils* hurt.
2. We are *welcome* to *practice* in the room after school.
3. I *seldom* see leaves on the old, *hollow* tree.
4. You should *allow* the child to *stammer* when she is angry.

RETEACHING STRATEGIES FOR SPELLING

Children who have made errors on the Unit Test may require reteaching. Use the following *Reteaching Strategies* and *Follow-up Masters 34A* and *34B* for additional instruction and practice of This Week's Words. (You may wish to assign *LEP Reteaching Follow-up Master 34* for reteaching of spelling words.)

A. Discovering Spelling Ideas

1. Say the following words as you write them on the chalkboard.

   stutter   winner   lumber   target

2. Ask the children how many consonants are found in the middle of each word. (two consonants)
3. Ask the children to identify which words have the same consonant letters in the middle (*stutter* and *winner*) and which have different consonant letters in the middle (*lumber* and *target*).
4. Ask the children how many vowel sounds are in each word. (two) Tell the children these words have two syllables, one for each vowel. Divide *mutter* and *lumber* into syllables. (mut|ter, lum|ber)
5. Ask the children to identify where each word is divided. (*stutter* – between the double consonants, *lumber* – between the different consonants) Ask the children to divide *winner* and *target* into syllables. (win|ner, tar|get)
6. Ask the children what they have learned about dividing words into syllables. (If a word has a double consonant in the middle, divide between the consonants. If a word has two different consonants in the middle, divide between the consonants.)

B. Word Shapes

1. Explain to the children that each word has a shape and that remembering the shape of a word can help them to spell the word correctly.
2. On the chalkboard, write the words *sunny* and *slumber*. Have the children identify "short," "tall," and "tail" letters.
3. Draw the configuration of each word on the chalkboard, and ask the children which word fits in each shape.

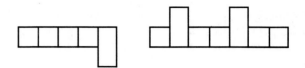

Use *Reteaching Follow-up Master 34A* to reinforce spelling generalizations taught in Unit 34.

Use *Reteaching Follow-up Master 34B* to reinforce spellings of This Week's Words for Unit 34.

Name

Reteaching Follow-up A   Discovering Spelling Ideas   UNIT **34**

THIS WEEK'S WORDS

butter	lesson	middle	number	perhaps
cattle	matter	rabbit	wonder	problem
dinner	happen	corner	forgot	funny

1. Study This Week's Words. Say each word to yourself. How many vowel sounds do you hear in each word? __two__

2. Each of This Week's Words has two syllables. There is a vowel sound in each syllable. Write each of This Week's Words in the column that tells about the consonants in the middle of the word. Divide each word into syllables.

words with double consonants	words with two different consonants
but|ter	for|got
din|ner	num|ber
fun|ny	per|haps
hap|pen	prob|lem
les|son	won|der
mat|ter	cor|ner
mid|dle	
rab|bit	
cat|tle	

3. Look at the words with double consonants. Where are they divided into syllables? __between the double consonants__

4. Look at the words with two different consonants. Where are they divided into syllables? __between the two consonants__

Reteaching • 57

Name

Reteaching Follow-up B   Word Shapes   UNIT **34**

THIS WEEK'S WORDS

butter	matter	corner	perhaps
cattle	happen	middle	problem
dinner	lesson	rabbit	number	wonder
		forgot	

Write each of This Week's Words in its correct shape. The first one has been done for you. Children may interchange answers that fit the same configuration.

1. f u n n y
2. p r o b l e m
3. m i d d l e
4. h a p p e n
5. c o r n e r
6. b u t t e r
7. n u m b e r
8. r a b b i t
9. m a t t e r
10. f o r g o t
11. w o n d e r
12. c a t t l e
13. d i n n e r
14. p e r h a p s
15. l e s s o n

58 • Reteaching

Another Syllable Pattern

PREVIEWING THE UNIT

Unit Materials

Instruction and Practice

Pupil Book	pages 150–153
Teacher's Edition	
Teaching Plans	pages 150–153
Enrichment Activities	
For the Classroom	pages 153A–153B
For the Home	page 153B
Reteaching Strategies	page 153C

Testing

Teacher's Edition	
Trial Test	pages 149E–149F
Unit Test	page 153B
Dictation Test	page 153B

Additional Resources

PRACTICE AND REINFORCEMENT
Extra Practice Master 35: This Week's Words
Extra Practice Master 35: Mastery Words
Extra Practice Master 35: Bonus Words
LEP Practice Master 35
Spelling and Language Master 35
Study Steps to Learn a Word Master

RETEACHING FOLLOW-UP
Reteaching Follow-up Master 35A:
  Discovering Spelling Ideas
Reteaching Follow-up Master 35B: Word
  Shapes
LEP Reteaching Follow-up Master 35

TEACHING AIDS
Spelling Generalizations Transparency 30

Visit our Web site
http://www.hbschool.com

Click on the SPELLING banner to find activities for this unit.

Learner Objectives

Spelling

- To spell words that have the V/CV syllable pattern.
- To recognize where V/CV words can be divided into syllables.

Reading

- To follow written directions.
- To recognize how words with the V/CV pattern are divided into syllables.
- To use a dictionary as a key to pronunciation.

Writing

- To write clues telling about a game.
- To use the writing process.
- To proofread for spelling, capitalization, and punctuation.
- To write legible manuscript and cursive letters.

Listening

- To follow oral directions.
- To listen to recognize how words can be divided into syllables.

Speaking

- To speak clearly to a group.
- To respond to a question.
- To express feelings and ideas about a piece of writing.
- To present game clues and interview questions.
- To contribute ideas and information in group discussions.

THIS WEEK'S WORDS

pilot
above
ahead
alike
alone
around
become
begin
behind
belong
below
beside
motor
paper
parade

MASTERY WORDS

again
ago
awake
away
because
tiger

BONUS WORDS

broken
final
machine
motel
pretend
reason
spider
total

Assignment Guide

This guide shows how you teach a typical spelling unit in either a five-day or a three-day sequence, while providing for individual differences. **Boldface type** indicates essential classwork. Steps shown in light type may be done in class or assigned as homework.

Five Days	● = average spellers ★ = better spellers ✓ = slower spellers	Three Days
Day 1	● ★ **Take This Week's Words Trial Test and correct** ● ✓ **Take Mastery Word Trial Test and correct** ● ★ **Read This Week's Words and discuss generalization on page 150**	**Day 1**
Day 2	● Complete Spelling Practice page 151 ● ✓ Complete Extra Practice Master 35: This Week's Words (optional) ✓ Complete Spelling on Your Own: Mastery Words page 153 ★ **Take Bonus Word Trial Test and correct**	
Day 3	● ★ ✓ **Complete Spelling and Language page 152** ● ★ ✓ Complete Writing on Your Own page 152 ● ★ ✓ Complete Proofreading page 152 ● ✓ Take Midweek Test (optional) ★ Complete Spelling on Your Own: Bonus Words page 153 ● ✓ Complete Spelling and Language Master 152 (optional)	**Day 2**
Day 4	● Complete Spelling on Your Own: This Week's Words page 153 ✓ Complete Extra Practice Master 35: Mastery Words (optional) ★ Complete Extra Practice Master 35: Bonus Words (optional)	
Day 5	● Take Unit Test on This Week's Words ● Complete Reteaching Follow-up Masters 35A and 35B (optional) ● ✓ **Take Unit Test on Mastery Words** ★ **Take Unit Test on Bonus Words**	**Day 3**

Enrichment Activities for the **classroom** and for the **home** included at the end of this unit may be assigned selectively on any day of the week.

INTRODUCING THE UNIT

Establish Readiness for Learning

Tell the children that they will continue to learn more about syllable patterns. In Unit 35 they will study words with the V/CV syllable pattern. Tell the children that they will apply the spelling generalizations to This Week's Words and use those words to write clues for a treasure hunt.

Assess Children's Spelling Ability

Administer the Trial Test before the children study This Week's Words. Use the test sentences provided. Say each word and use it in a sentence. Then repeat the word. Have the children write the words on a separate sheet of paper or in their spelling notebooks. Test sentences are also provided for Mastery and Bonus words.

Have the children check their own work by

listening to you read the spelling of the words or by referring to This Week's Words in the left column of the **Pupil Book.** For each misspelled word, have the children follow the **Study Steps to Learn a Word** on page 1 in the **Pupil Book** or use the copying master to study and write the words. Children should record the number correct on their **Progress Report.**

Trial Test Sentences

This Week's Words
1. *pilot* It takes more than one *pilot* to fly a big plane. *pilot*
2. *above* The plane flew *above* the clouds. *above*
3. *ahead* Sandy is *ahead* of me in line. *ahead*
4. *alike* The twins look *alike*. *alike*
5. *alone* People should never swim *alone*. *alone*
6. *around* Let's walk *around* the park. *around*

FOCUS

• Establishes objectives
• Relates to prior learning
• Sets purpose of instruction

7. *become*   The tadpoles will *become* frogs.   **become**

8. *begin*   The assembly will *begin* at ten o'clock.   **begin**

9. *behind*   Morty hid *behind* the tree.   **behind**

10. *belong*   These boots *belong* to Joey.   **belong**

11. *below*   The temperature fell *below* zero.   **below**

12. *beside*   Annie sat *beside* Dwight on the bus.   **beside**

13. *motor*   The *motor* in the hair dryer stopped working.   **motor**

14. *paper*   Rico needs some *paper* to draw a picture.   **paper**

15. *parade*   The band will march in the *parade*.   **parade**

Mastery Words

1. *again*   He will be back *again* soon. **again**

2. *ago*   Kevin left ten minutes *ago*.   **ago**

3. *awake*   Emily was wide *awake* at dawn.   **awake**

4. *away*   My parents are going *away* on a trip.   **away**

5. *because*   Gordon went to bed *because* he was sleepy.   **because**

6. *tiger*   My favorite zoo animal is the *tiger*. **tiger**

Bonus Words

1. *broken*   Sophie cut her hand on some *broken* glass.   **broken**

2. *final*   This is the *final* day of the circus.   **final**

3. *machine*   We called someone to fix the washing *machine*.   **machine**

4. *motel*   The new *motel* has a swimming pool.   **motel**

5. *pretend*   Irv likes to *pretend* he is a spaceman.   **pretend**

6. *reason*   Cherie had a good *reason* for being late.   **reason**

7. *spider*   The *spider* trapped a fly in its web.   **spider**

8. *total*   Add up all the numbers to find the *total*.   **total**

Apply Prior Learning

Have the children apply what they already know about syllable patterns by participating in the following activity.

Write the words *alike, behind, wagon,* and *broken* on the chalkboard. Ask the children to tell what is the same about all these words. Help them to recognize that each word has two vowel sounds with a consonant letter between those two sounds, and that each word has two syllables. Have volunteers come to the chalkboard and divide each word into syllables. Point out the V/CV pattern as they divide the words into syllables. Tell the children that in Unit 35 they will study words that have these syllable patterns. Explain that they can use these words in a variety of writing tasks; they can use the words in a note to a friend, in a letter, or in a story.

FOCUS

- Relates to prior learning
- Draws relationships
- Applies spelling generalizations to new contexts

FOR CHILDREN WITH SPECIAL NEEDS

Learning Difficulties

Dividing words into syllables and blending syllables together to form words may be particularly difficult for those children with auditory processing problems. The following activities may help the children to learn these skills.

Read This Week's Words aloud with the children. Read the words together a second time, clapping each syllable as you say it. Next, say a spelling word slowly and clap the syllables. Have the children tell how many syllables are in that word. Write the word on the chalkboard and ask a volunteer to divide the word into two syllables as the class says the word and claps the syllables once again. Continue this sequence with each of This Week's Words. You may wish to have the children write This Week's Words

and divide each word into syllables. Have them draw a line under the first syllable using one color crayon and a line under the second syllable using a different color crayon.

Limited English Proficiency

To help limited English proficient children work with the spelling generalizations for Unit 35, you may wish to refer to the booklet "Suggestions and Activities for Limited English Proficient Students."

TEACHING PLAN

Objective To spell words with the V/CV syllable pattern; to recognize how these words can be divided into syllables.

1. Direct the children's attention to the first drawing on page 150. Ask a child to read the word that appears on the planes. Help the children to recognize that the word *pilot* has one consonant letter between two vowel letters. Then direct their attention to the second drawing. Help the children to recognize that when the word *pilot* is divided into syllables, the consonant letter *l* is part of the second syllable.
2. Read the generalization on page 150 aloud.

You may wish to introduce the lesson by using **Spelling Generalizations Transparency 30.**

3. Have volunteers read This Week's Words aloud. As each word is read, have the children name the consonant letter that appears between two vowel sounds and indicate where the word would be divided into syllables.

You may wish to assign **LEP Practice Master 35** for reinforcement in writing spelling words.

35 Another Syllable Pattern

THIS WEEK'S WORDS

1. *pilot*
2. *above*
3. *ahead*
4. *alike*
5. *alone*
6. *around*
7. *become*
8. *begin*
9. *behind*
10. *belong*
11. *below*
12. *beside*
13. *motor*
14. *paper*
15. *parade*

This Week's Words

All the words this week have two syllables. Each word has one consonant letter between the two vowel sounds.

All of This Week's Words are divided into syllables before the consonant.

150

Extra Practice: This Week's Words

Name
Extra Practice   This Week's Words   UNIT 35

A. Find This Week's Words in the puzzle. Circle them. Write the words in the blanks as you find them. The words go across and down.

```
a l d p i l o t y d v a j f
x s b e g i n g k l a h u l
p o e y f h g p e x l e r q
b e l o w y d a c i o a q p
e d o j q u a r o u n d z c
h w n t v b m a v e e n c o
i g g b e s i d e x c p j m
n p a p e r z e a b o v e e
d a l i k e m o t o r c p e
```

Order may vary.

pilot	begin	below
around	beside	paper
above	alike	motor
behind	belong	parade
ahead	become	alone

B. Now draw a line between the two syllables in each word you wrote.

pilot	above	ahead	alike	alone
around	become	begin	behind	belong
below	beside	motor	paper	parade

Extra Practice • 147

Extra Practice: Mastery Words

Name
Extra Practice   Mastery Words   UNIT 35

Follow the directions.

1. First put an X through the five words that have just one syllable, like jump.
2. Next write the words with two syllables in the middle box.
3. Now draw a circle around the six words you wrote that have just one consonant letter after the first vowel.

again	place	tiger	those
ants	again tiger away		find
ago	until	candy	away
into	because awake		cold
also	listen	also	until
	ago	into	
listen	awake	because	candy

4. Write the words you circled. Draw a line between the two syllables in each word. Order may vary.

again	tiger	away
because	awake	ago

again	ago	awake	away	because	tiger

148 • Extra Practice

Spelling Practice

A. Add <u>a</u> or <u>be</u> to these words. Write This Week's Words.

1. come ___become___
2. side ___beside___
3. head ___ahead___
4. low ___below___
5. round ___around___
6. like ___alike___

B. Follow the directions. Use This Week's Words.

7. Add one of the syllables in the circle to each of the syllables in the box. Write five words.

(a
be)

gin	long	hind
bove		lone

___begin___ ___belong___ ___behind___

___above___ ___alone___

8. Write the four words that do not have <u>a</u> or <u>be</u> as the first syllable. Draw a line between the two syllables in each word.

___pa/per___ ___mo/tor___

___pa/rade___ ___pi/lot___

9. Write two pairs of words that are opposites. One word in each pair has the first syllable <u>a</u>. The other one has the first syllable <u>be</u>.

___above___ ___below___

___ahead___ ___behind___

C. The accented syllable is the one you say with more force. Write This Week's Words with these accented syllables.

10. pi ___pilot___
11. mo ___motor___
12. rade ___parade___
13. pa ___paper___

This Week's Words

pilot
above
ahead
alike
alone
around
become
begin
behind
belong
below
beside
motor
paper
parade

151

TEACHING PLAN

Objectives To add initial syllables and write words; to write words given syllables; to divide words with the V/CV pattern into syllables; to write antonyms.

1. Briefly review how This Week's Words can be divided into syllables before the middle consonant.
2. Discuss the directions on page 151. Items 1–7 require children to work with affixes and roots. To prepare them for Exercise **C,** remind the children that either the first or second syllable can be the accented syllable.
3. Have the children complete the activities independently. Remind them to use legible handwriting. For **Handwriting Models,** refer the children to page 258 in the **Pupil Book.**
4. To correct the children's work, have volunteers write the answers on the chalkboard. Let the children check their own work.

For reinforcement in writing spelling words, you may wish to assign *Extra Practice Master 35: This Week's Words.*

tra Practice: Bonus Words

Name
Extra Practice — Bonus Words — UNIT 35

A. Put the letters in the right order and write the Bonus words.

1. brenok ___broken___
2. ndeetpr ___pretend___
3. neasor ___reason___
4. chenima ___machine___
5. loatt ___total___
6. disper ___spider___
7. toelm ___motel___
8. nalif ___final___

B. Finish the story with Bonus words. Write your answers at the right.

Everything was going wrong. The washing __9__ wouldn't work. The dishwasher was __10__, too. When Mrs. Brooks found a __11__ in her desk drawer, that was the last straw.

"We need to get away, and that's __12__," she said to Mr. Brooks.

He agreed. "There's no __13__ why we shouldn't. Let's go to the mountains and __14__ we haven't a care in the world."

They drove to a __15__ in the mountains. After a weekend of __16__ peace and quiet, everything seemed much better.

9. ___machine___
10. ___broken___
11. ___spider___
12. ___final___
13. ___reason___
14. ___pretend___
15. ___motel___
16. ___total___

C. Write the Bonus words in alphabetical order.

___broken___
___final___
___machine___
___motel___
___pretend___
___reason___
___spider___
___total___

| pretend | machine | motel | fina |
| total | broken | reason | spider |

Extra Practice • 149

Summarize Learning

Have the children summarize what they have learned on pages 150 and 151. *Ask:*

- What did you learn about the V/CV syllable pattern? (Some words which have this syllable pattern are divided into syllables before the consonant.)
- What are some examples of words which have this syllable pattern? (pilot, above; accept other examples.)

TEACHING PLAN

SPELLING AND LANGUAGE

Objectives To write words in a sentence context; to describe a drawing.

1. Read the directions on page 152 aloud. Be sure the children understand that the sentences refer to the drawing and that they must select the words that describe the position of the shapes in the drawing.
2. Have the children complete the activity independently.
3. To correct the children's work, have volunteers read the completed sentences aloud. Let the children check their own work.

For extended practice in writing words in sentence context, you may wish to assign *Spelling and Language Master 35*.

WRITING ON YOUR OWN

Objectives To write clues telling about a game; to proofread for spelling.

1. Review the directions with the children.
2. As a **prewriting** activity, discuss a treasure hunt with the children. Have them generate ideas for clues and list them on the chalkboard. Then have the children **compose** their clues in a list. When they are ready to **revise**, remind the children to check for spelling. For additional help, you may also wish to refer them to the **Revising Checklist** on page 247 of the **Writer's Guide**. To **publish**, have the children exchange their lists with classmates and compare their ideas.

PROOFREADING

Objectives To proofread a sign for spelling errors; to write misspelled words correctly.

1. Read the directions on page 152.
2. Have the children read the sign independently, looking for errors. Then ask them to circle the misspelled words and write them correctly.

   If you are using the hardcover book, the children should simply locate the misspelled words and write them correctly in their notebooks.

THIS WEEK'S WORDS
pilot
above
ahead
alike
alone
around
become
begin
behind
belong
below
beside
motor
paper
parade

Spelling and Language • Where and How

Many of This Week's Words tell where or how. Look at these shapes. Use This Week's Words to finish the sentences.

1. The purple square is ___**beside**___ the green square.
2. The blue dot is ___**alone**___ in the corner.
3. A black line is ___**around**___ all the shapes.
4. The green square is ___**above**___ the red dots.

Writing on Your Own

Pretend you have invited friends to your house for a party. You are going to play Treasure Hunt. Write clues to tell your friends where they will find the treasure.

 WRITER'S GUIDE Did you write clearly so your friends can read the clues? If you need help writing any letters, turn to page 261.

Proofreading

1. Theo has six spelling mistakes in his sign. Circle each one.

> PET (PERADE) SATURDAY
> Bring all the pets that (bilong) to you!
> The fun will (begen) (arond) 2:00.
> Meet (behined) Walker School (biside) the swings.

2. Write the six misspelled words correctly.

PARADE	belong	begin
around	behind	beside

 WRITER'S GUIDE See the editing and proofreading marks on page 248.

152

Extra Practice: Spelling and Language

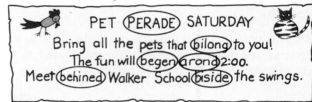

Name	UNIT
Spelling and Language	35

A. The underlined words in these sentences are wrong. Write the correct word on the line. Use This Week's Words.

1. Tanya was under the table, so she was <u>above</u> the table.
   below
2. Tanya was at the front of the line, so she was <u>in back</u> of everyone.
   ahead
3. Tanya was next to Leo, so she was <u>behind</u> Leo.   **beside**
4. Tanya looked just like her sister, so they were <u>different</u>.
   alike
5. Tanya hugged her brother, so she put her arms <u>above</u> her brother.
   around
6. Tanya was by herself, so she was <u>together</u>.   **alone**

B. Use This Week's Words to answer the questions.

7. What's the opposite of <u>ahead</u>?   **behind**
8. What's the opposite of <u>below</u>?   **above**
9. What's the opposite of <u>different</u>?   **alike**
10. What's the opposite of <u>behind</u>?   **ahead**
11. What's the opposite of <u>above</u>?   **below**

pilot	above	ahead	alike	alone
around	become	begin	behind	belong
below	beside	motor	paper	parade

150 • Extra Practice

Spelling on Your Own

THIS WEEK'S WORDS

First, write the words that go with the pronunciations.

1. /pā'pər/   2. /bi·gin'/   3. /pə·rād'/   4. /bi·lông'/

5. /pī'lət/   6. /bi·kum'/   7. /mō'tər/

O P 2 R S

✏ **SPELLING DICTIONARY** If you need help, use the pronunciation key on page 162.

Now write the other eight words. Look around your classroom. Use each of these eight words in a sentence. Tell what you see. Here is an example: "The clock is <u>above</u> the chalkboard."
See answers below.

MASTERY WORDS

again
ago
awake
away
because
tiger

Follow the directions. Use the Mastery words.

1. Write the word you use to tell why. _____ because

2. Write the word that has the sound /ī/. _____ tiger

3. Write the word with the letters <u>ai</u> but not the sound /ā/.

   again

Add <u>a</u> to each word. Write Mastery words.

4. go _____ ago   5. wake _____ awake

6. way _____ away   7. gain _____ again

BONUS WORDS

broken
final
machine
motel
pretend
reason
spider
total

1. Write all the Bonus words. Then draw a line to divide each word into syllables.
2. You say the second syllable of three of the words with more force. Write these words.
3. Write the six Bonus words that have a long vowel sound in the first syllable.
4. Write the four Bonus words that have /əl/ or /ən/.
5. Write a story for a friend. Use all the Bonus words. **See answers below.**

153

Spelling on Your Own Answers

THIS WEEK'S WORDS

1. paper 2. begin 3. parade 4. belong 5. pilot 6. become 7. motor
Children will write as directed. Be sure to check spelling.

BONUS WORDS

1. bro|ken, fi|nal, ma|chine, mo|tel, pre|tend, rea|son, spi|der, to|tal 2. machine, motel, pretend 3. broken, final, motel, reason, spider, total NOTE: *Pretend* should also be accepted as a correct answer. 4. broken, final, reason, total 5. Children will write as directed. Be sure to check spelling.

Summarize Learning

Have the children summarize what they have learned in this unit. *Ask:*

• What have you learned about using context to complete a sentence? (The sentence must be studied carefully in order to choose the correct word to complete the sentence.)

• What spelling generalizations have you learned? How did you use these generalizations?

TEACHING PLAN

Objectives To apply the unit spelling generalization to spell This Week's Words, Mastery words, and Bonus words independently.

THIS WEEK'S WORDS

1. Read the directions on page 153 aloud. Help the children get started by asking volunteers to read each pronunciation. Point out that the words for which pronunciations are not given are words that can be used to describe things or tell where they are.
2. Have the children complete the activity independently on a separate piece of paper.

MASTERY WORDS

1. Briefly review the unit generalization on page 150.
2. Have volunteers read the Mastery words aloud. As each word is read, have the children identify the consonant between the two vowel sounds and tell where the word would be divided into syllables.
3. Read the directions on page 153 aloud.
4. Have the children complete the activities independently.

BONUS WORDS

1. Briefly review the unit generalization on page 150 and the concept of stress and accent.
2. Have volunteers read the Bonus words aloud. Point out that the sound /sh/ is spelled with *ch* in *machine*.
3. Have the children complete the exercise independently on a separate piece of paper.

For reinforcement in writing spelling words, you may wish to assign *Extra Practice Master 35: Mastery Words* or *Bonus Words.*

CLOSING THE UNIT

Apply New Learning

Tell the children that if they misspell words with the V/CV syllable pattern in their writing, they should use one or more of the following strategies:

- think about the possible spelling for a sound within the word and use the dictionary to find the correct spelling.
- think of words that rhyme and compare in their minds how they are spelled.
- pronounce the word very carefully to see that the correct letter or letters have been used to spell the sounds in the word.

Transfer New Learning

Tell the children that when they encounter new words in their personal reading and in other content areas, they should learn the meaning of those words and then apply the generalizations they have studied to the spelling of those words. Tell them that once the words are familiar in both meaning and spelling, they should use the new words in their writing.

ENRICHMENT ACTIVITIES

Classroom activities and **home activities** may be assigned to children of all ability levels. The activities provide opportunities for children to use their spelling words in new contexts.

For the Classroom

To individualize classroom activities, you may have the children use the word list they are studying in this unit.

- *Basic:* Use **Mastery** words to complete the activity.
- *Average:* Use **This Week's Words** to complete the activity.
- *Challenging:* Use **Bonus** words to complete the activity.

1. **Language Arts/Writing Contrasting Sentences** Have the children choose some spelling words for which they can name antonyms. Then have them write contrasting pairs of sentences. To illustrate the activity, write the following on the chalkboard:

   Ann and Lee went *together*. I went _____. (alone)
   Al is *ahead* of me. I am _____ Al. (behind)

   After giving the correct spelling word to complete each of the model sentences, the children may make up sentences of their own. Then have them rewrite the sentences on another sheet of paper, leaving a blank in place of the spelling word. Children should then exchange papers and complete the sentences.

■ COOPERATIVE LEARNING: Have each group create a set of contrasting sentences using spelling words and their antonyms. Each member of the group should write sentences for a different spelling word. Tell the group members to check each other's sentences for clarity and effectiveness. When the group is satisfied with all the sentences, have one member rewrite them, leaving a blank in place of the spelling word. Then have the group share their sentences with classmates.

2. **Language Arts/Writing Questions** Have the children think of someone famous that they would like to meet. Tell them to write at least four questions that they would ask, using as many of their spelling words as possible. Remind the children of the question words *who, what, where, when, why,* and *how* as they prewrite and compose. Have the children identify the person they want to meet and then read aloud the questions they would ask.

■ COOPERATIVE LEARNING: Have each group write a series of questions that they would ask a famous person. Questions should contain as many spelling words as possible. Have the group decide upon the person they would like to meet. Then have each group member write a question. Remind the children of the question words *who, what, where, when, why,* and *how.* Have the group revise and proofread all the questions. Then have the group share their questions.

3. **Language Arts/Writing a Story** Have the children create a story for the imaginary character Captain Saturn, Space Pilot. First, direct their attention to page 252 of the **Writer's Guide** to read about stories. As a *prewriting* activity, have the children look over their spelling words and list possible adventure ideas and words that they might use to tell the story. Then have the children list their ideas for the following questions:

   Who are the main characters?
   What problem must they solve?
   Where does the story take place?
   When does the story take place?
   How is the problem solved?

Have the children use their notes to **compose** the story. Remind them to use as many spelling words as possible. Then have the children **revise** the story, making sure that it has a beginning, a middle, and an ending. The children should also **proofread** for spelling, capitalization, and punctuation. Tell the children to give the story a title. Some children may want to illustrate the story. **Publish** the children's stories in a class booklet.

■ COOPERATIVE LEARNING: Have each group create a story for the imaginary character Captain Saturn, Space Pilot. As a *prewriting* activity, have the children look over their spelling words for adventure ideas and words that might be used to tell the story. Then have them list their ideas for the questions above. When the group is ready to **compose,** have one person begin orally with an opening sentence. The other children should build on that sentence until the story is fully developed. Children should use as many spelling words as they can from all three lists. Have the group select one person to record the story. Other group members should **revise** the story, making sure that it has a beginning, a middle, and an ending. Each child should also proofread for spelling, capitalization, and punctuation. Have the group select one person to rewrite the story. Other children may wish to illustrate it. Each group can **publish** the story by having one child read it aloud.

For the Home

Children may complete these activities independently or with the assistance of a relative or friend in the home.

1. **Language Arts/Writing an Explanation for a Game** Have the children write an explanation of the game of hide-and-seek. Tell them to write their explanations as if they were for someone who has never played the game. Remind the children to use as many spelling words as possible.

2. **Language Arts/Writing a Description of an Object** Tell the children to review the words on all three spelling lists. Then have them use as many of these words as possible to describe something without actually naming it. After checking for correct spelling, capitalization, and punctuation, have the children share their descriptions with someone at home to see if he or she can guess what is being described.

3. **Social Studies/Writing Questions About Occupations** Tell the children to think of a job that interests them. Have them write five questions that they might ask a person with that job. Tell the children to use as many of their spelling words as possible. Present these example questions:

   Do you like being a *pilot?*
   Do pilots have to check the plane's *motor?*
   How does it feel to have clouds *above* and *below* you?

4. **Science/Explaining How Things Work** Ask the children to answer the following questions, using as many of their spelling words as they can:

   How do you think a car works?
   Where does a pilot fly?

Evaluating Spelling Ability

Unit Test

This Week's Words

1. **pilot** The *pilot* announced that we were about to land. *pilot*
2. **above** Ross dangled the string *above* the cat's head. *above*
3. **ahead** You go *ahead* and I will catch up. *ahead*
4. **alike** Ernie and his brother sometimes dress *alike.* *alike*
5. **alone** Thea stood all *alone* waiting for the bus. *alone*

6. **around** Books and toys are scattered all *around* the room. *around*
7. **become** A caterpillar will *become* a butterfly. *become*
8. **begin** Maria can *begin* the game by serving the first ball. *begin*
9. **behind** Gwen doesn't like to sit *behind* tall people. *behind*
10. **belong** Your bike doesn't *belong* in the kitchen. *belong*
11. **below** The Perlmanns live in the apartment *below* ours. *below*
12. **beside** Courtney can stand *beside* Louie. *beside*
13. **motor** The old car's *motor* made a lot of noise. *motor*
14. **paper** Write your name at the top of your *paper.* *paper*
15. **parade** There are elephants in the *parade.* *parade*

Mastery Words

1. **again** You must come over *again* soon. *again*
2. **ago** The tree was planted long *ago.* *ago*
3. **awake** Maxine is not *awake* yet. *awake*
4. **away** Lucas is going *away* soon. *away*
5. **because** The plant died *because* we forgot to water it. *because*
6. **tiger** That striped kitten looks like a *tiger.* *tiger*

Bonus Words

1. **broken** Our television set is *broken.* *broken*
2. **final** Maurice is studying for his *final* exams. *final*
3. **machine** We bought a new washing *machine.* *machine*
4. **motel** The Murphys stayed overnight in a *motel.* *motel*
5. **pretend** We can *pretend* it is a holiday. *pretend*
6. **reason** There is no *reason* to stay home. *reason*
7. **spider** A *spider* has eight legs. *spider*
8. **total** I have a *total* of eighteen dollars. *total*

Dictation Sentences

This Week's Words

1. The *pilot* saw the *parade* far *below* her.
2. This *paper* must *belong* to a child *around* here.
3. Go *ahead* and *begin,* and we will walk *behind* you.
4. I found the lost dog *alone beside* the road.
5. The birds in the tree *above* us all look *alike.*
6. Has the *motor become* too old to use?

Mastery Words

1. The *tiger* is *awake because* it is hungry.
2. He went *away again* a long time *ago.*

Bonus Words

1. The ice *machine* at the *motel* was *broken.*
2. A *spider* has a *total* of eight eyes.
3. I had a good *reason* for missing the *final* test.
4. Can you *pretend* that you are as tall as a tree?

Children who have made errors on the Unit Test may require reteaching. Use the following **Reteaching Strategies** and **Follow-up Masters 35A** and **35B** for additional instruction and practice of This Week's Words. (You may wish to assign **LEP Reteaching Follow-up Master 35** for reteaching of spelling words.)

A. Discovering Spelling Ideas

1. Say the following words as you write them on the chalkboard.

   before　　begin　　total

2. Ask the children to identify the number of vowel sounds in each word. (two) Tell them that these words have two syllables, one for each vowel sound.
3. Ask the children to identify the consonant that comes between the two vowel sounds in each word. (before – f, begin – g, total – the second t)
4. Divide *before* into syllables on the chalkboard. (be|fore) Ask the children to identify where the word was divided. (before the consonant between the two vowel sounds) Ask the children to divide *begin* and *total* following the same pattern as *before*. (be|gin, to|tal)
5. Ask the children what they have learned about dividing words into syllables. (Two-syllable words can be divided into syllables before the consonant between the two vowel sounds.)

B. Word Shapes

1. Explain to the children that each word has a shape and that remembering the shape of a word can help them to spell the word correctly.
2. On the chalkboard, write the words *paper* and *laser*. Have the children identify "short," "tall," and "tail" letters.
3. Draw the configuration of each word on the chalkboard, and ask the children which word fits in each shape.

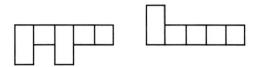

Use **Reteaching Follow-up Master 35A** to reinforce spelling generalizations taught in Unit 35.

Use **Reteaching Follow-up Master 35B** to reinforce spellings of This Week's Words for Unit 35.

Name _____

Reteaching Follow-up A　　　Discovering Spelling Ideas　UNIT **35**

THIS WEEK'S WORDS

pilot	alone	around	below	beside
above	begin	behind	motor	parade
ahead	alike	become	belong	paper

1. Study This Week's Words. Say each word to yourself. How many vowel sounds do you hear in each word? ____**two**____

2. Write each of This Week's Words. Underline the consonant that comes between two vowel sounds.

pi|lot	be|come
a|bove	be|long
a|head	be|low
a|like	mo|tor
a|lone	be|side
be|gin	pa|rade
a|round	pa|per
be|hind	

3. The word **decide** has a consonant between two vowel sounds. You divide **decide** into syllables like this: de/cide. Divide each of This Week's Words into syllables. Follow **decide** as a model.

4. What have you learned about dividing This Week's Words into syllables?

   Divide the words before the consonant between the two

   vowel sounds.

Reteaching • 59

Name _____

Reteaching Follow-up B　　　Word Shapes　UNIT **35**

THIS WEEK'S WORDS

pilot	alike	become	belong	motor
above	alone	begin	below	paper
ahead	around	behind	beside	parade

Write each of This Week's Words in its correct shape. The first one has been done for you. **Children may interchange answers that fit the same configuration.**

1. p a r a d e　　2. p i l o t
3. a r o u n d　　4. b e h i n d
5. b e s i d e　　6. a l i k e
7. b e l o w　　8. b e c o m e
9. a l o n e　　10. a h e a d
11. p a p e r　　12. a b o v e
13. m o t o r　　14. b e g i n
15. b e l o n g

60 • Reteaching

PREVIEWING THE UNIT

Unit Materials

Instruction and Practice

Pupil Book	pages 154–159
Teacher's Edition	
Teaching Plans	pages 154–159
Enrichment Activities	
For the Home	page 159A

Testing

Teacher's Edition	
Trial Test	pages 153E–153F
Unit Test	pages 159A–159B
Form A* Test 6	page T18
Form B* Test 4	page T20
End-of-Year Test*	page T22

*At the end of the year there are three testing options. If your grading period is six weeks, you may want to use **Form A**; if your grading period is nine weeks, you may want to use **Form B**. In addition, you may want to use the **End-of-Year Test** to assess spelling ability for Units 19–36.

Additional Resources

PRACTICE AND REINFORCEMENT
Review Master 36A: Units 31 and 32
Review Master 36B: Units 33 and 34
Review Master 36C: Unit 35 and Test
Exercise
Dictionary and Proofreading Master 6
Study Steps to Learn a Word Master 6
Mastery Words Review Master: Units 31–35
Bonus Words Review Master: Units 31–35

TESTING (optional)
Mastery Words Test: Units 31–35
Bonus Words Test: Units 31–35
Writing Test 6

TEACHING AIDS
Spelling and Writing Transparency 6
Home Letter 7

Visit our Web site
http://www.hbschool.com

Click on the SPELLING banner to find activities for this unit.

Learner Objectives

Spelling

- To review words that demonstrate these sound-letter relationships: /o͝o/oo; /o͞o/oo, ou, ew, o.
- To review words that demonstrate these sound-letter relationships: /ou/ou, ow; /oi/oi, oy.
- To review words that demonstrate these sound-letter relationships: /u/ou; /ou/ou; /ô/ough; /uf/ough.
- To review words that have the VC/CV syllable pattern.
- To review words that have the V/CV syllable pattern.

Reading

- To analyze a report.
- To find the main ideas in a report.
- To follow written instructions.

Writing

- To write a report.
- To use the writing process.
- To edit for clarity.
- To revise using editing and proofreading marks.
- To proofread for spelling, capitalization, and punctuation.
- To write legible manuscript and cursive letters.

Listening

- To recognize and write words given sound clues.
- To write words given pronunciations.
- To follow oral instructions.

Speaking

- To contribute ideas and information in group discussions.
- To express feelings and ideas about a piece of writing.
- To present a report.

REVIEW WORDS

UNIT 31
choose
noon
group
grew
stood
roof
tooth
flew

UNIT 32
brown
mouth
loud
enjoy
noise
sound
oil
point

UNIT 33
country
round
though
enough
thought
bought
touch
count

UNIT 34
lesson
matter
number
perhaps
problem
middle
happen
forgot

UNIT 35
ahead
begin
paper
parade
around
below
motor
behind

Assignment Guide

This guide shows how you teach a typical spelling unit in either a five-day or a three-day sequence, while providing for individual differences. **Boldface type** indicates essential classwork. Steps shown in light type may be done in class or assigned as homework.

Five Days	○ = average spellers ★ = better spellers ✓ = slower spellers	Three Days
Day **1**	**a** ● ★ ✓ **Take Review Words Trial Test and correct**	
Day **2**	**b** ● ★ ✓ Complete Spelling Review pages 154, 155, 156 ● ★ ✓ Complete Review Master 36A, 36B, 36C (optional) ✓ Complete Mastery Words Review Master: Units 31–35 (optional) ★ Complete Bonus Words Review Master: Units 31–35 (optional)	Day **1**
Day **3**	**c** ● ★ ✓ **Complete Spelling and Reading page 157**	
Day **4**	**d** ● ★ ✓ Complete Spelling and Writing pages 158–159 ● ★ ✓ Study Spelling and Writing Transparency 6 (optional) ● ★ ✓ Complete Dictionary and Proofreading Master 6 (optional)	Day **2**
Day **5**	**e** ● ★ ✓ **Take Review Word Unit Test** ✓ Take Mastery Words Test: Units 31–35 (optional) ★ Take Bonus Words Test: Units 31–35 (optional)	Day **3**

Enrichment Activities for the **home** included at the end of this unit may be assigned selectively on any day of the week.

INTRODUCING THE UNIT

Establish Readiness for Learning

Tell the children they will review words from the previous five units. In Unit 36 they will review:

- words with long, short, and other vowel sounds.
- words that have VC/CV syllable patterns.
- words that have V/CV syllable patterns.

Tell the children they will use some of the review words to write a report.

Assess Children's Spelling Ability

Administer the Trial Test before the children study the review words. Use the test sentences provided. Say each word and use it in a sentence. Then repeat the word. Have the children write the words on a separate sheet of paper or in their spelling notebooks.

Have the children check their own work by listening to you read the spelling of the words or by referring to the review words lists in the side boxes of the **Pupil Book.** For each misspelled word, have the children follow the **Study Steps to Learn a Word** on page 154 in

the **Pupil Book,** or use the copying master to study and write the words. Children shouldrecord the number correct on their **Progress Report.**

Trial Test Sentences

1. *choose* Help us *choose* a present for Thelma. *choose*
2. *noon* Tom will meet me at *noon* in the cafeteria. *noon*
3. *group* Mrs. Perez took a *group* of children to the beach. *group*
4. *grew* David *grew* a plant from a sweet potato. *grew*
5. *stood* We all *stood* up and cheered. *stood*
6. *roof* Our house has a new *roof*. *roof*
7. *tooth* The dentist looked at my *tooth*. *tooth*
8. *flew* The plane *flew* over the ocean. *flew*
9. *brown* Abigail's hair is light *brown*. *brown*
10. *mouth* The dog carried the stick in its *mouth*. *mouth*
11. *loud* Ken heard a *loud* crash. *loud*

12. **enjoy** I know you will *enjoy* that movie. **enjoy**
13. **noise** The car is making a funny *noise*. **noise**
14. **sound** I like the *sound* of a marching band. **sound**
15. **oil** Dad is changing the *oil* in the car. **oil**
16. **point** I broke the *point* on my pencil. **point**
17. **country** We drove to the *country* to buy fresh vegetables. **country**
18. **round** Anita shaped the clay into a *round* ball. **round**
19. **though** My dog is very lively, even *though* it is old. **though**
20. **enough** Are you strong *enough* to lift this box? **enough**
21. **thought** Everyone *thought* it was a wonderful idea. **thought**
22. **bought** Sam *bought* a new pair of shoes. **bought**
23. **touch** Don't *touch* that hot stove. **touch**
24. **count** Close your eyes and *count* to ten. **count**
25. **lesson** Tokie finished the math *lesson* first. **lesson**
26. **matter** Susan wondered what was the *matter* with Henry. **matter**
27. **number** Mindy cannot remember the telephone *number*. **number**
28. **perhaps** Mom said that *perhaps* we can go swimming tomorrow. **perhaps**
29. **problem** Let's try to solve this division *problem*. **problem**
30. **middle** Put the food in the *middle* of the table. **middle**
31. **happen** I don't know what will *happen* if we miss the train. **happen**
32. **forgot** Maude promised to come, but she *forgot*. **forgot**
33. **ahead** Wes was *ahead* of Judy in line. **ahead**
34. **begin** Summer vacation will *begin* soon. **begin**
35. **paper** Manuel needs some *paper* to write a letter. **paper**

36. **parade** Our town always has a *parade* on Memorial Day. **parade**
37. **around** Let's walk *around* the block. **around**
38. **below** They live in the apartment *below*. **below**
39. **motor** The boat has an electric *motor*. **motor**
40. **behind** Danielle sat *behind* us on the bus. **behind**

Apply Prior Learning

Have the children apply what they know about the generalizations for Units 31–35. Use the following activity.

Write these sentences on the chalkboard: The clown stood and shook the point of his pencil at me. Did you lose your balloon? A raccoon made that loud noise . The supermarket sells olive oil and brook trout. The country mouse visited his city cousin.

Have the children identify the vowel sound(s) in the underlined words and group them according to common elements. (/ou/: clown, loud, trout, mouse; /oo/: balloon, raccoon, lose; /oi/: oil, noise, point; /u/: cousin, country; /o͝o/: stood, shook, brook)

Next write these sentences on the chalkboard and have the children determine the common element in the underlined words. (They each have two vowel sounds.) I forgot today's lesson about number problems. The rabbit ate dinner. Have the children divide each underlined word into syllables. Have them add more words to each group and name each group according to the appropriate spelling generalization. Tell the children that they will review words that follow these generalizations and then use the words to write a report.

FOCUS

- Relates to prior learning
- Draws relationships
- Applies spelling generalizations to new contexts

TEACHING PLAN

Objectives To spell words that demonstrate these sound-letter relationships: /o͞o/oo; /ōo/oo, ou, ew, o; to spell words that demonstrate these sound-letter relationships: /ou/ou, ow; /oi/oi, oy.

1. Review the directions to the exercises on page 154. Remind the children that the answers to the exercises are to be found only among the sixteen review words on page 154.

2. Have the children complete the exercises independently. You may refer them to the **Writer's Guide** at the back of the **Pupil Book** for a review of the spelling generalizations for Units 31 and 32.

Review

Do these steps if you are not sure how to spell a word.

- **Say** the word. Listen to each sound. Think about what the word means.
- **Look** at the word. See how the letters are made. Try to see the word in your mind.
- **Spell** the word to yourself. Think about the way each sound is spelled.
- **Write** the word. Copy it from your book. Check the way you made your letters. Write the word again.
- **Check** your learning. Cover the word and write it. Did you spell it correctly? If not, do these steps until you know how to spell the word.

UNIT 31
choose
noon
group
grew
stood
roof
tooth
flew

UNIT 31 Follow the directions. Use words from Unit 31.

1. Write the five words spelled with oo. Circle the word that sounds like chews.

(choose)   noon   stood

roof   tooth

Add the letters to the words below that spell /ōo/. Write the words.

2. gr＿＿p ___group___   3. fl＿＿ ___flew___

4. gr＿＿ ___grew___

UNIT 32
brown
mouth
loud
enjoy
noise
sound
oil
point

UNIT 32 Follow the directions. Use words from Unit 32.

5. Write the four words with the vowel sound heard in out.

Word order may vary

brown   mouth

loud   sound

154

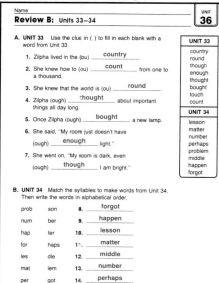

Review: Units 31 and 32

Name _____
Review A: Units 31–32

UNIT
36

A. UNIT 31 Write words from Unit 31 to complete the story. In the words you write, circle the letters that make an /ōo/ or /o͞o/ sound.

"It's __1__," Ramon said to his little brother Carlo. "Sit down so we can eat lunch. You can have a carrot that we __2__ in our garden." When Carlo bit into the carrot, he cried, "I've lost my __3__!" Just then, a __4__ of Ramon's friends walked by. Carlo __5__ up to show them his mouth. "Save your tooth, and make a wish," said one boy. "You can have anything in the world you __6__." Carlo held his tooth in his hand, looking at it. Just then, a bird __7__ off the __8__ and stole the tooth!

UNIT 31
choose
noon
group
grew
stood
roof
tooth
flew

UNIT 32
brown
enjoy
loud
mouth
noise
sound
oil
point

1. __n(oo)n__   2. __gr(ew)__
3. __t(oo)th__   4. __gr(ou)p__
5. __st(oo)d__   6. __ch(oo)se__
7. __fl(ew)__   8. __r(oo)f__

B. UNIT 32 Circle the four words in the paragraph that have an /ou/ sound. Underline the four words that have an /oi/ sound. Then write the words under the paragraph.

A girl with (brown) hair said, "I enjoy making noise. Sometimes I open my (mouth) and make a (loud) squeaky (sound) People point at me. They think I need oil for my squeak."

	/ou/ words		/oi/ words
9.	brown	10.	enjoy
11.	mouth	12.	noise
13.	loud	14.	point
15.	sound	16.	oil

Extra Practice • 151

Review: Units 33 and 34

Name _____
Review B: Units 33–34

UNIT
36

A. UNIT 33 Use the clue in ( ) to fill in each blank with a word from Unit 33.

1. Zilpha lived in the (ou) __country__

2. She knew how to (ou) __count__ from one to a thousand.

3. She knew that the world is (ou) __round__

4. Zilpha (ough) __thought__ about important things all day long.

5. Once Zilpha (ough) __bought__ a new lamp.

6. She said, "My room just doesn't have (ough) __enough__ light."

7. She went on, "My room is dark, even (ough) __though__ I am bright."

UNIT 33
country
round
though
enough
thought
bought
touch
count

UNIT 34
lesson
matter
number
perhaps
problem
middle
happen
forgot

B. UNIT 34 Match the syllables to make words from Unit 34. Then write the words in alphabetical order.

prob	son	8.	forgot
num	ber	9.	happen
hap	ter	10.	lesson
for	haps	11.	matter
les	dle	12.	middle
mat	lem	13.	number
per	got	14.	perhaps
mid	pen	15.	problem

152 • Extra Practice

Write the four words with the vowel sound heard in toy.

Word order may vary.

enjoy	noise
oil	point

UNIT 33 Follow the directions. Use words from Unit 33. Write the word that ends with each sound.

7. /ō/ ___though___   8. /ē/ ___country___

9. /f/ ___enough___   10. /d/ ___round___

UNIT 33

country
round
though
enough
thought
bought
touch
count

Write the words that rhyme with these words.

11. amount ___count___   12. much ___touch___

13. puff ___enough___   14. slow ___though___

Finish these sentences.

15. Maria ___bought___ a ticket to the show.

16. She ___thought___ that Elena would go with her.

UNIT 34 Follow the directions. Use words from Unit 34. Write the word that goes with each meaning. Then draw a line between the two syllables of each word you wrote.

17. something you solve ___prob|lem___

18. maybe ___per|haps___

19. It tells how many. ___num|ber___

20. did not remember ___for|got___

UNIT 34

lesson
matter
number
perhaps
problem
middle
happen
forgot

Write the words that have these double consonant letters. Draw a line between the two syllables.

21. dd ___mid|dle___   22. tt ___mat|ter___

23. pp ___hap|pen___   24. ss ___les|son___

155

TEACHING PLAN

Objectives To spell words that demonstrate these sound-letter relationships: /u/ou, /ou/ou, /ô/ough, /uf/ough; to spell words that have the VC/CV syllable pattern.

1. Review the directions to the exercises on page 155. Remind the children that the answers to the exercises are to be found only among the sixteen review words on page 155.
2. Have the children complete the exercises independently. You may refer them to the **Writer's Guide** at the back of the **Pupil Book** for a review of the spelling generalizations for Units 33 and 34.

⟳ EXTENDING THE LESSON

Have the children write sentences with review words from Units 33 and 34. Each sentence should contain at least one review word and other words that have the same vowel sound. An example is:

A loud clown had a round mouth.

Have the children use as many of their spelling words as they can and remind them to proofread their sentences for spelling.

Review: Unit 35

Name	UNIT 36

Review C: Unit 35 • Test Exercise

A. UNIT 35 In the story, circle the words that don't make sense. Then add a syllable to each word to make it correct. Write the new words on the lines. Use words from Unit 35.

The (per) says there will be a (pa) next week. It will (gin) in the morning. The people will walk (a) the park and (low) the bridge. Some clowns will walk (head) of the group. More clowns will follow (be) the group. The clowns will pull a car without a (mo).

UNIT 35

ahead
begin
behind
paper
parade
around
below
motor

1. ___paper___   2. ___parade___

3. ___begin___   4. ___around___

5. ___below___   6. ___ahead___

7. ___behind___   8. ___motor___

B. Write the words from Unit 35 that begin with be. Then draw a line between the syllables in each word.

be | gin   be | hind   be | low

C. UNITS 31–35 Fill in the circle below the word that is spelled wrong.

1	choose ⓐ	flew ⓑ	group ⓒ	rouf ●	6	point ⓐ	stood ⓑ	tooth ⓒ	grue ●
2	lowd ●	brown ⓑ	mouth ⓒ	sound ⓓ	7	noon ⓐ	enjoy ⓑ	noyse ●	oil ⓓ
3	rund ●	country ⓑ	bought ⓒ	touch ⓓ	8	thogh ●	enough ⓑ	thought ⓒ	count ⓓ
4	lesson ⓐ	problem ⓑ	hapen ●	forgot ⓓ	9	matter ⓐ	numbar ●	perhaps ⓒ	middle ⓓ
5	begin ⓐ	behined ●	below ⓒ	around ⓓ	10	ahead ⓐ	paper ⓑ	moter ●	parade ⓓ

Extra Practice • 153

TEACHING PLAN

Objective   To spell words that have the V/CV syllable pattern.

1. Review the directions to the exercises on page 156. Remind the children that the answers to the exercises are to be found only among the eight review words on page 156.
2. Have the children complete the exercises independently. You may refer them to the **Writer's Guide** at the back of the **Pupil Book** for a review of the spelling generalization for Unit 35.
3. Review the children's answers on pages 154–156 orally, or have volunteers write them on the chalkboard.

For reinforcement in writing words for Units 31–35, you may wish to assign **Review Masters 36A, 36B,** and **36C.**

WORDS IN TIME

Have a volunteer read **Words in Time** aloud. Tell the children that other words that name parts of machines also have interesting word histories.

As a COOPERATIVE LEARNING activity have each group compose a word history for a word that names a machine part, such as *gear, blade, wheel.* Ask the group to choose one word. Different children may use different resource materials, such as the dictionary, encyclopedia, or books on the origins of words. Have the children record the information and share it with one another. One child should use the information to write a word history. Another child can illustrate it by drawing a picture of the item or cutting a picture out of a magazine. One child should revise the word history, checking spelling, punctuation, and capitalization. The group may display its word history on the bulletin board.

UNIT 35

ahead
begin
paper
parade
around
below
motor
behind

UNIT 35   Follow the directions. Use words from Unit 35. Write the word that goes with each clue. Draw a line between the two syllables of each word you wrote.

25. I am written on and have /ā/.   pa|per

26. I mean "in a circle" and have /ou/.   a|round

27. I mean "in back of" and have /ī/.   be|hind

28. I start with /ə/ and mean "out in front."   a|head

29. I have marching bands and /ā/.   pa|rade

30. I have /ō/ and help things go.   mo|tor

Finish these sentences.

31. There's going to be a _____ parade _____ on Saturday.

32. Each float will be run by a _____ motor _____

33. Carmen read all about it in the _____ paper _____

34. It's going to _____ begin _____ at noon.

35. It's going to end _____ around _____ two o'clock.

36. Let's try to get there _____ ahead _____ of time.

37. Let's not stand _____ behind _____ any tall people.

WORDS IN TIME

The word <u>motor</u> comes from the old word <u>movere</u>. <u>Movere</u> meant "to move." Think about what things have a motor. Why do you think <u>movere</u> became the name for a motor?

156

Spelling and Reading

A Report

Read the following report. Look for the main idea in each paragraph.

How the Pilgrims Learned About Corn

Corn was first grown in America by American Indians. Hundreds of years ago, a group of American Indians called the Algonquians lived in what is now New England. Every summer, they grew enough corn to feed themselves for the year ahead.

When the Pilgrims first came to this country in 1620, they saw a field where the Algonquians had planted corn. The Pilgrims stood looking in wonder at the strange new food. They thought this food was amazing.

The Pilgrims wanted to learn how to plant corn. The Algonquians gave them lessons. This was very helpful to the Pilgrims. It meant they would not have so many food problems in the years ahead.

Write the answers to the questions. **See answers below.**

1. What does the writer of this report say the Algonquians did every summer? *Literal*
2. How did the Pilgrims learn to plant corn? *Literal*
3. Why did the Pilgrims have to be taught how to plant corn? *Interpretive*
4. How do you think the Algonquians and Pilgrims got along with each other? Give a reason for your answer. *Critical*

Underline the review words in your answers. Check to see that you spelled the words correctly.

157

Spelling and Reading Answers

1. The Algonquians grew enough corn to feed themselves for the year ahead. 2. The Algonquians gave them lessons. 3. They had never seen it before and did not know how to grow it. 4. Accept all reasonable answers. Possible answer: They probably got along well. The Algonquians were friendly in teaching the Pilgrims about planting corn.

On this page, students will read:
- This Week's Words from the preceding five units;
- words reviewed in this unit;
- words that follow the generalizations taught in the preceding five units.

TEACHING PLAN

Objectives To analyze and respond to a report; to identify main ideas in a report; to proofread written answers for spelling.

1. Tell the children that they will read a report that includes a number of spelling words from Units 31–35. Point out that a good report presents factual information about a subject. Tell them that writers carefully select the details to tell about each main idea in each paragraph of a report and that the information contained may come from books and magazines. Ask the children to recall any reports that stand out in their memory and to tell what characteristics made them outstanding. Explain that the report will serve as a model for their own writing.

2. Have the children read the report on page 157 to find out how the Pilgrims learned about corn. Tell them to look for the main idea in each paragraph and the details that tell why corn was so important, who helped the Pilgrims, and how they were helped.

3. Have the children answer the questions independently. Tell them to underline the review words in the answers and to proofread the answers for spelling.

4. Spot-check the children's answers as they work. Review answers orally.

TEACHING PLAN

Objectives   To recognize the purpose of a report; to identify the details used in a report; to evaluate the form of a report.

1. Have the children read the first paragraph of **Think and Discuss** on page 158. Ask them to look over the report again and decide if it fits the definition of a good report and to explain why or why not.
2. Have the children look at the illustration on page 158. Ask them to describe the scene and explain how it represents the information presented in the report.
3. Have the children read the rest of **Think and Discuss** independently and answer the questions. Ask them to give examples of other words and phrases that the writer could have used to tell about how the Pilgrims were helped and why it was so important for them.
4. Have the children read **Apply** at the bottom of page 158. Tell them that they will write a report using some of their spelling words. Explain that the audience for their report will be their classmates. Point out that each paragraph should have a topic sentence telling the main idea of the paragraph and that the detail sentences should tell about the topic sentence. Discuss with them the importance of using factual information as the basis for their detail sentences.

Spelling and Writing
A Report

Words to Help You Write

choose
enjoy
country
though
count
matter
number
problem
begin
below
around
ahead

Think and Discuss

In a report, a writer gives information about a subject. The information may come from books or magazines. A title tells what the report is about. On page 157 is a report one student wrote for a social studies class. What is the title of the report?^A

How many paragraphs are in the report?^B Each paragraph in a report has a topic sentence that tells the main idea of the paragraph. What is the topic sentence of the first paragraph?^C The other sentences in a paragraph are detail sentences. They tell more about the topic sentence. What does the writer tell about in the detail sentences in the first paragraph?^D

Look at the last paragraph. What is the topic sentence?^E What does the writer tell about in detail sentences in the third paragraph?^F

Apply

Write a **report** to share with your classmates. Follow the writing guidelines on the next page.

158

Summarize Learning

Have the children identify the characteristics of a good report. (use of factual information to tell about a subject; information presented in paragraph form with topic sentence and detail sentences in each paragraph; title telling about the subject)

Think and Discuss Answers

A. How the Pilgrims Learned About Corn B. three C. Corn was first grown in America by American Indians. D. The writer tells about the Algonquians and how they grew corn. E. The Pilgrims wanted to learn how to plant corn. F. The writer tells how the Pilgrims learned to plant corn from the Algonquians.

Prewriting

Choose a subject you find interesting.

- Use books and magazines to find three important ideas about the subject.
- List some facts about each of the three ideas.
- Arrange the three ideas in an order that makes sense.

Composing

Use the facts you listed to write the first draft of your report.

- Write one paragraph about each of the three ideas.
- Write a topic sentence and detail sentences for each paragraph. Use your list to write the detail sentences.
- Write a title that tells what the whole report is about.

Revising

Read your report and show it to a classmate. Follow these guidelines to improve your work. Use the editing and proofreading marks to show changes.

Editing

- Be sure you wrote a topic sentence for each paragraph.
- Be sure the detail sentences in each paragraph tell about the topic sentence.

Proofreading

- Check your spelling and correct any mistakes.
- Check your capitalization and punctuation.

WRITER'S GUIDE If you need help with capital letters and punctuation marks, turn to pages 255-257.

Copy your report onto clean paper. Write carefully and neatly.

Publishing

Share your report with your classmates. Draw a picture to go with your report, and post it on a class bulletin board.

159

Editing and Proofreading Marks	
≡	capitalize
⊙	make a period
∧	add something
⌃⸴	add a comma
⟋	take something away
◯	spell correctly
⁋	indent the paragraph
/	make a lowercase letter
～tr	transpose

TEACHING PLAN

Objectives To write a report; to edit a report; to proofread for spelling, capitalization, and punctuation.

1. **Prewriting** Have the children choose a subject which interests them. Have them formulate three ideas that they consider important about the subject. Explain that these will become the basis for the topic sentences of their paragraphs. Tell them to list details about each of the three ideas. Remind them that the details should be facts about the subject and that the information can come from books and magazines. Have them put their ideas in order. Suggest that they look over their spelling review words for additional words to use and that they use the **Spelling Thesaurus** on page 203 as well.

2. **Composing** Have the children write the topic sentences for each of the three paragraphs. Then have them complete the first drafts of the reports by writing detail sentences. Remind the children to write a title that tells the subject of the report.

3. **Revising (Editing and Proofreading)** Have each child ask a classmate to read the report. Have the reader check to see if the report is clearly written. Have the children consider their classmates' comments as they revise the reports. Tell them to follow the guidelines on page 159. Remind them to use the **Spelling Dictionary** to check their spelling. To help the children prepare a legible copy of their reports, have them consult the **Handwriting Models** in the **Writer's Guide** on page 258.

For reinforcement in editing and proofreading, you may wish to use *Spelling and Writing Transparency 6.*

4. **Publishing** Have the children share the articles with classmates.

Extra Practice: Dictionary/Proofreading

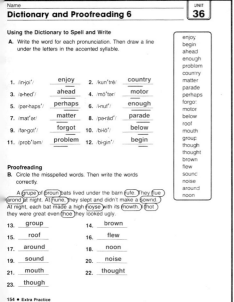

Dictionary and Proofreading 6 — UNIT 36

Using the Dictionary to Spell and Write

A. Write the word for each pronunciation. Then draw a line under the letters in the accented syllable.

1. /in·joi'/	enjoy	2. /kun'trē/	country	
3. /ə·hed'/	ahead	4. /mō'tər/	motor	
5. /pər·haps'/	perhaps	6. /i·nuf'/	enough	
7. /mat'ər/	matter	8. /pə·rād'/	parade	
9. /fər·got'/	forgot	10. /bi·lō'/	below	
11. /prob'ləm/	problem	12. /bi·gin'/	begin	

enjoy / begin / ahead / enough / problem / country / matter / parade / perhaps / forgot / motor / below / roof / mouth / group / though / thought / brown / flew / sound / noise / around / noon

Proofreading

B. Circle the misspelled words. Then write the words correctly.

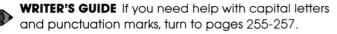

A grupe of broun bats lived under the barn rufe. They flue arond at night. At nune, they slept and didn't make a sound. At night, each bat made a high noyse with its mowth. I thot they were great even thoe they looked ugly.

13. group		14. brown	
15. roof		16. flew	
17. around		18. noon	
19. sound		20. noise	
21. mouth		22. thought	
23. though			

154 • Extra Practice

For additional practice in using a dictionary to spell and write and in proofreading, you may wish to assign *Dictionary and Proofreading Practice Master 6.*

ENRICHMENT ACTIVITIES

For the Home

Home activities may be assigned to children of all ability levels. The activities provide opportunities for children to use their spelling words in new contexts. The children may complete these activities independently or with the assistance of a relative or friend in the home.

1. **Fine Arts/Writing Interview Questions for a Composer** Explain to the children that Wolfgang Amadeus Mozart was a famous composer of the 1700's. Tell the children to imagine that they could talk to Mozart. Tell them to write two questions that he might ask about music today. Then have them write two questions that they might ask Mozart about music in the 1700's. Have the children share their questions with a friend or someone at home. Encourage the use of spelling words in the questions.

2. **Social Studies/Writing a Paragraph About Your Community** Tell the children to write a paragraph describing one aspect of the community in which they live. Direct their attention to page 249 of the **Writer's Guide** to read about paragraphs if necessary. As a prewriting activity, have them look over the review words in search of possible ideas and words that might be used. Tell them to list their ideas and then choose one as a topic. Topics might include physical characteristics and population of the community, transportation, recreational facilities, or types of industry in the community. After composing and revising their paragraphs, have the children share their paragraphs with a friend or someone at home.

3. **Language Arts/Writing Sentences with Rhyming Words** Tell the children to choose five spelling words and write several rhyming words for each. Then have them use as many of the rhyming words in one sentence as they can. Use these examples:

   I *found* something *round* on the *ground* that made a strange *sound*.
   It doesn't *matter* that the *hatter* got *fatter* while eating all the cookie *batter*.

   Tell the children to share their sentences with a friend or someone at home.

4. **Language Arts/Writing Clues for Spelling Words** Have the children choose five spelling words and write four clues for each. Clues should include the part of speech, the number of syllables, something about its spelling, and the meaning. Give this example for *touch*: This word can be a verb. It has one syllable. It begins with the same sound as *tomorrow*. It tells something you can do with your hands.

   When the children have completed their clues, tell them to have a friend or someone at home guess the spelling word.

EVALUATION

Unit Test

1. **choose**   Robbie will usually *choose* a hamburger with pickles.   **choose**
2. **noon**   We will meet under the big clock at *noon*. **noon**
3. **group**   Each *group* will draw part of the mural.   **group**
4. **grew**   The kittens *grew* bigger and bigger.   **grew**
5. **stood**   The statue *stood* in the hall.   **stood**
6. **roof**   Our *roof* leaked only when it rained.   **roof**
7. **tooth**   The baby has one little white *tooth*.   **tooth**
8. **flew**   The bat *flew* into the chimney.   **flew**
9. **brown**   Alyssa is wearing her new *brown* shoes.   **brown**
10. **mouth**   The nurse put the thermometer in my *mouth*. **mouth**
11. **loud**   That music is too *loud*.   **loud**
12. **enjoy**   They *enjoy* dancing to all sorts of music.   **enjoy**
13. **noise**   The strange *noise* grew louder and louder.   **noise**
14. **sound**   We heard the *sound* of footsteps echoing in the cave.   **sound**
15. **oil**   Many people like to cook with olive *oil*.   **oil**
16. **point**   Nora understood the *point* of the story.   **point**
17. **country**   People eat different foods in different parts of the *country*.   **country**

18. *round*   The cat stared at me with *round,* yellow eyes.   *round*

19. *though*   I eat spinach *though* I really don't like it.   *though*

20. *enough*   Peter is tall *enough* to reach the top shelf.   *enough*

21. *thought*   You *thought* you couldn't jump that high, but you did.   *thought*

22. *bought*   My parents *bought* a new car.   *bought*

23. *touch*   When you *touch* a snake, it feels cool.   *touch*

24. *count*   When I buy something, I always *count* my change.   *count*

25. *lesson*   I have a piano *lesson* at three o'clock.   *lesson*

26. *matter*   There is something the *matter* with this engine.   *matter*

27. *number*   Alex gave me his telephone *number.* *number*

28. *perhaps*   There are other beings, *perhaps,* on other planets.   *perhaps*

29. *problem*   We can solve this *problem* if we try.   *problem*

30. *middle*   Gary woke up in the *middle* of the night.   *middle*

31. *happen*   We waited and waited for something to *happen.* *happen*

32. *forgot*   Lee-Ann *forgot* her homework today.   *forgot*

33. *ahead*   If we look straight *ahead,* we can see the city in the distance.   *ahead*

34. *begin*   Angela will *begin* studying the violin.   *begin*

35. *paper*   Ben cut the *paper* into the shape of a snowflake.   *paper*

36. *parade*   The Scouts will march in the Columbus Day *parade* this year.   *parade*

37. *around*   Bushes cut in the shapes of animals grew all *around* the garden.   *around*

38. *below*   A river wound through the valley far *below* us.   *below*

39. *motor*   My father tried to start the *motor.* *motor*

40. *behind*   The puppy trailed *behind* us, exploring everything in sight.   *behind*

Mastery and Bonus Words Review and Assessment

For additional practice you may wish to assign **Mastery Words Review Master: Units 31–35** or **Bonus Words Review Master: Units 31–35.** To assess children's spelling ability with these words, use **Mastery Words Test: Units 31–35** or **Bonus Words Test: Units 31–35.**

Mastery Words Review

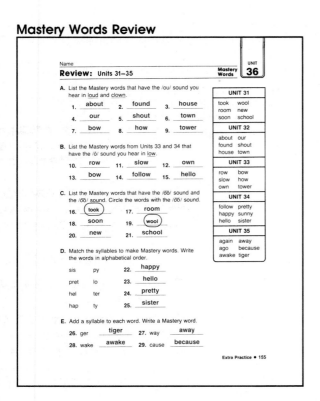

Bonus Words Review

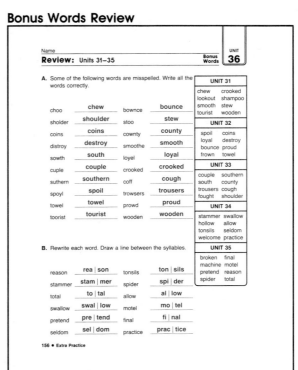

Mastery Words Test

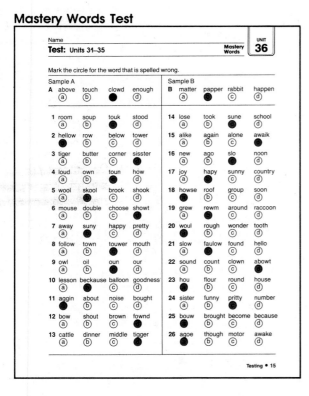

Bonus Words Test

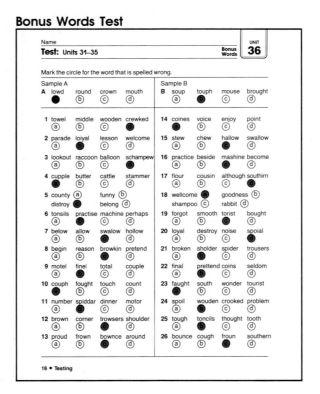

Mark the circle for the word that is spelled wrong.

Sample A					Sample B			
A kept	key	step	spel		**B** age	edge	dangur	large
ⓐ	ⓑ	ⓒ	⬤		ⓐ	ⓑ	ⓒ	ⓓ

1 broun	noon	sound	round		**11** mouth	bougt	group	sound
ⓐ	ⓑ	ⓒ	ⓓ		ⓐ	ⓑ	ⓒ	ⓓ
2 become	beegin	below	balloon		**12** oil	funny	voice	injoy
ⓐ	ⓑ	ⓒ	ⓓ		ⓐ	ⓑ	ⓒ	ⓓ
3 clown	kount	country	cloud		**13** touch	suond	loud	tooth
ⓐ	ⓑ	ⓒ	ⓓ		ⓐ	ⓑ	ⓒ	ⓓ
4 lose	roof	grew	floo		**14** papr	parade	number	dinner
ⓐ	ⓑ	ⓒ	ⓓ		ⓐ	ⓑ	ⓒ	ⓓ
5 raccoon	happen	leson	problem		**15** brought	tough	flew	groop
ⓐ	ⓑ	ⓒ	ⓓ		ⓐ	ⓑ	ⓒ	ⓓ
6 rabbit	corner	thought	forgott		**16** nois	pilot	belong	owl
ⓐ	ⓑ	ⓒ	ⓓ		ⓐ	ⓑ	ⓒ	ⓓ
7 cattle	midle	matter	double		**17** stod	brook	shook	cloud
ⓐ	ⓑ	ⓒ	ⓓ		ⓐ	ⓑ	ⓒ	ⓓ
8 soup	toothe	stood	shook		**18** rough	enugh	double	brought
ⓐ	ⓑ	ⓒ	ⓓ		ⓐ	ⓑ	ⓒ	ⓓ
9 flour	though	enough	tuoch		**19** wonder	flour	moter	mouse
ⓐ	ⓑ	ⓒ	ⓓ		ⓐ	ⓑ	ⓒ	ⓓ
10 butter	motor	numbur	wonder		**20** alone	alike	above	ahaed
ⓐ	ⓑ	ⓒ	ⓓ		ⓐ	ⓑ	ⓒ	ⓓ

FORM A TEST 6

Administering the Test

1. Tell the children that today they will take a spelling test on some of the words they have studied in Units 31–35. Pass out the test papers. Tell the children to leave them turned upside down until you are ready to begin.

2. Have the children turn their tests over. Direct their attention to Sample A. Point out that one of the four words is spelled incorrectly. Point out that circle *d* under the misspelling *s-p-e-l* is filled in.

3. Now direct the children's attention to Sample B. Have the children look for the incorrect spelling. Ask a child to tell you the word that is spelled incorrectly by spelling it correctly. (*d-a-n-g-e-r*) Then have the children fill in circle *c* in pencil.

4. After you have checked to see that all children have completed Sample B correctly, have the children proceed with the test.

Evaluating the Results

Use the following **Answer Key** to correct the children's tests and to determine whether they need more practice with particular units. The chart shows the units in which each answer word is taught.

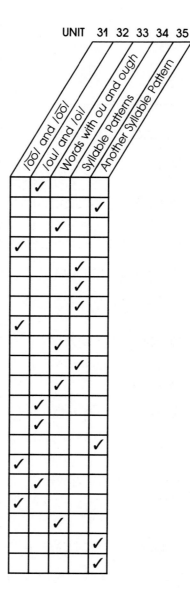

ANSWER KEY

#	a	b	c	d
1	●	b	c	d
2	a	●	c	d
3	a	●	c	d
4	a	b	c	●
5	a	b	●	d
6	a	b	c	●
7	a	●	c	d
8	a	●	c	d
9	a	b	c	●
10	a	b	●	d
11	a	●	c	d
12	a	b	c	●
13	a	●	c	d
14	●	b	c	d
15	a	b	c	●
16	●	b	c	d
17	●	b	c	d
18	a	●	c	d
19	a	b	●	d
20	a	b	c	●

Nine-Week Evaluation

Mark the circle for the word that is spelled wrong.

Sample A				Sample B			
A girl ⓐ	wurry ⓑ	hurt ⓒ	purpose ⓓ	**B** heart ⓐ	return ⓑ	harecut ⓒ	work ⓓ

1 nickle ⓐ	eagle ⓑ	table ⓒ	level ⓓ	**11** cloud ⓐ	mouth ⓑ	clown ⓒ	lowd ⓓ
2 people ⓐ	able ⓑ	perple ⓒ	camel ⓓ	**12** cousin ⓐ	cownt ⓑ	touch ⓒ	country ⓓ
3 bottle ⓐ	either ⓑ	letter ⓒ	suger ⓓ	**13** enuff ⓐ	thought ⓑ	flour ⓒ	double ⓓ
4 rode ⓐ	sail ⓑ	whoose ⓒ	mane ⓓ	**14** brought ⓐ	round ⓑ	bawght ⓒ	although ⓓ
5 reed ⓐ	son ⓑ	meet ⓒ	reid ⓓ	**15** numbur ⓐ	dinner ⓑ	matter ⓒ	butter ⓓ
6 main ⓐ	wun ⓑ	sale ⓒ	whose ⓓ	**16** cattle ⓐ	wonder ⓑ	middel ⓒ	corner ⓓ
7 stoud ⓐ	noon ⓑ	grew ⓒ	balloon ⓓ	**17** rabbit ⓐ	happy ⓑ	lessun ⓒ	funny ⓓ
8 flew ⓐ	tooth ⓑ	groop ⓒ	shook ⓓ	**18** moter ⓐ	became ⓑ	above ⓒ	alike ⓓ
9 poynt ⓐ	joy ⓑ	voice ⓒ	sound ⓓ	**19** alone ⓐ	around ⓑ	ahaed ⓒ	below ⓓ
10 mouse ⓐ	noyse ⓑ	oil ⓒ	enjoy ⓓ	**20** parade ⓐ	begin ⓑ	behind ⓒ	papar ⓓ

FORM B TEST 4

Administering the Test

1. Tell the children that today they will take a spelling test on some of the words they have studied in Units 28 – 35. Pass out the test papers. Tell the children to leave them turned upside down until you are ready to begin.

2. Have the children turn their tests over. Direct the children's attention to Sample A. Point out that one of the four words is spelled incorrectly. Point out the circle *b* under the misspelling *w-u-r-r-y* is filled in.

3. Now direct the children's attention to Sample B. Have the children look for the incorrect spelling. Ask a child to tell you the word that is spelled incorrectly by spelling it correctly. (*h-a-i-r-c-u-t*) Then have the children fill in circle *c* in pencil.

4. After you have checked to see that all children have completed Sample B correctly, have the children proceed with the test.

Evaluating the Results

Use the following **Answer Key** to correct the children's tests and to determine whether they need more practice with particular units. The chart shows the units in which each answer word is taught.

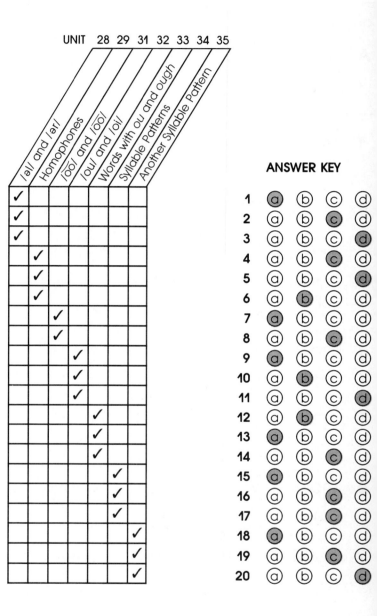

UNIT	28 /ål/ and /är/	29 Homophones	31 /o͞o/ and /o͝o/	32 /ou/ and /oi/	33 Words with ou and ough	34 Syllable Patterns	35 Another Syllable Pattern
1	✓						
2	✓						
3	✓						
4		✓					
5		✓					
6		✓					
7			✓				
8			✓				
9				✓			
10				✓			
11				✓			
12					✓		
13					✓		
14					✓		
15						✓	
16						✓	
17						✓	
18							✓
19							✓
20							✓

ANSWER KEY

1. (a)
2. (c)
3. (d)
4. (c)
5. (d)
6. (b)
7. (a)
8. (c)
9. (a) (d)
10. (b)
11. (d)
12. (b)
13. (a)
14. (c)
15. (a)
16. (c)
17. (c)
18. (a)
19. (c)
20. (d)

END-OF-YEAR TEST

This Week's Words

1. *everybody*   We thought *everybody* would be here by now.   *everybody.*
2. *sometimes*   Heavy traffic *sometimes* makes people late.   *sometimes*
3. *won't*   We promise we *won't* tell.   *won't*
4. *it's*   I hope *it's* warm and sunny tomorrow.   *it's*
5. *talk*   Let's *talk* about the story we just read.   *talk*
6. *taught*   Amy *taught* Megan how to play hopscotch.   *taught*
7. *learn*   Pedro wants to *learn* to play the guitar.   *learn*
8. *heard*   We *heard* the cat scratching at the door.   *heard*
9. *stairs*   These *stairs* go up to the attic.   *stairs*
10. *heart*   Your *heart* pumps blood through your body.   *heart*
11. *butterflies*   Monarch *butterflies* are orange and black.   *butterflies*
12. *marbles*   Ted put all his *marbles* in a plastic bag.   *marbles*
13. *knew*   Tracy *knew* he would enjoy day camp.   *knew*
14. *thumb*   Linda has a bandage on her *thumb.*   *thumb*
15. *half*   I ate the other *half* of the sandwich.   *half*
16. *family*   Mai is the youngest person in her *family.*   *family*
17. *library*   Let's go to the *library* and get some more books.   *library*
18. *people*   There were crowds of *people* at the beach.   *people*
19. *whose*   Do you know *whose* bike this is?   *whose*
20. *choose*   The librarian helped Laurie *choose* a book to read.   *choose*
21. *noise*   The lawn mower makes a lot of *noise.*   *noise*
22. *thought*   Vinnie *thought* his team would win.   *thought*
23. *enough*   It is not warm *enough* to go swimming today.   *enough*
24. *problem*   A dog that barks too much can be a *problem.*   *problem*
25. *parade*   The *parade* will start at noon.   *parade*

Mastery Words

1. *without*   Please don't leave *without* me.   *without*
2. *within*   There was another box *within* the first box.   *within*

3. *their*   Manny and Chad rode *their* bikes.   *their*
4. *draw*   Heide will *draw* a picture.   *draw*
5. *before*   They got there *before* we did.   *before*
6. *hurt*   Mary *hurt* her knee when she fell.   *hurt*
7. *work*   Dad has to *work* this Saturday.   *work*
8. *chair*   You may sit in this *chair.*   *chair*
9. *start*   Daryl will *start* work on Monday.   *start*
10. *listen*   Jessica will *listen* to the news on the radio.   *listen*
11. *know*   The children all *know* how to swim.   *know*
12. *attention*   Please try to pay *attention.*   *attention*
13. *city*   Our *city* has two swimming pools.   *city*
14. *dollar*   Duane earned a *dollar* by pulling weeds.   *dollar*
15. *hear*   We could *hear* a woodpecker nearby.   *hear*
16. *school*   Emma's *school* is having a picnic.   *school*
17. *about*   Claire read a book *about* a doctor.   *about*
18. *house*   The Halpern's *house* is by the river.   *house*
19. *happy*   Everyone was *happy* when our team won.   *happy*
20. *because*   We couldn't go *because* it was raining.   *because*

Bonus Words

1. *doesn't*   Our dog *doesn't* like the water.   *doesn't*
2. *daughter*   Mr. Ruiz is teaching his *daughter* how to swim.   *daughter*
3. *thirsty*   We were *thirsty* after playing in the sun.   *thirsty*
4. *worst*   This is the *worst* rainstorm we've had this year.   *worst*
5. *stories*   John reads *stories* to his little sister.   *stories*
6. *wrist*   Jenny twisted her *wrist* when she fell.   *wrist*
7. *factory*   Many people in town work at the *factory.*   *factory*
8. *travel*   The Bensons love to *travel* in the summer.   *travel*
9. *answer*   Please *answer* the telephone.   *answer*
10. *whole*   We spent the *whole* day at the amusement park.   *whole*
11. *towel*   George spread his *towel* on the sand.   *towel*
12. *proud*   Gina was *proud* that she had passed her swimming test.   *proud*
13. *cough*   The smoke from the fire made us *cough.*   *cough*
14. *practice*   The team has baseball *practice* twice a week.   *practice*
15. *reason*   Nell had a good *reason* for being late.   *reason*

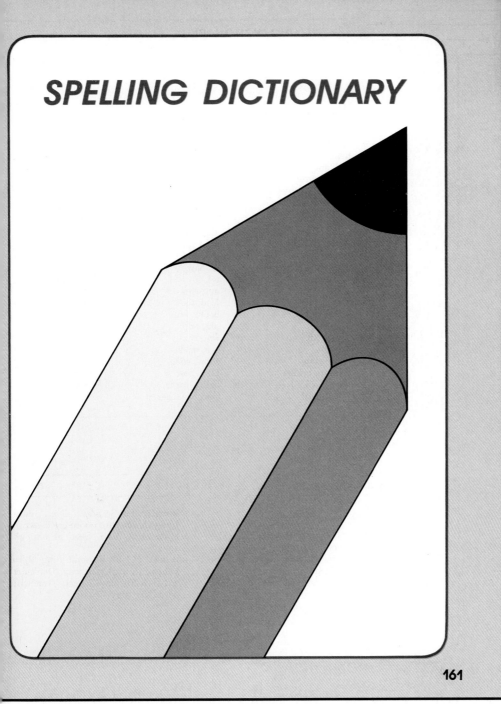

SPELLING DICTIONARY

161

PRONUNCIATION KEY

Remember these things when you read pronunciations:
- When you see ( ) around a sound, it means that sound is not always heard. /gran(d)′chīld′/
- This mark ′ comes after the syllable you say with the most force. This lighter mark ′ comes after the syllable you say with a little less force. /yes′tər·dā′/

/a/	act, cat	/m/	mother, room	/u/	up, come
/ā/	ate, rain	/n/	new, can	/û/	early, hurt
/â/	care, bear	/ng/	sing, hang	/yo͞o/	mule, few
/ä/	car, father	/o/	on, stop	/v/	very, five
/b/	bed, rub	/ō/	over, go	/w/	will
/ch/	chair, watch	/ô/	or, saw	/y/	yes
/d/	duck, red	/oi/	oil, toy	/z/	zoo, buzz
/e/	egg, hen	/ou/	out, cow	/zh/	treasure
/ē/	even, see	/o͞o/	food, too	/ə/	The schwa
/f/	fish, off	/o͝o/	book, pull		is the sound
/g/	go, big	/p/	pig, hop		these letters
/h/	hat, hit	/r/	ran, car		stand for:
/i/	if, sit	/s/	see, miss		a in ago
/ī/	ice, time	/sh/	show, wish		e in listen
/j/	jump, bridge	/t/	take, feet		i in giraffe
/k/	cat, look	/th/	thing, tooth		o in pilot
/l/	lost, ball	/th/	that, weather		u in circus

able	act

A

a·ble /ā′bəl/ *adj.* Having the skill: Jane is *able* to swim.

a·bout /ə·bout′/ *prep.* Having to do with: This story is *about* cats. —*adv.* Almost: Are you just *about* ready?

a·bove /ə·buv′/ *prep.* Over: Paul hung the picture *above* his desk.

a·corn /ā′kôrn/ *n.* Seed of an oak tree.

act /akt/ *v.* **1** To do something. **2** To behave in a certain way: Don't *act* silly. **3** To play a part: Tina will *act* in the play.

162

add	argue

—*n.* **1** Something done: Feeding birds is a kind *act*. **2** Part of a play: The third *act* was funny.

add /ad/ *v.* To put two or more numbers or things together.

a·dult /ə·dult′ *or* ad′ult/ *n.* A grown-up person.

af·ter /af′tər/ *prep.* **1** Later than: We got home *after* dark. **2** Following: Friday comes *after* Thursday.

a·gain /ə·gen′/ *adv.* Once more: Jenny and Scott played in the park *again*.

age /āj/ *n.* **1** The time someone or something has lived: Robin and Tom are the same *age*. **2** A period of time in history: We live in the space *age*.

—*v.* **aged, aging** To grow old.

a·go /ə·gō′/ *adj., adv.* In the past: I got my dog a year *ago*.

a·head /ə·hed′/ *adv.* In front; before: Miguel was *ahead* of me in line.

air /âr/ *n.* **1** What we breathe. **2** The sky: up in the *air*.

—*v.* To let air in: Open the window and *air* out the room.

a·larm /ə·lärm′/ *n.* A signal that warns of danger: fire *alarm*.

—*v.* To frighten: Loud noises *alarm* me.

a·like /ə·līk′/ *adj.* The same: The twins sometimes dress *alike*.

al·low /ə·lou′/ *v.* To permit: Dogs are not *allowed* on the beach.

a·lone /ə·lōn′/ *adj.* Without anyone or anything near.

—*adv.* Without help: Julia baked the cake *alone*.

al·so /ôl′sō/ *adv.* Too: Raymond *also* plays baseball.

al·though /ôl·thō′/ *conj.* Even if: *Although* I'm busy, I'll help you.

and /and/ *conj.* Also; added to.

an·gry /ang′grē/ *adj.* **angrier, angriest** Feeling anger; mad: The *angry* dog growled.

an·oth·er /ə·nuth′ər/ *adj.* **1** One more: May I have *another* apple? **2** A different one: Kurt moved to *another* city.

an·swer /an′sər/ *n.* **1** A reply. **2** A way of solving a problem: What is the *answer* to the riddle?

—*v.* To reply.

ant /ant/ *n.* A small crawling insect.

an·y /en′ē/ *adj.* No special one: *Any* coat will do.

an·y·one /en′i·wun′/ *pron.* No special person: *Anyone* can come.

an·y·thing /en′i·thing′/ *pron.* No special thing: I'll eat *anything*.

an·y·way /en′i·wā′/ *adv.* Anyhow: If it rains, we'll go *anyway*.

ap·ple /ap′əl/ *n.* A round fruit with a thin red, yellow, or green skin.

aren't /ärnt/ Are not.

ar·gue /är′gyōō/ *v.* **argued, arguing** **1** To disagree. **2** To give reasons for or against: Jim *argued* against skipping recess.

---

n. = **noun**, a naming word; **pron.** = **pronoun**, a word that takes the place of a noun; **v.** = **verb**, an action word; **adj.** = **adjective**, a describing word; **adv.** = **adverb**, a word that tells when, where, or how; **prep.** = **preposition**, such as *from, by with*; **conj.** = **conjunction**, such as *and, but, because*; **interj.** = **interjection**, such as *hello, oh.*

163

Spelling Dictionary

| arm | bedroom |

arm /ärm/ *n.* **1** The part of your body between your shoulder and hand. **2** A part of a chair.

a·round /ə·round'/ *adv.* Nearby: The cat is *around* here somewhere. —*prep.* On all sides: There is a fence *around* the house.

art /ärt/ *n.* **1** Drawing, painting, or making statues: Ms. Fong teaches *art.* **2** Great paintings or statues.

ar·tist /är'tist/ *n.* A person who draws, paints, or makes statues.

ask /ask/ *v.* To put a question to.

a·sleep /ə·slēp'/ *adj.* **1** Not awake. **2** Numb: My foot is *asleep.*

a·wake /ə·wāk'/ *adj.* Not sleeping.

a·way /ə·wā'/ *adj.* **1** At a distance: My school is a mile *away.* **2** In a different place: My parents are *away* from home.

a·while /ə·(h)wīl'/ *adv.* For a short time.

B

ba·by /bā'bē/ *n., pl.* **babies** A very young child. —*v.* **babied, babying** To treat gently: My brothers *baby* me.

back /bak/ *n.* The rear part of anything: the *back* of the room. —*v.* To cause to go backward: *Back* the car into the garage. —*adv.* **1** To the rear: Sit *back* in your chair. **2** In or to the place you came from: Go *back* home.

bake /bāk/ *v.* **baked, baking** To cook in an oven.

bal·loon /bə·loon'/ *n.* **1** A large bag filled with a gas: They floated over the sea in a *balloon.* **2** A small rubber sack filled with air; a toy: We blew up *balloons* for the party.

band·age /ban'dij/ *n.* Something you put over a cut or sore. —*v.* **bandaged, bandaging** To put on a bandage.

bar·ber /bär'bər/ *n.* A person who cuts hair.

bark¹ /bärk/ *n.* The sound a dog makes. —*v.* To make a sound like a dog.

bark² /bärk/ *n.* The outside covering of a tree.

barn /bärn/ *n.* A farm building.

bat¹ /bat/ *n.* A stick or club used for hitting balls. —*v.* **batted, batting 1** To hit with a bat. **2** To hit as if with a bat: The child *batted* the doll.

bat² /bat/ *n.* A mouselike animal with wings that flies at night.

beach /bēch/ *n., pl.* **beaches** The sandy shore of an ocean or lake.

bear /bâr/ *n.* A furry wild animal.

beat /bēt/ *v.* **1** To hit over and over: *beat* a drum. **2** To win a game. **3** To stir quickly: *Beat* the eggs. —*n.* The accent in music: That song has a good *beat.*

be·cause /bi·kôz'/ *conj.* For the reason that: We stayed home *because* it was snowing.

be·come /bi·kum'/ *v.* To grow to be: You *become* a teenager at thirteen.

bed·room /bed'room'/ *n.* A room for sleeping.

beet		bought

beet /bēt/ *n.* A red root vegetable.

be·fore /bi·fôr′/ *prep.* Coming ahead of: We took a walk *before* dinner. Alberto came *before* Loni in line. —*adv.* In the time that is over: Heidi never rode a horse *before*.

be·gin /bi·gin′/ *v.* **began, begun, beginning** To start: School *begins* in September.

be·have /bi·hāv′/ *v.* **behaved, behaving** **1** To act: The children *behaved* like grown-ups. **2** To act properly: Please *behave* yourself.

be·hind /bi·hīnd′/ *prep.* In back of: Kiyo hid *behind* a chair. —*adv.* In, at, or to the back: Luke stayed *behind* to finish his work.

be·long /bi·lông′/ *v.* **1** To be in the right place: Your hat *belongs* on your head. **2** To be someone's: This pencil *belongs* to Luis. **3** To be one of: I *belong* to a club.

be·low /bi·lō′/ *prep.* Lower than or under: A j goes *below* the line.

bend /bend/ *v.* **bent, bending** **1** To make something curve: June *bent* the clay into a C. **2** To stoop: *Bend* down to pick up the dime.

be·side /bi·sīd′/ *prep.* Next to: Ryan's bed is *beside* the wall.

be·tween /bi·twēn′/ *prep.* In the space dividing two things: Kim sat *between* Alice and Todd. Don't eat *between* meals.

bi·cy·cle /bī′sik·əl/ *n.* A vehicle with two wheels, pedals, and handlebars.

bike /bīk/ *n.* Short for *bicycle*.

bird /bûrd/ *n.* An animal with two wings and feathers that flies.

birth·day /bûrth′dā′/ *n.* The day you were born.

bite /bīt/ *v.* **bit, bitten** *or* **bit, biting** To cut with the teeth: Barbara *bit* into the apple. —*n.* **1** A small bit of food: Rita wants a *bite* of your pear. **2** A wound or sting gotten by biting.

blast /blast/ *n.* A loud noise: The horn made a loud *blast*. —*v.* To make a loud noise: The radio was *blasting*.

blend /blend/ *v.* To mix.

blow¹ /blō/ *v.* **blew, blown, blowing** **1** To move with force: The wind is *blowing*. **2** To push by blowing: The wind *blows* leaves around. **3** To send air out: *Blow* out the candles. **4** To make a sound by blowing: *Blow* your horn. **5** To clear by blowing: I *blew* my nose.

blow² /blō/ *n.* A hard hit.

blue·ber·ry /blo͞o′ber′ē/ *n., pl.* **blueberries** A round, bluish berry.

blue·bird /blo͞o′bûrd′/ *n.* A small bird with a blue back and wings.

boast /bōst/ *v.* To speak with too much pride; to brag: Jim *boasted* about winning the race.

bod·y /bod′ē/ *n., pl.* **bodies** **1** All of a person or animal: Good food is needed for a healthy *body*. **2** A whole part: a *body* of water.

born /bôrn/ *v.* Brought into the world: Joel was *born* in May.

both /bōth/ *adj., pron.* Two together: *Both* dogs ran. Then *both* stopped.

bot·tle /bot′(ə)l/ *n.* A narrow jar with a small opening at the top.

bought /bôt/ *v.* Past tense of *buy*.

act, āte, câre, ärt;   egg, ēven;   if, īce;   on, ōver, ôr;   bo͝ok, fo͞od;   up, tûrn;
ə = a in *ago*, e in *listen*, i in *giraffe*, o in *pilot*, u in *circus*;   yo͞o = u in *music*;   oil;   out;
chair; sing; shop; thank; that; zh in *treasure*.

165

bounce /bouns/ *v.* **bounced, bouncing** **1** To hit and spring back: The ball *bounced* off the wall. **2** To cause to bounce: Debra *bounced* the ball.

bow¹ /bou/ *v.* To bend your head or body forward.
—*n.* The act of bowing.

bow² /bō/ *n.* **1** A knot with loops: Tie the ribbon in a *bow*. **2** A thing used for shooting arrows.

brake /brāk/ *n.* What you use to stop a car or bicycle.

branch /branch/ *n., pl.* **branches** An armlike part of a tree.

brave /brāv/ *adj.* Not afraid.

break /brāk/ *v.* **broke, broken, breaking** To crack into pieces.
—*n.* A rest period: The workers took a ten-minute *break*.

bridge /brij/ *n.* Something built over a river or valley to allow people to get to the other side.

bright /brīt/ *adj.* **1** Giving off a lot of light: *bright* sun. **2** Cheerful: a *bright* smile. **3** Smart; clever.

bring /bring/ *v.* **brought, bringing** To carry to or to take along: I will *bring* Lee to the picnic.

bro·ken /brō′kən/ *v.* Past participle of *break*.
—*adj.* **1** Cracked in pieces: Sweep up the *broken* glass. **2** Not working: Our TV set is *broken*.

brook /brŏok/ *n.* A small stream.

brought /brôt/ *v.* Past tense of *bring*.

brown /broun/ *n., adj.* The color of chocolate.

bud·dy /bud′ē/ *n., pl.* **buddies** A close friend.

build /bild/ *v.* **built, building** To put pieces together; to make: Rhonda *built* a model airplane.

bump /bump/ *v.* To knock against: Geraldo *bumped* his head.
—*n.* **1** A swelling caused by bumping. **2** An uneven part: The car hit a *bump* in the road.

burn /bûrn/ *v.* **1** To be on fire. **2** To destroy by fire. **3** To hurt with fire or heat: He *burned* his hand.
—*n.* A wound caused by heat.

burst /bûrst/ *v.* **burst, bursting** **1** To break apart suddenly: The balloon *burst*. **2** To break out: We all *burst* into laughter.
—*n.* Something sudden: Kyle won with a *burst* of speed.

bur·y /ber′ē/ *v.* **buried, burying** **1** To put into the ground. **2** To hide or cover up: Kent *buried* his face in the pillow.

bush /bŏosh/ *n., pl.* **bushes** A small treelike plant.

bus·y /biz′ē/ *adj.* **1** Doing things: I'm *busy* making lunch. **2** Full of things to do: I had a *busy* day.

but·ter /but′ər/ *n.* A yellow spread made from cream, used on bread.
—*v.* To spread butter on.

but·ter·fly /but′ər·flī′/ *n., pl.* **butter-flies** An insect with four brightly colored wings.

buy /bī/ *v.* **bought, buying** To pay money and get something.
—*n.* Something you get for a low price: A pen for a dime is a *buy*.

C

cab·in /kab′in/ *n.* A small house made of wood.

cage /kāj/ *n.* A box or roomlike place made of wire or iron bars: Clean the bird *cage*.

calf

chin

calf /kaf/ *n., pl.* **calves** A young cow.

cam·el /kam′əl/ *n.* An animal with one or two humps on its back.

cam·er·a /kam′(ə·)rə/ *n.* A small machine used for taking pictures.

camp /kamp/ *n.* A place where people go for vacations: Helen went to summer *camp.*
—*v.* To stay outdoors in a tent or trailer: We *camped* by a pond.

can·dy /kan′dē/ *n., pl.* **candies** A sweet food made with sugar.

cane /kān/ *n.* **1** A stick people use to help them walk. **2** The woody stem of a plant.

can·not /kan′ot *or* ka·not′/ Can not.

can't /kant/ Can not.

card /kärd/ *n.* **1** A piece of stiff paper: a birthday *card.* **2** A card used for playing a game.

care /kâr/ *v.* **cared, caring** **1** To show interest or concern: Mabel *cares* about doing well. **2** To want or like: Would you *care* to come?

car·ry /kar′ē/ *v.* **carried, carrying** To take from one place to another: Flora *carried* her books to school.

cart·wheel /kärt′(h)wēl′/ *n.* Turning sideways to stand on your hands and then on your feet again.

cat /kat/ *n.* A small, furry animal.

catch /kach/ *v.* **caught, catching** **1** To get hold of: *Catch* the ball. **2** To trap: The spider *caught* a fly. **3** To discover or find: Mom *caught* me eating in bed. **4** To get an illness: Eric *caught* a cold.

cat·tle /kat′(ə)l/ *n. pl.* Cows, bulls, and steers.

cause /kôz/ *n.* A person or thing that makes something happen; reason: He was the *cause* of the trouble.
—*v.* **caused, causing** To make something happen: A traffic jam *caused* us to be late.

cent /sent/ *n.* A penny.

cer·tain /sûr′tən/ *adj.* **1** Entirely sure: I'm *certain* that I'm right. **2** Not just any: a *certain* one.

chair /châr/ *n.* A seat with a back.

chalk /chôk/ *n.* A powdery stick for writing on the board.

chance /chans/ *n.* **1** What may happen: There's a *chance* of rain. **2** A good time to do something: Amos has a *chance* to go to camp. **3** A risk: I never take *chances.*

chase /chās/ *v.* **chased, chasing** **1** To run after. **2** To drive away: Lucy *chased* the dog away.

cheek /chēk/ *n.* Either side of your face, below your eyes.

cher·ry /cher′ē/ *n., pl.* **cherries** A small, round, red fruit with a pit.

chew /chōō/ *v.* To grind up with your teeth: Always *chew* your food well.

child /chīld/ *n., pl.* **children** A young boy or girl.

chin /chin/ *n.* The part of your face below your mouth.

act, āte, câre, ärt; egg, ēven; if, īce; on, ōver, ôr; bŏŏk, fōōd; up, tûrn;
ə = a in *ago,* e in *listen,* i in *giraffe,* o in *pilot,* u in *circus;* yōō = u in *music;* oil; out;
chair; sing; shop; thank; that; zh in *treasure.*

167

Spelling Dictionary

choose /chōōz/ *v.* **chose, chosen, choosing** **1** To pick out. **2** To decide to do something: Ronald *chose* to go by himself.

chop /chop/ *v.* **chopped, chopping** **1** To cut with an ax: *Chop* down the tree. **2** To cut into small pieces: Ann is *chopping* onions.

church /chûrch/ *n., pl.* **churches** A building where people worship.

cir·cle /sûr′kəl/ *n.* A round shape. —*v.* **circled, circling** **1** To draw a circle around. **2** To move in a circle: The plane *circled* the field.

cir·cus /sûr′kəs/ *n., pl.* **circuses** A show with animals and clowns.

cit·y /sit′ē/ *n., pl.* **cities** A large town.

clap /klap/ *v.* **clapped, clapping** To hit your hands together. —*n.* A loud noise: We heard the *clap* of thunder.

class /klas/ *n., pl.* **classes** **1** A group of students. **2** People or things that are alike in some way: the middle *class*.

clay /klā/ *n.* **1** Mud that is used to make dishes. **2** Something like dough, used for modeling.

clear /klir/ *adj.* **1** Easy to see through. **2** Not cloudy or foggy: a *clear* sky. **3** Easy to understand. —*adv.* **1** In a clear way: I can hear you loud and *clear*. **2** All the way: *clear* across the room. —*v.* To take things away: Tomas *cleared* the table.

clev·er /klev′ər/ *adj.* **1** Showing skill: a *clever* idea. **2** Very smart: Seth is a *clever* child.

cliff /klif/ *n.* A high, steep rock.

climb /klīm/ *v.* **1** To go up: Ella *climbed* the stairs. **2** To go down, over, or into: Jason *climbed* into the car. —*n.* The act of climbing: It is a long *climb* up the mountain.

close[1] /klōz/ *v.* **closed, closing** **1** To shut: Please *close* the door. **2** To end: Erin *closed* her speech with a poem.

close[2] /klōs/ *adj.* **closer, closest** **1** Near. **2** Almost equal: a *close* race. —*adv.* **closer, closest** Near: Alan sat *close* to the window.

cloth·ing /klō′thing/ *n.* The things you wear.

cloud /kloud/ *n.* **1** A mass of tiny water drops that float in the sky. **2** Anything like a cloud: The car raised a *cloud* of dust.

clown /kloun/ *n.* A person in a circus who makes people laugh. —*v.* To act like a clown.

club /klub/ *n.* **1** A heavy stick. **2** A stick used to hit a ball: a golf *club*. **3** A group of people who join together: a book *club*.

coin /koin/ *n.* A piece of metal used as money.

cold /kōld/ *adj.* **1** Low in temperature. **2** Feeling cold: The children were *cold* and tired. —*n.* **1** A lack of heat: The *cold* made my face sting. **2** A sickness that makes you sneeze and cough.

col·lar /kol′ər/ *n.* **1** A fold of cloth that goes around your neck: The dress has a lace *collar*. **2** A band put on an animal's neck.

col·o·ny /kol′ə·nē/ *n., pl.* **colonies** **1** A group of people who settle in a new country: The first *colony* in America was in Virginia. **2** Ants living and working together.

| company | crooked |

com·pa·ny /kum′pə·nē/ *n., pl.*
companies **1** Guests: We are
having *company* for dinner. **2** A
business.

cop·y /kop′ē/ *n., pl.* **copies** **1** One
thing that looks just like another.
2 One of many things made at one
time: I have a *copy* of that book.
—*v.* **copied, copying** **1** To make
a copy. **2** To act like someone
else: Delia *copies* everything I do.

corn /kôrn/ *n.* A yellow grain that
grows on the ears of a tall plant.

cor·ner /kôr′nər/ *n.* Where two
walls, streets, or sides meet.
—*v.* To force into a corner; to trap:
The cat *cornered* the mouse.

cor·ral /kə·ral′/ *n.* A fenced-in place
where animals are kept.

cost /kôst/ *n.* The amount someone
charges or pays for something.
—*v.* **cost, costing** To have as its
price: The toy *costs* a dollar.

cough /kôf/ *v.* To push air out with a
sudden noise.
—*n.* The sound made by coughing.

count /kount/ *v.* **1** To find out how
many: *Count* the petals on the
daisy. **2** To name numbers in
order: *Count* from 1 to 10. **3** To
be sure of: You can *count* on me.

coun·try /kun′trē/ *n., pl.* **countries**
1 A nation. **2** The land outside of
cities and towns: There are many
farms in the *country*.

coun·ty /koun′tē/ *n., pl.* **counties**
An area within a state: A *county*
has its own local officials.

cou·ple /kup′əl/ *n.* **1** Two or a few:
Rosa has a *couple* of things to do.
2 Two people who belong together.

course /kôrs/ *n.* A group of classes: a
cooking *course*.
—**of course** Certainly.

court /kôrt/ *n.* **1** Where trials are
held. **2** Where tennis or basketball is played.

cous·in /kuz′(ə)n/ *n.* The son or
daughter of your uncle or aunt.

cov·er /kuv′ər/ *n.* Anything put over
something else: Nilda put a *cover*
on the frying pan.
—*v.* To be over or put something
over: Snow *covered* the ground.

co·zy /kō′zē/ *adj.* Warm and
comfortable: Matt felt *cozy* under
his blanket.

crash /krash/ *n.* **1** A loud noise.
2 One thing hitting something
else: a car *crash*.
—*v.* To hit with a loud noise: A
cup *crashed* on the floor.

crawl /krôl/ *v.* **1** To creep on hands
and knees. **2** To move slowly:
The cars *crawled* in heavy traffic.

cray·on /krā′on *or* krā′ən/ *n.* A
colored wax stick for drawing.

creek /krēk/ *n.* A small stream.

crook·ed /krŏŏk′id/ *adj.* **1** Not
straight. **2** Not honest: Their
plan sounds *crooked*.

act, āte, câre, ärt;   egg, ēven;   if, īce;   on, ōver, ôr;   bŏŏk, fōōd;   up, tûrn;
ə = a in *ago*, e in *listen*, i in *giraffe*, o in *pilot*, u in *circus*;   yōō = u in *music*;   oil;   out;
chair; sing; shop; thank; **th**at; zh in *treasure*.

Spelling Dictionary

crop

crop /krop/ *n.* Something that is grown on a farm: Corn is a *crop*.

crown /kroun/ *n.* A wreath or band worn by a king or queen.
—*v.* To make a person king or queen.

crumb /krum/ *n.* **1** A tiny piece of bread or cake. **2** A tiny bit: There wasn't a *crumb* of food left.

cry /krī/ *v.* **cried, crying** **1** To weep or sob. **2** To call out; to shout: Sam *cried* for help.
—*n., pl.* **cries** A shout.

cup /kup/ *n.* **1** A small, open bowl, usually with a handle, used mainly for drinking: I drink my milk from a *cup*. **2** The amount a cup will hold; cupful.
—*v.* **cupped, cupping** To shape like a cup: He *cupped* his hands to catch the falling water.

cup·board /kub'ərd/ *n.* A cabinet where dishes and food are kept.

D

dai·sy /dā'zē/ *n., pl.* **daisies** A white flower with a yellow center.

dance /dans/ *v.* **danced, dancing** To move in time to music.
—*n.* **1** A set of steps for dancing: The polka is a *dance*. **2** A party or gathering where people dance.

dan·ger /dān'jər/ *n.* Something that can hurt you: Fire is a *danger* to all of us.

daugh·ter /dô'tər/ *n.* What a girl or woman is to her parents.

do

de·cide /di·sīd'/ *v.* **decided, deciding** To make up your mind: Adam *decided* to stay at home.

deep /dēp/ *adj.* **1** Very far from the top: a *deep* hole. **2** Dark in color: Navy is a *deep* blue.
—*adv.* In, at, or to a deep place: Miners work *deep* in the earth.

de·lay /di·lā'/ *v.* **1** To make late: Rain *delayed* the game. **2** To put off: The O'Neals *delayed* their trip.

de·light /di·līt'/ *n.* Great joy.
—*v.* To give joy: Children *delight* their parents.

de·ny /di·nī'/ *v.* **denied, denying** To say that something is not true: He *denied* that he had been there.

desk /desk/ *n.* A table with drawers used for writing or studying.

de·stroy /di·stroi'/ *v.* To break or ruin: Fire can *destroy* a forest.

de·tail /di·tāl' *or* dē'tāl/ *n.* A small piece of information.

did·n't /did'(ə)nt/ Did not.

din·ner /din'ər/ *n.* The main meal of the day.

dish /dish/ *n., pl.* **dishes** **1** Something used to hold food. **2** A type of food: Spaghetti is my favorite *dish*.

di·vide /di·vīd'/ *v.* **divided, dividing** To make things or numbers into parts: Darin *divided* the clay into three pieces.

do /dōō/ *v.* **did, done, doing** **1** To carry out a task: Alex *did* his homework. **2** To get along: Ginny *does* well at school. **3** To be right: This pencil will *do*. **4** *Do* is used to ask questions: *Do* you like green apples? **5** *Do* can take the place of a verb already used: Helga skates better than I *do*.

170

doesn't

does·n't /duz′ənt/ Does not.

dol·lar /dol′ər/ *n.* A unit of money equal to 100 cents.

don't /dōnt/ Do not.

dot /dot/ *n.* A round mark: ·.
—*v.* **dotted, dotting** To mark with a dot: Remember to *dot* your i's.

dou·ble /dub′əl/ *adj.* **1** Twice as much; twice as large: a *double* meat burger. **2** Having two parts: a *double* feature.
—*v.* **doubled, doubling** To make twice as great: If you *double* 2, you get 4.

down·pour /doun′pôr′/ *n.* Heavy rain.

down·stairs /doun′stârz′/ *adv.* **1** Down the stairs. **2** On a lower floor: Tim is *downstairs*.

draw /drô/ *v.* **drew, drawn, drawing** To make a picture with a pencil or crayon.

draw·er /drôr/ *n.* A boxlike container that slides in and out.

dream /drēm/ *n.* **1** What goes through your mind when you are asleep. **2** Something you hope for: Al's *dream* is to be an actor.
—*v.* To have a dream.

drill /dril/ *n.* **1** A tool used for making holes. **2** An exercise: We had a fire *drill* today.
—*v.* **1** To make a hole with a drill. **2** To teach by giving a drill: Ms. Perkins *drilled* us in spelling.

drive /drīv/ *v.* **drove, driven, driving** **1** To run a car, bus, or truck. **2** To go or be carried in a car: Mr. Atkins *drove* me home.
—*n.* A ride: Let's go for a *drive*.

eagle

drop /drop/ *v.* **dropped, dropping** **1** To fall or let fall: Don't *drop* crumbs on the rug. **2** To leave out: *Drop* the e in race before you add ed.
—*n.* A tiny amount of liquid: I felt a *drop* of rain.

dry /drī/ *v.* **dried, drying** To remove water from: Joan *dried* the dishes.
—*adj.* Not wet: Use the *dry* towel.

duck /duk/ *n.* A bird with a flat bill and webbed feet that swims.
—*v.* To lower your head or move quickly: Sara *ducked* when I threw the ball.

dust /dust/ *n.* Tiny pieces of dirt.
—*v.* To wipe away dust: Peggy *dusted* the table.

dwell /dwel/ *v.* To live or make your home: Animals *dwell* in the forest.

E

each /ēch/ *adj., pron.* Every one: *Each* boy sings well. I gave a sandwich to *each*.
—*adv.* Apiece: Mom bought us two books *each*.

ea·gle /ē′gəl/ *n.* A hunting bird with sharp eyes and powerful wings.

act, āte, câre, ärt;   egg, ēven;   if, īce;   on, ōver, ôr;   bŏŏk, fōōd;   up, tûrn;
ə = **a** in *ago*, **e** in *listen*, **i** in *giraffe*, **o** in *pilot*, **u** in *circus;*   yōō = **u** in *music;*   oil;   out;
chair;   sing;   shop;   thank;   that;   zh in *treasure.*

171

Spelling Dictionary

ear¹ /ir/ *n.* What people and animals use for hearing.

ear² /ir/ *n.* Where grain grows on some plants: an *ear* of corn.

ear·ly /ûr′lē/ *adv., adj.* **earlier, earliest** **1** Near the beginning: I get up *early* in the morning. **2** Before the regular time: Josh got home *early*.

earn /ûrn/ *v.* **1** To get money for doing work. **2** To get by trying hard: Ellen *earned* the prize.

earth /ûrth/ *n.* **1** The planet we live on. **2** Ground or soil: We planted seeds in the *earth*.

east /ēst/ *n., adj., adv.* A direction; where the sun comes up.

eas·y /ē′zē/ *adj.* **easier, easiest** **1** Not hard to do. **2** Without worry or trouble: an *easy* life.

edge /ej/ *n.* **1** Where something ends: the *edge* of the paper. **2** The cutting side of a knife.

egg /eg/ *n.* **1** An oval body with a hard shell laid by female birds. **2** The food that is inside an egg.

eight /āt/ *n., adj.* The word for *8*.

ei·ther /ē′thər *or* ī′thər/ *adj., pron., conj.* One or the other: *Either* puzzle is fun. You may do *either.* *Either* do it now or do it later. —*adv.* Also: Mindy doesn't want to go *either.*

else /els/ *adj.* Other; besides: Do you want anything *else*?

emp·ty /emp′tē/ *adj.* Holding nothing: The box was *empty.* —*v.* **emptied, emptying** To make empty: Ben *emptied* his pockets.

en·e·my /en′ə·mē/ *n., pl.* **enemies** A person who tries to harm another, or a country that fights another country in war.

en·joy /in·joi′/ *v.* To take pleasure in: Lou *enjoys* playing the piano.

e·nough /i·nuf′/ *adj.* Having the amount needed: There is *enough* turkey for two meals. —*n.* All that is needed: There is *enough* for everyone.

en·vy /en′vē/ *n.* The desire to have what someone else has: Nadia's coat made me green with *envy.* —*v.* **envied, envying** To feel envy toward: Pat *envied* his brother.

e·ven /ē′vən/ *adj.* **1** Flat and smooth: The floor is *even.* **2** Steady; regular: She drove at an *even* speed. **3** On the same level: The top of the bush was *even* with my chin. **4** Equal: The score was *even.* —*adv.* Still: an *even* better idea. —*v.* **1** To make or become level: The road *evens* out here. **2** To make equal: The touchdown *evened* the score.

eve·ning /ēv′ning/ *n.* The early part of nighttime.

ev·er /ev′ər/ *adv.* At any time: Did you *ever* go to the zoo?

eve·ry /ev′rē *or* ev′ər·ē/ *adj.* Each one: You got *every* answer right.

eve·ry·bod·y /ev′rē·bod′ē/ *pron.* Each person; everyone.

eve·ry·day /ev′rē·dā′/ *adj.* **1** Taking place each day: an *everyday* job. **2** Not special: *everyday* clothes.

172

everywhere

eve·ry·where /ev′rē·(h)wâr′/ *adv.* In all places; all around.

eye /ī/ *n.* What people and animals use for seeing.
—*v.* **eyed, eying** *or* **eyeing** To watch: The cat *eyed* the bird.

F

face /fās/ *n.* **1** The front part of your head. **2** A look: Miko made a funny *face*.
—*v.* **faced, facing** **1** To turn toward: Everyone should *face* the teacher. **2** To have the front toward: Our house *faces* the road.

fac·to·ry /fak′tər·ē/ *n., pl.* **factories** A place where things are made.

faint /fānt/ *v.* To become weak and pass out.
—*adj.* **1** Dim; slight: There was a *faint* glow in the sky. **2** Weak.

fair¹ /fâr/ *adj.* **1** Following the rules; honest: It was a *fair* game. **2** Not good and not bad: My test mark was *fair*. **3** Clear; bright: The weather will be *fair* tomorrow.
—*adv.* In a fair way: Play *fair*.

fair² /fâr/ *n.* **1** A showing of farm animals and farm goods. **2** A sale of things: Our block had a *fair* to raise money.

fair·y /fâr′ē/ *n., pl.* **fairies** A tiny, make-believe being.

fall /fôl/ *v.* **fell, fallen, falling** **1** To drop down: Laura *fell* off the horse. **2** To pass into a state: George *fell* asleep.
—*n.* **1** The season after summer. **2** The act of falling: a bad *fall*.

fence

fam·i·ly /fam′ə·lē *or* fam′lē/ *n., pl.* **families** **1** Parents and their children. **2** Animals or plants that are related in some way: Lions are part of the cat *family*.

far /fär/ *adv., adj.* At a long way away: Our school is *far* from here.

farm /färm/ *n.* Land where crops are grown and animals are raised: My uncle grows corn on his *farm*.
—*v.* To have and run a farm.

fa·ther /fä′thər/ *n.* A male parent.

fawn /fôn/ *n.* A baby deer.

feast /fēst/ *n.* A large, special meal.
—*v.* To eat a feast.

fed /fed/ *v.* Past tense and past participle of *feed*.

feed /fēd/ *v.* **fed, feeding** To give food to: Jerry *fed* the birds.

feel /fēl/ *v.* **felt, feeling** **1** To touch. **2** To be aware of: I *feel* the wind blowing. **3** To be: Hal *feels* sad.

fell /fel/ *v.* Past tense of *fall*: Sandra *fell* and cut her knee yesterday.

felt /felt/ *v.* Past tense and past participle of *feel*.

fence /fens/ *n.* A wall of wood or wire put around a piece of land: He has a *fence* around his yard.

---

act, āte, câre, ärt;   egg, ēven;   if, īce;   on, ōver, ôr;   bŏŏk, fŏŏd;   up, tûrn;
ə = a in *ago*, e in *listen*, i in *giraffe*, o in *pilot*, u in *circus*;   yŏŏ = u in *music*;   oil;   out;
chair; sing; shop; thank; that; zh in *treasure*.

fight /fīt/ *n.* **1** A battle. **2** A bad quarrel.
—*v.* **fought, fighting** **1** To make war. **2** To quarrel. **3** To struggle against: Doctors *fight* disease.

fi·nal /fī′nəl/ *adj.* **1** Last: Today is the *final* day of school. **2** Not to be changed: My choice is *final*.

find /fīnd/ *v.* **found, finding** **1** To come upon: I *found* a watch at the beach. **2** To get back something lost: Mark *found* his glasses. **3** To learn: Allison *found* the answer to the math problem.

fin·ger /fing′gər/ *n.* One of the five parts that make up the end of your hand.

flag /flag/ *n.* A piece of cloth with special colors and designs on it.

flash /flash/ *n., pl.* **flashes** **1** A sudden bright light. **2** A short time: Russ finished in a *flash*.
—*v.* **1** To give a quick bright light: Lightning *flashed* in the sky. **2** To move quickly: Diane *flashed* by on her bike.

flat /flat/ *adj.* **flatter, flattest** **1** Smooth and level. **2** Without air: a *flat* tire.
—*adv.* In a flat way: Lie *flat* on your back.

flew /floo/ *v.* Past tense and past participle of *fly*[1].

float /flōt/ *v.* To rest on water or in the air: Eva can *float* on her back. The balloon *floated* away.
—*n.* A display in a parade.

flock /flok/ *n.* **1** A group of birds or animals: I saw a *flock* of geese today. **2** A large crowd: *Flocks* of people came to the park.

floor /flôr/ *n.* **1** The part of a room you stand on. **2** A story of a building: We live on the third *floor*.

flour /flour/ *n.* A fine powder made from wheat or other grain: My mother uses *flour* when she cooks.

fly[1] /flī/ *v.* **flew, flown, flying** **1** To go through the air: Birds can *fly*. **2** To wave in the air: The flags are *flying*. **3** To cause to float in the air: Betsy is *flying* her kite. **4** To go by plane.
—*n., pl.* **flies** In baseball, a ball hit high in the air.

fly[2] /flī/ *n., pl.* **flies** An insect with two wings that flies.

fog·gy /fog′ē/ *adj.* **foggier, foggiest** Full of fog or mist: It was so *foggy* that we could not see.

fold /fōld/ *v.* To bend one part over another: *Fold* the paper in half.

fol·low /fol′ō/ *v.* **1** To go along behind: The dog *followed* me home. **2** To come after: Fall *follows* summer. **3** To obey: Max *follows* orders well.

foot·ball /foot′bôl′/ *n.* **1** An oval ball. **2** A team game played with such a ball.

for·ev·er /fôr·ev′ər/ *adv.* Always: I'll be your friend *forever*.

for·get /fər·get′/ *v.* **forgot, forgotten, forgetting** **1** To fail to remember or think of. **2** To leave behind: Ken *forgot* his book.

174

forgot	give

for·got /fər·got′/ *v.* Past tense and past participle of *forget:* I *forgot* to do my homework last night.

fos·sil /fos′əl/ *n.* The mark of a very old plant or animal in a rock.

fought /fôt/ *v.* Past tense and past participle of *fight.*

found /found/ *v.* Past tense and past participle of *find:* Ben *found* the money he lost.

four /fôr/ *n., adj.* The word for *4.*

frame /frām/ *n.* A border around something: a picture *frame.*
—*v.* **framed, framing** To put something in a frame.

free /frē/ *adj.* **1** Not costing money. **2** Having liberty: You are *free* to leave when you want to.
—*v.* **freed, freeing** To let out of: They *freed* the fox from a trap.
—*adv.* Without paying: Parents may come *free* to the school play.

free·dom /frē′dəm/ *n.* Being free; liberty: Americans value *freedom.*

fresh /fresh/ *adj.* **1** Newly made or gotten: *fresh* fruit. **2** Clean and cool: *fresh* air.

from /frum, from, *or* frəm/ *prep.* **1** Starting at: We drove *from* Ohio to Iowa. **2** Sent or given by: I got a letter *from* my aunt.

frown /froun/ *v.* To look angry or sad.
—*n.* A sad or angry look.

fudge /fuj/ *n.* Soft chocolate candy.

fun·ny /fun′ē/ *adj.* **funnier, funniest** Able to make you laugh: Sue told a *funny* joke.

fur /fûr/ *n.* The hair on the skin of many animals.
—*adj.* Made of fur: a *fur* coat.

G

gar·den /gär′dən/ *n.* A place where flowers or vegetables are grown: We have roses growing in our *garden.*

gate /gāt/ *n.* The doorlike part of a fence or wall: The *gate* of the fence was open.

gath·er /gath′ər/ *v.* **1** To bring together: Simon *gathered* up the test papers. **2** To come together: The family members *gathered* for dinner.

geese /gēs/ *n.* Plural of *goose.*

gen·tle /jen′təl/ *adj.* Kind and tender: Be *gentle* when you pick up the baby.

gi·ant /jī′ənt/ *n.* In fairy tales, a very large, strong person.
—*adj.* Very large; huge: We saw a *giant* elephant at the circus.

gin·ger·bread /jin′jər·bred′/ *n.* A cake flavored with ginger.

gi·raffe /jə·raf′/ *n.* An animal with a very long neck and spotted skin.

girl /gûrl/ *n.* A female child.

give /giv/ *v.* **gave, given, giving** To hand over; to offer: *Give* me your hand.

act, āte, câre, ärt;   egg, ēven;   if, īce;   on, ōver, ôr;   book, food;   up, tûrn;
ə = a in *ago,* e in *listen,* i in *giraffe,* o in *pilot,* u in *circus;*   yoo = u in *music;*   oil;   out;
chair; sing; shop; thank; that; zh in *treasure.*

glad /glad/ *adj.* Pleased or happy: I'll be *glad* to come.

glass /glas/ *n., pl.* **glasses** **1** A clear material that breaks easily. **2** A drinking cup. **3** (*pl.*) Two pieces of glass or plastic used to help people see better.

gnat /nat/ *n.* A small biting or stinging fly.

good·ness /go͞od′nis/ *n.* The condition of being good: Caring for others is a sign of *goodness.*

goose /go͞os/ *n., pl.* **geese** A bird with a long neck that looks like a duck.

grab /grab/ *v.* **grabbed, grabbing** To take hold of suddenly: Chad *grabbed* my arm to stop me.

grade /grād/ *n.* **1** The school year or level: Mei is in the third *grade.* **2** A mark given in school: Rae gets good *grades* in school.

grand /grand/ *adj.* Large, important: The mayor lives in a *grand* house.

grand·fa·ther /gran(d)′fä′t͟hər/ *n.* Your father's or mother's father.

grand·moth·er /gran(d)′mu͟th′ər/ *n.* Your father's or mother's mother.

grape /grāp/ *n.* A fruit that grows in bunches on vines.

grass /gras/ *n.* A plant with green blades that covers the ground.

grew /gro͞o/ *v.* Past tense of *grow.*

groan /grōn/ *n.* A sound of pain.
—*v.* To make such a sound: Callie *groaned* because her arm hurt.

ground /ground/ *n.* Earth's surface; soil: The *ground* was wet.

group /gro͞op/ *n.* Several people or things together.
—*v.* To make a group: Darrel *grouped* his marbles by color.

grow /grō/ *v.* **grew, grown, growing** **1** To become larger or taller: Puppies *grow* very quickly. **2** To plant something: We *grow* tomatoes.

grown /grōn/ *v.* Past participle of *grow.*

guess /ges/ *n., pl.* **guesses** An idea you have without knowing for sure: I think it will rain, but that's just a *guess.*
—*v.* **1** To make a guess. **2** To suppose: I *guess* you are right.

gup·py /gup′ē/ *n., pl.* **guppies** A tiny, colorful fish.

gym /jim/ *n.* Short for *gymnasium.* A large room where people play games and exercise.

H

hair /hâr/ *n.* The threadlike strands that grow on your head.

hair·cut /hâr′kut′/ *n.* The cutting of hair or the way hair is cut.

half /haf/ *n., pl.* **halves** One of two equal parts.
—*adj.* Being half: a *half* hour.
—*adv.* Partly: Don is *half* asleep.

hand /hand/ *n.* **1** The end part of your arm. **2** One of the pointers on a clock or watch.
—*v.* To give or pass: Ken *handed* the money to the clerk.

hap·pen /hap′ən/ *v.* To take place: Nothing *happened* after you left.

hap·py /hap′ē/ *adj.* **happier, happiest** Full of joy; glad.

hard /härd/ *adj.* **1** Solid: *hard* as a rock. **2** Not easy: a *hard* test.
—*adv.* With effort or force: Penny works *hard.*

have·n't /hav′ənt/ Have not.

176

hay | **house**

hay /hā/ *n.* Grass that is cut and dried to feed animals.

head·ache /hed′āk′/ *n.* A pain in your head.

hear /hir/ *v.* **heard, hearing** To take in sounds through your ears.

heard /hûrd/ *v.* Past tense and past participle of *hear.*

heart /härt/ *n.* **1** The organ in your body that pumps blood. **2** Something that has this shape: ♡.

hel·lo /hə·lō′/ *interj.* A greeting.

help /help/ *v.* To be useful; to do what is needed: Ethel *helps* around the house.
—*n.* A person or thing that helps: Lena is a great *help* to Grandma.

here /hir/ *adv.* In or to this place: Let's sit *here.* Bring it *here.*

her·self /hər·self′/ *pron.* Her own self: She sang to *herself.*

he's /hēz/ **1** He is. **2** He has.

hid /hid/ *v.* Past tense of *hide*[1].

hide[1] /hīd/ *v.* **hid, hidden, hiding 1** To put out of sight: Gene *hid* the gift in the closet. **2** To hide oneself: Keisha *hid* behind a bush.

hide[2] /hīd/ *n.* The skin of an animal.

high /hī/ *adj.* **1** Far up. **2** Great in cost: The price is too *high.*
—*adv.* To a high place: The building reaches *high* in the sky.

high·way /hī′wā′/ *n.* A main road.

hike /hīk/ *n.* A long walk: We went for a *hike* in the woods.
—*v.* **hiked, hiking** To take a hike.

him·self /him·self′/ *pron.* His own self: He taught *himself* to skate.

hob·by /hob′ē/ *n., pl.* **hobbies** A special interest: Steve's *hobby* is collecting stamps.

hold /hōld/ *v.* **held, holding 1** To take and keep: Please *hold* my coat. **2** To keep in place: Glue will *hold* it together. **3** To keep back: *Hold* your breath. **4** To have: We *held* a meeting.

hole /hōl/ *n.* An open space in or through something solid.

hol·low /hol′ō/ *adj.* Empty inside: Squirrels live in that *hollow* tree.

hop /hop/ *v.* **hopped, hopping 1** To move the way a rabbit does. **2** To jump on one foot. **3** To jump over or into: Ted *hopped* into bed.

hope /hōp/ *v.* **hoped, hoping** To wish or expect: I *hope* to do well.
—*n.* **1** Trust that what you wish for will happen. **2** Something hoped for. **3** Cause for hope: Roxie is our team's only *hope.*

horn /hôrn/ *n.* **1** A hard bony growth on an animal's head: Cows have *horns.* **2** Something that makes a warning sound: a car *horn.* **3** A musical instrument.

horse /hôrs/ *n.* A four-legged animal with hoofs and a mane.

house /hous/ *n., pl.* **houses** /hou′zəz/ A building in which people live.

---

act, āte, câre, ärt; egg, ēven; if, īce; on, ōver, ôr; bŏŏk, fōōd; up, tûrn;
ə = a in *ago*, e in *listen*, i in *giraffe*, o in *pilot*, u in *circus*; yōō = u in *music*; oil; out;
chair; sing; shop; thank; that; zh in *treasure*.

how /hou/ *adv.* **1** In what way: *How* did you do it? **2** To what degree: *How* tall is Aaron?

hun·gry /hung′grē/ *adj.* Wanting or needing food.

hunt /hunt/ *v.* **1** To kill animals for food. **2** To look for: I *hunted* all over for my lost scarf.
—*n.* A search: a treasure *hunt.*

hur·ry /hûr′ē/ *v.* **hurried, hurrying** **1** To move or act quickly: Pam *hurried* to get home on time. **2** To make someone else move or act quickly: Don't *hurry* me.
—*n.* Eagerness to do something quickly: Grace was in a *hurry.*

hurt /hûrt/ *v.* To feel or cause pain or harm: Troy *hurt* himself.

I

ice /īs/ *n.* Frozen water: The pond turned to *ice* in the winter.
—*v.* **iced, icing** To put frosting on a cake.

ill /il/ *adj.* Feeling sick: I go to the doctor when I feel *ill.*

I'll /īl/ **1** I will. **2** I shall.

I'm /īm/ I am.

inch /inch/ *n., pl.* **inches** A unit of length.

in·sect /in′sekt/ *n.* A very small animal with six legs and often wings: Bees and flies are *insects.*

in·side /in′sīd′ *or* in′sīd′/ *adv.* Indoors.
—*prep.* In or within: Dan put his socks *inside* his shoes.
—*n.* The part that is inside: The *inside.* of the house is white.

in·to /in′tōō/ *prep.* **1** To the inside: Walk *into* the room. **2** To the form of: The ice turned *into* water.

in·vite /in·vīt′/ *v.* **invited, inviting** To ask someone to come: Joanne *invited* me to her party.

is /iz/ *v.* Form of the verb *to be.* You use *is* after names, words for one thing, and *he, she,* or *it.*

is·n't /iz′ənt/ Is not.

it's /its/ **1** It is. **2** It has.

J

jack·et /jak′it/ *n.* A short coat.

jam¹ /jam/ **jammed, jamming** *v.* To squeeze into a small space: He *jammed* his books into his bag.

jam² /jam/ *n.* Fruit cooked with sugar until thick: strawberry *jam.*

jar /jär/ *n.* A bottle with a wide top.

jaw /jô/ *n.* The upper or lower bone of a mouth: A whale has huge *jaws.*

jet /jet/ *n.* A kind of airplane.

job /job/ *n.* Work that is done, often for money.

join /join/ *v.* **1** To bring or come together: We all *joined* hands. **2** To become a member of a group.

joke /jōk/ *n.* Something that makes you laugh; a funny story.
—*v.* **joked, joking** To do or say something funny.

joy /joi/ *n.* Great happiness.

judge /juj/ *n.* **1** The person who makes decisions in a court of law. **2** The person who decides who wins a race or contest.
—*v.* **judged, judging** **1** To act as a judge in court. **2** To decide who wins: Liza *judged* the contest.

jug /jug/ *n.* A large bottle with a narrow neck and a handle.

juice /jōōs/ *n.* The liquid part of fruits, vegetables, or meat.

jump

known

jump /jump/ *v.* **1** To leap up or over: The cat *jumped* onto the window sill. **2** To jerk suddenly: Ken *jumped* when the phone rang. —*n.* A leap.

jun·gle /jung′gəl/ *n.* A thick forest where wild animals live.

just /just/ *adv.* **1** A little while ago: We *just* got here. **2** Barely: Alfredo got here *just* in time. **3** Only: I'm *just* tired. **4** Very: This meal is *just* delicious.

K

keep /kēp/ *v.* **kept, keeping** **1** To have and not give up: You may *keep* that pencil. **2** To hold back: *Keep* the dog off the sofa. **3** To continue: Let's *keep* trying.

kept /kept/ *v.* Past tense and past participle of *keep*.

ket·tle /ket′(ə)l/ *n.* **1** A large pot. **2** A pot with a spout; teakettle.

key /kē/ *n.* **1** A small metal thing used to open or close a lock. **2** Something that explains or gives answers: an answer *key* for a test. **3** One of the parts pressed on a piano or typewriter.

kick /kik/ *v.* To hit with your foot. —*n.* A blow with the foot: Lee gave the stone a hard *kick*.

kind·ness /kīnd′nis/ *n.* Being kind and nice: Nicky treats everyone with *kindness*.

kiss /kis/ *v.* To touch someone with your lips as a sign of love. —*n.* The act of kissing: Jake gave Grandma a hug and a *kiss*.

kitch·en /kich′ən/ *n.* The room where food is prepared.

kit·ten /kit′(ə)n/ *n.* A young cat.

knead /nēd/ *v.* To mix dough using your hands to push and squeeze.

knee /nē/ *n.* The joint in the middle of your leg and the area around it.

kneel /nēl/ *v.* **knelt** *or* **kneeled, kneeling** To go down on your knees.

knew /n(y)oō/ *v.* Past tense of *know*.

knife /nīf/ *n.* **knives** A tool with a sharp side for cutting.

knit /nit/ *v.* **knit** *or* **knitted, knitting** To make clothes using yarn and long needles.

knock /nok/ *v.* **1** To hit. **2** To make a pounding noise: *Knock* on the door. —*n.* A pounding noise: We heard a *knock* at the door.

knot /not/ *n.* A fastening made by tying ropes or string. —*v.* **knotted, knotting** To tie in a knot.

know /nō/ *v.* **knew, known, knowing** **1** To be sure: I *know* you are wrong. **2** To understand: Ira *knows* how to do it. **3** To be friends with: We *know* the Wilsons.

known /nōn/ *v.* Past participle of *know*.

act, āte, câre, ärt;   egg, ēven;   if, īce;   on, ōver, ôr;   boōk, foōd;   up, tûrn;
ə = **a** in *ago*, **e** in *listen*, **i** in *giraffe*, **o** in *pilot*, **u** in *circus*;   yoō = **u** in *music*;   oil;   out;
chair;   sing;   shop;   thank;   that;   zh in *treasure*.

179

L

la·dy /lā′dē/ *n., pl.* **ladies**   **1** A woman.   **2** A woman with good manners.

lake /lāk/ *n.* A body of water.

lamb /lam/ *n.* A young sheep.

land /land/ *n.*   **1** The part of Earth that is not covered by water.   **2** A country.

—*v.* To arrive on land: The airplane *landed* on the runway.

large /lärj/ *adj.* **larger, largest** Big in size or amount.

last¹ /last/ *adj.*   **1** Coming at the end: I ate the *last* piece.   **2** Just before this one: We saw the Itos *last* month.

—*adv.*   **1** Coming at the end: Bob woke up *last*.   **2** Most recently: When were you *last* at the zoo?

last² /last/ *v.* To go on: The picnic *lasted* all day.

late /lāt/ *adj., adv.* After or past a certain time: He came *late*.

lay¹ /lā/ *v.* **laid, laying** To put down: *Lay* your coats on the bed.

lay² /lā/ *v.* Past tense of *lie¹*.

learn /lûrn/ *v.*   **1** To get skill in or knowledge: Diego *learned* to play baseball.   **2** To find out: Janice *learned* why Nina left early.

leave /lēv/ *v.* **left, leaving**   **1** To go away.   **2** To let stay behind: Tad *left* his books at school.   **3** To let someone else do something: Just *leave* everything to me.

ledge /lej/ *n.* A narrow shelf: Put the plant on the window *ledge*.

left¹ /left/ *n.* The opposite of right.

—*adj., adv.* On or to the left: Give me your *left* hand. Turn *left*.

left² /left/ *v.* Past tense and past participle of *leave*.

leg /leg/ *n.*   **1** One of the parts of the body used to stand and walk.   **2** Something like a leg: a table *leg*.

less /les/ *adj.* Smaller in number or amount: Teddy has *less* money.

—*n.* An amount: I did *less* than I planned to do.

—*adv.* In a smaller amount: This book costs *less* than that one.

les·son /les′(ə)n/ *n.* Something to be learned or taught: Peter did the math *lesson*.

let /let/ *v.* To allow: Will your parents *let* you go to the zoo?

let's /lets/ Let us: *Let's* go now.

let·ter /let′ər/ *n.*   **1** One of the parts of the alphabet.   **2** A written message: I mailed a *letter*.

lev·el /lev′əl/ *adj.* Smooth or even: The ground is *level* over there.

li·brar·y /lī′brer′ē *or* lī′brə·rē/ *n., pl.* **libraries** A place where books are kept.

lie¹ /lī/ *v.* **lay, lain, lying** To rest in a flat position: Sandy is *lying* on the couch.

lie² /lī/ *n.* Something told that is not true: Jessie told me a *lie*.

—*v.* **lied, lying** To tell a lie.

life /līf/ *n., pl.* **lives**   **1** The state of being alive: There are no signs of *life* on Mars.   **2** The period of being alive: I have lived here all my *life*.   **3** A way of living: Firefighters have a dangerous *life*.

lift /lift/ *v.* To pick up and raise: Conchita *lifted* her little sister.

—*n.* A ride: We got a *lift* home.

light¹ /līt/ *n.*   **1** Brightness: We cannot see without *light*. **2** Something that gives light.

—*v.* **lit** *or* **lighted, lighting**   **1** To give light: The lantern *lighted* our

| light | | manage |

path.   **2** To set fire to: Mom will *light* the candles.
—*adj.* Pale in color: a *light* color.

light² /līt/ *adj.* Not heavy: as *light* as a feather.

limb /lim/ *n.* A branch of a tree.

line /līn/ *n.*   **1** A straight mark. **2** A row: There was a long *line* of people at the checkout counter.

li·on /lī′ən/ *n.* A large, powerful animal of the cat family.

list /list/ *n.* A group of things written down in order: Mom takes a shopping *list* to the market.
—*v.* To make a list.

lis·ten /lis′(ə)n/ *v.* To pay attention; to try to hear: *Listen* carefully.

live¹ /liv/ *v.* **lived, living**   **1** To be alive: Grandpa *lived* for eighty years.   **2** To make your home: They *live* in Iowa.

live² /līv/ *adj.* Being alive.

load /lōd/ *n.* Something carried: A mule can carry a heavy *load*.
—*v.* To fill or put on: Lisa *loaded* her camera. The movers *loaded* the furniture on the truck.

look·out /lŏŏk′out′/ *n.*   **1** The act of watching out: Be on the *lookout* for a ship with a yellow flag.   **2** A person who watches.

lose /lŏŏz/ *v.* **lost, losing**   **1** To be unable to find: Lori *lost* her scarf. **2** To fail to keep: Don't *lose* your temper.   **3** To fail to win.

loud /loud/ *adj.* Not quiet; noisy.

love /luv/ *n.* A strong feeling.
—*v.* **loved, loving**   **1** To have a deep feeling for: Parents *love* their children.   **2** To like very much: Cindy *loves* to swim.

low /lō/ *adj.*   **1** Not high: The truck cannot go under the *low* bridge. **2** Not loud: a *low* voice.

loy·al /loi′əl/ *adj.* Faithful: Our dog is very *loyal*.

luck·y /luk′ē/ *adj.* **luckier, luckiest** Having or bringing good luck: You were *lucky* to win.

lunch /lunch/ *n.* The meal eaten in the middle of the day.

M

ma·chine /mə·shēn′/ *n.* Something that does work: a sewing *machine*.

mag·ic /maj′ik/ *n.* The art of pretending to do things that are not possible.
—*adj.* Able to work magic: I will wave my *magic* wand.

mail /māl/ *n.* Letters and packages handled by the post office.
—*v.* To send a letter or package.

main /mān/ *adj.* Most important: Oak Avenue is the *main* street.

man·age /man′ij/ *v.* **managed, managing**   **1** To get by: How did you *manage* to do that alone? **2** To be in charge: Ms. Ramos *manages* a store.

---

act, āte, câre, ärt;   egg, ēven;   if, īce;   on, ōver, ôr;   bŏŏk, fŏŏd;   up, tûrn;
ə = a in *ago*, e in *listen*, i in *giraffe*, o in *pilot*, u in *circus*;   yŏŏ = u in *music*;   oil;   out;
chair;   sing;   shop;   thank;   that;   zh in *treasure*.

Spelling Dictionary

mane /mān/ *n.* The long hair on a horse's neck or around a male lion's face.

mar·ble /mär′bəl/ *n.* **1** A small glass ball used for games. **2** A hard stone used for buildings and statues: The floors are of *marble*.

mar·ket /mär′kit/ *n.* **1** A place where things are bought and sold: The farmer brought his fruit to *market*. **2** A store that sells food: We buy our food at the *market*.

mar·ry /mar′ē/ *v.* **married, marry·ing** **1** To become husband and wife. **2** To join as husband and wife: The judge *married* my aunt and uncle.

mat·ter /mat′ər/ *n.* Something that troubles you: What is the *matter*? —*v.* To be of importance: Doing well in school *matters* to me.

may /mā/ *v.* **1** To have permission to: You *may* leave the room. **2** To be possible: It *may* rain today.

may·be /mā′bē/ *adv.* Perhaps; possibly: *Maybe* we can go to the park tomorrow.

meal /mēl/ *n.* Food eaten at one time: I eat three *meals* a day.

mean[1] /mēn/ *v.* **meant, meaning** **1** To want to: I didn't *mean* to trip you. **2** To have as its sense: What does this word *mean*?

mean[2] /mēn/ *adj.* Cruel.

mean·while /mēn′(h)wīl′/ *adv.* At the same time.

mea·sles /mē′zəlz/ *n.* A disease that makes your skin break out in red spots.

meat /mēt/ *n.* The flesh of animals used as food.

meet /mēt/ *v.* **met, meeting** **1** To come together: Let's *meet* at the corner. **2** To get to know: I *met* Charlie only a year ago.

melt /melt/ *v.* To get soft or become liquid: Butter *melts* on hot toast.

mem·o·ry /mem′ər·ē/ *n., pl.* **memories** **1** The ability to remember: Eliza has a very good *memory* for names. **2** What is remembered: I have happy *memories* of my vacation.

mess /mes/ *n.* A dirty or not neat condition: Your room is a *mess*. —*v.* To make untidy: Don't *mess* up the living room.

mid·dle /mid′(ə)l/ *n.* The center or halfway point.

mid·night /mid′nīt′/ *n.* Twelve o'clock at night.

milk /milk/ *n.* A white liquid from cows or other female animals. —*v.* To get milk from: Davey helped the farmer *milk* the cows.

mis·take /mis·tāk′/ *n.* Something that is done wrong: Karen made a *mistake* on the spelling test.

more /môr/ *adj.* **1** Greater in number or amount: Rex has *more* pencils than I have. **2** Additional: I bought *more* pencils today. —*n.* A greater amount: *More* of my pencils are new. —*adv.* **1** In a greater amount: I write *more* now. **2** Again: Tell me once *more*.

morning   **notice**

morn·ing /môr′ning/ *n.* The time of day from sunrise until noon.

mo·tel /mō·tel′/ *n.* A place where travelers can stay overnight.

mo·tor /mō′tər/ *n.* The engine that makes cars and other machines go. —*adj.* Run by a motor: a *motor* boat.

mouse /mous/ *n., pl.* **mice** A small animal with a pointed nose and a long tail: Our cat catches *mice*.

mouth /mouth/ *n.* **1** The opening in your face used for speaking and eating. **2** An opening like a mouth: the *mouth* of a jar.

move /mōōv/ *v.* **moved, moving** **1** To go from one place to another: The car *moved* down the street. **2** To change where you live: The Engels *moved* to Grant Street. **3** To change position: The sleeping child didn't *move*.

my·self /mī·self′/ *pron.* My own self: I saw *myself* in the mirror.

N

nail /nāl/ *n.* **1** A thin pointed piece of metal used to hold wood together. **2** The thin, hornlike layer at the end of a finger or toe: Stop biting your *nails*. —*v.* To put something together with nails.

name /nām/ *n.* What someone or something is called. —*v.* **named, naming** **1** To give a name: They *named* the baby Inga. **2** To tell the name of: Can you *name* all fifty states?

nap /nap/ *n.* A short sleep. —*v.* **napped, napping** To sleep for a short time: The baby *naps* every afternoon.

nar·row /nar′ō/ *adj.* Not wide: The road was too *narrow* for two cars.

neat /nēt/ *adj.* **1** Clean and tidy. **2** Clever: That's a *neat* trick.

neck /nek/ *n.* The part of your body between your head and shoulders.

new /n(y)ōō/ *adj.* **1** Not old. **2** Started a short time ago: The *new* school year started last week.

news·pa·per /n(y)ōōz′pā′pər/ *n.* Sheets of paper with news stories on them: We read about the parade in the *newspaper*.

nice /nīs/ *adj.* **nicer, nicest** Pleasant; kind.

nick·el /nik′əl/ *n.* A coin worth five cents.

night /nīt/ *n.* The time between sunset and sunrise.

nine /nīn/ *n., adj.* The word for *9*.

nine·teen /nīn′tēn′/ *n., adj.* The word for *19*.

ninth /nīnth/ *n., adj.* Next after eighth.

noise /noiz/ *n.* Sound, especially loud sound: The crowd made a lot of *noise*.

noon /nōōn/ *n.* Twelve o'clock in the daytime.

north /nôrth/ *n., adj., adv.* A direction; the opposite of south.

not /not/ *adv.* In no way: I did *not* go.

no·tice /nō′tis/ *v.* **noticed, noticing** To see; to pay attention to: Do you *notice* anything different?

---

act, āte, câre, ärt;   egg, ēven;   if, īce;   on, ōver, ôr;   bŏŏk, fōōd;   up, tûrn;
ə = **a** in *ago,* **e** in *listen,* **i** in *giraffe,* **o** in *pilot,* **u** in *circus;*   yōō = **u** in *music;*   oil;   out;
chair;   sing;   shop;   thank;   that;   zh in *treasure.*

num·ber /num′bər/ *n.* **1** A unit in math. **2** An amount: I have a *number* of things to do.
—*v.* To give numbers to: Fay *numbered* the pages of her book.

O

oak /ōk/ *n.* **1** A tree that bears acorns. **2** The wood of this tree.
—*adj.* Made of oak.

o·bey /ō·bā′/ *v.* To do as you are told: My dog *obeys* me.

odd /od/ *adj.* **1** Strange, unusual: That is an *odd* house. **2** Not able to be divided by 2: *odd* numbers.

off /ôf or of/ *prep.* Away from: The pillow fell *off* the bed.
—*adv.* Not on: Take *off* your coat.

oil /oil/ *n.* A greasy liquid.
—*v.* To put oil on: We *oiled* the gate so it would not squeak.

old /ōld/ *adj.* **1** Having lived for a long time: Grandpa is an *old* man. **2** Of age: Thomas is eight years *old*. **3** Not new: James wore *old* jeans. **4** Known for a long time: Keith and Otis are *old* friends.

once /wuns/ *adv.* **1** One time: We go on a trip *once* a year. **2** At one time (in the past): I *once* saw a purple and red car.

on·ly /ōn′lē/ *adv.* Just: You have *only* one hour to play.
—*adj.* Alone: He is the *only* boy on the team.

on·to /on′tōō/ *prep.* **1** Upon the top of: The cat jumped *onto* the table. **2** To and upon: The team came *onto* the field.

oth·er /uth′ər/ *adj.* **1** Different: Do you want this crayon or the *other* one? **2** More: Do you want *other* books to read besides this one?

—*pron.* A different person or thing: Ricardo likes to help *others*.

our /our/ *pron.* Belonging to us: *Our* house is yellow.

our·selves /our·selvz′/ *pron.* Us and no one else: We made it *ourselves*.

out·side /out′sīd′ or out′sīd′/ *adv.* Outdoors: We played *outside*.
—*n.* The part that is out: We painted the *outside* of the house.
—*prep.* Out of: Put your boots *outside* the door.
—*adj.* On the outside: The *outside* shell of a nut is hard.

o·ver /ō′vər/ *prep.* On top of.
—*adv.* **1** Above. **2** Again: You must write your paper *over* because it is messy. **3** To a certain place: Bring it *over* here.
—*adj.* Finished: School is *over* at three o'clock.

owl /oul/ *n.* A night bird with large eyes and a hooked beak.

own /ōn/ *v.* To have in your possession: I *own* a bicycle.
—*adj.* Belonging to: my *own* room.

P

pack /pak/ *n.* A large bundle to be carried by a person or animal.
—*v.* **1** To put things in a package, box, or suitcase. **2** To crowd or fill up: People *packed* into the bus.

package		paw

pack·age /pak′ij/ *n.* **1** Something wrapped up or tied up: We mailed a *package* to my brother at camp. **2** The box that holds something: The directions are on the *package*.

pad·dle /pad′(ə)l/ *n.* A short oar.
—*v.* **paddled, paddling** **1** To use a paddle to move a boat. **2** To move your hands and feet in water: The children *paddled* about in the lake.

page /pāj/ *n.* One of the sheets of paper in a book or magazine.

paid /pād/ *v.* Past tense and past participle of *pay*.

pain /pān/ *n.* Ache; soreness.

paint /pānt/ *n.* Colored liquid that is spread on something to make it that color.
—*v.* **1** To spread paint on. **2** To make a picture with paint.

pair /pâr/ *n.* Two people or things that go together: a *pair* of shoes.

pan·cake /pan′kāk′/ *n.* A thin flat cake fried in a pan.

pane /pān/ *n.* A sheet of glass put in the frame of a window: This window has a broken *pane*.

pa·per /pā′pər/ *n.* **1** Material used for writing, printing, and wrapping things. **2** A piece of paper with writing on it: Barney handed in his *paper*. **3** A newspaper.
—*adj.* Made of paper: Joy made a *paper* airplane.

pa·rade /pə·rād′/ *n.* A march of people with bands and floats.
—*v.* **parade, parading** To show off: He *paraded* around in his costume.

par·ent /pâr′ənt/ *n.* A person's mother or father.

park /pärk/ *n.* Land with trees, grass, and playgrounds.
—*v.* To put a car somewhere and leave it: *Park* the car over there.

part /pärt/ *n.* **1** A piece of a whole. **2** Share: We all must do our *part*. **3** A role in a play. **4** Where hair is divided after combing: The *part* in Lynn's hair is crooked.
—*v.* **1** To divide into pieces. **2** To make a part in your hair.

par·ty /pär′tē/ *n., pl.* **parties** **1** A group of people gathered together to have fun. **2** A group of people who work to elect government leaders: the Democratic *party*.

paste /pāst/ *n.* A thick, white mixture used to stick things together.
—*v.* **pasted, pasting** To fasten with paste.

pat /pat/ *n.* A light touch.
—*v.* **patted, patting** To touch lightly: *Pat* the dog's head.

patch /pach/ *n., pl.* **patches** A piece of cloth used to cover a hole or weak spot: Mom put *patches* on the knees of my jeans.
—*v.* **1** To put back together: Dad *patched* together the broken bowl. **2** To put a patch on.

path /path/ *n.* A walk or trail.

pause /pôz/ *n.* A short stop.
—*v.* **paused, pausing** To make a pause: The speaker *paused* to drink some water.

paw /pô/ *n.* An animal's foot with nails or claws.

---

act, āte, câre, ärt;   egg, ēven;   if, īce;   on, ōver, ôr;   bŏŏk, fōōd;   up, tûrn;
ə = a in *ago*, e in *listen*, i in *giraffe*, o in *pilot*, u in *circus*;   yōō = u in *music*;   oil;   out;
chair; sing; shop; thank; that; zh in *treasure*.

Spelling Dictionary

pay /pā/ *v.* **paid, paying** To give money for something: Dad *paid* for my bike.
—*n.* Money you get for doing a job: Mom gets her *pay* on Fridays.

peace /pēs/ *n.* **1** A condition without war. **2** Calmness: Let's have some *peace* and quiet.

peach /pēch/ *n., pl.* **peaches** A round fruit with a fuzzy, yellowish-pink skin and a large seed or pit.

pear /pâr/ *n.* A fruit with a green or yellowish-brown skin. A pear is round at the bottom and smaller near the stem.

pearl /pûrl/ *n.* A small, round white gem formed inside an oyster shell.

pen[1] /pen/ *n.* A writing tool that uses ink.

pen[2] /pen/ *n.* A small, fenced area for animals: Put the pigs in the *pen*.

pen·cil /pen'səl/ *n.* A writing tool that has a stick of graphite inside wood.

pen·ny /pen'ē/ *n., pl.* **pennies** A coin worth one cent.

peo·ple /pē'pəl/ *n.* Plural of *person*.

per·haps /pər·haps'/ *adv.* Maybe; possibly: *Perhaps* I'll go with you.

per·son /pûr'sən/ *n., pl.* **people** *or* **persons** A human being.

pet /pet/ *n.* A tame animal kept in or near the house.

—*v.* **petted, petting** To stroke or pat: Our dog loves to be *petted*.

pick /pik/ *v.* **1** To choose: *Pick* the color you want. **2** To take or pull off with your fingers: I *picked* an apple off the tree.

pick·le /pik'əl/ *n.* A cucumber soaked in salt water or vinegar.

pic·ture /pik'chər/ *n.* **1** A painting, drawing, or photograph. **2** A movie.

piece /pēs/ *n.* **1** A part of a whole thing. **2** An amount of something: a *piece* of cheese.

pil·low /pil'ō/ *n.* A bag filled with feathers or other soft material: I rested my head on the *pillow*.

pi·lot /pī'lət/ *n.* The person who steers or guides an airplane.

pin /pin/ *n.* **1** A thin, pointed piece of wire used to fasten things together: The *pins* are in the sewing box. **2** A piece of jewelry fastened to a pin.
—*v.* **pinned, pinning** To fasten with a pin.

pi·rate /pī'rit/ *n.* A person who attacks and robs ships at sea.

pitch·er[1] /pich'ər/ *n.* A bottle with a spout for pouring.

pitch·er[2] /pich'ər/ *n.* A baseball player who throws the ball for the batter to hit.

place /plās/ *n.* **1** A certain space or area: Put an X in the right *place*. **2** A city, town, or other area: Elmwood is a nice *place* to live.
—*v.* **placed, placing** To put: *Place* your hands on your head.

plan /plan/ *n.* **1** An idea for doing or making something: We have a *plan* for earning money. **2** (*pl.*) Arrangements: vacation *plans*.

186

—*v.* **planned, planning** 1 To make a plan: *plan* a party. 2 To intend: We *plan* to visit Grandma.

plan·et /plan′it/ *n.* Any of the large bodies that move around the sun: Earth is a *planet*.

plant /plant/ *n.* A living thing that grows in soil or water.
—*v.* To put seeds or plants in the soil: We *planted* vegetables.

play·ground /plā′ground′/ *n.* An outside area for play.

plot /plot/ *n.* 1 A small piece of land: They will use that *plot* for a garden. 2 A secret plan. 3 The events in a story: That book has an exciting *plot*.
—*v.* **plotted, plotting** To plan something in secret.

pock·et /pok′it/ *n.* A small pouch sewn into clothing to hold money and other things.

point /point/ *n.* 1 The sharp end of something: The pencil has a sharp *point*. 2 A dot. 3 A unit in scoring: Our team has ten *points*.
—*v.* 1 To show or indicate: The teacher *pointed* out my mistakes. 2 To aim or direct.

po·lar /pō′lər/ *adj.* Having to do with the North or South Pole: *Polar* bears live in *polar* regions.

po·lice /pə·lēs′/ *n.* A group of people who work to keep order and make people obey the law.

po·lite /pə·līt′/ *adj.* Having good manners; not rude: It is *polite* to say "please."

po·ny /pō′nē/ *n., pl.* **ponies** A very small horse.

pop /pop/ *n.* A sudden sharp noise: The balloon broke with a loud *pop*.
—*v.* **popped, popping** To make or cause a sudden noise.

porch /pôrch/ *n., pl.* **porches** A covered opening to a house or building: the front *porch*.

prac·tice /prak′tis/ *v.* **practiced, practicing** To do something over and over so you can do it better.
—*n.* Doing something over and over to learn it better: Playing the piano well takes lots of *practice*.

pre·pare /pri·pâr′/ *v.* **prepared, preparing** To get or make ready: Dad is *preparing* dinner.

pre·tend /pri·tend′/ *v.* To make believe: Let's *pretend* that we are on a spaceship.

pret·ty /prit′ē/ *adj.* **prettier, prettiest** Attractive; pleasant.

price /prīs/ *n.* The amount of money something costs.

prin·cess /prin′sis/ *n.* The daughter of a king or queen.

print /print/ *n.* 1 Letters and words marked on paper with ink: This book has large *print*. 2 A mark made by pressing: Our feet left *prints* in the snow.
—*v.* 1 To put letters and words on paper: That machine *prints* newspapers. 2 To write letters as in print: *Print* your name here.

prize /prīz/ *n.* Something won in a contest or game.

prob·lem /prob′ləm/ *n.* Something to be solved: Rabbits in the garden are a *problem*. There were ten *problems* on the test.

act, āte, câre, ärt;   egg, ēven;   if, īce;   on, ōver, ôr;   bŏŏk, fōōd;   up, tûrn;
ə = **a** in *ago*, **e** in *listen*, **i** in *giraffe*, **o** in *pilot*, **u** in *circus*;   yōō = **u** in *music*;   oil;   out;
chair; sing; shop; thank; that; zh in *treasure*.

prom·ise /prom′is/ *n.* Words that show you will or you will not do something: I made a *promise.*
—*v.* **promised, promising** To give a promise.

prompt /prompt/ *adj.* Right on time: A *prompt* person is never late.

prop /prop/ *n.* Something that is used to hold something else up.
—*v.* **propped, propping** To hold something up with a prop: Paula *propped* up the plant with a stick.

proud /proud/ *adj.* Thinking well of: Sonia's parents are *proud* of her.

pud·ding /po͝od′ing/ *n.* A soft dessert made with milk and eggs.

pud·dle /pud′(ə)l/ *n.* A small pool of water: There were *puddles* in the street after the rain.

pull /po͝ol/ *v.* **1** To draw something forward or toward yourself: The dogs *pulled* the sled. **2** To take or tear out: Dad is *pulling* weeds.

pump·kin /pump′kin *or* pung′kin/ *n.* A large, round orange fruit: Did you buy a Halloween *pumpkin?*

pup·py /pup′ē/ *n., pl.* **puppies** A very young dog.

pur·ple /pûr′pəl/ *n., adj.* A color that is a mixture of blue and red.

pur·pose /pûr′pəs/ *n.* A plan or aim: The *purpose* of this book is to teach spelling.

push /po͝osh/ *v.* To press against and move something: Polly *pushed* the chair under the table.
—*n.* The act of pushing: That *push* almost knocked Stan over.

puz·zle /puz′əl/ *n.* Something that is confusing or hard to do: Elsa likes to figure out *puzzles.*
—*v.* **puzzled, puzzling** To confuse: The secret message *puzzled* us.

Q

quick /kwik/ *adj.* Done in a short time; fast: a *quick* shower.

quite /kwīt/ *adv.* **1** Completely: I am *quite* happy now. **2** Really: Alvin lives *quite* near me.

R

rab·bit /rab′it/ *n.* A small animal with long ears and a fluffy tail.

rac·coon /ra·ko͞on′/ *n.* A small, grayish-brown animal with a bushy tail. A raccoon has black marks on its face like a mask.

race¹ /rās/ *n.* A contest of speed: Iris won the swimming *race.*
—*v.* **raced, racing** **1** To take part in a race. **2** To move fast: I *raced* to the door.

race² /rās/ *n.* A group of people who are similar in the way they look.

rail·road /rāl′rōd′/ *n.* The track that trains move on.

rai·sin /rā′zən/ *n.* A dried grape.

ranch /ranch/ *n., pl.* **ranches** A large farm where cattle or horses are raised.

rath·er /rath′ər/ *adv.* **1** More willingly: I'd *rather* go tomorrow. **2** Instead: You should ask Philip *rather* than me.

reach /rēch/ *v.* **1** To touch or get hold of: Can you *reach* the top

188

read | **rough**

shelf ? **2** To arrive at: He *reached* home before dark.

read /rēd/ *v.* **read** /red/, **reading** **1** To get meaning from letters and words. **2** To say aloud something that is written: Please *read* us a story.

re·al·ly /rē′lē *or* rē′ə·lē/ *adv.* **1** In fact: Did that *really* happen? **2** Very; truly: Grandpa was *really* happy to see us.

rea·son /rē′zən/ *n.* **1** Explanation; excuse: What *reason* do you have for being late? **2** Cause: Being sleepy is a *reason* for going to bed.

re·cess /rē′ses/ *n., pl.* **recesses** A short break from work: Let's play hopscotch during *recess*.

re·cite /ri·sīt′/ *v.* **recited, reciting** To repeat something learned by heart: Len can *recite* lots of poems.

reed /rēd/ *n.* The hollow stem of certain kinds of grass.

re·pair /ri·pâr′/ *v.* To fix or mend. —*n.* (often pl.) The act of repairing: Our car needs *repairs*.

re·turn /ri·tûrn′/ *v.* **1** To come or go back. **2** To give back: Ned *returned* his library book.

ride /rīd/ *v.* **rode, ridden, riding** **1** To sit on something and make it move: to *ride* a bike. **2** To be carried along: to *ride* on a bus. —*n.* **1** A trip made when riding. **2** Something such as a merry-go-round that you ride for fun.

right /rīt/ *adj.* **1** Good and just: the *right* thing to do. **2** Correct: the *right* answer. **3** The opposite of left: your *right* hand.

—*adv.* **1** According to what is good and just: You did *right* to tell him. **2** Correctly: Ed spelled the word *right*. **3** To the right: Turn *right*. **4** Exactly: Put the books *right* here. **5** With no delay: Go *right* to bed.

rise /rīz/ *v.* **rose, risen, rising** **1** To stand or get up. **2** To move higher: The sun *rises* in the east.

riv·er /riv′ər/ *n.* A large stream of water.

rob·in /rob′in/ *n.* A bird with a reddish-orange breast.

rock¹ /rok/ *n.* A stone; something that is very hard.

rock² /rok/ *v.* To move back and forth: I *rocked* the baby to sleep.

rode /rōd/ *v.* Past tense of *ride*.

roll /rōl/ *v.* **1** To turn over and over: The stone *rolled* down the hill. **2** To move on wheels: The wagon *rolled* down the street. —*n.* **1** Something wrapped around itself: a *roll* of paper towels. **2** A small loaf of bread.

roof /ro͞of/ *n.* The top of a building.

room /ro͞om/ *n.* **1** Space: There's *room* for five people in the car. **2** An area within a house separated off by walls.

rose¹ /rōz/ *n.* A sweet-smelling flower that has thorns on its stem.

rose² /rōz/ *v.* Past tense of *rise*.

rough /ruf/ *adj.* **1** Not smooth; uneven: A cat's tongue feels *rough*. **2** Not gentle; rugged: Football can be a *rough* game. —*adv.* Not gently or carefully: Don't play *rough*.

---

act, āte, câre, ärt;　egg, ēven;　if, īce;　on, ōver, ôr;　bŏŏk, fŏŏd;　up, tûrn;
ə = a in *ago*, e in *listen*, i in *giraffe*, o in *pilot*, u in *circus*;　yŏŏ = u in *music*;　oil;　out;
chair;　sing;　shop;　thank;　that;　zh in *treasure*.

round /round/ *adj.* Having a shape like a circle or ball.
—*adv., prep.* **1** To move in a circle: The wheels turned *round.* **2** On all sides; around: The children sat *round* the teacher.
—*v.* To make round: We *rounded* the corners of the paper.

row¹ /rō/ *v.* To move a boat in water using oars.

row² /rō/ *n.* A line of things or people: We all stood in a *row.*

rub /rub/ *v.* **rubbed, rubbing** To press and move one thing against another: *Rub* the cat's back.

S

safe /sāf/ *adj.* **1** Free from danger or harm: Find a *safe* place to hide. **2** Not hurt: Sal was *safe.* **3** Careful: Mrs. Lopez is a *safe* driver.
—*n.* A metal box for keeping money and valuable things.

sail /sāl/ *n.* A piece of strong cloth that catches wind to move a boat.
—*v.* **1** To move on water or in air: The boat *sailed* into the bay. **2** To travel in a boat. **3** To run a sailboat: Brad is learning to *sail.*

sale /sāl/ *n.* **1** The act of selling: The clerk rang up the *sale.* **2** Selling things at low prices: The store is having a *sale* on boots.

same /sām/ *adj., pron.* Alike: Tammi and I bought the *same* shoes.

sand·wich /sand'wich *or* san'wich/ *n., pl.* **sandwiches** Two slices of bread with food between them.

save /sāv/ *v.* **saved, saving** **1** To take away from danger: The brave woman *saved* the child. **2** To keep money for a later time: Danny is *saving* for a bike. **3** To avoid waste: *Save* energy.

scent /sent/ *n.* A smell or odor: Flowers have a nice *scent.*

school /skōōl/ *n.* **1** A place where you learn. **2** The time when teaching is done: Let's play soccer after *school.*

scold /skōld/ *v.* To speak in an angry way: Dad *scolded* me for lying.

scratch /skrach/ *v.* **1** To mark with something sharp or rough: The cat *scratched* the table. **2** To scrape something that itches.
—*n., pl.* **scratches** A mark left by scratching.

scrub /skrub/ *v.* **scrubbed, scrubbing** To clean by rubbing very hard: *Scrub* the bathtub.

search /sûrch/ *v.* To look for or through: I'm *searching* for Nan.
—*n., pl.* **searches** The act of searching: We didn't find any shells during our *search.*

secret		should

se·cret /sē′krit/ *n.* Something you must not tell anyone else.
—*adj.* Known only to a few people: a *secret* meeting place.

see /sē/ *v.* **saw, seen, seeing** **1** What you do with your eyes. **2** To understand: I *see* what you mean. **3** To find out: *See* what he's doing.

seed /sēd/ *n.* The tiny thing from which a plant or tree grows.

seen /sēn/ *v.* Past participle of *see.*

sel·dom /sel′dəm/ *adv.* Not very often: Darrell is *seldom* late.

sell /sel/ *v.* **sold, selling** To give something in return for money: Mr. Roberts *sold* his car for $2,000.

send /send/ *v.* **sent, sending** To cause to go: We *sent* the dog home.

sent /sent/ *v.* Past tense and past participle of *send:* I *sent* my uncle a birthday card.

sen·tence /sen′təns/ *n.* A group of words that makes sense by itself.

shack /shak/ *n.* A small building, usually one in bad condition.

shad·ow /shad′ō/ *n.* The dark image made when a person or thing blocks the light.

shake /shāk/ *v.* **shook, shaken, shaking** **1** To move something back and forth or up and down quickly: *Shake* your head. **2** To tremble: Gerry *shook* with fear.

shall /shal/ *v.* A word used with other verbs to talk about the future: What *shall* I do next?

sham·poo /sham·pōō′/ *n.* A soap used to wash hair.
—*v.* To wash hair.

shape /shāp/ *n.* **1** The form of something: The *shape* of a ball is round. **2** The condition of someone or something: He is in good *shape.*
—*v.* **shaped, shaping** To give form to something: I *shaped* the clay into a ball.

she /shē/ *pron.* A word used in place of a girl's or woman's name.

shell /shel/ *n.* A hard outside covering: Turtles have *shells.*

she's /shēz/ She is.

shine /shīn/ *n.* Brightness.
—*v.* **shined, shone, shining** **1** To give off light: The stars *shine* at night. **2** To polish or make bright: *Shine* your shoes.

shook /shŏŏk/ *v.* Past tense of *shake.*

shop /shop/ *v.* **shopped, shopping** To look for things and buy them.
—*n.* A place where things are sold.

short /shôrt/ *adj.* **1** Not long: a *short* time. **2** Not tall. **3** Not enough: You are a nickel *short.*
—*n., pl.* **shorts** Pants that come above the knees.

should /shŏŏd/ *v.* Past tense of *shall.* Ought to: You *should* go home.

---

act, āte, câre, ärt;   egg, ēven;   if, īce;   on, ōver, ôr;   bŏŏk, fōōd;   up, tûrn;
ə = a in *ago,* e in *listen,* i in *giraffe,* o in *pilot,* u in *circus;*   yōō = u in *music;*   oil;   out;
chair;   sing;   shop;   thank;   that;   zh in *treasure.*

Spelling Dictionary

shoul·der /shōl′dər/ *n.* The part of your body where your arm joins your body.

shout /shout/ *n.* A sudden, loud yell: They heard a *shout* for help.
—*v.* **1** To make a sudden, loud yell. **2** To talk loud.

shov·el /shuv′əl/ *n.* A tool used for digging.
—*v.* To use a shovel: Bonnie *shoveled* the snow.

shut /shut/ *v.* **shut, shutting 1** To close: *Shut* the door. **2** To turn off: *Shut* off the light.

shy /shī/ *adj.* Quiet; not at ease with strangers: The *shy* boy was afraid to ask for help.

sick /sik/ *adj.* **1** Having an illness. **2** Tired of something: Oliver is *sick* of playing the same games.

sight /sīt/ *n.* **1** The act of seeing: The *sight* of home made him smile. **2** The ability to see. **3** What is seen: The sunset is a beautiful *sight*. **4** View; area reached by sight: out of *sight*.

sil·ver /sil′vər/ *n.* A shiny, whitish-gray metal.
—*adj.* **1** Made of silver: a *silver* ring. **2** Having the color of silver.

since /sins/ *prep., adv., conj.* From then until now: Rita has been here *since* Monday. I have seen her every day *since*. We have had fun *since* she came.

sing /sing/ *v.* **sang, sung, singing** To make music with your voice.

sir /sûr/ *n.* A title of respect used for a man.

sis·ter /sis′tər/ *n.* A girl who has the same parents as you do.

sit /sit/ *v.* **sat, sitting** To take a seat: Maury *sat* on the floor.

six /siks/ *n., adj.* The word for 6.

skate /skāt/ *n.* A boot or shoe with a metal blade or four small wheels attached to the bottom.
—*v.* **skated, skating** To move on skates: We *skate* in the park.

skin /skin/ *n.* The outside covering of people, animals, fruits, and vegetables.
—*v.* **skinned, skinning** To scrape off skin: Larry *skinned* his knee.

skirt /skûrt/ *n.* A piece of clothing that hangs from the waist.

sky /skī/ *n., pl.* **skies** The air above Earth: Planes fly in the *sky*.

slope /slōp/ *v.* **sloped, sloping** To be at an angle: That roof *slopes* down almost to the ground.
—*n.* A hillside: The children went down the *slope* on their sleds.

slow /slō/ *adj.* Not fast: A turtle walks at a *slow* pace.
—*v.* To make or become slower: The car *slowed* down.
—*adv.* In a slow or careful way: Cars should go *slow* near schools.

small /smôl/ *adj.* Little; not large: A mouse is a *small* animal.

smash /smash/ *v.* **1** To break into pieces. **2** To crash into.

smell /smel/ *v.* **1** To get the scent of something through your nose: *Smell* the flowers. **2** To give off a scent: Garbage *smells* awful.
—*n.* **1** The sense used to recognize odors: Dogs have a good sense of *smell*. **2** An odor.

smile /smīl/ *v.* **smiled, smiling** To raise the corners of your mouth to show that you are happy: Peter *smiled* when he heard the joke.
—*n.* The act of smiling: Mrs. Gregor gave us a friendly *smile*.

192

smoke	split

smoke /smōk/ *n.* The dusty cloud that rises from anything burning.
—*v.* **smoked, smoking** To give off smoke: The fire *smoked*.

smooth /smōōth/ *adj.* Without bumps or lumps: New sidewalk is *smooth*.
—*v.* To make something smooth.

snail /snāl/ *n.* A slow-moving animal with a shell on its back.

snake /snāk/ *n.* A reptile with no legs that moves by crawling.

sneeze /snēz/ *v.* **sneezed, sneezing** To blow air out through your nose and mouth: Dust makes me *sneeze*.
—*n.* The act of sneezing: A *sneeze* can be a sign of a cold.

snow /snō/ *n.* Small, white flakes of frozen water.
—*v.* To fall as snow: Does it *snow* here in the winter?

soft /sôft/ *adj.* **1** Not hard: My pillow is *soft*. **2** Quiet; not loud: a *soft* voice.

sold /sōld/ *v.* Past tense and past participle of *sell:* My father *sold* his car yesterday.

some·times /sum′tīmz′/ *adv.* Now and then: *Sometimes* we eat out.

son /sun/ *n.* What a boy or man is to his parents.

soon /sōōn/ *adv.* In a little while.

sound /sound/ *n.* Anything that can be heard: Don't make a *sound*!
—*v.* **1** To make a sound: *Sound* the horn. **2** To seem: It *sounds* right to me.

soup /sōōp/ *n.* A liquid food made with water or milk, meat or fish, and vegetables.

south /south/ *n., adj., adv.* A direction; the opposite of north.

south·ern /suth′ərn/ *adj.* **1** Of or from the south. **2** Toward the south: the *southern* part of the state.

space /spās/ *n.* **1** The unlimited area that holds the universe: The rocket traveled through *space*. **2** A limited area: a parking *space*.

speak /spēk/ *v.* **spoke, spoken, speaking 1** To say words; to talk. **2** To make a speech: Our teacher *spoke* at the meeting.

spell /spel/ *v.* **1** To say or write the letters of a word. **2** To stand for sounds: <u>C</u>-<u>a</u>-<u>r</u> spells <u>car</u>.

spider /spī′dər/ *n.* An animal that has eight legs and spins a web.

spill /spil/ *v.* **1** To let fall or run out: Lenny *spilled* his milk. **2** To fall or flow: Water *spilled* on the floor.

split /split/ *v.* **split, splitting 1** To cut lengthwise: We *split* logs for the fire. **2** To share.

act, āte, cáre, ärt;   egg, ēven;   if, īce;   on, ōver, ôr;   bŏŏk, fōōd;   up, tûrn;
ə = a in *ago,* e in *listen,* i in *giraffe,* o in *pilot,* u in *circus;*   yōō = u in *music;*   oil;   out;
chair;   sing;   shop;   thank;   that;   zh in *treasure.*

193

spoil /spoil/ *v.* **1** To ruin: The rain *spoiled* our day at the beach. **2** To become bad: Milk *spoils* if it is not kept cold. **3** To give someone everything he or she wants: Grandma *spoils* the baby.

spoke¹ /spōk/ *v.* Past tense of *speak*.

spoke² /spōk/ *n.* Part of a wheel.

spot /spot/ *n.* **1** A mark or stain: A leopard has *spots*. **2** A place: The park is my favorite *spot*.
—*v.* **spotted, spotting** To notice: Ann *spotted* a deer in the woods.

spray /sprā/ *n.* Water or other liquid in fine drops: Mom uses hair *spray*.
—*v.* To send out liquid in fine drops: *Spray* water on the plants.

spread /spred/ *v.* **spread, spreading** **1** To open completely: The bird *spread* its wings. **2** To smooth on: Zelda *spread* jelly on her toast.

spring /spring/ *v.* **sprang** *or* **sprung, springing** To leap suddenly: The dog *sprang* at me.
—*n.* **1** The season after winter. **2** A flow of water out of the ground.

spy /spī/ *n., pl.* **spies** A person who watches other people secretly.
—*v.* **spied, spying** **1** To keep watch secretly: They *spied* on our club meeting. **2** To catch sight of: I *spied* Morgan in the corner.

stair /stâr/ *n.* A step that goes from one level to another: Jack ran up the *stairs*.

stalk /stôk/ *n.* A stem of a plant.

stam·mer /stam′ər/ *v.* To pause while you are talking or repeat sounds without wanting to: When she is nervous, Hilary *stammers*.

stamp /stamp/ *n.* **1** A small piece of paper with glue on the back: Put a *stamp* on the letter. **2** A tool that makes a mark: a rubber *stamp*.
—*v.* **1** To put your foot down hard: The angry boy *stamped* his foot. **2** To mark with a stamp.

stand /stand/ *v.* **stood, standing** **1** To take or keep an upright position. **2** To put up with: I can't *stand* the smell of paint.

star /stär/ *n.* **1** A shining body that appears in the sky at night. **2** A shape with five or six points: ☆ ☆ **3** An actor or actress who plays the main part.
—*v.* **starred, starring** To play the main part.

stare /stâr/ *v.* **stared, staring** To look hard, often without blinking: The dog *stared* at the cat.
—*n.* A long, hard look.

start /stärt/ *v.* **1** To begin. **2** To turn on: Dad *started* the car.

state /stāt/ *n.* **1** The way something is: The dogs were in an excited *state*. **2** An area within a country: There are fifty *states* in the United States.

stay /stā/ *v.* To remain: You can *stay* for one more hour.

step /step/ *n.* **1** A movement made by lifting your foot and putting it down in another place. **2** A stair: We sat on the front *steps*.

—*v.* **stepped, stepping** **1** To move by taking steps: Please *step* over here. **2** To put your foot down on: Don't *step* on the bug.

stew /st(y)oo/ *n.* A thick soup made with meat and vegetables.

stick[1] /stik/ *n.* A thin piece of wood.

stick[2] /stik/ *v.* **stuck, sticking** **1** To prick with something sharp: I *stuck* myself with a needle. **2** To fasten with glue or paste. **3** To put: I *stuck* the book in my desk.

still /stil/ *adj.* Quiet: The house is *still* because everyone is asleep.
—*adv.* **1** Not moving: Sit *still* during dinner. **2** To this time: Aaron is *still* sick.

stir /stûr/ *v.* **stirred, stirring** To mix.

stone /stōn/ *n.* A small piece of rock.

stood /stood/ *v.* Past tense and past participle of *stand*.

stop /stop/ *v.* **stopped, stopping** **1** To come or bring to a halt: The cars *stopped* at the light. **2** To leave off doing something: *Stop* talking to Sara. **3** To keep from doing something: I *stopped* Tamara from leaving.
—*n.* **1** The act of stopping: The plane makes a *stop* in Denver. **2** The place where something stops: a bus *stop*.

sto·ry[1] /stôr'ē/ *n., pl.* **stories** **1** An account that tells what happened. **2** A tale: Harvey loves adventure *stories*.

sto·ry[2] /stôr'ē/ *n. pl.* **stories** A floor in a building or house.

stove /stōv/ *n.* Something used for cooking or heating.

strange /strānj/ *adj.* **1** Odd; unusual: You look *strange* in that costume. **2** Not known: There is a *strange* dog in our yard.

strap /strap/ *n.* A thin piece of leather or cloth used to close or hold something.

straw /strô/ *n.* **1** Dried grass or stalks: We put *straw* in the stalls for the horses. **2** A thin tube used for sucking up a drink.

street /strēt/ *n.* A road.

strike /strīk/ *v.* **struck, striking** **1** To hit: The car *struck* a tree. **2** To tell time by sounding a bell: The clock *struck* one.
—*n.* In baseball, a swing that misses the ball.

string /string/ *n.* A thin rope or cord: Rudy tied the box with *string*.
—*v.* **strung, stringing** To put on a string: It's fun to *string* beads.

stroll /strōl/ *v.* To walk in a slow, easy way.
—*n.* A slow walk: Caroline took a *stroll* in the park.

strong /strông/ *adj.* **1** Powerful; not weak: It takes a *strong* person to lift a heavy box. **2** Not easily broken: This rope is *strong*.

struck /struk/ *v.* Past tense and past participle of *strike*.

stud·y /stud'ē/ *v.* **studied, studying** To work to learn something.

stuff /stuf/ *n.* Lots of different things: Put this *stuff* away.
—*v.* To pack in; to fill: Annie *stuffed* the bag with presents.

sud·den /sud'(ə)n/ *adj.* Quick; without warning: a *sudden* stop.

act, āte, câre, ärt;   egg, ēven;   if, īce;   on, ōver, ôr;   book, food;   up, tûrn;
ə = a in *ago*, e in *listen*, i in *giraffe*, o in *pilot*, u in *circus*;   yoo = u in *music*;   oil;   out;
chair;   sing;   shop;   thank;   that;   zh in *treasure*.

Spelling Dictionary

sug·ar /sho͝og′ər/ *n.* Something used to make food sweet.

suit /so͞ot/ *n.* A set of clothes made up of a jacket and pants or a jacket and skirt.
—*v.* To be right for: Let's meet at a time that *suits* everyone.

sum·mer /sum′ər/ *n.* The season that comes after spring.

sun·ny /sun′ē/ *adj.* **sunnier, sunniest** Filled with sunshine; bright: It was a *sunny* afternoon.

sup·ply /sə·plī′/ *v.* **supplied, supplying** To give what is needed: Dad *supplied* the money.
—*n., pl.* **supplies** Things that are needed to do something: Notebooks and pencils are school *supplies*.

sup·pose /sə·pōz′/ *v.* **supposed, supposing** To think or believe: I *suppose* I can go.

sur·prise /sə(r)·prīz′/ *v.* **surprised, surprising** To do something unexpected: Jo's parents *surprised* her with a puppy.
—*n.* **1** The feeling caused by something unexpected: We all giggled with *surprise*. **2** Something not expected: Mom had a *surprise* for me when I got home.

swal·low /swol′ō/ *v.* To make food or drink go from your mouth into your stomach.

swap /swop/ *v.* **swapped, swapping** To trade or exchange: Clyde *swapped* his yo-yo for a whistle.

swift /swift/ *adj.* Quick; fast: A deer is a *swift* animal.

swim /swim/ *v.* **swam, swimming** To use your arms and legs to move along in water.

T

ta·ble /tā′bəl/ *n.* **1** A piece of furniture that has a flat top and is held up by legs. **2** A list or chart: a *table* of numbers.

tag¹ /tag/ *n.* A small piece of paper or cloth: a price *tag*.
—*v.* **tagged, tagging** To follow closely: Her brother *tagged* along.

tag² /tag/ *n.* A game in which you chase and try to touch others.
—*v.* **tagged, tagging** To touch someone with your hand.

take /tāk/ *v.* **took, taken, taking** **1** To get hold of: *Take* my hand. **2** To use: I *take* the bus to school. **3** To bring: We *took* the clock to the repair shop. **4** To receive: Jon *took* the message.

talk /tôk/ *v.* To say words.
—*n.* A conversation: Dad and I had a *talk* about airplanes.

tall /tôl/ *adj.* The opposite of short: Are you *tall* enough to reach the top shelf?

tap /tap/ *v.* **tapped, tapping** To hit or touch lightly: Lonnie *tapped* his pencil on the desk.
—*n.* A light touch: Ethan felt a *tap* on his shoulder.

tape /tāp/ *n.* **1** A long, narrow strip with one sticky side. **2** A plastic strip used to record sounds.
—*v.* **taped, taping** **1** To put tape on something. **2** To record on tape: We *taped* the school concert.

taste

thumb

taste /tāst/ *v.* **tasted, tasting** **1** To get the flavor of something: The cook *tasted* the soup. **2** To have a flavor: The soup *tasted* salty.
—*n.* The flavor of something: Sugar has a sweet *taste.*

taught /tôt/ *v.* Past tense and past participle of *teach:* My mother *taught* me how to tie my shoes.

teach /tēch/ *v.* **taught, teaching** To help someone learn.

teach·er /tē′chər/ *n.* A person who helps others learn: Mr. Collins is my music *teacher.*

team /tēm/ *n.* **1** A group of people who work or play together: Our baseball *team* won the game. **2** Animals that do work together: The sled was pulled by a *team* of dogs.

test /test/ *n.* A way to find out how much someone has learned: I have a spelling *test* tomorrow.
—*v.* To give a test; to try out: I *tested* the watch to see if it worked.

that's /thats *or* thəts/ That is.

their /thâr/ *pron.* Belonging to them.

there /thâr/ *adv.* At or to that place: Let's go *there* for dinner.

there's /thârz/ There is.

they /thā/ *pron.* More than one person or thing: *They* are friends.

they're /thâr/ They are: *They're* going to the park on Saturday.

think /thingk/ *v.* **thought, thinking** **1** To use your mind to remember, to imagine, or to solve a problem: Greg is *thinking* of the answer to the question you asked him. **2** To believe: I *think* you are right.

thirst·y /thûrs′tē/ *adj.* Needing or wanting something to drink.

those /thōz/ *adj., pron.* Plural of *that;* the ones there: *Those* pencils are mine. These pencils are longer than *those.*

though /thō/ *conj.* In spite of the fact that: I like tennis, *though* I don't play it well.
—*adv.* However: Juan took the medicine. He didn't like it, *though.*

thought¹ /thôt/ *n.* An idea: Think happy *thoughts.*

thought² /thôt/ *v.* Past tense and past participle of *think.*

thou·sand /thou′zənd/ *adj., n.* The word for *1,000.*

three /thrē/ *n., adj.* The word for *3.*

throat /thrōt/ *n.* The back part of your mouth: a sore *throat.*

thumb /thum/ *n.* The short, thick finger on one side of your hand.

act, āte, câre, ärt;   egg, ēven;   if, īce;   on, ōver, ôr;   bŏŏk, fōōd;   up, tûrn;
ə = **a** in *ago,* **e** in *listen,* **i** in *giraffe,* **o** in *pilot,* **u** in *circus;*   yōō = **u** in *music;*   oil;   out;
chair;   sing;   shop;   thank;   that;   zh in *treasure.*

197

Spelling Dictionary

tick·le /tik'əl/ *v.* **tickled, tickling** To touch someone in a way that makes the person laugh.

ti·ger /tī'gər/ *n.* A large animal of the cat family. A tiger has an orange body with black stripes.

tire¹ /tīr/ *n.* The rubber that goes around a wheel.

tire² /tīr/ *v.* **tired, tiring** To make or become weak or sleepy.

ti·tle /tīt'(ə)l/ *n.* The name of a book, a song, or something else: The *title* of the poem was "The Children's Hour."

to /tōō/ *prep.* **1** In the direction of: Les went *to* his room. **2** Until: We are at school from 9 *to* 3. **3** On: Tape the card *to* the box.

to·day /tə·dā'/ *n.* This day; the present time: *Today* is Friday. —*adv.* On this day: Susan worked hard *today*.

to·geth·er /tə·geth'ər/ *adv.* **1** With each other: The children played *together*. **2** Into one: Neila knotted the ropes *together*.

ton·sil /ton'səl/ *n.* One of two oval-shaped tissues in the throat: Marcia had her *tonsils* taken out.

too /tōō/ *adv.* **1** Also. **2** More than enough: It is *too* cold to swim.

took /tōōk/ *v.* Past tense of *take*.

tooth /tōōth/ *n., pl.* **teeth** **1** One of the hard white parts in your mouth used to bite and chew.

2 Anything like a tooth: The comb has a broken *tooth*.

top¹ /top/ *n.* **1** The highest part: Touch the *top* of your head. **2** A cover or lid: a bottle *top*. —*adj.* Highest; best: The book is on the *top* shelf. Vera is the *top* student in her class. —*v.* **topped, topping** **1** To put on top: I *topped* my cereal with fruit. **2** To do or be better: Hank's score *topped* mine.

top² /top/ *n.* A toy that spins.

to·tal /tōt'(ə)l/ *n.* The whole amount: Add the numbers to find the *total*. —*adj.* Complete: The story he told was a *total* lie. —*v.* To add: You must *total* the numbers to find the answer.

touch /tuch/ *v.* **1** To put your hand or another part of your body on or against something: Don't *touch* the hot stove. **2** To be up against: The sofa *touches* the wall.

tough /tuf/ *adj.* **1** Strong; rugged. **2** Hard to chew. **3** Hard to do: It's *tough* to get up early.

tour·ist /tōōr'ist/ *n.* A person who travels and visits other places.

tow·el /toul *or* tou'əl/ *n.* Cloth or paper used to dry something.

tow·er /tou'ər/ *n.* A tall, narrow building or part of a building.

town /toun/ *n.* A small city.

Spelling
Dictionary

trail

until

trail /trāl/ *n.* **1** A path. **2** The marks left by a person or animal.
—*v.* To follow behind: Jacob *trailed* everyone in the race.

train /trān/ *n.* A line of railroad cars.
—*v.* To teach: I *trained* my dog to roll over.

tramp /tramp/ *v.* **1** To walk with a heavy step: Mino *tramped* down the stairs. **2** To walk or wander: We *tramped* around in the woods.
—*n.* A person who wanders about and has no home.

trap /trap/ *n.* **1** A thing used to catch animals. **2** A trick to catch people off guard: The police set a *trap* for the robbers.
—*v.* **trapped, trapping** To catch and hold: Spider webs *trap* flies.

trav·el /trav′əl/ *v.* To go from one place to another: We *traveled* to Canada.

trick /trik/ *n.* **1** Something done to fool or cheat. **2** Something clever or skillful: magic *tricks*.
—*v.* To fool or cheat: They *tricked* Chet into thinking they had left.

trip /trip/ *n.* A journey or vacation.
—*v.* **tripped, tripping** To stumble or make fall: Andrea *tripped* over a rock. Hal stuck out his foot and *tripped* Anton.

trou·sers /trou′zərz/ *n., pl.* A pair of pants.

try /trī/ *v.* **tried, trying** **1** To make an effort. **2** To test: *Try* the soup to see if it needs salt.
—*n., pl.* **tries** A chance: You have three *tries* to hit the target.

tun·nel /tun′əl/ *n.* A narrow way under a river or a mountain.

turn /tûrn/ *v.* **1** To move around: He *turned* over in his sleep. **2** To change direction: We *turned* right at the corner. **3** To change: The leaves *turned* brown and then fell off the trees.
—*n.* A time or chance: It's your *turn* to do the dishes.

tur·tle /tûr′təl/ *n.* A slow-moving animal with a hard shell.

U

un·cle /ung′kəl/ *n.* **1** Your mother's or father's brother. **2** Your aunt's husband.

un·less /un·les′/ *conj.* Except if: We won't go *unless* you go too.

un·til /un·til′/ *prep., conj.* Up to the time of or when: I slept *until* nine o'clock. We played outside *until* it got dark.

act, āte, câre, ärt; egg, ēven; if, īce; on, ōver, ôr; bŏŏk, fōōd; up, tûrn;
ə = a in *ago*, e in *listen*, i in *giraffe*, o in *pilot*, u in *circus*; yōō = u in *music*; oil; out;
chair; sing; shop; thank; that; zh in *treasure*.

199

Spelling Dictionary

use /yo͞oz/ *v.* **used, using** **1** To put into action. **2** To finish: Alex *used* up all the paint.
—*n.* /yo͞os/ **1** The act of using. **2** Reason: There is no *use* crying.
—**used to** **1** Familiar with: I'm *used to* getting up early. **2** Did in the past: Miro *used to* live here.

V

val·ley /val′ē/ *n.* A low area between mountains or hills.

vil·lage /vil′ij/ *n.* A small town.
voice /vois/ *n.* **1** The sound made through the mouth. **2** The ability to make sounds: Helene lost her *voice* and could not sing.
vote /vōt/ *n.* A formal choice.
—*v.* **voted, voting** To choose by a vote: Americans *vote* for a President every four years.

W

wag /wag/ *v.* **wagged, wagging** To move quickly: Dogs *wag* their tails.
—*n.* A wagging motion: The dog knocked over the lamp with a *wag* of its tail.
walk /wôk/ *v.* **1** To go on foot. **2** To make to walk: *Walk* the dog. **3** To walk with: *Walk* me home.
—*n.* **1** The act of walking: We took a *walk*. **2** The distance walked: It is a long *walk* home.

want /wont *or* wônt/ *v.* To wish for: Sheila *wants* a new pair of skates.
wash /wôsh *or* wäsh/ *v.* To clean with soap and water.
—*n.* Clothing washed at one time: Elyse helped me fold the *wash*.
was·n't /wuz′ənt *or* woz′ənt/ Was not.
wave /wāv/ *v.* **waved, waving** **1** To flutter: The flags *waved* in the wind. **2** To move your hand to greet or to signal.
—*n.* **1** A moving ridge of water. **2** The act of waving your hand.

we /wē/ *pron.* I and others: *We* all went camping.
weak /wēk/ *adj.* Not having strength: A cold makes me *weak*.
weath·er /weth′ər/ *n.* The state of the air: The *weather* has been warm and sunny all week.
wel·come /wel′kəm/ *v.* **welcomed, welcoming** To greet gladly: Our dog *welcomed* us home.
—*n.* A friendly greeting: Aunt Katie gave me a warm *welcome*.
—*adj.* Freely allowed: You are *welcome* to borrow my book.
we'll /wēl/ **1** We will. **2** We shall.
we're /wir/ We are.
weren't /wûrnt *or* wûr′ənt/ Were not.
west /west/ *n., adj., adv.* A direction; where the sun goes down.

200

what's /(h)wots *or* (h)wuts/ What is.

wheel /(h)wēl/ *n.* A round thing that turns in a circle to move a car, wagon, bicycle, or similar thing.

wheth·er /(h)weth′ər/ *conj.* If: Let me know *whether* you will come or not.

which /(h)wich/ *adj., pron.* What one or ones of several: *Which* book did you read? *Which* do you like best?

whirl /(h)wûrl/ *v.* To spin or make to spin around very fast: The skaters *whirled* around on the ice.

who /hoo/ *pron.* **1** What person: *Who* is ready? **2** That: Anyone *who* came got a prize.

who·ev·er /hoo·ev′ər/ *pron.* Any person who: *Whoever* comes will have a good time.

whole /hōl/ *adj.* Complete; all of: The *whole* class got A's.
—*n.* The entire thing.

who's /hooz/ **1** Who is: *Who's* ready for recess? **2** Who has: *Who's* got my notebook?

whose /hooz/ *pron.* Belonging to which person: *Whose* book is this?

why /(h)wī/ *adv.* For what reason.

wide /wīd/ *adj.* **wider, widest** **1** Far from side to side: The puddle was too *wide* to jump across. **2** Having a distance from side to side: My desk is one meter *wide*.
—*adv.* All the way: *wide* open.

wild /wīld/ *adj.* **1** Living or growing in nature; not tame: a *wild* animal. **2** Crazy or hard to believe: a *wild* story.

will /wil/ *v.* **would** A word used with other verbs to tell what is going to

happen or what can be: Our school *will* be closed tomorrow. The car *will* hold five people.

win /win/ *v.* **won, winning** To do better than all others: Peter *won* the race.

wind¹ /wind/ *n.* **1** Moving air: The *wind* blew my hat off. **2** Breath: I had the *wind* knocked out of me.

wind² /wīnd/ *v.* **wound, winding** **1** To wrap around: Sharon *wound* the yarn into a ball. **2** To make a machine go by turning a part of it: I forgot to *wind* my watch. **3** To turn and twist: The road *winds* through the mountains.

win·dow /win′dō/ *n.* An opening in a wall that lets in air and light.

wipe /wīp/ *v.* **wiped, wiping** To clean or dry by rubbing: Please *wipe* your feet on the mat.

wise /wīz/ *adj.* **wiser, wisest** Having or showing good sense: My parents gave me *wise* advice.

wish /wish/ *n., pl.* **wishes** A hope or desire: My *wish* came true.
—*v.* **1** To hope for something: Mara *wished* for a pony. **2** To make a wish: Have you ever *wished* on a star?

with·out /with·out′ *or* with·out′/ *prep.* With no: Mother cooks *without* salt.

won /wun/ *v.* Past tense and past participle of *win*.

won·der /wun′dər/ *v.* To want to know: I *wonder* where he is.

won't /wōnt/ Will not.

wood /wood/ *n.* What makes up the trunk and branches of a tree.

---

act, āte, câre, ärt;   egg, ēven;   if, īce;   on, ōver, ôr;   book, food;   up, tûrn;
ə = a in *ago*, e in *listen*, i in *giraffe*, o in *pilot*, u in *circus*;   yoo = u in *music*;   oil;   out;
chair;   sing;   shop;   thank;   that;   zh in *treasure*.

201

Spelling Dictionary

wooden · yourself

wood·en /wŏŏd′(ə)n/ *adj.* Made of wood: *wooden* toys.

wool /wool/ *n.* **1** The hair of sheep: The sheep's *wool* is soft. **2** Yarn or cloth made from sheep's hair: My coat is made of *wool*.
—*adj.* Made of wool: a *wool* scarf.

word /wûrd/ *n.* **1** A sound or group of sounds that has meaning. **2** The letters that stand for a word.

work /wûrk/ *n.* **1** The effort needed to do something: Pulling weeds is hard *work*. **2** A job: My mother goes to *work* every morning.
—*v.* **1** To make an effort: Doug *works* hard. **2** To have a job: Dad *works* for the newspaper. **3** To run: That radio does not *work*.

world /wûrld/ *n.* **1** Earth: Blake would like to travel around the *world*. **2** Everything; the universe.

wor·ry /wûr′ē/ *v.* **worried, worrying** To be or make someone uneasy or upset: Mom will *worry* if I don't go straight home.
—*n., pl.* **worries** Something that makes you worry.

worst /wûrst/ *adj.* Most bad: I made the *worst* mistake of all.

worth /wûrth/ *prep.* **1** Good enough for: The zoo is a place *worth* visiting. **2** Having the same value: A quarter is *worth* twenty-five cents.
—*n.* Value: We got our money's *worth*.

would /wŏŏd/ *v.* Past tense of *will*. *Would* is often used to talk about wants and to ask polite questions: I *would* like another sandwich. *Would* you help me?

wrap /rap/ *v.* **wrapped, wrapping** To put a cover around something: Theo *wrapped* the present.

wreck /rek/ *v.* To destroy: The storm *wrecked* our tree house.
—*n.* Something that has been ruined: That car is a *wreck*.

wren /ren/ *n.* A small songbird.

wrist /rist/ *n.* The place where your hand joins your arm: Carol wears a watch on her *wrist*.

write /rīt/ *v.* **wrote, written, writing** **1** To make letters and words. **2** To be an author: Diane is *writing* a book.

writ·ten /rit′(ə)n/ *v.* Past participle of *write*.

wrote /rōt/ *v.* Past tense of *write*: George *wrote* a letter to his aunt.

Y

yard¹ /yärd/ *n.* The land around a building: the front *yard*.

yard² /yärd/ *n.* A measure equal to 3 feet or 36 inches.

your /yôr *or* yŏŏr/ *pron.* Belonging to you: Is this *your* pencil?

you're /yŏŏr *or* yôr/ You are: *You're* a very nice person.

your·self /yôr·self′ *or* yŏŏr·self′/ *pron., pl.* **yourselves** Your own self: Help *yourself* to an apple.

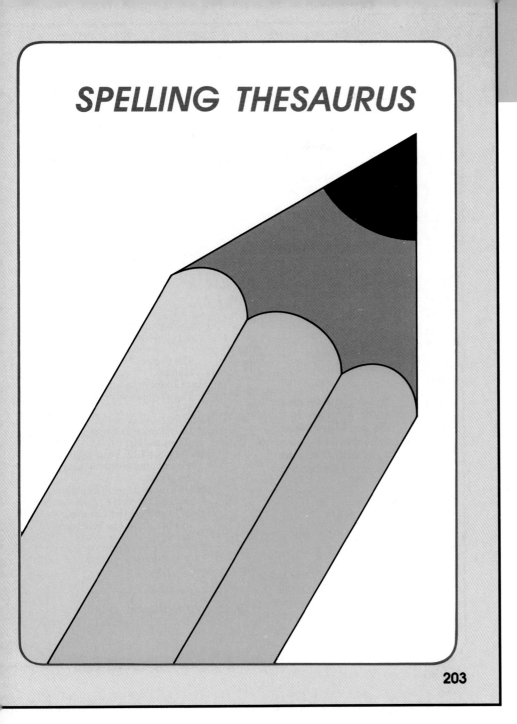

SPELLING THESAURUS

203

Spelling Thesaurus

What Is a Thesaurus?

A **thesaurus** lists words and their synonyms. Like a dictionary, a thesaurus lists words in alphabetical order. Each of these words is called an **entry word.** A list of synonyms follows the entry word. Sometimes a thesaurus lists antonyms.

Look at the parts of this thesaurus entry for the word *move.*

The **entry word** is in red letters. It is followed by the part of speech and a definition. An **example sentence** shows how the word can be used.

> move *v.* To go from one place to another. Our family is going to move to another city.

Synonyms for the entry word are in *slanted* letters. Each synonym is followed by a definition and an example sentence.

> *climb* To go up. The men plan to *climb* to the top of the mountain.
> *crawl* To creep on hands and knees. The baby can *crawl* to her blanket.
> *dance* To move in time to music. The students will *dance* at the party.
> *hurry* To move or act quickly. *Hurry* to the exit when the fire alarm sounds.
> *race* To move fast. Some rabbits *race* into the bushes when they are afraid.
> *skate* To move on ice. The children *skate* on the frozen pond.
> *travel* To go from one place to another. I want to *travel* on a train.

If an **antonym** is given, it is printed in dark letters.

> **ANTONYMS: stay, stop**

How to Use Your Spelling Thesaurus

Suppose you are writing a story that tells about how a runner moves. You read over your work and see you have used the word *move* too many times. You decide to use the Spelling Thesaurus to find some synonyms. Here are the steps you should follow.

1. Look for the word in the Thesaurus Index. The Index lists every word in the Spelling Thesaurus.
2. Find the word in the Index. This is what you will find:
   move *v.*
   The red letters tell you that *move* is an entry word.
3. Turn to the correct page in the Spelling Thesaurus and read the entry carefully. Choose the synonym or synonyms that will make your writing clearer and stronger. Not every synonym will fit in the context of your story.

Remember: Not every synonym will have the meaning you want. Look at the sample entry for *move* on page 206. Which synonyms for *move* would fit best in the paragraph about a runner?

- Sometimes you may find a word listed in the Index like this:
   hurry move *v.*
   This means you will find the word *hurry* listed as a synonym under the entry word *move*. Since *hurry* is not printed in red, you can tell that it is not an entry word. If you look for *hurry* in the Spelling Thesaurus as an entry word under the letter *H,* you will not find it!

- You will also see some lines in the Index that look like this:
   stay move *v.*
   This means that *stay* is listed as an antonym under the entry word *move*.

205

Spelling Thesaurus

A

adventurous brave *adj.*
afraid brave *adj.*
agree argue *v.*
aim point *v.*
alarm *n.*
amusing funny *adj.*
ancient old *adj.*
area space *n.*
argue *v.*
ask *v.*
attractive pretty *adj.*
avenue street *n.*
award prize *n.*

B

bang beat *v.*
bare empty *adj.*
bark sound *n.*
bathe swim *v.*
beam shine *v.*
beat *v.*
beautiful pretty *adj.*
begin stop *v.*
bell alarm *n.*
bend *v.*
bent crooked *adj.*
bit part *n.*
bite part *n.*
blank empty *adj.*
blast sound *n.*
blend *v.*
bold brave *adj.*
boulder rock *n.*
brave *adj.*
break *v.*
break repair *v.*
bright *adj.*
bright clever *adj.*
bright dark *adj.*

bright faint *adj.*
bright foggy *adj.*
brisk cold *adj.*
broad narrow *adj.*
brook river *n.*
build *v.*
build destroy *v.*
bumpy rough *adj.*
bundle package *n.*
burst break *v.*
bury cover *v.*
bury find *v.*

C

cabin house *n.*
call shout *v.*
calm still *adj.*
carry fall *v.*
carry hold *v.*
carton package *n.*
catch find *v.*
catch trap *v.*
chant sing *v.*
charming nice *adj.*
chat talk *v.*
cheer shout *v.*
cheerful happy *adj.*
chief main *adj.*
choppy rough *adj.*
clap sound *n.*
class group *n.*
clear *adj.*
clear easy *adj.*
clear foggy *adj.*
clever *adj.*
climb move *v.*
clip trim *v.*
cloudy clear *adj.*
club group *n.*
coach teacher *n.*
cold *adj.*

comfort hurt *v.*
construct build *v.*
cool cold *adj.*
corner trap *v.*
correct repair *v.*
correct right *adj.*
cover *v.*
cover find *v.*
crack break *v.*
crash sound *n.*
crawl move *v.*
creek river *n.*
crooked *adj.*
crop trim *v.*
crowd group *n.*
cruel mean *adj.*
crumb part *n.*
crush destroy *v.*
cry shout *v.*
curl bend *v.*
curve bend *v.*
curved crooked *adj.*
cut hurt *v.*

D

dance move *v.*
daring brave *adj.*
dark *adj.*
dark bright *adj.*
dazzling bright *adj.*
decide *v.*
delight *n.*
delightful happy *adj.*
desire want *v.*
destroy *v.*
destroy build *v.*
destroy repair *v.*
determine decide *v.*
different odd *adj.*
difficult easy *adj.*
dim bright *adj.*

Spelling Thesaurus

dim dark *adj.*
dim faint *adj.*
direct point *v.*
dirt ground *n.*
disagree argue *v.*
discover find *v.*
discuss talk *v.*
drag pull *v.*
drag push *v.*
drawing picture *n.*
dream plan *v.*
drop fall *v.*
drop hold *v.*
dull bright *adj.*
dull dark *adj.*
dwell live *v.*

E

earth ground *n.*
easy *adj.*
empty *adj.*
end stop *v.*
enormous large *adj.*
even flat *adj.*
exact right *adj.*
explain argue *v.*

F

fable story *n.*
faint *adj.*
fair clear *adj.*
fall *v.*
fall hold *v.*
familiar odd *adj.*
fast quick *adj.*
fearless brave *adj.*
feathery soft *adj.*
filled empty *adj.*
find *v.*
find cover *v.*

fine clear *adj.*
fine narrow *adj.*
firm strong *adj.*
fix break *v.*
fix destroy *v.*
flash shine *v.*
flat *adj.*
float fly *v.*
float swim *v.*
fluffy light *adj.*
fluffy soft *adj.*
flutter fly *v.*
fly *v.*
foggy *adj.*
foggy clear *adj.*
forceful strong *adj.*
form make *v.*
friendly nice *adj.*
frightened brave *adj.*
frosty cold *adj.*
full empty *adj.*
funny *adj.*

G

gentle nice *adj.*
giant large *adj.*
give hold *v.*
glad happy *adj.*
glare shine *v.*
glitter shine *v.*
gloomy dark *adj.*
gloomy foggy *adj.*
glow shine *v.*
glowing bright *adj.*
grab fall *v.*
grab hold *v.*
grand large *adj.*
grasp hold *v.*
gray foggy *adj.*
great large *adj.*
groan sound *n.*

ground *n.*
group *n.*

H

halt stop *v.*
handsome pretty *adj.*
happiness delight *n.*
happy *adj.*
hard easy *adj.*
hard soft *adj.*
harm hurt *v.*
hazy foggy *adj.*
heal hurt *v.*
healthy ill *adj.*
heavy light *adj.*
hide cover *v.*
hide find *v.*
high *adj.*
highway street *n.*
hike walk *v.*
hold *v.*
hold fall *v.*
hollow empty *adj.*
home house *n.*
hooked crooked *adj.*
hop jump *v.*
hope desire *v.*
horn alarm *n.*
hot cold *adj.*
house *n.*
huge large *adj.*
hum sing *v.*
hunt see *v.*
hurried quick *adj.*
hurry move *v.*
hurt *v.*
hut house *n.*

I

idea plan *n.*

207

Spelling Thesaurus

ill adj.
important main adj.
incorrect right adj.
inquire ask v.
intelligent clever adj.

J

jar shake v.
join meet v.
jolly funny adj.
joy delight n.
judge decide v.
jump v.

K

keep hold v.
kind mean adj.
kind nice adj.
knead blend v.
knock beat v.

L

lake n.
land ground n.
lane street n.
large adj.
lay place v.
leading main adj.
leap jump v.
leave meet v.
legend story n.
level flat adj.
light adj.
light faint adj.
lighted dark adj.
live v.
locate find v.
long high adj.
long want v.

look see v.
loud still adj.
lovely pretty adj.
low high adj.
lumpy rough adj.

M

main adj.
make build v.
march walk v.
mean adj.
mean nice adj.
medal prize n.
meet v.
mend break v.
mend destroy v.
mend repair v.
merry happy adj.
messy neat adj.
mighty strong adj.
misty foggy adj.
mix blend v.
modern old adj.
move v.

N

narrow adj.
narrow large adj.
neat adj.
new old adj.
nice adj.
nice mean adj.
noise sound n.
noisy still adj.
notice see v.

O

odd adj.
old adj.

open cover v.
open empty adj.
orderly neat adj.

P

package n.
paddle swim v.
painting picture n.
part n.
patch repair v.
path street n.
pause stop v.
peaceful still adj.
pebble rock n.
photograph picture n.
picture n.
piece part n.
place v.
place space n.
plain easy adj.
plain pretty adj.
plan n.
pleasant pretty adj.
pleasure delight n.
plod walk v.
plodding quick adj.
plot plan n.
point v.
poke pull v.
poke push v.
pond lake n.
pool lake n.
pop sound n.
press pull v.
press push v.
pretty adj.
principal main adj.
prize n.
proper right adj.
puddle lake n.
pull v.

208

Spelling Thesaurus

pull push *v.*
push *v.*
push pull *v.*
put place *v.*

Q

question ask *v.*
quick *adj.*
quiet still *adj.*
quit stop *v.*

R

race move *v.*
rattle shake *v.*
recent old *adj.*
remove place *v.*
repair *v.*
repair break *v.*
repair destroy *v.*
reward prize *n.*
right *adj.*
river *n.*
road street *n.*
rock *n.*
rock shake *v.*
room space *n.*
rough *adj.*
rough flat *adj.*
rude nice *adj.*
ruin build *v.*
ruin destroy *v.*
ruin repair *v.*

S

sad funny *adj.*
sad happy *adj.*
sadness delight *n.*

scared brave *adj.*
scrap part *n.*
scream shout *v.*
search see *v.*
section part *n.*
see *v.*
serious funny *adj.*
set place *v.*
settle decide *v.*
settle live *v.*
shack house *n.*
shake *v.*
shape build *v.*
sharp faint *adj.*
shear trim *v.*
shine *v.*
shiny bright *adj.*
shiver shake *v.*
short high *adj.*
shout *v.*
shove pull *v.*
shove push *v.*
sick ill *adj.*
signal alarm *n.*
simple easy *adj.*
sing *v.*
sink fall *v.*
siren alarm *n.*
skate move *v.*
sketch picture *n.*
slap beat *v.*
slight faint *adj.*
slow quick *adj.*
small large *adj.*
smart clever *adj.*
smash break *adj.*
smooth easy *adj.*
smooth flat *adj.*
smooth rough *adj.*
snare trap *v.*
soar fly *v.*
soft *adj.*

soil ground *n.*
sorrow delight *n.*
sound *n.*
space *n.*
sparkle shine *v.*
speak talk *v.*
speedy quick *adj.*
spill fall *v.*
spill hold *v.*
spin turn *v.*
split break *v.*
spot see *v.*
spring jump *v.*
squeal shout *v.*
stare see *v.*
start stop *v.*
stay live *v.*
stay move *v.*
step walk *v.*
still *adj.*
stir blend *v.*
stone rock *n.*
stop *v.*
stop move *v.*
stormy clear *adj.*
story *n.*
straight crooked *adj.*
straighten bend *v.*
strange odd *adj.*
stream river *n.*
street *n.*
strike beat *v.*
stroll walk *v.*
strong *adj.*
strong faint *adj.*
stumble fall *v.*
stupid clever *adj.*
sturdy strong *adj.*
sunless dark *adj.*
swift quick *adj.*
swim *v.*
swirl turn *v.*

209

T

tale story *n.*
talk *v.*
tall high *adj.*
tap beat *v.*
teacher *n.*
team group *n.*
tear break *v.*
thin narrow *adj.*
thought plan *n.*
tidy neat *adj.*
tight narrow *adj.*
tiny large *adj.*
tough strong *adj.*
tow pull *v.*
tow push *v.*
towering high *adj.*
track street *n.*
trail street *n.*
trainer teacher *n.*
tramp walk *v.*
trap *v.*
travel move *v.*
tremble shake *v.*
trim *v.*
trim neat *adj.*
trip fall *v.*

tug pull *v.*
tug push *v.*
tumble fall *v.*
tumble hold *v.*
turn *v.*
twirl turn *v.*
twist bend *v.*

U

ugly pretty *adj.*
uncover cover *v.*
uncover find *v.*
uneven flat *adj.*
unhappy happy *adj.*
unite meet *v.*
unkind mean *adj.*
untidy neat *adj.*
unusual odd *adj.*
unwell ill *adj.*
used old *adj.*
usual odd *adj.*

W

walk *v.*
want *v.*

warm cold *adj.*
weak strong *adj.*
weightless light *adj.*
well ill *adj.*
whirl turn *v.*
whisper shout *v.*
whistle sing *v.*
whole part *n.*
wide large *adj.*
wide narrow *adj.*
wind bend *v.*
wind turn *v.*
wipe clean *v.*
wish want *v.*
worn old *adj.*
wound hurt *v.*
wrap cover *v.*
wreck build *v.*
wreck destroy *v.*
wreck repair *v.*
wrong right *adj.*

Y

yell shout *v.*

alarm	blend

A

alarm *n.* Something that warns of danger. All homes should have a smoke *alarm*.
bell Something that makes a ringing sound when rung. The school *bell* rang three times at the fire drill.
horn Something that makes a warning sound. Mrs. Lopez honked her car *horn* at the dog in the street.
signal A sign used to send a message. A red light is a *signal* for a car to stop.
siren Something that gives out a loud whistle. A fire truck *siren* tells all cars to stop.

argue *v.* To give reasons for or against. No one on the team will *argue* with the umpire.
disagree To have a different opinion. Margaret thought the book was funny, but I had to *disagree*.
explain To give reasons for. Dr. Wall can *explain* why an ice pack will help your sore ankle.
ANTONYM: agree

ask *v.* To put a question to. Be sure to *ask* for help if you need it.
inquire To ask questions to get information. Max should *inquire* about a job at the library.
question To ask a question or questions. Did you *question* the teacher about the homework assignment?

B

beat *v.* To hit over and over. The drummer *beat* the drum.
bang To beat or hit hard and noisily. Babies love to *bang* on pots and pans.
knock To hit. *Knock* on the front door of my house when you arrive.
slap To hit or strike. Terry watched the waves *slap* the shore.
strike To hit. *Strike* the rug with a stick to shake out the dust.
tap To hit or touch lightly. If the cabin door is locked, *tap* on the window.

bend *v.* To make something curve. Steel is not easy to *bend*.
curl To become twisted. Amy likes to *curl* her hair.
curve To bend into or take the form of a curve. This road must *curve* around the lake.
twist To curve or bend. The tree branches *twist* around each other.
wind To run or move in a turning way. The runners had to *wind* through the trees.
ANTONYM: straighten

blend *v.* To mix. The artist must *blend* white paint with blue to make that color.
knead To mix dough using your hands; to push and squeeze. First *knead* the bread dough, and then form it into loaves.

211

Spelling Thesaurus

mix To stir in order to blend. *Mix* the muffin batter and pour it into a pan.

stir To mix. *Stir* the orange juice before you drink it.

brave *adj.* Not afraid. The brave scouts hiked to the top of the trail.

adventurous Liking adventure. The *adventurous* sailors began their trip across unknown seas.

bold Having courage. The astronaut Neil Armstrong was a *bold* man.

daring Brave and adventurous. The *daring* swimmer stepped into the river.

fearless Without fear. The *fearless* tigers search the jungle for food.

ANTONYMS: **afraid, frightened, scared**

break *v.* To crack into pieces. Glass will break easily.

burst To break apart suddenly. A balloon will *burst* when pricked with a pin.

crack To break or split apart. I like to *crack* peanuts open.

smash To break into pieces. Don't drop the plate, or it will *smash*.

split To cut or break lengthwise. We *split* logs for firewood.

tear To pull apart or rip. The thorns on the bushes can *tear* your shirt.

ANTONYMS: **fix, mend, repair**

bright *adj.* Giving off a lot of light. Do not look directly at the bright sun.

dazzling Blinding because of too much light. There is a *dazzling* light at the top of the lighthouse.

glowing Shining because of great heat. The *glowing* coals mean the fire is not out.

shiny Bright. The *shiny* stones sparkled in the water.

See also **clever.**

ANTONYMS: **dark, dim, dull**

build *v.* To put pieces together. Beavers build their homes with mud and sticks.

construct To make by putting parts together. The members plan to *construct* a clubhouse.

form To make or shape. Lava will *form* a cone around a volcano's center.

make To put parts together or to shape. Alex can *make* a kite with paper, sticks, and string.

shape To form. The birds *shape* their nests like small bowls.

See also **make.**

ANTONYMS: **destroy, ruin, wreck**

C

clear *adj.* Not cloudy or foggy. Sue looked for the plane in the clear sky.

fair Clear and bright. The weather report said it will be a *fair* weekend.

fine Not cloudy; clear. We had *fine* weather for our picnic.

ANTONYMS: **cloudy, foggy, stormy**

clever		delight

clever *adj.* Very smart. A fox is known as a clever animal.
bright Smart; clever. Emma had a *bright* idea.
intelligent Smart; bright. The *intelligent* dog found its way home.
smart Bright; clever. The *smart* dog knows many tricks.
ANTONYM: stupid

cold *adj.* Low in temperature. Winters in the northern United States are cold
brisk Cool. The *brisk* fall air makes leaves turn many colors.
cool Slightly cold. Bears like to live in *cool* places.
frosty Cold enough to make frost. Victor handed me a *frosty* glass of juice.
ANTONYMS: hot, warm

cover *v.* To be over or put something over. Cover your head with a hat or scarf in cold weather.
bury To hide or cover up. Dogs often *bury* a favorite bone or toy.
hide To put out of sight. Mice *hide* from owls in the tall grass.
wrap To put a cover around something. Please *wrap* the food in foil to keep it fresh.
ANTONYMS: find, open, uncover

crooked *adj.* Not straight. The line you drew is crooked
bent Made crooked by bending. The tree branches were *bent* toward the sun.

curved Bent in the shape of a curve. The *curved* train track goes around the mountain.
hooked Curved like a hook. A lobster has a *hooked* claw.
ANTONYM: straight

D

dark *adj.* Without light. Bears sleep in dark caves.
dim Without enough light. In *dim* light, the black pupil of the eye grows larger to let light in.
dull Not bright or clear. Many fish live in *dull* water.
gloomy Dark and dismal. We play games inside on a *gloomy* day.
sunless Without sun or sunlight. The plant cannot live in that *sunless* corner.
ANTONYMS: bright, lighted

decide *v.* To make up your mind. You must decide which book to read first.
determine To decide firmly. The umpire must *determine* if the pitch was a strike.
judge To decide who wins. Our teacher will *judge* which is the most interesting science project.
settle To decide or determine. Let's *settle* on a safe place to build a campfire.

delight *n.* Great joy. The children squealed with delight as they played in the swimming pool.
happiness A feeling of joy. I could see the *happiness* on my friend's face when he smiled.

213

joy Great happiness. *Joy* spread through the crowd as the firefighter carried a child from the burning house.

pleasure A feeling of enjoyment or delight. I take *pleasure* in doing any job well.

ANTONYMS: sadness, sorrow

destroy *v.* To break or ruin. Too little rain can destroy a farm crop.

crush To press or squeeze out of shape. Squirrels *crush* nuts with their teeth.

ruin To destroy. If you ride over a nail, you may *ruin* your tire.

wreck To destroy. An ocean wave could *wreck* the sand castle.

ANTONYMS: build, fix, mend, repair

E

easy *adj.* Not hard to do. This book is easy to read.

clear Easy to understand. This map shows a *clear* way to the airport.

plain Easy to understand. Always give *plain* turn signals from your bike.

simple Easy to understand or do. A dog can learn *simple* tricks.

smooth Without any difficulties or troubles. Scouts should mark a *smooth* trail to a camp.

ANTONYMS: difficult, hard

empty *adj.* Holding nothing. When the big van drove away, the house was empty

bare Empty. The room is *bare*.

blank Not completed or filled out. Please write your name in the *blank* space.

hollow Empty on the inside. Chris carved on the *hollow* pumpkin.

open Not filled. There is an *open* seat in the front of the train.

ANTONYMS: filled, full

F

faint *adj.* Dim. A faint beam of light showed through the dark forest.

dim Without enough light. Abraham Lincoln read by *dim* firelight.

light Not great. A *light* snow fell.

slight Small in amount. In the quiet house, Pat heard the *slight* creak of the door.

ANTONYMS: bright, sharp, strong

fall *v.* To drop down. A gymnast learns how to fall safely.

drop To fall or let fall. We watched the monkey *drop* the banana to the ground.

sink To go down. Soap with air in it does not *sink* in the bathtub.

spill To fall or flow. The rocks will soon *spill* into the river.

stumble To miss a step in walking or running. Don't *stumble* over the roller skates.

trip To stumble or make fall. Be careful not to *trip* on the stairs.

tumble To fall. A baby may *tumble* when she first tries to walk.

ANTONYMS: carry, grab, hold

214

find	ground

find *v.* To come upon. Sandra cannot find her book.

catch To discover or find. I try to catch words that I spelled wrong.

discover To learn or find out. The sailors hope to *discover* a treasure chest.

locate To find. You can *locate* the pears in the fruit and vegetable section.

uncover To make known. Scientists may *uncover* new facts about the sun.

ANTONYMS: bury, cover, hide

flat *adj.* Smooth and straight. Baseball is played on a flat field.

even Flat and smooth. Greg built a table with an *even* top.

level Smooth or even. Skate on the *level* sidewalk.

smooth Without bumps or lumps. The worker used a board to make the cement *smooth*.

ANTONYMS: rough, uneven

fly *v.* To go through the air. Many airplanes fly higher than birds.

float To rest on water or in the air. The soap bubbles *float* above our heads.

flutter To move quickly. Look at the butterfly *flutter* through the garden.

soar To rise high into the air. The eagle will *soar* over the lake looking for food.

foggy *adj.* Full of fog or mist. Drivers often turn on their car lights on a foggy day.

gloomy Dark; dismal. The ship sailed through the *gloomy* night.

gray Dark or dull. The *gray* skies warned us that a rainstorm was coming.

hazy Full of haze. Clouds filled the *hazy* sky.

misty Of or like mist. Ted couldn't see through the *misty* windows.

ANTONYMS: bright, clear

funny *adj.* Able to make you laugh. Do you think the comic strip is funny?

amusing Causing fun or laughter. Sid looked *amusing* dressed up as a pumpkin.

jolly Full of life and merriment. Everyone laughed at the *jolly* clown.

ANTONYMS: sad, serious

G

ground *n.* Earth's surface; soil. The spaceship is expected to touch ground in January.

dirt Loose earth. The groundhog leaves a mound of *dirt* at the door of its home.

earth The softer, loose part of the land. Flower bulbs must be covered with *earth*.

land The part of Earth that is not covered by water. Our world has more water than *land*.

soil The ground in which plants grow. The farmer pulled a carrot out of the *soil*.

215

Spelling Thesaurus

group *n.* Several people or things together. A *group* of fish is called a school.

class A group of persons or things that have something in common. The music *class* is preparing for a concert.

club A group of people who do things together. The students formed a *club* to walk their dogs together.

crowd A large number of people gathered closely together. A *crowd* gathered around the visiting astronauts.

team A group of people who work or play together. The students formed *teams* to make science projects.

H

happy *adj.* Full of joy; glad. The story has a *happy* ending.

cheerful Happy, joyous. The *cheerful* clown rode around the tent in a wagon.

glad Pleased or happy. The child was *glad* to see his father.

delightful Giving joy or pleasure. Ruthie wrote a *delightful* story about her visit to her aunt's farm in the country.

merry Full of fun and laughter. The Glee Club sings *merry* songs on holidays.
ANTONYMS: sad, unhappy

high *adj.* Far up. Les could hardly reach the *high* walls with his paintbrush.

long Extending quite far between ends. The kite was tied to a *long* string.

tall More than usual height. There are sixty floors in the *tall* building.

towering Like a tower. The coast redwood is a *towering* tree.
ANTONYMS: low, short

hold *v.* To take and keep. That glass pitcher can *hold* two quarts of water.

carry To take from one place to another. Mother cats *carry* their kittens in their mouths.

grab To grasp suddenly and forcefully. It is not polite to *grab* something from someone else.

grasp To take hold of firmly. A newborn baby can *grasp* onto your finger.

keep To have and not give up. Please *keep* my fish while I am away.
ANTONYMS: drop, fall, give, spill, tumble

house *n.* A building in which people live. Would you like to study at my *house* after school?

cabin A small house made of wood. This *cabin* was built with logs.

home The place where a person or animal lives. That bird makes its *home* in our tree.

hut A small house or cabin. The children built a *hut* on the beach.

shack A small building. Tony uses the *shack* as a workshop.

216

hurt	light

hurt *v.* To feel or cause pain or harm. Angela hurt her ankle when she fell.
cut To make an opening in something with a sharp edge. James *cut* his finger on the broken glass.
harm To do damage to. The dentist said that too much sugar will *harm* my teeth.
wound To hurt by cutting through the skin. Did Matt *wound* his chin when he fell off his bike?
ANTONYMS: comfort, heal

I

ill *adj.* Feeling sick. Two third-grade students are ill today.
sick Having an illness. The *sick* child has the mumps.
unwell Not well; sick. Peter has felt *unwell* since he ate.
ANTONYMS: healthy, well

J

jump *v.* To leap up or over. Try to jump over the puddle.
hop To move the way a rabbit does. Some birds *hop* but others walk.
leap To jump or spring. How far can a frog *leap?*
spring To leap suddenly. Watch the basketball player *spring* for the ball.

L

lake *n.* A body of water. The boat is in the lake
pond A body of still water smaller than a lake. Frogs and tadpoles live in the *pond.*
pool A small body of still water. The swan saw itself in the *pool* of water.
puddle A small pool of water. The car drove through the *puddle* and splashed me.

large *adj.* Big in size or amount. The United States is a large country.
enormous Unusually large or great. People travel across the ocean on *enormous* ships.
giant Very large. Some elephants have *giant* ears.
grand Large; important. The big house looks *grand.*
great Very large. A *great* hot-air balloon passed in the sky.
huge Very large. The Rocky Mountains are *huge.*
wide Far from side to side. Before trains, covered wagons carried people across the *wide* desert.
ANTONYMS: narrow, small, tiny

light *adj.* Not heavy. The mail carrier delivered a light package.
fluffy Light and frothy. *Fluffy* clouds dotted the sky.
weightless Having no weight. The *weightless* astronauts floated through the spaceship.
ANTONYM: heavy

217

live	narrow

live *v.* To make a home. Does Cleo still live nearby?

dwell To live in a home. Tuna fish *dwell* in warm ocean waters.

settle To come to make a home. When did you *settle* in this town?

stay To remain. Maria will *stay* with her aunt for the summer.

M

main *adj.* Most important. The main reason you are here is to find a book to read.

chief Most important. The *chief* job for worker ants is to build homes.

important Having much value. Fruits are an *important* part of a healthy diet.

leading Most important. Nebraska is a *leading* farm state.

principal First in rank or importance; chief; main. Judy plays the *principal* part in the school play.

mean *adj.* Cruel. The mean giant scared the little boy.

cruel Eager or willing to give pain to others. Who could ever be *cruel* to a puppy?

unkind Mean or cruel. Valerie does not say *unkind* words about her friends.

ANTONYMS: kind, nice

meet *v.* To come together. The Mississippi River and the Red River meet in Louisiana.

join To bring or come together. I'm going to *join* my friends at the movie theater.

unite To join together. The families *unite* once a year for a party.

ANTONYM: leave

move *v.* To go from one place to another. Our family is going to move to another city.

climb To go up. The men plan to *climb* to the top of the mountain.

crawl To creep on hands and knees. The baby can *crawl* to her blanket.

dance To move in time to music. The students will *dance* at the party.

hurry To move or act quickly. *Hurry* to the exit when the fire alarm sounds.

race To move fast. Some rabbits *race* into the bushes when they are afraid.

skate To move on ice. The children *skate* on the frozen pond.

travel To go from one place to another. I want to *travel* on a train.

ANTONYMS: stay, stop

N

narrow *adj.* Not wide. Cars must cross the narrow bridge one at a time.

fine Very thin. A *fine* line shows the state borders on a map.

thin Not fat or plump. The *thin* dog looks hungry.

| neat | | part |

tight Fitting closely. The mouse ran into the *tight* space between the walls.
ANTONYMS: broad, wide

neat *adj.* Clean and tidy. I hang up my clothes to keep my room neat.
orderly Neat and tidy. Sean can always find his books because he has an *orderly* desk.
tidy Neat and orderly. My father hangs tools on the wall to keep the garage *tidy*.
trim Neat, smart, or tidy. The gardener clipped the row of *trim* bushes.
ANTONYMS: messy, untidy

nice *adj.* Pleasant, kind. I like going to my dentist because she is a very nice woman.
charming Pleasing or delightful. "Cinderella" is a *charming* fairy tale.
friendly Showing friendship or kindness. We moved to a *friendly* neighborhood.
gentle Kind and tender. A bunny is a *gentle* pet.
kind Gentle or friendly. A *kind* police officer helped me find my new school.
ANTONYMS: mean, rude

O

odd *adj.* Strange, unusual. Many people thought the artist painted odd pictures.

different Unusual. That's a *different* way of dancing.
strange Odd or unusual. An anteater is a *strange* animal that eats ants.
unusual Not usual or ordinary. These flowers have an *unusual* smell.
ANTONYMS: familiar, usual

old *adj.* Not new. The old house on the corner needs repair.
ancient Very old. Some *ancient* buildings were built more than 2000 years ago.
used That has belonged to another. The store sells new and *used* books.
worn Damaged by much use. My *worn* red sweater is still the most comfortable.
ANTONYMS: modern, new, recent

P

package *n.* The box that holds something. Jake opened a package of writing paper.
bundle A package. Lisa's books made a heavy *bundle*.
carton A cardboard container. Please pack the books in a *carton*.

part *n.* A piece of a whole. Which part of the book did you like best?
bit A small part. The girl threw a *bit* of bread to the duck.
bite A small bit of food. Rebecca tried a *bite* of the unusual fish.

219

picture

prize

crumb A tiny piece. My dog ate the *crumb* off the floor.

piece A part of a whole thing. There is one *piece* missing from the puzzle.

scrap A little piece. Please throw away the *scrap* of paper.

section A separate part. Paul reads the news *section* of the newspaper every day.

ANTONYM: whole

picture *n.* A painting, drawing, or photograph. The artist drew my picture.

drawing A picture, design, or sketch made by drawing lines and by shading areas. A map is a *drawing* of an actual place in the world.

painting A picture made with paints. The artist did that famous *painting*.

photograph A picture made with a camera. John took my *photograph* with his camera.

sketch An unfinished drawing. The *sketch* seemed to show a man's sad face.

place *v.* To put. Please place the dishes on the table.

lay To put or place. The teacher said to *lay* the books on our desks.

put To set, lay, or place. Harry *put* his letters in the mailbox.

set To put in a certain place. Fred *set* the goldfish bowl on the table.

See also **space.**

ANTONYM: remove

plan *n.* An idea for doing or making something. Carlos had a plan to become a doctor.

dream Something you hope for. Terry's *dream* is to become president.

idea A thought. Henry has an *idea* for the school play.

plot The events of a story. The *plot* of that book is exciting.

thought An idea. Amy wrote down every *thought* in her journal.

point *v.* To show or indicate. The scientist asked us to point to the North Star.

aim To direct at something. You should *aim* the hose at the garden.

direct To tell or show the way. Can you *direct* me to the nurse's office?

pretty *adj.* Attractive; pleasant. Healthy, strong teeth will give you a pretty smile.

attractive Pleasing. Sweet-smelling flowers are *attractive* to bees.

beautiful Very lovely. It was a *beautiful* day at the beach.

handsome Looking pleasing. The *handsome* colt won a prize in the horse show.

lovely Beautiful. Martina has a *lovely* singing voice.

ANTONYMS: plain, ugly

prize *n.* Something won in a contest or game. Otis won first prize in the spelling contest.

220

| pull | right |

award A prize. He received an *award* for his painting.

medal An award for an outstanding act. Mary received a *medal* for her school work.

reward A gift given for working hard or doing something special. Cindy will give a *reward* to the person who finds her lost dog.

pull *v.* To draw something forward or toward yourself. Brian had to pull the wagon all the way home.

drag To haul or pull away. A beaver can *drag* small logs to a stream to build a dam.

tow To pull or drag by a rope or chain. A truck will *tow* the car to the garage.

tug To pull at with effort. The cat likes to *tug* at the ball of string.

ANTONYMS: poke, press, push, shove

push *v.* To press against and move something. Please push me on the swing.

poke To push in, out, or through. That bottle might *poke* a hole in the bag.

press To act upon by weight or pressure. Please *press* the first-floor button on the elevator.

shove To move by pushing from behind. We were not able to *shove* the wagon up the hill.

ANTONYMS: drag, pull, tow, tug

Q

quick *adj.* Done in a short time; fast. A shortcut is a quick way home.

fast Moving or acting with speed. Andrew passed everyone on the street. He is a *fast* walker.

hurried Made, done, or acting in haste. A *hurried* job is likely to be poorly done.

speedy Swift, fast, rapid. I would like a *speedy* answer.

swift Moving very fast. The *swift* horses galloped across the field.

ANTONYMS: plodding, slow

R

repair *v.* To fix or mend. She tried to repair the broken watch.

correct To change to make right. The glasses will *correct* your eyesight.

mend To repair. Tom will *mend* the tear in the tent.

patch To put a patch on. Please *patch* the hole in the roof before it rains.

ANTONYMS: break, destroy, ruin, wreck

right *adj.* Correct. Who can give me the right answer?

correct Exact; right. What is your *correct* shoe size?

exact Completely right. I had the *exact* change for the phone.

proper Correct. Set the oven for the *proper* temperature.

ANTONYMS: incorrect, wrong

221

river *n.* A large stream of water. The Mississippi is the longest river in the United States.
brook A natural stream. Rosie liked to wade across the *brook*.
creek A stream. We caught some fish in the *creek*.
stream A small body of flowing water. Many goldfish live in the *stream*.

rock *n.* A stone; something that is very hard. The pillow felt as hard as a rock.
boulder A large rock or stone. The sea lion sat on a *boulder* near the edge of the ocean.
pebble A small, smooth stone. Joan filled the bottom of the fishbowl one *pebble* at a time.
stone A small piece of rock. The boy skimmed a *stone* over the water.
See also **shake.**

rough *adj.* Not smooth. Sandpaper can smooth the rough edges of cut wood.
bumpy Having or making bumps. The car bounced along the *bumpy* road.
choppy Full of short, rough waves. The *choppy* sea was not safe for small boats.
lumpy Covered with or having lumps. I couldn't sleep on the *lumpy* bed.
ANTONYM: smooth

S

see *v.* What you do with your eyes. Your eyes have many parts that help you see.
hunt To look carefully. Birds *hunt* for worms in the early morning.
look To turn the eyes to see or try to see something. Will you help me *look* for my book?
notice To see; to pay attention to. Did you *notice* Adam's new jacket?
search To look for. Scientists *search* the sky for new stars.
spot To notice. The park ranger can *spot* a rattlesnake from many feet away.
stare To look hard, often without blinking. Mickey will *stare* at the sky until he sees a shooting star.

shake *v.* To move something back and forth or up and down quickly. A wet dog will shake the water off its fur.
jar To cause to tremble or shake. Strong thunder can *jar* the windows in our house.
rattle To make or cause a series of quick, sharp noises. The monkey likes to *rattle* coins in a can.
rock To move back and forth. I tried to *rock* the baby to sleep.
shiver To shake. Jane started to *shiver* when she went out into the cold.
tremble To shake. I started to *tremble* when I saw Max in his monster mask.

shine		sound

shine *v.* To give off light. Does the sun shine all the time?

beam To send out rays of light. The light from the lighthouse will *beam* across the sea.

flash To give a quick, bright light. The car's headlights *flash* on and off.

glare To give off a bright, blinding light. The baseball player wears a cap to keep the *glare* out of his eyes.

glitter To sparkle brightly. Raindrops *glitter* in the sunlight.

glow To shine because of great heat. We watched the fire *glow* in the darkness.

sparkle To give off sparks or flashes. A diamond will *sparkle* when light shines on it.

shout *v.* To make a sudden loud yell. We heard the umpire shout "Safe!"

call To speak in a loud voice. Please *call* your brother to dinner.

cheer To urge or encourage. The fans *cheer* for their favorite team.

cry To call out. Some animals *cry* at the full moon.

scream To make a long, loud cry. Did the baby *scream* when his toy fell to the floor?

squeal To give a long, high cry. Pigs *squeal* in their pens.

yell To shout; scream; roar. The children *yell* on the playground.

ANTONYM: whisper

sing *v.* To make music with your voice. Jordan likes to sing in the shower.

chant To sing to a chant. The Glee Club learned to *chant* the poem.

hum To sing with closed lips. Many people *hum* while they work.

whistle To make a sound by forcing breath through the teeth and lips. Andrea can *whistle* a tune.

soft *adj.* Not hard. A pillow is soft.

feathery Light as a feather. The sky was filled with *feathery* clouds.

fluffy Light and frothy. The whipped cream was *fluffy*.

ANTONYM: hard

sound *n.* Anything that can be heard. We heard the sound of firecrackers on July Fourth.

bark The sound a dog makes. The dog's *bark* is very loud.

blast A loud noise. The foghorn sounded a *blast* over the dark ocean.

clap A loud noise. Did you hear that *clap* of thunder?

crash A loud noise. The trash can fell over with a *crash*.

groan A sound of pain. With a *groan*, Manuel rubbed his sore arm.

noise Sound; especially loud sound. The three cooks made a lot of *noise* banging the pots.

pop A sudden sharp noise. The balloon made a loud *pop* when it broke.

space *n.* A limited area. Patty
made a space on her shelf for
her award.
area An open space. Many parks
have an *area* for camping.
place A city, town, or other area.
The people chose a *place* to
build a new library.
room Space. The closet has *room*
for more boxes.

still *adj.* Quiet. The classroom was
still during the test.
calm Quiet; peaceful; still. The sea
was *calm* after the storm.
peaceful Quiet; calm. The sky
looked *peaceful* after the storm
ended.
quiet Having or making no noise.
The baby became *quiet* and fell
asleep.
ANTONYMS: loud, noisy

stop *v.* To come or bring to a halt.
Our teacher told us to stop
writing and put our pencils
down.
end To come or bring to an end.
The show will *end* with our
song.
halt To stop. We should *halt* to let
our friends catch up.
pause To make a short stop. Paul
had to *pause* to catch his
breath.
quit To stop. Please *quit* singing
that same song over and over.
ANTONYMS: begin, start

story *n.* A tale. I would like to read
a story about people or animals.
fable A short story teaching a
lesson. In one *fable,* a fox tricks
a crow into giving him some
cheese.
legend A story handed down from
earlier times. People long ago
had more than one *legend* about
how things in nature happened.
tale A story. Melissa tells a funny
tale about how she found her
turtle.

street *n.* A road. Our street does
not have a sidewalk.
avenue A broad street. Ben took a
walk down the *avenue.*
highway A main road. Trucks use
that *highway* to bring goods to
the city.
lane A narrow path or road. My
grandfather's house is the last
on the *lane.*
path A road or trail. Follow the
path to the clubhouse.
road An open way which vehicles,
persons, or animals travel to
get from one place to another.
Cars and trucks blocked the
road into town.
track A path. The many footprints
showed the *track* was still used.
trail A path. Karen followed the
narrow *trail* along the lake.

strong *adj.* Powerful; not weak.
The strong man lifted the
bricks.
firm Strong, steady. Americans
have *firm* ideas about freedom.

224

| swim | | trim |

forceful Strong. Washington was a *forceful* leader.

mighty Very strong. A *mighty* tractor pushed away the hills of mud.

sturdy Strong. The *sturdy* house did not shake in the wind.

tough Strong; rugged. Stuart wore a *tough* pair of shoes on his long hike.

ANTONYM: weak

swim *v.* To use your arms and legs to move along in water. Carol is learning to swim.

bathe To go into a body of water. In summer, we *bathe* in the river.

float To rest on top of water. The raft can *float* on the lake.

paddle To move your hands and feet in water. Most dogs will *paddle* across water.

T

talk *v.* To say words. Myra will talk to the class about her idea.

chat To talk in a relaxed way. My grandmother likes to *chat* with her friends.

discuss To talk over. The teacher said tomorrow we will *discuss* the meaning of the poem.

speak To say words. May I *speak* to Nora, please?

teacher *n.* A person who helps others learn. I am learning to play the violin from a music teacher.

coach A teacher or trainer, as for pupils, athletes, or actors. The *coach* taught the new player how to throw the football.

trainer A person who trains. The horse *trainer* pulled on the reins, and the horse stopped.

trap *v.* To catch and hold. The spider tries to trap a fly in its web.

catch To take in a trap or by means of a hook. Dad and I didn't *catch* anything on our fishing trip.

corner To force into a corner; to trap. The riders want to *corner* the wild horses in a valley.

snare To trap or catch with a rope loop that jerks tight. The farmers hope to *snare* the fox tonight.

trim *v.* To cut to make neat. The mother liked to trim the girl's hair.

clip To trim. The vet came to *clip* the poodle's hair for the summer.

crop To trim. The man wants to *crop* the dead limbs from the trees.

shear To cut hair or fleece. We *shear* the sheep for their wool, which is used in clothing and rugs.

See also **neat.**

225

turn

turn *v.* To move around. The wheels turn when a car moves.

spin To turn or whirl about. The child's pinwheel did not *spin* because there wasn't a breeze.

swirl To move or cause to move with a whirling or twisting motion. The fallen leaves *swirl* in the wind.

twirl To turn around quickly. Watch Lynn *twirl* her baton in the air.

whirl To spin or make spin around very fast. The dancers *whirl* across the floor.

wind To turn and twist. The ivy will soon *wind* up the tree trunk.

W

walk *v.* To go on foot. A baby learns to walk at about one year old.

hike To take a long walk. We should *hike* back to camp before we are too tired to walk.

want

march To walk with even steps. The high school band will *march* in the parade.

plod To walk heavily or with great effort. Martin must *plod* up a snowy hill to his home.

step To move by taking steps. Please *step* to the end of the line.

stroll To walk in a slow, easy way. Many people *stroll* in the park on Sunday.

tramp To walk with a heavy step. After the storm, we had to *tramp* through the mud.

want *v.* To wish for. Barney may want eggs for breakfast.

desire To want very badly. They all *desire* to become teachers.

hope To want and expect. I *hope* the weather will be warm tomorrow.

long To want greatly. I *long* to have a puppy.

wish To hope for something. We *wish* we were home now.

226

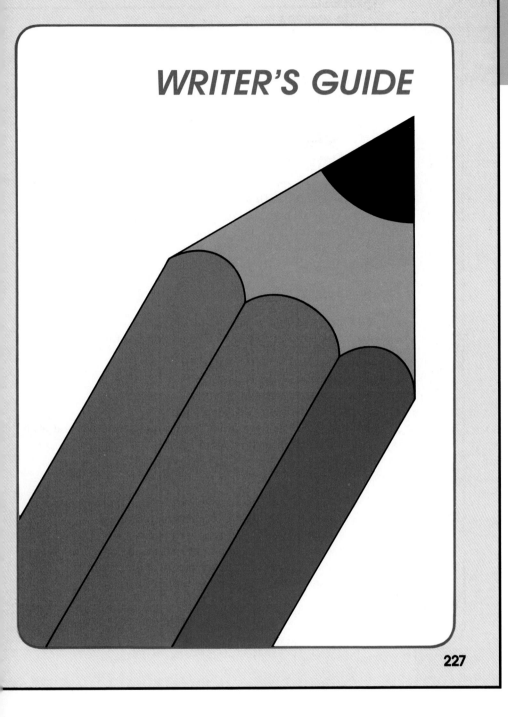

WRITER'S GUIDE

227

SPELLING RULES

Unit 1: **Short Vowel Sounds**

The short vowel sounds are usually spelled with one vowel letter.

- /a/ is spelled with **a,** as in happy.
- /e/ is spelled with **e,** as in pen.
- /i/ is spelled with **i,** as in hid.
- /o/ is spelled with **o,** as in dot.
- /u/ is spelled with **u,** as in sunny.

Unit 2: **Double Letters**

Some words end with a consonant sound that is spelled with double consonant letters after a short vowel sound.

- /l/ is spelled with **ll,** as in drill.
- /f/ is spelled with **ff,** as in cliff.
- /s/ is spelled with **ss,** as in less.
- /d/ is spelled with **dd,** as in odd.
- ☐ Some words do not have a short vowel sound but end with two consonant letters, as in roll.

Unit 3: **Verbs**

- If a verb ends with one vowel letter and one consonant letter, double the last letter before adding ed.
  chop—chopped   trip—tripped
- If a verb ends with one vowel letter and one consonant letter, double the last letter before adding ing.
  step—stepping   tap—tapping

228

Unit 4: Consonant Clusters

A **consonant cluster** is two or three consonant letters that are written together. All of the consonant sounds are heard.

- **cl** as in <u>cl</u>ose
- **dr** as in <u>dr</u>ive
- **fl** as in <u>fl</u>oor
- **pr** as in <u>pr</u>int
- **sn** as in <u>sn</u>ow
- **st** as in <u>st</u>ar
- **tr** as in <u>tr</u>ick
- **str** as in <u>str</u>ing
- **spr** as in <u>spr</u>ay

Unit 5: More Consonant Clusters

Consonant clusters often come at the end of words.

- **ct** as in a<u>ct</u>
- **st** as in we<u>st</u>
- **ft** as in li<u>ft</u>
- **nd** as in gra<u>nd</u>
- **ld** as in chi<u>ld</u>
- **lk** as in mi<u>lk</u>
- **mp** as in bu<u>mp</u>

Unit 7: More Letters Than Sounds

Some consonant sounds are spelled with more than one letter.

- The first sound in <u>th</u>at is spelled **th,** as in <u>w</u>ea<u>th</u>er.
- The first sound in <u>ch</u>ild is spelled **ch** or **tch,** as in <u>wh</u>ich and ki<u>tch</u>en.
- The first sound in <u>sh</u>ould is spelled **sh,** as in cra<u>sh</u>.
- The last sound in si<u>ng</u> is spelled **ng** or **n,** as in stro<u>ng</u> and a<u>n</u>gry.

229

Unit 8: **Plurals**

A word that names just one thing is **singular.** A word that names more than one thing is **plural.** Here are two ways to make a word plural.

- Add <u>s</u> to most words.
    robin—robins
- Add <u>es</u> to the words that end with <u>s</u>, <u>ss</u>, <u>sh</u>, or <u>ch</u>.
    circus—circuses
    guess—guesses
    bush—bushes
    ranch—ranches

Unit 9: **The Sound /j/**

Here are four ways to spell /j/.

- with **j** at the beginning of a word, as in <u>juice</u>
- with **g** before **e** or **i,** as in <u>gentle</u> and <u>giraffe</u>
- with **ge** at the end of a word, as in <u>cage</u>
- with **dge** after a short vowel sound, as in <u>bridge</u>

Unit 10: **The Sound /k/**

Here are three ways to spell /k/.

- with **c** or **k** at the beginning of a word, as in <u>cane</u> or <u>key</u>
- with **k** after a long vowel sound, as in <u>speak</u>
- with **ck** after a short vowel sound, as in <u>neck</u>

230

Unit 11: The Sound /s/

Here are four ways to spell /s/.

- with **s,** as in <u>s</u>uit
- with **c,** as in pen<u>c</u>il
- with **ce** at the end of a word, as in on<u>ce</u>
- with **ss,** as in mi<u>ss</u>

Unit 13: Verbs That End with <u>e</u>

- If a verb ends with <u>e</u>, drop the <u>e</u> before adding <u>ed</u>.
    skate—skated   hike—hiked
- If a verb ends with <u>e</u>, drop the e before adding <u>ing</u>.
    invite—inviting   live—living

Unit 14: The Vowel Sound /ā/

Here are five ways to spell /ā/.

- with **a-consonant-e,** as in br<u>ave</u>
- with **ai,** as in p<u>ai</u>d
- with **ay** at the end of a word, as in cl<u>ay</u>
- ☐ with **ey** at the end of a word, as in ob<u>ey</u>
- ☐ with **eigh,** as in <u>eigh</u>t

Unit 15: The Vowel Sound /ē/

Here are four ways to spell /ē/.

- with **ea,** as in t<u>ea</u>m
- with **ee,** as in ch<u>ee</u>k
- with **e,** as in <u>e</u>ven
- with **y** at the end of a word with more than one syllable, as in reall<u>y</u>

Unit 16: The Vowel Sound /ī/

Here are five ways to spell /ī/.

- with **i**-consonant-**e**, as in <u>bite</u>
- with **igh**, as in <u>fight</u>
- with **i**, as in <u>lion</u>
- with **y** at the end of a syllable or word, as in <u>myself</u>
- □ with **uy**, as in <u>buy</u>

Unit 17: The Vowel Sound /ō/

Here are four ways to spell /ō/.

- with **o**-consonant-**e**, as in <u>rose</u>
- with **oa**, as in <u>load</u>
- with **o**, as in <u>both</u>
- with **ow**, as in <u>window</u>

Unit 19: Compound Words

- A **compound word** is formed by putting two smaller words together.

  bed + room = bedroom   foot + ball = football

Unit 20: Contractions

- A **contraction** is a short way of writing two words together. Some of the letters are left out. An **apostrophe** (') takes their place.

  I <u>do</u> <u>not</u> have to work today.
  I <u>don't</u> have to work today.

  I hope <u>we</u> <u>will</u> be invited.
  I hope <u>we'll</u> be invited.

232

Unit 21: **The Sounds /ô/ and /ôr/**

Here are three ways to spell /ô/.

- with **a,** as in <u>walk</u>
- with **aw,** as in <u>jaw</u>
- with **au,** as in <u>cause</u>

Here are two ways to spell /ôr/.

- with **or,** as in <u>short</u>
- with **our,** as in <u>course</u> and <u>four</u>

Unit 22: **The Sounds /ûr/**

Here are four ways to spell /ûr/.

- with **ir,** as in <u>skirt</u>
- with **ur,** as in <u>burn</u>
- with **ear,** as in <u>earth</u>
- with **or,** as in <u>world</u>

Unit 23: **The Sounds /är/ and /âr/**

Here are two ways to spell /är/.

- with **ar,** as in <u>barn</u>
- □ with **ear,** as in <u>heart</u>

Here are two ways to spell /âr/.

- with **air,** as in <u>fair</u>
- with **ear,** as in <u>pear</u>

233

Unit 25: **More Plurals**

A **plural noun** names more than one thing.

- To form the plural of most nouns, add s.
    grade—grades   wheel—wheels
- To form the plural of nouns ending with a consonant and y, change the y to i and add es.
    fairy—fairies   guppy—guppies

Unit 26: **"Silent" Letters**

- When the sound of a letter is not heard, we call it a "silent" letter.
    knock   lamb   wrote

Unit 27: **Words That End with y**

- To form the plural of nouns ending with a consonant and y, change the y to i and add es.
    library—libraries
- If a verb ends with a consonant and y, change the y to i before adding ed.
    carry—carried
- If a verb ends with a consonant and y, just add ing.
    cry—crying

Unit 28: **The Sounds /əl/ and /ər/**

Here are two ways to spell /əl/.

- with **le,** as in bottle
- with **el,** as in nickel

234

Here are two ways to spell /ər/.

- with **er,** as in <u>summer</u>
- with **ar,** as in <u>sugar</u>

Unit 29: **Homophones**

- Homophones are words that sound alike but are spelled differently and have different meanings.
  break   brake

Unit 31: **The Sounds /o͝o/ and /o͞o/**

Here is one way to spell /o͝o/.

- with **oo,** as in <u>shook</u>

Here are four ways to spell /o͞o/.

- with **oo,** as in <u>balloon</u>
- with **ou,** as in <u>soup</u>
- with **ew,** as in <u>grew</u>
- □ with **o,** as in <u>lose</u>

Unit 32: **The Sounds /ou/ and /oi/**

Here are two ways to spell /ou/.

- with **ou,** as in <u>cloud</u>
- with **ow,** as in <u>crown</u>

Here are two ways to spell /oi/.

- with **oi,** as in <u>point</u>
- with **oy,** as at the end of <u>joy</u>

235

Unit 33: **Words with ou and ough**

The letters <u>ou</u> stand for three different sounds.

- The letters **ou** sound like the **u** in <u>much</u>, as in <u>touch</u>.
- The letters **ou** sound like the **ou** in <u>round</u>.
- With **gh, ou** sounds like the end of <u>paw</u>, as in <u>bought</u>.

The letters <u>ough</u> stand for two sounds.

- The letters **ough** rhyme with **oh,** like the **ough** in <u>though</u>.
- The letters **ough** rhyme with **uf,** like the **ough** in <u>rough</u>.

Unit 34: **Syllable Patterns**

- When a word has the same two consonant letters in the middle, divide the word into syllables between the two consonant letters that are the same.
    - cat·tle   din·ner   les·son
- Some words have two different consonant letters in the middle. Divide these words into syllables between the two consonant letters.
    - for·got   per·haps   won·der

Unit 35: **Another Syllable Pattern**

- When a word has one consonant letter between the two vowel sounds, divide the word into syllables before the consonant.
    - a·like   be·long   pa·per

236

TROUBLESOME WORDS TO SPELL

again	friend	mother	Thanksgiving
always	from	Mrs.	that's
am	fun	much	the
and	good	name	their
aunt	grammar	nice	then
baby	had	now	there
balloon	has	on	time
basketball	have	once	to
because	he	one	today
bought	here	our	tomorrow
boy	him	out	too
brother	his	party	train
brought	home	people	two
can	hope	play	vacation
children	house	please	very
cousin	I'm	pretty	we
day	in	said	were
didn't	it	saw	when
dog	know	sent	white
don't	like	snow	with
everybody	little	some	write
father	made	sometimes	writing
fine	make	store	you
football	me	teacher	your
for			

237

LANGUAGE: A Glossary of Terms and Examples

Grammar

Sentences

- A **sentence** is a group of words that tells a complete thought. Every sentence begins with a capital letter.
- The **subject** of the sentence is the part about which something is being said.

  The bicycle is here. Sally sees it.
- The **predicate** is all the words that tell something about the subject.

  The bicycle stopped. It is parked on the grass.
- A **statement** tells something. It ends with a period (**.**).

  I cut my finger.
- A **question** asks something. It ends with a question mark (**?**).

  Did you tell the secret?
- A **command** gives an order or a direction. It ends with a period (**.**).

  Go home.
- An **exclamation** shows strong feeling. It ends with an exclamation mark (**!**).

  What a great idea you have!

Nouns

- A **noun** is a word that names a person, place, or thing.
- A **common noun** names any person, place, or thing. It begins with a small letter.

  pumpkin   sister   floor   cabin

- A **proper noun** names a special person, place, or thing. A proper noun begins with a capital letter.

      Mrs. Takara   California
- A **singular noun** names one person, place, or thing.
- A **plural noun** names more than one person, place, or thing.
- To form the plural of most nouns, add <u>s</u>.

      dot—dots   pen—pens
- To form the plural of nouns ending in <u>s</u>, <u>ss</u>, <u>x</u>, <u>ch</u>, or <u>sh</u>, add <u>es</u>.

      circus—circuses   six—sixes   watch—watches
      class—classes   dish—dishes
- To form the plural of nouns ending with a consonant and <u>y</u>, change the <u>y</u> to <u>i</u> and add <u>es</u>.

      cherry—cherries   party—parties

Verbs

- An **action verb** is a word that shows an action. It is found in the predicate of a sentence.

      eat   scratch   dash   call
- A **linking verb** connects the subject with words in the predicate. It tells what the subject <u>is</u> or <u>is like</u>. The following forms of <u>be</u> are often used as linking verbs.

      am   is   are   was   were
- You add <u>ing</u> to make a verb that can be used with these linking verbs. These verbs tell what <u>is</u> or <u>was</u> happening.

      I am <u>carrying</u> it for her.
      We were <u>studying</u> together.
      I am <u>inviting</u> John to the party.
      They are <u>skating</u> at the lake.
      She is <u>hiking</u> up the mountain.

239

- A **helping verb** helps the main verb tell about an action.
  The following words are often used as helping verbs.

am	is	are	was
were	have	has	had

Verb Tenses

- **Present time verbs** tell about actions that are
  happening now.

  The curtains open.

  The people clap and cheer.
- **Past time verbs** tell about actions in the past. Most past
  time verbs end in ed.

  Abby walked quickly.   Her dog raced ahead.

  The dog hurried.   Abby chased it.

Irregular Verbs

- **Irregular verbs** are verbs that do not add ed to show
  past time. Some of these verbs are on the chart.

Verb	Present	Past
begin	begin(s)	began
choose	choose(es)	chose
grow	grow(s)	grew
shake	shake(s)	shook

Adjectives

- An **adjective** is a word that describes a noun.

  I have an old wagon.

240

Vocabulary

Compound Words

- A **compound word** is formed by putting two smaller words together.

  newspaper   haircut   football

Contractions

- A **contraction** is a short way of writing two words together. Some of the letters are left out. An apostrophe (') takes their place.

  I <u>can not</u> go to the party.
  I <u>can't</u> go to the party.

Homophones

- **Homophones** are words that sound alike. They are spelled differently and have different meanings.

  knot—not   brake—break

Rhyming Words

- **Rhyming words** end in the same sound.

  bake—lake   girl—whirl

Time-Clue Words

- **Time-clue words** help readers put a story in order.

  once   soon   when   before   after   finally

241

DICTIONARY: A Glossary of Terms and Examples

Alphabetical Order

- The order of letters from <u>A</u> to <u>Z</u> is called **alphabetical** order. Words in a dictionary are listed in alphabetical order. These words are in alphabetical order.

  bluebird
  crayon
  pirate
  pocket
  space
  spider

Guide Words

- There are two **guide words** at the top of each dictionary page. The word on the left is the first word on the page. The word on the right is the last word. All the other words on the page are in alphabetical order between those words.

package	paw

pack·age /pak′ij/ *n.* **1** Something wrapped up or tied up: We mailed a *package* to my brother at camp. **2** The box that holds something: The directions are on the *package*.
pad·dle /pad′(ə)l/ *n.* A short oar.
—*v.* **paddled, paddling 1** To use a paddle to move a boat. **2** To move your hands and feet in water: The children *paddled* about in the lake.

par·ent /pâr′ənt/ *n.* A person's mother or father.
park /pärk/ *n.* Land with trees, grass, and playgrounds.
—*v.* To put a car somewhere and leave it: *Park* the car over there.
part /pärt/ *n.* **1** A piece of a whole. **2** Share: We all must do our *part*. **3** A role in a play. **4** Where hair is divided after combing: The *part* in Lynn's hair is crooked.

242

Entry Word

- On a dictionary page, an **entry word** is a word in dark print that is followed by its meaning or meanings. Entry words appear in alphabetical order.

> **chew** /choo/ *v.* To grind up with your teeth: Always *chew* your food well.
> **child** /chīld/ *n., pl.* **children** A young boy or girl.
> **chin** /chin/ *n.* The part of your face below your mouth.

Pronunciation

- A **pronunciation** is given after each entry word in a dictionary. It is a special way of writing a word that shows how to say the word.

an·y   /en′ē/

Definition

- A **definition** tells what a word means in the dictionary. Many words have more than one definition.

> **move** /moov/ *v.* **moved, moving**
> **1** To go from one place to another: The car *moved* down the street.
> **2** To change where you live: The Engels *moved* to Grant Street.
> **3** To change position: The sleeping child didn't *move*.

243

Pronunciation Key

- A **pronunciation key** shows how to read the pronunciation.

act, āte, câre, ärt;   egg, ēven;   if, īce;   on, ōver, ôr;   bŏŏk, fōōd;   up, tûrn;
ə = a in *ago*, e in *listen*, i in *giraffe*, o in *pilot*, u in *circus*;   yōō = u in *music*;   oil;   out;
chair; sing; shop; thank; that; zh in *treasure*.

Syllables

- A word is made up of several parts called **syllables.** Each syllable has a vowel sound.
- In a word with two or more syllables in the dictionary, the **accent mark** (′) in the pronunciation shows which syllable is said with the most force.
- The syllable with the accent mark is called the **accented syllable.**

244

WRITER'S GUIDE

COMPOSITION
Guides for the
Writing Process

Writer's
Guide

COMPOSITION

Guides for the Writing Process

Prewriting

Use this checklist to plan your writing.

- Think about what you want to write.
- Think about why you are writing.
- Think about who will read your work.
- Ask yourself questions about your idea.
- Make a plan.
- Read over your plan.
- Add more ideas to your plan as you think of them.

Here are some prewriting plans.

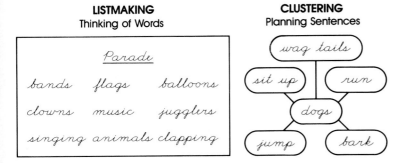

LISTMAKING
Thinking of Words

Parade

bands   flags   balloons

clowns   music   jugglers

singing animals clapping

CLUSTERING
Planning Sentences

wag tails

sit up   run

dogs

jump   bark

245

Writer's
Guide

COMPOSITION
Guides for the
Writing Process

WRITER'S GUIDE

CHARTING
Sensory Details

See	Hear	Taste	Feel	Smell
beach	waves crashing	salty water	hot sand	fresh air
picnic	people talking	sour lemonade	cool grass	meat cooking

MAPPING
Drawing a Plan

	friends	
Justin		Maria
shy	get lost on a hike	friendly

walk through the woods

meet a forest ranger

takes them back to school bus

246

Composing

Use this checklist as you write.

- Read over your plan.
- Use your plan.
- Write quickly.
- Do not worry about mistakes.
- Remember that you may get more ideas as you write.
- Add new ideas as you think of them.
- Think about why you are writing.
- Think about who will read what you write.

Revising

Use this checklist when you edit and proofread your work.

Editing

- Read over your work.
- Be sure your sentences make sense.
- Check that each sentence is a complete thought.
- Be sure each paragraph has a clear topic sentence.
- Check that all the detail sentences support the main idea.
- Be sure the words are lively and interesting.

Proofreading

- Be sure you used capital letters correctly.
- Be sure you used periods, question marks, and exclamation points correctly.
- Check the spelling of each word.
- Be sure you used each word correctly.
- Be sure the first line of each paragraph is indented.
- Be sure your handwriting is neat and readable.

Writer's Guide

Editing and Proofreading Marks

- Use **editing and proofreading marks** when you revise your writing. These marks help you see the changes you want to make.
- Remember that you can go back and change words or sentences as many times as you want or need to.

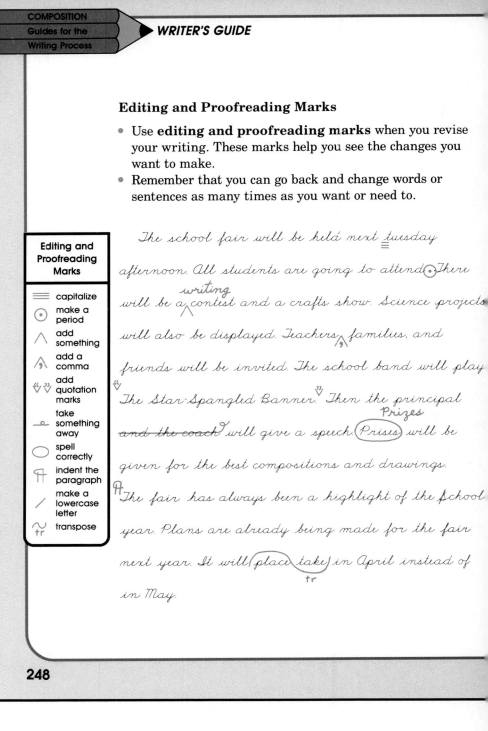

Editing and Proofreading Marks	
≡	capitalize
⊙	make a period
∧	add something
⋀	add a comma
⌄⌄	add quotation marks
ℯ	take something away
◯	spell correctly
¶	indent the paragraph
/	make a lowercase letter
∿tr	transpose

The school fair will be held next ̲t̲uesday afternoon⊙ All students are going to attend⊙ There will be a ^writing contest and a crafts show. Science projects will also be displayed. Teachers⋀ families, and friends will be invited. The school band will play ⌄The Star-Spangled Banner⌄ Then the principal ~~and the coach~~ will give a speech⊙ ◯Prizes◯ will be given for the best compositions and drawings. ¶ The fair has always been a highlight of the school year. Plans are already being made for the fair next year. It will ∿place take∿ in April instead of in May.

A Glossary of Terms and Examples

Kinds of Sentences

- A **sentence** is a group of words that tells a complete thought. Every sentence begins with a capital letter.
- A **statement** tells something. It ends with a period (.).

    I cut my finger.
- A **question** asks something. It ends with a question mark (**?**).

    Did you tell the secret?
- A **command** gives an order or a direction. It ends with a period (.).

    Go home.
- An **exclamation** shows strong feeling. It ends with an exclamation mark (**!**).

    What a great idea you have!

Paragraph

- A **paragraph** is a group of sentences that tell about one main idea.
- The **topic sentence** tells the main idea of the paragraph.
- The first line of a paragraph is indented.

Descriptive Paragraph

- A paragraph that describes a person, place, or thing is called a **descriptive paragraph.**
- A descriptive paragraph begins with a topic sentence. This sentence tells what the paragraph is about.
- Other sentences in the paragraph are the **detail sentences.** These sentences use clear and colorful words to describe the topic.

An example of a descriptive paragraph is on the next page.

249

**Writer's
Guide**

COMPOSITION
Guides for the
Writing Process

WRITER'S GUIDE

Here is an example of a descriptive paragraph.

> *It was the day after the big snowfall. Clean, white snow glistened in the bright sunlight. Long, sparkling icicles hung from roofs. Laughing children ran out of their houses. The cold, crisp air stung their cheeks. They carried bright red sleds in their arms.*

How-to Paragraph

- A **how-to paragraph** gives directions on how to do something.
- The topic sentence tells what the paragraph is about.
- The paragraph tells what materials are needed.
- Detail sentences explain the steps of how to do something.
- **Time-clue words,** words that help the reader follow the correct order, are also used. <u>First</u> and <u>last</u> are some examples of time-clue words.

Here is an example of a how-to paragraph.

> *Making play dough is easy. You need a cup of water, some food coloring, a cup of salt, two cups of flour, two tablespoons of oil, a bowl, and a big spoon. First, put the water in the bowl. Second, add the food coloring to the water and stir with the spoon. Next, add the salt, the flour, and the oil to the water mixture. Last, stir the mixture with the spoon until it is smooth.*

250

Friendly Letter

- A **friendly letter** has five parts.
- The **heading** contains the letter writer's address and the date. A comma is used between the name of the city and the state and between the day and the year.
- The **greeting** welcomes the person who receives the letter. The greeting begins with a capital letter. The greeting is followed by a comma.
- The **body** of the letter contains the message.
- The **closing** is the end of the letter. The first word is capitalized. A comma follows the closing.
- The **signature** is the written name of the person who wrote the letter.

Here is an example of a friendly letter.

> 1508 N.E. 49th St.
> Gladstone, Missouri 64118   **Heading**
> September 28, 20--
>
> Dear Mike,   **Greeting**
>   Thanks for your letter. I'm glad you are
> having fun with your grandparents. Dad   **Body**
> and I went fishing yesterday. Wish you could
> have been with us. See you soon.
>
>   Sincerely,   **Closing**
>   Dave   **Signature**

251

Journal

- A **journal** is something for you to write in every day. You can write about what happens to you each day.
- Each journal entry starts with the day and date.

Here is an example of a journal entry.

Saturday, October 13, 20—

Today was my ninth birthday. Mom and Dad invited my friends over for a surprise party. I was happy to see my friends. I thought everyone had forgotten my birthday.

Story

- A **story beginning** sets the scene for the action in the story. It tells <u>who</u> the story is about. It tells <u>what</u> is happening. It tells <u>where</u> it is happening and <u>when</u> it is happening.
- The **middle of the story** tells what happens to the characters. Sentences in a story must be in order so that the story makes sense.
- The **ending of the story** should tell how the characters solve their problems. It should answer the question <u>why</u>. Make sure the ending finishes the story.
- A story has a title. The first word and each important word begins with a capital letter.

See the example of a story on page 253.

> ### A Ride in a Big Truck
>
> Last summer I was riding with Dad in his big truck. We came to a tunnel in the city. We drove into the tunnel, and suddenly we were stuck. The tunnel was too low for the truck! Dad didn't know what to do. Then I had a good idea. I told Dad that maybe he should let some air out of our tires. A big smile came onto Dad's face. He let some air out of each tire. Then we drove out of the tunnel. Dad was proud of me, and I was proud of myself too.

News Story
- A **news story** is written to give readers information.
- The most important information in a news story is presented first.
- The answers to the questions <u>who</u>, <u>what</u>, <u>when</u>, <u>where</u>, and <u>how</u> are included at the beginning of the news story.
- A **headline** is a title that gives a short statement of the content of the story. The first word and each important word begin with a capital letter.

Here is an example of the beginning of a news story.

> ### Bantam Circus Comes to Mayfield
>
> A crowd of more than 1,000 people enjoyed the opening of the Bantam Circus last night at the County Fairgrounds. The circus, which has shows daily at 7:00 P.M. through Saturday, donated the money from last night's performance to three Mayfield charities.

253

Report

- A **report** presents facts about a topic.
- Before writing a report, take notes.
- Use your notes to make an **outline.** An outline has a title and lists the most important ideas from the notes.
- Write a paragraph for each main topic of the outline.

Here is an example of a title and first paragraph from a report.

A Comparison of Spiders and Insects

People often call spiders insects. but spiders are different from insects in many ways. Spiders have eight legs. Insects have only six legs. A spider's body has two sections. An insect's body has three sections. Spiders have no wings. Most insects have two wings.

Rhyming Poem

- The last words in many lines of poetry end in the same sound. When words end in the same sounds, they rhyme.

Here is an example of a rhyming poem.

The falling snowflakes make no sound
as they softly touch the ground
Like a mother dressed in white
come to kiss her babe goodnight.

254

MECHANICS: A Glossary of Rules

Capital Letters

Names and Titles of People and I

- Begin the name of a person with a capital letter.
    Douglas Dunn   Marsha Billings
- Begin titles of a person such as Ms., Mrs., Mr., and Dr. with a capital letter.
- Capitalize initials that take the place of names.
    Dorothy J. Arthur   Jackie E. Smith
- Always capitalize the word I.

Names of Places

- Begin each important word in the name of a town, city, state, or country with a capital letter.
    Enfield, New York
- Begin each important word in the name of a street and its abbreviation with a capital letter.
    Green St.

Names of Days, Months, and Holidays

- Begin the name of a day of the week or its abbreviation with a capital letter.
    Monday   Mon.   Wednesday   Wed.
- Begin the name of a month or its abbreviation with a capital letter.
    December   Dec.   August   Aug.
- Begin each important word in the name of a holiday with a capital letter.
    Washington's Birthday   Thanksgiving

255

Names of Books, Stories, Poems, and Television Shows

• Use a capital letter to begin the first, last, and all important words in the title of a book, story, poem, or television show.

<u>The Wind in the Willows</u>   "Sleeping Beauty"

Sentences

• Use a capital letter to begin a sentence.

That book is mine.

Punctuation

Period

• Use a period (.) at the end of a statement or command.

I see you.   Go away.

• Use a period (.) after an abbreviation.

Wed.   Ave.   A.M.   Dr.

• Use a period (.) after a numeral before the main topic in an outline.

I. United States
II. Mexico

Comma

• Use a comma (,) between the city and the state.

Baton Rouge, Louisiana   Albany, New York

• Use a comma (,) between the day and the year.

January 1, 1916

• Use a comma (,) after the greeting in a friendly letter and after the closing of any letter.

Dear Sara,   Your friend,

256

Question Mark

- Use a question mark (?) at the end of a question.
    Did they stay long?

Exclamation Point

- Use an exclamation point (!) at the end of an exclamation.
    What a pretty child!

Quotation Marks and Underline

- Use quotation marks (" ") before and after the title of a story or poem.
    "Cinderella"   "My Dog"
- Use quotation marks around a speaker's words when writing conversation.
    Marianne said, "I'm going home."
- Underline the title of a book or television show.
    <u>Encyclopedia Brown</u>   <u>The Cosby Show</u>

Apostrophe and Colon

- Use an apostrophe (') to show that one or more letters have been left out in a contraction.
    he's   we'll
- Add an apostrophe (') and an <u>s</u> to singular nouns to show possession.
    Fran's toy   student's book
- Add an apostrophe (') to plural nouns that end in <u>s</u> to show possession.
    the boys' bicycles   the Smiths' house
- Use a colon (:) between the hour and the minutes in the time of day.
    4:00   6:45   11:30

257

HANDWRITING: Alphabet and Common Errors

Uppercase Manuscript Alphabet

Lowercase Manuscript Alphabet

**Writer's
Guide**

Uppercase Cursive Alphabet

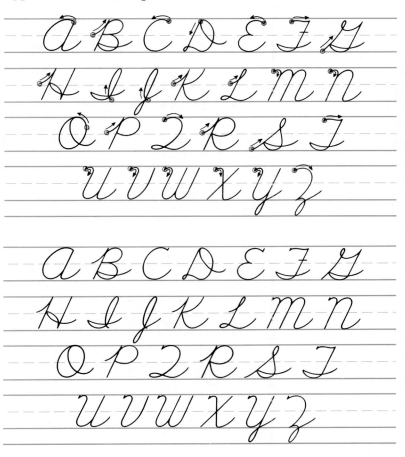

Lowercase Cursive Alphabet

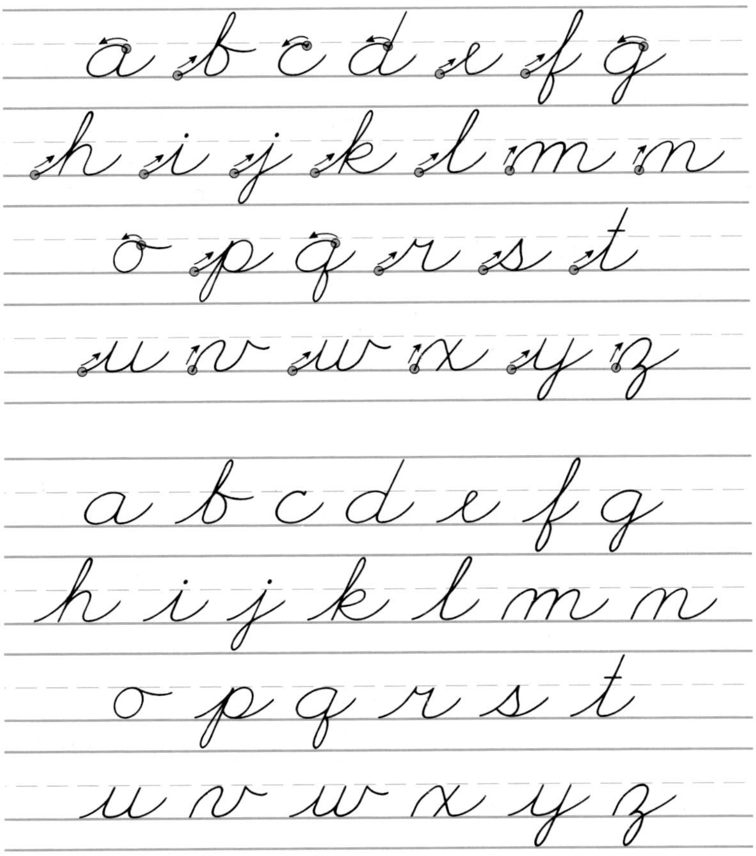

a b c d e f g
h i j k l m n
o p q r s t
u v w x y z

a b c d e f g
h i j k l m n
o p q r s t
u v w x y z

261

Common Errors–Manuscript Letters

- Write the letters correctly.

Be sure to retrace almost to the midline.
The **r** could look like **v.**

Wrong   Right

v   *r*

Be sure to start at the midline.
The **m** could look like cursive **n.**

Wrong   Right

m   *m*

Be sure not to loop in the retrace.
The **p** could look like cursive **p.**

Wrong   Right

p   *p*

Be sure to close the circle and retrace.
The **d** could look like cursive **cl.**

Wrong   Right

d   *d*

Be sure to close the circle.
The **g** could look like cursive **cj.**

Wrong   Right

g   *g*

262

Wrong   Right

q   q

Be sure to use the slant right stroke.
The **q** could look like **g.**

Wrong   Right

ie   u

Be sure not to loop in the retrace stroke.
The **u** could look like cursive **ie.**

Wrong   Right

K   k

Be sure to start the second stroke at the
midline. The **k** could look like uppercase **K.**

Wrong   Right

I   I

Be sure to use the across strokes.
The **I** could look like lowercase **l.**

Wrong   Right

O   Q

Be sure to add the slant stroke.
The **Q** could look like **O.**

263

Wrong	Right	
C	G	Be sure to use the across stroke at the midline. The **G** could look like **C**.
U	U	Be sure not to retrace. The **U** could look like cursive **U**.
O	D	Be sure to use a straight downstroke and retrace. The **D** could look like **O**.
w	W	Be sure to start at the top line. The **W** could look like lowercase **w**.

264

Common Errors–Cursive Letters

● Write the letters correctly.

Wrong	Right	Be sure not to loop. The **i** could look like **e.**

Be sure not to loop. The **i** could look like **e.**

Wrong	Right	Be sure to make a loop. The **e** could look like **i.**

Be sure to make a loop. The **e** could look like **i.**

Wrong	Right	Be sure to touch the top line. The **l** could look like **e.**

Be sure to touch the top line. The **l** could look like **e.**

Wrong	Right	Be sure the slant stroke returns to the bottom line. The **u** could look like **v.**

Be sure the slant stroke returns to the bottom line. The **u** could look like **v.**

Wrong	Right	Be sure not to loop. The **u** could look like **ee.**

Be sure not to loop. The **u** could look like **ee.**

Wrong	Right	Be sure to close the circle stroke. The **bi** could look like **lr.**

Be sure to close the circle stroke. The **bi** could look like **lr.**

265

Wrong	Right	Be sure to retrace with the overcurve. The **h** could look like **lr.**
tr	*h*	

Wrong	Right	Be sure to retrace to the midline. The **p** could look like **jo.**
jp	*p*	

Wrong	Right	Be sure to touch the midline twice. The **tri** could look like **tu.**
tri	*tri*	

Wrong	Right	Be sure to close the circle stroke. The **a** could look like **u.**
a	*a*	

Wrong	Right	Be sure to close the circle stroke. The **d** could look like **cl.**
d	*d*	

Wrong	Right	Be sure to loop left. The **g** could look like **q.**
q	*g*	

266

ong	Right	
m	*m*	Be sure to make cursive **m** look like manuscript **m**.
ong	Right	Be sure to make the straight slant in the right direction. The **ve** could look like **re**.
ve	*ve*	
ong	Right	Remember **P** does not join other letters. The **P** could look like **R**.
Re	*Pe*	
rong	Right	Be sure to touch the stem. The **K** could look like **H**.
K	*K*	
rong	Right	Be sure to start at the top line. The **N** could look like lowercase **n**.
n	*N*	
rong	Right	Remember **V** has no joining stroke. The **V** could look like **U**.
Ua	*Va*	

267

Remember **W** only joins with **h.**
The **We** could look like **Ule.**

Wrong   Right

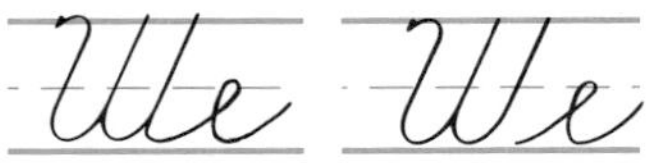

Be sure to start at the top line.
The **X** could look like lowercase **x.**

Wrong   Right

Be sure not to cross **T.**
The **T** could look like **F.**

Wrong   Right

Be sure to close the circle and not loop.
The **A** could look like **Cl.**

Wrong   Right

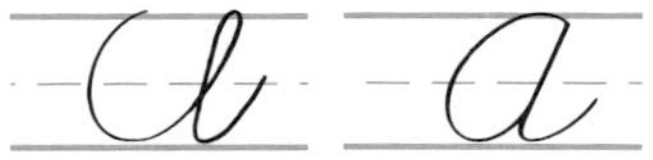

Be sure the joining stroke curves to the
midline. The **Ol** could look like **Al.**

Wrong   Right

Be sure to start at the midline and
undercurve to the top line. The **L** could
look like **Q.**

Wrong   Right

268

Be sure to slant the first stroke.
The **S** could look like **G**.

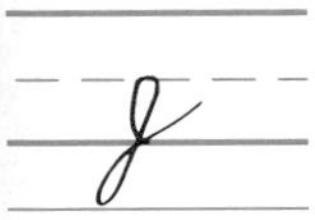

Wrong   Right

Be sure to curve to the top line.
The **J** could look like **g**.

Wrong   Right

269

This list shows all the words taught in Levels 1-6 of **Harcourt Brace Spelling.** Words in color are taught in this book. Each word is coded according to level.

FOR EXAMPLE: **string** 3-4; 4-14M; 2-27B means that **string** is a
Unit word in Level 3, Unit 4
Mastery word in Level 4, Unit 14
Bonus word in Level 2, Unit 27.

A

abandon 5-22B
ability 6-25
able 3-28
abnormal 6-16B
about 2-32; 3-32M; 1-25B
above 3-35; 5-25M
abrupt 6-1B
absence 6-1; 4-1B
abuse 6-10
accent 6-29; 5-35M
accept 4-13B
accidentally 5-25
according 5-7
account 5-31
accuse 4-9
ache 5-7
achieve 6-3
acorn 3-21B
acquaint 6-5B
across 2-11; 4-11M
act 3-5
action 5-11; 6-8M
activity 6-25
actor 4-25
add 3-2; 2-11B
addition 5-29; 6-25M
additional 6-23
addresses 5-8; 6-4M; 4-3B
adequate 6-33
adjective 5-35
adjust 6-7
adjustment 6-25B
admitted 6-33; 5-25B
adopt 6-1B
adore 6-16
adult 3-5B
adverb 5-35
advice 5-5B
advise 5-5B
affectionate 6-8B
afford 6-16
afraid 4-5; 5-25M; 2-20B
after 2-35; 3-28M; 1-19B
again 2-17; 3-35M
against 6-1; 5-1B
age 3-9; 5-10M
agent 5-10
ago 2-26; 3-35M

agree 4-5; 6-3M
agreement 5-29
agricultural 5-26B
ahead 3-35
aid 4-5; 6-17M
ailment 6-2
aim 4-5
air 3-23
airline 5-23
airmail 6-11
aisle 6-2
alarm 4-22; 3-23B
album 6-1
alert 4-23
algae 6-17B
algebra 6-27B
alike 3-35
all 1-32; 2-31M
alleys 5-8B
allies 5-8B
allow 5-17; 3-34B
allowance 6-9B
almanac 6-34B
alone 3-35
along 2-27
alphabet 4-9
already 6-11; 4-28B
also 2-26; 3-17M
altered 6-13B
although 3-33
always 2-31B
am 1-17; 2-5M
amendment 5-26
among 4-2; 6-1M
amount 5-14
amuse 6-10; 4-20B
amusement 5-29; 4-34B
anatomy 6-17B
anchor 5-7
ancient 5-11
and 2-5; 3-1M; 1-10B
angle 6-27
angry 3-7; 2-27B
animal 4-27; 6-28M
ankle 5-22; 4-26B
anniversary 4-17B
announcement 6-9B
annoy 5-14; 6-9M
annoying 5-25
another 3-7; 2-35B
answer 4-25; 3-28B
ant 2-5

antipollution 6-17
ants 3-25M
any 3-15
anyhow 4-28
anymore 5-23
anyone 3-19; 4-28M
anything 3-19M
anyway 3-19; 4-35M
apart 6-32
apartment 6-32; 5-19B
apologize 6-7B
apology 6-28
appeared 6-13
appetite 6-34
applaud 6-14
apple 3-1; 5-1M; 2-5B
applying 5-13
appoint 6-9; 5-14B
appointment 6-25
appreciate 6-35
approval 6-33
April Fools' Day 4-17
apron 5-22
Apt. (apartment) 4-13
aquarium 6-5B
Arbor Day 4-17
archery 5-19B
are 1-17; 2-33M
area 5-34; 6-34M
aren't 3-20B
argue 5-19; 3-23B
argument 5-19B
arise 5-5
arithmetic 6-35
arm 2-33; 3-23M
armor 5-21
around 3-35
arrange 5-10
arrangement 6-25
arrive 5-2
arrow 4-11
art 3-23
artificial 6-35B
artist 4-34; 3-23B
artistic 5-34
as 2-5
ashamed 5-11; 4-14B
ask 3-11
asleep 3-15; 5-3M; 2-21B

assembly 5-17B
assign 6-19; 4-7B
assignment 6-34
assure 5-11
astonishment 6-25
astronomy 6-28B
at 1-19; 2-5M
ate 2-19
athletics 6-34; 4-35B
atlas 6-1B
attack 5-25
attention 4-35; 6-8M
attitude 5-34B
attraction 6-25B
auction 6-14B
auditorium 6-14B
aunt 4-1
authentic 6-14B
author 6-21; 5-21B
authority 6-14B
autobiography 6-32; 5-35B
autograph 6-32
automatic 6-32
automation 6-14B
automobile 6-32
automotive 6-32
autos 6-4
autumn 6-19
available 6-2B
Ave. (avenue) 4-13
avenue 6-28
average 6-27
aviator 6-35
avoid 5-14; 4-19B
awake 3-14; 3-35M
award 5-19
aware 4-22
away 2-20; 3-35M
awful 6-14; 2-31B
awhile 3-16B
axle 6-5

B

baby 1-25; 3-27M
back 3-10; 4-9M
background 6-11; 4-28B
backward 6-33
bacon 4-26
bacteria 6-17B
bad 2-5
badge 4-10
badly 4-33M

baffle 5-32B
bag 2-1
baggage 5-17
bake 2-19; 3-13M; 1-23B
baker 4-34
bakeries 5-8
balance 6-31; 4-31B
ball 2-11; 2-31M
ballet 5-17B
balloon 3-31; 4-20M; 2-28B
ballot 5-32B
bamboo 5-15B
banana 4-35
band 2-1; 2-27M
bandage 4-1
bandages 3-8B
bank 2-27
banquet 6-5B
barbecue 6-34; 4-22B
barber 4-22; 5-19M; 3-23B
barefoot 5-23; 4-22B
bargain 5-22B
bark 3-23; 5-19M
barn 3-23; 4-22M
barrel 5-22
baseball 4-28; 5-23M
basic 5-33
basin 5-33
basketball 4-28; 6-11M
bat 3-3
batch 4-15B
batches 6-4
bath 4-14
bathe 4-15
batteries 5-8; 4-3B
battle 4-26
bazaar 5-5B
be 1-20; 2-1M
beaches 3-8; 4-3M
bear 3-23; 2-1B
beat 3-29
beautiful 4-33; 5-34M
beautifully 6-23
because 2-31; 3-35M
become 3-35
bed 1-14; 2-7M
bedroom 3-19; 5-23M
bee 1-20B

been 2-17
beet 3-29
before 2-33; 3-21M; 1-19B
beggar 6-21
begged 4-8; 6-13M
begin 3-35
beginning 4-11B
behave 5-2; 4-4B
behaving 3-13B
behind 3-35
beige 6-3B
believe 6-3
belong 3-35
below 3-35; 5-25M
benches 4-3
bend 3-5; 5-9M
beneficial 6-8B
benefit 6-28
beside 3-35; 5-31M
best 2-7; 2-13M
better 4-29; 2-7B
between 3-15; 5-3M; 2-17B
bewilder 6-1B
bicycle 5-5; 3-11B
big 1-11; 2-8M
bike 2-22; 3-16M; 1-26B
billboard 6-11; 4-28B
biography 5-35
bird 2-34; 3-22M
birds' 4-21
birth 4-23
birthday 3-22; 4-17M
biscuit 5-7B
bite 3-16; 5-2M
blanket 5-32; 2-27B
blast 5-9; 3-4B
bleakest 6-20B
blend 5-9; 3-5B
blew 2-28
blind 4-7
blink 2-27B
blister 6-29
block 5-9
bloom 4-20
blow 3-17; 4-7M
blown 6-2
blueberries 3-25B
blueberry 4-11
bluebird 3-22
blunder 5-1

copied 5-13M
copper 4-11
copy 3-27
cord 6-16
cordial 6-16B
corduroy 6-9B
corn 3-21; 4-22M
corner 3-34;
   4-25M; 2-33B
corral 3-21B
correction 6-8
corridor 6-33B
cost 3-10; 5-25M;
   2-10B
costume 4-29
cotton 4-11
couch 5-14
cough 4-9; 3-33B
could 2-29
couldn't 4-21
count 3-33
counter 5-31;
   6-26M
counting 4-8;
   6-13M
countless 5-31
country 3-33;
   5-26M
county 5-14;
   5-26M; 3-33B
couple 3-33B
courage 6-15
course 3-21
court 6-16; 3-21B
courteous 6-15B
courtesy 6-15
cousin 3-33;
   4-31M
cover 3-28; 5-21M
cow 2-4; 2-32M
coward 5-14;
   4-19B
cower 6-9; 5-14B
cozy 5-5; 3-15B
crack 5-7M
cracked 4-8
crank 5-9
crash 3-7; 5-11M;
   2-15B
crawl 2-31; 3-21M
crayon 3-14B
creak 5-3
cream 4-5
creamier 6-20
create 6-29
creative 6-34;
   4-35B
credit 5-33
creek 3-10B
crew 5-15
criticism 6-33
crook 5-15; 4-9B
crooked 3-31B
crop 4-1; 5-9M;
   3-1B
cross 2-11
crossing 5-4M
crowd 4-19
crown 3-32
cruel 4-20B
cruelest 6-20

crumb 6-19
crumbs 3-26B
crumpled 6-1
crunchy 5-9
crush 4-14
crust 5-9; 4-2B
crutches 5-8B
cry 3-27; 1-22B
crying 4-16
crystal 4-27
cube 4-20; 6-10M
culture 5-10
cunning 5-17B
cup 2-4; 3-10M;
   1-13B
cupboard 5-23;
   3-19B
curb 5-20; 6-15M
cure 6-10
curiosity 6-25
curious 6-10
curl 4-23
curtain 5-22
curve 5-20
custom 4-29
customer 5-7
cut 1-13; 2-4M
cute 4-20
cylinder 6-21B

D

dad 1-10; 2-2M
daily 5-2
daisy 5-5; 3-15B
damage 5-25;
   6-33M
damp 4-1; 6-1M
dancing 3-13;
   5-13M
danger 3-9;
   5-10M
dangerous 5-34;
   6-34M
dare 4-22
darkness 5-29
daughter 6-14;
   3-21B
dawn 6-14
day 1-31; 2-20M
daylight 4-29
deaf 5-1
dealer 5-21
dear 2-2; 2-34M;
   4-13M
debate 5-2
debt 5-16B
decay 4-27
deceive 6-3B
decide 3-11;
   5-5M
decimal 6-27
decision 6-8
deck 5-7
decorate 6-28M
decorating 5-13
decoration 6-25
decrease 5-25;
   6-26M
dedicate 6-28
deep 2-21; 3-15M
defeat 5-25

defend 5-9
definite 6-28
definition 6-26
delay 3-14B
delaying 5-13;
   4-16B
delicate 6-28
delicious 5-11;
   6-8M
delight 3-16B
delivered 6-13
democratic
   6-35B
denominator
   6-27
dent 5-9
deny 5-2; 3-27B
department 5-29
departure 6-32
depend 5-25;
   6-33M
depositing 6-13B
depth 6-1; 4-2B
desert 4-9
deserve 6-15;
   4-23B
design 6-19
designer 4-34B
desire 5-2; 4-4B
desk 2-7
desks 3-8; 5-8M
dessert 5-17;
   4-11B
destination 6-8
destroy 4-19;
   3-32B
detailed 6-2
details 3-25B
determine 6-34;
   4-35B
development
   6-25
devour 6-9; 5-14B
diagonal 6-27B
diagram 6-28B
dialogue 5-35B
diameter 6-27
diaries 5-8; 4-3B
dictate 6-26B
dictionary 5-35
did 1-11; 2-8M
didn't 3-20;
   4-21M
diet 6-29
different 4-11
difficult 5-17
dig 2-8; 1-11B
digestion 4-27;
   6-25M
digestive 6-17B
dimming 5-4B
dinner 3-34;
   5-17M; 2-2B
direction 5-11
director 6-21;
   4-25B
dirt 4-23
disagree 5-27
disappear 5-27
disapprove 5-15
disaster 6-21B

disconnect 5-27B
discount 5-31;
   6-26M
discourage 5-27B
discussion 5-29
disease 6-2; 4-5B
disguise 6-33
dish 2-15
dishes 3-8M
dishonest 5-27
dislike 5-27
disloyal 6-9
dismayed 5-13B
dismissal 5-34B
disobey 5-27
dispenser 6-32B
displays 5-8B
disposal 6-17
dissatisfy 5-27;
   6-35M
distance 5-5;
   4-10B
distraction 6-26B
ditch 4-15
divide 4-4; 6-31M
divided 3-13B
dividend 6-27
division 6-8
dizzy 5-17
do 2-28; 3-20M
dock 6-1
doctor 2-35;
   4-25M
dodge 4-10;
   6-7M
does 2-2; 2-17M
doesn't 3-20B
dog 2-10; 1-17B
dollar 2-35;
   3-28M
dominoes 6-4
done 2-9
donkeys 5-8
don't 3-20; 4-21M
door 2-33
dot 3-1
double 3-33;
   5-22M
doubled 5-13;
   6-26M
doubt 5-14
doubtful 5-28;
   6-19M; 4-33B
down 1-19; 2-32M
downpour 3-21B
downstairs 3-19B
downtown 4-28
dozen 4-26
Dr. (doctor) 4-13
Dr. (drive) 4-13
draft 5-9
dragon 5-33
drain 5-2
draw 2-31; 3-21M
drawer 3-4
drawing 4-34
dream 3-15; 2-21B
dreaming 4-8B
drenched 6-1;
   4-2B
dress 2-7; 2-14M

drew 5-15
dried 4-16
drift 5-1
drill 3-2
drilling 4-34M
drink 2-27
drive 3-4
driver 4-34
driving 4-16
drizzle 5-17
drop 3-3; 2-10B
dropped 5-4
drown 4-19; 6-9M
drowsy 5-25;
   6-33M
drug 4-2
drugstore 4-28
dry 2-23; 3-27M;
   1-22B
duck 2-4
ducks 3-8M
dull 4-11
dump 4-2
during 4-14
dusk 5-1
dust 3-5; 5-1M;
   2-13B
duty 4-20
dwarf 5-19B
dwell 5-1; 3-1B

E

E. (east) 4-13
each 2-16; 3-7M
eagle 3-28
earliest 6-20
early 3-22; 2-34B
earn 3-22; 6-15M
ears 3-25
earth 3-22; 2-15B
earthquake 6-11;
   4-28B
easel 5-3B
easier 6-20M
easily 6-23; 4-33B
east 3-5
easy 2-21; 3-15M
eat 1-29; 2-21M
eavesdrop 6-11;
   5-23B
echoes 6-4
eclipse 4-27
ecology 6-17
economy 5-26B
edge 3-9
editor 5-21
education 5-29
egg 2-11; 3-2M
eight 3-14; 2-20B
either 3-28
electing 5-4
election 5-26
Election Day 4-17
electric 5-34
electricity 6-25
elephant 5-34;
   6-28M
elevator 6-28
eligible 6-35B
else 3-1; 5-5M
embarrass 5-17B

emblem 5-1B
emergency 6-15;
   4-23B
emotional 6-26
emperor 5-34
employed 5-13;
   4-19B
employer 6-9
empty 3-27; 2-21B
encore 6-16
encouragement
   5-29B
end 2-7
endangered
   6-17; 4-27B
endless 5-28
enemy 5-34;
   6-28M; 3-27B
energetic 6-33B
energy 6-17;
   4-27B
engine 4-10;
   6-7M
enjoy 3-32; 5-31M
enjoyable 5-14
enjoyed 4-16M
enjoyment 4-34;
   5-29M
enlargement
   6-25B
enormous 5-25
enough 3-33
enter 5-31
entire 5-2; 4-4B
entrance 5-31;
   6-26M
entry 5-31; 6-26M
envelope 5-34
envied 5-13
environment
   6-17; 4-27B
envy 3-27B
equal 4-26;
   5-22M; 6-27M
equality 6-25
equation 6-8;
   6-27M
equator 6-5;
   4-25B
equipment 4-34;
   6-25M
erode 5-3B
error 6-21; 4-25B
evaporate 6-35
even 3-15; 5-22M
evening 3-15B
ever 2-35; 3-28M
every 3-15; 1-32B
everybody 3-19
everyday 4-28;
   6-11M; 3-19B
everywhere 5-23;
   3-19B
evil 5-22
exact 6-5
examination
   5-29B
examine 6-5
example 6-5
excellent 4-35;
   6-5M

helper 4-34M
helpful 5-28M
helping 4-8M
helpless 5-28
hen 1-14; 2-7M
her 2-34
herb 5-20
herbicide 6-17
herd 5-20
here 2-17; 2-34M;
    3-29M; 1-19B
here's 4-21B
heroes 6-4
hers 4-21
herself 3-19;
    4-23M
he's 3-20
hesitated 5-13B
hibernate 4-7B
hibernation 6-35
hid 3-1
hide 3-16; 2-22B
high 2-23; 3-16M
highway 3-16B
highways 5-8
hiked 3-13
hiking 4-34M
hill 1-11; 2-11M
him 2-8; 1-11B
himself 3-19;
    5-23M
hinder 5-1B
hinge 5-10
his 2-8
historian 6-16B
historical 5-31B
history 5-31B
hit 2-8; 1-11B
hoard 6-16B
hoarse 6-16; 4-22B
hobbies 4-3;
    3-25B
hoist 6-9B
hold 2-26; 3-5M
hole 4-4; 3-29B
holidays 4-17
hollow 3-34B
home 1-26; 2-25M
homophone 5-35
honest 5-16;
    6-19M
honor 5-16
hood 5-15
hook 4-9
hop 1-16; 3-3M
hope 2-25; 4-4M;
    1-26B
hopeless 5-28
hoping 3-13
horizontal 6-23B
horn 3-21
horror 5-21
horse 3-21
horseback 5-23;
    4-28B
hose 4-9
hospital 5-22
hot 1-16B
hotel 4-31
hottest 6-20
hour 5-16; 6-19M

house 2-32;
    3-32M
how 2-32; 3-33M
howl 4-19; 5-14M
huge 4-20; 6-10M
humanity 6-25B
humid 4-27;
    6-10M
humidity 4-27;
    6-35M
humor 5-21
humorous 6-10B
hunger 5-32
hungry 3-7; 2-27B
hunt 3-1; 4-2M
hunter 4-25; 6-17M
hurdle 5-20
hurl 6-15
hurricane 4-27
hurry 3-27; 4-31M
hurrying 4-16
hurt 2-34; 3-22M
husband 5-32
Hwy. (highway)
    4-13
hydrogen 5-2
hygiene 6-3
hymn 6-19

I

I 1-17; 2-23M
ice 3-11; 4-27M
I'd 4-21
idea 4-35; 5-34M
if 2-8
ignore 6-16
I'll 3-20; 4-21M
ill 3-2
I'm 3-20
image 6-7
imagination 5-11B
imagine 5-10
imitate 6-28B
imitation 6-35
immature 6-10B
immediately
    6-23B
immense 5-5B
immune 6-10B
impatient 6-22;
    5-27B
imperfect 6-15B
impersonal 6-22B
impolite 6-22
import 6-32
importance 4-35
impossible 6-22
improvement
    4-34; 6-25M
in 1-19; 2-8M
inaccurate 5-27B
incapable 6-22B
inches 3-8
incomplete 5-27;
    6-22M
incorrect 5-27
increase 5-25;
    4-5B
Independence
    Day 4-17

independent
    6-35B
industrial 5-26B
industry 6-34;
    4-35B
inflate 5-2B
information 6-26
initial 6-8
inquire 5-7
insect 5-9; 3-5B
insecure 6-22
inside 3-19M
inspect 6-26
inspector 6-21B
install 6-14
instead 5-1B
instrument 6-25
insulate 6-34
interest 6-34;
    4-35B
interior 5-25B
intermission
    6-35B
interrupt 5-17B
intestine 6-17B
into 3-19M
introduction 6-33
invention 4-35;
    6-34M
inventor 5-21
investigate 5-2B
invisible 6-22
invitation 6-35;
    4-13B
invite 3-13
invited 4-16
irrigation 5-26B
irritate 6-33B
is 2-8; 3-20M
island 4-7
isn't 3-20
issue 5-11
it 1-11; 2-8M
it's 3-20
its 4-21
itself 5-23
I've 4-21

J

jacket 4-9; 3-10B
jam 3-9
jammed 5-4
jar 2-3; 2-33M;
    3-9M
jaw 3-21
jazz 5-17
jest 5-9B
jet 2-3; 3-9M
jewelry 5-15B
jewels 5-15
job 2-10; 3-9M
jogger 5-21
join 5-14; 6-7M;
    3-9B
joint 4-19
joke 3-17; 5-3M;
    2-3B
journal 6-15;
    5-35B
journey 6-15

joy 3-32; 1-31B
joyful 4-19; 5-31M
Jr. (junior) 4-13
judge 3-9; 6-7M
judgment 5-29B
jug 3-9
juggle 5-17
jugs 4-3M
juice 3-9; 5-5M
jumble 6-7
jump 2-9; 3-9M;
    1-13B
jungle 5-32; 3-9B
junior 6-7
junk 6-7
just 2-9; 3-9M
justice 5-26
juvenile 6-7B

K

keep 2-4; 3-10M
kennel 5-17
kept 3-10
kettle 4-26; 3-10B
key 3-10; 2-4B
khaki 6-19B
kick 3-10; 4-9M;
    2-4B
kind 2-23; 4-7M
kindness 3-10;
    5-29M
kiss 3-2
kitchen 3-7; 2-16B
kite 2-4; 2-22M
kitten 3-10;
    4-26M; 2-4B
knapsack 5-16B
knead 5-16;
    3-26B
knee 3-26; 4-5M
kneel 5-16; 3-26B
knew 3-26
knife 3-26B
knight 5-16
knit 3-26
knives 5-8
knob 5-16; 6-19M
knock 3-26;
    5-16M
knoll 6-19B
knot 3-26; 5-16M
knotting 5-4B
knotty 5-16
know 2-25; 3-26M
knowledge 5-16
known 3-26;
    5-16M
knuckle 5-16B

L

label 5-22
labor 5-21B
Labor Day 4-17
lady 3-27
lake 3-14; 2-19B
lamb 3-26
lamp 4-1
lands 3-25
language 6-7;
    4-10B
lantern 5-32

large 3-9; 2-3B
largest 4-16;
    6-20M
lassos 6-4B
last 2-5; 3-1M
late 2-19; 3-14M;
    1-23B
lately 4-33; 6-23M
laugh 4-9; 2-17B
laughing 5-4
laundry 6-14
lawn 6-14
lawyer 6-14B
lay 3-14
leader 5-31;
    6-32M
leadership 5-31
learn 3-22; 6-15M;
    2-34B
leather 4-15
leave 2-21; 4-5M
led 1-14B
ledge 4-10; 3-9B
left 2-3; 3-5M
leg 2-7; 3-1M
legal 5-33B
legend 5-33B
legislature 6-35B
leisure 6-8B
lemon 4-26
length 4-14
lenses 6-4; 4-3B
less 3-2
lesson 3-34;
    4-26M
let 1-14; 2-3M
let's 3-20
letter 3-28; 4-13M;
    2-35B
lettuce 4-10
level 3-28; 4-26M
liar 6-29B
liberty 5-26
library 3-27
license 5-5
lied 5-13
life 3-16; 4-4M;
    2-22B
lift 3-5; 4-1M; 2-8B
lights 3-8M
like 1-26; 2-22M
likely 4-33; 6-23M
likeness 5-29;
    6-25M
limb 6-19; 3-26B
limelight 6-11B
limit 5-33
Lincoln's Birthday
    4-17
line 3-16; 5-2M
lion 3-16; 4-26M;
    2-23B
liquid 5-7B
listen 3-11;
    3-26M; 2-17B
lists 3-8; 4-3M
literature 5-35B
little 1-32; 2-11M
live 2-3
livelier 6-20;
    4-16B

living 3-13
load 3-17
loaded 4-8
loaves 5-8
location 6-25
lock 2-10B
lodge 6-7; 4-10B
logic 5-33B
loneliest 6-20;
    4-16B
lonesome 5-3;
    4-4B
long 2-27
look 1-28; 2-29M
looked 4-8
lookout 3-31B
loose 5-15
lose 3-31
losses 4-3; 6-4M
lost 2-10
lot 2-10; 1-16B
loud 3-32; 5-14M
loudly 4-33M
love 4-13M
loved 3-13
lovely 4-33
low 2-25; 3-17M
loyal 4-19; 5-14M;
    3-32B
loyalty 5-14
luck 2-9
lucky 3-10; 5-7M;
    2-4B
luggage 5-32B
lumber 6-21
lunar 5-21
lunch 2-16; 3-7M
lungs 6-17B
lying 5-13

M

machine 4-15;
    3-35B
machinery 6-35
mad 2-1
made 1-23;
    2-19M
magazine 6-28
magic 3-9; 5-33M
magnet 4-27
magnify 5-2B
mail 3-14; 4-5M;
    2-1B
mailed 5-4
main 3-29
maintain 6-26;
    5-2B
major 5-31B
majority 5-31B
make 1-23;
    2-19M
making 4-16M
mammal 5-17
mammoth 6-29;
    5-32B
man 2-5; 1-10B
manage 5-10;
    3-13B
manager 5-34;
    4-34B
mane 3-29

ridge 6-7
right 2-23; 3-16M
rigid 5-33
ring 2-27
riot 6-29B
ripe 4-4; 6-3M
rival 6-33
river 3-1; 3-28M
road 2-26; 1-29B
roar 4-22; 6-16M
roast 4-7; 2-26B
roasting 5-4
robin 2-1B; 4-31M
robins 3-8
robot 5-33
rock 3-1
rocket 5-7
rocking 4-34M
rode 3-29
rodeos 6-4B
roll 3-2
roof 3-31; 4-20M
room 2-28; 3-31M
roommate 6-11;
  5-23B
root 4-27
rope 1-26; 2-25M
rose 3-17
rough 3-33; 4-9M
round 3-33; 2-32B
row 2-25; 3-33M
royal 4-19; 6-9M
rub 2-9; 3-3M
ruin 6-29
rumor 6-21; 4-20B
run 1-13; 2-9M
runner 5-31M
rural 5-22B
rustle 5-16

s

S. (south) 4-13
sad 1-10B
saddest 6-20
saddle 5-22
sadness 5-25
safe 3-14; 2-19B
safely 4-33M
safer 4-16; 6-20M
said 1-25; 2-17M
sail 3-29
sailing 4-8
sailor 4-25
salad 4-31; 5-33M
salary 6-28
sale 3-29
Sally's 4-21
salmon 6-19
salute 6-31
salvage 5-10B
same 2-19;
  3-14M; 1-23B
sample 5-32
sandal 5-22
sandwiches 4-3;
  3-8B
sat 1-10; 2-5M
satisfying 5-13B
saucer 5-21;
  6-14M
sausage 6-14

save 2-19; 3-13M;
  1-23B
saw 1-32; 2-31M
say 1-31; 2-3M
saying 4-16M
scared 4-16;
  5-25M
scarves 5-8
scene 4-10
scenery 4-35
scent 4-10; 3-29B
schedule 5-7B
school 2-28;
  3-31M; 1-32B
science 4-10
scientific 6-35
scientist 4-34
scissors 5-17B
scold 3-17B
scoop 5-15
scooter 4-20
scorch 6-16;
  4-15B
scout 4-19
scowl 5-14
scrap 5-1; 4-1B
scrape 4-4
scratch 4-15; 3-4B
scrawny 6-14B
screamed 4-8
screen 5-3; 4-5B
scribble 6-26B
scrub 3-3B
scrubbing 5-4
sculptor 6-21B
S.E. (southeast)
  4-13
seals 4-3
search 6-15;
  3-22B
season 5-5
secret 3-11B
section 4-29
secure 6-10
security 6-25
see 1-20; 2-3M
seed 2-3; 3-11M
seek 4-9
seemed 4-8
seen 3-15; 4-5M
seize 6-3; 4-9B
seldom 4-29;
  6-29M; 3-34B
selection 5-11
self 4-2
selfish 6-23; 4-14B
senate 6-31B
senator 6-28
sensational 6-23
sense 5-5
sensible 5-34B
sent 2-7; 3-11M
sentence 3-11;
  5-35M
separate 6-28B
sergeant 5-19
serious 5-34
serve 6-15M
served 5-13
service 5-5; 4-10B
set 2-7

settle 4-11
settlement 5-29
settlers 5-17
several 4-26;
  6-23M
severe 6-31
severest 6-20B
sewing 4-34
shack 5-11; 3-7B
shade 4-14
shadow 4-7;
  6-31M; 3-17B
shake 2-19B
shall 3-1
shampoo 5-15;
  3-31B
shapes 3-25
share 4-22
sharp 4-14
sharpest 6-20
she 1-34; 2-15M
sheep 2-15; 6-4M;
  1-28B
sheepish 6-23
she'll 4-21
shell 3-2; 4-11M;
  2-11B
shellacked 6-13B
shelter 5-11
shelves 5-8
shepherd 5-16
sherbet 5-11B
sheriff 5-17; 4-11B
she's 3-20
shield 6-3B
shift 5-1; 4-1B
shine 3-7; 4-14M;
  2-15B
shiny 4-33; 5-11M
shirt 4-23
shock 5-7
shoe 2-15; 2-28M
shone 4-14
shook 3-31;
  5-15M; 2-29B
shop 2-10; 2-15M;
  1-34B
shopped 3-3B
shopping 4-8
shore 4-14; 6-16M
short 3-21; 5-11M;
  2-33B
should 2-29;
  3-26M
shoulder 6-2;
  3-33B
shout 3-7; 3-32M;
  2-15B
shouting 5-4
shovel 3-28;
  4-31M
show 1-34; 2-25M
shower 5-11
shown 4-14
shriek 6-3B
shrill 5-9B
shrub 5-9
shrunk 5-9
shut 2-15; 3-7M;
  1-34B

shy 3-16; 5-11M;
  2-23B
sick 2-4; 3-10M
sickness 5-29
side 2-22; 1-26B
sidewalk 4-28;
  5-31M
siege 6-3B
sight 3-16; 4-7M;
  2-23B
sign 5-31B
signal 4-26
signature 5-31B
silent 5-33B
silver 5-32; 3-11B
similar 6-21B
simplest 6-20;
  4-16B
simplify 6-33B
since 4-10; 3-11M
sincerely 5-5;
  4-13B
sincerity 6-25B
sing 2-27; 3-7M
single 5-32
singular 5-35
sir 3-22; 4-23M
sister 2-35; 3-34M
sit 2-8; 3-1M;
  1-11B
situation 6-8
six 3-11
skate 3-13; 2-19B
skater 4-34
skeleton 4-27
sketches 5-8B
ski 5-3
skinned 3-3; 5-4M
skirt 3-22; 5-20M
sky 2-23; 3-27M;
  1-22B
slang 4-14B
slant 5-9
sleep 1-28; 2-13M
sleepless 5-28
sleepy 5-25;
  6-33M
sleigh 6-3
slid 4-1
slide 2-22B
slight 4-7B
slimmer 6-20B
sling 4-14
slipped 4-8
slippers 4-11
slippery 4-35
slither 4-15B
slogan 5-22B
slope 3-17B
slow 2-25; 3-33M
slumber 6-29
small 2-14; 3-4M
smash 5-1; 3-1B
smell 3-2; 4-2M
smile 2-14B
smiling 3-13
smoke 4-4; 3-10B
smooth 5-15;
  3-31B
smother 4-15B
smudge 5-9B

snack 6-1; 4-1B
snag 5-1
snail 5-2; 3-14B
snake 3-14; 5-2M;
  2-19B
snapping 5-4
snobbish 6-23
snow 3-4; 4-27M
so 1-22; 2-26M
soak 4-7; 5-3M
soap 2-26; 4-7M
soar 4-22
social 5-11; 6-8M
society 5-26B
soda 4-31
soft 2-10; 3-11M
softness 5-29M
soil 5-14
solar 6-17
sold 3-17
solemn 6-19
solid 5-1; 6-1M
solution 6-25
solve 6-1
some 2-9; 1-25B
somebody 6-11
sometimes 3-19;
  4-28M
son 3-29; 2-9B
song 2-10
soon 2-3; 2-28M;
  3-31M
soothe 6-33B
sorrow 5-25
sound 3-32;
  4-19M; 2-32B
sounding 5-4
soup 3-31
source 6-16
south 4-19; 3-33B
southern 3-33B
southwest 4-28
soybean 6-9;
  4-19B
space 4-4; 5-2M;
  3-4B
spacecraft 5-23B
spade 5-2
sparkle 5-32B
speak 3-10; 4-9M
speaker 5-21
special 5-11;
  4-17B
species 6-17;
  4-27B
speeches 4-3
speechless 5-28
spell 3-2; 2-7B
spelling 4-8M
spend 4-2; 6-1M;
  2-7B
spider 4-31;
  5-33M; 3-35B
spies 3-25; 4-3M
spill 3-2
spinach 4-15
spirit 6-31; 4-1B
splash 4-14;
  5-11M
splendid 6-29

splint 5-9
split 4-1; 3-4B
spoil 3-32B
spoiled 5-4
spoke 3-17; 2-25B
spoken 4-31
sponge 5-1B
spool 4-20
spoon 4-20; 2-28B
sports 6-16
spot 2-14; 3-3M;
  1-16B
spray 3-4
spread 4-2; 3-4B
spring 3-4; 4-1M
sprinkle 5-32
squad 6-5
squall 6-14B
square 5-7; 6-5M;
  6-27M
squeak 6-2
squeeze 5-3; 4-5B
squirm 6-5; 4-23B
squirrel 5-17
squirting 6-13
St. (street) 4-13
stable 5-32
stage 4-10
stairs 3-23
stalk 6-14; 3-21B
stammer 3-34B
stamp 5-9; 3-5B
stand 2-13
star 3-4
starch 4-22B
starches 6-4
stare 3-13; 2-13B
start 2-33; 3-4M;
  3-23M
starve 5-19
state 3-4; 5-26M
statehood 5-26
statement 5-35
station 5-9B
stationary 6-8M
stationery 5-11B
stay 2-20; 3-4M;
  1-31B
stayed 4-16
staying 5-13M
steadier 6-20;
  4-16B
steal 4-5
steam 4-5; 6-2M
steel 5-3
steep 4-5; 2-13B
steering 6-13;
  4-34B
step 3-3; 5-9M;
  2-7B
stepped 4-8;
  6-13M
stereos 6-4
stern 4-23
stew 3-31B
stick 3-4; 2-13B
sticky 4-33M
still 2-13; 3-2M
sting 4-1
stingy 6-33
stir 4-23; 5-20M

stirring 3-3B
stitches 5-8; 4-3B
stock 5-1; 4-1B
stockholder 6-11B
stole 4-4
stomachs 4-3
stone 2-25
stones 3-25M
stood 3-31; 5-15M; 2-29B
stool 4-20
stop 1-16; 2-10M
stopped 3-3; 5-4M
storage 5-10
store 2-13; 4-22M
stories 4-3; 5-35M; 3-25B
storm 6-16
story 1-25; 2-13M
stout 6-9
stove 3-17; 5-3M; 2-25B
stow 6-2; 4-7B
straight 4-5; 2-20B
strange 4-10; 3-9B
strap 4-1; 3-1B
straw 3-21; 6-14M; 2-31B
stream 5-3
streamlined 6-11; 5-23B
street 2-21; 1-28B
streets 3-25M
strength 4-14B
strenuous 6-34B
stress 5-17
strike 5-2
string 3-4; 4-14M; 2-27B
stroll 3-17B
strong 3-7; 6-14M; 2-27B
struck 4-2; 3-1B
struggling 5-13B
stubborn 5-17
studied 5-13
study 3-27
studying 5-13
stuff 3-2; 4-2M; 2-11B
stumble 5-32B
stunned 5-4B
stunt 4-2
sturdy 6-15; 4-23B
style 5-2
stylish 6-23B
subject 5-35
submerge 6-15B
subscription 5-29B
succeeded 6-13B
successful 5-17B
sudden 4-11; 3-2B
suddenly 4-35; 5-34M
sufficient 6-33
suffix 6-5; 5-35B
sugar 3-28; 5-21M; 2-35B
suggest 4-10

suggestion 5-29
suit 3-11
summer 3-28; 4-11M; 2-9B
sun 1-13B
sunny 3-1; 3-34M; 2-3B
sunset 4-29
sunshine 4-28
superstition 5-29B
supervision 6-8B
supper 4-29; 5-21M
supply 3-27B
suppose 5-17M; 3-13B
supposed 5-13
surface 6-15; 4-23B
surgery 6-7B
surplus 5-20B
surprise 4-4; 3-13B
surround 6-9; 5-14B
survival 6-17
suspenders 6-21B
suspense 6-32B
suspenseful 5-28B
sustain 6-2B
swallow 5-32; 6-29M; 3-34B
swap 3-3B
swapped 5-4; 4-8B
swarm 5-19
sweater 4-25; 2-35B
sweet 2-14B
sweetest 6-20
swell 4-11
swept 5-1
swerve 5-20
swift 4-1; 3-1B
swim 2-14; 3-4M
swimmer 5-21; 4-25B
swirl 5-20
swollen 5-22; 4-26B
syllable 5-35
system 6-1

T

table 3-28; 4-26M
tagging 3-3; 5-4M
tail 2-20
tailor 5-21
take 1-23
talent 6-31; 4-31B
talk 3-21; 2-31B
tall 2-31; 3-21M
tangle 5-32
tape 3-13
tapping 3-3
tardiness 5-29
tardy 5-19
target 5-32
tariff 5-26
task 4-1; 5-9M
taste 3-13; 4-4M
tasteless 5-28M

tasty 4-33
taught 3-21; 6-14M; 2-31B
tax 6-5M
taxes 5-8; 4-3B
taxi 6-5
teach 2-21; 4-5M
teacher 3-7; 5-10M
team 3-15; 5-3M
teaspoon 4-28
teeth 2-15; 4-14M
telegram 6-32
telegraph 6-32
telescope 6-32
televise 6-32
television 6-32
tell 2-2; 2-7M
temporary 6-33; 5-25B
ten 2-2; 1-14B
tender 5-32
tenor 6-31
tense 5-5
tents 4-3
term 4-23
terminal 6-15; 4-23B
terrible 5-34
test 3-5; 4-2M; 2-7B
than 2-16
thank 2-15; 4-13M
thankful 4-33; 5-28M
Thanksgiving 4-17
that 1-34; 2-16M
that's 3-20
the 1-17; 2-16M
their 2-16; 3-20M
theirs 4-21
them 2-16; 4-15M; 1-34B
themselves 4-28
then 2-16; 1-34B
there 2-17; 3-20M; 1-19B
therefore 4-22B
there's 3-20
thermometer 6-26B
thermos 6-26B
thermostat 6-15B
these 2-16; 4-15M
thick 4-9
thin 4-14
thing 2-15
think 2-27; 4-14M; 1-25B
thinner 6-20
this 1-34; 2-16M
those 2-25; 3-17M
though 3-33
thought 3-33; 2-17B

thoughtful 5-28; 4-14B
thread 4-14
threat 5-1; 4-2B
three 2-21; 1-20B
thrift 5-9
thriftiest 6-20B
throat 5-3; 3-17B
throne 5-9B
throughout 6-11; 5-23B
throw 4-7; 6-2M; 2-25B
thumb 3-26; 2-15B
thunder 5-1; 4-2B
ticket 5-7; 4-9B
tickle 4-26; 3-10B
tie 2-23
tiger 3-16; 3-35M; 2-23B
tight 4-7
time 2-22; 1-26B
timid 5-1
tire 2-22
tires 3-25M
tissue 5-11
title 3-16B
to 2-28; 3-29M
toad 2-26
toast 4-7; 2-26B
today 3-14; 2-2B
together 3-7; 4-35M; 2-16B
told 2-26
tomatoes 6-4
tomb 6-19
tomorrow 4-7
tonight 4-7
tonsils 4-29; 3-34B
too 2-28; 3-29M
took 2-29; 3-31M
tool 4-20
tooth 3-31; 4-20M
top 2-10; 3-1M; 1-16B
topic 6-31
tore 4-22
torn 2-33
tornadoes 6-4
tortoise 6-9
tosses 4-3
total 5-33; 3-35B
touch 3-33
touchdown 6-11; 4-28B
touching 6-13; 4-8B
tough 3-33
tourist 4-34; 3-31B
tournament 5-29B
toward 5-19
towel 5-14; 3-32B
tower 2-32; 3-33M
town 2-32; 3-32M
toy 1-31; 2-32B
track 4-1; 2-14B
tractor 4-25
trader 6-21
traditional 6-23B
traffic 5-9

tragedy 6-28
trail 3-14; 2-20B
train 2-20; 1-29B
trainer 4-25
trains 3-25M
traitor 6-21; 4-25B
traits 6-2B
tramp 5-1; 3-5B
trample 5-9B
transferred 6-13
transfusion 6-8B
transportation 6-32
trap 2-5B
trapped 3-3; 4-8M
travel 3-28B
traveler 4-34
trays 5-8
treasure 6-8
treat 4-5; 4-17M; 2-21B
treaty 5-26
tree 1-20; 2-14M
trek 5-9B
tremble 5-32B
trial 6-29
triangle 6-27
triangular 6-27B
trick 3-4; 5-9M; 2-8B
tried 4-16
trimmed 4-8
triumph 6-29
triumphant 6-34B
tropical 6-28
trotting 5-4; 4-8B
troublesome 5-25
trousers 3-33B
truck 2-9; 4-2M
true 2-14; 2-28M
truly 4-33; 4-13B
trumpet 6-29
trunk 2-27
trust 4-2; 2-13B
truthful 5-28; 4-14B
try 2-23; 3-27M; 1-22B
tulip 4-20
tuna 4-20
tunnel 4-29; 5-22M; 3-28B
turkey 5-20
turn 2-34; 3-22M
turnpike 6-11; 5-23B
turtle 4-26; 3-22B
tutor 5-21
twice 4-4; 2-22B
twin 4-1
twine 5-2
twist 5-1; 4-1B
two 2-2B
type 5-2
typical 6-33
tyrant 5-2B

U

unable 4-32
unbelievable 5-27B

unbutton 5-27
uncertain 4-32B
uncles 3-8
uncomfortable 5-27B
uncover 5-27
understood 5-15
underwater 5-23; 6-35M
unexpected 4-32B
unhappy 4-32; 5-27M
uniform 6-16B
unit 4-20
universe 6-10; 4-20B
university 5-20B
unkind 4-32; 5-27M
unless 3-2
unlike 4-32; 5-27M
unload 5-27
unlock 5-27
unlucky 4-32; 5-27M
unmade 4-32
unpaid 4-32
unpleasant 5-27; 4-32B
unreal 4-32M
unroll 4-32M
unsafe 4-32
unselfish 5-27
untie 4-32M
until 2-9; 3-1M
unusual 4-32
up 1-19; 2-9M
upsetting 6-13B
upstairs 4-28; 6-11M
urban 6-15B
urgent 5-20B
us 1-13; 2-9M
use 2-17; 3-13M
useful 4-20M
useless 5-28
usual 6-8
usually 6-23; 4-33B

V

vacation 4-35; 5-11M
Valentine's Day 4-17
valley 3-2B
valleys 5-8
vanish 4-31
vapor 6-21
varied 5-13B
variety 6-35
vast 5-25
vegetable 5-32
vegetarian 6-7B
veil 6-3
vein 6-3
verb 5-35
verse 5-20
version 6-8
vertical 6-23B

very 2-2
Veterans Day 4-17
victory 5-25
view 6-10
vigorous 6-33B
village 4-10; 5-26M; 3-2B
villain 6-29B
vinegar 6-21
violet 6-34
violin 6-28
virus 5-33B
vision 6-8
visit 5-33M; 2-2B
visited 4-8
visitor 4-25; 6-21M
vocabulary 5-35
voice 3-32; 4-19M
volcanoes 6-4
vote 5-3; 3-17B
vow 6-9; 5-14B
voyage 5-14

W

W. (west) 4-13
wage 6-7
wagging 3-3
waist 5-2; 6-3M; 4-5B
wait 1-29; 2-20M
walk 3-21; 3-26M; 2-31B
wall 2-31
walnut 6-14
want 2-17; 3-5M; 1-32B

warehouse 5-23B
warmth 5-19
warning 5-19
wart 5-19B
was 1-17; 2-17M
wash 3-21; 2-2B
Washington's Birthday 4-17
wasn't 4-21; 3-20B
watch 2-16; 4-15M
watching 4-8
water 2-31; 2-35M
watered 6-13; 4-8B
waterproof 5-23
wave 2-19; 3-13M
way 1-31; 2-20M
we 1-20; 2-21M
weak 3-15
weakness 5-29
wealthier 6-20
weapon 6-31
weather 3-7; 4-27M; 2-16B
wedge 6-7B
wee 1-20B
weekend 5-23
weigh 6-3
welcome 4-29; 3-34B
we'll 3-20
well 2-7; 2-11M
went 2-2; 2-27M
we're 3-20; 4-21M
were 2-17; 2-34M; 1-17B

weren't 3-20B
west 3-5
wet 1-14; 2-2M
whale 1-35
wharf 5-19
what 2-17; 1-32B
whatever 6-11
what's 3-20B
wheat 4-5; 1-35B
wheels 3-25
when 2-17; 1-35B
whenever 5-23
where 2-17; 2-34M
wherever 5-23; 4-28B
whether 4-15; 3-7B
which 3-7; 4-15M
while 1-35
whimper 6-21
whirl 5-20; 3-22B
whisper 5-32
whistle 5-22; 4-26B
white 1-35
who 2-28; 3-26M
whoever 3-19B
whole 4-4; 6-19M; 3-29B
wholesale 6-11B
whose 3-29; 4-21M
why 2-23; 3-16M; 1-22B
wide 2-22; 3-16M
width 4-14
wild 3-5

wilderness 4-35; 6-34M
west 3-5
wildlife 6-17; 4-29B
will 1-11; 3-20M
wind 3-5; 4-27M
windmill 5-23
window 3-17; 5-32M; 2-25B
windshield 6-11B
windy 4-33; 6-23M
winner 4-34; 6-1M
winter 2-35; 4-25M
wipe 3-13
wise 3-16; 5-5M; 2-22B
wish 2-15; 1-34B
wishes 3-8M
with 1-34; 2-15M
withdrew 5-15B
within 3-19M
without 3-19M
wittiest 6-20B
wives 5-8
woke 4-4; 2-25B
wolves 5-8
woman 2-2
women 6-4M
women's 4-21
won 3-29; 2-9B
wonder 3-34; 2-9B
wondered 6-13
wonderful 5-34; 6-34M

won't 3-20; 4-21M
wood 2-29; 3-29M; 1-28B
woodcut 6-11B
wooden 4-26; 3-31B
wool 2-29; 3-31M
woolen 5-15
word 2-34; 3-22M
work 2-34; 3-22M; 1-32B
worker 4-34M
workshop 6-11
world 3-22; 5-26M; 2-34B
worm 5-20
worried 4-16; 5-13M
worry 3-22; 5-20M
worrying 4-16
worship 5-20
worst 5-20; 3-22B
worth 3-22B
worthless 5-28
worthwhile 5-20B
would 2-29; 3-29M
wrapped 5-4; 4-8B
wrapping 3-3B
wreath 5-16
wreck 5-16; 3-26B
wren 3-26
wrestle 5-16; 6-19M

wriggle 5-16B
wring 5-16
wrinkle 5-16
wrist 5-16; 3-26B
wristwatches 6-4; 5-8B
write 2-22; 3-26M
writing 4-34; 5-35M
written 3-26; 5-16M
wrong 4-14; 5-16M; 2-17B
wrote 3-26; 4-4M

Y

yard 3-23; 4-22M; 2-2B
year 2-34
yes 1-14; 2-2M
yesterday 4-35; 5-34M
yet 2-7
yield 6-3B
yolk 6-19
you 1-17; 2-28M
young 2-27
your 2-2
you're 4-21; 3-20B
yours 4-21
yourself 3-19; 4-28M
you've 4-21B

Z

zone 4-9

Lowercase Letters

Start slightly below the midline, circle left along the midline, around to the bottom line, slant up to the midline and close; retrace straight slant to the bottom line; undercurve. (short letter talk: around, slant, undercurve)

Start at the bottom line, undercurve to the top line; loop and straight slant to the bottom line, circle up to the right and tie to the stem at the midline; high curve. (short letter talk: undercurve, loop, slant, circle and tie, high curve)

Start at the midline, slight slant to the left, circle left up to the midline, around to the bottom line and up; leave the letter open. (short letter talk: check, up and around)

Start slightly below the midline, circle left along the midline to the bottom line, slant up to the top line; retrace straight slant to the bottom line; undercurve. (short letter talk: around, up high, retrace slant, undercurve)

Start at the bottom line, undercurve to the midline; loop and straight slant to the bottom line; undercurve. (short letter talk: undercurve, loop, slant, undercurve)

Start at the bottom line, undercurve to the top line; loop and straight slant to the descender line; loop to the right and up, tie to the stem at the bottom line; undercurve. (short letter talk: undercurve, loop, slant low, loop up and tie, undercurve)

Start slightly below the midline, circle left along the midline to the bottom line, slant up to the midline and close; retrace straight slant to the descender line; loop to the left and up, cross at the bottom line. (short letter talk: around, slant low, loop up and cross)

Start at the bottom line, undercurve to the top line; loop and straight slant to the bottom line; retrace; overcurve to the midline, round it and slant to the bottom line; undercurve. (short letter talk: undercurve, loop, slant, up-and-over, undercurve)

Start at the bottom line, undercurve to the midline; straight slant to the bottom line; undercurve: dot it slightly above the midline. (short letter talk: undercurve, slant, undercurve; dot it)

Start at the bottom line, undercurve to the midline; straight slant to the descender line; loop to the left and up, cross at the bottom line: dot it slightly above the midline. (short letter talk: undercurve, slant low, loop up and cross; dot it)

Start at the bottom line, undercurve to the top line; loop and straight slant to the bottom line; retrace; overcurve to the midline and make a small loop back to the stem; slant to the bottom line, undercurve. (short letter talk: undercurve, loop, slant, loop back, slant, undercurve)

Start at the bottom line, undercurve to the top line; loop and straight slant to the bottom line; undercurve. (short letter talk: undercurve, loop, slant, undercurve)

Start at the bottom line, overcurve to the midline, round it and straight slant to the bottom line; retrace; overcurve to the midline, round it and straight slant to the bottom line; retrace; overcurve to the midline, round it and straight slant to the bottom line; undercurve. (short letter talk: up-and-over, slant, up-and-over, slant, up-and-over, slant, undercurve)

Start at the bottom line, overcurve to the midline, round it and straight slant to the bottom line; retrace; overcurve to the midline, round it and straight slant to the bottom line; undercurve. (short letter talk: up-and-over, slant, up-and-over, slant, undercurve)

(continued on next page)

281

Lowercase Letters continued

Start slightly below the midline, circle left along the midline to the bottom line, up to the midline and close; high curve. (short letter talk: around, close, high curve)

Start at the bottom line, undercurve to the midline; straight slant to the descender line; loop to the left and up, circle up and around touching the midline, the bottom line, and the stem; undercurve. (short letter talk: undercurve, slant low, loop up and around, undercurve)

Start slightly below the midline, circle left along the midline to the bottom line, slant up to the midline and close; straight slant to the descender line; loop to the right and up, tie to the stem at the bottom line; undercurve. (short letter talk: around, slant low, loop up and tie, undercurve)

Start at the bottom line, undercurve to the midline; high curve to the midline; straight slant to the bottom line; undercurve. (short letter talk: undercurve, high curve, slant, undercurve)

Start at the bottom line, undercurve to the midline; slight retrace down and curve around touching the bottom line and the stem; undercurve. (short letter talk: undercurve, retrace and curve around, undercurve)

Start at the bottom line, undercurve to the top line; straight slant to the bottom line; undercurve: straight across a little above the midline. (short letter talk: undercurve, slant, undercurve; cross it)

Start at the bottom line, undercurve to the midline; straight slant to the bottom line, round it and undercurve to the midline; retrace straight slant to the bottom line; undercurve. (short letter talk: undercurve, slant, undercurve, slant, undercurve)

Start at the bottom line, overcurve to the midline, round it and straight slant to the bottom line, round it and undercurve to the midline; high curve. (short letter talk: up-and-over, slant, undercurve, high curve)

Start at the bottom line, undercurve to the midline; straight slant to the bottom line; round it and undercurve to the midline; retrace; straight slant to the bottom line, round it and undercurve to the midline; high curve. (short letter talk: undercurve, slant, undercurve, slant, undercurve, high curve)

Start at the bottom line, overcurve the midline, round it and slant right to the bottom line, undercurve; start at the midline, straight slant left to the bottom line. (short letter talk: up-and-over, slant, undercurve; slant)

Start at the bottom line, undercurve to the midline; straight slant to the bottom line, round it and undercurve to the midline; straight slant to the descender line; loop to the left and up, cross at the bottom line. (short letter talk: undercurve, slant, undercurve, slant low, loop up and cross)

Start at the bottom line, overcurve to the midline, round it and straight slant to the bottom line; curve right and down to the descender line, loop to the left and up, cross at the bottom line. (short letter talk: overcurve, slant, curve, slant low, loop up and cross)

Uppercase Letters

Start slightly below the top line, circle left along the top line, around to the bottom line, slant up to the top line and close; retrace; straight slant to the bottom line; undercurve. (short letter talk: top line, around, slant, undercurve)

Start at the midline, undercurve to the top line; straight slant to the bottom line; start at the top line, straight slant to the bottom line; overcurve to the left of the midline touching the first stroke, undercurve and cross. (short letter talk: midline, undercurve, slant; top line, slant, overcurve, undercurve and cross)

Start at the midline, undercurve to the top line; straight slant to the bottom line; retrace and circle up and around touching the top line, the midline, and the stem; circle around, touching the bottom line and the stem halfway between the bottom line and the midline; undercurve. (short letter talk: midline, undercurve, slant, retrace and around, around, undercurve)

Start at the bottom line, curve up to the left to the top line; slant down to the left to the bottom line, curve up halfway between the bottom line and the midline; undercurve and cross. (short letter talk: bottom line, curve up, slant down, curve up, undercurve and cross)

Start at the top line, slight slant to the left, circle left along the top line, around to the bottom line and up; leave the letter open. (short letter talk: top line, check, up and around)

Start at the bottom line, curve up to the left to the top line; slant down to the left to the descender line; loop to the left and up, cross at the bottom line. (short letter talk: bottom line, curve up, slant down low, loop up and cross)

Start at top line, straight slant to the bottom line; loop and curve along the bottom line, around and up to touch the top line and meet the starting point, curve in to the midline and curve out. (short letter talk: top line, slant, loop and curve, around and up, curve in and curve out)

Start at the midline, undercurve to the top line; straight slant to the bottom line; start at the top line; curve in and touch the stem at the midline; slant to the bottom line, undercurve. (short letter talk: midline, undercurve, slant; top line, curve in, slant, undercurve)

Start at the top line, slight slant to the left, circle left along the top line, around to the midline, stopping slightly to the left of the starting point, curve around farther to the left, touching the bottom line and up. (short letter talk: top line, check, around and around)

Start at the midline, undercurve to the top line; loop and straight slant to the bottom line; loop and undercurve. (short letter talk: midline, undercurve, loop and slant, loop and undercurve)

Start at the top line, slight slant to the left; make a slight double curve right across the top line; straight slant down to the left, curve up to halfway between the bottom line and the midline; undercurve and cross; straight across a little above the midline. (short letter talk: top line, check, double curve, slant, curve up, undercurve and cross; cross it)

Start at the top line, slight slant to the left, curve right up to the top line, straight slant to the bottom line; retrace and overcurve to the top line, straight slant to the bottom line; retrace and overcurve to the top line, straight slant to the bottom line, undercurve. (short letter talk: top line, check, curve, slant, retrace and up-and-over, slant, retrace and up-and-over, slant, undercurve)

Start at the bottom line, slant up to the right to the top line; make a loop and high curve to the top line; slant down to the left; curve around, touching the bottom line and the stem halfway between the bottom line and the midline; undercurve. (short letter talk: bottom line, slant, high curve, slant, around, undercurve)

Start at the top line, slight slant to the left, curve right up to the top line, straight slant to the bottom line; retrace and overcurve to the top line, straight slant to the bottom line, undercurve. (short letter talk: top line, check, curve, slant, retrace and up-and-over, slant, undercurve)

(continued on next page)

Uppercase Letters

Start slightly below the top line, circle left along the top line to the bottom line, up to the top line and close; curve in to the midline and curve out. (short letter talk: top line, around, close, curve in and curve out)

Start at the midline, undercurve to the top line; straight slant to the bottom line; retrace and circle up and around touching the top line, the midline, and the stem. (short letter talk: midline, undercurve, slant, retrace, and around)

Start at the top line, slight slant to the left, curve right up to the top line, round it to the bottom line; loop and undercurve. (short letter talk: top line, check, up-and-over, loop and undercurve)

Start at the midline, undercurve to the top line; straight slant to the bottom line; retrace and circle up and around touching the top line, the midline, and the stem; slant to the bottom line, undercurve. (short letter talk: midline, undercurve, slant, retrace and around, slant, undercurve)

Start at the bottom line, slant up to the right to the top line; loop, cross, and curve down and around, touching the bottom line and the stem halfway between the bottom line and the midline; undercurve. (short letter talk: bottom line, slant, loop and cross, curve down and around, undercurve)

Start at the top line, slight slant to the left; make a slight double curve right across the top line; straight slant down to the left, curve up to halfway between the bottom line and the midline; undercurve and cross. (short letter talk: top line, check, double curve, slant, curve up, undercurve and cross)

Start at the top line, slight slant to the left, curve right up to the top line, straight slant to the bottom line, round it and curve to the top line; retrace to the bottom line, undercurve. (short letter talk: top line, check, curve, slant, curve, slant up, retrace, undercurve)

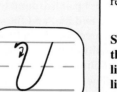

Start at the top line, slight slant to the left, curve right up to the top line, straight slant to the bottom line, round it and slant to the top line. (short letter talk: top line, check, slant, curve, slant up)

Start at the top line, slight slant to the left, curve right up to the top line, straight slant to the bottom line, round it and slant to the top line; retrace to the bottom line, round it and slant to the top line. (short letter talk: top line, check, curve, slant, curve, slant up, retrace, curve, slant up)

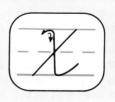

Start at the top line, slight slant to the left, curve right up to the top line, slant right to the bottom line, undercurve; start at the top line, straight slant left to the bottom line. (short letter talk: top line, check, curve, slant, undercurve; cross it)

Start at the top line, slight slant to the left, curve right up to the top line, straight slant to the bottom line, round it and slant to the top line; retrace to the descender line; loop to the left and up, cross at the bottom line. (short letter talk: top line, check, curve, slant, curve, slant up, retrace, loop up and cross)

Start at the top line, slight slant to the left, curve right up to the top line, round it and slant to the bottom line; curve right along the bottom line and down to the descender line, loop to the left and up, cross at the bottom line. (short letter talk: top line, check, up-and-over, slant, curve, slant low, loop up and cross)

Letras minúsculas

Comiencen un poco debajo de la línea del medio, hagan medio círculo hacia la izquierda por la línea del medio, hagan medio círculo hacia la línea de abajo, oblicuo hacia arriba hasta la línea del medio y cierren; repasen oblicuo derecho hasta la línea de abajo; curva por bajo. (forma breve: medio círculo, oblicuo, curva por bajo)

Comiencen en la línea de abajo, hagan una curva por bajo hasta la línea de arriba; lazo y oblicuo derecho hasta la línea de abajo, hagan medio círculo hacia la derecha y cierren al perfil en la línea del medio; hagan una curva alta. (forma breve: curva por bajo, lazo, oblicuo, medio círculo y cerrar, curva alta)

Comiencen en la línea del medio, oblicuo corto hacia la izquierda, hagan medio círculo hasta la línea del medio, hagan medio círculo hasta la línea de abajo y arriba; dejen abierta la letra. (forma breve: revés alto, arriba y medio círculo)

Comiencen un poco debajo de la línea del medio, hagan medio círculo hacia la izquierda por la línea del medio hasta la línea de abajo, oblicuo hacia arriba hasta la línea de arriba; repasen oblicuo derecho hasta la línea de abajo; hagan una curva por bajo. (forma breve medio círculo, arriba alto, repasar oblicuo, curva por bajo)

Comiencen en la línea de abajo, hagan una curva por bajo hasta la línea del medio; lazo y oblicuo derecho hasta la línea de abajo, hagan una curva por bajo. (forma breve: curva por bajo, lazo, oblicuo, curva por bajo)

Comiencen en la línea de abajo, hagan una curva por bajo hasta la línea de arriba; lazo y oblicuo derecho hasta la línea descendente; lazo hacia la derecha y arriba, cierren al perfil en la línea de abajo; hagan una curva por bajo. (forma breve: curva por bajo, lazo, oblicuo bajo, lazo arriba y cerrar, curva por bajo)

Comiencen un poco abajo de la línea del medio, hagan medio círculo hacia la izquierda por la línea del medio hasta la línea de abajo, oblicuo hacia arriba hasta la línea del medio y cierren; repasen oblicuo derecho hasta la línea descendente; lazo hacia la izquierda y arriba, crucen en la línea de abajo. (forma breve: medio círculo, oblicuo bajo, lazo arriba y cruzar)

Comiencen en la línea de abajo, hagan una curva por bajo hasta la línea de arriba; lazo y oblicuo derecho hasta la línea de abajo; hagan una curva por cima hasta la línea del medio, hagan medio círculo y oblicuo hasta la línea de abajo; repasen; hagan una curva por bajo. (forma breve: curva por bajo, lazo, oblicuo, arriba y por encima, curva por bajo)

Comiencen en la línea de abajo, hagan una curva por bajo hasta la línea del medio; oblicuo derecho hasta la línea de abajo; hagan una curva por bajo; pongan un punto un poco encima de la línea del medio. (forma breve: curva por bajo, oblicuo, curva por bajo; punto)

Comiencen en la línea de abajo, hagan una curva por bajo hasta la línea del medio; oblicuo derecho hasta la línea descendente; lazo hacia la izquierda y arriba, crucen en la línea de abajo; pongan un punto un poco encima línea del medio. (forma breve: curva por bajo, oblicuo bajo, lazo arriba y cruzar; punto)

Comiencen en la línea de abajo, hagan una curva por bajo hasta la línea de arriba; lazo y oblicuo derecho hasta la línea de abajo; repasen hagan una curva por arriba hasta la línea del medio y hagan un lazo pequeño hacia atrás hasta el perfil; oblicuo hasta la línea de abajo, curva por bajo. (forma breve: curva por bajo, lazo, oblicuo, lazo atrás, oblicuo, curva por bajo)

Comiencen en la línea de abajo, hagan una curva por bajo hasta la línea de arriba; lazo y oblicuo derecho hasta la línea de abajo; hagan una curva por bajo. (forma breve: curva por bajo, lazo, oblicuo, curva por bajo)

Comiencen en la línea de abajo, hagan una curva por arriba hasta la línea del medio, hagan medio círculo y oblicuo derecho hasta la línea de abajo; repasen; hagan una curva por arriba hasta la línea del medio, hagan medio círculo y oblicuo derecho hasta la línea de abajo; repasen; hagan una curva por arriba hasta la línea del medio, hagan medio círculo y oblicuo derecho hasta la línea de abajo; hagan una curva por bajo. (forma breve: arriba y por encima, oblicuo, arriba y por encima, oblicuo, arriba y por encima, oblicuo, curva por bajo)

Comiencen en la línea de abajo, hagan una curva por arriba hasta la línea del medio, hagan medio círculo y oblicuo derecho hasta la línea de abajo; repasen hagan una curva por arriba hasta la línea del medio, hagan medio círculo y oblicuo derecho hasta la línea de abajo; hagan una curva por bajo. (forma breve: arriba y por encima, oblicuo, arriba y por encima, oblicuo, curva por bajo)

Letras minúsculas   continuación

Comiencen un poco abajo de la línea del medio, hagan medio círculo hacia la izquierda por la línea del medio hasta la línea de abajo, arriba hasta la línea del medio y cierren; hagan una curva alta. (forma breve: medio círculo, cerrar, curva alta)

Comiencen en la línea de abajo, hagan una curva por bajo hasta la línea del medio; oblicuo derecho hasta la línea descendente; lazo a la izquierda y arriba, hagan medio círculo hacia arriba y hagan medio círculo tocando la línea del medio, la línea de abajo, y el perfil; hagan una curva por bajo. (forma breve: curva por bajo, oblicuo bajo, lazo arriba y medio círculo, curva por bajo)

Comiencen un poco abajo de la línea del medio, hagan medio círculo hacia la izquierda por la línea del medio hasta la línea de abajo, oblicuo hacia arriba hasta la línea del medio y cierren; oblicuo derecho hasta la línea descendente; lazo a la derecha y arriba, cerrar al perfil en la línea de abajo; hagan una curva por bajo. (forma breve: medio círculo, oblicuo bajo, lazo arriba y cerrar, curva por bajo)

Comiencen en la línea de abajo, hagan una curva por bajo hasta la línea del medio; hagan una curva alta hasta la línea del medio; oblicuo derecho hasta la línea de abajo; hagan una curva por bajo. (forma breve: curva por bajo, curva alta, oblicuo, curva por bajo)

Comiencen en la línea de abajo, hagan una curva por bajo hasta la línea del medio; repasen abajo un poco y hagan medio círculo tocando la línea de abajo y el perfil; hagan una curva por bajo. (forma breve: curva por bajo, repasar y medio círculo, curva por bajo)

Comiencen en la línea de abajo, hagan una curva por bajo hasta la línea de arriba; oblicuo derecho hasta la línea de abajo; hagan una curva por bajo; línea recta un poco encima de la línea del medio. (forma breve: curva por bajo, oblicuo, curva por bajo; línea recta)

Comiencen en la línea de abajo, hagan una curva por bajo hasta la línea del medio; oblicuo derecho hasta la línea de abajo, hagan medio círculo y curva por bajo hasta la línea del medio; derecho oblicuo hasta la línea de abajo; hagan una curva por bajo. (forma breve: curva por bajo, oblicuo, curva por bajo, oblicuo, curva por bajo)

Comiencen en la línea de abajo, hagan una curva por arriba hasta la línea del medio, hagan medio círculo y derecho oblicuo hasta la línea de abajo, hagan medio círculo y una curva por bajo hasta la línea del medio, hagan una curva alta. (forma breve: arriba y por encima, oblicuo, curva por bajo, curva alta)

Comiencen en la línea de abajo, hagan una curva por bajo hasta la línea del medio; oblicuo derecho hasta la línea de abajo, hagan medio círculo y una curva por bajo hasta la línea del medio; repasen; oblicuo derecho hasta la línea de abajo, hagan medio círculo y una curva por bajo hasta la línea del medio; hagan una curva alta. (forma breve: curva por bajo, oblicuo, curva por bajo, oblicuo, curva por bajo, curva alta)

Comiencen en la línea de abajo, hagan una curva por arriba hasta la línea del medio, hagan medio círculo y oblicuo hacia la derecha hasta la línea de abajo, hagan una curva por bajo; comiencen en la línea del medio, oblicuo derecho hacia la izquierda hasta la línea de abajo. (forma breve: arriba y por encima, oblicuo, curva por bajo; oblicuo)

Comiencen en la línea de abajo, hagan una curva por bajo hasta la línea del medio; oblicuo derecho hasta la línea de abajo, hagan medio círculo y una curva por bajo hasta la línea del medio; derecho oblicuo hasta la línea descendente; lazo a la izquierda y arriba, crucen en la línea de abajo. (forma breve: curva por bajo, oblicuo, curva por bajo, oblicuo bajo, lazo arriba y cruzar)

Comiencen en la línea de abajo, hagan una curva por arriba hasta la línea del medio, hagan medio círculo y oblicuo derecho hasta la línea de abajo; hagan una curva hacia la derecha y abajo hasta la línea descendente, lazo hacia la izquierda y arriba, crucen en la línea de abajo. (forma breve: curva por arriba, oblicuo, curva, oblicuo bajo, lazo arriba y cruzar)

Letras mayúsculas

Comiencen un poco debajo de la línea de arriba, hagan medio círculo hacia la izquierda por la línea de arriba hasta la línea de abajo, oblicuo hacia arriba hasta la línea de arriba y cierren; repasen oblicuo derecho hasta la línea de abajo; hagan una curva por bajo. (forma breve: línea de arriba, medio círculo, oblicuo, curva por bajo)

Comiencen en la línea del medio, hagan una curva por bajo hasta la línea de arriba; oblicuo derecho hasta la línea de abajo; repasen y hagan medio círculo arriba tocando la línea de arriba, la línea del medio y el perfil; hagan medio círculo, tocando la línea de abajo y el perfil medio espacio entre la línea de abajo y la línea del medio; hagan una curva por bajo. (forma breve: línea del medio, curva por bajo, oblicuo, repasar y medio círculo, medio círculo y curva por bajo)

Comiencen en la línea de arriba, oblicuo corto hacia la izquierda, hagan medio círculo hacia la izquierda por la línea de arriba hasta la línea de abajo y arriba; dejen la letra abierta. (forma breve: línea de arriba, revés alto, arriba y medio círculo)

Comiencen en la línea de arriba, oblicuo derecho hasta la línea de abajo; lazo y hagan una curva por la línea de abajo, un medio círculo y arriba hasta tocar la línea de arriba y dar con el punto de partida, curva adentro hasta la línea del medio y curva para fuera. (forma breve: línea de arriba, oblicuo, lazo y curva, medio círculo y arriba, curva adentro y curva para fuera)

Comiencen en la línea de arriba, oblicuo corta hacia la izquierda, hagan medio círculo hacia la izquierda por la línea de arriba, medio círculo hasta la línea del medio, deténganse un poco a la izquierda del punto de partida, hagan una curva más allá hacia la izquierda, tocando la línea de abajo y arriba. (forma breve: línea de arriba, revés alto, medio círculo y medio círculo)

Comiencen en la línea de arriba, oblicuo corto hacia la izquierda; hagan una curva doble corta por la línea de arriba; oblicuo derecho hacia abajo hacia la izquierda, hagan una curva hacia arriba medio espacio entre la línea de abajo y la línea del medio; curva por bajo y crucen; línea recta un poco encima de la la línea del medio. (forma breve: línea de arriba, revés alto, curva doble, oblicuo, curva arriba, curva por bajo y cruzar; línea recta)

Comiencen en la línea de abajo, oblicuo hacia arriba hacia la derecha hasta la línea de arriba; lazo y hagan una curva alta hasta la línea de arriba; oblicuo hacia abajo hacia la izquierda; hagan medio círculo, tocando la línea de abajo y el perfil medio espacio entre la línea de abajo y la línea del medio; hagan una curva por bajo. (forma breve: línea de abajo, oblicuo, curva alta, oblicuo, medio círculo, curva por bajo)

Comiencen en la línea del medio, hagan una curva por bajo hasta la línea de arriba; oblicuo derecho hasta la línea de abajo; comiencen en la línea de arriba, oblicuo derecho hasta la línea de abajo; hagan una curva por arriba a la izquierda hasta la línea del medio tocando la primera plumada, hagan una curva por bajo y crucen. (forma breve: línea del medio, curva por bajo, oblicuo; línea de arriba, oblicuo curva por arriba, curva por bajo y cruzar)

Comiencen en la línea de abajo, curva hacia arriba hacia la izquierda hasta la línea de arriba; oblicuo hacia abajo hacia la izquierda hasta la línea de abajo; hagan una curva hacia arriba medio espacio entre la línea de abajo y la línea del medio; hagan una curva por bajo y crucen. (forma breve: línea de abajo, curva arriba, oblicuo abajo, curva por bajo y cruzar)

Comiencen en la línea de abajo, hagan una curva hacia arriba hacia la izquierda hasta la línea de arriba; oblicuo hacia abajo hacia la izquierda hasta la línea descendente; lazo hacia la izquierda y hacia arriba, crucen en la línea de abajo. (forma breve: línea de abajo, curva arriba, oblicuo bien abajo, lazo arriba y cruzar)

Comiencen en la línea del medio, hagan una curva por bajo hasta la línea de arriba; oblicuo derecho hasta la línea de abajo; comiencen en la línea de arriba; hagan una curva hacia dentro tocando el perfil en la línea del medio; oblicuo hasta la línea de abajo, hagan una curva por bajo. (forma breve: línea del medio, curva por bajo, oblicuo; línea de arriba, curva adentro, oblicuo, curva por bajo)

Comiencen en la línea del medio, hagan una curva por bajo hasta la línea de arriba; lazo y oblicuo derecho hasta línea de abajo; lazo y hagan una curva por bajo. (forma breve: línea del medio, curva por bajo, lazo y oblicuo, lazo y curva por bajo)

Comiencen en la línea de arriba, oblicuo corto hacia la izquierda, hagan una curva hacia arriba hacia la derecha hasta la línea de arriba, derecho oblicuo hasta la línea de abajo; repasen y hagan una curva por arriba hasta la línea de arriba, oblicuo derecho hasta la línea de abajo; repasen y hagan una curva por arriba hasta la línea de arriba, oblicuo derecho hasta la línea de fondo, hagan una curva por bajo. (forma breve: línea de arriba, revés alto, curva, oblicuo, repasar y arriba y por encima, oblicuo, repasar y arriba y por encima, oblicuo, curva por bajo)

(continúa en la siguiente página)

Letras mayúsculas

Comiencen en la línea de arriba, oblicuo corto hacia la izquierda, hagan una curva hacia arriba hacia la derecha hasta la línea de arriba, derecho oblicuo hasta la línea de abajo; repasen y hagan una curva por arriba hasta la línea de arriba, oblicuo derecho hasta la línea de abajo, hagan una curva por bajo. (forma breve: línea de arriba, revés alto, curva, oblicuo, repasar y arriba y por encima, oblicuo, curva por bajo)

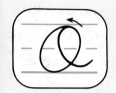

Comiencen un poco debajo de la línea de arriba, hagan medio círculo hacia la izquierda por la línea de arriba hasta la línea de abajo, arriba hasta la línea de arriba y cierren; hagan una curva hacia dentro hasta la línea del medio y hagan una curva para fuera. (forma breve: línea de arriba, medio círculo, cerrar, curva hacia dentro y curva hacia fuera)

Comiencen en la línea del medio, hagan una curva por bajo hasta la línea de arriba; oblicuo derecho hasta la línea de abajo; repasen y hagan medio círculo hacia arriba tocando la línea de arriba, la línea del medio y el perfil. (forma breve: línea del medio, curva por bajo, oblicuo, repasar, y medio círculo)

Comiencen en la línea de arriba, oblicuo corto hacia la izquierda, hagan una curva hacia arriba hacia la derecha hasta la línea de arriba, medio círculo hasta la línea de abajo; lazo y hagan una curva por bajo. (forma breve: línea de arriba, revés alto, arriba y por encima, lazo y curva por bajo)

Comiencen en la línea del medio, hagan una curva por bajo hasta la línea de arriba; oblicuo derecho hasta la línea de abajo; repasen y hagan medio círculo arriba tocando la línea de arriba, la línea del medio, y el perfil; oblicuo hasta la línea de abajo, hagan una curva por bajo. (forma breve: línea del medio, curva por bajo, oblicuo, repasar y medio círculo, oblicuo, curva por bajo)

Comiencen en la línea de abajo, oblicuo hacia arriba hacia la derecha hasta la línea de arriba; lazo, crucen, y hagan una curva hacia abajo y medio círculo, tocando la línea de abajo y el perfil medio espacio entre la línea de abajo y la línea del medio; hagan una curva por bajo. (forma breve: línea de abajo, oblicuo, lazo y crucen, curva abajo y medio círculo, curva por bajo)

Comiencen en la línea de arriba, oblicuo corto hacia la izquierda; hagan una curva doble corta por de la línea de arriba; oblicuo derecho hacia abajo hacia la izquierda, hagan una curva hacia arriba medio espacio entre la línea de abajo y la línea del medio; hagan una curva por bajo y crucen. (forma breve: línea de arriba, revés alto, curva doble, oblicuo, curva arriba, curva por bajo y cruzar)

Comiencen en la línea de arriba, oblicuo corto hacia la izquierda, hagan una curva hacia arriba hacia la derecha hasta la línea de arriba, derecho oblicuo hasta la línea de abajo, medio círculo y hagan una curva hasta la línea de arriba; repasen hasta la línea de abajo, hagan una curva por bajo. (forma breve: línea de arriba, revés alto, curva, oblicuo, curva, oblicuo arriba, repasar, curva por bajo)

Comiencen en la línea de arriba, oblicuo corto hacia la izquierda, hagan una curva hacia arriba hacia la derecha hasta la línea de arriba, derecho oblicuo hasta la línea de abajo, hagan medio círculo y oblicuo hasta la línea de arriba. (forma breve: línea de arriba, revés alto, curva, oblicuo, curva, oblicuo arriba)

Comiencen en la línea de arriba, oblicuo corto hacia la izquierda, hagan una curva hacia arriba hacia la derecha hasta la línea de arriba, derecho oblicuo hasta la línea de abajo, hagan medio círculo y oblicuo hasta la línea de arriba; repasen hasta la línea de abajo, medio círculo y oblicuo hasta la línea de arriba. (forma breve: línea de arriba, revés alto, curva, oblicuo, curva, oblicuo arriba, repasar, curva, oblicuo arriba)

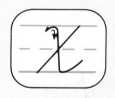

Comiencen en la línea de arriba, oblicuo corto hacia la izquierda, hagan una curva hacia arriba hacia la derecha hasta la línea de arriba, oblicuo hacia la derecha hasta la línea de abajo, hagan una curva por bajo; comiencen en la línea de arriba, oblicuo derecho hacia la izquierda hasta la línea de abajo. (forma breve: línea de arriba, revés alto, curva, oblicuo, curva por bajo; cruzarlo)

Comiencen en la línea de arriba, oblicuo corto hacia la izquierda, hagan una curva hacia la derecha hasta la línea de arriba, oblicuo derecho hasta la línea de abajo, hagan medio círculo y oblicuo hasta la línea de arriba; repasen hasta la línea descendente; lazo hacia la izquierda y arriba, crucen en la línea de abajo. (forma breve: línea de arriba, revés alto, curva, oblicuo, curva, oblicuo arriba, repasar, lazo arriba y cruzar)

Comiencen en la línea de arriba, oblicuo corto hacia la izquierda, hagan una curva hacia arriba hacia la derecha hasta la línea de arriba, hagan medio círculo y oblicuo hasta la línea de abajo; hagan una curva a la derecha por la línea de abajo y abajo hasta la línea descendente, lazo hacia la izquierda y arriba, crucen en la línea de abajo. (forma breve: línea de arriba, revés alto, arriba y por encima, oblicuo bajo, lazo arriba y cruzar)

NOTES

NOTES

NOTES

NOTES

NOTES

NOTES

NOTES

NOTES

NOTES

NOTES

NOTES